The **Rough Guide** to

The Greek Islands

written and researched by

**Lance Chilton, Marc Dubin, Nick Edwards,
Mark Ellingham, John Fisher and Natania Jansz**

with additional contributions by

Don Bapst, Andrew Benson, Geoff Garvey and Irwin Lane

**ROUGH
GUIDES**

NEW YORK • LONDON • DELHI
www.roughguides.com

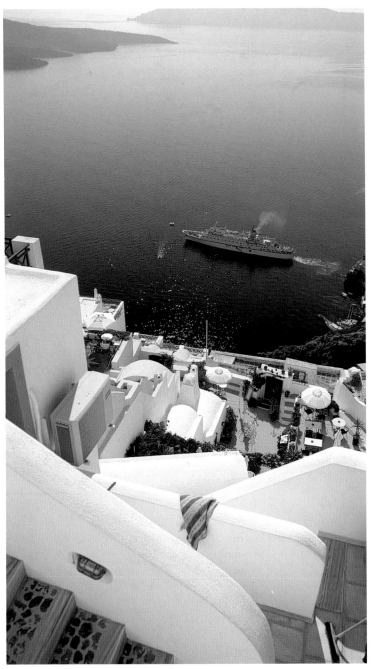

△ Santoríni (Thíra)

Introduction to

The Greek Islands

It would take a lifetime of island-hopping to really get to know the more than 160 permanently inhabited Greek islands, let alone the countless smaller gull-roosts which dot the Aegean and Ionian seas. At the right time of year or day, they conform remarkably well to their fantastic travel-poster image; any tourist board would give its eye-teeth for the commonplace vision of purple-shadowed island silhouettes floating on a cobalt-and-rose horizon.

Closer to hand, island **beaches** come in all shapes, sizes and consistencies, from discrete crescents framed by tree-fringed cliffs straight out of a Japanese screen painting, to deserted, mile-long gifts deposited by small streams, where you could imagine enacting Crusoe-esque scenarios among the dunes. But inland there is always civilization, whether the tiny cubist villages of the remoter outposts or burgeoning resorts as cosmopolitan – and brazen – as any in the Mediterranean.

What amazes most first-time visitors is the islands' relative **lack of pollution**. If you're used to the murky waters of the open Mediterranean as sampled in Spain, Israel or much of Italy, the Aegean will come as a revelation, with forty-foot visibility the norm, and all manner of sea creatures to view, from starfish and octopuses on the bottom to vast schools of fish.

The sea is also a **watersports** paradise: the joys of snorkelling and kayaking are on offer to novices, and some of the best windsurfing areas in the world beckon. Yacht charter, whether bare-boat or skippered, is big business,

Fact file

• Greece is the southernmost country of the Balkan peninsula, with a **surface area** of 131,957 square kilometres (50,949 square miles) divided into 52 provinces. No other country, with the obvious exceptions of Indonesia and the Philippines, has so many islands, though they form only about ten percent of Greece's total territory. The **population** is overwhelmingly **Greek-speaking** and 96 percent are **Greek Orthodox** in religious affiliation, with noticeable Catholic, Sunni Muslim, Jewish and evangelical Christian minorities, plus (mostly on the mainland) pockets of Turkish-, Romany- and Macedonian-speakers. Around one million live out on the islands, and nearly half of these live in towns of over five thousand people.

• Per "native" population of 10.2 million, Greece has the highest proportion of immigrants in Europe – officially 800,000 but potentially 1.1 million, most of these Albanian.

• Since 1974 Greece has been a **parliamentary republic**, with the president as (largely ceremonial) head of state and a 300-seat, single-chamber parliament led by a prime minister. Before being voted out in March 2004, PASOK, the (approximately) social democratic ruling party, completed its third consecutive term in office, something hitherto unheard of in the perennially unstable – and historically rightist – Greek political world.

• **Tourism** is the country's main foreign-currency earner, with over ten million visitors from overseas in a good year. **Shipping**, which used to occupy second place, is in crisis and has been replaced by **agricultural products**, especially olive oil and olives, citrus, wine and raisins.

particularly out of Rhodes, Kálymnos, Lefkádha, Póros and Pireás; indeed, the Greek islands are rated on a par with the Caribbean for quality sailing itineraries. And during the months when the sea is too cold or the weather too blustery, many islands – not necessarily the largest ones – offer superb **hiking** on surviving mule-trails between hill villages, or up the highest summits.

Although more protected than the Greek mainland from invasions, the various archipelagos have been subject to a staggering variety of **foreign influences**. Romans, Arabs, Byzantines, crusading Knights of St John, Genoese, Venetians, French, English, Italians and Ottomans have all controlled different islands since the time of Alexander the Great. The high tide of empire has left behind countless **monuments**: frescoed Byzantine churches and monasteries, the fortified Venetian towns of the Cyclades and the Ionians, the more conventional castles of the Genoese and Knights in the northern and eastern Aegean and Dodecanese, Ottoman bridges and mosques, and the Art Deco or mock-Renaissance edifices of the Italian Fascist administration.

Constructions from many of these eras are often juxtaposed with – or even superimposed on – the cities and temples of ancient Greece, which provide the foundation in all senses for claims of an enduring Hellenic **cultural identity** down the centuries; museums, particularly on Crete, Corfu, Rhodes, Sámos, Híos, Lésvos and Límnos, amply document the archeological evidence. But it was medieval Greek peasants, fishermen and shepherds, working without an indigenous ruling class or formal Renaissance to impose models of taste or patronize the arts, who most tangibly contributed to our idea of Greekness with their songs and dances, costumes, weaving and vernacular architecture. Much of this has vanished in recent decades, replaced by an avalanche of electric-*bouzoúki*-instrumental cassettes, "genuine museum copies" and tacky souvenir shops, but enough remains in isolated pockets for visitors to marvel at Greek popular culture's combination of form and function.

Of course, most Greek-island visits are devoted to more hedonistic pursuits: going lightly dressed, swimming in balmy waters at dusk, talking and drinking under the stars until 3am. Such pleasures amply compensate for certain enduring weaknesses in the Greek **tourism "product"**: don't go expecting orthopedic mattresses, state-of-the-art plumbing, Cordon-Bleu cuisine or attentive service. Except at a limited number of upmarket facilities in new or restored buildings, hotel and *pension* rooms can be box-like, campsites tend to be of the rough-and-ready sort, and the food at its best is fresh and simply presented.

Boatyards

Even in the more touristed islands, a remarkable number of traditional boatyards (*karnáyia*) still survive. Small craft are built in the time-honoured way, with the keel and framework assembled first from seasoned pine – which abounds in Greek coastal regions – and then overlaid with planking. You can often spot *karnáyia* from some distance by the bright-orange *mínio*, or red-lead paint, applied to the exposed wood – long illegal in most of the EU but still the preservative of choice in Greece. Equipment can be low-tech and most techniques unchanged over centuries, with wooden trellising and launching rollers the rule; serious accidents caused by hulls lurching the wrong way at the wrong time are not unheard of.

The Greek islanders

To attempt an understanding of the islanders, it's useful to realize how recent and traumatic were the events that created the modern Greek state and **national character** – the latter a blend of extroversion and pessimism not entirely due to Greece's strategic position between the West and the Middle East.

Until the early 1900s, Crete, the east Aegean and the Dodecanese – nearly half the islands described in this book – remained under Ottoman or Italian rule. Meanwhile, many people from these "unredeemed" territories lived in Asia Minor, Egypt, western Europe or the northern Balkans. The Balkan Wars of 1912–13, Greece's 1917–18 World War I involvement fighting Bulgaria, the Greco-Turkish war of 1919–22, and the organized **population exchanges** which followed each of these conflicts had profound, brutal effects. Orthodox refugees from Turkey suddenly made up a noticeable proportion of the population of Crete and the northeast Aegean (especially Límnos, Lésvos and Sámos), and with the forced or voluntary departure of their Levantines, Muslims and (during World War II) Jews, these islands lost their multicultural traits.

Even before the last world war, the Italian occupation of the Dodecanese was characterized by progressively stricter suppression of Greek Orthodox identity, but in general the war years in most other island groups were not quite so dire as on the mainland. Neither was the 1946–49 civil war that followed, nor the 1967–74 dictatorship, so keenly felt out in the Aegean, though benign neglect was about the best many islands could expect until the 1960s. Given the chance to emigrate to Australia, Canada or Africa, many entrepreneurial islanders did so, continuing a trend of **depopulation** which ironically had accelerated earlier in the twentieth century, following political union of the northeast Aegean and Dodecanese with the Greek mainland. The uncomfortably close memory of catastrophe, continuing misrule and scarce opportunity at home spurred yet another diaspora.

The advent of **tourism** in the 1960s arguably saved a number of islands from complete desolation, though local attitudes towards this deliverance have been decidedly ambivalent. It galls local pride to have become a class of seasonal service personnel, and the encounter between outsiders and villagers has often been corrosive to a deeply conservative rural society. Though younger Greeks are happily adaptable as they rake in the proceeds at resort areas, tourists still need to be sensitive in their behaviour towards the older generation. The mind boggles imagining the reaction of black-clad elders to nude bathing, or even scanty apparel, in a country where – despite being increasingly out of step with majority sentiment – the Orthodox Church remains an all-but-established faith and self-appointed guardian of national identity. In the presence of ubiquitous Italian-style espresso bars, Internet cafés and ATMs, it's easy to be lulled into thinking that Greece became thoroughly European the moment it joined the EU – until a flock of sheep is paraded along the main street at high noon, and the 1pm ferry shows up at 3pm, or not at all.

Where to go

There is no such thing as a "typical" Greek island; each has its distinctive personality, history, architecture, flora – even a unique tourist clientele. Landscapes vary from the lush

Wayside shrines

Throughout Greece you'll see, by the side of the road, small shrines or *ikonostáses* which usually hold a saint's icon, an oil lamp, a few floatable wicks and a box of matches. Unlike in Latin America, they don't necessarily mark the spot where someone met their end in a motoring accident (though just occasionally they do); typically they were erected by a family or even one individual in fulfilment of a vow, or *támma* , to a particular saint to reciprocate for any favours granted, in particular being spared death in a road mishap. *Ikonostáses* come in various sizes and designs, from spindly, derrick-like metal constructions to sumptuous, gaily painted models of small cathedrals in marble and plaster which you can practically walk into. Often they indicate the presence of a larger but less convenient (and often locked) church off in the countryside nearby, dedicated to the same saint, and act as a substitute shrine where the devout wayfarer can reverence the icon it contains.

The Evil Eye

Belief in the Evil Eye (in Greek, simply *tó Máti* or "the Eye") is pan-Mediterranean and goes at least as far back as Roman times, but nowhere has it hung on so tenaciously as in Greece (and neighbouring coastal Turkey). In a nutshell, whenever something attractive, valuable or unusual – an infant, a new car, a prized animal – becomes suddenly, inexplicably indisposed, it is assumed to be *matisméno* or "eyed". Blue-eyed individuals are thought most capable of casting this spell, always unintentionally or at least unconsciously (unlike *máyia*, wilful black magic). The diagnosis is confirmed by discreet referral to a "wise woman", who is also versed in the proper counter-spell. But prevention is always better than cure, and this involves two main strategies. When admiring something or someone, the admirer – blue-eyed or otherwise – must mock-spit ("*phtoo, phtoo, phtoo!*") to counteract any stirrings of envy which, according to anthropologists, are the root-cause of the Eye. And the proud owners or parents will protect the object of admiration in advance with a blue amulet, hung about the baby's/animal's neck or the car's rear-view mirror, or even painted directly onto a boat-bow.

cypress-and-olive-swathed Ionians to the bare, wind-scoured ridges of the Cyclades and Dodecanese, by way of subtle gradations between these extremes in the Sporades and northeast Aegean. Setting aside the scars from a few unfortunate man-made developments, it would be difficult to single out an irredeemably ugly island; all have their adherents and individual appeal, described in the chapter introductions.

Perhaps the best strategy for initial visits is to sample assorted islands from contiguous archipelagos – Crete, the Dodecanese, the Cyclades and the northeast Aegean are all reasonably well connected with each other, though the Sporades, Argo-Saronic and Ionian groups offer limited (or no) possibilities for island-hopping, and usually involve a long traipse across the mainland to get to. If time and money are short, the best place to visit is well-preserved **Ídhra** in the Argo-Saronic Gulf, just a short ride from Pireás (the main port of Athens), but an utterly different place once the day-cruises have gone; neighbouring **Spétses** has similar architectural charm and more accessible beaches. Of the Sporades, **Skýros** and **Skópelos** remain the most traditional and aesthetic, with forests, pale-sand beaches and well-preserved capitals. Among the Cyclades, cataclysmically volcanic **Santoríni (Thíra)** and **Mýkonos** with its perfectly preserved harbour town rank as must-see spectacles, but fertile, mountainous **Náxos** and gently rolling **Sífnos** have life more independent of cruise-ship tourism and seem more amenable to long stays. For true aficionados, dramatically cliff-girt **Amorgós** or **Folégandhros**, rocky **Sýros** with its UNESCO-recognized harbour town, artistic **Tínos** or lonely **Anáfi** and its balmy, south-facing beaches are less obvious but equally satisfying choices. **Crete** could (and does) fill an entire Rough Guide to itself, but the highlights have to be **Knossos** and the nearby **archeological museum** in Iráklion, the other Minoan palaces at **Phaestos** and **Ayía Triádha**, and the west in general – **Réthymnon** with its intact old town, the proud city of **Haniá**, with its hinterland extending to the relatively unspoilt southwest coast, reachable via the fabled **Samarian Gorge**. **Rhodes**, with its unique old town, is capital of the Dodecanese, but picturesque, Neoclassical **Sými** opposite and austere **Pátmos**, the island of Revelation, are far more manageable. **Kárpathos**, marooned between Rhodes and Crete, has some of the best beaches and walking in the Dodecanese, while **Léros** and **Níssyros** will appeal to those looking for characterful, unspoilt islands that don't necessarily have superb coastline. From Pátmos or Léros, it's easy to continue north via **Sámos** – still one of the most attractive islands despite recent fires – and **Híos**, with striking medieval architecture, to balmy, olive-cloaked **Lésvos**, perhaps the most traditional of all islands in its way of life. The Ionian islands are, probably more than any other region except Crete and Rhodes, package-holiday territory, but if you're exiting Greece towards Italy, stop off at **Corfu** to savour the Venetian-style main town, which along with neighbouring **Paxí** islet escaped damage from the 1953 earthquake which devastated the southern Ionians. Little **Ith[á]ki**, easiest reached from the mainland, is relatively untouristed, given a lack of beaches, though big brother **Kefaloniá** is now well and truly in the spotlight owing to spectacular scenery – and exposure in Louis de Bernière's blockbuster novel, *Captain Corelli's Mandolin*.

When to go

Most islands and their inhabitants are far more agreeable, and resolutely Greek, outside the **busiest period** of early July to late August, when crowds of foreigners or locals, soaring temperatures and the effects of the infamous **meltémi** can detract considerably from enjoyment. The *meltémi* is a cool, fair-weather wind which originates in high-pressure systems over the far north Aegean, gathering momentum as it travels southwards and assuming near-gale magnitude by the time it reaches Crete. North-facing coasts there, and throughout the Cyclades and Dodecanese, bear the full brunt; its howling is less pronounced in the north or east Aegean, where continental landmasses provide some shelter for the islands just offshore. In the Ionian archipelago, an analogous northwest wind off the Adriatic is called the **maïstros**.

You won't miss out on **warm weather** if you come between late May and mid-June – when a wide variety of garden produce and fish is still available – or in September, when the sea is warmest for swimming, though at these times you'll find little activity on the northernmost islands of Thássos, Límnos and Samothráki. During October you'll probably hit a week's stormy spell, but for much of that month the "little summer of Áyios Dhimítrios", the Greek equivalent of **Indian summer**, prevails. While autumn choice in restaurants and nightlife can be limited, the light is softer, and going out at midday becomes a pleasure rather than an ordeal. The only black spot on visits from late August through September are swarms of **flies** and a few aggressive **wasps**, especially in districts with an appreciable grape harvest. The most reliable venues for late-autumn or early-winter breaks are Rhodes and relatively balmy southeastern Crete, where swimming in December is not unheard of.

December to March are the **coldest** and least comfortable months, particularly on the Ionian islands, typically the rainiest patch in Greece from November onwards (though global warming has meant recent wet summers as well). The high peaks of northerly or lofty islands wear a brief mantle of **snow** around the turn of the year, with Crete's mountainous spine staying partly covered into April. Between January and April the glorious lowland wild flowers start to bloom, beginning in the southeast Aegean. April weather is notoriously unreliable, though the air is crystal-clear and the landscape **green** – a photographer's dream. May is more settled, though the sea is still a bit cool for prolonged dips.

Other factors that affect the timing of a Greek-island visit have to do with the level of tourism and the related **amenities** provided. Service standards, particularly in tavernas, invariably slip under peak-season pressure, and room rates are at their highest from July to September. If you can only visit during midsummer, reserve a package well in advance, or plan an itinerary off the beaten track. Between November and April, you have to contend with pared-back ferry and plane schedules (and almost nonexistent hydrofoil or catamaran departures), plus skeletal facilities when you arrive. However, you will find fairly adequate services to the more populated islands, and at least one hotel and taverna open in the port or main town of all but the tiniest isles.

Average temperatures (°F) and rainfall (days)

	Jan Max	Jan Min	March Max	March Min	May Max	May Min	July Max	July Min	Sept Max	Sept Min	Nov Max	Nov Min
Crete (Haniá)	60	46	64	48	76	56	86	68	82	64	70	54
rainfall	17		11		5		0		3		10	
Cyclades (Mýkonos)	58	50	62	52	72	62	82	72	78	68	66	58
rainfall	14		8		5		0.5		1		9	
Ionian (Corfu)	56	44	62	46	74	58	88	70	82	64	66	52
rainfall	13		10		6		2		5		12	
Dodecanese (Rhodes)	58	50	62	48	74	58	86	70	82	72	68	60
rainfall	15		7		2		0		1		7	
Sporades (Skiáthos)	55	45	58	47	81	58	82	71	75	64	62	53
rainfall	12		10		3		0		8		12	
East Aegean (Lésvos)	54	42	60	46	76	60	88	70	82	66	64	50
rainfall	11		7		6		2		2		9	

things not to miss

It's not possible to see everything that the Greek Islands have to offer in one trip – and we don't suggest you try. What follows is a selective taste of the islands' highlights: outstanding buildings, superb ancient sites and natural wonders. They're arranged in five colour-coded categories, which you can browse through to find the very best things to see, and experience. All highlights have a page reference to take you straight into the Guide, where you can find out more.

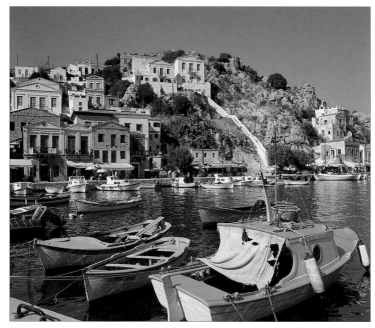

01 Harbour, Sými Page **319** • The mansions of Sými's picturesque harbour, built with wealth from the sponge trade, are part of an architecturally protected area.

02 Váï beach, Crete Page **249** • A superb beach, fringed by a wild date-palm grove.

03 Windsurfing off Vassilikí, Lefkádha Page **519** • Located in a vast, cliff-flanked bay, Vassilikí is one of Europe's biggest windsurf centres.

04 Hiking in the Samarian Gorge Page **272** • The magnificent Samarian Gorge is the longest in Europe.

xv

05 **Lindos acropolis, Rhodes** Page **306** • From the Hellenistic acropolis of Lindos, high above the modern village, you look north along the length of Rhodes island.

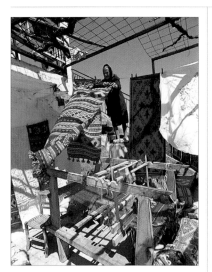

06 **Village weaver, near Lasíthi Plateau** Page **240** •
Traditional crafts, such as weaving and embroidery, still flourish in parts of Crete.

07 **Beaches and water-sports** Page **75** • Greece's expansive coast provides a multitude of opportunities for getting into the water, or just lying next to it.

08 Melissáni Cave, Kefaloniá Page 526 • Take a boat trip to the underwater Melissáni Cave, and admire the rock formations and play of light on the cave walls.

09 View over Firá Page 196 • The island capital of Firá is one of several villages that teeter at the edge of Santoríni caldera cliff.

10 Chapel of Metamórfosis, Dhíkeos peak, Kós
Page 343 • A hike up 846-metre Dhíkeos peak to the Metamórfosis chapel rewards you with excellent panoramic views.

ACTIVITIES | CONSUME | EVENTS | NATURE | SIGHTS |

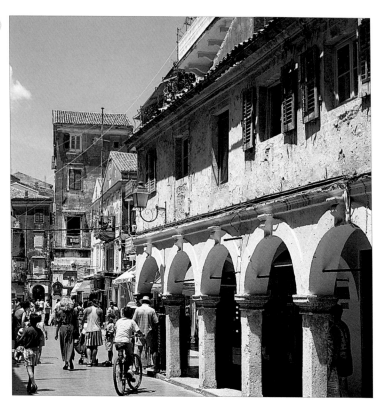

11 **Kérkyra (Corfu) old town** Page **494** • With its elegant Venetian architecture and fine museums, Corfu's capital is the cultural heart of the Ionians.

12 **Tomatoes drying, Híos** Page **407** • Strings of sun-drying tomatoes are a common sight in autumn in Híos's mastic villages.

13 Nightlife Page **64** • The after-dark scene in the most popular island resorts is lively, varied and long.

14 Getting out on the water Page **76** • The Greek archipelagos are an excellent place to sail, island-hop or simply spend a day on a boat.

15 Loggerhead sea turtle Page **541** • The Ionian islands harbour one of the Mediterranean's main concentrations of the endangered loggerhead sea turtle.

xix

16 Sámos Page **379** • Despite recent fires, Sámos remains arguably the most verdant and beautiful of the east Aegean islands.

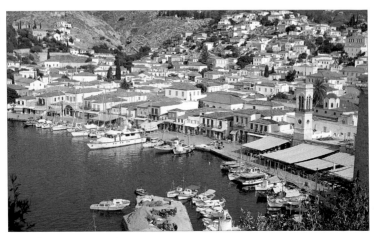

17 **Ídhra** Page **103** • Ídhra's perfect horseshoe-shaped harbour is surrounded by grand eighteenth-century mansions.

18 **Kárpathos: view south from Ólymbos village** Page **293** • The view south from windswept, remote Ólymbos gives a good idea of the rugged coast of unspoilt northern Kárpathos.

19 **Monastery of Ayíou Ioánnou Theológou, Pátmos** Page **367** • Built in honour of St John the Divine, this huge monastery is a warren of interconnecting courtyards, chapels, stairways, arcades, galleries and roof terraces.

20 Hozovio-tíssas monastery, Amorgós Page **184** • With its vast walls gleaming white at the base of a sheer orange cliff, the Hozoviotíssas monastery is a dramatic sight.

21 Greek food and wine Page **57** • Fresh and simple food and wine, enjoyed alfresco, are one of Greece's greatest pleasures.

22 Naoússa harbour, Páros Page **165** • Páros's second port, Naoússa is still very much a traditional working harbour.

23 Knossos palace, Crete Page 222 • The most restored, vividly coloured and ultimately the most exciting of Crete's Minoan palaces.

24 Temple of Aphaea, Égina Page 96 • The beautiful fifth-century-BC Temple of Aphaea is one of the most complete and visually complex ancient buildings in Greece.

25 Volcano floor, Níssyros Page **333** • No stay on Níssyros would be complete without a visit to the island's dormant volcano.

26 Haniá old town water-front, Crete Page **263** • Haniá displays haunting vestiges of its Venetian and Ottoman past.

27 Ápella beach, Kárpathos Page **293** • One of the most scenic of Kárpathos's east-coast beaches.

28 Longós, Paxí Page **514** • The prettiest coastal village on verdant, largely unspoilt Paxí.

29 Mólyvos, Lésvos Page **427** • The castle-crowned village of Mólyvos ranks as one of the most beautiful on Lésvos.

30 Dovecotes on Tínos Page **142** • Distinctive, ornate dovecotes, introduced by the Venetians, punctuate the island of Tínos.

Contents

Using this Rough Guide

We've tried to make this Rough Guide a good read and easy to use. The book is divided into five main sections, and you should be able to find whatever you want in one of them.

Color section

The front colour section offers a quick tour of the Greek Islands. The **introduction** aims to give you a feel for the islands, with suggestions on where to go. We also tell you what the weather is like and include a basic country fact file. Next, our authors round up their favourite aspects of the Greek Islands in the **things not to miss** section – whether it's great food, amazing sights or a special hotel. Right after this comes the Rough Guide's full **contents** list.

Basics

You've decided to go and the Basics section covers all the **pre-departure** nitty-gritty to help you plan your trip. This is where to find out which airlines fly to your destination, what paperwork you'll need, what to do about money and insurance, about Internet access, food, security, public transport, car rental – in fact just about every piece of **general practical information** you might need.

Guide

This is the heart of the Rough Guide, divided into user-friendly chapters, each of which covers a specific island group. Every chapter starts with a list of **highlights** and an **introduction** that helps you to decide where to go, depending on your time and budget. Likewise, introductions to the various towns and smaller areas within each chapter should help you plan your itinerary. We start most town accounts with information on arrival and accommodation, followed by a tour of the sights, and finally reviews of places to eat and drink, and details of nightlife. Longer accounts also have a directory of practical listings. Each chapter concludes with **public transport** details for that region.

Contexts

Read Contexts to get a deeper understanding of how Greece ticks. We include a brief **history**, articles about **wildlife** and **music**, together with a detailed further-reading section that reviews dozens of **books** relating to Greece and the islands.

Index + small print

Apart from a **full index**, which includes maps as well as places, this section covers publishing information, credits and acknowledgements, and also has our contact details in case you want to send in updates and corrections to the book – or suggestions as to how we might improve it.

Chapter list and map

Contents

Colour section i–xxiv

Basics 7–86

Guide 87–552

Contexts

CONTENTS

Language

small print and Index

Basics

Basics

Getting there

It's 2000 miles (or more) from the UK and Ireland to many points in Greece, so for most north European visitors flying is the only viable option. There are direct flights to a variety of Greek airports from all the major British airports; flying time is three and a half to four and a half hours, depending on your start point and Greek destination. Road or rail alternatives from the UK take a minimum of three days, and are only worth considering if you plan to visit Greece as part of an extended trip through Europe. The most popular route is down through Italy, then across to Greece by ferry. The old overland route through former Yugoslavia will remain tricky for the foreseeable future, but a much longer route via Hungary, Romania and Bulgaria is still possible.

Only two carriers currently fly direct to Greece from North America, so most North Americans travel to a gateway European city, then pick up an onward connecting flight with an associated airline. You may discover that it's cheaper to arrange the final Greece-bound leg of the journey yourself, in which case your only criterion will be finding a suitable, good-value North America–Europe flight; such onward flights from the UK are detailed on pp.10–13.

It's fairly easy to track down flights from Australia to Athens, less so from New Zealand. But given most people's travel plans, you might be better off with a Round-the-World (RTW) ticket that includes Greece. If London is your first destination in Europe, and you've picked up a reasonably good deal on a flight there, it's probably best to wait until you reach the UK before arranging your onward travel to Greece.

Airfares to Greece from Europe and North America always depend on the **season**, with the highest in effect from June to early September (plus Easter week), when the weather is best; fares drop during the "shoulder" seasons – April/May and late September/October – and you'll get the best prices during the low season, November to March (excluding Christmas and New Year weeks when prices are hiked up and seats are at a premium). Note also that flying on weekends from North America ordinarily adds $50 or so to the round-trip fare; price ranges quoted assume midweek travel.

Australian and New Zealand fares have their low season from mid-January to the end of February and October/November; high season is mid-May to August, plus December to mid-January; and shoulder season the rest of the year.

You can often cut costs by going through a **specialist flight agent** – either a consolidator, who buys up blocks of tickets from the airlines and sells them at a discount, or a **discount agent**, who in addition to dealing with discounted flights may also offer special student and youth fares and a range of other travel-related services such as travel insurance, rail passes, car rentals, tours and the like. Some UK agents specialize in **charter flights**, which may be cheaper than anything available on a scheduled flight, but again departure dates are fixed and withdrawal penalties are high. For Greece, you may even find it more cost-effective (especially from the UK) to pick up a **package deal**, with accommodation included, from one of the tour operators listed on p.14.

Booking flights online

Many airlines and discount travel websites offer you the opportunity to book your tickets online, cutting out the costs of agents and middlemen. **Good deals** can often be found through discount or auction sites, as well as through the airlines' own websites. Even if you don't end up actually buying your ticket online, the websites are worth a visit to clue you up on what the prevailing published economy fares are. However, the airlines' own sites tend to give you a choice of only nonchangeable/nonrefundable and full economy fares – for the numerous options in between, you'll have to ring them. The cheapest of the airlines' published fares, designated by a bewildering "alphabet soup" of capital letters, require a minimum stay of three days away, and over a Saturday night, with a typical maximum period of thirty or sixty days, and make you liable to penalties (including total loss of ticket value) if you miss your outbound departure or change your return date. Some airlines also issue "student" tickets to those under 26, often extending the maximum stay to a year. There is also a number of "Senior" or "Golden" fares available for those over 60. When exploring a quoted fare on a website, always click the "Rules" link – all conditions will be spelled out in small print.

Some of the general travel sites like Expedia or Travelocity offer substantially discounted "special bargain" fares – the problem with some of these is you don't get to see the scheduling, or the airlines used, until after you've bought the ticket. Any reputable site will have a secure, encrypted facility for making credit-card payments – if it doesn't, you're probably better off not using the site to purchase.

Online booking agents and general travel sites

Ⓦ **www.cheapflights.co.uk (UK & Ireland)**, **www.cheapflights.com** (US), **www.cheapflights.ca** (Canada) or **www .cheapflights.com.au** (Australia & New Zealand) The most comprehensive source of flight deals: not a booking site itself, but maintains links to the travel agents offering the deals.
Ⓦ **www.cheaptickets.com** Discount flight specialists (US only).
Ⓦ **www.etn.nl/discount.htm** A hub of consolidator and discount agent web links, maintained by the nonprofit European Travel Network.
Ⓦ **www.expedia.co.uk** (UK & Ireland), **www.expedia.com** (US) or **www.expedia.ca** (Canada) Discount airfares, all-airline search engine and daily deals.
Ⓦ **www.geocities.com/thavery2000** An extensive list of airline websites and US toll-free numbers.

Ⓦ **www.kelkoo.co.uk** Useful UK-only price-comparison site, checking several sources of low-cost flights (and other goods and services) according to specific criteria.
Ⓦ **www.lastminute.com** (UK & Ireland), **www.lastminute.com.au** (Australia) or **www.lastminute.co.nz** (New Zealand) Good holiday-package and flight-only deals available at very short notice.
Ⓦ **www.opodo.co.uk** Popular and reliable source of cheap UK airfares. Owned by, and run in conjunction with, nine major European airlines.
Ⓦ **www.priceline.co.uk** or **www.priceline.com** Bookings from the UK/US only. Name-your-own-price auction website that can knock around forty percent off standard website fares. You can't choose the airline or flight times (although you do specify dates) and the tickets are nonrefundable, nontransferable and nonchangeable.
Ⓦ **www.skyauction.com** Bookings from the US only. Auctions tickets and travel packages using a "second bid" scheme. The best strategy is to bid the maximum you're willing to pay, since if you win you'll pay just enough to beat the runner-up regardless of your maximum bid.
Ⓦ **www.travel.com.au** and **wwww.travel.co.nz** Australia t☎300 130 482 or 02/9249 5444, New Zealand ☎0800 468 332. Comprehensive online travel companies, with discounted fares.
Ⓦ **www.travelocity.co.uk** (UK & Ireland), **www.travelocity.com** (US) or **www.travelocity.ca** (Canada) Destination guides, hot web fares and deals for car rental, accommodation and lodging as well as fares.
Ⓦ **www.travelselect.com** A subsidiary of lastminute.com (see above) that is useful and fairly easy to use, but without most of the guff and banner adverts of the better-known sites. Linked to walk-in travel agency in the UK (London storefront) if you want to talk to a human.
Ⓦ **www.travelshop.com.au** Australian website offering discounted flights, packages, insurance and online bookings.
Ⓦ **www.zuji.com.au** Another Aussie site with destination guides, hot fares and great deals for car rental, accommodation and lodging.

Flights from the UK and Ireland

Most of the cheaper flights from Britain and Ireland to Greece are **charters**, which are sold either with a package holiday or (less commonly) as a flight-only option. The flights have fixed and unchangeable outward and

Connections at Athens airport

Missing connections at Eleftherios Venizelos Airport is a distinct possibility, due to the airport's poor internal signage and its enormous size (claimed third largest in the world). Mad dashes down nightmarishly endless concourses and up escalators (there are a few well-concealed lifts for luggage trolleys) add further stress.

Printed airport rules stipulate a minimum of 55 minutes between your incoming flight's arrival and onward flight's departure, but some airlines – for example Olympic – insist on a **minimum leeway** of 90 minutes. Given Olympic's habitual late arrivals, the carrying out of lengthy security checks even for transfer passengers and the fact that all aircraft for domestic flights are parked a very long shuttle-coach-ride distant on the runway, prudence would dictate observing this rule when buying fares. Some, but not all, ticketing systems won't let you book an itinerary if the layover is too short.

You may find (if desk staff in your departing country are in a cooperative mood) that you can have your **luggage checked through** to your final domestic destination, even if your international- and domestic-leg airlines are different. Do this at the outset as a precaution, and even if your inbound flight is hideously late, you stand a good chance of getting yourself and your carry-on to the end of your itinerary as planned, even if your checked baggage only shows up the next day.

return dates, and usually a maximum stay of four weeks.

For longer stays or more flexibility, or if you're travelling out of season (when few charters are available), you'll need a **scheduled flight** with a major airline. As with charters, these are offered under a wide variety of fares, and are again often sold off at a discount by agents. Useful advertisements for discounted flights are found in the weekend-supplement travel sections of newspapers like *The Independent*, *The Guardian*, *The Observer*, *The Telegraph* and *The Sunday Times*, as well as weekly listings magazines such as *Time Out*. So far the only no-frills airline serving Greece is easyJet; the main advantage in using them is the ability to secure economical one-way fares.

Although Athens remains the prime destination for cheap fares, there are also **direct flights** from Britain to (on the Greek mainland) Thessaloníki (for Thássos and the Sporades), Kavála (for Thássos and the northeast Aegean), Préveza (Áktio; for Lefkádha) and direct to the islands of Crete, Rhodes, Kós, Corfu, Mýkonos, Zákynthos, Kefalloniá, Skiáthos, Sámos, Santoríni, Lésvos and Límnos. With any flight to Athens, you can buy a **domestic connecting flight** on Olympic or Aegean Airlines to one of almost two dozen Greek island airports.

Charter flights

Travel agents throughout Britain sell **charter flights** to Greece, which usually operate from late April or early May to late October or early November (depending on destination); late-night departures and early-morning arrivals are common, though you may have a choice of more civilized hours. Even the high-street chains frequently promote "flight-only" deals, or discount all-inclusive holidays, when their parent companies need to offload their seat allocations. The main charter airlines which offer flight-only to Greece are Excel, Thomas Cook, and TUI; you can book tickets on these on the phone or through their websites, and you may find that flight-only deals are rare indeed at peak season. Round-trip purchases are usually mandatory, and four weeks away is generally the maximum period.

Compared to the cost of flights via Athens, you can pay dearly for the convenience of a direct service to the holiday island of your choice. **Sample return fares** at high season range from a reasonable £230 (Gatwick to Rhodes or Corfu) up to a hefty £300 (Manchester to Zákynthos or Kefalloniá, Gatwick to Lésvos). Sámos is even pricier at £240–340 from Gatwick, depending on season. For many islands, you may well find two-stop scheduled services via Athens are much cheaper.

The greatest variety of **flight destinations** tends to be from London Gatwick and Manchester. In summer, if you book in advance, you should have a choice of most of the Greek regional airports listed above. Flying from elsewhere in Britain (Birmingham, Bristol, Cardiff, East Midlands, Luton, Stansted, Glasgow or Newcastle), or looking for last-minute discounts, you'll find options more limited, most commonly to Athens, Corfu, Rhodes, Kós and Crete.

Summer charters operate **from Dublin and Belfast** to Athens and there are additional services to Mýkonos, Rhodes, Crete and Corfu. A high-season charter from Dublin to Athens costs upwards of €317 return, while a week's package on one of the above islands costs from €635 per person for two weeks.

If you travel to Greece on a charter flight, you may visit another, **non-EU country** (eg Turkey) only as a day-trip; if you stay overnight, you will possibly invalidate your ticket. This rule is justified by the Greek authorities because they subsidize charter airline landing fees, and are therefore reluctant to see tourists spending their money outside Greece. Whether you go along with that rationale or not, there is no way around it, since the Turkish authorities clearly stamp all passports, and the Greeks usually check them. We have, however, had reports of charter-flight-only patrons flying to Kós, happily spending a week in Turkish Bodrum, and then returning without incident, but it would be wise to double-check if the rule is still in effect.

Student/youth charters can be sold as one-way flights only. By combining two one-way charters you can, therefore, stay for over a month. Student/youth charter tickets are available to anyone under 26, and to all card-carrying full-time students under 32.

Finally, remember that **reconfirmation** of return charter flights is vital and should be done at least 72 hours before departure. If you've travelled out with a package company, this service will usually be included as part of the rep's duties, but you should not assume that it has been done. Personal

visits to the airline's representative office are best, as phone numbers given on ticket wallets are typically constantly engaged.

Scheduled flights

The advantages of some **scheduled flights** are that they can be booked well in advance, have longer ticket validities (from thirty days up to a year), involve fewer of the typical restrictions applicable to charters, and often leave at more pleasant hours. However, many of the cheaper, short-duration fares do have minimum/weekend-stay requirements, and also severe restrictions on date changes or refunds hardly different from charters. As with charters, discount fares on scheduled flights are available from high-street travel agents, as well as from a number of specialist flight and student/youth agencies – though it's always well worth contacting the airlines direct, using the telephone numbers and websites on opposite page. Most airlines offer per-person discounts of £5–10 for booking return journeys on their website, with e-confirmation and e-ticketing to the fax or email address of your choice. Unlike charters, scheduled tickets usually don't require reconfirmation for the return leg. As of writing, there are no direct scheduled services to any Greek island from Britain or Ireland, though Rhodes, Corfu and Crete are often mooted to receive some in the future.

The national carrier **Olympic Airways**, notorious as the least punctual airline in the skies, was forced to scale back operations between the UK and Greece in 2003–04. They now offer just two daily services (noon and late afternoon) from London Heathrow to Athens, as well as two weekly red-eye flights to Athens from Manchester, and four to five weekly evening departures from London Gatwick to Thessaloníki. **British Airways** still offers two to three daily flights from Heathrow to Athens (most mornings, plus always noon and evening), as well as one morning flight from Gatwick in summer. Both airlines have a range of fares (Olympic is usually slightly more expensive), and even in July and August, discount flight agents or websites (including BA's own) can come up with deals, valid for sixty days away, for as low as £170 return, including tax; more realistically, you'll pay around £220 return during high season from London, £300 from Manchester. It may be worth avoiding the very lowest fare tiers if you want to be flexible, as no return date changes are allowed on these. In the spring (except around Easter) or autumn, return fares to Athens run to about £150 including taxes, and in winter dip to about £125. As this route is common-rated between these airlines, you'll also be able to book onward connections simultaneously to domestic Greek airports, though discounts will apply only if using Olympic on all legs of the journey. Note that flights from British regional airports route through Heathrow in the first instance, with a supplement applicable (£70–80). Olympic has a code-sharing partnership with bmi (see opposite), which should ease the pain (and possibly the cost) of connections from Scotland and the north of England in particular.

Olympic and British have both lost business to a pair of relative newcomers, easyJet and Hellas Jet. Potentially the cheapest, no-frills service is provided by **easyJet**, with several flights daily out of Luton and Gatwick to Athens; fares vary from £29 to £159 one way, tax included, with the exact amount depending on the season, how far in advance you book and availability for the particular flight – a last-minute booking for three weeks from the end of August will probably result in a combined return fare of £210, over Christmas/New Year's £290. Departures also vary with time of year, but typically there are two daily from Luton, in the early afternoon and late in the evening, and at least one from Gatwick in the early morning, with an additional early evening flight April to October. While there's no on-board meal service (although drinks and snacks are sold), you can change your ticket after booking for a small fee, provided space is available.

The newest airline on the scene is **Hellas Jet**, a subsidiary of Cyprus Airways which began operations in 2003 and quickly garnered a reputation for decent service and competitive fares. They offer a daily red-eye service from Heathrow to Athens, as well as a somewhat pricier but very convenient daily late morning service from Gatwick. Their fares run from £95–120 in low season to £210 in high season.

Irish travellers will find year-round scheduled services with **Aer Lingus** and British Airways operating from both Dublin and Belfast via Heathrow or Manchester to Athens, or from Dublin via Heathrow on **bmibaby** and Olympic, but you'll find them pricey compared to charters. Travelling to London and buying a separate ticket when you get there is an alternative if direct flights from Ireland are in short supply, and may sometimes save you a little money, but on the whole it's rarely worth the time and effort. Budget flights to London from Ireland are offered by bmibaby, Aer Lingus and Ryanair.

Scheduled airlines

Aer Lingus UK ☎0845 084 4444, Republic of Ireland ☎0818 365 000, ⊕www.aerlingus.com.
bmi ☎0870 607 0555, ⊕www.flybmi.com.
bmibaby UK ☎0870 264 2229, Republic of Ireland ☎01/435 0011, ⊕www.bmibaby.com.
British Airways UK ☎0870 850 9850, Republic of Ireland ☎1800 626 747, ⊕www.ba.com.
easyJet ☎0870 000 000, ⊕www.easyjet.com.
Hellas Jet ☎0870 751 7222, ⊕www.hellas-jet.com.
Olympic Airways ☎0870 606 0460, ⊕www.olympic-airways.co.uk.
Ryanair UK ☎0871 246 0000, Republic of Ireland ☎0818 303 030, ⊕www.ryanair.com.

Flight and travel agents in the UK and Republic of Ireland

Aran Travel International Galway ☎091/562595. Good-value flights to all parts of the world.
Avro ☎0870 458 2841, ⊕www.avro.co.uk. Seat-only sales on flights to Corfu, Crete (Iráklion and Haniá) and Rhodes from most UK airports.
Excel Airways ☎0870 998 9898, ⊕www.excelairways.com. Flight-onlys to almost every major charter-served airport in Greece, mostly from Gatwick and Manchester but often Glasgow, Birmingham and East Midlands as well.
Flightline International ☎0870 040 1757, ⊕www.flightlineinternational.com. A general search agency, not linked to a particular company. Will find just about any flight-only charter offered out of British and Irish airports to Greece, with quotes and buying facility.
Greece & Cyprus Travel Centre ☎0121/355 6955, ⊕www.greece-cyprus.co.uk. Competent flight consolidator for Olympic and Hellas Jet in

particular; a myriad of fares to suit every need, including one-ways.

Joe Walsh Tours Dublin ☎01/676 0991, ⓦwww.joewalshtours.ie. General budget fares agent.

McCarthys Travel Republic of Ireland ☎021/427 0127, ⓦwww.mccarthystravel.ie. General flight agent.

North South Travel ☎01245/608291, ⓦwww.northsouthtravel.co.uk. Friendly, competitive flight agency, offering discounted fares worldwide – profits are used to support projects in the developing world, especially the promotion of sustainable tourism.

Rosetta Travel Belfast ☎028/9064 4996, ⓦwww.rosettatravel.com. Flight and holiday agent, specializing in deals direct from Belfast.

STA Travel ☎0870 160 0599, ⓦwww.statravel.co.uk. Worldwide specialists in low-cost flights and tours for students and under-26s. A dozen branches across England, especially on or near university campuses.

Thomas Cook ☎0870 750 0316, ⓦwww.thomascook.com. Good selection of flight-onlys to Corfu, Kefalloniá, Zákynthos, Kós, Lésvos, Santoríni, Skiáthos, Sámos and Rhodes from a half-dozen UK airports.

Thomson ☎0870 165 0079, ⓦwww .thomson-holidays.com. Limited flight-only deals to Corfu, Rhodes, Iráklion (Crete), Zákynthos, Kós, Sámos, Kefalloniá, Skiáthos and Kavála (for Thássos) on TUI, its parent-company airline.

Trailfinders UK ☎020/7938 3939, ⓦwww.trailfinders.com; Republic of Ireland ☎01/677 7888, ⓦwww.trailfinders.ie. One of the best-informed and most efficient agents for independent travellers; branches in all the UK's largest cities, plus Dublin.

Packages and tours

Virtually every British **tour operator** includes Greece in its programme, though with many of the larger, cheap-and-cheerful outfits you'll find choices limited to the established resorts – notably the islands of Rhodes, Kós, Lésvos, Crete, Skiáthos, Zákynthos and Corfu. If you buy one of these at a last-minute discount, especially in spring or autumn, you may find it costs little more than a flight – and you can use the accommodation included as much or as little as you want.

For a more low-key and genuinely "Greek" resort, however, it's better to book your holiday through one of the **specialist agencies**

listed below. Most of these are fairly small-scale operations, providing competitively priced packages with flights (unless otherwise stated) and often more traditional village-based accommodation. They also make an effort to offer islands without overdeveloped tourist resorts. Such agencies tend to divide into two types: those which, like the major chains, contract a block of accommodation and flight seats (or even their own plane) for a full season, and an increasing number of bespoke agencies which tailor holidays at your request, making all transport and accommodation arrangements on the spot. These can work out somewhat more expensive, but the quality of flights and lodging is often correspondingly higher.

The **walking** holiday operators listed opposite either run trekking groups of ten to fifteen people plus an experienced guide, or provide customers with a printed, self-guiding itinerary, and arranged accommodation at the end of each day. Walks tend to be day-long hikes from one or more bases, or point-to-point treks staying in village accommodation en route. Camping out is not usually involved.

Sailing holidays usually involve small flotillas of four- to eight-berth yachts, stopping at different anchorages each night, or are shore-based, with instruction in small-craft handling. All levels of experience are catered for. Prices start at around £415 per person, flights included, in a group of four on a thirty-foot boat for a one-week flotilla. Alternatively, confident sailors can simply arrange to charter a yacht from the designated agencies below.

Villa or village accommodation holidays

Cachet Travel ☎020/8847 3847, ⓦwww.cachet-travel.co.uk. Attractive range of villas and apartments, in the more unspoilt south and west of Crete, plus Sámos.

CV Travel ☎0870 787 9712, ⓦwww.cvtravel .co.uk. Quality villas, mostly on Corfu and Paxí but also Itháki, Spétses, Pátmos, Alónissos, Crete and Thíra.

Direct Greece ☎0870 516 8683, ⓦwww.direct -greece.co.uk. Moderately priced villas, apartments and restored houses on Rhodes, Hálki, Kálymnos, Kefalloniá, Lésvos, Corfu, Lefkádha, Santoríni and Crete.

Greek Islands Club Ⓦwww
.greekislandsclub.com. Extremely high-quality villas
throughout the Ionian and Sporades islands; also
Pátmos, Thíra and Crete.
Greek Sun Holidays ℡01732/740317
Ⓦwww.greeksun.co.uk. Good-value package
holidays in the Dodecanese, northeast Aegean and
Cyclades; also tailor-made island-hopping itineraries.
Hidden Greece/Simply Simon ℡020/7839
2553 Ⓦwww.hidden-greece.co.uk. Two bespoke
agencies, each running for forty-plus years, have
joined forces, arranging accommodation on and
transport to 35 less-visited islands in the Cyclades,
northeast Aegean and Dodecanese.
Island Wandering ℡01580/860733, Ⓦwww
.islandwandering.com. Tailor-made island-hopping
itineraries between most Greek archipelagos; deals
range from prebooked accommodation only (this
tends to be on the basic side) to mini-tours, with
local ferry or air transfers arranged.
Laskarina Holidays ℡01629/822203,
Ⓦwww.laskarina.co.uk. Top-end villas, quality hotels
and restored houses on Skópelos, Alónissos, Hálki,
Sými, Tílos, Kálymnos, Télendhos, Léros, Lipsí,
Pátmos, Ikaría and Sámos; excellent customer service.
Planet Holidays ℡0870 066 0909,
Ⓦwww.planet-holidays.net. Four- and five-star
hotels on the most popular islands.
Pure Crete ℡020/8760 0879, Ⓦwww
.pure-crete.com. Characterful, converted cottages
and farmhouses in western Crete.
Skopelos Villas ℡01689/877938,
Ⓦwww.skopelos-villas.co.uk. Villa holidays on
Skópelos and Skiáthos.
Sunvil Holidays ℡020/8568 4499,
Ⓦwww.sunvil.co.uk/greece. Durable and
consistently high-quality outfit specializing in
upmarket hotels and villas in the Ionian islands, the
Sporades, western Crete, Límnos, Sámos, Ikaría and
Pátmos. Also walking holidays on Amorgós.
Tapestry Holidays ℡020/8235 7788, Ⓦwww
.tapestryholidays.com. Top-rated Turkey specialists
now branched out into quality villas, hotels and
restoration inns on Kefalloniá, Skópelos and Itháki.
Travel à la Carte ℡01635/863030,
Ⓦwww.travelalacarte.co.uk. Established Corfu
specialist, now diversified into beach and rural villas
on Hálki, Paxí and Sými as well.
Travelux ℡01580/765000,
Ⓦwww.travelux.co.uk. Long-established Lefkádha
and Meganíssi villa specialists.

Walking and horse-riding holidays

ATG Oxford ℡01865/315678, Ⓦwww
.atg-oxford.co.uk. Somewhat pricey but high-
standard guided walks on Crete and Náxos.

Equitour ℡01993/849489, Ⓦwww.equitour
.co.uk. Horse-riding holidays on Corfu.
Exodus ℡020/8675 5550, Ⓦwww.exodus.co.uk.
One-week treks on Évvia/Skýros, or the White
Mountains of Crete; also sail-walk two-week tours
through the Cyclades and one week multi-activity
trips.
Explore Worldwide ℡01252/760 000,
Ⓦwww.exploreworldwide.com. Treks on Crete and
Corfu; also island-wanderer trips, mostly in the
Cyclades, mixing *kaïki*-sailing with light walking
ashore.
Jonathan's Tours Ⓦwww.jonathanstours.com.
Family-run walking holidays on Crete (where
Jonathan has 15 years' experience), Sámos, Lésvos
and Lefkádha.
Ramblers Holidays ℡01707/331133,
Ⓦwww.ramblersholidays.co.uk. Walking holidays
on Crete and Sámos.
Sherpa Expeditions ℡020/8577 2717,
Ⓦwww.sherpa-walking-holidays.co.uk. Self-
guiding itineraries on Kefalloniá/Itháki and Crete.
Walks Worldwide ℡01524/262255,
Ⓦwww.walksworldwide.com. Escorted treks on
Corfu.

Nature and wildlife holidays

Marengo Guided Walks ℡01485/532710,
Ⓦwww.marengowalks.com. Annually changing
programme of easy walks guided by ace botanist
Lance Chilton; typical one-week offerings may
include Sámos, Sými, Kálymnos, northern Lésvos,
Crete and Thássos.
Naturetrek ℡01962/733051, Ⓦwww.naturetrek
.co.uk. Fairly pricey but expertly led one- or two-
week natural history tours; past island offerings have
included springtime birds and flora on Sámos.

Sailing holidays

Nautilus Yachting ℡01732/867445, Ⓦwww
.nautilus-yachting.co.uk Bareboat yacht charter out
of Athens, Corfu, Lefkádha, Kós, Rhodes, Sámos and
Skiáthos; also flotilla holidays from Lefkádha.
Seafarer Cruising & Sailing ℡020/7406 1747,
Ⓦwww.seafarercruises.com. Seven-day set cruises
in the central Aegean on motor-sailers/motor-yachts;
also a different itinerary on a luxurious larger craft.
Setsail Holidays ℡01737/764443,
Ⓦwww.setsail.co.uk. Bareboat charters across the
country, flotillas from Póros along the Peloponnesian
coast.
Sportif ℡01273/844919, Ⓦwww.sportif-uk.com.
Windsurfing packages on Kós, Rhodes and
Kárpathos. Instruction clinics in conjunction with
nearby accommodation.

Sunsail ☏ 023/9222 2222, ⊛ www.sunsail.com. Resort-based tuition in dinghy sailing, yachting and windsurfing at five locations in Greece, mostly in the Ionian islands; one- or two-week flotilla sailings, good facilities for nonsailing children.
Templecraft ☏ 01273/812333, ⊛ www.templecraft.com. Bareboat charters across the Ionians, out of Rhodes for the Dodecanese, and out of Athens for the Argo-Saronic islands.

Special interest holidays

The Greek Experience ☏ 023/9283 0312, ⊛ www.greekexperience.com. Folk dance, art, creative writing and Greek language workshops on Kýthira.
Peligoni Club ☏ 01243/511499, ⊛ www.peligoni.com. Painting, yoga, Pilates, photography workshops based on a scattered cluster of villas and cottages in northern Zákynthos.
Skyros Holidays ☏ 020/7267 4424, ⊛ www.skyros.com. Holistic health, fitness, crafts and "personal growth" holidays at two centres on the island of Skýros, as well as prestigious writers' workshops tutored by big names.

By rail from the UK, Ireland and the rest of Europe

Travelling **by train** from Britain or Ireland to Greece takes two and a half to three and a half days and fares work out vastly more expensive than flights. However, with an InterRail or Eurail Pass you can take in Greece as part of a wider train trip around Europe.

Routes

The most practical route from Britain crosses France and Italy before embarking on the ferry from Bari or Brindisi to Pátra (Patras) or Corfu (Kérkyra). Book seats well in advance, especially in summer (for ferry information, see the box on pp.18–19).

Until 1990, the all-overland route through **former Yugoslavia** was the most popular; for obvious reasons this is a nonstarter for the foreseeable future, recent hopeful developments in Serbia notwithstanding. A more roundabout alternative from Budapest runs via **Bucharest** and **Sofia** to **Thessaloníki**, which is advised as your first Greek stop, since Athens is six to seven hours further on the train.

It is not possible to buy a through train **ticket** from Britain to Greece; should you attempt to piece together the various sectors (London–Paris, Paris–Italy, Italy–Greece), you'll find that just outbound exceeds £300. It is actually much cheaper to cross Europe on an InterRail pass (see below), and if you wish to return by land (rather than flying back one-way on easyJet) to purchase another InterRail pass in Greece.

Rail passes

An **InterRail pass** offers unlimited travel (except for express-train supplements and reservation fees) on a zonal basis with 28 European rail networks. These passes are only available to **European residents**, and you will be asked to provide proof of residency before being allowed to purchase one. The passes come in over-26 and (cheaper) under-26 versions; you can save £5 by booking via the InterRail website ⊛ www.inter-rail.co.uk

To reach Greece from the UK you'll need a one-month pass valid for at least two zones; Greece falls in Zone G, together with Italy, Turkey and Slovenia, plus many of the Italy–Greece ferries (though not out of Venice). To reach Italy from Britain, you'll need to purchase a Zone E pass to cross France; to reach northern Greece via central Europe, you'll need so many other zones (C, D and H) that you'll be obliged to buy an all-zone pass. InterRail passes do not allow free travel between Britain and the continent, although they make you eligible for discounts on rail travel in Britain and Northern Ireland, the cross-Channel ferries, and the London–Paris Eurostar service.

For North Americans, Australians and New Zealanders, a **Eurail Pass** will not pay for itself if you're planning to stick to Greece. This pass, which must be purchased before arrival in Europe, allows unlimited free first-class train travel in Greece and sixteen other countries, and is available in increments of fifteen days, 21 days, one month, two months and three months. If you're under 26, you can save money with a Eurail Youthpass, which is valid for second-class travel or, if you're travelling with one to four other companions, a joint Eurail Saverpass, both of which are available in the same increments as the Eurail Pass. You stand a better chance of getting your money's worth out of a Eurail Flexipass, which is good for ten or fifteen days' travel within a two-month period. This, too, comes in first-class, under-26/second-class (Eurorail Youth Flexipass) and group (Eurail Saver Flexipass) versions.

Rail contacts

UK and Ireland

The Man in Seat 61 ⓦ www.seat61.com. Named after British rail buff Mark Smith's favourite seat on the Eurostar, this noncommercial site expertly offers practical advice for planning a train journey from the UK to just about anywhere in Eurasia. You can't buy tickets here, but all the necessary links are provided.
Rail Europe UK ☏ 0870 584 8848, ⓦ www .raileurope.co.uk. Discounted rail fares for under-26s on a variety of European routes; also agents for InterRail and Eurostar.

North America

DER Travel ☏ 1-888 337-7350, ⓦ www.dertravel.com/rail. Eurail and many individual country passes.
European Rail Services Canada ☏ 1-800 205-5800 or 416/695-1211, ⓦ www.europeanrailservices.com. Eurail and many individual country passes.
Europrail International Inc Canada ☏ 1-888 667-9734, ⓦ www.europrail.net. Eurail, and many individual country passes.
Rail Europe US ☏ 1-877 257-2887, Canada ☏ 1-800 361-RAIL, ⓦ www.raileurope.com. Official North American Eurail Pass agent; also sells most single-country passes.

Australia and New Zealand

CIT World Travel Australia ☏ 02/9267 1255 or 03/9650 5510, ⓦ www.cittravel.com.au. Eurail rail passes.
Rail Plus Australia ☏ 1300 555 003 or 03/9642 8644, ⓦ ww.railplus.com.au. Sells Eurail passes.
Trailfinders Australia ☏ 02/9247 7666, ⓦ www.trailfinder.com.au. All European passes.

By car from the UK and Ireland

If you have the time and inclination, **driving to Greece** can be a pleasant proposition. Realistically, though, it's really only worth considering if you have at least a month to spare, are going to stay in Greece for an extended period, or want to take advantage of various stopovers en route. The most popular route is down through France and Italy to catch one of the Adriatic ferries. A longer alternative through eastern Europe (Hungary, Romania and Bulgaria) is just about feasible.

The fastest way to get across to the continent is the **Eurotunnel** service via the Channel Tunnel; the alternative is one of the time-honoured ferry crossings (see below). Eurotunnel operates shuttle trains 24 hours a day, for cars, motorcycles, buses and their passengers. The service runs continuously between Folkestone and Coquelles, near Calais, with up to four departures per hour (only one per hour midnight–6am) and takes 35min (45min for some night departure times), though you must arrive at least 30min before departure. It is possible to turn up and buy your ticket at the toll booths (after exiting the M20 at junction 11a), though at busy times booking is advisable. **Rates** depend on the time of day, time of day and length of stay; it's cheaper to travel between 10pm and 6am, while the highest fares are reserved for weekend departures and returns in July and August. For current information, contact the Eurotunnel Customer Services Centre at ☏ 0870 535 3535, ⓦ www.eurotunnel.com.

The traditional cross-Channel options for most travellers are the **ferry or hovercraft** links between Dover and Calais or Boulogne (the quickest and cheapest routes), Ramsgate and Dunkerque, or Newhaven and Dieppe. Irish drivers will prefer routes bypassing Britain, direct to Roscoff or Cherbourg, or from the southwest of England to St-Malo or Caen.

Ferry prices vary according to the time of year and, for motorists, the size of your car. The Dover–Calais/Boulogne runs, for example, start at about £245–340 open return for a car with up to five passengers, though this range can nearly double in peak season.

Ferries crossing the Channel and the Irish Sea

Brittany Ferries UK ☏ 08705 360360, ⓦ www.brittanyferries.com; Republic of Ireland

021/427 7801, www.brittanyferries.ie. Portsmouth to Caen, St Malo or Cherbourg; Poole to Cherbourg; Plymouth to Roscoff; Cork to Roscoff.
Hoverspeed UK 0870 240 8070, www.hoverspeed.co.uk. Dover to Calais; Newhaven to Dieppe.
Irish Ferries Britain 0870 517 1717, Northern Ireland 0800 018 2211, Republic of Ireland 1890 313 131, www.irishferries.com. Dublin to Holyhead; Rosslare to Pembroke, Cherbourg and Roscoff.
P&O Ferries UK 0870 520 2020, www.poferries.com. Dover to Calais; Hull to

Zeebrugge (Belgium); Portsmouth to Cherbourg; Portsmouth to Le Havre.
P&O Irish Sea UK 0870 242 4777, Republic of Ireland 1800 409 049, www.poirishsea.com. Larne to Cairnryan; Larne to Troon; Larne to Fleetwood; Dublin to Liverpool; Dublin to Mostyn; Dublin to Cherbourg; Rosslare to Cherbourg.
P&O Stena Line 0870 600 0600, www.posl.com. Dover to Calais.
Sea France 0870 571 1711, www.seafrance.com. Dover to Calais.
Stena Line 0870 570 7070, Republic of Ireland 01/204 7777, www.stenaline.co.uk. Rosslare

Italy–Greece ferries

Note: all timings are approximate.

From Ancona ANEK to Pátra (20hr 30min) usually via Igoumenítsa (15hr), 5 weekly Jan–March, almost daily April–Dec with ANEK; Blue Star daily except Tues year-round to Igoumenítsa (15hr) and Pátra (21hr), daily year-round direct to Pátra (19hr); Minoan to Pátra (20hr 30min) via Igoumenítsa (15hr), daily May–Oct; Superfast daily year-round to Igoumenítsa (15hr) and Pátra (21hr), or direct to Pátra (19hr). Sailings at 1.30pm, 4.30pm, 5pm, 7pm.

From Bari Minoan to Pátra (14hr) via Igoumenítsa (8hr), sometimes via Corfu, daily mid-June to mid-Sept; Superfast daily year-round to Igoumenítsa (9hr 30min) and Pátra (15hr 30min); Ventouris to Igoumenítsa (11hr 30min) via Corfu (10hr), up to 6 weekly June–Sept, 3 weekly otherwise, sailings at 4pm, 8pm on Minoan and Superfast; Ventouris highly variable at 7–11pm.

From Brindisi Agoudimos to Igoumenítsa, 6 weekly most of year (8hr); Blue Star almost daily year-round to Corfu (7hr) and Igoumenítsa (8hr 30min); Fragline to Corfu/Igoumenítsa (8–9hr 30min) almost daily April to early Oct; Med Link Lines to Pátra (10hr direct) via Kefaloniá (11hr), every other day April–Sept, 4–6 weekly July & Aug.

There's a fairly even division between late-morning and late-evening departures, with slightly faster craft on the daytime sailings. Agoudimos departs at 10am or 9pm, Blue Star at 10.30am most days, Fragline at 8.30–9pm and Med Link at 7–8pm.

From Trieste ANEK to Igoumenítsa (24hr) and Pátra (32hr), 4 weekly mid-Oct to mid-April, daily except Thurs otherwise, also via Corfu (26hr). Variable departure from Trieste 1pm–7pm.

From Venice Blue Star to Igoumenítsa (24hr 30min) and Pátra (34hr), 4 weekly year-round, also calling at Corfu April–Dec; Minoan to the same ports (20hr 30min and 28hr 30min respectively on high-speed craft), also stopping at Corfu, daily May–Oct. Departures at noon or 7pm on Blue Star, 3pm on Minoan.

Sample fares
Prices below are one-way high/low season fares, port taxes included. Substantial reductions apply on many lines from Ancona, Brindisi or Bari for both InterRail or Eurail pass-holders, and for those under 26. Discounts of 30–50 percent are usually available on return tickets, even in peak season. Many companies allow you to sleep in your van on board, sparing you the cost of a cabin berth; ask about reduced "camping" fares.

Igoumenítsa from Bari or Brindisi: deck class €40–46/22–24; car from €48–56/20–22.

Fishguard; Dun Laoghaire or Dublin to Holyhead;
Belfast to Stranraer.

Via Italy

For motorists heading for the Ionian islands,
it has always made most sense to drive **via
Italy** – and whatever your final destination,
taking a ferry on the final leg makes for a
more relaxed journey. Initial routes down to
Italy through **France** and **Switzerland** are
very much a question of personal taste. One

of the most direct is Calais–Reims–Geneva–
Milan and then down the Adriatic coast to
the Italian port of your choice. Even on the
quickest autoroutes (with their accompanying tolls), the journey will involve two
overnight stops.

Once in **Italy**, you've a choice of five
ports. Regular car and passenger ferries link
Ancona, Bari and Brindisi with Igoumenítsa
(the port of Epirus in western Greece) and/or
Pátra (at the northwest tip of the
Peloponnese and the closest port to

Pátra from Ancona: deck class €68–80/52–80; car from €98–108/66–74.
Pátra from Bári: deck class €56/34; car from €67/36.
Pátra from Brindisi: deck class €50/40; car from €55/35.
Pátra from Trieste: deck class €68/52; car from €98/72.
Pátra from Venice: deck class €64/46; car from €112/61.

Italian agents
The dialling code for Italy is ☎39; when ringing from overseas you must include
the initial '0' of the local area code.
Agoudimos Brindisi: c/o Hellas Ferry Lines, ☎ & ℱ0831/548044.
ANEK Ancona: Stazione Marittima ☎071/207 2275; Trieste: Via Rossini 2
☎040/322 0561, ℱ322 0142.
Blue Star Brindisi: ☎0831/548 115; Ancona: Stazione Marittima ☎ & ℱ071/207
0218; Venice: Stazione Marittima 123 ☎041/277 0559, ℱ277 0367.
Fragline Brindisi: Costa Morena ☎ & ℱ0831/548 318.
Med Link Lines Brindisi: c/o Discovery Shipping, Costa Morena ☎ & ℱ0831/548 116.
Minoan Lines Ancona: Via Astagno 3 ☎071/201 708, ℱ201 933; Bari: c/o P.
Santelia, Via Latilla 15 ☎080/521 0266, ℱ528 9716; Venice: Stazione Marittima
123 ☎041/2407177, ℱ2447503.
Superfast Ferries Ancona: Via XXIX Settembre 2/0 ☎071/202 033, ℱ202 219;
Bari: Corso A. de Tullio 6 ☎080/521 1416, ℱ572 0427.
Ventouris Bari: c/o P. Lorusso & Co, Stazione Marittima Booths 18–20
☎080/5217609, ℱ5217734.

Ferries on the Internet
All of the shipping companies have websites, as given below. Viamare Travel Ltd
(☎020/7431 4560, ⓦwww.viamare.com) is the UK agent for most of these
companies.
Agoudimos Lines ⓦwww.agoudimos-lines.com
ANEK ⓦwww.anek.gr
Blue Star ⓦwww.bluestarferries.com
Fragline ⓦwww.fragline.gr
Med Link Lines ⓦwww.mll.gr
Minoan Lines ⓦwww.minoan.gr
Superfast ⓦwww.superfast.com
Ventouris ⓦwww.ventouris.grto

Athens). Most sail via the island of Corfu, and most years one company calls at Kefailoniá en route to Pátra during July and August (southbound) only; you can stop over at no extra charge if you get these halts specified on your ticket. Generally, these ferries run year-round, but services are reduced December to April. Ferries also sail less regularly from Venice and Trieste to Pátra via Igoumenítsa/Corfu. For more details see the box on pp.18–19.

From any Italian port, a crossing to Pátra costs the same as to Igoumenítsa or Corfu; the **cheapest** of all the crossings is from Brindisi to Igoumenítsa, which line does not continue to Pátra. However, drivers will discover that the extra cost in Italian motorway tolls and fuel offsets the Brindisi or Bari route's savings over those from Ancona, Trieste or Venice; the shipping companies are well aware of this and set their prices accordingly.

In summer, it is essential to **book tickets** a few weeks ahead, especially in the peak July–August season. During the winter you can usually just turn up at the main ports (Brindisi and Ancona have the most reliable departures at that time of year), but it's still wise to book a few days in advance if you are taking a car or want a cabin. A few phone calls or internet searches before leaving home are, in any case, advisable, as the range of fares is considerable; if you do just turn up at the port, it's worth spending some time shopping around the agencies.

Via Hungary, Romania and Bulgaria

Avoiding former Yugoslavia involves a pretty substantial diversion through Hungary, Romania and Bulgaria. Too exhausting and too problematic at the best of times, this is not a drive to contemplate unless you actively want to see some of the countries en route. However, it's all simpler than it was, with visas easier to obtain at the borders, if you haven't fixed them in advance.

From **Budapest**, the quickest route through **Romania** is via Timis šoara, then on towards Sofia in Bulgaria and across the Rila mountains to the border at Kulata. Once at the Greek border, you have a ninety-minute drive to Thessaloníki or Kavála. Bear in mind

that road conditions are often poor and border formalities extensive. Contact the relevant embassies and the AA for more advice.

Flights from North America

The Greek national airline, Olympic Airways, flies **direct to Athens** out of New York (JFK), Montréal and Toronto. The airline – and also its domestic competitor Aegean – can offer reasonably priced add-on flights within Greece, especially to the Greek islands. Delta is the only North American carrier currently offering any direct service to Athens, though American Airlines, Air Canada and US Airways have code-sharing agreements with Olympic, and thus quote through fares to/from Boston, Chicago, Dallas/Fort Worth, Denver, Los Angeles, Miami, San Francisco, Tampa, Vancouver and Washington DC.

Another option is picking up any suitable flight to Europe and making your way to Greece by train, in which case a Eurail Pass makes a reasonable investment – details are given on p.16.

Nonstop flights to **Athens** out of **New York-JFK** on Olympic (5–7 weekly) start at around US$600 round-trip in winter, rising to around $1100 in summer for a maximum thirty-day stay. Delta has several weekly summertime direct services from New York-JFK to Athens, but even discount fares are pricey at around $1450. Sometimes, but not always, one-stop flights are less expensive; winter flights on BA via London can be around $550. Travelling during the May and October "shoulder seasons" will also yield significant savings.

Common-rating (ie price-fixing) agreements between different airlines means that fares to **Athens** from the **Midwest, Deep South** or the **West Coast** don't vary much; from Chicago, Miami, Denver or Los Angeles you're looking at $1200–1500 high season, $650–820 in winter, something in between at shoulder season. These tickets typically involve the use of American Airlines, US Airways, United, Air France, Alitalia, Iberia and Swiss, via their European gateway cities. With little to distinguish these itineraries price-wise, you might examine the stopover time at their respective European hubs, as these often differ by several hours. You may be better off getting a domestic add-on to New York and heading directly to Athens from there.

As with the US, airfares from **Canada** to **Athens** vary depending on where you start your journey, and whether you take a direct service. Olympic flies out of Toronto, with a stop in Montréal, three to four times weekly for return fares of just under CDN$1400 in winter, climbing to nearly CDN$2500 in summer. Indirect flights from Montréal on Lufthansa via a German hub can cost about the same in summer, but much more during low season. From Calgary or Vancouver, there are no direct flights; expect to pay CDN$2050–3000 during low/high seasons respectively, on such combinations as Air Canada/Lufthansa via Germany or Air Canada/Olympic via London.

Airlines

Air Canada ☎1-888 247–2262, ⓦwww.aircanada.com.
Air France ☎1-800 237-2747, Canada ☎1-800/667-2747, ⓦwww.airfrance.com.
Alitalia ☎1-800 223-5730, Canada ☎1-800 361-8336, ⓦwww.alitalia.com.
American Airlines ☎1-800 433-7300, ⓦwww.aa.com.
British Airways ☎1-800 AIRWAYS, ⓦwww.ba.com.
Delta Air Lines domestic ☎1-800 221-1212, international ☎1-800 241-4141, ⓦwww.delta.com.
Iberia ☎1-800 772-4642, ⓦwww.iberia.com.
KLM/Northwest US domestic ☎1-800 225-2525, international ☎1-800 447-4747, ⓦwww.klm.com.
Lufthansa US ☎1-800 645-3880, Canada ☎1-800/563-5954, ⓦwww.lufthansa.com.
Olympic Airways ☎1-800 223-1226 or 718/896-7393, ⓦwww.olympic-airways.gr.
Swiss ☎1-877 FLY-SWISS, ⓦwww.swiss.com.
United Airlines domestic ☎1-800 241-6522, international ☎1-800 538-2929, ⓦwww.united.com.
US Airways domestic ☎1-800 428-4322, international ☎1-800 622-1015, ⓦwww.usair.com.
Virgin Atlantic Airways ☎1-800 862-8621, ⓦwww.virgin-atlantic.com.

Travel companies

Air Brokers International ☎1-800 883-3273 or 415/397-1383, ⓦwww.airbrokers.com. Consolidator and specialist in RTW tickets.
Airtech ☎212/219-7000, ⓦwww.airtech.com. Standby seat broker; also deals in consolidator fares and courier flights.
Educational Travel Center ☎1-800 747-5551 or 608/256-5551, ⓦwww.edtrav.com. Low-cost fares worldwide, student/youth discount offers, Eurail passes.
Flightcentre US ☎1-866 WORLD-51, ⓦwww.flightcentre.us, Canada ☎1-888 WORLD-55, ⓦwww.flightcentre.ca. Rock-bottom fares worldwide.
New Frontiers US ☎1-800 677-0720 or 212/986-6006, ⓦwww.newfrontiers.com. Discount firm, specializing in travel from the US to Europe.
STA Travel US ☎1-800 329-9537, Canada ☎1-888/427-5639, ⓦwww.statravel.com. Worldwide specialists in independent travel; also student IDs, travel insurance, car rental, rail passes, etc.
Student Flights ☎1-800 255-8000 or 480/951-1177, ⓦwww.isecard.com/studentflights. Student/youth fares, plus student IDs and European rail and bus passes.
TFI Tours ☎1-800 745-8000 or 212/736-1140, ⓦwww.lowestairprice.com. Consolidator with global fares.
Travel Avenue ☎1-800 333-3335, ⓦwww.travelavenue.com. Full-service travel agent that offers discounts in the form of rebates.
Travel Cuts US ☎1-800 592-CUTS, Canada ☎1-888 246-9762, ⓦwww.travelcuts.com. Popular, long-established student-travel organization, with worldwide offers.
Travelers Advantage ☎1-877 259-2691, ⓦwww.travelersadvantage.com. Discount travel club, with cashback deals and discounted car rental. Membership required ($1 for 3 months' trial).
Travelosophy US ☎1-800 332-2687, ⓦwww.itravelosophy.com. Good range of discounted and student fares worldwide.

Specialist tour operators

Adventures Abroad ☎1-800 665-3998 or 604/303-1099, ⓦwww.adventures-abroad.com. Offers fairly bland ten-day "Poetic Greek Isles tour" in spring or autumn.
Classic Adventures ☎1-800 935-5000, ⓦwww.classicadventures.com. Two good offerings, at about $2600 land only: spring or autumn rural cycling tours of "classical Greece", crossing the north Peloponnese to Zákynthos in eleven days, or a pedal through the archeological sites and medieval towns of Crete, in twelve days.

Hellenic Adventures ☎1-800 851-6349 or 612/827-0937, ⓦwww.hellenicadventures.com. Small-group, human-scale tours, led by an enthusiastic Greek-American: the east Aegean isles, sailing in the Cyclades, plus Crete. Good info on the website for independent travellers too.
Valef Yachts ☎1-800 223-3845, ⓦwww .valefyachts.com. Offers a choice of fixed, seven-day motor-yacht cruises around the Dodecanese, the Sporades plus Halkidhiki, the Cyclades, the Argo-Saronics plus the Argolid, or the Ionian islands; a bit rushed, but affordable at $900–1500 per person. Also very expensive bareboat charter (sailing or motor yacht); pick your craft from the online brochure.

Flights from Australia and New Zealand

With the huge Greek-emigrant community in Australia, it's absolutely staggering that Olympic suspended all direct air links to Greece in October 2002 – a measure of its woes (though there are now code-shared stopping services with Gulf Air). Neither are there any direct flights from New Zealand – you'll have to get yourself to Southeast Asia or a North American hub for onward travel. Tickets purchased direct from the airlines tend to be expensive; travel agents or Australia-based websites offer much better deals on fares and have the latest information on limited specials and stopovers.

If Greece is only one stop on a longer journey, you might consider buying a **Round-the-World** (RTW) fare. At present only the more expensive, fifteen-stop "Global Explorer" (roughly A$3400) offered by the One World airline group includes Athens. RTW fares from any point in Australia are usually common-rated, ie the price is the same from whichever Australian airport you commence travel. From New Zealand, allow almost NZ$4000 for the same programme.

For a **simple return fare**, you may have to buy an add-on internal flight to reach the international gateways of **Sydney** or **Melbourne**. Tickets are valid for one year; at the time of writing, high-season departures could be had for A$2270–2500 on such airlines as Lufthansa, Singapore Airways, Thai Airways, Gulf Air or Austrian Airlines plus Lauda Air, for multi-stop itineraries via Southeast Asia, the Middle East and a European hub. For $A2270, you could fly east-bound via North America on a combination of United Airlines, Air Canada and Lufthansa. Leaving at low season means fares of A$1547–1736 on Singapore Airlines, Thai Airways, Lufthansa or Qantas plus Royal Jordanian.

From **Auckland**, the usual routes to Athens are either westbound several times weekly via Bangkok, Sydney or Singapore, or eastbound almost daily via Los Angeles with Air New Zealand on the first leg. At high season count on paying NZ$2449–2729 on Singapore Airlines, Emirates, Thai Airways or (for an east-bound itinerary) Air New Zealand plus Lufthansa. During low season prices aren't much different: NZ$2199–2349 for travel on Thai Airways, Emirates or (again going east) Air New Zealand plus Lufthansa.

Airlines

Aeroflot ☎02/9262 2233, ⓦwww.aeroflot.com.au.
Air New Zealand Australia ☎13 24 76, ⓦwww.airnz.com.au; New Zealand ☎0800 737 000, ⓦwww.airnz.co.nz.
Alitalia Australia ☎02/9244 2445, New Zealand ☎09/308 3357, ⓦwww.alitalia.com.
British Airways Australia ☎1300 767 177, New Zealand ☎0800 274 847, ⓦwww.ba.com.
Egyptair Australia ☎02/9241 5696, ⓦwww.egyptair.com.eg.
Emirates Australia ☎1300 303 777 or 02/9290 9700, New Zealand ☎09/377 6004, ⓦwww.emirates.com.
Gulf Air Australia ☎02/9244 2199, New Zealand ☎09/308 3366, ⓦwww.gulfairco.com.
Lufthansa Australia ☎1300 655 727, New Zealand ☎0800 945 220, ⓦwww.lufthansa.com.
Qantas Australia ☎13 13 13, New Zealand ☎0800 808 767 or 09/357 8900, ⓦwww.qantas.com.
Royal Jordanian Australia ☎02/9244 2701, New Zealand ☎03/365 3910, ⓦwww.rja.com.jo.
Singapore Airlines Australia ☎13 10 11, New Zealand ☎0800 808 909, ⓦwww .singaporeair.com.
Thai Airways Australia ☎1300 651 960, New Zealand ☎09/377 3886, ⓦwww.thaiair.com.

Travel agents

Flight Centre Australia ☎13 31 33, ⓦwww.flightcentre.com.au; New Zealand ☎0800 243 544, ⓦwww.flightcentre.co.nz.
STA Travel Australia ☎1300 733 035, New Zealand ☎0508/782 872, ⓦwww.statravel.com.

Student Uni Travel Australia ☎02/9232 8444, ⓦwww.sut.com.au; New Zealand ☎09/379 4224, ⓦwww.sut.co.nz.
Trailfinders Australia ☎02/9247 7666, ⓦwww.trailfinders.com.au.

Specialist agents and tour operators

Kompas Holidays Australia ☎07/3222 3333 or 1800 269 968, ⓦwww.kompasholidays.com.au.

Scores for its Greek island-hopping programme, covering eleven of the better-known islands; they arrange hotels (three-day minimum stay per island) and all ferry transfers.

Sun Island Tours Australia ☎02/9283 3840, ⓦwww.sunislandtours.com.au. An assortment of island-hopping, fly-drives, cruises and guided land-tour options, as well as upscale accommodation on selected islands.

Departure points: Athens, Pireás and main ports

As detailed in the "Getting there" section, you may well find yourself travelling to the islands via Athens. This is not necessarily a hardship. The Greek capital is, admittedly, no holiday resort, with its predominantly concrete architecture and air pollution, but it has modern excitements of its own, as well as superlative ancient sites. A couple of nights' stopover will allow you to take in the Acropolis, the ancient agora and major museums, wander around the old quarter of Pláka and the bazaar area, and sample some of the country's best restaurants and clubs. Morning arrival in Athens would allow you time for a look at the Acropolis and Pláka, before heading down to the port of Pireás (Piraeus) to catch one of the overnight ferries to Crete or the Dodecanese.

Not all the islands are accessible from Pireás, so we've given brief accounts of other useful mainland ports below.

Athens

Athens' **airport** – Eleftherios Venizelos – at Spáta, some 26km east of the city, opened in March 2001, replacing the far more convenient (if tiny) one south of town at Ellinikó. There are ample banking facilities in the arrivals hall, including several ATMs. By mid-2004, a **light-rail line** should whisk you from Eleftherios Venizelos airport to Stavrós station, new terminus of the metro network. Until the rail link opens, take #E94 express **bus** (every 15–30min 6am–midnight) from outside arrivals to metro station Ethnikí Ámyna and then continue by metro. Alternatively, take the #E95 express bus all the way to central Sýndagma square (every 25–35min around the clock), or the #E96

express bus to Pireás (Piraeus) port (every 20–40min), going via the beach suburbs; this service may continue even after the light rail link opens. All three services cost €2.90, but for the price you automatically get a one-day travelcard valid on all Athens public transport. Tickets should be bought from a booth beside the stops, or, if this is closed, can be purchased on the bus; make sure you have small change.

A **taxi** to Athens or Pireás should cost no more than €20 – at most times of the day your driver will find it quickest to head south-west to Vári and Voúla, and then north through the southerly beach suburbs rather than struggle through traffic in the northeastern suburbs. This amount should include a €2 airport surcharge and €0.20 for each item of luggage, but make sure the meter is working (fares begin at €0.70, minimum fare €1.50) and visible from the start – double or even quintuple overcharging of newcomers is the norm.

For those who have stopped off in Athens for the day or overnight, it's about 9km from the city centre to the ferry port of **Pireás**. The easiest way to get there is by **taxi**, which should cost around €5–7, depending on your start-point and how many bags you have. You may find that you have fellow passengers in the cab: this is permitted, and each drop-off will pay the full fare. Otherwise, Line 1 of the **metro** (Kifissiá–Pireás) will get you there swiftly, passing through Omónia and Monastiráki stations and depositing you, at the port, within moderate walking distance of many boat-berths.

All international **trains** arrive at the Stathmós Laríssis, just to the northwest of the city centre. You can take yellow trolley bus (#1) or the metro immediately outside to reach Sýndagma square.

Accommodation

Finding **accommodation** in Athens is usually not a problem except during midsummer – though it's always best to phone ahead. A small selection of places is listed below, ranging from hostels to fairly comfortable hotels.

For a quick stay, **Pláka**, the oldest quarter of the city, is the obvious area. It spreads south of Sýndagma square, lies within easy walking range of the Acropolis and has lots of outdoor restaurants and cafés. It's possible to stay in the port of Pireás, too, though there's no real need, and you might as well make the most of your time in Athens. All the listings below are in Pláka, except for *Marble House* and *Art Gallery*, which are just south in Veïkoú/Koukáki district, and the *Tempi* which is just north of Monastiráki square and station.

Hostels and budget inns

John's Place Patróöu 5, Pláka ☎210 32 29 719. **②** doubles; also multi-bed rooms.
Marble House Pension in a quiet alley off Anastasíou Zínni 35, Koukáki ☎210 92 34 058. **③**
Phaedra Herefóndos 16, Pláka ☎210 32 27 795. **③**
Student's Inn Kydhathinéon 16 ☎210 32 44 808. Pricey dorms, some triples at **④**
Tempi Eólou 29 ☎210 32 13 175. **③**

Thisseus Inn Thisséos 10 ☎210 32 45 960. **②** doubles, also triples and quads.

Mid-range hotels

Acropolis House Kódrou 6–8 ☎210 32 22 344. **④**
Adonis Kódrou 3 ☎210 32 49 737. **④**
Art Gallery Pension Erekhthíou 5, Veïkoú ☎210 92 38 376. **⑤**
Kouros Kódrou 11 ☎210 32 27 431. **④**
Nefeli Iperídhou 16, Pláka ☎210 32 28 044. **③**

Eating

Pláka is bursting with touristy **restaurants**, most of them very pleasantly situated but poor value. Three with nice sites *and* good food are *Iy Ipiros*, actually on Platía Ayíou Filíppou in the Monastiráki flea market, for *mayireftá*; *O Thanasis*, nearby at Mitropóleos 69, for dynamite souvláki and kebabs; and *Baïraktaris*, around the corner at Platía Monastirakíou 2, with more carnivorous fare and occasional live acoustic music. *Eden*, at Liossíou 12, is one of the city's few vegetarian restaurants.

The city and sights

Central Athens is a compact, easily walkable area. Its hub is **Sýndagma square** (Platía Syndágmatos), flanked by the Parliament building, banks and a few airline offices. Pretty much everything you'll want to see in a fleeting visit – the Acropolis, Pláka, the major museums – lies within twenty to thirty minutes' walk of here. Just east of the square, too, are the **National Gardens** – the nicest spot in town for a siesta.

Walk south from Sýndagma, along Níkis or Filellínon streets, and then briefly west, and you'll find yourself in Pláka, the surviving area of the nineteenth-century, pre-Independence village. Largely pedestrianized, it is a delightful area just to wander around – and it is the approach to the Acropolis. For a bit of focus to your walk, take in the fourth-century BC **Monument of Lysikratos**, used as a study by Byron, to the east, and the Roman-era **Tower of the Winds** (Aéridhes), to the west. The latter adjoins the Roman Forum. Climb north from the Tower of the Winds and you reach **Anafiótika**, with its whitewashed Cycladic-style cottages (built by workers from the island of Anáfi) and the eclectic **Kanellopoulou Museum** (Tues–Sun 8am–3pm; €2).

Head north from the Roman Forum (April–Sept daily 8am–7pm; Oct–March Tues–Sun 8.30am–3pm; €2), along Athinás or Eólou streets, and you come to an equally characteristic part of the city – the **bazaar** area, which shows Athens in its Near Eastern lights. **Platía Monastirakíou** is worth a look beyond its metro station to its Ottoman mosque (now a museum of ceramics). On Sundays a genuine **flea market** sprawls to its west, out beyond the tourist shops promoted as "Athens Flea Market".

Even with a few hours to spare between flight and ferry, you can squeeze in a visit to the **Acropolis** (daily: April–Sept 8am–7pm; Oct–March 8am–4.30pm; site and museum €12). The complex of temples, rebuilt by Pericles in the "Golden Age" of the fifth century BC, is focused on the famed Parthenon. This, and the smaller Athena Nike and Erechtheion temples are given context by a small museum housing some of the original relief art left behind by Lord Elgin.

If you have more time, make your way down to the **Theatre of Dionysos**, on the south slope (daily: summer 8am–7pm; winter 8.30am–3pm; €2 or joint Acropolis ticket), and/or to the Ancient (Classical Greek era) **agora** (southeastern entrance down the path from the Areopagus; northern entrance on Adhrianoú; daily: summer 8am–7pm; winter 8.30am–3pm; €4 or joint Acropolis ticket), presided over by the Doric **Thiseion**, or Temple of Hephaestus.

Athens' major museum is the **National Archeological Museum** on Patissíon 28, due to reopen summer 2004 after a lengthy refit. Its highlights include the Mycenaean (*Odyssey*-era) treasures, Classical sculpture and, upstairs, the brilliant Minoan frescoes from Santoríni (Thíra).

Two other superb museums are the **Benáki** (Mon, Wed, Fri & Sat 9am–5pm, Thurs 9am–midnight, Sun 9am–3pm; €6, temporary exhibitions €3), a fascinating personal collection of ancient and folk treasures, and the **Goulandhris Museum of Cycladic and Ancient Greek Art** (Mon & Wed–Fri 10am–4pm, Sat 10am–3pm; €3.50), with its wonderful display of figurines from the Cycladic island civilization of the third millennium BC.

Pireás

Pireás (Piraeus), the port of Athens, is the southwesternmost stop on Line 1 of the **metro** which you can board at Platía Viktorías, Omónia or Monastiráki squares. The journey takes about 25 minutes – trains run from 6am to midnight – with a flat fare of €0.60 (€0.70 if you've used Line 2 or Line 3 as well). If you're travelling by **rail** from Pátra, the train continues through Athens down to Pireás.

You can buy **ferry and catamaran tickets** from agencies at the harbour in Pireás, or in central Athens (there are several outlets on Lefóros Amalías, which runs south of Sýndagma square). Wherever you buy tickets, make sure you ask around the agencies and get a ferry that makes a reasonably direct run to your island destination. There may be little choice to obscure islands, but ferries to the Cyclades and Dodecanese can take very different routes.

For the Argo-Saronic islands, you take a Hellas Flying Dolphin or Saronic Dolphin **hydrofoil**, both companies departing from the Aktí Tzelépi quay in central Pireás. These are twice as fast and around twice the cost, but conventional ferries to the islands beyond Égina are scarce. Tickets can be bought in advance in Athens – worth doing in high season – or an hour before departure at booths on the quay.

Other mainland ports

Although Pireás has a wide choice of ferry, catamaran and hydrofoil connections, certain islands can (or must) be reached from other ports on the mainland. Below is a quick run-through of the more important and useful.

Note also that there are two islands – **Évvia** (northeast of Athens) and **Lefkádha** in the Ionian islands – that require no ferry, and can be reached by bus, and in Évvia's case also by train.

Alexandhróupoli

The third northern port (6hr by bus from Thessaloníki) has daily ferries and summer-only hydrofoils to Samothráki, plus at least one weekly departure to Límnos and other northeast Aegean isles. It's a somewhat unenticing place to stay, though if you get stuck the *Lido* at Paleológou 15 (☎25510 28808) represents by far the best budget-hotel value.

Igoumenítsa

Many ferries from Italy call at Igoumenítsa, stopping at **Corfu** en route. There are regular shuttles across to Corfu, to both the main town and also Lefkími in the south, plus one or two daily services to **Paxí**. Hotel vacancies are plentiful as nobody stays more than a night; the *Stavrodhromi* (☎26650 22343) is a reliable, friendly cheapie, 500m inland at Soulíou 14.

Kavála

The second port of northern Greece (3hr by bus from Thessaloníki) offers fast access to **Thássos**, either direct by hydrofoil, or from the nearby roll-on-roll-off shuttle point at Keramotí. There are also links to **Límnos** and other **northeast Aegean** islands, as well as (only in summer) to **Samothráki**. The city has a line of good tavernas in the old quarter below the castle, but pleasant, affordable hotels are in short supply. In ascending order of comfort and price, try the *Akropolis* (☎2510 223 543) at Venizélou 29, the *Nefeli* at Erythroú Stavroú 50 (☎2510 227 441) or the *Esperia* (☎2510 229 621) at Erythroú Stavroú 42, opposite the archeological museum.

Kyllíni

This small port, south of Pátra (buses), is the main departure point for the Ionian island of **Zákynthos**, and in summer has boats to Póros on **Kefalloniá**. Little point in staying, if you time things right.

Kými

This is technically an island port – on Évvia (see Chapter Six) – but is mentioned here as it is the main port for **Skýros** in the Sporades. Kými can be reached from Athens by bus, which should be timed to dovetail with ferry departures. If you miss the

connection, staying options are limited to two fairly expensive hotels.

Lávrio

This tiny port, south of Athens (and reachable by bus from the Mavromatéon terminal; 1hr 15min) has daily ferries to **Kéa**, the closest of the Cyclades, less often to **Kýthnos**, Kéa's neighbour, as well as three weekly departures to Áyios Efstrátios and Límnos. Lávrio is set to expand greatly in the near future, eclipsing Rafína as the main east-coast port of Attikí.

Neápoli

A small, undistinguished port at the southern foot of the Peloponnese, with ferry and hydrofoil connections to Ayía Pelayía on **Kýthira**, and local boats to the islet of **Elafónissos**.

Párga and Astakós

These two small ports, south of Igoumenítsa, have daily ferries to, respectively, **Paxí** and **Kefalloniá** in the Ionian. Párga is a popular, crowded resort, more pleasant (and with more accommodation vacancies, mostly studios) off-season; Astakós is rarely busy but has few places to stay – buses from Athens tend to dovetail with ferry departures, currently just once daily, which call at **Itháki** too.

Pátra (Patras)

Pátra is the major port of the Peloponnese, and the main jump-off for Italy and most of the **Ionian islands**. Easiest access from Athens is on the train (Stathmós Peloponíssou terminal; 4hr), since the Pátra station is right by the boat terminals. The city itself is uninteresting, so plan on moving out the same day, if possible. Reasonable budget hotels include the *El Greco*, Ayíou Andhréou 145 (☎2610 272 931) or the *Atlanta* at Zaïmi 10 (☎2610 220 098).

Ráfina

Another small port near Athens (again reachable by bus from the Mavromatéon terminal;

40min). Connections are to the **Cyclades** or nearby **Évvia**.

Thessaloníki

The northern capital is a busy mainland port. There are useful long-haul ferries to **Kós** and **Rhodes** via **Sámos**; to the northeastern Aegean islands; and to **Crete** via select Sporades and **Cyclades**. In summer only there are departures to Skíathos, Skópelos and Alónissos in the **Sporades**. It's worth exploring the Byzantine churches, especially the Áyios Yeóryios Rotónda and tiny Ósios Dhavíd, as well as the Archeological Museum. Hotels are plentiful if mostly uninspiring, noisy and often vastly overpriced; worthwhile exceptions include the *Tourist* on Mitropóleos 21 (☎2310 270 501); the *Nea Mitropolis* at Syngroú 22 (☎2310 525 540); the *Bill* at Syngroú 29, corner Amvrossíou (☎2310 537 666); and the *Orestias Castorias* at Agnóstou Stratiótou 14 (☎2310 276 517).

Vólos and Áyios Konstandínos

Vólos is the major port city – modern and rather grim – of Thessaly, in central Greece.

It is easiest reached from Athens by bus (Mavromatéon terminal; 4hr), though there's also a couple of through express trains daily, via Lárissa. Ferries and hydrofoils run regularly to the **Sporades** – Skiáthos, Skópelos and Alónissos. Try to complete your journey the same day; failing that, pleasantly situated budget hotels include the *Roussas* (☎24210 21732) at Iatroú Tzánou, 1km east of the dock, or the *Iasson* right by the dock (☎24210 26075). **Áyios Konstandínos** is an alternative but less active port for the **Sporades**, again with buses from Athens (Mavromatéon terminal; 2hr 30min).

Yíthio

This elegant Peloponnese town has ferries most days to the isolated island of Kýthira, plus a few times weekly to Kíssamos in western Crete. It's a 4–5hr haul here by bus from Athens (Kifissoú 100 terminal), changing at Spárti. Budget hotels or pensions in town include the Matina, Vassiléos Pávlou 19 (T27330 22518); the Saga on Tzanetáki, opposite Kranae islet (T27330 23220); and the Kranae, Vassiléos Pávlou 17 (T27330 24394).

Red tape and visas

UK and all other EU nationals (plus those of Norway, Switzerland and Iceland) need only a valid passport for entry to Greece; you are no longer stamped in on arrival or out upon departure, and (in theory at least) EU nationals enjoy uniform civil rights with Greek citizens. US, Australian, New Zealand, Canadian and most non-EU Europeans receive mandatory entry and exit stamps in their passports and can stay, as tourists, for ninety days (cumulative) in any six-month period. Such nationals arriving from another EU state not party to the Schengen Agreement may not be stamped in routinely at minor Greek ports, so it's best to make sure this is done in order to avoid unpleasantness on exit. Your passport must be valid for three months after your arrival date.

If you are planning to **travel overland**, you should check current visa requirements for Romania and Bulgaria at their closest consulates; transit visas for most of these territories are at present issued at the borders, though at a higher price than if obtained in advance at a local consulate.

Unless of Greek descent, visitors from **non-EU** countries are currently not, in practise, being given extensions to tourist visas by the various Aliens' Bureaux in Greece, though in theory these are available for the hefty sum of €450. You must leave not just Greece but the entire Schengen Group – essentially the entire EU as it was before May 2004, minus Britain and Eire, plus Norway and Iceland – and stay out until the maximum-90-days-in-180 rule as set forth above is satisfied. If you **overstay** your time and then leave under your own power – ie are not deported – you'll be hit with a huge spot fine upon departure, probably in the region of €450, and possibly be banned from re-entering for a period of time; no excuses will be entertained except (just maybe) a doctor's certificate stating you were immobilized in hospital. It cannot be overemphasized just how exigent Greek immigration officials have become on this issue.

By EU law, EU nationals are allowed to stay indefinitely in any EU state (with certain exceptions in force for the ten new members who joined in May 2004), but to be sure of avoiding any problems, it's best to get a five-year **residence permit** (*ádhia paramonís*) and (if appropriate) a work permit – for both, see "Finding work", p.77. If you're not employed (self- or otherwise), you will be required to prove that you have sufficient resources to support yourself, and health insurance (either UK-based for expats, or locally in Greece). The usual ways to demonstrate solvency are pink, personalized bank **exchange receipts** given whenever you import money by wire or travellers' cheques; confirmation by your home state National Insurance authorities that you have a pension eligibility; or a Greek **savings account passbook** – the pages of the passbook in particular should be photocopied and given to the police.

Residence/work permits for non-EU nationals can now only be obtained on application to a Greek embassy or consulate outside of Greece; you have a much better chance of securing one if you are married to a Greek, or have permanent-resident status in another EU state, but even then there will be wrangles and delays.

Greek embassies abroad

Australia 9 Turrana St, Yarralumla, Canberra, ACT 2600 ☎02/6273 3011.
Britain 1A Holland Park, London W11 3TP ☎020/7221 6467, ⊛www.greekembassy.org.uk.
Canada 80 Maclaren St, Ottawa, ON K2P 0K6 ☎613/238-6271.
Ireland 1 Upper Pembroke St, Dublin 2 ☎01/676 7254.
New Zealand 5–7 Willeston St, Wellington ☎04/473 7775.
USA 2221 Massachusetts Ave NW, Washington, DC 20008 ☎202/939-5800, ⊛www.greekembassy.org.

Information, maps and websites

The National Tourist Organization of Greece (Ellinikós Organismós Tourismoú, or EOT; GNTO abroad, ⓦwww.gnto.gr) maintains offices in most European capitals, plus major cities in North America and Australia (see below for addresses). It publishes an array of free, glossy, regional pamphlets, invariably five to ten years out of date, which are OK for getting an idea of where you want to go, even if the actual text should be taken with a spoonful of salt. Also available from the EOT are a reasonable foldout map of the country and a number of (equally outdated) brochures on special interests and festivals.

Tourist offices

In Greece, you will find official **EOT offices** in many of the larger towns and resorts, where in addition to the usual leaflets, you can find weekly **schedules** for the inter-island **ferries** – hardly one-hundred-percent reliable, but useful as a guideline. EOT staff should be able to advise on **bus** and **train** departures as well as current opening hours for local sites and museums, and occasionally can give assistance with accommodation – though there have been scandals in the provinces concerning certain staff taking backhanders to steer potential clients towards particular outfits.

Where there is no EOT office, you can get information (and often a range of leaflets) from **municipally run** tourist offices, for example those in Kós, Rhodes and Mólyvos – these can be highly motivated and better than the EOT branches. In the absence of any of these, you can visit the **Tourist Police**, essentially a division (often just a single room) of the local police station. They can sometimes provide you with lists of rooms to let, which they regulate, but they're really where you go if you have a **serious complaint** about a taxi, accommodation or an eating establishment.

Greek national tourist offices abroad

Australia 51 Pitt St, Sydney, NSW 2000 ☎02/9241 1663, Ⓔhto@tpg.com.au.
Canada 91 Scollard St, 2nd Floor, Toronto, ON M5R 1GR, ☎416/968-2220, Ⓔgrnto.tor@sympatico.ca.
UK 4 Conduit St, London W1R 0DJ ☎020/7734 5997, ⒺEOT-greektouristoffice@btinternet.com.
USA 645 5th Ave, New York, NY 10022 ☎212/421-5777.

Maps

Maps in Greece are an endless source of confusion and often outright misinformation. Each cartographic company seems to have its own peculiar system of transcribing Greek letters into the Roman alphabet – and these, as often as not, do not match the semi-official transliterations on the road signs, which again may not match, even in the same region.

The most reliable **general touring maps** of the Greek islands are those published by Athens-based **Road Editions** (ⓦwww .road.gr) and rivals **Anavasi** ⓦwww .mountains.gr/anavasi). Road Editions products, at scales of 1:25,000 to 1:100,000, are widely available in Greece at selected bookstores and kiosks, including their own retail outlets in Athens (Ippokrátous 39), Thessaloníki (Proxénou Koromilá 41), Pátra (Zaïmi 20) and Iráklion (Hándhakos 29), as well as at a surprising number of petrol stations and general tourist shops countrywide. Anavasi products are available in better Athens bookstores, at their own shopfront at Stoá Arsakíou 6A in central Athens, as well as on the islands they cover, which include most of the Cyclades and Sporades at scales of 1:25,000–1:40,000. In Britain both brands are found at Stanfords (see p.31) and the Hellenic Book Service (see p.31); in case of difficulty, contact (in Britain) Portfolio (☎020/8579 7748). In the

US, they're sold exclusively through Map Link (see address, opposite) or Omni Resources (☎910/227-8300, ⓦwww .omnimap.com). An also-ran for the islands, with coverage only of Crete, Sýros, and a few others, is **Emvelia Editions** (ⓦwww .emvelia.gr). They have just one retail outlet in Athens – Ellinoekdhotiki, at Navarínou 12 – and very sporadic sales points overseas – notably the Hellenic Book Service in London – but this situation is bound to improve.

Having extensively field-tested all three brands, there's no clear answer as to which is best. Road Editions products are more intelligently folded and easier to read, but often lack detail; Emvelia tends to show more villages in a busier format. Both are somewhat out-of-date in the matter of current road surfaces, though Road has recently updated most of its maps, originally issued in 1997–98. Anavasi maps are waterproof and almost rip-proof, and tend to be even newer than Road – they're almost always the top choice for the few islands they cover thus far. In short, none is anywhere near perfect, but, based on large-scale military maps not available to the public, they're the best you will find, and where two companies cover the same island, you may want to buy both.

Where Road, Anavasi or Emvelia products are unavailable, good second choices are the **GeoCenter** maps *Greece and the Islands* and *Greek Islands/Aegean Sea*, which together cover the country at a scale of 1:300,000. The single-sided foldup Freytag-Berndt 1:650,000, with an index, is very nearly as good, and easier to use when driving. All of these are widely available in Britain and North America (see the list of map outlets, opposite), though much less easily in Greece.

Hiking/topographical maps

Hiking/topographical maps are gradually improving in quality and availability, with both Road and Anavasi loosening the stranglehold which the Army has long excercised on detailed information. Anavasi's GPS-compatible, CD-ROM-available series is considered more accurate than Road – with better-verified road and path networks – and

their larger-scale products for the islands they cover are detailed enough to walk with.

Both Road and Anavasi products are based on the older (1970s) maps of the **Yeografikí Ipiresía Stratoú** (Army Geographical Service, or YIS). If you want to obtain these for islands not covered by Road or Anavasi, visit the **YIS** at Evelpídhon 4, north of Aréos Park in Athens, on Monday, Wednesday or Friday from 8am to noon only. All foreigners must leave their passport with the gate guard; EU citizens may proceed directly to the sales hall. Other nationals will probably have to go upstairs for a vetting interview; if you don't speak reasonably good Greek, it's best to have a Greek friend get them for you. As of writing, YIS maps covering Crete, the Dodecanese, the east Aegean, northern Corfu and Skýros are still off-limits to all foreigners, as well as Greeks.

A German company, **Harms**, has five maps at 1:80,000 scale which cover Crete from west to east and show, with about fifty percent accuracy, many hiking routes.

Finally, for hiking in particular areas of Crete, Corfu, Sámos, Rhodes, Sými, Kálymnos, Thássos and Lésvos, map-and-guide booklets published by **Marengo Publications** in England also prove very useful. Stanfords keeps a good stock of these, or order from Marengo direct at 17 Bernard Crescent, Hunstanton PE36 6ER ☎01485/532710, ⓦwww.marengowalks.com.

Map outlets

UK and Ireland

Blackwell's Map and Travel Shop 53 Broad St, Oxford OX1 3BQ ☎01865/792792, ⓦwww.bookshop.blackwell.co.uk. Branches in Bristol, Cambridge, Cardiff, Leeds, Liverpool, Newcastle, Reading and Sheffield.

The Map Shop 30A Belvoir St, Leicester LE1 6QH ☎0116/247 1400.

National Map Centre 22–24 Caxton St, London SW1H 0QU ☎020/7222 2466, ⓦwww.mapsnmc.co.uk.

National Map Centre Ireland 34 Aungier St, Dublin ☎01/476 0471, ⓦwww.mapcentre.ie.

Newcastle Map Centre 55 Grey St, Newcastle upon Tyne NE1 6EF ☎0191/261 5622, ⓦwww.traveller.ltd.uk.

Stanfords 12–14 Long Acre, London WC2
☏ 020/7836 1321, ⊛ www.stanfords.co.uk. Also at
39 Spring Gardens, Manchester ☏ 0161/831
0250, and 29 Corn St, Bristol ☏ 0117/929 9966.
The Travel Bookshop 13–15 Blenheim Crescent,
London W11 2EE ☏ 020/7229 5260,
⊛ www.thetravelbookshop.co.uk.
Traveller 55 Grey St, Newcastle upon Tyne
☏ 0191/261 5622, ⊛ www.newtraveller.com.

US and Canada

110 North Latitude US ☏ 336/369-4171,
⊛ www.110nlatitude.com.
Book Passage 51 Tamal Vista Blvd, Corte
Madera, CA 94925, plus newer outlet in San
Francisco ☏ 1-800 999-7909,
⊛ www.bookpassage.com.
Distant Lands 56 S Raymond Ave, Pasadena, CA
91105 ☏ 1-800 310-3220,
⊛ www.distantlands.com.
Globe Corner Bookstore 28 Church St,
Cambridge, MA 02138 ☏ 1-800 358-6013,
⊛ www.globecorner.com.
Longitude Books 115 W 30th St #1206, New
York, NY 10001 ☏ 1-800 342-2164,
⊛ www.longitudebooks.com.
Map Link Inc. 30 S La Patera Lane, Unit 5, Santa
Barbara, CA 93117 ☏ 805/692-6777,
⊛ www.maplink.com.
Map Town 400 5 Ave SW #100, Calgary, AB, T2P
0L6 ☏ 1-877/921-6277, ⊛ www.maptown.com.
Travel Bug Bookstore 3065 W Broadway,
Vancouver, BC, V6K 2G9 ☏ 604/737-1122,
⊛ www.travelbugbooks.ca.
World of Maps 1235 Wellington St, Ottawa, ON,
K1Y 3A3 ☏ 1-800 214-8524,
⊛ www.worldofmaps.com.

Australia and New Zealand

Map Centre ⊛ www.mapcentre.co.nz.
Mapland 372 Little Bourke St, Melbourne
☏ 03/9670 4383, ⊛ www.mapland.com.au.
Map Shop 6–10 Peel St, Adelaide ☏ 08/8231
2033, ⊛ www.mapshop.net.au.
Map World 371 Pitt St, Sydney ☏ 02/9261 3601,
⊛ www.mapworld.net.au. Also at 900 Hay St,
Perth ☏ 08/9322 5733.
Map World 173 Gloucester St, Christchurch
☏ 0800 627 967, ⊛ www.mapworld.co.nz.

Greece on the Internet

Greece is strongly represented on the
Internet, with many bilingual English-Greek
websites offering information on nearly every
conceivable subject. Some of it, however, is

little more than propaganda – anything to do
with Macedonia, for example, is liable to be
extremely polemic in tone. Almost every heavily visited island will have its own website,
though some of these, in bizarre dialects of
"Gringlish", are barely readable, while others –
mastered by expatriate residents – are fluent
enough but either obsolete or vague on
specifics so as to avoid raising local hackles.
Country-wide and regional sites recommended below are reasonably balanced, current and literate. To read Greek characters on
a website, you may have to select "Unicode"
in "Character Set" under the "View" pull-down
menu in Internet Explorer – selecting "Greek"
shows accented vowels as a "?" character.

News, views and printed matter

⊛ aegeantimes.net A good digest of current
Greece-, Turkey- and Cyprus-related news stories from
around the world. You have to log in to post comments
– not for the thin-skinned as debate gets heated.
⊛ www.athensnews.gr The online edition of the
Athens News, Greece's longest-running quality English-
language newspaper, with the day's top stories.
⊛ www.ekathimerini.com The online edition of
the abridged English translation of *Kathimerini*, one
of Greece's most respected dailies. It's fully archived
for years back, and has an excellent search facility.
⊛ www.hellenicbooks.com The website of the
UK's premier Greek bookstore. It posts full,
opinionated reviews of its stock, offers the possibility
of buying online, and has witty descriptions of every
island.

Greek culture

⊛ www.culture.gr The Greek Ministry of Culture's
website. Good alphabetical gazetteer to monuments,
archeological sites and museums; lots of info about
the more obscure sites.
⊛ www.geocities.com/rebetology Basically the
site of an annual *rebétika*-related conference and
festive gathering on Ídhra, but also posts interesting
papers and snippets in its archive.
⊛ www.kemo.gr The last word on Greece's
minority communities, without the usual ranting
polemics – many academic but readable papers
posted for free download.

Travel in Greece

⊛ www.ferries.gr Maintained by a Cretan travel
agency, this sites makes a good stab at showing all

domestic (and international) ferry schedules, organized by company, though inevitably some info is a couple of months old. Unlike the gtp site (see below), you can make bookings.

ⓦ**www.greektravel.com** A subjective, North-American-orientated but useful site maintained by North Carolinan Matt Barrett, who's been visiting Greece for over three decades. It contains selected recommendations, destination thumbnails, tricks and shortcuts, plus hundreds of links to affiliated sites.

ⓦ**www.gtp.gr** The website of *Greek Travel Pages*, the fat (and expensive) printed manual on every Greek travel agent's desk. Mostly used for its ferry schedules (also kept on a separate site, ⓦ**www.gtpweb.com**). Completely revamped in 2001, it's still not one-hundred-percent reliable.

ⓦ**www.ktel.org** Bilingual website of the KTEL, or national bus syndicate, which posts – page glitches permitting – fairly reliable schedules. Coverage has increased recently to include the entire mainland and larger (but not smaller) islands.

Greek destinations

ⓦ**www.foi.org.uk** The site of Friends of the Ionian, which encourages sustainable, off-the-beach tourism; lots on the environment, natural history and local walks.

ⓦ**www.ionian-islands.com** A good if rather commercial site with lots of links to accommodation, travel and eating establishments.

ⓦ**www.island-ikaria.com** Literate, interesting, well-organized and fairly current, covering everything from hot springs to festivals.

ⓦ**www.kalymnos-isl.gr** The island's official website, with the English pages edited by expatriate radio journalist and author Faith Warn. Thoroughly revamped in early 2004.

ⓦ**www.leros.org** A bit of "Gringlish" to contend with, but clearly devised with love, giving a fun, thorough flavour of the island's landscapes, people and traditional architecture.

ⓦ**www.lesvos.com** An excellent overview of Lésvos, with useful (if not entirely current) hotel and restaurant recommendations.

ⓦ**www.parosweb.com** Good all-purpose site for the island, with plenty of news on and for visitors and expats, an events calendar and the usual accommodation, property and dining info.

ⓦ**www.saronicnet.com** Accommodation (hotels and villas) and activities (diving, donkey-trekking) on Ídhra, Spétses and Póros – three separate sites best accessed through this portal.

ⓦ**www.skiathosinfo.com** Excellent info on getting to Skiáthos and what you'll find on arrival, as well as literally hundreds of useful links to sites on the Sporades specifically and Greece in general.

ⓦ**stigmes.gr/br** An English-summary online edition of what's claimed to be Crete's leading monthly magazine, plus lots of links to other Crete-related sites.

ⓦ**www.symivisitor.com** Current news for aficionados; a range of accommodation, restaurant and beach profiles, presented by the publishers of the monthly island newspaper.

ⓦ**www.west-crete.com** Cretophiles' favourite site, with all travel/cultural topics (including trekking and naturist beaches) and links to helpful businesses; not restricted to the west of the island.

Greek weather

ⓦ**forecast.uoa.gr** A good one-stop site, maintained by the University of Athens physics faculty. An eccentric, limited selection of reporting stations, however; for much of Greece you click on a thumbnail image of the entire country which must be enlarged to read conditions at specific places.

ⓦ**www.poseidon.ncmr.gr** A Greek oceanographer's site maintained by the National Centre for Marine Research which profiles Aegean weather meticulously, including groovy graphics of sea currents and surface winds, based on satellite imaging. It's slowish but sophisticated, good for yachties, and reports one topic (rain, temperature, wind-speed, etc) at a time.

Insurance

Even though EU health care privileges apply in Greece (see p.34 for details), you'd do well to take out an insurance policy before travelling to cover against theft, loss, illness or injury. Before paying for a whole new policy, however, it's worth checking whether you are already covered: some all-risks homeowners' or renters' insurance policies *may* cover your possessions when overseas, and many private medical schemes (such as BUPA or WPA in the UK) offer coverage extensions for abroad.

In Canada, provincial health plans usually provide partial cover for medical mishaps overseas, while holders of official student/teacher/youth cards in Canada and the US are entitled to meagre accident coverage and hospital inpatient benefits. **Students** will often find that their student health coverage extends during the vacations and for one term beyond the date of last enrolment. Most **credit-card issuers** also offer some sort of vacation insurance, which is often automatic if you pay for the holiday with their card. However, it's vital to check just what these policies cover – frequently only death or dismemberment in the UK.

After exhausting the possibilities above, you might want to contact a **specialist travel insurance** company, or consider the travel insurance deal we offer (see box, below). A typical travel insurance policy usually provides cover for the **loss** of baggage, tickets and – up to a certain limit – cash,

cards or cheques, as well as **cancellation** or curtailment of your journey. Most of them exclude so-called **dangerous sports** unless an extra premium is paid: in the Greek islands this means motorbiking, windsurfing, sea-kayaking and often sailing, with most visitors engaging in one or the other at some point. Many policies can be chopped and changed to exclude coverage you don't need – for example, sickness and accident benefits can often be excluded or included at will. If you do take medical coverage, ascertain whether benefits will be paid as treatment proceeds or only after return home, whether there is a **24-hour medical emergency number**, and how much the deductible is (sometimes negotiable). When securing baggage cover, make sure that the **per-article limit** – typically under £500 in the UK – will cover your most valuable possession. Travel agents and tour operators in the UK are likely to **require travel**

Rough Guide travel insurance

Rough Guides Ltd offers a low-cost travel insurance policy, especially customized for our statistically low-risk readers by a leading British broker, provided by the American International Group (AIG) and registered with the British regulatory body, GISC (the General Insurance Standards Council). There are five main Rough Guides insurance plans: **No Frills** for the bare minimum for secure travel; **Essential**, which provides decent all-round cover; **Premier** for comprehensive cover with a wide range of benefits; **Extended Stay** for cover lasting four months to a year; and **Annual Multi-Trip**, a cost-effective way of getting Premier cover if you travel more than once a year. Premier, Annual Multi-Trip and Extended Stay policies can be supplemented by a "Hazardous Pursuits Extension" if you plan to indulge in sports considered dangerous, such as scuba-diving or trekking. For a policy quote, call the Rough Guide Insurance Line: toll-free in the UK ☎0800 015 09 06 or ☎+44 1392 314 665 from elsewhere. Alternatively, get an online quote at ⓦwww.roughguides.com/insurance.

insurance when you book a package holiday, though they can no longer insist that you buy their own – however, you will be required to sign a declaration saying that you have a policy with a particular company.

If you need to make a **medical claim**, you should keep receipts for medicines and treatment, and in the event you have anything stolen or lost, you must obtain an **official statement** from the police or the airline which lost your bags. In the wake of growing numbers of fraudulent claims, most insurers won't even entertain one unless you have a police report. There is usually also a **time limit** for submitting claims after the end of your journey.

Health

British and other EU nationals are officially entitled to free medical care in Greece upon presentation of an E111 form, available from most post offices. In June 2004, this and most other E-forms are set to be replaced by a Europe-wide benefits "Smart Card". "Free", however, means admittance only to the lowest grade of state hospital (known as a *yenikó nosokomío*), and does not include nursing care, special tests or the cost of medication. If you need prolonged medical care, you should make use of private treatment which, while slightly less expensive than elsewhere in western Europe, is where your travel insurance policy (see p.33) comes in handy. The US, Canada, Australia and New Zealand have no formal healthcare agreements with Greece (other than allowing for free emergency trauma treatment).

There are no required **inoculations** for Greece, though it's wise to ensure that you are up to date on tetanus and polio. The **water** is safe pretty much everywhere, though you will come across shortages or brackish supplies on some of the drier and more remote islands. Bottled water is widely available if you're feeling cautious.

Specific hazards

The main health problems experienced by visitors have to do with **overexposure to the sun**, and the odd nasty from the sea. To combat the former, don't spend too long in the sun, cover up limbs, wear a hat, and drink plenty of fluids in the hot months to avoid any danger of **sunstroke**; remember that even hazy sun can burn. For sea-gear, goggles or a dive mask for swimming and footwear for walking over wet or rough rocks are useful.

Hazards of the deep

In the sea, you may have the bad luck to meet an armada of **jellyfish** (*tsoúkhtres*), especially in late summer; they come in various colours and sizes ranging from purple "pizzas" to invisible, minute creatures. Various over-the-counter remedies for jellyfish stings are sold in resort pharmacies; baking soda or diluted ammonia also help to lessen the sting. The welts and burning usually subside of their own accord within a few hours; there are no deadly man-of-war species in Greek waters.

Less vicious but more common are black, spiky **sea urchins** (*ahini*), which infest rocky shorelines year-round; if you step on or graze one, a sewing needle (you can crudely sterilize it by heat from a cigarette lighter) and olive oil are effective for removing spines; if you don't extract them they'll fester. You can take your revenge by eating the roe of the reddish–purple ones, which is served as a delicacy in a few seafood restaurants.

Stingrays and skates (Greek names include *platý*, *seláhi*, *vátos* or *trígona*), which mainly frequent bays with sandy bottoms where they can camouflage themselves. Though shy, they can give you a nasty lash with their barbed tail if trodden on, so shuffle your feet a bit when entering the water.

When snorkelling in deeper water, especially around Crete, the Dodecanese, or the east Aegean, you may happen upon a brightly coloured **moray eel** (*smérna*) sliding back and forth out of its rocky lair. Keep a respectful distance – their slightly comical air and clown-colours belie an irritable temper and the ability to inflict nasty bites or even sever fingers.

Sandflies, dogs, mosquitoes and wasps

If you are sleeping on or near a **beach**, it's wise to use insect repellent, either lotion or wrist/ankle bands, and/or a tent with a screen to guard against **sandflies**. Their bites are potentially dangerous, as these flies spread leishmaniasis, a parasitic infection characterized by chronic fever, listlessness and weight loss. It's difficult to treat, requiring long courses of medication.

In Greece, the main reservoirs for leishmaniasis are **dogs**. Transmission of the disease to humans by fleas has not been proven, but it's wisest not to befriend strays as they also carry echinococcosis, a debilitating liver fluke. In humans these form nodules and cysts which can only be removed surgically.

Mosquitoes (*kounóupia*) in Greece carry nothing worse than a vicious bite, but they can be infuriating. The most widespread solution are the small electrical devices (trade names Vape-Net or Bay-Vap) that vaporize an odourless insecticide tablet; many accommodation proprietors supply them routinely, and if you see them supplied on your night-table it's a good bet they'll be needed. Insect repellents such as Autan are available from most general stores and kiosks.

Wasps and **hornets** (*sfigónes*, *sfíkes*) are common, particularly during the vintage season (Aug–Oct) when they're attracted by all the fermenting grape-mess. Some mind their own business, others are very aggressive, even dive-bombing swimmers some distance out to sea. One of the best repellent measures (used by tavernas) is coffee grounds set alight.

Creepy-crawlies

Adders (*ohiés*) and **scorpions** (*skorpii*) are found throughout the Greek islands (except, oddly, Astypálea); both creatures are shy – scorpions in particular are nocturnal – but take care when climbing over dry-stone walls where snakes like to sun themselves, and don't put hands or feet in places, like shoes, where you haven't looked first. Wiggly, fast-moving, six-inch **centipedes** which look like a rubber toy from Hong Kong should also be treated with respect, as they pack a nasty bite.

The number of annual deaths from **snakebite** in Europe is very small. Many snakes will bite if threatened, whether they are venomous or not. If a bite injects venom, then swelling will normally occur within thirty minutes. If this happens, get medical attention, keep the bitten part still, and make sure all body movements are as gentle as possible. If medical attention is not nearby then bind the limb firmly to slow the blood circulation, but not so tightly as to stop the blood flow.

Many reptiles, including snakes, can harbour **Salmonella** bacteria, so should be handled cautiously and preferably not at all. This applies particularly to tortoises.

In addition to munching its way through a fair fraction of Greece's surviving pine forests, the **pine processionary caterpillar** – taking this name from the long, nose-to-tail convoys which individuals form at certain points in their life cycle – sports highly irritating hairs, with a poison worse than a scorpion's. If you touch one, or even a tree-trunk they've been on recently, you'll know all about it for a week, and the welts may require antihistamine lotion or pills to heal.

Plants

If you snap a **wild-fig** shoot while walking in the countryside, take care not to come in contact with drops of the highly irritant **sap**. The immediate antidote to this alkaloid is a mild acid, like lemon juice or vinegar; left unneutralized, fig "milk" raises welts which take a month to heal. Severe allergic reactions have to be treated with strong steroids, either topical cream (available from pharmacies) or intravenously in hospital casualty wards.

Pharmacies, drugs and contraception

For **minor complaints** it's enough to go to the local **farmakío** (pharmacy). Greek pharmacists are highly trained and dispense a number of medicines which elsewhere could only be prescribed by a doctor. In the larger towns and resorts there'll usually be one who speaks good English. Pharmacies are usually closed evenings and Saturday mornings, but all should have a monthly schedule (in both English and Greek) on their door showing the complete roster of night and weekend duty pharmacists in town.

Greeks are famously hypochondriac, so pharmacies are veritable Aladdin's caves of **arcane drugs and sundry formulas** – just about everything available in North America and northern Europe is here, and then some, at affordable prices. **Homeopathic** and **herbal** remedies are quite widely available, too, now sold in most larger pharmacies alongside more conventional products.

If you regularly use any form of **prescription drug**, you should bring along a copy of the prescription, together with the generic name of the drug; this will help should you need to replace it, and also avoids possible problems with customs officials. In this regard, it's worth being aware that **codeine is banned** in Greece. If you import any you might find yourself in serious trouble, so check labels carefully; it's the core ingredient of Panadeine, Veganin, Solpadeine, Codis and Empirin-Codeine, to name just a few common compounds.

Hayfever sufferers should be prepared for the early Greek pollen season, at its height from April to June. Pollen from Aleppo and Calabrian pine in April/May can be particularly noxious. If you're taken by surprise, you'll be able to get tablets at a pharmacy, but best to come prepared.

Contraceptive pills are more readily available every year, but don't count on getting these – or spermicidal jelly/foam – outside of a few large island towns, over-the-counter at the larger *farmakía*; Greek women tend not to use any sort of birth control systematically, and have an average of four abortions during their adult life. **Condoms**, however, are inexpensive and ubiquitous – just ask for *profylaktiká* (the slangy terms *plastiká* or *kapótes* are even better understood) at any pharmacy or corner *períptero* (kiosk).

Women's hygienic supplies are sold sometimes in pharmacies, much more often in supermarkets, near the toilet paper and diapers. Napkins ("Always" brand) are ubiquitous; tampons can be trickier to find in remoter spots, especially on the smaller islands.

Doctors and hospitals

You'll find English-speaking **doctors** in any of the bigger towns or resorts. For an **ambulance**, phone ☎166. In **emergencies**, treatment is given free in **state hospitals** (ask for the *thálamos atihimáton* – casualty ward), though you will only get the most basic level of nursing care. Staff attitudes vary: we've been attended to very satisfactorily on several occasions, but if you're the latest in a series of inebriated foreigners to fall of a hotel balcony in a given resort, your reception may be cavalier at best. Greek families routinely take in food and bedding for relatives, so as a tourist you'll be at a severe disadvantage. Somewhat better are the ordinary state-run **outpatient clinics** (*yiatría*) attached to most public hospitals and also found in rural locales. These operate on a first-come, first-served basis, so go early; usual hours are 8am to noon, though it's sometimes possible to get seen by someone between 1 and 5pm.

Costs, money and banks

The cost of living in Greece has increased remarkably since it joined the EU and subsequently adopted the euro. The days of renting an island house for a monthly pittance are ancient history, and food prices at corner shops now differ little from those of other EU member countries. However, outside the established resorts, travel between and around the islands remains reasonably priced, with the cost of restaurant meals, short-term accommodation and public transport still cheaper than anywhere in northern or western Europe except parts of Portugal.

Prices depend on where and when you go. Larger tourist resorts and the trendier small islands (such as Sými, Sífnos, Ídhra, Paxí and Pátmos) are more expensive, and costs everywhere increase sharply in July, August and at Christmas, New Year and Easter. **Students** with an International Student Identity Card (ISIC) can get discounted (sometimes free) admission at many archeological sites and museums; those **over 65** can rely on site-admission discounts of 25 to 30 percent, as well as similar discounts for transport (which may apply at age 60). These, and other occasional discounts, tend to be more readily available to EU nationals.

Some basic costs

On most islands a **daily per-person budget** of £26–28/US$44–47 will get you basic accommodation, breakfast, picnic lunch, a short ferry or bus ride and a simple evening meal, as one of a couple. Camping would cut costs marginally. On £50/US$80 a day you could be living quite well, plus sharing the cost of renting a large motorbike or small car.

Inter-island **ferry fares**, a main unavoidable expense, are subsidized by the government in an effort to preserve remote island communities. To give you some idea of prices, the cheapest cabin for the overnight journey from Athens to Sámos, a twelve-hour trip, costs about €35, while a deck-class ticket for the four-hour trip from Rhodes to Kós costs about €10. For €5–8 you can catch a short-hop ferry to the numerous small islands that lie closer to Rhodes, Kós and Sámos, the most likely touchdown points if you're flying to the Dodecanese or east Aegean on a direct charter; a cheap cabin from Pireás to Rhodes, one of the longest single ferry journeys in Greece, will set you back €46. Local ferries in the Cyclades are a bit pricier for the sea miles travelled; Páros or Náxos to Thíra in the Cyclades costs about €9.

The simplest double **room** generally costs around €25–30 a night, depending on the location and the plumbing arrangements. Bona-fide single rooms are rare, and cost about seventy percent of double rates. Organized **campsites** are little more than €4 per person, with similar charges per tent and perhaps 25 percent more for a camper van. With discretion you can camp for free in the more remote, rural areas.

A basic taverna **meal** with local wine can be had for around €11–14 a head. Add a better bottle of wine, seafood or more careful cooking, and it could be up to €19–22 a head; you'll rarely pay more than that. Sharing seafood, Greek salads and dips is a good way to keep costs down in the better restaurants, and even in the most developed of resorts, with inflated "international" menus, you'll often be able to find a more earthy but decent taverna where the locals eat.

Youth and student discounts

Various official and quasi-official **youth/ student ID cards** soon pay for themselves in savings. Full-time students are eligible for the International Student ID Card (ISIC; Ⓦ www.isiccard.com), which entitles the bearer to special air, rail and ferry fares and discounts at museums, theatres and other attractions. For Americans there's also a health benefit, providing token medical coverage and a per-day stipend for hospital stays up to two months. The card costs $22 for Americans, CDN$16 for Canadians, A$16.50 for Australians, NZ$21 for New Zealanders, £6 in the UK, and €12.70 in the Republic of Ireland.

You only have to be 26 or younger to qualify for the **International Youth Travel Card**, which costs US$22/£7 and carries the same benefits. Teachers qualify for the **International Teacher Identity Card (ITIC)**, offering similar discounts and costing US$22, CDN$16, A$16.50 and NZ$21 and £6. All these cards are available in the US from STA and Travel CUTS and, in Canada, Hostelling International; in the UK, Australia and New Zealand from STA.

Several other travel organizations and accommodation groups also sell their own cards, good for various discounts. A university photo ID might open some doors, but is not as easily recognizable as the ISIC cards, although the latter are often not accepted as valid proof of age.

Money

Greece is one of twelve EU countries that changed over to a single currency, the **euro** (€), in February 2002. The fixed conversion rate used was 340.75 dhrachmas (*dhrakhmés*) to one euro; people still commonly quote prices in dhrachmas, and many till receipts continue to show the value in both currencies. Rounding up of odd euro equivalents of drachma prices has prevailed since February 2002, effectively making the country two to three percent more expensive in 2003 than in early 2002 even before inflation was taken into account. Greek shopkeepers have not been bothering much with shortfalls of 10 cents or less, whether in their favour (especially) or yours. You will be able to exchange any leftover drachma paper notes until March 2012, at branches of the Bank of Greece.

For the most up-to-date **exchange rates** of the US dollar or the pound sterling against the euro, consult the very useful currency speculators' website, ⓦwww.oanda.com.

Euro notes exist in denominations of 5, 10, 20, 50, 100, 200 and 500 euro, and coins in denominations of 1, 2, 5, 10, 20 and 50 cents and 1 and 2 euro. Each country in the euro-zone strikes its own coins (just one face is distinctive), but the other side – and all notes – are uniform throughout Europe. See p.79 for a discussion of counterfeit notes.

Banks and exchange

Greek **banks** are normally open Monday to Thursday 8.30am–2.30pm and Friday 8.30am–2pm. Always take your passport with you as proof of identity and be prepared for at least one long queue. Outside these times, the largest hotels and travel agencies can often provide an exchange service, albeit sometimes with hefty commissions. On small islands with no full-service bank, "authorized" bank agents will charge yet another extra fee (1–2 percent) to cover the cost of posting a travellers' cheque to the main branch.

A number of authorized brokers for exchanging foreign cash have emerged in Athens and other major tourist centres. When changing small amounts, choose those bureaux that charge a flat percentage commission (usually one percent) rather than a high minimum. There's also a small number of 24-hour automatic **foreign-note-changing machines** in a few resorts, but a high minimum commission tends to be deducted.

In 1998, the Greek **post office** abandoned the business of changing money – a nuisance, as many tiny islands have a post office but no bank. If you have a UK-based **Girobank** account, you may be able to use your chequebook to get money at the affiliated Tahydhromiko Tamievtirio (Postal Savings Bank), often run from the same premises.

There is no need to **purchase euro** beforehand unless you're arriving at some ungodly hour in one of the remoter frontier posts, or on a Sunday.

Travellers' cheques

The safest, though most expensive, way to carry money is as **travellers' cheques**. These can be obtained from banks (even if you don't have an account) or from offices of Thomas Cook and American Express; you'll usually pay a commission of between one and two percent, though enquire about any special commission-free deals from your travel agent or your home bank. You can cash the cheques at most banks, though rarely elsewhere. Each travellers' cheque encashment in Greece will incur a minimum commission charge of €1.20–2.40 depending on the bank for amounts of up to €60 equivalent, so you won't want to make too many small-value transactions. For greater amounts, a set percentage applies. Make sure you keep the purchase agreement and a record of cheque serial numbers safe and separate from the cheques themselves. In the event that cheques are lost or stolen, the issuing company will expect you to report the loss forthwith; most companies claim to replace lost or stolen cheques within 24 hours.

Credit cards and ATMs

Major **credit cards** are not usually accepted by cheaper tavernas or hotels, but they're almost essential for renting cars, for buying Olympic Airways tickets and for expensive souvenirs. Major travel agents may also claim to accept them, though a **three-percent surcharge** is often levied on the purchase of ferry (as opposed to air) tickets.

Credit/debit cards are also handy for withdrawing money from the growing network of Greek **ATMs**; you'll just need to know the PIN numbers for your cards. Larger airports (such as Athens, Haniá or Iráklion on Crete, Rhodes, Lésvos, Kós, Corfu and Thessaloníki) have at least one ATM in the arrivals hall, and almost any town or island with a population larger than a few thousand (or a substantial tourist traffic) also has them. The best distributed are those of the National Bank/Ethniki Trapeza, the Trapeza Pireos/Bank of Piraeus, and the Commercial Bank/Emboriki Trapeza, which happily and interchangeably accept Visa, MasterCard, Visa Electron, Plus and Cirrus cards; those of the equally widespread Alfa Trapeza/Alpha Bank are somewhat more restrictive, accepting only American Express and Visa-affiliated cards.

ATM transactions with **debit cards** linked to a current (checking) account via the Plus/Cirrus systems attract charges of 2.25 percent on the sterling/dollar transaction value, subject to a minimum of £1.75, making them the **least expensive** way of getting money in Greece as long as you withdraw more than £80 equivalent in euro (currently about €115). By contrast, using **credit cards** at an ATM is one of the **most expensive** ways of obtaining cash: a cash advance per-transaction fee of £2 minimum typically applies in the UK, plus a "foreign transaction" surcharge of up to 2.75 percent on the total, depending on the card issuer; the "tourist" (not the more favourable "interbank") exchange rate will also be applied.

Wiring money

In an emergency you can arrange to have substantial amounts of **money wired** from your home bank, to a bank in Greece. Receiving funds by SWIFT transfer takes a minimum of two, and up to ten, working days. From the UK, a bank charge of 0.03 percent, with a minimum of £17, maximum £35, is typically levied for two-day service; some building societies charge a £20 flat fee irrespective of the amount. If you choose this route, your home bank will need the address and (ideally) the branch number of the bank where you want to pick up the money. It's unwise to transfer more than the equivalent of €10,000; above that limit, as part of measures to combat money-laundering, the receiving Greek bank will begin asking awkward questions and imposing punitive commissions.

Having money wired from home using one of the **companies** listed below is never convenient; local affiliate offices are thin on the ground in Greece although you may find that main post offices (in provincial capitals) are the designated receiving points for Western Union. It is also more expensive than using a bank. However, the funds should be available for collection at Amex's, Thomas Cook's or Western Union's local representative office within hours, sometimes minutes, of being sent.

Money-wiring companies

Thomas Cook US ☎1-800 287-7362, Canada ☎1-888 823-4732, Britain ☎01733/318 922, Northern Ireland ☎028/9055 0030, Republic of Ireland ☎01/677 1721, ⊛www.thomascook.com.

Travelers Express MoneyGram US ☎1-800 955-7777, Canada ☎1-800 933-3278, UK ☎0800 018 0104, Republic of Ireland ☎1850 205 800, Australia ☎1800 230 100, New Zealand ☎0800 262 263, ⓦwww.moneygram.com.

Western Union US and Canada ☎1-800 325-6000, Australia ☎1800 501 500, New Zealand ☎0800 270 000, UK ☎0800 833 833, Republic of Ireland ☎1800 395 395, ⓦwww.westernunion.com.

B

BASICS | Getting around

Getting around

Island-hopping is an essential feature of a Greek holiday; the ferry network – supplemented in season by hydrofoils and catamarans – is extensive, and will eventually get you to any of the 166 inhabited isles. Planes are relatively expensive, at three to four times the cost of a deck-class ferry ticket and almost twice as much as the cheapest cabin berth. They are, however, useful for saving time at the start or finish of a visit, providing critical links between smaller islands and Athens, Thessaloníki, Rhodes and Crete. On the islands themselves, buses provide skeletal connections, which most tourists choose to supplement by renting a scooter, motorbike or car.

Sea transport

There are several different varieties of vessel for sea travel: **roll-on-roll-off** (ro-ro) barge short-haul ferries, nicknamed *pondófles* or "slippers" in Greek, designed to shuttle mostly vehicles short distances; medium-sized to large **ordinary ferries** (which operate the main services); **high-speed catamarans**, also medium-sized to large, which match hydrofoils in speed but carry a certain number of cars; **hydrofoils**, which carry only passengers; and local **kaïkia** (small boats which do short hops and excursions in season). Costs are very reasonable on the longer journeys, though proportionately more expensive for shorter, inter-island connections. Short-haul lines with monopolies – for example Alexandhroúpoli–Samothráki and Kými–Skýros – are invariably overpriced.

We've indicated most of the **ferry, catamaran and hydrofoil connections**, both on the maps (see opposite for a general pattern) and in the "Travel details" at the end of each chapter. Don't take our listings as exhaustive or wholly reliable, however, as schedules are notoriously erratic, and must be verified each year; details given are

essentially for departures between late June and mid-September. **Out-of-season** departure frequencies are severely reduced, with many islands connected only once or twice a week. However, in spring or autumn those ferries that do operate are often compelled by the transport ministry to call at extra or unusual islands, making possible some interesting connections.

The most reliable, up-to-date information is available from the local **port police** (*limenarhío*), which in Attikí maintains offices at Pireás (☎210 45 11 310), Rafína (☎22940 28888), Lávrio (☎22920 25249) and on or near the harbours of all fair-sized islands. Smaller places may only have a *limenikós stathmós* (marine station), often just a single room with a VHF radio. Their officers rarely speak much English, but keep complete schedules posted – and, meteorological report in hand, are the final arbiters of whether a ship will sail or not in stormy weather conditions.

Only the largest companies produce regular **schedule** sheets, which may not be adhered to as the season wears on. The only attempt at an all-inclusive Greek ferry

Adapted from an original drawing by Phil Green

TURKEY

Alexandhroúpoli

Samothráki

Kavála Keramotí

Thássos

Límnos

Lésvos

Híos

Sámos

Ikaría

Fourní

Agathoníssi

Lipsí

Léros

Pátmos

Kálymnos

Kós

Nissyros

Tílos

Symi

Kastellórizo

Rhodes

Hálki

Kárpathos

Kássos

Sitía

Áyios Nikólaos

Anáfi

Astypálea

Amorgós

Dhonoússa

Koufoníssi

Skhinoússa

Iráklia

Náxos

Íos

Thirassía/Thíra

Folégandhros

Síkinos

Kími

Skýros

Áyios Efstrátios

Tínos

Andhros

Mýkonos

Síros

Kéa

Kýthnos

Séri fos

Sífnos

Kímolos

Mílos

Paros

Réthymnon

Haniá

CRETE

Iráklion

Thessaloníki

Vólos

Áyios Konstandínos

Áyios Nikólaos

Évio

Kými

Skíathos
Skópelos
Alónissos

Rafína

Lávrio

ATHENS

PIREÁS

Égina

Angístri
Méthana
Póros

Idhra

Ermióni

Spétses

Pórto Héli

Leonídhio

Kyparíssi

Yérakas

Monemvasía

Neápoli

Kýthira

Elafónisos

Ýthio

Andikýthira

Kastélli

Háni

Kastélli

Paleohóra

Gávdhos

Hóra
Stakíon

GREECE

Corfu
Town

Igoumenítsa

Párga

Lefkími

Paxí

Vassilikí
(Lefkádha)

Astakós

Fiskárdho

Kefalloniá

Áyios Nikólaos

Pessádha

Argostóli

Itháki

Sámi

Pátra

Póros

Kyllíni

Zákynthos
Town

Zákynthos

**GREEK FERRIES, CATAMARANS
& HYDROFOILS**

Shading of lines indicates
frequency of sailings in summer

━━━ Daily
━━━ 4 to 6 per week
━━━ 1 to 3 per week

B

The wreck of the Express Samina – and beyond

On September 27, 2000, around midnight in gale conditions, the **Express Samina**, oldest ship in the domestic fleet, slammed full speed into the Pórtes rocks outside Páros harbour in the Cyclades, and sank within minutes. The bridge was unstaffed by senior officers, all of whom were elsewhere watching a football match on television. The British and Greek navies, exercising in the area, plus swarms of fishing boats from Páros, together plucked most of the 500-plus aboard from the water, including numerous foreign tourists, but 82 passengers drowned. It was the worst **maritime disaster** in Greece since the ferry *Iraklion* went down in December 1966, with 226 casualties.

Skipper Vassilis Yiannakis, previously at the helm in the collision and sinking of the *Nireus* (in 1991) and the first mate were quickly remanded in custody to await trial. Once the furore had died down, the pair seemed on reflection to be easy scapegoats, and at the time of writing no trial date had been set, with prosecutors still unable to decide what charges to file. The boat had formerly been owned by Agapitos Lines, one of several shipping companies swallowed up by Minoan Flying Dolphins in its several-year drive to acquire dominance of the Greek passenger-ferry industry and a near-monopoly on sailings to the Cyclades and the Dodecanese. In this they had been assisted by a previous merchant-marine minister in the PASOK government, who also became a focus of opprobrium, along with Minoan Flying Dolphins' management (one of whom, general manager Pandelis Sfinias, committed suicide on November 30 by jumping from the sixth floor of his Pireás headquarters).

It also emerged that the 34-year-old *Express Samina* was the worst but by no means the only rust-bucket in the Greek domestic fleet, well past its scrap-by date. EU regulations normally require ships to be retired after 27 years of service, but Greek shipping interests had wheedled an extension to 35 years from Brussels. With an effective **monopoly** and regulated fares, there was little incentive to keep boats up to date. Greek newspapers quickly tallied eighteen ferries 29 years old or older. The age of the *Express Samina* was a critical factor in her rapid sinking; newer craft have multiple airtight compartments, so that a single breach in the hull will not be fatal, but the *Express Samina* had just a single compartment, and was effectively doomed the moment the rocks tore a three-metre gash in her side (though the crew having left bulkhead doors open did not help). Most lifesaving equipment, from the ancient, cork-buoyed lifejackets to the snail-slow lifeboats, was inadequate or scarcely used at the critical hour. Only the

guide is the yearly *Greek Travel Routes, Domestic Sea Schedules*, co-produced by the GNTO and the Greek travel agents' manual the *Greek Travel Pages*, and rarely available before July. You're better off referring to the websites listed on pp.31–32.

Regular ferries

On most **ferry** routes, your only consideration will be getting a boat that leaves on the day, and for the island, that you want. However, when sailing from **Pireás**, the main port of Athens, to the Cyclades or Dodecanese islands, you should have a choice of at least two, often three, sailings

and may want to bear in mind a few of the factors below.

Though spanking-new **boats** are still a rarity, you will more often than not be surprised to encounter a former English Channel or Scandinavian fjord ferry, rechristened and enjoying a new lease of life in the Aegean.

Routes taken and the speed of the boats can vary enormously. A journey from Pireás to Thíra, for instance, can take anything from four and a half (high-speed "cat") to fourteen ("milk-run" conventional ferry) hours. Prior to buying a ticket it's wise to establish how many stops there will be before your island, and the estimated time year before, an inspection engineer had resigned in protest that his verdict on the boat as unseaworthy was being ignored by Minoan.

The government had to be seen to be doing something, and so made a show of granting some minor routes to Minoan's competitors during the weeks following the sinking, and pushed for a **thirty-year limit** on service time for boats in early 2001 (now in fact the rule). It's in the medium term, however, that the fallout from the disaster has had most effect. The oldest members of the domestic fleet were instantly confined to port, pending safety inspections – which several did not pass, leaving a shortfall. Those ships that could be brought into compliance with EU standards were refitted, but clean bills of health – and exceptional exemptions to the age-limit rule – were often issued in an arbitrary and biased manner.

Investigations still proceed at glacial pace, and Minoan Flying Dolphins remains the target of a vast number of civil suits for wrongful death, and also a criminal investigation – not, perhaps, unrelated to the directors' July 2001 decision to rechristen the company Hellas Flying Dolphins. *Express Samina* survivors' claims for compensation for their lost property remain unpaid pending resolution of the wrongful-death suits.

In the prevailing climate of protecting profits (and one's legal behind) before service, matters are likely to get worse before they get better. Only a few newly commissioned ferries – such as NEL's high-speed catamarans *Aeolos Express, Aeolos Kenderis* and *Aeolos Express II* – have taken to the water since the disaster. **Loopholes** in the law allows substandard craft to continue operating under the following conditions: if their destination is a non-EU country (ie Turkey), if they run on a chartered basis rather than scheduled, and if they decline to collect government subsidies for an unprofitable line. The entire fleet of Miniotis Lines, which provides critical links in the northeast Aegean, passed the legal age limit in 2003, and it remains to be seen if new boats will come on-stream in 2004 or whether the services will just lapse. Terrified of another public-relations nightmare in the run-up to Greece's hosting of the 2004 Olympics, the port police became far stricter about confining boats to port in marginal weather conditions. The only hope of improvement will be after 2005, when cabotage (whereby only Greek-registered lines can provide domestic ferry service) ends, opening competition to the likes of P&O or Fred Olsen. In the meantime, many islands of the Dodecanese, northeast Aegean and Ionian archipelagos, left poorly served by the removal of boats and lines, are depending on new, subsidized peripheral air links provided by Olympic Aviation.

of arrival. Many agents act just for one specific boat (they'll blithely tell you that theirs is the only available service), so you may have to ask around to uncover alternatives. Especially in high season, early arrival is critical in getting what may be a very limited stock of accommodation.

Regular ferry **tickets** are, in general, best bought on the day of departure, unless you need to reserve a cabin berth or space for a car. Buying tickets in advance will tie you down to a particular craft at a particular time – and innumerable factors can make you regret that. Most obviously there's bad weather, which, particularly off-season, can play havoc with the schedules, causing some small boats to remain at anchor and others to alter their routes drastically. (The ticket price is refunded if a boat fails to sail.) There are only three periods of the year – March 23–25, the week before and after Easter, and most of August – when ferries need to be booked at least several days in advance. Around the times of elections – whether national, municipal, or European – there will also be a crunch for the best cabins, as Greeks are required to return to their home precinct to vote.

Obligatory, personalized advance ticketing, a rule especially enforced since the *Express Samaina* disaster, means that you cannot buy your ticket on board. Staff at the gangway will bar you from embarking if you don't have a ticket (the only furtive exceptions seem to be the short-haul, roll-on-roll-off services, for example from Igoumenítsa to Corfu, or the central mainland to Évvia). In many cases there may not even be a last-minute sales booth at the quayside. **Fares** for each route are currently set by the transport ministry and should not differ among ships or agencies (though they're marginally more *towards* Pireás as opposed to *from*). There is usually a twenty-percent discount on round-trip fares.

The cheapest class of ticket, which you'll be automatically sold unless you specify otherwise, is **deck class**, variously called *tríti* or *gámma thési*. This gives you the run of most boats except for the upper-class restaurant and bar. On the shorter, summer journeys the best place to be, in any case, is on deck – space best staked out as soon as you get on board. However, boats acquired recently seem, with their glaring overhead lights and moulded-plastic bucket seats, expressly designed to frustrate those attempting to sleep on deck. In such cases it's well worth the few extra euro for a **cabin bunk**, especially if you can share with friends (cabins are usually quadruple, occasionally triple or double). Class consciousness is the rule, so deck-class passengers may find themselves firmly locked out of second-class facilities at night to prevent them from crashing on the plush sofas, and may have to make do with pullman-type seats. **First-class** cabins usually cost scarcely less than a plane flight and are not terrific value – the main difference between first and second being the presence of a bathroom in the cabin, and a better location. Most cabins, incidentally, are overheated or overchilled, and pretty airless; ask for an *exoterikí* (outer) cabin if you want a porthole (though these are always bolted shut).

All bookings are now computerized, and supposedly have accurate space allocations that preclude **overbookings**, but occasionally you may be sold a cabin berth at an intermediate port only to find that they are "full" when the boat arrives. Pursers will usually not refund you the difference between a cabin and third class. Your first- or second-class fare entitles you to a bunk, and this is clearly stated (in Greek) on the verso of your

ticket. Make a scene if necessary until you are accommodated – there are often cabins in the bilge, set aside for the crew but generally unused, where you can sleep.

Motorbikes and cars get issued extra tickets, in the latter case four to five times the passenger deck-class fare, depending on size. Car fees are roughly proportionate to distance: for example Sámos–Ikaría cost €26–30 depending on port and direction, while Sámos–Pireás is about €74. This obviously limits the number of islands you'll want to drag a car to – it's really only worth it for the larger ones like Crete, Rhodes, Híos, Lésvos, Sámos, Corfu or Kefalloniá. Even with these, unless you're planning a stay of more than four days, you may find it cheaper to leave your car on the mainland and rent another on arrival. Technically, written permission is required to take rental motorbikes and cars on ferries, though in practice few crew will quiz you on this.

Some ferries sell a limited range of **food on board**, though it tends to be overpriced and mediocre. Honourable exceptions are the meals served by all ferries to Crete on their overnight sailings. On the short, daytime hops between the various islands of the Argo-Saronic, Cyclades and Sporades, it's a good idea to stock up beforehand with your own provisions; most ferries on these lines offer nothing other than biscuits, greasy, cling-wrapped pizzas, coffee and soft drinks.

Hydrofoils and catamarans

Hydrofoils – commonly known as *dhelfínia* or "Flying Dolphins" – are roughly twice as fast (and at least twice as expensive) as ordinary ferries. However, they're a useful alternative to regular ferries if you are pushed for time, and their network can also neatly fill gaps in ferry scheduling. Their main drawback (aside from frequent engine breakdowns) is that they were originally designed for cruising on placid Russian or Polish rivers, and are quite literally out of their depth on the open sea; thus they are extremely sensitive to bad weather, and even in moderate seas are not for the seasick-prone. Most of these services don't operate – or are heavily reduced – from October to June and are prone to arbitrary cancellation if not enough passengers turn up. You are generally not allowed to transport scooters or bicycles on hydrofoils.

At present, hydrofoils operate among the **Argo-Saronic** islands close to Athens, between Kavála and Thássos, between Alexandhroúpoli and **Samothráki**, between Lávrio and **Kéa**, among certain of the other **Cyclades** (Ándros, Tínos, Mýkonos, Páros, Náxos, Amorgós, the minor islets, Íos and Santoríni), and in the **Dodecanese** and east Aegean among Rhodes, Kós, Kálymnos, Léros, Lipsí and Pátmos, with regular forays up to Sámos, Agathoníssi, Ikaría and Foúrni. The principal mainland ports are Aktí Tselépi in Pireás, Rafína, Vólos and Áyios Konstandínos, as well as Igoumenítsa, Kavála and (seasonally) Alexandhroúpoli. Services in the Argo-Saronic are run by Hellas Flying Dolphins and Saronic Dolphins; in the Cyclades by Hellas Flying Dolphins; and in the Dodecanese or east Aegean by Kyriakoulis Maritime. You may see craft with other livery, but we have excluded them from "Travel details", as they are chartered by tour agencies and do not offer scheduled services controlled by the Ministry of Transport.

Catamarans attempt to combine the speed of hydrofoils with the (relative) reliability and vehicle-carrying capacity of larger ferries. The fact that they are new and sleek, purpose-built in France or Scandinavia, has not prevented numerous breakdowns, since they are constantly playing catch-up to fill in weather-cancelled itineraries and thus miss necessary maintenance. **Inside** they are rather soulless: ruthlessly air-conditioned, with no deck seating and with Greek TV blaring at you from numerous screens – paying a few euro extra for *dhiakikriméni thési* (upper class) gets you a better view and less crowding, but there's no escaping the TV. Cabins are non-existent and food facilities even more unappetizing than on conventional ferries – bring snacks. Car fares are normal, though passenger **tickets** are at least double a comparable ferry journey, ie similar to hydrofoil rates.

Small ferries, kaïkia and taxi boats

In season, **kaïkia** (caiques) and **small ferries** of a few hundred tonnes' displacement sail between adjacent islands and to a few of the more obscure ones. These can be extremely useful and often very pleasant, but are no cheaper than mainline services. In fact, if they're classified as tourist agency charters, and not passenger lines controlled by the transport ministry, they tend to be quite expensive, with pressure to buy return fares (one-ways are almost always available). The more consistent *kaïki* links are summarized in the "Travel details" section of each chapter, though inevitably departures depend on the whims of local boat-owners, so the only firm information is to be had on the quayside. *Kaïkia* and small ferries, despite appearances, have a good safety record. EU regulations, however, mean that many of these smaller boats are doomed for trivial reasons such as not having a second lavatory. Likely to survive are the swarms of **taxi boats** that are a feature of Sými and Itháki, among other spots; these exist to shuttle clients on set routes to remote beaches or ports which can only be reached arduously, if at all, overland. Costs on these are generally reasonable, usually per person but occasionally per boat.

Domestic flights

State-run Olympic Airways and its subsidiary Olympic Aviation at present operate most of the **domestic flights** within Greece. They cover a fairly wide network of islands, and while most routes are to and from Athens or Thessaloníki, there are some very useful peripheral ones centred on Rhodes, Corfu and Crete. Privately run Aegean has cherry-picked the high-volume, high-profit routes from Athens and Thessaloníki to Crete (Haniá and Iráklion), Thíra, Mytilíni, Mýkonos, Rhodes, Kós, Híos, Corfu, Kavála, Ioánnina and Alexandhroúpoli. **Tickets** for both airlines are most easily obtained from travel agents (their own high-street outlets are thin on the ground). Aegean often undercuts Olympic price-wise, and surpasses it service-wise, though flight frequencies tend to be sparse.

Olympic **schedules** can be picked up at their offices abroad (see "Getting there" for contact details in the relevant countries) or through their branch offices and representatives in Greece, which are maintained in almost every town or island of any size.

Aegean's are easiest to get from their desks at major airports. Both airlines publish English-language schedules twice yearly (spring and autumn).

Fares for flights to and between the islands, including the domestic airport tax, work out around three to four times the cost of a ferry journey, but on certain inter-island hauls that are poorly served by boat (Rhodes–Kastellórizo or Corfu–Kefalloniá, for example), you should consider this time well bought.

Island flights are often full in peak season; if they're an essential part of your plans, it is worth trying to make a **reservation** at least a week to ten days in advance. If a flight you've set your heart on is full, **waiting lists** exist – and are worth signing on to at the airport check-in counter; experience has shown that there are almost always one or two no-shows or cancellations. Domestic air tickets are nonrefundable, but you can change your flight, space permitting, without penalty as late as a couple of hours before your original departure.

Incidentally, the only surviving Olympic-run **shuttle buses** between the main town and the airport are on Kós, Límnos and Kastellórizo; others have long since been axed as a cost-cutting exercise. Elsewhere (Híos, Rhodes), municipally run services have picked up the slack, but otherwise you're at the mercy of the taxi-drivers who congregate outside the arrivals gate.

Like ferries, flights are subject to **cancellation** in very bad weather, since many services are on small 50- or 68-seat ATR turbo-prop planes, smaller De Havilland 38-seaters, or the even tinier Dornier 18-seaters, none of which will fly in strong winds or (depending on the destination airport) after dark. Despite these uncertainties, a flight on a Dornier puddle-jumper is a highly recommended experience. You can watch the crew, who are often on first-name terms with passengers, flicking switches in the cockpit; virtually every seat has a view, and you fly low enough to pick out every island feature – you might even select beaches in advance.

Size restrictions also mean that the 15-kilo baggage weight limit can be fairly strictly enforced, especially on the Dorniers; if, however, you've just arrived from overseas or purchased your ticket outside Greece, you are allowed the 20–23-kilo standard international limit. All services operated on the domestic network are **non-smoking**.

Contacts for Greek domestic airlines

Aegean Countrywide ☎801 11 20 000, Venizelos Airport ☎210/35 34 294 or 210 35 30 101, Ⓦwww.aegeanair.com.
Olympic Airways/Aviation Countrywide ☎801 11 44 444, Venizelos Airport ☎210 35 65 529, Ⓦwww.olympic-airways.gr.

Island ground transport

Most islands have some kind of bus service, but many visitors prefer to rent a two- or four-wheeler. Even if you just do this for a day, you can get the measure of a small or medium-sized island and work out where you'd like to be based.

Buses

Bus services on the **major routes** are highly efficient and frequent. On **secondary roads** they're less regular, with long gaps, but even the remotest villages will be connected – at least on weekdays – by a school or market bus to the island (or in Crete, provincial) capital. These often depart for the capital before dawn, returning there between 1.30 and 3pm. On the islands there are usually buses to connect the port and main town for ferry arrivals or departures.

The network is nationally run by a single syndicate known as the **KTEL** (Kratikó Tamío Ellinikón Leoforíon). However, even in medium-sized towns there can be several scattered terminals for services in different directions, so make sure you have the right station for your departure.

Buses are traditionally two-toned cream-and-green, being slowly replaced by hi-tech, navy-and-green models. They are amazingly **prompt** as a rule, so be there in plenty of time for scheduled departures. On small island routes, it's generally first come, first served, with some standing allowed, and tickets dispensed on the spot by an *ispráktoros* or conductor. However, these tickets tend to be issued only up to the next major town, where you'll have to alight briefly and purchase an onward fare (there is always enough time for this).

Motorbikes, scooters and bicycles

The cult of the **motorcycle** is highly developed in Greece, presided over by a jealous deity apparently requiring regular human sacrifice. Accidents among both foreign and local bikers are routine occurrences, with annual fatalities edging into two figures on the busier islands. Some package companies have even taken to warning clients in print against renting motorbikes (thereby making a bit extra on organized overland excursions), but with caution and common sense – and an eye to increasingly enforced regulations – riding a two-wheeler through a resort should be a lot safer than piloting one through London or New York.

Many tourists come to grief on rutted dirt tracks or astride mechanically dodgy machines. In other cases **accidents** are due to attempts to cut corners, in all senses, or by riding two to an underpowered scooter simply not designed to propel such a load. Don't be tempted by this apparent economy – you won't regret getting two separate scooters, or one powerful 100cc bike to share – and remember that you're likely to be charged an exorbitant sum for any repairs if you do have a wipeout. Also, verify that your travel insurance policy covers motorcycle accidents.

One worthwhile precaution is to wear a **crash helmet** (*krános*); many rental outfits will offer you (an admittedly ill-fitting) one, and some will make you sign a waiver of liability if you refuse it. Helmet-wearing is in fact required by law, with a €78 fine levied for failure to do so; on some smaller islands (eg Léros) the rule is laxly enforced, on others (eg Sámos and Corfu) random police roadblocks do a brisk commerce in citations, and foreign renters are most definitely not exempt.

Reputable establishments demand a full **motorcycle driving licence** for any engine over 90cc (the law actually stipulates "over 50cc"), and you will usually have to leave your passport as security. For smaller models, any driving licence will do. Failure to

carry the correct license on your person attracts a €86 fine.

Fines of any sort are to be paid within ten working days at the municipal cashier's (*dhimotikó tamío*); proof of payment then needs to be taken to the police station to have the citation cancelled. Non-payment will be followed by a court date being set, and the Greek authorities – so dilatory in other respects – are amazingly efficient at translating summons into foreign languages and forwarding them to your overseas address. No-shows are automatically convicted, and a conviction will make re-entry to Greece awkward at best.

Small **motor scooters** with automatic transmission, known in Greek as *mihanákia*, or *papákia* (little ducks) after their characteristic noise, are good transport for all but the hilliest islands. They're available for rent on many islands for €13–20. Prices can be bargained down out of peak season, or if you negotiate for a longer period of rental.

Before riding off, make sure you check the bike's **mechanical state**, since many are only cosmetically maintained. Bad brakes and worn or oil-fouled spark plugs are the most common defects; dealers often keep the front brakes far too loose, with the commendable intention of preventing you going over the handlebars. If you break down it's your responsibility to return the machine, so take down the phone number of the rental agency in case it gives out in the middle of nowhere. Better outlets often offer a free retrieval service.

The latest generation of **scooters**, such as Piaggio, Vespa or Peugeot, is practical enough, but thirsty on fuel; make sure there's a kick-start as backups to the battery, since ignition switches commonly fail. Bungee cords (a *khtapódaki* or "little octopus" in slang) for tying down bundles are supplied on request, while capacious baskets are also often a feature. The ultra-trendy, low-slung models with fat, small-radius tyres, however, are unstable on anything other than the smoothest, flattest island roads. Especially if you intend to go off-road, always choose traditionally designed bikes with large-radius, nobbly, narrow tyres, if available. Again, if you're going to spend every day of your vacation astride a *mihanáki*, consider bringing or buying cyclists' or motorcyclists' **gloves**; they'll be hot and silly-looking in mid-summer, but if you lose all the skin off your hands when you go for a spill, the wounds take months to heal, and leave huge scars.

In the family of true **motorbikes** with manual transmissions, and safer tyres (as described above), the favourites, in descending order of reliability, are the Honda 50, Yamaha Townmate and Suzuki FB Birdie; gears are shifted with an easy-to-learn left-foot pedal action, and (very important) these can all be push-started if the starting crank fails. For two riders, the least powerful safe model at nominal extra cost is the Honda Cub 90cc or Yamaha 80 Townmate. Best of all is the attractive Honda Astrea 100 and its rival-brand clones, very powerful but scarcely bigger than older models. If you've got the proper license and off-road experience, dirt-bikes of 125cc and up can also be found in most resorts.

Cycling

Cycling in Greece is not such hard going as you might imagine (except in midsummer), especially on one of the mountain bikes that are rapidly supplanting the old bone-shakers at rental outfits; they rarely cost more than €7 a day. You do, however, need steady nerves, as roads are generally narrow with no verges or bike lanes (except on Kós), and many Greek drivers consider cyclists a lower form of life, on a par with the snakes regularly found run over.

If you have your own mountain or touring bike (the latter not rented in Greece), you might consider taking it along by **train** or **plane** (it's free if within your 20–23kg international air allowance, but always arrange it in writing with the airline beforehand to avoid huge charges at check-in). Once in Greece you should be able to take a bike for free on most of the ferries, in the guard's van on most trains (for a small fee – it goes on a later goods train otherwise), and with a little persuasion in the luggage bays of buses. Any small spare parts you might need, however, are best brought along, since specialist bike shops are only found in the largest island towns.

Driving and car rental

Automobiles have obvious advantages for getting to the more inaccessible parts of larger islands, but this is not an especially cheap Mediterranean country in which to **rent a car**. If you intend to drive **your own vehicle** to and through Greece, via EU member states, it's worth knowing that Green Cards are no longer required; insurance contracted in any EU member state is valid in any other, but in many cases this is only third-party cover – the statutory legal minimum. Competition in the industry is so intense, however, that many UK insurers will throw in full, pan-European cover for free or for a nominal sum, for up to sixty days; shop around if necessary.

EU citizens bringing their own cars are, in theory, free to circulate in the country for six months, or until their home-based road tax or insurance expires, whichever comes first. Plain-clothes inspectors at highway checkpoints and ferry-docks have lately been waving down cars without visible **tax discs**, and they're empowered to impound them immediately. You must always be able to prove that the car has been in Greece for less than six months (the dated ticket for any ferry you may have arrived on from Turkey or Italy is considered sufficient). Besides the annoyance of impoundment, **fines** for overstaying are horrendous, and **import duties** run anywhere from 50 to 120 percent of the value of the car, depending on its age. If you're resident and don't officially import your car, you're only allowed to use an EU-plated car for six-month periods each year (you choose the time period) – the rest of the time it must be stored off-road, under customs seal.

Other, **non-EU** nationalities will get a **carnet** for their vehicle entered in their passport; the carnet normally allows you to keep a vehicle in Greece for up to six months, exempt from road tax. It is difficult, though not impossible, to leave the country without the vehicle; the nearest customs post will seal it for you (while you fly back home for a family emergency, for example) but you may possibly have to pay storage if you don't have access to off-street parking, and also find a Greek national to act as your **guarantor**. This person will assume all financial liabilities arising from ownership of the car should you ultimately abandon it.

Car rental

Car rental on the islands starts at around €330 a week in high season for the smallest, A-group vehicle from a one-off outlet or local chain, including unlimited mileage, tax and insurance. Overseas tour operators' and international chains' brochures threaten alarming rates of €440 for the same period but, except in August, no rental company expects to fetch that price for a car. Outside peak season, at the smaller local outfits, you can often get terms of about €35 per day, all inclusive, with even better rates for three days or more. **Comparison shopping** among agencies in the larger resorts can yield a variation in quotes of up to twenty percent for the same conditions over a four-to-seven-day period; the most negotiable variable is whether or not kilometres in excess of one hundred per day (a common hidden catch) are free. Open **jeeps**, which are increasingly popular, begin at about €82 per day, rising to as much as €97 at busy times and places.

Brochure prices in Greece almost never include tax, **collision damage waiver** (CDW) and personal insurance. It is strongly recommended that you pay a few extra euro a day for "Super Collision Damage Waiver", "Franchise Waiver" or "Liability Waiver Surcharge", as it is variously called, or you could be hit with a €300–350 fee for even the tiniest scratch or missing mud-flap. Be careful of the hammering that cars get on dirt tracks; tyres, windshield and the underside of the vehicle are almost always excluded from even supplementary insurance policies. All agencies will want either a **credit card** or a large **cash deposit** up front; minimum age requirements vary from 21 to 23. **Driving licences** issued by any EU state are honoured, but an International Driving Licence is required by all other drivers, including Australians, New Zealanders and North Americans. This must be arranged before departure, since ELPA (the Greek motoring association) doesn't issue IDLs to foreign nationals.

In peak season, you may get a better price through one of the **overseas booking companies** that deal with local firms than if you negotiate for rental in Greece itself. Competitive companies in Britain include Suncars and Transhire. Autorent, Budget, Payless, EuroHire, European, Kosmos, National/Alamo, Reliable, Eurodollar and Just are dependable Greek, or smaller international, chains with branches in many towns; all are considerably cheaper than the biggest international operators such as Hertz or Avis but it is always worthwhile visiting all the international chains' websites for a quote, and with a Frequent Flyer discount code you may well match prices of the discount booking companies noted above. Specific local recommendations, mostly based on author experience, are given in the guide.

In terms of **models**, the more competitive companies tend to offer the Subaru M80 or Vivio, the Fiat Cinquecento or Seisento and the Suzuki Swift 1000 as A-group cars, and Opel (Vauxhall) Corsa 1.2, Fiat Uno/Punto, Peugeot 106, Daewoo Matiz, Hyundai Atos, Citroën Saxo, Renault Clio/Twingo or Nissan Micra in the B group. Any more than two adults, with luggage, will generally require B category, in which the Atos and the Clio are the most robust models. The badly designed, underpowered Suzuki Alto 600 or 800, Fiat Panda 750/900 and Seat Marbella should be avoided if offered as A-group cars, and indeed have been phased out by the more reputable agencies. The standard four-wheel-drive option is a Suzuki jeep (1.3- or 1.6-litre), mostly open-top – great for bashing down steep, rutted tracks to remote beaches.

Car-rental agencies

Britain

Avis ☎0870 606 0100, ⊛www.avis.com.
Budget ☎0800 181 181,
⊛www.budget.com.
Hertz ☎0870 844 8844, ⊛www.hertz.com.
National ☎0870 536 5365,
⊛www.nationalcar.co.uk.
Sixt ⊛www.e-sixt.com.
Suncars ☎0870 500 5566, ⊛www.suncars.com.
Thrifty ☎01494/751 600, ⊛www.thrifty.com.
Transhire ☎0870 789 8000,
⊛www.transhire.com.

Ireland

Avis Northern Ireland ☎028/9024 0404,
Republic of Ireland ☎01/605 7500,
🖥www.avis.ie.
Budget Republic of Ireland ☎0903/277 11,
🖥www.budget.ie.
Cosmo Thrifty Northern Ireland ☎028/9445
2565, 🖥www.thrifty.com.
Hertz Republic of Ireland ☎01/676 7476,
🖥www.hertz.ie.
Sixt Republic of Ireland ☎1850 206 088,
🖥www.irishcarrentals.ie.
Thrifty Republic of Ireland ☎1800 515 800,
🖥www.thrifty.ie.

North America

Alamo ☎1-800 522-9696, 🖥www.alamo.com.
Auto Europe US ☎1-800 223-5555,
Canada ☎1-888 223-5555,
🖥www.autoeurope.com.
Avis US ☎1-800 331-1084, Canada ☎1-800
272-5871, 🖥www.avis.com.
Budget ☎1-800 527-0700,
🖥www.budgetrentacar.com.
Dollar US ☎1-800 800-4000, 🖥www.dollar.com.
Europe by Car ☎1-800 223-1516,
🖥www.europebycar.com.
Hertz US ☎1-800 654-3001, Canada ☎1-800
263-0600, 🖥www.hertz.com.
National ☎1-800 227-7368,
🖥www.nationalcar.com.
Thrifty ☎1-800 367-2277, 🖥www.thrifty.com.

Australia

Avis ☎13 63 33 or 02/9353 9000,
🖥www.avis.com.au.
Budget ☎1300 362 848, 🖥www.budget
.com.au.
Dollar ☎02/9223 1444, 🖥www.dollarcar.com.au.
Hertz ☎13 30 39 or 03/9698 2555,
🖥www.hertz.com.au.
National ☎13 10 45, 🖥www.nationalcar.com.au.
Thrifty ☎1300 367 227, 🖥www.thrifty.com.au.

New Zealand

Apex ☎0800 93 95 97 or 03/379 6897,
🖥www.apexrentals.co.nz.
Avis ☎09/526 2847 or 0800 655 111,
🖥www.avis.co.nz.
Budget ☎09/976 2222, 🖥www.budget.co.nz.
Hertz ☎0800 654 321, 🖥www.hertz.co.nz.
National ☎0800 800 115,
🖥www.nationalcar.co.nz.
Thrifty ☎09/309 0111, 🖥www.thrifty.co.nz.

Motoring organizations

UK and Ireland

AA UK ☎0870 600 0371, 🖥www.theaa.com.
AA Ireland Dublin ☎01/617 9988,
🖥www.aaireland.ie.
RAC ☎0800 550 055, 🖥www.rac.co.uk.

North America

American Automobile Association (AAA)
☎1-800 AAA-HELP, 🖥www.aaa.com. Each state
has its own branch of this club – check the phone
book for local address and phone number.
Canadian Automobile Association (CAA)
☎613/247-0117, 🖥www.caa.com. Again, each
region has its own club – check the phone book for
local address and phone number.

Australia and New Zealand

AAA Australia ☎02/6247 7311,
🖥www.aaa.asn.au.
AA New Zealand ☎09/377 4660,
🖥www.nzaa.co.nz.

Driving in Greece

As in all of continental Europe, you drive **on
the right** in Greece. The country has the
highest **accident rate** in the EU after
Portugal, and on the larger tourist islands it's
easy to see why. Driving habits amongst
locals can be atrocious: overtaking is erratic,
tailgating and barging out heedlessly from
side-roads are preferred pastimes, lane lines
go unheeded, turn signals go unused, and
motorbikes hog the road or weave from side
to side. **Drunk driving** is also a major problem; Sunday afternoons in rural areas are
particularly bad, and for the same reason
you should be extra vigilant when driving late
at night at weekends or on holidays. Well-
publicized police campaigns are underway
to combat the problem, with radar guns
being deployed against speeders as well.

Matters are made worse by poor **road
conditions**: signposting is absent or badly
placed, pavement markings are faded,
asphalt can turn into a one-lane surface or a
dirt track without warning on secondary
routes, and you're heavily dependent on
magnifying mirrors at blind intersections in
congested villages. Uphill drivers insist on
their **right of way**, as do those first to

approach a one-lane bridge; **flashed head-lights** usually mean the opposite of what they do in the UK or North America, here signifying that the other driver insists on coming through or overtaking.

Parking in the biggest island towns is uniformly a nightmare owing to congestion and high vehicle numbers. **Pay-and-display** systems as in the UK are the rule, and it's not always clear where you obtain tickets from (sometimes a kiosk, sometimes a machine). They tend to be strip-type, where you pop out the date and starting hour from pre-punched cardboard stock.

Wearing a **seatbelt** is compulsory – you will be fined for non-observance at the many checkpoints – as is keeping a first-aid kit in the boot (many rental companies skimp on this), and children under the age of 10 are not allowed to sit in the front seats. It's illegal to drive away from any kind of accident, and in cases where serious injury has resulted you can be held at a police station for up to 24 hours. If this happens, you have the right to ring your consulate immediately to summon a lawyer; don't make a statement to anyone who doesn't speak, and write, very good English. In practice, once police are informed that there was no personal injury, they rarely come out to investigate.

Tourists with proof of AA/RAC/AAA membership are given free road assistance from ELPA, the Greek equivalent, which runs **breakdown services** on several of the larger islands; in an emergency ring their road assistance service on ☎104. Many car rental companies have an agreement with ELPA's equally widespread competitors Hellas Service (☎1057) and Express Service (☎154); however, you will always get a faster response if you dial the local number for the island you're stranded in (ask for these in advance). Any breakdown service is prohibitively expensive to summon on your own – over €140 to enrol as an "instant member" for a year.

Running a vehicle

Petrol/gasoline currently costs €0.69–0.83 per litre for regular unleaded (*amólyvdhi*), super unleaded or super lead-replacement; diesel costs €0.57–0.64 per litre.

Lead-replacement fuel for older cars without catalytic converters is called "Neo Super" or "Super 2002", the year leaded fuel was phased out.

It is easy to run short of fuel **after dark or at weekends** in both rural and urban Greece; most stations close at 8pm sharp, and nearly as many are shut all day Sunday. There will always be at least one pump per district open on a rota basis, but it's not always apparent which one it is. This is not so much of a problem on the major highways, but it is a factor everywhere else. So always fill up, or insist on full rental vehicles at the outset, and if you've brought your own car, keep a full petrol can at all times. Some stations which claim to be open around the clock are in fact automated-only at night – you have to use bill-taking machines, which don't give change. If you fill your tank without having exhausted your credit, punch the button for a receipt and get change the next day during attended hours (assuming you're still in the area).

Petrol stations run by multinational companies (BP, Mobil, Shell and Texaco) usually take **credit cards**; Greek chains like EKO, Elda, Eteka, Jetoil, Revoil and Elinoil usually don't (except in tourist areas). The tiny, generic-petrol stations of the EP (Eleftherο Pratirio) chain are always the cheapest around. Shell is the most expensive major chain, BP tends to be much less.

In terms of **maintenance**, the easiest car models to have serviced and buy parts for in Greece are VWs (including combi and Transporter vans), Mercedes, BMWs, Audis, Opels, Ladas, Skodas and virtually all French, Italian, Korean and Japanese makes. British models are a bit more difficult, but you should be fine as long as you haven't brought anything too esoteric like a Hillman Minx – the Mini is, for example, still a cult vehicle in Greece, Fords are present (though not common), and the Opel is of course the continental brand of Vauxhall.

In general, both mechanics' **workshops** and **parts retailers** are clustered at the approach and exit roads of all major towns, usually prominently signposted. For the commonest makes, emergency spares like fan belts and cables are often found at surprisingly remote service stations, so don't hesitate to ask at an unlikely-looking spot. Rural mechanics are okay for quick patch-up jobs like snapped clutch cables, but for major problems it's best to limp into the nearest sizable town to find a mechanic who is factory-trained for your make.

Hitching

Hitching carries the usual risks and dangers, and is inadvisable for women travelling alone, but, overall, Greece is one of the safer countries in which to do it. It's fairly reliable, too, as a means of getting around in remote areas, so long as you're not overly concerned about time; lifts are fairly frequent but tend to be short.

Hitching is easiest in remote areas of the larger islands; at its best, it's a useful way of picking up some Greek beyond a restaurant vocabulary. While you'll often get lifts from Greeks eager to display or practise their English, there will be as many instances where to communicate you're forced to try the language. In the more thinly populated rural areas, you'll see appreciable numbers of elderly Greeks waving down a ride – you'll be doing a useful service by picking them up, and reciprocating in some small way for the hospitality which is still often the rule in isolated regions.

Taxis

Greek **taxis** are among the cheapest in the EU – so long as you get an honest driver who switches the meter on and doesn't use high-tech devices to doctor the reading. Use of the meter is mandatory within city or town limits, where Tariff "1" applies, while in rural areas or between midnight and 5am, Tariff "2" is in effect. On certain islands, such as Kálymnos and Léros, set rates apply on specific fixed routes for "collective" taxis – these only depart when full. Otherwise, throughout Greece the meter starts at €0.75, though the minimum fare is €1.50; any baggage not actually on your lap is charged at €0.20 apiece. Additionally, there are surcharges of €2 for leaving or entering an airport, and €0.60 for leaving a harbour area. If you summon a taxi by phone on spec, there's a €1.50 charge, while a pre-arranged rendezvous is €2.10 extra; in either case the meter starts running from the moment the driver begins heading towards you. All categories of supplemental charges must be set out on a laminated card affixed to the dashboard. For a week or so before and after Orthodox Easter, and Christmas, a *filodhórima* or gratuity of about ten percent is levied. Any or all of these extras will legitimately bump up the basic meter reading of about €8 per ten rural kilometres.

Accommodation

There are huge numbers of beds for tourists in the Greek islands, so most of the year you can rely on turning up pretty much anywhere and finding a room – if not in a hotel, then in a private house or block of rooms (the standard island accommodation). Only from late July to early September, at Christmas/New Year, and around Easter, the country's high seasons, are you likely to experience problems. At these times, if you don't have accommodation reserved well in advance, you'd be wise to keep well off the main tourist trails, turning up at each new place early in the day and taking whatever is available – you may be able to exchange it for something better later on.

Out of season, you face a slightly different problem: most private rooms – and camp-sites – operate only from late April or early May to October, leaving hotels your only option. During winter you may have no choice but to stay in the main towns or ports. There will often be very little life outside these places anyway, with all the seasonal beach bars and restaurants closed. On many smaller islands, you will often find just one hotel – and perhaps one or two tavernas – staying open year-round. Be warned also that any resort or harbour hotels which do operate through the winter are likely to have a certain number of **prostitutes** as long-term guests; licensed prostitution is legal in Greece, and the management in many places consider this is the most painless way to keep the bills paid.

Hotels

Hotels in the larger resorts are often contracted out on a seasonal basis by foreign package-holiday companies, though there are often vacancies available (especially in spring or autumn) for walk-in trade. The tourist police set official **categories** for hotels, which range from "L" (Luxury) down to the rarely encountered "E" class; all except the top category have to keep within set price limits. The letter system is supposed to be replaced with a star grading system as in other countries, but the process, while already begun, is being resisted; L is five-star, E is no-star, etc. While they last, letter ratings are supposed to correspond to **facilities** available, though in practice categorization often depends on location within a resort, number of rooms and "influence" with the tourism authorities – there are so-called E-class hotels with under nine rooms which are plusher than nearby C-class outfits. It is mandatory for D-class hotels to have at least some rooms with

---

Hot water

A key variable in both rooms and hotels is the type of water heating. Rooftop **solar units** (*iliaká*) are more popular than electric **immersion heaters** (*thermosífona*). Under typical high-season demand, however, solar-powered tanks tend to run out of hot water during the post-beach shower crunch at 6pm, with no more available until the next day. A heater, either as a backup or primary source, is more reliable; proprietors may either jealously guard the boiler controls or entrust you with its workings, which involves either a circuit breaker or a rotary switch turned to "I" for fifteen minutes. You should never shower with a *thermosífono* powered up (look for the glow-lamp indicator on the tank) – besides the risk of shock from badly earthed plumbing, it would be fairly easy to empty smaller tanks and burn out the heating element.

Accommodation price codes

Throughout the book we've categorized accommodation according to the following **price codes**, which denote the cheapest available double room in high season. All prices are for the room only, except where otherwise indicated in accounts. Many hotels, especially those in 4 category and over, include breakfast in the price; you'll need to check this when booking. During low season, rates can drop by more than fifty percent, especially if you are staying for three or more nights. Exceptions are during the Christmas/New Year and Easter weeks when you'll pay high-season prices. Single rooms, where available, cost around seventy percent of the price of a double.

❶ Up to €25
❷ €26–35
❸ €36–50

❹ €51–70
❺ €71–90
❻ €91–120

❼ €121–170
❽ €171 plus and upwards

Note: Youth hostels typically charge €7–9 for a dormitory bed.

attached baths; C-class must be completely en suite, and additionally have a bar or designated breakfast area. The presence of a pool and/or tennis court will attract a B-class rating, while A-category hotels should have a restaurant, bar, conference/business facilities and extensive common areas. Often these, and the L outfits (essentially self-contained complexes), back onto a quasi-private beach.

In terms of **food**, C-class hotels are required only to provide the most rudimentary of continental breakfasts – you may choose not to take, or pay, for it – while B-class and above will usually offer some sort of buffet breakfast including cheese, cold cuts, sausages, eggs and so on. With some outstanding exceptions, noted in the Guide, lunch or supper at hotel-affiliated restaurants is bland and poor value.

Private rooms

The most common island-resort accommodation is **privately let rooms** (*dhomátia*). Like hotels, these are regulated and officially divided into three classes (A down to C), according to facilities. These days the bulk of them are in new, purpose-built, low-rise buildings, but a few are still actually in people's homes, where you'll occasionally be treated to disarming hospitality.

Licensed rooms are almost always scrupulously clean, whatever their other amenities. At their (now all-but-vanished) **simplest**,

you'll get a bare, concrete-floored room, with a hook on the back of the door and toilet facilities outside in the courtyard. At the **fancier** end of the scale, they are modern, fully furnished places with an en-suite bathroom and a fully equipped kitchen shared by guests. Between these extremes there will be a choice of rooms at various prices – owners will usually show you the most expensive first. Some of the cheap places will also have more expensive rooms with en-suite facilities – and vice versa, with rare singles often tucked under stairways or in other less desirable corners of the building. Price and quality are not necessarily directly linked, so always ask to see the room before agreeing to take it.

Areas to **look for rooms**, along with recommendations of the best places, are included in the Guide. As often as not, however, the rooms find you: owners descend on ferry or bus arrivals to fill any space they have, sometimes waving photos of the premises. Many island municipalities have acted, or are moving, to outlaw this practice, owing to widespread bait-and-switch tactics and the pitching of unlicensed rooms. In smaller places you'll often see rooms advertised, sometimes in German (*Zimmer*); the Greek signs to look out for are "ΕΝΙΚΙΑΖΟΜΕΝΑ DHOMÁTIA" or "ΕΝΙΚΙΑΖΟΝΤΕΗ DHOMÁTIA". In the more developed island resorts, where package holidaymakers predominate, *dhomátia* owners will often require you to stay for at least three days, or even a week.

It has become standard practice for rooms proprietors, like hotel staff, to ask to keep your **passport** – ostensibly "for the tourist police", who do require customer particulars – but in reality to prevent you skipping out with an unpaid bill. Some owners may be satisfied with just taking down your details, as is done in hotels, and they'll almost always return the documents once you get to know them, or if you need them for another purpose.

If you are **stranded**, or arrive very late in a remote island village, you may very well find that there is someone with an unlicensed room prepared to earn extra money by putting you up. This should not be counted on, but things work out more often than not. Otherwise, the most polite course is to have a meal or drink at the taverna or *kafenío* and then, especially in summer, enquire as to the possibility of sleeping either in the vacant schoolhouse or in a spare room at the *kinotikó grafío* (community records office).

Old-fashioned, 1970s-vintage rooms on the remoter islets, occasionally still without private bath, tend to fall into the ❶ price category. Standard, en-suite rooms without cooking facilities weigh in at ❷; newer, well-amenitied rooms and self-catering studios occupy the top end of the ❸ niche, along with the more modest C-class hotels, the better among these edging into ❹. Category ❺ corresponds fairly well to the better-value B-class hotels and the humbler designer inns in popular centres like the trendier Cyclades, while ❻ tallies with most of B-class and the really state-of-the-art restoration projects. ❼–❽ means A- and L-class, and the sky's the limit here – €300 is by no means unheard of these days.

Prices in any establishment should by law be displayed on the back of the door of your room, or over the reception desk. If you feel you're being overcharged at a place which is officially registered, threaten to report it to the tourist office or police, who will generally adopt your side in such cases. A hotelier is free to offer a room at any amount under the official rate, but it's an offence to charge one euro-cent over the permitted price for the **current season**. Depending on location,

there are up to three of these: typically October to May (low), June to mid-July, plus September (mid) and mid-July through August (high). Small amounts over the posted price may be legitimately explained by municipal tax or out-of-date forms. More commonly you will find that you have bargained so well, or arrived so far out of high season, that you are actually paying far less than the maximum prices – which are in any case optimistically pitched for a few high-traffic days in the year.

In **winter**, officially from November 1 until early April, private rooms – except in Ródhos Old Town and the biggest towns of Crete – are closed pretty much across the board to keep the few open hotels in business. There's no point in traipsing about hoping to find exceptions; most owners obey the system very strictly. If they don't, the room-owners will find you themselves and, watching out for hotel rivals, guide you back to their place.

Villas and long-term rentals

The easiest – and usually most economical – way to arrange a **villa rental** is through one of the package-holiday companies detailed on p.14. They represent some superb places, from fairly simple to luxurious, and costs can be very reasonable, especially if shared between a few people. Several of the companies we list will arrange **"multi-centre"** stays on two islands over two weeks.

On the islands, a few local travel agents arrange villa rentals, though they are often places the overseas companies gave a miss on or could not fill. **Out of season**, you can sometimes get a good deal on villa or apartment rental for a month or more by asking around locally, though in these days of EU convergence and the increasing desirability of the islands as year-round residences, "good deal" means anything under €180 per month for a large studio (*garsoniéra*) or €250 for a small one-bedroom flat.

Hostels and monasteries

The Greek islands are not exactly packed with **youth hostels** (*xenón neótitos* in the singular), – just a few on Thíra, Rhodes and

Crete, mostly not officially recognized by the IYHF. Those that do exist tend, with honourable exceptions, to be pretty run-down and/or filthy, and thus a far cry from similar north European institutions. Competition from unofficial "student hostels" and inexpensive rooms means that they are not as cost-effective as elsewhere in Europe. It's best to have a valid IYHF card, but you can often buy one on the spot, or maybe just pay a little extra for your bed. Dorms tend to have four to six beds; most hostels have a curfew at 11pm or midnight, and many places only open in spring and summer.

The tradition of offering hospitality to travellers (of the appropriate sex) at Greek **monasteries** and **convents** is more common on the mainland than on the islands, so you should always ask locally before heading out to one for the night. Also, dress modestly – shorts for men and women, and short skirts are total anathema – and try to arrive early in the evening, not later than 8pm or sunset (whichever is earlier).

Camping

Officially recognized campsites range from ramshackle compounds behind a beach to highly organized and rather soulless complexes, formerly run by EOT prior to privatization. Most places cost about €4.50 a night per person, slightly less per tent and €8 per camper van, but at the fanciest sites, rates for two people plus a tent can almost equal the price of a basic room. The Panhellenic Camping Association regularly (but not annually) publishes a booklet covering most officially recognized Greek campsites and the facilities they offer; it's available from many EOT offices.

Camping rough – outside authorized campsites – is such an established element of Greek travel that few people realize that it's officially illegal. Since 1977 "freelance" camping, as EOT calls it, has actually been forbidden by a law originally enacted to harass gypsies, and regulations are increasingly enforced. Another drawback is the increased prevalence of theft in rural areas, often by bands of refugees from Albania and other north Balkan states. All told, you will feel less vulnerable inside a tent, camper van or even a rock-cave – not that rain is likely during the long Greek summer, but some protection is essential from wind, sun, insects (see "Health", p.34) and stray animals raiding your food. You will always need at least a light sleeping bag, since even summer nights can get cool and damp; a foam pad is also recommended for pitching on harder ground.

If you do camp rough, it's vital to exercise sensitivity and discretion. Police will crack down on people camping (and especially littering) around popular tourist beaches, particularly when a large community of campers develops. Off the beaten track, however, nobody is very bothered, though it is always best to ask permission locally in the village taverna or café. During high season, when everything – even the authorized campsites – may be full, attitudes towards camping rough are more relaxed, even in the most touristed places. At such times the best strategy is to find a sympathetic taverna, which in exchange for regular patronage will probably be willing to guard small valuables and let you use their facilities.

Eating and drinking

Greeks spend a lot of time socializing outside their homes, and sharing a meal is one of the chief ways of doing it. The atmosphere is always relaxed and informal, and pretensions (and expense-account prices) are rare outside of the more chi-chi parts of Athens and certain major resorts. Greeks are not prodigious drinkers – tippling is traditionally meant to accompany food – though since the mid-1990s a whole range of bars and pubs has sprung up, both in tourist resorts and as pricey music halls at the outskirts of the major towns.

Breakfasts, picnic fare and snacks

Greeks don't generally eat **breakfast**, so the only egg-and-bacon kind of places are in resorts where foreigners congregate, or where there are returned North American- or Australian-Greeks. Such spots can sometimes be fairly good value (€5–7 for the works, maybe even with "French" filter coffee), especially if there's competition. More indigenous alternatives are yogurts at a *galaktopolío* (milk bar), or cheese pies and pretzel rings from a bakery (see "Snacks", p.58).

Picnic fare

Picnic fare is good, cheap and easily available at bakeries and *manávika* (fruit-and-veg stalls). **Bread**, alas, is often of minimal nutritional value and inedible within a day of purchase. It's worth paying extra at the bakery (*foúrnos* or *psomádhiko*) for *olikís* (wholemeal), *sikalísio* (rye bread), *oktásporo* (eight-grain) or even *enneásporo* (nine-grain), the latter types most commonly baked where large numbers of Germans or Scandinavians are about. When buying **olives**, go for the fat Kalamáta or Ámfissa ones; they're more expensive, but tastier. However, locally gathered olives – especially the slightly shrivelled *hamádhes* or fully ripened, ground-gathered olives – often have a distinctive nutty taste, compensating for large kernels. The best **honey** is reckoned to be the pure-thyme variety from the more barren islands (such as Límnos, Náxos, Kálymnos and Astypálea), although it's about double the price of ordinary honeys.

Honey is an ideal topping for the famous local **yogurt**. All of the larger island towns have at least one dairy shop where locally produced yogurts are sold in plastic or (better) clay containers of various sizes. Sheep-milk yogurt is richer and sweeter, scarcely requiring honey; cows milk yoghurt is tarter but more widely available. Side by side with these will be *krémes* (custards) and *ryzógala* (rice puddings) in one-serving plastic containers.

Feta cheese is ubiquitous – sometimes, ironically, imported from Holland or Denmark, though this is being clamped down on, and local brands are usually better and not much more expensive. The goat's-milk variety can be very dry and salty, so ask for a taste before buying. If you have access to a fridge, leaving the cheese overnight in a plastic container filled with water will solve both problems, though if left too long like this the cheese simply dissolves. This sampling advice goes for other indigenous cheeses as well, the most palatable of which are the expensive gruyère-type *graviéra*.

Despite membership of the EU, plus growing personal incomes and exotic tastes, Greece imports very little garden produce from abroad, aside from bananas and a few mangoes. **Fruit** in particular is relatively expensive and available only by season, though in the more cosmopolitan spots it is possible to find such things as avocados (light-green Fuerte variety from Crete are excellent) for much of the year. Reliable picnic fruits include *yiarmádhes*, a breed of giant peach available during August and September; *krystália*, tiny, hard green pears that ripen a month or two later and are heavenly; and the *himoniátiko* melon (called casava in North America) which appears at the same time, in its yellow, puckered skin with green flecks. Greece also has a burgeoning kiwi industry, and while the first crop in October coincides with the end of the tourist season, availability carries over into the following May. Less portable, but succulent, are **figs** (*sýka*); there's a crop of small fruits in May, followed by larger ones in August. Salad **vegetables** are more reasonably priced; besides the famous, enormous tomatoes (June–Sept), there is a bewildering variety of springtime greens, including rocket, dill, enormous spring onions and lettuces. Useful expressions for shopping are *éna tétarto* (250g) and *misó kiló* (500g).

Snacks

Traditional **snacks** can be one of the distinctive pleasures of Greek eating, though they are being increasingly edged out by an obsession with Western junk/fast food at nationwide chains such as *Goody's* (burgers), *Everest* and *Grigoris Mikroyevmata* (assorted), *Roma Pizza* and *Theios Vanias* (baked pastries) – somewhat less insipid for being homegrown. However, independently produced kebabs (*souvlákia*) are widely available, and in most larger resorts and towns you'll find *yíros* – doner kebab with garnish in thick, doughy *píta* bread that's closer to Indian naan bread.

Other common snacks include *tyrópites* (cheese pies – the best are the *striftés* or *kouroú* if available) and *spanokópites* (spinach pies), which can usually be found at the baker's, as can *kouloúria* (crispy pretzel rings sprinkled with sesame seeds) and *voutímata* (dark biscuits heavy on the molasses, cinnamon and butter). Pizza can be very good as well, sold *al metro* (by the piece).

Restaurants

Greek cuisine and **restaurants** are simple and straightforward. There's usually no snobbery about eating out; everyone does it regularly, and it's still reasonable – typically €10–15 per person for a substantial (non-seafood) meal with a measure of house wine. Even if the cooking is simple, you

should expect it to be wholesome; Greeks are generally fussy about freshness and provenance.

That said, there's a lot of **lazy cooking** about – especially in resorts, where menus are dominated by bad pizza, spaghetti bolognese, chops. and "tourist moussaká" – a dish heavy with cheap potato slices, and nary a crumb of mince.

Of late you find growing numbers of what the Greeks call "**kultúra**" restaurants, often pretentious attempts at Greek nouvelle cuisine with speciality wine lists, which tend to be long on airs and graces, and (at €19–28 a head) short on value. The exceptions which succeed have been singled out in the text.

When choosing a restaurant, the usual best strategy is to go where the Greeks go. And, despite increasing EU labour regulations limiting staff hours, they go late: 2pm to 3.30pm for **lunch**, 9pm to 11pm for **supper**. You can eat earlier, but you're likely to get indifferent service and cuisine if you frequent establishments catering to the tourist schedule. Chic appearance is not a reliable guide to quality; often the more ramshackle, traditional outfits represent the best value. One good omen is the waiter bringing a carafe of refrigerated water, unbidden, rather than pushing you to order bottled stuff.

In busy resort areas, it's wise to keep a wary eye on the **waiters**, who are inclined to urge you into ordering more than you want, then bring things you haven't ordered. Although cash-register receipts are required in all establishments, these are often only for the grand total, and itemized **bills** will be in handwritten Greek script. Where prices are printed on menus, you'll be paying the right-hand (higher) of the two columns, inclusive of all taxes and usually service charge, although a small extra tip of about ten percent directly to the waiter is hugely appreciated – and usually not expected.

Bread costs extra, but consumption is not obligatory; unless it is assessed as part of the cover charge, you have the right to send it back without paying for it. You'll be considered deviant for refusing it, but so much Greek bread is inedible sawdust that there's little point in paying extra unless you actually want to use it as a scoop for dips.

Children are always welcome, day or night, at family tavernas, and Greeks don't mind in the slightest if they play tag between the tables or chase the **cats** running in mendicant packs – which you should not feed, as signs often warn you. They are wild and pretty desperate, and you'll need a doctor's visit and tetanus jab if they whack at a dangled bit of food and claw your hand instead.

Estiatória

There are two basic types of restaurant: the *estiatório* and the **taverna**. Distinctions between the two are slight, though the former is more commonly found in large towns and tends to have the slightly more complicated dishes termed *mayireftá* (literally, "cooked"). With their long hours, old-fashioned-tradesmen's clientele and tiny profit margins, *estiatória* (sometimes know as *inomayiría*) are, alas, something of a vanishing breed.

An *estiatório* will generally feature a variety of such oven-baked casserole dishes as moussakás, *pastítsio*, meat or game stews like *kokinistó* and *stifádho*, *yemistá* (stuffed tomatoes or peppers), the oily vegetable casseroles called *ladherá* and oven-baked meat and fish. Usually you go into the kitchen and point at the desired steam trays to choose these dishes.

Batches are cooked in the morning and then left to stand, which is why this *mayireftá* food is often **lukewarm** or even cold. Greeks don't mind this (most actually believe that hot food is bad for you), and dishes like *yemistá* are actually enhanced by being allowed to cool off and stand in their own juice. Similarly, you have to specify if you want your food with little or no oil (*horís ládhi*), but once again you will be considered a little strange since Greeks regard olive oil as essential to digestion.

Desserts (*epidhórpia* in formal Greek) of the pudding-and-pie variety don't exist at *estiatória*, and yogurt or cheese are only occasionally served. Fruit, however, is always available in season; watermelon (often on the house), melon and grapes are the summer standards. Autumn treats worth asking after include *kydhóni* or *akhládhi stó foúrno*, baked quince or pear with some sort

of syrup or nut topping. Sometimes you may be offered a complementary slice of sweet semolina halva (*smigdhalísios halvás*).

Tavernas and psistariés

Tavernas range from the glitzy and fashionable to rough-and-ready ones with seating under a reed canopy, behind a beach. Really primitive ones have a very limited (often unwritten) menu, but the more established will offer some of the main *mayireftá* dishes mentioned above, as well as the standard taverna fare. This essentially means **mezédhes** (hors-d'oeuvres) or **orektiká** (appetizers) and **tís óras** (meat and fish, fried or grilled to order).

Psistariés or grill-houses serve spit-roasted lamb, pork or goat (generically termed *kondosoúvli*), grilled chicken (*kotópoulo skáras*) or *kokorétsi* (grilled offal roulade). They will usually have a limited selection of *mezédhes* and salads (*salátes*), but no *mayireftá* at all.

Since the idea of courses is foreign to Greek cuisine, starters, main dishes and salads often arrive together unless you request otherwise. The best thing is to order a selection of *mezédhes* and salads to share, in true Greek fashion. Waiters encourage you to take the *horiátiki saláta* – the so-called Greek **salad**, including feta cheese – because it is the most expensive. If you only want tomato, or tomato and cucumber, ask for *domatosaláta* or *angourodomáta*. *Láhano-karóto* (cabbage-carrot) and *maroúli* (lettuce) are the typical winter and spring salads respectively.

The most interesting **mezédhes** are *tzatzíki* (yogurt, garlic and cucumber dip), *melitzanosaláta* (aubergine/eggplant dip), *kolokythákia tiganitá* (courgette/zucchini slices fried in batter) or *melitzánes tiganités* (aubergine/eggplant slices fried in batter), *yígandes* (white haricot beans in vinaigrette or hot tomato sauce), *tyropitákia* or *spanakópites* (small cheese and spinach pies), *revythókeftedhes* or *pittaroúdhia* (chickpea patties similar to falafel), *okhtapódhi* (octopus) and *mavromátika* (black-eyed peas).

Among **meats**, *souvláki* (shish kebab) and *brizóles* (chops) are reliable choices, often locally produced. In both cases, pork (*hirinó*) is usually better and cheaper than veal (*moskharísio*). The best *souvláki*, though not often available, is lamb (*arnísio*). At *psistariés*, meaty lamb shoulder chops (*kopsídha*) are more substantial than the scrawny rib chops called *païdhákia*; roast lamb (*arní psitó*) and roast kid (*katsíki stó fournó*) are considered *estiatório* fare. *Keftédhes* (breadcrumbed meatballs), *biftékia* (similar, but meatier) and the spicy, home-made, coarse-grain sausages called *loukánika* are cheap and good. *Kotópoulo* (chicken), especially grilled, is widely available but typically battery-farmed in Epirus or on Évvia. Other dishes worth trying are stewed goat (*gídha vrastí*) or baked goat (*katsíki stó foúrno*) – goat in general is a wonderfully healthy meat, typically free-range, undosed with antibiotics or hormones.

As in *estiatória*, traditional tavernas offer fruit rather than sticky **desserts**, though nowadays these are often available, along with coffee, in tavernas frequented by foreigners.

Fish and seafood

Seaside *psarotavérnes* offer **fish**, though for the inexperienced, ordering can be fraught with peril. Summer visitors get a relatively poor choice of fish, most of it frozen, farmed or imported from Egypt and North Africa. Drag-net-trawling is prohibited from the end of May until the beginning of October, when only lamp-lure (*grí-grí*), trident, "doughnut" trap (*kýrtos*) and multi-hook line (*paragádhi*) methods are allowed. During these warmer months, such few fish as are caught tend to be smaller and dry-tasting, and are served with a tureen of *ladholémono* (oil and lemon juice) sauce. Taverna owners often comply only minimally with the requirement to

indicate when seafood is **frozen** (look for the abbreviation "kat.", "κ" or just an asterisk on the Greek-language side of the menu).

Given these considerations, it's often best to set your sights on the **humbler**, seasonally migrating or perennially local species. The cheapest consistently available fish are *gópes* (bogue), *atherína* (sand smelts) and *marídhes* (picarel), eaten head and all, best rolled in salt and sprinkled with lemon juice. In the Dodecanese, *yermanós* (same as Australian leatherback), which first came through the Suez canal from the Indian Ocean in the 1890s, is a good frying fish which appears in spring; *gávros* (anchovy) and *sardhélles* (sardines) are late summer treats, at their best in the northeast Aegean. In the north Aegean or the Sporades, *pandelís* or *sykiós* (Latin *Corvina nigra*, in French "corb") is caught in early summer, and is highly esteemed since it's a rock-dweller not a bottom feeder – and therefore a bit pricier than the preceding. In autumn especially you may encounter *psarósoupa* (fish broth) or *kakaviá* (a bouillabaisse-like stew).

Less esteemed species tend to **cost** about €27–38 per kilo; choicer varieties of fish, such as *barboúni* (red mullet), *tsipoúra* (gilt-head bream), *lavráki* (seabass) or *fangrí* (common bream), will be expensive if wild – about €45 per kilo and up, depending on what the market will bear. If the price seems too good to be true, it's almost certainly **farmed**. Prices are usually quoted by the kilo (less often by the portion), and should not be much more than double the street-market rate. Standard procedure is to go to the glass-fronted cooler and pick your own specimen, then have it weighed (uncleaned) in your presence. If you are concerned that you may be later overcharged, which

Vegetarians

If you are **vegetarian**, you may be in for a hard time, and will often have to assemble a meal from various *mezédhes*. Even the excellent standbys of yoghurt with honey, *tzatzíki* and Greek salad begin to pall after a while, and many of the supposed "vegetable" dishes on menus are cooked in stock or have pieces of meat added to liven them up. Wholly or largely vegetarian restaurants, however, are slowly on the increase in touristy areas; they are highlighted in the Guide where appropriate.

sometimes happens, have the amount confirmed orally or on a slip of paper.

Cheaper **seafood** (*thalassiná*) such as *kalamarákia* (fried baby squid, usually frozen) and *okhtapódhi* (octopus) are a summer staple of most seaside tavernas, and occasionally *mýdhia* (mussels), *kydhónia* (cockles) and *garídhes* (small prawns) will be on offer at reasonable prices. Keep an eye out, however, to freshness and season – mussels in particular are a common cause of stomach upsets or even mild poisoning.

As the more favoured species have become overfished, **unusual seafoods**, formerly the exclusive province of the poor, are putting in a greater appearance on menus. Ray or skate (variously known as *platý*, *seláhi*, *trígona* or *vátos*) can be fried or used in soup, and is even dried for decoration. Sea urchins (*ahiní*) are also a humble (and increasingly rare) favourite, being split and emptied for the sake of their (reputedly aphrodisiac) roe that's eaten raw. Only the reddish ones are gravid; special shears are sold for opening them if you don't fancy a hand full of spines. Many a quiet beach is littered with their halved carapaces, evidence of an instant Greek picnic.

Wines

Both *estiatória* and tavernas will usually offer you a choice of bottled **wines**, and many still have their own house variety: kept in barrels, sold in bulk by the quarter-, half- or full litre, and served either in glass flagons or the brightly coloured tin "monkey-cups" called *kantária*. Not as many tavernas stock their own wine as once did, but it's worth asking whether they have wine *varelísio* (barrelled) or *hýma* (in bulk). Per-litre prices range from €4.50 (Ikaría) to €6 or even €8 (Corfu), with smaller measures priced (more or less) proportionately. Non-resinated wine is almost always more than decent. **Retsina** – pine-resinated wine, a slightly acquired taste – is also available straight from the barrel, though the bottled brands Yeoryiadhi from Thessaloníki, Liokri or Malamatina from central Greece (the latter often cut with soda water), and Cambas from near Athens, are all excellent and likely to be more consistent in quality.

Among the **bottled wines** available **nationwide**, Cambas Attikos, Boutari Lac des Roches, any white from Zítsa and the Rhodian CAIR products (especially the Moulin range) are good, inexpensive whites, while Boutari Naoussa and Kourtakis Apelia are decent, mid-range reds. If you want a better but still moderately priced red, go for the Merlot of either Boutari and Tsantali, or Averof Katoï from Epirus.

If you're travelling around **wine-producing islands**, however, you may as well go for **local bottlings**; the best available guide to the emerging Greek domaines and vintners is Nico Manessis' *The Illustrated Greek Wine Book* (see p.623 of Contexts for ordering information). Almost anything produced on Límnos is decent; the Alexandrine muscat is now used for whites, the local *límnio* grape for reds and rosés. Santoríni, another volcanic island, has a number of premium white products such as Ktima Arghyrou and Boutari Nykhteri, and the Gentilini Robola white of Kefalloniá is justly esteemed. Páros (Moraïtis) and Náxos also both have acceptable local vintages, while Crete is now beginning to have labels superior to the bog-standard Logado, such as Economou (Sitía) and Lyrarakis (Iráklion). On Rhodes, Alexandhris products from Émbonas are well thought of, as is the Emery label with its Villaré white, and CAIR's dry white "2400".

Curiously, island red wines (except for Rhodes's CAIR Moulin and Emery Cava) are almost uniformly mediocre; in this respect you're better off choosing **reds from the mainland**. Carras from Halkidhikí does the excellent Porto Carras, while Ktima Tselepou offers a very palatable Cabernet-Merlot blend. Antonopoulos Yerontoklima (Pátra), Ktima Papaïoannou Nemea (Peloponnese), and Tsantali Rapsani (Thessaly) are all superb, velvety reds – and likely to be found only in the better *kultúra* tavernas or *káves* (bottle shops). Antonopoulos, Tselepos (Mantinia domaine), Spyropoulos (again Mantinia) and Papaïoannou also do excellent **mainland whites**, especially the Spyropoulos Orino Mantinia, sometimes found organically produced.

Other **premium micro-wineries** on the mainland whose products have long been fashionable, in both red and white, include the vastly overrated Hatzimihali (Atalánti, central Greece), the outstanding

Dhiamandákou (near Náoussa, red and white), Athanasiadhi (central Greece), Skouras (Argolid) and the two rival Lazaridhi vintners (Dhráma, east Macedonia), especially their superb Merlots. For any of these you can expect to pay €7–11 per bottle in a shop, double that at a taverna.

Last but not least, CAIR on Rhodes makes its very own "**champagne**" ("naturally sparkling wine fermented en boteille", says the label), in both brut and demi-sec versions. It's not Moët & Chandon quality by any means, but at less than €6 per bottle, who's complaining?

Cafés, cake shops and bars

The Greek eating and drinking experience encompasses a variety of other places beyond restaurants. Most importantly, there is the institution of the **kafenío**, found in every town, village and hamlet in the country. In addition, you'll come across **ouzerís**, **zaharoplastía** (Greek patisseries) and **barákia**.

The kafenío

The **kafenío** (plural *kafenía*) is the traditional Greek coffee shop or café. Although its main business is "Greek" (Middle Eastern) coffee – prepared *skéto* or *pikró* (unsweetened), *métrio* (medium) or *glykó* (sweet) – it also serves spirits such as ouzo (see opposite), brandy (usually Metaxa or Botrys brand, in three grades), beer, the sage-based tea known as *alisfakiá*, juices and soft drinks. Another refreshing drink sold in cafés is *kafés frappé*, iced, jigger-shaken instant coffee with or without milk and sugar – uniquely Greek despite its French-sounding name. Like Greek coffee, it is always accompanied by a welcome glass of cold water. One quality fizzy soft drink to single out is the Vólos-based Epsa, with its Orangina-like bottles and high juice content. A refreshing curiosity – confined to Corfu and Paxí – is *tsitsibýra* (ginger beer), a holdover from the nineteenth-century British occupation of the Ionian islands; cloudy, greyish-white and fizzy, it tastes vaguely of lemon and the sour beginnings of fermentation.

Usually the only **edibles** available are "spoon sweets" or *glyká koutalioú* (sticky,

syrupy preserves of quince, grape, fig, citrus fruit or cherry) and the traditional, now-vanishing *ipovrýhio*, a piece of mastic submerged in a glass of water like a submarine – which is what the word means in Greek.

Like tavernas, *kafenía* range from the plastic, chrome and sophisticated to the old-fashioned, spit-on-the-floor or mock-retro variety, with marble or brightly painted metal tables and straw-bottomed chairs. An important institution anywhere in Greece, they form the pivot of life in the country villages. You get the impression that many men spend most of their waking hours there. Greek women are rarely to be seen in the more traditional places – and foreign women may sometimes feel uneasy or unwelcome in these establishments. Even in holiday resorts, you will find that there is at least one coffeehouse that the local men have reserved for themselves.

Some *kafenía* close at siesta time, but many remain open from early in the morning until late at night. The chief summer socializing time is 6–8pm, immediately after the siesta. This is the time to take your predinner ouzo, as the sun begins to sink and the air cools down.

Ouzo, tsípouro, mezédhes, ouzerís and mezedhopolía

Ouzo, *tsípouro* (confined to Thássos and the Sporades) and *tsikoudhiá* (Crete) are simple spirits of up to 48 percent alcohol, distilled from grape-mash residue left over from wine-making, and then usually flavoured with herbs such as anise or fennel. There are nearly thirty name brands of ouzo, with the best reckoned to be from Lésvos and Sámos; inferior ones are either weak (such as the Rhodian Fokiali, at forty percent) or spiked with molasses or grain alcohol to "boost" them.

When you order, you will be served two glasses: one with the ouzo, and one full of water to be tipped into your ouzo until it turns a milky white. You can drink it straight, but the strong, burning taste is hardly refreshing if you do. It is increasingly common to add **ice cubes** (*pagáki*), a bowl of which will be provided upon request. The next measure up from a glass is a *karafáki* – a deceptively small 200ml vial, and the favourite means of delivery for *tsípouro* – which will very rapidly render you legless if you don't alternate tippling with snacks.

A much smoother variant of ouzo is **soúma**, found chiefly on Rhodes and Sámos, but in theory anywhere grapes are grown. The smoothness is deceptive – two or three glasses of it and you had better not have any other firm plans for the afternoon.

Until the 1980s, every ouzo you ordered was automatically accompanied by a small plate of **mezédhes** on the house: bits of cheese, cucumber, tomato, a few olives, sometimes octopus or even a couple of small fish. Unfortunately, these days "*oúzo mezédhes*" is a separate, more expensive option on a price list. Often, however, they are not featured on any formal menu, but if you order a *karafáki* you will automatically be offered a small selection of snacks.

Though they are confined to the better resorts and select neighbourhoods of the larger islands and towns, one kind of drinking establishment specializes in ouzo and *mezédhes*. These are called **ouzerí** (same in the Greek plural, we've added 's' to the hybrid throughout the Guide). In some towns you may also come across **mezedhopolía**, basically a bigger, more upmarket kind of *ouzerí*. *Ouzerís* and *mezedhopolía* are well worth trying for the marvellous variety of *mezédhes* they serve (though numbers of mediocre tavernas have counterfeited the name). At the genuine article, several plates of *mezédhes* plus drinks will effectively substitute for a more involved meal at a taverna (though it usually works out more expensive if you have a healthy appetite). Faced with an often bewilderingly varied menu, you might opt for the *pikilía* (medley, assortment) available in several sizes, the largest and most expensive one usually heavy on the seafood. At other *ouzerís* the language barrier may be overcome by the waiter wielding an enormous *dhískos* or tray laden with all the current cold offerings – you pick the ones you like the look of, though you'll still have to "blind"-order hot entrées to follow.

Sweets, breakfast and western coffee

Similar to the kafenío is the **zaharoplastío**, a cross between café and patisserie, serving coffee, alcohol, yoghurt with honey and sticky cakes.

The better establishments offer an amazing variety of pastries, cream-and-chocolate confections, honey-soaked Greco–Turkish sweets like *baklavás*, *kataïfi* (honey-drenched "shredded wheat"), *loukoumádhes* (deep-fried batter puffs dusted with cinnamon and dipped in syrup), *galaktoboúreko* (custard pie) and so on.

If you want a stronger slant towards the dairy products and away from the pure sugar, seek out a *galaktopolío*, where you'll often find *ryzógalo* (rice pudding – rather better than the English canned variety), *kréma* (custard) and locally made *yiaoúrti* (yogurt), best if it's *próvio* (from sheep's milk).

Ice cream, sold principally at the gelaterie which have swept over Greece of late (*Dhodhoni* and *Häagen Dazs* are the posh chains), can be very good and almost indistinguishable from Italian prototypes. A scoop (*baláki*) costs €1–1.50; you'll be asked if you want it in a cup (*kypelláki*) or a cone (*konáki*), and whether you want toppings like *santí* (whipped cream) or nuts. By contrast, the mass-produced brands like Delta or Evga are pretty average, with the exception of Skandalo and Nirvana labels. A sign reading "PAGOTÓ POLÍTIKO" or "KAÏMÁKI" means that the shop concerned makes its own Turkish-style ice cream – as good as or better than the usual Italian version.

Both *zaharoplastía* and *galaktopolía* are more family-oriented places than the *kafenío*, and many also serve a basic **continental breakfast** of *méli mé voútyro* (honey poured over a pat of butter) or jam (all kinds are called *marmeládha* in Greek; ask for *portokáli* – orange – if you want proper marmalade) with fresh bread or *friganiés* (melba-toast-type slivers). You are also more likely to find approximations of British **tea** here, as obscure Sri Lankan or Madagascan brands of bag, often left to stew in a metal pot.

"Nes"(café) has become the generic term for all instant **coffee**, regardless of brand; it's generally pretty vile, provoking migraines in the susceptible, and since the mid-1990s there's been a nationwide reaction against it. Even in the smallest provincial capital or resort there will be at least one trendy café which does a range of foreign-style coffees – filter, dubbed *fíltros* or *gallikós* (French); cappuccino; and espresso – at overseas prices. A more enticing, recent innovation is *freddoccino*, a cappuccino-based alternative to the traditional cold frappé. Outside of the largest towns, properly made versions of these drinks will be harder to find and many will come from instant packets.

Bars – and beer

Bars (*barákia* in the plural), once confined to towns and holiday resorts, are now found all over Greece. They range from clones of Parisian cafés or Spanish bodegas to seaside cocktail bars, with music or TV running all day. At their most sophisticated, however, they are well-executed theme venues in ex-industrial premises or Neoclassical houses that can hold their own against close equivalents in Spain or London, with western (currently techno, dub or ambient) soundtracks.

For this and other reasons, drinks are invariably more expensive than in a café – count on €5–8. Bars are, however, most likely to stock a range of **beers**, mostly foreign labels made locally under licence at just one or two breweries on the central mainland. Genuine **local brews** available include Mythos, a smooth lager in a green bottle, put out by the Boutari vintners; Pils Hellas, a sharp pilsner; and last but not least, the resurrected Fix, for years until its demise in 1980 Greece's only beer, though not (according to those who remember) much better the second time around than the first.

Greece also finally has a **microbrewery**, the Athens-based Craft: they make a tasty pilsner and an amber lager, but distribution is not wide.

Kronenberg 1664 and Kaiser are two of the more common quality **foreign-licence** varieties, with the latter available in both light and dark. Bland, inoffensive Amstel and the increasingly rare, yeasty Henninger are the two cheapies; the Dutch themselves claim that Amstel is better than the one available in Holland, and Amstel also makes a very palatable, strong (seven percent) **bock**. Heineken, still referred to as a "*prássini*" by bar and taverna staff after its green bottle, despite the advent of Mythos, is too sharp for many. Recently a wave of even pricier, imported German beers, such as Bitburger, Fisher and Warsteiner (plus a few British ones), has washed over the fancier resorts. Incidentally, try not to get stuck with the one-third-litre cans, vastly more **expensive** (and more of a rubbish problem) than the returnable half-litre bottles. On ferry-boats or in remote locales you may not have a choice, however.

Mineral water, mostly still, typically comes as half-litre and one-and-a-half litre plastic bottles. The ubiquitous Loutraki brand is not esteemed by the Greeks themselves, who prefer various brands from Crete and Epirus. In the better tavernas there has been a backlash against plastic bottles – which constitute a tremendous litter problem – and you can now get it in one-litre glass bottles. Souroti is about the only brand of sparkling (*aerioúho* in Greek) water.

Communications

Greece's postal system is adequate, especially for outgoing mail. Service provided by OTE (Organismós Tiliepikinoníon tís Elládhos, the telecoms entity) has improved drastically since the 1990s, under the twin threats of privatization and competition from thriving local mobile networks. Mobile phone users are well looked after, with signals in all but the remotest corners of the country. A few Internet facilities are found in major towns and resorts.

Postal services

Post offices are open Monday to Friday from 7.30am to 2pm, though certain main branches have hours until the evening and on Saturday morning.

Airmail letters from the mainland take three to seven days to reach the rest of Europe, five to twelve days to get to North America, and a bit longer for Australia and New Zealand. Generally, the larger the island (and the planes serving its airport), the quicker the service. Postal rates for up to 20g are a uniform €0.65 to all overseas destinations. For a modest fee (about €3) you can shave a day or two off delivery time to any destination by using the **express service** (*katepígonda*). **Registered** (*systiméno*) delivery is also available for a similar amount, but proves quite slow unless coupled with express service.

If you are sending large purchases or excess baggage home, note that **parcels** should and often can only be handled in the main provincial or county capitals. This way, your bundle will be in Athens, and on an international flight, within a day. Always present your box open for inspection, and come prepared with tape and scissors – most post offices will sell cardboard boxes, but nothing to actually close the package. An array of services are available: air parcel (fast and expensive), surface-air lift (a couple of weeks slower but much cheaper), insured, and proof of delivery among others.

For a simple letter or card, a stamp (*grammatósimo*) can also be purchased at an authorized postal agency (usually a stationery store). Ordinary **post boxes** are bright yellow, express boxes dark red, but it's best to use only those by the door of an actual post office, since days may pass between collections at other street-corner or wall-mounted boxes. If you are confronted by two slots, "ESOTERIKÓ" is for domestic mail, "EXOTERIKÓ" for overseas. Often there are more: one box or slot for mail into Athens and suburbs, one for your local province, one for "other" parts of Greece, and one for overseas; if in doubt, ask someone.

The **poste-restante** system is reasonably efficient, especially at the post offices of larger towns. Mail should be clearly addressed and marked "poste restante", with your surname underlined, to the main post office of whichever town you choose. It will be held for a month and you'll need your passport to collect it.

Phones

Making **telephone calls** is relatively straightforward. All land-line exchanges are now digital, and you should have few problems reaching any number from either overseas or within Greece.

Call boxes, poorly maintained and invariably sited at the noisiest street corners, work only with phonecards; these come in three sizes – 1000, 5000 and 10,000 units – and are available from kiosks and newsagents. Not surprisingly, the more expensive cards are the best value in terms of euro per unit. Despite numbers hopefully scribbled on the appropriate tabs, call boxes cannot be rung back; however, green, countertop cardphones kept by many hotels can be rung.

A more economic type of pre-paid calling card, which can also be used on private subscriber lines, is the **Hronokarta**, which comes in three denominations. To use one, dial 0808, then at the prompt enter the 12-digit card number. Charges are about half that of conventional telecards.

Other options for calling include a bare handful of **counter coin-op phones** in bars, *kafenía* and hotel lobbies; these should take small euro coins – five-cent, ten-cent, twenty-cent and fifty-cent denominations – and, unlike kerbside phone boxes, can be rung back. Most of them are made in northern Europe and bear instructions in English. You'll probably want to avoid making long-distance calls **from hotel rooms**, as a minimum one-hundred-percent surcharge will be slapped on – more often triple or quadruple the basic rate.

For **international** (*exoterikó*) **calls**, it's best to use kerbside cardphones. **Faxes** are best sent from post offices and some travel agencies – at a price; receiving a fax may also incur a small charge.

Overseas phone calls with a 1000-unit card will **cost**, approximately, €0.40 per minute to all EU countries and much of the rest of central Europe, North America and Australia – versus €0.24 per minute on a private subscriber line. There is no particular cheap rate for overseas calls to these destinations, and dialling countries with problematic phone systems like Russia, Israel or Egypt is obviously rather more. Calling **within Greece**, ordinary **rates** are €0.11 per minute on a subscriber line, rather more from a cardphone; a twenty-percent discounted rate applies daily from 10pm to 8am, and from 10pm Saturday until 8am Monday.

Mobile phones

Mobile phones are an essential fashion accessory in Greece, which has the highest per-capita usage in Europe outside of

Useful phone codes and numbers

Phoning Greece from abroad
Dial the international access code (given below) + 30 (country code) + ten-digit number

Australia ☎0011	New Zealand ☎00
Canada ☎011	UK ☎00
Ireland ☎010	USA ☎011

Phoning abroad from Greece
Dial the country code (given below) + area code (minus any initial 0) + number

Australia ☎0061	New Zealand ☎0064
Canada ☎001	UK ☎0044
Ireland ☎00353	USA ☎001

Specialty Greek phone prefixes

Local call rate ☎0801	Toll-free/Freefone ☎0800

Useful Greek telephone numbers

Ambulance ☎166	Police/Emergency ☎100
Fire brigade, urban ☎199	Speaking clock ☎141
Forest fire reporting ☎191	Tourist police ☎171 (Athens);
Operator ☎132 (Domestic)	☎210 171 (elsewhere)
Operator ☎139 (International)	

Phone charge-card operator access numbers from Greece
NB: These can only be accessed from private subscriber lines.

AT&T USA Direct ☎00 800 1311	British Telecom ☎00 800 4411
Australia ☎00 800 6111	Canada Direct ☎00 800 1611
Australia (Optus) ☎00 800 6121	MCI ☎00 800 1211
Bell Atlantic ☎00 800 1821	NTL ☎00 800 4422
Bell South ☎00 800 1721	Sprint ☎00 800 1411

Italy – in a population of roughly 11 million, there are claimed to be nearly 7 million mobile handsets in use. There are four **networks** at present: Panafon-Vodafone, Telestet-TIM, Cosmote and newcomer Q-Telecom. Calling any of them from Britain, you will find that costs are exactly the same as calling a fixed phone – so you won't need to worry about ringing them when given as alternative numbers for accommodation – though of course such numbers are pricey when rung locally.

Coverage countrywide is fairly good, though there are a few "dead" zones on really remote islets. **Pay-as-you-go**, contract-free plans are heavily promoted in Greece (such as Telestet B-Free and Panafon-Vodafon À La Carte), and if you're going to be around for a while – for example, studying, or working for a season in the tourist industry – an outlay of €90 or less will see you to a decent apparatus and your first calling card. This lasts up to a year – even if you use up your talk time you'll still have an incoming number, along with a voice-mail service. Top-up calling cards – starting from denominations of €8–9 depending on the network – are available at all *períptera*.

If you want to use your **home-based mobile abroad**, you'll need to check with your phone provider whether it will work. North American users will only be able to use tri-band rigs in Greece. Any GSM mobile from the UK, Australia or New Zealand should work fine in Greece.

In the UK you'll have to inform your service network before going abroad to get international access ("**roaming**") switched on. You may get charged extra for this depending on the terms of your package and where you are travelling to. You will also be charged extra to have **incoming calls** forwarded

abroad, as the people calling you will be paying the usual rate; discount plans are available with most providers to reduce the cost of forwarding the call to you overseas by as much as seventy percent. If you want to **retrieve messages** while you're away, you'll probably have to ask your provider for a special access number, as your one-stroke "mail" key may not always work abroad.

Experience has shown that the Greek network selected out of the four existing ones for roaming purposes makes little difference in terms of **call charges**: depending on the length of chat, these can equal £0.70 VAT exclusive per minute, whether to Greek numbers or back to Britain (including voice-mail retrieval). To get round this you can buy a Greek-based pay-as-you-go **SIM** upon arrival in the country (roughly €15–20), and substitute it for the UK-based SIM in your phone. UK providers may tell you that this can't be done, but you are legally entitled to the phone-unblock code from the manufacturer after (usually) six months of use. Otherwise, have a phone shop in Greece free up the phone with a simple five-minute computer procedure.

Email and Internet

Internet cafés are the easiest places to check web-based email accounts (for example ⓦwww.yahoo.com and ⓦwww.hotmail.com) and locations are included throughout the Guide. Rates tend to be about €6 per hour maximum, often less, with half-hour or even ten-minute increments available.

If you are carrying your own **laptop**, you will need about 2m of North American-standard cable (UK cables will not work), lightweight and easily purchasable in Greece, with RJ-11 male terminals at each end. The Greek **dial tone** is discontinuous and thus not recognized by most modems – instruct it to "ignore dial tone". Many newer hotel rooms have RJ-11 **sockets**, but some older ones still have their phones hard-wired into the wall. You can often get around this problem with a female-female **adaptor**, either RJ-11- or 6P6C-configured, available at better electrical retailers. They weigh and cost next to nothing, so carry both (one is sure to work) for making a splice between

---

Greek phone numbers

During 2002, all Greek phone numbers changed to a system resembling the French one, in which you are obliged to dial all ten numbers of a subscriber, including the former area code, wherever you may be. All land lines begin with 2, all mobiles begin with 6.

your cable and the RJ-11 end of the cable between the wall and phone (which you simply unplug). You will usually have to dial an initial "9" or "0" to get around the hotel's central switchboard for a proper external dial tone.

Compuserve and AOL definitely have **points of presence** in Greece, but more obscure ISPs may also have a reciprocal agreement with Greek-based ISPs such as forthnet.gr, otenet.gr and germanosnet.gr, so ask your provider for a list of any available dial-up numbers. **Piggybacking charges**

tend to be fairly high, but for a modest number of minutes per day, still work out rather less than patronizing an Internet café. **Greek ISPs** are very flexible about subscription periods, offering packages of anything from a month to a year (averaging €10–12 per month for unlimited access, with just a few euro-cents per hour surfing charges. So if you're travelling for a while with a laptop, consider signing up; otenet.gr in particular allows you to retrieve mail from any other POP3 account for the price of dialing their nationwide number.

The media

Although the Greek press and airwaves have been relatively free since the fall of the colonels' dictatorship in 1974, nobody would ever propose the Greek media as a paradigm of responsible or objective journalism. Papers are almost uniformly sensational, state-run radio and TV often biased in favour of the ruling party, and private channels imitative of the worst American programming.

British **newspapers** are fairly widely available in Greece at a cost of €1.75–2.50 for dailies, or €4 and up for Sunday editions. You'll find one-to-two-day-old copies of *The Times*, *The Telegraph*, *The Independent* and *The Guardian*'s European edition, plus a few of the tabloids, in all the resorts as well as in major towns. American and international alternatives include turgid *USA Today* and the more readable *International Herald Tribune*, the latter including as a major bonus a free though somewhat abridged English translation of the respected Greek daily *Kathimerini* (online at ⓦ www.ekathimerini .com; see also opposite). Among numerous foreign **magazines**, *Time* and *Newsweek* are also widely available.

There are relatively few surviving **locally produced** English-language magazines or papers. Expensive, glossy *Odyssey* is produced every other month by and for wealthy diaspora Greeks, and differs little from the average in-flight magazine. By far the best of

the English-language **newspapers** is the four-colour *Athens News* (weekly every Friday, online at ⓦ www.athensnews.gr; €1.80) in colour with good features and Balkan news, plus entertainment and arts listings, available in most resorts.

Before setting out from the **UK**, there are two **Greece-specific periodicals** well worth consulting. One is the *Anglo-Hellenic Review* (£2), published twice yearly by the Anglo-Hellenic League; it has excellent essays by renowned scholars, and good reviews of recently issued books on Greek topics. Obtain it either from the Hellenic Book Service (see p.31) or The Hellenic Centre, 16/18 Paddington St, London W1M 4AS. The other is the Greek London Embassy's almost monthly newsletter, *Greece: Background-News-Information*. Though clearly pro-government to the point of verging on propaganda, it's well written (even humorous), giving a lively overview of events in the country over the past few weeks. To register on their mailing list (free), contact them on ☏020/7727 3071, 🖷7727 8960 or email 🖃officepress@ greekembassy.org.uk.

Greek publications

Many papers have ties (including funding) with specific **political groups**, which bias tends to decrease the already low quality of Greek dailies. Among these, only the **centrist** *Kathemerini* – whose former proprietress Helen Vlahos attained heroic status for her defiance of the junta – approaches the standards of a major European newspaper. *Eleftherotypia*, once a PASOK mouthpiece, now aspires to more independence, and has links with Britain's *The Guardian*; *Avriani* has taken its place as the PASOK cheerleading section. *Ta Nea* is a highly popular, MOR tabloid, much loved for its extensive small ads. On the far **Left**, *Avyi* is the Eurocommunist/Synaspismós forum with literary leanings, while *Rizospastis* acts as the organ of the KKE (unreconstructed Communists). *Ethnos* became notorious some years back for receiving covert funding from the KGB to act as a disinformation bulletin. At the other end of the political spectrum, *Apoyevmatini* generally supports the **centre-right** Néa Dhimokratía party, while *Estia's* no-photo format and reactionary politics are both stuck somewhere at the beginning of the twentieth century. The ultra-nationalist, lunatic fringe is staked out by paranoid *Stohos* ("Our Goal: Greater Greece; Our Capital: Constantinople"). With the generally fish-wrap quality of most newspapers, you wouldn't think there'd be room for a designated **gutter press**, but there is: *News Traffic* and *Espresso*.

Among **magazines** that are not merely translations of overseas titles, *Takhydhromos* is the respectable news-and-features weekly, *Ena* is more sensationalist, *Klik* a crass rip-off of Britain's *The Face*, while *To Pondiki* (The Mouse) is a satirical weekly revue in the same vein as Britain's *Private Eye*; its famous covers are spot-on and accessible to anyone with minimal Greek. More specialized niches are occupied by low-circulation titles such as *Adhesmatos Typos* (a slightly rightist, muckraking journal) and *Andi*, an intelligent bi-weekly somewhat in the mould of Britain's *New Statesman*.

Radio

If you have a **radio** on your personal stereo, playing dial roulette can be rewarding. Greek music programmes are always accessible (if variable in quality), and since abolition of the government's former monopoly of wavelengths, regional stations have mushroomed; indeed the airwaves are now positively cluttered as every island town sets up its own studio and transmitter. The two state-run channels are ER1 (a mix of news, talk and popular music) and ER 2 (strictly popular music).

On heavily touristed islands like Rhodes, Corfu and Crete, there will usually be at least one station on the FM band trying its luck at English-moderated programming by and for foreigners. The Turkish state radio's Third Channel is also widely (if somewhat unpatriotically) listened to on border islands for its classical, jazz and blues programmes. The **BBC World Service** broadcasts on short wave throughout Greece; 6.18, 9.41, 15.07 and 12.09 MHz are the most common frequencies. However, short-wave services are being phased out in many parts of the world, so consult ❀www.bbc.co.uk/worldservice, for current frequencies.

Television

Television first appeared in Greece in 1965, but it only became dominant during the 1967–74 junta, with the ruling colonels using it as a means of social control and to purvey anodyne variety revues, sports events and so on. As in many countries, it transformed the Greeks from a nation of live performers and coffee-house habitués to introverted stay-at-homes, which dovetailed nicely with the junta's "family values".

Greece's centralized, government-controlled **TV stations**, ET1, NET and (out of Thessaloníki) ET3, nowadays lag behind private, mostly rather right-wing channels – Antenna, Star, Alpha, Alter and Makedonia TV – in the ratings. On NET, news summaries in English are broadcast daily at 6pm. Programming on all stations has evolved little since junta days, tending to be a mix of soaps (especially Italian, Spanish and Latin American), game shows, westerns, B-movies and sports. All foreign films and serials are broadcast in their original language, with Greek subtitles. Most private channels operate around the clock; public stations broadcast from around 7am or 8am until just after midnight. Numerous **cable**

and satellite channels are received, including CNN, MTV, Filmnet, Euronews (in English), French TV5 and Italian Rai Due. The range available depends on the area (and hotel) you're in.

Opening hours, public holidays and visitor attractions

It's difficult to generalize about Greek opening hours, which change constantly. The traditional timetable starts at a relatively civilized hour, with shops opening between 8.30 and 9am, then runs through until lunchtime, when there is a long break for the hottest part of the day. Most places, except banks and government offices, may then reopen in the mid- to late afternoon. Tourist areas tend to adopt a slightly more northern European timetable, with shops and offices, as well as the most important archeological sites and museums, usually open throughout the day.

Business and shopping hours

Most **government agencies** are open to the public on weekdays from 8am to 2pm. In general, however, you'd be optimistic to show up after 1pm expecting to be served the same day, as queues can be long. Private businesses, or anyone providing a service, frequently operate a straight 9am-to-5/6pm schedule. If someone is actually selling something, then they are more likely to follow a split shift as detailed below.

Shopping hours during the hottest months are theoretically Monday, Wednesday and Saturday from approximately 9am to 2.30pm, and Tuesday, Thursday and Friday from 8.30am to 2pm and 6 to 9pm. During the cooler, shorter-day months the morning schedule shifts slightly forward, the evening session a half or even a full hour back. There are, however, many exceptions to these rules by virtue of holidays and professional idiosyncrasy, so it's best not to count on getting anything done except from Monday to Friday, between 9.30am and 1pm. It's worth noting that **delis** and **butchers** are not allowed to sell fresh meat during summer afternoons (though

some flout this rule); similarly **fishmongers** are only open in the morning until they sell out (usually by noon), as are **pharmacies**, which additionally are shut on Saturday (except for the duty pharmacist).

All of the above opening hours will be regularly thrown out of sync by the numerous public holidays and festivals – or the equally numerous strikes, which can be general or profession-specific. The most important holidays, when almost everything will be closed, are listed opposite.

Ancient sites and monasteries

All the major **ancient sites** are now fenced off and, like most **museums**, charge **admission fees** ranging from a token €2 to a whopping €12, with a usual fee of around €3. At most of them reductions of 25 to 30 percent apply to senior citizens, and 50 percent to students with proper identification – students from the EU with proper ID will often get in free. In addition, entrance to all state-run sites and museums is **free** to all EU nationals on Sundays and public holidays from November to March – non-EU nationals are unlikely to be detected as such

Public holidays

January 1
January 6
March 25
First Monday of Lent (variable
    Feb/March; see below)
Easter weekend (variable April/May;
    see below)
May 1
Pentecost or Whit Monday (fifty
    days after Easter; see below)
August 15
October 28
December 25 and 26

Variable religious feasts
Lenten Monday
2004   February 23
2005   March 14
Easter Sunday
2004   April 11
2005   May 1
Whit/Pentecost Monday
2004   May 31
2005   June 20

unless they go out of their way to advertise the fact.

Opening hours vary from site to site. As far as possible, individual times are quoted in the text, but bear in mind that these change with exasperating frequency, and at smaller sites may be subject to the whim of a local *fýlakas* or site guard. Unless specified, the times quoted are generally summer hours, in effect from around late May to the end of September. Reckon on similar days but later opening and earlier closing in winter. Usually, the **last admission ticket** is sold fifteen to twenty minutes before the cited closing time.

Along with your ticket, most sites and museums will provide a little colour **folding pamphlet** prepared by the *Tamío Arheoloyikón Porón* (Archeological Receipts Fund); this usually includes an accurate if potted history and site or gallery plan, and we've found them to be uniformly excellent, in stark contrast to the often miserable labelling of the sites or galleries themselves. Serious students will therefore want to invest in **site guides** or **museum catalogues**, which have often been expertly compiled by the excavating archeologists or curators.

Smaller sites generally close for a long lunch and **siesta** (even where they're not supposed to), as do **monasteries**. The latter are generally open from 9am to 1pm and 5 to 8pm (3.30 to 6.30pm in winter) for limited visits. Most monasteries impose a fairly strict **dress code** for visitors: no shorts on either sex, with women expected to cover their arms and wear skirts; the necessary wraps are sometimes provided on the spot.

It's free to take **photos** of open-air sites, though museum photography and the use of videos or tripods anywhere requires an extra fee and written permit. This usually has to be arranged in writing from the nearest Department of Antiquities (Eforía Arheotíton). It's also worth knowing that Classical studies students can get a free annual pass to all Greek museums and sites by presenting themselves at the office on the rear corner (Tossítsa/Bouboulínas) of the National Archeological Museum in Athens – take documentation, two passport-sized photographs and be prepared to say you're a teacher.

Festivals and cultural events

Many of the big Greek popular festivals have a religious basis, so they're observed in accordance with the Orthodox calendar. Give or take a few saints, this is similar to the regular Catholic liturgical year, except for Easter, which can fall as many as five (but usually one or two) weeks to either side of the western festival – in 2001 and 2004 the two coincided (a very rare event). Other festivals are cultural in nature, with the highlight for most people being to catch a performance of Classical drama in one of the country's ancient theatres. There's also a full programme of cinema and concerts, with something on offer in even the smallest town at some point during the year.

Easter

Easter is by far the most important festival of the Greek year – infinitely more so than Christmas – and taken much more seriously than it is anywhere in western Europe, aside from Spain. From Wednesday of Holy Week until the following Monday, the state radio and TV networks are given over solely to religious programmes.

The **festival** is an excellent time to be in Greece, both for its beautiful religious ceremonies and for the days of feasting and celebration that follow. The mountainous island of **Ídhra** with its alleged 360 churches and monasteries is the prime Easter resort, but unless you plan well in advance you have no hope of finding accommodation at that time. Other famous Easter celebrations are held at Corfu, Pyrgí on Híos, Ólymbos on Kárpathos and St John's monastery on Pátmos.

The first great public ceremony takes place on **Good Friday** evening as the Descent from the Cross is lamented in church. At dusk the *Epitáfios*, Christ's funeral bier, lavishly decorated by the women of the parish (in large villages there will be more than one, from each church), leaves the sanctuary and is paraded solemnly through the streets. In many places, Crete especially, this is accompanied by the burning of effigies of Judas Iscariot.

Late **Saturday** evening sees the climax in a majestic *Anástasis* Mass to celebrate Christ's triumphant return. At the stroke of midnight all the lights in every crowded church are extinguished, and the congrega-

tion plunged into the darkness which envelops Christ as He passes through the underworld. Then there's a faint glimmer of light behind the altar screen before the priest appears, holding aloft a lighted taper and chanting *Avtó to Fós* . . . ("This is the Light of the World"). Stepping down to the level of the parishioners, he touches his flame to the unlit candles of the nearest worshippers, intoning *Dévteh, léveteh Fós* ("Come, take the Light"). Those at the front of the congregation and on the aisles do the same for their neighbours until the entire church – and the outer courtyard, standing room only for latecomers – is ablaze with burning candles and the miracle reaffirmed.

Even the most committed agnostic is likely to find this moving. The traditional greeting, as fireworks (and dynamite) explode all around you in the street, is *Khristós anésti* ("Christ is risen"), to which the response is *Alithós anésti* ("Truly He is risen"). In the week up to Easter Sunday you should wish people *Kaló Páskha* ("Happy Easter"); on or after the day, you say *Khrónia pollá* ("Many happy returns").

Worshippers then take the burning **candles** home through the streets; they are said to bring good fortune to the house if they arrive still burning. On reaching the front door it is common practice to make the sign of the cross on the lintel with the flame, leaving a black smudge visible for the rest of the year. The forty-day **Lenten fast** – still observed by the devout and in rural areas – is traditionally broken early on Sunday morning with a meal of *mayerítsa*, a soup made from lamb tripe, rice, dill and lemon. The rest of the lamb will be roasted on a spit for Sunday lunch, and festivities often take place through the rest of the day.

The Greek equivalent of **Easter eggs** are hard-boiled eggs (painted red on Holy Thursday), which are baked into twisted, sweet bread-loaves (*tsouréki*) or distributed on Easter Sunday. People rap their eggs against their friends' eggs, and the owner of the last uncracked egg is considered lucky.

The festival calendar

Most of the other Greek festivals are celebrations of one or other of a multitude of **saints**; the most important are detailed below. A village or church bearing the saint's name is a fair guarantee of some sort of observance – sometimes right across the town or island, otherwise quiet, local and consisting of little more than a special liturgy and banners adorning the chapel in question. Saints' days are also celebrated as **name days**; if you learn that it's an acquaintance's name day, you wish them *Khrónia pollá* ("Many years", as in "Many happy returns"). Also listed are a few more secular holidays, most enjoyable of which are the pre-Lenten carnivals.

In addition to the specific dates mentioned, there are literally scores of **local festivals**, or *paniyíria*, celebrating the patron saint of the main village church. With hundreds of possible name-saints' days (calendars list two or three, often obscure, for each day) you're unlikely to travel around Greece for long without stumbling on something.

It is important to remember the concept of the *paramoní*, or **eve of the festival**. Most of the events listed below are celebrated on the night before, so if you show up on the morning of the date given you will very probably have missed any music, dancing or drinking.

January 1
New Year's Day (Protokhroniá) in Greece is the feast day of Áyios Vassílios (St Basil). The traditional New Year greeting is *Kalí khroniá*.

January 6
Epiphany (Áyia Theofánia, or Fóta for short), when

the *kalikántzari* (hobgoblins) who run riot on earth during the twelve days of Christmas are rebanished to the nether world by various rites of the Church. The most important of these is the blessing of baptismal fonts and all outdoor bodies of water. At lakeside, seaside or riverside locations, the priest traditionally casts a crucifix into the deep, with local youths competing for the privilege of recovering it.

Pre-Lenten carnivals
These – known in Greek as *Apokriá* or *Aporkriés* – span three weeks, climaxing during the seventh weekend before Easter. *Katharí Dheftéra* (Lenten Monday) of the first carnival week is always seven weeks before Easter Sunday. The Ionian islands, especially Kefalloniá, are also good for carnival, as is Ayiássos on Lésvos, while the outrageous Goat Dance is enacted on Skýros in the Sporades.

March 25
Independence Day and the feast of the Annunciation (*Evangelismós* in Greek) is both a religious and a national holiday, with, on the one hand, military parades and dancing to celebrate the beginning of the revolt against Turkish rule in 1821, and on the other church services to honour the news given to Mary that she was to become the Mother of Christ. There are major festivities on Tínos, Ídhra (Hydra) and any locality with a monastery or church named Evangelístria or Evangelismós.

April 23
The feast of **Áyios Yeóryios** (St George), the patron of shepherds, is a big rural celebration, with much feasting and dancing at associated shrines and towns. Good venues include the island of Skýros, of which George is patron saint. If April 23 falls before Easter, ie during Lent, the festivities are postponed until the Monday after Easter.

May 1
May Day (*Protomayiá*) is the great urban holiday when townspeople traditionally make for the countryside to picnic, returning with bunches of wild flowers. Wreaths are hung on their doorways or balconies until they are burnt in bonfires on Saint John's Eve (June 23). There are also large demonstrations by the Left, claiming the *Ergatikí Protomayiá* (Working-Class First of May) as their own.

May 21
The feast of **Áyios Konstandínos** (St Constantine) and his mother, **Ayía Eléni** (St

Helen), the first pro-Orthodox Byzantine rulers. It's widely celebrated as the name day for two of the more popular Christian names in Greece.

May/June

The Monday of Áyio Pnévma (the Holy Spirit, Whit Monday in UK, Pentecost Monday in the US) marks the descent of same to the assembled disciples, fifty days after Easter. Usually a modest liturgy is celebrated at rural chapels of the Holy Spirit, gaily decked out with pennants; at Pagóndas village on Sámos, there's a musical festival.

June 29–30

The joint feast of Áyios Pétros and Áyios Pávlos (SS Peter and Paul), two of the more widely celebrated name days, is on the 29th. Celebrations often run together with that for the Gathering of (all) the Holy Apostles (Áyii Apóstoli), on the 30th.

July 17

The feast of Ayía Marína: a big event in rural areas, as she's an important protector of crops. Ayía Marína village on Kássos especially will be en fête. Between mid-July and mid-September there are religious festivals every few days, especially in the rural areas, and what with these, the summer heat and a mass exodus from the big cities, ordinary business slows or even halts.

July 20

The feast of Profítis Ilías (the Prophet Elijah) is widely celebrated at the countless hill- or mountain-top shrines of Profítis Ilías – nowadays, as on Sámos, with a 4WD trip up to the mountain of the same name with sound systems cranked up and barbecue spits turning on arrival.

July 26

Ayía Paraskeví is celebrated in parishes or villages bearing that name.

August 6

Metamórfosis toú Sotíros (Transfiguration of the Saviour) provides another excuse for celebrations, particularly at Khristós Ráhon village on Ikaría, and at Plátanos on Léros. On Hálki the date is marked by messy food-fights with flour, eggs and squid ink, so beware.

August 15

Apokímisis tís Panayías (Assumption or Dormition of the Blessed Virgin Mary). This is the day when people traditionally return to their home village, and in most places there will be no accommodation available on any terms. Even

some Greeks will resort to sleeping in the streets. There is a great pilgrimage to Tínos, and major festivities at Páros, at Ayiássos on Lésvos, on Lipsí and at Ólymbos on Kárpathos.

August 29

Apokefálisis toú Prodhrómou (Beheading of John the Baptist). Popular pilgrimages and celebrations at Vrykoúnda on Kárpathos.

September 8

Yénnisis tís Panayías (Birth of the Virgin Mary) sees special services in churches dedicated to the event, and a double cause for rejoicing on Spétses where they also celebrate the anniversary of the battle of the straits of Spétses, which took place on September 8, 1822. A re-enactment of the battle takes place in the harbour, followed by fireworks and feasting well into the night. Elsewhere, there's a pilgrimage of childless women to the monastery at Tsambíka, Rhodes.

September 14

A last major summer festival, the Ípsosis toú Stavroú (Exaltation of the Cross).

September 24

The feast of Áyios Ioánnis Theológos (St John the Divine), observed on Níssyros and Pátmos, where at the saint's monastery there are solemn, beautiful liturgies the night before and early on the morning.

October 26

The feast of Áyios Dhimítrios (St Demetrius), another popular name day. In rural areas the new wine is traditionally broached on this day, a good excuse for general inebriation.

October 28

Óhi Day, the year's major patriotic shindig – a national holiday with parades, folk-dancing and speeches to commemorate Metaxas's apocryphal one-word reply to Mussolini's 1940 ultimatum: Óhi! ("No"!).

November 8

Another popular name day, the feast of the Archangels Michael and Gabriel (Mihaíl and Gavríl, or tón Taxiárhon), marked by rites at the numerous churches named after them, particularly at the rural monastery of Taxiárhis on Sými, and the big monastery of Mandamádhos, Lésvos.

December 6

The feast of Áyios Nikólaos (St Nicholas), the

patron of seafarers, who has many chapels dedicated to him.

December 25

A much less festive occasion than Greek Easter, Christmas (*Khristoúyenna*) is still an important religious feast celebrating the birth of Christ, and in recent years it has started to take on more of the trappings of the western Christmas, with decorations, Christmas trees and gifts. December 26 is not Boxing Day as in England but the Sýnaxis tís Panayías, or Gathering of the Virgin's Entourage.

December 31

New Year's Eve (*Paramoní Protokhroniás*), when, as on the other twelve days of Christmas, a few children still go door-to-door singing the traditional *kálanda* (carols), receiving money in return. Adults tend to sit around playing cards, often for money. A special baked loaf, the *vassilópitta*, in which a coin is concealed to bring its finder good luck throughout the year, is cut at midnight.

Cultural festivals

As well as religious festivals, Greece has a full range of **cultural festivals,** including a few on the more popular islands. The most durable are listed below:

Itháki Music Festival (July)
Ippokrateia Festival Kós (July–Aug)
Lesviakó Kalokéri Lésvos (July–Aug)
Manolis Kalomiris Festival, Sámos (July–Aug)
Réthymnon Renaissance Festival (July–Aug)
Sými Festival (July–Sept)
Lefkádha Arts Jamboree (Aug)
Iráklion Festival (early Aug)
Thíra Music Festival (Aug–Sept)
Rhodes Festival (Aug–Oct)

Cinema

Greek **cinemas** show a large number of American and British movies, always in the original soundtrack with Greek subtitles, though fly-posters tend to be Greek-only. **Indoor** screenings are affordable, currently €6–8 depending on location and plushness of facilities; they shut from mid-May to late September unless they have air-conditioning or a roll-back roof. Accordingly in summer vast numbers of **outdoor** cinemas operate; an outdoor movie (marginally cheaper) is worth catching at least once for the experience alone, though it's best to opt for the early screening (about 9pm) since the sound on the 11pm show gets turned down or even off to avoid complaints of noise from adjacent residences.

Sports and outdoor pursuits

The Greek seashore offers endless scope for watersports, with windsurfing-boards for rent in most resorts and, less reliably, waterskiing and parasailing facilities. On land, the greatest attraction lies in hiking; often the smaller, less developed islands are better for this than the larger ones criss-crossed by roads.

In terms of spectating, the twin Greek obsessions are **football** (soccer) and **basketball**, with **volleyball** a close third in popularity.

Watersports

The years since the mid-1980s have seen a massive growth in the popularity of **windsurfing** in Greece. The country's bays and coves are ideal for beginners, and boards

can be rented in literally hundreds of resorts. Particularly good areas, with established schools, include Vassilikí on Lefkádha island, Kéfalos on Kós, Zákynthos, western Náxos, Kokkári on Sámos, several spots on Lésvos, Corfu's west coast and numerous locales on Crete. You can almost always pay for an initial period of instruction, if you've not tried the sport previously. Board rental rates are very reasonable – about €10 an hour.

Waterskiing is available at a number of the larger resorts, and a fair few of the smaller ones too. By the crippling rental standards of the ritzier parts of the Mediterranean it is a bargain, with twenty minutes' instruction often available for around €13–16. At many resorts, parasailing (*parapént* in Greek) is also possible; rates start at €18 a go.

A combination of steady winds, appealing seascapes and numerous natural harbours have long made Greece a tremendous place for **sailing**. Holiday companies offer all sorts of packaged and tailor-made cruises (see p.15 in "Getting there"). In Greece, small boats and motorized dinghies are rented out by the day at many resorts. Spring and autumn are the most pleasant and least expensive seasons; *meltémi* winds make for pretty nauseous sailing between late June and early September, and summer rates for the same craft can be three times as high as shoulder-season prices.

Because of the potential for pilfering submerged antiquities, **scuba-diving** is severely restricted, its legal practice in the islands confined to certain coasts around Ídhra, Kálymnos, Rhodes, Skiáthos, Corfu, Zákynthos and Mýkonos. For more information and an update on new, approved sites, contact the Union of Greek Diving Centres (☎210 92 29 532 or 210 41 18 909).

Walking

Young urban Greeks have only recently become used to the notion that anyone should want to **walk** for pleasure, yet if you have the time and stamina it is probably the single best way to see the quieter islands. For more detail, you may want to acquire specific hiking guidebooks; see p.621 in Contexts. See also p.30 for details of hiking maps available, and p.15, p.21 and p.23 for details of companies offering walking holidays on the islands.

Football and basketball

Football (soccer) is far and away the most popular sport in Greece – both in terms of participating and watching. The most important (and most heavily sponsored) teams are Panathanaïkós and AEK of Athens, Olympiakós of Pireás and PAOK of Thessaloníki. The only major team on the islands is the Cretan Ofí. If you're interested, matches (usually played on Wednesday nights and Sunday afternoons) are easy enough to catch from September to May. In mid-autumn you might even see one of the Greek teams playing European competition. At the time of writing Greece had qualified for the Euro 2004 finals in Portugal – the first time since 1980 – beating Northern Ireland 1-0 in Athens.

The nation's **basketball** team is one of the continent's strongest and won the European Championship in 1987 – cheered all the way with enormous enthusiasm. At private-club level, many of the football teams maintain basketball squads – Panathanaïkós were European champions in 1996, 2000 and 2002, and Olympiakós back in 1997.

Finding work

Since Greece's full accession to the European Union in early 1993, a citizen of any EU state has (in theory) the right to work in Greece. In practice, however, there are a number of bureaucratic hurdles to overcome. Formerly, the most common job for foreigners was teaching English in the numerous private cramming academies (*frondistíria*), but lately severe restrictions have been put on the availability of such positions for non-Greeks, and you'll probably have more luck finding something in the commercial or leisure-oriented trade. Similarly, that other long-standing fallback of long-haul backpackers, picking fruit or greenhouse vegetables, is now the exclusive province of immigrant males.

Short-term work

EU membership notwithstanding, short-term work in Greece is always on an unofficial basis and for this reason it will generally be where you can't be seen by the police or you're badly paid – or, more often, both. The influx, since 1990, of between 800,000 and 1.1 million (estimates differ) immigrants from various poor countries has resulted in a surplus of unskilled labour and severely depressed wages.

Tourism-related work

Most women working casually in Greece find jobs in **bars** or **restaurants** around the main resorts. Men, unless they are "trained" chefs, will probably find it harder to find any work, even washing up.

If you're waiting or serving, most of your wages will probably have to come from tips but you may well be able to get a deal that includes free food and lodging; evening-only hours can be a good shift, leaving you a lot of free time. The main drawback may be the machismo and/or chauvinist attitudes of your employer. (Ads in the local press for "girl bar staff" are certainly best ignored; see "Personal safety" on p.79).

Corfu, with its big British slant, is an obvious choice for bar work; Rhodes, Kós, Crete, Skiáthos, Páros, Íos and Santoríni are also promising. Start looking, if you can, around April or May; you'll get better rates at this time if you're taken on for a season.

On a similar, unofficial level you might be able to get a sales job in **tourist shops** on Corfu, Ídhra, Rhodes or Crete, or (if you've the expertise) helping out at one of the **windsurfing** schools that have sprung up all around the coast. **Yacht marinas** can also prove good hunting-grounds, though less for the romantic business of crewing than of scrubbing down and repainting. Again, the best possibilities are likely to be on Rhodes, Corfu or Kálymnos; the Zéa port at Pireás is actually the biggest marina, but non-Greek owners don't tend to rest up there for long.

Perhaps the best type of tourism-related work, however, is that of courier/greeter/group co-ordinator for a **package holiday company**. All you need is EU nationality and language proficiency compatible with the clientele, though knowledge of Greek is a big plus. English-only speakers are pretty well restricted to places with a predominantly British package trade, namely Crete, Rhodes, Skiáthos and the Ionian islands.

Many such staff are recruited through ads in newspapers issued outside Greece, but it's by no means unheard of to be hired on the spot in April or May. A big plus, however you're taken on, is that you're usually guaranteed about six months of steady work, often with use of a car thrown in, and that if things work out you may be re-employed the following season with an explicit contract and better wages.

Selling and busking

You may do better by working for yourself. Travellers report rich pickings during the tourist season from **selling jewellery** on island beaches, or on boats – craftware from Asia is especially popular with Greeks. Once you've managed to get the stuff past the customs officials (who will be sceptical, for instance, that all those trinkets are presents for friends), there rarely seem to be problems with the local police, though it probably pays to be discreet.

Busking can also be quite lucrative. Playing in resort pedestrian zones, it's possible to make up to €10 in a two-hour session.

Documentation for long-term employment

If you plan to work professionally for someone else, you first visit the nearest Department of Employment and collect two forms: one an **employment application** which you fill in, the other for the formal offer of work by your prospective employer. Once these are vetted, and revenue stamps (*hartósima*, purchased at kiosks) applied, you take them to the Aliens' Bureau (*Ypiresía Allodhapón*) or, in its absence, the central police station, to support your application for a **residence permit** (*ádhia paramonís*). For this, you will also need to bring your passport, six photographs, more *hartósima* and a stable address (not a hotel). Permits are given for terms of five years.

You should allow four to six weeks for all the formalities to be completed; the bottleneck is usually the required **health examination** at the nearest public hospital. There you will be chest-X-rayed for signs of TB, blood-tested for hepatitis B and C, HIV and a couple of other nasties, and have a (farcical) evaluation by a neurologist or psychiatrist for signs of mental disorder; this is all done at a reasonable cost. Once you've assembled all the results, you'll have to trot these over yourself to the local public health office, where a periodic (once weekly at best) meeting of its administrative council will vet and endorse these, and issue you with a certificate of approval. Finally you take this to the local police or Aliens' Bureau, which should have your permit ready, free of charge other than for a few more *hartósima*, within three working days.

As a **self-employed professional**, you must satisfy the requirements of the Greek

state with equivalent qualifications to native Greeks plying the same trade. You should also befriend a good accountant, who will advise you on which of the several varieties of incorporation are to your advantage; trading under a fictitious name is vastly more expensive tax-wise than doing business as a private person. You will need to sign on with **TEBE**, the Greek National Insurance scheme for self-employed people (analogous to Class 4 National Insurance contributions in the UK). If you are continuing to contribute to a social insurance scheme in a country which has reciprocal agreements with Greece (all EU states do), this must be proved in writing – a tedious and protracted process.

Once you're square with TEBE, visit the tax office or *eforía* to be issued a **tax number** (abbreviated "ah-fi-mi" in Greek, similar to a UK Schedule D number) which must be cited in all transactions. To be issued one of these, you need to bring a birth certificate which shows the full unmarried names of *both* your parents. You will be required to prepare receipt and invoice books with your tax number professionally printed on them, or have a rubber stamp made up for applying that number to every sheet. The tax office will also determine which rate of **VAT** (the "fi-pi-ah") you should pay for each kind of transaction; VAT returns must be filed every two months, which is where that friendly accountant comes in handy again.

EU nationals who do not intend to work in Greece but still need a residence permit (such as second-property-owners needing to set up a bank account) will still get a **residence permit** fairly easily, but must present evidence of financial solvency and health insurance.

At present, undocumented **non-EU nationals** who wish to work in Greece do so surreptitiously, with the ever-present risk of denunciation to the police and instant deportation. Having been forced to accept large numbers of EU citizens looking for jobs in a climate of rising unemployment, Greek immigration authorities are cracking down hard on any suitable targets, be they Albanian, African, Swiss or North American. That old foreigners' standby, teaching English, is now available only to holders of

TEFL certificates – preferably Greeks, non-EU nationals of Greek descent and EU nationals in that order. If you are a non-EU foreign national of Greek descent, you are termed *omólogos* (returned Greek diaspora member) and in fact have tremendous employment, taxation and residence rights and privileges – you can, for example, open your very own *frondistírio* without any qualifications, something starkly evident in the often abysmal quality of language instruction in Greece.

Crime and personal safety

As in the past, Greece remains one of Europe's safest countries, with a low crime rate and a deserved reputation for honesty. If you leave a bag or wallet at a café, you'll most likely find it scrupulously looked after, pending your return. Similarly, Greeks are relatively relaxed about leaving possessions unlocked or unattended on the beach, in rooms or on campsites. The biggest hazards on beaches, oddly, are free-ranging goats – who will eat just about anything left accessible – and the wake of passing cruise ships or ferries, which can wash all your possessions out to sea with little or no warning.

Recent years, however, have seen a large increase in **theft** and **crimes against persons** at archeological sites, in towns, remote villages and resorts, so it's wise to lock things securely and treat Greece like any other European destination. In particular, there has been a huge rise in pickpocketing on the old section of the **Athens metro** (not the new extension, which is heavily policed).

There are other ways to lose your money – most notably getting stuck with **counterfeit euro notes** (at the moment €100 and €200 ones abound). The currency changeover has proven to be a bonanza for forgers – which has led to the introduction of (useless) electronic bill scanners in many shops. The best tests are done by the naked eye: genuine notes all have a hologram strip or (if over €50) patch at one end, there's a watermark at the other, and a security thread embedded in the middle. If you end up being given a duff note, you'll have to lump it – if you unwittingly try to pass it on, or report it in good faith to the police, you'll still be assumed party to the scam, and face a session of interrogation at the very least.

See p.66 for **emergency phone numbers**.

Police and specific offences

There is a single, nationwide **police force**, the *Elliniki Astynomia*, rather than the division into urban corps and rural gendarmerie normal in most of Europe. Greek cops are gruff at the best of times, frequently unpleasant otherwise, and many have little regard for foreigners. Police practice often falls short of northern European norms, and fit-ups or beatings in custody are not unknown.

You are required to **carry suitable ID** on you at all times (except when in bathing costume) – either a passport or a driving licence.

Otherwise, the most common causes of a brush with authority are nude bathing or sunbathing, camping outside an authorized site, public inebriation or lewd behaviour, and taking photos in forbidden areas.

Nude bathing is legal on only a very few beaches (most famously on Mýkonos), and is deeply offensive to the more traditional Greeks – exercise considerable sensitivity to local feeling and the kind of place you're in. It is, for example, very bad etiquette to swim or sunbathe nude within sight of a church, of which there are many along the Greek coast. Generally, if a beach has become fairly well established as naturist, or is well secluded, it's highly unlikely that the police are going to come charging in. Where they do get bothered is if they feel a place is turning into a "hippie beach" or nudity is getting too overt on mainstream tourist stretches. Most of the time, the only action will be a warning, but you can officially be arrested straight off – facing up to three days in jail and a stiff fine.

Topless (sun)bathing for women is technically legal nationwide, but specific locales often opt out of the "liberation" by posting signs, which should be heeded.

Very similar guidelines apply to **camping rough**, which has been theoretically illegal nationwide since 1977 (see "Accommodation", p.56). Even for this you're still unlikely to incur anything more than a warning to move on. The only real risk of arrest is if you are told to clear off and fail to do so. In either of the above cases, even if the police do take any action against you, it's more likely to be a brief spell in their cells than any official prosecution.

The **hours between 3 and 5pm**, the midday *mikró ípno* (siesta), are sacrosanct – one does not make phone calls to strangers or any sort of noise (especially with motorcycles) at this time. **Quiet** is also mandated by law **between midnight and 8am** in residential areas.

The well-publicized ordeal of twelve British plane-spotters who processed slowly through Greek jails and courts in 2001–02 on espionage charges should be ample incentive to **take no pictures** at all in and **around airports or military installations**. The latter are usually well festooned with signs of a bellows camera with a red 'X' through it. "No pictures at all" includes farewell snaps near the runway; most civilian airports double as air-force bases, and you don't know what the authorities will claim was in your viewfinder.

Any sort of **disrespect** towards the Greek state or Orthodox Church in general, or Greek civil servants in particular, may be construed as offences in the most literal sense, so it's best to keep your comments on how things are working (or not) to yourself. Every year a few foreign louts find

themselves in deep trouble over a drunken indiscretion. This is a society where verbal injuries count, with an appreciable backlog of court cases dealing with the alleged public utterance of *malákas* (wanker).

In the non-verbal field, ripped or soiled clothes and untucked-in shirts are considered nearly as insulting. Don't expect a uniformly civil reception if dressed in **grunge attire**, since Greeks will interpret this in one of two possible ways, neither reflecting well on you. Poverty is an uncomfortably close memory for many, and they may consider that you're making light of hard times. More to the point, the cult of fashion victim-hood is developed to near-Italian levels in Greece; if you clearly have so little self-respect as to appear slovenly and dishevelled in public, why should any Greek respect you?

Public drunkenness of the sort which fuelled the much-publicized crimes at Faliráki in 2003 (see p.305) has always been held in contempt in Greece, where the inability to hold one's liquor is considered unmanly. Inebriation will be considered an aggravating factor if you're arrested for something else, not an excuse.

Drug offences are treated as major crimes, particularly since there's a mushrooming local use and addiction problem. The maximum penalty for "causing the use of drugs by someone under 18", for example, is life imprisonment and an astronomical fine. Theory is by no means practice, but foreigners caught in possession of even small amounts of marijuana do get long jail sentences if there's evidence that they've been supplying the drug to others. Moreover, you could be inside for well over a year awaiting a trial date, with little or no chance of bail being granted.

If you get arrested for any offence, you have a right to contact your **consulate**, who will arrange a lawyer for your defence. Beyond this, there is little they can, or in most cases will, do. There are honorary British consulates on Rhodes, Crete and Corfu.

Personal safety

Thousands of women travel independently in Greece without being **harassed** or feeling intimidated. With the recent sea-change in local mores – specifically, a vast increase in the "availability" of young Greek women to young local men, up to and including living together before marriage – much of the traditional Mediterranean-macho impetus for trying one's luck with foreign girls has faded. Any hassle you do get is likely to be from a dwindling minority of professionally single Greek men, known as *kamákia* (fish harpoons), who migrate in summer to the beach bars and discos of the main resorts and towns, specifically in pursuit of "liberated, fun-loving" tourists.

Indigenous Greeks, who become increasingly protective of you as you become more of a fixture in any one place, treat these outsiders with contempt; their obvious stakeouts are waterfront cafés, beach bars and dance clubs. Words worth remembering as unambiguous responses include *pápsteh* ("stop it"), *afístemeh* ("leave me alone") and *fíyeteh* ("go away"), the latter intensified if followed by "*dhrómo!*" (road, as in "Hit the road!").

Sadly, foreign women stand as much or more chance of being **sexually assaulted** at certain notorious resorts (Kávos, Corfu; Faliráki, Rhodes) by northern European men as they do by ill-intentioned locals. With too many people seemingly checking their common sense in at the departing airport, the UK Foreign Office has been obliged to

remind them in print not to go out barcrawling alone, nor to go home alone, or to accept late-night rides from strangers.

Hitching at any time of the day is not advisable for lone women travellers, but **camping** is generally not a problem, though away from recognized sites it is often wise to attach yourself to a local family by making arrangements to use nearby private land. In the remoter islands you may feel more uncomfortable travelling alone. The intensely traditional Greeks may have trouble understanding why you are unaccompanied, and might not welcome your presence in their exclusively male *kafenía* – often the only place where you can get a drink. Travelling with a man, you're more likely to be treated as a *xéni*, a word meaning both (female) stranger and guest.

Lone men need to be aware of one longestablished racket in the largest island ports. You may be approached by dubious gents asking the time, or your origins, and then offering to take you for a drink in a nearby bar. This is invariably staffed with hostesses (who may also be prostitutes), whose main job is to convince you to treat them to drinks. At the end of the night you'll be landed with an outrageous bill, some of which goes towards the hostess's "commission"; physical threats are brought to bear on reluctant payers.

Travellers with disabilities

It is all too easy to wax lyrical over the attractions of Greece – the stepped, narrow alleys, the ease of travel by bus and ferry, the thrill of clambering around the great archeological sites – without remembering that they are potential hazards for anyone who has difficulty in walking, is wheelchair-bound or suffers from other disabilities.

It is possible, however, to enjoy an inexpensive and trauma-free holiday in Greece with a little forward planning. Much existing or readily available information is out of date – you should always try to double-check; a

number of addresses of contact organizations are detailed below. The Greek National Tourist Office is a good first step as long as you have specific questions to put to them; they publish a useful questionnaire which you could send to hotels or owners of apartment/villa accommodation.

Contacts for travellers with disabilities

UK and Ireland

Access Travel 6 The Hillock, Astley, Lancashire M29 7GW ☎01942/888 844, ⓦwww.access-travel.co.uk. A tour operator that can arrange flights, transfer and accommodation. This is a small business, personally checking out places before recommendation. They can guarantee accommodation standards on Rhodes in particular. ATOL bonded.

Holiday Care 7th Floor, Sunley House, 4 Bedford Park, Croydon, Surrey CR0 2AP ☎0845 124 9971, ⓦwww.holidaycare.org.uk. Provides lists of accessible accommodation abroad. Information on financial help for holidays available.

Irish Wheelchair Association Blackheath Drive, Clontarf, Dublin 3 ☎01/833 8241, ⓦwww.iwa.ie. Useful information provided on travelling abroad with a wheelchair.

Tripscope The Vassall Centre, Gill Avenue, Bristol BS16 2QQ ☎0845 758 5641, ⓦwww.tripscope.org.uk. This registered charity provides a national telephone information service offering free advice on UK and international transport for those with a mobility problem.

US and Canada

Access-Able ⓦwww.access-able.com. Online resource for travellers with disabilities.

Directions Unlimited 123 Green Lane, Bedford Hills, NY 10507 ☎1-800 533-5343 or 914/241-1700. Tour operator specializing in custom tours for people with disabilities.

Mobility International USA 451 Broadway, Eugene, OR 97401; Voice and TDD ☎541/343-1284, ⓦwww.miusa.org. Information and referral services, access guides, tours and exchange programmes. Annual membership $35 (includes quarterly newsletter).

Society for the Advancement of Travelers with Handicaps (SATH) 347 5th Ave, New York, NY 10016 ☎212/447-7284, ⓦwww.sath.org. A nonprofit educational organization that has actively

represented travellers with disabilities since 1976.

Wheels Up! ☎1-888 389-4335, ⓦwww.wheelsup.com. Provides discounted airfare, tour and cruise prices for disabled travellers, also publishes a free monthly newsletter and has a comprehensive website.

Australia and New Zealand

ACROD (Australian Council for Rehabilitation of the Disabled) PO Box 60, Curtin ACT 2605 ☎02/6283 3200, TTY 02/6282 4333, ⓦwww.acrod.org.au. Provides lists of travel agencies and tour operators for people with disabilities.

Disabled Persons Assembly 4/173–175 Victoria St, Wellington, New Zealand ☎04/801 9100 (also TTY), ⓦ www.dpa.org.nz. Resource centre with lists of travel agencies and tour operators for people with disabilities.

Planning a holiday

There are **organized tours** and **holidays** specifically for people with disabilities; many companies in Britain will advise on the suitability of holidays or villas advertised in their brochures.

It might be useful to make a list of all the facilities that will make your life easier while you are away so that you can fully brief travel agencies, insurance companies, airlines and other travel operators of your **needs**. If you use a wheelchair, it's advisable to have it serviced before you go, and carry a repair kit. Before purchasing **travel insurance**, ensure that people with a pre-existing medical condition are not excluded. A **medical certificate** of your fitness to travel, provided by your doctor, is also extremely useful; some airlines or insurance companies may insist on it.

You should also carry extra supplies of any required **drugs** and a prescription including the generic name in case of emergency. It's probably best to assume that any special equipment, drugs or clothing you may require is unavailable in Greece and will need to be brought with you.

Senior travellers

Travellers over sixty are accorded every respect in Greece; you are, for example, rather less likely to be grumbled or shouted at by the famously irate Athens bus drivers or harbour officials. Seniors are entitled to discounts at state-run attractions of twenty-five to thirty percent; long-term bus passes in the major cities are similarly discounted; and, without making much effort to publicize the fact, Olympic Airways (and quite possibly its new private competitors) also offer discounts on full fares on domestic flights. Keep proof of age to hand for all these benefits.

Contacts for senior travellers

UK

Saga Holidays ☏0800 096 0074, ⊛www.saga .co.uk. The country's biggest and most established specialist in tours and holidays aimed at older people.

US

American Association of Retired Persons 601 E St NW, Washington, DC 20049 ☏1-800 424-3410, ⊛www.aarp.org. Can provide discounts on accommodation and vehicle rental. Membership open to US and Canadian

residents aged 50 or over for an annual fee of US$12.50.

Elderhostel 75 Federal St, Boston, MA 02110 ☏1-877426-8056, ⊛www.elderhostel.com. Runs a worldwide network of educational and activity programmes, cruises and homestays for people over 60 (companions may be younger). Programmes generally last a week or more and costs are in line with those of commercial tours.

Saga Holidays 222 Berkeley St, Boston, MA 02116 ☏1-800 343-0273, ⊛www.sagaholidays.com. Specializes in worldwide group travel for seniors.

Vantage Travel ☏1-800 322-6677, ⊛www.vantagetravel.com. Specializes in worldwide group travel for seniors.

Travelling with children

Children are worshipped and indulged in Greece, arguably to excess, and present few problems when travelling. As elsewhere in the Mediterranean, they are not segregated from adults at meal times and early on in life are inducted into the typical late-night routine. So you'll see plenty of kids at tavernas, expected to eat (and up to their capabilities, talk) like adults. Outside of certain all-inclusive resorts, however (see "Contacts" on p.84) there are very few amusements specifically for kids – certainly nothing like Disney World Paris.

Most ferry-boat lines and airlines in Greece offer some sort of **discount** for children, ranging from fifty to one hundred percent depending on their age; hotels and rooms won't charge extra for infants, and levy a

modest surcharge for "third" beds which the child occupies by him/herself.

Baby foods and **nappies** (diapers) are readily available and reasonably priced; private rooms establishments and luxury hotels are more likely to offer some kind of **babysitting** service than the mid-range, C-class hotels.

Contacts for travellers with children

UK and Ireland

Club Med ☎0700 258 2932, ⓦwww.clubmed.co.uk. Specializes in purpose-built holiday resorts, with kids' club, entertainment and sports facilities on site; has villages in the Greek islands on Corfu, Évvia and Kós.

Mark Warner Holidays ☎020/7761 7000, ⓦwww.markwarner.co.uk. Holiday villages with children's entertainment and childcare laid on. Island villages in Greece include those at Platý on Límnos.

Simply Travel ☎020/8541 2280, ⓦwww.simply -travel.com. Upmarket tour company offering villas and hotels in the less touristy parts of Greece. May be able to provide qualified, English-speaking nannies to come to your villa and look after the children.

US

Travel With Your Children 40 5th Ave, New York, NY 10011 ☎212/477 5524 or 1-888 822-4388. Publish a regular newsletter, *Family Travel Times*, ⓦwww.familytraveltimes.com, as well as a series of books on travel with children including *Great Adventure Vacations With Your Kids*.

Gay and lesbian travellers

In modern Greece overtly gay behaviour in public remains taboo for men in rural areas. There is, however, a sizeable gay contingent in Athens, Thessaloníki and Pátra, plus a fairly obvious scene at certain resorts like Ídhra, Rhodes and Mýkonos. Skála Eressoú on Lésvos, the birthplace of Sappho, is (appropriately) an international mecca for lesbians. Even in Athens, however, most gay nightlife is underground (often literally so in the siting of clubs), with no visible signage for nondescript, heavily soundproofed doorways.

Homosexuality is legal over the age of 17, and (male) bisexual behaviour common but rarely admitted; the law code itself, however, still contains perjorative references to passive partners. Greek men are terrible flirts, but cruising them is a semiotic minefield and definitely at your own risk – references in gay guides to "known" male cruising grounds should be treated sceptically. "Out" gay Greeks are rare, and "out" local lesbians rarer still; foreign same-sex couples will be regarded in the provinces with some bemusement but accorded the standard courtesy as foreigners.

Contacts for gay and lesbian travellers

UK

ⓦwww.gaytravel.co.uk Online gay and lesbian travel agent, offering good deals on all types of holiday. Also lists gay- and lesbian-friendly hotels around the world.

Dream Waves Holidays ☎0870 042 2475, ⓦwww.gayholidaysdirect.com. Specializes in exclusively gay holidays, including skiing trips and summer sun packages.

Madison Travel 118 Western Rd, Hove, East Sussex NN3 1DB ☎01273/202532, ⓦwww .madisontravel.co.uk. Established travel agents specializing in packages to gay- and lesbian-friendly mainstream destinations, and also to gay/lesbian destinations.

Respect Holidays 74 Haverstock Hill, London NW3 2BE ☎020/7485 8855, ⓦwww.respect -holidays.co.uk. Offers exclusively gay packages to all popular European resorts.

US and Canada

Damron Company PO Box 422458, San Francisco, CA 94142 ☎1-800 462-6654 or 415/255-0404, ⓦwww.damron.com. Publisher of the *Men's Travel*

Guide, a pocket-sized yearbook full of listings of hotels, bars, clubs and resources for gay men; the *Women's Traveler*, which provides similar listings for lesbians; and *Damron Accommodations*, which provides detailed listings of over 1000 accommodations for gays and lesbians worldwide. All of these titles are offered at a discount on the website. ⓦ**www.gaytravel.com** ☎1-800 GAY-TRAVEL. The premier site for trip planning, bookings, and general information about international gay and lesbian travel.

International Gay & Lesbian Travel Association 4331 N Federal Hwy, Suite 304, Ft Lauderdale, FL 33308 ☎1-800 448-8550, ⓦwww.iglta.org. Trade group that can provide a list of gay- and lesbian-owned or -friendly travel agents, accommodation and other travel businesses.

Australia and New Zealand

Gay and Lesbian Travel Australia ⓦwww.galta.com.au. Directory and links for gay and lesbian travel in Australia and worldwide.

Parkside Travel ☎08/8274 1222, ⓔparkside@herveyworld.com.au. Gay travel agent associated with local branch of Hervey World Travel; all aspects of gay and lesbian travel worldwide.

Silke's Travel ☎1800 807 860 or 02/8347 2000, ⓦwww.silkes.com.au. Long-established gay and lesbian specialist, with the emphasis on women's travel.

Tearaway Travel ☎1800 664 440 or 03/9510 6644, ⓦwww.tearaway.com. Gay-specific business dealing with international and domestic travel.

Directory

Addresses In Greece streets are cited in the genitive case, usually with no tag like "Street" or "Avenue"; the number always follows. Thus something described as 36 Venizelos Avenue in Roman-alphabet letterhead comes out as Venizélou 36, and it's this convention which we've adopted throughout the book. The practice is different with *platía* (square, plaza) and *leofóros* (avenue), which always appear before the name. Postcodes are five-digit, nationwide, and precede the municipality concerned, eg 831 00 Sámos.

Bargaining This isn't a regular feature of touristic life, though you'll find it possible with private rooms and certain hotels out of season. Similarly, you should be able to negotiate discounted rates for vehicle rental, especially for longer periods. Services such as shoe, watch and camera repair don't have iron-clad rates, so use common sense when assessing charges (advance written estimates are not routine practice).

Departure tax This is levied on all international ferries – currently €5–8 per person and per car or motorbike, usually (but not always) included within the quoted price of the ticket. To non-EU states (eg Turkey) it's €12–15 per person, sometimes arbitrarily levied twice (on entry and exit). There's also an airport departure tax of €12 for all EU/EEA destinations, €22 for all non-EU destinations, but this is always included in the price of the ticket – there's no collection at the airport itself. Many small regional flights (eg Léros–Astypálea) are exempt from this in an attempt to boost tourism to less visited regions. Additionally, a special tax (originally conceived of to fund construction of Venizelos airport), nicknamed the *spatósima* locally, is levied within the ticket price of all flights leaving Athens: €7.79 for Greek destinations, €10.30 for non-Greek ones.

Electricity Voltage is 220 volt AC throughout the country. Wall outlets – rarely abundant enough – take double round-pin plugs as in the rest of continental Europe. Three-to-two-pin adapters should be purchased beforehand in the UK, as they can be difficult to find locally; standard 5-, 6- or 7-amp models permit operation of a hair dryer or travel iron.

If necessary, you can change the fuse to a higher rating back in the UK; beware, they're physically smaller than the 13-amp ones popped into all three-prong plugs, and you may have to go to a specialist electrical dealer for them. Unless they're dual voltage, North American appliances will require both a step-down transformer and a plug adapter (the latter easy to find in Greece).

Films Fuji and Kodak print films are reasonably priced and easy to have processed – "One Hour Foto" places abound in resorts. APS film is also widely sold and processed. Kodak and Fuji E6 slide films can be purchased, again at UK prices or better, in larger towns, but the only place on the islands where you can get them processed is Iráklion (Crete), so you'll probably have to wait till you get home.

Greek-language courses The longest established outlet is The Athens Centre, Arhimídhous 48, Méts, 116 36 Athens (☎210 70 12 268, ⓦwww.athenscentre.gr). One to try on Crete is Lexis, 48 Dhaskaloyiánni, 73100 Haniá (☎ & ⓕ28210 55673, ⓔlexis-glacc@cha.forthnet.gr). There are always adverts in the *Athens News* for other schools, which come and go.

Laundries *Plindíria*, as they're known in Greek, are prominent in the main resort towns; sometimes an attended service wash is available for little or no extra charge over the basic cost of €6–7 per wash and dry. Self-catering villas or *dhomátia* will usually be furnished with a drying line and a selection of plastic wash-tubs (*skáfes*) or a bucket (*kouvás*). In hotels, laundering should be done in a more circumspect manner; management can object if you use bathroom washbasins, Greek wall-mounting being what it is, or do more than a few socks and undies. It's best to use the flat pans of showers for both washing and hanging up to dry.

Períptera These are street-corner kiosks, or sometimes a hole-in-the-wall shopfront. They sell everything from pens to disposable razors, stationery to soap, sweets to condoms, cigarettes to plastic crucifixes, yogurts to milk-in-cartons – and are often open when nothing else is.

Time As throughout the EU, Greek summer time begins at 2am on the last Sunday in March, when the clocks go forward one hour, and ends at 2am the last Sunday in October when they go back. Be alert to this, as the change is not well publicized, leading scores of visitors to miss planes and ferries every year. Greek time is thus always two hours ahead of Britain. For North America, the difference is seven hours for Eastern Standard Time, ten hours for Pacific Standard Time, with an extra hour plus or minus for those weeks in April when one place is on daylight saving and the other isn't. A recorded time message (in distinctly slow Greek, 24-hour convention) is available by dialling ☎141.

Toilets Public toilets are usually in parks or squares, often subterranean; otherwise try a bus station. Except in areas frequented by tourists, public toilets tend to be pretty filthy – it's best to use those in restaurants and bars. Remember that throughout Greece, you drop paper in the adjacent wastebins, *not* in the bowl.

Useful things to bring A high-quality, porcelain-lined canteen or drinking-water bottle; a small alarm clock for early buses and ferries; a flashlight/torch (power outages on the way back from island tavernas are common); pocket knife (Swiss Army type or similar), with tweezers, mini-screwdriver and other similar accessories (these are now widely sold in Greece at hunting/fishing shops); ear plugs for noisy ferries or hotels; and good-quality tea bags if you must have a cuppa.

Guide

Guide

1

The Argo-Saronic

CHAPTER 1 # Highlights

* **Temple of Aphaea, Égina**
The best preserved Archaic
temple on any island, set
on a pretty pine-wooded
hill. See p.96

* **Apónissos, Angístri** Swim
from an almost Caribbean-
like beach, a stone's throw
from Athens. See p.100

* **Póros Town** Climb up the
clocktower for a view over
the Argo-Saronic gulf and

the Peloponnese. See
p.101

* **Ídhra Town** A perfect
horseshoe-shaped harbour
surrounded by grand eigh-
teenth-century mansions.
See p.104

* **Spétses** Some of the best
beaches in the Argo-
Saronics, plus a grand
capital, full of majestic old
houses. See p.106

△ Moored yachts at Spétses harbour front

The Argo-Saronic

The rocky, volcanic **Argo-Saronic** islands, most of them barely an olive's
throw from the Argolid, differ to a surprising extent not just from the
mainland but from one another. Less surprising – given their proximity
to the mainland – is their massive popularity, with Égina (Aegina)
almost becoming an Athenian suburb at weekends. Ídhra (Hydra), Póros and
Spétses are not far behind in summer, though their visitors tend to be predominantly cruise- and package-tourists. More than any other group, these
islands are at their best out of season, when populations fall dramatically and
the port towns return to a quieter, more provincial life.

    Égina, important in antiquity and more or less continually inhabited since
then, is the most fertile of the group, famous for its pistachio nuts, as well as for
one of the finest ancient temples in Greece. Its main problem – the crowds –
can be escaped by avoiding weekends, or taking the time to explore its satellite isle, **Angístri**.

    The three southerly islands, **Spétses**, **Ídhra** and **Póros**, are pine-cloaked
and comparatively infertile. They were not extensively settled until medieval
times, when refugees from the mainland – principally Albanian Christians –
established themselves here. In response to the barrenness of their new
homes the islanders adopted piracy as a livelihood. The seamanship and huge
fleets thus acquired were placed at the disposal of the Greek nation during
the War of Independence. Today, foreigners and Athenians have replaced
locals in the rapidly depopulating harbour towns; windsurfers and sailboats
are faint echoes of the massed warships and *kaïkia* once at anchor.

    The closest island of the Argo-Saronic group, **Salamína**, is virtually a suburb
of Pireás, just over a kilometre offshore to its east, and almost touches the industrial city of Mégara to the west. It is frequented by Athenian weekenders or is a
base for commuting to the capital, but sees very few foreign visitors. Despite its
proximity to the metropolis, it is noted for its distinct folk dances and costumes.

Salamína

Salamína (Salamís) is the quickest possible island hop from Athens. Take the
metro to the end of the line in Pireás and then one of the green buses marked
Pérama to the shipyard port of Pérama, just west of Pireás, and a ferry (daily
5am–midnight; €0.50) will whisk you across to the little port of **Paloúkia** in
a matter of minutes. The ferry crosses the narrow strait where, in 480 BC, the
Greek navy trounced the Persian fleet, despite being outnumbered three to

▲ The Cyclades & Crete

▼ Monemvasiá & Kýthira

one; this battle is said by some to be more significant than the battle of Marathon, ten years earlier.

On arrival in Paloúkia, you won't be rewarded by pristine or isolated beaches or an island with the same picturesque attraction as any in, say, the Cyclades a few hours sailing further onwards, but you will find a fairly slow-paced worka-day retreat with a number of surprisingly large bays supporting quite rural communities. The water quality in the Saronic Gulf has improved immeasur-ably in recent years and you will frequently find pockets of bathers happily splashing in the clear waters – especially in the bays to the less-exposed west side of the island.

Paloúkia, Salamína Town and Selínia

By the ferry dock in **PALOÚKIA** is a bus station, with services to the contiguous capital Salamína Town (3km) and beyond, though the large selec-tion of signed destinations can be confusing.

SALAMÍNA TOWN (also known as Kouloúri) is home to 26,000 of the island's 31,000 population. It's a busy, functional place, with a couple of banks, a fish market and a long palm-tree laced promenade facing Salamína Bay. Pretty much uniquely for an island town – and emphasizing the absence of tourists – there is no bike or scooter rental outlet, and also no hotel. Bus services link most points on the island to Salamína Town. **Iliaktí beach**, some 5km to the west, is pleasant enough, as is the coastal strip running through the resorts of **Áyios Ioánnis** and **Résti**, on the way to which, a growing numbers of locals can be seen quite happily taking to the waters.

Buses marked **Faneroméni** run to the port at the northwest tip of the island, the **Voudóro peninsula**, where there are hourly ferries across to Lákki Kaloyírou, near Mégara on the Athens–Kórinthos road. En route, the bus passes close by the frescoed seventeenth-century **monastery of Faneroméni** (6km from Salamína), rather majestically sited above the gulf.

Around 6km to the south of Paloúkia is the popular local town of **SELÍNIA**, which supports a fairly lively, though low-key tourist scene. It can also be reached direct by bus from Paloúkia. This is the main summer resort, with a pleasant waterfront, a bank, several tavernas and two inexpensive but quiet pleasant hotels, the *Akroyali* (T210 46 73 263; ❸) and the *Votsalakia* (T210 46 71 334; ❸).

Eándio and the south

South from Salamína Town, the road edges the coast towards Eándio (6km; regular buses). There are a few tavernas along the way and opportunites to swim, though a well-organized and fenced-off public beach is now up and running just outside Eándio. **EÁNDIO** itself is quite a pleasant village, with a little pebble beach and the island's best **hotel**, the *Gabriel* (T210 46 62 275; ❸), which overlooks the bay.

Two roads continue from Eándio. The one to the southeast runs to the unassuming village resorts of Peráni and Paralía (both around 4km from Eándio). The more interesting route is southeast towards **Kanákia** (8km from Eándio; two buses daily), over the island's pine-covered mountain, and passing (at around 5km) the photogenic monastery of **Ayíou Nikolaou Lemoníon**. Shortly after the monastery, an unmarked and fairly rough dirt road leads left, up and down to the south coast passing through the isolated coastal settlements of **Saterlí** and **Kolónes** before emerging at the small-scale resort of **Peristéria** (5km). This is a much more attractive settlement than the littered, exposed beach and scruffy huts of Kanákia itself, which has an end-of-the-world feel to it.

Égina (Aegina)

Égina was a major power in Classical times, rivalling Athens. It carried trade to the limits of the known world, maintained a sophisticated silver coinage system (the first in Greece) and had prominent athletes and craftsmen. During the fifth century BC, however, the islanders made the political mistake of siding with their fellow Dorians, the Spartans. Athens seized on this as an excuse to act on a long-standing jealousy; her fleets defeated those of the islanders in two separate sea battles and, after the second, the population was expelled and replaced by more tractable colonists.

Subsequent history was less distinguished, with the pattern of occupation familiar to central Greece – by Romans, Franks, Venetians, Catalans and

ÉGINA
(AEGINA)

Souvála

Mesagrós
Paleohóra   **Temple
of Aphaea**
• Livádhi   Ómorfi Áyios   Ayía
Ekklisía Nektários   Marína
                            Alónes •
ÉGINA
TOWN   Yiannákidhes •
              Theotókou
       Khryssoleondissis
Fáros   Lazáridhes

                    Pahiá Ráhi •   • Pórtes
Marathónas •   Anitséou •
              Ellaníou Dhiós
                        ▲ Mt Óros
                                    • Vláhidhes
        Eyinítissa •
                                    Kípi
            • Pérdhika   Sfendoúri
    Moní Islet   0   3 km

▼ Méthana, Póros, Ídhra & Spétses

◀ Angístri

Turks – before the War of Independence brought a brief period as seat of government for the fledgling Greek nation. For a time it was a prison island and only comparatively recently has it shaken off the consequent unfavourable reputation. The grim Égina prison still stands behind the stadium, but is currently used as a stray-dog shelter. These days, the island is most famous for its **pistachio orchards**, whose thirsty trees lower the water table several feet annually – hence the notices warning you of the perennial water crisis.

Athenians regard Égina as a beach annexe for their city, being the closest place to the capital most of them would swim at, though for tourists it has a monument as fine as any in the Aegean in its beautiful fifth-century-BC **Temple of Aphaea**. This is located on the east coast, close to the port of **Ayía Marína**. Hydrofoils are more frequent than ferries, run from the same quay in Pireás as the conventional boats, and cost hardly any more. If you plan to stay, make sure your boat docks at **Égina Town**, the island capital. Ferries and hydrofoils also call at **Souvála**, a Greek weekend retreat on Egina's north coast and generally devoid of interest to outsiders.

Égina Town

A solitary column of the Temple of Apollo beckons as your ferry or hydrofoil steams around the point into the harbour at **ÉGINA TOWN**. The island's capital, it makes an attractive base, with some grand old buildings from the time (1826–28) when it served as the first capital of Greece during the War of Independence. And for somewhere so close to Athens, it isn't especially overrun by foreign tourists, although accommodation prices are high, particularly at weekends.

The **long harbour** waterfront combines the workaday with the pictur-esque, but is nonetheless appealing: fishermen talk and tend their nets, and *kaïkia* selling produce from the mainland bob at anchor. North of the port, behind the small town beach, a lone column on a low hill, known, logically enough, as **Kolóna** (Column) marks the remains of the Temple of Apollo and the ancient acropolis. Near the entrance to the ruins (Tues–Sun 8.30am–3pm; €3), a small but worthwhile **Sanctuary of Apollo archeology museum** has finds from the extensive excavations that have revealed five thousand years and ten layers of settlement; a free pamphlet gives a history and explains the objects on display. On the north flank of Kolóna hill there's an attractive bay with a very small, sandy **beach** – the best spot for swimming in the immedi-ate vicinity of the town.

The town's other sights include the restored **Markélos Tower**, seat of the first Greek government, uphill from the middle of the harbour, near the large **Church of Áyios Nikólaos**. The frescoed thirteenth-century church of **Ómorfi Ekklisía** is a fifteen-minute walk east of the port. In the suburb of Livádhi, just to the north, a plaque marks the residence of **Nikos Kazantzakis**, when he was writing his most celebrated book, *Zorba the Greek*.

Practicalities

The **bus station** is on the spacious Platía Ethneyersías, just north of the ferry arrival point, with excellent services to most villages; buy your tickets before you get on the bus. Horse buggies (€15 per 15min) and taxis are found nearby. The **post office** is across the square, and the **tourist police** post (☏22970 23333) is immediately behind it in the same building as the regular police. Several offices on and behind the main waterfront rent cars, scooters, motorbikes and mountain bikes – Égina is large and hilly enough to make a motor worthwhile for anything other than a pedal to the beaches towards Pérdhika. Four **banks** line the main waterfront. Aegina Island Holidays (☏22970 26430) on the waterfront near the church, offers excur-sions to the Epidaurus theatre festival on the mainland, handles tickets for the hydrofoils to Souvála and Ayía Marína, and books accommodation. You can access the **Internet** at Prestige, at the junction of Ródhi and Eákou. Foreign-language papers can be found at Kalezi, mid-way along the waterfront.

Accommodation

Good inexpensive **accommodation** is available in the *Ilektra* rooms (☏22970 23360, ☏22970 26715; ❷) on Leonárdhou Ladhá, northwest of the square. On the seafront between the square and the Kolóna are the *Avra* (☏22970 22303, ☏22970 23917; ❸) and the friendly *Plaza Hotel* (☏22970 25600; ❷), where seaview rooms may be a bit noisy. The pleasantly situated *House of Peace* (☏22970 23790, ✉the_house_of_peace@yahoo.com), on the corner of Kánari and Aphrodíti, has rooms and apartments all looking on to a garden shaded by palm and pistachio trees. Up above the Markélos Tower is the ochre- and orange-coloured *Traditional Pension* (*Eyinitiko Arhondiko*; ☏22970 24968, ☏22970 24156; ❹) and on the other side of the church the *Stone House* (*To Petrino Spiti*; ☏22970 23827) has pleasant studios for three (❹). Housed in a former sponge factory, the prominent *Hotel Brown* (☏22970 22271, ✉brownhotel@aig.forthnet.gr; ❺), on the southern waterfront, is a fine upmarket choice with smaller rooms and more spacious apartments, all looking out onto a leafy garden.

Eating and entertainment

There are enough reasonable **tavernas** in the town: directly behind the fish market on P. Irióti is *Psarotaverna Agora*, particularly good for inexpensive seafood and with outdoor seating on the cobbles in summer. Nearby is *Steki*, another unadorned fish taverna, which does great grilled sardines and octopus. On the north side of the harbour and near the *Avra* hotel, small *Lekkas* is excellent for no-nonsense meat grills by the waterside, while the adjoining *Flisvos* offers excellent charcoal-grilled fish and meat dishes. Two blocks back from the waterfront on Koumoundoúrou, *To Patitiri* ("Wine Press") gives you the chance to dine in a secluded, leafy courtyard (dinner only). Finally, the popular *To Karafaki ouzerí* on pedestrianized P. Irióti is a congenial spot for a *mezédhes*-style dinner, washed down with an ouzo or six.

In terms of **nightlife**, Égina Town boasts two summer **cinemas**: the Olympia near the football grounds before the *Miranda* hotel, and the newer Akroyiali at the south end of the harbour on the Pérdhika road, which shows quality foreign films; the winter cinema, the Titina, is by the park of the medieval tower-house, a block below the OTE.

Live music is best caught at one of two places: the *En Egini* (☎22970 22922), at Spýrou Ródhi 44, and *Kyvernio* (☎22970 25801), at Mitropóleos 4; both kick off at midnight on Fridays and Saturdays and feature live Greek acts. Reservations are recommended at both places if you want to secure a table. *To Ellinikon*, 1km south of the harbour and still on the waterfront, is a flashy **bar**, all decked out in silver and chrome.

Áyios Nektários and Paleohóra

Áyios Nektários, a whitewashed modern convent situated around 6km east of Égina Town, was named in honour of the Greek Orthodox Church's most recent and controversial saint, Anastasios Kefalas, a rather high-living monk who died in 1920 and was canonized in 1962. An oversized church – the largest in Greece – was recently completed on the main road below. Opposite the convent car park, a partly paved road leads up into the hills towards the seventeenth-century convent of Khryssoleondísis – primarily worth seeing for its views.

Paleohóra, a kilometre or so further east, was built in the ninth century as protection against piracy, but failed singularly in this capacity during Barbarossa's 1537 raid. Abandoned in 1827 following Greek independence, Paleohóra is now utterly deserted, but possesses the romantic appeal of a ghost village. You can drive right up to the site: take the turning left after passing the new large church and keep going about 400m. Some twenty of Paleohóra's reputed 365 churches and monasteries – one for every saint's day – remain in a recognizable state, and can be visited, but only those of Episkopí (locked), Áyios Yeóryios and Metamórfosis (on the lower of the two trails) retain frescoes of any merit or are in any state of preservation. Little remains of the town itself; when the islanders left, they simply abandoned their houses and moved to Égina Town.

The Temple of Aphaea

The Doric **Temple of Aphaea** (daily 8.15am–7pm €4) lies 12km east of Égina Town, among pines that are tapped to flavour the local retsina, and beside a less aesthetic radio mast. It is one of the most complete and visually complex ancient buildings in Greece, its superimposed arrays of columns and lintels evocative of an Escher drawing. Built in the fifth century BC to replace a destroyed sixth-century original, it slightly predates the Parthenon. The dedication is unusual: Aphaea was a Cretan nymph who had fled from the lust of King Minos, and seems to have been worshipped almost exclusively on Égina. As recently as two centuries ago, the temple's pediments were intact and virtually perfect, depicting two battles at Troy. However, like the Elgin marbles they were "purchased" from the Turks – this time by Ludwig I of Bavaria, which explains their current residence in Munich's Glyptothek museum.

Hourly **buses** from Égina Town to Ayía Marína stop at the temple, or you could walk from Ayía Marína along the path that takes up where Kolokotróni leaves off, but rented transport allows you to stop at the monastery of Áyios Nektários and at the island's former capital of Paleohóra.

The east: Ayía Marína and Pórtes

The island's major package resort of **AYÍA MARÍNA**, another 3km on, sits on the east coast of the island, south of the Aphaea temple ridge. The concentrated tackiness of its jam-packed high street rivals anything found on Corfu: signs abound for Guinness and cider, burger bars and salaciously named cocktails. The beach is packed and overlooked by constantly sprouting, half-built hotels, and the water, while now adequately clean, is rather shallow and more suited to children than adults.

Beyond the resort, the paved road continues south 8km to **PÓRTES**, a low-key shore hamlet. Among the uneasy mix of new summer villas-in-progress (no short-term accommodation) and old basalt cottages, are scattered a few tiny fish tavernas – the otherwise undistinguishable *Galanopetra* and the *Akroyiali* have the best position overlooking the small harbour – with a functional beach between the two fishing anchorages. The road climbs to the village of Anitséou, just below a major saddle on the flank of Mount Óros, and then forges west towards the scenic village of **Pahiá Ráhi**, almost entirely rebuilt in traditional style by foreign owners. From here it is possible to take a very rough, single-lane, winding track down to the main west-coast road at Marathónas (see below), though you are better advised to stick to the longer, paved and tree-lined route that heads back to Égina Town and then to loop back to Marathónas along the coastal road.

Mount Óros

Just south of the saddle between Pahiá Ráhi and Anitséou, mentioned below, are the foundations of the shrine of **Ellaníou Dhiós**, with the monastery of Taxiárhis squatting amid the massive masonry. The 532-metre summit cone of **Mount Óros**, an hour's walk from the highest point of the road, is capped by the modern chapel of Análipsi (the Ascension) and has views across the entire island and much of the Argo-Saronic Gulf.

Gerald Thompson's *A Walking Guide to Aegina*, available locally, describes in detail a series of walks across the range of mountains and wooded valleys between Mount Óros and the Aphaea temple and down to the port of Souvála, all avoiding main roads.

The west: Marathónas, Pérdhika and Moní islet

The road due south of Égina Town running along the west coast of the island is served by regular buses (8–10 daily). Small but sprawling **MARATHÓNAS**, 5km from Égina, has the biggest of the west coast's small and rather scruffy sand beaches, and is tolerable enough, with a scattering of rooms, tavernas and cafés along the shore.

PÉRDHIKA, 9km along at the end of the coastal road, scenically set on its little bay, is the most pleasant and picturesque village on the island and certainly has the best range of nonpackaged **accommodation** outside Égina Town. There are rooms on the main road, and just off it; immediately before the waterfront, is the well-priced *Hotel Hippocampus* (☎22970 61363; ❸), and nearer the harbour, is *Antzi Studios* (☎22970 61233; ❷), spotted in high summer by the bougainvillea draped over the blue-and-white painted facade.

The back streets of the elongated village are nonetheless rather characterless, but its attractive, pedestrianized waterfront esplanade reveals a relaxed, seaside-holiday atmosphere, very different from the rest of the island. Here, overlooking a panorama of Moní islet and the Peloponnese, are a dozen **tavernas** and cafés among which *Remetzo* is good for lobster, spaghetti and grills. The *Café Kiosk* sells snacks and breakfast and *To Proreon*, prettily decorated with pots and plants, is best for atmosphere. Athenians who sail here, tend to gravitate to *Andonis,* perhaps the most popular fish taverna of the bunch.

The only other diversion at Pérdhika is a trip to the pale-limestone offshore islet of **Moní** (10min; several departures daily; €4 return). There are no facilities on the island and most of it is fenced off as a nature conservation area. It's really only worth the trip for a swim in wonderfully clear water, as Pérdhika bay itself is fairly small and the water very shallow.

Angístri

Angístri, fifteen minutes by catamaran from Égina, is small enough to be overlooked by most island-hoppers, though it is now in many foreign holiday brochures. The island fosters an uneasy coexistence between Athenian and German old-timers, who bought property here years ago, and British newcomers on package trips. Beaches, however, remain better and less crowded than on Égina, and out of season the pine-covered island succumbs to a leisurely village pace, with many islanders still making a living from fishing and farming. Headscarves worn by the old women indicate the islanders' Albanian ancestry, and until recently, they still spoke Arvanítika – a dialect of medieval Albanian with Greek accretions – amongst themselves.

Boats and catamarans to Angístri from Égina leave from the main quay, while the local *Angistri Express* boat departs from a separate point south of the main harbour. Boats and catamarans from Égina and Pireás call only at Skála. **From Pireás**, a regular ferry runs at least twice daily in season (via Égina) and once a day out of season, taking two and a half hours; the *Keravnos I* and *Keravnos II* catamarans run four times a day, via Égina, and take 55 minutes.

Skála and Mýlos

The essentially modern resort of **SKÁLA** is dominated by many new apartment buildings and hotels with little to distinguish them, spreading west halfway along the north shore of the island. The popular town beach, Angístri's only sandy one, nestles against the protected south shore of this headland, below the big white church. Just inland of the ferry dock is the attractive hotel *Yana* (T 22970 91228; ❷), sharing a pool with the *Alter Ego* self-catering apartments; both are run by the helpful Nektarios (Nick) Panou of Skala Travel (T 22970 91356, F 22970 91342), who can also arrange reservations for other **accommodation**. On summer weekends you would be well advised to reserve ahead. For **food**, there's *Mandraki* near the harbour, or *Gionis* at the north end of the beach near the church; neither are that special but the latter has pleasant shaded tables under the trees.

Both **scooters** and **mountain bikes** are available for rent; Limenária, near the end of the trans-island road, is less than 8km distant, so in cooler weather you can comfortably cross Angístri on foot or by bike. A road to the left of the harbour leads within fifteen minutes to the *Angistri Club*, with a disco-bar on the rocks above the sea, and the nearby *Alkyoni* taverna. From there, it's another ten minutes' walk to the secluded **Halikádha** pebble beach backed by crumbling cliffs and pine-covered hills; along with Apónissos (see p.100), this is the best that the island has to offer, and is clothing-optional.

Metóhi, the hillside hamlet just above Skála, was once the main village, and in recent years has been completely bought up and restored by foreigners and Athenians; *Taverna Parnassos* dishes up good-value grills and *mayireftá* and has a good view down towards Skála.

Ever-spreading Skála threatens in the future to merge with **MÝLOS** (Megalohóri), just 1.5km west along the north coast. Once you penetrate a husk of new construction, you find an attractive, traditional Argo-Saronic-style village centre. Although there's no decent beach nearby, it makes an alternative base to Skála, with plenty of rented **rooms** and some **hotels**. The *Milos Hotel* (T 22970 91241; ❷) is a good, well-positioned choice and *Sailor* and *Konaki* are recommended places to **eat**.

The rest of the island

In summer, four daily **buses** connect Skála and Mýlos with Limenária on the far side of the island – or you could hike from Metóhi along a winding dirt road through the pine forest, with views across to Égina and the Peloponnese. The excellent paved west-coast road takes you past the turning for **Dhragonéra**, a broad, pine-shaded pebble beach with a dramatic panorama across to the mainland.

LIMENÁRIA is a small farming community set at the edge of a fertile plateau in the southeast corner of the island, and still largely unaffected by tourism. There are two tavernas – *Tasos* is very good – and a few rooms. A half-hour walk west of Limenária, on the old path which parallels the road, will bring you past a shallow salt lake, to the little hamlet of **APÓNISSOS**, connected via a small causeway to the tiny islet of the same name, with the larger island of **Dhoroússa** beyond. The *Aponisos Taverna* is the only place to **eat** here and, while the service is rather indifferent, the food is reasonably cheap and good; the location is superb, overlooking a couple of small beaches with azure-blue water.

Póros

Separated from the mainland by a 450-metre strait, **Póros** ("the ford") barely qualifies as an island, and far more than any other Argo-Saronic island it is package-tour territory. Its proximity to Pireás also means a weekend Athenian invasion. The island town has character though, and the topography is interesting: Póros is in fact two islands, **Sferiá** (Póros Town) and the much more extensive **Kalávria**, separated from each other by a shallow engineered canal, which is now silting up.

In addition to its regular ferry and hydrofoil connections with Pireás and the other Argo-Saronics, Póros has frequent boats shuttling across from the workaday mainland port of **Galatás** in the Peloponnese (5min; €0.30), and there's a car ferry every twenty minutes from near the Naval Academy. These allow for some interesting excursions – locally to ancient Troezen near Trizína, and the nearby Devil's Bridge. Further afield, day-trips to Náfplio or to performances of ancient drama at the great theatre of Epidaurus (Epídhavros) are possible by car, or by taking an excursion, available through travel agents in Póros Town (see opposite).

Póros Town

Ferries from the Argo-Saronics or from Galatás drop you at **PÓROS**, the main town on the island, which rises steeply on three sides of the tiny volcanic Sferiá. The harbour and town are picturesque, and the cafés and waterfront lively. Fishermen sell their catch direct from the boat and it is possible to arrange fishing trips. Particular sights are the hilltop clocktower and a small, well-labelled **archeological museum** (Mon–Sat 8.30am–3pm; free), with items from the mainland site of Troezen and elsewhere.

Near the main ferry dock is the helpful Family Tours (T 22980 23743, F 22980 24480), which has a variety of rooms available. Also on the waterfront are three other **travel agents**: Marinos Tours (T 22980 23423), sole agents for the Hellas Flying Dolphin hydrofoils and with well-priced local maps, Hellenic Sun Travel (T 22980 25901) and Saronic Gulf Travel (T 22980 24555).

All these agencies **exchange** money, arrange **accommodation** in rented rooms and handle **tours** off the island. If you want to look around on your own, quieter places to stay are up on the hill behind the clocktower, although prices are generally on the high side. To the right of the road to Kalávria you'll find two reasonable hotels: *Dimitra* (T 22980 25981, F 22980 25653; ❷) and *Dionysos* (T 22980 23953; ❸), at Papadhopoúlou 78. *Sto Roloi* (T 22980 25508, E storoloi@otenet.gr; ❹–❺) is Póros's answer to a boutique hotel. This turn-of-the-century private house now takes in discerning guests up on the hill close to the clocktower (*to rolói*).

Down on the quayside, among the cafés, bars, crêperies and souvenir shops facing Galatás, good-value **restaurants** include *Taverna Poseidon* on the north promenade and *Kathestos tis Yefsis*, which has a children's menu, on the south promenade. *Moskhoyiannis* has traditional Greek food in the souvenir lane which runs between the Alpha Bank and the post office square. A well-signed lane from near the car-ferry quay leads gently up, past the police station to the upper square. Here, by the Áyios Yeóryios cathedral are a cluster of good tavernas: *Platanos, Perasma, Dimitris* – the last run by a local butcher and offering excellent meat. The *Karavolos* ("Snail"; look out for signs) is another popular option, and unsurprisingly has snails on the menu.

The *Poseidon XL* is a cocktail and music **bar**, 3km from Póros Town high up on a hill overlooking the port. It enjoys stunning night-time views while *Maskes* at the eastern end of the promenade is a buzzing music **club**.

Additional facilities around the waterfront include **scooter** and **bicycle** rental outlets (you can take either across on boats to the mainland), four **banks**, a **post office**, the summer-only Diana **cinema** above the small shopping centre and the helpful **tourist police** (mid-May to Sept; T 22980 22462). **Internet** access and foreign-language newspapers are available at the Kendro Typou on Douzína on the north promenade.

Kalávria

Most of Póros's **hotels** are to be found on Kalávria, the main body of the island, just across the canal beyond the Naval Cadets' Training School. They stretch for a couple of kilometres on either side of the bridge, with some of those to the west in Neório ideally situated to catch the dawn chorus – the Navy's marching band. If you'd rather sleep in, head beyond the first bay where the fishing boats tie up. Two kilometres from the bridge, in **Megálo Neório**, is the pleasant *Pavlou* hotel (T 22980 22734, F 22980 22735; ❹–❺), a larger beach and a watersports centre.

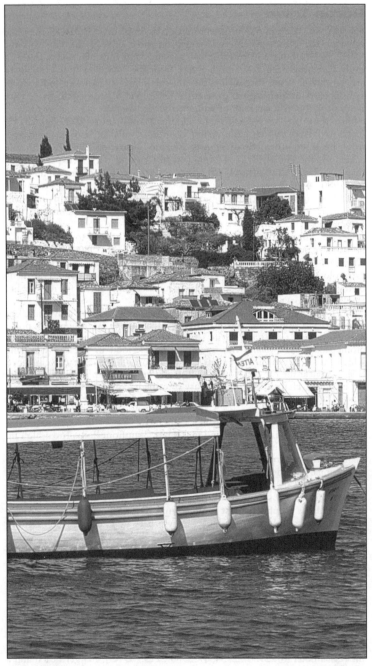

△ Póros harbou

Alternatively, turn right through **Askéli**, where posh hotels and villas face good clear water. Two **bus** routes run half-hourly from Póros Town waterfront to Askéli and Zoödhóhou Piyís, and to Neório.

The monastery of Zoödhóhou Piyís and Temple of Poseidon

At the end of the four-kilometre stretch of road through Askéli lies the eighteenth-century **monastery of Zoödhóhou Piyís** ("Life-giving Spring") whose monks have fled the tourists and been replaced by a caretaker. It's a pretty spot, with a couple of summer tavernas at the beach below.

From here you can either walk up across to the northern side of the island through the pines, or bike along the road. Initially, Kalávria appears to be mostly pine forest, but the far side has fertile plateaus, olive terraces, small deserted beaches in narrow inlets and magnificent panoramic views. Foot or bike routes lead you to a saddle in the hills and the few columns and ruins that make up the sixth-century-BC **Temple of Poseidon**. Keep your eyes open or you may miss them; look for a small blue caretaker's hut. It was here that Demosthenes, fleeing from the Macedonians after taking part in the last-ditch resistance of the Athenians, took poison rather than surrender. The road leads on, back down in a circular route to the canal and Sferiá.

Ídhra (Hydra)

The port and town of **Ídhra**, with tiers of substantial greystone mansions and white-walled, red-tiled houses climbing up from a perfect horseshoe harbour, are a beautiful spectacle. The whole island is treated as a national monument, blessedly free of traffic – except for an occasional garbage truck – making it one of the most peaceful and refreshing destinations in Greece. Unfortunately, thousands of others think so too, so the town's busy from Easter until September. In summer, especially with the midday crush of cruise-ship day-trippers and the weekend invasion of Athenians, it's packed to the gills; the front becomes one long outdoor café and souvenir stall, the hotels are full and the discos flourish. Once a fashionable artists' colony, established in the 1960s as people restored the grand old houses, it has experienced a predictable metamorphosis into one of the more popular resorts in Greece. Good beaches are also notably scarce. But this acknowledged, a visit is still recommended, especially out of peak season and during the week.

Ídhra Town and around

The waterfront of **ÍDHRA TOWN** is lined with mansions, most of them built during the eighteenth century, on the accumulated wealth of a remarkable merchant fleet of 160 ships which traded as far afield as America and, during the Napoleonic Wars, broke the British blockade to sell grain to France. Fortunes were made and the island also enjoyed a special relationship with the Turkish Porte, governing itself and paying no tax, but providing sailors for the sultan's navy. These conditions naturally attracted Greek immigrants from the less-privileged mainland, and by the 1820s the town's population was nearly 20,000 – an incredible figure when you reflect that today it is under 3000. During the War of Independence, Hydriot merchants provided many of the ships for the Greek forces and consequently many of the commanders.

The **mansions** (*arhondiká*) of these merchant families, designed by Venetian and Genoese architects, are still the great monuments of the town. A town map is available locally, if you are interested in seeking them out – some are labelled at the entrance with "*Oikía*" (home) and the family name. On the western waterfront, and the hill behind, are the **Voulgaris** mansion, with its interesting interior, and the **Tombazis** mansion, used as a holiday hostel for arts students. Set among pines above the restored windmill on the western point, the **Koundouriotis** mansion was the home of George Koundouriotis, a wealthy shipowner who fought in the War of Independence and whose great grandson, Pavlos Koundouriotis, was president of republican Greece in the 1920s. It is being refurbished as a museum with EU funding. On the eastern waterfront are the **Kriezis** mansion, the **Spiliopoulos** mansion and the **Tsamados** mansion – now the national merchant navy college which you can sometimes visit between lectures. The **historical archives museum** is also on the eastern waterfront (Tues–Sun 9am–2.30pm; €3).

Ídhra is also reputedly hallowed by no fewer than 365 churches – a total claimed by many a Greek island, but here with some justice. The most important is the church of **Panayía Mitropóleos**, set in a monastic courtyard by the port, with a distinctive clocktower and a **Byzantine museum** (Tues–Sun 10am–5pm; €2).

Ídhra festivals

On the second or third weekend in June, Ídhra Town celebrates the **Miaoulia**, in honour of Admiral Andreas Miaoulis whose **fire boats**, packed with explosives, were set adrift upwind of the Turkish fleet during the War of Independence. The highlight of the celebrations is the burning of a boat at sea as a tribute to the sailors who risked their lives in this dangerous enterprise.

On an altogether more peaceful note, the **International Puppet Theatre Festival** takes place here at the end of July and appeals to children of all ages.

Easter is a particularly colourful and moving experience. Ídhra's prosperity allows for grand celebrations, with a special emphasis on performances of choral music. Reservations must be made well ahead of time for all of these festivals.

Practicalities

The town is small and compact, but away from the waterfront, the streets and alleyways are steep and maps slightly ambiguous, so finding your way around can be difficult (the map in the free *This Summer in Hydra* will help). There are several **banks** along the waterfront, and the **tourist police** (daily mid-May to mid-Oct 9am–10pm; ☎22980 52205) are on Vótsi. The **post office** and a **laundry** are on the small market square, behind the National bank. The **ferry** and **hydrofoil** offices are upstairs on the eastern waterfront, about 10m beyond the Studio Hydra shop.

There are a number of **pensions** and **hotels** along, or just behind, the waterfront in Ídhra Town. The ones in the back streets often bear small almost indistinguishable stone or wooden signs, so you may have to ask around for directions. The *Amarillis* at Tombázi 15 (☎22980 53611, ☏22980 52249; ➍) is a good small hotel with comfortable rooms and private facilities. There are a couple of old mansions beautifully converted into hotels: *Angelica*, several blocks up at Miaoúli 42 (☎22980 53202, ✉angelicahotel@hotmail.com; ➎), and *Hydra*, steeply uphill at Voulgari 8 (☎ & ☏22980 52102, ✉hydrahotel @aig.forthnet.gr; ➍).

There's no shortage of **restaurants** and cafés around the waterfront, but for good tavernas you would do better to head a little inland. The *Garden* taverna, known for well-prepared meat dishes, is on the road heading up from the hydrofoil dock, while friendly *To Steki*, 300m inland on a street perpendicular from mid-quay, is excellent for *mayireftá*. Close by and on the west side of the *Amarillis Hotel* is the small *Barba Dimas* taverna, which has wonderful *mezédhes*, snails and fish. Further up on the same road, *To Kryfo Limani* is a pleasant taverna in a small garden, while further yet will bring you excellent and economically priced home cooking at the *Yeitoniko* (also known as *Manolis & Christina's*), which has tables on its roof and a small verandah. For a splurge you might want to try the classy *Moita* (☎22980 52020) near the OTE, which serves up interesting spins on seafood.

To sample the **nightlife** you might start at a portside bar: try the *Pirate* or *To Roloi*; the *Amalour* is a funky, ethnic style bar and the *Ydronetta*, built in and around the "canons" on the west side of the port, is a sophisticated café bar from where you'll get the best view of the sun setting.

Beaches around Ídhra Town

The town's only sandy beach is at **MANDHRÁKI**, 1.5km east of the harbour along a concrete road; it's the private domain of the *Miramare Hotel* (☎22980 52300; ➎), although the windsurfing centre is open to all.

On the opposite side of the harbour, to the southwest, a paved coastal path leads around to **KAMÍNI**, about a twenty-minute walk. Just as you reach Kamíni, on the right is a small *pension*, *Antonia* (☎22980 52481; ➌). On the left, across the street, Eleni Petrolekka has a popular rival *pension* and apartments (☎22980 52701; ➌). Also on the left is the *Kondylenia* restaurant, with fresh fish and wonderful views of the sunset. About 50m up the dry, paved streambed to the left is *Christina's*, a fine traditional Greek fish taverna.

Thirty minutes' walk beyond Kamíni (or a boat ride from the port) will bring you to **VLYHÓS**, a small hamlet with three tavernas, rooms, a small beach and a rebuilt nineteenth-century bridge. The *Marina* taverna enjoys sunset views from the water's edge, near the small jetty, while *Enalion* on the east side is a cool, chilled-out place that plays jazz sounds. Within the settlement, the attractive *Antigone* rooms (☎22980 53228, ☏22980 53042; ➍) and café offer you an accommodation choice. If you don't fancy the walk back, small boats ferry passengers (€1.50) back to Ídhra port every half hour or so. Swimming here, in the lee of an offshore islet, is good. Further to the west is the steep-sided island of **Dhokós**, large, but only seasonally inhabited by goatherds and people tending their olives.

The rest of the island

There are no motor vehicles on Ídhra, except for a few trucks to cart away rubble and rubbish, and no surfaced roads away from the port; the island is mountainous and its interior accessible only by foot or hoof. The net result is that most tourists don't venture beyond the town, so by a little walking you can find yourself in a dramatically different kind of island. The pines devastated by forest fires in 1985 have mostly grown back.

Following the streets of the town upwards and inland behind the *Angelica*, you reach a path which winds up the mountain for about an hour's walk to the **monastery of Profitis Ilías** and the **convent of Ayía Efpraxía**. Both are beautifully situated; the nuns at the convent (the lower of the two) offer hand-woven fabrics for sale. A path continues behind Profitis Ilías to a saddle overlooking the south coast and a steeply descending *kalderími* onwards to scattered houses and chapels near the sea. From the saddle, a faint path climbs to the right for twenty minutes to the 588-metre summit of Mount Éros, the Argo-Saronic islands' highest viewpoint. To the east of Profitis Ilías are four more monasteries, the nearest to town being **Ayía Triádha**, occupied by a few monks (no women admitted). From here a path continues east for two more hours to the cloister of **Zourvás** in the extreme east of the island.

A dirt road continues west of Vlyhós, past a busy boat-repair yard, to **Episkopí**, a high plateau planted with olives and vineyards and dotted by a scattering of homes (no facilities), and then climbs above Mólos Bay, the property of an Athenian hospital owner, and closed to the public. From Episkopí itself, vague tracks lead to the southwestern extreme of the island, on either side of which the bays of **Bísti** and **Áyios Nikólaos** offer solitude and good swimming. Bísti has a pebble beach with rocks for swimming off at one side; Áyios Nikólaos has a small sand beach.

The best cove of the many on the south coast is **Limnióniza** (beyond Ayía Triádha), with a pebble beach and pine trees; the overland access path is long (1hr 15 min from town) and rough, though well-marked and obvious.

Points on the coast, especially Bísti and Áyios Nikólaos, can be reached much more easily by **water taxis** (€6–10), which will drop you off and then pick you up again at any time you arrange.

Spétses

Spétses was the island where the author John Fowles once lived and which he used, thinly disguised as Phraxos, as the setting for *The Magus*. It is today very popular with well-to-do Athenians and with foreigners, and seems to have risen above the bad 1980s reputation earned by an unhealthy proportion of cheap package tours and lager louts. The architecture of Spétses Town is distinct and distinguished, though less photogenic than that of Ídhra. Lacking any dramatic topography, and despite a bout of forest-fire devastation in 1990, hints of the landscape described by Fowles are still to be seen: "away from its

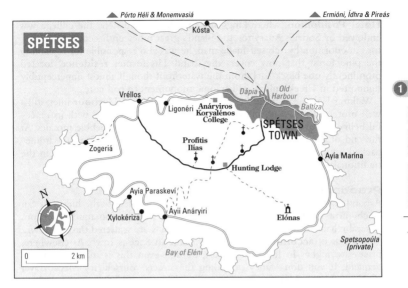

inhabited corner [it is] truly haunted . . . its pine forests uncanny". Remarkably, at Áyii Anáryiri, Spétses' best beach, development has been restrained to a scattering of holiday villas.

Spétses Town

SPÉTSES TOWN is the island's port – and its only settlement. It shares with Ídhra the same history of late-eighteenth-century mercantile adventure and prosperity, and the same leading role in the War of Independence, which made its foremost citizens the aristocrats of the newly independent Greek state. Pebble-mosaic courtyards and streets sprawl between 200-year-old mansions, whose architecture is quite distinct from the Peloponnesian styles across the water. Though homeowners may bring private cars onto the island, their movement inside the town limits is prohibited. A few taxis supplement the horse-drawn buggies, whose bells ring cheerfully night and day along the long waterfront. Motorbikes, scooters and noisy three-wheel mini-trucks are the preferred mode of transport, and career continuously through the town streets, making life almost as difficult for pedestrians as if cars had been allowed.

The sights are principally the majestic old houses and gardens, the grandest of which is the magnificent Mexis family mansion, built in 1795 and now used as the **local museum** (Tues–Sun 8.30am–2.15pm; €2), housing displays of relics from the War of Independence that include the bones of the Spetsiot admiral-heroine Laskarina Bouboulina. One of Bouboulina's homes, to the rear of the cannon-studded main harbour known as the **Dápia**, has been made into a **museum** (daily morning and late afternoon; €4) by her descendants and is well worth visiting. Guided tours (30min) are given in English several times a day.

Just outside the town, Fowles aficionados will notice **Anáryiros Koryalénos College**, a curious Greek re-creation of an English public school where the author was employed and set part of his tale; it is now vacant, save for the occasional conference or kids' holiday programme. Like the massive waterfront

Hotel Posidonion, where kings and presidents once slept, the college was endowed by Sotirios Anaryiros, the island's great nineteenth-century benefactor. An enormously rich self-made man, he was also responsible for replanting the pine forest that now covers the island. His former **residence**, located prominently one block back from the waterfront though almost imperceptibly signposted in Greek only, is a Pharaonic monument to bad taste.

Walking 1.5km east from the Dápia, you pass the **Old Harbour** inlet, still a well-protected mooring, and the church of **Áyios Nikólaos** with its graceful belfry, "Freedom or Death" memorial and some giant pebble mosaics. At the end of the road, you reach the **Baltíza** inlet where, among the sardine-packed luxury yachts, half a dozen boatyards continue to build *kaïkia* in the traditional manner.

Practicalities

A good way to get around the island is by bike, and, despite the hills, you can reach most points or make the 25km circuit without too much exertion. Several reliable **bike-** and **scooter-rental** outlets are scattered through town.

All kinds of **accommodation** are available in Spétses Town. As elsewhere, prices are higher in July and August, though even this is subject to actual demand. If you don't fancy pounding the streets yourself, try Alasia Travel (T 22980 74098), Melédon Tourist and Travel Agency (T 22980 74497) or Pine Island Tours (T 22980 72464), all by the Dápia. Simple but comfortable hotels include *Faros* (T 22980 72613, F 22980 72614; ❸) on Platía Oroloyíou ("Clocktower Square"), *Stelios* (T 22980 72971; ❸) on the waterfront, and *Star* (T 22980 72214, F 22980 27872; ❺), which is quieter because its pebble-mosaic pavement makes it off-limits to vehicles.

A few hotels – the *Faros* (see above), the *Alexandris* (T 22980 72211; ❸), above the petrol station, and the waterfront *Klimis* (T 22980 72334; ❹) – stay open all winter. You might even want to spring for the renovated *Posidonion* (T 22980 72308, F 22980 72209; ❺) on the western waterfront, or a few steps further will bring you to *Nissia* (T 22980 75000, E nissia@otenet.gr; ❺), perhaps the classiest hotel on the island with its 31 individual island-style studio apartments.

In Spétses Town, **food** and **drink** tend to be more expensive than elsewhere. Among the better and more economical options are *Roussos*, by the town beach, which is honest and unfussy, or the *Lazaros* taverna, about 500m up the main road from from the Dápia, which is also well-priced and has superior food. For fish, go to the long-established *Patralis* near the water in Kounoupítsa, west towards the *Spetses* hotel. More upmarket and better quality places are situated towards the old harbour including the *Tarsanas* – a good fish taverna, or the *Liotrivi* and *Exedra*, both close to each other overlooking the water among the boatyards at Baltíza. All three tend to be patronized mainly by discerning Greek diners and offer a Greek-Mediterranean cuisine.

By day, *To Kafenio*, near the Flying Dolphin office at the Dápia, remains steadfastly traditional, with drinks and lunchtime *mezédhes* – a good place to watch and wait for your ferry. By night, clubbers head for *Tsitsiano* or *Remezzo* in the Old Harbour, and the places at the other end of town around Kounoupítsa. You can catch a string quartet over cocktails at the rather elegant *To Balkoni* nearer the Dápia.

The **post office** is near the *Roussos* taverna, while a couple of **banks** are behind the Dápia, near the *Roumani* hotel. There's also a **laundry** behind Platía Oroloyíou. You can use the **Internet** at Delfinia Net Café abutting the town beach.

Around the island

For **swimming** you need to get clear of the town. Beaches within walking distance are at various spots beyond the Old Harbour, at **Ayía Marína** (twenty minutes east, with the very pleasant *Paradise* restaurant), and several other spots half an hour away in either direction. The tempting smaller isle of **Spetsopoúla**, just offshore from Ayía Marína, is off-limits: it's the private property of the heirs of shipping magnate Stavros Niarchos.

For heading further afield, you'll need to hire a **bike** or **scooter**, or use the **kaïkia** rides from the Dápia, which run to beaches around the island in summer. A very expensive alternative are **water taxis**, though they can take up to ten people. **Walkers** might want to go over the top of the island to Áyii Anáryiri; forest fires have ravaged much of the southern side's pines between Ayía Marína and Áyii Anáryiri, though happily the trees are now growing back. There is a **bus** service (€1) to Áyii Anáryiri from near the *Roussos* taverna, running several times a day in season. Routes out of town start from beyond the *Lazaros* taverna, and pass the forest service firewatch tower. Brave the precariously attached steps and you're rewarded with the island's highest and best viewpoint.

West from Spétses Town

Heading west from the Dápia around the coast, the road is now paved all around the island. The forest that survived the fires stretches from the central hills right down to the western shores and makes for a beautiful coastline with little coves and rocky promontories, all shaded by trees. *Blueberry Hill Restaurant and Café Bar* at Ligonéri, run by a Greek-American woman, provides wonderful respite from the bustle of town. You can swim below and then have lunch or dinner under the pines. A regular bus service runs to Ligonéri in season from in front of the *Hotel Posidonion*. A timetable is posted at the stop.

Vréllos is the next place you come to, at the mouth of a wooded valley known locally as "Paradise". Here you'll find a cool, pine-tree copse overlooking a small pebbly beach. The coastline onwards is dotted with coves and in a few places there are small, seasonal tavernas – there's a good one at **Zogeriá**, for instance, where the scenery and rocks more than make up for the small beach.

Working your way anticlockwise around the coast towards Áyii Anáryiri you reach **Ayía Paraskeví** with its small church and beach – one of the most beautiful coves on Spétses and an alternate stop on some of the *kaïki* runs. There's a small taverna and watersports here in summer. Further round still, you'll come to the as yet unheralded **Xylokériza beach**, a well-tended, white-pebbled strand in a sheltered bay. There's a beach bar and small cafeteria serving light snacks. This is a more satisfactory stop than the better known, and consequently more populated, Áyii Anáryiri beach further on.

Áyii Anáryiri

Áyii Anáryiri, on the south side of the island is the most popular beach. It consists of a beautiful, long, sheltered bay of fine sand. Gorgeous first thing in the morning, it fills up later in the day with bathers, windsurfers and, at one corner, speedboats driving waterskiers. There's a good seafront taverna *Manolis* and another, *Tasos*, just behind, run by one of the island's great eccentrics. You can bed down at *Pension Nerantzoula* (☎22980 72527; ❷), a small unit set in a shaded, leafy garden 100m from the beach.

Travel details

Ferries

From the central harbour at Pireás at least 13 boats daily run to Égina (1hr 30min–2hr); 3 daily to Angístri (2hr 30min); 5 daily to Póros (2hr 45min); 2 daily to Ídhra (3hr 30min) and 1 daily to Spétses (4hr 30min). In addition there are 3 boats daily to Souvála (2hr).

Most of the ferries stop on the Peloponnesian mainland at Méthana (between Égina and Póros) from where it is possible to board. There are also shuttle boats between Póros and Galatás (5min) from dawn until late at night, taxi-boats between Spétses and Pórto Héli, and 4 daily ferries between Spétses and Kósta.

NB: There are more ferries at weekends and fewer out of season (although the service remains good). Departures from Pireás are, on average, hourly with only the 8am departure going all the way down to Spétses from where it returns at 3.15pm. The last departure (for Égina) is at 8pm (9pm on Sundays). The longer-haul, closed-hull boats are much faster than the landing craft ferries that service only Égina and Angístri and are a much better choice to get to/from Égina.

Ferry schedules are posted at the ticket offices on the quay though you can pick up your own copy from the pursor's office on board the ferries. The general information number for the Argo-Saronic ferries is ☎210 41 71 190.

Hydrofoils and catamarans

Approximately hourly hydrofoil services depart from Aktí Tselépi at Pireás for Égina 7am–8pm in season, 8am–7pm out of season (40min). In addition, approximately hourly hydrofoil or catamaran (same price) departures leave the same quay for Póros (1hr), Ídhra (1hr 30min), Spétses (2hr 10min) and Pórto Héli (2hr 25min). There are also 2–3 services a day to Ermióni (2hr). Hydrofoil services are offered by Hellas Flying Dolphins (☎210 41 99 200, ⓦwww.dolphins.gr) and Saronic Dolphins (☎210 42 24 980).

There 5 are departures daily (6 on weekends) from Pireás to Angístri (via Égina) with either the *Keravnos I* or *Keravnos II* catamaran leaving also from Aktí Tselépi in Pireás. For further information call ☎210 41 13 108 or ☎22970 91163.

NB: Services are heavily reduced out of season, though all the routes between Pórto Héli and Pireás still run. Hydrofoils are usually twice as fast and twice as expensive as ordinary boats.

2

The Cyclades

N

0   100 km

CHAPTER 7 # Highlights

* **Boat tour around Mílos** The best way to take in the geological diversity of this volcanic island. See p.131

* **Mýkonos Town** Labyrinthine lanes filled with restaurants, boutiques and nightlife. See p.148

* **Delos** The Cyclades' sacred centre and holiest ancient site, birthplace of Apollo and Artemis. See p.153

* **Ermoúpolis, Sýros** Once Greece's busiest port, the elegant capital of the Cyclades is now a UNESCO heritage site. See p.157

* **Church of Ekatondapylianí, Parikía, Páros** An imposing and ornate Byzantine church incorporating an impressive number of architectural styles. See p.162

* **Tragéa, Náxos** This fertile inland plain, covered with orchards, shelters most of the villages on the Cyclades' largest island. See p.176

* **Hóra, Folégandhros** Free of traffic and sitting atop a spectacular cliff, this capital has a handsome old kástro. See p.192

* **Caldera of Thíra** A geographical wonder, this crater left by a colossal volcanic explosion averages five miles in diameter. See p.194

△ Dovecotes, Tínos

2

The Cyclades

N amed, most probably, after the circle they form around the sacred island of Delos, the **Cyclades** (Kykládhes) is the most satisfying Greek archipelago for island-hopping. On no other group do you get quite such a strong feeling of each island as a microcosm, each with its own distinct traditions, customs and path of modern development. Most of these self-contained realms are compact enough to explore in a few days, giving you a sense of completeness and identity impossible on, say, Crete or most of the Ionian islands.

The islands do share some features, with the majority of them (Ándhros, Náxos, Sérifos and Kéa excepted) being arid and rocky; most also share the "Cycladic" style of brilliant-white Cubist architecture. The extent and impact of tourism, though, is markedly haphazard, so that although some English is spoken on most islands, a slight detour from the beaten track – from Íos to Síkinos, for example – can have you groping for your Greek phrasebook.

But whatever the level of tourist development, there are only three islands where it has come completely to dominate their character in season: **Íos**, the original hippie-island and still a paradise for hard-drinking backpackers, **Thíra**, the major island in the volcanic cluster of Santoríni and a dramatic natural backdrop for luxury cruise liners, and **Mýkonos**, by far the most popular of the group, with its teeming old town, selection of nude beaches and sophisticated restaurants, clubs and hotels. After these two, **Páros** and **Náxos** are the most popular, with their beaches and main towns drastically overcrowded at the height of the season, which in the Cyclades is late July to late August. To avoid the hordes altogether – except in August, when nearly everywhere is overrun and escape is impossible – the most promising islands are **Síkinos**, **Kímolos** or **Anáfi**, though the once-tranquil **Minor Cyclades** around Náxos have become fashionable destinations for well-heeled Athenians in recent years, as have nearby **Amorgós**, and **Folégandhros** to the west, with its unspoilt capital. For a different view of the Cyclades, visit **Tínos** and its imposing pilgrimage church, a major spiritual centre of Greek Orthodoxy, or **Sýros** with its elegant townscape and (like Tínos) large Catholic minority. Due to their closeness to Athens, adjacent **Ándhros**, **Kéa**, **Kýthnos** and **Sérifos** are predictably popular – and relatively expensive – weekend havens for Greeks, while **Sífnos** remains a popular destination for upmarket tourists of all nationalities. The one major ancient site is **Delos** (Dhílos), certainly worth making time for: the commercial and religious centre of the Classical Greek world, it's visited most easily on a day-trip, by *kaïki* or jet boat from Mýkonos.

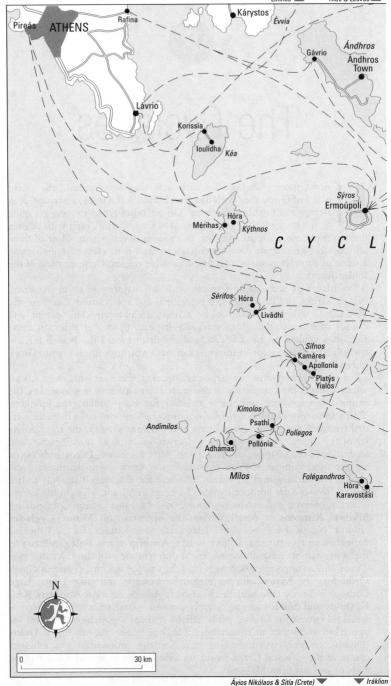

Límnos ▲   Híos & Lésvos ▲

Pireás   ATHENS   Rafina   Kárystos
                                          Évvia

                                    Gávrio   Ándhros
                                              Ándhros
                                               Town

Lávrio

     Korissía

       Ioulidha   Kéa

                                         Sýros
                                       Ermoúpoli

        Hóra
   Mérihas   Kýthnos   C   Y   C   L

              Sérifos   Hóra
                       Livádhi

                         Sífnos
                        Kamáres
                            Apollonía
                            Platýs
                             Yialós

                   Kímolos
     Andímilos   Psathí
                    Pollónia   Políegos
         Adhámas

        Mílos   Folégandhros
                             Hóra
                           Karavostási

N

0   30 km

Áyios Nikólaos & Sitía (Crete) ▼   ▼ Iráklion

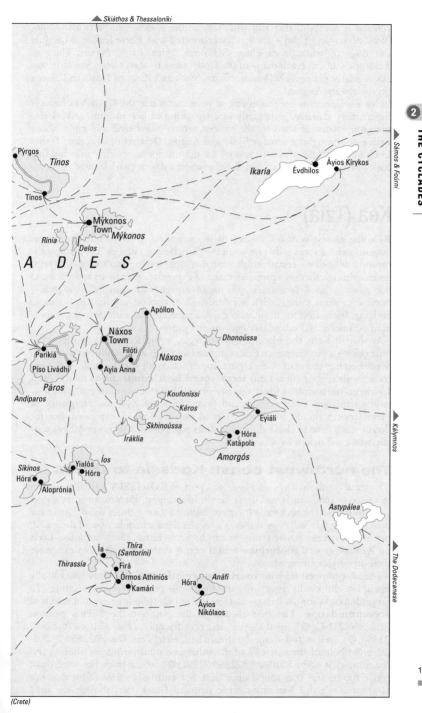

Skiáthos & Thessaloníki

Sámos & Foúrni

Kálymnos

The Dodecanese

2

THE CYCLADES

Pýrgos

Tínos

Tínos

Ikaría   Évdhilos   Áyios Kírykos

Mýkonos Town   Mýkonos

Rínia

Delos

A   D   E   S

Náxos Town

Parikiá   Filóti   Dhonoússa

Píso Livádhi   Náxos

Páros   Ayía Ánna

Andíparos   Koufoníssi

Kéros

Skhinoússa   Eyiáli

Iráklia   Hóra   Katápola

Amorgós

Íos

Síkinos   Yialós   Hóra

Hóra   Aloprónia

Astypálea

Ía   Thíra (Santoríni)

Thirassía   Firá

Órmos Athiniós   Anáfi

Kamári   Hóra

Áyios Nikólaos

115

(Crete)

When it comes to **moving on**, many of the islands – in particular Mílos, Páros, Náxos and Thíra – are handily connected with Crete (easier in late July and August), while from Tínos, Mýkonos, Sýros, Páros, Náxos, Thíra or Amorgós, you can reach many of the Dodecanese by direct boat. Similarly, you can regularly get from Mýkonos, Náxos, Sýros and Páros to Ikaría and Sámos (in the eastern Aegean).

One consideration for the timing of your visit is that the Cyclades often get frustratingly **stormy**, particularly in early spring or late autumn, and it's also the group worst affected by the *meltémi*, which blows sand and tables about with ease throughout much of July and August. Delayed or cancelled ferries (even in the height of tourist season) are not uncommon, so if you're heading back to Athens to catch a flight, leave yourself a day or two's leeway.

Kéa (Tziá)

Kéa, the closest of the Cyclades to the mainland, is extremely popular in August and on weekends year-round with Athenian families. Their impact is mostly confined to certain small coastal resorts, leaving most of the interior quiet, although there is a preponderance of expensive apartments and villas and not as many good tavernas as you might expect (and virtually no nightlife) because so many visitors self-cater. Midweek or outside August, Kéa is a more enticing destination for those who enjoy a rural ramble, with its rocky, forbidding perimeter and inland oak and almond groves.

As ancient Keos, the island and its strategic, well-placed harbour supported four cities – a pre-eminence that continued until the nineteenth century when Sýros became the main Greek port. Tourists account for the bulk of the sea traffic with regular (in season) **ferry/speed boat connections** to and from Lávrio on the mainland (only a ninety-minute bus ride from Athens), plus sporadic catamarans and ferries to and from Sýros and Kýthnos. Frequency of these services should improve as Lávrio port capacity is expanded, but for details you'll have to check directly with its port police as agents in Athens usually won't sell tickets to Kéa.

The northwest coast: Korissía to Otziás

The small northern ferry and hydrofoil port of **KORISSÍA** has fallen victim to uneven expansion; if you don't like its looks upon disembarking, try to get a bus to Písses (16km), Otziás (6km) or Ioulídha (6km). Buses usually meet the boats; during July and August there's a regular fixed schedule around the island, but at other times public transport can be very elusive. There are a few **taxis** on Kéa and several **motorbike-rental** outfits at the port, all more expensive than on neighbouring islands.

The ill-equipped seafront **tourist information** office is only sporadically open, but the kindly agents for any hydrofoils or catamarans operating (To Stegadhi bookshop), sell maps and guides, and can phone around in search of **accommodation**. The best choices at the port are the *Nikitas* pension (T22880 21193; ❸), open all year and very friendly; *Hotel Korissia* (T22880 21484; ❹), well inland along the stream bed; *Hotel Tzia Mas* (T22880 21305; ❹), right behind the east end of the otherwise uninspiring port beach; and the somewhat noisy *Karthea* (T22880 21222; ❹), which does, however, boast single rooms and year-round operation. For **eating**, a series of nondescript tavernas along the waterfront serve standard Greek fare, though the only

Lávrio

Piréas

Kýthnos

KÉA

Otziás

Ayía Iríni

Vourkári

Korissía

IOULÍDHA
(HÓRA)

Panayía Kastrianí

Ayía Marína

Elliniká

Písses

Káto Meriá

Koúndouros

Stavroudháki

Kambí

Hávouna

Karthaía

N

0   2 km

THE CYCLADES | Kéa

2

standout is *Apothiki*, a great place to splurge on hearty dishes like chicken
souvláki wrapped in bacon. There's good swimming at **Yialiskári**, a small,
eucalyptus-fringed beach between Korissía and Vourkári; along the way, at
the northern edge of Korissía, *Keos Katoikies* (☎22880 84002,
🅦www.keos.gr; ❼), and the swanky *Hotel Brillante Zoi* (☎22880 22685; ❻),
offer plush amenities and a peaceful setting. The *Yialiskari* rooms (☎22880
21197; ❸), not far from the beach, are basic, but far better value. The nearby
Tastra beach bar-café is currently something of the hub of nightlife on the
island, having lured revellers from now more residential Korissía and Ioulídha
in recent years.

VOURKÁRI, a couple of kilometres to the north, is more compact and
arguably more attractive than Korissía, serving as the favourite hangout of the
yachting set. A few expensive **tavernas**, including the nationally renowned
Giannis Maroulis and *Konstantina Marouli*, serve up fresh seafood, and there's a very
good *ouzerí* – *Strofi tou Mimi* – located where the road cuts inland towards Otziás.
Despite a few nondescript bars, the nightlife here, as on the rest of the island,
consists primarily of hanging out in tavernas long after plates have been cleared.

Another 4km to the east, past the picked-over ruins of the Minoan palace
Ayía Iríni that lie virtually unnoticed on the peninsula north of the island's

117

main harbour, **OTZIÁS** has a small beach that's a bit better than the one at Korissía, though more exposed to prevailing winds; facilities are limited to a couple of tavernas and a fair number of apartments for rent. Kéa's only functioning monastery, the eighteenth-century **Panayía Kastrianí**, is an hour's walk along a dirt road from Otziás. Although more remarkable for its fine setting on a high bluff than for any intrinsic interest, the hostel at the monastery (T 22880 24348) is the cheapest accommodation deal on the island, albeit rather basic, isolated and not dependably open. From here you can take the pleasant walk on to the island capital, Ioulídha, in another two hours.

Ioulídha

IOULÍDHA (ancient Ioulis), aka Hóra, was the birthplace of the renowned early-fifth-century-BC poets Simonides and Bacchylides. With its numerous red-tiled roofs, Neoclassical buildings and winding flagstoned paths, it is by no means a typical Cycladic village, but, beautifully situated in an amphitheatric fold in the hills – accessible from Korissía by paved road or on foot over the ancient stone paths that connected the towns during the island's heyday – it is architecturally the most interesting settlement on the island, and the best base for exploring it. Accordingly Ioulídha has "arrived" in recent years, with numerous bars and bistros, much patronized in August and on weekends, but during other times it's quiet, its narrow lanes excluding vehicles. The **archeological museum** (Tues–Sun 8.30am–3pm; free) displays surprisingly extensive finds from the four ancient city-states of Kéa, although the best items were long ago spirited away to Athens. The lower reaches of the town stretch across a spur to the **kástro**, a tumbledown Venetian fortress incorporating stones from an ancient temple of Apollo. Fifteen minutes' walk northeast, on the path toward Panayía Kastrianí, you pass the **Lion of Kea**, a sixth-century-BC sculpture carved out of an outcrop of rock, six metres long and three metres high. There are steps right down to the lion, but the effect is most striking from a distance.

Along with a **post office** and **bank agent**, there are a couple of **pensions** in Ioulídha, the best of which is the comfortable *Ioulis* (T 22880 22177; ❺), with its own terrace restaurant, up in the *kástro*. Choices for **eating** and **drinking** tend to be of a generally higher quality than in Korissía; however, unless you arrive during a busy period, you may find many places closed for the season. *Iy Piatsa*, just as you enter the lower town from the car park, has a variety of tasty dishes, while up on the *platía*, *Rolando's* serves a full range of fish plates best enjoyed with the ubiquitous ouzo; neighbouring *To Kalofagadhon* is the best place for a full-blown meat feast. The aptly named *Panorama* serves up pastries and coffee and is a good place to watch the sun set. Once a hub of nightlife, the central town shuts down early these days, though the vice-mayor, Antonakis Zoulos, happens to be one of the most accomplished traditional musicians in Greece, so you could stop at the town hall to ask where he'll be performing next. Full-on *bouzoúki* nights occur regularly at bars, cafés and tavernas in town or back at the port.

The south

About 8km southwest of Ioulídha, reached via a mix of tracks and paths, or by mostly paved road, the crumbling Hellenistic watchtower of **Ayía Marína** sprouts dramatically from the grounds of a small nineteenth-century monastery. Beyond, the paved main road twists around the startling scenic head of the lovely agricultural valley at **PÍSSES**, emerging at a large and little-developed beach. There are two tavernas, plus a pleasant **campsite**, *Camping Kea*, which has good turfy ground and also runs the studios (☎22880 31302) further inland. Of the tavernas, the best is *To Akroyiali*, with a good range of dishes and some decent house wine, as well as rooms to rent upstairs (☎22880 31301 or 22880 31327; ❸).

Beyond Písses, the asphalt – and the bus service – peter out along the 5km road south to **KOÚNDOUROS**, a sheltered, convoluted bay popular with yachters; there's a taverna behind the largest of several sandy coves, none cleaner or bigger than the beach at Písses. The luxury *Kea Beach* hotel (☎22880 31230; ❻) sits out on its own promontory with tennis courts, pool, and a hamlet of dummy windmills built as holiday homes. At the south end of the bay, *St George Bungalows* (☎22880 31277; ❸) has smart rooms at very reasonable prices, as well as its own taverna which is recommended. A further 2km south at Kambí, there's a nice little beach and a good taverna, *To Kambí*.

Besides the very scant ruins of ancient Poiessa near Písses, the only remains of any real significance from Kéa's past are fragments of a temple of Apollo at **ancient Karthaia**, tucked away on the southeastern edge of the island above Póles Bay, with an excellent deserted twin beach that's easiest reached by boat. Otherwise, it's a good three-hour round-trip walk from the hamlet of Stavroudháki, some way off the lower road linking Koúndouros, Hávouna and Káto Meriá. Travelling by motorbike, the upper road, which plies more directly between Písses and Káto Meriá, is worth following as an alternative return along the island's summit to Ioulídha; it's paved between Ioulídha and Káto Meriá, and the entire way affords fine views over the thousands of magnificent oaks which are Kéa's most distinctive feature.

Kýthnos (Thermiá)

Though one of the duller and most barren of the Cyclades, a short stay on **Kýthnos**, which owes its alternative name, Thermiá, to its renowned hotsprings, is a good antidote to the exploitation likely to be encountered elsewhere. Few foreigners bother to visit, and the island is even quieter than Kéa, particularly to the south where hikes from Dhryopídha, with its colourfully tiled roofs, to coastal coves are the primary diversion. It's a place where Athenians come to buy land for villas, go spear-fishing and sprawl on generally mediocre beaches without having to jostle for space. You could use it as a first or last island stop; in August there are several **ferry connections** a week with Kéa and Lávrio, a frequent ferry and catamaran service to and from Sérifos, Sífnos and Pireás, plus further direct ferry and catamaran connections with Mílos and Kímolos.

Mérihas and around

In good weather, boats dock on the west coast at **MÉRIHAS**, a rather functional ferry and fishing port with most of the island's facilities. This fact almost obliges you to stay here, and makes Mérihas something of a tourist ghetto, but it's redeemed by proximity to the island's best beaches. The closest beach of any repute is **Episkopí**, a 500-metre stretch of averagely clean grey sand with a single taverna, thirty minutes' walk north of the town; you can shorten this considerably by sticking to coast-hugging trails and tracks below the road. Far better are the adjacent beaches of **Apókroussi**, which has a

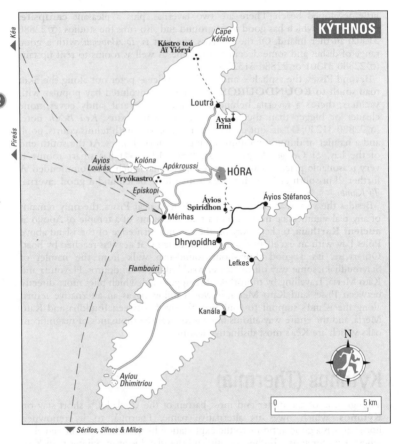

◄ Kéa

◄ Pireás

KÝTHNOS

Cape
Kéfalos

Kástro toú
Aï Yióryi

Loutrá

Ayía
Irini

Áyios
Loukás   Kolóna   Apókroussi

Vryókastro

Episkopí

Mérihas

HÓRA

Áyios
Spirídhon

Áyios Stéfanos

Dhryopídha

Lefkes

Flamboúri

Kanála

Áyiou
Dhimitríou

N

0   5 km

▼ Sérifos, Sífnos & Milos

canteen, and **Kolóna**, the latter essentially a sandspit joining the islet of Áyios Loukás to Kýthnos. These lie about an hour's walk northwest of Episkopí, and are easiest reached by boat trip from the harbour. Between the two beaches lie the sparse ruins of the tenth-century fortified town of **Vryókastro**. Camping is generally tolerated, even on Martinákia beach, the nearest to Mérihas, which has a taverna of the same name.

Owners of **accommodation** often meet the ferries in high season. There are numerous rooms to let, but they tend to be large and equipped for visiting families, so they can be on the expensive side – although with some opportunity for bargaining during the week. Out of season, owners are often not on the premises, but a contact phone number is usually posted. Few places have sea views, one exception being the rooms maintained by Yannoulis Larentzakis (☎22810 32247; ❸), near the ferry dock, which has the added bonus of being open all year round. A little inland, behind the small bridge on the seafront, *Panayiota* (☎22810 32268; ❹) and *Studios Panorama* (☎22810 32184; ❹) are decent choices; and there are plenty of other rooms and studios of similar price and quality along the same road. The Milos Express agency may be able to help you find a room (☎22810 32104, ℻22810 32291).

The best **restaurants** are *Ostria*, a classic fish taverna on the waterfront, *Gialos*, specializing in lamb dishes, and *To Kandouni*, furthest from the ferry, a tasty grill with specialities such as *sfougáto* ("Cretan omelette"). There's also a bakery on the road to Dhryopídha.

The **bus service**, principally to Loutrá, Hóra, Dhryopídha and Kanála, is reasonably reliable, in season at least; the only motorbike rental is through the main Milos Express agency and is noticeably more expensive than on many islands. The Cava Kythnos shop doubles as the official **National Bank** outlet (exchange all day, credit cards accepted for a three-percent fee), and is the agent for catamaran tickets and the boat to Kéa.

Hóra and Loutrá

HÓRA lies 6km northeast of Mérihas, set in the middle of the island. Tilting south off an east–west ridge, and laid out to an approximate grid plan, it's an awkward blend of Kéa-style gabled roofs, Cycladic churches with dunce-cap cupolas, and concrete monsters. Hóra supports a **post office** (open only until noon); the closest accommodation at present is at Loutrá. You can **eat** at the friendly *To Kentro* taverna near the small, central square, at the folksy *To Steki tou Detzi* grill, or at *Messaria*, whose specialities include rabbit in wine sauce.

The much-vaunted resort of **LOUTRÁ** (3km north of Hóra and named after its thermal baths) is scruffy, its nineteenth-century spa long since replaced by a sterile modern construction. The best **taverna**, *Katerini*, is a little out on a limb in the neighbouring bay to the west. Otherwise there are a few seafront bars and tavernas offering basic services, such as showers, to yachting crews. There is no shortage of places to sleep: **pensions** such as *Delfini* (☎22810 31430; ❹), *Meltemi* (☎22810 31271; ❺) and *Porto Klaras* (☎22810 31276, ⓦwww.porto-klaras.gr; ❹) are acceptable choices. The new *Kythnos Bay* (☎22810 31218; ❻), meanwhile, is probably the most comfortable option. You can also stay in the state-run *Xenia* baths complex (☎22810 31217; ❹), where a twenty-minute bath plus basic check-up – blood pressure, heart rate and weight – costs about €5. The small bay of Ayía Iríni, just a kilometre east of Loutrá, and north of the church from which it takes its name, is a more pleasant place to swim and boasts the decent *Trehandiri* taverna on the hill above the bay. About a ninety-minute walk from Loutrá, on Cape Képhalos, lie the picturesque ruins of the medieval **Kástro toú Áï Yióryi**, abandoned in the mid-seventeenth century.

Dhryopídha and the south

You're handily placed in Hóra to tackle the most interesting thing to do on Kýthnos: the beautiful **walk** south to Dhryopídha. It takes about ninety minutes, initially following the old cobbled way that leaves Hóra heading due south; critical junctions in the first few minutes are marked by red paint dots. The only reliable water source is a well in the valley bottom, reached after thirty minutes, just before a side trail to the triple-naved **chapel of Áyios Spyrídhon** which has recycled Byzantine columns. Just beyond this, you collide with a bulldozed track between Dhryopídha and Áyios Stéfanos, but purists can avoid it by bearing west towards some ruined ridgetop windmills and picking up secondary paths for the final forty minutes of the hike.

More appealing than Hóra by virtue of spanning a ravine, **DHRYOPÍDHA**, with its pleasing tiled roofs, is reminiscent of Spain or Tuscany. A surprisingly large place, it was once the island's capital, built around a famous cave, the Katafiki, at the head of a well-watered valley. Tucked away behind the cathedral is a tiny **folklore museum** that opens erratically in high season. Beside the cathedral is a cheap *psistariá*, *To Steki*. Some people let rooms in their houses, but the nearest official accommodation is 6km south at Kanála.

KANÁLA is a good alternative to Loutrá. There are some rooms in the older settlement up on the promontory and a good taverna, *Louloudhas*, with a huge terrace overlooking the larger western beach, **Megáli Ámmos**, which also has rooms and a combination snack-bar and taverna. Three of the nicer **pensions** in the area are *Nikos Bouritis* (☏22810 32195; ❹), *Nikos Filippaios* (☏22810 32653; ❹) and the B&B *Margarita* (☏22810 32265; ❹), with the latter warmly recommended for its home-like atmosphere.

From Kanála, a succession of small coves extends up the east coast as far as **ÁYIOS STÉFANOS**, a small coastal hamlet. Southwest of Dhryopídha, reached by a turning off the road to Kanála, **Flamboúri** is the most presentable beach on the west coast. The extension of the asphalted road southwards makes the double bay of **Ayíou Dhimitríou** more accessible than before; although not too exciting, there are a couple of tavernas and rooms to rent in high season.

Sérifos

Sérifos has long languished outside the mainstream of history and modern tourism. Little has happened here since the legendary Perseus returned with Medusa's head, in time to save his mother, Danaë, from being ravished by the local king Polydectes – turning him, his court and the green island into stone. Many would-be visitors are deterred by the apparently barren, hilly interior, which, with the stark, rocky coastline, makes Sérifos appear uninhabited until the ferry turns into Livádhi bay. Though newly paved roads have made the interior more accessible in recent years, the island is best recommended for serious **walkers**, who can head for several small villages in the under-explored interior, plus some isolated coves. Modern Serifots love seclusion, and here, more than anywhere else in the Cyclades, you will find farmsteads miles from anywhere, with only a donkey path to their door. Many people still keep livestock and produce their own wines, and many also cultivate the wild narcissus for export.

Few islanders speak much English; even a few select words of amateur Greek will come in handy and will be warmly received. American yachties drop anchor here in some numbers, to take on fresh water which, despite appearances, Sérifos has in abundance.

Livádhi and the main beaches

Most visitors stay in the port, **LIVÁDHI**, set in a wide greenery-fringed bay and handy for most of the island's beaches. The usually calm bay here is a magnet for island-hopping yachts, whose crews chug to and fro in dinghies all day and night. It's not the most attractive place on Sérifos and mosquitoes abound, but Livádhi and the neighbouring cove of Livadhákia are certainly the easiest places to find rooms and any amenities you might need, all of which are very scarce elsewhere.

Unfortunately, the long **beach** at Livádhi is nothing to write home about: the sand is hard-packed and muddy, and the water weedy and prone to intermittent jellyfish flotillas – only the far northeastern end is at all usable. Turn left up the main business street, or climb over the southerly headland from the cemetery, to reach the neighbouring, far superior **Livadhákia**. This goldensand beach, shaded by tamarisk trees, offers snorkelling and other watersports, as well as an acceptable taverna. If you prefer more seclusion, five minutes' stroll across the headland to the south brings you to the smaller **Karávi** beach, which is cleaner and almost totally naturist, but has no shade or facilities.

A slightly longer 45-minute walk north of the port along a bumpy track leads to **Psilí Ámmos**, a sheltered, white-sand beach considered the best on the island. Accordingly it's popular, with two rival tavernas that tend to be full in high season. Naturists are pointed – via a ten-minute walk across the headland – towards the larger and often deserted **Áyios Ioánnis** beach, but this is rather exposed with no facilities at all, and only the far south end is inviting. Both beaches are theoretically visited by *kaïkia* from Livádhi, as are two nearby sea caves, but don't count on it. Additionally, and plainly visible from arriving ferries, two more sandy coves hide at the far southeastern flank of the island opposite an islet; they are accessible on foot only, by a variation of the track to Psilí Ámmos. The more northerly of the two, **Áyios Sóstis**, has a well with fresh water and is the most commonly used beach for secluded camping.

Practicalities

The helpful Krinas Travel (☎22810 51448, Ⓔcoralli@mail.otenet.gr), near the jetty, sells **catamaran** and **boat** tickets. The public **bus stop** and posted schedule are at the base of the yacht and fishing-boat jetty. **Buses** connect Livádhi with Hóra, 2km away, some ten times daily, but only manage one or two daily trips to Megálo Livádhi, Galaní and Kállitsos. You can rent a **bike** or **car** from Blue Bird (☎22810 51511), next to the filling station on the main street, or from Krinas Travel.

Accommodation

Accommodation proprietors don't always meet ferries, with the exception of the *Coralli Camping Bungalows* (see p.124), which regularly sends a minibus; in high season you'll have to step lively off the boat to get a decent bed. The most rewarding hunting grounds are on the headland above the ferry dock, or

Livadhákia beach; anything without a sea view will be a notch cheaper. Up on the headland, the *Pension Cristi* (☏22810 51775; ❹) has an excellent, quiet position overlooking the bay as does the *Naias Hotel* (☏22810 51749, ⓦwww.naiasserifos.gr; ❺); the nearby *Areti* (☏22810 51479; ❻) is a little smarter but less friendly. Alternatively, down in the flatlands, the inexpensive seafront rooms of *Anna Kolokytha* (☏22810 51263; ❸) and *Fani* (☏22810 51746; ❸) are friendly and spotlessly clean, though the rooms at the front get some traffic noise. The *Hotel Anna* (☏22810 51666; ❹), above the pizzeria by the yacht harbour, is another fall-back, while slightly cheaper rooms can be found at the far end of the bay at *Margarita Alexopoulou* (☏22810 51321; ❸).

Livadhákia, ten to fifteen minutes' walk south, offers more nocturnal peace, choice and quality, though it has a more touristy feel and the mosquitoes are positively ferocious – make sure your room is furnished with electric vapour pads. One of the oldest and largest complexes of rooms and apartments, close to the beach and with verdant views, is run by Vaso Stamataki (☏22810 51346; ❷). Newer and higher-standard choices include the *Hotel Helios* (☏22810 51066; ❹), just above the road as you arrive at Livadhákia, and, further along, the *Medusa* (☏22810 51127; ❸). Cheaper are the rooms in adjacent buildings just after *Helios*: *Georgia* (☏22810 51336; ❷) and *Roula* (☏22810 51545; ❸) – the latter has sea views. Further along are *Dorkas* (☏22810 51422, Ⓕ22810 52182; ❹) and, right by the beach above a restaurant, *Alexandros* (☏22810 51119; ❸). Near the built-up area, beside one of only two public access tracks to the beach and behind the best patch of sand, *Coralli Camping Bungalows* (☏22810 51500, ⓦwww.coralli.gr; ❹), has a restaurant, bar, shop and landscaped camping area.

Eating and nightlife

As on most islands, **tavernas** near the quay tend to be slightly pricier, but *Mokkas* fish taverna is recommended. Walk up the beach and meals get less expensive; the two best traditional tavernas are the busy *Perseus* and *Cyclades*. Another 500m brings you to *Stamatis*, a favourite with locals for inexpensive home-style food. At the extreme northeast end of the beach, *Sklavenis* (aka *Margarita's*) has a homely feel and courtyard seating, but the food can be overly deep-fried and quite pricey. For crêpes, ice cream, and *loukoumádhes* try *Meli*, in the commercial centre by the port police.

Nightlife is surprisingly lively, and most of it is clustered in or near a mini-mall on the seafront just up from the yacht jetty, so you should be able to quickly find something to suit your taste. *Alter Ego*, at the back, offers more typically Greek music as does nearby *Ayia Menta*; *Vitamin C* and *Karnayio* are two popular café-bars next door, while *Mouses* and *Metalleio* are full-on dance bars.

Hóra

If you don't fancy catching a bus from Livádhi to **HÓRA**, you can always walk, if you're travelling light; it's a pleasant if steep forty minutes up a cobbled way, with the *kalderími* leading off from a bend in the road about 300m out of Livádhi. By late September, you'll have no choice, since the bus – like nearly everything else – ceases operation for the winter.

Quiet and atmospheric, Hóra teeters precariously above the harbour and is one of the least spoiled villages of the Cyclades. The best sights are to be found on the town's borders: tiny churches cling to the cliff-edge, and there are breathtaking views across the valleys below. At odd intervals along its alleyways, you'll find part of the old castle making up the wall of a house, or a marble statue leaning incongruously in one corner. A pleasant diversion is the hour-long **walk** down to **Psilí Ámmos**: start from beside Hóra's cemetery and aim for the lower of two visible pigeon towers, and then keep close to the phone wires, which will guide you towards the continuation of the double-walled path descending to a bend in the road just above the beach.

Among several **tavernas** near the central *platía*, the nicest are *Petros* and *Stavros* (also known as the *Panorama Restaurant* for its view), which can arrange **rooms** too (☎22810 51303; ❷). The island's **post office** is found in the lowest quarter, and a few more expensive rooms for rent lie about 200m north of town, on the street above the track to the cemetery.

The north

North of Hóra, the island's high water-table sometimes breaks the surface to run in delightful rivulets swarming with turtles and frogs, though in recent years many of the open streams seem to have dried up. Reeds, orchards and even the occasional palm tree still take advantage of the unexpected moisture, even if it's no longer visible. This is especially true at **KÁLLITSOS** (Kéndarhos), reached by a ninety-minute path from Hóra, marked by fading red paint splodges along a donkey track above the cemetery. Once at Kállitsos (no facilities), a paved road leads west for 3km to the fifteenth- to seventeenth-century **monastery of Taxiarhón**, designed for sixty monks but presently home only to one of the island's two parish priests – part of a dying breed of farmer-fisherman monks. If he's about, the priest will show you treasures in the monastic church, such as an ivory-inlaid bishop's throne, silver lamps from Egypt (to where many Serifots emigrated during the nineteenth century) and the finely carved *témblon*.

As you loop back towards Hóra from Kállitsos on the asphalt, the fine villages of Galaní and Panayía (named after its tenth-century church) make convenient stops. In **GALANÍ** you can sometimes get simple **meals** at the central store, which also sells excellent, tawny-pink, sherry-like wine; its small-scale production in the west of the island is highly uneconomic, so you'll find it at few other places on Sérifos. Below the village, trails lead to the remote and often windswept beach of **Sykaminiá**, with no facilities and no camping allowed; a better bet for a local swim is the more sheltered cove of **Platýs Yialós** at the extreme northern tip of the island, reached by a partly paved track (negotiable by scooter) that branches off just east of Taxiarhón. The neighbouring beach has a taverna that may have a couple of very basic rooms available in season. The church at **Panayiá** is usually locked, but comes alive on its feast day of Xilopanayía (August 16). Traditionally, the first couple to dance around the adjacent olive tree, would be the first to marry that year, but this led to unseemly brawls so the priest always goes first these days.

The southwest

A little way south of Panayía, you reach a junction in the road. Turn left to return to Hóra, or continue straight towards **Megálo Horió** – the site of ancient Seriphos, but with little else to recommend it. A few kilometres detour off the main road to Megálo Horió, **Avéssalos** is one of the island's least explored beaches, making up for its relatively uninspiring landscape with sheer peace and quiet. **Megálo Livádhi**, further on from Megálo Horió, is a remote and quiet beach resort 8km west of Hóra, with two lovely tavernas whose tables are practically on the beach. *Iy Marditsa* taverna has some simple rooms behind the beach (☎22810 51003; ❷). Iron and copper ore were once exported from here, but cheaper African deposits sent the mines into decline and today most of the idle machinery rusts away, though some gravel–crushing still goes on. At the north end of the beach, there's a monument to four workers killed during a protest against unfair conditions in 1916. An alternate turning just below Megálo Horió leads to the small mining and fishing port of **Koutalás**, a pretty sweep of bay with a church-tipped rock, and a long if narrow beach. It has become rather a ghost settlement and the workers' restaurants have all closed down, but there is one snack-bar/taverna, catering mainly to yachting crews. Above the port are the scant ruins of a medieval **kástro**. The winding track above the village leads to Livádhi, and apart from the pleasant **Gánema** beach, which has a taverna of the same name, there are no places to rest or buy refreshments on the long journey back.

Sífnos

Sífnos is a more immediately appealing island than its northern neighbours since it's prettier, more cultivated and has some fine architecture. This means that it's also much more popular, and extremely crowded in July or August, when rooms are very difficult to find. Take any offered as you land or come armed with a reservation. In keeping with the island's somewhat upmarket clientele, camping rough is forbidden, while nudity is tolerated only in isolated coves.

The island's modest size – no bigger than Kýthnos or Sérifos – makes it eminently explorable. The **bus service** is excellent, most of the roads quite decent, and there's a network of paths that are fairly easy to follow. Sífnos has a strong tradition of pottery (existence of which has been noted as early as the third century BC) and has long been esteemed for its distinctive cuisine (intrinsically linked to the development of pottery, which allowed for the more sophisticated preparation of baked dishes), though its perhaps best appreciated today for its many beautifully situated **churches** and **monasteries**.

Ferry connections are more frequent to Sífnos than to the other more northerly islands. In season, the *Express Milos* and *Express Pegasus* ply a regular shuttle via Kýthnos and Sérifos, then on to Mílos and Kímolos before heading east to Folégandhros, Síkinos, Íos and Thíra, from where the course is reversed back to Pireás. Links with the central Cyclades are far less frequent, with occasional high-season ferries to Páros or Sýros, as well as a high-speed service to Thíra.

Kamáres

KAMÁRES, the island's port, is tucked away at the foot of high, bare cliffs in the west, which enclose a beach. A compact resort with concrete blocks of villas edging up to the base of the cliffs, Kamáres's seafront road is crammed with bars, travel agencies, ice-cream shops and restaurants. You can store luggage at the Aegean Thesaurus **travel agency** while hunting for a room (proprietors tend not to meet boats); they also change money and can book accommodation throughout the island.

Accommodation is relatively expensive, though bargaining can be productive outside peak season. Try the reasonable *Hotel Stavros* (T22840 33383, F22840 31709; ❹) or, further along above the town beach, the friendly *Boulis Hotel* (T22840 32122, F22840 32381; ❹). Above the *Boulis*, the welcoming *Makis* **campsite** (T & F02840 32366) has good facilities and good-value air-conditioned rooms (❸). Continue past the *Makis* and turn right up from the end of the beach to find newer, quieter accommodation in Ayía Marína, including the *Moshka Pension* (T22840 31719; ❸), and the *Delphini Hotel* (T22840 33740, F22840 33741; ❼), which has its own pool.

The best **restaurants** are *Meropi Kambourakis*, ideal for a pre-ferry lunch; the *Boulis* (under the same management as the *Boulis Hotel*) with its collection of huge retsina barrels; *O Argyris* fish taverna; *Apsendi*, on the waterfront, serving a selection of international cheeses; the *Kamares ouzerí* and *Kyra Margena* at the far end of the beach in Ayía Marína. Kamáres also has a little **nightlife**; try *Collage Bar*, good for a sunset cocktail, and *Follie-Follie*. The best place to **hire a scooter or car** is at Dionysos.

Apollonía and Artemónas

A steep twenty-minute bus ride (hourly service until late at night) takes you up to **APOLLONÍA**, the centre of Hóra, an amalgam of three hilltop villages which have merged over the years into one continuous community. With white buildings, flower-draped balconies, belfries and pretty squares, it is eminently scenic, though not self-consciously so. On the central *platía* itself, the **folk museum** (daily 9.30am–2pm & 6–10pm; €1) is worth a visit. As well as an interesting collection of textiles, lace, costumes and weaponry, there are paintings by Nikolaos Tselemendi, a celebrated cookery teacher.

Radiating out from the *platía* is a network of stepped marble footways and the main pedestrian street, flagstoned Odhós Stylianoú Prókou, which leads off to the south, lined with shops, restaurants, bars and churches, including the cakebox cathedral, **Áyios Spyrídhon**, and the eighteenth-century church of **Panayía Ouranoforía** (commonly transliterated as Yeraniofórou and many variations thereof), which stands in the highest quarter of town, incorporating fragments of a seventh-century-BC temple of Apollo and a relief of St George over the door. **Áyios Athanásios**, next to Platía Kleánthi Triandafýlou, has frescoes and a wooden *témblon*. Some 3km southeast, a short distance from the village of Exámbela, you'll find the active monastery of **Vrýssis** which dates from 1612 and is home to a good collection of religious artefacts and manuscripts.

ARTEMÓNAS, fifteen minutes north of Apollonía on foot, is worth a morning's exploration for its churches and elegant Venetian and Neoclassical houses. **Panayía Gourniá** (the key is kept next door) has vivid frescoes; the clustered-dome church of **Kohí** was built over an ancient temple of Artemis (also the basis of the village's name); and seventeenth-century **Áyios Yeóryios** contains fine icons. Artemónas is also the point of departure for **Herónissos**, an isolated hamlet with a few tavernas and potteries behind a deeply indented, rather bleak bay at the northwestern tip of the island. The road there is paved now, and you may find occasional boat trips from Kamáres, though these are only worth the effort on calm days.

Practicalities

The **post office** and **bus stop** edge onto Apollonía's central *platía*. The **bank** and **police station** are located on the main road leading north out of town. There are **rooms** scattered all over the village, making them hard to find; however, there are some obvious choices along the road towards Fáros (thus a bit noisy), *Margarita Giamaki* (☎22840 31032; ❸) being fairly representative. The *Hotel Sifnos* (☎22840 31624, ⓕ22840 33068; ❹), on the main pedestrian street, is the most traditional in its architecture and furnishing, and is operated by the friendly Diaremes family. All the central hotels are sure to be noisy when the nearby clubs are open during the summer, and if you want quieter premises with a better view, be prepared to pay more: *Margarita Kouki* (☎22840 31894; ❸), above the luxurious *Hotel Petali* (☎22840 33024, ⓔpetali @vernicos.gr; ❼), north of the square on the pedestrian lane, is a welcome exception. Probably your best bet is to look on the square for the main branch of the excellent travel agency, Aegean Thesaurus (☎22840 31151, ⓔaegean@thesaurus.gr), which can book you into rooms of all categories and even handles reservations for other islands and Athens. They sell a worthwhile package consisting of an accurate topographical map, bus/boat schedules and a short text on Sífnos for about €2; they can also book you on hiking tours or Greek folk-dancing lessons. Next door is a rarity on the Greek islands, a **motorbike-rental** company that also rents push-bikes, Moto Giannis (☎22840 31151).

There are a number of **restaurants** in Apollonía, including *Iy Orea Sifnos*, with good food despite its kitsch decor, on the central square. On the main pedestrian street, the charmingly decorated *Odos Oneiron* offers eclectic upscale dishes, while the more reasonably priced *Adiexodos* serves great *mezédhes* on its terrace with a view; *Cafe Sifnos* does something for nearly every taste and is open all day. There are several tavernas up in the backstreets: *To Apostoli to Koutouki* is quite good for standard Greek fare and very reasonable; probably the best and most famous place to eat on the island, owing to its highly rated chef, is *Liotrivi* (*Manganas*) on the square up in Artemónas, where there's also an excellent bakery.

Most of the **nightlife** can be found on the main pedestrian street south of the square, where you'll find *Sfera* and the long-standing *Argo*. The *Camel Club*, on the road to Fáros, is another popular place for late-night action. For *rebétika* music there's the *Aloni*, just above the crossroad to Kástro.

The east coast

Most of Sífnos's coastal settlements are along the less precipitous eastern shore, within a modest distance of Apollonía and its surrounding cultivated plateau. These all have good bus services, and a certain amount of food and accommodation, **Kástro** being far more appealing than the resorts of **Platýs Yialós** and **Fáros** which can get very overcrowded in July and August.

Kástro

An alternative east-coast base that seems the last place on Sífnos to fill up in season, **KÁSTRO** can be reached on foot from Apollonía in 35 minutes, all but the last ten on a clear path threading its way east via the hamlet of Káto Petáli. Built on a rocky outcrop with an almost sheer drop to the sea on three sides, the ancient capital of the island retains much of its medieval character. Parts of its boundary walls survive, along with a full complement of sinuous, narrow streets graced by balconied, two-storey houses and some fine sixteenth- and seventeenth-century churches with ornamental floors. Venetian coats of arms and ancient wall-fragments can still be seen on some of the older dwellings; there are the remains of the ancient acropolis (including a ram's head sarcophagus by one of the medieval gates), as well as a small **archeological museum** (Tues–Sun 8am–2.30pm; free), which does not always stick closely to the official opening hours, installed in a former Catholic church in the higher part of the village.

Among the several **rooms**, the modernized *Aris Rafeletos* apartments (T & F 22840 31161; ❹) are open all year. More basic, but boasting gorgeous views, the friendly *Maximos* (T 22840 33692; ❸) is another good option. Nationally renowned *To Astro* and *Leonidas* are the obvious **tavernas** to try out, while the *Kavos Sunrise* café-bar is laid-back and has a fantastic view. On the edge of town, the *Castello* disco-bar is a livelier hangout.

There's nothing approximating a beach in Kástro; for a swim you have to walk to the nearby rocky coves of **Serália** (to the southeast, and with more rooms) and **Paláti**. You can also hike – from the windmills on the approach road near Káto Petáli – to either the sixteenth-century monastery of **Khryssostómou** or along a track opposite the cliff face that overlooks the church of the **Eptá Martýres** (Seven Martyrs); nudists sun themselves and snorkel on and around the flat rocks below.

Platýs Yialós

From Apollonía, there are almost hourly buses to the resort of **PLATÝS YIALÓS**, some 12km distant, near the southern tip of the island. Despite claims to be the longest beach in the Cyclades, the sand can get very crowded. Diversions include a pottery workshop, but many are put off by the continuous row of snack-bars and rooms to rent, which line the entire stretch of beach, and also the strong winds which plague it. **Rooms** are expensive, although the comfortable *Pension Aggeliki* (T 22840 71288, F 22840 31931; ❸), near the bus stop, is more reasonably priced, while the *Hotel Efrossyni* (T 22840 71353, F 22840 71235; ❺), next door, is comfortable, and breakfast is included in the price. The local **campsite** (T 22840 71286) is rather uninspiring – a stiff hike inland, shadeless and on sloping, stony ground. Among several fairly pricey **tavernas** are *Ariadne*, with a nicely shaded verandah, *Foni*, a friendly fish taverna that hosts live music acts some evenings, and *Kalimera*, with French-influenced Greek cuisine.

A more rewarding walk uphill from Platýs Yialós brings you to the convent of **Panayía toú Vounoú** (though it's easy to get lost on the way without the locally sold map); the caretaker should let you in if she's about.

Fáros and around

Less crowded beaches are to be found just to the northeast of Platýs Yialós (though unfortunately not directly accessible along the coast). **FÁROS**, again with regular bus links to Apollonía, makes an excellent fall-back base if you don't strike it lucky elsewhere. A small and friendly resort, it has some of the cheapest **accommodation** on the island, as well as a couple of smarter places, including *Fabrica* (T 22840 71427, W www.fabrica-sifnos.com; ❻), which maintains two charming properties, one housed in a historic eighteenth-century stone structure. *To Kyma* is a pleasant seafront **taverna**, and the smart *On the Rocks*, perched on the headland at the far end of **Fasoloú beach**, serves a tasty selection of snacks as well as full meals. The chef at *Zambelis*, meanwhile, claims to have served as personal chef to Christina Onassis. The closest beaches are not up to much: the town strand itself is muddy, shadeless and crowded, and the one to the northeast past the headland is not much better. Head off in the opposite direction, however, through the older part of the village, and things improve at **Glyfó**, a longer, wider family beach about twenty minutes away.

Continuing from Glyfó, a fifteen-minute cliffside path leads to the beach of **Apokoftó**, with a couple of good tavernas, and, up an access road, to the *Hotel Flora* (T 22840 71278; ❾), which has superb views. The shore itself tends to collect seaweed, however, and a rock reef must be negotiated to get into the water. Flanking Apokoftó to the south, marooned on a sea-washed spit and featuring on every EOT poster of the island, is the disestablished, seventeenth-century **Khryssopiyís monastery**. According to legend, the cleft in the rock appeared when two village girls, fleeing to the spit to escape the attentions of menacing pirates, prayed to the Virgin to defend their virtue. The friendly nearby **taverna** bearing the name of the monastery and known locally as *Lebesis* specializes in reasonably priced lamb dishes and has a lovely, shaded terrace.

The interior and Vathý

Apollonía is a good base from which to start your explorations of more remote Sífnos. You can rent **bikes** at Moto Apollo, beside the petrol station on the road to Fáros, but the island is best explored on foot.

Taking the path out from Katavatí (the district south of Apollonía) you'll pass, after a few minutes, the beautiful empty **monastery of Firáyia** and – fifteen minutes along the ugly modern road – the path climbing up to **Áyios Andhréas**, where you'll be rewarded with tremendous views over the islands of Sýros, Páros, Íos, Folégandhros and Síkinos. Just below the church is an enormous Bronze Age archeological site.

Even better is the all-trail walk to Vathý, around three hours from Katavatí and reached by bearing right at a signed junction in Katavatí. Part way along, you can detour on a conspicuous side-trail to the **monastery of Profítis Ilías**, on the very summit of the island, with a vaulted refectory and extensive views.

Vathý

A fishing village on the shore of a stunning funnel-shaped bay, **VATHÝ** is the most attractive and remote base on the island. However, the highway there has been recently improved, so it's poised for development, with a new luxury hotel with a huge pool. There are an increasing number of **rooms**, the best deals probably being at *Manolis* taverna (☏22840 71111; ❷), or those attached to the tiny **monastery of the Archangel Gabriel**. Unusually, camping rough meets with little objection from the locals, a reflection of their friendly attitude towards outsiders. For **food**, *Manolis* does excellent grills and has a fascinating gyrating clay oven in the courtyard; *Okeanida* has good *mezédhes* such as chickpea balls and cheesy aubergine patties; while *Tò Tsikali* behind the monastery has farm-fresh cheese and rabbit dishes.

Now that there are regular **buses** (8 daily in high season, 2 daily at other times), *kaïkia* run less frequently than they once did from Kamáres. It is possible to walk to Platýs Yiálos in ninety minutes, but the path is not well marked. At the far end of the bay, a traditional pottery still functions.

Mílos

Volcanic **Mílos** is geologically diverse with weird rock formations, hot springs, good beaches and sensational views. Minoan settlers were attracted by obsidian, and other products of its volcanic soil made the island one of the most important of the Cyclades in the ancient world. Today, the quarrying of barite, perlite and porcelain has left deep scars on the landscape but given the island a relative prosperity and independence. With more **beaches** than any other island in the Cyclades, Mílos hasn't had to tart itself up to court tourism – in itself a good reason to stay several days.

You get a good preview of the island's **geological wonders** as your ferry enters Mílos Bay, one of the world's most striking natural harbours, shaped by a series of ancient explosions. Off the north coast, accessible only by excursion boat, the Glaroníssia (Seagull Isles) are shaped like massed organ pipes, and there are more strange formations on the southwest coast at Kléftiko. Inland, too, you frequently come across odd, volcanic outcrops, and thermal springs burst forth.

Like most volcanic islands, Mílos is quite fertile: away from the summits of **Profítis Ilías** in the southwest and lower hills in the east, a gently undulating countryside is intensively cultivated to produce grain, hay and orchard fruits. The island's domestic architecture, with its lava-built, two-up-two-down houses, isn't as immediately impressive as its more pristine neighbours, but is charming nonetheless.

Adhámas

The main, lively port of **ADHÁMAS**, known as Adhámandas to locals, was founded by Cretan refugees fleeing a failed rebellion in 1841. With a handsome marble-paved esplanade around its natural headland, it's now among the most attractive ports in the Cyclades with all the requisite facilities.

Towards the south beach, the **Mining Museum of Mílos** (summer daily 9am–2pm & 6–9pm; free) houses an extensive collection of mining tools, minerals, and geological maps of Mílos. Near the quayside, the small but interesting **Ecclesiastical Museum** (sporadically open in summer; free) is housed in the century-old Áyia Triádha church. You can take a **boat tour** around the

MÍLOS & KÍMOLOS

island on one of three boats; weather permitting, these normally leave at 9am and make several stops at otherwise inaccessible swimming spots like the magnificent Kléftiko, with a late lunch on Kímolos (see p.134 and p.136).

There are several **banks** and a **post office** near the Ecclesiastical Museum, as well as the hub of the island's **bus services**, which run hourly to Pláka, nine times daily in high season to Pollónia, seven times daily to Paleohóri via Zefyría and to Provatás. The taxi rank is nearby – call ☎22870 22219 to book. Some visitors arrive by plane from Athens; most seats, however, are reserved by the local mining industry. Olympic Airways is located near the National Bank, near Adhámas port; the **airport** is 5km southeast of the port, close to Zefyría.

During high season, the highly organized **tourist office** opposite the ferry dock (☎22870 22445) has a daily updated list of available rooms around the island and a handy brochure, while Milos Travel (☎22870 22000, Ⓦwww.milostravel.gr) is another good resource for finding somewhere to stay, and also offers coastal boat trips, car rental, maps and ferry tickets. Most **accommodation** is concentrated on the hill above the harbour and on or just off the main road to Pláka, and ranges from moderately priced addresses with shared facilities, such as the rooms of Anna Gozadinou (☎22870 22364; ❸), to smart rooms with TV and all mod cons, such as *Thalassitra* (☎22870 23422, Ⓦwww.sunnymilos.com; ❺). Some of the best hotels include the *Delfini* (☎22870 22001; ❸), one block behind the town beach to the left from the ferry landing; the smart, central, double-glazed *Portiani Hotel* (☎22870 22940,

ⓕ22870 22766; ❻) and the luxury *Santa Maria Village* (☎22870 21949, ⓕ22870 22880; ❼), 300m behind the beach. The **campsite** (☎22870 31410, ⓕ22870 31412) at Hivadholímni beach (see p.135) on the south shore of the bay also has bungalows (❹); its minibus meets ferries. Closer to town, **Frangomnímata beach** (near the memorial to French sailors and soliders who died here in 1897) is just a ten-minute walk northwest, though camping here is discouraged.

Flisvos, near the jetty, is a good place to **eat**. Of the three adjacent tavernas along the seafront towards the long tamarisk-lined beach south of town, *Navagio*, specializing in fish, is the best value. Just off the main street inland, *Pitsounakia* is a good cheap *psistariá* with a pleasant courtyard. Apart from the obvious string of cafés along the main seafront drag, *Akri*, above the jetty, is a trendier **bar**, with a pleasant verandah. *Vibera La Betina* and *Malion* are other current hotspots where the music ranges from deafening Western rock or techno (usually at the former) to Greek pop or the odd live *bouzoukí* night (often at the latter).

The northwestern villages and ancient Melos

The main appeal of Mílos is in an area that has been the island's focus of habitation since Classical times, where a cluster of villages huddle in the lee of a crag, 4km northwest of the harbour.

PLÁKA (**MÍLOS**) is the largest of these communities and the official capital of the island. Behind the lower car park, at the top of the approach boulevard through the newer district, the **archeological museum** (Tues–Sun 8.30am–3pm; €3) contains numerous obsidian implements, plus a whole wing of finds from ancient Phylakope (see p.136), whose highlights include a votive lamp in the form of a bull and a rather Minoan-looking terracotta goddess. Labelling is scant, but you'll no doubt recognize the plaster-cast copy of the *Venus de Milo*, the original of which was found on the island in 1820. The statue was promptly delivered to the French consul for "safekeeping" from the Turks; her arms were knocked off in the melée surrounding her abduction. This was the last the Greeks saw of *Venus* until a copy was belatedly forwarded from the Louvre in Paris. Up in a mansion of the old quarter, the **folk museum** was closed for renovations at the time of writing but is scheduled to open in summer 2004 when it will display artefacts related to the history of arts, crafts and daily life on Mílos.

A stairway beginning near the police station leads up to the old Venetian **Kástro**, its slopes clad in stone and cement to channel precious rainwater into cisterns. The enormous chapel of **Panayía Thalassítra** looms near the summit, where the ancient Melians made their last stand against the Athenians before the massacre of 416 BC. Today it offers one of the best views in the Aegean, particularly at sunset in clear conditions.

Pláka has a **post office** and a **motorbike-rental** outfit near the archeological museum. There are **rooms** available scattered around the village, with those on the west side offering spectacular views. Among the nicest of these are the pretty studios of Stratis Vourakis (☎22870 21702; ❹). Dimitri Moraitis (☎22870 41353; ❺) has newly refurbished rooms in the house where the *Venus de Milo* was allegedly hidden following its discovery, and Maria Kentrota (☎22870 21572; ❸) has a couple of charming, if basic, studios close to the archeological museum. There are also three or four blocks of modern accommodation overlooking the busy approach road. A number of *ouzerís* make Pláka a good base for **eating**: highly recommended are *Arhondoula*, serving excellent seafood dishes, and slightly more upscale *Alisachni*, offering classic Greek dishes with a modern flair.

The attractive village of **TRYPITÍ** (meaning "perforated"), that takes its name from the cliffside tombs nearby and covers a long ridge a kilometre south of Pláka, is another good base if you're after a village environment. There are a few modest **rooms**, two of which are just down the steep street from the tiny *platía* below the main church. The best places to **eat** are *Glaronisia* and *Ergina*, which features oven-roasted goat and cuttlefish. From Trypití, it's a pleasant 45-minute walk down to Adhámas via Skinópi on the winding old *kalderími*, which begins on the saddle linking Trypití with the hamlet of Klimatovoúni.

TRIOVÁSSALOS and its twin **PÉRAN TRIOVÁSSALOS** are more workaday and less polished than Pláka or Trypití. There are "rooms to rent" signs out here as well, but the places will inevitably be noisier. Péran also offers a naïve pebble mosaic in the courtyard of **Áyios Yeóryios church** – created in 1880, it features assorted animal and plant motifs.

Local sites and the coast

From Pláka's archeological museum, signs point you towards the **early Christian catacombs** (Tues–Sun 8.30am–3pm; free), 1km south of Pláka and just 400m from Trypití village; steps lead down from the road to the inconspicuous entrance. Some 5000 bodies were buried in tomb-lined corridors stretching some 200m into the soft volcanic rock, making them the largest catacombs in Greece; only the first 50m is illuminated and accessible by boardwalk. Don't miss the adjacent ruins of **ancient Melos**, extending down from Pláka almost to the sea. There are huge Dorian walls, the usual column fragments lying around and, best of all, a well-preserved Roman **amphitheatre** (unrestricted access) some 200m west of the catacombs by track, then trail. Only seven rows of seats remain intact, but these look out evocatively over Klíma to the bay. Between the catacombs and the theatre is the signposted spot where the *Venus de Milo* was found in what may have been the compound's gymnasium.

At the very bottom of the vale, **KLÍMA** is the most photogenic of several fishing hamlets on the island, with its picturesque boathouses tucked underneath the principal living areas. There's no beach to speak of, and only one place to stay – the impeccably sited, if a little basic *Panorama* (T 22870 21623, F 22870 22112; ❹), with an acceptable balcony taverna.

Pláthiena, 45 minutes' walk northwest of Pláka, is the closest proper beach, and thus is extremely popular in summer. There are no facilities, but the beach is fairly well protected and partly shaded by tamarisks. Head initially west from near the police station on the marked footpath towards **ARETÍ** and **FOURKOVOÚNI**, two more cliff-dug, boathouse-hamlets very much in the Klíma mould. Although the direct route to Pláthiena is signposted, it no longer goes via Fourkovoúni; both hamlets are reached by side-turnings off the main route, which becomes a jeep track as you approach Fourkovoúni. By moped, access to Pláthiena is only from Plakés, the northernmost and smallest of the five northwestern villages.

The south

The main road to the south of the island splits at **Kánava junction**, a dreary place at first glance owing to the large power plant here. But opposite this, indicated by a rusty sign pointing seaward, is the first of Mílos's **hot springs**, which bubble up in the shallows and are much enjoyed by the locals.

Taking the left or easterly fork leads to **ZEFYRÍA**, hidden among olive groves below the bare hills; it was briefly the medieval capital until an eighteenth-century epidemic drove out the population. Much of the old town is still deserted, though some life has returned, and there's a magnificent seventeenth-century church.

South of here it's a further 8km down a winding road to the coarse-sand beach of **Paleohóri**. Actually a triple strand totalling 800m in length, it's indisputably the island's best; clothing's optional at the westerly cove, where steam vents heat both the shallow water and the rock overhangs onshore. There are a number of **places to stay**, such as the inland *Broutzos* (☎22870 31267; ●), the purpose-built rooms at the *Vihos Artemis* restaurant (☎22870 31222; ●) nearer the beach, and the rooms of both *Maria Tsirigotaki* (☎22870 31231; ●) and *Panayiota Vikeli* (☎22870 31228; ●) The place to **eat** is *Pelagos*, which has a large raised patio.

The westerly road from Kánava junction leads past the airport gate to **Hivadholímni**, considered to be the best beach on Mílos bay itself. Not that this is saying much: Hivadholímni is north-facing and thus garbage-prone, with shallow sumpy water offshore, although there is a taverna, a disco-bar and a sizeable community of campers during the summer. It's better to veer south to **Provatás**, a short but tidy beach, closed off by colourful cliffs to the east. Being so easy to get to, it hasn't escaped some development: there are two rooms establishments plus, closer to the shore, a newer, luxury complex, *Golden Milos Beach* (☎22870 31307, ☎22870 31309; ●). The best value for food and accommodation is the *Maïstrali* (☎22870 31420, ☎22870 31164; ●).

Several kilometres before Provatás, a road forks east through a dusty white quarry to the trendy and popular beach of **Firipláka**. Further east, **Tsigrádho** beach is accessible by boat, or by the novel means of a rope hanging down a crevice in the cliff face. Two kilometres west of Provatás, you'll see a highway sign for **Kípos**. Below and to the left of the road, a small **medieval chapel** dedicated to the Kímisis (Assumption) sits atop foundations far older – as evidenced by the early Christian reliefs stacked along the west wall and a carved, cruciform baptismal font in the *ierón* behind the altar screen. At one time a spring gushed from the low-tunnel cave beside the font – sufficiently miraculous in itself on arid Mílos. A few minutes to the west, unspoilt **Yérondas** beach is easily accessed, though little visited by tourists.

For the most part **Hálakas**, the southwestern peninsula centred on the wilderness of 748-metre Profitis Ilías, is uninhabited and little built upon, with the exception of the **monastery of Sidherianós**. The roads are memorable, if a little tiring, and several spots are worth making the effort to see. **Emboriós** on the east side of the peninsula has a fine little beach and a great local taverna with a few cheap rooms run by Manoulis Koliarkis (☎22870 21389; ●). On the mostly rugged west coast, **Triádhes** is one of the finest and least spoilt beaches in the Cyclades, but you'll have to bring your own provisions. **Kléftiko** in the southwest corner is only reachable by boat (from Kípos via Yérondas or from Adhámas, see p.131), but repays the effort to get there with its stunning rock formations, semi-submerged rock tunnels and colourful coral.

The north coast

From either Adhámas or the Pláka area, good roads run roughly parallel to the **north coast** which, despite being windswept and largely uninhabited, is not devoid of interest. **Mandhrákia**, reached from Péran Triovássalos, is another boathouse settlement, and **Sarakíniko**, to the east, is a sculpted inlet with a sandy seabed and a summer beach café. Nearby **Mitakás** beach is difficult to find along an unmarked trail from the main road but worth the search for its seclusion. A few kilometres further east, the little hamlet of **Páhena** is not shown on many maps, though it has another lovely beach. For **rooms** in the area try Terry's Travel (☎22870 22640, ⊛terrysmilostravel.com; ❸). Still heading east, the remains of three superimposed Neolithic settlements crown a small knoll at **Fylakopí** (ancient Phylakope); the site was important archeologically, but hasn't been maintained and is difficult to interpret. Just before the site is another of Mílos's coastal wonders: the deep-sea inlet of **Papáfranga**, set in a ravine and accessible through a gap in the cliffs.

Pollónia

POLLÓNIA, 12km northeast of Adhámas, is immensely popular with windsurfers, and a diving centre has further increased its popularity among watersports enthusiasts. Pollónia is essentially a small harbour protected by a storm-lashed spit of land on the northeast, where self-catering units are multiplying rapidly, fringed by a long but narrow, tamarisk-lined beach to the rear, and closed off on the south by a smaller promontory on which the tiny original settlement huddles. Besides the town beach, the only other convenient, half-decent beach is at **Voúdhia**, 3km east, where you will find more of the island's hot springs, although it is effectively spoiled by its proximity to huge mining works, which lend it the desolate air of a *Mad Max* location.

On the quay are several **tavernas** and a couple of very mediocre café/snack-bars. Inland and south of here you'll find a concentration of **accommodation**, more simple rooms and fewer apartments, most with the slight drawback of occasional noise and dust from quarry trucks. Among the highest-quality units here are the *Kapetan Tasos Studios* (☎22870 41287, ⓕ22870 41322; ❹), with good views of the straits between Mílos and Kímolos; *Flora* (☎22870 41249; ❹), on the road towards the spit, is another option, as are *Efi* rooms (☎22870 41396, ⓕ22870 41310; ❹), above the far end of the beach, *Andreas* (☎ & ⓕ22870 41262; ❹) has triple studios with stunning views and easy access to the quiet neighbouring bay. Pollónia has no bank or post office, but the friendly Axios Rent A Car office (☎ & ⓕ22870 41234) can change money and advise you on accommodation matters. A **motorbike rental** place and a well-stocked supermarket complete the list of amenities. There is a huge map fixed on a metal frame near the bus stop, which shows all the facilities and gives telephone numbers.

Getting to Kímolos may be the main reason you're here. The *Tria Adhelfia* makes the trip daily year-round at 6.45am and 2pm, returning from Kímolos an hour later. During high season there is also ferry boat, ensuring at least five crossings a day.

Kímolos

Of the three islets off the coast of Mílos, Andímilos is home to a rare species of chamois, Políegos has more ordinary goats, but only **Kímolos** has any human habitation. Volcanic like Mílos, with the same little lava-built rural cottages, it profits from its geology and used to export chalk (*kimolía* in Greek) until the supply was exhausted. Fuller's earth is still extracted locally, and the fine dust of this clay is a familiar sight on the island, where mining still outstrips fishing and farming as an occupation. Rugged and barren in the interior, it has some fertile land on the southeast coast where wells provide water, and this is where the population of about eight hundred is concentrated.

Kímolos is sleepy indeed from September to June, and even in August sees few visitors. This is probably just as well, since there are fewer than a hundred beds on the whole island, and little in the way of other amenities.

Psathí, Hóra and Goúpa

Whether you arrive by ferry, or by *kaïki* from Pollónia, you'll dock at the hamlet of **PSATHÍ**, which is pretty much a nonevent except for the excellent *Tò Kyma* ("The Wave") **taverna** midway along the beach, specializing in fried octopus. The laissez-faire attitude towards tourism on the island is demonstrated by the fact that **ferry tickets** are only sold outside the expensive café at the end of the jetty, an hour or so before the anticipated arrival of the boat. The *Tria Adhelfia* and another open ferry come and go from Pollónia on Mílos from the base of the jetty five times a day in summer. A minibus runs from the port to the capital, which can also be reached by foot in about fifteen minutes.

Around the bay, there are a few old windmills and dazzlingly white **HÓRA** perched on the ridge above them. The magnificent, two-gated sixteenth-century **kástro** here is one of the best preserved of such fortresses built against marauding pirates in the Cyclades; the perimeter houses are intact and inhabited, though its heart is a jumble of romantic ruins. Just outside the *kástro* to the north stands the conspicuously unwhitewashed, late-sixteenth-century church of **Khryssóstomos**, the oldest and most beautiful on the island. Near the church, the new premises of the **archeological museum**, with pottery from the Geometric to the Roman period, are currently under construction and are due to open in 2004.

There are a few adequate **rooms** near the port, most reserved through the same number (℡22870/51392; **②–④**) at which you can also inquire about other rooms around Kímolos. Better situated **accommodation** options include Margaro Petraki's rooms (℡22870 51314; **②**), tucked away in the rather unglamorous maze of backstreets, or try those of Apostolos Ventouris (℡22870 51329; **②**) above his *kafenío* nearby. Sofia Ventouris (℡22870 51219; **⑤**) has a few new studios with sea views, close to the church. For **meals**, aside from a couple of basic *psistariés* and a café-bar, the aptly named *Panorama*, near the east gate of the *kástro*, is the most elaborate and consistently open taverna. *Meltemi*, to the west of the village, is another good taverna, which also has some rooms (℡22870 51360; **③**). Finally, there are a couple of boat agencies, and a **post office** in the west of the village.

East of Hóra, a ten-minute walk brings you to **GOÚPA**, a traditional fishing village with a few **tavernas**. Just at its base, **Rémma** beach remains unspoilt despite its accessibility, as does **Klíma**, just off the main dirt road to Prássa to the north.

Around the island

During summer at least, the hamlet of **ALYKÍ** on the south coast is a better bet for staying than Psathí and Hóra; it only takes about thirty minutes to walk there on the paved road that forks left from the port. Alykí is named after the saltpan that sprawls between a rather mediocre beach offering no shade or shelter, but where you'll find the **rooms** of *Sardi* (℡22870 51458; **③**) and *Pasamichalis* (℡22870 51340; **③**), as well as a few simple **tavernas**. You can stroll west one cove to **Bonátsa** for better sand and shallow water, though you won't escape the winds. Passing another cove you come to the even more attractive beach of Kalamítsi, with better shade and a decent taverna. To the east, between Alykí and Psathí, the smaller, more secluded beach of **Skála** is better for camping, which is generally tolerated here.

The 700m coarse-sand beach of **Elliniká** is a 45-minute walk west of Alykí: starting on the road, bear left – just before two chapels on a slope – onto a narrower track which runs through the fields at the bottom of the valley. Divided by a low bluff, the beach is bracketed by two capes and looks out over Dhaskalió islet and across to harder-to-reach Kambána beach, home of nesting turtles; Elliniká tends to catch heavy weather in the afternoon, and there are no facilities here.

Another road leads northeast from Hóra to a beach and radioactive springs at **Prássa**, 7km away. The route takes in impressive views across the straits to Políegos, and there are several shady peaceful coves where it's possible to camp out. Innumerable goat tracks invite exploration of the rest of the island; in the far northwest, on Kímolos's summit, are the ruins of an imposing Venetian fortress known as **Paleókastro**.

Ándhros

Ándhros, the second largest and northernmost of the Cyclades, is also one of the most verdant, making it a great place for serious walkers. Thinly populated but prosperous, its fertile, well-watered valleys and gorges have sprouted scores of Athenian holiday villas whose red-tiled roofs and white walls stand out among the greenery. Some of the more recent of these have robbed many of the villages of life and atmosphere, turning them into scattered settlements with no nucleus, and creating a weekender mentality manifest in noisy Friday and Sunday evening traffic jams at the ferry dock. The island doesn't cater to independent travellers, and it can be difficult to find a bed during August, especially at weekends. On the positive side, the permanent population is distinctly hospitable; traditionally working on ships, they are only too happy to try out their English on you. Together with some of the more idiosyncratic reminders of the Venetian period, such as the *peristereónes* (pigeon towers) and the *frákhtes* (dry-stone walls, here raised to the status of an art form), it is this friendliness that lends Ándhros its charm.

Ferries connect the island with Rafína on the mainland, only an hour from Athens or fifteen minutes from the airport by bus and, in season, you can loop back onto the central Cycladic routes via Mýkonos, Tínos or Sýros. A bus usually meets arriving ferries and runs to Batsí and on to Hóra at least six times a day in the high season.

Northern and western Ándhros

All ferries and catamarans arrive at the main port, **GÁVRIO**, a moderately attractive holiday resort. Few venture onto the adjacent windswept beach, although there are plenty more attractive alternatives just to the south, where you'll find some of the area's better accommodation. A converted dovecote houses a sporadically functioning **tourist office**, and there are half a dozen ferry **ticket agents**, a **bank**, and a **post office** on the waterfront.

The cheapest **accommodation** is in the basic *Galaxias* (☎ 22820 71228; ❸), which serves as a late-arrival fall-back. There are more room and

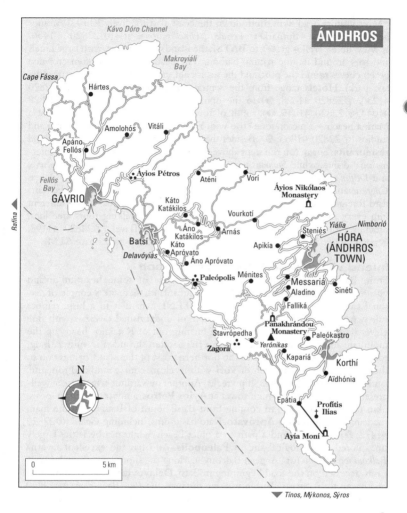

ÁNDHROS

Kávo Dóro Channel

Cape Fássa

Makroyiáli Bay

Hártes

Amolohós • Vitáli

Apáno Fellós

Fellós Bay

GÁVRIO

Rafina

• Áyios Pétros

Aténi • Vorí

Áyios Nikólaos Monastery

Káto Katákilos

Vourkoti

Batsí

Áno Katákilos

Arnás

Steniés

Yiália — Nimborió

HÓRA (ÁNDHROS TOWN)

Delavóyiás

Káto Apróvato

Áno Apróvato

Apikía

Paleópolis

Ménites

Messariá

Aladino

Sinéti

Falliká

Stavrópedha

Panakhrándou Monastery

Yerónikas

Paleókastro

Zagorá

Kapariá

Korthí

Aïdhónia

Epátia

Profitis Ilías †

Ayía Moní

N

0   5 km

▼ Tínos, Mýkonos, Sýros

studio outfits along and above the main coastal road to Batsí: *Aktio* (☎22820 71607, ℻22820 71773; ❹) is fairly representative, while *Andros Holiday Hotel* (☎22820 71384, ℻22820 71097; ⓦwww.androsholiday.com; ❼) is a good upmarket choice. **Restaurants** worth trying include the good if basic *Estiatorio o Valmas*, *Tria Asteria*, and the popular *En Gavrio ouzerí*. **Nightlife** revolves around a string of nondescript cafés and bars along the harbourfront and at Áyios Pétros beach several kilometres south. Along the same stretch the excellent *Yiannouli* taverna is worth checking out for lunch.

Around 3km northwest of the port are two beaches, one with holiday villas and a taverna, the other hidden beyond the headland and popular with rough campers. Beyond Apáno Fellós, the countryside is empty except for a few hamlets inhabited by the descendants of Albanians who settled here and in southern Évvia some six hundred years ago.

Most visitors head 8km south down the coast, past the lively Khryssí Ámmos beach, and the upmarket *Perrakis Hotel* above it (T 22820 71456, W www.hotelperrakis.gr; **7**), to **BATSÍ**, the island's main resort, with large hotels and bars around its fine natural harbour. The beautiful though often crowded beach curves round the port, and the sea is cold, calm and clean (except near the taxi park). **Hotels** range from the central, comfortable *Chryssi Akti* (T 22820 41236, F 22820 41628; **5**) to the upmarket *Aneroussa Beach Hotel* (T 22820 41044, F 22820 41045; **7**), south of town past the Stivári area towards Ayía Marína beach – a picturesque cove with *Yiannoulis Mastrozannes* fish taverna and studios (T 22820 41963; **3**). Besides these there are plenty of other rooms and **restaurants**: *Sirocco* (on the steps above the port) serves a curious range of international dishes, while *Stamatis* is an established taverna with a nice atmosphere, and *Delfinia* has a pleasant, sheltered balcony. There are several café-bars, such as *Capriccio* and *Nameless*, a half a dozen or so loud indoor bars featuring the standard foreign/Greek musical mix, and even an outdoor cinema with a different film every night in the summer. For information on walking tours, free local brochures or other travel needs, go to Greek Sun Travel (T 22820 41198, E greeksun@traveling.gr), upstairs near the taxi park; two banks have ATMs.

Inland villages and Delavóyais beach

From Batsí you're within easy walking distance of some beautiful inland villages. At **KÁTO KATÁKILOS**, one hour inland, there are a couple of seasonal **tavernas**; a rough track leads to **ATÉNI**, a hamlet in a lush, remote valley. **ÁNO KATÁKILOS** has a couple of undervisited tavernas with fine views across the village. A right-hand turning out of Katákilos heads up the mountain to **ARNÁS**, whose lone taverna is often shrouded in mist. A long, rough hike down from Arnás to the northern coast of the island, brings you to the secluded, sheltered beach of **Vorí** with its clean, course sand and romantic landscape featuring several shipwrecks. Another rewarding trip is to a well-preserved, twenty-metre-high tower at **Áyios Pétros**, a mystery even to locals, 5km from Gávrio or 9km coming from Batsí. South of Batsí along the main road are **Káto** and **Áno Apróvato**. Káto has rooms, including *Galini* (T 22820 41472; **2**), a taverna and a path to a quiet beach, while nearby is the largely unexplored archeological site of **Paleópolis**. Áno has the excellent taverna *Balkoni tou Aigaiou* (or "Aegean Balcony"). Along the shore here, though just as easily accessed on the road beginning in Batsí, **Delavóyias** beach is something of a haven for naturists. Within walking distance, the *Blue Bay Village* (T 22820 41150, F 22820 41922; **5**) has simple, comfortable rooms as well as a pool.

Hóra and around

A bus service links the west coast with **HÓRA**, aka **ÁNDHROS TOWN**, 35km from Gávrio. With its setting on a rocky spur cutting across a huge bay, the capital is the most attractive place on the island. Paved in marble and schist from the still-active local quarries, the buildings around the bus station are grand nineteenth-century affairs, and the squares with their ornate wall fountains and gateways are equally elegant. The hill quarters are modern and rather exclusive, while the small port on the west side of the headland has a yacht supply station and ferry landing. There are beaches on both sides of the headland, the better of which is Parapórti, to the east, though it's somewhat exposed to the *meltémi* winds in summer.

The few **hotels** in town are on the expensive side and tend to be busy with holidaying Greeks, although you could try the traditional *Aegli* (T 22820

22303; ❸), opposite the big church on the main walkway. Most rooms are clustered behind the long **Nimborió beach** northwest of town, and range from good clean rooms like those of *Villa Stella* (☎22820 22471; ❸) to modern apartments such as the *Alcioni Inn* (☎22820 23652, ⓕ22820 24522; ❺). The *Paradise Hotel* (☎22820 22187, ⓦwww.paradiseandros.gr; ❼), with its swimming pool and tennis court, is the best upmarket choice, while the hillside *Stagira* (☎22820 23525, ⓕ22820 24502; ❼), just outside of town, is the best spot for a romantic retreat. For **eating**, most cafés are up in Hóra: *Plátanos* has a generous *mezédhes* selection that can be enjoyed with an ouzo under the plane trees, the appropriately named *O Stathmos* right by the bus station is good, and there's a decent *psistariá* on the main drag. The nicest fish taverna is *Nona*, tucked away at the town end of the beach at the old Plakoura harbour, while *Cabo del Mar* is pricey but good, with an unsurpassed view. *Nostaglia Ouzeri* has a pleasant shaded terrace.

Nimborió beach is the epicentre of the island's **nightlife**, such as it is, with a few thumping discos that start with Western music and shift into Greek pop into the wee hours of the morning. There's a **post office** and **bank** around town, a couple of **travel agents** and three **motorbike rentals** behind the beach.

From the square right at the end of town you pass through an archway and down to windswept **Platía Ríva**, with its statue of the unknown sailor scanning the sea. Beyond, lies the thirteenth-century Venetian **kástro**, precariously joined to the mainland by a narrow-arched bridge, which was damaged by German munitions in World War II. Don't be discouraged by the stark modern architecture of the **archeological museum** (Tues–Sun 8.30am–2.30pm; €2), on the main street – it proves to be well laid out and labelled, with instructive models. Its prize item is the fourth-century "Hermes of Andros", reclaimed from a prominent position in the Athens archeological museum. Behind it, the **Modern Art Museum** (Wed–Mon 8am–2.30pm, also 6–8pm in summer; €3) has a sculpture garden and a permanent collection with works by Picasso, Matisse, Kandinsky, Chagall and others, as well as temporary shows.

Hiking is particularly inviting south and west from Ándhros, where there are lush little river valleys. One obvious destination is **MÉNITES**, a hill village just up a green valley choked with trees and straddled by stone walls. The church of the **Panayía** may have been the location of a temple of Dionysos, where water was turned into wine; water still flows continuously from the local rocks. Nearby, is the medieval village of **MESSARIÁ**, with the deserted twelfth-century Byzantine church of **Taxiárhis** below, the picturesque setting for a nine-day festival of the Virgin Mary that begins on August 15. The finest monastery on the island, **Panakhrándou**, is only an hour's (steep) walk away, via the village of Falliká: reputedly tenth-century, it's still defended by massive walls but occupied these days by just three monks. It clings to an iron-stained cliff southwest of Hóra, to which you can return directly with a healthy two-to three-hour walk down the creek valley, guided by red dots.

Hidden by the ridge directly north of Hóra, the prosperous nineteenth-century village of **STENIÉS** was built by the vanguard of today's shipping magnates; just below, at Yialiá, there's a small pebble beach with a taverna. Nearby on the road to Strapouriés is a wonderful taverna, *Bozakis*, which boasts a view all the way down to the coast and excellent food. Beyond Steniés is **APIKÍA**, a tidy little village, which bottles Sariza-brand mineral water for a living; there are a few **tavernas**, including *O Tassos*, which has a lovely garden setting and specialities such as goat and rabbit. There are a very limited number of **rooms** here, including *Paraskeyi Tsoumezi* (☎22820 23130; ❸), near Yialiá beach, as well as the *Pighi Sariza Hotel* (℡22820 23799, ℻22820 22476; ❺). The road is now asphalted up to Vourkotí and even past this point is quite negotiable via Arnás to the west coast. There are some stunning views all along this road but bike-riders need to take care when the *meltémi* is blowing – it can get dangerously windy.

Southern Ándhros

On your way south, you might stop at **Zagorá**, a fortified geometric town – unique in having never been built over – that was excavated in the early 1970s. Located on a desolate, flat-topped promontory with cliffs falling away on three sides, it's worth a visit for the view alone. With your own transport, the sheltered cove of **Sinéti** south of Hóra is also worth a detour.

The village of **KORTHÍ** is a friendly place which is slowly waking up to its tourist potential. Set on a large sandy bay, cut off from the rest of the island by a high ridge and so relatively unspoilt, it is pleasant enough to merit spending the night at the austere-looking *Hotel Korthion* (℡22820 61218; ❸). There are also several good **tavernas**, including *To Vintsi tis Yitsas* at the waterfront. You could also take in the nearby convent of **Zoödhóhou Piyís** (open to visitors before noon), with illuminated manuscripts and a disused weaving factory.

To the north is **PALEÓKASTRO**, a tumbledown village with a ruined Venetian castle and a legend about an old woman who betrayed the stronghold to the Turks, then jumped off the walls in remorse, landing on a rock now known as "Old Lady's Leap". In the opposite direction out of Korthí are **AÏDHÓNIA** and **KAPARIÁ**, dotted with pigeon towers (*peristereónes*) left by the Venetians.

Tínos

Tínos still feels like one of the most Greek of the larger islands in the Cyclades. A few foreigners have discovered its beaches and unspoiled villages, but most visitors are Greek, here to see the church of **Panayía Evangelístria**, a grandiose shrine erected on the spot where a miraculous icon with healing powers was found in 1822. A local nun, now canonized as Ayía Pelayía, was directed in a vision to unearth the relic just as the War of Independence was getting underway, a timely coincidence which served to underscore the links between the Orthodox Church and Greek nationalism. Today, there are two major annual pilgrimages, on March 25 and August 15, when, at 11am, the icon bearing the Virgin's image is carried in state down to the harbour over the heads of the faithful.

The Ottoman tenure here was the most fleeting in the Aegean. **Exóbourgo**, the craggy mount dominating southern Tínos and surrounded by most of the island's sixty-odd villages, is studded with the ruins of a Venetian citadel that defied the Turks until 1715, long after the rest of Greece had fallen. An enduring legacy of the long Venetian rule is a persistent **Catholic minority**, which accounts for almost half the population, and a sectarian rivalry said to be responsible for the numerous graceful belfries scattered throughout the island – Orthodox and Catholic parishes vying to build the tallest. The sky is pierced, too, by distinctive and ornate **dovecotes**, even more in evidence here than on Ándhros. Aside from all this, the inland village architecture is striking and there's a flourishing folk-art tradition that finds expression in the abundant local marble. The islanders have remained open and hospitable to the relatively

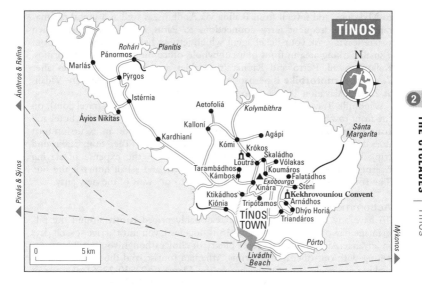

few foreigners and the steady stream of Greek visitors who touch down here, and any mercenary inclinations seem to be satisfied by booming sales in religious paraphernalia to the faithful.

Tínos Town and the southern beaches

At **TÍNOS TOWN**, trafficking in devotional articles certainly dominates the streets leading up from the busy waterfront to the Neoclassical **church** (daily 8am–8pm) that towers above. Evangelistrías in particular overflows with holy-water vessels, votive candles, and plastic icons, while parallel Megaloháris, which points a slightly more direct approach to the church, is relatively clear of shops, making room for the long, thick pad that has been bolted to the street in sympathy of devotees who crawl to the church uphill on their hands and knees from the harbour every day. Approached via a massive marble staircase, the famous **icon** inside the church is all but buried under a dazzling array of jewels; below is the crypt (where the icon was discovered) and a mausoleum for the sailors drowned when the Greek warship *Elli*, at anchor off Tínos during a pilgrimage, was torpedoed by an Italian submarine on August 15, 1940. Museums around the courtyard display more objects donated by the faithful (who inundate the island for the two big annual festivals), as well as icons, paintings and work by local marble sculptors.

The shrine aside – and all the attendant stalls, shops and bustle – the port is none too exciting, with just scattered inland patches of nineteenth-century buildings. You might make time for the **Archeological Museum** (Tues–Sun 8.30am–3pm; €2) on the way up to the church, whose collection includes a fascinating sundial from the local Roman sanctuary of Poseidon and Amphitrite (see p.145).

Practicalities

Ferries dock at any of three different **jetties**; which one depends on weather conditions. There are at least four boats a day from Pireás via Sýros going on

to Mýkonos, and several from Rafína via Ándhros, as well as a useful catamaran, and less frequent ferry connections to Páros, Náxos and Thíra. When
you're leaving, ask your ticket agent which jetty to head for. **Buses** leave from
a small parking area in front of a cubbyhole-office on the quay, to Pánormos,
Kallóni, Stení, Pórto and Kiónia (timetables available here; no buses after
7.30pm). A **motorbike** is perhaps a more reliable means of exploring – Vidalis
at Zanáki Alavánou 16 is a good rental agency.

Windmills Travel (T & F 22830 23398, E info@windmills-travel.com), on
the front towards the new jetty, can help with information as well as hotel and
tour bookings; they even have a book exchange. In season an excursion boat
does day-trips taking in Delos (see p.153) and Mýkonos (Tues–Sun; €20 round
trip); this makes it possible to see Delos without the expense of staying
overnight in Mýkonos, but only allows you two and a half hours at the site.
The **tourist police** are located on the road to the west of the new jetty.

Accommodation

To have any chance of securing a reasonably priced **room** around the pilgrimage day of March 25 (August 15 is hopeless), you must arrive several days
in advance. At other times, there's plenty of choice, though you'll still be competing with out-of-season pilgrims, Athenian tourists and the ill and disabled
seeking a miracle cure. Of the hotels, the *Eleana* (T 22830 22561; ❸), east of
the quay about 200m inland from the Commercial Bank and taxi stand, is a
good budget option, as are the rooms of Andreas Plytas (T 22830 24721; ❸).
Slightly pricier options include the *Avra* (T 22830 22242; ❸), a Neoclassical
relic on the waterfront, and the *Vyzantio* (T 22830 22421, F 22830 22422; ❹),
three blocks inland on the road to Pórto. The *Favie Suzanne* (T 22830 22693,
F 22830 25993; ❹), across the small square is probably a bit quieter, while the
newly renovated *Hotel Tinion* (T 22830 22261, F 22830 24754; ❺), behind the
post office, is a stylish 1920s hotel. The *Vyzantio* (above) and the *Meltémi*
(T 22830 22881, F 22830 23000; ❸) at Filipóti 7, near Megalohárís, are the
only places open out of season. Finally, there is a smart hotel, the *Aeolos Bay*
(T 22830 23410; ❺) with a swimming pool, near the beginning of the beach
road east of the promontory, and just out of town, *Anna's Rooms* (T 22830
22877, F 22830 23651; ❷) represents better value. Otherwise, beat the crowds
by staying at *Tinos Camping*, which also has a few nice rooms to let (T 22830
22344; ❷); follow the signs and it's a ten-minute walk from the port.

Eating and drinking

As usual, most seafront **restaurants** are rather overpriced and indifferent, with
the exception of a friendly *psitopolió* right opposite the bus station, and the
smarter *Xinari* restaurant and pizzeria on Evangelistrías. About midway along
the port near the *Leto Hotel*, behind the dolphin fountain, there are three excellent tavernas: *Kanilio*, with tasty pork in mustard sauce (*hirinó mé moustárda*);
Metaxi Mas, a *mezedopolío* that has a remarkably varied menu, including delicious *hortokeftédhes* (vegetable croquettes); and *Palea Palladha*, justifiably proud
of its grilled *loukániko*, sharp local feta and smooth house wine. Nearby there's
a small bakery, *Psomi Horiatiko*, and across from both is the Palládha, the public
square where every morning there's a farmer's **market** with local fruit and
vegetables. For late-night snacks, try *Edesma* (meaning "food"), which stays
open till 5am.

There are a few **bars**, mostly in a huddle near the new quay. Sleek *Fevgatos*
has sophisticated decor, *Koursaros* on the corner plays rock music, and *Pyrsos* is
pretty lively with a mixture of international hits and Greek music. *Kaktos*,

meanwhile, has dancing on a terrace with ocean views, while *Sivilla* blends Greek and world music in a cozy setting. At 3am all bars in Tínos Town close, but for those not ready to hit the sack, *Papyros* and *La Casa* clubs stay open until dawn playing mainly Greek music.

Southern beaches

Kiónia, 3km northwest (hourly buses in summer), is the site of the **Sanctuary of Poseidon and Amphitrite** which was discovered in 1902; the excavations yielded principally columns (*kiónia* in Greek), but also a temple, baths, a fountain and hostels for the ancient pilgrims. The **beach** is functional enough, lined with rooms to rent and snack-bars, but it's better to walk past the large *Tinos Beach Hotel* (☎22830 22626, ℱ22830 23153; ❼), the last stop for the bus, and follow an unpaved road to a series of sandy coves beyond.

The beach beyond the headland east of town starts off rocky but improves if you walk 500m further along. Further east, **Pórto** (six buses daily) boasts two good beaches, with a couple of good tavernas as well as **rooms** at the reasonably priced restaurant belonging to *Akti Aegeou* (☎22830 24248, ℱ22830 23523; ❺), on the first beach of Áyios Pandelímon, as well as the smart studios of *Porto Raphael* (☎22830 22403, ℱ22830 23913; ❸), above Áyios Ioánnis. *Porto Tango* (☎22830 24410, ℱ22830 24416; ❼) is an excellent upmarket hotel here, with a lovely pool setting.

Northern Tínos

A good beginning to a foray into the interior is to take the stone stairway – the continuation of Odhós Ayíou Nikoláou – that passes behind and to the left of the Evangelistrías. This climbs for ninety minutes through appealing countryside to **KTIKÁDHOS**, a fine village with a good seaview taverna, *Drosia*. You can either flag down a bus on the main road or stay with the trail until Xinára (see p.146).

Heading northwest from the junction flanked by Ktikádhos, Tripótamos and Xinára, there's little to stop for – except the fine **dovecotes** around Tarambádhos – until you reach **KARDHIANÍ**, one of the most strikingly set and beautiful villages on the island, with its views across to Sýros from amid a dense oasis. The cliff-hugging *O Dinos* here serves shellfish with a prime sunset view. **ISTÉRNIA**, just a little beyond, is not nearly so appealing but there is some accommodation on offer, including the *Lameras Hotel* (☎22830 31215; ❷). The *Tavsternia* taverna commands stunning panoramic views and there are a few café-bars perched above the turning for **Órmos Isterníon**, a comparatively small but overdeveloped beach.

Five daily buses along this route finish up at **PÝRGOS**, a few kilometres further north and smack in the middle of the island's marble-quarrying district. A beautiful village, its local artisans are renowned throughout Greece for their skill in producing marble ornamentation; ornate fanlights and bas-relief plaques crafted here adorn houses throughout Tínos. Pýrgos is also home to the School of Arts, and the **Museum of Tinian Artists** (daily 10.30am–1.30pm & 5.30–7pm; €2, ticket also valid for Yiannoulis Halepas Museum) contains numerous representative works from some of the island's finest artists. Nearby, the **Yiannoulis Halepas Museum** (same hours; €2, ticket also valid for Museum of Tinian Artists) is devoted exclusively to the work of the artist who was born in this home and who is generally recognized as the most important Neoclassical Greek sculptor. There are two *kafenía* and a snack-bar on the attractive shady *platía*, and one acceptable **taverna** opposite the bus station.

Pýrgos is popular in summer, and if you want to stay there are some new **studios** for rent on the main road coming into the village; alternatively ask the locals on the *platía*.

The marble products were once exported from **PÁNORMOS** harbour, 4km northeast, which has a tiny, commercialized beach. Better is **Roharí** beach on the northwest side of the bay, accessible by foot or *kaïki*, with its deep clear waters and massive waves. The tiny island it faces is called Planítis or "the Planet." An alternative to pricey hotels such as the *Planítis View* (T 22830 31552, F 22830 31650; ◎) that dominate Pánormos, are the decent rooms of the *O Markos* taverna (T 22830 31336; ❸).

Around Exóbourgo

The ring of villages around **Exóbourgo** mountain is another focus of interest on Tínos. The fortified pinnacle itself (570m), with ancient foundations as well as the ruins of three Venetian churches and a fountain, is reached by steep steps from **XINÁRA** (near the island's major road junction), the seat of the island's Roman Catholic bishop. Most villages in north central Tínos have mixed populations, but Xinára and its immediate neighbours are purely Catholic; the inland villages also tend to have a more sheltered position, with better farmland nearby – the Venetians' way of rewarding converts and their descendants. Yet **TRIPÓTAMOS**, just south of Xinára, is a completely Orthodox village with possibly the finest architecture in this region – and has accordingly been pounced on by foreigners keen to restore its historic properties.

At **LOUTRÁ**, the next community north of Xinára, there's an Ursuline convent and a good folk art museum (summer only 10.30am–3.30pm; free) in the old Jesuit monastery; to visit, leave the bus at the turning for Skaládho. From Krókos, 1km northwest of Loutrá, which has a scenically situated taverna, it's a forty-minute walk to **VÓLAKAS** (also transliterated as Vólax), one of the most remote villages on the island, a windswept oasis surrounded by bony rocks. Here, half a dozen elderly Catholic basketweavers fashion some of the best examples in Greece. There is a small folklore museum (free) which you have to ask the lady living in the house opposite the entrance to open, and the charming outdoor Fontaine Theatre which in August hosts visiting theatre groups from all over Greece. Accommodation is hard to come by, but there are a couple of places to eat, including the recommended *O Rokos* and *I Volax* **tavernas**.

At Kómi, 5km beyond Krókos, you can take a detour for **KOLYMBÍTHRA**, a magnificent double beach: one part wild, huge and windswept (temporary residence to pink flamingos migrating to Africa during May), the other sheltered and with a couple of tavernas including *Kolibithra Beach* (T 22830 51213), which also has rooms (❹). The bus to Kalloní goes on to Kolymbíthra twice a day in season; out of season you'll have to get off at Kómi and walk 4km.

From either Skaládho or Vólakas you go on to Koúmaros, where another long stairway leads up to Exóbourgo, or skirt the pinnacle towards the agricultural villages of **FALATÁDHOS** and **STENÍ** which appear as white speckles against the fertile Livádha valley. Falatádhos has a number of whitewashed churches, the most notable of which is **Áyios Ioánnis** for its marble decoration. There is also a **House of Exhibitions** (changing hours; free), which shows contempory art in summer. The village has a number of excellent restaurants including *Lefkes* taverna and *To Katoï*, specializing in grilled dishes. From Stení, which has fewer amenities but plenty of postcard-perfect whitewashed buildings to admire, you can catch the bus back to the harbour (7 daily). On the way down, try to stop off at one of the beautiful settlements just below the important twelfth-century **convent of Kekhrovouníou**, where Ayía Pelayía had her vision. Particularly worth visiting are **TRIANDÁROS** and **DHÝO HORIÁ**, which has a fine main square where cave-fountains burble. If you have your own transport, there are quite wide and fairly negotiable tracks down to some lovely secluded bays on the east of the island from the area of Steni. One such is **Sánta Margaríta**; given the lack of tourist development here, it's a good idea to take something to drink.

This is hardly an exhaustive list of Tiniot villages; armed with a map and good walking shoes for tackling the many old trails that still exist, you could spend days within sight of Exóbourgo and never pass through the same hamlets twice. Take warm clothing out of season, especially if you're on a scooter, since the forbidding mountains behind Vólakas and the Livadhéri plain keep things noticeably cool.

Mýkonos

Originally visited only as a stop on the way to ancient Delos, **Mýkonos** has become easily the most popular (and the most expensive) of the Cyclades. Boosted by direct air links with Britain and domestic flights from Athens, it sees more than a million tourists pass through in a good year (half of them in August alone), producing some spectacular overcrowding in high summer on Mýkonos's 75 square kilometres. But if you don't mind the crowds, or you come in the shoulder season, the prosperous capital is still one of the most beautiful of all island towns, its immaculately whitewashed houses concealing hundreds of little churches, shrines and chapels.

The sophisticated nightlife is pretty hectic, amply stimulated by Mýkonos's former reputation as *the* gay resort of the Mediterranean – a title that has been surrendered to Sitges in Spain. Today, gay tourists are well in the minority on the island until September, when the gay clientele is present in full force. The locals (more than 10,000 at last estimate, more than half of them Albanian immigrants) take it all in their stride, ever conscious of the important revenue generated by their laissez-faire attitude. When islanders first opened up to the artsy tourists who began appearing on Mýkonos in the 1960s, they guessed their eccentric visitors were sharing cigarettes due to lack of funds. Since then, a lot of the innocence has evaporated, and the island certainly isn't unspoilt, but Mýkonos does offer excellent (if crowded) beaches, picturesque windmills and a rolling arid interior. Best of all, the well-organized local tourist industry does everything in its power to see that beaches are more cared for and that transportation runs more frequently than on most neighbouring islands. A local ban on the construction of large international chain restaurants and hotels has done much to preserve the landscape, as does the presence of the second largest biological cleaning plant in Greece. The legality of scuba diving, a rarity in Greece, means that there are dive centres on virtually every beach.

Mýkonos Town

Don't let the crowds put you off exploring **MÝKONOS TOWN**, the archetypal postcard image of the Cyclades. Its sugar-cube buildings are stacked around a cluster of seafront fishermen's dwellings, with every nook and cranny scrubbed and shown off. Most people head out to the beaches during the day, so early morning or late afternoon are the best times to wander the maze of narrow streets. The labyrinthine design was intended to confuse the pirates who plagued Mýkonos in the eighteenth and early nineteenth centuries, and it still has the desired effect.

Getting lost in the convoluted streets and alleys of town is half the fun of exploring, although there are a few places worth seeking out. Coming from the ferry quay you'll pass the **Archeological Museum** (Tues–Sat 9am–3.30pm, Sun 10am–3pm; €2) on your way into town, which displays some good Delos pottery; the town also boasts a **Maritime Museum** displaying various nautical artefacts, including a lighthouse re-erected in the back garden (Tues–Sun 10.30am–1pm & 6.30–9pm; €3). Next door is **Lena's House** (Mon–Sat 6–9pm, Sun 5–7pm; free), a completely restored and furnished middle class home from the nineteenth century. At the base of the Delos jetty, the **Folklore Museum** (Mon–Sat 5.30–8.30pm, Sun 6.30–8.30pm; free), housed in an eighteenth-century mansion crams in a larger-than-usual collection of bric-a-brac, including a vast four-poster bed. The museum shares the same promontory as the old Venetian *kástro*, the entrance to which is marked by Mýkonos's oldest and best-known church, **Paraportianí**, which is a fascinating asymmetrical hodgepodge of four chapels amalgamated into one.

The shore leads to the area known as **Little Venice** because of its high, arcaded Venetian houses built right up to the water's edge. Together with the adjoining **Alefkándhra** district, this is a dense area packed with art galleries, trendy bars and discos. Away from the seafront, behind Platía Alefkándhra, are Mýkonos's two **cathedrals**: Roman Catholic and Greek Orthodox. Beyond, the famous **windmills** look over the area, a little shabby but ripe for photo opportunities. South of here, sleepier **Vídha**, which runs along a tiny beach, has seen the recent arrival of accommodation spilling over from the rest of town.

MÝKONOS TOWN

0   100 m

▲ Toúrlos & Áyios Stéfanos

❶ North Bus Station

Accommodation Centre
Tourist Police

Island Ferries

Ⓐ

Archeological Museum

AYIOU STEFANOU

POLYKANDHRIOTI

Ⓑ

▶ Áno Méra

Boats to Delos

KAMBANI

❷
❸

PLATIA M. MAVROYENOUS

Folklore Museum

Kástro

❹

❻ ❺

KAMBANI

❼
❽ ❾

KAMBANI

National Bank & Port Police

AYIOU IOANNOU

MAVROYENI

ZOUGANELI

AY. ANARYRON

❿

Paraportiani

LITTLE VENICE

DHRAKOPOULOU

LIDHORIKA

DHILOU

ARHONDIKONOI MATOYIANNI

KALOYERA

AY. YERASIMOU

❶❶

Ⓒ

Ⓓ

N

Maritime Museum

LITOU

ALEFKÁNDHRA

❶❷

❶❸

❶❺ ❶❻

❶❼

MITROPOLEOS

Mykonos Accommodation Center

❶❽

ENOPLON DHYNAMEON

TOURLIANI

ROHARI

❶❹

Windmills

❶❾

Car Park

IPIROU

AY. EFTHIMOU

XENIAS

LÁKKA

❷⓿

Ⓔ

Laundry

✉

South Bus Station

AYIOU IOANNOU

Ⓕ

VÍDHA

Ⓖ

Ⓗ **Scooter Rental**

Scooter Rental

Ⓘ

Scooter Rental

Scooter Rental

Ⓙ

Ⓚ

▼ Megáli Ammos   ▼ Órnos & Airport

RESTAURANTS, CAFÉS & BARS

Aigli	19	Kastro	10
Aroma	11	Katerina's	10
Astra	19	Kostas	15
Camares	3	La Mer	10
Caprice	10	Montparnasse	
Celebrities	11	Piano Bar	10
Edem	14	Nikos Taverna	8
Cafe Express	5	Pasta Fresca	6
Irish Bar	7	El Pecado	4
Kalua	2	Pelican	12

Porta	9
Sea Satin	17
Skandinavian	
Bar-Disco	7
Space	20
Spiro's	13
White Shark	11
Yacht Club	1
Yiavroutas	
Estiatorio	16

ACCOMMODATION

Adonis	G
Belvedere	F
Elysium	J
Geranium	K
Pension Marina	H
Philippi	D
Semeli	E
Stelios Pension	A
Terra Maria	C
La Veranda	B
Villa Giovanni	I

Practialities

There is some accommodation information at the recently expanded **airport** (about 3km southeast of town) and at the new **northern port** where large cruise ships dock (a few kilometres north of town in Toúrlos), but unless you know where you're going it's easier to take a bus or taxi into town, and sort things out there. The vast majority of visitors arrive by ferry at the **jetty** at the north end of town, where a veritable horde of room-owners pounces on the newly arrived. The scene is actually quite intimidating, and so, if you can avoid the grasping talons, it is far better to go a 100m further, where a row of offices deals with official hotels, rented rooms and camping information, or go into the heart of town to the extremely helpful Mykonos Accommodation Center (T 22890 23160, W mykonos-accommodation.com) on Enóplon Dhynaméon near the Maritime Museum.

Easier to find, but less accommodating, the local **accommodation centre** (open high season only) can be found up from the ferry stalls next to the **tourist police** near the old ferry landing, in front of which is the **north bus station** for Toúrlos, Áyios Stéfanos, Eliá and Áno Méra. The harbour curves around past the dull, central Polikandhrióti beach, where you're likely to catch a glimpse of a pelican, the island's beloved mascot.

The **south bus station**, for beaches to the south, is across town, not far from Lákka square where the **post office**, Olympic Airways office and several **motorbike** agencies can be found. Buses to all the most popular beaches and resorts run frequently until the early hours. **Taxis** run from Platía Mavroyénous on the seafront and from the south bus station, and their rates are fixed and quite reasonable; try Mykonos Radio Taxi (T 22890 22400). There are countless advertiser-based tourist **publications** circulating throughout Mýkonos during high season, the best of which is the free Mýkonos Sky Map available from most agents and hotels.

Catamaran and ferry tickets are sold at several separate and uncooperative **travel agencies** on the harbour front. Check out the various possibilities, and if your boat leaves from the new harbour, catch the bus up from the old ferry landing across from the Eurobank.

Accommodation

Accommodation prices in Mýkonos rocket in the high season to a greater degree than almost anywhere else in Greece. For a good deal, try the comfortable *Stelios Pension* (T 22890 24641, F 22890 26779; ❸), set away from the central bustle of town on steps leading up from the OTE office. More central, both the *Terra Maria* at Kaloyéra 18 (T 22890 24212, F 22890 27112; ❺) and the *Philippi* at Kaloyéra 25 (T 22890 22294, F 22890 24680; ❺) have clean rooms with garden views. There are plenty of very expensive hotels like the *Semeli* (T 22890 27466, F 22890 27467; ❼) above town on Ayíou Ioánnou, which has a pool, whirlpool and very tastefully decorated rooms, or the *Belvedere* (T 22890 25122, E belvedere@myk.forthnet.gr; ❻), next door, which is a relative bargain when you can find a room. A few slightly out of the way gems are *La Veranda* (T 22890 23670; ❼), located on the hillside above town, with rooms set around a small pool, and the *Adonis* (T 22890 22434, F 22890 23449; ❼), in the Vídha area, with views of the windmills from some of its nicely appointed rooms. Unsurprisingly, most accommodation is extremely gay-friendly: *Geranium* (T 22890 24620, F 22890 24624; ❼) is almost exclusively gay, as is nearby *Elysium* (T 22890 23952, F 22890 23747; ❼), the latter with a poolside bar that's also a popular setting for a late afternoon cocktail. Two recommended **pensions** are on the south side of town above the bus station: *Villa Giovanni* (☏ 22890 22485, ℻ 22890 23485; ❻) and *Pension Marina* (☏ 22890 24960, ℻ 22890 26213; ❺) on Ayíou Ioánnou and Lákka. There are two **campsites**: *Mykonos Camping* (☏ & ℻ 22890 24578, ⓦ www.mycamp.gr) above Paránga beach is smaller and has a more pleasant setting than nearby *Paradise Camping* on Paradise beach (☏ 22890 22129, ⓦ www .paradisemykonos.com), however, the latter also has bungalows (❺). Both are packed in season, and dance music from the 24-hour bars on Paradise beach makes sleep difficult. The overpriced campsite restaurants serving poor food are best avoided. Hourly bus services to Paránga and Paradise beaches continue into the early hours but can get overcrowded.

Eating

Even **light meals** and **snacks** are expensive in Mýkonos, but there are several bakeries, supermarkets and fruit stalls, some concentrated near the south bus station. The area around Alefkándhra is a promising place to head for a full **meal**: *Pelican*, behind the two cathedrals on the *platía*, is pricey but well sited. *Kostas*, also nearby, has competitive prices, a good wine list including barrelled wine (not easily found on Mýkonos) and friendly service. Less than fifty metres further along Mitropóleos, the small *Yiavroutas Estiatorio* is probably the least expensive and most authentically Greek place on the island, again with good barrelled wine. *Magic Garden* serves Mediterranean dishes in a verdant setting, while under the windmills, *Sea Satin Market* prepares upscale seafood in a trendy setting that turns clubby after midnight. *Edem*, meanwhile, close to Panakhrándou, offers poolside dining. *Nikos Taverna*, near the port at Little Venice, is the most famous restaurant on the island, packing every inch of its terrace with customers, which can have a detrimental effect on service. *Pasta Fresca Barkia*, on the waterfront, serves excellent home-made pasta and pizza and is a great spot for people watching. For **late–night** snacks, most of the cafés on Kambáni stay open until the small hours, and *Cafe Express* is open all night.

Nightlife

Nightlife in town is every bit as good as it's cracked up to be – and every bit as pricey. *Aigli* and *Astra* are two chic cafés by day that turn clubby by night; their terraces are divided by the tiny landmark of **Tría Pigádhia** (Three Wells), which local legend claims a maiden must drink from before she will find her husband. Today's revellers at places such as *Skandinavian Bar-Disco* and the nearby *Irish Bar* seem to prefer more modern strategies. More sophisticated bars on Andhroníkou Matoyiánni and Enóplon Dhynaméon (which are collectively referred to by some as "Fifth Avenue" for the nightly fashion parade along its cobblestone catwalk) include *White Shark*, *Aroma*, and *Celebrities*, while *Space*, on Lákka square, is the largest club on the island. Little Venice's *Katerina's*, *Caprice*, *Montparnasse Piano Bar* and *Kastro* are ideal for sunset cocktails; the first serves delicious fresh fruit juices, and the last plays classical music and is popular with a gay crowd. Back (northeast) towards the harbour, *La Mer* is a popular disco/bar playing a lively mix of Greek and dance music, while *Porta* is a popular gay haunt near *Kounelas* restaurant. Stylish lounge-style clubs along the waterfront include *El Pecado*, *Camares* and *Kalua*. *Cavo Paradiso*, near *Paradise Camping*, is the after-hours club where die-hard party animals of all persuasions come together, though another late-night party at the characterless *Yacht Club* on the jetty is increasingly popular due to its proximity to town.

The beaches

The closest **beaches** to town are those to the north, at **Toúrlos** (only 2km away but horrid) and **Áyios Stéfanos** (4km, much better), both developed resorts and connected by a very regular bus service to Mýkonos Town. There are tavernas and rooms to let (as well as package hotels) at Áyios Stéfanos, away from the beach; *Mocambo Lido* taverna at the far end of the bay has a pleasant setting and good food.

Other nearby destinations include southwest peninsula resorts, with undistinguished beaches tucked into pretty bays. The nearest to town, 1km away, is **Megáli Ámmos**, a good beach backed by flat rocks and pricey rooms, but nearby Kórfos bay is disgusting, thanks to the town dump and machine noise. Buses serve **Ornós**, an average beach, and **Áyios Ioánnis**, a dramatic bay with the new super-deluxe *St John Hotel* (☎22890 28752, ⦻www.saintjohn.gr; ❽) and a tiny, stony beach, which achieved its moment of fame as a location for the film *Shirley Valentine*.

The south coast is the busiest part of the island. *Kaïkia* ply from town to all of its beaches, which are still regarded to some extent as family strands by the Greeks. You might begin with **Platýs Yialós**, 4km south of town, though you won't be alone: one of the longest-established resorts on the island, it's not remotely Greek any more, the sand is monopolized by hotels, and you won't get a room to save your life between June and September. **Psaroú**, next door to the west, is very pretty – 150m of white sand backed by foliage and calamus reeds, crowded with sunbathers. Here you'll find *N'Ammos*, an elegant fish **restaurant** on the waterfront. Other beach facilities include a diving club (☎22890 24808, ⦻www.dive.gr), waterskiing and windsurfer rental, but again you'll need to reserve well in advance to secure **rooms** between mid-June and mid-September. Try *Soula Rooms* (☎& ⓕ22890 22006; ❺), a surprisingly calm property on the beach.

Just over the headland to the east of Platýs Yialós is **Paránga beach**, actually two beaches separated by a smaller headland, the first of which has a decent taverna with some basic rooms and is quieter than its noisy neighbour, which is home to a loud beach bar and *Mykonos Camping*. A dusty footpath beyond Platýs Yialós crosses the fields and caves of the headland across the clifftops past Paránga, and drops down to **Paradise beach**, a crescent of golden sand that is packed in season. Here, as on many of Mýkonos's most popular beaches, it can be difficult to find an opening big enough to fit a towel, and what little space you manage to find clear of people is likely to be taken up by straw umbrellas, which can be rented (usually along with two accompanying loungers) for about €5. Behind the beach are shops, self-service restaurants and the noisy 24-hour beach bars of *Paradise Camping*. The next bay east contains **Super Paradise** (officially "Plindhrí") beach, accessible by footpath or by *kaïki*. One of the most fun beaches on the island, it has a decent taverna and two bars at opposite ends of the beach pumping out cheesy summer hits. One half of the beach is very mixed, getting progressively more gay as you walk away from where the *kaïkia* dock towards the beach bar perched in the hills, below which the beach is almost exclusively gay and nudist.

One of the best beaches on Mýkonos is **Eliá**, the last port of call for the *kaïkia*. A broad, sandy stretch with a verdant backdrop, it's the longest beach on the island, though split in two by a rocky area, and almost exclusively gay late in the season. To retreat from the crowds, follow the bare rock footpath over the spur (look for the white house) at the end of the beach that cuts upwards for grand views east and west and then winds down to **Kaló Livádhi** (seasonal bus service), a stunning beach adjoining an agricultural valley scattered with little farmhouses; even here there's a restaurant (a good one at that) at the far end of the beach. **Ayía Ánna**, further on, boasts a shingle beach and taverna, with the cliffs above granting some fine vistas. **Kalafáti**, still further east, is more of a tourist community, its white-sand beach supporting a few hotels, restaurants and a disco. There's a local bus service from here to Áno Méra (see below), or you can jump on an excursion boat to **Tragoníssi**, the islet just offshore, for spectacular coastal scenery, seals and wild birds. The rest of the east coast is more difficult to reach: there are some small beaches, really only worth the effort if you crave solitude, and the region is dominated by the peak of Profítis Ilías, sadly spoilt by a huge radar dome and military establishment. **Liá**, roughly 12km east of Eliá, is smaller but delightful, with bamboo windbreaks and clear water, plus another good taverna.

The **north coast** suffers persistent battering from the *meltémi*, plus tar and litter pollution, and for the most part is bare, brown and exposed. **Pánormos Bay** is the exception to this, with the lovely, relatively sheltered beaches of **Pánormos** and **Áyios Sóstis** along its western edge. Despite a good restaurant, a relaxed beach bar and the rather conspicuous *Albatros Club Hotel* (☎22890 25130, ☎22890 25361; ⑥) on Pánormos, these beaches remain the least crowded on the island, and although they are not served by buses, are becoming increasingly popular.

Áno Méra

From Pánormos Bay, it's an easy walk to the only other settlement of any size on the island, **ÁNO MÉRA**, where you should be able to find a **room**. The village prides itself on striving to maintain a traditional way of life, although the result is rather pseudo and wishy-washy: the so-called traditional *kafenío* has long since ditched Greek coffee for cappuccino and traditional sweets for "icecream special". There are, however, several acceptable **restaurants** on the *platía*, of which *Daniele at Basoulas* is currently the most popular for its wide range of Mediterranean dishes; (you'll also find a large **hotel** here, *Ano Mera* (☎22890 71215, ☎22890 71276; ⑦). The red-roofed church near the square is the sixteenth-century **monastery of Panayía Tourlianí**, where a collection of Cretan icons and the unusual eighteenth-century marble baptismal font are worth seeing. It's not far, either, to the late twelfth-century **Paleokástro monastery** (also known as Dárga), just north of the village, in a magnificent green setting on an otherwise barren slope. To the northwest are more of the same dry and wind-buffeted landscapes, though they do provide some enjoyable, rocky walking with expansive views across to neighbouring islands – head to Áyios Stéfanos for buses back to the harbour.

Delos (Dhílos)

The remains of **ancient Delos**, Pindar's "unmoved marvel of the wide world", though skeletal and swarming now with lizards and tourists, give some idea of the past grandeur of this sacred isle a few sea-miles west of Mýkonos. The ancient town lies on the west coast on flat, sometimes marshy ground that rises in the south to **Mount Kýnthos**. From the summit – an easy walk – there's a magnificent view across the Cyclades.

The first excursion boats to Delos leave the small port near the west end of Mýkonos harbour daily at 8.30am (€6 round trip), except Mondays

DELOS

Stadium

Gymnasium

Lake House

Sacred Lake

N

0   100 m

Lion Terrace

Roman Wall

Agora of the Italians

Tourist Pavilion

Museum

Apollo Temples

Sanctuary of Dionysos

House of the Naxians   SANCTUARY OF APOLLO

Sacred Harbour

Sacred Way

Agora of the Competialists

Boats

Commercial Harbour

House of Hermes

Syrian Gods

House of Dionysos

Terrace of the Foreign Gods

House of Cleopatra

House of the Trident

Egyptian Gods

THEATRE QUARTER

Theatre

House of the Dolphins

House of the Masks

Sacred Cave

Warehouses

Mt Kýnthos 113m

when the site is closed. You have to return on the same boat, but in season each does the trip several times and you can choose what time you leave. The last return is usually about 3pm, and you'll need to arrive early if you want to make a thorough tour of the site. In season a daily *kaïki* makes return trips from the beaches (€10) with pick-up points at Platýs Yialós and Órnos, but only allows you three hours on the island. Check ahead with operators of Delos excursion boats or look for posters advertising evening concerts and other special performances that occasionally animate the ancient site in season.

Some history

Delos's ancient fame was due to the fact that Leto gave birth to the divine twins Artemis and Apollo on the island, although its fine harbour and central position did nothing to hamper development. When the Ionians colonized the island around 1000 BC it was already a cult centre, and by the seventh century BC it had become the commercial and religious centre of the **Amphictionic League**. Unfortunately Delos also attracted the attention of Athens, which sought dominion over this prestigious island; the wealth of the Delian Confederacy, founded after the Persian Wars to protect the Aegean cities, was harnessed to Athenian ends, and for a while Athens controlled the Sanctuary of Apollo. Athenian attempts to "purify" the island began with a decree that no one could die or give birth on Delos – the sick and the pregnant were taken to the islet of Rínia – and culminated in the simple expedient of banishing the native population.

Delos reached its peak in the third and second centuries BC, after being declared a free port by its Roman overlords. In the end, though, its undefended wealth brought ruin: first Mithridates (88 BC), then Athenodorus (69 BC) plundered the treasures and the island never recovered. By the third century AD, Athens could not even sell it, and for centuries, every passing seafarer stopped to collect a few prizes.

The site

As you land at **the site** (Tues–Sun 8.30am–3pm; €5), the Sacred Harbour is on your left, the Commercial Harbour on your right and straight ahead lies the **Agora of the Competialists**. Competialists were Roman merchants or freed slaves who worshipped the Lares Competales, the guardian spirits of crossroads; offerings to Hermes would once have been placed in the middle of the agora, their position now marked by a round and a square base. The **Sacred Way** leads north from the far left corner; it used to be lined with statues and the grandiose monuments of rival kings. Along it you reach three marble steps which lead into the **Sanctuary of Apollo**; much was lavished on the god, but the forest of offerings has been plundered over the years. On your left is the Stoa of the Naxians, while against the north wall of the House of the Naxians, to the right, a huge statue of Apollo stood in ancient times. In 417 BC the Athenian general Nikias led a procession of priests across a bridge of boats from Rínia to dedicate a bronze palm tree; when it was later blown over in a gale it took the statue with it. Three **Temples of Apollo** stand in a row to the right along the Sacred Way: the Delian Temple, that of the Athenians and the Porinos Naos, the earliest of them, dating from the sixth century BC. To the east towards the museum you pass the **Sanctuary of Dionysos**, with its marble phalluses on tall pillars.

The best finds from the site are in Athens, but the **museum** still justifies a visit, if only to see the famous **lions**, their lean bodies masterfully executed by Naxians in the seventh century BC to ward off intruders who would have been unfamiliar with the fearful creatures, as they are not indigenous to the area. Of the original nine, three have disappeared and one – captured by Venetians in the seventeenth century – adorns the Arsenale in Venice. To the north stands a wall that marks the site of the **Sacred Lake** where Leto gave birth, clinging to a palm tree, guarded by excellent reproductions of the lions. On the other side of the lake is the City Wall, built in 69 BC – too late to protect the treasures.

Set out in the other direction from the Agora of the Competialists and you enter the residential area, known as the Theatre Quarter. Many of the walls and roads remain, but there is none of the domestic detail that brings other such sites to life. Some colour is added by the mosaics: one in the House of the Trident, and better ones in the House of the Masks, most notably a vigorous portrayal of Dionysos riding on a panther's back. The theatre itself seated 5500 spectators, and, though much ravaged, offers some fine views. Behind the theatre, a steep path leads past the Sanctuaries of the Foreign Gods and up Mount Kýnthos for spectacular views back down over the ruins and out to the surrounding Cyclades.

Sýros

Don't be put off by first impressions of **Sýros**. From the ferry it can seem vaguely industrial, but away from the Neório shipyard things improve quickly. Very much a working island with only a relatively recent history of tourism, it is among the most Greek of the Cyclades and the most populous island in the group. It might also come as a refreshing change from its more touristic

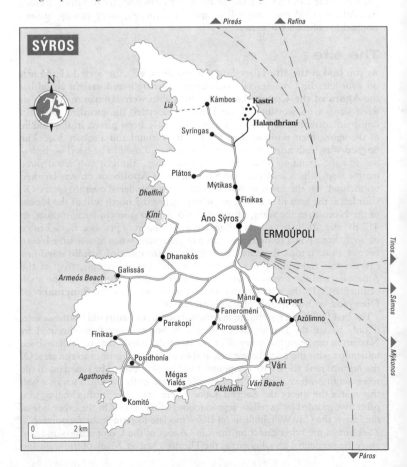

neighbours. Of course, outsiders do come to the island; in fact there's a thriving permanent foreign community, and the beaches are hardly undeveloped, but everywhere there's the underlying assumption that you're a guest of an inherently private people.

Ermoúpoli

The main town and port of **ERMOÚPOLI** was founded during the War of Independence by refugees from Psará and Híos, becoming Greece's chief port in the nineteenth century. Although Pireás outstripped it long ago, Ermoúpoli

▲ Áno Sýros   ▲ Vrondádho & Anástasis Church

ERMOÚPOLI

VAPÓRIA

Áyios Nikólaos

Apollon Theatre

PLATIA VARDHAKA

Mitrópolis

Archeological Museum

Town Hall

PLATIA MIAOULI

PLATIA TSIROPINA

Bank

Market

KI & KYR STEFANOU

PROTOPAPADHAKI

ANDIPAROU

Laundry

PLATIA KANARI

Accommodation Kiosks

Bus Station

Ferry Quay

Teamwork Agency

0   100 m

RESTAURANTS & BARS

Aegean Casino	14
Ais Ithoki	5
Archontariki	1
Boheme del Mar	9
La Dolce Vita	12
Fresh Corner	13
Inopneymata	7
Kimbara	8
Liquid	8
Manousos	2
Mojo	8
Petrino	6
Piramatiko	3
Psaropoula Ouzeri	11
Severo	8
Vakhos	4
Yiannena Estiatorio	10

N

ACCOMMODATION

Dream	G
Hermes	F
Kastro	E
Nisaki	H
Omiros	B
Paradise	D
Sea Colours Apartments	C
Syrou Melathron	A

▼ Neório Shipyard, Southern Villages

is still the largest town in the Cyclades, and the archipelago's capital. Medieval Sýros was largely a Catholic island, but an influx of Orthodox refugees during the War of Independence created two distinct communities; now almost equal in numbers, the two groups today still live in their respective quarters occupying two hills that rise up from the sea. They do, however, commonly celebrate each others' festivals, lending vibrant mix of culture that gives the island its colour.

Ermoúpoli itself, the **lower town**, is worth at least a night's stay, with grandiose buildings a relic of its days as a major port. The long, central **Platía Miaoúli** is named after an admiral of the revolution whose statue stands there, and in the evenings the population parades in front of its arcades, while children ride the mechanical animals. Up the stairs to the left of the town hall is the small **Archeological Museum** (Tues–Sun 8.30am–3pm; free), with three rooms of finds from Sýros, Páros and Amorgós. To the left of the clocktower more stairs climb up to **Vrondádho**, the hill that hosts the Orthodox quarter. The wonderful church of the **Anástasis** stands atop the hill, with its domed roof and great views over Tínos and Mýkonos – if it's locked, ask for the key at the priest's house.

Up from the right of the square you'll find the **Apollon Theatre**, a copy of Milan's La Scala, which occasionally hosts performances. Up from it is the handsome Orthodox church of **Áyios Nikólaos**, and beyond it to the right is **Vapória**, where the island's wealthiest shipowners, merchants and bankers built their mansions.

On the taller hill to the left, is the intricate medieval quarter of **Áno Sýros**, with a clutch of Catholic churches below the cathedral of St George. There are fine views of the town below, and, close by, the **Cappuchin monastery of St Jean**, founded in 1535 to do duty as a poorhouse. It takes about 45 minutes of tough walking up Omírou to reach this quarter, passing the Orthodox and Catholic cemeteries on the way – the former full of grand shipowners' mausoleums, the latter with more modest monuments and French and Italian inscriptions (you can halve the walking time by taking a shortcut onto the stair-street named Andhréa Kárga, part of the way along). Once up here it's worth visiting the local art and church exhibitions at the **Vamvakaris museum** (daily 10.30am–1pm & 7–10pm; €1.50), and the **Byzantine museum** attached to the monastery.

Heading west from Ermoúpoli, on the road leading from the ferry quay to Kíni, accessible by bus, the **Industrial Museum** (Mon & Wed–Sun 10am–2pm, also Thurs–Sun 6–9pm; €2.50, Wed free) traces the history of the island's ship-building, mining and other many industries through a well-labelled series of artefacts and exhibitions.

Practicalities

The harbour is still busy, though nowadays it deals with more tourists than industrial shipping; Sýros is a major crossover point on the ferry-boat routes. There are several **travel agencies** for various ferries and hydrofoils, the most helpful of which is TeamWork (☎22810 83400, ✉teamwork@otenet.gr). Also on the harbourfront is the **bus station**, along with the **tourist police** and several **motorbike-rental** places, of which Apollon on Andíparou, one block behind the seafront, is recommended. Odhós Híou, the **market** street, is especially lively on Saturday when people come in from the surrounding countryside to sell fresh produce. The town's only **Internet café**, *Bizanas*, is on Platía Miaoúli in the base of the town hall.

Accommodation

TeamWork agency (see opposite), on the waterfront, is a useful source of information and able to help with your accommodation needs. In the summer you might try the kiosk belonging to the Rooms and Apartments Association of Sýros (℡22810 87360), also on the waterfront. Keeping step with a growing level of tourism, **rooms** have improved in quality and number in recent years; many are in garishly decorated, if crumbling, Neoclassical mansions. Good choices include *Kastro* rooms, Kalomenopóulou 12 (℡22810 88064; ❸), *Dream*, on the seafront near the bus station (℡22810 84356, ℻22810 86452; ❹), and *Paradise*, Omírou 3 (℡22810 83204, ℻22810 83581; ❸). Particularly recommended are newly renovated *Hotel Nisaki* (℡22810 88200, ℻22810 82000; ❺), on Papadhám behind the port authority, with great views of the harbour, and the traditionally decorated rooms of *Sea Colours Apartments* (℡22810 88716, ℻22810 83508; ❹), located at Áyios Nikólaos beach, another quiet corner of town. A notch up in price and quality is the well-sited *Hotel Hermes* (℡22810 83011, ℻22810 87412; ❻) on Platía Kanári, overlooking the port. A more stylish traditional hotel is the *Omiros* (℡22810 84910, ℻22810 86266; ❼) set back from the harbour in the direction of Áno Sýros or, for luxury, try the *Syrou Melathron* (℡22810 86495, ℻22810 87806; ❼), beyond Áyios Nikólaos in Vapória. Up in Áno Sýros, the island's most unique accommodation at *Anemomilos* (℡210 93 15 773; ❼), features deluxe apartment-style lodging in a renovated windmill.

Eating

Numerous shops sell *loukoúmia* (Turkish delight), *madoláta* (nougats) and *halvadhópita* (sweetmeat pie) for which the island is famed.

The most authentic and reasonably priced of the harbour **eateries** are the *Yiannena Estiatorio* on Platía Kanári and the popular *Psaropoula Ouzeri*. On Platía Miaoúli, the *Manousos* taverna is a good traditional place, as are a number of other tavernas to the east of the square, including *Petrino*, *Ais Ithoki*, *Inopneymata* and *Archontariki*; *Archontariki* serves a special casserole of mushrooms and ham baked in cheese. Another respected traditional taverna is *Vakhos*, near the market, with specialities like rabbit casserole, and haddock in garlic sauce. *La Dolce Vita*, on steps leading up Filini near where the ferries dock, is an excellent Italian restaurant; for snacks resist the glitzy *Goody's* hamburger-joint and have a *yíros* at the more authentic *Fresh Corner* nearby. In Áno Sýros, the *Artemision* taverna is fine and affords excellent views, and legendery *Lilis* is a beloved local place once frequented by Vamvakaris himself (see below).

Nightlife

Sýros still honours its contribution to the development of **rebétika**; *bouzoúki*-great Markos Vamvakaris hailed from here, and a *platía* in Áno Sýros has been named after him on which a tiny, sporadically open **museum** respects his honour. **Taverna–clubs** such as *Xanthomalis* (up in Áno Sýros and open only in winter) with music at weekends, now take their place beside a batch of more conventional disco-clubs down near the Apollon Theatre. There are several other (often expensive) *bouzoúki* bars scattered around the island, mostly strung along routes to beach resorts. The seafront has a rash of lively **bars** in apparent competition for the title of trendiest. *Mojo*, *Severo*, *Kimbara*, and *Liquid* are currently the main contenders, though less self-consciously hip *Boheme del Mar* has the best atmosphere. *Piramatiko*, on Platía Miaoúli, meanwhile, is often heaving, playing a loud and varied mix from indie to house; across the square in the Internet café *Bizanas* there is a popular **pool** hall. The big venue for night-owls is *Turquoise*, a huge **club** in a converted warehouse out past the Neório shipyard opposite the turning to Vári. The *Aegean Casino* on the seafront is open till 6am for those who have money to burn (and are sufficiently well dressed).

Around the island

The main loop road (to Gallissás, Fínikas, Mégas Yialós, Vári and back), and the road west to Kíni, are good: **buses** ply the routes hourly in season, and run until late. Elsewhere, expect potholes, especially to the **north** where the land is barren and high, with few villages. The main route north from Áno Sýros is quite easily negotiable by bike, provided you don't mind the hills; en route, the village of **Mýtikas** has a decent taverna just off the road. A few kilometres further on, the road forks, with the left turn leading, after another left, to the small settlement of **Syríngas**, where there's an interesting cave to explore. Straight on leads to **Kámbos**, from where a path leads down to Liá beach; the right fork eventually descends to the northeast coast and the early-Cycladic cemetery **Halandhrianí**. Most of the finds from the nineteenth-century excavation of the site are now in Athens, though there is still an unexcavated settlement here. On **Kastrí** hill, to the north, are the remains of one of the Cyclades' most ancient fortified habitations dating from the third millennium BC.

The well-trodden route **south** offers more tangible and accessible rewards. Closest to the capital, fifteen minutes away by bus, is the twin-beach coastal settlement of **KÍNI**. Good accommodation can be found at the *Sunset Hotel* (T & F 22810 71211; ❹), with the excellent *Zalounis* taverna just below. **Dhelfíni**, just to the north, is also a fine pebbly beach, dramatically accessed on a rather awkward footpath.

GALISSÁS, a few kilometres south, but reached by different buses, is fundamentally an agricultural village, but has been taken over since the mid-1980s by backpackers attracted by the island's only **campsite** *Two Hearts* (T 22810 42052, W www.twohearts-camping.com). The site has good facilities and sends minibuses to all boats. There is also a surplus of unaesthetic **rooms**, which at least makes bargaining possible, and six bona fide hotels, of which the cheapest are *Semiramis I & II* (T 22810 42067; ❺) and the excellent *Françoise* (T 22810 42000; ❺), though the *Benois* (T 22810 42833; ❻) is decent value, with buffet breakfast included. Among the many **eating** choices, *To Iliovasilema*, next to *Benois*, is an acceptable fish taverna, and *Cavos*, part of a luxury complex, the *Dolphin Bay Hotel* (T 22810 42924; F 22810 42843; ❼), has great views overlooking the bay. *Argo* is a great place for live Greek music. Galissás's identity crisis is exemplified by the proximity of bemused, grazing dairy cattle, a heavy-metal music **pub** and upmarket handicraft shops. Still, the locals are welcoming, and if you feel the urge to escape, you can rent a scooter, or walk ten minutes past the headland to the nudist beach of **Armeós**, where there's fresh spring water. Note that buses out are erratically routed; to be sure of making your connection you must wait at the high-road stop, not down by the beach.

A pleasant forty-minute walk or a ten-minute bus ride south from Galissás brings you to the more mainstream resort of **FÍNIKAS**, purported to have been settled originally by the Phoenicians (although an alternative derivation could be from *fínikas*, meaning "palm tree" in Greek). The **beach** is narrow and gritty, right next to the road but protected to some extent by a row of tamarisk trees; the pick of the **hotels** is the *Cyclades* (T 22810 42255, F 22810 43178;

❻), and there is an acceptable restaurant just in front, while the *Amaryllis* **rooms** (☎ 22810 42894, ℱ 22810 43681; ❺) are slightly cheaper. The fish taverna *Barbalias* on the seafront is recommended.

Fínikas is separated by a tiny headland from its neighbour **POSIDHONÍA** (or Delagrazzia), a nicer spot with some idiosyncratically ornate mansions and a bright blue church right on the edge of the village. It's worth walking ten minutes further south, past the naval yacht club and its patrol boat to **Agathopés**, with a sandy beach and a little islet just offshore. Komitó, at the end of the road leading south from Agathopés, is little more than a stony beach fronting an olive grove. **Accommodation** around Posidhonía ranges from the smart *Possidonion* hotel (☎ 22810 42100, ℱ 22810 42220; ❻) on the seafront to basic rooms inland. *Meltemi* is a good seafood **taverna**.

The road swings east to **MÉGAS YIALÓS**, a small resort below a hillside festooned with brightly painted houses. The long, narrow beach is lined with shady trees and there are pedal boats for hire. Of the **room** set-ups, *Mike and Bill's* (☎ 22810 43531; ❸) is a reasonable deal, and the pricier *Alexandra Hotel* (☎ 22810 42540; ❺), on the bay, enjoys lovely views. **VÁRI** is more – though not much more – of a town, with its own small fishing fleet. Beach-goers are in a goldfish bowl, as it were, with tavernas and **rooms** looming right overhead, but it is the most sheltered of the island's bays, something to remember when the *meltémi* is up. The *Kamelo* hotel (☎ 22810 61217, ℱ 22810 61117; ❹) provides the best value, while the *En Plo* beach **bar** is a fun spot in season. The adjacent cove of **AKHLÁDHI** is far more pleasant and boasts two small good-value hotels, including the *Ahladi Hotel* (☎ 22810 61400; ❹), on the seafront, and has one taverna.

Páros and Andíparos

Gently and undramatically furled around the single peak of Profitis Ilías, **Páros** has a little of everything one expects from a Greek island: old villages, monasteries, fishing harbours, a labyrinthine capital, nice beaches and varied nightlife. Parikía, the *hóra*, is the major hub of interisland ferry services, so that if you wait long enough you can get to just about any island in the Aegean. However, the island can be touristy and expensive, so it's touch-and-go when it comes to finding rooms and beach space in August, when the attractive inland settlements and the satellite island of **Andíparos** handle the overflow. The August 15 festival here is one of the best such observances in Greece, with a parade of flare-lit fishing boats and fireworks delighting as many Greeks as foreigners, though it's a real feat to secure accommodation around this time.

Parikía and around

PARIKÍA sets the tone architecturally for the rest of Páros, with its ranks of typically Cycladic white houses punctuated by the occasional Venetian-style building and church domes. The busy waterfront is jam-packed with bars, restaurants, hotels and ticket agencies. Continue inland from the **windmill** past the tourist information office and taxi station to reach **Mavroyénous Square**, around which you'll find a maze of houses designed to thwart both the wind and pirates, and the telephone office, police station (and tourist police), banks and Olympic Airways office.

Just beyond the central clutter, though, to the left (southeast) of the windmill, the town has one of the most architecturally interesting churches in the

Aegean – the **Ekatondapylianí**, or "The One Hundred Gated". What's visible today was designed and supervised by Isidore of Miletus in the sixth century, but construction was actually carried out by his pupil Ignatius. Legend tells that it was so beautiful on completion that the master, consumed with jealousy, grappled with his apprentice on the rooftop and both of them fell to their deaths. They are portrayed kneeling at the column bases across the court-yard, the old master tugging at his beard in repentance and his rueful pupil clutching a broken head. The church was substantially altered after a severe earthquake in the eighth century, but its essentially Byzantine aspect remains, its shape an imperfect Greek cross. Enclosed by a great wall to protect its icons from pirates, it is in fact three interlocking churches; the oldest, the chapel of Áyios Nikólaos to the left of the apse, is an adaptation of a pagan building dating from the early fourth century BC. To the right of the courtyard, the **Byzantine Museum** (daily 9am–9pm; €1.50) displays a collection of icons. Behind Ekatondapylianí, the **Archeological Museum** (Tues–Sun 8am–3pm; €2) has a fair collection of antique bits and pieces, its prize exhibits being a fifth-century winged Nike and a piece of the *Parian Chronicle*, a social and cul-tural history of Greece up to 264 BC engraved in marble. Nearby are the exposed, excavated ruins of an **ancient cemetery** used from the eighth century BC until the second century AD, and a few hundred metres east of town lie a smattering of **archaeological sites** including the ruins of a sculpture and pottery workshop from the Hellenistic period as well as an ancient sanctuary.

These sights apart, the real attraction of Parikía is simply to wander the town itself, especially along the meandering **old market street**. Arcaded lanes lead past Venetian-influenced villas, traditional island dwellings and ornate wall-fountains. The town culminates in a seaward Venetian **kástro**, whose surviving east wall incorporates a fifth-century-BC round tower and is constructed using masonry pillaged from a temple of Athena. Part of the base of the temple is still visible next to the beautiful, arcaded church of Áyios Konstandínos and Ayía Eléni which crowns the highest point, from where the fortified hill drops sharply to the quay in a series of hanging gardens.

Practicalities

Ferries dock in Parikía by the windmill; the **bus stop** is 100m or so to the left. Bus routes extend to Náoussa in the north, Poúnda (for Andíparos) in the west, Alykí in the south and Dhryós on the island's east coast (with another very useful service between Dhryós and Náoussa). Be aware that there are two Poúnda stops on Páros, one being the west coast port, the other a beach on the way to Dhryós on the east coast (see p.168). Buses to Náoussa carry on running hourly through the night, while other services stop around midnight. The **airport** is around 12km south of town, close to Alykí – from where ten daily buses run to Parikía.

Most of the island is flat enough for bicycle rides, though you'll be hard pressed to find any push-bikes; motorbikes are more common and are available for rent at several places in town. Forget-Me-Not, along the seafront west of the bus stop, offers a professional and friendly service. Polos Tours, left of the windmill, is one of the more together and friendly **travel agencies**, issuing air tickets when Olympic is shut, and acting as agents for virtually all the boats. Luggage can be left at Santorineos Travel, 50m beyond Polos Tours.

Accommodation

As for **accommodation**, Parikía is a pleasant and central base, but absolutely mobbed in summer. You'll be met off the ferry by locals offering rooms, even at the most unlikely hours; most rooms and hotels are to the left of the windmill, and some can be a long walk. One of the best deals to be had is at the basic *Pension Festos* (☎22840 21635, ℱ22840 24193; ❷) on the backstreets inland, while the *Apostolopoulos Apartments* (☎22840 21338, ℱ22840 21928; ❹) and *Rena Rooms* (☎22840 22220, ℠www.cycladesnet.gr/rena; ❹) are somewhat more upscale options. Of the hotels, the family-run *Argonauta* (☎22840 21440, ℠argonauta.gr; ❹), at the back of Platía Mavroyénous near the National Bank, is highly recommended, as are the apartments maintained by the same family in the Livádhia area to the north of town. Other acceptable hotels include the *Dina* (☎22840 21325, ℱ22840 23525; ❸), further inland, in the market; the *Oasis* (☎22840 21227, ℱ22840 25141; ❹), near the windmill; and the small, family-run *Kypreou* (☎22840 21383; ❹) across from Ekatondapyliani church. Set back from the harbour on the road leading towards Cinema Rex (see p.164), the *Hotel Anna Platanou* (☎22840 21751, ℠www.annaplatanou.gr; ❹; ask for the ten percent discount for Rough Guide readers) is a smart, family-run property with clean, spacious rooms; *Villa Katerina* (☎22840 21864, ℠www.villakaterina.gr; ❹) is another comfortable option. *Koula Camping* (☎22840 22081, ℱ22840 22740), along the seafront east of the bus stop, has good facilities but can get noisy. *Krios Camping* (☎22840 21705, ⓦvirtuals.compulink.gr/krios), across the bay to the north has a nice beach.

Eating, drinking and nightlife

Most of the **eating** establishments in Parikía are along the waterfront to the right (south) of the windmill. Parian Products Farmers' Union, near the police station, is a lovely wine and cheese shop perfect for stocking up for a beach picnic. *Magic*, near the *kástro*, is a good place for breakfast, and *Hibiscus*, next to the town hall, offers generous-sized, wood-oven-baked pizzas. *Plaza*, on the waterfront, has excellent pasta, pizza and Greek dishes. Inland, *Argonauta Restaurant*, near the hotel of the same name, across from the National Bank, is dependably good, and further back in the market is the popular taverna, *Garden of Dionysos*. Excellent but pricey *Apollon*, nearby, is set in a converted 1920 olive press. The most elegant setting for Greek food in town, though, is *Dafni* with its white furnishings set in a leafy garden. A recent trend has seen an influx of crêperies: *Creperie Karpovzi* is the best of the lot, with intimate decor and an eclectic after-hours crowd. *May Tey* serves average Chinese food at moderate mark-up, while Italian dishes can be found at *Cavo D'Oro* in the Livádhia area. *Trata*, behind the ancient cemetery left of the windmill, is recommended for fish; *Ragousis Bakery*, behind the National Bank, is a good place for sandwiches and pastries; and beyond it you'll find the *Happy Green Cow*, a nice vegetarian café.

Parikía has a wealth of **pubs**, **bars** and low-key **discos**. The most popular cocktail bars extend along the seafront, mostly to the south of the windmill, tucked into a series of open squares and offering competing but staggered "happy hours", so that you can drink cheaply for much of the evening. A rowdy crowd favours the conspicuous *Saloon D'Or*, while the *Pirate Bar*, behind the town hall, features jazz and blues. *Evinos* and *Pebbles* are more genteel, the latter pricey but with good sunset views and classical music. Loungey *Kentrikon Central*, near the *Argonauta Hotel*, plays a more eclectic range of music. The "theme" pubs are a bit rough and ready for some – most outrageous are *Sex Club* and the *Dubliner/Paros Rock Complex*, comprising four bars, a snack section, disco and seating area. *Alga*, near the waterfront, on the other hand, is easily the trendiest of the newer places in town, with smart, contemporary decor.

Finally, a thriving cultural centre, Arhilohos (near Ekatondapylianí) caters mostly to locals, with occasional **film** screenings – there are also two open-air cinemas, Neo Rex and Paros, where foreign films are shown in season.

Around Parikía

If you're staying in Parikía, you'll want to get out into the surroundings at some stage, if only to the beach. The most rewarding **excursion** is the hour's walk along the road starting just past the museum up to the **Áyii Anáryiri** monastery. Perched on the bluff above town, this makes a great picnic spot, with cypress groves, a gushing fountain and some splendid views.

There are **beaches** immediately north and south of the harbour, though none are particularly attractive when compared with Páros's best. In fact, you might prefer to avoid the northern stretch altogether and head **south** along the asphalt road instead. The first unsurfaced side-track you come to leads to a small, sheltered beach; fifteen minutes further on is **PARASPÓROS**, with an attractively landscaped and relatively quiet **campsite** (☎22840 21100) and beach near the remains of an ancient temple to Asklepios (see p.341), the god of healing and son of Apollo. Continuing for 45 minutes (or a short hop by bus) brings you to arguably the best of the bunch, **AYÍA IRÍNI**, with good sand and a taverna next to a farm and shady olive grove.

Off in the same direction, but a much longer two-hour haul each way, is **PETALOÚDHES**, the so-called "Valley of the Butterflies", a walled-in oasis where millions of Jersey tiger moths perch on the foliage during early summer (June–Sept 9am–8pm; €2). The trip pays more dividends when combined with a visit to the eighteenth-century nunnery of **Khristoú stoú Dhássous**, at the crest of a ridge twenty minutes to the north. Only women are allowed in the sanctuary, although men can get as far as the courtyard. The succession of narrow drives and donkey paths linking both places begins just south of Parikía. Petaloúdhes can be reached from Parikía by bus (in summer), by scooter or on an overpriced excursion by mule.

Náoussa and around

The second port of Páros, **NÁOUSSA** is a major resort town developed around a charming little port. Modern concrete hotels and attendant trappings have all but swamped its original character, though down at the small harbour fishermen still tenderize octopuses by thrashing them against the walls, and with a little patience you can still find some of its winding, narrow alleys and simple Cycladic houses. The local **festivals** – an annual Fish and Wine Festival on July 2, and an August 23 shindig celebrating an old naval victory over the Turks – are still celebrated with enthusiasm; the latter tends to be brought forward to coincide with the August 15 festival of the Panayía. Most people are here for the local beaches (see p.166) and the relaxed nightlife; there's really only one attraction, a **museum** (daily 9am–1.30pm & 7–9pm; free) in the monastery of Áyios Athanásios, with an interesting collection of Byzantine and post-Byzantine icons from the churches and monasteries around Náoussa.

Despite encroaching development, the town is noted for its nearby beaches and is a good place to head for as soon as you reach Páros. Because it's newer and more fashionable than Parikía, accommodation is more expensive. There is a helpful local council **information centre** just over the bridge, west from the harbour, and Nissiotissa Tours (☎22840 51480, ℱ22840 51189), off the left side of the main square, which can help you find a room, though it specializes in transport. The *Sea House* (☎22840 52198; ❺) on the rocks above Pipéri beach was the first place in Náoussa to let **rooms** and has one of the best locations. Out of season you should haggle for reduced prices at the *Madaki* (☎22840 51475; ❺), just over the bridge west of the harbour, and at the basic, but well-located *Stella* (☎22840 52198; ❸), several blocks inland from the old harbour. If you don't mind a five-minute climb, the friendly *Papadakis* (☎22840 52504, ℱ22840 51269; ❻) has excellent views, and nearby *Katerina Rooms* (☎22840 52326; ❺), are another comfortable option. Most elegant is the boutique **hotel** *Heaven* (☎22840 51549, ⓦwww.heaven-naoussa.gr; ❼), which is also set back away from the harbour, as is *Manos Hotel* (☎22840 51114, ⓦwww.hotelmanos.gr; ❻), which has a lovely pool. There are two **campsites** in the vicinity: the relaxed and friendly *Naoussa* (☎22840 51565), out of town towards Kolymbíthres (see p.166), and the newer *Surfing Beach* (☎22840 51013, ℱ22840 51937) at Sánta María, northeast of Náoussa; both run courtesy minibuses to and from Parikía.

Most of the harbour **tavernas** are decent, specializing in fresh fish and seafood, though there are more interesting places to eat at along the main road leading inland from just beside the little bridge over the canal. *Glaros*, with good barrelled unresined wine, and the *Vengera* opposite, stay open until the early morning hours. Bars cluster around the old harbour: *Linardo* and *Agosta* play dance music, *Camaron* plays mainly Greek music, and *Café Sante*, inland, off the main drag, is a relaxed spot, as is popular *Athinae*. There are several big clubs up from the bus station, including *Nostos* and *Privilege,* popular with a younger late-night crowd.

Local beaches

Pipéri beach is a couple of minutes' walk west of Náoussa's harbour; there are other good-to-excellent beaches within walking distance, and a summer *kaïki* service to connect you for about €4 round trip. To the west, an hour's hike brings you to **Kolymbíthres** ("Basins"), where there are three tavernas and the wind- and sea-sculpted rock formations from which the place draws its name. A few minutes beyond, **Monastíri** beach, below the abandoned Pródhromos monastery, is similarly attractive, and partly nudist. If you go up the hill after Monastíri onto the rocky promontory, the island gradually shelves into the sea via a series of flattish rock ledges, making a fine secluded spot for diving and snorkelling, as long as the sea is calm. Go northeast and the sands are better still, the barren headland spangled with good surfing beaches. **Langéri** is backed by dunes; the best surfing is at **Sánta María**, a trendy beach connected with Náoussa by road, which also has a couple of tavernas, including the pleasant *Aristofanes*; and **Platiá Ámmos** perches on the northeastern tip of the island.

The northeast coast and inland

AMBELÁS hamlet marks the start of a longer trek down the **east coast**. Ambelás itself has a good beach, a small taverna and some rooms and hotels, of which the *Hotel Christiana* (☎22840 51573, ℻22840 52503; ❸) is good value, with great fresh fish, local wine in the restaurant and extremely friendly proprietors. From here a rough track leads south, passing several undeveloped stretches on the way; after about an hour you reach **Mólos beach**, impressive and not particularly crowded. **MÁRMARA**, twenty minutes further on, has rooms to let and makes an attractive place to stay, though the marble that the village is built from and named after has largely been whitewashed over.

If Mármara doesn't appeal, then serene **MÁRPISSA**, just to the south, might – a maze of winding alleys and ageing archways overhung by floral balconies, all clinging precariously to the hillside. There are rooms here too: *Afendakis* (☎ & ℻22840 41141; ❷) has clean and modern rooms and furnished apartments (❻), and you can while away a spare hour climbing up the conical Kéfalos hill, on whose fortified summit the last Venetian lords of Páros were overpowered by the Ottomans in 1537. Today the monastery of **Áyios Andónios** occupies the site, but the grounds are locked; to enjoy the views over eastern Páros and the straits of Náxos fully, pick up the key from the priest in Márpissa before setting out (ask in the minimarket of his whereabouts). On the shore nearby, **PÍSO LIVÁDHI** was once a quiet fishing village, but has been dominated by rampant construction in the name of package tourism. The main reason to visit is to catch a (seasonal) *kaïki* to Ayía Ánna on Náxos; ask at the friendly Perantinos Travel Agency (☎22840 41135) near the bus stop if you need to **stay** overnight here. *Hotel Andromache* (☎22840 41387, ℻22840 41733; ❺) is a good place behind the beach, as is the *Akteon Hotel* (☎22840 41873, ℻22840 41733; ❺) at **Logarás beach** next door. The *Captain Kafkis Camping* (☎ & ℻22840 41479) – a small quiet **campsite** – is out of town on the road up to Márpissa. For a meal try *Vrochas* **taverna**, and head to the *Anchorage* café/bar for afternoon snacks or night-time cocktails.

Inland

The road runs west from Píso Livádhi back to the capital. A medieval flag-stoned path once linked both sides of the island, and parts of it survive in the east between Mármara and the villages around Léfkes. **PRÓDHROMOS**, encountered first, is an old fortified farming settlement with defensive walls girding its nearby monastery, while **LÉFKES** itself, an hour up the track, is perhaps the most beautiful and unspoilt settlement on Páros. The town, whose name means "poplars", flourished from the seventeenth century on, its popu-lation swollen by refugees fleeing from coastal piracy; indeed it was the island's *hóra* during most of the Ottoman period. Léfkes's marbled alleyways and amphitheatrical setting are unparalleled, and also undisturbed by motorbikes, which are forbidden in the middle of town. The central **church** that dominates the town's landscape is made largely of local marble and contains an impressive collection of icons, though it is most often closed; the views over the hill-hug-ging cemetery behind it and across the interior to the sea are the most remark-able on the island. Despite the few rooms, a disco (*Akrovatis*), a taverna on the outskirts and the presence of two oversized hotels – the *Hotel Pantheon* (T 22840 41646, F 22840 41700; ❺), a large 1970s hotel at the top of the village, and *Lefkes Village* (T 22840 41827, F 22840 42398; ❼), a beautiful hotel on the outskirts, with stunning views – the area around the main square has steadfastly resisted change; the central *kafenío* and bakery observe their siestas religiously, and reserved local residents seem to prefer that tourists remain along the coastal resorts.

Thirty minutes further on, through olive groves, is **KÓSTOS**, a simple village and a good place for lunch in a taverna. Any traces of path disappear at **MARÁTHI**, on the site of the ancient marble quarries which once supplied much of Europe. Considered second only to Carrara marble, the last slabs were mined here by the French in the nineteenth century for Napoleon's tomb. From Maráthi, it's easy enough to pick up the bus on to Parikía, but if you want to continue hiking, strike south for the monastery of **Áyios Minás**, twenty minutes away. Various Classical and Byzantine masonry fragments are worked into the walls of this sixteenth-century foundation, and the friendly custodians can put you on the right path up to the convent of **Thapsaná**. From here, other paths lead either back to Parikía (two hours altogether from Áyios Minás), or on up to the island's summit for the last word in views over the Cyclades.

The south of the island

There's little to stop for south of Parikía until **POÚNDA**, 6km away, and then only to catch the ferry to Andíparos (see p.168). What used to be a sleepy hamlet is now a concrete jungle, and neighbouring **ALYKÍ** appears to be permanently under construction. The **airport** is close by, making for lots of unwelcome noise; redeeming features include good-value accommodation at the *Young Inn* (T 697 64 15 232, W www.young-inn.com; ❷) and an excellent beachside restaurant, by the large tamarisk tree. The end of the southern bus route is at Angeriá, about 3km inland of which is the **convent of Áyii Theodhóri**. Its nuns specialize in weaving locally commissioned articles and are further distin-guished as *paleomeroloyítes*, or old-calendarites, meaning that they follow the medieval Orthodox (Julian) calendar, rather than the Gregorian one.

Working your way around the **south coast**, there are two routes east to Dhryós. Either retrace your steps to Angeriá and follow the (slightly inland) coastal road, which skirts a succession of isolated coves and small beaches, or keep on across the foothills from Áyii Theodhóri – a shorter walk. Aside from an abundant water supply (including a duck pond) and surrounding orchards, **DHRYÓS** village is mostly modern and characterless, lacking even a well-defined *platía*. Follow the lane signed "Dhryós Beach", however, and things improve a bit.

Between here and Píso Livádhi to the north are several sandy coves – Khryssí Aktí ("Golden Beach"), Tzirdhákia, Mezádha, Poúnda (not to be confused with the port of the same name on the opposite coast) and Logarás – prone to pummelling by the *meltémi*, yet all favoured to varying degrees by campers and by windsurfers making a virtue out of necessity. **KHRYSSÍ AKTÍ** is now thoroughly overrun with tavernas, room complexes and the whole range of watersports; there are also tavernas at Logarás, but other facilities are concentrated in Dhryós, which is still the focal point of this part of the island.

Andíparos

Andíparos was once quiet and unspoiled, but now the secret is definitely out. The waterfront is lined with new hotels and apartments, and in high season it can be full, though in recent years families seem to be displacing the young, international crowd. The island has managed to hold on to a friendly small-island atmosphere and still has a lot going for it, including good sandy beaches and an impressive cave, and the rooms and hotels are less expensive than on Páros.

Most of the population of eight hundred live in the large low-lying northern **village**, across the narrow straits from Páros, the new development on the outskirts concealing an attractive traditional settlement around the *kástro*. A long, flag-stoned pedestrian street forms its backbone, leading from the jetty to the Cycladic houses around the outer wall of the *kástro*, which was built by Leonardo Loredano in the 1440s as a fortified settlement safe from pirate raids – the Loredano coat of arms can still be seen on a house in the courtyard. The only way into the courtyard is through a pointed archway from the *platía*, where several cafés are shaded by a giant eucalyptus. Inside, more whitewashed houses surround two churches and a cistern built into the surviving base of the central tower.

Andíparos's **beaches** begin right outside town: **Psaralíki**, just to the south with golden sand and tamarisks for shade, is much better than Sifnéïko (aka "Sunset") on the opposite side of the island. Villa development is starting to follow the newly paved road down the east coast, but has yet to get out of hand. **Glýfa**, 4km down, is another good beach and, further south, **Sorós** has rooms and tavernas. On the west coast there are some fine small sandy coves at **Áyios Yeóryios**, the end of the road, and another long stretch of sand at **Kalóyeros**. *Kaïkia* make daily trips round the island and, less frequently, to the uninhabited islet of Dhespotikó, opposite Áyios Yeóryios.

The great **cave** (summer daily 10.45am–3.45pm; €3) in the south of the island is the chief attraction for day-trippers. In these eerie chambers the Marquis de Nointel, Louis XIV's ambassador to Constantinople, celebrated Christmas Mass in 1673 while a retinue of five hundred, including painters, pirates, Jesuits and Turks, looked on; at the exact moment of midnight explosives were detonated to emphasize the enormity of the event. Although electric light and cement steps have diminished its mystery and grandeur, the cave remains impressive. Tour buses (€3 round trip) and public buses (€1 one way) run from the port every hour in season; bus services and opening hours are reduced out of season, and in winter you'll have to fetch the key for the cave from the mayor or village council (☎22840 61218).

Practicalities

To get here, you have a choice of **boats** from Parikía (hourly in season, weather permitting; 40min), arriving at the jetty opposite the main street, or the car ferry from Poúnda (every 30min; 10min), arriving 150m to the south.

There are plenty of **hotels** along the waterfront, including *Anargyros* (☏22840 61204; ❸), which has good, basic rooms. More upmarket places to the north of the jetty include *Mantalena* (☏22840 61206; ❺) and *Artemis* (☏22840 61460; ❺), while inland there are some cheaper rooms as well as the *Hotel Galini* (☏22840 61420; ❺) to the left of the main street. The popular **campsite** (☏22840 61221) is a ten-minute walk northeast along a track, next to its own nudist beach; the water here is shallow enough for campers to wade across to the neighbouring islet of Dhipló. For peace and quiet with a degree of comfort try *Oliaros* (☏22840 25305, ℻22840 25304; ❹) at Áyios Yeóryios, a long stretch of beach with several tavernas, of which *Captain Pipinos* is recommended.

The best of the waterfront **tavernas** is *Anargyros*, below the hotel of the same name. The main street leads up beside it, and *Klimataria*, 100m inland off to the left, has tables in a pleasant garden, though it's only open at night. *The Internet Cafe*, also on the main street, has excellent coffee, as does *Romvi's* on the water-front. There are plenty of **bars** around the eucalyptus-filled *platía*, where a festive atmosphere prevails at night. *Café Margarita* is a pleasant street-side hang-out on the way up to this *platía*, and the *Nautica* is probably the liveliest of the waterfront spots. For quiet music and views of the mountains try *Yam*, an out-door restaurant and bar near the *Klimataria*. A short-schedule **bank**, a **post office**, a cinema and several **travel agents** round up the list of amenities.

Náxos

Náxos is the largest and most fertile of the Cyclades, and, with its green and mountainous highland scenery, seems immediately distinct from many of its neighbours. The difference is accentuated by the **unique architecture** of many of the interior villages: the Venetian Duchy of the Aegean, which ruled from the thirteenth to the sixteenth century, left towers and fortified mansions scattered throughout the island, while medieval Cretan refugees bestowed a singular character upon Náxos's eastern settlements.

Today Náxos could easily support itself without tourists by relying on its pro-duction of potatoes, olives, grapes and lemons, but it has thrown in its lot with mass tourism, so that parts of the island are now almost as busy and commer-cialized as Páros in season. But the island certainly has plenty to see if you know where to look: the highest mountains in the Cyclades, intriguing central valleys, a spectacular north coast and marvellously sandy beaches in the south-west. It is also renowned for its wines, cheese – sharp *kefalotýri* and milder *grav-iéra* – and *kítron*, a sweet liqueur distilled from the fruit of this citrus tree.

Náxos Town

A long causeway, built to protect the harbour to the north, connects **NÁXOS TOWN** (or Hóra) with the islet of Palátia – the place where, according to legend, Theseus abandoned Ariadne on his way home from Crete. The famous stone **Portára** that has greeted visitors for 2500 years is the portal of a temple of Apollo, built on the orders of the tyrant Lygdamis in the sixth century BC, but never completed. Most of the town's life goes on down by the

NÁXOS

Páros ◀

Ikaría & Sámos ▶ Dhonoússa ▶

Abrámi ♨ Ayiá Apóllon
Hília Vrýssi
Faneroménis ‡ Myrísis
Amití
Koronídha Liónos
Áyiou Ioánnou Galíni Kóronos
Khryssostómou ‡ Engarés
NÁXOS Kouronohóri Kinídharos
TOWN
(Hóra) Melanés Móni
Áyios Prokópios Glinádho Flério Panayía
Mýli Dhrossianí
Áyii Apáno Kalóxilos Apíranthos
Ayía Ánna Galanádho Kástro
Potamiá Akádhimos Moutsoúna
Tripodhes
Áyios Matthéos ‡ Sangrí Ayii Filóti
Káto Sangrí Apóstoli
Pláka Áno Sangrí Dhanakós
TRAGÉA
▲ Mt Zás
Kastráki
Psilí Ámmos
▲ Apalírou
Ÿ. Ioánnis Pýrgos
PYRGÁKI Himárou
Alíko ▲ Kavaláris
Áno
Pyrgáki ▲ Plotsóri Pánormos Koufoníssi
Ayiássos
Káto
Kálandou Koufoníssi
Kéros

N

0   5 km

Íos & Thíra ◀ Amorgós ▶

Iráklia & Skhinoússa ▼

crowded port esplanade or just behind it; back streets and alleys behind the
harbour lead up through low arches of the old town, Bourgos, to the fortified
kástro from where Marco Sanudo and his successors ruled over the Cyclades.
Only two of the *kástro*'s original seven towers remain, though the **north gate**
(approached from Apóllon and known as the Traní Portá or "Great Gate")
survives as a splendid example of a medieval fort entrance. The Venetians'
Catholic descendants, now dwindled to a few old ladies, still live in the old
mansions which encircle the site, many with ancient coats of arms above crumbling doorways. One of these, the **Domus Della-Rocca-Barozzi** (daily
10am–3pm & 7.30–10.30pm; €3), is open to the public and offers the best
views from the *kástro*; the guided tour (€5) even includes a tasting from the
family's wine cellar, and live classical concerts often animate the adjoining
courtyard on summer evenings. Other brooding relics survive in the same area:
a seventeenth-century Ursuline convent and the Roman Catholic cathedral,
restored in questionable taste in the 1950s, though still displaying a thirteenth-
century crest inside. Nearby, was one of Ottoman Greece's first schools, the
French School; opened in 1627 for Catholic and Orthodox students alike, its

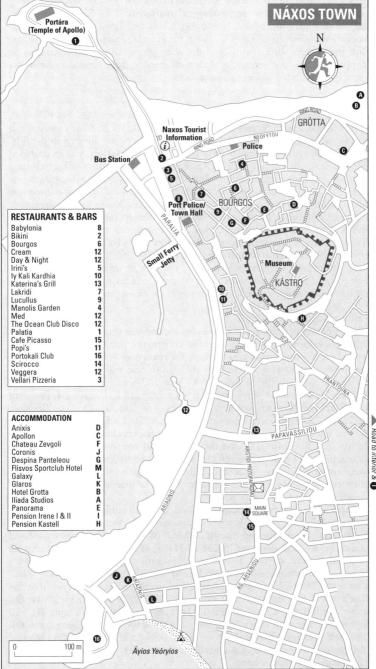

NÁXOS TOWN

Portára
(Temple of Apollo) ❶

GRÓTTA

Ⓐ
Ⓑ

Ⓒ

RING ROAD

NEOFYTOU

Naxos Tourist
Information
ⓘ
❷

Police

Bus Station

❸
❺

❹

Ⓗ

❼
❽

❻

BOURGOS

Ⓓ
Ⓔ

Port Police/
Town Hall

❾
Ⓖ

Ⓕ

PARALIA

Small Ferry
Jetty

Museum

❿
⓫

KÁSTRO

Ⓗ

RESTAURANTS & BARS

Babylonia	8
Bikini	2
Bourgos	6
Cream	12
Day & Night	12
Irini's	5
Iy Kali Kardhia	10
Katerina's Grill	13
Lakridi	7
Lucullus	9
Manolis Garden	4
Med	12
The Ocean Club Disco	12
Palatia	1
Cafe Picasso	15
Popi's	11
Portokali Club	16
Scirocco	14
Veggera	12
Vellari Pizzeria	3

ACCOMMODATION

Anixis	D
Apollon	C
Chateau Zevgoli	F
Coronis	J
Despina Panteleou	G
Flisvos Sportclub Hotel	M
Galaxy	L
Glaros	K
Hotel Grotta	B
Iliada Studios	A
Panorama	E
Pension Irene I & II	I
Pension Kastell	H

PRANTOUNA

⓬

⓭

PAPAVASSILIOU

ARIADNIS

ARISTIDOU PROTOPAPADAKI

AG. ARSENIOU

MAIN
SQUARE

⓮

⓯

Ⓙ
Ⓚ

ARIADNIS

Ⓛ

⓰

Áyios Yeóryios

0   100 m

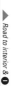 Road to interior & ❶

Ⓜ   Airport ▼

pupils included, briefly, Nikos Kazantzakis (see p.618). The school building now houses an excellent **archeological museum** (Tues–Sun 8.30am–3pm; €3), with finds from Náxos, Koufoníssi, Kéros and Dhonoússa, including an important collection of Early Cycladic figurines. Archaic and Classical sculpture and pottery dating from Neolithic through to Roman times are also on display. On the roof terrace, a Hellenistic mosaic floor shows a nereid (sea nymph) surrounded by deer and peacocks.

Practicalities

Náxos is served by a tiny **airport**, located just a few minutes' bus ride from Náxos Town. Large **ferries** dock along the northerly harbour causeway; all small boats and the very useful *Express Skopelitis* ferry use the jetty in the fishing harbour, not the main car-ferry dock. The **bus station** is at its landward end; buses run five times a day to Apóllon (€3.40), with one of the morning services going via Engarés and Abrámi, which is much quicker though not any cheaper. There are six buses a day to Apíranthos via Filóti, two of these going on to Moutsoúna on the east coast. Buses run (every 30min 8am–midnight) to Áyios Prokópios, Ayía Ánna and as far as the *Maragas* campsite on Pláka beach, and four times a day to Pyrgáki. Printed timetables are available from the bus station. More convenient are the **day-tours** of Náxos (€18) that can be booked at **Naxos Tourist Information** (☎22850 25201, ℻22850 25200), on the seafront near the jetty, which offers a wealth of information. It's also the best place to book special tours to the Minor Cyclades as well as accommodation, since the proprietor maintains some of the finest properties on the island.

Accommodation

There's plenty of accommodation in Náxos and you should have no problem finding somewhere to stay. Once you've run the gauntlet of touts on the jetty, there are three basic areas to look for **rooms** in Náxos Town: in the old quarter near the *kástro*, where they are hard to find and relatively expensive; up to the left (north) of town in Grótta; and south of town near Áyios Yeóryios beach, where they are most abundant and less expensive, but with significant night-time noise from clubs and discos. *Despina Panteleou* (☎22850 22356; ❸) and *Pension Kastell* (☎22850 23082, ⓦwww.kastell.gr; ❸) are good choices near the *kástro*. In Grótta, try *Iliada Studios* (☎22850 23303, ℻22850 24687; ❹), on the cliff beyond town, with good views out to sea. Just out of the centre, off the main road to the interior, try the clean, spacious *Pension Irene* (☎22850 23169, ℮irenepension@hotmail.com; ❸), with two locations, one with a nice pool. The friendly proprietors meet guests regularly at the ferry jetty.

Hotel choices near the *kástro* include the charming traditional *Chateau Zevgoli* (☎22850 22993, ⓦwww.naxostownhotels.com; ❼), with antique-furnished, air-conditioned rooms, *Anixis* (☎22850 22932, ⓦwww.hotel-anixis.gr; ❼) and *Panorama* (☎22850 24404; ❺). Across from the cathedral you'll find one of the newest and best, the *Apollon* (☎22850 22468, ⓦwww.naxostownhotels.com; ❻). Up in Grótta there's the friendly *Hotel Grotta* (☎22850 22215, ⓦwww.hotelgrotta.gr; ❺), while near Áyios Yeóryios beach you'll find economical *Coronis* (☎22850 22297, ℻22850 23984; ❸), more comfortable *Glaros* (☎22850 23101, ⓦwww.hotelglaros.com; ❺), and the more upscale *Galaxy* (☎22850 22422, ⓦwww.hotel-galaxy.com; ❼). The self-sufficient *Flisvos Sportclub Hotel* (☎ & ℻22850 24308, ⓦwww.flisvos-sportclub.com; ❼), has a windsurf centre offering rental of boards, sails, catamarans, as well as lessons.

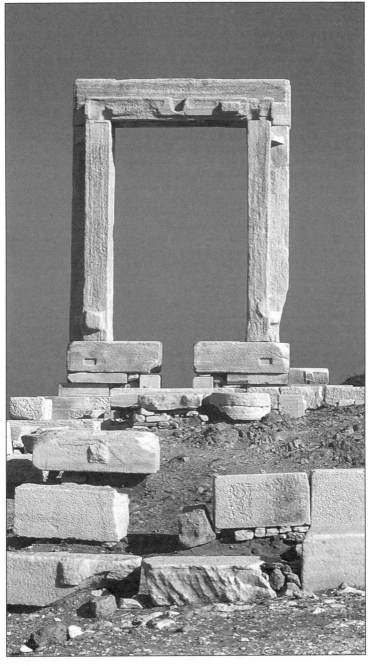

△ Temple of Apollo, Náxos

Eating, drinking and nightlife

One of the best quayside breakfast bars is the *Bikini* crêperie; the nearby *Vellari Pizzeria* is a great spot for a quick meal while waiting for a ferry. Further along to the south are a string of relatively expensive but simple oven-food **tavernas** – *Irini's*, close to the jetty, is generally regarded as the best of the lot, while *Iy Kali Kardhia* is typical, serving acceptable casserole dishes washed down with barrelled wine. Nearby, *Popi's*, is a veritable institution, specializing in lamb raised on the proprietor's own land; inside there's a wine, *kítron* and cheese shop. *Cafe Picasso*, near the main square, serves Mexican food (evenings only), while *Scirocco*, close by, is excellent, though known as much for the long queue to get in, as its traditional meals. A short stroll north of the square, *Katerina's Grill*, is as good for people watching as for its Greek dishes. *Manolis Garden*, near the ancient agora, is one of the most pleasant of the Bourgos tourist eateries, and intimate *Lucullus*, nearby, is the most romantic as well as the oldest. *Portokali Club* on the headland to the south of town is a club, café and restaurant with good views over Áyios Yeóryios bay, though its construction over a prime natural setting caused some local controversy. The best place to watch the sunset is from the *Palatia* fish taverna near Portára, which, despite its location, is surprisingly reasonable and serves great food. There's a good **bakery** about midway along the harbour front. For local cheese, wine, *kítron*, spices and other dried comestibles, head for Tirokomika Proionia Naxou, a delightful old store on Papavassilíou.

Much of the evening action goes on at the south end of the waterfront, where you'll find café-bars and clubs such as *Day & Night*, *Cream*, *Veggera*, *Med* and the *Ocean Club Disco*. Near the jetty, the island's first gay bar, *Babylonia*, is discreetly situated on an upper level. *Lakridi*, behind the town hall, plays jazz and classical music. There's also an open-air **cinema**, the Cine Astra, on the road to the airport at the southern end of town; it's a fair walk out, but the Ayía Ánna bus stops here.

The southwestern beaches

The **beaches** around Náxos Town are worth sampling. For some unusual swimming just to the **north** of the port, beyond the causeway, **Grótta** is easiest to reach. Besides the caves after which the place is named, the remains of submerged Cycladic buildings are said to be visible, though only when you're out in the water. The finest spots, though, are all **south** of town, the entire southwestern coastline boasting a series of excellent **beaches** accessible by regular bus. **ÁYIOS YEÓRYIOS**, a long sandy bay fringed by the southern extension of the hotel "colony", is within walking distance. There's a line of cafés and tavernas at the northern end of the beach, and a windsurfing school, plus *Camping Naxos* (☎22850 23500), which isn't recommended; try the far more attractively sited ones on Pláka beach (see opposite). A word of warning for campers: although this entire coast is relatively sheltered from the *meltémi*, the plains behind are boggy and you should bring along mosquito repellent.

Buses take you to **ÁYIOS PROKÓPIOS** beach, with plenty of reasonably priced hotels, rooms and basic tavernas, plus the upmarket *Hotel Lianos Village* (☎22850 26366, ✉lianos-village@nax.forthnet.gr; ⑦), with its pleasant pool setting. *Anessio* and *Colosseo* are two excellent restaurants here, and *Kahlua* and *Splash* are good cafés. Rapid development along this stretch means that this resort has blended into the next resort of **AYÍA ÁNNA**, further along the busy road; here you will find accommodation of similar price and quality. The seaview *Iria Beach Hotel* (☎22850 42600, ⓦwww.iria-beach.com; ⑤) and the nearby *Kouros Hotel* (☎22850 29151, ℻22850 29153; ❸) are comfortable options. *Kabouras, Hios* and *Gorgona* **tavernas** are all excellent traditional places with good prices; *Bar Bagianni* on the road from Áyia Ánna to Áyios Prokópios is also recommended. Moving along the coast, away from the built-up area, the beach here is nudist.

Beyond the headland, stretch the five kilometres of **PLÁKA** beach, a vegetation-fringed expanse of white sand. Things are not so built up here, and parts of the beach are nudist (past *Plaka* campsite). There are two suitably laid-back and friendly **campsites** here: *Maragas* (☎ & ℻22850 24552), which also has double rooms (❷), and the newer *Plaka* (☎22850 42700, ℻22850 42701), a little further along, which is small and quiet with a few inexpensive bungalows (❷). The *Hotel Orkos Village* (☎22850 75321, Ⓦwww.orkos-naxos.com; ❻) has apartments in an attractive location, on a hillside above the coast between Pláka beach and Mikrí Vígla, and the *Plaza Beach Hotel* (☎22850 29400, Ⓦwww.plazabeachhotel.gr; ❼) is a glittering new mega-resort at the southern end of the beach that is likely to push the nudists further out. Good **tavernas** in the vicinity of Pláka are *Golden Beach, Paradiso*, and *Galini*, while *Amore Mio* is the most romatic spot for dining with views of the coast. The nearby *Waffle House* has a tasty range of home-made ice cream.

For real isolation, go to the other side of the Mikrí Vígla headland which begins at the southern edge of Pláka beach, along a narrow footpath across the cliff-edge, to **KASTRÁKI** beach; towards the middle of the beach, *Areti* (☎22850 75292; ❺) has apartments and a restaurant, but the fresh food at *Axiotissa* **taverna** is unbeatable. A few people camp around the taverna on the small headland a little further down. In summer, this stretch – all the way from Mikrí Vígla down to Pyrgáki – attracts camper vans and windsurfers from all over Europe. On the **Alíko** promontory to the south of Kastráki there is a small nudist beach known locally as "Hawaii Beach" for the vibrant blue colour of its waters.

From Kastráki, it's a couple of hours' walk up to the Byzantine castle of **Apalírou** which held out for two months against the besieging Marco Sanudo. The fortifications are relatively intact and the views magnificent. **Pyrgáki** beach has a couple of tavernas and a few rooms; four kilometres further on is **Ayiássos** beach.

The rest of the **southern coast** – virtually the whole of the southeast of the island – is remote and mountain-studded; you'd have to be a dedicated and well-equipped camper/hiker to get much out of the region.

Central Náxos and the Tragéa

Although buses bound for Apóllon (in the north) link up the central Naxian villages, the core of the island – between Náxos Town and Apíranthos – is best explored by motorbike or on foot. Much of the region is well off the beaten track, and can be a rewarding excursion if you've had your fill of beaches; Christian Ucke's *Walking Tours on Naxos*, available from bookshops in Náxos town, is a useful guide for hikers.

Once out of Hóra, you quickly arrive at the neighbouring villages of **GLINÁDHO** and **GALANÁDHO**, forking respectively right and left. Both are scruffy market centres: Glinádho is built on a rocky outcrop above the Livádhi plain, while Galanádho displays the first of Náxos's fortified mansions and an unusual "double church". A combined Orthodox chapel and Catholic sanctuary separated by a double arch, the church reflects the tolerance both by the Venetians during their rule, and by the locals, each other's religions.

Continue beyond Glinádho to **TRÍPODHES** (ancient Biblos), 9km from Náxos Town. Noted by Homer for its wines, this old-fashioned agricultural village has nothing specific to offer, but you can enjoy a coffee at the shaded *kafenío*. The start of a long but rewarding walk is a rough road (past the parish church) which leads down the colourful Pláka valley, past an old watchtower and the Byzantine church of **Áyios Matthéos** ("mosaic pavement"), and ends at the glorious Pláka beach (see p.175).

To the east, the twin villages of **SANGRÍ**, on a vast plateau at the head of a long valley, can be reached by continuing to follow the left-hand fork past Galanádho, a route which allows a look at the domed eighth-century church of **Áyios Mámas** (on the left), once the Byzantine cathedral of the island but neglected during the Venetian period and now a sorry sight. Either way, **Káto Sangrí** boasts the remains of a Venetian castle, while **Áno Sangrí** is a comely little place, all cobbled streets and fragrant courtyards. Thirty minutes' stroll away, on a path leading south out of the village, are the partially reconstructed remains of a Classical temple of Demeter.

The Tragéa

From Sangrí, the road twists northeast into the **Tragéa** region, scattered with olive trees and occupying a vast highland valley. It's a good jumping-off point for all sorts of exploratory rambling, and **HALKÍ** is a fine introduction to what is to come. Set high up, 16km from the port, it's a noble and silent town with some lovely churches, including the **Panayía Protóthronis** church, with its eleventh- to thirteenth-century frescoes; it only opens to visitors in the morning. Nearby are the romantic ruins of the seventeenth-century Venetian **Grazia-Barozzi Tower**. Tourists wanting to stay here are still something of a rarity, although you can usually get a **room** in someone's house by asking at the store. *Yiannis* **taverna** is the focal point of village activity and has a good selection of fresh *mezédhes* to enjoy with a glass of ouzo. Nearby is the distillery and shop of Vallindras Naxos Citron, whose charming proprietors explain the process of producing *kítron* followed by a little tasting session. The olive and citrus plantations surrounding Halkí are crisscrossed by paths and tracks, the groves dotted with numerous Byzantine chapels and the ruins of fortified *pýrgi* or Venetian mansions.

The road from Halkí heads north to **MONÍ**. Just before the village, you pass the sixth-century monastery of **Panayía Dhrossianí**, a group of stark, grey-stone buildings with some excellent frescoes; the monks allow visits at any time, though you may have to contend with coach tours from Náxos Town. Moní itself enjoys an outstanding view of the Tragéa and surrounding mountains, and has four tavernas, plus some rooms. The main road leads on to Kinídharos, with an old marble quarry above the village; a few kilometres beyond, a signpost points you down a rough track to the left, to **FLÉRIO** (commonly called Melanés). The most interesting of the ancient marble quarries on Náxos, this is home to two famous **koúri**, dating from the sixth century BC, that were left recumbent and unfinished because of flaws in the material. Even so, they're finely detailed figures, over five metres in length. One of the statues lies in a private, irrigated orchard; the other is up a hillside some distance above, and you will need to seek local guidance to find it.

From Flério you could retrace your steps to the road and head back to Hóra via Mýli and the ruined Venetian castle at Kouronohóri, both pretty hamlets connected by footpaths. If you're feeling more adventurous, ask to be directed south to the footpath which leads over the hill to the Potamiá villages. The first of these, **ÁNO POTAMIÁ**, has a fine taverna and a rocky track back towards the Tragéa. Once past the valley, the landscape becomes craggy and barren, the forbidding Venetian fortress of **Apáno Kástro** perched on a peak just south of the path. This is believed to have been Sanudo's summer home, but the fortified site goes back further, if the Mycenaean tombs found nearby are any indication. From the fort, paths lead back to Halkí in around an hour. Alternatively, you can continue further southwest down the Potamiá valley towards Hóra, passing first the ruined **Cocco Pýrgos** – said to be haunted by one Constantine Cocco, the victim of a seventeenth-century clan feud – on the way to **MÉSO POTAMIÁ**, joined by some isolated dwellings with its twin village **KÁTO POTAMIÁ**, nestling almost invisibly among the greenery flanking the creek.

At the far end of the gorgeous Tragéa valley, **FILÓTI**, the largest village in the region, lies on the slopes of Mount Zás (or Zeus) which, at 1000m, is the highest point in the Cyclades. Under the shade of the plane trees on the main *platía* are several pleasant *kafenía*, as well as *Babulas Grill-Restaurant* (℡22850 31426; ②), which has the best rooms in the village. To get an idea of the old village, climb the steps up the hill starting at the *platía*. A turning at the southern end of the village is signposted to the **Pýrgos Himárou**, a remote twenty-metre Hellenistic watchtower, and **Kalándou** beach on the south coast; beyond the turning the road is unpaved. There are no villages in this part of the island, so bring supplies if you're planning to camp. From the village, it's a round-trip walk of three to four hours on mostly unmarked trails to the summit of **Zás**, a climb which rewards you with an astounding panorama of virtually the whole of Náxos and its Cycladic neighbours. Save yourself the rather tedious walk along the main Filóti–Apóllon road by taking the bus towards Apóllon and asking the driver to let you off at the Dhánakos turning, where the waymarked final approach trail begins just beside a small chapel on your right. There is also a marked turn-off to the Zás Cave, a pleasant place for a picnic, but not the best point from which to tackle the steep ascent to the summit.

Apíranthos

APÍRANTHOS (Apérathos in local dialect), a hilly, winding 10km beyond the cave, shows the most Cretan influence of all the interior villages. It is a good quiet place to stay for a few days, and being high in the mountains is noticeably cooler and greener than the coast. There are four small **museums** and two Venetian fortified mansions, while the square contains a miniature church with a three-tiered bell tower. Ask to be pointed to the start of the spectacular **path** up over the ridge behind; this ends either in Moní or Kalóxilos, depending on whether you fork right or left respectively at the top. Cafés and tavernas on the main street look out over a terraced valley below; the nationally renowned **taverna** *Leftheri*, here, is generally regarded as one of the best restaurants on the island. **Rooms** are available but are not advertised – ask in the cafés or in the embroidery shop.

Apíranthos has a beach annexe of sorts at **Moutsoúna**, 12km east. Emery mined near Apíranthos used to be transported here by means of an aerial funicular and then shipped out of the port. The industry collapsed in the 1980s, and the sandy cove beyond the dock now features a growing colony of holiday villas and the excellent *Ostria* taverna. An unpaved road heads south along the coast to a remote sandy beach at **Psilí Ámmos** – ideal for self-sufficient campers, but you must take enough water. From here a track carries on to relatively secluded **Pánormos** beach in the southeastern corner of the island.

Northern Náxos

The route through the mountains from Apíranthos to Apóllon is very scenic, and the road surface is in good condition all the way. Jagged ranges and

②

hairpin bends confront you before reaching Kóronos, the halfway point, where a road off to the right threads through a wooded valley to **Liónas**, a tiny and very Greek port with a pebble beach. You'd do better to continue, past Skadhó, to the remote, emery-miners' village of **KORONÍDHA** which is a pleasing, vine-covered settlement – the highest village on the island and the original home of *kítron* liqueur.

Back on the main road, a series of slightly less hairy bends leads down a long valley to **APÓLLON**, a small resort with two beaches: a tiny and crowded stretch of sand backed by cafés and restaurants, and a longer and quieter stretch of shingle, popular mainly with Greek families. The only major attraction is a **koúros**, approached by a path from the main road just above the village. Lying *in situ* at a former marble quarry, this largest of Náxos's abandoned stone figures is just over ten metres long, but, compared with those at Flério, disappointingly lacking in detail. Here since 600 BC, it serves as a singular reminder of the Naxians' traditional skill; the famous Delian lions (see p.155) are also made of Apollonian marble. Not surprisingly, bus tours descend upon the village during the day, and Apóllon is now quite a popular little place. The local festival, celebrated on August 28–29, is one of Náxos's best.

It's easy to make a round trip of the north coast and inland villages by bus from Náxos Town. The coastal road is spectacularly beautiful, going high above the sea for most of the way, making it more like parts of Crete or the mainland than other islands. Ten kilometres past the northern cape sprouts the beautiful **Ayiá** *pýrgos*, or tower, another foundation (in 1717) of the Cocco family. There's a tiny hamlet nearby, and, 7km further along, a track leads off to **Abrámi** beach, an idyllic spot with a highly recommended family-run taverna and **rooms** to let, *Pension and Restaurant Efthimios* (☎22850 63244, ⓔabram@can.gr; ②). Just beyond the hamlet of Hília Vrýssi is the abandoned **monastery of Faneroménis**, built in 1606. Carrying on along the coastal road you will reach Engarés valley, at the foot of which is another quiet beach, **Amití**, which can be reached via one of two dirt tracks, the most obvious being the one leading down from Galíni, only 6km from Hóra. Inland from Galíni, the unspoiled town of **Engarés** is home to the excellent *Haris* taverna, while *Vasilis* in equally undervisited **Melanés** serves chickens and game raised on site. On the final stretch back to the port, you pass a unique eighteenth-century Turkish fountain-house and the fortified monastery of **Ayíou Ioánnou Khryssostómou**, where a couple of aged nuns are still in residence. A footpath from the monastery and the road below lead straight back to town.

Minor Cyclades

Four of the six small islands in the patch of the Aegean between Náxos and Amorgós have slid from obscurity into fashion in recent years. The group is known commonly as the Minor Cyclades and includes **Áno Koufoníssi**, **Skhinoússa**, **Iráklia** and **Dhonoússa**. The islands' new popularity is hastening the development of better facilities and higher prices, but with little room for expansion and only limited ferry service, they've managed to avoid the mass tourism of the rest of the Cyclades. For real peace and quiet – what the Greeks call *isykhiá* – visit outside of August or make the crossing from Áno Koufoníssi to **Kéros**, with no permanent population but an important archeological site, and **Káto Koufoníssi**, inhabited only by goatherds.

▲ *Amorgós*

Dhonoússa (see inset) ▲

MINIC CYCLADES

Andikéri

Kéros

• Dhaskalió

Áno Koufoníssi

Pori

114m ▲

Harakópou
Finíkas

Hóra

Káto Koufoníssi

Panayía †

Neró

3 km

0

N

Skhinoússa

Hóra

Mersíni

Tsigoúri

Livádhi

Dhonoússa

Skyloníssi

▲ Papás
383m

Haravyí

Kalotarítissa

Mersíni

Stavrós *Kéndros* *Livádhi*

Iráklia

Áyios Yeóryios

Livádhi

Pigádhi

Panayía (Hóra)

▲ *Papás*
419m

Áyios Athanásios

Vourkária

🏛 *Áyios Ioánnis
Cave*

Alimiá

Karvounólakos

Náxos ▲

Though a Pireás-based **ferry** has been known to call at the islands – linking them with Náxos and Amorgós and (sometimes) Páros and Sýros – the small, local *Express Skopelitis* is a more frequent fixture, leaving the little ferry quay in Náxos almost daily in August to head to most of the islets. At other times of year, don't arrive unless you're in no hurry to push on.

Koufoníssi and Kéros

Áno Koufoníssi (usually referred to simply as Koufoníssi) is the most populous island of the group, and is reachable by ferries from Náxos several times per week in high season, outside of which you might better use the private vessel of Prasinos Excursions from Pánormos (T22850 71438; €20–50 per person depending on size of group). With some of the least-spoiled beaches in the Cyclades, the island is attracting increasing numbers of Greek and foreign holidaymakers. Small enough to walk round in a morning, the island can actually feel overcrowded in July and August.

The old single-street village of **HÓRA**, on a low hill behind the harbour, is being engulfed by new room and hotel development, but still has a friendly, small-island atmosphere. A map by the jetty shows where to find all the island's **rooms**: the popular restaurant and pension *Melissa* (T & F22850 71454; ❺) is a good choice near the harbour. The most upmarket options include *Hotel Aegeon* (T & F22850 74050; ❺), by the village beach; *Katerina Studios* (T22850 71670, F22850 71455; ❸); and *Ostria Village* (T & F22850 71671; ❺), both east of the village. Basic *Akroyiali* (T22850 71685; ❸) is on the front just beyond the beach; Yeoryia Kouveou has beautifully situated rooms at *Hondros Kavos* (T22850 71707, F22850 71441; ❸), outside the village to the east; and the *Petros Club* (T & F22850 71728; ❺) is in a quiet position inland, with excellent views.

Koufoníssi is noted for its fish **tavernas**; *Remezzo*, up in Hóra, has excellent food and a cozy atmosphere, while *Captain Nicola* at the bay is cheaper than most and has a fine array of seafood. Nearby *To Steki Tis Marias* is a good breakfast place with a few rooms (❷), and has views over the narrow channel to Káto Koufoníssi. The most popular nightspot is *Soroccos*, a lively café-bar on the front, while good alternatives include *Ta Kalamia*, with a quieter choice of music and *Nikitas*, which has excellent views. *To Palio Fanari*, to the west of the village, is the club favoured by locals, playing a mix of dance and Greek music. The ticket agency is on the main street, and there is a "post office" (limited hours) just north of the town hall.

All the good beaches are in the southeast of the island, getting better as you go east along a dirt path that skirts the coastline along the edge of low cliffs. **Fínikas**, a ten-minute walk from the village, is the first of four wide coves with gently shelving golden sand, where there are rooms and a good taverna. Further east is **Harakópou**, which has a windswept **campsite** (T22850 71683) with cane shade and rather poor facilities on the headland before the next beach, **Thános**. Next is **Platiá Poúnda**, where caves have been hollowed out of the cliffs. Further east, the path rounds a rocky headland to **Porí**, a much longer and wilder beach, backed by dunes and set in a deep bay. It can be reached more easily from the village by following a track heading inland through the low scrub-covered hills.

KÁTO KOUFONÍSSI, the practically uninhabited island to the southwest, has a seasonal taverna and some more secluded beaches; a *kaïki* shuttles people across until late in the evening. A festival is held here on August 15, at the church of the Panayía. The island of **Kéros** is harder to reach, but if there is a willing group of people keen to visit the ancient site, a boat and boatmen can be hired for around €50 for the day.

Skhinoússa

A little to the southwest, the island of **Skhinoússa** is just beginning to awaken to its tourist potential. Boats dock at the small port of Mersíni, which has one *pension* (☎22850 71159; ❹) and a couple of cafés; a road leads up to **HÓRA**, aka Panayía, the walk taking just over ten minutes. As you enter the village, the well-stocked **tourist centre** is one of the first buildings you'll come across. The principal ferry agent, the centre has a metred phone and sells both Greek and foreign press.

Accommodation is mostly in fairly simple rooms, such as *Anesi* (☎22850 71180; ❷), *Agnadema* (☎22850 71987, ⓕ22850 74077; ❷), above the bakery of the same name, and the pleasant *Provaloma* (☎22850 71936; ❷), which also has a taverna. The rooms belonging to Anna (☎22850 71161; ❷) are particularly recommended, as is the modern *Hotel Sunset* (☎22850 71948; ❹), which enjoys stunning views of the harbour. The 2002-built *Iliovasilema Hotel* (☎22850 71948, ⓦwww.schinousa.gr/iliovasilema; ❻) is a sign of things to come for the tiny island as it increases in popularity as a destination. The main concentration of **restaurants**, cafés and bars is along the main thoroughfare. *Panorma* and *Margarita* offer traditional diners some of the best views on the island.

There are no fewer than sixteen **beaches** dotted around the island, accessible by a lacework of trails. **Tsigoúri** is a ten-minute walk southwest from Hóra; largely undeveloped except for the *Tsigouri Beach Villas* (☎22850 71175, ⓕ22850 71176; ❸), which has a good taverna with great views. The only other beach with any refreshments is **Almyrós**, a half-hour southeast of Hóra, which has a simple canteen.

Iráklia

Iráklia (pronounced Iraklía by locals), the westernmost of the Minor Cyclades, has just over 100 permanent residents. As the first stop on the ferry service from Náxos, the island is hardly undiscovered by tourists, but with fewer amenities than some of its neighbours, it retains the romantic, ramshackle feel of a more secluded retreat.

Ferries call at **ÁYIOS YEÓRYIOS**, a small but sprawling settlement behind a sandy tamarisk-backed beach. *Anna's Place* (☎ & ⓕ22850 71145; ❷) has rooms with shared cooking facilities; *Villa Glafkos* (☎22850 71892; ❸) and *Maïstrali* (☎22850 71807, ⓔnickmaistrali@in.gr; ❸) are other accessible, roomy alternatives. Dhimitrios Stefanidhis (☎22850 71484; ❷), *Sohoro Rooms* (☎22850 71565; ❷), *Anthi & Angelo's* (☎22850 71486; ❷), and Alexandra Tournaki (☎22850 71482; ❷), meanwhile, all have acceptable rooms nearby. *O Pefkos* is a pleasant **taverna**, with tables shaded by a large pine tree. Two agencies sell tickets for **ferries**, but there are no banks in town, nor are there bus or taxi services. The recommended *Perigiali* taverna also has a small shop selling maps showing the mule path to a fine **cave** of Ayíos Ioánnis on the west side of the island.

Livádhi, the best beach on the island, is a fifteen-minute walk southeast of town. There is shade, but bring refreshments, as the taverna might not be open. The village of Livádhi, deserted since 1940, stands on the hillside above, its houses ruined and overgrown; among the remains are Hellenistic walls incorporated into a later building, and fortifications from the time of Marco Sanudo. Marietta Markoyianni (☎22850 71252; ❷) has rooms on the beach; *Zografos Rooms* (☎22850 71946, ⓕ22850 71956; ❹), above the road to Panayía, has fine views but is rather remote.

PANAYÍA or HÓRA, an unspoiled one-street village at the foot of Mount Papás, is another hour's walk inland along the paved road. It has a bakery/mini-market, two café/shops and an excellent *ouzerí*, but no rooms. A track to the east heads down to Pigádhi, a rocky beach with sea urchins, at the head of a narrow inlet. To the west, a track from the near-deserted hamlet of **Áyios Athanásios** leads back to the port.

The **cave of Áyios Ioánnis** lies behind the mountain, at the head of a valley leading to Vourkária bay. From Panayía, follow a signposted track west before zigzagging up to a saddle well to the north of the summit, with views over Skhinoússa, Koufoníssi, Kéros, Náxos and Amorgós; the path drops down to the south around the back of the mountain. A painted red arrow on the left indicates the turning to the cave, just over an hour's walk from Panayía. A church bell hangs from a cypress tree above the whitewashed entrance; inside there's a shrine, and the cave opens up into a large chamber with stalactites and stalagmites. It can be explored to a depth of 120m and is thought to be part of a much larger cave system, yet to be opened up; a festival is held here every year on August 18.

The main trail continues beyond the cave to a small sandy beach at **Alimiá** but this can be reached more easily with the beach-boat from Áyios Yeóryios. In season, the boat sails daily to either Skhinoússa, Alimiá or the nearby pebble beach of Karvounólakos.

Dhonoússa

Dhonoússa is a little out on a limb compared with the other Minor Cylclades, and ferries call less frequently. Island life centres on the pleasant port settlement of **STAVRÓS**, spread out behind the harbour and the village beach.

Rooms, most without signs, tend to be booked up by Greek holiday-makers in August; try Maria Prasinos (☎22850 51578; ❹), with rooms along a lane behind the church; *Iliovasilema* (☎22850 51570; ☎22850 51607; ❹), which also has a decent restaurant; or *Firoa* (☎22850 51658; ❸), 150m away from the centre. There are a few **tavernas** in town, all of them reasonable and good. The **ticket agency** above the harbour changes **money** at astronomically high rates and has been known to be less than accommodating, so you would be wise to bring enough with you.

The hills around Stavrós are low and barren and scarred by bulldozed tracks, but a little walking is repaid with dramatic scenery and a couple of fine beaches. Campers and nudists head for **Kéndros**, a long and attractive stretch of sand fifteen minutes to the east, although shade is limited and there are no facilities. A road has been built on the hillside above, replacing the donkey track to the farming hamlets of Haravyí and Mersíni; these have more hens and goats in the streets than people, and there are no cafés, shops or rooms. **Mersíni** is an hour's walk from Stavrós and has a welcome spring beneath a plane tree, the island's only running water. A nearby path leads down to Livádhi, an idyllic white sand beach with tamarisks for shade. In July and August, there's often a beach-boat from the port.

The road to **KALOTARÍTISSA**, on the northeast coast, is now paved and no longer an especially attractive walk. You might want to head inland from Stavrós toward Papás, the island's highest point, from where a valley drops down rapidly to the tiny village with a simple taverna that sometimes has a room to rent. There are two small pebble beaches and a path that continues above the coast to Mersíni. It takes four to five hours to walk round the island.

Amorgós

Amorgós, with its dramatic mountain scenery and laid-back atmosphere, is attracting visitors in increasing numbers; most ferries and catamarans call at both Katápola in the southwest and Eyiáli in the northeast – with these destinations, rather than Amorgós, on schedules – and there is a regular bus service between both ports. The island can get extremely crowded in midsummer, the numbers swollen by French people paying their respects to the film location of Luc Besson's *The Big Blue*, although few actually venture out to the wreck of the *Olympia*, at the island's west end, which figured so prominently in the movie. In general it's a low-key, escapist clientele, happy to have found a relatively large, interesting and uncommercialized island with excellent walking.

Katápola and around

KATÁPOLA, set at the head of a deep bay, is actually three separate hamlets: **Katápola** proper on the south flank, **Rahídhi** on the ridge at the head of the gulf and **Xilokeratídhi** along the north shore. There is a beach in front of Rahídhi, but the beach to the west of Katápola is better, though not up to the standards of Eyiáli in the northeast. In season there is also a regular *kaïki* to nearby beaches at **Maltézi** and **Plákes** (€2–3 return) and a daily *kaïki* to the islet of **Gramvoússa** off the western end of Amorgós (€6–8 return).

Prekas is the one-stop **boat-ticket agency**, and there are several **motorbike-rental** outlets including the friendly Corner Rentabike (☏22850 71867), though the local bus service is more than adequate and the walking trails are delightful. The **bus** shuttles almost hourly until 11pm between Katápola and Hóra, the island capital; several times daily it continues to Ayía Ánna via Hozoviotíssas monastery, and once a day (9.45am) out to the "Káto Meriá", made up of the hamlets of Kamári, Arkessíni and Kolofána.

There are plenty of small **hotels** and **pensions** and, except in high summer when rooms are almost impossible to find, proprietors tend to meet those boats arriving around sunset – though not necessarily those that show up in the small hours. A good clean place next to the beach at the western end of Katápola is *Eleni Rooms* (T & F 22850 71543; ❹); *Dimitri's Place* in Rahídhi (T 22850 71309; ❷) is a compound of interconnecting buildings in an orchard with shared cooking facilities. The smart traditional *Hotel Minoa* (T 22850 71480, F 22850 71003; ❺), on the waterfront, may be a bit too noisy for some, who might try the *Valsamitis* (T 22850 71148, F 22850 71147; ❺), off the northeast corner of the port. South of the port you'll find the *Hotel Anna* (T 22850 71218, F 22850 71084; ❷), with a lovely setting and basic cooking facilities. There are several similarly priced *pensions* further east, including *Sofia* (T 22850 71493, F 22850 71494; ❷). The **campsite** (T & F 22850 71257) is well signed between Rahídhi and Xilokeratídhi.

In Katápola proper, *Mourayio* is the most popular **taverna** in town; alternatively try the *Psaropoula* or *Minos*. There are four tavernas close to the campsite near Xilokeratídhi, of which the first is a friendly fish taverna, and of the others around the corner *Vitzentzos* is by far the best. What **nightlife** there is focuses on a handful of cafés and pubs. A bar called *Le Grand Bleu* in Xilokeratídhi regularly shows *The Big Blue* on video but there are other less obvious and less expensive places to drink, such as *The Blue Moon Bar* next door.

Steps, and then a jeep track, lead south out of Katápola to the remains of **ancient Minoa**, which are apt to disappoint close up: some polygonal wall, four or five courses high, the foundations of an Apollo temple, a crumbled Roman structure and bushels of unsorted pottery shards. The setting, however, with views encompassing Hóra and ancient Arkessíni, is memorable. Beyond Minoa, the track dwindles to a trail, continuing within a few hours to Arkessíni (see opposite) via several hamlets – a wonderful **excursion** with the possibility of catching the bus back.

Hóra and around

HÓRA, accessible by an hour-long path beginning from behind the Rahídhi campsite, is one of the best-preserved settlements in the Cyclades, with a scattering of tourist shops, cafés, tavernas and rooms. Dominated by a rock plug wrapped with a chapel or two, the thirteenth-century Venetian fortifications look down on countless other bulbous churches including the tiny **Áyios Fanoúrios**, and a line of decapitated windmills beyond. Of the half-dozen or so **places to stay**, *Pension O Ilias* (T 22850 71277; ❷) is recommended. *Liotrivi* restaurant, down the steps from the bus stop, is probably the best place to **eat** in town. In addition to a pair of traditional tavernas, *Kastanis* and *Klimataria*, there are several typical café-bars, including *Kallisto* and *Zygos*, which boasts good views from its rooftop terrace. Also in the upper square is the island's main **post office**.

From the top of Hóra, near the upper telecoms tower, a wide cobbled *kalderími* drops down to two major attractions, effectively short-cutting the road and taking little longer than the bus to reach them. Bearing left at an inconspicuous fork after fifteen minutes, you'll come to the spectacular **monastery of Hozoviotíssas** (daily 8am–1pm; donation expected, modest dress required), which appears suddenly as you round a bend, its vast wall gleaming white at the base of a towering orange cliff. Only four monks occupy the fifty rooms now, but they are quite welcoming considering the number of visitors who file through; you can see the eleventh-century icon around which the monastery was founded, along with a stack of other treasures. Legend has it that during the Iconoclastic period, a precious icon of the Virgin was committed to the sea by beleaguered monks at Hózova, in the Middle East, and it washed up safely at the base of the palisade here. The view from the *katholikón*'s terrace overshadows all for most visitors, and to round off the experience, you are ushered into a comfy reception room and treated to a sugary lump of *loukoúmi*, a fiery shot of *kítron* and a cool glass of water.

The far southwest

The right-hand trail leads down, within forty minutes, to the pebble **beaches** at **Ayía Ánna**. Skip the first batch of tiny coves in favour of the path to the westernmost bay, where naturists cavort, almost in scandalous sight of the monastery far above. As yet there are no tavernas here, nor a spring, so bring food and water for the day.

For alternatives to Ayía Ánna, take the morning bus out toward modern Arkessíni, alighting at **Kamári** hamlet (where there's a single taverna) for the twenty-minute path down to the adjacent beaches of **Notiná**, **Moúros** and **Poulopódhi**. Like most of Amorgós's south-facing beaches, they're clean, with calm water, and here, too, a freshwater spring dribbles most of the year. The road is paved as far as **Kolofána**, where there is one place with **rooms**. From here unpaved roads lead to the western tip of the island, and remote beaches at Káto Kámbos and at Paradhísa, facing the islet of Gramvoússa.

Archeology buffs will want to head north from Kamári to Vroútsi, start of the overgrown hour-long route to **ancient Arkessini**, a collection of tombs, six-metre-high walls and houses out on the cape of Kastrí. The main path from Minoa also passes through Vroútsi, ending next to the well-preserved Hellenistic fort known locally as the "Pýrgos", just outside modern **ARKESSÍNI**. The village has a single taverna with rooms, and, more importantly, an afternoon bus back to Hóra and Katápola.

The northeast

The energetically inclined can walk the four to five hours from Hóra to Eyiáli, either continuing on the faint trail just beyond Hozoviótissas, or taking the scenic and sheltered valley track through Terláki and Rikhtí. The two routes, and the modern jeep road, more or less meet an hour out of Hóra. Along most of the way, you're treated to amazing views of **Nikouriá islet**, nearly joined to the main island, and in former times a leper colony. The only habitations en route are the summer hamlet of **Asfodhilítis**, with well water but little else for the traveller, and **Potamós**, a double village you encounter on the stroll down towards Eyiáli bay.

EYIÁLI is smaller than Katápola but more picturesque, so it's gaining in popularity. The road inland, behind the harbour, leads to a group of **hotels** of similar price and quality including *Pension Christine* (☎22850 73236, ℱ22850 73109; ②), *Akrogiali* (☎22850 73263, ℱ22850 73249; ③) and the *Aegean* (☎22850 73206; ②). Above on the main road is *Filoxenia* (☎22850 73453, ℱ22850 73007; ④), which has fully equipped kitchens. Along the beach is the *Lakki Village* (☎22850 73253, ℱ22850 73244; ④) and behind this the pleasant *Pension Askas* (☎22850 73133, ℱ22850 73333; ④) – both of which have their own shaded tavernas. Next to *Pension Askas* there is a very friendly official **campsite**, *Eyiáli Camping* (☎22850 73050, ℱ22850 73236), usually less crowded than the one in Katápola. Overlooking the bay on the road up to Tholária is a luxury hotel with a swimming pool, the *Aegialis* (☎22850 73393, ⓦwww.amorgos-aegialis.com; ⑦). For **eating out**, *Limani* (aka *Katerina's*) on the single inland lane, is packed until midnight by virtue of its excellent food and barrel wine. Other places tend to be pricier and of inferior quality, with the exception of the tiny *12 Acropolis* restaurant, which also maintains a small guesthouse (ⓦwww.12acropolis.gr; ②). Besides a few seasonal music **bars**, nightlife is focused around the *Corte Club* at the *Egialis* hotel and *Disco The Que* on the beach. For a more active adventure, you can take advantage of the **diving** centre, Dive Ventures (☎22850 73611), which organizes daily boat and shore dives.

The main Eyiáli **beach** is more than serviceable, getting less weedy and reefy as you stroll further north, the sand interrupted by the remains of a Roman building jutting into the sea. A trail here leads over various headlands to three clothing-optional bays: the first sandy, the second mixed sand and gravel, the last shingle. There are no facilities anywhere so bring along what you need.

There is a **bus service** up to each of the two villages visible above and east of Eyiáli, with eight departures daily up and down (a timetable is posted by the harbour bus stop), but it would be a shame to miss out on the beautiful **loop walk** linking them with the port. A path starting at the far end of the beach heads inland and crosses the road before climbing steeply to **THOLÁRIA**, named after vaulted Roman tombs found around Vígla, the site of ancient Eyiáli. Vígla is on a hill opposite the village but there is little to see beyond the bases of statues and traces of city walls incorporated into later terracing. Another path winds down behind the hill to a tiny pebble beach at Mikrí Vlihádha far below. There are a few **taverna-cafés**, including a handsome wooden-floored establishment near the church, and several places to stay, including some comfortable **rooms** (reserve through *Pension Lakki* in Eyiáli), the large and upmarket *Vigla* (☎22850 73288, ℉22850 73332; ❻) and the *Thalassino Oneiro* (☎22850 73345; ❸), which has a fine restaurant and an extremely friendly owner.

LANGÁDHA is another hour's walk along a path starting below Tholária; to the left of the trail is the chapel of Astrátios with an altar supported by the capital of a Corinthian column. Past here there are views down to the inlet of Megáli Vlihádha and, on a clear day, across to Ikaría in the north. The path descends through the village of Stroúmbos, abandoned apart from a few houses restored as holiday homes, and into a small gorge before climbing the steps up to Langádha. The place is home to a sizeable colony of expatriates – reflected in the German-Greek cooking at the beautifully located *Nikos'* **taverna** at the lower end of the village, which also runs the attached **hotel** (☎22850 73310, ℉22850 73368; ❹). The *Artemis Pension* (☎ & ℉22850 73315, ⓦwww.artemis-pension.gr; ❹) is another comfortable option.

Beyond Langádha, another rocky path leads around the base of the island's highest peak, the 821-metre-high **Kríkellos**, passing on the way the fascinating church of **Theológos**, with lower walls and ground plan dating to the fifth century. Somewhat easier to reach, by a slight detour off the main Tholária–Langádha trail, are the church and festival grounds of **Panayía Panohorianí** – not so architecturally distinguished but a fine spot nonetheless.

Íos

Though not terribly different – geographically or architecturally – from its immediate neighbours, no other island attracts the same vast crowds of young people as **Íos**. Attempts are being made, however, to move the island's tourism upmarket. Buildings are now painted white with blue trim, instead of garish psychedelic hues, camping rough is discouraged, and Greece's early closing laws (3am except Fri & Sat) are enforced, so bars no longer stay open all night. (There is still, however, a lingering problem with *bómba*, a cheap local drink that gets you drunk fast and then makes you sick. It might be worth resisting drinks that are suspiciously cheap.)

The only real villages – **Yialós**, **Hóra** and **Mylopótamos** – are in one small corner of the island, and development elsewhere is somewhat restricted by poor roads. As a result there are still some very quiet beaches with just a few rooms to rent. Yialós has one of the best and safest natural harbours in the Cyclades, with a paved esplanade.

Most visitors stay along the arc delineated by the port – at Yialós, where you'll arrive (there's no airport), in Hóra above it or at the beach at Mylopótamos; it's a small area, and you soon get to know your way around. **Buses** constantly shuttle between Koumbára, Yialós, Hóra and Mylopótamos, with a daily service running roughly from 8am to midnight; you should never have to wait more than fifteen minutes during high season, but at least once try the short walk up (or down) the stepped path between Yialós and Hóra. Various travel offices run their own buses to the beaches at Manganári and Ayía Theodhóti; they sell return tickets only and are a bit expensive. To rent your **own transport**, try Jacob's Car and Bike Rental (☏22860 91047) in Yialós or Vangelis Bike Rental (☏22860 91919) in Hóra; unlike most of the other islands, here you'll need a valid motorcycle licence. For a motorboat, head to Mylopótamos where Ios Boat Rental (☏22860 91301, ⓦwww.iosboat.com) requires no licence, just a credit card. For a quick escape from the party atmosphere at the height of the season, try one of the daily excursions to Síkinos on the beautiful *Leigh Browne* sailing vessel parked in the harbour, which departs at 10.30am and returns at 5pm, weather and passengers permitting (€20).

Despite its past popularity, **sleeping on the beach** on Íos is discouraged these days. Crime and police raids are becoming more frequent as the island strains under the sheer impact of increasing youth tourism, and the police have been known to turn nasty. They prefer you to sleep in the official campsites and, given the problem of theft, you should probably take their advice.

Yialós and Hóra

From **YIALÓS** quayside, **buses** turn around just to the left, while Yialós **beach** – surprisingly peaceful and uncrowded – is another five minutes' walk in the same direction. You might be tempted to grab a room in Yiálos as you arrive: owners meet the ferries, hustling the town's **accommodation**, and there are also a couple of kiosks by the jetty that will book rooms for you. In shoulder season you can bargain for prices considerably lower than those listed below, but the town won't be in full swing. *Hotel Mare Monte* (T & F 22860 91585; ○), about halfway down the beach, has clean modern rooms and a small pool; *Galini Rooms* (T & F 22860 91115; ○), down a lane behind the beach, is a good quiet choice, if a little out of the way. One of the best choices is the quiet family-owned *Golden Sun* (T & F 22860 91110; ○), about 300m up the road to Hóra, which has a large pool. There are more rooms on the stepped path from Yialós to Hóra, although they can be noisy at night: smarter, quieter options include *Armadoras* (T 22860 91201, F 22860 91253; ○), with a pleasant pool and bar, and the newly renovated *Hotel Poseidon* (T 22860 91091, W www.poseidonhotelios.gr; ○), located directly under the windmill on the hill dominating the port, and featuring a pool and bar. *Ios Camping* (T 22860 91329) is friendly and clean and has a rather luxurious swimming pool and café area. Yialós has other essentials, including a reasonable supermarket and a few **tavernas**. The *Octopus Tree*, a small *kafenío* by the fishing boats, serves cheap fresh seafood caught by the owner, while on the front heading towards the beach, the *Waves Restaurant* does good Indian food; *Enigma* is a warm, intimate space serving cuisine from Cyprus. A twenty-minute stroll over the headland at **KOUMBÁRA**, there's a smaller and less crowded beach, with a rocky islet to explore, and the *Polydoros* taverna, one of the better places to eat on Íos – well worth the walk or bus ride; here you'll also find the excellent *Filippos* fish taverna and the lively *La Luna* café-bar on the beach.

Hóra

HÓRA (aka Íos Town), a twenty-minute walk up behind the port, is one of the most picturesque towns in the Cyclades, filled with meandering arcaded lanes and whitewashed chapels, though it's overwhelmed by crowds of young revellers in the high season. It divides naturally into two parts: the old town climbing the hillside to the left as you arrive, and the newer development to the right.

The **Archeological Museum** (Tues–Sun 8.30am–3pm; €2), in the yellow town hall, is part of an attempt to attract a more diverse range of visitors to the island. The **outdoor theatre** of Odysseus Elytis, behind the windmills, provides a beautiful setting in which to enjoy concerts and plays, details of which can be found at the travel agent/information booth next to the archeological museum.

There are plenty of basic **rooms** in the old part, although the bars can make sleep difficult. Your best strategy for a modicum of quiet is to wend your way up to the left where you find several establishments, including *Francesco's* (T & F 22860 91223; ○). Lower down, there's the *Hotel Philippou* (T 22860 91290; ○), above the National Bank and next to the cathedral. Your best chances for affordable rest will be found in the newer quarter: *Markos Pension* (T 22860 91059, F 22860 91060; ○; ask for the ten percent discount for Rough Guide readers), with a poolside bar; *Lofos (The Hill) Pension* (T 22860 91481, F 22860 91205; ○), to the right up from the Rollan supermarket; *Village Twins* (T 22860 91155; ○), up to the left before the *Scorpion Club*; and the friendly *Four Seasons Pension* (T 22860 91308, F 22860 91136; ○), up from Vangelis Bike Rental.

Every evening in summer, Hóra is the centre of the island's **nightlife**, its streets throbbing with music from ranks of competing discos and clubs – mostly free, or with a nominal entrance charge, though drinks tend to be expensive. Most of the smaller **bars** and pubs are tucked into the thronging narrow streets of the old village on the hill, offering something for everyone – unless you just want a quiet drink – and you'll have no trouble finding them. A welcome exception to the techno-pop dancing fodder can be found at the *Ios Club*, perched right up on the hill, which plays quieter music, has reasonable food and is a good place to watch the sunset. The larger **dancing clubs** are clustered near the bus stop and include the *Star Club*, *Scorpion*, *Disco 69* and *Sweet Irish Dream*, while *Voodoo* and *Orange* up in town have more of a loungey feel till late in the evening.

Eating is a secondary consideration but there are plenty of cheap and cheerful *psistariés* and takeaway joints: sound choices include the Italian restaurant *Pinocchio*, *The Nest* taverna, and the *Lord Byron mezedhopolíon* in an alley up to the left in the old quarter – it's open year round and tries hard to re-create a traditional atmosphere, with old *rebétika* music and some good, unusual Greek food.

Around the island

The most popular stop on the island's bus routes is **MYLOPÓTAMOS** (universally abbreviated to Mylópotas), the site of a magnificent beach and a mini-resort. Due to the large number of young travellers in Íos, **camping** is a popular option. *Far Out Beach Club* (☎22860 91468, ⓦwww.faroutclub.com), is the better of the campsites, with an attractive setting and excellent facilities, including an air-conditioned cafeteria, but it's very popular and can get noisy and crowded. *The Purple Pig* (☎22860 91302, ⓦwww.purplepigstars.com), a friendly Australian-run backpackers' complex, by the road up to Hóra, has clean bungalows (❶–❷), good camping facilities and plenty of other pleasurable distractions, including its own club and a poolside bar. Up the road at the far end of the beach, *Gorgona* (☎ & ⓕ22860 91307; ❹), *Dracos* (☎22860 91281; ❹) and *Hotel Ios Plage* (☎ & ⓕ22860 91301, ⓦwww.iosplage.com; ❺) have reasonable rooms, the last with an excellent restaurant on its terrace. *Hotel Katerina* (☎22860 91614, ⓕ22860 91858; ❺), nicely situated by a pool looking over the bay, and the luxurious *Ios Palace Hotel* (☎22860 91269; ❻), above the near end of the beach, are among the most upmarket choices besides the two expensive hotels maintained by *Far Out* (☎22860 91468, ⓦwww.faroutclub.com; ❻), the *Far Out Village Hotel*, next to the *Far Out Beach Club* (see above), and the *Far Out Hotel*, up on the hill on the road approaching Mylopótamos. On the rocks, beyond the *Ios Palace*, the *Harmony Restaurant* is one of the better places to eat, serving pizzas and Mexican food. The restaurants and self-service cafés behind the beach are uninspiring, and only the *Faros Café* rates a mention for staying open through the night to cater for the crowds returning from Hóra in the early hours. Mylopótamos itself has surprisingly little in the way of nightlife.

From Yialós, daily boats depart at around 10am (returning in the late afternoon; €12 return) to **Manganári** on the south coast, where there's a beach and a swanky hotel; you can also get there by scooter. Most people go from Yialós to Manganári by private buses run by travel agencies (€5 return), which leave Yialós about 11am, calling at Hóra and Mylopótamos and return later in the afternoon; the condition of the road, however, makes the boat a much more pleasant option. Once predominantly nudist, shedding clothes here is now officially discouraged though still very much in practice. There's more to see, and a better atmosphere at **Ayía Theodhóti** up on the east coast. You can get there on a paved road across the island – the daily excursion bus costs €3 return. A couple of kilometres south of Ayía Theodhóti is Paleókastro, a ruined Venetian castle which encompasses the remains of a marble-finished town and a Byzantine church. In the unlikely event that the beach – a good one and mainly nudist – is too crowded, try the one at **Psathí**, 14km to the southeast. Frequented by wealthy Athenians, this small resort has a couple of pricey tavernas, although *Alonistra* fish taverna is a cheaper, excellent exception. Another decent beach is at **Kálamos**: get off the Manganári bus at the turning for Kálamos, which leaves you with a four-kilometre walk.

"**Homer's**" **tomb** can be reached by motorbike along a safe unpaved road that is scheduled to be paved in the near future (turning left from the paved road to Ayía Theódhoti 4.5km from Hóra). The town itself has long since slipped down the side of the cliff, but the rocky ruins of the entrance to a tomb remain, as well as some graves – one of which is claimed to be Homer's, but which in reality probably dates only to the Byzantine era.

Síkinos

Síkinos has so small a population that the mule ride or walk up from the port to the village was only replaced by a bus late in the 1980s and, until the new jetty was completed at roughly the same time, it was the last major Greek island where ferry passengers were still taken ashore in launches. With no dramatic characteristics, nor any nightlife to speak of, few foreigners make the short trip over here from neighbouring Íos and Folégandhros or from sporadically connected Páros, Náxos or Thíra. There is now a **bank** with an ATM on the island as well as a **post office** up in Kástro-Hóra, and you can sometimes change cash at the store in Aloprónia.

Aloprónia and Kástro-Hóra

Such tourist facilities as exist are concentrated in the little harbour of **ALOPRÓNIA**, with its long sandy beach and extended breakwater and jetty. More and more formal **accommodation** is being built here, but it's still possible to camp or just sleep out under the tamarisks behind the beach. For rooms, try *Flora* (☏ 22860 51214; ❷), near the main road leading to Hóra, *Loukas* (☏ 22860 51076), which has rooms (❷) and studios (❹) around town, or the recommended *The Rock* (☏ 22860 51186; ❷), above the *Rock Cafe*; alternatively, the comfortable and traditional *Hotel Kamares* (☏ 22860 51234, Ⓕ 22860 51281; ❸) has a nicer setting than the conspicuous *Porto Sikinos* luxury complex (☏ 22860 51247, Ⓕ 22860 51220; ❻). The handful of **tavernas** and **café-bars** in town are virtually all affiliated with the properties listed above and bear the same names, *Loukas* taverna being the most affordable if the most standard option.

The double village of **KÁSTRO-HÓRA** is served by the single island bus, which shuttles regularly from early morning till quite late in the evening between the harbour and here, though the route should soon be extended to Episkopí with the completion of the new road. On the ride up, the scenery turns out to be less desolate than initial impressions suggest. Draped across a ridge overlooking the sea, Kástro-Hóra makes for a charming day-trip, and the lovely oil-press **museum** (evenings in summer; free), run privately by a Greek-American, is highly recommended. A partly ruined monastery, **Zoödhóhou Piyís** ("Life-giving Spring", a frequent name in the Cyclades), crowns the rock above. The architectural highlight of the place, though, is the central quadrangle of **Kástro**, a series of ornate eighteenth-century houses arrayed defensively around a chapel square, their backs to the exterior of the village. There are only a few basic **rooms** in town, reserved through the Divoli family (☏ 22860 51263 or 22860 51212; ❶) or Antonios Margetis (☏ 22860 51253; ❸). A good selection of **food** is available, along with fine local wine, at both *Klimataria* and *To Steki tou Garbi* next door. The *kafenía* up here are very traditional affairs and you might feel more welcome at the café-bars *Kastro* or *Platía*.

Around the island

West of Kástro-Hóra, an hour-plus walk (or vehicle ride) takes you through a landscape lush with olive trees to **Episkopí**, where elements of an ancient temple-tomb have been ingeniously incorporated into a seventh-century church – the structure is known formally as the Iróön, though it's now thought to have been a Roman mausoleum rather than a temple of Hera. Ninety minutes from Kástro-Hóra, in the opposite direction, lies **Paleokástro**, the patchy remains of an ancient fortress. The beaches of **Áyios Yeóryios** and **Áyios Nikólaos** are reachable by a regular *kaïki* from Aloprónia; the former is a better option because it has the daytime *Almira* restaurant. It is possible to walk to them, but there is no real path at the later stages. A more feasible journey by foot is to the pebble beach at **Áyios Pandelímonas**: just under an hour's trail walk southwest of Aloprónia, it is the most scenic and sheltered on the island, and is also served by a *kaïki* in season.

Folégandhros

The cliffs of **Folégandhros** rise sheer in places over 300m from the sea – until the early 1980s as effective a deterrent to tourists as they always were to pirates. It was used as an island of political exile right up until 1974, but life in the high, barren interior has been eased since the junta years by the arrival of electricity and the construction of a lengthways road from the harbour to

Hóra and beyond. Development has been given further impetus by the recent exponential increase in tourism and the mild commercialization this has brought.

A veritable explosion in accommodation for most budgets, and improvement in ferry arrival times, means there is no longer much need for – or local tolerance of – sleeping rough on the beaches. The increased wealth and trendiness of the heterogeneous clientele is reflected in fancy jewellery shops, an arty postcard gallery and a helipad. Yet away from the showcase Hóra and the beaches, the countryside remains mostly pristine, and is largely devoted to the spring and summer cultivation of barley, the mainstay of many of the Cyclades before the advent of tourism. Donkeys and donkey paths are also still very much in evidence, since the terrain on much of the island is too steep for vehicle roads.

Karavostási and around

KARAVOSTÁSI, the rather unprepossessing port whose name simply means "ferry stop", serves as a last-resort base; it has several **hotels** but little atmosphere. Best value if you do decide to stay is *Hotel Aeolos* (☎22860 41205, ℻22860 41336; ❸), while the *Poseidon* (☎22860 41272, ℻22860 41008; ❹) throws in breakfast at its decent restaurant, *To Kati Allo*, and the *Vrahos Hotel* (☎22860 41450, ℻22860 41304; ❹) has some nice rooms on the far side of the bay. *Iy Kali Kardhia* **taverna** above the harbour is recommended, and there are a couple of pleasant beach **bars** including the *Smyrna Ouzeri*, housed in a converted boathouse. There are many buses a day in summer to Hóra, three continuing to Áno Meriá; if you're feeling adventurous try Jimmy's **motorbike rental** (☎22860 41448), which is cheaper than its counterparts in Hóra.

The closest **beach** is the smallish, but attractive enough, sand-and-pebble **Vardhiá**, signposted just north over the headland. Some fifteen minutes' walk south lies **Livádhi**, a rather average beach with tamarisk trees and the island's official **campsite**, *Livadhi Camping* (☎ & ℻22860 41204), which is good and friendly, although the hot water supply can be erratic.

Easily the most scenic beach on Folégandhros, a 300-metre stretch of pea-gravel with an offshore islet, is at **Katergó**, on the southeastern tip of the island. Most people visit on a boat excursion from Karavostássi or Angáli, but you can also get there on foot from the hamlet of Livádhi, a short walk inland from Loustriá. Be warned, though, that it's a rather arduous trek, with some nasty trail-less slithering in the final moments.

Hóra

The island's real character and appeal are to be found in the spectacular **HÓRA**, perched on a clifftop plateau some 45 minutes' walk from the dock; an hourly high-season **bus** service (6 daily spring/autumn) runs from morning until late at night. Locals and foreigners – hundreds of them in high season – mingle at the cafés and tavernas under the almond, flowering Judas and pepper trees of the two main *platíes*, passing the time undisturbed by traffic, which is banned from the village centre. Towards the cliff-edge, and entered through two arcades, the defensive core of the medieval **kástro** is marked by ranks of two-storey houses, whose repetitive, almost identical stairways and slightly recessed doors are very appealing.

From the square where the bus stops, a zigzag path with views down to both coastlines climbs to the cragtop, wedding-cake church of **Kímisis Theotókou**, nocturnally illuminated to grand effect. Beyond and below it hides the **Khryssospiliá**, a large cave with stalactites, accessible only to proficient climbers; the necessary steps and railings have crumbled away into the sea, although a minor, lower grotto can still be visited by *kaïki* from the port.

Practicalities

Accommodation in and around Hóra seems slightly weighted to favour over hotels rooms, with concentrations around the bus plaza at the eastern entrance to the village and at the western edge. Many of the tavernas and shops advertise rooms in their windows; otherwise try the purpose-built complex run by Yianoullis Yerardis (☎22860 41235; ❸), east of the bus stop. The nearby *Hotel Polikandia* (☎22860 41322, ⓕ22860 41323; ❹) has an engaging proprietress and lower rates off-season. The most luxurious facilities are at the cliff-edge *Anemomilos Apartments* (☎22860 41309, ⓕ22860 41407; ❺), immaculately appointed and with stunning views; the new *Meltemi* (☎22860 41328, ⓕ22860 41425; ❺), just opposite, has clean, comfortable rooms. The only hotel actually within Hóra is the traditional *Castro* (☎ & ⓕ22860 41230, ⓔddcastro@otenet.gr; ❻), built in 1212 and fully renovated in 1992, with three rather dramatic rooms looking directly out on an alarming drop to the sea. At the western edge of Hóra near the police station, a dense cluster of rooms tend to block each other's views; the least claustrophobic are the *Folgeandros Apartments* (☎22860 41239, ⓔfoleaps@ath.forthnet.gr; ❹), which has properties at several locations. By the roadside on the way to Áno Meriá, the *Fani-Vevis* (☎22860 41237; ❹), in a Neoclassical mansion overlooking the sea, seems to function only in high season; 100m beyond the smart *Kifines Studios* (☎ & ⓕ22860 41274; ❺).

Hóra's dozen or so **restaurants** are surprisingly varied. The *Folegandros ouzerí* in water-cistern plaza, is fun, if a bit eccentrically run. Breakfast can be enjoyed on the adjacent Platía Kondaríni at *Iy Melissa*, which does good fruit and yogurt, omelettes and juices. *Iy Piatsa* has a nightly changing menu of well-executed Greek dishes, while their neighbour and local hangout *O Kritikos* is notable only for its grills. *Iy Pounda* near the bus stop is the most traditional place and has a small garden. Hóra is inevitably beginning to sprawl unattractively at the edges, but this at least means that the burgeoning **nightlife** – a few dance bars along with a number of music pubs and *ouzerí*s – can be exiled to the north, away from most accommodation. *Avissos* and *Patitiri* are two hip, lively bars, while *Kellari* is a rustic and charming wine bar where the atmosphere is more relaxed. A **post office** (no bank) completes the list of amenities, though the single **ferry agent** also does money exchange, as does the friendly and competent Italian-run Sottovento agency (☎22860 41444, ⓔsottovento94@hotmail.com), which offers a wide range of services.

The rest of the island

Northwest of Hóra, a narrow, paved road threads its way towards **ÁNO MERIÁ**, the other village of the island; after 4km you pass its first houses, clustered around the three churches of Áyios Pandelímonas, Áyios Yeóryios and Áyios Andhréas. The **folk museum** (daily 5–8pm; donation requested), on a nineteenth-century farm near the town's entrance, traces the history of the island's people. **Tavernas**, which operate in high season only, include the traditional standbys: *O Mimis*, *Tou Mitsaki*, and *Iliovasilema*.

Up to six times a day in high season, a **bus** trundles out here to drop people off at the footpaths down to the various sheltered beaches on the southwest shore of the island. Busiest of these is **Angáli** (aka Vathý), where there are a few simple summer-only tavernas, reached by a fifteen-minute walk along a dirt road from the bus stop. Near to Angáli are the better of the few basic **rooms** available in the northern part of the island: *Irini* (☎22860 41190; ❷) and *Panagiotis* (☎22860 41301; ❷).

Nudists should take the paths which lead twenty minutes east or west to **Firá** or **Áyios Nikólaos** beaches respectively; the latter in particular, with its many tamarisks, coarse sand and view back over the island, is Katergó's only serious rival in the best-beach stakes. At Áyios Nikólaos, a lone taverna operates up by the namesake chapel; Firá has no facilities at all. From the *Iliovasilema* taverna, a motorable track continues north to a point from where a 500-metre path takes you down to the pleasant little bay of **Ambéli**.

Santoríni (Thíra)

As the ferry manoeuvres into the great caldera of **Santoríni** the land seems to rise up and clamp around it. Gaunt, sheer cliffs loom hundreds of feet above, nothing grows or grazes to soften the awesome view, and the only colours are the reddish-brown, black and grey pumice striations layering the cliff face of **Thíra**, the largest island in this mini-archipelago, and the location of all but the smallest of its modern settlements. The landscape tells of a history so dramatic and turbulent that legend hangs as fact upon it.

From as early as 3000 BC, the island developed as a sophisticated outpost of Minoan civilization, until sometime between 1647 and 1628 BC (according to latest estimates) when catastrophe struck: the volcano-island erupted, its heart sank below the sea, leaving a crater (caldera) 10km in diameter, and earthquakes reverberated across the Aegean. Thíra was destroyed and the great Minoan civilization on Crete was dealt a severe blow. At this point, the island's history became linked with legends of Atlantis, the "Happy Isles Submerged by Sea". Plato insisted that the legend was true, and Solon dated the cataclysm to 9000 years before his time – if you're willing to accept a mistake and knock off the final zero, a highly plausible date.

These apocalyptic events, though, scarcely concern modern tourists, who come here to take in the spectacular views, stretch out on the island's dark-sand beaches and absorb the peculiar, infernal geographic features; as recently as a century ago, Thíra was still reckoned to be infested with vampires. Though not quite as alarming as the undead, the tourism industry has managed to bleed away much traditional island life, creating in its wake a rather expensive and stagey playground. There is one time-honoured local industry, however, that has benefited from all the outside attention: **wine**. Santoríni is one of Greece's most important producers, and the fresh, dry white wines it is known for (most from the *assýrtiko* grape for which the region is known) are the perfect accompaniment to the seafood served in the many restaurants and tavernas that hug the island's postcard-perfect cliffs.

Arrival and departure

Ferries dock at the somewhat grim port of **Órmos Athiniós**; **Skála Firás** and **Ía** in the north are reserved for local ferries, excursion *kaïkia* and cruise ships. **Buses**, astonishingly crammed, connect Athiniós with the island capital Firá and, less frequently, with Ía and the main beaches at Kamári and Périssa. Disembark quickly and take whatever bus is going, if you want to avoid a long wait or a tedious hike up. You'll be accosted at Athiniós by people offering rooms all over the island; in the summer it might be a good idea to pay attention to them, given the scramble for beds, in Firá especially. From Skála Firás, you have the traditional route of 580 steps (about 45 minutes) up to Firá – not too difficult a walk, if you don't mind mule manure – or you can go by mule (€3, negotiable in off-season) or cable car (summer only 6.40am–10pm, every 20min; €3), so exhilarating a ride that you may want to take it for fun. The **airport** is on the east side of the island, near Monólithos; there is a regular shuttle-bus service to the Firá bus station, which runs until 10pm.

When it comes to **leaving** – especially for summer/evening ferry departures – it's best to buy your ticket in advance. Note, too, that although the bus service stops around midnight, a shared taxi isn't outrageously expensive (about €6 from Firá to Athiniós). Incidentally, **ferry information** from any source is notoriously unreliable on Thíra and rival agencies don't inform you of alternatives – Nomikos Travel (☎22860 23660), with seven branches, is the largest, though Pelikan (☎22860 22220) is also recommended. In any case, it's wise to enquire about your options at several agencies and triple-check departure times before working your way back to the port. If you do get stranded in Athiniós, there's no place to stay, and the tavernas are pretty awful, though there is Intenet access at *@thinios.com café*. With time on your hands, it's probably worth calling for a taxi (☎22860 22555) or zigzagging the 3.5km up to the closest village, **MEGALOHÓRI**, where there are a few diversions including several tavernas, the hip *Art Café*, and the exclusive *Villa Vedema Hotel* (☎22860 81796, ⓦwww.vedema.gr; ❽), one of the island's finest properties.

Firá

Half-rebuilt after a devastating earthquake in 1956, **FIRÁ** (also known as Thíra or Hóra) still clings precariously to the edge of the enormous caldera, affording astonishing views. You will, of course, have to pay for such a beautiful setting. It's so thoroughly commercialized and, in summer, so inundated with cruise-ship passengers and day-trippers that it can get overwhelming; it is definitely worth phoning for accommodation in advance.

However, the view is still thrilling, and Firá also has several excellent museums. The **Archeological Museum** (Tues–Sun 8am–2.30pm; €3 includes entrance to Museum of Prehistoric Thíra), near the cable car to the north of town, has a collection which includes a curious set of erotic Dionysiac figures. At the other end of town, between the cathedral and bus station, the **Museum of Prehistoric Thíra** (Tues–Sun 8.30am–3pm; €3 inludes entrance to Archeological Museum), a newly opened museum housed in a handsome building, has interesting displays of fossils, Cycladic art, and astonishing finds from Akrotíri. The handsome **Megaro Ghyzi** (Mon–Sat 10.30am–1.30pm & 5–8pm, Sun 10.30am–4.30pm; €3) above the the Archeological Museum in an old mansion owned by the Catholic diocese of Santoríni, has been restored as a cultural centre, and has a good collection of old prints and maps as well as photographs of the town before and after the 1956 earthquake. Further north along the caldera, the **Thíra Foundation**, housed in galleries carved into the cliffside, contains superb life-size 3D colour photo reproductions of the frescos of Akrotíri (daily 10am–8pm; €3). Towards the back of the town, north of the main square, is the extensive **Lignos Folklore Museum** (daily 10am–2pm & 6–8pm; €3), which features a completely furnished nineteenth-century house with period winery, cavern, garden, and workshops, as well as a gallery and historical archive.

Practicalities

Buses leave Firá from just south of Platía Theotokopoúlou to Périssa, Perívolos, Kamári, Monólithos, Akrotíri, Órmos Athiniós and the airport. **Taxis** go from near the bus station, within steps of the main square. If you want to see the whole island in a couple of days, a rented **motorbike** might do, though you must be very careful – especially since local drivers seem to enjoy antagonizing tourists on difficult and precipitous roads; try Moto Chris at the top of the road that leads down to *Santoríni Camping* (see opposite). The Firá branch of Nomikos Travel (see p.195), opposite the OTE, is friendly and organizes **excursions** and trips to ancient Thíra and Thirassía in conjunction with Kamari Tours (☎22860 31390).

Accommodation

For a caldera-view **hotel** in Firá consider the excellent *Loucas* (☎22860 22480, ⒺIoucasason@ath.fortnet.gr; ❼), a traditional hotel with barrel-ceilinged caves – to prevent collapse during an earthquake – carved into the cliffside, and a beautiful new pool; or the nearby *Kavalari* (☎22860 22455, Ⓔkavalhtl@otenet.gr; ❼). The most stylish option, however, is the boutique-style *Theoxenia Hotel* (☎22860 22740, ⓦwww.theoxenia.net; ❼). There are plenty of rooms without caldera views at the back of town. *Villa Rena* (☎22860 28130, ⓔrena@santorini.org; ❻), which has a large pool, and *San Georgio* (☎22860 23516, ⓕ22860 25755; ❺), just north of the main square, are two quiet, comfortable places managed by the same family with the help of an accommodating staff (ask for the ten percent discount for Rough Guide readers at either property). *Costa Marina Villas* (☎22860 28923, ⓕ22860 28926; ❻) and the *Pelican Hotel* (☎22860 23113, ⓕ22860 23514; ❻) are other roomy options, as is the smart *Villa Haroula* (☎22860 24226; ❼), on the road down to *Santorini Camping* (☎22860 22944, ⓕ22860 25065), the nearest **campsite** to town. (The best campsite on the island is near Akrotíri village; see p.200.) The *Thíra Youth Hostel* (☎22860 22387) is on the road to Ía; it can get noisy at night.

Eating, drinking and nightlife

FIROSTEFÁNI, between Firá and Imerovígli, has slightly less expensive rooms with views over the caldera, though as the area gets trendier by the minute, it's hardly a bargain destination. Good properties include *Hotel Mylos* (☎22860 23884; ❻), *Hotel Galini* (☎22860 22095, ⓦwww.galinihotel.gr; ❻) and *Mina Villas* (☎22860 25650; ❻). For something more stylish, *Manos Apartments* (☎22860 23202; ❼) is highly recommended. Another good location, where you don't have to pay as much for the (caldera) view, is **KARTERÁDHOS**, a small village about twenty minutes' walk southeast of Firá, where you'll find pleasant *Hotel Albatross* (☎22860 23435, ⓕ22860 23431; ❻), the charming *Cyclades* (☎22860 24543, ⓦwww.cycladeshotel.com; ❻) and the welcoming *Pension George* (☎ & ⓕ22860 22351, ⓔgeorge@santorini.org; ❸).

Firá's **restaurants** are primarily aimed at the tourist market, but for dependably good food with a sensational view (and prices to match) find *Aris*, below the *Loucas* hotel, or *Flame of the Volcano*, the last of the caldera-side restaurants north past the cable-car station (towards Firostefáni). On Erythroú Stavroú, the first street up from the main square, *Nikolas* is an old and defiantly traditional taverna, but it can be hard to get a table; the best moderately priced choice is *Naoussa*, further north on the same street, upstairs on the right. Nearby *Sphinx* offers exotic pasta dishes with a Greek twist, while *Calderimi*, near the cathedral, serves excellent Italian/Mediterranean food. Otherwise try *Koutouki* on 25-Martíou, the road to Ía; the welcoming *Mama's Cyclades*, a little further up on the same road; or *Aktaion* with slightly *nouvelle* interpretations of Greek classics in Firostefáni.

Most of the **nightlife** can be found northwest of the central square on Erythroú Stavroú: *Town Club*, *Tango*, *Canava* and, above, *Enigma* and *Koo*. The best bars from which to admire the caldera are *Franco's* and *Palia Kameni*, two rather exclusive and pricey cocktail bars with unbeatable locations. More laid back, but set back from the caldera, is the *Kira Thira* bar, which also offers a wine-tasting package. A good breakfast or afternoon snack can be found at *Corner Crêpes*, near the main square, or at the slightly trendier *Diverso* on the square itself.

The north

Once outside Firá, the rest of Thíra comes as a nice surprise, although development is beginning to encroach. The volcanic soil is highly fertile, with every available space terraced and cultivated: wheat, tomatoes (most made into paste), pistachios and grapes are the main crops (see p.200 for information on Santoríni's wines), all still harvested and planted by hand.

A satisfying – if demanding – approach to Ía, 12km from Firá in the northwest of the island, is to walk the stretch from **IMEROVÍGLI**, 3km out of Firá, using a spectacular footpath along the lip of the caldera; the walk takes around two hours. Jutting up from the side of the cliff is the conspicuous conical rock of **Skáros**, once the site of an important settlement and Venetian fortress, the scant remains of which can still be seen today; known also as Castle Rock, it can be mounted along a steep but obvious trail for unsurpassed views over the caldera and back to Thíra. Imerovígli is crowded with luxury, caldera-side **apartments** such as *Chromata* (☎22860 24850; ❼) and *Astra* (☎22860 23641; ❼), requiring reservations well in advance; *Katerina* (☎22860 22708, ℱ22860 23398; ❺) is a more moderately priced hotel, with caldera views from the large balcony/bar area only. Between the *Katerina* and *Chromata*, *Altana* is a small caldera-side **café** whose position and relaxed atmosphere make for a pleasing breakfast spot. Continuing to Ía, you'll pass Toúrlos, an old Venetian citadel on Cape Skáros.

Ía and around

ÍA, the most delightful village on the island, was once a major fishing port of the Aegean, but it has declined in the wake of economic depression, wars, earthquakes and depleted fish stocks. Partly destroyed in the 1956 earthquake, the town has been sympathetically reconstructed, its pristine white houses clinging to the cliff face. Apart from the caldera and the village itself, there are a couple of things to see, including the **Naval Museum** (daily except Tues 10am–2pm & 5–8pm; €3) and the very modest remains of a Venetian castle. Ía is a fine, and quieter, alternative to Firá, with a **post office** and several **bike-rental** offices (of which Mortor Fun is particularly good), as well as a couple of travel agencies – Karvounis (☎22860 71290, ✉mkarvounis@otenet.gr), on the pedestrial street, is the older and more reliable.

Much of the town's **accommodation** is in its restored old houses, including the traditional *Hotel Lauda* (☎22860 71204, ℱ22860 71274; ❻), the *Hotel Anemones* (☎22860 71220; ❺), the *Hotel Fregata* (☎22860 71221; ❺) and the luxurious *Perivolas Traditional Houses* (☎22860 71308, ⓌWwww.perivolas.gr; ❼), which are cut into the cliff near a pool suspended at its edge. Near the bus terminal, also reachable by the main road that continues round to the back end of the village, is an excellent hostel – the *Oia Youth Hostel* (☎22860 71465), with a terrace and shady courtyard, a good bar, clean dormitories and breakfast included.

Generally, the further you go along the central ridge towards the new end of Ía, the better value the **restaurants**: the *Anemomilos* and *Laokastri* are two such examples. *Blue Sky* is an excellent, affordable taverna in the centre of things, but expect queues. For a splurge, *1800* is generally regarded as the finest restaurant in town, serving a highly refined Mediterranean cuisine. **Nightlife** revolves around sunset-gazing, for which people are coached in from all over the island, creating traffic chaos and driving up prices, though the sunset is no different seen from Ía than from Firá when all is said and done. Slightly removed from the sunset tourist stampede, the pleasant *Alitana* is on the road leading down to the youth hostel.

Below the town, 200-odd steps switchback hundreds of metres down to two small harbours: **Ammoúdhi**, for the fishermen, and **Arméni**, where the excursion boats dock. Both have excellent fish tavernas. *Sunset* taverna at Ammoúdhi is recommended, and at Arméni there is a taverna which specializes in grilled octopus lunches. **FINIKIÁ**, 1km east of Ía, is a very quiet and traditional little village. *Lotza Rooms* (☎22860 71051; ❸) are located in an old house in the middle of the village, while *Hotel Finikia* (☎22860 71373, ℱ22860 71118; ❺), above the village near the main road, is a smarter option. Just north of Ía is **Baxédhes** beach, with a few tavernas including the *Paradhisos*, which has good food and reasonable prices. It's a quiet alternative to Kamári and Périssa (see opposite), though it's not much of a beach until you reach a secluded cape Koloubus, about 1km east, where ancient tombs have been discovered carved into the rock.

The east, coast and inland

Beaches on Thíra, to the east and south, are bizarre – long black stretches of volcanic sand which get blisteringly hot in the afternoon sun. They're no secret, and in the summer, the crowds can be a bit overpowering.

Closest to Firá, **MONÓLITHOS** has a couple of tavernas including the excellent *Mario* and *Galini*. To the south is the pricier *Domata*, serving fusion cuisine that gives Latin food a Greek flair. Further south, **KAMÁRI** has surrendered lock, stock and barrel to the package-tour operators and there's not a piece of sand that isn't fronted by concrete villas. Nonetheless it's quieter and cleaner than most, with some beachfront **accommodation**, including *Hotel Nikolina* (☎22860 31702, ℱ22860 32664; ❸), with basic but cheap rooms towards the southern end of the beach, as well as the *White House* (☎22860 31441; ❹) and the friendly *Sea Side Rooms* (☎22860 33403, ⓦwww.seaside.gr; ❹) further along the beach. *Rose Bay Hotel* (☎22860 33650, ℱ22860 33653; ❼) is a far pricier option, with a pleasant pool setting, set back away from the noisy beach thoroughfare.

Psistaria O Kritikos, a taverna-grill frequented by locals rather than tourists, is one of the best places to **eat** on the island. It's a long way out of Kamári on the road up to Messariá, and too far to walk, but the bus stops outside. There are plenty of cafés and restaurants behind the beach, though many are expensive or uninspiring. *Saliveros*, in front of the *Hotel Nikolina*, has taverna food at reasonable prices, and *Almira*, next to *Sea Side Rooms*, is a smarter restaurant and only a little more expensive. Kamári is a family resort with little in the way of clubs and nightlife, but there is a good open-air **cinema** near the campsite, and in summer, buses run until 1am, so there's no problem getting back to Firá after seeing a film. West of Kamári, is **Panayía Episkopi**, the most important Byzantine monument on the island. Built in the eleventh century, it was the setting of centuries of conflict between Orthodox Greeks and Catholics, but is most notable today for its carved iconostasis of light blue marble with a white grain.

Things are scruffier at **PÉRISSA**, around the cape. Because of its attractive situation and abundance of cheap rooms, it's noisy and crowded with backpackers. *Camping Perissa Beach* (☎22860 81343) is right behind the beach and has plenty of shade but is also next to a couple of noisy late-night bars. There is also a youth hostel on the road into Périssa: *Anna* (☎22860 82182, ℱ22860 81943; ❷) has dorm beds as well as a few simple studios closer to the beach. There are plenty of cheap rooms in the same area and some upmarket hotels behind the beach; the modern *Meltemi Hotel* (☎22860 81325, ⓦwww.meltemivillage.gr; ❻) is a sensible choice. The beach itself extends almost 7km to the west, sheltered by the occasional tamarisk tree, with beach bars dotted along at intervals. *Dichtia* and *Aquarius* are two excellent restaurants here.

Kamári and Périssa are separated by the Mésa Vounó headland, on which stood **ancient Thira** (Tues–Sun 8.30am–2.30pm; €3), the post-eruption settlement dating from the ninth century BC. Excursion buses go up from Kamári (€15), staying two hours at the site (ask at Kamari Tours behind the beach) but you can walk the **cobbled path** starting from the square in Kamári by the Argo General Store. The path zigzags up to a whitewashed church by a **cave**, containing one of Thíra's few freshwater springs, before crossing over to meet the road and ending at a saddle between Mésa Vounó and Profitis Ilías, where a refreshments van sells expensive drinks. From here, the path to the site passes a chapel dating back to the fourth century AD before skirting round to the Temenos of Artemidoros with bas-relief carvings of a dolphin, eagle and lion representing Poseidon, Zeus and Apollo. Next, the trail follows the sacred way of the ancient city through the remains of the agora and past the theatre. Most of the ruins (dating mainly from Hellenistic and Roman times) are difficult to place, but the site is impressively large and the views are awesome. The site can also be reached by a path from Périssa, and either way it's less than an hour's walk.

Inland

Inland about 2km, on the paved road west lies **EMBÓRIO**; though virtually ignored by tourists, it's Santoríni's largest village, with a goldmine of whimsical island architecture and the important remnants of the medieval Venetian fortress that once dominated the landscape.

North of here, **PÝRGOS** is one of the oldest settlements on the island, a jumble of old houses and alleys that still bear the scars of the 1956 earthquake. It climbs to another Venetian fortress crowned by several churches and you can clamber around the battlements for sweeping views over the entire island and its Aegean neighbours. A thirty-minute hike up the steep, winding road to the south leads to the monastery of **Profítis Ilías**, now sharing its refuge with Greek radio and TV pylons and the antennae of a NATO station. With just one monk remaining to look after the church, the place only really comes to life for the annual Profítis Ilías festival, when the whole island troops up here to celebrate. The views are still rewarding, though, and from near the entrance to the monastery an old footpath heads across the mountainous ridge in about an hour to ancient Thíra.

By way of contrast, **MESSARIÁ** – a thirty-minute stroll north – has a skyline consisting solely of massive church domes that lord it over the houses huddled in a ravine. The **Arhondikó Aryírou** (daily 9am–2pm & 4.30–7pm; €4) is a fully restored nineteenth-century mansion combining Neoclassical elements with island architecture.

Southwest of here, along the road to Akrotíri, are scattered a few of Santoríni's most important **wineries**, the largest of which, *Santo* and *Boutari*, offer the most comprehensive tours (€2–3), complete with multi-media presentations. Slightly more hidden are smaller wineries, such as *Canava Roussos, Antoniou* and *Koutsoyianopoulos* – the last is also home to the exceptional **Wine Museum** (daily 12–8pm; €1.70 inclues tasting) – which offer a more intimate glimpse at the wine-making process. Whatever the scale of the tour, none is complete without a taste of Santoríni's prized dessert wine, **visánto** (remniscent of the *vin santo* of Tuscan fame), among the finest wines produced in Greece. Tour prices at the smaller wineries (€2–5) usually include tastings, while samples are available from the larger wineries for a nominal fee.

Akrotíri and the south coast

Evidence of the Minoan colony that once thrived here has been uncovered at the ancient site of Minoan Thira at **Akrotíri** (Tues–Sat 8.30am–2.30pm; €5), at the southwestern tip of the island. Tunnels through the volcanic ash uncovered structures, two and three storeys high, first damaged by earthquake, then buried by eruption; Professor Marinatos, the excavator and now an island hero, was killed by a collapsing wall and is also buried on the site. Only a small part of what was the largest Minoan city outside of Crete has been excavated thus far and there's currently precious little to see as walkways are being constructed and a protective roof installed, completion of which is estimated to finish in several years time. Lavish frescoes once adorned the walls, however, and Cretan pottery was found stored in a chamber; most of the frescoes are currently exhibited in Athens, though you can see excellent reproductions at the Thíra Foundation in Firá (see p.196). Visit early to avoid crowds and heat.

Akrotíri itself can be reached by bus from Firá or Périssa. The newest and best campsite on the island, *Caldera View Camping* (☎22860 82010, ℗22860 81889) is situated here, as is the excellent *Glaros* taverna, on the way to Kókkini Ámmos beach, which has fine food, though the equally good *Dolphins Taverna* is better situated on the water. Kókkini Ámmos is about 500m from the site and is quite spectacular with high reddish-brown cliffs above sand the same colour (the name means "red sand"). There's a drinks stall in a cave hollowed into the base of the cliff. It's a better beach than the one below the site, but gets crowded in season.

The south coast

More secluded black-sand beaches lie under the surreal, pockmarked pumice stone that dominates the lunar coast around **Cape Exomýtis** at the island's southern extremity. Both **Vliháda** to the west and **Áyios Yeóryios** to the east of the cape, are accessed by decent roads branching off from the main one to Embório, though no buses run here and there are no amenities to speak of. West of ancient Akrotíri, a lighthouse marks the tip of **Cape Akrotíri**, which offers excellent views of the Kaméni islets and Thirassía.

The Kaméni islets and Thirassía

From either Firá or Ía, boat excursions and local ferries run to the charred volcanic islets of **Paleá Kaméni** and **Néa Kaméni**, and on to the relatively unspoilt islet of Thirassía, which was once part of Thíra until shorn off by an eruption in the third century BC. At Paleá Kaméni you can swim from the boat to hot springs with sulphurous mud, and Néa Kaméni, with its own mud-clouded hot springs, features a demanding hike to a smouldering, volcanically active crater.

To escape Thíra's tourist throngs, **Thirassía** is an excellent destination, except during the lunch-hour, tour-boat rush. At other times, the island is one of the quietest in the Cyclades, with views as dramatic as any on Thíra. The downside is that there is no sandy beach, no nightlife and nowhere to change money, though there is an ATM.

Most tour boats head for **Kórfos**, a stretch of shingle backed by fishermen's houses and high cliffs. It has a few tavernas, including *Tonio* which stays open when the day-trippers have gone, but no rooms. From Kórfos a stepped path climbs up to **MANOLÁS**, nearly 200m above. Donkeys are still used for transport, and stables can be seen in both villages. Manolás straggles along the edge of the caldera, an untidy but attractive small island village that gives an idea of what Thíra was like before tourism arrived there. It has a bakery, a couple of shops and the friendly *Panorama* and *Candouni* tavernas that open for the midday rush. Dhimitrios Nomikos has **rooms** (☎22860 29102; ❷) overlooking the village from the south.

The best **excursion** from Manolás is to follow the unmade road heading south; about halfway along you pass the church of Profítis Ilías on a hilltop to the left. From here an old and overgrown trail descends through the deserted caldera-side village of **Kerá**, before running parallel with the road to the

monastery of the Kímisis above the southern tip of the island. Minoan remains were excavated in a pumice quarry to the west of here in 1867, several years before the first discoveries at Akrotíri, but there is nothing to be seen today.

Ferries run to Thirassía from Órmos Athiniós four times a week in season and three times a week through the winter. There is no problem taking a car or rental bike over, but fill up with petrol first. **Day-tours**, arranged through any of the travel companies in Firá and Ía, take in a hike up to the active crater of Néa Kaméni and a dip in the hot springs at Paleá Kaméni, then stay two or three hours on Thirassía. Prices range from €10 for transport on a large ferry to about €30 for a more intimate guided tour on a traditional *kaiki*. The glass-bottom *Calypso* makes the same excursion for €18 and hovers over the volcanic reefs at the end of each journey to allow passangers a peak at the depths of Santoríni's flooded crater, while an outing on the *Great Blue Santoríni* submarine is quicker, at a greater depth and at a considerably higher fare of €50.

Anáfi

A ninety-minute boat ride to the east of Thíra, **Anáfi** is the last stop for ferries and is something of a travellers' dead end, with no high-season ferries on to Crete or the Dodecanese and no bank. Not that this is likely to bother most of the visitors, who intentionally come here for weeks in midsummer to take over the island's beaches with a vengeance.

At most other times the place seems idyllic, and indeed may prove too sleepy for some: there are no bona fide hotels, scooters, discos or organized excursions, and donkeys are still the main method of transport in the interior. Anáfi, though initially enchanting, is a harsh place, its mixed granite/limestone core overlaid by volcanic rock spewed out by Thíra's eruptions. Apart from the few olive trees and vines grown in the valleys, the only plants that seem to thrive are prickly pears.

The harbour and Hóra

The tiny harbour hamlet of **ÁYIOS NIKÓLAOS** has a single taverna, *Akroyiali Popi's*, with a few rooms (℡22860 61218; ❶). Jeyzed Travel (℡22860 61253, ℱ22860 61352) can provide information as well as issue ferry tickets, change money and book rooms. In August there are enough Greek visitors to fill all the rooms on the island, so it's a good idea to book ahead. Most places to stay are in Hóra. In season a bus runs from the harbour every two hours or so, 9am to 11pm, to stops at both ends of the village.

HÓRA itself, adorning a conical hill overhead, is a stiff, 25-minute climb up the obvious old mule path which shortcuts the modern road. Exposed and blustery when the *meltémi* is blowing, Hóra can initially seem a rather forbidding ghost town. This impression is slowly dispelled as you discover the hospitable islanders taking their coffee in sheltered, south-facing terraces, or under the anti-earthquake barrel vaulting that features in domestic architecture here.

For accommodation, try the modern, purpose-built **rooms** of *Anafi* (℡22860 61271; ❷), *Pelagos* (℡22860 61240; ❷), or *Anatoli* (℡ & ℱ22860 61279; ❷). More pleasant are those of *Illiovasilema* (℡22860 61280; ℱ22860 61238; ❹) and *Panorama* (℡ & ℱ22860 61292; ❸) at the east edge of the village, with stunning views south to the islets of Ftená, Pahiá and Makriá, and the distinctive monolith at the southeastern corner of Anáfi. Evening **diners** seem to divide their custom between the simple, welcoming *To Steki*, with reasonable food and barrel wine served on its terrace, and the more upmarket *Alexandhra's* on the central walkway. *Armenaki* is a lively taverna/*ouzerí* which hosts regular *bouzoúki* nights. Otherwise nightlife is limited mostly to *Mylos*, in a converted windmill in the village. Several shops, a bakery and a **post office** round up the list of amenities.

East along the coast: beaches and monasteries

The glory of Anáfi is a string of south-facing beaches starting under the cliffs at Áyios Nikólaos. Rough campers head for **KLISÍDHI**, a short walk to the east of the harbour, which has 200m of tan, gently shelving sand. Above the calamus-and-tamarisk oasis backing the beach, there are two cafés and a taverna, including the *Margaritas*, with popular rooms (℡22860 61237; ❷) and the *Villa Apollon* (℡22860 61348; ❹) on the hillside. Klisídhi can be reached by road but it's quicker to take the clifftop path starting behind the power station at the harbour. East of here the beaches can only be reached by foot or boat.

From a point on the paved road just east of Hóra, the **main path** skirting the south flank of the island is signposted "Kastélli – Paleá Hóra – Roúkouna – Monastíri". The primary branch of this trail roller-coasters in and out of several agricultural valleys that provide most of Anáfi's produce and fresh water. Just under an hour along, beside a well, you veer down a side trail to **Roúkounas**, easily the island's best beach, with some 500m of broad sand rising to tamarisk-stabilized dunes, which provide welcome shade. A single taverna operates up by the main trail in season; the suggestively craggy hill of **Kastélli**, an hour's scramble above the taverna, is the site both of ancient Anafi and a ruined Venetian castle.

Beyond Roúkounas, it's another half-hour on foot to the first of the exquisite half-dozen **Katelímatsa** coves, of all shapes and sizes, and 45 minutes to

Monastíri beach – all without facilities, so come prepared. Nudism is banned on Monastíri, because of its proximity to the monasteries.

The monasteries

Between Katelímatsa and Kálamos, the main route keeps inland, past a rare spring, to arrive at the **monastery of Zoödhóhou Piyís**, some two hours out of Hóra. A ruined temple of Apollo is incorporated into the monastery buildings to the side of the main gate; according to legend, Apollo caused Anáfi to rise from the waves, pulling off a dramatic rescue of the storm-lashed Argonauts. The courtyard, with a welcome cistern, is the venue for the island's major festival, celebrated eleven days after Easter. A family of cheesemakers lives next door and can point you up the start of the spectacular onward path to **Kalamiótissa**, a little monastery perched atop the abrupt pinnacle at the extreme southeast of the island. It takes another hour to reach, but is eminently worthwhile for the stunning scenery and views over the entire south coast. Kalamiótissa comes alive only during its September 7–8 festival; at other times, you could haul a sleeping bag up here to witness the amazing sunsets and sunrises, with your vantage point often floating in a sea of cloud. There is no water up here, so bring enough with you. It's a full day's outing from Hóra to Kalamiótissa and back; you might wish to take advantage, in at least one direction, of the excursion **kaïki** that runs from Áyios Nikólaos to Monastíri (6 times daily in high season). There is also a slightly larger mail and supplies boat that takes passengers to and from Thíra (Órmos Athiniós) twice a week, supplementing the main-line ferries to Pireás, though the journey takes two hours and is regularly cancelled in season due to winds.

Travel details

Ferries

Most of the Cyclades are served by main-line ferries from Pireás. Boats for Kéa, and less often Kýthnos depart from Lávrio. There are daily services from Rafína to Ándhros, Tínos and Mýkonos, with less frequent sailings to Sýros, Páros, Náxos and Amorgós, and the north and east Aegean. All three ports are easily reached by bus from Athens. From May to September there are also a few weekly sailings from Thessaloníki to the most popular islands.

The frequency of sailings given below is intended to give an idea of services from late June to early September, when most visitors tour the islands. During other months, expect departures to be at or below the minimum level listed, with some routes cancelled entirely.

All agents are required to issue computerized tickets, using a computerized booking system. This was designed to conform to EU regulations and prevent the overcrowding of ferries so common in the past. It means that, in high season (particularly August), certain popular routes may be booked up days in advance, so it is important to check availability on arrival in Greece and book your outward and in-bound pre-flight tickets well ahead (particularly those returning to Pireás from the most popular islands). That said, agents are notoriously ill-equipped with advance information on ferry schedules, and purchasing a ticket too far in advance can lead to problems with delayed or cancelled boats. There is usually more space on ferries sailing between islands than to and from Pireás.

Amorgós 6–8 ferries weekly to Náxos and Páros, one of these continuing to Rafína rather than Pireás; 3–4 weekly to Sýros; 2–3 weekly to Tínos and Mýkonos; 2–3 weekly to Ándhros, Koufoníssi, Skhinoússa, Iráklia and Dhonoússa; 2–3 weekly to Astypálea.

Anáfi 6–8 weekly to Pireás (12hr 30min), mostly via Thíra (1hr 30min), Íos, Náxos, Páros; 1 weekly to Sýros, Síkinos and Folégandhros; 2 weekly mail boats to Thíra (2hr).

Ándhros At least 3 daily to Rafína (2hr), Tínos (2hr) and Mýkonos; 4 weekly to Sýros; 2 weekly to Amorgós and Náxos; 1–4 weekly to Páros.

Dhonoússa 3–4 weekly to Amorgós; 2–3 weekly to Náxos, Koufoníssi, Skhinoússa,

Iráklia and Páros; 1 weekly to Pireás, Mýkonos, Tínos and Sýros.

Íos At least 3 daily to Pireás (10hr), Páros (5hr), Náxos (3hr) and Thíra (several of which continue to Anáfi); 4–5 weekly to Síkinos and Folégandhros; 1 weekly to Crete; 1 weekly to Mílos, Kímolos, Sérifos and Sífnos; 2–3 weekly to Sýros and Kássos; 1 daily to Mýkonos.

Kéa 1–3 daily to Lávrio (1hr 30min); 4 weekly to Kýthnos; 2 weekly to Sýros.

Kímolos 2 daily *kaïkia* to Mílos (Pollónia) year-round, 5 in summer; 2–5 weekly to Mílos (Adhámas), Sífnos, Sérifos, Kýthnos and Pireás (7hr); 2 weekly to Folégandhros, Síkinos and Thíra.

Koufoníssi, Skhinoússa, Iráklia 2–3 weekly to Náxos; 1–2 weekly to Páros, Sýros and Tínos and Mýkonos; 1 weekly to Dhonoússa, Amorgós and Pireás.

Kýthnos 4–12 weekly to Pireás (3hr 15min); 4–8 weekly to Sérifos, Sífnos, Kímolos and Mílos; 3–4 weekly to Thíra and Folégandhros; 1–2 weekly to Síkinos, Sýros, Íos and Kéa.

Mílos At least daily to Pireás (8hr); Thurs–Sat to Sífnos (2hr), Sérifos and Kýthnos; 2–5 daily *kaïkia* or 4–6 weekly ferries to Kímolos; 2–3 weekly to Folégandhros, Síkinos, Íos and Thíra; 2 weekly to Sýros; 2 weekly to Crete (Áyios Nikólaos or Sitía); 2 weekly to Kássos and Kárpathos; 1 weekly to Hálki and Rhodes.

Mýkonos At least 2 daily to Pireás (5hr), Rafína (3hr 30min), Tínos (1hr), Ándhros (2hr 30min) and Sýros (2hr); 2–3 weekly to Amorgós; 2 weekly to Crete (Iráklion), Skiáthos and Thessaloníki; 1–2 weekly to Dhonoússa, Koufoníssi, Skhinoússa and Iráklia; 1 weekly to Foúrni; 3–4 weekly to Ikaría and Sámos; daily to Íos, Náxos and Páros; daily (except Mon) excursion boats to Delos.

Náxos At least 3 daily to Pireás (8hr), Páros (1hr), Íos and Thíra; 6–8 weekly to Sýros; 5–7 weekly to Amorgós; 3 weekly to Crete (Iráklion); 5–6 weekly to Amorgós; 4–5 weekly to Tínos; 5 weekly to Síkinos and Folégandhros; 2 weekly to Ándhros and Rafína; 3 weekly to Anáfi; 3–4 weekly to Rhodes; 4–6 weekly to Ikaría and Sámos; 2–3 weekly to Astypálea; 1–2 weekly to Kássos and Kárpathos; 1 weekly to Kós and Foúrni; 2–3 weekly to Skiáthos and Thessaloníki; 3–6 weekly to Iráklia, Skhinoússa, Koufoníssi and Dhonoússa.

Páros At least 3 daily to Pireás (7hr), Andíparos, Náxos, Íos, Thíra; 6–8 weekly to Sýros and Tínos; 4 weekly to Iráklion (Crete); 5–7 weekly to Ikaría and Sámos; 4–6 weekly to Síkinos, Folégandhros and Amorgós; 4 weekly to Rafína and Ándhros; 2–3 weekly to Skiáthos, Thessaloníki and Rhodes; 4–6

weekly to Anáfi; 1–2 weekly to Foúrni, Kós, Kássos and Kárpathos; 2–3 weekly to Astypálea; 2–4 weekly to Koufoníssi, Skhinoússa, Iráklia and Dhonoússa; 1 weekly to Vólos; 3–6 weekly to Ikaría and Sámos; at least 1 daily to Mýkonos; at least hourly (from Parikía) to Andíparos in summer, dropping to 3 weekly in winter. There is also a car ferry from Poúnda to Andíparos at least hourly throughout the year.

Sérifos and Sífnos 5–12 weekly to Pireás (4hr 30min), Kýthnos and each other; 5–10 weekly to Mílos; 2–5 weekly to Kímolos; 2–3 weekly to Folégandhros, Síkinos and Thíra; once weekly to Íos; 2 weekly to Sýros; twice weekly from Sífnos to Páros.

Síkinos and Folégandhros 6 weekly between each other, and to Pireás (10hr); 2 weekly to Sýros, Kýthnos, Sérifos, Sífnos, Mílos and Kímolos; 3–6 weekly to Íos, Thíra, Páros and Náxos.

Sýros At least 2 daily to Pireás (4hr), Tínos (1hr), Mýkonos (2hr), Náxos and Páros; at least 2 weekly to Rafína (3hr 30min) and Ándhros; 3 weekly to Amorgós and the islets behind Náxos; 2–4 weekly to Íos and Thíra; 1 weekly to Síkinos and Folégandhros; 4–7 weekly to Ikaría and Sámos; 2–3 weekly to Astypálea; 2 weekly to Kéa, Kýthnos, Sérifos, Sífnos, Mílos and Kímolos; 1 weekly to Pátmos and Lipsí; 2–3 weekly to Skiáthos and Thessaloníki.

Thíra At least 3 daily to Pireás (10–12hr), Páros, Íos and Náxos; 5–6 weekly to Iráklion, Crete (5hr) and Thessaloníki; 6–8 weekly to Síkinos and Folégandhros; 4–6 weekly to Anáfi and Sífnos; daily to Mýkonos; 6–8 weekly to Sýros; 3–5 weekly to Tínos and Skiáthos; 2–4 weekly to Mílos and Kímolos; 1–2 weekly to Kárpathos, Kássos and Sérifos; 2 weekly to Rhodes; 4–6 weekly to Thirassía (plus lots of expensive daily excursion boats in season); 2 weekly mail boats to Anáfi.

Tínos At least 2 daily to Pireás (5hr), Rafína (4hr), Ándhros, Sýros and Mýkonos; 3–4 weekly to Páros and Náxos; 3 weekly to Thíra and Iráklion (Crete); 1–3 weekly to Skiáthos and Thessaloníki; 3 weekly to Amorgós; 1 weekly to Íos, Koufoníssi, Skhinoússa, Iráklia and Dhonoússa; also excursion boats calling at Delos and Mýkonos, 1 daily most days.

Other services

To simplify the lists above, certain strategic catamaran and small-boat services have been omitted. Of these, the *Express Skopelitis* plies daily in season between Mýkonos and Amorgós, spending each night at the latter and threading through all of the minor isles between it and Náxos, as well as Náxos and Páros (Píso Livádhi), in the course of a week; however, it's unreliable and often over-crowded – for current info call ☎22850 71256. The *Seajet* catamaran – a small-capacity (and expensive) jet-boat (☎210 414 1250 for details) – operates daily during summer out of Rafína and connects Sýros, Ándhros, Tínos, Mýkonos, Páros, Náxos and Thíra. The long-haul, full-sized *Blue Star* ships shave a few hours off the travel time to some of the most popular Cyclades (through the hubs of Páros and Náxos) for only slightly more than the price of standard tickets and much less than the cost of catamaran services.

Cycladic routes are pretty well mapped out by the three companies – Minoan Flying Dolphins, Speed Lines and Cruises (Santorini Dolphin) and Dolphin Sea Line, with regular services from Pireás, Thíra and Rafína respectively. Catamaran travel is expensive; however, when time is an issue, or for more regular connections to some of the less commonly serviced routes such as the minor islets around Náxos, these handy high-speed craft are a welcome addition to the conventional fleet.

Flights

There are **airports** on **Páros**, **Mýkonos**, **Thíra**, **Smros**, **Mílos** and **Náxos**. In season, or during storms when ferries are idle, you have little chance of getting a seat on any flight at less than three days' notice, and tickets are predictably expensive. Expect off-season (Oct–April) frequencies to drop by at least eighty percent. Flights are on Olympic unless otherwise stated.

Athens to: Mílos (1–2 daily; 45min); Mýkonos (4–5 daily on Olympic; 3–4 daily on Aegean; 40min); Náxos (6 weekly; 45min); Páros (2–3 daily; 40min); Sýros (3–6 weekly on Olympic, 35min); Thíra (5–6 daily on Olympic; 3–4 daily on Aegean).

Mýkonos to: Rhodes (2 weekly; 55min); Thessaloníki (2 weekly on Olympic, daily on Aegean; 1hr 20min); Thíra (4 weekly; 30min).

Thíra to: Rhodes (2–5 weekly; 50min); Thessaloníki (2 weekly on Olympic, 1 daily on Aegean; 1hr 20min).

Crete

Highlights

Museum,
world's foremost
...um. See p.216

✳ **Minoan sites** Knossos is the most exciting, but Malia, Phaestos, Zakros and other archeological ruins across the island are also worth a visit. See p.222, p.228, p.234 and p.250

✳ **Beach resorts** Although those on the Iráklion coast are overcrowded, Mátala, Paleohóra, Plakiás and Sitía still have bags of charm and excellent strands. See p.229

✳ **Lasíthi Plateau** This green and fertile high mountain plateau has picturesque agricultural villages and unique

white cloth-sailed windmills. See p.240

✳ **The Dhiktean cave** Mythological birthplace of Zeus, the Dhiktean cave is stunningly situated on the Lasíthi Plateau. See p.241

✳ **Haniá and Réthymnon old towns** These atmospheric centres display haunting vestiges of their Venetian and Turkish pasts and are a joy to wander around. See p.263 and p.254

✳ **Samarian Gorge** A magnificent gorge: the longest in Europe, offering a chance to see brilliant wildflowers, golden eagles and perhaps a Cretan ibex. See p.272

△ Haniá old town

3

Crete

Crete (Kríti) is a great deal more than just another Greek island. In many places, especially in the cities or along the developed north coast, it doesn't feel like an island at all, but rather a substantial realm in its own right – a mountainous, wealthy and surprisingly cosmopolitan one. But when you lose yourself among the mountains, or on the lesser-known coastal reaches of the south, it has everything you could want of a Greek island and more: great beaches, remote hinterlands and hospitable people.

In **history**, Crete is distinguished above all as the home of Europe's earliest civilization. It was only at the beginning of the twentieth century that the legends of King Minos and of a Cretan society that ruled the Greek world in prehistory were confirmed by excavations at **Knossos** and **Phaestos**. Yet the **Minoans** had a remarkably advanced society, the centre of a maritime trading empire as early as 2000 BC. The artworks produced on Crete at this time are unsurpassed anywhere in the ancient world, and it seems clear that life on Crete in those days was good. This apparently peaceful culture survived at least three major natural disasters. Each time the palaces were destroyed, and each time they were rebuilt on a grander scale. Only after the last destruction, probably the result of an eruption of Santoríni and subsequent tidal waves and earthquakes, do significant numbers of weapons begin to appear in the ruins. This, together with the appearance of the Greek language, has been interpreted to mean that Mycenaean Greeks had taken control of the island. Nevertheless, for nearly 500 years, by far the longest period of peace the island has seen, Crete was home to a culture well ahead of its time.

The Minoans of Crete probably came originally from Anatolia; at their height they maintained strong links with Egypt and with the people of Asia Minor, and this position as meeting point and strategic fulcrum between east and west has played a major role in Crete's subsequent history. Control of the island passed from Greeks to Romans to Saracens, through the Byzantine empire to Venice, and finally to Turkey for more than two centuries. During World War II, the island was **occupied** by the Germans and attained the dubious distinction of being the first place to be successfully invaded by paratroops.

Today, with a flourishing **agricultural economy**, Crete is one of the few islands that could probably support itself without tourists. Nevertheless, **tourism** is heavily promoted. The northeast coast in particular is overdeveloped, and though there are parts of the south and west coasts that have not been spoilt, they are getting harder to find. By contrast, the high mountains of the interior are still barely touched, and one of the best things to do on Crete is to **rent a vehicle** and explore the remoter villages.

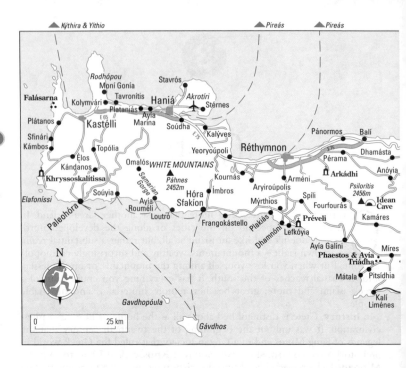

Every part of Crete has its loyal devotees and it's hard to pick out highlights, but generally if you want to get away from it all you should head west, towards **Haniá** and the smaller, less well-connected places along the south and west coasts. It is in this part of the island that the White Mountains rise, while below them yawns the famous **Samarian Gorge**. The **far east**, around **Sitía**, is also relatively unscathed with a string of isolated beaches worth seeking out to the south of the over-popular **Váï beach**, which lures crowds attracted by its famous palm grove. However, Sitía's new international airport, currently under construction, could change things significantly here in the next few years.

Whatever you do, your first main priority will probably be to leave **Iráklion** (Heraklion) as quickly as possible, having paid the obligatory, and rewarding, visit to the **Archeological Museum** and nearby **Knossos**. The other great Minoan sites cluster around the middle of the island: **Phaestos** and **Ayía Triádha** to the south (with Roman **Gortys** to provide contrast), and **Malia** on the north coast. Almost wherever you go you'll find a reminder of the island's history, whether it's the superbly preserved Minoan town of **Gourniá** near the cosmopolitan resort of **Áyios Nikólaos**, the exquisitely sited palace of **Zakros** in the far east, or the lesser sites scattered around the west. Unexpected highlights include Crete's Venetian forts at **Réthymnon** and **Frangokástello**; its hundreds of frescoed Byzantine churches, most famously at **Kritsá**; and, at Réthymnon and Haniá, the cluttered old Venetian and Turkish quarters.

Crete has by far the longest summers in Greece, and you can get a decent tan here right into October and swim at least from May until November. The one seasonal blight is the *meltémi*, a northerly wind which regularly blows harder here and more continuously than anywhere else in Greece – the best of several reasons for avoiding an **August** visit if you can. It's far from an ill wind, however, as it also lowers humidity and makes the island's higher summer temperatures more bearable.

Iráklion, Knossos and central Crete

Many visitors to Crete arrive in the island's capital, **Iráklion** (Heraklion), but it's not an outstandingly beautiful city, nor one where you'll want to stay much longer than it takes to visit the **Archeological Museum** and nearby **Knossos**. Iráklion itself, though it has its good points – superb fortifications, a fine market, atmospheric old alleys and some interesting lesser museums – is for the most part an experience in survival: despite a recent makeover of central areas by the city hall it remains modern, raucous, traffic-laden and overcrowded.

The area immediately around the city is less touristy than you might expect, mainly because there are few decent beaches of any size on this central part of the coast. To the west, mountains drop straight into the sea virtually all the way to Réthymnon, with just two significant coastal settlements: **Ayía Pelayía**, a sizeable resort, and **Balí**, which is gradually becoming one. Eastwards, the main resorts are at least 30km away, at **Hersónissos** and beyond, although there is a string of rather unattractive developments all the way there. Inland, there's agricultural country, some of the richest on the island, a cluster of Crete's better vineyards, and a series of wealthy but rather dull villages. Directly behind the capital rises **Mount Ioúktas** with its characteristic profile of Zeus; to the west the Psilorítis massif spreads around the peak of **Mount Psilorítis** (Ídha) the island's highest mountain. On the south coast there are few roads and little development of any kind, except at **Ayía Galíni** in the southwest, a nominal fishing village long since swamped with tourists, and **Mátala**, which has thrown out the hippies that made it famous and is now crowded with package-trippers. **Léndas** has to some extent occupied Mátala's old niche.

Despite the lack of resorts, there seem constantly to be thousands of people trekking back and forth across the centre of the island. This is largely because of the superb archeological sites in the south: **Phaestos**, second of the Minoan palaces, with its attendant villa at **Ayía Triádha**, and **Gortys**, capital of Roman Crete.

Iráklion

The best way to approach **IRÁKLION** is by sea, with Mount Ioúktas rising behind it and the Psilorítis range to the west. As you get closer, it's the city walls that first stand out, still dominating and fully encircling the oldest part of town; finally you sail in past the great **Venetian fortress** defending the harbour entrance. Unfortunately, big ships no longer dock in the old port but at great modern concrete wharves alongside, which neatly sums up Iráklion itself. Many of the old parts have been restored from the bottom up, but they're of no relevance to the bustle and noise that characterizes much of the city today. In recent times, however, Iráklion's administrators have been giving belated attention to dealing with some of the image problems, and large tracts of the centre – particularly the focal Platía Eleftherías – have been landscaped and refurbished with the aim of presenting a less daunting prospect to the visitor.

Orientation, arrival and information

Virtually everything you're likely to want to see in Iráklion lies within the walled city, and even here the majority falls into a relatively small sector – the northeastern corner. The most vital thoroughfare, **25-Avgoústou**, links the harbour with the commercial city centre. At the bottom it is lined with shipping and travel agencies and rental outlets, but further up these give way to banks, restaurants and stores. **Platía Venizélou** (or Fountain Square), off to the right, is crowded with cafés and restaurants; behind Venizélou lies **El Greco Park** (actually a rather cramped garden), with more bars, while on the opposite side of 25-Avgoústou are some of the more interesting of Iráklion's older buildings. Further up 25-Avgoústou, **Kalokerinoú** leads down to Haniá Gate and westwards out of the city; straight ahead, **Odhós–1821** is a major shopping street, and adjacent 1866 is given over to the animated **market**, perhaps the best on the island. To the left, Dhikeosínis heads for the city's main square, **Platía Eleftherías**, paralleled by the pedestrian alley, Dedhálou, lined with many of the city's swankier fashion stores and the direct link between the two squares. The revamped Elefthérias is very much the traditional centre of the city, both for traffic – which swirls around it constantly – and for life in general; it is ringed by more expensive tourist cafés and restaurants and comes alive in the evening with crowds of strolling locals.

Points of arrival

Iráklion **airport** is right on the coast, 4km east of the city. **Bus** #1 leaves for Platía Elefthérias every few minutes from the car park in front of the terminal; buy your ticket (€0.70) at the booth before boarding. There are also plenty of **taxis** outside (which you'll be forced to use when the buses stop at 11pm), and prices to major destinations are posted here and in the domestic departures hall – it's about €6–8 to the centre of town, depending on traffic. Get an agreement on the fare before taking a cab and beware if the driver extols the virtues of a particular place to stay and offers to drop you there – he'll usually be getting a kickback from the proprietors. To avoid such hassles ask to be dropped at the central Platía Elefthérias, from where everything is in easy walking distance.

There are two main **bus stations** (often titled A and B on maps). Bus station A straddles both sides of the main road between the ferry dock and the Venetian harbour. Buses run from here **west** to Réthymnon and Haniá and **east** along the coastal highway to Hersónsissos, Mália, Áyios Nikólaos, and Sitía as well as **southeast** to Ierápetra and points en route. Local bus #2 to Knossos also leaves from here (south side of the main road). Buses for the **southwest** (Phaestos, Mátala and Ayía Galíni) and along the inland roads west (Týlissos, Anóyia) operate out of terminal B, just outside Haniá Gate, a very long walk from the centre up Kalokerinoú (or jump on any bus heading down this street). From the wharves where the **ferries** dock, the city rises directly ahead in steep tiers. If you're heading for the centre, for the Archeological Museum or the tourist office, cut straight up the stepped alleys behind the bus station onto Dhoúkos Bofór and to Platía Elefthérias; this will take about fifteen minutes. For accommodation though, and to get a better idea of the layout of Iráklion's main attractions, it's simplest to follow the main roads by a rather more roundabout route. Head west along the coast, past the major eastbound bus station and on by the Venetian harbour before cutting up towards the centre on 25-Avgoústou.

Information

Iráklion's **tourist office** (Mon–Fri 9am–2.30pm; ☏2810 228 225, ☏2810 226 020) is located just below Platía Elefthérias, opposite the Archeological Museum at Zanthoudhídhou 1. A sub-office at the **airport** (April–Sept daily 9am–9pm) is good for basic information and maps. The **tourist police** – more helpful than most – are at Dhikeosínis 10 (☏2810 283 190), halfway between Platía Elefthérias and the market.

Accommodation

Finding a **room** can be difficult in season. The best place to look for inexpensive places is in the area around Platía Venizélou, along Hándhakos and towards the harbour to the west of 25-Avgoústou. Other concentrations of affordable places are around El Greco Park and in the streets above the Venetian harbour. Better hotels mostly lie closer to Platía Elefthérias, to the south of Platía Venizélou and near the east- and westbound bus stations.

IRÁKLION

S. VENIZELOU

Áyios Andhréas
Bastion

SKORDHILON

1879

6

@

Prioulí
Fountain

SAVATHIANON

MAKARIOU

SFAKION

AYION DHEKON

OEDHIOHAKI

KALOKERINOU

PLATÍA
EKATERÍNIS

Áyios Minas

Pantokratóros
Bastion

Cathedral

Haniá Gate

KARDIOTISSIS

South/West
Bus Station (B)

62 MARTYRÓN

PLASTIRA

Haniá & Festós

TOMBAZI

THERISSOU

YIANNIKOU

ROMANOU

PLASTIRA

THENON

N

Kazantzakis'
Tomb

KONDILAKI

0   250 m

Martinengo
Bastion

ACCOMMODATION

Dedalos	I
Hellas	H
Kris	E
Kronos	A
Lato	B
Mirabello	F
Olympic	J
Rea	G
Vergina	C
Youth Hostel	D

Venetian Fortress

Venetian Harbour

S. VENIZELOU

Áyios Petros

Historical Museum

GAZI

Arsenáli

EPIMENIDHOU

Ferry Dock

East/West Bus Station (A)

DHOUKOS BOFOR

Airport & the east

El Greco Park

Áyios Títos

Loggia

Sabbionera Bastion

PLATIA VENIZELOU

MIRABELOU

Archeological Museum

Morosini Fountain

San Marco

MILATOU

SAPOUTIE

ZANTHOUDHIDHOU

IKAROU

Ayía Ekateríni

Market

Tourist Police

PLATIA ELEFTHERIAS

PLATIA DHASKALOYIANNI

Bembo Fountain

PLATIA KORNAROU

PLATIA ARKADHIOU

Public Gardens

Vitouri Bastion

PEDHIADHOS

Pórta Kenoúria

Southeast Bus Terminal

PLATIA KYPROU

Jesus Bastion

RESTAURANTS

Bougatsa Kirkor	10
Fos Fanari	3
Geroplatanos	8
I Avli Tou Deikaliona	4
Ippokampos	1
Kapetanios	5
Katsina	2
Loukoulos	9
The Mexican	6
Pagopoleion	7
Taverna Giovanni	11

Knossós & Natural History Museum

There are no **campsites** near Iráklion. The nearest sites both lie to the east of the city: *Creta Camping* at Káto Goúves (☎28970 41400), 16km east, and *Caravan Camping* (☎28970 22901) at Hersónissos, 28km east.

Dedalos Dhedhálou 15 ☎2810 244 812, ✉daedalos@internet.gr. Recently refurbished hotel with balcony rooms overlooking this pedestrianized shopping street which is tranquil at night. All rooms are en suite and equipped with TV and three have air con (€4 surcharge); fans available for the rest on request. ❸

Hellas Hándhakos 24 ☎2810 288 851, ℱ2810 284 442. Hostel-type place with simple doubles, and dormitory rooms (€7 per bed) favoured by younger travellers. Also has a roof garden and snack-bar. ❶

Kris Dhoúkos Bofór 2, near the Venetian harbour ☎2810 223 211. Studio rooms with kitchenette, fridge, great balcony views and friendly female proprietor. ❸

Kronos Agaráthou 2, west of 25-Avgoústou ☎2810 282 240, ℱ2810 285 853. Pleasant, friendly and modern hotel with en-suite, sea-view balcony rooms. ❹

Lato Epomenídhou 15 ☎2810 228 103, ⊛www.lato.gr. Stylish and luxurious hotel where air-con rooms have minibar, TV and fine balcony views over the Venetian harbour (the higher floors have the better views). Breakfast included. ❻

Mirabello Theotokopoúlou 20 ☎2810 285 052, ⊛www.mirabello-hotel.gr. Good-value, family-run

hotel featuring balcony rooms with or without bath and most with air con and TV. In a quiet street just north of El Greco Park. ❸–❹

Olympic Platía Kornárou ☎2810 288 861, ℱ2810 222 512. Overlooking the busy *platía* and the famous Bembo fountain. One of the many hotels built in the 1960s, but one of the few that has been refurbished; rates include breakfast. ❻

Rea Kalimeráki 1 ☎2810 223 638, ☎2810 242 189. A friendly, comfortable and clean *pension* in a quiet street. Some rooms with washbasins, others with own shower. ❷

Vergina Hortátson 32 ☎2810 242 739. Basic but pleasant rooms with washbasins in a quiet street and set around a courtyard with a giant banana tree. ❶

Youth Hostel Výronos 5 ☎2810 286 281, ✉heraklioyouthhostel@yahoo.com. Formerly Iráklion's official youth hostel, it has been stripped of its HI status. It is in fact a good place to stay, family run and very friendly and helpful. There's plenty of space and some beds (albeit illegal) on the roof if you fancy sleeping out under the stars. Private rooms (€25) as well as dormitories (€10 per bed); hot showers, breakfast and other meals available.

The Town

A good place to start your explorations of the town is the focal Platía Venizélou, crowded most of the day with Iraklian youth patronizing outdoor cafés (marginally cheaper than those on Eleftherías), and with travellers who've arranged to meet in "Fountain Square". The **Morosini Fountain**, which gives the square its popular name, is not particularly spectacular at first glance, but on closer inspection is really a very beautiful work; it was built by Venetian governor Francesco Morosini in the seventeenth century, incorporating four lions which were some three hundred years old even then. From the *platía* you can strike up Dhedhálou, a pedestrianized street full of fashion and tourist shops, or continue on 25-Avgoústou to a major traffic junction at Platía Nikifoúrou Foka. To the right, Kalokerinoú leads west out of the city, the market lies straight ahead along Odhós-1866, and Platía Eleftherías is a short walk to the left up Dhikeosínis.

Platía Eleftherías and the Archeological Museum

Platía Eleftherías, with seats shaded by palms and eucalyptuses, is very much the traditional heart of the city: traffic swirls around it constantly, and on summer evenings strolling hordes jam its cafés and restaurants. Most of Iráklion's more expensive shops are in the streets leading off the *platía*.

The **Archeological Museum** (April–Sept Mon 12–7pm, Tues–Sun 8am–7pm; Oct–March daily 8am–5pm; €6) is nearby. Almost every important

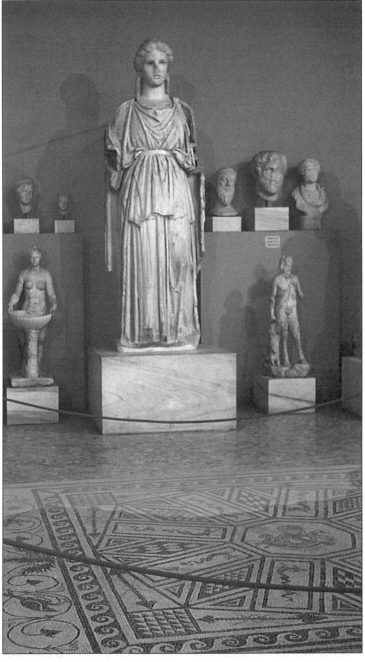

217

△ Archeological Museum interior, Iráklion

prehistoric and Minoan find on Crete is included in this fabulous, if bewilderingly large, collection. The museum tends to be crowded, especially when a guided tour stampedes through, but it's worth taking time over. You can't hope to see everything, nor can we attempt to describe it all (several good museum guides are sold here; the best probably being the glossy ones by J.A. Sakellarakis or Andonis Vasilakis), but highlights include the **mosaics** in Room 2 (the galleries are arranged basically in chronological order), the famous **inscribed disc** from Phaestos in Room 3 (itself the subject of several books), most of Room 4, especially the magnificent bull's head **rhyton** (drinking vessel), the **jewellery** in Room 6 (and elsewhere) and the engraved steatite **black vases** in Room 7. Save some of your time and energy for upstairs, where the **Hall of the Frescoes**, with intricately reconstructed fragments of the wall paintings from Knossos and other sites, is especially wonderful. A long-overdue **renovation** of the Archeological Museum was planned to begin in early 2004, and should place the collection at the forefront of museum presentation in Greece. However, once work is under way and whilst it is in progress, there will inevitably be some frustration for visitors as rooms are closed and items moved around.

Walls and fortifications

The massive **Venetian walls**, in places up to 15m thick, are the most obvious evidence of Iráklion's later history. Though their fabric is incredibly well preserved, access is virtually nonexistent. It is possible, just, to walk along them from Áyios Andhréas Bastion over the sea in the west, as far as the Martinengo Bastion where lies the **tomb of Nikos Kazantzakis**, Cretan author of *Zorba the Greek*, whose epitaph reads: "I believe in nothing, I hope for nothing, I am free." At weekends, Iraklians gather here to pay their respects and enjoy a free view of the soccer matches played by one of the city's two team's in the stadium below. If the walls seem altogether too much effort, the **port fortifications** are very much easier to see. Stroll out along the jetty (crowded with courting couples after dark) and you can get inside the sixteenth-century **Venetian fortress** (Tues–Sun 8.30am–3pm; €2) at the harbour entrance, emblazoned with the Venetian Lion of St Mark. Standing atop this, you can begin to understand how Iráklion (or Candia as it was known until the seventeenth century) withstood a 22-year siege before finally falling to the Ottomans. On the landward side of the port, the Venetian **arsenáli** (arsenals) can also be seen, their arches rather lost amid the concrete road system all around.

Churches and other museums

From the harbour, 25-Avgoústou will take you up past most of the town's other highlights. The **church of Áyios Títos**, on the left as you approach Platía Venizélou, borders a pleasant little *platía*. Byzantine in origin but substantially rebuilt by the Venetians, it looks magnificent principally because, like most of the churches here, it was adapted by the Turks as a mosque and only reconsecrated in 1925; consequently it has been renovated on numerous occasions. On the top side of this *platía*, abutting 25-Avgoústou, is the Venetian **city hall** with its famous loggia, again almost entirely rebuilt. Just above this, facing Platía Venizélou, is the **church of San Marco**, its steps usually crowded with the overflow of people milling around in the *platía*. Neither of these last two buildings has found a permanent role in its refurbished state, but both are generally open to house some kind of exhibition or craft show.

Slightly away from the obvious city-centre circuit, but still within the bounds of the walls, there are a couple of lesser museums worth seeing if you have the time. First of these is the excellent collection of **icons** in the **church of Ayía Ekateríni** (Mon–Sat 8.30am–1.30pm, plus Tues, Thurs & Fri 5–7pm; €2), an ancient building just below the undistinguished cathedral, off Kalokerinoú. The finest here are six large scenes by Miháïl Damaskinos (a near-contemporary of El Greco) who fused Byzantine and Renaissance influences. Supposedly both Damaskinos and El Greco studied at Ayía Ekateríni in the sixteenth century, when it functioned as a sort of monastic art school.

The **Historical Museum** (Mon & Wed–Fri 9am–5pm, Tues & Sat 9am–2pm; €3; ⓦ www.historical-museum.gr) is some way from here, down near the waterfront opposite the now closed and crumbling *Xenia* hotel. Its display of folk costumes and jumble of local memorabilia includes the reconstructed studies of both Nikos Kazantzakis and Emanuel Tsouderos (the latter both Cretan statesman and former Greek prime minister). There's enough variety to satisfy just about anyone, including the only El Greco painting on Crete, the untypical *View of Mount Sinai and the Monastery of St Catherine*.

A **Natural History Museum** (Sept–June Mon–Fri 9am–3pm, Sun 9am–5pm; July–Aug daily 9am–8pm; €4.50; ⓦ www.nhmc.uoc.gr) is definitely worth the trek out to visit it. Covering three floors, as well as the usual flora and fauna displays, it has exhibits detailing the island's geological evolution, the arrival of man and the environment as it would have appeared to the Minoans. The museum lies 2km south of the Pórta Kenoúria (a gate in the walls) along the road to Knossos. Bus #2 from Platía Eleftherías will drop you there (ask for the "Pagrito School" stop) or take a taxi (about €3).

The beaches

Iráklion's **beaches** are some way out, whether east or west of town. In either direction they're easily accessible by bus: #6 heads west from the stop outside the *Astoria* hotel in Platía Eleftherías; #7 east from the stop opposite this, under the trees in the centre of the *platía*.

Almyrós (or Ammoudhári) to the west has been subjected to a degree of development, comprising a campsite, several medium-size hotels and one giant one (the *Zeus Beach*, in the shadow of the power station at the far end), which makes the beach hard to get to without walking through or past something built up.

Amnissós, to the east, is the better choice, with several tavernas and the added amusement of planes swooping in immediately overhead to land. This is where most locals go on their afternoons off; the furthest of the beaches is the best, although new hotels are encroaching here, too. Little remains to indicate the once-flourishing port of Knossos here, aside from a rather dull, fenced-in dig. If you're seriously into antiquities, however, you'll find a more rewarding site in the small Minoan villa, known as **Nírou Háni** (Tues–Sun 8.30am–3pm; free) at Háni Kokkíni, the first of the full-blown resort developments east of Iráklion.

Eating

Big city though it is, Iráklion disappoints when it comes to eating, and since the advent of the euro, genuine budget places are getting harder to find. The cafés and tavernas of *platíes* **Venizélou** and **Eleftherías** are essential places to sit and watch the world pass, but their food is expensive and mediocre. One striking exception is *Bougatsa Kirkor*, by the Morosini Fountain in Venizélou, where you can sample authentic Cretan *bougátsa* – a creamy cheese pie sprinkled with sugar and cinnamon; alternatively, try a plate of *loukoumádhes* (dough fritters), available from a number of cafés (*Aktarika* is good) near the junction of Dhikeosínis and 25-Avgoústou. A more atmospheric option is to head for the little alley, **Fotíou Theodhosáki**, which runs through from the market to Odhós Evans. It is entirely lined with the tables of rival taverna owners, certainly authentic and catering for market traders and their customers as well as tourists. Compared with some, they look a little grimy, but are by no means cheap, which can come as a surprise.

A relaxed and economical lunchtime venue in the **centre** of town is *Geroplatanos* with tables on the leafy Platía Ayíou Títou beside the church of the same name. Across from here is one of Iráklion's most stylish bars, *Pagopoleion* ("Ice Factory"), also good for lazy terrace breakfasts and snacks; attached is an excellent restaurant and although medium priced, the food is consistently good – their recommended *mezedhákia* buffet (Sat & Sun 1–4pm) allows you to fill a plate for around €5. *Pagopoleion* is the creation of photographic artist Chrissy Karelli, who has preserved a strident inscription on one wall, left by the Nazi occupiers who used local labour to run what was then Iráklion's only ice factory. Still near the centre, just off Eleftherías on **Platía Dhaskaloyiánni** (where the post office is), are some authentic and inexpensive *ouzerís*: try *Ta Asteria* or *40 Kymata*; by day the *platía* is a pleasant and relaxing venue, if not for a meal then to sit at one of its cafés, which transform into more raucous and crowded music bars after dark. Nearer Venizélou, try exploring some of the backstreets to the east, off Dhedhálou and behind the loggia. The *Taverna Giovanni*, on the alley Koráï parallel to Dhedhálou, is one of the better tavernas in Iráklion, although the pricey food and an expensive wine list seem aimed more at Iráklion's smart set than the casual visitor. Should you have a craving for non-Greek food, there is Italian at the equally expensive *Loukoulos*, almost opposite the *Taverna Giovanni*, which has a leafy courtyard. More reasonable prices are on offer at the very good and popular new taverna-*ouzerí I Avli tou Deikaliona* (☎2810 244 215), Kalokerinoú 8, at the rear of the Historical Museum, where you may need to book to get a table on their attractive terrace. Mexican tacos and beers are on offer at *The Mexican*, Hándhakos 71, on the west side of the central zone – an area with many lively bars and cafés.

The **waterfront** is dotted with fish tavernas with little to recommend them. Instead, turn left at the bottom of 25-Avgoústou and cross the road to *Ippokampos*, which specializes in excellent-value fish dishes and *mezédhes* at moderate prices. Deservedly popular with locals, it's often crowded late into the evening: you may have to wait in line or turn up earlier than the Greeks eat to get an outdoor table. For simple and cheap seafood *mezédhes*, slightly south from here, *Katsina*, at Marineli 12, is a simple and friendly *ouzerí* with outdoor tables on a small *platía*; this alley has a whole bunch of similar places popular with locals, and at the southern end, *Fos Fanari*, opposite the pint-sized chapel of Áyios Dimítrios is also worth a try.

For **snacks** and **takeaways**, there's a group of *souvláki* and other fast-food stalls clustering around the top of 25-Avgoústou near the entrance to El Greco Park, which is handy if you need somewhere to sit and eat. For *tyrópita* and *spanakópita* (cheese or spinach pies) and other pastries, sweet or savoury, there are no shortage of *zaharoplastía* and places such as *Everest* – just north of the Morosini Fountain – which does takeaways of these as well as lots of other savouries. If you want to buy your own food, the **market** on Odhós-1866 is the place to go; it's an attraction in itself, and does a great line in modestly priced Cretan herbs (including saffron) to take home.

Drinking, nightlife and entertainment

Iráklion is a bit of a damp squib as far as **nightlife** goes, certainly when compared with many other towns on the island. If you're determined, however, there are a few city-centre possibilities, and plenty of options if all you want to do is sit and **drink**. In addition, there are a number of **cinemas** scattered about: check the posters on the boards by the tourist police office.

Bars

The city's most animated **bars** are located around **Platía Koráï** behind Dhedhálou (up from *Taverna Giovanni* listed opposite) and along the alley of the same name to the west. On summer nights these places are packed with Iráklion's younger set. *Flash* and *To Avgo* are the most popular venues on the *platía* itself while along the alley are places such as *Rebels* and glitzy *Korais*, which has a plant-festooned terrace, movie-screens and music and attracts big crowds. Another scene is opening up along Milatou – parallel with and slightly north of Koráï – where a new spectacular bar, *Mayo*, has opened and is currently *the* place to be seen. Slightly north again, *Pagopoleion* (see opposite) is a less frenetic after-dark alternative with a DJ and laid-back Latin and modern Greek sounds. After 10pm, a lively bar scene also fans out into the streets around Hándhakos; among a number of new-style places *Jasmin*, Ayiostefanitón 6, is tucked in an alley on the left, midway down Hándhakos, and serves a variety of teas (including the Cretan *dhíktamo* – a panacea used by the ancients) with easy jazz and rock as background music. Nearby, *Orionas*, at Psaromíligon 15, is a music and drinks bar on two floors which has a varied programme of live music at weekends including jazz, blues, reggae and rock acts.

In and around **Platía Venizélou**, there are many bars, again some are very fashionable, with *Andromeda* and *Aktarika* being a couple of the most popular. These represent a new breed of *kafenío* emerging in Iráklion, attracting a younger crowd: the drinks are **cocktails** rather than *rakí* and the music is Western or modern Greek. There are similar bars along Kandanoléon, off El Greco Park, and on the east side of the park itself.

Clubs and discos

For **discos** and **clubs** proper, there is a large selection, playing Western music, interspersed with Greek tunes (not the type played for tourists). *Privelige* is the most popular, down towards the harbour at the bottom of Dhoúkos Bofór, below the Archeological Museum. The nearby *Envy* provides competition, and (outside high summer) along Ikárou, downhill from Platía Eleftherías, another group of clubs is gathered, including *Minoica*, *Korus Club* and *Athina*, all playing similar music and popular with young Iraklians.

Listings

Airlines Aegean, Dhimokratias 11 (☎2810 344 394) and Olympic, Platía Eleftherías (☎2810 229 191) are the main scheduled airlines with connecting flights to Athens and other parts of Greece. Charter airlines flying into Iráklion mostly use local travel agents as their representatives.

Airport For airport information call ☎2810 228 402. Bus #1 runs from Platía Eleftherías to the airport every few minutes; buy a ticket (€0.70) from the booth outside the *Astoria Hotel* first.

Banks There are now ATMs all over town, but the main bank branches are on 25-Avgoústou.

Car and bike rental 25-Avgoústou is lined with rental companies, but you'll often find cheaper rates on the backstreets; it's always worth asking for discounts. For cars and bikes, good places to start include: Blue Sea, Kosmá Zótou 7, near the bottom of 25-Avgoústou (☎2810 241097), which gives a twenty percent discount to Rough Guide readers, and Sun Rise, 25-Avgoústou 46 (☎2810

221 609). For cars try: Reliable, Epimenidou 8 off the east side of the same street (☎2810 344 212); Motor Club, Platía Ánglon 1 at the bottom of 25-Avgoústou facing the port (☎2810 222408); and Ritz in the *Hotel Rea*, Kalimeráki 1 (☎2810 223638). All offer free delivery to hotels and airport.

Ferry tickets Available from Minoan Lines, 25-Avgoústou 78 (☎2810 229 646, ⓦ www.minoan.gr), which handles the islands and Athens; and ANEK Lines, 25-Avgoústou 33 (☎2810 222 481), for Athens only; also try any of the travel agents listed opposite. Another source for tickets and ferry information is the long-established Paleologus Travel, 25-Avgoústou 5 (☎2810 346 185); their comprehensive websites (ⓦ www.ferries.gr, ⓦ www.greekislands.gr) are excellent.

Hospital Most central is the hospital on Apollónion, southwest of Platía Kornárou (☎2810 229713), between Albér and Moussoúrou.

Internet Iráklion now has a number of Internet cafés located in and around the city centre. Netcafé, Odhós-1878 4 (daily 10am–2am; €2.40 for 1hr) is good; other central places with similar charges and hours are Internest, Mihelidhaki 23, Konsova, Dhikeosínis 25, and Gallery Games, Koraï 14.

Laundry Washsalon, Hándhakos 18 (Mon–Sat 8.30am–9pm) is reliable and also does service washes (€6 for 6kg). Laundry Perfect at Malikoúti 32, north of the Archeological Museum, will do the same for €5.80 (Mon–Sat 9am–9pm).

Left luggage Offices in Station A (daily 6.30am–8pm; €1 per bag per day), but not Station B, as well as a commercial agency at Hándhakos 18 (daily 24hr; large locker €1.50 per large locker per day). You can also leave bags at the youth hostel (even if you don't stay there) for €1.50 per bag per day. If you want to leave your bag while you go off on a bike for a day or two, the rental company should be prepared to store it.

Newspapers and books For English-language newspapers and novels, Bibliopoleio, almost opposite the Morosini Fountain on Platía Venizélou, is the most central. The excellent Planet International Bookstore, on four floors behind Platía Venizélou at the corner of Hándhakos and Kydhonías, has the island's biggest stock of English-language titles and is a great place to browse.

Pharmacies Plentiful on the main shopping streets – at least one is open 24hr on a rota basis; the others will have a sign on the door indicating which it is. There are traditional herbalists in the market.

Post office Main office in Platía Dhaskaloyiánnis, off Platía Eleftherías (Mon–Fri 7.30am–8pm).

Taxis Major taxi ranks in Platía Eleftherías and by the Morosini Fountain, or call ☎2810 210 102 or 2810 210 168. Prices displayed on boards at the taxi stands.

Toilets In El Greco Park and the public gardens near the cathedral, or at the bus stations; there's also an excellent one at the Archeological Museum (no entrance charge).

Travel agencies Budget operators and student specialists include the extremely helpful Blavakis Travel, Platía Kallergón 8, just off 25-Avgoústou by the entrance to El Greco Park (☎2810 282 541), and Prince Travel, 25-Avgoústou 30 (☎2810 282 706). For excursions around the island, villa rentals and so on, the bigger operators are probably easier: Creta Travel Bureau, Epimenídhou (☎2810 227002) and Adamis Tours, 25-Avgoústou 23 (☎2810 346202). The latter is also the local American Express agent.

Knossos

KNOSSOS, the largest of the **Minoan palaces**, reached its cultural peak more than three thousand years ago, though a town of some importance persisted here well into the Roman era. It lies on a low, largely man-made hill some 5km southeast of Iráklion; the surrounding hillsides are rich in lesser remains spanning 25 centuries, starting at the beginning of the second millennium BC.

Just over a century ago the palace existed only in mythology. Knossos was the court of the legendary King Minos, whose wife Pasiphae bore the Minotaur, half-bull, half-man. Here the labyrinth was constructed by Daedalus to contain the monster, and youths were brought from Athens as human sacrifice until Theseus arrived to slay the beast and, with Ariadne's help, escape its lair. The discovery of the palace, and the interplay of these legends with fact, is among the most amazing tales of modern archeology. Heinrich Schliemann, the German excavator of Troy, suspected that a major Minoan palace lay under the

Within the map image:

Royal Road

Theatral Area

PALACE OF KNOSSOS

North Entrance

Lustral Basin

Bull Relief

N

West Court

Giant "Pithoi"

Storage Pits

Throne Room

Workshops

Site Entrance

Piano
Nobile

Storerooms

● Statue
West Entrance

Central Court

Grand
Stairway

Royal Apartments

Priest-King
Fresco

South House

0   25 m

Southeast House

3

CRETE | Knossos

various tumuli here, but was denied the necessary permission to dig by the local Ottoman authorities at the end of the nineteenth century. It was left for Sir Arthur Evans, whose name is indelibly associated with Knossos, to excavate the site, from 1900 onwards.

The #2 and #4 local **buses** set off every ten minutes from Iráklion's city bus stands (adjacent to the eastbound bus station), proceed up 25-Avgoústou (with a stop just south of Platía Venizélou) and out of town on Odhós-1821 and Evans. This is also the route you should take if **driving** (follow the signs from Platía Eleftherías); there's a free car park downhill on the left, immediately before the site entrance, which will enable you to avoid paying for the private car parks dotting the road before this. A **taxi** from the centre will cost around €5. At Knossos, outside the fenced site, stands the *caravanserai* where ancient wayfarers would rest and water their animals. Head out onto the road and you'll find no lack of watering holes for modern travellers either – a string of rather pricey tavernas and tacky souvenir stands. There are several **rooms** for rent here, and if you're really into Minoan culture, there's a lot to be said for staying out this way to get an early start. Be warned, though, that this zone is expensive and unashamedly commercial.

The British School at Athens has a useful website (Ⓦ www.bsa.gla.ac.uk /knossos/vrtour) dedicated to Knossos with detail on the history of the site and excavations in addition to a virtual tour.

The site

As soon as you enter the **Palace of Knossos** (daily: April–Sept 8am–7pm; Oct–March 8.30am–3pm; €6) through the West Court, the ancient ceremonial

223

entrance, it is clear how the legends of the labyrinth grew up around it. Even with a detailed plan, it's almost impossible to find your way around the complex with any success, although a series of **timber walkways** now channels visitors around the site, severely restricting the scope for independent exploration. If you're worried about missing the highlights, you can always tag along with one of the constant guided tours for a while, catching the patter and then back-tracking to absorb the detail when the crowd has moved on. Outside the period December to February you won't get the place to yourself, whenever you come, but exploring on your own does give you the opportunity to appreciate individual parts of the palace in the brief lulls between groups.

Knossos was liberally "restored" by Evans, and these restorations have been the source of furious controversy among archeologists ever since. It has become clear that much of Evans's upper level – the so-called *piano nobile* – is pure conjecture. Even so, his guess as to what the palace might have looked like is certainly as good as anyone's, and it makes the other sites infinitely more mean-ingful if you have seen Knossos first. Without the restorations, it would be almost impossible to imagine the grandeur of the multistorey palace or to see the ceremonial stairways, strange, top-heavy pillars and gaily painted walls that distinguish the site. For some idea of the size and complexity of the palace in its original state, take a look at the cutaway drawings (wholly imaginary but probably not too far off) on sale outside.

Royal Apartments

The superb **Royal Apartments** around the central staircase are not guess-work, and they are plainly the finest of the rooms at Knossos. The **Grand Stairway** itself (now closed to public access) is a masterpiece of design: not only a fitting approach to these sumptuously appointed chambers, but also an integral part of the whole plan, its large well bringing light into the lower storeys. Light wells such as these, usually with a courtyard at the bottom, are a constant feature of Knossos and a reminder just how important creature com-forts were to the Minoans, and how skilled they were at providing them.

For evidence of this luxurious lifestyle you need look no further than the **Queen's Suite** (now viewed behind glass screens), off the grand **Hall of the Colonnades** at the bottom of the staircase (reached by descending a timber walkway). Here, the main living room is decorated with the celebrated **dol-phin fresco** (a reproduction; the original is now in the Iráklion Archeological Museum) and with running friezes of flowers and abstract spirals. On two sides it opens out onto courtyards that let in light and air; the smaller one would probably have been planted with flowers. The room may have been scattered with cushions and hung with plush drapes, while doors and further curtains between the pillars would have allowed for privacy, and provided cool shade in the heat of the day. Remember, though, that all this is speculation and some of it is pure hype; the dolphin fresco, for example, was found on the courtyard floor, not in the room itself, and would have been viewed from an upper bal-cony as a sort of trompe l'oeil, like looking through a glass-bottomed boat. Whatever the truth, this is an impressive example of Minoan architecture, the more so when you follow the dark passage around to the queen's **bathroom** (now only partially visible behind a screen). Here is a clay tub, protected behind a low wall (and again probably screened by curtains when in use), and the famous "flushing" toilet (a hole in the ground with drains to take the waste away – it was flushed by throwing a bucket of water down).

The much-perused **drainage system** was a series of interconnecting terra-cotta pipes running underneath most of the palace. Guides to the site never fail to point these out as evidence of the advanced state of Minoan civilization, and they are indeed quite an achievement, in particular the system of baffles and over-flows to slow down the runoff and avoid any danger of flooding. Just how much running water there would have been, however, is another matter. Although the water supply was, and is, at the bottom of the hill, and even the combined efforts of rainwater catchment and hauling water up to the palace can hardly have been sufficient to supply the needs of more than a small elite, the discovery of rem-nants of an aqueduct system carrying water to the palace from springs on nearby Mount Ioúktas could mean that this was not the only water supply.

The Grand Stairway ascends to the floor above the queen's domain, and a set of rooms generally regarded as the **King's Quarters** (currently not on view). These are chambers in a considerably sterner vein; the staircase opens into a grandiose reception chamber known as the **Hall of the Royal Guard** (aka Hall of the Colonnades), its walls decorated in repeated shield patterns. Immediately off here is the **Hall of the Double Axes** (aka the King's Room), believed to have been the ruler's personal chamber, a double room that would allow for pri-vacy in one portion while audiences were held in the more public section. Its name comes from the double-axe symbol carved into every block of masonry.

The Throne Room and the rest of the palace

At the top of the Grand Stairway (you will need to retrace your steps up the timber staircase), you emerge onto the broad **Central Court**, a feature of all the Minoan palaces. Open now, this would once have been enclosed by the walls of the buildings all around. On the far side, in the northwestern corner of the courtyard, is the entrance to another of Knossos's most atmospheric sur-vivals, the **Throne Room**. Here, a worn stone throne – with its hollowed shaping for the posterior – sits against the wall of a surprisingly small chamber; along the walls around it are ranged stone benches, suggesting a king ruling in council, and behind there's a reconstructed fresco of two griffins. Just how much rebuilding took place here can be gauged from the fact that when the throne was unearthed the surrounding ruins cleared its back by only a few centimeters: the ceiling and rooms above are all the creation of Evans's "recon-stitution", as he preferred to describe his imaginative reconstructions. Anyway, in all probability in Minoan times this was the seat of a priestess rather than a ruler (there's nothing like it in any other Minoan palace), and its conversion into a throne room seems to have been a late innovation wrought by the invad-ing Mycenaeans, during their short-lived domination prior to the palace's final destruction in the fourteenth century BC. The Throne Room is now closed off with a wooden gate, but you can lean over this for a good view, and in the antechamber there's a wooden copy of the throne on which everyone used to perch to have their picture taken, but this is now also off limits.

The rest you'll see as you wander, contemplating the legends of the place which blur with reality. Try not to miss the giant *pithoi* in the northeast quad-rant of the site, an area known as the palace workshops; the storage chambers which you see from behind the Throne Room, and the reproduced frescoes in the reconstructed room above it; the fresco of the Priest-King looking down on the south side of the central court, and the relief of a charging bull on its north side. This last would have greeted you if you entered the palace through its north door; you can see evidence here of some kind of gatehouse and a lustral bath, a sunken area perhaps used for ceremonial bathing and purification. Just outside this gate is the **theatral area**, an open space a little like a stepped amphitheatre, which may have been used for ritual performances or dances. From here the **Royal Road**, claimed as the oldest road in Europe, sets out. At one time, this probably ran right across the island; nowadays it ends after about a hundred yards in a brick wall beneath the modern road. Circling back around the outside of the palace, you get more idea of its scale by looking up at it; on the south side are a couple of small reconstructed Minoan houses which are worth exploring.

Beyond Knossos

If you have transport, the drive beyond Knossos can be an attractive and enjoyable one, taking minor roads through much greener country, with vineyards draped across low hills and flourishing agricultural communities. If you want specific things to seek out, head first for **MYRTIÁ**, an attractive village with the small **Kazantzakis Museum** (March–Oct daily 9am–7pm; Nov–Feb Sun only 10am–3pm; €3) in a house where the writer's parents once lived. **ARHÁNES**, at the foot of Mount Ioúktas, is a much larger and wealthy farming town that was also quite heavily populated in Minoan times. There are plenty of places to eat here on an animated central square, but no places to stay. None of the three archeological sites here is open to the public, but **Anemospiliá**, 2km northwest of the town (directions from the archeological museum on p.216), can be visited and has caused huge controversy since its excavation in the 1980s: many traditional views of the Minoans, particularly that of Minoan life as peaceful and idyllic, have had to be rethought in the light of the discovery of an apparent human sacrifice. Close to Arhánes' main square, an excellent **archeological museum** (Tues–Sun 8.30am–3pm; free) displays finds from here and other nearby excavations, including the strange ceremonial dagger seemingly used for human sacrifice. From Arhánes you can also drive (or walk with a couple of hours to spare) to the summit of Mount Ioúktas to see the imposing remains of a Minoan **peak sanctuary** and enjoy spectacular panoramic **views** towards Knossos (with which it was linked) and the northern coast beyond. At **VATHÝPETRO**, south of the mountain, is a **Minoan villa and vineyard** (Tues–Sun 8.30am–3pm; free), which once controlled the rich farmland south of Arhánes. Inside, a remarkable collection of farming implements was found, as well as a unique **wine press** which remains *in situ*. Substantial amounts of the farm buildings remain, and it's still surrounded by fertile vines (Arhánes is one of Crete's major wine-producing zones) three and a half thousand years later – making it probably the oldest still-functioning vineyard in Europe, if not the world. Continuing southeast for 2km soon brings you to another agricultural village, **HOUDHÉTSI**, where you'll find the remarkable **Museum of Musical Instruments of the World** (daily 9am–3pm & 5.30–8.30pm; €3; ⓦ www.labyrinthmusic.gr). Founded by Irish *lýra* player Ross Daly who is famed in Crete and lives here, the museum consists of a collection of mainly string and percussion instruments (many very rare) from across the globe. To locate the museum head for *Bar Paranga* at the top (or south end) of the village – the museum is opposite. Should it not be open during these times ring the English-speaking guardian, Eleni Arvanti, from the public phone alongside the bar, and she will open it up for you (ⓣ 2810 743 634).

Southwest from Iráklion: sites and beaches

If you take a **tour** from Iráklion (or one of the resorts), you'll probably visit the **Gortys**, **Phaestos** and **Ayía Triádha** sites in a day, with a lunchtime swim at **Mátala** thrown in. Doing it by public transport, you'll be forced into a rather more leisurely pace, but there's still no reason why you shouldn't get to all three and reach Mátala within the day; if necessary, it's easy enough to hitch the final stretch. **Bus services** to the Phaestos site are excellent, with some nine a day to and from Iráklion (fewer run on Sun), five of which continue to or come from Mátala; there are also services direct to Ayía Galíni. If you're arriving in the afternoon, plan to visit Ayía Triádha first, as it closes early.

The route to Áyii Dhéka

The road from Iráklion towards Phaestos is a pretty good one by the standards of Cretan mountain roads, albeit rather dull. The country you're heading towards is the richest agricultural land on the island, and right from the start the villages en route are large and businesslike. In the biggest of them, **Ayía Varvára**, there's a great rock outcrop known as the **Omphalos** (Navel) of Crete, supposedly the very centre of the island.

Past here, you descend rapidly to the fertile fields of the Messará plain, where the road joins the main route across the south near the village of **ÁYII DHÉKA**. For religious Cretans Áyii Dhéka is something of a place of pilgrimage; its name, "The Ten Saints", refers to ten early Christians martyred here under the Romans. The old Byzantine church in the centre of the village preserves the stone block on which they are supposed to have been decapitated and in a crypt below the modern church on the village's western edge you can see the martyrs' (now empty) tombs. It's an attractive village to wander around, with several places to eat and even some **rooms** – try *Dimitris Taverna* (℡28920 31560; ❶), where you can both stay and eat, which has excellent value en-suite, air-conditioned rooms with views above the restaurant and a splendid new terrace at the rear below.

Gortys and around

Within easy walking distance of Áyii Dhéka, either through the fields or along the main road, sprawls the site of **Gortys** (daily 8am–7pm; €4), ruined capital of the Roman province that included not only Crete but also much of North Africa. After a look at the plan of the extensive site at the entrance, cutting across the fields to the south of the road will give you some idea of the scale of this city, at its zenith in approximately the third century AD. An enormous variety of remains, including an impressive **theatre**, and a couple of **temples** are strewn across your route and more spectacular discoveries are being unearthed by the archeologists who return to dig each summer. Even in Áyii Dhéka you'll see Roman pillars and statues lying around in people's yards or propping up their walls.

There had been a settlement here from the earliest times and evidence of a Minoan site has been enearthed on the acropolis, but the extant ruins date almost entirely from the Roman era. Only now is the site being systematically excavated by the Italian Archeological School. At the main entrance to the **fenced site**, to the north of the road, are the ruins of the still impressive **basilica of Áyios Títos**; the eponymous saint converted the island to Christianity and was its first bishop. Beyond this is the **odeion** which houses the most important discovery on the site, the **Law Code**. These great inscribed blocks of stone were incorporated by the Romans from a much earlier stage of the city's development; they're written in an obscure early Greek-Cretan dialect, and in a style known as *boustrophedon* (ox-ploughed), with the lines reading alternately in opposite directions like the furrows of a ploughed field. At 10m

227

by 3m, this is reputedly the largest Greek inscription ever found. The laws set forth reflect a strictly hierarchical society: five witnesses were needed to convict a free man of a crime, only one for a slave; raping a free man or woman carried a fine of a hundred staters, violating a serf only five. A small **museum** in a loggia (also within the fenced area) holds a number of large and finely worked sculptures found at Gortys, more evidence of the city's importance.

Míres

Some 20km west of Gortys, **MÍRES** is an important market town and focal point of transport for the fertile Messará plain: if you're switching buses to get from the beaches on the south coast to the archeological sites or the west, this is where you'll do it. There are good facilities including a **bank**, a few **restaurants** and a couple of **rooms**, though there's no particular reason to stay unless you are waiting for a bus or looking for work (it's one of the better places for agricultural jobs). A useful **Internet** café, Net Escape, near the bus stop will allow you to send a few emails while awaiting onward connections. Heading straight for Phaestos, there's usually no need to stop.

Phaestos (Festós)

The **Palace of Phaestos** (daily 8am–7pm; €4) was excavated by the Italian Federico Halbherr (also responsible for the early work at Gortys) at almost exactly the same time as Evans was working at Knossos. The style of the excavations, however, could hardly have been more different. Here, to the approval of most traditional archeologists, reconstruction was kept to an absolute minimum – it's all bare foundations, and walls which rise at most a metre above ground level. This means that despite a magnificent setting overlooking the plain of Messará, the palace at Phaestos is not as immediately arresting as those at Knossos or Malia. Much of the site is fenced off and, except in the huge central court, it's almost impossible to get any sense of the place as it was; the plan is almost as complex as at Knossos, with none of the reconstruction to bolster the imagination.

It's interesting to speculate why the palace was built halfway up a hill rather than on the plain below – certainly not for defence, for this is in no way a good defensive position. Psychological superiority over the peasants or reasons of health are both possible, but it seems quite likely that it was simply the magnificent view that finally swayed the decision. The site looks over Psilorítis to the north and the huge plain, with the Lasíthi mountains beyond it, to the east. Towards the top of Psilorítis you should be able to make out a small black smudge: the entrance to the Kamáres cave (see p.240).

On the ground closer at hand, you can hardly fail to notice the strong similarities between Phaestos and the other palaces: the same huge rows of storage jars, the great courtyard with its monumental stairway, and the theatre area. Unique to Phaestos, however, is the third courtyard, in the middle of which are the remains of a **furnace** used for metalworking. Indeed, this eastern corner of the palace seems to have been home to a number of craftsmen, including potters and carpenters. Oddly enough, Phaestos was much less ornately decorated than Knossos; there is no evidence, for example, of any of the dramatic Minoan wall-paintings.

The **tourist pavilion** near the entrance serves drinks and **food**, as well as the usual postcards, books and souvenirs. The nearby village of **ÁYIOS IOÁNNIS**, along the road towards Mátala, has economical **rooms**, including some at *Taverna Ayios Ioannis* (☎28920 42006; ❶), which is also a good place to eat charcoal-grilled *kounélli* (rabbit) and lamb.

Ayía Triádha

Some of the finest artworks in the museum at Iráklion came from **Ayía Triádha** (daily: May–Sept 10am–4.30pm; Oct–April 8.30am–3pm; €3), about a 45-minute walk (or a short drive) from Phaestos. No one is quite sure what this site is, but the most common theory has it as some kind of royal summer villa. It's smaller than the palaces, but if anything even more lavishly appointed and beautifully situated. In any event, it's an attractive place to visit, far less crowded than Phaestos, with a wealth of interesting little details. Look out in particular for the row of **stores** in front of what was apparently a marketplace, although recent thinking tends towards the idea that these were constructed after the villa had declined, possibly in the Mycenaean period. The remains of a **paved road** that probably led down to a harbour on the Gulf of Messará can also be seen running alongside the royal villa. The sea itself looks invitingly close, separated from the base of the hill only by Timbáki airfield (mainly used for motor racing these days), but if you try to drive down there, it's almost impossible to find your way around the unmarked dust tracks. There's a fourteenth-century **church** – dedicated to Áyios Yeóryios – at the site, worth visiting in its own right for the remains of ancient frescoes (key available from the ticket office).

Mátala and around

MÁTALA has by far the best-known **beach** in Iráklion province, widely promoted and included in tours mainly because of the famous **caves** cut into the cliffs above its beautiful sands. These are believed to be ancient **tombs** first used by Romans or early Christians, but more recently inhabited by a sizeable hippie community. You'll still meet people who will assure you that this is *the* travellers' beach on Crete, although today, the town is full of package tourists and tries hard to present a respectable image. The caves have long since been cleared and cleaned up and these days are a fenced-off **archeological site** (April–Sept daily 10am–7pm; €2) and locked up every evening.

A few people still manage to evade the security, or sleep on the beach or in the adjacent campsite, but on the whole the place has changed entirely. The years since the early 1980s have seen the arrival of crowds and the develop-ment of hotels, restaurants and even a disco to service them; early afternoon, when the tour buses pull in for their swimming stop, sees the beach packed to overflowing. If you're prepared to accept Mátala for what it is – a resort of some size – you'll find the place more than bearable. The town beach is beautiful, and if the crowds get excessive, you can climb over the rocks in about twenty minutes (past more caves, many of which are inhabited through the summer) to another excellent stretch of sand, known locally as "Red Beach". In the evening, when the trippers have gone, there are waterside bars and restaurants looking out over invariably spectacular sunsets.

The chief problems concern prices and crowds: rooms are both expensive and oversubscribed, and food is good but not cheap. If you want **accommoda-tion**, try looking up the little street to the left as you enter town, just after the *Zafiria* hotel (☎28920 45112, ✉info@zafiria-matala.com; ❸), where there are several rooms for rent, such as *Matala View* (☎28920 45114, ✉matalaview@hotmail.com; ❶), the pleasant and modern *Fantastik* (☎28920 45362, ℻28920 45492; ❶) and the equally good *Hotel Nikos* (☎28920 45375, ⓦwww.kreta-inside.com; ❷). If these are full, then everywhere closer in is likely to be as well, so head back out along the main road where places tend to fill up last, or try the **campsite**, *Camping of Matala* (☎28920 45720), next to the beach above the car park; *Kommos Camping* (☎28920 45596) is a nicer site, but a few kilometres out of Mátala and reached by heading back towards Pítsidia and turning left along a signed track. There are places to **eat and drink** all over the main part of town, and it's worth seeking out the *Skala* fish taverna on the south side of the bay for fresh seafood and a great view. Nightlife is con-fined to a solitary summer **disco**, *Kandari*, plus a couple of music bars on the main square. On the south side of the bay the two most popular music bars are the *Marinero*, and *Tommy's Music Bar* above it. **Internet** access is available inside the stylish *Kafeneio* bar on the main square. Impossible to miss are most other facilities, including various stores and a bookshop (with international press), currency exchange, car and bike rental, travel agents, post office and a covered market where tourist tat has almost squeezed out the fruit and veg stalls.

Around Mátala: Pitsídhia and Kalamáki

One way to enjoy a bit more peace is to stay at **PITSÍDHIA**, about 5km inland. This has long been a well-used option, so it's not quite as cheap as you might expect, but there are plenty of rooms, lively places to eat and even music bars. If you decide to stay here, the beach at **KALAMÁKI** is an alternative to Mátala. Both beaches are approximately the same distance to walk, though there is a much better chance of a bus or a lift to Mátala. Kalamáki has devel-oped somewhat, with a number of **rooms** – *Psiloritis* (☎28920 45693, ℻28920 45249; ❶) is a good bet – and a couple of tavernas, but it's still a rather unfin-ished, soulless little place. The beach stretches for miles, surprisingly wild and windswept, lashed by sometimes dangerously rough surf. At the southern end (more easily reached by a path off the Pitsídhia–Mátala road) lies **Kommos**, once a Minoan port serving Phaestos and now the site of a major archeological excavation. It's not yet open to the public, but you can peer into the fenced-off area to see what's been revealed so far, which is pretty impressive: dwellings, streets, hefty stonework and even the ship sheds where repairs on the Minoan fleet were carried out.

Iráklion's south coast

South of the Messará plain are two more beach resorts, **Kalí Liménes** and **Léndas**, with numerous other little beaches along the coast in between, but nothing spectacular. **Public transport** is very limited indeed; you'll almost always have to travel via Míres (see p.228). If you have your own transport, the roads in these parts are all passable and newly sealed, but most are very slow going; the Kófinas hills, which divide the plain from the coast, are surprisingly precipitous.

Kalí Liménes

While Mátala itself was an important port under the Romans, the chief harbour for Gortys lay on the other side of Cape Líthinon at **KALÍ LIMÉNES**. Nowadays, this is once again a significant port – for oil tankers. This has rather spoiled its chances of becoming a major resort, and there are few proper facilities, but some people like Kalí Liménes: it's certainly off the beaten track and the constant procession of tankers gives you something to look at while beach lounging. There are a couple of places offering **rooms** – the best is the seafront *Taverna Panorama* (℡28920 97517; ❸; April–Nov) which also has a decent **taverna** attached. The coastline is broken up by spectacular cliffs and, as long as there hasn't been a recent oil spill, the beaches are reasonably clean and totally empty.

Léndas

LÉNDAS, further east along the coast, is far more popular, with a couple of buses daily from Iráklion and a partly justified reputation for being peaceful (sullied by considerable summer crowds). Many people who arrive think they've come to the wrong place, as at first sight the village looks shabby, the beach is small, rocky and dirty, and the rooms are frequently all booked. A number of visitors leave without ever correcting that initial impression, but the attraction of Léndas is not the village at all but on the other (west) side of the headland. Here, there's a vast, excellent sandy strand named **Dhytikós** (or Dhiskós) **beach**, part of it usually taken over by nudists, with a number of taverna/bars overlooking it from the roadside. The beach is a couple of kilometres from Léndas, along a rough track; if you're walking, you can save time by cutting across the headland. A considerably more attractive prospect than staying in Léndas itself is **camping** on the beach to the west of the village, or with luck getting a **room** at one of the few beach tavernas – try *Villa Tsapakis* (℡28920 95378, ⓦwww.villa-tsapakis.gr; ❷), with sea-view rooms and reductions for longer stays. They will also change money on a credit card here (a useful service in this part of Crete where banks and ATMs are nonexistent) and have their own **taverna**, *Odysseas*, nearby. After you've discovered the beach, even Léndas begins to look more welcoming, and at least it has most of the facilities you'll need, including a couple of minimarkets, both of which will change money, a dual-screen **Internet** café on the main square, and numerous places to **eat and drink**: the outstanding *Taverna El Greco* (℡28920 95322) with a leafy terrace above the beach on the east side of the village is one of the best restaurants on the whole south coast.

Once you've come to terms with the place, you can also explore some deserted beaches eastwards, and the scrappy remains of **ancient Lebena** on a hilltop overlooking them. There was an important Asklepion (temple of the god Asklepios) here around some now-diverted warm springs, but only the odd broken column and fragments of mosaic survive in a fenced-off area on the village's northern edge.

East of Iráklion: the package-tour coast

East of Iráklion, the startling pace of **tourist development** in Crete is all too plain to see. The merest hint of a beach is an excuse to build at least one hotel, and these are outnumbered by the concrete shells of resorts-to-be. It's hard to find a room in this monument to the package-tour industry, and it can be expensive if you do. That said, there are one or two highlights amidst the dross which are well worth a visit. Beyond the teenage-package resort of Mália a fine **Minoan palace** will transport you back three and a half millennia or, if you're looking for splendid isolation, the twin sea hamlets of **Sísi** and **Mílatos** are refreshingly out of sync with the rest of this coast.

Goúrnes and Goúves

As a general rule, the further east you go, the better things get: when the road detours all too briefly inland, the more alluring Crete of olive groves and stark mountains asserts itself. You certainly won't see much of it at **GOÚRNES**, where an abandoned former US Air Force base still dominates much of the coastline, awaiting a plan for its redevelopment, or at nearby Káto Goúves, where there's a **campsite**, *Camping Creta* (☎28970 41400), sharing a boundary with the former base. From here, however, you can head inland to the old village of **GOÚVES**, a refreshing contrast, and just beyond to the **Skotinó cave**, one of the largest and most spectacular on the island (about an hour's walk from the coast; open all hours; free).

Hersónissos (Límin Hersoníssou)

Heading east from Goúves you'll pass the turn-off for the new E75 Hersónissos bypass which cuts inland, and shortly after the turning for the direct route up to the Lasíthi Plateau. Carry straight on and you'll roll into the first of the really big resorts, **HERSÓNISSOS** (or, more correctly, Límin Hersoníssou; Hersónissos is the village in the hills just behind, also overrun by tourists).

Hersónissos was once just a small fishing village; today it's the most popular of Crete's package resorts. If what you want is plenty of video-bars, tavernas, restaurants and Eurodisco nightlife, then this is the place to come. The resort has numerous small patches of sand beach between rocky outcrops, but a shortage of places to stay in peak season.

The focal main street, two-kilometre long Odhós Elefthériou Venizélou, is a seemingly endless ribbon of bars, travel agents, tacky jewellery and beachwear shops, amusement arcades and – during the daytime at least – nose-to-tail traffic jams. North of here, along the modern seafront, a solid line of restaurants and bars is broken only by the occasional souvenir shop; in their midst you'll find a small pyramidal Roman **fountain** with broken mosaics of fishing scenes, the only real relic of the ancient town of Chersonesos. Around the headland above the harbour and in odd places along the seafront, you can see remains of Roman harbour installations, mostly submerged.

Beach and clubs excepted, the distractions of Hersónissos comprise **Lychnostatis Open-Air Museum** (Mon–Fri & Sun 9.30am–2pm; €4), a surprisingly rewarding "museum" of traditional Crete, on the coast at the eastern edge of the town; a small aquarium, **Aqua World** (April–Oct daily 10am–6pm; €5), just off the main road at the west end of town, up the road almost opposite the *Hard Rock Cafe*; the watersports paradise **Star Water Park** (daily: April & May 10am–6pm; June–Sept 10am–7pm; €15 full day, €10 half-day; reductions for under-12s) near the beach at the eastern end of the resort; and, a few kilometres inland, the competing **Aqua Splash Water Park** which has similar features and prices.

A short distance inland are the three **hill villages** of Koutoulafári, Piskopianó and "old" Hersónissos, which all have a good selection of tavernas, and are worth searching out for accommodation.

Practicalities

Hersónissos is well provided with all the back-up **services** you need to make a holiday go smoothly. Banks, bike and car rental and post office are all on or just off the main drag, Elefthériou Venizélou, as are the taxi ranks. There are a number of **Internet** cafés: *Cafe Neon*, Elefthériou Venizélou 40, and the central *Internet Cafe*, 10, alongside the church both have plenty of screens. **Buses** running east and west leave from the main bus stop on Venizélou every thirty minutes.

Finding somewhere to stay can verge on the impossible in July and August. Much of the **accommodation** here is allocated to package-tour operators and what remains for casual visitors is among the priciest on the island. To check for availability of accommodation generally, the quickest and best option is to enquire at one of the many travel agencies along Venizélou, such as Zakros Tours (☎28970 22317) at no. 46. The town's most reasonably priced (for Hersónissos) central options include *Zorba's Hotel*, Beach Road (☎28970 22134, ⓦwww.hersonissos.com/zorbas; ❸) and *Virginia*, Máchis Krítis 18 (☎ & ⓕ28970 22455; ❸), but be prepared for a fair amount of noise. One place to try on the western edge as you enter the town is *Hotel Ilios* (☎28970 22500, ⓕ28970 22582; ❹), just back from the main road, which has a rooftop pool. There are two good **campsites**: one at the eastern end of town, *Caravan Camping* (☎28970 24718), which also has several reed-roofed bungalows, and *Camping Hersonissos* (☎28970 22902), just to the west of town. The well-run *"paleó"* (old) **youth hostel** is no longer affiliated to the IYHF and charges €10 for a bed with use of kitchen; it's sited at the extreme eastern end of Venizélou (☎28970 24567), a little beyond *Caravan Camping* (see above) and serves meals.

Despite the vast number of **eating places**, there are few in Hersónissos worth recommending, and the tavernas down on the harbourfront should be avoided. One of the few Greek tavernas that stands out is *Kavouri* along Arhéou Theátrou, but it's fairly expensive; a cheaper in-town alternative for some delicious and inexpensive Cretan cooking is *Taverna Creta Giannis*, Kaniadháki 4, just off the south side of Venizélou slightly east of the church. Nearby, and also definitely worth a try, is *Passage to India*, an authentic and extremely good Indian restaurant; it lies on Petrákis, another side street just off the main street near the church. Heading out of town on the Piskopianó road, near the junction to Koutoulafári, the friendly *Fegari* taverna also serves good Greek food at reasonable prices. Sitting at your table overlooking the street below you can view the steady trek of clubbers heading down the hill to the bars and night-clubs of Hersónissos. The hill villages have the greatest selection of tavernas, particularly Koutoulafári, where you can have a relaxed evening amongst the narrow streets and small *platíes*.

Hersónissos is renowned for its **nightlife**, and there's certainly no shortage of it. A night's partying kicks off around the **bars** ringing the harbour, which is packed with promenaders and the overspill from countless noisy music bars from 10pm through to the early hours. After midnight, the larger **disco-clubs** and **pubs** in the streets leading up to and along Elefthériou Venizélou are the places to be seen. Currently the most popular music clubs are *Aria* (open July–Aug only), the island's largest, on the main road at the west end of town, *Arena*, also on Venizélou, and *Camelot* and *New York*, both near the harbour. The *Hard Rock Café*, close to *Aria* on Venizélou, has a terrace where clubbers chill out between venues. If you fancy a quiet drink then you've come to the wrong resort, but you could try *Kahluai Beach Cocktail Bar* or *Haris Ouzo & Raki Place* (beneath the *Hotel Virginia*). There is an open-air **cinema** showing original-version films at the *Creta Maris* hotel at the west end of the town and close to the beach.

Stalídha

STALÍDHA is a Cinderella town, sandwiched in between its two louder, brasher and some would say uglier sisters, Mália and Hersónissos, but it is nei-ther quiet nor undeveloped. This rapidly expanding beach resort, with more than sixty tavernas and bars and a few discos, can offer the best of both worlds, with a friendlier and more relaxed setting, a better beach (and usual array of watersports) and very easy access to its two livelier neighbours. The town essentially consists of a single, relatively traffic-free street which rings the seafront for more than two miles, before the apartment blocks briefly become fewer and further, until the mass development of Mália begins.

Finding a place to stay can be difficult, since **accommodation** is almost entirely in studio and apartment blocks which are booked by package compa-nies in high season. Out of season, however, you may well be able to negotiate a very reasonable price for a studio apartment complete with swimming pool; ask in the central travel agencies first, as they will know what is available, and expect to pay around ❷–❸ for two. Finding somewhere to **eat** is less difficult as there are plenty of rather ordinary tavernas, the best and most authentic being *Maria's*, the *Hellas Taverna* and the more upmarket *Blue Sea Restaurant*, all at the western end of the seafront.

Stalídha is completely overshadowed by its neighbours when it comes to **nightlife**, though you can dance at *Bells* disco, on the main coast road, or at *Rhythm*, on the beach; the music bars *Sea Wolf Cocktail Bar* and *Akti Bar* are near each other along the beach.

Mália

The E-75 Hersónissos bypass is currently being extended to detour around Mália and when the new stretch opens in 2004 you will need to turn off this to enter the resort proper. Similar to the other resorts along this stretch of coast, much of **MÁLIA** is carved up by the package industry, so in peak season finding a place to stay is not always easy. The town's focus is a T-junction (where the **bus** drops you) and from where the beach road – a kilometre-long strip lined with bars, clubs, games arcades, tavernas and souvenir shops – heads north to the sea and beaches. South of this junction the older village presents a slightly saner image of what Mália used to be, but even here rampant commercialism is making inroads.

Practicalities

The best **accommodation** options, especially if you want any sleep, are among the numerous rooms and pensions signposted in the old town, such as *Esperia* (☎28970 31086; ❸), up a side road slightly east of the T-junction. Backtracking from the junction, along the main Iráklion road, there are a number of reasonably priced pensions on the left and right including *Hibiscus* (☎28970 31313, ⓕ28970 32042; ❸), which has rooms and studios with kitchenette and fridge around a pool in a garden behind. If you really want to be in the centre of things, try *Kostas* (☎28970 31101; ❸), a family-run pension incongruously located behind the mini-golf at the end of the beach road. Otherwise, on arrival visit one of the travel companies along the main road – such as Stallion Travel, Venizélou 128 (☎28970 33690) – to enquire about accommodation availability. All the other things you're likely to need – **banks** with ATMs, **post office** and food shops – are strung out along the main street near the junction, but the town's best **Internet** access, *Internet Cafe*, is bang in the middle of the beach road madness (about a third of the way down on the right).

Eating in Mália is unlikely to be a problem as **restaurants** jostle for your custom at every step, especially along the beach road. None is particularly good here, and a few are diabolical. The best places for a meal are around Platía Ayíou Dhimitríou, a pleasant square beside the church in the centre of the old village to the south of the main road. Here, you could try *Kalimera* or *Petros*, or the pleasant *Kalesma* with a delightful terrace, perhaps after an aperitif at *Bar Yiannis* just north of the church or *Ouzeri Elizabeth* alongside it, where they serve local wine from the barrel. A little harder to find, and to the west of the square, *Apolafsi* is a good-quality small family taverna which is slightly less pricey than the others.

The beach road comes into its own at night, when the profusion of **bars**, **discos** and **clubs** erupt into a pulsating cacophony. The aptly named *Zoo* is one of the most frenetic, and once past midnight the internal walls part to reveal an even larger dance area. Other popular venues (many British-owned and -run) along the strip include *Cloud Nine*, *Cosmos*, *Midway*, *Zig-Zag*, *Apollo*, and *Arthur's Camelot*. There are also a clutch of "English pubs" with names like *Newcastle* and *Camden*. Unfortunately, a good night's clubbing is frequently spoiled by groups of drunken youths pouring out of these bars and getting into brawls. At one point the situation got so bad that tour operators threatened to pull out of the resort if action wasn't taken to deal with the hooligans – all rather ironical as it was they who were shipping them in by the plane-load on cut-price packages. Recent years have seen a police clampdown on such activities as drinking on the street, and the situation has considerably improved.

The Palace of Malia

Much less imposing than either Knossos or Phaestos, the **Palace of Malia** (daily 8.30am–3pm; €4), 2km east of Mália town, in some ways surpasses both. For a start, it's a great deal emptier and you can wander among the remains in relative peace. While no reconstruction has been attempted, the palace was never reoccupied after its second destruction in the fifteenth century BC, so the ground plan is virtually intact. It's much easier to comprehend than Knossos and, if you've seen the reconstructions there, it's easy to envisage this seaside palace in its days of glory. There's a real feeling of an ancient civilization with a taste for the good life, basking on the rich agricultural plain between the Lasíthi mountains and the sea.

From this site came the famous **gold pendant** of two bees (which can be seen in the Iráklion Archeological Museum or on any postcard stand), allegedly part of a horde that was plundered and whose other treasures can now be found in the British Museum in London. The beautiful leopard-head axe, also in the museum at Iráklion, was another of the treasures found here. At the site, look out for the strange indented stone in the central court (which probably held ritual offerings), for the remains of ceremonial stairways and for the giant *pithoi*, which stand like sentinels around the palace. To the north and west of the main site, archeological digs are still going on as the **large town** which surrounded the palace comes slowly to light, and part of this can now be viewed via an overhead walkway.

Any passing **bus** should stop at the site, or you could even rent a **bike** for a couple of hours as it's a pleasant, flat ride from Mália town. Leaving the archeological zone and turning immediately right, you can follow the road down to a lovely stretch of clean and relatively peaceful **beach**, backed by fields, scrubland and a single makeshift taverna, which serves good fresh fish. From here you can walk back along the shore to Mália or take a bus (every 30min in either direction) from the stop on the main road.

Sísi and Mílatos

Head **east** from the Palace of Malia, and it's not long before the road leaves the coast, climbing across the hills towards Áyios Nikólaos. If you want to escape the frenetic pace of all that has gone before, try continuing to Sísi or Mílatos. These little shore villages are bypassed by the main road as it cuts inland, and are still very much in the early stages of tourist development. The larger of the two, **SÍSI**, is charmingly situated around a small harbour overlooked by balcony bars and more tavernas. The opening of the resort's first disco bar (*Faros*) and the large holiday complex (*Kalimera Krita*), a couple of kilometres to the east, are a sure sign that more development is on its way; there's even a **post office**, confirming the resort status. **Accommodation** is mainly in studios and apartments; it's best to ask in the travel agencies and bars for details of availability. There's also a small pension, *Elena* (no phone; ❶) just behind the harbour, and a shady **campsite** with pool and taverna (☎28410 71247) signposted on the way in. Among a cluster of seafront **tavernas** all specialising in freshly caught fish, the *Fisherman's Place* is worth a try.

In quieter **MÍLATOS**, rooms can be found in the old village, 2km inland, but the seaside settlement – despite a rather pebbly beach – is more desirable. A number of the seafront tavernas let out rooms and, outside the peak season when there's little chance of a bed, the friendly *Rooms Taverna Sokrates* (☎28410 81375; ❷) is worth a try and does decent **food**, especially fish, netted by the village boats. Despite their pebbly main **beaches**, the resorts make for a refreshing change of pace, and there are some fine, deep aprons of sand in the rocky coves beyond the resort centres.

West of Iráklion: around Psilorítis

Most people heading west from Iráklion speed straight out on the **E75 coastal highway**, nonstop to Réthymnon. If you're in a hurry this is not such a bad plan; the road is fast and spectacular, hacked into the sides of mountains which for the most part drop straight to the sea, though there are no more than a couple of places where you might consider stopping. By contrast, the old roads inland are agonizingly slow, but they do pass through a whole string of **attractive villages** beneath the heights of the Psilorítis range. From here you can set out to explore the **mountains** and even walk across them to emerge in villages with views of the south coast.

The coastal route towards Réthymnon

Leaving the city, the **new highway** runs behind a stretch of highly developed coast, where the hotels compete for shore space with a cement works and power station. As soon as you reach the mountains, though, all this is left behind and there's only the clash of rock and sea to contemplate. As you start to climb, look out for **Paleókastro**, hovering beside a bridge which carries the road over a small cove; the castle is so weathered as to be almost invisible against the brownish face of the cliff.

Ayía Pelayía and Fódhele

Some 3km below the highway, as it rounds the first point, lies the resort of **AYÍA PELAYÍA**. It looks extremely attractive from above but, once there, and especially in July and August, you're likely to find the narrow, taverna-lined beach packed to full capacity. This is not somewhere to roll up in high season without reserved **accommodation**, although in quieter times *Zorba's Apartments* (T & F 2810 256 072, E zorbas@freemail.gr; ➍), along the nameless main street behind the beach or, on the road above it, the excellent-value *Danai Rooms* (T 2810 285 936; ➊), with air-conditioned, en-suite rooms with kitchenette and fridge, should have space. Opposite *Zorba's Apartments*, the Pangosmio travel agency (T 2810 811 402, F 2810 811 424) may be able to come up with something, even at the last minute in high season. Out of season you might find a real bargain apartment and, despite the high-season crowds, the resort maintains a dignity long since lost in Mália and Hersónissos, and even a certain exclusivity; a couple of Crete's most luxurious hotels, including the enormous *Peninsula* (T 2810 811 313, W www.peninsula.gr; ➐), nestle on the headlands just beyond the main town beach. There are plenty of **minimarkets** for buying picnic food and **Internet** access is available at *Netcafé Atlas*, next door to *Zorba's Apartments*.

Not far beyond Ayía Pelayía, there's a turning inland to the village of **FÓDHELE**, allegedly El Greco's birthplace. A plaque from the University of Valladolid (in Spain) acknowledges the claim and, true or not, the community has built a small tourist industry on that basis. There are a number of craft shops and some pleasant tavernas where you can sit outside along the river. A peaceful 1km walk (or drive) takes you to the spuriously titled **El Greco's House** (May–Oct Tues–Sun 9am–5pm; €1.50), exhibiting a few reprints of his works and not much more, and the more worthwhile and picturesque fourteenth-century Byzantine **church of the Panayía** (Tues–Sun 9am–3.30pm; free) with frescoes, opposite. None of this amounts to very much but it is a pleasant, relatively unspoilt village if you simply want to sit in peace for a while. A couple of **buses** a day run here from Iráklion, and there's the odd tour; if you arrive on a direct bus, the walk back down to the highway (about 3km), where you can flag down a passing service, is not too strenuous.

Balí and Pánormos

BALÍ, on the coast approximately halfway between Iráklion and Réthymnon, also used to be tranquil and undeveloped, and by the standards of the north coast it still is in many ways. The village is built around a trio of small coves, some 2km from the highway (a hot walk from the bus), and is similar to Ayía Pelayía except that the beaches are not quite as good and there are no big hotels, just an ever-growing proliferation of studios, apartment buildings, rooms for rent and a number of smaller hotels. You'll have plenty of company here and it has to be said that Balí has become a package resort too popular for its own good. The third and best beach, known as "Paradise", no longer really deserves the name; it's a beautiful place to splash about, surrounded by mountains rising straight from the sea, but there's rarely a spare inch on the sand in high season.

Continuing along the coast, the last stop before you emerge on the flat stretch leading to Réthymnon is at **PÁNORMOS**. This makes a good stopover if you're in search of somewhere more peaceful and authentic. The small sandy beach can get crowded when boats bring day-trippers from Réthymnon, but most of the time the attractive village remains relatively unspoiled, and succeeds in clinging to its Cretan identity. There are several decent **tavernas** – try *Taverna Panorama* in the heart of the village or *Sofoklís* near the harbour – and **rooms** places, one large hotel and the very comfortable *Pension Lucy* (T 28340 51328, ➌), which has also sprung a seafront offshoot with balcony studio rooms and apartments.

Inland towards Mount Psilorítis

Of the **inland routes**, the old main road (via Márathos and Dhamásta) is not the most interesting. This, too, was something of a bypass in its day and there are few places of any size or appeal, though it's a very scenic drive. If you want to dawdle, you're better off on the road which cuts up to **Týlissos** and then goes via **Anóyia**. It's a pleasant ride through fertile valleys filled with olive groves and vineyards, a district (the Malevísi) renowned from Venetian times for the strong, sweet Malmsey wine.

Týlissos and Anóyia

TÝLISSOS has a significant archeological site (daily 8.30am–3pm; €2) where three Minoan houses were excavated; unfortunately, its reputation is based more on what was found here (many pieces in the Iráklion Archeological Museum) and on its significance for archeologists than on anything which remains to be seen. Still, it's worth a look, if you're passing, for a glimpse of Minoan life away from the big palaces, and for the tranquillity of the pine-shaded remains.

ANÓYIA is a much more tempting place to stay, especially if the summer heat is becoming oppressive. Spilling prettily down a hillside close below the highest peaks of the mountains, it looks traditional, but closer inspection shows that most of the buildings are actually concrete; the village was destroyed during World War II and the local men rounded up and shot – one of the German reprisals for the abduction of General Kreipe by the Cretan Resistance. The town has a reputation as a **handicrafts** centre (especially for woven and woollen goods), skills acquired both through bitter necessity after most of the men had been killed, and in a conscious attempt to revive the town. At any rate it worked, for the place is thriving today – thanks, it seems, to a buoyant agricultural sector made rich by stockbreeding, and the number of elderly widows keen to subject any visitor to their terrifyingly aggressive sales techniques.

Quite a few people pass through Anóyia during the day, but not many of them **stay**, even though there are some good *pensions* and rented rooms in the upper half of the town, including the flower-bedecked *Rooms Aris* (T 28340 31460, F 28430 31058; ❷) and the nearby *Aristea* (T 28340 31459; ❷), which has an ebullient female proprietor, en-suite rooms with spectacular views, and rates that include breakfast.

The town has a very different, more traditional ambience at night, and the only problem is likely to be finding a **place to eat**: although there are plenty of snack-bars and so-called tavernas, most have extremely basic menus, more or less limited to spit-barbecued lamb, which is the tasty local speciality served up by the grill places on the lower square. If you can face it, a steep hike to the top of the village will bring you to *Taverna Skalomata* offering well-prepared taverna standards, some pretty good barbecued lamb, plus a fine view.

Mount Psilorítis and its caves

Heading for the mountains, a smooth road ascends the 21km from Anóyia to an altitude of 1400m on the **Nídha plateau** at the base of Mount Psilorítis. Here, the *Taverna Nida* (T 28340 31141; April–Sept daily; Oct–May Sat & Sun only) serves up hearty mountain dishes featuring lamb, pork and chicken, and has a couple of **rooms** (❶), which makes it a good base for hikes in the surrounding mountains. A short path leads from the taverna to the celebrated **Idean cave** (Idhéon Ándhron), a rival of that on Mount Dhíkti (see p.241) for the title of Zeus's birthplace, and certainly associated from the earliest of times with the cult of Zeus. The remnants of a major archeological dig carried out inside – including a miniature railway used by archeologists to remove tonnes of rock and rubble – still litter the site giving the place a rather unattractive prospect. When you enter the cave down concrete steps into the depths, it turns out to be a rather shallow affair, devoid even of natural wonders, with little to see.

The taverna also marks the start of the way to the top of **Mount Psilorítis** (2456m), Crete's highest mountain, a climb that for experienced, properly shod hikers is not at all arduous. The route (now forming a stretch of the E4 Pan-European footpath) is well marked with the usual red dots and paint splashes, and it should be a six- to seven-hour return journey to the **chapel of Tímios Stavrós** ("Holy Cross") at the summit, although in spring, thick snow may slow you down.

If you're prepared to camp on the plateau (it's very cold, but there's plenty of available water) or find rooms at the taverna, you could continue on foot next day down to the southern slopes of the range. It's a beautiful hike and also relatively easy, four hours or so down a fairly clear path to **Vorízia** where there is no food or accommodation, although **KAMÁRES**, 4km west, has both: for **rooms**, the very cheap, very basic and unsigned (you'll need to ask for it) *Hotel Psiloritis* (☏28920 43290; ●) should have a bed, and the best **place to eat** is the *Taverna Bournelis* at the village's western end. If you're still interested in caves, there's a more rewarding one above Kamáres, a climb of some five hours on a good, but aggressively steep path; if you're coming over from Nídha, the cave actually makes a rather shorter detour off the main traverse path. The start of the route is just to the left of the *Taverna Bournelis* and the proprietors here can advise on the ascent (in Greek and German only). There is at least one daily **bus** from here down to Míres and alternate (more difficult) routes to the peak of Psilorítis if you want to approach from this direction.

Eastern Crete

Eastern Crete is dominated by **Áyios Nikólaos**, and while it is a highly developed resort, by no means all of the east is like this. Far fewer people venture beyond the road south to **Ierápetra** and into the eastern isthmus, where only **Sitía** and the famous beach at **Váï** ever see anything approaching a crowd. Inland, too, there's interest, especially on the extraordinary **Lasíthi Plateau**, which is worth a night's stay if only to observe its abidingly rural life.

Inland to the Lasíthi Plateau

Leaving the palace at Malia, the highway cuts inland towards **NEÁPOLI**, soon beginning a spectacular climb into the mountains. Set in a high valley, Neápoli is a market town little touched by tourism. There is one excellent **hotel**,

Neapolis (☎28410 33967, Ⓦwww.neapolis-hotel.gr; ➋), some rooms, a modern church and a folk museum. Beyond the town, it's about twenty minutes before the bus suddenly emerges high above the Gulf of Mirabéllo and Áyios Nikólaos, the island's biggest resort. If you're stopping, Neápoli also marks the second point of access to the **Lasíthi Plateau**.

Scores of bus tours drive up here daily to view the "thousands of white-cloth-sailed windmills" which irrigate the high plain ringed by mountains, and most groups will be disappointed. There are very few working windmills left, and these operate only for limited periods (mainly in June), although most roadside tavernas seem to have adopted many of those made redundant as marketing features. The drive alone is worthwhile, however, and the plain is a fine example of rural Crete at work, every inch devoted to the cultivation of potatoes, apples, pears, figs, olives and a host of other crops; stay in one of the villages for a night or two and you'll see real life return as the tourists leave. There are plenty of easy rambles around the villages as well, through orchards and past the rusting remains of derelict windmills.

You'll find **rooms** in the main village of **TZERMIÁDHO**, where the *Hotel Kourites* (☎28440 22194; ➋) is to be found on the eastern edge, in **ÁYIOS YEÓRYIOS** – where there's a **folk museum**, and the economical and friendly *Hotel Dias* (☎28440 31207; ➊) – and **PSYKHRÓ**, where the *Hotel Zeus* (☎28440 31284; ➋) lies close to the Dhiktean cave.

The Dhiktean cave

Psykhró is the most visited village on the plateau, as it's the base for visiting Lasíthi's other chief attraction: the birthplace of Zeus, the **Dhiktean cave** (daily 8am–7pm; €4; ask for the free information leaflet on the cave). In legend, Zeus's father, the Titan Kronos, was warned that he would be overthrown by a son and accordingly ate all his offspring; however, when Rhea gave birth to Zeus in the cave, she fed Kronos a stone and left the child concealed, protected by the Kouretes, who beat their shields outside to disguise his cries. The rest, as they say, is history (or at least myth). There's an obvious path running up to the cave from Psykhró, near the start of which (beyond the car park) the mule handlers will attempt to persuade you the ascent is better done on one of their steeds (costing a hefty €10). In reality, it's hardly a particularly long or dauntingly steep hike to the cave entrance.

The cave has been made more "visitor friendly" in recent years, with the introduction of concrete steps in place of slippery stones, and electric lighting instead of flashlamps and candles. Inevitably some of the magic and mystery has been lost and the "guides", who used to make the visit much more interesting with their hilarious and preposterous tales, have now been banned, presumably in the interests of accuracy and decorum. Thus you will now have to pick out for yourself the stalactites and stalagmites formed in the image of the breasts of Rhea where the infant Zeus was suckled, as well as the baby Zeus himself – a feat verging on the impossible for someone lacking a Cretan imagination.

One of the cave guardians, Petros Zarvakis, is also a wildlife expert and leads **guided wild-flower and bird-spotting hikes** (April–Sept) into the mountains surrounding the plain, and also to the summit of Mount Dhíkti; if he is not on duty at the cave entrance or at the taverna in the car park, he can be contacted on ☎28440 31600 or 694 56 16 074. **Buses** run around the plateau to Psykhró direct from Iráklion and from Áyios Nikólaos via Neápoli. Both roads offer spectacular views, coiling through a succession of passes guarded by lines of ruined windmills.

Áyios Nikólaos and around

ÁYIOS NIKÓLAOS ("Ag Nik" to the majority of its British visitors) is set around a supposedly bottomless **salt lake**, now connected to the sea to form an inner harbour. It is supremely picturesque and has some style and charm, which it exploits to the full. There are no sights as such but the excellent **archeological museum** (Tues–Sun 8.30am–3pm; €3) and an interesting **folk museum** (Mon–Fri & Sun 11am–4pm; €3) are both worth seeking out. The lake and port are surrounded by restaurants and bars, which charge above the odds, and whilst the resort is still very popular, some tourists are distinctly surprised to find themselves in a place with no decent beach at all.

There are swimming opportunities further north however, where the pleasant low-key resort of **Eloúnda** is the gateway to the mysterious islet of

ÁYIOS NIKÓLAOS

RESTAURANTS & BARS

Auoas	1
Itanos	7
Cafe Migomis	4
Ofou To Lo	8
Pelagos	3
I Pita Tou Riga	2
Sarris	9
La Strada	6
Twins	5

ACCOMMODATION

Angelos	C
Atlantis	I
Coral	A
Eva	E
Green House	G
Marilena	B
Mediterranean	D
Rooms Mary	F
Sgouros	H

Spinalónga, and some great backcountry to the north – perfect to explore on a scooter. Inland from Áyios Nikólaos, **Kritsá** with its famous frescoed church and textile sellers is a tour-bus haven, but just a couple of kilometres away, the imposing ruins of **ancient Lato** are usually deserted.

Áyios Nikólaos practicalities

The **tourist office** (daily: July–Aug 8am–10pm; Sept–June 8am–9pm; ☎28410 22357), situated between the lake and the port, is one of the best on the island for information about accommodation. The **bus station** is now situated to the northwest end of town near the archeological museum. You'll find the greatest concentration of **stores** and **travel agents** on the hill between the bridge and Platía Venizélou (along the streets 25-Martíou, Koundoúrou and pedestrianized 28-Oktovríou), and the main **ferry agent**, Plora Travel (☎28410 25868), on the corner of 28-Oktovríou and K. Sfakianáki. The **post office** (Mon–Sat 7.30am–2pm) is halfway up 28-Oktovríou on the right. To **hire a motorbike**, **scooter** or **mountain bike** try the reliable Mike Manolis (☎28410 24940), who has a pitch along Modhátsou. Good **car-rental** deals are available at Club Cars, 28-Oktovríou 24 (☎28410 25868), near the post office. Various **boat trips** to points around the gulf (such as Spinalónga and Eloúnda; about €12) leave from the west side of the harbour. **Internet** access is available at Peripou, 28-Oktovríou 25 (daily 9.30am–2am; €4.50 per hour or €1.50 for 15min), and Cafe du Lac at no. 17 on the same street.

Accommodation

Since many of the package companies have pulled out in recent years the town is no longer jammed solid as it once was, though in the peak season you won't have so much choice. One thing in your favour is that there are literally thousands of **rooms**, scattered all around town. The tourist office normally has a couple of boards with cards and brochures about hotels and rooms, including their prices. If the prices seem very reasonable it is because many are for the low season. The nearest **campsite** is *Gournia Moon*, 17km away (see p.247).

Angelos AktiAktí S. Koundoúrou 16 ☎28410 23501, ℮28410 23501. Welcoming small hotel offering excellent air-con balconied rooms with TV and fine views over the Gulf. ❸

Atlantis Aktí Atlantidhos 15, near the town beach ☎28410 28964, ℮p.mixalis@mailcity.com. Nothing special, but handy enough, offering en-suite rooms with fridges, fans and balconies. Also has a snack-bar below serving cheap breakfasts. ❷

Coral Aktí S. Koundoúrou ☎28410 28363, ⓦwww.hermes-hotels.gr. One of Áyios Nikólaos's leading in-town hotels offering air-con rooms with sea views, fridges, balconies and satellite TV, plus a rooftop pool and bar. When things are slack, prices can fall by up to 25 percent. Rates include breakfast. ❻

Hotel Eva Stratigoú Kóraka 20 ☎28410 22587. Decent simple rooms in a misnamed *pension* close to the centre. ❷

Green House Modhátsou 15 ☎28410 22025. Probably the best cheap place to stay in town; clean with shared facilities. ❶

Marilena Érythrou Stavroú 14 ☎28410 22681, ℮28410 24218. Not the bargain it once was, but it's still a pleasant place to stay; some rooms with sea view and balcony. ❸

Rooms Mary Evans 13, near the Kitroplatía ☎28410 24384. Very friendly place with en-suite balcony rooms (some with sea view); access to fridge and use of kitchen. Also has some apartments nearby costing slightly more. ❷

Mediterranean S. Dhávaki 27 ☎28410 23611. Clean, economical en-suite rooms with fridges and fans, and close to the lake. ❷

Sgouros Kitroplatía ☎28410-28931. Modern hotel overlooking one of the town's beaches, and close to plenty of tavernas. ❸

Eating

At least when it comes to eating there's no chance of missing out, even if some of the prices are fancier than the restaurants. There are tourist-oriented **tavernas** all around the lake and harbour and little to choose between them, apart from the different perspectives you get on the passing fashion show. Have a drink here perhaps, or a mid-morning coffee, and choose somewhere else to eat. The places around the Kitroplatía are generally fairer value, but again you are paying for the location.

Auoas Paleológou 44. This taverna serves good, traditional Cretan dishes in and under a plant-covered trellised courtyard, where food and wine prices are among the lowest in town.

Itanos Kýprou 1, off the east side of Platía Venizélou. Popular with locals, this taverna serves Cretan food and wine and has a terrace across the road.

Café Migomis Nikoláou Plastíra 22. Pleasant café high above the bottomless lake with a stunning view. Perfect (if pricey) place for breakfast, afternoon or evening drinks.

Ofou To Lo Kitroplatía. Best of the moderately priced places on the seafront here: the food is consistently good.

Pelagos Stratigoú Kóraka, just back off the lake behind the tourist office ☏ 28410 25737. A

stylish fish taverna with the best garden terrace in town, serving excellent food reflected in the prices.

I Pita Tou Riga Paleológou 24, close to the lake. Excellent Lilliputian snack-bar/restaurant serving imaginative fare – salads, filled pitta breads and some Asian dishes; has a small terrace up steps across the road.

Sarri's Kýprou 15. Great little economical neighbourhood café-diner especially good for breakfast fare and *souvláki*, all served on a leafy terrace.

La Strada Nikoláou Plastíra 5. Authentic Italian fare and good-value pizza and pasta, should you fancy a change of cuisine.

Twins Fronting the harbour. Handy pizzeria, fast-food outlet and coffee bar, open all hours. Their "small" pizzas measure a giant 40cm in diameter.

Drinking and nightlife

After you've eaten you can get into the one thing which Áyios Nikólaos undeniably does well: **bars and nightlife**. Not that you really need a guide to this – the bars are hard to avoid, and you can just follow the crowds to the most popular places centred around the harbour and 25-Martíou. For a more relaxed drink you could try *Hotel Alexandros* on Paleológou (behind the tourist office), with a rooftop cocktail bar overlooking the lake, which after dark metamorphoses into a 1960s-to-1980s period music bar. A similar pace rules at *Zygos* on the north side of the lake which serves low-priced cocktails and ices until the small hours. One curiosity worth a look in the harbour itself is *Armida* (April–Oct), a bar inside a beautifully restored century-old wooden trading vessel, serving cocktails and simple *mezédhes*.

Quiet drinking, however, is not what it's all about in the **disco-bars**. *Lipstick* on the east side of the harbour is the only genuine full-blown dance club, while the nearby *Rule Club* (above the *Creta Cafe*) doesn't hit its stride until the small hours when the pubs and restaurants close. There are raucous music bars to try at the bottom of 25-Martíou ("Soho Street") where it heads up the hill – *Rififi*, *Royale*, *Oxygen, Cellar* and *Roxy* all get going after sunset, while around the corner on M. Sfakianáki *Santa Maria* is a popular place with locals. Across the harbour *Aquarius* and *Charlie Chan* both get lively, while *Sorrento* is another "golden-oldies" music bar frequented by a north-European crowd.

The coast north of Áyios Nikólaos

North of Áyios Nikólaos, the swankier hotels are strung out along the coast road, with upmarket restaurants, discos and cocktail bars scattered between them. **ELOÚNDA**, a resort on a more acceptable scale, is about 8km out along this road. **Buses** run regularly, but if you feel like renting a **scooter** it's a spectacular ride, with impeccable views over a gulf dotted with islands and moored supertankers. Ask at the bookshop near the post office, on the central square facing the sea, about the attractive *Milos* and *Delfinia* **rooms**, studios and apartments (☏28410 41641, ⓦwww.pediaditis.gr; ❷–❸), which come with sea views and, at the *Milos*, a pool. You could also try the friendly *Pension Oasis* (☏28410 41076, Ⓕ28410 41128; ❶), which has en-suite rooms with kitchenette and is just off the square, behind the church. There are quite a few similar places along the same road, or ask at one of the many travel agents around the main square for help finding a room or apartment; try the friendly Olous Travel (☏28410 41324, Ⓕ28410 41132), which also gives out **information** and changes money and travellers' cheques. For **eating**, *Britomares*, in a plum spot in the centre of the harbour, the nearby *Poulis* and the even pricier ultra-chic *Ferryman* (tellingly with a menu in English only) are the town's best tavernas, but more economical fish and *mezédhes* are to be had at the simple *Ouzeri Maritsa* below the church tower at the north end of the square. **Nightlife** tends to be generally low key, and centres around café terraces and cocktail bars. The *Hellas* café, on a backroad behind the beach, has live Greek music at weekends.

Just before the centre of the village, a road (signposted) leads downhill to a natural causeway leading to the ancient "sunken city" of **Olous**. Here you'll find restored windmills, a short length of canal, Venetian salt pans and a well-preserved dolphin **mosaic**, inside a former Roman basilica, but nothing of the sunken city itself beyond a couple of walls in about two feet of water. Swimming here is good however – but watch out for sea urchins.

From Eloúnda, *kaïkia* run half-hourly in high season (€8 return) to the fortress-rock of **Spinalónga**. As a bastion of the Venetian defence, this tiny islet withstood the Turkish invaders for 45 years after the mainland had fallen; in more recent decades and until 1957, it served as a leper colony. As you look around at the roofless shells of houses once inhabited by the unfortunate lepers, and the boat which brought you disappears to pick up another group, an unnervingly real sense of the desolation of those years descends. **PLÁKA**, back on the mainland, and 5km north of Eloúnda, used to be the colony's supply point; now it is a haven from the crowds, with a small pebble beach and a couple of ramshackle fish **tavernas**, one of which, *Taverna Spinalonga*, can arrange a boat to take you across to Spinalónga (April–Sept) for about €6 return. There are **boat trips** daily from Áyios Nikólaos to Olous, Eloúnda and Spinalónga (costing around €12–15), usually visiting at least one other island along the way.

Inland to Kritsá and Lató

The other excursion everyone takes from Áyios Nikólaos is to **KRITSÁ**, a "traditional" village about 10km inland. Buses run at least every hour from the bus station, and despite the commercialization it's still a good trip: the local **crafts** (weaving, ceramics and embroidery basically, though they sell almost everything here) are fair value, and it's also a welcome break from living in the fast lane at "Ag Nik". In fact, if you're looking for somewhere to stay around here, Kritsá has a number of advantages: chiefly availability of **rooms**, better prices and something at least approaching a genuinely Cretan atmosphere; try *Argyro* (☏ & Ⓕ28410 51174; ❷), with pleasant rooms – some en suite – around a courtyard on your way into the village. The small *platía* at the centre of the village is the focus of life and there are a number of decent places **to eat** here, too: the central *Saridhakis* is a cool place to sit out under a plane tree or you could head for the bakers for tempting *tyrópita* (cheese pies) or currant breads. One of the best-situated tavernas is *Castello*, also in the centre, and there are a few others near where the bus stops.

On the approach road, some 2km before Kritsá, is the lovely Byzantine **church of Panayía Kyrá** (daily 8.30am–3pm; €3), inside which survives perhaps the most complete set of Byzantine frescoes in Crete. The fourteenth- and fifteenth-century works have been much retouched, but they're still worth the visit. Excellent (and expensive) reproductions are sold from a shop alongside. Just beyond the church, a surfaced road leads off for 3km to the archeological site of **Lato** (Tues–Sun 8.30am–3pm; free), where the substantial remains of a Doric city are coupled with a grand hilltop setting. The city itself is extensive, but largely neglected, presumably because visitors and archeologists on Crete are more concerned with the Minoan era. Ruins aside, you could come here just for the views: west over Áyios Nikólaos and beyond to the bay and Olous (which was Lato's port), and inland to the Lasíthi mountains. At the time of writing a ticket office and café were being constructed at the site entrance, suggesting that a charge will be imposed in the near future.

The eastern isthmus

The main road south and then east from Áyios Nikólaos is not a wildly exciting one, essentially a drive through barren hills sprinkled with villas and skirting above the occasional sandy cove. The stretch of the E75 northern highway beyond Ístro is now undergoing major **engineering works** intended to by-pass the archeological site of Gourniá and the coastal town of Pahía Ámmos making the route to Ierápetra more direct. The long-term aim is to continue the new road east all the way to Sitía, linking up with the new airport there, but this is still some years away. Five kilometres east of Ístro, along a newly completed stretch of the E75, an exit on the left is signed for the **monastery of Faneroméni**. The way bends around to cross the E75 on a viaduct before heading inland along a track (partly asphalted in its early stage) that climbs dizzily skywards for 6km, giving spectacular views over the Gulf of Mirabéllo along the way. The **view** from the monastery over the gulf is one of the finest in Crete. To get into the rather bleak-looking monastery buildings, knock loudly. You will be shown up to the chapel, built into a cave sanctuary, and the frescoes – although late – are quite brilliant.

Gourniá, Pahiá Ámmos and Mókhlos

Back on the coast road, it's another 2km to the site of **Gourniá** (Tues–Sun 8.30am–3pm; €2), slumped in the saddle between two low peaks. The most completely preserved **Minoan town**, its narrow alleys and stairways intersect a throng of one-roomed houses (of which only the ground-floor walls survive – they would have had at least one upper floor) centred on a main square, and the rather grand house of what may have been a local ruler or governor. Although less impressive than the great palaces, the site is strong on revelations about the lives of the ordinary people – many of the dwellings housed craftsmen (who worked with wood, metal and clay), who left behind their tools and materials to be found by the excavators. Its desolation today (you are likely to be alone save for a dozing guardian) only serves to heighten the contrast with what must have been a cramped and raucous community 3500 years ago.

It is tempting to cross the road here and take one of the paths through the wild thyme to the sea for a swim. Don't bother – the bay and others along this part of the coastline act as a magnet for every piece of floating detritus dumped off Crete's north coast. There is a larger beach (though with similar problems), and rooms to rent, in the next bay along at **PAHIÁ ÁMMOS**, about twenty minutes' walk, where there is also an excellent seafront fish taverna, *Aiolus*; in the other direction, there's the campsite of *Gournia Moon* (☎28420 93243; May–Sept), with its own small cove and a swimming pool.

This is the narrowest part of the island, and from here a fast road cuts across the isthmus to Ierápetra (p.251) in the south. In the north, the route on towards Sitía is one of the most exhilarating in Crete. Carved into cliffs and mountainsides, the road teeters above the coast before plunging inland at Kavoúsi. Of the beaches you see below, only the one at **MÓKHLOS** is at all accessible, some 5km below the main road. This sleepy seaside village has a few rooms, a hotel or two and a number of **tavernas** – *Tò Bogazi* is good – squatting along its tiny harbour; if you find yourself needing a **place to stay**, you could try the rooms at the clean and simple *Pension Hermes* (☎28430 94074; ❶) behind the waterfront, which are the cheapest in the village, or there's *Hotel Sofia* (☎28430 94738, ℻28430 94238; ❷) on the harbour itself for a bit more en-suite luxury. Nearer Sitía the familiar olive groves are interspersed with vineyards used for creating wine and sultanas, and in late summer the grapes, spread to dry in the fields and on rooftops, make an extraordinary sight in the varying stages of their slow change from green to gold to brown.

Sitía

SITÍA is the port and main town of the relatively unexploited eastern edge of Crete. It's a pleasantly scenic if unremarkable place, offering a plethora of waterside restaurants, a long sandy beach and a lazy lifestyle little affected even by the thousands of visitors in peak season. There's an almost Latin feel to the town, reflected in (or perhaps caused by) the number of French and Italian tourists, and it's one of those places that tends to grow on you, perhaps inviting a longer stay than intended. For entertainment there's the **beach**, providing good swimming and windsurfing, and in town a mildly interesting **folklore museum** (Mon–Sat 10am–1pm; €2), a Venetian fort and Roman fish tanks to explore, plus an excellent **archeological museum** (Tues–Sun 8.30am–3pm; €2). As part of a government push to increase tourism at this end of the island, a new **international airport** (set to open in 2004) is being constructed on a plateau above the town, and will most likely have a big impact on Sitía itself as well as the surrounding area.

Practicalities

The bus drops you at the **bus station** (actually an office on the street) on the southwest fringe of the centre and close to the town's main **supermarket**, useful for stocking up on provisions. There are plenty of cheap pensions and **rooms** within easy walking distance, especially in the streets around the folklore museum and beyond here towards the ferry port. For economical rooms, try *Pension Venus*, I. Kondhiláki 60 (☎28430 24307; ❶), or *Arhontiko*, I. Kondhiláki 16 (☎28430 28172; ❶); en-suite accommodation is available at *Rooms Apostolis*, N. Kazantzákis 27 (☎28430 22993; ❷), and *Nora*, Rouseláki 31 (☎28430 23017, ℮norahotel@yahoo.gr; ❸), near the ferry port. An upmarket option in the centre is *Itanos*, Platía Iróön Polytekhníou (☎28430 22146, ℡ww.forthnet.gr/internetcity/hotels/itanos; ❹), with balconied sea-view

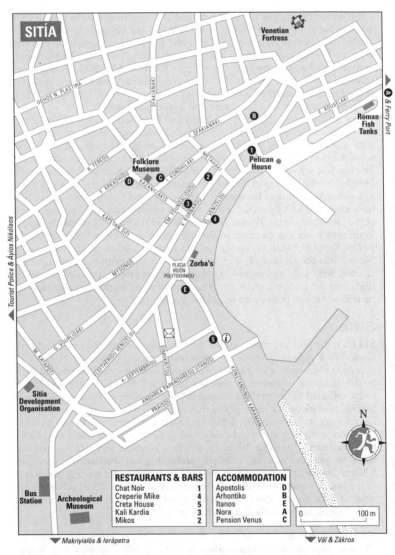

SITÍA

Venetian Fortress

ODHOS N. PLASTIRA

SFAKIANAKI

E. ROUSELAKI

Roman Fish Tanks

A & Ferry Port

I. SFAKIANAKI

B

R. FEREOU

Folklore Museum

KONDHILAKI

P. METAXAKI

1

Pelican House

V. ARKADHIOU

C

2

KAZANTZAKIS

EM. FOUNDALIDHOU

D

KAPETAN SIFI

V. KORNAROU

3

EL. VENIZELOU

4

MYSONOS

PLATIA IROÓN POLYTEKHNIOU

Zorba's

E

Tourist Police & Ágios Nikólaos

G. YOURLIDAKI

ELEFTHERIOU VENIZELOU

DIMOKRITOU

5

i

4-SEPTEMBRIOU

ANDHREA PAPANDHREOU

PRAISOU

ITANOS

KONSTANDINOU KARAMANLI

N

Sitía Development Organisation

Bus Station

Archeological Museum

RESTAURANTS & BARS		ACCOMMODATION	
Chat Noir	1	Apostolis	D
Creperie Mike	4	Arhontiko	B
Creta House	5	Itanos	E
Kali Kardia	3	Nora	A
Mikos	2	Pension Venus	C

0   100 m

▼ *Makriyialós & Ierápetra*   ▼ *Váï & Zákros*

rooms on the town's main square. Should you have problems finding somewhere to stay, the **tourist office** (Mon–Fri 9.30am–2.30pm & 5.30–9pm, Sat 10.30am–2.30pm & 5–8pm; ☎28430 28300), on the seafront at the start of the beach road, should be able to help, or there's the **tourist police** at Mysónos 24 (daily 7.30am–2.30pm; ☎28430 24200), who also provide limited tourist information; both can supply a good town map. A colourful weekly **market** takes place on Tuesdays between 7am and 2pm along Odhós N. Plastira to the northwest of the centre.

For **food**, the waterside places are relatively expensive; the best-value choices near here are *Kali Kardia*, M. Foundalídhou 28, two blocks in from the waterfront for tasty *mezédhes* and *Creta House*, at the start of the beach road (Konstandínou Karamanlí), serving traditional island dishes. Just behind the seafront, the popular *Mikos*, V. Kornárou 117, serves up charcoal-grilled meat and a potent local wine. At the north end of the seafront *Chat Noir*, Galanáki 3, is a newish arrival that does the usual standard dishes well and has a small seafront terrace. Good crêpes are to be had at *Creperie Mike*, Venizélou 162, to the east of the focal *Zorba's* restaurant on the seafront. **Nightlife** centres on a few bars and discos near the ferry dock and out along the beach. The town's monster disco-club, *Planitarion*, attracts crowds from all over the east. It's a couple of kilometres beyond the ferry port, and is best reached by taxi. The in-town alternative is *Oasis*, a stylish new bar near the start of the beach road with an attractive terrace, popular with a younger crowd. Sitía's main bash is the summer-long Kornaria **cultural festival** featuring concerts, dance and theatre by Greek and overseas participants.

Onward to Váï beach and Palékastro

Leaving Sitía along the beach, the Váï road climbs above a rocky, unexceptional coastline before reaching a fork to the **monastery of Toploú** (daily 9am–7pm; €2.50). The monastery's forbidding exterior reflects a history of resistance to invaders, but doesn't prepare you for the gorgeous flower-decked cloister within. The blue-robed monks keep out of the way as far as possible, but in quieter periods their cells and refectory are left discreetly on view. In the church is one of the masterpieces of Cretan art, the eighteenth-century icon *Lord Thou Art Great* by Ioánnis Kornáros. Outside you can buy enormously expensive reproductions.

   Váï beach itself features alongside Knossos or the Lasíthi plateau on almost every Cretan travel agent's list of excursions. Not surprisingly, it is now covered in sunbeds and umbrellas, though it is still a superb beach. Above all, it is famous for its palm trees, and the sudden appearance of the grove is indeed an exotic shock; lying on the fine sand in the early morning, the illusion is of a Caribbean island – a feature seized upon by countless TV-commercial makers seeking an exotic location on the cheap. As everywhere, notices warn that "camping is forbidden by law", and for once the authorities seem to mean it – most campers climb over the headlands to the south or north. If you do sleep out, watch your belongings, since this seems to be the one place on Crete with crime on any scale. There's a compulsory car park (€2.50), a café and an expensive taverna at the beach, plus toilets and showers. Because of its status as a nature reserve there is **no accommodation** here whatsoever; the nearest place offering a bed for the night is Palékastro (see below). By day you can find a bit more solitude by climbing the rocks or swimming to one of the smaller beaches which surround Váï. **Ítanos**, twenty minutes' walk north by an obvious trail, has a couple of tiny beaches and some modest ruins from the Classical era.

   PALÉKASTRO, an attractive farming village some 9km south, makes a good place to stopover. Although its beaches can't begin to compare with those at Váï, you'll find several modest places with **rooms** – among them *Hotel Hellas* (☎28430 61240, @hellas_h@otenet.gr; ❷), which offers en-suite facilities and food, and the good-value *Váï* (☎28430 61414; ❶), with rooms above a taverna at the west end of the village, on the Sitía road. The extensive **beaches** provide plenty of space to **camp** out without the crowds, but you should respect local sensitivities, keeping away from the main strands and responsibly disposing of any rubbish. Add in a **tourist office** (April–Oct daily 9am–10pm; ☎28430 61546) on the main street, a small **folk museum** (May–Oct Tues–Sun

8.30am–1pm & 5–8.30pm; €1.50), a number of reasonable **tavernas**, a few **bars** and even a **dance-club**, *Design*, and the place begins to seem positively throbbing. The sea is a couple of kilometres down a dirt track, effortlessly reached with a **scooter** hired from Moto Kastri (☏ 28430 61477), on the eastern edge of the village along the Váï road. Palékastro is also the crossroads for the road south to Zákros and your own transport presents all kinds of beach and exploration possibilities.

Zákros

ÁNO ZÁKROS (Upper Zákros) lies a little under 20km from Palékastro. There are several tavernas and a simple hotel, the *Zakros* (☏ & ℉ 28430 93379; ②), which has some rooms with bath and great views from its rear rooms; it also offers guests a free minibus service to the Minoan palace and beach. The Minoan palace is actually at Káto ("lower") Zákros, 8km further down towards the sea. Most buses run only to the upper village, but in summer, a couple do run every day all the way to the site; it's usually not difficult to hitch if your bus does leave you in the village. Two kilometres along the road you can, if on foot, take a short cut through an impressive **gorge** (the "Valley of the Dead", named for ancient tombs in its sides). The gorge entrance is signed "Dead's Gorge" next to an information board and car-park area with a steep path leading down to the trail, which then follows a stream bed for 4km to reach the sea near the Minoan palace (see below). It's a solitary but magnificent hike, brightened especially in spring with plenty of plant life.

The **Palace of Zakros** (daily: July–Oct 8am–7pm; Nov–June 8am–3pm; €3) was an important find for archeologists; it had been occupied only once, between 1600 and 1450 BC, and was abandoned hurriedly and completely. Later, it was forgotten almost entirely and as a result was never plundered or even discovered by archeologists until very recently. The first major excavation began only in 1960; all sorts of everyday objects, such as tools, raw materials, food and pottery, were thus discovered intact among the ruins, and a great deal was learned from being able to apply modern techniques (and knowledge of the Minoans) to a major dig from the very beginning. None of this is especially evident when you're at the palace, except perhaps in a particularly simple ground plan, so it's as well that it is also a rewarding visit in terms of the setting. Although the site is set back from the sea, in places it is often marshy and waterlogged – partly the result of eastern Crete's slow subsidence, partly the fault of a spring which once supplied fresh water to a cistern beside the royal apartments, and whose outflow is now silted up. In wetter periods, among the remains of narrow streets and small houses of the town outside the palace and higher up, you can keep your feet dry and get an excellent view down over the central court and royal apartments. If you want a more detailed overview of the remains, buy the guide to the site on sale at the entrance.

The delightful village of **KÁTO ZÁKROS** is little more than a collection of tavernas, some of which rent out rooms around a peaceful beach and minuscule fishing anchorage. It's a wonderfully restful place, but is often unable to cope with the volume of visitors seeking accommodation in high season, and as rooms are rarely to be had on spec you'd be wise to ring ahead. You should also be aware that villagers are far more hostile these days to wild camping after years of problems, and you should be sensitive to their concerns. Reliable rooms can be found at *Poseidon* (☏ 28430 26896; ②), which has fine sea views, and the friendly *George Villas* (☏ & ℉ 28430 26883, ✉ georgevillas @sit.forthnet.gr; ③), 600m behind the archeological site along a driveable track. Otherwise ask at the *Taverna Akrogiali* (☎28430 26893, ✉akrogiali @sit.forthnet.gr; ❷) on the seafront which acts as an agent for many other room options.

Ierápetra and the southeast coast

The main road from Sitía to the south coast is a cross-country, roller-coaster ride between the east and west ranges of the **Sitía mountains**. One of the first places it hits on the south coast is the sprawling resort of **Makryialós** soon followed by the bustling town and resort of **Ierápetra**. More tranquil hideaways lie further west at the charming pint-sized resorts of **Mýrtos** and **Keratókambos** and the slightly less inviting **Árvi** and **Tsoútsouras**.

Makryialós

Although originally comprised of two distinct villages, the larger **MAKRYIALÓS** (🖥www.makrigialos.gr) has gobbled up its neighbour Análipsi to form a single and unfocused resort, whose only real plus point is a long strand with fine sand which shelves so gently you feel you could walk the two hundred nautical miles to Africa. Unfortunately, since the early 1990s it has been heavily developed, so while still a very pleasant place to stop for a swim or a bite (the outstanding mid-priced *Porfira* taverna on the sea is recommended; open evenings only), it's not somewhere you're likely to find cheap **rooms**. Signed up a side road inland, on the road coming in from the east, stone-built *Hamlet Cottages* (☎28430 51434; ❹) come complete with kitchen and terrace. Up the same track and nearby is *White River Cottages* (☎28430-51120; ✉wrc@sit.forthnet.gr; ❹), where an abandoned hamlet of traditional stone dwellings (originally Áspro Pótamos or "White River") has been restored as a warren of charming studios and apartments with a focal pool.

From here to Ierápetra there's little reason to stop; the few beaches are rocky and the coastal plain submerged under ranks of polythene-covered greenhouses. Beside the road leading into Ierápetra are long but exposed stretches of sand, including the appropriately named "Long Beach", where you'll find a **campsite**, *Camping Koutsounari* (☎28420 61213), which offers plenty of shade and has a taverna and minimarket.

Ierápetra

IERÁPETRA itself is a bustling modern supply centre for the region's farmers. It also attracts a fair number of package tourists and the odd backpacker looking for work in the prosperous surrounding agricultural zone, especially out of season. The tavernas along the tree-lined seafront are scenic enough and the EU blue-flagged beach stretches a couple of miles east. But as a town, most people find it pretty uninspiring, despite an ongoing modernization programme which has cleaned up the centre and revamped the seafront. Although there has been a port here since Roman times, only the **Venetian fort** guarding the harbour and a crumbling Turkish minaret remain as reminders of better days. What little else has been salvaged is in the one-room **Archeological Museum** (Tues–Sun 8.30am–2.30pm; €2) near the post office.

The town hall on the main square Platía Kanoupáki, or the library next door, should be able to provide a copy of the detailed town map (but not much else) which will help you find your way around. If you want to stay, head up

Kazantzákis from the chaotic bus station, and you'll find a friendly welcome and good-value, apartment-style **rooms** with kitchenette at *Rooms Popy* at no. 27 (T 28420 24289, F 28420 27772; ❷), or equal comfort in the nearby *Cretan Villa*, Lakérdha 16 (T 28420 28522, W www.cretan-villa.com; ❷–❸), a beautiful 180-year-old house. More central and economical is the *Hotel Ersi*, Platía Eleftherías 20 (T 28420 23208; ❶), which will also rent you a seafront apartment nearby for not much more than the cost of a room. The cheapest seafront rooms option is *Katerina*, (T 28420 28345, F 28420 28519; ❷) at the eastern end of the strand.

You'll find places to **eat** and **drink** all along the waterfront, the better of them, such as *Taverna Napoleon* and *Gorgona*, being towards the Venetian fort. **Nightlife** centres on a clutch of **clubs**, **bars** and fast-food places along central Kyrba, behind the promenade. Ierápetra has two **Internet cafés**, *Orfeas* (T 28420 24407; €6 per hour), Koundouriótou 25, just north of the museum, also serving good breakfasts, and the cheaper *Internet Café* inside the *Cosmos Hotel*, Koundoúrou 16, slightly north of Platía Eleftherías (T 28420 25900; €3.60 per hour).

West from Ierápetra

Heading **west** from Ierápetra, the first stretch of coast is grey and dusty, the road jammed with trucks and lined with drab ribbon development and plastic greenhouses. There are a number of small resorts along the beach, though little in the way of public transport. If travelling under your own steam, there is a scenic detour worth taking at Gría Lygiá: the road on the right for Anatolí climbs to Máles, a village clinging to the lower slopes of the **Dhíkti range**. Here would be a good starting point for **walking** through some stunning mountain terrain (the E4 Pan-European footpath which crosses the island from east to west passes just 3km north of here). Otherwise, the dirt road back down towards the coast (signposted Míthi) has spectacular views over the Libyan Sea, and eventually follows the Mýrtos river valley down to Mýrtos itself.

Mýrtos and Árvi

MÝRTOS, 18km west of Ierápetra, is the first resort that might actually tempt you to stop, and it's certainly the most accessible, just off the main road with numerous daily **buses** from Ierápetra and a couple direct to Iráklion. Although developed to a degree, it nonetheless remains tranquil and inexpensive, with lots of young travellers (many of whom often sleep on the beach, to the irritation of locals). There are plenty of **rooms** possibilities, amongst which you could try the central *Rooms Angelos* (T 28420 51091; ❷) and *Nikos House* (T 28420 51116, W www.nikoshouse.cz; ❷), or the less expensive *Rooms Despina* (T 28420 51524; ❷) at the back of the village near the bus stop. A useful travel agent, Magic Tours (T 28420 51203, W www.welcometo-magic.com) on the central main street is a good source of **information**, and also **changes money**, rents **cars**, sells boat and plane tickets and operates a taxi service to Iráklion and Haniá airports. Just off the road from Ierápetra a couple of kilometres east of the village (and signed) are a couple of excavated hilltop **Minoan villas** you might want to explore: Néa Mýrtos and Pýrgos. Some of the finds from these sites – in addition to a folklore section with tools, kitchen and farming implements once used by the villagers – are displayed in a new village **museum** (Mon–Fri 9am–2pm; €1.50), located to the side of the church.

After Mýrtos the main road turns inland towards Áno Viánnos, then continues across the island towards Iráklion; several places on the coast are reached by a series of recently asphalted roads replacing the former rough tracks. **ÁRVI** is a resort of similar size to Mýrtos, although it lacks the latter's charm. The beach, flanked by a new harbour development, hardly justifies it, but it's an interesting little excursion (with at least one bus a day) if only to see the bananas and pineapples grown here and to experience the microclimate – noticeably warmer than neighbouring zones, especially in spring or autumn – that encourages them. For **rooms** you could try the central *Pension Gorgona* (☎28950 71353; ❷) or, beyond the river at the east end of the beach, the cheaper *Taverna Kyma* (☎28950 71344; ❷).

Beyond Árvi

KERATÓKAMBOS, reached on a side road 4km from Áno Viánnos, has a rather stony beach and, although popular with Cretan day-trippers, is a great place to escape the tourist grind for a spell. It has a range of **rooms**, though they're not easy to come by in August. Try the *Morning Star* taverna (☎28950 51209; ❶) which has rooms with and without bath, or the comparable *Taverna Kriti* (☎28950 51231, ℻28950 51456; ❷) next door; the **food** at both places is tasty too.

TSOÚTSOUROS (ⓦwww.tsoutsouros.com), 10km west as the crow flies and now linked by an eleven-kilometre-long asphalted road to the major highway further north, is similar to its neighbour with a line of tavernas, hotels and rooms places arching behind a seafront and yacht harbour, to the east and west of which are a couple of decent if pebbly, grey-sand **beaches**. **Accommodation** may be available here when the other resorts are full: *Rooms Mihalis* (☎28910 92250; ❶) or the good-value *San Georgio Hotel* (May–Sept ☎28910 92322; ❷) further east are both worth trying. There are no facilities for changing money at either place, although both have a couple of **supermarkets**, handy for gathering picnic ingredients.

If you hope to continue across the **south** of the island, be warned that there are no buses, despite completion of the road towards Míres after years of work. It's an enjoyable rural drive, but progress can be slow; there's very little traffic if you're trying to hitch.

Réthymnon and around

The relatively low, narrow section of Crete which separates the Psilorítis range from the White Mountains in the west seems at first a nondescript, even dull part of the island. Certainly in scenic terms it has few of the excitements that the west can offer; there are no major archeological sites and many of the villages seem modern and ugly. On the other hand, **Réthymnon** itself is an attractive and lively city, with some excellent beaches nearby. And on the south coast, in particular around **Plakiás**, there are beaches as fine as any Crete can offer, and as you drive towards them the scenery and villages improve.

Réthymnon

Since the early 1980s, **RÉTHYMNON** has seen a greater influx of tourists than perhaps anywhere else on Crete, with the development of a whole series of large hotels extending almost 10km along the beach to the east. For once, though, the middle of town has been spared, so that at its heart Réthymnon remains one of the most beautiful of Crete's major cities (only Haniá is a serious rival) with an enduringly provincial air. A wide sandy beach and palm-lined promenade border a labyrinthine tangle of Venetian and Turkish houses lining streets where ancient minarets lend an exotic air to the skyline. Dominating everything from the west is the superbly preserved outline of

RÉTHYMNON

Haniá

Spíli

Iráklion

Bus Station

PERIFERIAKOS

PERIFERIAKOS

IGOUMENOU GAVRIIL

SYNDAGMATOS

Fortress

MAVILI

KORONAIOU PANOU

I. MELISSINOU

KATEHAKI

NIKIFOROU FOKA

SABATHIOU

HIMARAS

MESOLONGIOU

SALAMINOS

DAMVERGI

PLATIA PLASTIRA

Public Gardens

TSANTALIDHOU

DHIMITRAKAKI

Historical & Folk Art Museum

Porta Guora

Nerandzés Mosque

PETIHAKI

Archeological Museum

DHASKALAKI

PLATIA MARTYRON

ETHNIKIS ANDISTASIS

Minaret

SOULIOU

RADHAMANTHIOS

PLEXOUDI

Loggia

Rimóndi Fountain

Inner Harbour

Ferry Dock

OTE

VERNARDOU

ARKADHIOU

MOATSOU

VERNARDOU K.

DHIMOKRATIAS

V. KALERGI

ELEFTHERIOU VENIZELOU

Veli Pasha Mosque

Kara Pasha Mosque

(due to relocate)

KOUNDOURIOTOU

VERNARDI K.

PLATIA IRÓON POLYTEKNIOU

HORTATZI

K. YIAMBOUDHAKI

SOFOKLI VENIZELOU

E. PORTALIOU

PAPANDHREOU

0   250 m

ACCOMMODATION

Atelier	A
Barbara Dokimaki	I
Byzantine	G
Fortezza	B
Rooms George	C
Ideon	F
Leo	E
Olga's	D
Sea Front	K
Youth Hostel	H
Zania	J

RESTAURANTS & BARS

Agrimia	8
Castelvecchio	4
Fanari	7
O Gounos	1
Kyria Maria	6
Mesostrati	10
To Pigadi	5
O Pontios	3
O Psaras	2
Samaria	12
Stella's Kitchen	9
O Zefyros	11

the **fortress** built by the Venetians after a series of pirate raids had devastated the town.

The Town

With a **beach** right in the heart of town, it's tempting not to stir at all from the sands, but Réthymnon repays at least some gentle exploration. For a start, you could try checking out the further reaches of the beach itself. The waters protected by the breakwaters in front of town have their disadvantages – notably crowds and dubious hygiene – but less sheltered sands stretch for miles to the east, crowded at first but progressively less so if you're prepared to walk a bit.

Away from the beach, you don't have far to go for the most atmospheric part of town, immediately behind the **inner harbour**. Almost anywhere here, you'll find unexpected old buildings, wall fountains, overhanging wooden balconies, heavy, carved doors and rickety shops, many still with local craftsmen sitting out front, gossiping as they ply their trades. Look out especially for the **Venetian loggia**, which houses a shop selling high quality and expensive reproductions of Classical art; the **Rimóndi fountain**, another of the more elegant Venetian survivals; and the **Nerandzés mosque**, the best preserved in Réthymnon but currently serving as a music school and closed to the public. When (seemingly endless) repairs are completed it should again be possible to climb the spiral staircase to the top of the **minaret** for a stunning view over the town. Simply by walking past these three, you'll have seen many of the liveliest parts of Réthymnon. Ethnikís Andístasis, the street leading straight up from the fountain, is the town's **market** area.

The old city ends at the Porta Guora at the top of Ethnikís Andístasis, the only surviving remnant of the city walls. Almost opposite are the quiet and shady **public gardens**. These are a soothing place to stroll, and in the latter half of July the **Réthymnon Wine Festival** is staged here. Though touristy, it's a thoroughly enjoyable event, with spectacular local dancing as the evening progresses and the barrels empty. The entrance fee includes all the wine you can drink, though you'll need to bring your own cup or buy one of the souvenir glasses and carafes on sale outside the gardens.

The museums and fortress

A little further up the street from the Nerandzés mosque at M. Vernárdhou 28, a beautifully restored seventeenth-century Venetian mansion is the home of the small but tremendously enjoyable **Historical and Folk Art Museum** (Mon–Sat 9am–2pm & 6–8pm; €3). Gathered within four, cool, airy rooms are musical instruments, old photos, basketry, farm implements, an explanation of traditional ceramic and breadmaking techniques, smiths' tools, traditional costumes and jewellery, lace, weaving and embroidery (look out for a traditional-style tapestry made in 1941 depicting German parachutists landing at Máleme), pottery, knives and old wooden chests. It makes for a fascinating insight into a fast-disappearing rural (and urban) lifestyle, which survived virtually unchanged from Venetian times to the 1960s, and is well worth a look.

Heading in the other direction from the fountain you'll come to the fortress and **Archeological Museum** (Tues–Sun 8.30am–3pm; €3), which occupies a building almost directly opposite the entrance to the fortress. This was built by the Turks as an extra defence, and later served as a prison, but it's now entirely modern inside: cool, spacious and airy. Unfortunately, the collection is not particularly exciting, and really only worth seeing if you're going to miss the bigger museums elsewhere on the island.

The massive **Venetian fortress** (Sat–Thurs 8.30am–7pm; Nov–March closes 6pm; €2.90) is a must, however. Said to be the largest Venetian castle ever built, this was a response, in the last quarter of the sixteenth century, to a series of **pirate raids** (by Barbarossa among others) that had devastated the town. Inside is now a vast open space dotted with the remains of all sorts of barracks, arsenals, officers' houses, earthworks and deep shafts, and at the centre a large domed building that was once a church and later a **mosque** (complete with a surviving but sadly defaced *mihrab*). It was designed to be large enough for the entire population to take shelter within the walls. Although much is ruined, it remains thoroughly atmospheric, and you can look out from the walls over the town and harbour, or in the other direction along the coast to the west. It's also worth walking around the outside of the fortress, preferably at sunset, to get an impression of its fearsome defences, plus great views along the coast; there's a pleasant resting point around the far side at the *Sunset* taverna.

Practicalities

The **bus station** in Réthymnon is by the sea to the west of the town centre just off Periferiakós, the road which skirts the waterfront around the fortress. If you arrive by **ferry**, you'll be more conveniently placed, over at the western edge of the harbour. At the time of writing, the **tourist office** (Mon–Fri 8am–2.30pm, Sat 10am–4pm; ☎28310 29148, ⓦwww.rethymnon.com) backed onto the main town beach, although it was due to relocate in 2004; the office provides maps, timetables and accommodation lists. To access the **Internet** head for the *Galero Internet Cafe* (daily 9am–midnight; €3.50 per hour, €1 for 15min), beside the Rimóndi fountain in the old town, or *Cafe-Bar Internet*, Platía Martýron 4, near the Porta Guora on the south edge of the old town, with similar prices.

Accommodation

There's a great number of places to stay in Réthymnon, and only at the height of the season are you likely to have difficulty finding somewhere, though you may get weary looking. The greatest concentration of **rooms** is in the tangled streets west of the inner harbour, between the Rimóndi fountain and the museums; there are also quite a few places on and around Arkadhíou and Platía Plastíra.

The nearest **campsite**, *Camping Elizabeth* (☎28310 28694), lies 4km east of town; take the bus for the hotels (marked *Scaleta/El Greco*) from the long-distance bus station to get there. It's a pleasant, large site on the beach, with all facilities.

Atelier Himáras 32 ☎28310 24440, ⓔatelier@ret.forthnet.gr. Pleasant en-suite rooms place run by a talented potter, who has her studio in the basement and sells her wares in a shop on the other side of the building. ❷
Barbara Dokimaki Platía Plastíra 14 ☎ & ⓕ28310 24581. Strange warren of a rooms place, with one entrance at the above address, just off the seafront behind the *Ideon*, and another on Dambérgi; ask for the newly refurbished top-floor studio rooms, which have balconies and kitchenettes. ❸
Byzantine Vospórou 26, near the Porta Guora ☎28310 55609, ⓦwww.byzantineret.gr. Pleasant

rooms in a renovated Byzantine palace. The tranquil patio bar is open to all. ❸
Fortezza Melissinoú 16, near the fortress ☎28310 55551, ⓦwww.fortezza.gr. Stylish, top-of-the-range hotel with almost everything you'd expect for the price, including air-con rooms, pool and restaurant. Rates include breakfast. ❺
Rooms George Makedhonías 32 ☎28310 50965. Decent en-suite rooms (some with fridge), near the Archeological Museum. ❷
Ideon Platía Plastíra 10 ☎28310 28667, ⓦwww .hotelideon.gr. High-class hotel with a brilliant position just north of the ferry dock; little chance of space without pre-booking in season, though. ❺

Leo Vafé 2 ☏28310 26197. Good hotel with lots of wood and a traditional feel; the price includes breakfast, and there's a bar. ❷

Olga's Pension Soulíou 57 ☏28310 54896, ⓕ28310 29851. The star attraction at this very friendly *pension* on one of Réthymnon's most touristy streets is the resplendent flower-filled roof garden. ❸

Sea Front Arkadhíou 159 ☏28310 51981, eⒺlotia@ret.forthnet.gr. Rooms with sea views

and balconies in an attractively refurbished mansion with ceiling fans and lots of wood. ❸

Youth Hostel Tombázi 41 ☏28310 22848, ⓦwww.yhrethymno.com. The cheapest beds (€7) in town. Large, clean, and very friendly and popular, it has food, showers, clothes-washing facilities and a multilingual library. ❶

Zania Pávlou Vlástou 3 ☏28310 28169. *Pension* right on the corner of Arkadhíou; a well-adapted old house, but only a few rooms. ❶

CRETE | Réthymnon

Eating and drinking

Immediately behind the town beach are arrayed the most touristy **restaurants**, the vast majority being overpriced and of dubious quality. One that maintains some integrity (and reasonable prices) is the *Samaria* taverna. Around the inner **harbour** there's a second, rather more expensive, group of tavernas, specializing in fish, though as often as not the intimate atmosphere in these places is spoiled by the stench from the harbour itself; *O Zefyros* is one of the less outrageously pricey and maintains reasonable standards. Not far from here and slightly west of Platía Plastíra, *Taverna Fanari* at Makedhonías 5 is a good-value little restaurant serving up tasty lamb and chicken dishes. Another good option in this zone is *Taverna Castelvecchio*, Himáras 29, a long-established family taverna next to the fortress which has a pleasant terrace with view over the town and offers some vegetarian choices.

The cluster of *kafenía* and tavernas by the **Rimóndi fountain** and the newer places spreading into the surrounding streets generally offer considerably better value than the inner harbour, and a couple of the old-fashioned *kafenía* serve magnificent yogurt and honey. Places to try include *Kyria Maria* at Moskhovítou 20, tucked down an alley behind the fountain (after a meal, everyone gets a couple of Maria's delicious *tyropitákia* with honey on the house); *Agrimia*, a reliable standard on Platía Petiháki, slightly east of the fountain; and the *Cul de Sac* and *Galero* cafés overlooking the fountain which are relatively expensive, but a great place to people-watch over a coffee. Slightly west of the fountain a cluster of upmarket restaurants set their terrace tables in the narrow streets of the old town. The prices and reputations of some of these are inflated but a newcomer, *Tò Pigadi*, Xanthoúdhidhou 31, offers excellent, reasonably priced food and service on its attractive terrace with an ancient well (*pigádi*). For a slightly cheaper option try *O Psaras* (The Fisherman), a simple, friendly taverna by the church at the junction of Nikifórou Foká and Koronéou. A good lunchtime stop close to the Archeological Museum is *O Pontios*, Melissinoú 34, a simple place with tables outside and an enthusiastic female proprietor. Healthy, home-baked lunches can also be had at *Stella's Kitchen*, a simple café (with some vegetarian options) linked to *Olga's Pension* at Soulíou 55, where meals can be enjoyed up on the leafy roof garden. Tucked behind the church on Platía Martíron, *Mesostrati* is a pleasant little neighbourhood *ouzerí*/taverna serving well-prepared Cretan country dishes and has a small terrace. A noisier evening alternative is *Taverna O Gounos*, Koronéou 6 in the old town; the family who run it perform live *lyra* every night, and when things get really lively the dancing starts.

If you want takeaway food, there are numerous **souvláki** stalls, including a couple on Arkadhíou and Paleológou and another at Petikháki 52, or you can buy your own ingredients at the **market** stalls set up daily on Ethnikís Andistásis below the Porta Guora. There are small general stores scattered everywhere, particularly on Paleológou and Arkadhíou; east along the beach road you'll even find a couple of minimarkets. The **bakery** *Iy Gaspari* on Mesolongíou, just behind the Rimóndi fountain, sells the usual cheese pies, cakes and the like, and it also bakes excellent brown, black and rye bread. There's a good *zaharoplastío*, *N.A. Skartsilakos*, at Paleológou 36, just north of the fountain, and several more small cafés which are good for breakfast or a quick coffee.

Nightlife

Nightlife is concentrated in the same general areas as the tavernas. At the west end of Venizélou, in the streets behind the inner harbour, the overflow from a small cluster of noisy music bars – *Venetsianako*, *Dimman* and *Xtreme* – begins to spill out onto the pavement as partygoers gather for the nightly opening of the *Fortezza Disco* in the inner harbour itself, which is the glitziest in town, flanked by its competitors *Metropolis*, *NYC*, *Nitro* and the nearby *Opera Club* a little way down Salamínos. Heading up this street, a string of more subdued cocktail bars – *Petalouda*, *Memphis*, *Santan* and *Pasodia* – cater for those in search of a quieter drink, as does *Notas*, at Himáras 27 near the *Fortezza* and facing the *Atelier pension*, which puts on live (acoustic) guitar and song every night. A new bar scene popular with the local student community has recently taken root around Platía Plastíra, above the inner harbour, where music bars include *Karma*, *Art*, *Da Cappo* and *Enzzo*, all with expansive terraces.

Around Réthymnon

While some of Crete's most drastic resort development spreads ever eastwards out of Réthymnon, to the west a sandy coastline, not yet greatly exploited, runs all the way to the borders of Haniá province. But of all the short trips that can be made out of Réthymnon, the best known and still the most worthwhile is to the **monastery of Arkádhi**.

Southeast to Arkádhi

The **monastery of Arkádhi** (daily 8am–8pm; €2), some 25km southeast of the city and immaculately situated in the foothills of the Psilorítis range, is also something of a national Cretan shrine. During the 1866 rebellion against the Turks, the monastery became a rebel strongpoint in which, as the Turks gained the upper hand, hundreds of Cretan independence fighters and their families took refuge. Surrounded and, after two days of fighting, on the point of defeat, the defenders ignited a powder magazine just as the Turks entered. Hundreds (some sources claim thousands) were killed, Cretan and Turk alike, and the tragedy did much to promote international sympathy for the cause of Cretan independence. Nowadays, you can peer into the roofless vault where the explosion occurred and wander about the rest of the well-restored grounds. Outside the entrance a modern monument displays the skulls of many of the victims. The sixteenth-century **church** survived, and is one of the finest Venetian structures left on Crete; other buildings house a small **museum** devoted to the exploits of the defenders of the (Orthodox) faith. The monastery is easy to visit by public bus or on a tour.

West to Aryiroúpolis, Yeoryoúpoli and beyond

Leaving Réthymnon to the west, the main road climbs for a while above a rocky coastline before descending (after some 5km) to the sea, where it runs alongside sandy **beaches** for perhaps another 7km. An occasional hotel offers accommodation, but on the whole there's nothing but a line of straggly bushes between the road and the windswept sands. If you have your own vehicle, there are plenty of places to stop for a swim, with rarely anyone else around – but beware of some very strong currents.

One worthwhile detour inland is to **ARYIROÚPOLIS**, a picturesque village perched above the Mousselás river valley and the seat of ancient Lappa, a Greek and Roman town of some repute. The village is famous for its **springs** which gush dramatically from the hillside and provide most of the city of Réthymnon's water supply. Among a number of **places to stay** try *Rooms Argiroupolis* (☎28310 81148, ☎28310 81149; ❷ including breakfast), near the springs, *Rooms Zografakis* (☎28310 81269; ❷ including breakfast), or – with great views from its air-conditioned rooms and taverna terrace – the excellent-value *Agnantema* (☎28310 81172; ❶) in the upper village. For **places to eat**, you're spoilt for choice, with five tavernas at the springs and a bar (serving tasty *mezédhes*) in the upper village, together with tavernas at *Zografakis* and *Agnantema*, the latter enjoying a spectacular terrace view down the river valley. A shop under the arch in the main square, named Lappa Avocado and selling local products of the region including olive oil and avocado-based skin products, can provide a free **map** detailing a surprising number of churches, caves and ancient remains to see in and around the village, including an outstanding third-century **Roman mosaic**. An interesting **folklore museum** (daily 10am–7pm; free) – signed from the main square – is worth a look for its collection of tapestries, farm implements, photos and ephemera collected by the Zografakis family who have lived here for countless generations. There are numerous fine **walks** in the surrounding hills, on which the proprietor of Lappa Avocado, who speaks English, will advise. Although little more than 20km from Réthymnon and easy to get to with your own transport, Aryiroúpolis is also served by **buses** from Réthymnon's bus station (Mon–Fri only) currently leaving at 11.30am and 2.30pm, and in the reverse direction at 7am, 12.30 and 3.30pm.

Back on the coastal route, if you are looking for a place to relax for a while, probably the best base is **YEORYOÚPOLI** just across the provincial border in Haniá, where the beach is cleaner, wider and further from the road. There's been a distinct acceleration in the pace of development at Yeoryoúpoli over the last few years and it's now very much a resort, packed with rooms to rent, small hotels, apartment buildings, tavernas and travel agencies. But everything remains on a small scale, and the undeniably attractive setting is untarnished, making it a very pleasant place to pass a few days, as long as you don't expect to find many vestiges of traditional Crete. Most of the new beachfront places are exclusively for package tourists, so it's best to head along the roads down towards the beach from the central *platía*. Here, you'll find *Andy's Rooms* (☎28250 61394; ❷), and *Cretan Cactus* (☎28250 61449; ❷), close to the beach; on the far side of the bridge across the river, *Anna* (☎28250 61376; ❶) offers some of the best value in town. *Taverna Paradise* (☎28250 61313; ❷), towards the river from the square, has more rooms and tasty food. *Taverna Babis*, in the other direction, is also good.

Within walking distance inland – though it can also be visited on the tourist train from Yeoryoúpoli – is **Kournás**, Crete's only freshwater lake, set deep in a bowl of hills and almost constantly changing colour. There are a few tavernas with rooms to rent along the shore here (bring mosquito repellent), or you could try for a bed in the nearby hill village of **MATHÉS** where the *Villa Kapasa* (☎28250 61050, ⓦwww.villa-kapasas.com; ❷) has some very pleasant en-suite rooms around a garden. *Taverna Mathes*, the village taverna has great terrace views and good food. A few kilometres uphill from the lake in **KOURNÁS** village, the *Kali Kardia* taverna is another great place to sample the local lamb and sausages.

Beyond Yeoryoúpoli, the main road heads inland, away from a cluster of coastal villages beyond Vámos. It thus misses the Dhrápano peninsula, the setting for the film of *Zorba the Greek*, with some spectacular views over the sapphire Bay of Soúdha and several quiet beaches. **Kókkino Horió**, the movie location, and nearby **Pláka** are indeed postcard-picturesque (more so from a distance), but **Kefalás**, inland, outdoes both of them. On the exposed north coast there are good beaches at **Almyrídha** and **Kalýves**, and off the road between them. Both have been discovered by package operators; accommodation is mostly in apartments and rooms are scarce, although there are a few mid-range and more upmarket hotels. Almyrídha is the more pleasant, with a string of good fish tavernas (try *Dimitri's*) along the beach that make for an enjoyable lunch stop. If you want to stay here try *Marilena's Pension* (☎28250 32202; ❷), on the seafront to the east, or the more central, modern *Almira Apartments* (☎28250 61376; ❸).

South from Réthymnon

There are a couple of alternative routes south from Réthymnon, but the main one heads straight out from the centre of town, an initially featureless road due south across the middle of the island towards **Ayía Galíni**. About 23km out, a turning cuts off to the right for **Plakiás** and **Mýrthios**, following the course of the spectacular Kourtaliótiko ravine.

Plakiás and the south coast

PLAKIÁS has undergone something of a boom in recent years and is no longer the pristine village all too many people arriving here expect. That said, it's still quite low key, with a satisfactory beach and a string of good tavernas around the dock. There are hundreds of **rooms**, but at the height of summer you'll need to arrive early if you hope to find one; the last to fill are generally those furthest inland, heading towards the youth hostel. Good places to try include *Gio-ma Taverna* (☎28320 32003, ⓦgioma.gr; ❶), on the seafront by the harbour, or the excellent balcony rooms at *Ippokambos* (☎28320 31525, ⓔamoutsos@otenet.gr; ❶), slightly inland on the road to the enjoyably relaxed **youth hostel** (☎28320 32118, ⓦyhplakias.com; dorms €7), which is 500m inland and signed from the seafront. *Pension Afrodite* (☎28320 31266; ❷) is a quiet spot with pleasant apartments, off the road to the hostel.

Once you've found a room there's not a lot else to discover here. Every facility you're likely to need is strung out along the waterfront or on the few short streets off it, including a **post office** (Mon–Fri 7.30am–2pm), **bike rental**, ATMs and **money exchange**, several **supermarkets** and even a **laundry**. Places to eat are plentiful too. The attractive **tavernas** on the waterfront in the centre are a little expensive; the pick of them are *Sofia* and *Christos* (next to *Gio-ma*) for fish. You'll eat cheaper further inland – seek out *Taverna Medousa* at the east end of town, reached up the road inland past the post office and then right. On the way here you'll pass *Nikos Souvlaki* which dishes up the least expensive meals in town, often accompanied by live *bouzoúki* music in the evenings. Beyond the harbour at the west end of town, a line of waterfront places enjoy spectacular sunsets – *Sunset* and *Glaros* are both worth a try.

Mýrthios

For a stay of more than a day or two, **MÝRTHIOS**, in the hills behind Plakiás, also deserves consideration. Originally put on the map for legions of younger travellers by a legendary youth hostel, it's now distinctly pricey, but there are some great apartments and wonderful views. And you'll generally find locals still outnumbering the tourists. To **stay**, check out the classy *Anna Apartments* (☎697 33 24 775, ⓦannaview.com; ❸), while for food the long-established *Plateia Taverna* has had a complete makeover but still serves up excellent food. A car is an advantage here, although the Plakiás bus will usually loop through Mýrthios (be sure to check – otherwise, it's less than five minutes' walk from the junction). It takes twenty minutes to walk down to the beach at Plakiás, a little longer to Dhamnóni.

Dhamnóni and Skhinariá

Some of the most tempting **beaches** in central Crete hide just to the east of Plakiás, though unfortunately they're now a very poorly kept secret. These three splashes of yellow sand, divided by rocky promontories, are within easy walking distance and together go by the name **Dhamnóni**. At the first, Dhamnóni proper, there's a taverna with showers and a wonderfully long strip of sand, but there's also a lot of new development including a number of nearby rooms for rent and a huge and ugly Swiss-owned holiday village, which has colonized half of the main beach. At the far end, you'll generally find a few people who've dispensed with their clothes, while the little cove which shelters the middle of the three beaches (barely accessible except on foot) is entirely nudist. Beyond this, **Ammoúdhi** beach has another taverna, *Ammoudi* (☎28320 31355; 3), with good rooms for rent, and slightly more of a family atmosphere. **Skhinariá** beach, just around the corner, is a considerable distance by road via the village of Lefkóyia. A popular diving spot, in summer it attracts Greek families, but is otherwise quiet. There's a decent taverna here, *Lybian Star.*

Préveli and "Palm Beach"

Next in line along the coast is **PRÉVELI**, some 6km southeast of Lefkóyia, served by two daily **buses** from Réthymnon (check current times with any tourist office). It takes its name from a **monastery** (April & May daily 8am–7pm; June–Oct Mon–Sat 8am–1.30pm & 3.30–8pm, Sun 8am–8pm; in winter, knock for admission; €2.50) set high above the sea which, like every other in Crete, has a proud history of resistance, in this case accentuated by its role in World War II as a shelter for marooned Allied soldiers awaiting evacuation off the south coast. There are fine views and a new monument – to the left as you approach – commemorating the rescue operations and depicting a startling life-size, rifle-toting abbot and an allied soldier cast in bronze. The evacuations took place from "**Palm Beach**", a sandy cove with a small date-palm grove and a solitary drink stand where a stream (actually the Megapótamos river) feeds a little oasis. The beach usually attracts a summer camping community and is now also the target of day-trip boats from Plakiás and Ayía Galíni. Sadly, these groups between them deposit heaps of rubbish, often leaving this lovely place filthy, and despite an ongoing clean-up campaign it seems barely worth the effort. The easiest way to get to "Palm Beach" from the monastery is to follow a newly asphalted road that leaves the main road 1km before the monastery itself. This leads, after a further kilometre, to a **pay car park** (€1.50) where you'll need to leave any transport. From here, a marked path clambers steeply down over the rocks – about a twenty-minute descent to the beach. Should you not wish to return this way (although you'll have little option if you've brought transport), you can avoid the arduous steep climb by taking a track on the east side of the beach which follows the river valley 2km back to a stone bridge, where there are cafés. You should be able to get one of the two daily buses to drop you at this bridge. All this said, **boat trips** from Plakiás and Ayía Galíni will get you here with a great deal less fuss.

Spíli and Ayía Galíni

Back on the main road south, the pleasant country town of **SPÍLI** lies about 30km from Réthymnon. A popular coffee break for coach tours passing this way, Spíli warrants time if you can spare it. Sheltered under a cliff are narrow alleys of ancient houses, all leading up from a *platía* with a famous 24-spouted **fountain** that replaced a Venetian original. If you have your own transport, it's a worthwhile place to stay, peacefully rural at night but with several good **rooms** for rent. Try the *Green Hotel* (☎28320 22225; ❷), on the main road, or the charming *Rooms Herakles* (☎28320 22411, Ⓔheraclespapadakis @hotmail.com; ❷, reductions for more than one night) just behind, the eponymous proprietor of which can advise on some superb **walks** in the surrounding hills and also rents out **mountain bikes**. There are two **banks** along the main street (with ATMs) and **Internet** access is possible at *Cafe Babis*, close to the fountain.

The ultimate destination for most people on this road is **AYÍA GALÍNI**. If heading here was your plan, maybe you should think again since this picturesque "fishing village" is so busy in high season that you can't see it for the tour buses, hotel billboards and British package tourists. It also has a beach that is much too small for the crowds that congregate here. Even so, there are a few saving graces – mainly some excellent restaurants and bars, a lively nightlife scene, plenty of rooms and a friendly atmosphere that survives and even thrives on all the visitors. Out of season, when the climate is mild, it can be quite enjoyable too, and from November to April, despite competition from immigrant workers, a number of long-term travellers spend the winter packing tomatoes or polishing cucumbers here. If you want somewhere to stay, start looking at the top end of town, around the main road: the economical *Hotel Minos* (☎28320 91292; ❶), with superb views, is a good place to start, with the nearby *Hotel Idi* (☎28320 91152, Ⓕ28320 91082; ❷) and *Hotel Hariklia* (☎ & Ⓕ28320 91257; ❷) as backups, but there are dozens of possibilities, and usually something to be found even at the height of summer.

The coastal plain east of Ayía Galíni, hidden under acres of polythene greenhouses and burgeoning concrete sprawl, must be among the ugliest regions in Crete, and **Timbáki** the dreariest town. Since this is the way to Phaestos and back to Iráklion, you may have no choice but to grin and bear it.

The Amári Valley

An alternative route south from Réthymnon, and a far less travelled one, is the road which turns off on the eastern fringe of town to run via the **Amári Valley**. Very few buses go this way, but if you're driving it's well worth the extra time. There's little specifically to see or do (though hidden away are a number of richly frescoed Byzantine churches), but it's an impressive drive under the flanks of the mountains and a reminder of how, in places, rural Crete continues to exist regardless of visitors. The countryside here is delightfully green even in summer, with rich groves of olive and assorted fruit trees, and if you **stay** (there are rooms in Thrónos and Yerákari), you'll find the nights are cool and quiet. It may seem odd that many of the villages along the way are modern: they were systematically destroyed by the German army in reprisal for the 1944 kidnapping of General Kreipe.

Haniá and the west

The substantial attractions of Crete's westernmost quarter are enhanced by its relative lack of visitors, and despite the now-rapid spread of tourist development, the west is likely to remain one of the emptier parts of the island. This is partly because there are no big sandy beaches to accommodate resort hotels, and partly because it's so far from the great archeological sites. But for mountains and empty (if often pebbly) beaches, it's unrivalled.

Haniá itself is an excellent reason to come here, but the immediately adjacent coast, especially to the west of the city, is overdeveloped and not particularly exciting; if you want beaches head for the south coast. **Paleohóra** is the only place which could really be described as a resort, and even this is on a thoroughly human scale; others are emptier still. **Ayía Rouméli** and **Loutró** can be reached only on foot or by boat; **Hóra Sfakíon** sees hordes passing through but few who stay; **Frangokástello**, nearby, has a beautiful castle and the first stirrings of development. Behind these lie the **White Mountains** (Lefká Óri) and, above all, the famed walk through the **Samarian Gorge**.

Haniá

HANIÁ, as any of its residents will tell you, is spiritually the capital of Crete, even if the official title was passed back (in 1971) to Iráklion. For many, it is also by far the island's most attractive city, especially if you can catch it in spring, when the White Mountains' snowcapped peaks seem to hover above the roofs. Although it is for the most part a modern city, you might never know it as a tourist. Surrounding the small outer harbour is a wonderful jumble of half-derelict **Venetian streets** that survived the wartime bombardments, and it is here that life for the visitor is concentrated. Restoration and gentrification, consequences of the tourist boom, have made inroads of late, but it remains an atmospheric place.

Arrival, information and orientation

Large as it is, Haniá is easy to handle once you've reached the centre; you may get lost wandering among the narrow alleys of the old city but that's a

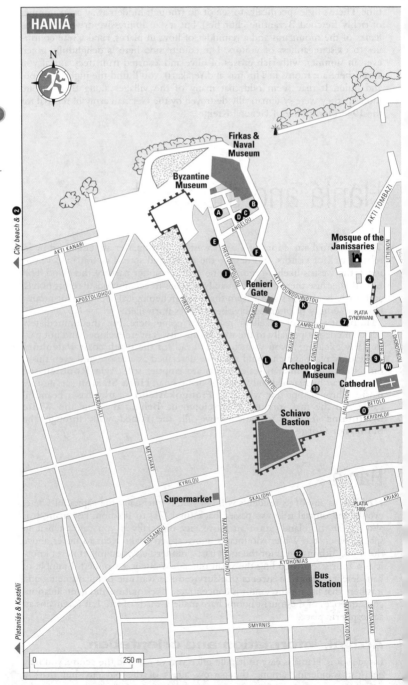

Firkas &
Naval
Museum

Byzantine
Museum

Mosque of the
Janissaries

AKTI TOMBAZI

AKTI KANARI

ANGELOU

A

D C

B

E

THEOTOKOPOULOU

F

AKTI KOUNDOURIOTOU

LITHINON

APOSTOLIDHOU

I

Renieri
Gate

4

PIREOS

DHIMOS

K

8

ZAMBELIOU

SKUFON

PLATIA
SYNDRIVANI

7

KONDHILAKI

E. DHOROTHEOU

ISODHION

PARHALI

L

Archeological
Museum

PORTOU

10

HALIDHON

Cathedral

9

M

METAHAKI

Schiavo
Bastion

BETOLO

SKRIDHLOF

O

KYRILOU

KISSAMOU

MANOUSOYANAKIDHOU

Supermarket

SKALIDHI

PLATIA
1866

KRIARI

KYDHONIAS

12

Bus
Station

ZMVRAKAKKIDON

SFAKIANAKI

SMYRNIS

0   250 m

ACCOMMODATION

Amphora	F
Casa Veneta	I
To Dhiporto	O
El Greco	E
Fidias	N
Kastelli	G
Lucia	K
Maro	L
Meltemi	B
Nikos	J
Pension Nora	A
Port	H
Rooms Stella	D
Thereza	C
Vranas Studios	M

RESTAURANTS

Akrogiali	2
Anaplous	5
Aroma	4
Apostolis	1
Ela	10
Iordanis Bougatsa	11&12
Karnayio	3
Rudi's Bierhaus	6
Souvlaki Alusides	7
Tamam	8
Tholos	9

Inner Harbour

SARPIDHONOS

Port Police

PLATIA KATEHAKI

AKTI ENOSEOS

Arsenali

KALERGON

KASTÉLLI

KANEVAROU

ANDHROUTSOU

SIFAKA

SPIÁNTZA

Minoan Excavation

SFAKA

San Rocco

VOURDOUBA

MINOOS

KARAOLI

DHASKALOYIANNIS

PLATIA 1821

Ayios Nikólaos

AKTI MIAOULI

SARPAKI

Anaryíri Minaret

POTIE

DHALIANI

Minaret

TSOUDHERON

NIKIFOROU FOKA

KYPROU

Market

PLATIA S. VENIZELOU

ELEFTHERIOU VENIZELOU

YIANNARI

N. PLASTIRA

VELOUDHAKIDHON

APOKORONOU

TRIKOUPI

ANDHREA

Stadium

KORAI

PAPANDHREOU

TZANAKAKI

Public Gardens

KARAISKAKI

Dhimarhío

KORNAROU

SOLOMOU

SFAKIANAKI

Akrotiri ▶

Platía Eleftherías ▶

Platía Eleftherías ▶

▼ new road, Soúdha, Réthymnon & Iráklion

265

relatively small area, and you're never far from the sea or from some other obvious landmark. The **bus station** is on Kydhonías, within easy walking distance from the centre – turn right out of the station, then left down the side of Platía-1866 and you'll emerge at a major road junction opposite the top of Halídhon, the main street of the old quarter leading straight down to the Venetian harbour. Arriving by **ferry**, you'll anchor about 10km east of Haniá at the port of Soúdha: there are frequent buses from here which will drop you by the **market** on the fringes of the old town, or you can take a taxi (around €8); there are also KTEL buses to Réthymnon and Kastélli meeting most ferries. From the **airport** (15km east of town on the Akrotíri peninsula) taxis (around €10) will almost certainly be your only option, though it's worth a quick check to see if any sort of bus is meeting your flight. The very helpful **tourist office** is in the *dhimarhío* (town hall) at Kydhonías 29 (Mon–Fri 8am–2.30pm ☎28210 36155, ℻28210 36205), four blocks east of the bus station.

Accommodation

There are thousands of **rooms** to rent in Haniá and, unusually, quite a few luxurious **hotels**. Though you may face a long search for a bed at the height of the season, eventually everyone does seem to find something. The nearest **campsite** within striking distance is *Camping Hania* (☎28210 31138), some 4km west of Haniá behind the beach, served by local bus. The site is rather small, and hemmed in by new development, but it has a pool and all the facilities just a short walk from some of the better beaches.

Harbour area

Perhaps the most desirable rooms of all are those overlooking the **harbour**, which are sometimes available at reasonable rates: be warned that this is often because they're very noisy at night. Most are approached not direct from the harbourside itself but from the streets behind; those further back are likely to be more peaceful. Theotokopoúlou and the alleys off it make a good starting point. The nicest of the more expensive places are here, too, equally set back but often with views from the upper storeys. In recent years the popularity of this area has led to anyone with a room near the harbour tarting it up and attempting to rent it out at a ridiculously inflated price. You'll often be touted in the street for these and it's wise not to commit yourself until you've made some comparisons.

Amphora 2 Párodos Theotokopoúlou 20 ☎28210 93224, ⓦamphora.gr. Large, traditional hotel in Venetian mansion, and beautifully renovated; worth the expense if you get a view, but probably not for the cheaper rooms without one. Good restaurant below, see p.269. ❺
Casa Veneta Theotokopoúlou 57 ☎28210 90007, ℻28210 75931. Very well-equipped, comfortable studios and apartments with friendly owner. Good value. ❹
El Greco Theotokopoúlou 47–49 ☎ 28210 94030 ⓔhotel@elgreco.gr. Comfortable hotel with nicely furnished if rather small rooms; all amenities including TV. Some have balconies and there's a seasonal roof terrace. ❹
Lucia Aktí Koundouriótou ☎28210 90302, ℻28210 91843. Harbourfront hotel with balcony

rooms; less expensive than you might expect for one of the best views in town, and reasonably soundproof. ❸
Maro B Párodos Porto 5 ☎28210 54981. Probably the cheapest rooms in the old town, hidden away in a quiet, unmarked alley off Portou not far from the Schiavo bastion. Basic but friendly and clean. ❷
Meltemi Angélou 2 ☎28210 92802. First of a little row of *pensions* in a great situation on the far side of the harbour near the Naval Museum; perhaps noisier than its neighbours, but excellent views and a good café downstairs (see p.269). ❹
Pension Nora Theotokopoúlou 60 ☎ 28210 72265. Charming, simple rooms in an old wooden Turkish house, some with shared bath. Pleasant breakfast café below. ❷

Rooms Stella Angélou 10 ☎ 28210 73756.
Creaky, eccentric old house above an eclectic gift
shop, with plain, clean rooms. ④
Thereza Angélou 8 ☎ & Ⓕ 28210 92798.
Beautiful old house in a great position, with
stunning views from roof terrace and some of
the rooms; classy decor, too. Slightly more
expensive than its neighbours but deservedly
so; unlikely to have room in season unless you
book. ⑥

The old town: east of Halídhon

In the eastern half of the old town, rooms are far more scattered, usually
cheaper, and in the height of the season your chances are much better over
here. **Kastélli**, immediately east of the harbour, has some lovely places with
views from the heights. Take one of the alleys leading left off Kanevárou if you
want to try these, but don't be too hopeful since they are popular and often
booked up.

To Dhiporto Betólo 41, one block north of
Skridhlóf ☎ 28210 40570. Pleasant, good-value
rooms all with air con, TV and fridge; some triples
and singles. ③
Fidias Kalinákou Sarpáki 8 ☎ 28210 52494.
Signposted from the cathedral, this favourite backpackers' meeting place has been going forever
and has the real advantage of offering single
rooms or fixing shares. Recently renovated to add
en-suites, but still has the cheapest beds in town.
Bed in shared three-bed room €8–10. ②
Kastelli Kanevárou 39 ☎ 28210 57057,
Ⓔ kastelistudios@chania-cci.gr. A comfortable,
modern, reasonably priced *pension* and very quiet
at the back. All rooms come with fans and anti-
mosquito machines. The owner is exceptionally
helpful and also has a few apartments and a
beautiful house (for up to five people) to rent. ③
Nikos Dhaskaloyiánnis 58 ☎ 28210 54783. One of
several rooms places along this street near the
inner harbour; good-value, relatively modern
rooms, all with shower. Same owner has economical studios nearby with kitchen and fridge. ③
Port Sífaka 73, just off Dhaskaloyiánnis ☎ 28210
59484. Clean, quiet modern place with good-size,
en-suite rooms. ③
Vranas Studios Ayíon Dhéka and Kalinákou
Sarpáki, near the cathedral ☎ & Ⓕ 28210 58618.
Pleasant, spacious studio-style rooms with TV, air
con, fridge and kitchenette. ④

The City

Haniá has been occupied almost continuously since Neolithic times, so it
comes as a surprise that a city of such antiquity should offer little specifically
to see or do. It is, however, a place which is fascinating simply to wander
around, stumbling upon surviving fragments of city wall, the remains of
ancient Kydonia which are being excavated, and odd segments of Venetian
or Turkish masonry.

Kastélli and the harbour

The **port** area is as ever the place to start, the oldest and the most interesting
part of town. It's at its busiest and most attractive at night, when the lights from
bars and restaurants reflect in the water and crowds of visitors and locals turn
out to promenade. By day, things are quieter. Straight ahead from Platía
Syndriváni (also known as Harbour Square) lies the curious domed shape of
the **Mosque of the Janissaries**, built in 1645 (though heavily restored since)
and the oldest Ottoman building on the island. It is occasionally open as a
gallery, housing temporary exhibitions in the messy structures that adjoin the
original mosque, although there are plans to demolish these.

The little hill that rises behind the mosque is **Kastélli**, site of the earliest
habitation and core of the Minoan, Venetian and Turkish towns. There's not a
great deal left, but archeologists believe that they may have found the remains
of a Minoan palace (logically, there must have been one at this end of the
island), and the "lost" city of Kydonia, in the **excavations** being carried out –

and open to view – along Kanevárou. It's also here that you'll find traces of the oldest **walls**; there were two rings, one defending Kastélli alone, a later set encompassing the whole of the medieval city. Beneath the hill, on the inner (eastern) harbour, the arches of sixteenth-century **Venetian arsenals**, a couple of them beautifully restored, survive alongside remains of the outer walls.

Following the esplanade around in the other direction leads to a hefty bastion which now houses Crete's **Naval Museum** (daily 9am–4pm; €2). The collection consists of model ships and other naval ephemera tracing the history of Greek navigation, plus a section on the 1941 **Battle of Crete** with fascinating artefacts, and poignant photos depicting the suffering here under the Nazis. You might want to wander in through the gate beside the museum anyway for a (free) look at the seaward fortifications and the platform from which the modern Greek flag was first flown on Crete (in 1913). Walk around the back of these restored bulwarks to a street heading inland and you'll find the best-preserved stretch of the outer walls. Just behind the Naval Museum at the top of Theotokopoúlou lies the new **Byzantine Museum** (Tues–Sun 8.30am–3pm; €2, combined ticket with Archeological Museum €3), with a small but interesting collection of mosaics, icons and jewellery from the various periods of Byzantine rule. Continue up Theotokopoúlou and explore the alleys off it to discover some of the most attractive parts of the old town, with widespread restoration and plenty of fascinating small shops.

Halídhon and beyond

Behind the harbour lie the less picturesque but more lively sections of the old city. First, a short way up Halídhon on the right, is Haniá's **Archeological Museum** (Tues–Sun 8.30am–3pm; €2), housed in the Venetian-built church of San Francesco. Damaged as it is, especially from the outside, this remains a beautiful building and it contains a fine little display, covering the local area from Minoan through to Roman times. In the garden, a huge fountain and the base of a minaret survive from the period when the Ottomans converted the church into a mosque; around them are scattered various other sculptures and architectural remnants. The nearby **Folklore Museum** (Mon–Sat 9am–3pm & 6–9pm; €1.50) is worth a look as much for its setting, on a fine courtyard that is also home to Haniá's Roman Catholic church, and the mansion itself as for its contents

The **cathedral**, ordinary and relatively modern, is just a few steps further up Halídhon on the left. Around it are some of the more animated shopping areas, particularly **Odhós Skrídhlof** ("Leather Street"), lined with the shops of traditional leathermakers plying their trade, with streets leading up to the back of the market beyond. In the direction of the Spiántza quarter are ancient alleys with tumbledown Venetian stonework and overhanging wooden balconies; though gentrification is spreading apace, much of the quarter has yet to feel the effect of the city's modern popularity. There are a couple more **minarets** too, one on Dhaliáni, and the other in Platía-1821, which is a fine traditional square to stop for a coffee.

From the top of Halídhon, or beyond the market (well worth a visit, see p.271), spread the broad, traffic-choked streets of the **modern city**. You may venture out here for business – travel agencies and banks lie in this direction, along with the post office, bus station and shops, but few tourists stay long. And in truth there's little reason to linger. On Tzanakáki, not far from the market, you'll find the **public gardens**, a park with strolling couples, a few caged animals (including *krí-krí* or Cretan ibex) and a café under the trees; there's also an open-air auditorium which occasionally hosts live music or local festivities.

Locals tend not to hang around here this part of town either – though they are drawn to the seafront cafés of Aktí Miaoúli, east of the old city, and to the seafood tavernas behind the beach (see below).

The beaches

Haniá's beaches all lie to the west of the city. For the packed and recently cleaned-up **city beach**, this means no more than a ten-minute walk following the shoreline from the Naval Museum, but for more extensive spaces you're better off taking the local bus (#21) out along the coast road. This leaves from the east side of Platía-1866 and runs along the coast as far as **Kalamáki beach**. Kalamáki and the previous stop, **Oásis beach**, are again pretty crowded but they're a considerable improvement over the beach in Haniá itself. In between, you'll find plenty of alternatives, though some of these are quite a walk from the bus stop. Further afield there are even finer beaches at **Ayía Marína** (see p.272) to the west, or **Stavrós** (p.271) out on the Akrotíri peninsula, either of which can be reached by KTEL buses from the main station.

Eating

You're never far from something to **eat** in Haniá: in a circle around the harbour is one restaurant, taverna or café after another. These tend to be pricey, though, and the quality at many leaves a lot to be desired. Away from the water, there are plenty of slightly cheaper possibilities on Kondhiláki, Kanevárou and most of the streets off Halídhon. For snacks or lighter meals, the cafés around the harbour generally serve cocktails and fresh juices at exorbitant prices, though breakfast (especially "English") can be good value. For more-traditional places, try around the market and along Dhaskaloyiánnis (*Synganaki* here is a good traditional bakery serving *tyrópita* and the like, with a cake shop next door). Fast food is also increasingly widespread.

Akrogiali Aktí Papanikolí 19, behind the city beach ☎ 28210 73110. Worth the walk, or short taxi ride, to this excellent, reasonably priced seafront fish taverna. Always packed with locals, so may be worth booking – though there are plenty of alternatives along the street.
Amphora Aktí Koundouriótou, under the *Hotel Amphora*. One of the most reliable places on the outer harbour, with good, simple Greek food.
Anaplous Sífaka 37. A couple of blocks west of Platía-1821, *Anaplous* occupies a stylishly "restored" ruin of a Turkish mansion bombed in the war. Serves both *mezédhes* and full meals to live guitar music.
Apostolis Aktí Enóseos 6 & 10, inner harbour. The fish tavernas at the inner end of the harbour are rated much higher by locals than those further round – some locals claim *Apostolis 2*, practically the last, and just a couple of doors down from its seemingly identical sister restaurant, is the best of all. The fish is excellent, but pricey.
Aroma Aktí Tombázi 4, next to the Mosque of the Janissaries. Pleasant café with great harbour view to savour over lazy breakfasts or late drinks.

Mousses, nearby at the corner of Kanevárou, is equally good, and open 24 hours.
Ela Top of Kondhiláki. Standard taverna food with live Greek music accompaniment to enliven your meal in yet another roofless taverna town-house.
Iordanis Bougatsa Kydhonías 96, opposite the bus station. This place serves little except the tra-ditional creamy *bougátsa*, a sugar-coated cheese pie to eat in or take away. Another branch is at Apokorónou 24, between the market and the tourist office.
Karnayio Platía Kateháki 8. Set back from the inner harbour near the port police. Not right on the water, but one of the best harbour restaurants nonetheless. The nearby *Faka* is also good.
Meltemi Angélou 2. Slow, relaxed terrace bar beneath the rooms place of the same name; good for breakfast, and where locals (especially expats) sit whiling the day away or playing *tavli*.
Rudi's Bierhaus Sífaka 24. Haniá's beer shrine: Austrian Rudi Riegler's bar stocks more than a hundred of Europe's finest beers to accompany very tasty *mezédhes*.

Souvlaki Alusides Zambelíou. The most popular *souvláki* and fast food in the old town.

Tamam Zambelíou. Excellent, fashionable place with adventurous Greek menu including much vegetarian food. Unfortunately only a few cramped tables outside, and inside it can get very hot.

Service can be slow.

Tholos Ayíon Dhéka 36. Slightly north of the cathedral, *Tholos* is another "restaurant in a ruin", this time Venetian/Turkish, with a wide selection of Cretan specialities.

Bars and nightlife

Haniá's **nightlife** has more than enough venues to satisfy most night-owls. The majority of the touristy clubs and disco bars are gathered in the area around the harbour, whilst there are plenty of terrace bars along both harbourfronts, with more scattered throughout the old quarter. Young locals, however, tend to start their evenings in the bars and cafés along Aktí Miaoúli, east of the harbour, and Sarpidhónos, which leads from the inner harbour in that direction. Around midnight, most move on to clubs, either in town or out along the coast, especially in Plataniás.

As everywhere, places go in and out of fashion, and names change frequently, but the venues generally remain where they were – in the old town **bars** you're occasionally reminded of the proximity of the Soúdha NATO bases by an influx of rowdy servicemen. Reliable places around the harbour include the *Four Seasons*, a very popular bar by the port police, and several bars, including long-running *Scorpio*, in an alley starting behind the Mosque of the Janissaries. Nearby here, on upper floors, are the laid-back *Point* bar (above *Mousses* café) and *Plateia*, with live Greek music. At the opposite or western end of the harbour *Fagotto*, Angélou 16, is a pleasant, laid-back jazz bar, often with live performers. Of the places on **Aktí Miaoúli**, try *Ellinikon* or *Mythologia*, though most seem almost interchangeable.

Currently king of the **clubs** is *Tessara Tetarta* (the *Four Quarters*), on Aktí Kanári by the municipal swimming pool just before the town beach, though don't expect much action before 1am. Rivals include *Daz*, down an alley off the top of Halídhon, under the Schiavo bastion, and *Premier*, a big, bright place on Tsoudherón behind the market.

A venue offering more traditional entertainment is the *Café Kriti*, Kalergón 22, at the corner of Andhroyíou, basically an old-fashioned *kafenío* where there's **Greek music** and **dancing** virtually every night. It's also worth checking for events at the open-air auditorium in the public gardens, and for performances in restaurants outside the city, which are the ones the locals will go to. Look for posters, especially in front of the market and in the little *platía* across the road from there.

For **films**, you should also check the hoardings in front of the market. There are open-air screenings at Attikon, on Venizélou out towards Akrotíri, about 1km from the centre, and occasionally in the public gardens.

Listings

Airlines Olympic, with scheduled daily flights between Haniá and Athens plus frequent flights to Thessaloníki, has an office at Tzanakáki 88 (Mon–Fri 9am–4pm; ☎28210 57701–3) opposite the public gardens. Aegean (to Athens only) is at Venizélou 12 (☎28210 51100) across from the market. For airport information call ☎28210 63264.

Banks and exchange The main branch of the National Bank of Greece is directly opposite the market with two ATMs, and there's a cluster of banks with more ATMs around the top of Halídhon. You'll also find plenty of out-of-hours exchange places on Halídhon, in the travel agencies.

Bike and car rental Possibilities everywhere, especially on Halídhon, though these are rarely the best value. For bikes, Summertime, Dhaskaloyiánnis 7, slightly northeast of the market (☎28210 45797, ⓦstrentals.gr) has a huge range, including mountain bikes. Bike Trekking, Karaóli 15 (☎28210 20143) has organized mountain-biking tours. For cars, look along Halídhon – two reliable local companies are Hermes, Tzanakáki 52 (☎28210 54418) or Tellus Rent a Car, Halídhon 108, opposite Platía-1866 (☎28210 91500). Good deals for *Rough Guide* readers are available from El Greco Cars at the *El Greco* hotel (☎28210 60883, ⓔcars@elgreco.gr).

Boat trips A number of boats make daily trips from Haniá, mainly to the nearby islands of Áyii Theódori and Lazarétta, for swimming and *krí-krí* (ibex) spotting: you're unlikely to escape the attentions of their stalls around the harbour. The *Evagelos* glass-bottomed boat, for example, makes this trip three times daily, with an all-day alternative on Saturdays to the Rodhópou peninsula (for information call ☎694 58 74 283); the *MS Irini* (☎28210 52001) is a more traditional vessel.

Diving Blue Adventures Diving, Dhaskalioyánnis 69 (☎28210 40403), runs daily diving and snorkelling trips.

Ferry tickets From any travel agent, or the ANEK line office is on Venizélou, right opposite the market (☎28210 27500); Blue Star at Platía-1866 14 (☎28210 75444).

Internet There are plenty of Internet cafés including: Kathodon, Isodhíon 10 at Karaoli; the more tranquil Vranas, Ayíon Dhéka beneath *Vranas Studios* (see p.267; minimum 1hr, though credit given) and Café Notos, on the outer harbour under the *Hotel Notos*.

Laundry There are plenty to choose from, including Speedy Laundry (☎28210 88411; 9am–9pm), junction of Koronéou and Korkídhi, just west of

Platía-1866, who will collect and deliver your load if you call; Afrodite, Ayíon Dhéka 22 (daily 8.30am–8.30pm) in the old town and Fidias, Kalinákou Sarpáki 6 (next to the *pension* of the same name; Mon–Sat 9am–9pm). All do service washes for around €6.

Left luggage The bus station has a left-luggage office open 6am–8.30pm; €1–2 per item per day depending on size.

Market and supermarkets To buy food, head for the entertaining market which has fresh fruit and vegetables, meat and fish, bakers, dairy stalls and general stores for cooked meats, tins, etc; on Saturday mornings there's a wonderful line of stalls along Minóos, inside the eastern city wall, where local farmers sell their produce. Several small stores by the harbour *platía* sell cold drinks and food, which are expensive but open late. Small supermarkets can be found on Platía-1866 and the larger Marinopolos supermarket is at the top of Pireos, outside the western wall, close to the Schiavo bastion.

Post office The main post office is on Tzanakáki (Mon–Fri 7.30am–8pm, Sat 9am–1pm).

Taxis The main taxi ranks are in Platía-1866. For radio taxis try ☎18300 or 28210 94300.

Tourist police Inconveniently located at Iraklíou 23 in the southern suburb of Koubés (☎28210 53333 or 28210 28708).

Travel agencies El Greco Travel, on Kydhonías near the bus station (☎28210 86015), and Tellus Travel, Halídhon 108, opposite Platía-1866 (☎28210 91500), are both good for inexpensive bus tickets, flights and standard excursions. For cheap tickets home try Bassias Travel, Halídhon 69 (☎28210 44 295), very helpful for regular tickets too. They also deal in standard excursions. Other travel agents for tours and day-trips are everywhere.

Around Haniá: the Akrotíri and Rodhópou peninsulas

Just north of Haniá, the **Akrotíri peninsula** loops around to protect the Bay of Soúdha and a NATO military base and missile-testing area. In an ironic twist, the peninsula's northwestern coastline is fast developing into a luxury suburb; the beach of Kalathás, near Horafákia, long popular with jaded Haniotes is surrounded by villas and apartments. **STAVRÓS**, further out, has not yet suffered this fate, and its **beach** is absolutely superb if you like the calm, shallow water of an almost completely enclosed lagoon. It's not very large, so it does get crowded, but rarely overpoweringly so. There's a makeshift taverna/*souvláki* stand on the beach, and a couple of tavernas across the road, but for accommodation you need to search slightly south of here, in the area around **Blue beach**, where there are plenty of apartment buildings but no low-budget accommodation in summer whatsoever. On Blue beach you could try *Zorba's Apartments* (T 28210 52525; ③).

Inland are the **monasteries** of **Ayía Triádha** (daily 9am–7pm; €1.50) and **Gouvernétou** (daily 7am–2pm & 4–8pm; free). The former is much more accessible and has a beautiful seventeenth-century church inside its pink-and-ochre cloister, though ongoing renovations – the latest has turned one building into an olive-oil factory where the monks produce and bottle their own oil – on occasions make the normally peaceful enclosure more like a building site. Four kilometres north of Gouvernétou – which is in a far better state of preservation and where traditional monastic life can still be observed – you can clamber down a craggy path to the amazing and abandoned ruins of the **monastery of Katholikó**, built into a craggy ravine, and the remains of its narrow (swimmable) harbour.

West to Rodhópou

The coast to the west of Haniá was the scene of most of the fighting during the German invasion in 1941 and at Máleme there's a big German cemetery; the Allied cemetery is in the other direction, on the coast just outside Soúdha. There are also beaches and considerable tourist development along much of this shore. At **Ayía Marína** there's a fine sandy beach and an island offshore said to be a sea monster petrified by Zeus before it could swallow Crete. Seen from the west, its "mouth" still gapes open.

Between **Plataniás** and **Kolymvári** an almost unbroken strand unfurls, exposed when the wind blows and by no means all sandy, but deserted for long stretches between villages. The road here runs through mixed groves of calamus reed (Crete's bamboo) and oranges; the windbreaks fashioned from the reeds protect the ripening oranges from the *meltémi*. At Kolymvári, the road to Kastélli cuts across the base of another mountainous peninsula, **Rodhópou**. Just off the main road here is a monastery, **Goniá** (summer Mon–Fri & Sun 8am–12.30pm & 4–8pm, Sat 4–8pm; winter daily 3.30–5.30pm; free; respectable dress required), with a view most luxury hotels would envy. Every monk in Crete can tell tales of his proud ancestry of resistance to invaders, but here the Turkish cannon balls are still lodged in the walls to prove it, a relic of which the good fathers are far more proud than any of the icons.

South to the Samarian Gorge

From Haniá the **Samarian Gorge** (May–Oct; €5 for entry to the national park) can be visited as a day-trip or as part of a longer excursion to the south. At 16km, it claims to be Europe's longest gorge and is startlingly beautiful. In the June to August period (ring Haniá tourist office or check at the bus station for other times) **buses** leave Haniá bus station for the top at 6.15am, 7.30am, 8.30am and 2pm (this latter service changes to 4.30pm outside school holidays), depositing you at the gorge entrance and then collecting you at the port of Hóra Sfakíon for the return trip to Haniá. You can also get the boat and bus back via Soúyia or Paleohóra and if this is your intention you should specify when you buy your ticket: otherwise, for the three early buses, you'll normally be sold a return trip (valid from Hóra Sfakíon at any time). Should you take the last bus you will need to spend a night at Ayía Rouméli (the end of the gorge) as you will not get through the gorge in time for the last boat. It's well worth catching the earliest bus to avoid the full heat of the day while walking through the gorge, though be warned that you will not be alone – there are often as many as five coachloads setting off before dawn for the nail-biting climb into the White Mountains. There are also direct early-morning buses from Iráklion, Réthymnon, Soúyia and Paleohóra as well as bus tours from virtually everywhere on the island, adding up to a couple of thousand plus walkers on most days during high season.

Despite all the crowds, the walk *is* hard work, especially in spring when the stream is a roaring torrent. Early and late in the season, there is a danger of **flash floods**, which are not to be taken lightly: in 1993, a number of walkers perished when they were washed out to sea. For this reason the first and last three weeks of the season are entirely dependent on the weather and you will only be allowed into the gorge if the authorities deem it safe. If in doubt (and to save yourself a wasted journey), phone the Haniá Forest Service's **gorge information number** (☎28210 67140) or the gorge office (☎28210 67179) for information. Should you arrive after 4pm you will only be allowed into the first couple of kilometres from each end of the gorge and the wardens ensure that no one remains in the gorge overnight, where camping is strictly forbidden.

Omalós

One way to avoid an early start from the north coast would be to stay at **OMALÓS**, in the middle of the mountain plain from which the gorge descends. There are plenty of **tavernas** and some ordinary **rooms** for rent – the friendly no-frills *Samaria pension* (☎28210 67168; ❶) is the cheapest – plus a clutch of surprisingly fancy **hotels**; the *Hotel Gigilos* (☎28210 67181; ❷) is good value and its proprietor will drive you the 5km to the top of the gorge next morning if you stay overnight. However, since the village is some way from the start of the path, and the first buses arrive as the sun rises, it's almost impossible to get a head start on the crowds. Some people sleep out at the top (where there's a bar-restaurant in the *Tourist Lodge* and kiosks serving drinks and sandwiches), but a night under the stars here can be a bitterly cold experience. The one significant advantage to staying up here would be if you wanted to undertake some other **climbs** in the White Mountains, in which case the Kallérgi mountain hut (☎28210 33199 or ☎693 66 57 954; €12 per person) is about an hour's hike (signed) from Omalós or ninety minutes from the top of the gorge; you can also drive up there from Omalós.

The gorge

The **gorge** itself begins at the *xylóskalo*, or "wooden staircase", a stepped path plunging steeply down from the southern lip of the Omalós plain. Here, at the head of the track, opposite the sheer rock face of Mount Gíngilos, the crowds pouring out of the buses disperse rapidly as keen walkers march purposefully down while others dally over breakfast, contemplating the sunrise. You descend at first through almost alpine scenery: pine forest, wild flowers and very un-Cretan greenery – a verdant shock in the spring, when the stream is at its liveliest. Small churches and viewpoints dot the route, and about halfway down you pass the abandoned village of **Samariá**, now home to a wardens' station, with picnic facilities and filthy toilets. Further down, the path levels out and the gorge walls close in until at the narrowest point (the *sidherespórtes* or "iron gates") one can practically touch both tortured rock faces at once, and, looking up, see them rising sheer for almost a thousand feet.

At an average pace, with regular stops, the walk down takes five or six hours (though you can do it far quicker), and the upward trek considerably longer. It's strenuous – you'll know all about it next day – the path is rough, and solid shoes are vital. On the way down, there is plenty of water from springs and streams (except some years in Sept and Oct), but nothing to eat. The park that surrounds the gorge is a refuge of the Cretan wild ibex, the *krí-krí*, but don't expect to see one; there are usually far too many people around.

Villages of the southwest coast

When you finally emerge from the gorge, it's not long before you reach the singularly unattractive village of **AYÍA ROUMÉLI**, which is all but abandoned until you reach the beach, a mirage of iced drinks and a cluster of tavernas with **rooms** for rent. On arrival, it's best to buy your boat tickets straightaway if you want to be sure of the sailing you want (though in theory they guarantee that no one will be left behind, and that the buses will wait for the boat). If you plan to stay on the south coast, you should get going as soon as possible for the best chance of finding a room somewhere nicer than Ayía Rouméli. From May to October there are three boats daily to Loutró and Hóra Sfakíon (11.30am, 3.45pm and 6pm, plus 9am June–Sept), and a sailing to Soúyia and Paleohóra daily at 4.45pm.

If you are planning on staying down here, bring enough cash – the Visa-only ATM in Hóra Sfakíon is the only one between Paleohóra and Plakías. Drivers heading for Soúyia should also ensure their tanks are full – there's no fuel there.

Loutró

For tranquillity, it's hard to beat **LOUTRÓ**, two-thirds of the way to Hóra Sfakíon, and accessible only by boat or on foot. The chief disadvantage of Loutró is its lack of a real beach; most people swim from the rocks around its small bay. If you're prepared to walk, however, there are **deserted beaches** along the coast to the east which can also be reached by hired **canoe**. Indeed, if you're really into walking there's a **coastal trail** through Loutró which covers the entire distance between Ayía Rouméli and Hóra Sfakíon (now part of the E4 Pan-European footpath), or you could take the daunting zigzag path up the cliff behind to the mountain village of **Anópoli**. Loutró itself has a number of **tavernas** and **rooms**, though not always enough of the latter in peak season. Call the *Blue House* (T 28250 91127; ❶) if you want to book ahead; this is also the best place to eat. Slightly more upmarket accommodation is on offer at the nearby *Hotel Porto Loutro* (T 28250 91433, W hotel portoloutro.com; ❷), which also hires out canoes and runs full-day **cruises** on its own boat to Palm beach and the island of Gávdhos; prices should be posted outside. There's space to **camp** out on the cape by a ruined fort, but due to a long history of problems, you should be aware that campers are not very popular in the village. If you're determined to camp, head for the **beaches** and coves to the east (such as Sweetwater) and west (Mármara) of the resort which can be reached on foot, or more comfortably by canoe or daily boats from the harbour.

Hóra Sfakíon and beyond

HÓRA SFAKÍON is the more usual terminus for walkers traversing the gorge, with a regular boat service along the coast to and from Ayía Rouméli. Consequently, it's quite an expensive and not an especially welcoming place; there are plenty of **rooms** and some decent **tavernas**, but for a real beach you should jump straight on a bus (currently running at 11am and 6pm April–Sept) going toward Plakiás (see p.260). Plenty of opportunities for a dip present themselves en route, one of the most memorable at **Frangokástello**, named after a crumbling Venetian attempt to bring law and order to a district that went on to defy both Turks and Germans. The foursquare, crenellated and imposing thirteenth-century **castle**, isolated a few kilometres below a chiselled wall of mountains, looks like it's been spirited out of the High Atlas or Tibet. The place is said to be haunted by ghosts of Greek rebels massacred here in 1829: every May, these *dhrossoulítes* ("dewy ones") march at dawn across the coastal plain and disappear into the sea near the fort. The rest of the time Frangokástello is peaceful enough, with a superb beach and a number of tavernas and rooms, but there's not a lot to do. The greatest concentration of rooms is immediately below the castle – try *Maria's Studios* (☎28250 92159; ❷) or *Kali Kardia* (☎28250 92123; ❶) for example. Slightly further east, and less influenced by tourism or modern life, are the attractive villages of **Skalotí** and **Rodhákino**, where basic lodging and food can be found in the villages proper or their seafront offshoots a couple of kilometres to the south.

Soúyia

In quite the other direction from Ayía Rouméli, less regular boats also head to **SOÚYIA** and on to Paleohóra. Soúyia, until World War II merely the anchorage for Koustoyérako inland, is a low-key resort, with a long, grey pebble beach and mostly modern buildings (except for a church with a sixth-century Byzantine mosaic as the foundation). Since the completion in 1990 of the paved road to Haniá, the village has started to expand; even so, except in the very middle of summer, it continues to make a good fall-back for finding a room or a place to camp, eating cheaply and enjoying the beach when the rest of the island is swarming with visitors.

Rooms right on the seafront tend to be both pricier and noisier than elsewhere: instead try the street inland from the eastern edge of town, overlooking the riverbed, where the friendly *Lissos* (☎28230 51244; ❷) offers good en-suite rooms, or the many places on the road as it comes into Soúyia, such as *Captain George* (☎28230 51133; ❸), where there are some larger apartments, or the peaceful *El Greco*, set further back (☎28230 51186; ❷). Since the local travel agent closed, there's no one centre for **information**. Your hotel should be able to fill you in on how to walk the beautiful Ayía Iríni **gorge** or hike over to the nearby ancient site of **Lissós**. Otherwise, bus tickets are sold at *Snacks Roxana*, near the bottom of the main road, while the two supermarkets opposite can arrange taxi boats to local beaches (get one to bring you home from Lissós, for example). Boat tickets are sold at the *períptero* on the seafront, and the boats leave from the dock at the western end of the beach. For **food**, *Rembetiko* has a pleasant garden terrace just off the main street, while the seafront is packed with possibilities. The German-run *Omikron* taverna has a more northern-European ambience and offers some **vegetarian** choices, *Café Lotos* provides Internet access.

Kastélli and the western tip

Apart from being Crete's most westerly town, and the end of the main E65 coastal highway, **KASTÉLLI** (Kíssamos, or Kastélli Kissámou as it's variously known) has little obvious attraction. It's a busy town with a rocky central **beach** (although there's an excellent sandy beach to the west) visited mainly by people using the boat that runs twice weekly to the island of Kýthira and the Peloponnese. The very ordinariness of Kastélli, however, can be attractive: life goes on pretty much regardless of outsiders, and there's every facility you might need. The town was important in antiquity, though sadly the recently excavated **mosaics** signed around the centre have all been buried under a layer of earth to protect them, while the new **museum** (located in the refurbished former Venetian governor's residence on the main square), planned to display finds from these digs and others nearby, has yet to open thanks to wrangling over the status of the contents – it will possibly begin operating by May 2004.

As regards **practicalities**, you'll find most of what you need around the main square, Platía Kastellíou. The bus station is here, as are a couple of cafés; banks, shops and travel agencies (for ferry tickets or car rental) lie east of the square along Skalídhi (another group can be found around Platía Venizélou, on the main road through town). The harbour itself is a good 2km west of town – a significant walk if you're heavily laden, or an inexpensive taxi ride. For **rooms**, *Koutsounakis* (℡28220 23416; ❸) and more basic *Vergerakis* (aka *Jimmy's*; ℡28220 22663; ❶) are both right by Platía Kastellíou; for more facilities and a beachside location, the excellent *Hotel Galini Beach* (℡28220 23288, ⓦgalinibeach.com; ❸) is at the pebbly, eastern end of the seafront near the sports stadium, or *Maria Beach* (℡28220 22610, ⓦmariabeach.gr; ❸) has a whole variety of rooms and apartments on the town's sandy western beach. Heading north from the main square brings you to the beach promenade where there are a number of **tavernas** – *Papadakis* is worth a try – and late-night drinking and music **bars** popular with the local younger set, particularly at weekends.

Falásarna to Elafoníssi

To the west of Kastélli lies some of Crete's loneliest, and, for many visitors, finest coastline. The first place of note is **Falásarna**, where the scant ruins of an ancient city are ignored by most visitors in favour of some of the best beaches on Crete, wide and sandy with clean water. There's a handful of **tavernas** and an increasing number of **rooms** for rent: *Sunset* (℡28220 41204; ❶), at the end of the paved road near the archeological site, is among the better choices for both. Plenty of people **camp** out here too; if you join them, be sure to take any litter away with you. Rubbish, occasional tar and crowds of locals on summer weekends can always be escaped if you're prepared to walk, and the beaches are worth it. The nearest real town is **Plátanos**, 5km up a paved road, serviced by a couple of daily buses; the town has supermarkets and a bank and ATM.

Further south, the western coastline is far less discovered. **SFINÁRI** is a quiet village with a number of rooms to rent on the road down to a quiet pebble beach. At the bottom are a couple of tavernas – try *Captain Fidias* – which offer

---

A round trip

If you have transport, a circular drive from Kastélli, via the west coast and back by the inland route through Élos and Topólia, makes for a stunningly scenic circuit. Near the sea, villages cling to the high mountainsides, apparently halted by some miracle in the midst of calamitous seaward slides. Around them, olives ripen on the terraced slopes, the sea glittering far below. Inland, especially at **ÉLOS**, the main crop is the chestnut, whose huge old trees shade the village streets.

South of **TOPÓLIA**, the chapel of Ayía Sofía is sheltered inside a cave which has been used as a shrine since Neolithic times. Cutting south just before Élos, a spectacular paved road continues through the high mountains towards Paleohóra. On a motorbike, with a sense of adventure and plenty of fuel, it's great: the bus doesn't come this way, villagers still stare at the sight of a tourist, and a host of small, seasonal streams cascade beside or under the asphalt.

free camping. **KÁMBOS** is similar, but even less visited, its beach a considerable walk down a hill (or a very steep drive). **Accommodation** is available at the good-value *Rooms Hartzulakis* (☎28220 44445; ●) on the edge of a long gorge which also leads down to the sea; the same place has a terrace taverna with great views, and you should be able to get information about walking locally. Beyond them both is the **monastery of Khryssoskalítissa**, increasingly visited by tours from Haniá and Paleohóra, but well worth the effort for its isolation and nearby beaches; the bus gets as far as Váthy, from where the monastery is another two hours' walk away, although you could try hitching – with a fair chance of success – as many of the tourist cars are bound to be heading for the same destination.

Five kilometres beyond Khryssoskalítissa, the tiny uninhabited islet of **Elafoníssi** lies marooned on the edge of a gloriously scenic turquoise lagoon. It's all too easy to get here now, a fact reflected in the huge number of visitors who do, by car, with coach tours, or on a boat from Paleohóra. The pinky-white sand, the warm, clear lagoon and the islet to which you can easily wade still look magnificent, but you certainly won't have it to yourself. There's a single, inadequate portable toilet and a number of stalls selling cold drinks and basic food, while a kilometre or so up the road are a couple of taverna/rooms places – *Elafonissi* (☎28220 61274; ●) is the better of them. For a day-trip, though, it's best to bring your own supplies.

Kándanos and Paleohóra

The easiest route to the far southwest leaves the north coast at Tavronítis, 22km west of Haniá, heading for Paleohóra; several buses follow this route from Haniá every day, and although this road also has to wind through the western outriders of the White Mountains, it lacks the excitement of the alternatives to either side. **KÁNDANOS**, at the 58-kilometre mark, has been entirely rebuilt since it was destroyed by the Germans for its fierce resistance to their occupation. The original sign erected when the deed was done is preserved on the war memorial in the central square: "Here stood Kándanos, destroyed in retribution for the murder of 25 German soldiers, and never to be rebuilt again." The pleasantly easy-going and once-again substantial village had the last laugh.

When the beach at **PALEOHÓRA** finally appears below it is a welcome sight. The little town is built across the base of a peninsula, its harbour and a beach known as "Pebble Beach" on the eastern side, the wide sands ("Sandy Beach") on the other. Above, on the outcrop, Venetian ramparts stand sentinel. These days Paleohóra has developed into a significant resort, but it's still thoroughly enjoyable, with a main street filling with tables at night as diners spill out of the restaurants, and with a pleasantly chaotic social life. You'll find a helpful **tourist office** (Mon & Wed–Sun 10am–1pm & 6–9pm; ☎28230 41507) in the town hall on Venizélos, the official name of the main street; they have full accommodation lists and provide a decent **map** which is useful for finding food and accommodation locations.

There are plenty of **places to stay** (though not always many vacancies in high season) – try *Castello Rooms* (☎28230 41143; ●), at the southern end of Sandy beach; the alleys behind here, beneath the castle, have many more simple rooms places. *Villa Marise* (☎28230 42012; ●) enjoys probably the best location in town, right on the sandy beach more or less opposite the post office, and has a variety of well-equipped rooms, apartments and studios for up to six people. Probably the least expensive rooms in town are at *Anonymous* (☎28230 41509; ●), with shared bathrooms and kitchen, and a very friendly atmosphere.

There's also a fair-sized **campsite**, *Camping Paleohora* (☎28230 41120), 2km north of "Pebble Beach"; if you are tempted to sleep on the main "Sandy Beach" – one of the best on the south coast, with showers, trees and acres of sand – be prepared for trouble from police and local residents who are no longer willing to tolerate it. The windsurfing school/rental place that used to attract many people to Paleohóra no longer operates, though conditions remain excellent and there are plans to open a kite-surfing centre. There are plenty of alternative entertainments, though, from dolphin-watching trips to excursions into the hills to Azoyirés, or a five-to-six-hour hike along the coastal path to Soúyia.

For **eating** and **drinking**, tavernas, bars and cafés are to be found throughout the resort, particularly along the roads behind the two beaches. A good place to try for some imaginative **vegetarian** specials is *The Third Eye*, just out of the centre towards Sandy beach. Other decent in-town eating places include *Pizzeria Niki*, off the south side of Kontekáki (the road running from east to west at the south end of Venizélos), and *The Wave* at the south end of "Pebble Beach", serving good fish on a seaside terrace. As Paleohóra publicizes itself as a "family" resort there's an unwritten curfew around 11pm when the bars lower their sounds, so if you're looking for some untamed nightlife you've definitely come to the wrong place. Even *Palehora Club*, at the extreme north end of "Pebble Beach" close to the campsite, has had to close its outdoor **dance** floor, though the action continues till late indoors. In the other direction, just beyond the end of the "Sandy Beach", the *Castaway Club* has a more chilled vibe, as well as a pool, open throughout the day. A great little open-air **cinema**, Cine Attikon, is tucked away in the northern backstreets; most of their films are in English and programmes (which change daily) are posted outside the tourist office.

Almost everything else you're likely to need is located in the centre of town. **Banks** (with ATMs), **travel agents**, a **laundry**, **mountain-bike** and **car-rental** companies and **Internet** access (at Er@to Cafe or Notos Travel) are all along Venizélos, while the **post office** is on the road behind "Sandy Beach". There are two **pharmacies** on Kontekáki and there's a **health centre** in the street parallel to Venizélos to the west. **Boats** run from Paleohóra to Elafoníssi, to the island of Gávdhos and along the coast to Soúyia and Ayía Rouméli; Notos Travel (☎28230 42110), on Venizélos, and E-Motion (☎28230 41755), on Kondekáki by the harbour, are good sources of information and tickets. They also have information about other trips – to walk the **Samarian Gorge**, for example, although you can also do that independently by catching the bus leaving daily at 6am throughout the summer, and a boat back from Ayía Rouméli.

Gávdhos

The island of **Gávdhos**, some fifty kilometres of rough sea south of Paleohóra, is the most southerly landmass in Europe. Gávdhos is small (about 10km by 7km) and barren, but it has one major attraction: the enduring **isolation** which its inaccessible position has helped preserve. This may not last much longer, as a big new port is under construction, together with a new electricity plant and asphalted roads. Providing you avoid the crowds in August, if all you want is a beach to yourself and a taverna to grill your fish, this remains the place for you. But not for much longer.

For the moment not too much has changed, and it is usually possible to turn up on spec and find a bed, but travel agents in Paleohóra (see opposite) will arrange a room if you want one and also provide current ferry information. There's a semi-permanent community of campers and would-be "Robinson Crusoes" resident on the island throughout the summer – in addition to the six indigenous families who live here year round. Largely because water is often difficult to obtain most people choose to base themselves near to one of the three largest beaches and at the most popular of all, **SARAKÍNIKO**, there's a slew of beachfront **tavernas** – *Taverna Gerti & Manolis* have **rooms** (T28230 41103; ❶) – in addition to a squatters' community spreading a shanty town of unsightly breezeblock summer dwellings behind the beach.

Travel details

Buses

The following are the main routes only. For the latest timetables and complete route and fare information for the west of the island, visit the website at ⓦbus-service-crete-ktel.com. There are also plenty of unofficial websites with time-tables for the east: the official central timetable at ⓦwww.ktel.org rarely seems to work.

Áyios Nikólaos to: Iráklion (22 daily, 6 via Iráklion Airport 6.15am–9.45pm; 1hr 30min); Kritsá (11 daily 6am–8pm; 30min); Lasíthi plateau (1 daily at 2pm, returning 7am; 2hr); Sitía (7 daily 6.15am–8.30pm; 1hr 30min).

Haniá to: Hóra Sfakíon (3 daily 8.30am–2pm; 2hr); Omalós (Samarian Gorge; 4 daily 6.15am–2pm; 1hr 15min); Paleohóra (5 daily 8.30am–6pm; 2hr); Iráklion via Réthymnon(25 daily, 2 via old road 5.30am–9pm; 2hr 30min total).

Iráklion to: Ayía Galíni (8 daily 6.30am–6.30pm; 2hr 15min), Áyios Nikólaos (20 daily 6.15am–8.30pm; 1hr 30min), Phaestos (8 daily 7.30am–4.30pm; 1hr 30min), Ierápetra (8 daily 6.30am–7.30pm; 2hr 30min).

Kastélli to: Haniá (15 daily 6am–8.30pm; 1hr 15min).

Réthymnon to: Ayía Galíni via Spíli (5 daily 5.30am–2.15pm; 45min–1hr 30min), Plakiás (5 daily 6.15am–4.30pm; 1hr 15min).

Ferries

For the latest timetables for domestic and interna-tional ferries from and to Crete visit ⓦwww .cretetravel.com or ⓦwww.ferries.gr

Áyios Nikólaos and Sitía 3–4 sailings a week to Pireás (12hr), 2–3 ferries a week to Kássos, Kárpathos, Hálki and Rhodes; 2–3 weekly to Mílos.
Haniá Daily overnight to Pireás with ANEK (9–11hr) or Blue Star (5hr 45min).
Hóra Sfakíon 5 ferries daily to Loutró/Ayía Rouméli (1hr/2hr 30min); 3–4 weekly to Gávdhos (1hr 30min) in season.
Iráklion 2 ferries daily to Pireás (12hr); 1 daily fast ferry to Pireás (6hr); 2 ferries weekly to Thessaloníki; 1 daily ferry to Thíra (4hr), also fast boats and hydrofoils (2hr 30min); daily ferries to Páros in season; 1–2 weekly to Mýkonos and Íos; weekly to Náxos, Tínos & Skíathos.
Kastélli (Kíssamos) 2 ferries weekly to Kýthira/Pireás (3hr 30min/12hr), one of them via Yíthio (6hr); 1 ferry weekly to Kalamáta (7hr 30min).
Paleohóra 2–3 boats a week in season to Gávdhos. Also daily sailings to Elafoníssi and Soúyia/Ayía Rouméli.
Réthymnon Daily ferries to Pireás (11hr 30min); seasonal day-trips to Thíra.

Flights

Haniá to: Athens (3–4 daily on Olympic; 3 daily on Aegean), Thessaloníki (3 weekly on Olympic).
Iráklion to: Athens (5–7 daily on Olympic; 6 daily on Aegean), Rhodes (4 weekly, summer only, on Olympic; 1–2 daily on Aegean), Thessaloníki (2 weekly on Olympic; 2 daily on Aegean).
Sitía to: Alexandhroúpoli (3 weekly on Olympic); Athens (3 weekly on Olympic); Préveza (3 weekly on Olympic).

The Dodecanese

CHAPTER 4　Highlights

* **Northern Kárpathos** Old walking trails take you between traditional villages. See p.293

* **Ródhos old town** Superbly preserved medieval streets, inextricably linked with the Knights of Saint John. See p.300

* **Lindos Acropolis, Rhodes** A pleasing blend of ancient and medieval culture, with great views over the town. See p.306

* **Thárri monastery, Rhodes** Superb Byzantine frescoes in the oldest religious foundation on the island. See p.310

* **Sými** The officially protected harbour and hillside village teem with trippers during the day, but a stay overnight is rewarding. See p.319

* **Volcano of Níssyros** The craters of the dormant volcano still hiccup, with the most recent activity in 1933. See p.330

* **Brós Thermá, Kós** Relax in the shoreline hot springs, which flow into the sea, protected by a boulder ring. See p.341

* **Mount Dhíkeos, Kós** The hike up is worthwhile for the views over the Dodecanese. See p.342

* **Hóra, Astypálea** The windswept island "capital" is perched dramatically above the sea and has a beautiful Venetian kástro. See p.348

△ Hóra, Astypálea

The Dodecanese

T he furthest Greek island group from the mainland, the **Dodecanese** (Dhodhekánisos) lie close to the Turkish coast – some of them, such as Kós and Kastellórizo, almost within hailing distance of Anatolia. Because of this position, and their remoteness from Athens, these islands have had a turbulent history: they were the scene of ferocious battles between German and British forces in 1943–44, and were only finally included in the modern Greek state in 1948 after centuries of occupation by Crusaders, Ottomans and Italians. Even now the threat (real or imagined) of invasion from Turkey is very much evident in the form of numerous military bases and smaller watch-points. Despite certain high-level civilian rapprochements which have taken place between Greece and Turkey in recent years, the Greek army and air force clearly prefer to keep their powder dry.

Whatever the rigours of the various occupations, their legacy includes a wonderful blend of architectural styles and of Eastern and Western cultures. Medieval Rhodes is the most famous, but almost every island has some Classical remains, a Crusaders' castle, a clutch of traditional villages and abundant grandiose public buildings. For these last the Italians, who occupied the Dodecanese from 1912 to 1943, are mainly responsible. In their determination to beautify the islands and turn them into a showplace for fascism they undertook public works, excavations and reconstruction on a massive scale; if historical accuracy was often sacrificed in the interests of style, only an expert is likely to complain. A more sinister aspect of the Italian administration was the attempted forcible Latinization of the populace: spoken Greek and Orthodox observance were banned in progressively stricter increments between the mid-1920s and 1936. The most tangible reminder of this policy is the (rapidly dwindling) number of older people who can still converse – and write – more fluently in Italian than in Greek.

Aside from this bilingualism, the Dodecanese themselves display a marked topographic and economic schizophrenia. The dry limestone outcrops of **Kastellórizo**, **Sými**, **Hálki**, **Kássos** and **Kálymnos** have always been forced to rely on the sea for their livelihoods, and the wealth generated by this maritime culture – especially during the nineteenth century – fostered the growth of attractive port towns. The sprawling, relatively fertile giants **Rhodes** (Ródhos) and **Kós** have recently seen their traditional agricultural economies almost totally displaced by a tourist industry grown up around good beaches and nightlife, as well as some of the most exciting historical monuments in the Aegean. **Kárpathos** lies somewhere in between, with a lightly forested north grafted on to a rocky limestone south; **Tílos**, despite its lack of trees, has ample water, though the green volcano-island of **Níssyros** does not. **Léros** shelters

Karlóvassi & Vathý (Sámos)

Pythagório

Ikaría

Sámos

Foúrni

Pátmos   Arkí

Skála   Agathoníssi

Hóra

Lipsí

Léros   Farmakoníssi

Ayía Marína

Lakkí   Xirókambos

Myrtiés   Kálymnos

Télendhos   Psérimos

Póthia

Bodrum

Mastihári

Kós   Marmaris

Kós

Kardhámena

Astypálea   Kéfalos

Yialí   Datça

Astypálea   Mandhráki   Sými

Níssyros   Sými

Megálo Horió

Tílos   Livádhia   Ródhos

Kámiros

Skála

Emborió

Hálki

Monólithos   Líndhos

Yennádhi

Kattaviá   Rhodes

(Ródhos)

Ólymbos   Dhiafáni

Mesohóri   Kárpathos

Pigádhia

Frý

Kássos

TURKEY

N

0   50 km

Pireás

Pireás

Pireás

Kastellórizo

Rhodes

TURKEY

Kaş

Rhó   Meyísti

Kastellórizo

(Meyísti)

N

0   10 km

Sitía & Áyios Nikólaos (Crete)

softer contours and more amenable terrain than its map outline would suggest, while **Pátmos** and **Astypálea** at the fringes of the archipelago offer architecture and landscapes more typical of the Cyclades.

The largest islands in the group are connected by regular **ferries and catamarans**, and none (except for Kastellórizo, Astypálea and Tílos) is hard to reach. Rhodes is the main transport hub, with connections with Crete, the northeastern Aegean, the Cyclades and the mainland as well. Kálymnos and Kós are jointly an important secondary terminus, with a useful ferry based on

Kálymnos, hydrofoil services using Kós and Kálymnos as a focus and transfer point, and excursion boats based on Kós providing a valuable supplement to larger ferries arriving at uncivil hours.

Kássos

Like Psará islet in the northeast Aegean, **Kássos** contributed its large fleet to the Greek revolutionary war effort, and likewise suffered appalling consequences. In late May 1824, an Ottoman army sent by Ibrahim Pasha, Governor of Egypt, besieged the island; on June 7, aided perhaps by a traitor's tip as to the weak point in Kássos's defences, the invaders descended on the populated north-coastal plain, slaughtered most of the inhabitants and put houses, farms and trees to the torch.

Barren and depopulated since then, Kássos attracts few visitors, despite regular air links with Rhodes and Kárpathos, and being a port of call on ferry lines from those isles to Crete. Numerous sheer gorges slash through lunar terrain, with fenced smallholdings of midget olive trees providing the only permanent relief. Springtime grain crops briefly soften the usually empty terraces, and livestock somehow survives on a thin furze of thornbush. What remains of the population is grouped together in five villages facing Kárpathos, leaving most of the island uninhabited and uncultivated. Until very recently, there was little sign here of the wealth brought into other islands by diaspora Greeks or – since Kássos hasn't much to offer them – tourists; amidst the occasional new concrete monster, crumbling houses and disused hillside terraces poignantly recall better days. A long pattern of serving as roving pilots, or residence in Egypt (Kassiots were instrumental in digging the Suez Canal), has been eclipsed by subsequent emigration to the US. Thus American-logo T-shirts and baseball caps are *de rigueur* summer fashion, and the conversation of vacationing expatriates is spiked with Americanisms.

Kássos can be a nuisance to reach, despite the recent completion of a new jetty at Frý (pronounced "free"), replacing the old, inadequate one at Boúka fishing port; in extreme wind conditions, ferries may still not be able to dock. In such cases, you disembark at Kárpathos and fly the remaining distance in a dual-prop, fifty-seater aircraft. The air ticket plus a taxi fare to Kárpathos airport isn't much more than the fare charged by Finíki (Kárpathos)-based excursion boats which can manoeuvre into Boúka in most weathers. The airport lies 1km west of Frý, an easy enough walk, otherwise a cheap (€1.50) ride in one of the island's three taxis. Except in July and August, when a few rental motorbikes and boat excursions are offered, the only method of exploring the island's remoter corners is by hiking along fairly arduous, shadeless paths and roads. Place-name signposting tends to be in Greek only, and in Kassiot dialect at that – the islanders clearly aren't expecting many non-Kassiot visitors.

Frý and Emboriós

Most of the appeal of the capital, **FRÝ**, is confined to the immediate environs of the wedge-shaped fishing port of **Boúka**, protected from the sea by two crab-claws of breakwater and overlooked by the cathedral of Áyios Spyrídhon. Inland, Frý is engagingly unpretentious, even down-at-heel; there are no concessions to tourism, and little attempt has been made to prettify an essentially scruffy little town that's quite desolate out of season. Somewhat overpriced

accommodation is found at the seafront hotels *Anagenissis* (☎22450 41495, ⓦwww.kassos-island.gr; ❷) and, just behind with fewer views, the less expensive, all-en-suite *Anessis* (☎22450 41201, Ⓕ22450 41730; ❷). The manager of the *Anagenissis* also has a few pricier apartments, and runs the all-in-one travel agency just below (though Olympic Airways has its own premises two doors down). Both hotels tend to be noisy owing to morning bustle on the waterfront – and the phenomenal number of small but lively fast-food joints and café-bars in town, some right underneath. During high season a few **rooms** operate; these tend to be more expensive and mostly located in the suburb of Emboriós, fifteen minute's walk east. There's no full-service **bank**, but there is a stand-alone ATM.

Outside of peak season, Frý can support only one full-service **taverna**: *O Mylos*, overlooking the intermittent harbour works. Luckily it's excellent and reasonable, with a good variety of daily-special *mayireftá* at lunch and sometimes fish grills by night. From late June to early September at least one taverna, perched above Boúka, will be functioning, or try *To Meltemi ouzerí*, on the way to Emboriós. In Emboriós itself, only *Ta Tessera Adherfia* by the palm-tree church shows any sign of life outside of summer. Shops in Frý, including two fruit stalls, are fairly well stocked for self-catering.

Local beaches

Frý's town **beach**, if you can call it that, is at **Ammouá** (Ammoudhiá), a thirty-minute walk beyond the airstrip along the coastal track. This sandy cove, just before the landmark chapel of Áyios Konstandínos, is often caked with seaweed and tar, but persevere five minutes more and you'll find much cleaner pea-gravel coves. The determined can swim off the little patch of sand at **Emboriós**, along with the resident ducks, and there's a more private pebble stretch off to the right. But having got this far, you may as well continue ten to fifteen minutes along the shore, first along an old track, then on a path past the last house, for a final scramble to the base of the **Pouthená** ravine, where there's another secluded pebble cove. Otherwise, it's worth shelling out for high-season boat excursions to far better beaches on a pair of islets visible to the northwest, **Armathiá** and **Makrá**. There are no amenities (or shade) on either islet, so come prepared.

The interior

At the edges of the agricultural plain just inland from Frý cluster a number of villages, linked to each other by road; all are worth a passing visit, and can be reached by foot in a single day.

Larger in extent and more rural than Frý, **AYÍA MARÍNA**, 1500m inland and uphill, is most attractive seen from the south, arrayed above olive groves; one of its two belfried churches is the focus of the island's liveliest festival, on July 17. Some fifteen minutes beyond the hamlet of Kathístres, a further 500m southwest, the cave of **Ellinokamára** is named for the late Classical, polygonal wall completely blocking the entrance; its ancient function is uncertain, perhaps a cult shrine or tomb complex. To reach it, turn south at the two restored windmills in Ayía Marína, then right (west) at the phone-box junction; carry on, straight and down (not level and left) until you see a red-dirt path going up the hillside to a crude, stone-built pastoral hut. Some modern masonry walls enclose the start of this path, but once at the hut (the cave is more or less underneath it) you're compelled to hop a fence to visit – there are no gates. From Ellinokamára another, fainter path – you'll probably need a guide, or at least detailed directions – continues for ninety minutes in the same direction to the larger, more natural cave of **Seláï**, with impressive stalactites in the rear chamber.

Generally, walking opportunities on Kássos are poor – trails are few, unmarked and in poor condition, with no shade and few reliable water sources. An exception is the forty-minute path from Arvanitohóri to Póli, which is clearly walled in and enjoyable, shortcutting the road effectively – it starts at the base of the village, where two trees occupy planter wells. **PÓLI**, somewhat impoverished and resolutely agricultural, is the site of a badly deteriorated ancient and medieval acropolis – a few stretches of fortification remain – and marks the start of a four-kilometre road leading southeast to **Áyios Mámas**, signposted in dialect as "**Áï Mámas**", one of two important rural monasteries, perched spectacularly overlooking the sea. Alternatively, from Póli you can descend – again on walled-in path for the first twenty minutes, then dirt track – to **PANAYÍA**, famous for its now-neglected mansions (many of Kássos's wealthiest ship captains hailed from here) and for the oldest surviving church on the island, the eighteenth-century **Panayía tou Yióryi**.

Between Ayía Marína and Arvanitohóri, another road – formerly just a dirt track, but paved over in the late 1990s – veers off southwest from the road linking the two villages towards the rural monastery of **Áyios Yeóryios Hadhión**. The pleasure of walking this route, however, has been rather diminished by the paving process, so you'll probably want to hire a taxi, rent a scooter if available or hitch a lift in at least one direction. At the beginning of the route you skirt the narrows of a fearsome gorge, and from there on you are unlikely to see another living thing aside from goats, sheep or an occasional Eleonora's falcon. After about an hour, the Mediterranean appears to the south, a dull expanse ruffled only by the occasional ship bound for Cyprus and the Middle East. When you finally reach a fork, adopt the upper, right-hand turning, following derelict phone lines towards Áyios Yeóryios Hadhión (signed as "**Áï Yeóryi**"), 12km (3hr on foot) from Frý. This is busiest at its late-April festival time, but during the warmer months there's a resident caretaker who runs a small snack/drinks bar. There are a few open guest cells (ask nicely, donation expected) and cistern water here if you need to fill up canteens; the only other water en route is a well at the route's high point.

From the monastery it's another 3km on dirt track – motorbikes can make it most of the way – to **Hélatros** ("Hélathros" on older maps), a lonely cove at the mouth of one of the larger, more forbidding Kassiot canyons. The sand-and-gravel beach itself is small and mediocre, but the water is pristine and – except for the occasional fishing boat – you'll probably be alone. The lower, left-hand option at the fork is the direct track to Hélatros, but this is only 2km shorter and, following severe winter storm damage, impassable to any vehicle and all but the most energetic hikers; since the paving of the upper road to Áï Yeóryi, it is likely to have got even worse.

Kárpathos

A long, narrow island marooned between Rhodes and Crete, wild **Kárpathos** has always been something of an underpopulated backwater, although it is the third largest of the Dodecanese. A habitually cloud-capped mountainous spine rises to over 1200m, and divides the more populous, lower-lying south from an exceptionally rugged north. A magnificent, windswept coastline of cliffs and

KÁRPATHOS

N

Saría

Palátia

Rhodes, Háki & Sými

Trístomo

Vrykoúnda

Avlóna

Vanánda

Dhiafáni

Ólymbos

Fýsses

Papá Miná

Ayía
Marína

Forókli

Áyios Minás

Agnóndia

Spóa

Áyios Nikólaos

Mesohóri

Ápella

Lefkós

Mýrtonas

Kyrá Panayiá

Paralía Lefkoú

Kalilímni
1215m

Katódhio

Potáli

Aháta

Voládha

Stés

Ádhia

Óthos

Apéri

Pylés

Vróndi

Pigádhia

Finíki

Menetés

Arkássa

Ammopí

Áyios Nikólaos
Tihiasméni
Trahanamós

Makrýs Yialós

Áyios Ioánnis

Amfiárti

Kássos & Crete

Kássos

0   5 km

promontories has begun to attract significant numbers of Scandinavian and German package tourists, who arrive on several direct international charters weekly. Since the 1990s, these clients have more or less monopolized several resorts in the southern part of the island, pushing independent travellers up to the remote north of the island. Despite this development, Kárpathos remains saddled with a deficient road system – only partly paved, unspeakable otherwise – and often expensive taverna food, which offsets reasonable room prices. Most island-hoppers come here for a glimpse of the traditional village life in the far north, and for the numerous superb, secluded beaches lapped by the proverbial crystalline water.

The island's **interior** isn't the most alluring: the central and northern uplands were badly scorched by forest fires in the 1980s, and agriculture plays a slighter role than on any other Greek island of comparable size. The Karpathians are too well off to bother much with farming; massive emigration to America and the resulting remittance economy has transformed Kárpathos into one of the wealthiest Greek islands.

Kárpathos's four Classical **cities** figure little in ancient chronicles. Alone of the major Dodecanese, the island was held by the Genoese and Venetians after the Byzantine collapse and so has no castle of the crusading Knights of St John, nor any surviving medieval fortresses of consequence. The Ottomans couldn't be bothered to settle or even garrison it; instead they left a single judge or *kadi* at the main town, making the Greek population responsible for his safety during the many pirate attacks.

Pigádhia (Kárpathos Town)

The island capital of **PIGÁDHIA**, often known simply as Kárpathos, nestles at the south end of scenic **Vróndi Bay**, whose sickle of sand extends 3km northwest. The town itself, curling around the jetty and quay where ferries and excursion boats dock, is as drab as its setting is beautiful; an ever-increasing number of concrete blocks contributes to the air of a vast building site, making the Italian-era port police and county governmental buildings seem like heirlooms by comparison. Although there's nothing special to see, Pigádhia does offer just about every facility you might need, albeit with a definite package-tourism slant.

Practicalities

Olympic Airways (book a week in advance at peak season – planes to Rhodes and Kássos have just 46 seats) is at the west end of Apodhímon Karpathíon, the "Street of the Overseas Karpathians", but the office has very restricted hours, so everyone buys their tickets from Possi Travel (☎22450 22235) on the front. They're also sole agents for LANE, currently the only shipping line to call at Pigádhia. The **post office** is on Ethnikís Andístasis, while several **banks** have ATMs.

Accommodation

Most ferries are met by people offering **self-catering studios**, though they may be forbidden from touting on the quay itself. Unless you've arranged something in advance, you might consider such offers – the town is so small that no location will be too inconvenient, though the best place to stay is on the hillside above the bus terminal. More luxurious places lie north, towards and behind **Vróndi** beach to either side of the ruined fifth-century basilica of **Ayía Fotiní**, but tend to be occupied by package groups. Three of the best

When it comes to exploring the island, there are regular **buses** to Ammopí, and also Pylés, via Apéri, Voládha and Óthos, some of these looping back via Arkássa. Paralía Lefkoú sees two daily services in season, plus there's one daily bus (in term time only) to Spóa via Mesohóri, as well as sporadic service to Ápella and Kyrá Panayiá. The "station" (just a stop with a destination-placard) is at the corner of 28-Oktovríou and Dhimokratías, a couple of blocks back from the front. Set-rate, unmetered **taxis**, with a terminal in the municipal car park a bit further up Dhimokratías, aren't too expensive to get to these and other points (such as the airport, 17km away) on the paved road system, but charge a fortune to go anywhere else. Upwards of ten outfits **rent cars**, though you may have to try every one to find an available vehicle; rates are vastly over the odds, though available models have improved of late. Agencies to try include Circle (☎22450 22690), which may give discounts to *Rose Studios* (see below) clients; Avis (☎22450 22702), at the north edge of town, which will deliver to the airport; Drive (☎22450 61249), a branch of the reliable Rhodes chain; and Trust, based in Ammopí, which will deliver and collect in Pigádhia (☎22450 81060). Car rental from/to the airport (which will save you a €20 return in taxi transfers) must be arranged in advance; the two booths there are otherwise unstaffed. Moto Carpathos (☎22450 22382), near the town hall (*dhimarhío*), has the largest fleet of scooters for rent. Be warned that the only fuel on the island is to be found at two pairs of stations just to the north and south of town, and that tanks on smaller scooters are barely big enough to permit completing a circuit of the south, let alone head up north – which is, in any case, expressly forbidden by most outfits for both bikes and non-4WD cars.

Northern Kárpathos is most pleasantly and usually reached **by boat**. Two rival *kaḯkia* are moored side by side on the jetty, offering all-in **day-tours** to Dhiafáni and Ólymbos for around €15 (pay on board); the *Chrisovalandou III* is more attractive and stable in heavy sea than the *Karpathos II*. Less well publicized is the fact that you can use these boats to travel **one-way** between the north and the south in either direction – the standard rate for this is €8. Departures are typically 8.30am northbound, 4.30pm southbound. It's also worth knowing about the tiny **mail boat** which once or twice weekly reverses this pattern: southbound from Dhiafáni at 8am, northbound from Pigádhia at 3pm (one-way fare again €8). Various agents can also offer trips to Kássos and to isolated east-coast beaches without facilities (bring lunch if not included).

---

hillside premises are perennially popular *Rose Studios* (☎22450 22284, @rose studios@hotmail.com; ❷), whose well-kept, partly air-conditioned rooms with fridge and hot-plate are run by a kindly family and need to be booked in advance; the courteous *Amaryllis Studios* (☎22450 22375; ❸), slightly downhill and east, with enormous if rather plain air-con units; and the helpful *Elias Rooms* (☎22450 22446, @eliasrooms.tripod.com; ❷; mid-May to Sept only) just above the *Hotel Karpathos*, with variable, mostly en-suite rooms in a converted older house. Lower down, the central *Hotel Karpathos* itself (☎22450 22347; ❸) has fair-sized, well-kept 1970s rooms with air con, fridges and TVs. For more comfort, the only other hotel that caters in any way to nonpackage guests is the helpful *Atlantis*, opposite the Italian "palace" (☎22450 22777, @htatlantis@yahoo.com; ❹ July–Aug B&B, ❷–❸ otherwise).

Eating and drinking

Many of Pigádhia's waterfront **tavernas**, where defrosted *yíros* and chips reign supreme, are undistinguished and overpriced; quality and value improve significantly as you head east towards the ferry dock. Near the end of the strip are a pair of worthy choices: *Anna*, good for nonfarmed fish, and the best all-rounder, *Iy Orea Karpathos*, with palatable local bulk wine, *trahanádhes* soup, spicy sausages, marinated artichokes and great spinach pie – you can, as the locals do, use it as an *ouzerí* and just order *orektiká*. One block inland, the clear winner is *To Ellinikon*, a *mezedhopolío* that caters all year round to a local clientele with hot and cold *orektiká*, meat and good desserts. If *yíros* and chips it must be, then by far the best place for the fresh kind, own-sourced, is 2003-opened *Ovelistirio tis Erasmias*, one block inland. Trendy, musical **café-bars** such as *Oxygen* and *Escape* offer taped sounds from perches overlooking the bay; *Centro Café*, rather than music, imports decent *gelato* from Rhodes. Among several **Internet cafés**, most established is *Café Galileo* on Apodhímon Karpathíon. At Vróndi there are two serviceable lunchtime tavernas at the southerly, town end: *To Limanaki* and the *Seaside Snack Bar*.

Southern and western Kárpathos

The southern extremity of Kárpathos, towards the airport, is extraordinarily desolate and windswept. There are a few relatively undeveloped sandy beaches – in particular **Makrýs Yialós** – on the southeast coast in the region known as Amfiárti, but they're only really attractive to foreign windsurfers who come to take advantage of the prevailing northwesterlies. Most people go no further in this direction than **AMMOPÍ** (sometimes transliterated as "Amoopi"), just 7km from Pigádhia. This, together with the development at Vróndi and Arkássa, is the closest thing on Kárpathos to a purpose-built beach resort. Three sand-and-gravel, tree- or cliff-fringed coves are bordered by half a dozen **tavernas** and increasing numbers of **hotels** and **studios**. Quietest among the latter, not completely dominated by packages, are the highly recommended, well-designed *Vardes Studios* (℡22450 81111 or 697 21 52 901; ❸), with distant sea views and orchard setting, and the more bleakly positioned *Sunflower Studios* (℡ & ℻22450 81019, ✉hotelsunflower@yahoo.com; ❸). Of the tavernas, the *Golden Beach* behind the middle cove is acceptable, the only one the locals will be seen in.

West out of Pigádhia the road climbs steeply 9km up to **MENETÉS**, an appealing village draped in the lee of a ridge, with some handsome old houses and a spectacularly sited – though hideous – church. There are two **tavernas** here (*Koula* and *Dionysos*) and a World War II memorial with sweeping views north.

Arkássa, Finíki and Ádhia

Beyond Menetés, you descend to **ARKÁSSA**, on the slopes of a ravine draining to the west coast, with excellent views to Kássos en route. Despite just one good nearby beach interrupting a mostly rocky shore, Arkássa has been heavily developed, with hotels and restaurants sprouting in clusters. Much of the **accommodation** is aimed squarely at the package market, but independent travellers could try for various facilities inland from **Áyios Nikólaos** beach signposted just south, a 200-metre stretch of sand – rare hereabouts. These include the *Seaside Studios* (℡22450 61421; ❹); the higher-standard *Montemar Studios* (℡22450 61394; ❹), almost one-bedroom apartments, though kitchens are rudimentary; and – right behind the beach – the *Glaros* (℡22450 61015, ℻22450 61016; ❹), five package-free studios and an attached, full-service **taverna** run by a Karpathian-American from Virginia. Other, mediocre eateries lie north of the ravine in the village centre; among the **bars**, *Retro* has Internet access.

A few hundred metres south of where the ravine meets the sea, a signposted cement side road leads briefly to the whitewashed chapel of **Ayía Sofía**, marooned amidst various remains of Classical and Byzantine Arkessia. These consist of several mosaic floors with geometric patterns, including one running diagonally under the floor of a half-buried chapel, emerging from the walls on either side. The Paleókastro headland beyond was the site of Mycenaean Arkessia; the walk up is again signposted, but scarcely worth it for the sight of a few stretches of polygonal wall and a couple of tumbled columns.

The tiny fishing port of **FINÍKI**, just a couple of kilometres north, offers a minuscule beach, fairly regular excursions to Kássos, half a dozen tavernas and several **rooms/studios** establishments. Accommodation includes *Giavasis Studios* (☎22450 61365; ❷), on the road to the jetty, or for more comfort and value the well-designed and -built *Arhontiko Studios* up on the main bypass road (☎22450 61473, ⓕ22450 61054; ❸). Skip the overpriced port **tavernas** here in favour of well-loved *Kostas*, 1km north under two tamarisks at Áyios Yeóryios monastery above reefy Kamarákia beach; it's open all day until 10pm, offering such delights as expertly grilled swordfish and chips made of home-grown courgettes.

Some 7km north of Finíki along the coast road, the Karpathian forest resumes at **ÁDHIA** hamlet, giving rise to the name of the *Pine Tree Restaurant*, which has baked bread, lentil soup and octopus *makaronádha* washed down by sweet Óthos wine. There are also six **rooms** and **studios** off to one side, overlooking the orchard and the sea (☎697 73 69 948, ⓔpinetree_adia @hotmail.com; ❷).

Paralía Lefkoú and Mesohóri

Dense forest continues much of the way to the turning for the attractive resort of **PARALÍA LEFKOÚ**, shore annexe of the inland hamlet of Lefkós. This is a delightful place for flopping on the beach, and marks the furthest point you can reach from Pighádhia on a small motorbike and return safely without running out of fuel. Any effort to get here will be rewarded by the striking topography of cliffs, hills, islets and sandspits surrounding a triple bay. There are now over two dozen places to stay, and perhaps half as many tavernas, but package companies tend to monopolize the better **accommodation** from June to September. About the only exception is the spartan but en-suite *Sunweek Studios* (☎22450 71025; ❷), on the seaward promontory. You'll have better luck at **Potáli**, the stonier, fourth bay just south of the access road; here try for the excellent, quiet and spacious *Akroyiali Studios* (☎22450 71263, ⓕ22450 71178; ❸), with balconies overlooking the beach, or the smaller *Lefkosia Studios* close to the road (☎22450 71176 or 22450 71148; ❸), which have the plus of the attached *Orama Café*, serving luscious fruit juices and muesli or egg breakfasts. **Tavernas** at the main resort can disappoint: *Tou Kalymniou to Steki* on the promontory is only just okay as a fish/seafood *ouzerí*, leaving the kindly *Blue Sea* as the best option, thanks to pizzas, meat-rich *mayireftá* and pancake breakfasts.

Back on the main road, you climb northeast through the densest surviving patches of pine forest to **MESOHÓRI**. The village tumbles down towards the sea around narrow, stepped alleys, coming to an abrupt halt at the edge of a flat-topped bluff dotted with three tiny, ancient chapels and separated from the village proper by a vast oasis of orchards. These are nurtured by the fountain (best water on the island) underneath the church of **Panayía Vryssianí**, wedged against the mountainside just east and invisible from the end of the access road. On the stair-street leading to this church is an excellent taverna, the *Dhramoundana*, remarkably reasonable for Kárpathos, and featuring local capers, sausages and marinated "sardines" (really a larger fish, *ménoula*). The paved main road continues over the island's watershed to Spóa, overlooking the east coast (see below).

Central Kárpathos

The **centre** of Kárpathos supports a quartet of villages blessed with superb hillside settings, ample running water – and a cool climate, even in August. Nearly everyone here has "done time" in North America, then returned home with their nest eggs. New Jersey, New York and Canadian car plates tell you exactly where repatriated islanders struck it rich – often fabulously so (the area has the highest per capita income in Greece). West-facing **PYLÉS** is the most attractive, set above another spring-fed oasis, while **ÓTHOS**, noted for its sweet, tawny-amber wine, excellent bread and slender sausages, is the highest (approx 400m) and chilliest, on the flanks of 1215-metre Mount Kalilímni. On the east side of the ridge you find **VOLÁDHA** with its tiny Venetian citadel and a trio of nocturnal tavernas. From the smart new track-and-footie stadium below **APÉRI**, the largest, lowest and wealthiest settlement, you can drive 6km along a very rough road to the dramatic pebble beach of **Aháta**, with just a rather modest snack-bar.

Beyond Apéri, the road up the **east coast** is being paved up to Spóa, passing above beaches most easily accessible by boat trips from Pigádhia. **Kyrá Panayiá** is the first encountered, reached via a paved but twisty, four-kilometre side road through Katódhio hamlet. There's a surprising number of villas and rooms in the ravine behind the 150m of fine gravel and sheltered, turquoise water; the beach taverna is, alas, mediocre. **Ápella** is the best of the beaches you can reach by road, though there's a final short path from the single taverna-rooms (the only facility) at the road's end to the scenic 300-metre gravel strand. The end of this route is **SPÓA**, high above the shore just east of the island's spine, with a snack-bar and more reliable *kafenío* at the edge of the village which might make better meal stops than the overpriced *Votsalo* down at **Áyios Nikólaos**, 5km below, a small hamlet with an average beach and the overgrown ruins of a Paleo-Christian basilica to explore.

Northern Kárpathos

Although connected by a rutted dirt road with Spóa, much the easiest (and usual) way to get to northern Kárpathos is by sea. Inter-island ferries call at Dhiafáni two or three times a week in season, or passengers use the above-cited smaller tour *kaïkia* from Pigádhia daily. The journey time on the smaller boats is about ninety minutes, with boats met at Dhiafáni by buses for the eight-kilometre transfer up to the traditional village of **Ólymbos**, the main attraction in this part of the island, along with good walking opportunities. If you can't tear yourself away from the sea, coastal **Dhiafáni** makes a better base, with excellent **beaches** within walking distance to either side.

Ólymbos and around

Originally founded as a pirate-safe refuge in Byzantine times, windswept **ÓLYMBOS** straddles a long ridge below slopes studded with mostly ruined windmills. Two restored ones, beyond the main church, grind wheat and barley during late summer only, though one is kept under sail during any tourist season. The village has long attracted foreign and Greek ethnologists, who treat it as a living museum of peasant dress, crafts, dialect and music long since gone elsewhere in the Greek islands. It's still a very picturesque place, yet traditions are vanishing by the year. Nowadays it's only the older women and those working in the several tourist shops who wear the striking and magnificently colourful traditional dress – an instant photo opportunity in exchange for persistent sales pitches for the trinkets, many of them imported.

After a while you'll notice the prominent role that the women play in daily life: tending gardens, carrying goods on their shoulders or herding goats. Nearly all Ólymbos men emigrate or work outside the village, sending money home and returning only on holidays. The long-isolated villagers also speak a unique dialect, said to maintain traces of its Doric and Phrygian origins – thus "Ólymbos" is pronounced "Élymbos" locally. Live vernacular music is still heard regularly and draws crowds of visitors at **festival** times, in particular Easter and August 15, when you've little hope of finding a bed.

Among places to **stay**, the friendly *Rooms Restaurant Olymbos* (☎22450 51252 or 22450 51009; ❷), near the village entrance, has rooms with baths or unplumbed ones with traditional furnishings, while the *Café-Restaurant Zefiros*, near the centre and run by two young sisters, manages the eight-room, en-suite *Hotel Astro* (☎22450 51421; ❸ B&B), with breakfast given in the restaurant. There are a few other places to **eat**, such as *O Mylos/Windmill*, occupying one of the restored mills and offering locally made wine and home-style specialities – though resorting with distressing frequency to the microwave.

From the village, the superb west-coast beach at **Fýsses** is a sharp 35-minute drop below, first cross-country, later by path. Most **local hikes**, however, head more gently north or east, many of them on waymarked paths, though you'll have to stay overnight in the area to enjoy them. The easiest option is the ninety-minute walk back down to Dhiafáni, beginning just below the two working windmills. The way is well marked, with water en route. It eventually drops to a ravine amidst extensive forest, though the last half-hour is mostly over bulldozed riverbed. You could also tackle the trail north to the ruins and beach at **Vrykoúnda** ("Vrougoúnda" in dialect), via sparsely inhabited **AVLÓNA**, set on a high upland devoted to grain. The father of the *Rooms Olymbos* management has opened an annexe here, *Restaurant Avlona*, on the through road, with four en-suite rooms (☎22450 51046; ❶) in the hamlet centre, an ideal base for committed walkers. From Ólymbos, it's just under three hours' walk one way to Vrykoúnda, which offers traces of Hellenistic/Roman Brykous, the remote cave-shrine of John the Baptist on the promontory and good swimming. **Trístomo**, a Byzantine anchorage in the far northeast of Kárpathos, can also be reached on a magnificent cobbled way beginning above Avlóna; the return is by the same way. There's also a fine ninety-minute marked path from Avlóna down to Vanánda beach (see opposite).

Dhiafáni and beaches

Although its popularity is growing – especially since the 1996 completion of a dock for large ferries – rooms in **DHIAFÁNI** are still inexpensive, and the pace of life slow outside of August. There are plenty of places at which to stay and eat, a stand-alone **ATM** at the base of the jetty, and even a small travel agency. The obvious *Mayflower Hotel* (☎22450 51228; ❶), opposite the quay, has shared bathrooms, as does *Pansion Delfini* (☎22450 51391; ❶), up on the southern hillside. Top of the heap in all senses is 2003-built *Hotel Studios Glaros* (☎22450 51501, ⓕ22450 51259; ❸) further up the same slope, with some of its sixteen huge units having four beds. On the front, the most interesting **taverna** is Italian-run *Iy Gorgona/L'Angolo*, featuring light dishes, wonderful desserts, proper coffees, and *limoncello digestif*.

Boat trips are offered to various nearby **beaches**, as well as to the Byzantine site of Palátia on the uninhabited islet of **Saría** or through the narrow strait to Trístomo anchorage and the ruins of Vrykoúnda. There are several coves within walking distance. Closest is **Vanánda**, a stony beach with an eccentrically managed campsite snack-bar in the oasis behind. To get there, follow the pleasant signposted path north through the pines, but don't believe the signs that say ten minutes – it's over thirty minutes away, shortcutting the more recent road. **Papá Miná**, with a few trees and cliff-shade, lies an hour's walk away via the cairned trail taking off from the road to the ferry dock. With a jeep you can reach three other superb beaches below the 18km of dirt road between Spóa and Ólymbos. The closest, also with path access from Ólymbos, is 250-metre long **Forókli** (clothing optional). Some 7km further towards Spóa, there's the turning for the even worse track down to **Áyios Minás** (bear left at fork partway along) and **Agnóndia** (bear right), equally pristine.

Rhodes (Ródhos)

It's no accident that **Rhodes** is among the most visited of the Greek islands. Not only is its east coast lined with numerous sandy beaches, but the capital's nucleus is a beautiful and remarkably preserved medieval city, the legacy of the crusading Knights of St John who used the island as their main base from 1309 until 1522. Unfortunately this showpiece is jammed to capacity with over a million tourists in a good season, as against about 111,000 permanent inhabitants (including many foreigners). Of transient visitors, Germans, Brits, Swedes, Italians and Danes predominate, though they tend to arrive in different months of the year.

Ródhos Town's medieval Old Town is very much the main event, but the rest of this sizeable island also repays exploration. **Líndhos**, with its ancient acropolis and (occasionally) atmospheric village, ranks second place on most people's lists. The beaches of the southwest coast – particularly near **Haráki** and **Yennádhi** – and isolated monuments of the interior, such as castles near **Monólithos** and **Kritiniá**, and frescoed churches at **Thárri** and **Asklipió**, are also worth pointing a car towards. Adrenalin junkies will (literally) want to go to extremes at the far south cape, **Prassoníssi**, one of the best windsurfing venues in Europe.

Some history

Blessed with an equable climate and strategic position, Rhodes was important from earliest times despite a lack of good harbours. The best natural port spawned the ancient town of Lindos which, together with the other city-states Kameiros and Ialyssos, united in 408 BC to found the new capital of **Rodos** (Rhodes) at the northern tip of the island. At various moments the cities allied themselves with Alexander, the Persians, Athenians or Spartans as prevailing conditions suited them, generally escaping retribution for backing the wrong side by a combination of seafaring audacity, sycophancy and burgeoning wealth as a trade centre. Following the failed siege of Demetrios Polyorketes in 305 BC, Rhodes prospered even more, displacing Athens as the major venue for rhetoric and the arts in the east Mediterranean.

Decline set in when Rhodes became involved in the Roman civil wars, and Cassius sacked Rhodes; by late imperial times, it was a backwater, a status confirmed by numerous barbarian raids during the Byzantine period. The Byzantines were compelled to cede the island to the Genoese, who in turn

RHODES

Sými ▲

Marmaris (Turkey) ►

Kastellórizo ►

Kós, Kálymnos, Léros & Pátmos ◄

Ialyssos (Filérimos)

RÓDHOS TOWN

Kritiká · Ixiá
Triánda
Kremastí
Paradhísi
Theológos
Kalavárdha Fánes
Soroní
Páno Kalamónas
Maritsá
Dhamatría
Tris · Pastídha
Koskinoú
Asgoúrou
Réni Koskinoú
Thérmes Kallithéas
Kallithéa Bay
Faliráki
Kalythiés · Ladhikó
Traganoú
Afándou
Kameiros
Petaloúdhes
Psínthos
Sálakos
Mt. Profítis Ilías 798m
Dhimyliá
Eleoússa
Arhípoli
Kápi
Platánia
Eptá Piyés
Cape Vayiá
Kolýmbia
Tsambíka
Alimniá
Kopriá
Kámiros Skála
Kastéllo
Kritinía
Apóllona
Áyios Nikólaos Foundouklí
Arhángelos
Émbona
Artamíti
Malóna
Stegná
Áyia Agáthi
Feraklós
Mássari
Haráki
Mt. Atávyros 1215m
Láerma
Kálathos
Vlyhá
Tomb of Kleoboulos
Glyfádha
Mt. Akramýtis 825m
Cape Armenístis
Siánna
Áyios Isidhoros
Thárri
Pylónas
Lárdhos
Líndhos
St. Paul
Monólithos
Ístrios
Profýlia
Péfki
Foúrni
Áyios Yeóryios Várdhas
Apolakkiá
Arnítha
Váti
Asklipió
Glýstra
Kiotári
Skiádhi
Mesanagrós
Yennádhi
Kteniá
Lahaniá
Hokhlakás
Kattaviá
Áyios Pávlos
Plimýri
Cape Vígla
Prassoníssi

N

0 ——— 10 km

surrendered it to the Knights of St John. The second great siege of Rhodes, during 1522–23, saw Ottoman Sultan Süleyman the Magnificent oust the stubborn knights, who retreated to Malta; Rhodes once again lapsed into relative obscurity, though heavily colonized and garrisoned, until its seizure by the Italians in 1912.

Arrival and information

All international and inter-island **ferries** and the *Dodekanisos Express* **catamaran** dock at the middle of Rhodes' three ports, the commercial harbour of Kolóna; the only exceptions are local **boats** to and from Sými, all excursion craft, the *Sea Star* catamaran and the **hydrofoils**, which use the yacht harbour of Mandhráki. Its entrance was supposedly once straddled by the Colossus, an ancient statue of Apollo built to celebrate the end of the 305-BC siege; today two columns surmounted by bronze deer are less overpowering replacements.

The **airport** is 13km southwest of town, by the village of Paradhísi; public buses bound for Paradhísi, Kalavárdha, Theológos or Sálakos pass the stop (look for the perspex-and-wood kiosk) on the main road opposite the northerly car-park entrance fairly frequently between 6am and midnight (fare €1.50). A taxi into town will cost €12–21, plus bags and airport supplement, depending on the time of day. **Buses** for both the west and east coasts of Rhodes – sleek air-con turquoise-and-blue models displacing the old orange-and-white ones – leave from two almost adjacent terminals on Papágou and Avérof, just outside the Italian-built New Market (a tourist trap, to miss without regret). Between the lower eastern station and the **taxi** rank at Platía Rimínis there's a **municipal tourist office** (June–Sept Mon–Sat 8am–9.30pm, Sun 9am–3pm), while some way up Papágou on the corner of Makaríou stands the more reliable **EOT office** (Mon–Fri 7.30am–2.30pm); both dispense bus and ferry schedules, the latter also providing a list of standard taxi fares, complete with complaint form. Rhodes taxi drivers have a deservedly poor reputation – overcharging of new arrivals is routine, as is refusing to take you to your chosen hotel, while steering you to inconvenient accommodation that gives them kickbacks.

Ródhos Town

Ancient Rodos, which lies underneath nearly all of the modern city, was laid out by one Hippodamus in the grid layout much in vogue at the time, with planned residential and commercial quarters. Its perimeter walls totalled nearly 15km, enclosing nearly double the area of the present town, and the Hellenistic population was said to exceed 100,000 – a staggering figure for late antiquity, as against 50,631 at the last modern census.

The contemporary town divides into two unequal parts: the compact **old walled city**, and the **New Town** which sprawls around it in three directions. The latter dates from the Ottoman occupation, when Greek Orthodox natives – forbidden to dwell in the old city – founded several suburb villages or *marásia* in the environs, which have since merged. Commercialization is predictably rampant in the walled town, and in the modern district of Neohóri ("Niohóri" in dialect), west of Mandhráki yacht harbour; the few buildings that aren't hotels are souvenir shops, car-rental or travel agencies and bars – easily sixty to seventy in every category.

Accommodation
Hotels and pensions at all price levels abound in the Old Town, mostly in the quad bounded by Omírou to the south, Sokrátous to the north, Perikléous to the east and Ippodhámou to the west. There are also a few possibilities worth considering in Neohóri, especially if you're bound for the airport or to Sými at an early hour. During crowded seasons, or late at night, it's prudent to either ring ahead or be prepared to accept the offers of proprietors meeting the ferries and change base next day if necessary – as it frequently is, since standards amongst quay-touted premises tend to be low.

RÓDHOS TOWN

ACCOMMODATION

Andreas	O
Apollo Tourist House	K
Casa Antica	C
Hotel Esperia	D
Ganymedes	M
La Luna	E
Marco Polo Mansion	H
Hotel Mediterranean	A
New Village Inn	B
Niki's	J
Pink Elephant/	
Roz Elefandas	N
S. Nikolis	L
Spot	I
Via-Via	G
Youth Hostel	F

RESTAURANTS, BARS & CLUBS

Anatolikes Nostimies	21
Iy Aporia	20
L'Auberge Bistrot	19
Bekir Karakuş	8
Blue Lagoon Pool Bar	4
Christos' Garden	3
Colorado Entertainment Centre	2
El Divino	6
Fotis Melathron	10
Kafé Besara	15
Khristos Estiatorio (O Vlahos)	28
Loutra Badoz	16
Mango Bar	18
Ta Marasia	22
O Meraklis	12
Metaxi Mas	29
Mikes	9
Niohori	1
Orhan	13
Resalto	11
Iy Rogmi tou Khronou	17
Roló?̈	7
Sakis	27
Stani	24
To Steki tou Heila	26
To Steki tou Tsima	25
To Steno	23
Sticky Fingers	5
Il Vecchio Forno	14

Old Town

Andreas Omírou 28D ☎22410 34156,
🌐www.hotelandreas.com. Perennially popular
(reservations needed) and under the dynamic new
management of Belgian-American Constance
Rivemal, this is one of the more imaginative old-
house restoration-*pensions*, thoroughly refurbished
in 2003. En-suite rooms in a variety of formats
(including family-size, and a spectacular "penthouse"). Terrace bar with views for excellent
breakfasts and evening drinks; two-night minimum
stay, credit cards accepted, indeed vital for
advance booking. Open late March–Oct 31. ❹ low
season, ❻

Apollo Tourist House Omírou 28C ☎22410
32003, 🌐www.apollo-touristhouse.com. Just five
en-suite rooms are to emerge from a thorough
overhaul of this old budget standby in 2004 by
owner Umberto; the self-catering kitchen makes it
good for longer stays. ❸

Ganymedes Perikléous 68 ☎694 24 51 874,
🌐www.hotel-ganymedes.com. Above a ground-
floor French patisserie (which provides breakfast)
are four very sweet rooms in pastel shades, with
faux antiques and modern baths; three are airy
with views, the interior one is best as a single. ❸

La Luna Ierokléous 21 ☎ & ℱ22410 25856.
Clean, wood-trimmed if plain (no en suites) *pension* in a converted old Turkish house, complete
with still-functioning *hamam* (Turkish bath), open
to guests. Garden bar for breakfast, by the citrus
and banana trees. ❸

Marco Polo Mansion Ayíou Fanouríou 42 ☎ &
ℱ22410 25562, 🌐www.marcopolomansion
.web.com. Superb 1999 conversion of an old
Turkish mansion, again with a *hamam* on site, but
here all rooms are en suite and exquisitely
furnished with antiques from the nearby gallery
of the same name, plus cotton pillows and handmade mattresses. Large buffet breakfasts are
provided by Spyros and Efi in the garden snack-
bar, which functions primarily for residents but is
open to guests. One-week minimum stay, reservations mandatory; part open in winter by arrangement. B&B rates ❹–❼

Niki's Sofokléous 39 ☎22410 25115, ℱ22410
36033. Some rooms can be on the small side, but
all are en suite, most have air con, and upper-
storey ones have fine views from balconies.
There's a washing machine, common terrace and
very friendly, helpful management to round things
off. Someone will wait up for late-night arrivals;
credit cards accepted. ❸

Pink Elephant/Roz Elefandas Officially Irodhótou
42 but actually on Timahídhas ☎ & ℱ22410
22469, 🌐www.pinkelephantpension.com. Simple

but clean rooms occupying several levels of a
modernized old building, near the traditional red-
light district; roof deck with sunning and covered
sections. Discount for singles. ❸–❹

S. Nikolis Ippodhámou 61 ☎22410 34561,
🌐www.s-nikolis.gr. Wide variety of premises in
the west of the Old Town. Hotel rates (❺) include
breakfast, TV and air con; there's also a cheaper,
unattended old-house *pension* (❷). The independent honeymoon suites (❼) and the self-catering
apartments (❺) are among the finest restoration
results in the Old Town, the latter interconnecting
to accommodate groups or families. Booking
essential, and accepted only with credit-card
number. Open April–Nov.

Spot Perikléous 21 ☎ & ℱ22410 34737. Yet
another old-town hotel under a new generation of
management, this modern building has cheerfully
painted en-suite rooms of varying formats with
textiles on the walls, representing superb value.
Internet facilities, optional air con and free luggage
storage. Open March–Nov. ❸

Via-Via Lysipoú 2, alley off Pythagóra ☎ &
ℱ22410 77027, 🌐www.hotel-via-via.com.
Efficiently but congenially run hotel; most one- to
four-person rooms are en suite but two share a
bath, and two have air con. All are simply but
tastefully furnished, with ongoing improvements.
Self-catering kitchen, roof terrace for breakfast
with an eyeful of the Ibrahim Pasha mosque
opposite. Three grades of breakfast offered, from
continental to full brunch. Open all year except
Jan. ❸–❹

Youth Hostel Eryíou 12 ☎22410 30491. Both
three- to five-bunk dorms and doubles (❷) in this
courtyarded hotel with kitchen facilities; €9 for a
bunk, but non-YHA-affiliated.

Neohóri

Casa Antica Amarándou 8 ☎22410 26206.
Double and quad studios in a made-over 150-
year-old house, with clean, white-tile decor, courtyard and roof terrace. Near some of the better
Neohóri tavernas. ❹

Hotel Esperia Yeoryíou Gríva 7 ☎22410 23941,
ℯesperia@esperia-hotels.gr. Well-priced, well-
run B-class hotel in a quiet location overlooking a
little plaza. Small-to-medium size, though salubrious and tasteful rooms with showers. Open all
year. ❹

Hotel Mediterranean Kó 35 ☎22410 24661,
🌐www.mediterranean.gr. Beachfront hotel in a
superb location; though nominally A-class, it's less
expensive than you'd think, especially if booked
through the recommended travel agent (see
p.305). The street-level snack-bar/café is very

popular around the clock with nonresidents as well. ❹ low season, ❻ New Village Inn Konstandopédhos 10 ☎ 22410 34937, ✉ newvillageinn@rho.forthnet.gr.

Whitewashed, somewhat grotto-like en-suite rooms "refreshed" yearly, friendly Greek and American management; singles available at a good rate. Open most of the year. ❸

The Old Town

Simply to catalogue the principal monuments and attractions cannot do full justice to the infinitely more rewarding **medieval city**. There's ample gratification to be derived from slipping through the eleven surviving gates and strolling the streets, under flying archways built for earthquake resistance, past the warm-toned sandstone and limestone walls painted ochre or blue, and over the *hokhláki* (pebble) pavement.

Dominating the northernmost sector of the city's fourteenth-century fortifications is the **Palace of the Grand Masters** (summer Mon 12.30–6.40pm, Tues–Fri 8am–6.40pm; winter Mon 12.30–3pm, Tues–Sun 8.30am–3pm; €6, or joint €10 ticket includes all museums in this section). Largely destroyed by an ammunition depot explosion set off by lightning in 1856, it was reconstructed by the Italians as a summer home for Mussolini and Victor Emmanuel III ("King of Italy and Albania, Emperor of Ethiopia"), neither of whom ever visited Rhodes. The exterior, based on medieval engravings and accounts, is passably authentic, but inside, free rein was given to Fascist delusions of grandeur: a marble staircase leads up to rooms paved with Hellenistic mosaics from Kós, and the ponderous period furnishings rival many a northern European palace. The ground floor is home to the splendid **Medieval Exhibit** and **Ancient Rhodes, 2400 Years** gallery (same hours and admission ticket), together the best museums in town. The medieval collection highlights the importance of Christian Rhodes as a trade centre, with exotic merchandise placing the island in a trans-Mediterranean context. The Knights are represented with a display on their sugar-refining industry and a gravestone of a Grand Master; precious manuscripts and books precede a wing of post-Byzantine icons, moved here permanently from Panayía Kástrou (see opposite). Across the courtyard in the north wing, "Ancient Rhodes" overshadows the official archeological museum by explaining the everyday life of the ancients, arranged topically (beauty aids, toys, cookware, worship and so on); highlights include a Hellenistic floor mosaic and a household idol of Hecate, goddess of the occult. On Tuesday and Saturday afternoons, there's supplementary self-guiding access of the **city walls** (one hour starting at 2.45pm; €6 or joint €10 ticket), beginning from a gate next to the palace and finishing at the Koskinoú gate.

The heavily restored **Street of the Knights** (Odhós Ippotón) leads due east from the Platía Kleovoúlou in front of the palace; the "Inns" lining it housed the Knights of St John, according to linguistic and ethnic affiliation, until the Ottoman Turks compelled them to leave for Malta after a six-month siege in which the defenders were outnumbered thirty to one. Today the Inns house various government offices and cultural institutions vaguely appropriate to their past, with occasional exhibitions, but the whole effect of the Italians' renovation is predictably sterile and stagey (indeed, nearby streets were used in the 1987 filming of *Pascali's Island*).

At the bottom of the hill, the Knights' Hospital has been refurbished as the **Archeological Museum** (summer Tues–Sun 8am–6.40pm; may close 2.30pm winter; €3 or joint ticket), though the arches and echoing halls of the building somewhat overshadow the appallingly labelled and presented contents – largely painted pottery dating from the sixth and seventh centuries BC. Behind the second-storey sculpture garden, the Hellenistic statue gallery is more accessible; in a rear corner stands the so-called "Marine Venus", beloved of Lawrence Durrell, but lent a rather sinister aspect by her sea-dissolved face – in contrast to the friendlier *Aphrodite Bathing*. Virtually next door is the **Decorative Arts Collection** (Tues–Sun 8.30am–3pm; €2 or joint ticket), gleaned from old houses across the Dodecanese; the most compelling artefacts are carved cupboard doors and chest lids painted in naïve style with mythological or historical episodes.

Across the way stands the **Byzantine Museum** (Tues–Sun 8am–6.40pm; €1.50 or joint ticket), housed in the old cathedral of the Knights, who adapted the Byzantine shrine of Panayía Kástrou for their own needs. Medieval icons and frescoes lifted from crumbling chapels on Rhodes and Hálki, as well as photos of art still *in situ*, constitute the exhibits; it's worth a visit since most of the Byzantine churches in the Old Town and outlying villages are kept locked. The highlight of the collection is a complete fresco cycle from the domes of Thárri monastery (see p.310) dating from 1624, removed in 1967 to reveal much older work beneath.

If instead you head south from the Palace of the Grand Masters, it's hard to miss the most conspicuous Turkish monument in Rhodes, the rust-coloured **Süleymaniye mosque**. Rebuilt in the nineteenth century on foundations three hundred years older, it's currently closed and under scaffolding like many local Ottoman monuments, though it's soon to emerge from its lengthy refit in all its candy-striped glory. The Old Town is in fact well sown with mosques and *mescids* (the Islamic equivalent of a chapel), many of them converted from Byzantine shrines after the 1522 conquest, when the Christians were expelled from the medieval precinct. A couple of these mosque, such as the 2002-renovated Ibrahim Pasha mosque on Plátonos, are still used by the sizeable **Turkish-speaking minority** here, some of them descended from Muslims who fled Crete between 1898 and 1913. Their most enduring civic contributions are, opposite the Süleymaniye, the **Ottoman Library** (Mon–Sat 9.30am–4pm; tip to custodian), with a rich collection of early medieval manuscripts and Korans, and the imposing, still-functioning **hamam**, or Turkish bath, on Platía Ariónos up in the southwest corner of the medieval city (Mon–Fri 11am–6pm, Sat 8am–6pm; €1.50; at time of writing men and women attend alternate days while the women's section is closed for repairs). Heading downhill from the Süleymaniye mosque, you come to **Odhós Sokrátous**, once the heart of the Ottoman bazaar, and now the "Via Turista", packed with fur and jewellery stores pitched at cruise-ship tourists. Beyond the tiled central fountain in Platía Ippokrátous, Odhós Aristotélous leads into the **Platía tón Evréon Martýron** ("Square of the Jewish Martyrs"), named in memory of the large local community that was almost totally annihilated during the summer of 1944; a black granite column in the centre honours them. Of the four synagogues that once graced Rhodes, only the ornate, arcaded **Kal Kadosh Shalom** (daily 10am–5pm; donation) on Odhós Simíou just to the south survives. It's maintained essentially as another memorial to the approximately 1800 Jews of Rhodes and Kós sent from here to the concentration camps; plaques in French – the language of educated Ottoman Jews across the east Aegean – commemorate the dead. At the rear of the building, a one-room **museum**, set up by a Los Angeles attorney of Jewish Rhodian descent, features archival photos of the community's life on Rhodes and in its far-flung diaspora in the Americas and Africa.

About 2km southwest of Mandhráki, the sparse, unenclosed remains of **Hellenistic Rhodes** – a restored theatre and stadium, plus a few columns of an Apollo temple – perch atop Monte Smith, the hill of Áyios Stéfanos renamed after a British admiral who used it as a watchpoint during the Napoleonic wars.

Neohóri

The pointy bit of **Neohóri** is surrounded by a continuous **beach**, complete with deckchairs, parasols and showers, particularly on the more sheltered east-facing section called **Élli**. At the northernmost point of the island an **Aquarium** (daily: April–Sept 9am–9pm; Oct–March 9am–4.30pm; €3), officially the "Hydrobiological Institute", offers some diversion with its subterranean maze of seawater tanks. Upstairs is a less enthralling collection of half-rotten stuffed sharks, seals and even a whale. Some 200m southeast stand the **Murad Reis mosque**, an atmospherically neglected Muslim cemetery, and the equally dilapidated **Villa Cleobolus**, where Lawrence Durrell lived from 1945 to 1947. Just a few paces northwest of this, the Italian-built Albergo delle Rose (*Hotel Rodon*) was refurbished and pressed into service in 1999 as the **Casino of Rhodes**, Greece's third largest, and unusually, open to locals as well as visitors.

Eating and drinking

Eating well for a reasonable price in and around Ródhos Town is a challenge, but not an insurmountable one. As a general rule, the remoter and further south you go, the better value you'll find – so touristy, alas, has the Old Town become. Unless otherwise stated, the following restaurants are open all year round.

Old Town

L'Auberge Bistrot Praxitélous 21 ☎22410 34292. Genuine, popular, French-run bistro with excellent Frenchified food: allow €18 per person for a starter, main course and dessert, plus wine from a well-selected Greek list, jazz soundtrack included. Summer seating in the courtyard of this restored medieval inn; inside under the arches during cooler months. Open late March to late Dec for supper daily except Mon; book in high season.

Fotis Melathron Little alley off Apelloú and Sokrátous ☎22410 24272. Housed in a converted Turkish mansion, this is considered the top *kultúra* restaurant in the Old Town. Sample fare: cyclamen *dolmádhes*, well-presented salads, squash flowers, crayfish nuggets, sweetbreads. The upstairs "snugs" are excellent for private parties of four to eight. It's usually a good idea to reserve. Their annexe *Fotis*, nearby at Menekléous 8, does very fresh fish and nothing else other than perhaps *ahinosaláta* (urchin roe) and rocket salad; budget €70 for two with wine at either establishment.

O Meraklis Aristotélous 30. A *patsatzídhiko* (tripe-soup kitchen) that's only open 3–8am for a motley clientele of post-club lads, Turkish stall-holders, nightclub singers and travellers just stumbled off an overnight ferry. Great free entertainment, including famously rude staff, and the soup – the traditional Greek hangover cure – is good too.

Mikes (pronounced "mee-kess") Nameless alley behind Sokrátous 17. Inexpensive hole-in-the-wall, serving only grilled fish, salads and wine; outdoor tables, galley-like kitchen.

Orhan Evdhóxou 49. Orhan himself has passed on, but his widow and daughters continue a tradition of inexpensive home-style cooking from a limited menu; pleasant patio seating.

Il Vecchio Forno Sofokléous 5. Pizza *al metro* (by the slice) is all the rage in Greece now, and this little French/Greek-run place does it extremely well.

Neohóri

Anatolikes Nostimies Kapodhistríou 60, Akándia port. The name means "Anatolian Delicacies", and that's what's on offer at this Rhodian/Turkish-run grill: Turkish/Middle Eastern dips and starters, plus sixteen variations of kebab. Not much atmosphere, but friendly and reasonable; post-prandial hubble-bubble provided on request. Open 11am–midnight.

Iy Aporia Kolokotróni 5. Rough-as-guts little dive run by two ladies, basically a workmen's *kafenío* that serves very good and cheap food: fried fish, chops and salads, washed down by the usual refreshments and accompanied by taped folk/laïká music. Sit outside opposite grim industrial scenery for a sea breeze and even a sea view.

Khristos Estiatorio (O Vlahos) Klavdhíou Pépper 165, at the big bend, Zéfyros beach. This has abandoned its former hybrid identity as an *ouzerí* and is now a full-on restaurant. Great tzatziki, plus vegetable-strong *mayireftá* (cuttlefish with spinach, fish soup, eggplant *imam*) that sell out quickly. Not as cheap (€12–16) as formerly, but still worth the trek out.

Ta Marasia Ayíou Ioánni 155, just off the *platía* of the same name. Currently the most daring *ouzerí* in the town limits, operating out of a 1923-vintage house. The food's excellent, if not always very traditional (grilled oyster mushrooms, red cabbage, yogurt-and-nut salad), though there are more usual seafood platters like urchins and *rengosaláta*. Don't over-order, as portions tend to be generous.

Metaxi Mas Klavdhíou Pépper 115, Zéfyros beach. No sign or menu in English – look for the elevated boat – at this seafood *ouzerí* purveying various exotic titbits; count on €40 per couple with booze, slightly cheaper per person in a group – but still rather less than in the Old Town. Daily lunch and supper, Sun lunch only.

Niohori Ioánni Kazoúli 29, by the Franciscan monastery. Also known as "*Kiki's*" after the jolly proprietress, this homey, inexpensive local serves lunch and supper; best for grills, the meat sourced from their own farm.

Sakis Ipsilándou 27, Áyios Nikólaos. Genuine taverna with pleasant patio seating, equally popular with Rhodians and savvy expats. Excellent seafood and starters; it's possible to have three courses (including modest fish) and a beer for €14. Supper only.

Stani Ayías Anastasías 28, cnr Paleón Patrón Yermanoú, south of the Koskinoú Gate. Most central outlet of a chain of Rhodian Turkish confectioners, scooping out two dozen flavours of the best ice cream on the island, publicity for rival *Mike's* notwithstanding.

To Steki tou Heila Hatziangélou, corner Episkópi Kyrinías, near Zéfyros. Very popular seafood *ouzerí* which probably just pips the next listing for quality at similar prices, though the street's noisy. Rocket and onion salad, Sými shrimps, squid, marinated sardines, *fáva*, cockles (check price of last). Open daily, supper only.

To Steki tou Tsima Peloponnísou 22, around cnr from *Stani*. Very reasonable seafood *ouzerí*, with the stress on aficionados' shellfish titbits such as *foúskes* (fresh marine invertebrates), *spiníalo* (pickled version of same) and small fish not prone to farming – always ask about off-menu specials. No airs or graces (except for proper table napery), just patently fresh materials. Open daily, supper only.

To Steno Ayíon Anaryíron 29, 400m southwest of the Ayíou Athanasíou Gate. A genuinely welcoming *ouzerí*, with outdoor seating during the warmer months and superb menu (chickpea soup, courgette croquettes, sausages). A new injection of seafood has meant that prices have crept up – budget €18–20 per head.

Nightlife

The Old Town formerly had a well-deserved reputation for being tomb-silent at night; this has changed drastically since the late 1990s, with an entire alley (Miltiádhou) off Apelloú given over to a half-dozen loud **music bars** and **clubs**, frequented almost exclusively by Greeks and spilling over into adjacent lanes. There are other nuclei of activity on Sofokléous and Platía Ariónos, where music levels permit conversation. These are just appetizers for the estimated two hundred foreigner-patronized bars and clubs in Neohóri, where theme nights and various other gimmicks predominate. They are found mostly along the streets and alleys bounded by Alexándhrou Dhiákou, Orfanídhou, Lohagoú Fanouráki and Nikifórou Mandhilará.

Sedate by comparison, Ministry of Culture-approved **folk dances** (June–Oct Mon, Wed & Fri 9.20pm; €12) are presented with live accompaniment by the Nelly Dimoglou Company, performed in the landscaped "Old Town Theatre" off Andhroníkou, near Platía Ariónos. More of a technological extravaganza is the **Sound and Light** show, spotlighting sections of the city walls, staged in a garden just off Platía Rimínis. There's English-language narration nightly except Sunday, its screening time varying from 8.15pm to 10.15pm.

Thanks to a large contingent from the local university, there are several year-round **cinemas** showing first-run fare indoors or open-air according to season and air-con capabilities. Choose from among the summer-only outdoor cinema by the Rodon Municipal Theatre, next to the town hall in

Neohóri; the Metropol five-plex, southeast of the Old Town opposite the stadium, refurbished in 2001; and the nearby Pallas three-plex on Dhimokratías, refurbished in 1999.

Bekir Karakuş Sokrátous 76. Bags of atmosphere in this, the last traditional Turkish-run *kafenío* in the Old Town. Oriental-fantasy interior; tends to open after 11am.

Blue Lagoon Pool Bar 25-Martíou 2, Neohóri. One of the better theme bars, in this case a "desert island" with palm trees, waterfalls, live turtles and parrots, a shipwrecked galleon – and taped music. Open March–Oct 8.30am–3am.

Christos' Garden Dhilberáki 59, Neohóri. This combination art-gallery/bar/café occupies a carefully restored old house and courtyard with pebble-mosaic floors throughout. Incongruously classy for the area.

Colorado Entertainment Centre Orfanídhou 57, cnr Aktí Miaouli, Neohóri. Triple venue: "pub" with live in-house band (rock covers), "club" with taped sounds, and quiet upstairs chill-out bar.

El Divino Alexándhrou Dhiákou 5, Neohóri. Very classy, Greek-frequented "music bar" with garden seating and the usual range of coffees and alcohol. Open June–Oct.

Kafé Besara Sofokléous 11–13, Old Town. Congenial breakfast café/low-key boozer run by an Australian lady, with interesting mixed clientele and live Greek acoustic music some nights Oct–May.

Mango Bar Platía Dhoriéos 3, Old Town. Piped music and a variety of drinks at this durable bar on an otherwise quiet plaza; also a good source of breakfast after 8am, served under a plane tree.

Resalto Plátonos 6, opposite the mosque. Live Greek *rebétika* and *laïká* sounds, rather cheaper than nearby rival *Café Chantant*. Open Thurs–Sun only.

Iy Rogmi tou Khronou Platía Ariónos, Old Town. Taped music (not house or techno) at a reasonable level and a congenial crowd make this established bar worth a look; much the same crowd spills over to *Loutra Badoz* next door, which hosts live jazz some nights.

Rolóï Orféos 1, Old Town. The Baroque clock-tower erected by Ahmet Fetih Pasha in 1857 is now the focus of possibly the most exclusive café-bar in the Old Town. Admission charge (€3.50) to climb the tower, and steeply priced drinks, but you are paying for the terrific view.

Sticky Fingers Anthoúla Zérvou 6, Neohóri. Long-lived music bar with reasonable drinks; live rock several nights weekly from 10pm onwards. Fri & Sat only off-season.

Listings

Airlines Olympic Airways, Iérou Lóhou 9 ☎22410 24555; Aegean Airlines, Ethelondón Dhodhekanisíon 20 ☎22410 24400.

Bookshop Newsstand at Grigoríou Lambráki 23 is currently the only outlet for any quality foreign-language books.

Car rental Prices at noninternational chains are fairly standard at €41–44 per day, but can be bargained down to about €32–35 a day, all-inclusive, out of peak season and/or for long periods. Especially recommended is Drive, who change their cars every 12–18 months; they have several premises across the island, including at the airport (☎22410 81011) and the *Grand Hotel* in town (☎22410 26284). Other flexible outfits, all in the New Town, include Alamo/National, 28-Oktovríou 18 (☎22410 73570); Just/Ansa, Mandhilará 70 (☎22410 31811); Kosmos, Papaloúka 31 (☎22410 74374); and Payless, Íonos Dhragoúmi 29 (☎22410 26586).

Exchange Most conventional bank branches are near Platía Kýprou in Neohóri, plus there are various exchange bureaux keeping long hours. In the Old Town, there are two full-service banks with ATMs, plus a pair of stand-alone ATMs on Sokrátous.

Ferry agents ANES, Afstralías 88 (☎22410 37769), for catamaran and hydrofoil to Sými; DANE, Afstralías 92 (☎22410 43150), to Pireás via select Dodecanese; Dodhekanisos Navtiliaki, Afstralías 3, by the Shell station (☎22410 70590), for the *Dodekanisos Express* catamaran to most Dodecanese islands; Inspiration, Aktí Sakhtoúri 4 (base of main ferry dock; ☎22410 24294), for most GA boats to Dodecanese and Cyclades, plus DANE sailings; Kyriakoulis Maritime, Neoríon dock (☎22410 78052), for hydrofoils to Kós and all intervening islands; LANE, Alexándhrou Dhiákou 38 (☎22410 33607), to Crete via Háiki, Kárpathos, Kássos; for the *Sea Star* catamaran to Tílos and Níssyros, booth at Mandhráki port or ☎22410 78052. Weekly tourist office departure-schedule handouts are deeply unreliable; authoritative sailing information is available at the *limenarhío* (port police), on Mandhráki esplanade near the post office.

Internet cafés The most central and competitive of several are *Rock Style*, Dhimokratías 7, opposite the stadium, and *Mango Bar* (see "Nightlife" opposite).

Laundries House of Laundry, Erythroú Stavroú 2, Neohóri; Express, Kostí Palamá 5, behind New Market; Wash & Go, Plátonos 33, Old Town.

Motorbike rental Low-volume scooters will make little impact on Rhodes; sturdier Yamaha 125s, suitable for two people, start at about €20 a day. In the Old Town, Mandar Moto at Dhimosthénous 2, cnr Platía Evréon Martýron, has a large stable of medium-sized scooters suitable for short jaunts. Recommended outlets in Neohóri include Margaritis, Ioánni Kazoúli 23, with a wide range of late models up to 500cc, plus mountain bikes; or (to roll out in style) Rent a Harley at 28-Oktovríou 80 – classic models for two riders start at a whopping €105 per day.

Travel agencies Recommended in the Old Town is Castellania, Evripídhou 1–3, cnr Platía Ippokrátous (☎22410 75860), which can arrange all domestic air tickets, both domestic and international ferries, and also discount scheduled and charter flights abroad. In Neohóri, conveniently located Triton Holidays at Plastíra 9 (☎22410 21690, ✉info@tritondmc.gr) is excellent for all local travel arrangements, including catamaran, ferry and air tickets, plus the hydrofoil to Turkey. They also have a network of accommodation across the Dodecanese, and can book you an entire itinerary at attractive rates.

The east coast

Heading down the coast from the capital you have to go some way before you escape the crowds from local beach hotels, their numbers swollen by visitors using the regular buses from town or on boat tours out of Mandhráki. You should look in at the abandoned spa of **Thérmes Kallithéas**, a prize example of orientalized Art Deco dating from 1928–30, the work of a young Pietro Lombardi, who in his old age designed the European Parliament building in Strasbourg. Located 3km south of Kallithéa resort proper, down a paved track through pines, the buildings are set in a palm grove, though an EU-funded restoration begun in 1999 has ground to a halt. The concrete lido near the domed structure is popular, as are several nearby secluded coves framed by rock formations which often interpose themselves between the water and the sand, the latter furnished with sunbeds and (in most cases) snack-bars.

The former fishing village of **FALIRÁKI** has acquired considerable notoriety since the early 1990s as the "boozing and bonking" capital of the Dodecanese, a reputation reinforced by a string of rapes and, in August 2003, the fatal stabbing of one British youth and the arrest of several others on charges of public lewdness. All of this has been fuelled by a culture of pub crawls organized by tour reps, many of whom were also arrested and charged for taking kickbacks from bar owners. The British press indulged in an orgy of self-flagellation, while local authorities made pious noises about cleaning up the resort, with the alleged malefactors subject to (by the standards of any country, let alone Greece) extraordinarily speedy justice *pour encourager les autres*. The scenery just inland from Faliráki – arid, scrubby sandhills at the best of times – has been made that much bleaker by late 1980s fire damage that stretches way beyond Líndhos. The cape to the south, **Ladhikó** (45-minute path from Faliráki), shelters the more scenic bay of "Anthony Quinn", named in honour of the late actor whom Greeks took to their hearts following his roles in *Zorba the Greek* and *The Guns of Navarone* (the latter filmed locally).

The enormous mass of **Tsambíka**, 26km south of town, is the first place at which most nonpackage visitors will seriously consider stopping. Actually the very eroded flank of a once much-larger mountain, this promontory has a monastery on top offering unrivalled views along some 50km of coastline. From the main highway, a steep, 1500-metre cement drive leads to a small car park and a snack-bar, from which steps take you to the summit. The little monastery here is unremarkable except for its September 8 festival: childless women climb up – sometimes on their hands and knees – to be relieved of their barrenness, and any children born afterwards are dedicated to the Virgin with the names Tsambikos or Tsambika, which are particular to the Dodecanese. From the top you can survey **Kolýmbia** just to the north, a small beach to one side of a tiny, rock-girt cove, backed by a dozen, low-rise hotels. Shallow **Tsambíka Bay** on the south side of the headland (two-kilometre access road) warms up early in the spring, and the excellent beach, protected by owners of the Orthodox Church from permanent development – there's just a taverna, a half-dozen *kantína* caravans, and "watersports" – teems with people all summer.

The next beach south is gravelly **Stegná** with its mix of summer cottages for locals and accommodation for Germans, plus a couple of **tavernas** that attract a Greek clientele. Stegná is reached by a steep road east from the less reward-ing village of **ARHÁNGELOS**, just inland and overlooked by a crumbling castle. Though you can disappear into the warren of alleys between the main road and the citadel, the place is now firmly caught up in package tourism, with a full complement of banks, tavernas, minimarts and jewellery stores. Another overnight base on this stretch of coast, English-dominated this time, is **HARÁKI**, a pleasant if undistinguished two-street fishing port with mostly self-catering accommodation (generally ❸) overlooked by the stubby ruins of **Feraklós castle**, the last stronghold of the Knights to fall to the Turks. You can swim off the town beach if you don't mind an audience from the handful of waterfront cafés and tavernas, but most people head west out of town, then north 800m along a marked dirt track to secluded **Agáthi beach**.

Líndhos

LÍNDHOS, the island's second-ranking tourist attraction, erupts from barren surroundings 12km south of Haráki. Like Ródhos Old Town, its charm is heavily undermined by commercialism and crowds: up to half a million visi-tors in a typical year. At midday dozens of coaches park nose-to-tail on the narrow southerly access road, with even more on the drives down to the beaches. Back in the village itself, those few vernacular houses not snapped up by package operators have, since the 1960s, been bought up and refurbished by wealthy British, Germans and Italians. The old *agorá* or serpentine high street presents a mass of fairly indistinguishable bars, crêperies, mediocre restaurants and travel agents. Although high-rise hotels and all vehicular traffic have been prohibited inside the municipal boundaries, the result is a relentlessly com-mercialized theme park – hot and airless from June to August, but eerily deserted in winter.

Nonetheless, if you arrive before or after peak season, when the pebble-paved streets between the immaculately whitewashed houses are relatively empty of both people and droppings from the donkeys shuttling up to the acropolis (see below), you can still appreciate the beautiful, atmospheric setting of Líndhos. The most imposing fifteenth- to eighteenth-century **captains' residences** are built around *hokhláki* courtyards, their monumental doorways often fringed by intricate stonework, with the number of braids or cables supposedly corres-ponding to the number of ships owned. A few are open to the public, notably the **Papakonstandis Mansion**, the most elaborate and home to an unofficial museum (erratic hours, nominally daily 11am–2pm); entrance to the "open" mansions is free but some pressure will probably be exerted on you to buy something, especially lace and embroidery.

On the bluff looming above the town, the ancient acropolis with its Doric **Temple of Athena** (restorations ongoing until 2008) and imposing **Hellenistic stoa** is found inside the Knights' **castle** (summer Mon

12.30–6.40pm, Tues–Sun 8am–6.40pm; rest of year Tues–Sun 8.30am–3pm; €6) – a surprisingly felicitous blend of ancient and medieval culture. Though the ancient city of Lindos and its original temple dated from at least 1100 BC, the present structure was begun by local ruler Kleoboulos in the sixth century BC after a fourth-century fire.

Líndhos's north beach, once the main ancient harbour, is overcrowded and heavily commercialized; if you do base yourself here, quieter **beaches** are to be found one cove beyond at Pállas beach (with a nudist annexe around the headland), or 5km north at **Vlyhá Bay**. South of the acropolis huddles the small, perfectly sheltered **St Paul's harbour**, with excellent swimming; the apostle is said to have landed here in 58 AD on a mission to evangelize the island.

Practicalities

It used to be tempting fate to just turn up and hope for **accommodation** vacancies on spec, but since certain British tour companies pulled out of Líndhos in the late 1990s, it's something of a buyers' market. If you're not met at the bus stop under the giant fig tree by proprietors touting rooms, Pallas Travel (☎22440 31494) can arrange a room or even a whole villa for a small fee; just watch that you're not shoved into a windowless cell – ventilation is paramount here. The oft-cited backpackers' standby, *Pension Electra* (☎22440 31226; ❹) on the way to the north beaches, recently got an overhaul but remains overpriced.

Most local **restaurants** tend to be exploitative and serve bland fare, with a quick turnover in ownership. You may as well push the boat out at *Mavrikos* on the fig-tree square, founded in 1933 and in the same family ever since. *Mezédhes* such as *manoúri* cheese with basil and pine-nuts, sweet marinated sardines, or beets in goat-cheese sauce, are accomplished, as are main courses such as cuttlefish in wine sauce or expertly grilled fish; dipping into the excellent (and expensive) Greek wine list as well will add €18 minimum a bottle to the typical food charge of €21–26 per person. For snacks and desserts, try *Il Forno*, an Italian-run bakery, and *Gelo Blu*, the most genuine of several *gelaterie* here, also offering decadent cakes. The better of two **Internet cafés** is helpful and well-equipped Lindianet; The Link is a unique combination laundry and secondhand bookshop (Mon–Sat 9am–8pm). Líndhos has one amenity that would be the envy of much larger towns: a **spa** (Mon–Sat 1pm–9pm), offering the full range of services including all-day packages. Local **car-rental** rates tend to be cheaper than in Ródhos Town, though you've less choice in models. There are two proper **banks**, working normal hours, each with ATMs. And finally, Lindos Suntours (☎22440 31333) has a nice line in unclaimed one-way charter seats back to Britain, as does Village Holidays (☎22440 31486).

The west coast

Rhodes' **west coast** is the windward flank of the island, so it's damper, more fertile and more forested; most beaches, however, are exposed and decidedly rocky. None of this has deterred development, and as in the east the first few kilometres of the busy shore road down from the capital have been surrendered entirely to tourism. From Neohóri's aquarium down to the airport, the shore is fringed by an almost uninterrupted line of generic Mediterranean-*costa* hotels, though such places as Triánda, Kremastí and Paradhísi are still nominally villages, with real centres. This was the first part of the island to be favoured by the package operators, and tends to be frequented by a decidedly sedate, middle-aged/family clientele that doesn't stir much from the poolside.

There's not much inducement to stop until you reach the important archeological site of **KAMEIROS**, which together with Lindos and Ialyssos was one of the three Dorian powers that united during the fifth century BC to found the powerful city-state of Rhodes. Soon eclipsed by the new capital, Kameiros was abandoned and only rediscovered in 1859. As a result it is a particularly well-preserved Doric townscape, doubly worth visiting for its beautiful hillside site (summer Tues–Sun 8am–6.40pm; winter 8.30am–3pm; €4). While none of the individual remains is spectacular, you can make out the foundations of two small temples, the re-erected pillars of a Hellenistic house, a Classical fountain, and the stoa of the upper agora, complete with a water cistern. Because of the gentle slope of the site, there were no fortifications, nor was there an acropolis. On the beach below Kameiros there are several **tavernas**, highly commercialized but acceptable while waiting for one of the two daily buses back to town (if you're willing to walk 4km back to Kalavárdha you'll have a better choice of service).

At the tiny anchorage of **KÁMIROS SKÁLA** (aka Skála Kamírou) 15km south, there are five more touristy restaurants, which somewhat inexplicably have become the target of coach parties. Less heralded is the daily **kaïki** which leaves for the island of **Hálki** at 2.30pm, weather permitting, returning early the next morning; on Wednesdays there are day-trips departing at 9.30am and 11am, returning at 4pm, while on Sundays there's a single journey at 9am, back at 4pm. For a better **meal**, skip the circus here and proceed 400m southwest to off-puttingly named **Paralía Kopriá** ("Manure Beach"), where *Psarotaverna Johnny's* has good nonfarmed fish and *orektiká*, especially on Sundays when home-made *dolmádhes* and (seasonally) squash blossoms may be on the menu with the usual standards; it's been "discovered" and so is pricier than formerly, but still worth a stop.

A couple of kilometres south of Skála, the "Kastello", signposted as **Kástro Kritinías**, is from afar the most impressive of the Knights' rural strongholds, and the paved access road is too narrow and steep for tour buses. Close up it proves to be no more than a shell, but a glorious shell, with fine views west to assorted islets and Hálki. You make a "donation" to the formidable old woman at the car park in exchange for fizzy drinks, seasonal fruit or flowers.

Beyond Kritinía itself, a quiet hillside village with a few rooms and tavernas, the main road winds south through the dense forests below mounts Akramýtis and Atávyros to **SIÁNNA**, the most attractive mountain settlement on the island, famous for its aromatic pine-sage honey and *soúma*, a grape-residue distillate similar to Italian *grappa* but far smoother. The tiered, flat-roofed farmhouses of **MONÓLITHOS**, 4km southwest at the end of the public bus line, are scant justification for the long trip out here, and food at the four **tavernas** is indifferent owing to the tour-group trade, but the view over the bay is striking and you could use the village as a base by staying in rooms or at the *Hotel Thomas* (☎22410 22741 or 22460 61291; ❷), which has fair-sized rooms belying a grim exterior. Diversions in the area include yet another **Knights' castle**, 2km west of town, photogenically perched on its own pinnacle but enclosing even less inside than Kástro Kritinías, and the sand-and-gravel beaches (no facilities) at **Foúrni**, five paved but curvy kilometres below the castle. In the headland between the first and second beaches are some caves that were hollowed out by early Christians fleeing persecution.

The interior

Inland Rhodes is hilly, and the northern two-thirds still mostly wooded, despite the depredations of arsonists. You'll need a vehicle to see its highlights, especially as enjoyment resides in getting away from it all; no single site justifies the tremendous expense of a taxi or the inconvenience of trying to make the best of sparse bus schedules.

Ialyssos and the Valley of the Butterflies

Starting from the west-coast highway, turn inland at the central junction in Tríanda for the five-kilometre uphill ride to the scanty acropolis of ancient **Ialyssos** (Tues–Sun 8am–6.40pm; €3) on flat-topped, strategic Filérimos hill; from its Byzantine castle Süleyman the Magnificent directed the 1522 siege of Rhodes. Filérimos means "lover of solitude", after the tenth-century settlement here by Byzantine hermits. The existing **Filérimos monastery**, restored successively by Italians and British, is the most substantial structure here. As a concession to the Rhodian faithful, the church alone is usually open to pilgrims after the stated hours. Directly in front of the church sprawl the foundations of third-century **temples to Zeus and Athena**, built atop a far older Phoenician shrine. Below this, further towards the car park, lies the partly subterranean church of **Aï-Yeórgis Hostós**, a simple, barrel-vaulted structure with fourteenth- and fifteenth-century frescoes, not as vivid or well preserved as those at Thárri or Asklipió (see p.309). A little way southeast of the parking area, a hillside **Doric fountain** with a columned facade was only revealed by subsidence in 1926 – and is now off-limits owing to another landslip which has covered it again. Southwest of the monastery and archeological zone, a "Way of the Cross", with the fourteen stations marked out in copper plaques during the Italian era, leads to an enormous concrete crucifix, a 1995 replacement of an Italian-built one; you're allowed to climb out onto the cross-arms for a supplement to the already amazing view. Illuminated at night, the crucifix is clearly visible from the island of Sými and – perhaps more pertinently – "infidel" Turkey across the way.

The only highly publicized tourist "attraction" in the island's interior, **Petaloúdhes** or the **Butterfly Valley** (May–Sept daily 8.30am–sunset; April & Oct 9am–3pm; admission €3–5 depending on season), reached by a seven-kilometre paved side road bearing inland from the west-coast highway between Paradhísi and Theológos, is actually a rest stop for Jersey tiger moths. Only in summer do these creatures congregate here, attracted for unknown reasons by the abundant *Liquidambar orientalis* trees growing abundantly in this stream canyon. In season, the moths roost in droves on the tree trunks; they cannot eat during this final phase of their life cycle, must rest to conserve energy and die of starvation soon after mating. When sitting in the trees, the moths are a well-camouflaged black and yellow, but flash cherry-red overwings in flight.

Some 2km before Petaloúdhes, the **microwinery** (15,000–20,000 bottles annually) of Anastasia Triandafyllou is worth a stop for its Athiri whites and blended reds (open daily until 7pm). There's a popular **taverna** partway up the valley, by the roadside, but for even better fare continue all the way up the road to the edge of **PSÍNTHOS** village, where the friendly *Piyi Fasouli* serves excellent grills and appetizers at seating under plane trees beside the namesake spring; prices have climbed to about €16 a head, but it's still worth it for the quality of the ingredients.

Eptá Piyés to Profítis Ilías

Heading inland from Kolýmbia junction on the main east-coast highway, you've a four-kilometre walk or drive to **Eptá Piyés** ("Seven Springs"), a superb oasis with a tiny dam created by the Italians for irrigation. A trail, or a rather claustrophobic Italian aqueduct-tunnel, both lead from the vicinity of the springs to the reservoir.

Continuing inland, you reach neglected Rationalist structures at Eleoússa (built as the planned agricultural colony of Campochiaro in 1935–36) after another 9km, in the shade of the dense forest at the east end of Profítis Ilías ridge. Two other undisturbed villages, Platánia and Apóllona, nestle on the south slopes of the mountain overlooking the start of an area bereft of trees, but most people keep straight on 3km further from Eleoússa to the late Byzantine church of **Áyios Nikólaos Foundouklí** ("St Nicholas of the Hazelnuts"). The partly shaded site has a fine view north over cultivated valleys, and locals descend in force for picnics on weekends. The frescoes inside, dating from the thirteenth to the fifteenth centuries, could use a good cleaning, but various scenes from the life of Christ are recognizable.

Heading west from the church along mostly paved roads gets you finally to **Profítis Ilías**, where the Italian-vintage chalet-hotels *Elafos* and *Elafina* (now hosting childrens' summer camps) hide in deep woods just north of the 798-metre peak, Rhodes' third-highest point but out of bounds since it's a military area. However, there's good, gentle strolling below and around the summit, and a snack-bar on the through road is generally open in season.

Atávyros villages

All tracks and roads west across Profítis Ilías converge on the main road from Kalavárdha bound for **ÉMBONA(S)**, a large and architecturally nondescript village backed up against the north slope of 1215-metre **Mount Atávyros**. Émbona, with a half-dozen meat-oriented **tavernas** (try *Bakis* on the *platía*, which has its own butcher's), is more geared to handling tourists than you might expect, since it's the venue for summer "folk-dance tours" from Ródhos Town. The village also lies at the heart of the island's most important wine-producing districts, and CAÏR – the Italian-founded vintners' co-operative – produces a choice of acceptable mid-range varieties. However, products of the smaller, family-run Emery **winery** (daily 9am–4.30pm) at the northern outskirts are more esteemed. To get some idea what Émbona would be like without tourists, carry on clockwise around the peak past the Artamíti monastery, to less celebrated **ÁYIOS ISÍDHOROS**, with nearly as many vines and tavernas, a more open feel, and the **trailhead** for the five-hour return ascent of Atávyros. This path, beginning at the northeast edge of the village at a wooden placard and well marked with paint splodges, is the safest and easiest way up the mountain, which has extensive foundations of a Zeus temple on top.

Thárri monastery

The road from Áyios Isídhoros to Siánna is paved; not so the perennially rough one that curves for 12km east to Láerma, but it's worth enduring if you've any interest in Byzantine monuments. The **monastery of Thárri**, lost in pine forests 5km south, is the oldest religious foundation on the island, re-established as a living community of half a dozen monks in 1990 by the charismatic abbot Amfilohios. The striking *katholikón* (open daily, all day) consists of a long nave and short transept surmounted by barrel vaulting. Various recent cleanings have restored damp-smudged frescoes dating from 1300 to 1450 to their former exquisite glory. The most distinct, in the transept, depict the Evangelists Mark and Matthew, plus the Archangel Gabriel, while the nave boasts various acts of Christ, including such scenes as the *Storm on the Sea of Galilee*, *Meeting the Samaritan Woman at the Well* and *Healing the Cripple*.

The far south

South of a line connecting Monólithos and Lárdhos, you could easily begin to think you had strayed onto another island. Gone are most of the multi-star hotels and roads to match, and with them the bulk of the crowds. Gone too are most other tourist facilities and public transport. Only one or two daily buses (in season) ply to the depopulated villages here (Yennádhi has more services), approaching along the east coast; tavernas grace the more popular stretches of sand, but aside from the growing package enclaves of Lárdhos, Péfki and Kiotári, there are few places to stay.

Despite the shelving of plans for a second island airport in the area, new beachfront development mushrooms to either side of **LÁRDHOS**, itself solidly on the tourist circuit despite an inland position between Láerma and the peninsula culminating in Líndhos. The beach 2km away is gravelly and dull, so it's best to continue 3km to **Glýstra** cove, a small but delightful crescent, with umbrellas and a snack-bar. Four kilometres east of Lárdhos, **PÉFKI** (Péfkos on some maps) began life as the garden annexe and overflow for Líndhos, but is now a burgeoning package resort in its own right; the sea is clearer than at Lárdhos, with small, well-hidden beaches which are getting harder to find with all the new development on the clifftop.

Asklipió

Nine kilometres beyond Lárdhos, a paved side road heads 3.5km inland to **ASKLIPIÓ**, a sleepy village guarded by a crumbling castle and graced by the Byzantine church of **Kímisis Theotókou** (daily 9am–6pm; €1). The building dates from 1060, with a ground plan nearly identical to Thárri's, except that two subsidiary apses were added during the eighteenth century, supposedly to conceal a secret school in a subterranean crypt. The frescoes within are in better condition than those at Thárri owing to the drier local climate; they are also a bit later, though some claim that the final work at Thárri and the earliest here were executed by the same hand, a master from Híos.

The format and subject matter of the frescoes are equally rare in Greece: didactic "cartoon strips" that extend completely around the church in some cases, featuring extensive Old Testament stories in addition to the more usual lives of Christ and the Virgin. There's a complete sequence from Genesis, from the Creation to the Expulsion from Eden; note the comically menacing octopus among the fishes in the panel of the Fifth Day, and Eve subsequently being fashioned from Adam's rib. A *Revelation of John the Divine* takes up most of the south transept, while an enormous Archangel Michael dominates the north transept, with sword in right hand and a small soul being carried to judgement in his left. Pebble-mosaic flooring decorates both the interior and the vast courtyard. Two adjacent buildings house separate museums: an ecclesiastical exhibit, and a more interesting folklore gallery in an ex-olive mill, full of unlabelled rural craft tools and antiquated, belt-driven machinery.

To the southern tip

Back on the coast road, the beachfront hamlet of **KIOTÁRI** has mushroomed as a package venue for Germans and Italians since the mid-1990s, when the Orthodox Church elected to sell up its vast holdings here. You could stop for a meal at *Mourella*, far and away the best **taverna** here, and have a swim. But there's little local character remaining, so you'll most likely choose to continue 4km to **YENNÁDHI**, the only sizeable settlement on this coast, served by up to six buses daily. The older village core inland offers various amenities including **car rental**, a **post office**, some rooms (try *Betty Studios* by the pharmacy; ☎22440 43020; ❹) and a few **tavernas**; best of these is *Klimis*, one of three behind the seemingly endless sand-and-gravel beach, with good house wine, *mayireftá* and occasional fish grills.

From Yennádhi, a good road heads 7km inland, past baby pines slowly greening a fire-blasted landscape, to the oasis village of **VÁTI**. Here, much the superior of two **tavernas** is *To Petrino*, also doubling as the central *kafenío*; it's not cheap, but the quality of such country-style offerings as spicy *revíthia* soup, *hórta*, roast suckling pig and chocolate cake is such that mainly Greeks attend, especially at weekends (lunch and supper).

Some 10km south of Yennádhi, and 2km inland, **LAHANIÁ** village with its **hotel** of the same name (☎22440 46821; ❷) and smattering of private rooms makes another possible base. Abandoned after a postwar earthquake, since the 1980s its older houses have been mostly occupied and renovated by Germans on long-term lease agreements. On the main *platía* at the lower, eastern end of the village, the *Platanos* taverna has decent food and seating between the church and two wonderful fountains, one with an Ottoman inscription.

You can go directly from Lahaniá to **Plimýri**, an attractive sandy bay backed by dunes, with swimming in the clean, brisk water marred only by strong afternoon winds; the only facility is the indifferent **taverna** *Plimirri Beach* with mostly farmed fish on the menu, next to the **church of Zoödhóhou Piyís** (interior open May–Oct Sun only noon–5pm) which has ancient columns upholding its vaulted porch. Beyond Plimýri the road curves inland to **KATTAVIÁ**, over 100km from the capital, marooned amidst grain fields; the village, like so many in the south, is three-quarters deserted, the owners of the closed-up houses off working in Australia or North America.

There are a few **rooms** to rent, a vital **filling station** and several **tavernas** at the junction that doubles as the *platía* – most interesting of these are the brightly coloured *Martine's Bakaliko/Mayeriko* (closed Thurs), run by folk from Lahanía, which has some vegetarian dishes and attempts to use local organic ingredients when possible.

From Kattaviá a paved road leads on to **Prassoníssi**, Rhodes' southernmost extremity and a mecca for European **windsurfers**. The sandspit which tethers Prassoníssi ("Leek Island") to Rhodes was partially washed away by storms early in 1998, but enough remains to create flat water on the east side and up to two-metre waves on the west, ideal for different ability levels. Of the two **windsurfing schools** operating here, Polish-run Prasonisi Center (April–Oct; ☎22440 91044, ⓦwww.windsurfing-rodos.com) is keener and friendlier. They're geared up for one-week packages, and lodge their clients in one of the half-dozen food and accommodation outfits further inland. One which has been recommended for walk-in service, despite a sizeable allotment to the surf schools, is *Faros/Lighthouse Taverna Rooms to Let* (☎22440 91030, ⓦwww .lighthouse-hotel.com; ❺).

The far southwest

From Lahaniá it's also possible to head 9km northwest along a narrow paved road to the picturesque hilltop village of **MESANAGRÓS**. This already existed in some form by the fifth century AD, if foundations of a ruined basilica at the village outskirts are anything to go by. A smaller thirteenth-century chapel squats amidst mosaic-floor patches of the larger, earlier church, with a *hokhláki* floor and stone barrel arches (key from the nearby *kafenío*).

The onward road to Skiádhi monastery, 6km distant, is shown incorrectly on most maps. Take the Kattaviá-bound road initially, then bear right onto an unsigned dirt track after about 2km; the last 4km are quite badly surfaced. Known formally as Panayía Skiadhení, **Skiádhi monastery** – despite its undistinguished modern buildings – was founded in the thirteenth century to house a miraculous icon of the Virgin; in the fifteenth century a heretic stabbed the painting, and blood flowed from the wound in the Mother of God's cheek. The offending hand was, needless to say, instantly paralyzed; the fissure, and intriguing brown stains around it, are still visible. The immediate surroundings of the monastery are rather dreary since a fire in 1992, but the views west are stunning. Tiny **Khteniá** islet is said to be a petrified pirate ship, rendered into stone by the Virgin in answer to prayers from desperate locals. Except on September 7–8, the festival of the icon, you can stay the night by arrangement with the caretaker.

West of Kattaviá, the paved island loop road emerges onto the deserted, sandy southwest coast; Skiádhi can also be reached from this side as well, by another dirt road. Only strong swimmers should venture far offshore here, as it's exposed and tricky currents are the rule.

The nearest village is nondescript, agricultural **APOLAKKIÁ**, 7km north of the Skiádhi turning and equipped with **tavernas** popular among bike-tourers. Northwest, the road leads to Monólithos, while the northeasterly bearing leads quickly and pleasantly back to Yennádhi via Váti. Due north, just below an irrigation reservoir, the tiny frescoed Byzantine chapel of **Áyios Yeóryios Várdhas** (unlocked) is well worth the four-kilometre detour if you have your own transport.

Hálki

Hálki, a tiny (20 square kilometres), waterless, limestone speck west of Rhodes, is a fully fledged member of the Dodecanese, though all but about three hundred of the former population of three thousand emigrated (mostly to Rhodes or to Florida) in the wake of a devastating sponge blight during the early 1900s. Despite a renaissance through tourism in recent years, the island is tranquil compared with its big neighbour, with a slightly weird, subdued atmosphere owing to foreigners in their villas vastly outnumbering locals for much of the year. The big event of the day is the arrival of the regular afternoon *kaïki* from Kámiros Skála on Rhodes.

Hálki first attracted outside attention in 1983, when **UNESCO** designated it the "isle of peace and friendship" and the seat of regular international youth conferences. Some 150 crumbling houses were to be restored at UNESCO's expense as accommodation for delegates, but by 1987 just one hotel had been completed, and the only sign of "peace and friendship" was a stream of UNESCO and Athenian bureaucrats staging musical binges under the rubric of "ecological seminars". Confronted with an apparent scam, the islanders sent UNESCO packing and engaged two UK package operators (Laskarina and Direct Greece) to complete restorations and bring in paying guests. There is now in fact a third tour company present (CV Travel), and most of the ruins have been refurbished to the specifications of these companies.

Emborió

The skyline of **EMBORIÓ**, the island's port and only habitation, is pierced by the tallest freestanding clocktower in the Dodecanese and, a bit further north, the belfry of Áyios Nikólaos church. Emborió's restored houses are pretty much block-booked from April to October by the tour companies mentioned; independent travellers will be lucky to find anything at all on spec, even early or late in the season. Nonpackage **accommodation**, all requiring advance reservations, includes the delightful, en-suite *Captain's House* (☏22460 45201; ❷), which has the feel of an old French country hotel and whose English manageress Christine can point you in likely directions if she's full; *Pension Keanthi* (☏22460 45334; ❷), near the school, offering bland, pine-furnished rooms with high ceilings plus a few galleried studios (❸); and the municipally owned *Hotel Halki* (☏22460 49390; ❸) in the old sponge factory on the south side of the bay, which has chronic management and structural problems, most recent years operating summer only if at all. Of the half-dozen **tavernas** along the field-stoned, pedestrianized waterfront, *Remezzo* (aka *Takis*) is excellent for *mayireftá* and pizzas, *Maria* behind the post office has good grills, the Georgian-Greek-run place next to the *Steki* bar has some unusual dishes, while *Houvardas*, near the north end of the quay has proven reliable for *mayireftá* over the years. Amongst a similar number of bars and cafés, the standout has to be *Soula's* (aka "The Parrot Bar" after resident birds), near the base of the jetty, with puddings and home-made ice cream to die for. There's a **post office**, four well-stocked stores, two good bakeries cranking out a range of bread and pies, plus two **travel agencies** that sell boat tickets and change money (there's no bank or ATM); one of them, Zifos Travel (☏22460 45028, ✉zifos-travel @rho.forthnet.gr) often has a few vacancies amongst studios which they hold back from the UK companies.

The rest of the island

Three kilometres west lies the old pirate-safe village of **HORIÓ**, abandoned in the 1950s but still crowned by the Knights' castle. Except during the major August 14–15 festival, the church here is kept securely locked to protect its frescoes. Across the valley, the little monastery of **Stavrós** is the venue for the other big island bash on September 14. There's little else to see or do inland, though you can spend three hours **walking** across the island on the eight-kilometre road finally paved in 2002, as the extension of the cement "Tarpon Springs Boulevard" donated by the expatriate community in Florida. At the end (best arrange a ride out, and walk back) you'll reach the monastery of **Ayíou Ioánnou Prodhrómou**; the caretaker there can put you up in a cell (except around August 29, the other big festival date), but you'll need to bring supplies. The terrain en route is monotonous, but compensated by views over half the Dodecanese and Turkey.

Longish but narrow **Póndamos**, fifteen minutes' walk west of Emborió, is the only sandy beach on Hálki, and even this has had to be artificially supplemented. The sole facility is the somewhat pricey *Nick's Pondamos Taverna*, serving lunch daily, plus supper four evenings weekly. Small and pebbly **Yialí**, west of and considerably below Horió via a jeep track, lies an hour's hike away from Póndamos. A thirty-minute walk north of Emborió lies **Kánia**, with a rocky foreshore and a rather industrial ambience from both power lines and the island's only petrol pump to one side.

Since these three coves are no great shakes, it's worth signing on at Emborió quay for **boat excursions** to more remote beaches. More or less at the centre of Hálki's southern shore, directly below Horió's castle, **Trahiá** consists of two coves to either side of an isthmus; you can (just) reach this overland by rough path – soon to be bulldozed into a track – from Yialí. North-coast beaches figuring as excursion-boat destinations include the pretty fjord of **Aréta**, **Áyios**

Yeóryios just beyond, and the remote double bay of **Dhýo Yialí**. Of these, Aréta is the most attractive, and the only one accessible overland (90min one way) by experienced hillwalkers equipped with the *Chalki, Island of Peace and Friendship* map based on the old Italian topographical survey sheet.

Alimniá (Alimiá) islet

One of the more promoted local boat excursions visits **Alimniá (Alimiá) islet**, roughly halfway between Hálki and Rhodes. Despite more well-water and greenery and a better harbour than Hálki's, the deserted village here, overlooked by a few palm trees and yet another Knights' castle, was completely abandoned by the 1960s. The locals were initially deported during World War II after they admitted to assisting British commandos sent in April 1944 to sabotage the enemy submarines who used the deep harbour here. The seven commandos themselves were captured on the spot by the Nazis, bundled off first to Rhodes, then to Thessaloníki, where six were summarily executed as spies rather than regular prisoners of war; future Austrian premier and UN Secretary General Kurt Waldheim allegedly countersigned their death sentences.

Interesting history acknowledged, Alimniá is probably not a place you'd want to be stuck for an entire day. Excursions on offer are pricey (about €23, picnic lunch included), beach space very limited, the castle a hot, 45-minute walk up (the best thing to do here) and the crumbling village behind its salt marsh unedifying. If you snorkel in the outer bay beyond little Áyios Minás monastery, you might glimpse outlines of the Italian-built submarine pens to one side of the deep bay. The former inhabitants only show up to graze livestock, or on April 23, for the annual festival (Áyios Yeóryios).

Kastellórizo (Meyísti)

Kastellórizo's official name, Meyísti (biggest), seems more a stance of defiance than a statement of fact. While the largest of a tiny group of islands, it is actually the smallest of the Dodecanese, over seventy nautical miles from its nearest Greek neighbour (Rhodes) but barely more than a nautical mile off the Turkish coast at the narrowest straits. At night its lights are quite outnumbered by those of the Turkish town of Kaş, which lies across the bay and with whom Kastellórizo generally has excellent relations.

During the island's heyday (roughly 1860–1910) almost 10,000 people lived here, supported by a fleet of schooners that transported goods, mostly timber, from the Greek towns of Kalamaki (now Kalkan) and Andifelos (Kaş) on the Anatolian mainland opposite. But the withdrawal of island autonomy after the 1908 "Young Turk" revolution, the Italian seizure of the other Dodecanese (but not Kastellórizo) in 1912 and an inconclusive 1913–15 revolt against the Turks sent the island into decline. A French occupation of 1915–21 prompted destructive shelling from the Ottoman-held mainland, a harbinger of worse to come (see overleaf). Shipowners failed to modernize their fleets upon the advent of steam power, preferring to sell ships to the British for the Dardanelles campaign, and the new frontier between the island and republican Turkey, combined with the expulsion of all Anatolian Greeks in 1923, deprived any remaining vessels of their trade. During the 1930s the island enjoyed a brief renaissance when it became a major stopover point for French, British and Italian seaplanes, but events at the close of World War II put an end to any hopes of the island's continued viability.

When Italy capitulated to the Allies in the autumn of 1943, a few hundred Commonwealth commandos occupied Kastellórizo, departing of their own accord in spring 1944 – leaving the island deserted and vulnerable to the attentions of pirates. In early July, a harbour fuel dump caught (or was set on) fire and an adjacent arsenal exploded, taking with it more than half of the two thousand houses on Kastellórizo. Even before these events most of the population had left for Rhodes, Athens, Australia (especially Perth) and North America. Today there are just 342 official residents here by the last census (with only about 250 actually living permanently on Kastellórizo), largely maintained by remittances from over 30,000 emigrants and by subsidies from the Greek government, which fears that the island will revert to Turkey should their numbers diminish any further.

Yet Kastellórizo has a future of sorts, thanks partly to expat "Kassies" who have begun renovating their crumbling ancestral houses as retirement or holiday homes. Each summer, the population is swelled by returnees of Kassie ancestry, who occasionally celebrate traditional weddings in the **Áyios Konstandínos** cathedral at Horáfia, which incorporates ancient columns from Patara in Asia Minor. Access has also improved since the late 1980s: an airport (domestic flights only) was completed, larger aircraft laid on in 2003, and the harbour dredged to accommodate larger ferries, though the island has yet to be designated an official port of entry to Greece, which causes problems for both yachties and conventional travellers crossing from Turkey.

Perhaps the biggest boost in the island's fortunes, however, was serving as the location for the Italian film *Mediterraneo*, winner of the Oscar for Best Foreign Film in 1992, which has resulted in substantial numbers of Italian midsummer visitors (though the island in fact gets a broad spectrum of tourists). You will either love Kastellórizo and stay a week, or crave escape after a day; its detractors dismiss the island as a human zoo maintained by the Greek government for the edification of nationalists, while partisans celebrate an atmospheric, barely commercialized outpost of Hellenism.

Kastellórizo Town

The current population is concentrated in the northern town of **KASTELLÓRIZO** – supposedly the finest natural harbour between Beirut and Fethiye on the Turkish coast – and its little "suburb" of **Mandhráki**, just over the fire-blasted hill with its half-ruined Knights' castle. Its outer bulwark now houses the worthwhile local **museum** (Tues–Sun 7am–2.30pm; free), with displays including plates from a Byzantine shipwreck, frescoes rescued from decaying rural churches and a reconstruction of an ancient basilica on the site of today's gaudy, crumbling Áyios Yeóryios Santrapé church at Horáfia. Just below and beyond the museum, in the cliff-face opposite Psorádhia islet, is Greece's only **Lycian house-tomb**; it's well signposted from the shoreline walkway, up some steps beside the first wooden lamp standard.

Most of the town's surviving mansions are ranged along the waterfront, their tiled roofs, wooden balconies and blue or green shutters on long, narrow windows having obvious counterparts in the originally Greek-built houses of Kalkan and Kaş just across the water. Just one or two streets back, however, many properties are derelict – abandonment having succeeded where the World War I shelling, a 1926 earthquake and the 1944 explosions failed; sepia-toned posters and black-and-white postcards on sale of the town in its prime are poignant evidence of its later decline.

Practicalities

A single **bank**, with handy ATM, stands on the east quay; the **post office** is on the far side of the bay. The more reliable and competent of the town's two **travel agencies** is Papoutsis (☎22410 70630), which represents all ferries, and sells Olympic Aviation tickets. An eleven-seater **minibus** shuttles between town and airstrip at flight times (fare €1.50); excess passengers are accommodated in the lone **taxi**, which has to make two journeys, but it's likely another bus will soon be laid on to meet the larger aircraft.

It is possible to arrange a ride over **to Turkey** on one of four local boats, most reliably on Monday or Friday (8am departure). The standard day-return or one-way fee is €15, plus the cost of any visa required on the Turkish side, and you have to leave your passport with the authorities the day before. Although Kastellórizo is not yet a legal port of entry to Greece – it lacks a proper Schengen database computer, and customs stamps – police here cannot legally deny disembarkation to EU nationals arriving **from Kaş**, which is an official entry/exit point for Turkey.

Kastellórizo is not really geared up for large numbers of visitors, though **pensions** in the old houses have been upgraded to en-suite status, and prices have climbed sharply in recent years. If you're not met off the boat or airport shuttle-van, the best budget options include the large-roomed if basic *Pension Caretta* (☎22460 49028, ☞22460 49208; ❷), which also has a fine restored apartment (❸) for two, and the *Pension Asimina*, behind the arcaded Italian market (☎22460 49361; ❷). Excellent mid-range choices include *Karnayo* off the *platía* at the west end of the south quay (☎22460 49225, ☞22460 49266); air-conditioned rooms (❹), studios (❹) and an apartment sleeping four spread over two sensitively restored buildings, all wood and stone with furniture in matching taste. Also in this range, all the way round at the north end of the west quay, the *Pension Mediterraneo* (☎22460 49007 or 697 36 76 038, ⓦwww.mediterraneopension.org; ❸) has simple rooms well furnished with mosquito nets and wall art, half with sea view, plus an arcaded basement suite (❺) and optional breakfast with proprietress Marie's home-made marmalade. Relative luxury is available at the air-conditioned *Kastellorizo Hotel Apartments* (☎22460 49044, ⓦwww.kastellorizohotel.gr; ❺–❻), on the opposite side of the bay from the ferry jetty, offering quality-fitted studios or galleried maisonettes, some with sea view.

Apart from fish, goat meat and wild-fig preserves, plus whatever can be smuggled over from Kaş, Kastellórizo has to import foodstuffs and drinking water from Rhodes; prices when eating out can consequently be higher than usual, with the further pretext of the island's celebrity status. The two most conspicuous waterfront **tavernas** are not recommended – it's best to continue a few steps to *Tò Mikró Parisi* for affordable, and more likely fresher, seafood and meat grills. Other good quayside choices include *Kaz-Bar* (mid-May to mid-Oct) to the right of the market, where chef Colin and his mother preside over a chip-free zone, serving lots of greens, tabbouleh, spring rolls, chicken wings and other light dishes appropriate for summer; and the inexpensive but savoury *Akrothalassi*, purveying large grills and salads near the west end of the quay, by the church – it's popular at lunch, as they've the only shaded seating. One to recommend inland (still adorned with film posters – it served as the canteen for the *Mediterraneo* film crew) is *Ta Platania* (June to mid-Oct), opposite Áyios Konstandínos in Horáfia, good for daily-changing *mayireftá* (moussaka, green beans) and desserts, often home-made. There are more puddings and good breakfasts at *Zaharoplastio Iy Meyísti*, back on the waterfront. **Nightlife** spills out of the half-dozen *barákia* lining the quay, occasionally ending up in the water when tipplers overbalance at their tables.

The rest of the island

Kastellórizo's austere hinterland is predominantly bare rock, flecked with stunted vegetation; incredibly, two or three generations ago much of the countryside was carefully tended, producing wine of some quality and in quantity. A rudimentary paved road system links points between Mandhráki and the airport, plus there's an ugly new dirt track opened by the army to Áyios Stéfanos, but there aren't many specific places on it to visit and no scooters for rent. Karstic cliffs drop sheer to the sea, offering no anchorage for boats except at the main town, Mandhráki and Návlakas fjord (see below).

Rural monasteries and ruins

Heat permitting, you can hike up the obvious, zigzag stair-path, then south through fire-charred scrub to the rural **monastery of Ayíou Yeoryíou toú Vounioú**, 35 minutes away. The sixteenth-to-eighteenth-century church boasts fine rib-vaulting and a carved *témblon*, but its highlight is a crypt, with the frescoed, subterranean chapel of **Áyios Harálambos** off to one side; access is via a steep, narrow passage descending from the church floor – bring a torch and grubby clothes, and get the key first from Kostas the keeper, who lives behind the *Little Paris* taverna. Alternatively, a fifteen-minute track-walk west of the port leads to the peaceful monastery of **Ayías Triádhas**, perched on the saddle marked by the telecom tower, and an army base (off-limits) – one of many strongpoints which have sprouted here since the Ímia crisis (see p.577).

The onward path arrives after twenty minutes at the ancient citadel of **Paleókastro**, where you'll find masonry from Classical to medieval times, a warren of vaulted chambers, tunnels, cisterns plus another little monastery with a *hokhláki* courtyard. From any of the heights above town there are tremendous views north over sixty kilometres of Anatolian coast.

The shoreline and Rhó

Swimming is complicated by a total absence of decent beaches and an abundance of sea urchins and razor-sharp limestone reefs; the safest entries near town lie beyond the graveyard at Mandhráki and the cement jetty below the power plant at road's end – or people just dive from the lidos on the northwest quay. Once away from the shore, you're rewarded by clear waters with a rich variety of marine life. From Ayíou Yeoryíou toú Vounioú, you can continue 45 minutes further on foot, first on a useless modern bulldozer track, then on the original, French-built *kalderími*, to the multi-lobed fjord of **Návlakas**, a favourite mooring spot for yachts and fishing boats. The French built this cobbled way to facilitate offloading the components of a 120-millimetre gun battery here during World War I, safe from Ottoman artillery. Uniquely on Kastellórizo, this bay is sea-urchin-free, with freshwater seeps keeping the temperature brisk; there's superb snorkelling to 25-metre depths off the south wall.

Over on the southeast coast, accessible only by a 45-minute boat ride from town, the grotto of **Perastá** (Galázio Spílio) deserves a look for its stalactites and strange blue-light effects; the low entrance, negotiable only by inflatable raft, gives little hint of the enormous chamber within, with monk seals occasionally nesting in another adjacent cave. Ninety-minute rubber-raft trips (€8–10 depending on number of people) visit only the cave, or for about double that amount on a larger *kaïki*, you can take it in as part of a five-hour tour that includes Rhó islet.

Should you make the trip out to **Rhó**, the tomb of **Iý Kyrá tís Rhó** ("The Lady of Rhó"), aka Dhespina Akhladhiotis (ca. 1898–1982) – who resolutely hoisted the Greek flag each day on that islet in defiance of the Turks on the mainland – is the first thing you see when you dock at the sandy, northwestern harbour. From here a path heads southeast for 25 minutes to the islet's southerly port, past the side trail up to the intact Hellenistic fortress on the very summit. The islet has no facilities – just a few soldiers to prevent Turkish military landings or poachings of the hundreds of goats – so bring your own food and water.

Sými

Sými's most pressing problem, lack of fresh water, is in many ways also its saving grace. As with so many dry, rocky Dodecanese islands, water must be imported at great expense from Rhodes, pending completion of a reservoir in the distant future. Consequently, the island can't hope to support more than a handful of large hotels; instead, hundreds of people are shipped in daily during the season from Rhodes, relieved of their money and sent back. This arrangement suits both the Symiots and those visitors lucky enough to stay longer; many foreigners return regularly, or even own houses here.

Once beyond the inhabited areas, you'll find a surprisingly attractive island that has retained some forest cover of junipers, valonea oaks and even a few pines – ideal walking country in spring or autumn (though not midsummer, when temperatures are among the highest in Greece). Another prominent feature of the landscape are dozens of tiny monasteries, usually locked except on their patron saint's day, though their cisterns with a can on a string for fetching water are usually accessible.

Sými Town

SÝMI, the island's capital and only proper town, consists of **Yialós**, the excellent natural port, and **Horió**, on the hillside above. Incredibly, just over a century ago the place was richer and more populous (25,000) than Ródhos Town, its wealth generated by shipbuilding and sponge-diving, skills nurtured since pre-Classical times. Under the Ottomans, Sými, like most of the smaller Dodecanese, enjoyed considerable autonomy in exchange for a yearly tribute in sponges to the sultan; but the Italian-imposed frontier, the 1919–22 Greco-Turkish war, the advent of synthetic sponges and the gradual replacement of the crews by Kalymniots spelt doom for the local economy. Vestiges of past nautical glories remain in still-active boatyards at Pédhi and Haráni, but today the souvenir-shop sponges come entirely from overseas and, the recent boom notwithstanding, a significant number of the magnificent nineteenth-century mansions stands roofless and empty.

The approximately 2500 remaining Symiots are scattered fairly evenly throughout the mixture of Neoclassical and more typical island dwellings; despite the surplus of properties, many outsiders have preferred to build anew, rather than restore derelict shells accessible only by donkey or on foot. As on Kastellórizo, a wartime ammunition blast – this time set off by the retreating Germans – levelled hundreds of houses up in Horió. Shortly afterwards, the official Axis surrender of the Dodecanese to the Allies was signed here on May 8, 1945: a plaque marks the spot at the present-day *Restaurant Les Catherinettes*.

At the lively **port**, an architecturally protected area since the early 1970s, spice and sponge stalls plus a few jewellery shops throng with Rhodes-based

SÝMI

N

Nímos

Large Ferries

Hydrofoils
& Small Ferries

Análipsi ⛪

*Áyios
Isídhoros*

**Dhódheka
Spília** ⛪

Emborió *Haráni*

Tolí

**Taxiárhis Mihaḯl
Roukouniótis** ⛪

Sými

*Áyía
Marína*

Pédhi

*Áyios
Nikólaos*

**Áyios
Emilianós** ⛪

**Áyii
Anáryiri** ⛪

Maróni

Theológos ⛪

*Áyios Yeóryios
Dhyssálona*

**Áyios
Vassílios** ⛪

Lápathos

**Áyios
Prokópios** ⛪

Panayía Strateri ⛪

Nanoú

**Stavrós
Polémou** ⛪

**Megálos
Sotíros
(Nerás)** ⛪

**Byzantine
Wine Presses**

Marathoúnda

**Taxiárhis Mihaḯl
Panormítis** ⛪

0   5 km

trippers between 11am and 3.30pm, and the several excursion craft disgorging them envelop the quay with exhaust fumes. But just uphill, away from the water, the more peaceful pace of village life takes over, with livestock and chickens roaming free-range. Two massive stair-paths, the Kalí Stráta and Katarráktes, effectively deter many of the day-trippers and are most dramatic towards sunset; large, owl-haunted ruins along the lower reaches of the Kalí Stráta are lonely and sinister after dark, though these too are now undergoing restoration one by one.

A series of blue arrows through Horió leads to the excellent local **museum** (Tues–Sun 8.30am–2.30pm; €2). Housed in a fine old mansion at the back of the village, the collection concentrates on Byzantine and medieval Sými, with exhibits on frescoes in isolated, locked churches and a gallery of medieval icons, as well as antiquarian maps and the inevitable ethnographic wing. The nearby **Hatziagapitos Mansion** has been refurbished as an annexe; here, wonderful carved wooden chests are the main exhibits, along with fragmentary wall-paintings. On the way back to central Horió, the nineteenth-century pharmacy, with its apothecary jars and wooden drawers labelled for exotic herbal remedies, is worth a look.

At the very pinnacle of things, a **Knights' castle** occupies the site of Sými's ancient acropolis, and you can glimpse a stretch of Classical polygonal wall on one side. A dozen churches grace Horió; that of the Assumption, inside the fortifications, is a replacement of the one blown to bits when the Germans detonated the munitions cached there. One of the bells in the new belfry is the nose-cone of a thousand-pound bomb, hung as a memorial.

Practicalities

Two **catamarans** and a **hydrofoil** run daily to Sými from Ródhos Town, departing at least morning and late afternoon – sometimes evening too – on an *epivatikó* (scheduled service) basis. There are also daily departures on a more expensive *ekdhromikó* (excursion) basis at 9am, returning 3.45pm, but note that you're forbidden from taking large luggage on these. The *epivatiká* dock at Yialós's new south quay, conveniently near the taxi and bus stops, while the *ekdhromiká* all use the old north mooring by the clocktower. The hydrofoil *Aigli* leaves Mandhráki port in Rhodes at 7am, 10.30am or 5pm, takes 55 minutes to arrive, and costs about €10. Both Sými-based catamarans (*Symi II* and *Panormitis*), as well as the *Dodekanisos Express*, use the central Kolóna harbour of Rhodes, taking about the same time for the crossing and costing slightly less than the hydrofoil; the *Panormitis* (most days either at 9am or 6pm) is your more likely craft. A few times a week there are also mainline ferries in either direction, typically the cheapest of all (1hr 40min journey time). ANES, the outlet for *Panormitis/Symi II/Aigli* tickets, maintains a booth on the quay and an office in the marketplace lanes (☎22460 71444). Among **ferry** agents, DANE Lines and the *Dodekanisos Express* catamaran is handled by Symi Tours nearby (☎22460 71307).

There's no official tourism bureau, but the island's English-language advertiser-newsletter, *The Symi Visitor* (free; ⓦ www.symivisitor.com), is literate and has current island gossip with informative features. The **post office** in the official Italian "palace" is open standard hours; of the two **banks**, the Alpha is more efficient and has a ATM. During the season a small green **bus** (€0.70 flat fare) shuttles between Yialós and Pédhi via Horió on the hour (returning at the half-hour) until 11pm. There are also six **taxis** (allow €3 Yialós–Horió with baggage), and two pricey outlets for **motor-scooter** (minimum €18–24 daily) and **car rental** (a whopping €58–70 daily), though this is a perfect island for boat and walking excursions. A **laundry** operates in the grid of market lanes, resorted to by those whose hosts forbid washing clothes in rooms.

Accommodation

Accommodation for independent travellers is somewhat limited and proprietors tend not to meet arriving boats, though the situation isn't nearly so bad as on Hálki. Studios, rather than simple rooms, predominate, and package operators control most of these, though curiously you may have an easier time finding spots in July/August than during spring/autumn, considered the most pleasant seasons here. Despite asphyxiating summer heat, air conditioning and ceiling fans are rarely found – go for north-facing and/or balconied units when possible. If you're planning in advance, the *Symi Visitor* website (see above) is worth consulting.

Ο ΆΓΙΟΣ ΓΕΩΡΓΙΟΣ

△ Icon in shop, Rhodes

Albatros Marketplace ☎22460 71707 or 22460 71829. Partial sea views from this exquisite, small hotel; pleasant second-floor breakfast salon and air con. ❸

Aliki Haráni quay ☎22460 71665, ⊛www .simi-hotelaliki.gr. A complete overhaul of an 1895 mansion, and Sými's poshest hotel: tasteful rooms with wood floors and some antique furnishings, and large bathrooms, though only some have sea views. Breakfast included in price. ❻

Anastasia Behind the post office ☎22460 71364. Pleasantly set hotel, though with limited harbour views, this has parquet-floored rooms plus a couple of studios, with some package allotment however. ❸

Fiona At the top of the Kalí Stráta ☎22460 72088. Mock-traditional hotel building whose large airy rooms have double beds and stunning views; breakfast in mid-air on common balcony. ❹

Jean Manship C/o Jean & Tonic Bar ☎ & ⓕ02460 71819 8pm–1am Greek time. Jean manages three traditional houses in Horió, suitable for couples (❸–❹) or a group of up to six (€90 for the whole house), with stunning views.

Katerina Tsakiris Rooms Horió ☎22460 71813. Just a handful of very plain en-suite rooms with shared kitchen and grandstand view; reservations essential. ❸–❹

Kokona Rear of town, by church and quiet square ☎22460 71549, ⓕ22460 72620. Small hotel with just eight basic rooms (2 air con), though most have balconies and there's a breakfast patio by the belfry. ❹

Les Catherinettes Above eponymous restaurant, north quay ☎22460 72698, ⓔmarina-epe @rho.forthnet.gr. Creaky but spotless en-suite pension in a historic building with painted ceilings and sea-view balconies for most rooms; discounts for longer stays. ❸–❹

Niriidhes Apartments On Haráni–Emborió road, 2km from Yialós ☎22460 71784, ⓔnirapart@otenet.gr. Spacious if plain, 1994-built apartments spread over four buildings on a quiet, east-facing slope. Air con, phones, "private" beach below, friendly management; most units accommodate four people. ❺

Symi Visitor Accommodation ☎22460 72755, ⊛www.symivisitor.com. Managed by affable returned Greek-Australian Nikos Halkitis and partner Wendy Wilcox, who offer a variety of houses restored as double-occupancy studios in prime locations of Horió. Rates range from ❹ at The Cottages to ❻ at The Mule House, by way of ❺ at Vassilis; they also have pricier units such as the Villa Harani suitable for four to five persons.

Taxiarhis Apartments Edge of Horió overlooking Pédhi ☎22460 72012, ⓕ22460 72013. Secluded, well-designed row of studios and one-bedroom apartments with common areas and balconies, though some package patronage. Breakfast on request. ❹–❺

Villa Symeria Up the Kalí Stráta (contact Albatros Hotel). Restored mansion comprising two apartments with either air con or fans, suitable for up to four and six persons respectively. ❻

Eating and drinking

You're best off avoiding most **eateries** on the north and west quays of the port, where menus, ingredients, prices and attitudes have been terminally warped by the day-trip trade. Away from these areas, you've a fair range of choice among *kultúra* tavernas, old-style *mayireftá* places, a few genuine *ouzerís* and even a traditional *kafenío* or two.

Dhimitris South quay, near ferry mooring. Excellent, family-run seafood-stressing *ouzerí* with exotic items such as *hokhlióalo* (sea snails), *foúskes*, *spinóalo* and the indigenous miniature shrimps, along with the more usual dishes and lots of vegetarian starters.

Haritomeni Northeast edge of Horió, about halfway up the hill in kink of the road above Yialós filling station ☎22460 71686. Superb *ouzerí* with such fare as pork cheeks, *mydhopílafo* (mussels in rice), artichokes in egg-lemon sauce, stuffed aubergines and snails. Open all year: lovely terrace with views in summer, fireplace interior in winter. Reserve in peak season.

To Kantirimi North side main square, Yialós. A

good source of pancake or waffle breakfasts under the trees; becomes a snack café/bar later in the day.

Lefteris Top of the Kalí Stráta where it levels off into a small *platía*, Horió. The local characters' *kafenío*, well attended by all. The place for a coffee or an ice cream at any hour.

O Meraklis Rear of the bazaar. Polite service and fair portions of well-priced *mayireftá*, fresh fish and *mezédhes* make this a reliable bet April–Dec. Sample meal: beans, beets, dips, and roast lamb with potatoes as a tender main course.

Mythos South quay between bus and taxi stops, Yialós. Supper-only *ouzerí* that's reckoned among the best, and best-value, cooking on the island.

There is a menu, but let chef Stavros hit you with his Frenchified medley which includes salad, seafood starters (squid in basil sauce), duck with juniper berries, lamb slices, and home-made desserts. Budget €19–23 a head before dipping into the decent wine list. There's a roof-terrace annexe (*Akataion*; July–Sept), specializing in Italian dishes, about 150m down the quay. Credit cards accepted; open Easter–Oct.

Pahos West quay (no sign). The old-boys' *kafenío*, in operation since World War II, and still a classic spot for a sundown ouzo and people-watching.

Pahos himself has retired and can often be found sitting out front as a customer; otherwise it's unchanged.

Yiorgos Near top of Kalí Stráta in Horió. Jolly, much-loved institution maintaining consistent food quality since 1977, with summer seating on a pebble-mosaic courtyard. Service can be slipshod, and prices have crept up to Yialós levels, but perennial recipes include feta-stuffed peppers, spinach-rice, chicken in mushroom-wine sauce, and grilled fish when available. Open random lunchtimes in season, supper all year (indoors in winter).

Nightlife

Nightlife continues into the early hours and is somewhat biased towards Yialós. Up in Horió, convivial *Jean & Tonic* is the heart and soul of the bar scene, catering to a mixed clientele (visitors and expats until 3am, Greek restaurateurs 3am until dawn) most of the year; a short way down the Kalí Stráta, *Kali Strata* is a low-key place with unbeatable views and excellent, wide-ranging music. Down at Yialós, the *Harani Club* has the nicest interior and a mix of Greek and international music depending on the crowd; in the same alley, *Vapori* was the first outsider-owned bar here (in 1983), and continues the tradition with newspapers draped over chairs, breakfasts, and **Internet** access (three terminals). Elsewhere, *Katoi* on the south quay is a no-hassle bar favoured by locals, whilst *The Club* on the *platía* functions between midnight and dawn, and has a pool table. On the road to Pédhi, *Alethini* hosts live Greek music most Saturday nights from 11pm.

Around the island

Sými has no big sandy beaches, but there are plenty of pebbly stretches at the heads of the deep, protected bays which indent the coastline. **PÉDHI**, a short bus ride down from Horió, retains some of its former identity as a fishing hamlet, with enough water in the plain behind – the island's largest – to support a few vegetable gardens. The beach is poor, though, and patronage from yachts and the giant, overpriced *Pedhi Beach* hotel has considerably bumped up prices at several local **tavernas**, of which the most reasonably priced and authentic is fish specialist *Tolis*, tucked away by the boatyard at the north corner of the bay. Many will opt for another twenty minutes of walking via a rough but obvious path along the south shore of the almost landlocked bay to **Áyios Nikólaos**. The only all-sand cove on Sými, this offers sheltered swimming, tamarisks for shade and a mediocre taverna. Alternatively, a paint-splodge-marked path on the north side of the inlet leads in half an hour to **Ayía Marína**, where there's a minuscule beach, a shingle lido with sunbeds, a rather posh taverna-bar complete with lawn, and a monastery-capped islet to which you can easily swim.

Around Yialós, you'll find tiny Sými Paradise "beach" (still called **NOS** or Navtikós Ómilos Sýmis by most) ten minutes past the boatyards at Haráni, but there's sun here only until lunchtime – not a bad thing in high summer. You can continue along the cement-paved coast road, with steps leading down to rock slabs favoured by nudists, or cut inland from the Yialós *platía* past the abandoned desalination plant, to appealing **Emborió** (Nimborió) Bay, with a recently improved **taverna** (*Metapontis*) and an artificially sand-strewn beach a bit beyond. Inland from this lie Byzantine mosaic fragments under a protective shelter (follow signs to "Early Christian Basilica"), and, nearby, a catacomb complex known locally as **Dhódheka Spília**.

Plenty of other, more secluded coves are accessible by energetic walkers with sturdy footwear, or those prepared to pay a modest sum for the taxi-boats (daily in season 10am–1pm, returning 4–6pm; one-way fares available to the nearer bays cited above). These are the best method of reaching the southern bays of **Marathoúnda** and **Nanoú**, and the only method of getting to the spectacular fjord of **Áyios Yeóryios Dhyssálona**. Dhyssálona lacks a taverna and lies in shade after 1pm, while Marathoúnda is fringed by coarse, slimy pebbles (though it has a full-service taverna), making Nanoú the most popular destination for day-trips. The 200-metre beach there consists of gravel, sand and small pebbles, with a scenic backdrop of pines and a reasonable taverna (menu of squid, chips and salad) just behind. It's also possible to reach Nanoú overland, via Panayía Stateri chapel up on the main trans-island road, descending a scenic, forested gorge for some forty minutes; most of the old path from Horió to Panayía Stateri still exists, making a marvellous traverse of about three hours in total, leaving time for a meal and swim at Nanóu before the boat trip back to Yialós (at 4pm in the cooler months).

For more hiking adventures, you can cross the island from Horió in ninety minutes to **Áyios Vassílios**, the most scenic of the gulfs with its namesake little monastery and **Lápathos** beach; in about the same time to **Tolí**, a deserted, west-facing cove, also accessible from Emborió; or in three hours, partly through forest, from Yialós to **Áyios Emilianós** at the island's extreme west end, where another little monastery is tethered to the body of Sými by a causeway. On the way to the latter you should look in at the monastery of **Taxiárhis Mihaïl Roukouniótis** (daily 9am–2pm & 4–8pm), Sými's oldest, with naïve eighteenth-century frescoes and a peculiar ground plan: the current *katholikón* is actually superimposed on a lower, thirteenth-century structure abandoned after being burnt and pillaged by pirates during the 1400s, though a fine fresco of St Lawrence (Áyios Lavréntios) survives behind the altar screen. Resident, trilingual Father Amfilohios will gladly tell you anything else you might possibly wish to know about the place. However, the best frescoes on the island, of early-eighteenth-century vintage, are found at the monastery of **Megálos Sotíros**, on the road south to Panormítis, just before the drop down the escarpment. There's a resident keeper here, so the *katholikón* is usually open, in the middle of the arcaded, pebble-paved courtyard. The frescoes inside, devoted unsurprisingly to the life of the Saviour (*Sotír* in Greek), include a fine *Deposition*, with Joseph of Aramathea holding a winding sheet to receive the dead Christ, and a *Resurrection* with Jesus all but doing a jig on the sepulchre.

Panormítis monastery

The Archangel is also honoured at the huge monastery of **Taxiárhis Mihaïl Panormítis** near the southern tip of the island, Sými's biggest rural attraction and generally the first port of call for the excursion boats from Rhodes (confirm the itinerary if you wish to proceed direct to Yialós – some craft do). These allow only a quick thirty-minute tour; if you want more time, you'll have to come by scooter from Yialós (though the road down from the central escarpment is steep, with nine hairpin bends), or arrange to stay the night (€10 minimum donation) in the *xenónas* (inn) set aside for pilgrims. They monopolize it all summer, as Mihaïl has been adopted as the patron of sailors in the Dodecanese.

Like many of Sými's monasteries, Panormítis is of recent (eighteenth-century) vintage and was thoroughly pillaged during World War II, so don't expect too much of the building or its treasures. An appealing pebble-mosaic court surrounds the central *katholikón*, tended by the monk Gabriel and lit by an improbable number of oil lamps. It's also graced by a fine *témblon*, though the frescoes are recent and mediocre. One of the two small museums (€2 admits to both) contains a strange mix of precious antiques, exotic junk (stuffed crocodiles and koalas, elephant tusks), votive offerings, models of ships and a chair piled with messages-in-bottles brought here by Aegean currents – the idea being that if the bottle or toy boat arrived, the sender got their prayer answered. There's a small beach, a shop/*kafenío*, a bakery and a **taverna** (*Panormion*) popular with passengers of the many yachts calling in. Near the taverna stands a memorial commemorating three Greeks, including the monastery's abbot, executed in February 1944 by the Germans for aiding British commandos.

Tílos

The small, usually quiet island of **Tílos**, with an official population of about five hundred (dwindling to eighty in winter), is one of the least frequented and worst connected of the Dodecanese, though it can be visited on a day-trip by catamaran from Rhodes in peak season. Why anyone would want to come for just a few hours is unclear: while it's a great place to rest on the beach or go walking, there is nothing very striking at first glance. After a few days, however, you may have stumbled on several of the seven small **castles** of the Knights of St John which stud the crags, or found some of the inconspicuous medieval chapels clinging to the hillsides.

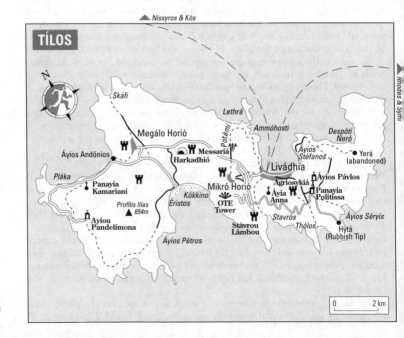

Tílos shares the characteristics of its closest neighbours: limestone **mountains** resembling those of Hálki, plus volcanic lowlands, pumice beds and red-lava sand as on Níssyros. Though rugged and scrubby on its heights, the island has ample water – from springs or pumped up from the agricultural plains – and clusters of oak and terebinth near the cultivated areas. From many points on the island you've startling views across to Kós, Sými, Turkey, Níssyros, Hálki, Rhodes and even (weather permitting) Kárpathos.

Since the mid-1990s, however, development on Tílos has threatened to reverse the conditions which many visitors have come to enjoy; besides the Dodge City atmosphere of Livádhia, a hyperactive bulldozing programme has scarred virtually every mountain in the east of the island. But a road from the telecom-tower hill, heading east along the summit ridge will thankfully not sully the beach at Áyios Séryis, where a fish-farm proposal is suspended indefinitely.

Getting around

Tílos's wide main road runs 7km from Livádhia, the port village, to Megálo Horió, the capital and only other significant habitation. A public **bus** links the two, and services are theoretically scheduled to coincide with ferry arrivals; at other times the sleek bus makes up to six runs daily along the Livádhia–Éristos stretch. There are also two **taxis**, or you can rent a **car** from outlets in Livádhia such as Drive and Tilos Travel. Stefanakis, also in Livádhia (℡ 22460 44310), has a monopoly on ferry tickets; Tilos Travel is arguably the more helpful, however (℡ 22460 44294, ⓦ www.tilostravel.co.uk), offering an accommodation booking service, boat excursions all season – providing there are sufficient passenger numbers – and scooter as well as car rental. For more active sea-going jaunts with kayaks or windsurfers, contact French-run Tilos Marine at Livádhia beach.

Many visitors come specifically to **walk**, assisted by the extremely accurate **map** prepared by Baz "Paris" Ward and sold locally – or by certified walking **guides** Iain and Lyn Fulton (℡ 22460 44128 or 694 60 54 593, ⓔ fulton@otenet.gr), who may take you on unusual itineraries not described or mapped in existing literature. A half-dozen critical sections of deteriorating trail or *kalderími* have been surveyed in preparation for cleaning and consolidation, so quality walking opportunities should improve in the future.

Livádhia

With its hastily paved streets, unfinished building sites and higgledy-piggledy layout, **LIVÁDHIA** makes a poor introduction to the island, but it remains the better equipped of the two settlements to deal with tourists, and is closer to the majority of remaining path-hikes. There are generally enough beds in the various **studios** and **hotels** to go around, but in peak season it's certainly worth phoning ahead. Truly budget options, dwindling by the year, are restricted to a few outfits on the shore just beyond the Italian "palace", for example *Galini* (aka *Paraskevi*; ℡ 22410 44280; ❷). Elsewhere along the bay lie newer, better-appointed choices: galleried, 2002-built *Blue Sky Apartments* above the ferry dock (apply to Tilos Travel; ❹); *Anastasia* (℡ 22460 44111; ❸), just behind the *Armenon* taverna, where a usual willingness to bargain offsets slightly small rooms, or *Pavlos and Nina* (℡ 22460 44011; ❸), overlooking the sea near the friendly *Eleni Beach Hotel* about halfway around the bay (℡ 22460 44062, ⓔ elenihtl@otenet.gr; ❹), whose large airy rooms require advance booking. The *Faros Hotel* (℡ 22460 44068; ❸) at the extreme end of Livádhia bay is widely praised for its calm atmosphere and hospitable managing family.

Inland, go for the well-appointed *Studios Irinna* (T 22410 44366; ❸), alias *Kula's*; or the *Hotel Irini* (T 22410 44293, F 22460 44238; W www .tilosholidays.gr; ❸–❹), 200m inland from mid-beach, with a popular pool, good breakfasts and pleasant lounge making up for somewhat small rooms. The same keen management has the *Studios Ilidi* on the west hillside (❹ for 2, ❺ for 4-person apartments).

Over a dozen **tavernas** operate around Livádhia in peak season; of these perhaps half merit consideration. Among the more authentic spots for a no-nonsense Greek feed are *Irina* (alias *Stefanos and Maria*), doling out inexpensive *mayireftá* right on the shore near the church; *Mihalis* with its popular garden tables, though quality varies and it's really best just for fish; *To Armenon* (alias *Nikos'*) on the shore road, an excellent and salubrious beach-taverna-cum-*ouzerí*, with octopus salad, white beans and the like; *Oniro* next door, for excellent grills; and inland on the way to *Armenon*, the cheap and cheerful *Oasis*, doing more competent grills and pizza in a secluded garden. For something different, go for French-Vietnamese-run *Calypso* on the west hillside (reserve on T 694 72 13 278; supper only), which excels at Creole-colonial dishes like *Martiniqueois* prawns *acras* or Vietnamese pork-and-mushroom vermicelli; vanilla custard, exotic rum-based cocktails and a cutting-edge music soundtrack round out the experience.

For **breakfast** (plus evening thin-crust pizzas and home-made desserts), Anglo-Italian *Joanna's Café*, just inland from the bakery is hard to beat, also with a long list of strong cocktails. *Iy Omonia*, under trees strung with light bulbs, near the post office, is the enduringly popular "traditional" alternative for a sundowner, breakfast or a tipple while waiting for a ferry, and also does inexpensive, generous *mezédhes*. Livelier, organized **nightlife** in or near Livádhia is limited to three bars: *Cafe Ino* on the shore near *Irina* for the trendy set, the *Bozi* at the far east end of the bay (nightly in summer, weekends otherwise) and a durable music pub in Mikró Horió (see below).

There's a **post office**, but as yet no bank or ATM, so come with sufficient cash or apply to either travel agency (Tilos Travel will do cash advances on plastic for a small commission, or currency exchange – sterling only). **Email** (but no Internet) facilities at Kosmos gift shop and several well-stocked **supermarkets** complete the roster of amenities.

Around Livádhia

From Livádhia you can walk an hour north along the obvious trail to the pebble bay of **Lethrá**, or in about the same time south on separate itineraries to the secluded coves of **Stavrós** or **Thólos**. The track to the former begins between the *Tilos Mare Hotel* and the *Castellania Apartments*, becoming a trail at the highest new house in the village; once up to the saddle with its paved road, you've a sharp drop to the beach – ignore over-eager cairning in the bed of the descending ravine, the true path is up on the right bank, indicated by red-painted surveyor's marks. The route to Thólos begins by the cemetery and the chapel of **Áyios Pandelímon** with its Byzantine *hokhláki* court, then curls around under the seemingly impregnable castle of **Agriosykiá**; from the saddle overlooking the descent to Thólos (25min; also surveyed in preparation for refurbishment), a route marked with cairns leads northwest to the citadel in twenty minutes. It's less than an hour's walk west, with some surviving path sections shortcutting the road curves, up to the ghost village of **Mikró Horió**, whose 1200 inhabitants left for Livádhia during the 1950s. The only intact structures are the church (locked except for the August 15 festival) and an old house which has been restored as a small-hours **music pub** and operates only during July and August, with a variable formula of Greek/foreign music, and a shuttle van laid on from the port.

Megálo Horió and Éristos

The rest of Tílos's inhabitants live in or near **MEGÁLO HORIÓ**, which has an enviable perspective over the vast agricultural *kámbos* stretching down to Éristos (see below), and is overlooked in turn by the vast castle of the Knights, containing a sixteenth-century chapel. The castle was built on the site of ancient Tílos, whose recycled masonry remains evident; reach it by a stiff, thirty-minute climb that begins on the lane behind the Ikonomou supermarket before threading its way through a vast jumble of cisterns, house foundations and derelict chapels – the remains of the much larger medieval Megálo Horió. Two more flanking fortresses stare out across the plain: the easterly one of **Messariá** helpfully marks the location of the **Harkadhió** cave (closed for ongoing excavations), where Pleiocene midget-elephant bones were discovered in 1971. A signposted 500-metre track goes there from the road, ending near a spring and modern amphitheatre (used for the summer festival) just below the cave-mouth, which was hidden for centuries until a World War II artillery barrage exposed it. The bones themselves have been transferred to a tiny, not very compelling **museum** in Megálo Horió, on the ground floor of the town hall (Mon–Fri 8am–2.30pm on application upstairs to the warden).

Best choices for **accommodation** in the village are the central *Milios Apartments* (☎22460 44204, ℻22460 442665; ❷–❸ depending on size) or *Studios Ta Elefandakia* (☎22460 44213; ❷), set among attractive gardens by the car park. The lone **taverna**, *Kastro*, has reasonable food and a terrace with views, but has proven unwelcoming to outsiders; there's a traditional **kafenío** by historic Taxiárhis church, and further up, the friendly, Athenian-run *Kafenio Ilakati* (late May to early Sept only; opens 7pm), with cakes and drinks.

South of and below Megálo Horió, signs direct you towards the three-kilometre paved side road to the long, pink-grey-sand **Éristos** beach, allegedly the island's best, though summer rubbish piles from rough campers can be disconcerting, and a reefy zone must be crossed entering the water. The far south end, where the reef recedes, is also a designated nudist zone, as are the two secluded, attractive coves at **Kókkino** south beyond the headland (accessible by path only). About halfway down the road on the right amongst the orchards is *Taverna-Rooms Tropikana* (☎22410 44020; ❶), nothing special in either respect, but the most reliable all-season venue for a snack near the beach. For more comfort, there's the *Eristos Beach Hotel* (☎22460 44024; ❸) – the rooms are good value, with a plusher (❹) annexe built in 2002.

The far northwest

The main road beyond Megálo Horió hits the coast again at somewhat grim **ÁYIOS ANDÓNIOS**, whose main bright spot is a **taverna**, the *Dhelfini*, packed at weekend lunch because of its fresh fish and frequented otherwise by the local fishermen. The remoter alternative, *Elpidha*, has fresh, basically presented squid or cuttlefish, and not much else. At low tide on the exposed, average beach you can find more lava-trapped skeletons strung out in a row – human this time, presumably tide-washed victims of a Nissyrian eruption in 600 BC, and discovered by the same archeologists who found the miniature pachyderms.

There's better, warm-water swimming at isolated **Pláka** beach, 2km west of Áyios Andónios, where people camp rough despite a total lack of facilities. The paved road finally ends 8km west of Megálo Horió at the fortified **monastery of Ayíou Pandelímona** (daily: summer 10am–7pm, winter 10am–4pm), founded in the fifteenth century for the sake of its miraculous spring, still the best water on the island. The settlement hosts the island's major festival of July 25–27; otherwise a resident caretaker operates a small snack/drinks café. The monastery's tower-gate and oasis setting, more than two hundred forbidding metres above the west coast, are the most memorable features, though an eminently photogenic inner courtyard boasts a *hokhláki* surface, and the church a fine marble floor. On the south *katholikón* wall, an early eighteenth-century fresco shows the founder-builder holding a model of the monastery, while behind the ornate altar screen, in the conch, hides another rare fresco of the Holy Trinity.

The public bus calls here perhaps once or twice a day. To vary the **return to Megálo Horió**, you can walk back much of the way on a signposted path; it's shown correctly on Baz Ward's map (see p.327), and ends at the minor monastery of Panayía Kamarianí near Áyios Andónios. Committed and experienced hill-walkers can tackle the challenging path which curls around the southwest flank of Profítis Ilías, Tílos's highest mountain, finishing three hours later near Áyios Pétros cove, with a further half-hour track-walking to Éristos (allow 5hr with stops). This begins, as signposted, beside the monastery; it's a well-surveyed route, with no real exposure or sharp drops, but there's only one spring along the way, rather disheartening scree at the start, and the wild feel of a remote traverse on a much larger island.

Níssyros

Volcanic **Níssyros** is noticeably greener than its southern neighbours Tílos and Hálki, and unlike them has proven wealthy enough to retain over eight hundred of its population year-round (down, though, from 10,000 in 1900). While remittances from abroad (particularly Astoria, New York) are significant, most of the island's income is derived from the offshore islet of Yialí, where a vast lump of **pumice** is slowly being quarried away by Lava Ltd. The concession fee collected from Lava by the municipality has engendered a huge public payroll and vast per-capita sums available to spend, making Níssyros something of a mini-Kuwait. Under the circumstances, the Nissyrians bother little with agriculture other than keeping cows and pigs; the hillside terraces meticulously carved out for grain and grapes lie fallow, and wine is no longer made here.

The main island's peculiar geology is potentially a source of other benefits: DEI, the Greek power company, spent the years between 1988 and 1992 sinking exploratory **geothermal** wells and attempting to convince the islanders of the benefits of cheap electricity. In 1993, a local referendum went massively against the project, as did (by a closer margin) a 1997 poll, and DEI, together with its Italian contractor, took the hint and packed up. The desalination plant scarcely provides enough fresh water to spur a massive growth in package tourism; the relatively few tourists (mostly German) who stay the night, as opposed to the day-trippers from Kós, still find peaceful villages with a minimum of concrete eyesores and a friendly if rather tight-knit population.

Níssyros also offers good **walking** opportunities through a countryside planted with oak and terebinth, on a network of trails fitfully marked and maintained with EU money; you may hear the contented grunting of pigs as they gorge themselves on acorns from the many oak trees. Autumn is a wonderful time, especially when the landscape has perked up after the first rains; the late-January almond-blossoming is much reduced owing to the early-1990s blight that devastated the trees, which are now making a slow comeback.

Mandhráki

MANDHRÁKI is the deceptively large port and island capital, with blue patches of sea visible at the end of narrow streets lined with tightly packed houses, whose brightly painted balconies and shutters are mandated by law. Except for the tattier fringes near the ferry dock, where multiple souvenir shops and bad tavernas pitched at day-trippers leave a poor first impression, the bulk of the place is cheerful and village-like, arrayed around the community orchard or *kámbos* and overlooked by two ancient fortresses.

Into a corner of the nearer of these, the fourteenth-century Knights' castle, is wedged the little monastery of **Panayía Spilianí**, built on this spot in accordance with instructions from the Virgin, who appeared in a vision to one of the first Christian islanders. The monastery's prestige grew after raiding Saracens failed to discover the vast quantities of silver secreted here in the form of a rich collection of Byzantine icons. During 1996–97, the Langadháki area just below was rocked by a series of earthquakes, damaging a score of venerable houses (mostly repaired now); the seismic threat is ever present, quite literally cutting the ground out from under those who erroneously dub the volcano "extinct". A new combination archeological-ethnographical-historical **museum** has been built on the *kámbos* with money partly donated by the Nissyrian founder of the Vitex paint company, and should be ready for visitors by the end of 2004.

As a defensive bastion, the seventh-century-BC Doric **Paleókastro** (unrestricted access), twenty minutes' well-signposted walk out of the Langadháki district, is infinitely more impressive than the Knights' castle, and ranks as one of the more underrated ancient sites in Greece. Once restoration scaffolding is removed, you should again be able to clamber up onto the massive, polygonal-block walls by means of a broad staircase beside the still-intact gateway.

Practicalities

The most useful of Mandhráki's four **travel agencies** is Dhiakomihalis (☎22240 31459), which acts as a representative for the *Nissos Kalymnos*, the catamarans and DANE boats, rents cars and exchanges money. Kentris (☎22420 31227), near the town hall, handles GA and NEL ferries, plus Olympic Airways tickets. There's a **post office** at the port and a single **bank** in town, but it has no ATM and levies stiff commissions, as does Dhiakomihalis; a stand-alone ATM at the harbour is unreliable. Also at the base of the jetty is the **bus stop**, with (theoretically) up to five daily departures to the hill villages and six to Pálli; otherwise, there are two set-rate **taxis** and two outlets for **scooter rental**, of which John and John (branch also in Pálli) provides the best service – rates begin at €12 per day. Besides Dhiakomihalis, there's also Manos K **car rental** by the single filling station (☎22420 31028).

Accommodation

You'll see a handful of port **hotels** on your left as you disembark; cheapest of these is the waterfront *Three Brothers* (☎22420 31344; ❷) and the *Romantzo* (☎22420 31340; ❶) across the way, with partial sea views, and fridges in the simple but well-kept rooms. For slightly more comfort, try the municipally run *Xenon Polyvotis* (☎22420 31011, ☎22420 31204; ❷–❸) just beyond, whose biggish, neutral-decor rooms have fans and (mostly) knockout sea views. In the town proper, the main budget option is the small, very simple, hillside *Hotel Ypapandi* (☎22420 31485 or visit *Taverna Panorama*; ❶), near Mandhráki's most comfortable accommodation, the *Hotel Porfyris* (☎22420 31376, ☎22420 31176; ❹), with a large swimming pool and breakfast terrace; many rooms, which have air con and fridges, overlook the sea and *kámbos*. There's little actually on the shore aside from *Studios Sunset-Iliovasilema* (☎22420 31159 or 697 21 41 344; ❸), adequate and quiet, near the converted windmill, or the very basic *Hotel Nissiros* under the castle (☎697 49 84 739; ❷).

Eating

Culinary **specialities** include pickled caper greens, honey, *pittiá* (chickpea croquettes) and *soumádha*, an almond-syrup drink widely sold in recycled wine bottles, which should be consumed within three months of purchase. When eating out, it's best to give all of the commercialized, shoddy shoreline **tavernas** a miss in favour of more genuine haunts inland. Top of the heap is evenings-only, musical *ouzerí Iy Fabrika* (closed Thurs), with indoor/outdoor tables by season and hearty fare by owner Manolis, also the miners' chef on Yialí. Pricier runners-up include *Panorama*, with bean and mushroom salad and suckling pig on offer, or *Irini* on lively, ficus-shaded Platía Ilikioméni, with more involved *mayireftá* unavailable elsewhere. Finally, little *Taverna Nissiros*, the oldest eatery in town, is always busy despite predictably average grill quality. Focuses of **nightlife** are Platía Ilikioméni, where *Randevou* is the best-stocked of the sweet-cafés, and a string of *barákia* on the shore at Lefkándio district, the most popular of these being the *Enallax*.

Beaches and Pálli

Beaches on Níssyros are in even shorter supply than water, so much so that tour agencies here occasionally peddle excursions to a sandy cove on **Áyios Andónios** islet, opposite the Yialí mines. Closer at hand, the short, black-rock beach of **Hokhláki**, behind the Knights' castle, is unusable if the wind is up. It's best to head east along the main road, passing the refurbished spa of **Loutrá** (hot mineral water baths 8–11am; only by doctor's referral) to the smallish, partly sheltered "**White Beach**" (properly Yialiskári), 2km along and dwarfed by an ugly hotel. The Loutrá spa is well worth a stop for its "snack-bar" at the far end of the building, really an **ouzerí** with generous portions of salads, fried appetizers, seafood and meat – though it's become pricey of late, especially the fish.

A kilometre or so further, 4km in total from Mandhráki, the fishing village of **PÁLLI** makes an excellent hangout at lunchtime, when the port fills with trippers. **Tavernas** are multiplying, but the newer ones have generated reader complaints of price-gouging, so it's best to stick with the two long-term favourites: the less expensive *Ellinis*, with spit-roasted meat by night, grilled fish in season and simple rooms upstairs (☎22420 31453; ❷), or the adjacent *Afroditi* (aka *Nikos & Tsambika*), with big portions of grills and *mayireftá*, Cretan bulk wine and excellent home-made desserts. The scooter-rental outlet, an excellent bakery cranking out brown bread and fine pies (branch in Mandhráki), and modest nightlife make Pálli also worth considering as a base. About the only other **accommodation** is the well-sited *Frantzis Studios* by the bakery (☎22420 31240; ❸), with well-kept units in slightly scruffy grounds. A tamarisk-shaded, dark-sand **beach**, kept well groomed, extends east of Pálli to the abandoned Pantelídhi spa, behind which the little grotto-chapel of **Panayía Thermianí** is tucked inside the vaulted remains of a Roman baths complex.

To reach Níssyros's best beaches, continue in this direction for an hour on foot (or twenty minutes by bike along the road), past an initially discouraging seaweed- and cowpat-littered shoreline, to the delightful cove of **Liés**, with a snack-bar, *Oasis* (July–Aug only). Just beyond here the paved road ends at a car park; in summer boat trips from Mandhráki call here too. Walking a further fifteen minutes along a trail over the headland brings you to the idyllic, 300-metre expanse of **Pahiá Ámmos**, with grey-pink sand heaped in dunes, limited shade at the far end and a large colony of rough campers in summer – plus the "boho" contingent from the previous night at *Iy Fabrika*.

The interior

Níssyros's central, dormant **volcano** gives the island its special character and fosters the growth of the abundant vegetation – and no stay would be complete without a visit. When excursion boats arrive from Kós, several agency coaches and usually one of the public buses are pressed into service to take customers into the interior. These tours tend to monopolize the crater floor between 11am and 2pm, so if you want solitude, use early-morning or late-afternoon scheduled buses to Nikiá (at least three daily continue to the crater floor), a scooter or your own two feet to get there.

The road up from Pálli winds first past the virtually abandoned village of **EMBORIÓS**, where pigs and free-ranging cattle (a major driving hazard) far outnumber people, though the place is slowly being bought up and restored by Athenians and foreigners. New owners are often surprised to discover natural saunas, heated by volcano steam, in the basements of the crumbling houses; at the outskirts of the village there's a signposted public **steam bath** in a grotto, its entrance outlined in white paint. If you're descending to Pálli from here, an old cobbled way starting at the sharp bend below the sauna offers an attractive short cut of the four-kilometre road, while another *kalderími* drops from behind *To Balkoni tou Emboriou* **taverna** (lunch & supper early May to late Sept, limited, if cheap, menu) to within a quarter-hour's walk of the craters.

NIKIÁ, the large village on the east side of the volcano's caldera, is, with fifty year-round inhabitants, more of a going concern, and its spectacular situation 14km from Mandhráki offers views out to Tílos as well as across the volcanic caldera. There are two places to **drink** (and, modestly, **eat**) here: *Platia* and *Iy Porta* (summer only, with superior food) on or near the engagingly round *hokhláki* plaza ringed by stone seating, itself called the Pórta and marked out in white paint for the steps of folk dances. By the bus turnaround area, signs point to the 45-minute **trail** descending to the crater floor; a few minutes downhill, you can detour briefly to the eyrie-like **monastery of Áyios Ioánnis Theológos**, which only comes to life at the September 25–26 evening festival. To **drive** directly to the volcanic area you must use the road which veers off just past Emboriós.

However you approach the **volcano**, a sulphurous stench drifts out to meet you as fields and scrub gradually give way to lifeless, caked powder. The sunken main crater of **Stéfanos** is extraordinary, a moonscape of grey, brown and sickly yellow; there is another, less-visited double crater (dubbed **Polyvótis**) to the west, equally dramatic, with a clear trail leading up to it from the access road. The perimeters of both are pocked with tiny blowholes from which jets of steam puff constantly and around which form little pincushions of pure sulphur crystals. The whole floor of the larger crater seems to hiss, and standing in the middle you can hear something akin to a huge cauldron bubbling away below you. According to legend this is the groaning of Polyvotis, a Titan crushed here by Poseidon under a huge rock torn from Kós. When there are tour groups around, a small, tree-shaded snack-bar operates in the centre of the wasteland, and a booth on the access road sporadically charges admission (€1) to the volcanic zone.

Since the 1991 destruction of the old direct *kalderími* between the volcano and Mandhráki, finding pleasant options for **walking** back to town requires a bit of imagination and possession of Beate and Jürgen Franke's locally available, GPS-drawn topographical map (free from various hotels or the town hall). First choice involves backtracking along the main crater access road for about 1km from the admission booth to find the start of a clear, crudely marked path which passes the volcanic gulch of **Káto Lákki** and the monastery of **Evangelístra** on its two-hour-plus course back to the port. You can lengthen the trip by detouring from Evangelístra south to **Profítis Ilías**, the island's summit, a two-hour round-trip – the route is well marked with cairns or white paint and was cleaned in 1998. An alternative approach to Evangelístra requires returning to Emboriós and leaving from the top of the village, near the cemetery and small castle, on a 45-minute course to the monastery – an enjoyable link, despite haphazard marking and cleaning. From Evangelístra, the onward route to Mandhráki briefly follows the now mostly paved road down before the marked path resumes, handily shortcutting hairpin bends.

Kós

After Rhodes, **Kós** is the second largest and most popular island in the Dodecanese, and there are superficial similarities between the two. Here also the harbour is guarded by an imposing castle of the Knights of St John; the streets are lined with grandiose Italian public buildings; and minarets and palm trees punctuate extensive Hellenistic and Roman remains. Although its hinterland for the most part lacks the wild beauty of Rhodes' interior, acre for acre Kós is the most fertile of the Dodecanese, blessed with rich soil and abundant ground water.

Mass **tourism** has largely displaced the old agrarian economy amongst the population of just over 28,000, and outside the main town and Kardhámena this is very much a family-holiday isle, where you can turn the kids loose on push bikes. Except for Kós Town and Mastihári, there aren't many independent travellers, and from early July to early September you'll be lucky to find any sort of room at all without reservations far in advance, or a prebooked package. The tourist industry is juxtaposed rather bizarrely with cows munching amid baled hay, and Greek Army tanks exercising in the volcanic badlands around the airport. All these peculiarities acknowledged, Kós is still definitely worth a few days' time while island-hopping: its handful of **mountain villages** are appealing, the tourist infrastructure excellent (including such amenities as regular city buses and cycle paths) and swimming opportunities are limitless – about half the island's perimeter is fringed by **beaches** of various sizes, colours and consistencies.

Kós Town

The town of **KÓS**, home to over half of the island's population, spreads in all directions from the harbour, with most of its charm residing in scattered ancient and medieval antiquities. Apart from the Knights' castle, the first thing you see on arrival, there's a wealth of Hellenistic and Roman remains, many of which were only revealed by an earthquake in 1933, and excavated subsequently by the Italians, who also planned and laid out the "garden suburb" extending either side of the central grid. Elsewhere, vast areas of open space alternate with a hotchpotch of Ottoman monuments and later mock-medieval or Rationalist-Modernist buildings.

The **castle** (Tues–Sun 8am–2.30pm; €3) is reached via a causeway over its former moat, now filled in and planted with palms (hence the avenue's Greek name, Finíkon). The existing double citadel, which was built in stages between 1450 and 1514, replaced an original fourteenth-century fort deemed incapable of withstanding advances in medieval artillery. A fair proportion of ancient Koan masonry has been recycled into the walls, where the escutcheons of several Grand Masters of the Knights of St John can also be seen.

Immediately opposite the castle entrance stands the riven trunk of Hippocrates' plane tree, its branches now propped up by scaffolding instead of the ancient columns of yore; at 700 years of age, it's not really elderly enough to have seen the great healer, though it has a fair claim to being one of the oldest trees in Europe. Adjacent are two Ottoman fountains (a dry hexagonal one and a working one spilling into an ancient sarcophagus) and the eighteenth-century **mosque of Hassan Pasha**, also known as the Loggia Mosque after the portico on one side; its ground floor – like that of the **Defterdar mosque** on Platía Eleftherías – is taken up by rows of shops.

KÓS & PSÉRIMOS

▲ Bodrum (Turkey)

Cape Skandhári

Cape Psalídhi

Cape Áyios Fokás

◄ Léros

Léros ►

Rhodes ►

Lámbi

Selvéri

Kós Town

Áyios Gavríl

Ambávris

Platáni
Kermedés (Kermedés)
Asómatos

Áyios Fokás

Brós Thermá

Marathoúnda

Avlákia

Vathý

Grafiótissa

Platý

Tingáki

Zipári

Evangelístria

Amanioú

A S F E N D H I O Ú

Áyios
Dhimítrios

Ziá

D Í K E O S

Khristós
846m

Nissyros & Tílos ►

Pséримos

Alykí

Marmári

Pylí

Linopótis

Harmýlio

Laqoúdhi

Paleó Pylí

Tolári

Kardhámena

Nissyros ►

Mastihári

Troúlos

Knights'
Castle

Áyios
Ioánnis

Andimáhia

Pláka

Limniónas

Áyios Stéfanos

Psílos Grémmos 'Sunny
'Markos Paradise' 'Bubble Magic'
Kamíla 'Camel'
Langádhes

Kamári

Kastrí

Kéfalos

Panayía
Palatianí

Astypalía

Zíni
362m

Látra
428m

Aspri
Pétra

Áyios
Theológos

Áyios Ioánnis
Thymianós

Cape Dhrépano

Cape Kríkello

N

0   5 km

Opposite the latter stands the Italian-built **Archeological Museum** (Tues–Sun 8am–2.30pm; €3), with a predictable Latin bias in the choice of exhibits. Four rooms of statuary are arrayed around an atrium with a mosaic of Hippocrates welcoming Asklepios to Kós; the most famous item, purportedly a statue of Hippocrates, is indeed Hellenistic, but most of the other highly regarded works (such as Hermes seated with a lamb) are Roman.

The largest single section of ancient Kós is the **agora**, a sunken, free-access zone containing a confusing jumble of ruins, owing to repeated earthquakes between the second and sixth centuries AD. More comprehensible are the so-called western excavations, lent definition by two intersecting marble-paved streets and the **Xystos** or restored colonnade of a covered running track. In the same area lie several floor mosaics, such as Europa being carried off by Zeus in the form of a bull; gladiators; a boar being speared; plus gods and muses, all viewable under protective canopies. To the south, across Grigoríou toú Pémptou, are a Roman-era **odeion**, garishly restored both during the 1930s and again in 2000, and the **Casa Romana** (shut for works until early 2005), a third-century-AD house built around three atria with surviving patches of mosaic floors showing panthers and tigers, plus assorted sea creatures.

Kós also retains a thoroughly commercialized **old town**, lining the pedestrianized street running from behind the market hall on Platía Eleftherías as far as Platía Dhiagóras and the isolated minaret overlooking the western archeological zone. One of the few areas of town to survive the 1933 earthquake, today it's crammed with expensive tourist boutiques, cafés and snack-bars. About the only genuinely old thing remaining here is a capped **Turkish fountain** with a calligraphic inscription, found where the walkway cobbles cross Odhós Venizélou.

Practicalities

Large **ferries and catamarans** anchor just outside the harbour at a special jetty by one corner of the castle; **excursion boats** to neighbouring islands sail right in and dock all along Aktí Koundouriótou. **Hydrofoils** tie up south of the castle at their own berth, on Aktí Miaoúli. Virtually all ferry and excursion-boat agents sit within 50m of each other at the intersection of pedestrianized Vassiléos Pávlou and the waterfront. Among the more helpful and genuinely representative of ferries and hydrofoils, not just expensive excursions, are Adris Nissia at Vassiléos Pávlou 2, and Exas opposite the National Bank at Andóni Ioannídhi 4 (☎22420 29900).

The **airport** is 24km southwest of Kós Town in the centre of the island; an Olympic Airways shuttle bus (€3) meets Olympic flights for a transfer to the town terminal, but if you arrive on any other flight you'll have to either take a taxi or head towards the giant roundabout outside the airport gate and find an orange-and-cream-coloured KTEL bus – they run from here to Mastihári, Kardhámena and Kéfalos as well as Kós Town. The **KTEL bus terminal** in town is a series of stops around a triangular park 400m back from the water, with an info booth adjacent at Kleopátras 7 (tickets on the bus). The municipality also runs a frequent **local bus** service, DEAS, through the beach suburbs and up to the Asklepion, with a ticket and information office at Aktí Koundouriótou 7. Push- or **mountain-bike** rental are popular options for getting around, given the island's relative flatness; if you want a **motor scooter**, try Moto Harley at Kanari, corner Neomartýrou Khrístou, while Autorent/Helen's at Vassiléos Pávlou 31 (☎22420 28882 or 694 44 50 062) or in Psalídhi suburb, at both the *Ramira* and *Okeanis* hotels, has a reputation for good-condition **cars**, as does AutoWay at Vassiléos Yeoryíou 22 (☎22420 25326).

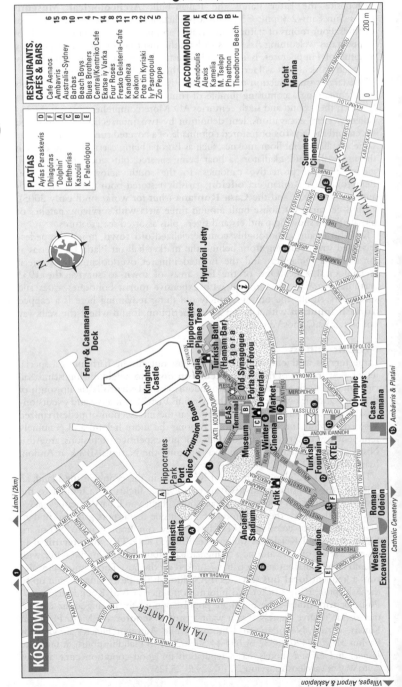

KÓS TOWN

PLATÍAS
Ayías Paraskevís	D
Dhiagóras	F
'Dolphin'	A
Eleftherías	C
Kazoúli	B
K. Paleológou	E

RESTAURANTS, CAFÉS & BARS
Café Aenaos	6
Ambavris	15
Australia-Sydney	9
Barbas	10
Beach Boys	1
Blues Brothers	4
Central/Kentriko Cafe	7
Ekatse iy Varka	14
Four Roses	8
Fresko Gelateria-Cafe	13
Kanadheza	11
Koakon	3
Pote tin Kyriaki	12
Iy Psaropoula	2
Zio Peppe	5

ACCOMMODATION
Afendoulis	E
Alexis	A
Kamelia	C
M. Tselepi	D
Phaethon	B
Theodorou Beach	F

G (200m), Campsite (1500m), Psalídhi, Áyios Fokás & Brós Thermá ▲

Yacht Marina

Summer Cinema

ITALIAN QUARTER

Hydrofoil Jetty

Ferry & Catamaran Dock

Knights' Castle

Hippocrates' Plane Tree
Turkish Bath (Hamam Bar)
Loggia
Agora
Old Synagogue
Pórta toú Fórou
Defterdar

Excursion Boats

Hippocrates Park
Police
Port

DEAS Termina
Museum
Winter Cinema
Market

Turkish Fountain
KTEL
Atik

Olympic Airways

Casa Romana

Hellenistic Baths

Ancient Stadium

Nymphaion

Western Excavations

Roman Odeion

ITALIAN QUARTER

N

200 m

0

▲ Lámbi (2km)

▼ Villages, Airport & Asklepíon

Catholic Cemetery ▼

Ambávris & Platáni ▼

The municipal **tourist office** at Vassiléos Yeoryíou 3 (May–Oct Mon–Fri 8.30am–2.30pm & 5.30–8.30pm; Nov–April no evening hours) keeps stocks of local maps, bus timetables and ferry schedules (the latter not to be trusted implicitly). For more involved information, head for the Newsstand **book shop/newsagent** just behind the archeological museum on Platía Kazoúli. No fewer than seven **banks** have ATMs, while the **post office** is at Vassiléos Pávlou 14. The most central and best-equipped **Internet café** is Cafe del Mare at Megálou Alexándhrou 4. **Laundries** include Happy Wash at Mitropóleos 20 and Laundromat Center at Alikarnassoú 124.

Accommodation

If you're just in transit, you're virtually obliged to **stay** in Kós Town, and even if you plan a few days on the island, it still makes a sensible base, as it is the public transport hub and has the greatest concentration of vehicle rental and nightlife. Be wary of touts which besiege most arriving sea-craft – their rooms are apt to be unlicensed, inconveniently remote and of dubious cleanliness. They may further claim to represent establishments listed below, and then take you elsewhere.

Good, licensed, budget choices in the centre include the deservedly popular *Pension Alexis* (☎22420 25594; ❷; March to early Nov), Irodhótou 9 at the corner of Omírou, across from the Roman agora, with wood-floored rooms, which share bathrooms and a self-catering kitchen. Alexis's ebullient sister Sonia keeps it now, whilst Alexis himself is found at the *Hotel Afendoulis* (☎22420 25321, ✉afendoulishotel@kos.forthnet.gr; ❸; April–Nov), about 600m south at Evrypýlou 1, with large, balconied en-suite rooms, a few family quads, optional fridges/air con, and breakfast available. If they're full, try the nearby *Hotel Kamelia*, at Artemisías 3 (☎22420 28983, ℻22420 27391; ❸; March–Oct); rear rooms have an orchard view. Other quiet possibilities include the air-conditioned *Hotel Phaethon* at Venizélou 75 (☎22420 28901; ❹) and the self-catering rooms let by Moustafa Tselepi (☎22420 28896; ❸), at Metsóvou 8 (enquire at Venizélou 35). For more comfort and a small private beach, *Theodhorou Beach*, 1200m from the centre at the end of town towards Psalídhi (☎22420 22280, ℻22420 23526; ❹) has generous-sized rooms not completely monopolized by packages, and attractive common areas. The well-appointed **campsite** (☎22420 23275; May to early Oct) lies another 1300m out towards Cape Psalídhi, and can be reached by either the DEAS bus service or its own minibus (which meets ferries).

Eating, drinking and nightlife

Despite an overwhelming first impression of Euro-stodge cuisine, it's easy to **eat** well and even reasonably in Kós Town, as long as you search inland, away from the harbour. The *Australia-Sydney* on Vassiléos Pávlou opposite the post office is a cheap and cheerful hole-in-the wall with a limited menu of daily dishes where two can eat for under €18, while the *Koakon (Andonis)*, on Ieroú Lóhou near the corner of Amerikís, offers *mayireftá* in a more salubrious environment without the usual multinational flags and photo-menus. In the east of town, *Barbas*, on Evrypýlou, opposite the *Hotel Afendoulis* offers excellent grills as well as the odd seafood touch like octopus salad, while *Kanadheza* diagonally opposite does creditable pizzas as well as grills and stays open all year. If your appetite doesn't stretch to a whole pizza, *Zio Peppe*, at Ríga Feréou 13, on the waterfront does it superbly by the slice. For fish, choose between *Iy Psaropoula*, at Averof 17, with mainly Greeks in attendance, and the even better *Ekatse iy Varka* by the isolated minaret on Platía Dhiagóra, with local species like *filípi* and a quaffable home-made rosé wine. Kós's sole *ouzerí* is tiny *Pote tin Kyriakí*, at Pissándhrou 9 (supper only; closed Sun, as the name says), which neither wants nor gets many tourists – there's only a Greek sign out; the creatively drawn menu (in school copy-books) has delights such as fried mussels and *dhákos* ("monk's" salad). Equal to any of these is *Ambavris* (May–Oct), 800m south out of town by the road from near Casa Romana, in the eponymous village. To order from their English-only à la carte menu is to miss the point of the place; take the hint about "Mezedes" and let the house bring on their best – this changes seasonally but won't much exceed €22 for six plates, drinks extra.

For **breakfast**, the *Central/Kentriko Cafe* on Platía Ayías Paraskevís behind the market hall does American pancakes, French toast and fresh fruit juices, though service and quality had suffered a bit at our last visit. You can join the largely Greek crowd at *Cafe Aenaos*, right under the Defterdar mosque, and people-watch while refilling your Greek coffee from the traditional *bríki* used to brew it up – they also do juices. *Fresko Gelateria-Cafe*, on the corner of Kleopátras and Ioannídhi, is the best place to wait for a bus while slurping decadent home-made ice cream. For a convivial **drink** on the water, try long-lived *Blues Brothers* on Aktí Koundouriótou, near the port police; equally durable music bars with dance floors include *Four Roses* on the corner of Arseníou and Vassiléos Yeoryíou, and *Beach Boys* at Kanári 57. If you prefer loud techno and house, look no further than the "Pub Lanes", officially Nafklírou and Dhiákou; every address is a bar, whose identity tends to change each season, so just choose according to the crowd and the noise level. Otherwise there is one active **cinema**, the Orfeas, with summer and winter (Oct–May) premises as shown on the map; the indoor premises also hosts concerts and other special events, as does *Apoplous* in Psalídhi, just past the *Theodhorou Beach* hotel.

The Asklepion and Platáni

Native son **Hippocrates** is justly celebrated on Kós; not only does he have a tree, a street, a park, a statue and an international medical institute named after him, but the **Asklepion** (summer Tues–Sun 8am–6.30pm; earlier closure winter; €3), 4km south of town, one of just three in Greece, is a major tourist attraction. A little fake green-and-white train shuttles up to the site regularly; otherwise take a DEAS bus up to Platáni (see opposite), from where the ruins are a further 15-minute walk. There is a small snack-bar at the Asklepion, or pause for lunch in Platáni en route.

The Asklepion was actually founded just after the death of Hippocrates, but it's safe to assume that the methods used and taught here were his. Both a temple to Asklepios (god of healing, son of Apollo) and a renowned curative centre, its magnificent setting on three artificial hillside terraces overlooking Anatolia reflects early recognition of the importance of the therapeutic environment. Until recently, two fountains provided the site with a constant supply of clean, fresh water, and extensive stretches of clay piping are still visible, embedded in the ground.

Today, very little remains standing above ground, owing to periodic earthquakes and the Knights' use of the site as a quarry. The lower terrace in fact never had many buildings, being instead the venue for the observance of the Asklepieia – quadrennial celebrations and athletic/musical competitions in honour of the healing god. Sacrifices to Asklepios were conducted at an **altar**, the oldest structure on the site, whose foundations can still be seen near the middle of the second terrace. Just to its east, the Corinthian columns of a

Hippocrates

Hippocrates (ca. 460–370 BC) is generally regarded as the father of scientific medicine, though the Hippocratic oath probably has nothing to do with him and is in any case much altered from its original form. Hippocrates was certainly born on Kós, probably at Astypalia near present-day Kéfalos, but otherwise details of his life are few and disputed; what seems beyond doubt is that he was a great physician who travelled throughout the Classical Greek world, but spent at least part of his career teaching and practising at the Asklepion on his native island. A vast number of medical writings have been attributed to Hippocrates, only a few of which he could have actually written; *Airs, Waters and Places*, a treatise on the importance of environment on health, is widely thought to be his, but others were probably a compilation from a medical library kept on Kós, which later appeared in Alexandria during the second century BC. This emphasis on good air and water, and the holistic approach of ancient Greek medicine, now seems positively contemporary.

second-century-AD **Roman temple** were partially re-erected by nationalistically minded Italians. A monumental **staircase** leads from the altar to the second-century-BC Doric temple of Asklepios on the topmost terrace, the last and grandest of a succession of the deity's shrines at this site.

About halfway to the Asklepion, the village of **PLATÁNI** (also Kermedés, from the Turkish name Germe) is, along with Kós Town, the remaining place of residence for the island's dwindling community of ethnic Turks. Until 1964 there were nearly three thousand of them, but successive Cyprus crises and the worsening of relations between Greece and Turkey prompted mass emigration to Anatolia, and a drop in the Muslim population to currently under a thousand. Several excellent, Turkish-run **tavernas** are to be found at and around the main crossroads junction, with a working Ottoman fountain: *Arap* (summer only); the slightly less touristy *Asklipios*; *Sherif*, across the way (summer only); and *Gin's Place* (all year), each offering Anatolian-style *mezédhes* (fried vegetables with yogurt, *bourekákia*, and so on) and kebabs better than most in Kós Town. Afterwards, retire across from *Arap* to *Zaharoplastio Iy Paradhosi* for the best ice cream on the island.

Just outside Platáni on the road back to the port, the island's neglected **Jewish cemetery** lies in a dark conifer grove, 300m beyond the well-kept Muslim graveyard. Dates on the Hebrew-Italian-script headstones stop after 1940, after which none of the local Jews were allowed the luxury of a natural death prior to their deportation in summer 1944. Their former synagogue or *hávra*, a wonderfully orientalized Rationalist specimen from 1934, at Alexándhrou Dhiákou 4, was refurbished in 1991 as a municipal events hall but now has a plaque commemorating its former use.

Eastern Kós

If you're looking for anything resembling a deserted **beach** near the capital, you'll need to make use of the DEAS bus line connecting the various resorts to either side of town, or else rent a vehicle; push-bikes can take advantage of the cycle paths extending as far east as Cape Psalídhi. Closest is **Lámbi**, 3km north towards Cape Skandhári with its military watchpoint, the last vestige of a vast army camp which has deferred to the demands of tourism – and supposed intra-NATO amity.

The bus line usually terminates at Áyios Fokás, 8km southeast of Kós Town, but sometimes continues an extra 4km to unusual and remote **Brós Thermá** (last service around 6pm); if you make the trip with your own transport be prepared to negotiate a dirt track for the final kilometre. Brós Thermá is known for its **hot springs** – best experienced at sunset or after – which issue from a grotto and flow through a trench into a shoreline pool protected by boulders, heating the seawater to an enjoyable temperature. Winter storms typically disperse the boulder wall, rebuilt every April, so that the pool changes from year to year. Just adjacent, the long-running *Psarotaverna Therma* does affordable seafood – especially parrotfish, swordfish and tuna, though the rest of the menu is unmemorable. There's also a newer drinks-and-ice-cream café right by the pool.

Tingáki and Marmári

The two neighbouring beach resorts of Tingáki and Marmári are separated from each other by the salt marsh of **Alykí**, which retains water until July after a wet winter. Between January and April, Alykí is host to hundreds of migratory birds, and most of the time you'll find tame terrapins to feed near the outlet to the warm, shallow sea. There's almost always a breeze along this coast, which means plenty of windsurf boards for hire at either resort; the profiles of Kálymnos, Psérimos and Turkey's Bodrum peninsula all make for spectacular scenery. If you're aiming for either of these resorts from town, especially on a bike of any sort, it's safest and most pleasant to go by the **minor road** which takes off from the southwest corner of town (follow initial signage for the Vassiliadhi supermarket); the entire way to Tingáki is paved, and involves the same distance as using the main trunk road and marked turn-off. Similarly, a grid of paved rural lanes links the inland portions of Tingáki and Marmári.

TINGÁKI, a busy beachside resort popular with Brits, lies 12km west of the harbour. Oddly, there's very little **accommodation** near the beach in the dozen or so medium-sized hotels and more numerous studios; most of these are scattered inland through fields and cow pastures. One of the better choices, if heavily subscribed to by packages, is the family-oriented *Hotel Ilios* (☎22420 69411; ❸), a well-designed bungalow complex. By far the best local **taverna** here, with pleasant seating indoors and out, is *Ambeli* (summer daily; winter Fri/Sat eve, Sun lunch), well signposted 2.5km east of the main beachfront crossroads; the best strategy is to avoid "mains" and order a pile of starters like *pinigoúri* (cracked wheat), *bekrí mezé*, or *yaprákia* (the local *dolmádhes*). Among **car-rental** outfits, Sevi (☎22420 69076) can be recommended, and will even deliver vehicles on request to Kós Town. The beach itself is white sand, long and narrow – it improves, and veers further away from the traffic of the frontage road, as you head southwest.

MARMÁRI, 15km from town, has a smaller built-up area than Tingáki, and the beach itself is broader, especially to the west where it forms little dunes. Most hotels here are monopolized by German tour groups, but you might hit on an on-spec vacancy at the B-class, 1997-built *Esperia* on the main access road down from the island trunk road (☎22420 42010, ⓕ22420 42012; ❹), in grassy surroundings.

The Asfendhioú villages

The main interest of inland Kós resides in the villages on **Mount Dhíkeos**, a handful of settlements collectively referred to as **Asfendhioú**, nestled amidst the island's only natural forest. Together these communities give a good idea of what Kós looked like before tourism and ready-mix concrete arrived, and all are now severely depopulated by the mad rush to the coast. They are accessible via the curvy side road from Zipári, 8km from Kós Town; a badly marked but paved minor road to Lagoúdhi; or by the shorter access road for Pylí.

The first Asfendhioú village you reach up the Zipári road is **Evangelístria**, where a major crossroads by the parish church and taverna of the same name leads to Lagoúdhi and Amanioú (west), Asómatos (east) and Ziá (uphill). On the way up from Zipári, the *Panorama* taverna is not too commercialized and open in winter as well. **ZIÁ**'s spectacular sunsets make it the target of up to six evening tour buses daily, though the village has barely a dozen families still resident, and its daytime tattiness seems to increase each tourist season. Best of the dozen **tavernas** here is the *Olympia*, at the start of the pedestrian walkway up to the church, open all year with such dishes as chickpeas, cracked wheat, *spédzofaï* (sausage and pepper stew), dark bread and good bulk wine; there's a good *pikilía* or medley of *mezédhes* "off-menu", especially at weekends when a local clientele predominates. Ziá is also the trailhead for the ascent of 846-metre **Dhíkeos peak**, a two-and-a-half-hour round-trip, initially on track but mostly by path. The route is fairly obvious, and the views from the pillbox-like summit **chapel of Metamórfosis** are ample reward for the effort. Up top, you can also ponder the esoteric symbolism of a giant crucifix fashioned out of PVC sewer pipe and filled with concrete.

East of Ziá or Evangelístria, roads converge at **ASÓMATOS**, home to about thirty villagers and a number of outsiders restoring abandoned houses; the evening view from the church of Arhángelos with its pebble mosaic rivals that of Zía, though there are no reliable facilities here. **ÁYIOS DHIMÍTRIOS**, 2km beyond along a fairly rough track, is marked by its old name of Haïhoútes on some maps, and is today completely abandoned except for a single house next to the attractive church; in the narthex, a small photo display documents a much larger population during the war years, when the village was a centre of resistance to the German occupation. You can continue from here on 3.5km of more rough road to the junction with the paved road linking Platáni with the municipal rubbish tip.

Pylí

PYLÍ can be reached via the paved road through Lagoúdhi and Amanioú, or from the duck-patrolled Linopótis pond on the main island trunk road. In the upper of its two neighbourhoods, 100m west of the partly pedestrianized square and church, the simple *Iy Palia Piyi* taverna serves inexpensive but appetizing meat grills and fried-vegetable *mezédhes* in a superb setting, beside a giant cistern-fountain (*piyí*), decorated with carved lion-head spouts. Pylí's other attraction is the so-called **Harmýlio** ("Tomb of Harmylos"), signposted near the top of the village as "Heroon of Charmylos". This consists of a subterranean, niched vault (fenced off), probably a Hellenistic family tomb; immediately above, traces of an ancient temple have been incorporated into the medieval chapel of Stavrós.

Paleó (medieval) **Pylí**, roughly 3km southeast of its modern descendant, was the Byzantine capital of Kós. Head there via Amanioú, keeping straight at the junction where signs point left to Ziá and Lagoúdhi. In any case, the castle should be obvious on its rock, straight ahead; the deteriorating road ends next to a spring, opposite which a stair-path leads within fifteen minutes to the roof of the fort. En route you pass the remains of the abandoned town tumbling southwards down the slope, as well as three fourteenth-century chapels with fresco fragments within; the first one encountered, Arhángelos, has the best-preserved scenes, though the third church (Ipapandí) is the most architecturally interesting.

Western Kós

Near the arid, desolate centre of the island, well sown with military installations, a pair of giant, adjacent roundabouts by the airport funnels traffic northwest towards **Mastihári**, northeast back towards town, southwest towards **Kéfalos**, and southeast to **Kardhámena**. Most visitors are after the south-coast **beaches**, reached from the Kéfalos-bound turning.

Mastihári and Andimáhia

The least developed, least "packaged" and least expensive of the northern shore resorts, **MASTIHÁRI** has a shortish, broad beach extending west, and a less attractive one at **Troúlos** 1.5km east. At the end of the westerly beach, inside a partly fenced enclosure, lie remains of the fifth-century basilica of **Áyios Ioánnis**, one of several on the island. If you want to **stay**, try quieter digs overlooking the west beach such as the simple *Hotel Kyma* (☎22420 59045; ❷) or the *Hotel Fenareti* (☎22420 59028, ℗22420 59129) further up the grade, with rooms (❷) and studios (❸) in a peaceful garden environment. *O Makis*, one street inland from the quay, and *Kali Kardia*, at the base of the jetty, are the best of a half-dozen **tavernas**, both well regarded for fresh fish, *mezédhes* and (at *Kali Kardia*) *mayireftá*. Mastihári is also the port for small roll-on-roll-off **ferries** to Kálymnos; there are three well-spaced departures in each direction most of the year, timed more or less to coincide with Olympic Airways flight schedules – though KTEL buses to or from Kós Town don't (perhaps deliberately) always dovetail well.

The workaday village of **ANDIMÁHIA**, 5km southeast of Mastihári, straggles over several ridges; the only concession to tourism is a much-photographed windmill on the main street, operating as a working museum (typically 8.30am–5pm) with its unfurled sails. If open, for a token fee you can climb up to the mast loft and observe its workings – which incidentally point downwind, not into the wind as popularly imagined. East of Andimáhia, reached via a marked, three-kilometre side road, an enormous, triangular **Knights' castle** overlooks the straits to Níssyros. Once through the imposing north gateway (unrestricted access), you can follow the well-preserved west parapet, and visit two interior chapels: one with a fresco of Áyios Khristóforos (St Christopher) carrying the Christ Child, the other with fine rib-vaulting. Electricity was provided and unsafe masonry was consolidated in 2001, since when the castle functions as an occasional concert venue.

Kardhámena

KARDHÁMENA, on the southeast coast 31km from Kós Town, is the island's largest package resort after the capital itself, with locals outnumbered twenty to one in season by visitors (mostly young Brits) intent on getting as drunk as possible as cheaply as possible. Runaway local development has banished whatever redeeming qualities the place may once have had, reducing it to a seething mass of off-licences, bars, trinket shops and excursion agencies. Pubs named the *Black Swan*, *Bonkers* or *Cheeky Monkeys* dispense imported beer, and you can easily find fish and chips. A hefty sand beach stretches to either side of the town, hemmed in to the east with ill-concealed military bunkers and a road as far as Tolári, home to the massive *Norida Beach* all-inclusive complex.

Kardhámena is most worth knowing about as a place to catch a **boat to Níssyros**. There are supposedly two daily sailings in season: the morning tourist excursion *kaïki* at either 9am or 9.30am, and another, less expensive, barely publicized one – the *Chrisoula* – at 2.30pm, but in practice the afternoon departure (at a minimum: Mon, Wed, Thurs & Fri; never Sun) can occur any time between 1.30pm and 6.30pm, depending on when the Nissyrians have finished their shopping.

Outside high season, there are generally a few **rooms** not taken by tour companies, and prices are not outrageous. For more comfort, the dead-central *Hotel Rio* (T 22420 91627; ❸), just inland from the seafront Platía Eleftherías, gets good reviews, and like most accommodation here is underpriced for its class. **Tavernas** are not very numerous, and by contrast surprisingly expensive; the most "Greek" is *Avli*, in an old house by the *Hotel Rio*.

South-coast beaches

The thinly populated portion of Kós southwest of the airport and Andimáhia boasts the most scenic and secluded beaches on the island, plus a number of minor ancient sites. Though given fanciful English names and shown as separate extents on tourist maps, the south-facing **beaches** form essentially one long stretch at the base of a cliff, most with sunbeds, a rudimentary snack-bar and a jet-ski franchise. **Magic**, officially Polémi, is the longest, broadest and wildest, with a taverna above the car park, no jet skis and a nudist zone at the east end. **Sunny**, signposted as Psilós Gremmós and easily walkable from Magic, has another taverna and jet skis; **Langádhes** is the cleanest and most picturesque, with junipers tumbling off its dunes and more jet skis. **Paradise**, often dubbed "Bubble Beach" because of volcanic gas vents in the tidal zone, is small and oversubscribed, with wall-to-wall sunbeds. Jet-ski-free **Camel** (Kamíla) is the shortest and loneliest, protected somewhat by the steep, unpaved drive in past its hillside taverna; the shore here is pure, fine sand, with good snorkelling to either side of the cove.

Uninterrupted beach resumes at **Áyios Stéfanos**, overshadowed by a huge Club Med complex, and extends 5km west to Kamári (see below). A marked public access road leads down to the beach just west of a small peninsula, crowned with the exquisite remains of two triple-aisled, sixth-century basilicas. Though the best preserved on the island, several columns have been toppled since the 1980s, and wonderful bird mosaics languish under a permanent layer of "protective" gravel. The basilicas overlook tiny but striking **Kastrí** islet with its little chapel; in theory it's an easy swim (sometimes wading) across from the westerly beach, with some of the best snorkelling on Kós around the rock formations, but you must run a gauntlet of boats from the local water-ski school.

The far west

Essentially the shore annexe of Kéfalos (see below), **KAMÁRI** is a sprawling package resort of rapidly multiplying breeze-blocks, pitched a few notches above Kardhámena; it's a major watersports centre and an alternative departure point for Níssyros (up to five days weekly in season). *Stamatia*, near the main roundabout, is the oldest and (relatively) most authentic **taverna** hereabouts; one independent **hotel** that can be recommended is the simple *Maria* (T 22420 71308; ❷), on the seafront west of the main road up to **KÉFALOS**, 43km from Kós Town. Squatting on a bluff looking down the length of the island, this is the end of the line for buses: a dull village but worth knowing about for its post office and as a staging point for expeditions into the rugged peninsula terminating dramatically at Cape Kríkello.

Main highlights of a half-day tour here, beginning along the widened ridge road south, include a Byzantine church incorporating an ancient temple, 1km beyond the village; the late Classical theatre (unrestricted access) – with two rows of seats remaining – and Hellenistic temple of **ancient Astypalia**, 500m further at the side-path signposted "Palatia"; and the cave of **Asprí Pétra** (inhabited during the Neolithic period), marked rather vaguely off the ridge road and requiring a half-hour walk to reach. A paved road west from just after Astypalia leads to an often windy beach and small chapel at **Áyios Theológos**, 7km from Kéfalos; the *Sunset Wave* taverna is a reliable option for a home-made sweet and coffee, though the fare in recent years has tended towards the hamburger-and-chips variety. Keeping to the main paved road until the end of the line brings you to the appealing (but usually locked) monastery of **Áyios Ioánnis Thymianós**, also 7km from the village.

About 1.5km north of Kéfalos on the road tracing the island's summit ridge, a paved side road covers the 2.7km to **Lim(n)iónas**, the only north-facing beach and fishing anchorage on this part of Kós. There's just one surviving fish **taverna** here, the rather commercialized *Limionas*; two compact sandy beaches sit either side of the peninsula.

Psérimos

Psérimos could be an idyllic little island were it not so close to Kós and Kálymnos. Throughout the season, both of these larger neighbours dispatch daily excursion boats, which compete strenuously to dock at the small harbour village of **AVLÁKIA**. In midsummer, day-trippers blanket the main sandy beach which curves around the bay in front of Avlákia's thirty-odd houses and huge communal olive grove; even during May or late September you're guaranteed at least a hundred outsiders daily (versus a permanent population of 25). There are two other, somewhat less attractive beaches to hide away on during the day: clean **Vathý** (sand and gravel), a well-marked, thirty-minute path-walk east, starting from behind the *Taverna Iy Pserimos*, or grubbier **Marathoúnda** (pebble), a 45-minute walk north on the main trans-island track. Nowhere on Psérimos, including the monastery of Grafiótissa (big festival Aug 15), is much more than an hour's walk away.

Even during the season there won't be too many other overnighters, since there's a limited number of beds available, and your reception at some of the more put-upon snack-bars may become warmer once it's clear that you're **staying**. Pick of the several small *pensions* is *Tripolitis* (☎22430 23196; ❷), upstairs from English-speaking *Nick and Anna's* café/snack-bar or the rooms above *Taverna Manola* on the opposite end of the beach (☎22430 51540; ❷), who also keep the plusher *Studios Kalliston* next door (❸). There's just one small, limited-stock **store**, since most of the island's supplies are brought in daily from Kálymnos. Eating out however, won't break the bank, and there's often fresh fish in the handful of **tavernas**; many of these have contracts with the tour boats, but *Taverna Manola* doesn't, and despite modest appearances proves very adept at *ouzerí* fare and seafood.

Nearly all the **boats** based on Kós and Kálymnos harbour operate triangle tours (approximately €20), which involve departure between 9.30am and 10am, followed by a stop for swimming on either Platý islet or adjacent Psérimos, lunch in Avlákia, or Póthia, the port of Kálymnos (or even on board), and another swimming stop at whichever islet wasn't visited in the morning. If you want to spend the entire day on Psérimos, you're much better off departing Póthia at 9.30am daily on the tiny *Nissos Pserimos*, returning at 4pm (€6 round-trip). The islanders themselves use this boat to visit Kálymnos for shopping and administrative business.

Astypálea

Geographically, historically and architecturally, **Astypálea** (alias Astropália) would be more at home among the Cyclades – on a clear day you can see Anáfi or Amorgós (to the southwest and northwest respectively) far more easily than any of the other Dodecanese. Moreover, Astypálea's inhabitants are descendants of medieval colonists from the Cyclades, and the island looks and feels more like these than its neighbours to the east.

Despite an evocative butterfly shape, Astypálea does not immediately strike you as especially beautiful. Many beaches along the bleak, heavily indented coastline often have reef underfoot and suffer periodic dumpings of seaweed. The heights, which offer limited walking opportunities, are windswept and covered in thornbush or dwarf juniper. Yet the herb *alisfakiá*, brewed as a tea, flourishes too, and hundreds of sheep and goats manage to survive – as opposed to snakes, which are (uniquely in the Aegean) entirely absent. Lush citrus groves and vegetable patches in the valleys signal a relative abundance of water, hoarded in a reservoir.

In antiquity the island's most famous citizen was Kleomedes, a boxer disqualified from an early Olympic Games for causing the death of his opponent. He came home so enraged that he demolished the local school, killing all its pupils. Things have calmed down a bit in the intervening 2500 years, and today Astypálea is renowned mainly for its **honey**, **fish and lobster** (which finds its way into the local dish of *astakomakaronádha*); the abundant local catch has only been shipped to Athens since the late 1980s, a reflection of traditionally poor **ferry links** in every direction. These have improved recently with the introduction of extra services towards Piréas via select Cyclades, and high-season links with Rhodes via a few intervening islets, but outside July or August you still risk being marooned here for a day or two longer than intended; you may need or want to take advantage of the newly inaugurated **flights** to Léros, Kós or Rhodes. There is, curiously, no conventional package tourism here since Laskarina Holidays deleted the island from their catalogue in 1995, frustrated by chronically unreliable connections to Kós and its major airport.

Despite this relative isolation, plenty of people find their way to Astypálea during the short, intense **midsummer season** (mid-July to the first Sept Sun before school starts), when the 1500 permanent inhabitants are all but over-run by upwards of 7000 guests a day. Most arrivals are Athenians, French or Italians, supplemented by large numbers of yachties and foreign owners of holiday homes in the understandably popular Hóra. At such times you won't find a bed without reserving well in advance, and camping rough is expressly frowned upon.

Skála and Hóra

The main harbour of **SKÁLA** or Péra Yialós dates from the Italian era (Astypálea was the first island the Italians occupied in the Dodecanese) and most of the settlement between the quay and the line of nine windmills is even more recent. Its only real bright spot is a 1998-inaugurated **archeological museum** (June–Sept Mon 10am–1pm & 7–10pm, Tues–Sun 8.30am–2.30pm & 5–11pm; Oct–May Tues–Sun 8am–2pm; free), a single well-lit room crammed with the best local finds spanning all historical periods from the Bronze Age to medieval times.

As you climb up beyond the port towards **HÓRA**, however, the neighbourhoods get progressively older and more attractive, their steep streets enlivened by the photogenic *poúndia*, or colourful wooden balconies-with-stairways of the whitewashed houses, which owe much to the building styles of Mýkonos and Tínos, the origins of the colonists brought to repopulate the island in 1413. The whole culminates in the thirteenth-century **kástro** (Mon–Fri mornings, closed Sat & Sun; free), one of the finest in the Aegean, erected not by the Knights but by the Venetian Quirini clan and subsequently modified by the Ottomans after 1537. Until well into the twentieth century over three hundred people lived inside the *kástro*, but depopulation and a severe 1956 earthquake combined to leave only a desolate shell today. The fine rib vaulting over the main west gate supports the church of Evangelístria Kastrianí, one of two intact here, the other being Áyios Yeóryios (both usually locked). Currently the *kástro* grounds are in the throes of a consolidation and restoration project undertaken by the Byzantine antiquities authority, designed to keep the perimeter fortifications from crumbling further.

Practicalities

Two **buses** run along the paved road between Hóra, Skála, Livádhia and Analípsi, frequently in July and August from 8am until 11pm, much less regularly out of season. The Análipsi-bound bus usually manages to dovetail well with arriving/departing aeroplanes. There are only two official set-rate **taxis**, far too few to cope with passenger numbers in season; fares are reasonable, for example €6 from Skála to the airport. Several places offer **scooters**, the most reliable being Lakis and Manolis (T22430 61263), with branches at Hóra and Skála dock; they also rent out a few pricey cars and jeeps, as does Vergoulis (T22430 61351) near the museum. Also near the museum, Astypalea Tours (T22430 61571) is the main travel agency, representing the *Nissos Kalymnos* as well. The island **map** sold locally is grossly inaccurate, even by lenient Greek-island standards, though in compensation rural junctions are adequately signposted. The **post office** and most shops are in Hóra, though the island's only **bank**, complete with ATM, is down in Skála by the port police.

Accommodation

Skála, and to a lesser extent Hóra, have **accommodation** ranging from spartan, 1970s-vintage rooms to new luxury studios; proprietors tend not to meet ferries unless arrangements have been made, even if they have vacancies. Owing to high-season harbour noise – particularly the sound of ferries dropping anchor at 3am – you might prefer more atmospheric restored studios or entire houses (❺ for two people peak season, ❸ low) up in Hóra if uninterrupted sleep is a priority; enquire at Kostas Vaïkousis' antique shop on the quay or reserve in advance on T22430 61430 or T697 74 77 800. Rather plusher are the 2000-built *Studios Kilindra* on the quiet west slope of Hóra (T22430 61966, Wwww.astipalea.com.gr; open all year), offering luxury amenities including a swimming pool – units accommodate two to three people, with the smallest at ❻, the suite ❽.

Otherwise, the obvious, bog-standard port **hotels** are the *Astynea* (T22430 61040, F22430 61041; ❸) and the somewhat cheaper but fairly well-kept *Paradisos* (T22430 61224, F22430 61450; ❸), both en-suite with sea views. Among backpackers' standbys on the east shore of the bay, the en-suite *Rooms Australia* above the restaurant of the same name (T22430 61067, F22430 59812; ❸) have been refurbished with fans or air con, also offering more comfortable studios closer to the water (❹), while remoter *Akti Rooms* (T22430 61856; ❹) are also well equipped and maintained. A small, basic, July–August-only **campsite** operates amongst calamus reeds and tamarisks behind Dhéftero Marmári Bay (see p.350), about 4km along the road to Análipsi, but (like much of the island) it can be mosquito-plagued any year after a wet winter.

Eating, drinking and nightlife

During August, nearly thirty **tavernas** and beach snack-bars operate across the island, few of them memorable and many concerned primarily with turning a quick profit. Among the more reliable Skála options, *Iy Monaxia* (aka *Viki's*), one block inland from the ferry jetty by the old power plant, has home-style cooking and stays open all year. The *Astropalia* (closes end Sept) on the hillside above the street up to Hóra, does good, if somewhat pricey, fish and not much else. Best of the lot, with even better seafood, and superbly prepared home-grown vegetable dishes, is the homey *Australia* (April–Nov), just inland from the head of the bay. Behind the *Hotel Paradhisos*, you'll find more careful cooking, polished presentation (and much higher prices) at *Aitherio* and *Maïstrali* (both open into Oct); it's pot-luck as to which is better any given night. Under the *Hotel Astynea*, the *Dapia Café* is good for full breakfasts, midday crêpes and novelty teas.

Most **nightlife** happens up in more atmospheric Hóra, where the esplanade between the windmills and the base of the *kástro* seems to be one solid café–bar. Of these, the favourites are the unsigned *Tou Nikola* (*Iy Mylí*) on the corner, with the island's characters in residence, and the *Ayeri Ouzeri* diagonally opposite, good also for a full-on meal. Around the corner by the town hall (*dhimarhío*), *Barbarosa* (supper all year, lunch only during high season) gives Greek standards a continental twist. All these are joined in season by music bars such as long-lived *Kastro*, best for conversation-level music, and the *Panorama* where the island's youth hang out until dawn.

Southwestern Astypálea

A twenty-minute walk (or a short bus journey) from Hóra brings you to **LIVÁDHIA**, a fertile valley draining to a popular, good beach with a generally indifferent collection of restaurants and cafés immediately behind. You can rent a **room or studio** just inland – for example at *Studios O Manganas* (T 22430 61468; ❹), on the frontage road, representing the highest standard here, or *Venetos Studios* (T 22430 61490, F 22430 61423; ❸; May–Sept), at the base of the westerly hillside, comprising several separate buildings scattered in a pleasant orchard. Among the half-dozen **tavernas**, *To Yerani* is the most consistently open (until Oct) and renowned for its excellent *mayireftá*; they also keep simple rooms adjacent (T 22430 61484; ❷).

If the busy beach here doesn't suit, continue southwest fifteen minutes on foot to three small single coves at **Tzanáki**, packed out with naturists in midsummer. The third large bay beyond Livádhia, more easily reached by motorbike, is **Áyios Konstandínos**, a partly shaded, sand-and-gravel cove with a good seasonal taverna. Around the headland, the lonely beaches of **Vátses** and **Kaminákia** are more usually visited by excursion boat from Skála, subject to weather and captain's whim; wooden *kaïki* the *Agios Georgios* is the most characterful. By land, Vátses has the easier dirt road in, some twenty minutes by scooter from Livádhia; it's one of the sandier island beaches, with a basic *kantína*, but prone to wind. The track to Kaminákia, 8.5km from Livádhia, is rough and steep for the final 2km – best to go in a car – but the sheltered, clean and scenic cove makes the effort worthwhile. There's a good, stone-clad **taverna** (July–Sept) here, overseeing a handful of sunbeds and offering honest rustic fare (salads and a dish of the day).

It's a two-hour walk or half-hour motorbike trip from Hóra to the oasis of **Áyios Ioánnis**, just under 10km distant. Proceed northwest along the signposted paved road beginning from the windmills, then keep left when a sidetrack goes right to Panayía Flevariotíssas monastery. Beyond this point the main track, briefly dampened by a spring seeping across the road surface, curls north towards farming cottages at Messariá before reaching a junction with gates across each option. Take the left-hand one, and soon the walled orchards of the uninhabited farm-monastery of Áyios Ioánnis come into view. From the balcony of the church, a steep, faint path leads down to the base of a ten-metre waterfall, though alas bathing pools below have silted up, and the cascade itself – apparently tapped for irrigation – is likely to be dry most years.

Northeastern Astypálea

Northeast of the harbour are three coves known as **Próto** (First), **Dhéftero** (Second) and **Tríto** (Third) **Mármari**, and marked as **Marmári A'**, **B'** and **C'** respectively on some maps. The first is home to the power plant and boatyards; the next hosts the campsite while the third, relatively attractive, also marks the start of the path east to the perfectly decent coves of unfortunately named **Mamoúni** ("bug" or "critter" in Greek). Beyond Tríto Marmári, the main beach at **Stenó** ("narrow", after the isthmus here), with sandy shore and shallows, a few tamarisks and a high-season *kantína*, is the best.

ANÁLIPSI, widely known as **Maltezána** after medieval Maltese pirates, is a nine-kilometre bus trip or taxi ride from Skála. Although the second-largest settlement on Astypálea, there's surprisingly little for outsiders save a narrow, exposed, packed-sand beach (there are better ones east of the main bay) and a nice view south to some islets. Despite this, blocks of **rooms/studios** (most open only July & Aug) sprout in ranks well back from the sea, spurred by the proximity of the airport, less than 1km away. A more reliable exception, and the largest **hotel** complex on the island, is the 48-unit *Maltezana Beach* (☎22430 61558, ⓦwww.maltezanabeach.gr; ❺ high, ❸ low season; Easter to late Sept), with large, well-appointed bungalow-rooms, a restaurant and a pool. There are about eight independent **tavernas** here, the most reliably open (Feb–Christmas) being *Analipsi* (aka *Ilias and Irini's*, after the managing couple) by the jetty, which doubles as the *kafenío* for the local fishermen and seemingly every passing worker on the island. The food – fried squid, bean soup – is simple but good; confirm prices and portion size of the often frozen seafood. For more careful preparation, there's *Ovelix* a few hundred yards inland (supper much of the year, lunch also July–Aug), specialists in grilled lobster and scaly fish. Proprietor Panayiotis – bearing a strong resemblance to the cartoon character, hence the name of the restaurant – also has a few basic rooms upstairs (☎22430 61260; ❷). Behind calamus reeds and eucalyptus near the fishing jetty lie the best-preserved mosaic floors on the island: those of the Byzantine **Tallarás baths**, with somewhat crude figures of zodiacal signs, the seasons personified, and a central androgynous figure (Time or Fortune) holding the cosmic orb.

The motorable dirt track ends 23km from Hóra at **Mésa Vathý** (invariably and erroneously shown on most maps as Éxo Vathý), a sleepy fishing village with a single **taverna** (*Iy Galíni*) and superb small-craft anchorage in what's an almost landlocked inlet. Frankly, though, it's not really worth the long, bumpy trip out overland, and to rub salt in the wound, the fish on the menu is usually frozen (as all too often on Astypálea). Following several accidents, this is no longer the **backup ferry port** in winter, when Skála is buffeted by the prevailing southerlies; at such times ships use the new deep-water quay at **Áyios Andhréas**, just west of Tríto Marmári.

Kálymnos

Most of the 17,000-strong population of **Kálymnos** lives in or around the large port of Póthia, a prosperous but not conventionally beautiful town, famed for its **sponge industry**. Unfortunately, almost all of the eastern Mediterranean's sponges were devastated by a mysterious disease in 1986, related to freak warm currents, and only a few of the fleet of thirty-odd boats are still in use. Warehouses behind the harbour continue to process and sell sponges, but most of these are imported from Asia and the Caribbean. There are also still numbers of elderly gentlemen about who rely on two canes, walking frames or even wheelchairs, stark evidence of the havoc wrought in their youth by nitrogen embolism (the "bends"), long before divers understood its crippling effects.

In response to the sponge blight (and a repeat outbreak in 1999), the island established a tourist industry – confined to one string of beach resorts – and

KÁLYMNOS & TÉLENDHOS

Glaroníssia

Léros (Xirókambos)

Léros (Lakkí)

Léros (Ayía Marína)

Kós & Psérimos

Kolonóstilos
Aptíki
Emboriós
Asprokykliá
Skália   Paliónissos
589m
Kalavrós
Aryinónda
Dhrasónda
Télendhos
Áyios
Konstandínos   Paradise
Pótha
Basilicas   Pláka   Pezónda
Télendhos   Armeós   Kyrá Psilí
Hokhlakás   Massoúri   609m
Melitsahás   Myrtiés   533m   Almyrés
Styménia
Platý-Yialós   Eliés   654m   Metóhi   Plátanos
Ayía   Pánormos   Prof. Ilías   Ͱína   Dhaskalió
Kyriakí   Linária   Dhámos   679m   Vathýs
Kandoúni   Early Basilicas
Stavroú   Péra Kástro   Aktí   Sarí
Árgos   Hóra   Póthia
Ayía Fotiní
Khryssoheriás
Ayía   Vothýni
Ekateríni
Kefála
Vlyhádhia
Bay
Nerá

0   2 km

Astypálea & Amorgós

also adapted most of its sponge boats for deep-sea fishing. But **tourism**
proved as fickle as sponges, and has essentially **collapsed** since the millennium. The nonfunctioning, half-built airport near Árgos village, two decades
a-building, and thus the continuing need for tedious transfers from Kós, was
the main excuse for a mass pull-out by most package companies, with more
set to follow in 2004. Given this crash in bucket-and-spade holidays, the island
could possibly reinvent itself as an off-season hiking and rock-climbing destination – it has some of the best cliffs in Greece, and a respectable surviving
path network.

Kálymnos essentially consists of two cultivated and inhabited valleys
sandwiched between three limestone ridges, harsh in the full glare of noon
but magically tinted towards dusk. The climate, especially in winter, is purported to be drier and healthier than that of neighbouring Kós or Léros, since
the quick-draining limestone strata, riddled with many caves, doesn't retain as
much moisture. The rock does, however, admit seawater, which has tainted

Póthia's wells; drinking water must be brought in by tanker truck from the Vathýs valley, and there are also potable springs at Kamári, Potamí district of Póthia and Hóra.

Since Kálymnos is the home port of the very useful local namesake ferry (see p.372), a minor hub for Kyriakoulis Maritime hydrofoils, and moreover where the long-distance ferry lines from the Cyclades and Astypálea join up with the main Dodecanesian routes, many travellers arrive unintentionally, and are initially most concerned with how to move on quickly. Yet Kálymnos has sufficient attractions to justify a stay of several days while island-hopping – or even longer, as the remains of the package industry at the western beaches suggest.

Póthia

PÓTHIA (sometimes pronounced Pothiá), without being obviously pictur-esque, is colourful and authentically Greek, its houses marching up the valley inland or arrayed in tiers up the sides of the mountains framing it. Your first and overwhelming impression will be of the phenomenal amount of noise engendered by traffic and the cranked-up sound systems of the half-dozen waterfront cafés. This is not entirely surprising, since with nearly 16,000 inhab-itants, Póthia has overtaken Kós Town as the second-largest municipality in the Dodecanese after Ródhos Town. Things get even louder on **Easter Sunday** evening, when competing teams stationed on the heights either side of town engage in an organized dynamite-throwing contest, with feasting and general merriment afterwards.

Perhaps the most rewarding way to acquaint yourself with Póthia is by wan-dering the **backstreets**, where elegant Neoclassical houses are surrounded by surprisingly large gardens, and craftsmen ply their trade in a genuine workaday bazaar. The Pothians particularly excel in iron-working, and all but the hum-blest dwellings in the eastern Evangelístria district are adorned by splendidly ornate banisters, balcony railings and fanlights. During the Italian occupation, many local houses were painted blue and white to irritate the colonial over-lords, and though the custom has all but died out, the Greek national colours still appear amongst more traditional pink and ochre buildings.

Of the two local museums, priority should be given to the **Municipal Nautical and Folklore Museum** (Mon–Fri 8am–1.30pm, Sat & Sun 10am–12.30pm; €1.50), on the seaward side of Khristós cathedral. A large photo in the foyer shows Póthia as it was in the 1880s, with no quay, jetty, roads or sumptuous mansions, and with most of the population still up in Hóra, while other photos document sponge fishing and the Allied liberation of 1945. Three-dimensional exhibits include horribly primitive divers' breathing apparatuses, and "cages" designed to keep propellers from cutting air lines, a constant fear.

Practicalities

All **boat** and **hydrofoil** agents, including the headquarters of the *Nissos Kalymnos*, plus a municipal **tourist information** booth (sporadic Mon–Fri hours), line the waterfront as you bear right out of the pier-area gate. Olympic Airways has a helpful representative agent at Patriárhou Maxímou 12, 200m inland from the quay. Finally, four **banks** on or just behind the waterfront have ATMs.

Buses run as far as Emboriós in the northwest and Vathýs in the east, from a stop beside the municipal "palace", with schedules helpfully posted near many stops, and departures in season fairly frequent. Tickets must be bought before-hand from authorized kiosks, and cancelled on board. Otherwise, you can use shared **taxis** from Platía Kýprou (more than KTEL rates, less costly than a normal taxi), or rent a **scooter** from reputable Scootermania (☎22430 51780), just back from the waterfront, near where it bends south. There's plenty of **car rental** available on the quay (eg, Avis, ☎22430 28990; Auto Market, as for Scootermania, or ☎697 28 34 628), though the island's compact enough that only families would need one.

Accommodation

Accommodation is rarely a problem, with a little booking office on the quay; as on Kós, beware of *dhomátia* touts as you disembark, since many of their premises are substandard, unlicensed or remote – often all three. The town's best, and quietest **hotel**, near the "archeological" museum, is the garden-set *Villa Themelina* (☎22430 22682, ☎22430 23920; ❷ B&B; open all year), housed in an early-twentieth-century mansion, plus modern studio and apartment annexes (❸–❹), with breakfast patio and a large swimming pool. The high-ceiling, bug-screened, wood-floored rooms in the main house make this Kálymnos's most elegant accommodation. The only comparable alternative, on the west quay but fairly quiet, is the *Arhondiko* (☎22430 24051, ☎22430 24149; ❷), another refurbished mansion whose somewhat plain rooms have TV, fridge and air con; some also have balconies. Two places in Amoudhára district (west of the harbour) are worth contacting in advance: the en-suite *Pension Greek House* (☎22430 29559; ❶) with volubly friendly management, some studios and kitsch decor; and considerably above this, the well-signposted, well-kept *Hotel Panorama* (☎22430 22917, ☎22430 23138; ❷; April–Oct), which has balconied rooms with views and a pleasant break-fast salon.

Eating

The best place for **eating out** used to be the line of seafood tavernas north-east along the waterfront past the Italian-built municipal "palace", but stan-dards have dipped and prices risen; the only spot here worth a mention is *Rembetiko*, which often has live music nights. Much the best seafood and Kalymnian specialties are found at *Taverna Pandelis*, tucked inconspicuously into a cul-de-sac behind the waterfront *Olympic Hotel*; this features daily, fresh-gathered shellfish like *foúskes* and *kalógnomes* (related to mussels) and wild scaly fish. Other alternatives include *mayireftá* at *Xefteris*, well signposted inland from Khristós cathedral, or excellent wood-fired pizzas at *Pizza Porto* and *Pizza Imia*, near each other at mid-quay. Fans of sticky cakes and home-made ice cream will want to attend the traditional *Zaharoplastio O Mihalaras* back on restaurant row; they've a more modern annexe near the ferry jetty. **Nightlife** venues are in a state of constant flux; *Neon* on the quay has three **Internet** terminals (€2/30min). A **cinema**, Cine Oasis, operates both summer and winter premises behind the traditional, column-facaded café-tearoom *Ai Musai*, on the front.

Around Póthia

Just over 1km northwest of Póthia, in the suburb of Mýli, is a castle of the Knights of St John, **Kástro Khryssoheriás** (unrestricted access). From the whitewashed battlements there are wonderful views southeast over town to Kós, and north towards Hóra and Péra Kástro. The former Kalymnian capital of **HÓRA** (aka

Horió), 1.5km further along the main road, is still a village of nearly three thousand inhabitants, and guards a critical pass in local geography, focus of settlement in every era. Steep steps lead up from its eastern edge to the nocturnally illuminated Byzantine citadel-town of **Péra Kástro** (daily May–Oct 10am–2pm; tip to guide), appropriated by the Knights of St John and inhabited until late in the eighteenth century. Inside the imposing gate heaps of rubble are slowly being repieced together; a guided tour by the warden visits five well-maintained, whitewashed chapels, containing late medieval fresco fragments.

Some 200m past the turning for Árgos en route to the northwest coast from Hóra, you can detour briefly left to visit two early Byzantine basilicas which are fairly representative, and among the easiest to find, of a vast number on Kálymnos. The more impressive of the two, accessed by whitewashed steps on the left just as the highway begins to descend, is that of **Khristós tís Ierousalím**, probably dating from the late fourth century, with its apse fully preserved; the three-aisled **Limniótissa** church in an adjacent field is larger but considerably less intact.

West coast resorts

From the basilicas, the road dips into a tree-shaded valley leading to the consecutive **beach resorts** of Kandoúni, Myrtiés and Massoúri, collectively referred to as "Brostá" by islanders. **KANDOÚNI**, some 200m of brown, hard-packed sand favoured by the locals, is the shore annexe of the rich agricultural valley-villages of **Pánormos** and **Eliés**. Kandoúni **accommodation** freed up by the departure of the tour companies includes the *Kalydna Island Hotel* (☎22430 47880; ❹), but for both bathing and staying you're probably better off at **LINÁRIA**, the north end of the same bay. A smaller cove set apart from Kandoúni proper by a rock outcrop, this has better sand and the possibility of **staying** at *Skopellos Studios* (☎22430 47155; ❸), on the slope below the church. There's just a single surviving shoreline taverna here, *Yiorgos*, following a landslide that destroyed its neighbour.

The next beach north, **PLATÝ-YIALÓS**, though again a bit shorter than Kandoúni, is arguably the best on the island: cleaner than its southern neighbours, more secluded, and placed scenically at the base of a cliff, opposite Ayía Kyriakí islet. A lone **taverna** (*Kyma/Wave*), right behind the sand at road's end, proves popular for simple, inexpensive lunches or sunset drinks (it closes shortly after). Among a handful of choices for **staying** on spec, long-time budget favourite is the Vavoulas family's *Pension Plati Gialos* (☎ & ℻22430 47029, ⓦwww.pension-plati-gialos.de), actually overlooking Linária, with spacious balconies, mosquito nets and a well-attended terrace bar; choose between simple, fan-equipped rooms (❷) or two family apartments (❸). For more comfort, *Mousselis Studios* (☎22430 47757; ❸) is just down the road towards the beach, with an acceptable restaurant.

The main road climbs from Pánormos up to a pass, where the *Hotel Kamari* (☎22430 47278, ℻22430 48130; ❷) is another non-packaged possibility, with views from most rooms, before descending in zigzags to meet the sea again 8km from Póthia at **MYRTIÉS**. Together with **MASSOÚRI** (1km north) and **ARMEÓS** (2km north and end of the line for most buses), it has been hardest hit by the Kalymnian tourism slump, so vacant and boarded-up premises abound. No great loss in many cases, as during their long tenure the package companies had a predictably dire effect on local **tavernas**; the best survivor, in Armeós, is meat specialists *Tsopanakos*. Armeós is also the local mecca for **rock-climbers**, with many of the most popular cliffs overhead and a small equipment shop (Climber's Nest) catering to them. The beach at Myrtiés is narrow, pebbly and cramped by development, though it does improve as you approach Massoúri. The closest all-sand beach to Myrtiés lies 500m south, at **Melitsahás** cove (Melitsáhas in dialect), which also has the only locally patronized **taverna** at its fishing anchorage, *Iy Dhrossia* (open all year), best for oysters, lobster and shrimp as well as scaly fish at affordable rates. On-spec **accommodation** is now fairly easy to find, if still beset as ever by road noise; remoter, quieter spots include the largish *Maria's Studios* (☏22430 48135 or 22430 28528; ❷), enjoying spectacular views from above Melitsahás, or *Studios Niki's* (☏22430 47201; ❷), up on the higher one-way bypass road between Myrtiés and Massoúri. Possibly this coast's most appealing feature is its position opposite the evocatively shaped islet of Télendhos (see below), which frames some of the most dramatic sunsets in Greece. It's also possible to go from Myrtiés directly to Xirókambos on Léros aboard the daily early-afternoon **kaïki**.

Some 5km beyond Massoúri, **ARYINÓNDA** has a clean pebble beach backed by a single **rooms** outfit, *Arginonta Beach* (☏22430 40000; ❶), with a friendly proprietor, and a few beach **tavernas**. It is also the trailhead for the spectacular two-and-a-half-hour walk inland and over two gentle passes to Metóhi in the Vathýs valley. From the bus stop and gravelled car-park area and small spring, head southeast on a path between rock walls which soon climbs the south flank of the ravine here, sporadically marked by paint dots. Don't believe sources which show the route emerging at Styménia, and be aware that in the future the municipality intends to bulldoze a road from just above the *Arginonta Beach* to Styménia, which may disrupt the first half-hour or more of the trail. You'll need a sun hat, stout shoes and a litre or two of water, as the next source is in Plátanos hamlet, beyond Metóhi.

The end of the bus line, **EMBORIÓS**, 20km from the port, offers a gravel-and-sand beach, which gets better as you head west, **accommodation** and a number of **tavernas**, including the long-running *Harry's Paradise*, with attached, air-conditioned garden apartments (☏22430 40061; ❸) in bland white-and-pine decor. If the twice-daily bus service fails you, there is usually a shuttle boat back to Myrtiés at 4pm (leaving the latter at 10am).

Télendhos

The trip across the strait to the striking, volcanic-plug islet of **TÉLENDHOS** is arguably the best reason to come to Myrtiés; little boat-buses shuttle to and fro regularly (8am–midnight, half-hourly each direction; €1.50). According to local legend, Télendhos is a petrified princess, gazing out to sea after her errant lover; the woman's-head profile is most evident at dusk. The hardly less pedestrian geological explanation has the islet sundered from Kálymnos by a cataclysmic earthquake in 554 AD; traces of a submerged town are said to lie at the bottom of the straits.

Home to about fifteen permanent inhabitants, Télendhos is car-free and blissfully tranquil, even more so since many package operators gave up allotments here. For cultural edification you'll find the ruined thirteenth-century **monastery of Áyios Vassílios** and an enormous, 1997-excavated **basilica of Ayía Triádha** up on the ridge, part way along the flagstoned, ten-minute path to **Hokhlakás** pebble beach, which is small but very scenic, with sunbeds for rent. **Pótha** and nudist **"Paradise"** on the other side of the islet are preferred by some.

There are about eight places to eat and a roughly equal number of **accommodation** establishments, most (but not all) linked to the tavernas. Places to stay that get uniformly positive reviews include: *Pension Studios Rita* (T 22430 47914, F 22430 47927), rooms (❶) and renovated-house studios (❷), managed by the namesake snack-bar/café; the simple but en-suite rooms above *Zorba's* (T 22430 48660; ❶); *Rinio Studios* (T 22430 23851; ❷), set a bit inland and built in 2003 to a high standard; or, north beyond Áyios Vassílios, the Greek-Australian-run *On the Rocks*, three superbly appointed rooms with double glazing and mosquito nets (T 22430 48260, W otr.telendos.com; ❸; April–Nov). If you want more (relative) luxury on Télendhos, it's fairly easy to secure a vacancy at the large *Hotel Porto Potha* (T 22430 47321, E portopotha @klm.forthnet.gr; ❷), set rather bleakly at the very edge of things but with a large pool and friendly managing family. Endorseable **tavernas** include *Barba Stathis*, en route to Hokhlakás; *Zorba's*, dab hands at sardines and goat in tomato sauce; *Plaka*, next to *On the Rocks*, good for inexpensive meat straight from grandpa's flock; and the slightly pricey, full-service taverna at *On the Rocks* itself, with lovely home-made desserts, and a bar that's the heart and soul of local **nightlife** (including "Greek Nights"). At one corner of the premises you can visit yet another Byzantine monument, the chapel of Áyios Harálambos, occupying a former bathhouse.

Vathýs

The first 4km east from Póthia seem vastly unpromising (power plant, rubbish tip, multiple gasworks, cement quarries, fish farms), until you round a bend and the ten-kilometre ride ends dramatically at **VATHÝS**, a long, fertile valley, carpeted with orange and tangerine groves, whose colour provides a startling contrast to the mineral greys and oranges higher up on Kálymnos. At the simple fjord port of **RÍNA**, more ruined basilicas flank the bay; near the southerly one is the best **accommodation** option, the helpful *Rooms Manolis* (T 22430 31300; ❶), simple but en suite and with sweeping views, set in landscaped terraces accessible by a lane behind *The Harbors* (see below). Some of the **tavernas** are pricier than you'd expect, owing to patronage from the numerous yachts that call here; the best choice, with shambolic service but good grilled fish, is *The Harbors*, the first place on the right at the road's end.

The steep-sided inlet has no beach to speak of, so people swim off the artificial lido on the far right; the closest pebble-coves reachable overland are **Aktí**, about 3km back towards Póthia, a functional pebble strand with sunbeds and a single snack-bar, and **Pezónda**, a little further north, reached by steep track (and then a 45-minute walk northwest) starting from Metóhi hamlet. At track's end another path heads east in fifteen minutes to the amazingly set little **monastery of Kyrá Psilí**, frequented only on August 15.

Boat excursions sometimes visit the stalactite cave of **Dhaskalió**, inhabited in Neolithic times, out towards the fjord mouth on its north flank, and the remoter, tiny beaches of **Almyrés** and **Dhrasónda**, accessible only by sea.

It's possible to **walk** back to Póthia along the old direct *kalderími* which existed before the coastal highway – a two-hour jaunt which begins in Plátanos hamlet. The route is tricky to find in this direction, however, so most people start in Póthia, at the church of Ayía Triádha behind the *Villa Themelina* hotel – the way is marked initially by red paint splodges.

The southwest

Climbing southwest out of Póthia towards Áyios Sávvas monastery, the most worthwhile halt is the privately run "**Folklore Museum-Traditional**

House of Kalymnos" (daily 9am–9pm; €1.50), a treasure trove of old-time furnishings and costumes. Some 6km southwest of Póthia, the small bay of **Vlyhádhia** is reached through a narrow ravine draining from the nondescript village of Vothýni. The sand-and-pebble beach here isn't really worth a special trip, since the bay is apt to be sumpy and at least some of the locals (who have blotted out all Roman-alphabet road signs) are resentful of foreigners. If you're interested in **scuba diving**, the Vlyhádhia area is one of the limited number of legal areas in Greece. Local divemaster Stavros Valsamidhes has also assembled an impressive **Museum of Submarine Finds** (Mon–Sat 9am–7pm, Sun 10am–2pm; free), which in addition to masses of sponges and shells offers a reconstructed ancient wreck with amphorae and World War II debris. Depending on your ability, dives (arrange on ☏22430 50662) may visit ancient wrecks *in situ*, as well as seal caves.

Póthia-based *kaïkia* make well-publicized excursions to the cave of **Kefála** just west of Vlyhádhia, the most impressive of half a dozen caverns around the island. You have to walk thirty minutes from where the boats dock, but the vividly coloured formations repay the effort; the cave was inhabited before recorded history, and later served as a sanctuary of Zeus (who is fancifully identified with a particularly imposing stalagmite in the biggest of six chambers).

Léros

Léros is so indented with deep, sheltered anchorages that during World War II it harboured, in turn, much of the Italian, German and British Mediterranean fleets. Unfortunately, many of these magnificent fjords and bays seem to absorb rather than reflect light, and the island's fertility – there are orchards and vegetable gardens a-plenty – can make Léros seem scruffy when compared with the crisp lines of its more barren neighbours. These characteristics, plus the island's lack of spectacularly good beaches, meant that until the late 1980s just a few thousand foreigners (mostly Italians who grew up on the island), and not many more Greeks, came to visit each year, mostly in August.

August is still mayhem, but the tourist profile is now broader, with a longer season; Scandinavian, British, Dutch and German package operators have long since "discovered" Léros and the company of islanders relatively unjaded by mass tourism. Foreign-visitor numbers have, however, levelled off or even dipped since the late 1990s, with matters unlikely to change until and unless the airport runway is lengthened to accommodate jets.

Not that Léros strenuously encourages mass tourism; various **prisons and sanatoriums** have dominated the Lerian economy since the 1950s, directly or indirectly employing about a third of the population. During the junta era, the island hosted a notorious detention centre at Parthéni, and today the mental hospital on Léros remains the repository for many of Greece's more intractable psychiatric cases; another asylum is home to hundreds of mentally handicapped children. The island's domestic image problem is compounded by its name, the butt of jokes by mainlanders who pounce on its similarity to the word *lerá*, connoting rascality and unsavouriness. *Thá tiliósto stí Léro* ("I'll end up in Léros") and *Thá soú páo Léro* ("I'll send you to Léros") are standard locutions on neighbouring islands for, respectively, self and others who are showing signs of mental wobbliness. In 1989, a major scandal emerged concerning the administration of the various

Lipsí & Pátmos

N

Blefoútis

Artemis
Temple
Parthéni
Reservoir

Kryfós

Áyios
Nikólaos

Álinda
Panayiés

Kokálli

Ayía Marína

Krithóni

Goúrna
Plátanos
Pandélli

Áyios
Isídhoros

Vromólithos

Ángyra

Dhrymónas
Lakkí

Kouloúki
Teménia

Merikiá
Katsoúni

Lepídha

Xirókambos

Pátmos

0   2 km

Kálymnos ▼   Kálymnos ▼   Kálymnos & Kós ▼

asylums, with EU maintenance and development funds found to have been embezzled by staff, and inmates kept in degrading conditions. A subsequent influx of EU inspectors, foreign psychiatrists and extra funding resulted in drastic improvements in patient treatment.

More obvious is the legacy of the **Battle of Léros** on November 12–16, 1943, when overwhelming German forces displaced a Commonwealth division which had landed on the island following the Italian capitulation. Bomb nose-cones and shell casings still turn up as gaily painted garden ornaments in the courtyards of churches and tavernas, or have been pressed into service as gateposts. Each year for three days following September 26, memorial services and a naval festival commemorate the sinking of the Greek battleships *Queen Olga* and *Intrepid* during the German attack.

Unusually for a small island, Léros has abundant ground water, channelled into cisterns at several points (currently, alas, not potable). These, plus low-lying ground staked with the avenues of eucalyptus trees planted by the Italians, make for an unusually active mosquito contingent, so come prepared. The island's main centres are concentrated enough to walk between, with sufficient hills to give cyclists a good work-out. There is an adequate bus service, plus several car-, scooter- and bicycle-rental outfits, of which Motoland (branches at Álinda and Pandélli) have proven reliable. If you rent a scooter, take extra care – Lerian roads are particularly narrow, potholed and gravel-strewn, and the low-slung, fat-tyred bikes on offer don't cope well.

Lakkí and Xirókambos

All large **ferries** arrive at the main port of **LAKKÍ**, originally constructed in 1935–38 as a model town to house 7500 civilian dependents of an adjacent Italian naval base. Boulevards far too wide for today's paltry amount of traffic are lined with some marvellous Rationalist edifices, including the round-fronted cinema (functioning once again), the church, the primary school, a shopping centre with a round atrium and the derelict remains of the Leros Palace Hotel.

Buses don't meet the ferries – instead there's a **taxi squadron** that charges set fares to standard destinations. If you arrive during business hours, consider renting a car or bike from Koumoulis, near the cinema. Few people stay willingly at any of the handful of listless hotels in Lakkí, preferring to head straight for the resorts of Pandélli, Álinda or Vromólithos (see opposite). There's just one proper – if not consistently open – **taverna**, *Tò Petrino*, inland next to the **post office**; three ATMs attached to as many **banks**; Kastis, the DANE agent (☎22470 22500); Leros Travel, the GA Ferries agent (☎22470 22154); and Aegean Travel a block inland (☎22470 26000), for Blue Star Ferries. The nearest approximation of a **beach** is at sand-and-gravel **Kouloúki**, 500m west, where there's a seasonal taverna and some pines for shade, though it's too close to the ferry jetty for most tastes. You can carry on another kilometre or so to **Merikiá**, a slight improvement, also with a taverna.

XIRÓKAMBOS, nearly 5km from Lakkí in the far south of the island, is the point of arrival for the afternoon *kaïki* from Myrtiés on Kálymnos (it goes back very early the following morning). Though billed as a resort, it's essentially a fishing port where folk also happen to swim – the beach here is poor to mediocre, improving as you head west. Top **accommodation** here is the *Hotel Efstathia* (☎22470 24099; ❹), actually studio apartments with huge, well-furnished doubles as well as family four-plexes, plus a large pool. You've a choice of three **tavernas** at the east end of things, where the road hits the shore. The island's **campsite** (☎22470 23372; May–Oct), with an in-house scuba-diving centre (☎694 42 38 490), is in an olive grove at the village of **LEPÍDHA**, 750m back up the road to Lakkí. Just north of the site, an access drive on the far side of the road leads up to a tiny acropolis with stretches of ancient masonry and sparse patches of early Christian mosaics.

Pandélli and Vromólithos

Just less than 3km north of Lakkí, Pandélli and Vromólithos together form an attractive and scenic resort, Álinda's (see p.362) only rival.

PANDÉLLI is still very much a working port, the cement jetty benefiting local fishermen as well as an increasing number of yachts that call here. A negligible beach is compensated for by a relative abundance of nonpackage **accommodation**, such as the *Pension Happiness* (☎22470 23498; ❷), where the road down from Plátanos meets the sea, or the newer *Pension Lavyrinthos*, directly opposite (☎22470 24165; ❷). For a higher standard, try *Niki Studios* (☎22470 25600; ❸) at the base of the road up to the castle – airy, Australian-Greek-run and with partial sea views. Up on the ridge dividing Pandélli from Vromólithos, the en-suite *Hotel Rodon* (☎22470 23524; ❷) is basic but friendly, with knock-out views and pricier studios downstairs. On summer nights there may be a faint strain of music from *Café del Mar*, perched on a rock terrace below (it operates as a daytime bar May–Oct); the other long-lived local **bar** is the civilized, English-Danish-run *Savana*, at the opposite end of Pandélli, with excellent music (you can nominate your favourite tracks). It stands beyond a row of waterfront **tavernas** that, alas, are mostly tourist traps of the first order. Exceptions include *Psaropoula*, with good fish and *mayireftá*; *Kafenio tou Tzouma*, a seafood *ouzerí*; and – up adjacent to *Hotel Rodon* – *Mezedhopolio Dimitris*, reckoned the best (and arguably best-sited) *ouzerí* on the island, scoring highly for delicacies such as chunky local sausages and *hánoum boúrek* (stuffed with *pastourmás* or cured meat) along with the usual dips.

VROMÓLITHOS boasts the best easily accessible **beach** on the island, car-free and hemmed in by hills studded with massive oaks. The shoreline is gravel and coarse sand, and the sea here is clean, but as so often on Léros you have to cross a rock pavement at most points before reaching deeper water. Two **tavernas** behind the beach trade more on their location than their cuisine, but the standard of **accommodation** here is higher than at Pandélli. Prime choices are *Tony's Beach*, spacious studio units set in equally extensive waterside grounds (☎22470 24743, ⓦ www.tonysbeachstudios.gr; ❹; June–Sept), and the stone-floored *Glaros*, just inland in pleasant grounds (☎22470 24358, ⓕ 22470 23683; ❹; May–Oct).

Plátanos and Ayía Marína

The Neoclassical and vernacular houses of **PLÁTANOS**, the island capital 1km west of Pandélli, are draped gracefully along a saddle between two hills, one of them crowned by the inevitable Knights' castle. Known locally as the **Kástro** (daily 8am–1pm, also May–Oct Wed, Sat & Sun 3–7pm; €1), this is reached either by a zigzagging road peeling off the Pandélli-bound road, or via a more scenic stair-path from the central square; the battlements, and the views from them, are dramatic, especially near sunrise or sunset. The medieval church of **Panayía tou Kástrou** inside the gate houses a small museum (additional €1), though its carved *témblon* and naïve oratory are more remarkable than the sparse exhibits, mostly icons and other liturgical items. The **archeological museum** (Tues–Sun 8am–2.30pm; free), down the road to Ayía Marína, is more interesting.

Plátanos is not really a place to stay or eat, although it's well sown with **shops** and **services**. The latter include Olympic Airways, south of the turning for Pandélli; a **post office**, down the road towards Ayía Marína; and two **banks** (one with an ATM). The single **bus** (schedule posted at the stop, opposite the island's main **taxi** rank) plies three or four times daily between Parthéni in the north and Xirókambos in the south.

Plátanos merges seamlessly with **AYÍA MARÍNA**, 1km north on the shore of a fine bay, still graced by a small, Italian-built public market building. If you're travelling to Léros on an excursion boat, catamaran, the small ferry *Nissos Kalymnos*, or hydrofoil, this will be your port of entry. Although accommodation here is very limited, it has some of the best places to **eat** on the island. Just west of the police station, on the water, *Mezedhopolio tou Kapaniri* (open all year) is a good, reasonable *ouzerí*, at its best after dark, with a wide-ranging menu including pizzas. Further west, there's the superior *Ouzeri Neromylos* (closed late Oct to mid-March), out by the marooned windmill, again serving a wide variety of dishes, especially seafood. Lively (for Léros) **nightlife** is provided by a half-dozen bars near the main junction, such as *Enallaktiko*, with a few **Internet** terminals, and *Apothiki New Face* on the quay. Kastis Travel nearby (☎22470 22140) handles all ticket sales for departing hydrofoils and the catamaran, plus there are two bank **ATMs**, one of them a stand-alone model on the quay.

Álinda and the north

ÁLINDA, 3km northwest of Ayía Marína, ranks as the longest-established resort on Léros, with development just across the road from a long, narrow strip of pea-gravel beach. It's also the first area for accommodation to open in spring, and the last to shut in autumn. Most of the **hotels** and **pensions** here are partly alotted to tour companies, but worthwhile establishments that keep rooms back for walk-ins include *Hotel Gianna* (T22470 23153; ❸), with fridge-equipped rooms plus a few studios overlooking the war cemetery, or – set back from mid-beach – the well-kept *Hotel Alinda* (T22470 23266, F22470 23383; ❸), with a decent restaurant and sunken Byzantine mosaic out front, plus spacious rooms (some air con). One to avoid is *Studios Diamantis*, whose thoroughly unpleasant management touts aggressively from their taxi and gift shop in Ayía Marína. At **Krithóni**, 1.5km south, more comfort is available at the island's top-flight accommodation: the *Crithoni's Paradise* (T22470 25120, F22470 24680; rooms ❻, suites ❼–❽; open all year), a mock-traditional low-rise complex with decent buffet breakfast, a large pool and all mod cons in the rooms. Álinda's independent **restaurant** options aren't brilliant, except for Italian-run *Osteria Da Giusi e Marcello* near the north end of the beach (supper only; closed early Jan to March), which does pizza, pasta and decadent desserts, accompanied by bulk and bottled Italian wine.

The **Allied War Graves Cemetery**, mostly containing casualties of the November 1943 battle, occupies a walled enclosure at the south end of the beach; immaculately maintained, it serves as a moving counterpoint to the holiday hubbub outside. The other principal sight at Álinda is the privately run **Historical and Ethnographic Museum** (May–Sept only, Tues–Sun 9am–1pm & 7–9pm; €3), housed in the unmistakable castle-like mansion of Paris Bellinis (1871–1957). Most of the top floor is devoted to the Battle of Léros: relics from the sunken *Queen Olga*, a wheel from a Junkers bomber, a stove made from a bomb casing. There's also a rather grisly mock-up clinic (mostly gynecological tools) and assorted rural impedimenta, costumes and antiques.

Alternative beaches near Álinda include **Panayiés**, a series of gravel coves (one naturist) at the far northeast of the bay, and **Goúrna**, the turning for which lies 1km or so off the trans-island road. The latter, Léros's longest sandy beach, is hard-packed and gently shelving, if wind-buffeted; a few sunbeds are provided by the single taverna. A separate road beyond the Goúrna turning leads to **Kokálli**, no great improvement beach-wise, but flanked to one side by the scenic islet of **Áyios Isídhoros**, which is tethered to the mainland by a causeway, its eponymous chapel perched on top.

Seven kilometres from Álinda along the main route north, a marked side-track leads left to the purported **Temple of Artemis**, on a slight rise just west of the airport runway. In ancient times, Léros was sacred to the goddess, and the temple here was supposedly inhabited by guinea fowl – the grief-stricken sisters of Meleager, metamorphosed thus by Artemis following their brother's death. All that remains now are some jumbled, knee-high walls, which are more likely to have been an ancient fortress, but the view is superb.

The tiny **airport** terminal itself is being expanded for a busier future, but it's still no place to be stuck a minute longer than necessary; if your midday flight to Astypálea or Rhodes is delayed (more likely than not), you can repair across the road to a **taverna**, *To Arhondiko*, for an acceptable if rather pricey lunch.

The onward route skims the shores of sumpy, reed-fringed Parthéni Bay, with its yacht dry dock and dreary, Italian-built army base (formerly the political prison), until the paved road ends 11km along at **Blefoútis**, a rather more inspiring sight with its huge, almost landlocked bay. The small beach (the rough Lerian norm) has tamarisks to shelter under and an adequate taverna, *Iy Thea Artemi*, for a *kalamári*-and-chips lunch.

Pátmos

Arguably the most beautiful and certainly the best known of the smaller Dodecanese, **Pátmos** has a distinctive, immediately palpable atmosphere. It was in a cave here that St John the Divine (in Greek, O Theológos or "The Theologian"), received the New Testament's Book of Revelation and unwittingly shaped the island's destiny. The monastery honouring him, founded here in 1088 by the Blessed Khristodhoulos (1021–93), dominates Pátmos both physically – its fortified bulk towering high above everything else – and, to a considerable extent, socially. While the monks inside no longer run the island unchallenged as they did for more than six centuries, their influence has stopped it going the way of Rhodes or Kós – though Pátmos now has no less than three nudist beaches, something unthinkable a decade or so ago. Despite vast numbers of visitors and the island's firm presence on the cruise, hydrofoil and yacht circuits, tourism has not been allowed to take Pátmos over completely. While there are several after-hours clubs around Skála, drunken rowdiness is virtually unknown. Package clients only outnumber independent visitors in certain years, and are pretty much confined to Gríkou and a handful of larger hotels at Skála and Kámbos. Day-trippers still exceed overnighters, and Pátmos seems an altogether different place once the last cruise-ship passengers have gone at sunset. Away from Skála, touristic development is appealingly subdued if not deliberately retarded, thanks to the absence of an airport – real-estate sales seem to be the major activity.

Skála and around

SKÁLA, with most of the island's population of about three thousand, seems initially to contradict any solemn, otherworldly image of Pátmos. The waterside, with its ritzy jewellery shops, cafés and clientele, is a bit too sophisticated for such a small town, and certain service staff more than a little world-weary. During peak season, the quay and commercial district swarm by day with trippers souvenir-hunting or being shepherded onto coaches for the ride up to the monastery; after dark there's still a considerable traffic in well-dressed cliques of visitors on furlough from the cruise ships anchored outside the bay. In winter (which here means by Oct 10), Skála assumes a ghost-town air as most shops and restaurants close, and their owners and staff go back to Rhodes or Athens.

Hóra, a bus or taxi ride up the mountain, would be a more attractive base, but has few rooms. Yet given time – especially in spring or autumn – Skála reveals some more enticing corners in the residential fringes to the east and west, where vernacular mansions hem in pedestrian lanes creeping up the hillsides. The modern town dates only from the 1820s, when the Aegean had largely been cleared of pirates, but at the summit of the westerly rise, **Kastélli**, you can see the extensive foundations of the island's ancient acropolis.

Practicalities

Almost everything of interest can be found within, or within sight of, the Italian-built municipal "palace": large ferries anchor opposite, the port police occupy the east end, the **post office** one of its corners, and the useless **tourist**

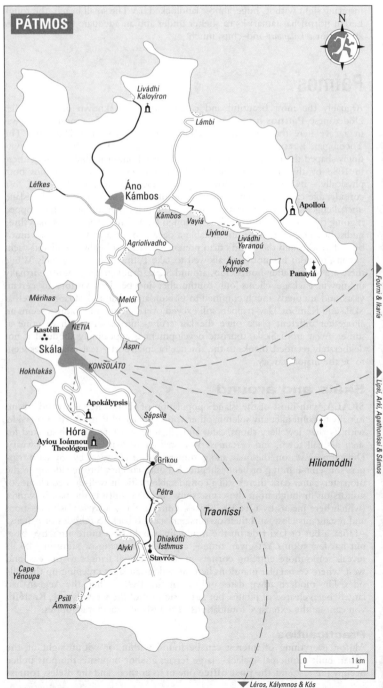

PÁTMOS

N

Livádhi
Kaloyíron

Lámbi

Léfkes

Áno
Kámbos

Apolloú

Kámbos   Vayiá

Liyínou

Agriolívadho

Livádhi
Yeranoú

Áyios
Yeóryios

Panayiá

Mérihas

Melóï

NETIÁ

Áspri

Kastélli

Skála

KONSOLÁTO

Hokhlakás

Apokálypsis

Sápsila

Hóra

Ayíou Ioánnou
Theológou

Gríkou

Hiliomódhi

Pétra

Traoníssi

Alykí

Dhiakófti
Isthmus

Stavrós

Cape
Yénoupa

Psilí
Ámmos

Fourní & Ikaría

Lipsí, Arkí, Agathoníssi & Sámos

Léros, Kálymnos & Kós

0   1 km

office (erratic hours) is tucked into an inconspicuous door in the front. There are two **banks**, each with an ATM. **Scooter rental** outfits are common, with lowish rates (€10 a day or less) owing to the modest size of the island. **Excursion boats** to Psilí Ámmos, Lipsí and Arkí/Maráthi all leave at about 10am from just in front of Astoria Travel and Apollon Travel, the two places handling hydrofoil tickets. GA Ferries and the *Nissos Kalymnos*/DANE (☎22470 32575) have separate agencies on, or just off, the central waterfront square; Blue Star Ferries and the *Dodekanisos Express* catamaran share an agency, Kyriaki Liapi (☎22470 29303) in Konsoláto district to the east.

Accommodation

Accommodation touts meet all ferries and hydrofoils, and their offerings tend to be a long walk distant and/or inland – not necessarily a bad thing, as no location is really remote, and anywhere near the waterfront, which doubles as the main road between Gríkou and Kámbos, will be noisy. Pátmos vernacular architecture is quite distinctive, but you wouldn't know it from most lodgings, bland if inoffensive rooms thrown up using EU money during the 1980s, with institutional (one might even say monastic) furnishings.

Establishments worth reserving in advance (they'll often send a van to fetch you) are scattered across several districts. In **central Skála**, good hotel choices include *Effie* (☎22470 32500, ℉22470 32700; ❸–❹), on the hillside above the municipal car park, with anodyne, pine-and-tile, heated/air-con rooms but the unusual virtue of all-year operation; the *Kastelli* a few paces higher on the same lane, with better views (☎22470 31361, ℉22470 31656; ❹); or the welcoming, well-appointed *Galini*, in a secluded cul-de-sac off the Hóra road (☎22470 31240, ℉22470 31705; ❹).

Konsoláto district, east of the centre near the fishing anchorage, has more high-quality digs, though the worst noise from fishing boats and ferries coming and going from 1 to 4am. Here you'll find the overpriced *Captain's House* (☎22470 31793, ℉22470 32277; ❺), with friendly management, above -average furnishings and affiliated car rental; and the better-value *Byzance*, a few steps inland (☎22470 31052, ⓦbyzancehotel.com; ❹), with premises spread over two buildings – go for the larger rooms with balconies looking onto a garden. Some 150m further towards Gríkou, the *Blue Bay* (☎22470 31165, ⓦwww.bluebay.50g.com; ❹–❺; April–Oct) is probably the best choice here, with helpful Australian-Greek management, reasonably furnished sea-view rooms with fridges and air con, plus relative calm for the area.

Netiá, the unglamorous area northwest between the power plant and Mérihas cove, is actually a good choice as a base. Various members of a Greek-Australian family run clustered establishments: the *Hotel Australis* (☎22470 31576, ℉22470 32284; ❸), with full breakfast for the price, on-site bike rental, and myriad small kindnesses that guarantee repeat clientele; their annexe the *Australis Apartments* (☎22470 32562, fax as above), accommodating four people; the adjacent *Villa Knossos* (☎22470 32189; ❹), whose rooms all have attractive terraces; or the more basic *Pension Sydney* up the hill (☎22470 31689; ❸), offering balconied rooms with fridge and fan. But the best standard in this area is provided by the *Hotel Asteri* (☎22470 32465, ℯpasca@otenet.gr; ❸–❺), unimprovably set on a knoll overlooking the bay, in a well-landscaped environment that's also a working farm – guests have home-produced honey, eggs and tomatoes at breakfast.

Pebbly **Hokhlakás** Bay, just a ten-minute walk southwest starting from the central market street, is perhaps the quietest district, with wonderful sunset views. Comfortable, welcoming options here include the hillside *Studios Yvonni*

(☎22470 32466, ⊛www.12net.gr/yvonni; ❹), whose management is most easily findable at the giftshop of the same name near the DANE agency; or the *Maria* down in the flatlands (☎22470 31201, ⑤22470 32018; ❹ high, ❷ low season; Easter to mid-Oct), where a pleasant front garden, air conditioning and big sea-view balconies make up for tiny bathrooms. Exposed Hokhlakás isn't very swimmable; if you're keen to stay nearer to a proper beach, head for the well-run, pleasantly set **campsite** *Stefanos-Flowers* at **Melóï**, 1.5km north of Skála, just down the slope from Pátmos's most exclusive digs, the *Porto Scoutari Hotel* (☎22470 33124, ⊛www.portoscoutari.com; ❺–❼), a sea-view bungalow complex open all year. Both individual spacious units and common areas are furnished with mock antiques and original art, all arrayed around a large pool.

Eating and drinking

Restaurant options in Skála have improved from an era of surplus *souvláki/yíros* joints or snack stalls, and not enough full-service, sit-down places. Easily the town's most distinctive is seafood-only *Ouzeri Tò Hiliomodhi* (open all year), just off the start of the Hóra road, with its vegetarian *mezédhes* and delicacies such as limpets (served live, be warned), grilled octopus and salted anchovies, with summer seating in a pedestrian lane. The best all-rounder (Easter to early Sept) is reckoned to be *Veggera*, opposite the yacht marina, with a VIP clientele, flawless presentation for the French-Mediterranean cooking, and per-head bills of about €35; reservations required on ☎22470 32988. Honourable mentions go to *The Old Harbour* (supper May–Oct), opposite the municipal car park and town beach, where the chef moonlights from his day job feeding the monks in Hóra with a meat-rich menu of "continental" specialties, and *Pandelis*, one lane inland behind Astoria Travel, where a wide-ranging menu of reliably good *mayireftá* make up for famously dour – if efficient – service.

Aside from these, you're best off heading a bit out of town; this is one island where the beach tavernas excel. Melóï has a decent *mayireftá* taverna, *Melloi* (alias *Stefanos*), reasonably priced and open early or late in the season, best at lunch (though it gets coach tours). Just over the hill at **Áspri** cove are two more, *Aspri* and *Kyma*: the former, just inland with a wider-ranging menu, stays open later in the season, but the latter (June–Aug only), fish specialists down on a concrete mole by the water, has more charm. At **Sápsila** cove, 2km southeast of Skála, *Benetos* (supper only except Mon, June to early Oct; summer reservations mandatory on ☎22470 33089, seatings at 6, 8 & 10pm) has since 1998 established a reputation as about the best eatery on the island due to its Mediterranean and Pacific-Rim fusion dishes, with a stress on seafood. Budget a minimum of €30 for drink and three courses, which may include roast vegetable terrine with balsamic vinegar and raisins, baked fish fillet with risotto and Hubbard squash, and lemon sorbet.

Back in town, the biggest and most durable **café-bar** is the wood-panelled, barn-like *Café Arion* on the waterside, where all sorts of people sit outside, dance, or prop up the long bar. Other **nightlife** venues include the pricey *Isalos*, inland from the Italian "palace", occasionally hosting live music, and the year-round *Konsolato* late-night bar, in the eponymous district. Skála has two **Internet cafés**: one inside the *Blue Bay Hotel*, (€1/10min), the other – *Millennium* (€5/hr) – on the main lane to Hokhlakás cove.

The monasteries and Hóra

Top of your sightseeing agenda is likely to be the monastery of Ayíou Ioánnou Theológou (St John), sheltered behind massive defences in the hilltop capital of Hóra. There's a regular KTEL bus up, or you can do a forty-minute walk by a beautiful old cobbled path. To find its start, proceed through Skála towards Hokhlakás, and once past the telecoms building and the *Millennium Internet Café* bear left onto a lane starting opposite an ironmonger's; follow this uphill to its end on the main road – immediately opposite you'll see the cobbled path. Just over halfway, you might pause at the **monastery of Apokálypsis** (daily 8am–1.30pm, also Tues, Thurs & Sun 4–6pm; free) built around the cave where St John heard the voice of God issuing from a cleft in the rock, and where he sat dictating his words to a disciple. In the cave wall, the presumed nightly resting place of the saint's head is fenced off and outlined in beaten silver.

This is merely a foretaste of the monastery of **Ayíou Ioánnou Theológou** (same hours and admission as Apokálypsis). In 1088, the soldier-cleric Ioannis "The Blessed" Khristodhoulos was granted title to Pátmos by Byzantine Emperor Alexios Komnenos; within three years he and his followers had completed the essentials of the existing monastery, the threats of piracy and the Selçuk Turks dictating a heavily fortified style. A warren of interconnecting courtyards, chapels, stairways, arcades, galleries and roof terraces, it offers a rare glimpse of a Patmian interior; hidden in the walls are fragments of an ancient Artemis temple which stood here before being destroyed by Khristodhoulos. Off to one side, the **treasury** (same hours; €6) doesn't quite justify its hefty entrance fee with its admittedly magnificent array of religious treasure, mostly medieval icons of the Cretan school. Pride of place goes to an unusual mosaic icon of Áyios Nikólaos, and the eleventh-century parchment chrysobull (edict) of Emperor Alexios Komnenos, granting the island to Khristodhoulos. Cruise-ship or coach-tour patrons can crowd out the place at midday, so wisely go early or late. The best time to show up, besides the famous Easter observances, is September 25–26 (Feast of John the Theologian) and October 20–21 (Feast of Khristodhoulos), both marked by solemn liturgies and processions of the appropriate icon.

Hóra

The promise of security afforded by St John's stout walls spurred the growth of **HÓRA** immediately outside the fortifications. It remains architecturally homogeneous, with cobbled lanes sheltering dozens of shipowners' mansions from the island's seventeenth- to eighteenth-century heyday. High, windowless walls and imposing wooden doors betray nothing of the opulence within: painted ceilings, pebble-mosaic terraces, flagstoned kitchens, and carved furniture. Inevitably, touristic tattiness disfigures the main approaches to the monastery gate, but away from the principal thoroughfares are lanes that rarely see traffic, and by night, when the monastery ramparts are floodlit to startling effect, it's hard to think of a more beautiful Dodecanesian village. Neither should you miss the **view** from Platía Lódza (named after the remnant of an adjacent Venetian *loggia*), particularly at dawn or dusk. Landmasses to the north, going clockwise, include Ikaría, Thýmena, Foúrni, Sámos with its brooding mass of Mount Kérkis, Arkí, and the double-humped Samsun Daǧ (ancient Mount Mykale) in Turkey.

Among several tavernas in Hóra, *Vangelis* on the inner square has a wonderful old jukebox, friendly service and view seating on various levels, but alas the cooking is no longer estimable; you'll probably eat better at *Lotza*, near the start of the monastery approach, with light meals, crêpes and desserts. There are, however, very few places to **stay**; foreigners here are mostly long-term occupants, who have bought up and restored almost half of the crumbling mansions since the 1960s. Finding a short-term room can be a pretty thankless task, even in spring or autumn; phone well ahead for reservations at the *dhomátia* of Yeoryia Triandafyllou (☏ 22470 31963; ❸), en suite with a communal terrace, or *Marouso Kouva* (☏ 22470 31026; ❸).

The rest of the island

Pátmos, as a locally published guide once memorably proclaimed, "is immense for those who know how to wander in space and time". Lesser mortals will find the island compact and easy to get around on foot or by bus, if not a scooter. Unfortunately, most paths have been destroyed by road-building and property development; a single **bus** offers surprisingly reliable service between Skála, Hóra, Kámbos and Gríkou – the main stop, with a posted timetable, is right in front of the main ferry dock.

After its extraordinary atmosphere and striking volcanic scenery, **beaches** are Patmos's principal attraction. From Hóra, a paved road (partly shortcut by a path) winds east to the sandiest part of rather overdeveloped and cheerless **GRÍKOU**, the main venue for Patmian package tourism – and shut tight as a drum come late September. The beach itself, far from the island's best, forms a narrow strip of hard-packed sand, giving way to large pebbles at **Pétra** beach immediately south, whose far end is colonized by nudists – and whose near side features much the best rural **taverna** on Pátmos, *Ktima Petra* (May–Sept), with brown bread, lush salads, good bulk retsina, carefully cooked *mayireftá*, plus grills after dark. Still later, it becomes a bar with a full cocktails list.

En route to Pétra, named for its peculiar volcanic monolith on the shore, you pass hillside *Flisvos* (aka *Floros*), now rather eclipsed by nearby *Ktima Petra* but going since the 1960s with a limited choice of inexpensive, savoury *mayireftá*, served on the terrace. They also have basic rooms (❷) and fancier apartments (❹) – reserve on ☏ 22470 31380, ℻ 22470 32094. Another good **accommodation** option here, though it periodically gets monopolized by "special interest" groups, is the hillside *Hotel Golden Sun* (☏ 22470 32318, ⓦ www.hotel-golden-sun.com; ❺; Easter–Sept), with most rooms facing the water.

From Hóra, you can ride a scooter over as far as the Dhiakoftí isthmus, beyond which a 25-minute walk southwest on the island's last surviving bona fide path leads to **Psilí Ámmos** beach. This is the only pure-sand cove on the island, with shade lent by tamarisks, nudism galore at the far south end and a good lunchtime **taverna** that occasionally does roast goat, freshly shot on the surrounding hills. There's also a summer *kaïki* service here from Skála, departing by 10am and returning at 5 or 6pm.

Northern Pátmos

More good beaches are to be found in the **north of the island**, tucked into the startling eastern shoreline (west-facing bays are uniformly unusable owing to wind and washed-up debris); most are accessible from side roads off the main route north from Skála. **Melóï** is handy and quite appealing, with tamarisks behind the slender belt of sand, and good snorkelling offshore. The first beach beyond Méloï, **Agriolívadho (Agriolivádhi)**, has mostly sand at its broad centre, kayak rental, and two tavernas, the better being fish specialist *O Glaros* on the south hillside. Hilltop Kámbos is the only other real village on Pátmos, the focus of scattered farms in little oases all around; **Kámbos** beach, 600m downhill, is popular with Greeks, and the most developed remote resort on the island, with seasonal watersports facilities and a taverna *Ta Kavourakia*, though its appeal is diminished by the road just inland and a rock shelf in the shallows.

East of Kámbos are several less-frequented coves, including pebble **Vayiá**, nudist, double-bay **Liyínou** and sand-and-gravel **Livádhi Yeranoú**, the latter with more tamarisks, an islet to swim out to and a very good, inexpensive namesake **taverna** with something of a cult following, doing simple seafood dishes, *keftédhes*, *hórta* and salads. From lower Kámbos you can also journey north to the bay of **Lámbi**, best for swimming when the prevailing wind is from the south, and renowned for an abundance of multicoloured volcanic stones – as well as another excellent beach **taverna** *Leonidas* (May to early Oct), with a wide range of fish, *mezédhes* and grilled meat.

Lipsí

Of the various islets to the north and east of Pátmos, **LIPSÍ** is the largest, most interesting and most populated, and the one that has the most significant summer tourist trade. The presence of a British package company (Laskarina), on-spec Italian and French travellers, and the island's appearance on both main-line and off-line ferry routes, mean that it's unwise to show up in peak season without a reservation (though rooms proprietors meet arrivals at other times).

During quieter months, however, Lipsí still makes an idyllic halt, its sleepy pace making plausible a purported link between the island's name and that of **Calypso**, the nymph who legendarily held Odysseus in thrall. Deep wells provide water for many small farms, but there is only one flowing spring, and pastoral appearances are deceptive – four times the relatively impoverished full-time population of about six hundred live overseas (many in Hobart, Tasmania). Most of those who remain cluster around the fine harbour, as does the majority of food and lodging.

Of late, however, Lipsí has acquired a definite – and unwanted – link with **Dhekaeftá Noemvríou/17 November**, Greece's (and Europe's) longest-lived terrorist organization (see p.574). In July 2002, the national anti-terrorist squad swooped on the island and apprehended the group's supremo, Alexandhros Yiotopoulos (alias Nikos Ikonomou), in the act of leaving for Sámos, eventual destination exile in Turkey. He had been living quietly here for 17 years in a faded-pink hilltop villa, now abandoned and shuttered following his December 2003 conviction on all charges and life sentencing; ironically Yiotopoulos was much liked by the islanders for his generosity and willingness to help with bureaucratic problems.

The port settlement

All arriving craft use the same dock at the far west end of the port settlement, the only significant habitation on Lipsí. Amongst **travel agents**, Lipsos Travels reps for GA Ferries and the *Dodekanisos Express*; Laid Back (phone as overleaf) sells tickets for the hydrofoil and *Nissos Kalymnos*; while Paradhisis Travel by the port police changes money and organizes popular excursions to neighbouring islands, though there's a free-standing **ATM** near Paradhisis. The **post office** is up a stairway on the attractive cathedral *platía*, opposite a hilariously eclectic **ecclesiastical museum** (unpredictable hours, best chances of admission 10am–1pm daily; free) featuring such "relics" as earth collected from Mount Tabor and water from the Jordan River, as well as archeological finds, medieval glazed ware and two faded letters of 1824 from Greek revolutionary hero Admiral Miaoulis.

A prime **accommodation** choice in all senses is Nikos' and Anna's welcoming *Apartments Galini* (☎22470 41212, ℻22470 41012; ❸), the first building you see above the ferry jetty; Nikos may take guests for fishing trips on request. Equally sought after, though less airy, are the *Studios Kalymnos* in a garden on the road north out of "town" (☎22470 41141, ℻22470 41343, ℮studios_kalymnos@lipsi-island.gr; ❸), run by Laid Back Holidays. Other good options not monopolized by package clients include *Rena's Rooms* (☎22470 41363 or 22470 41110; ❸), overlooking Liendoú beach, the *Flisvos Pension* at the east end of the port (☎22470 41261; ❷); and the *Glaros* (☎22470 41360; ❷) on the hillside behind the *Kalypso Hotel Restaurant*, with terrazo-floored 1980s rooms sharing cooking facilities. Top of the heap is the 1997-built *Aphrodite Hotel* (☎22470 41000 or 22470 41394; ❹), a studio-bungalow complex designed to accommodate package clients, though they're not adverse to walk-ins at slow times.

Among eight surviving **tavernas**, mostly on or just behind the quay, the best are indisputably *O Yiannis* (early May to early Oct), an excellent all-rounder with meat/seafood grills and *mayireftá* – the only one open at lunch out of peak season – and *La Nave da Massimo/The Boat* up in the village centre (supper only, May–Sept), specializing in grills and a few Italian dishes. Honourable mentions go to salubrious *Tholari*, at the east end of the bay (supper all year), and *Pefkos* on the quay near *O Yiannis*. On the waterfront to either side of the *Kalypso*, *kafenía* and *ouzerís* with idiosyncratic decor (especially *Asprakis*) offer *mezédhes* outdoors at twilight – an atmospheric and almost obligatory pre-supper ritual, where an ouzo and octopus chunk runs to €1.50. Later on, *The Rock* is the clear winner amongst a handful of **bars** for a congenial crowd and good taped music.

Around the island

The island's **beaches** are rather scattered, though none is more than an hour's walk distant. Closest to town, and sandiest, are **Liendoú** and **Kámbos**, but many visitors prefer the attractive duo of **Katsadhiá** and **Papandhriá**, adjacent sand-and-pebble coves 2km south of the port, with an extremely basic taverna, *Andonis* (May–Sept), just inland from a musical snack-café-bar run by Andonis's son, *Dilaila* (June–Sept), which dominates the main bay here and runs an informal pine-grove **campsite** (free but you must buy a meal from them daily).

An hour's walk along the paved road leading west from town brings you to protected **Platýs Yialós**, a small, shallow, sandy bay with a single taverna (mid-June to late Sept only). During these periods a pair of white transit vans provides a **minibus** service from the port to all the points cited above; otherwise you can rent a **scooter** from one of two outlets and point them towards isolated east-coast beaches. Of these, **Hokhlakoúra** consists of rather grubby shingle with no facilities, though nearby **Turkómnima** is better. A final ten-minute path scramble gets you from a rough track's end to **Monodhéndhri**, on the northeast coast, notable only for its lone juniper tree and nudist practice – though there's a superior, nameless cove just to the right.

A growing network of roads, paved or otherwise, rather limit opportunities for genuine path **walks** through the undulating countryside, dotted with blue-domed churches. The most challenging route heads west, high above the coast, from the far end of Kámbos bay to the bay of **Kímisi** (3hr round-trip), where the religious hermit Filippos, long a cult figure amongst foreign visitors, used to dwell in a tiny monastery above the shore, next to the single island spring. A particularly ugly road was bulldozed in from the north in 1999 and later paved, disturbing his solitude; Filippos moved to town and died, aged 85, in 2002.

Arkí and Maráthi

About two-thirds the size of Lipsí, **Arkí** is considerably more primitive, lacking drinking water, dynamo electricity (there are solar panels), ferry anchorage or much in the way of a village centre. Just 45 permanent inhabitants eke out a living here, mostly engaged in fishing, though catering for yacht parties attracted here by the superb anchorage is increasingly important. Arkí is a twice-or-thrice-weekly stop on the *Nissos Kalymnos*: if you want to disembark here, you should warn the crew in advance so they can radio for a shuttle service from the island. Most visitors arrive by the more reliable supply boat from Pátmos (or excursion craft from Lipsí), which actually dock at the quay. Of the three tavernas on the round harbourside *platía*, the better two – *Nikolas* (☎22470 32477) and *O Trypas* (☎22470 32230) – each control a handful of rooms (❷), but avoid August when Italians and Greeks snap up every vacancy in advance. *Nikolas* is more food-oriented, with home-made puddings, while *O Trypas* doubles as the happening music pub, courtesy of the owner's enormous collection of CDs and tapes.

You can swim at the "Blue Lagoon" of **Tiganákia** at the southeast tip of the island – excursions from Lipsí stop there – but there are no real beaches to speak of on Arkí. The nearest sandy, tamarisk-shaded one is just offshore on the islet of **Maráthi**, where another pair of **tavernas** caters to day-trippers who come several times a week from Pátmos or Lipsí. *Marathi* (☎22470 31580; ❷; nominally all year), run by the engaging Mihalis Kavouras, is the more traditional, cosy outfit, with waterside seating and simple, adequate rooms; *Pantelis* (☎22470 32609; ❷; June–Oct) is plusher but more commercially minded – and apt to lock the compound's outer gate at 11pm if you go drinking at his rival's bar.

Agathoníssi

The small, steep-sided, waterless islet of **Agathoníssi (Gaïdharo)** is too remote – much closer to Turkey than Pátmos, in fact – to be a really popular target of day-excursions, though a few are offered on Sámos. Intrepid German and Italian backpackers (some of whom return annually) form its main clientele, along with a steady trickle of yachts. Even though hydrofoil connections dovetail fairly well with appearances of the *Nissos Kalymnos*, you should count on staying for three days, especially if the wind's up. Despite the lack of springs (cisterns are ubiquitous, topped up by tanker shipments from Rhodes), the island is greener and more fertile than apparent from the sea; mastic, carob and scrub oak on the heights overlook two arable plains in the west. Just 146 people live here, down from several hundred before World War II, but those who've opted to stay seem determined to make a go of raising goats or fishing (more accurately fish-farming), and there are almost no abandoned or neglected dwellings.

Most of the population lives in the hamlet of **MEGÁLO HORIÓ**, just visible on the ridge above the harbour of **ÁYIOS YEÓRYIOS**, and level with tiny **Mikró Horió**. Except for two café-restaurants (*Dhekatria Adherfia* being the more reliable) in Megálo Horió, all amenities are in the port. Here the choice is between *Rooms Theoloyia Yiameou* (☎22470 29005; ❶), the vine-patioed *Hotel Maria Kamitsi* (☎22470 29003; ❶), or the 1999-built *Yiannis*

Rooms (☎22470 29062; ➋), of a slightly higher standard, run by the *Glaros* taverna. Worthy **eating/drinking** options in Áyios Yeóryios include local hangout *Limanaki*, with fish grills; and *Glaros*, perhaps the best all-rounder.

With no wheeled transport for rent, exploring involves **walking** along the cement- or dirt-road network, or following a limited number of tracks and paths. If you don't swim at the port, which has the largest beach, you can walk twenty minutes southwest along a track to shingle-gravel **Spiliás**, or continue another quarter-hour along a faint path over the ridge to **Gaïdhourávlakos**, where nudists enjoy a gravel-and-sand cove. Bays in the east of the island, all served by the paved road system (occasionally shortcut by trails), tend to be dominated by fish farms; **Pálli** is the most pristine of these, though usually visited by boat trip. At **Thóli** in the far southeast, an hour-plus trek away, you can see an arcaded Byzantine structure, probably a combination granary and trading post, and by far the most venerable sight on Agathoníssi.

Travel details

To simplify the lists below, some companies/boats have been left out. DANE provides a once-weekly link between Rhodes, Kós, Sámos and Thessaloníki in each direction, while GA also plies once weekly (north, then south) between Rhodes, Kós, Sámos, Híos, Lésvos, Límnos and Alexandhroúpoli.

Nissos Kalymnos

The small, slow but reliable Nissos Kalymnos (cars carried) is the most regular lifeline of the smaller islands (excepting Hálki, Kastellórizo and Kássos) – it visits them all at least twice a week between mid-March and mid-Jan. This ship can be poorly publicized on islands other than its home port; if you encounter difficulties obtaining information, you should phone the central agency on Kálymnos (☎22430 29612). In 2003, after years of no change, a new, somewhat user-hostile schedule was introduced, as follows:

Monday Leaves Kálymnos 7am heading south, via Kós, Níssyros, Tílos, Sými and Rhodes (arrival 4.30pm). Sails back north at 6pm, plying via the same islands (in reverse order), to arrive back at Kálymnos at 3.30am (Tues).

Tuesday Leaves Kálymnos immediately at 3.30am for Astypálea, arrives there 6.30am, returns immediately to Kálymnos (arrives 10am). Rest of day off.

Wednesday Leaves Kálymnos 7am for Léros (Ayía Marína port), Lipsí, Pátmos, Arkí, Agathoníssi, Sámos (Pythagório; arrives 2.15pm). Turns around more or less immediately and retraces steps through the same islands (in reverse order), arriving at Kálymnos at 10pm; departs immediately for Astypálea, arriving at 1am (Thurs), returning to Kálymnos at 4am.

Thursday Same schedule as Monday.

Friday Same schedule as Wednesday, but no journey to Astypálea.

Saturday Leaves Kálymnos at 7am for Astypálea, arrives there 10am, immediate return to Kálymnos. Rest of day off.

Sunday Same schedule as Friday.

Large ferries

Note that the following frequencies are only valid for the period mid-June to mid-Sept; in spring or autumn some of the more esoteric links, such as Astypálea to Níssyros, or Lipsí to Sámos, will not apply.

Astypálea 3 weekly to Kálymnos, Amorgós and Pireás on GA; 1 weekly to Náxos, Páros, Níssyros, Sýros, on GA; 1–2 weekly to Kós, Kálymnos, and Rhodes on DANE.

Hálki 2–3 weekly to Ródhos Town, Kárpathos (both ports), Kássos, Crete (Sitía & Áyios Nikólaos) and Mílos on LANE, all subject to cancellation in bad weather. Once-daily *kaïki* (6am) to Rhodes (Kámiros Skála).

Kálymnos Similar ferry service to Kós, but only 1 high-speed NEL service direct to Pireás, plus 3 daily roll-on-roll-off ferries, well-spaced, to Mastihári; daily morning *kaïki* to Psérimos; and a daily *kaïki* (1pm) from Myrtiés to Xirókambos on Léros.

Kárpathos (both ports) and **Kássos** 2–3 weekly with each other, Hálki, Crete (Áyios Nikólaos & Sitía), Mílos and Ródhos Town, on LANE.

Kastellórizo (Méyisti) 3 weekly to Rhodes, then Pireás indirectly, via select Dodecanese and Cyclades, on GA.

Kós 13–20 weekly to Rhodes and Pireás on GA, Blue Star or DANE; 11–12 weekly to Kálymnos, Léros and Pátmos on GA, Blue Star or DANE; 3 weekly to Pireás (1 with stop on Kálymnos) on NEL high-speed craft; 1 weekly to Tílos, Níssyros, Astypálea and Sými on DANE and GA; 1 weekly to Níssyros, Astypálea and Sými; 1 weekly to Níssyros, Tílos and Sými on GA; 1 weekly to Amorgós, Náxos, Páros, Mýkonos, Sýros on GA; 1 weekly to Amorgós, Sýros, Mýkonos on Blue Star; 3 daily roll-on-roll-off ferries year-round from Mastihári to Kálymnos; 4–7 weekly excursion kaïkia to Níssyros; 4–6 weekly islanders' kaïkia from Kardhámena to Níssyros.

Léros 6–11 weekly to Pireás, Pátmos, Kálymnos, Kós and Rhodes on GA or DANE; 1–2 weekly to Mýkonos on GA; 1 weekly to Níssyros on DANE; 1 weekly to Kós, Pátmos, Sýros and Rhodes on Blue Star; seasonal daily excursion boats from Ayía Marína to Lipsí and Pátmos (2pm), and from Xirókambos to Myrtiés on Kálymnos (7.30am).

Lipsí 1 weekly to Sámos (Vathý), Ikaría (Áyios Kýrikos), select Cyclades on Hellas Ferries.

Níssyros and Tílos 1 weekly with each other, Sými, Rhodes, Kastellórizo, Kós, Kálymnos, Astypálea, Amorgós, Náxos, Páros, Sýros, Pireás on GA; 1 weekly (Níssyros only) to Rhodes, Kálymnos, Léros, Pátmos, Pireás on DANE. Excursion boats between Níssyros and Kós as follows: to Kardhámena nearly daily at 3.30–4pm; 4–7 weekly to Kós Town (all of these are seasonal). The islanders' somewhat less expensive "shopping" kaïki the Chrisoula, leaves 4–5 times weekly at 7am. Unless you're bound for the airport it's not really cheaper to use Kardhámena services when you consider the cost of a bus to Kós Town – €7–8 to Kardhámena on an excursion boat, versus €10 to Kós.

Pátmos Similar ferry service to Léros, with the addition of tourist kaïkia to Sámos (Pythagório), Lipsí, Arkí and Maráthi on a daily basis; Mon–Thurs only to Arkí in low season.

Rhodes 13-18 weekly to Kós, Kálymnos and Pireás on GA, Blue Star or DANE; 1–2 daily to Léros and Pátmos on GA, Blue Star or DANE; 2–3 weekly to Hálki, Kárpathos, Kássos, Crete (Sitía & Áyios Nikólaos), Mílos on LANE; 3 weekly to Mýkonos on GA or Blue Star; 1 weekly to Sými, Tílos, Níssyros on GA; 2 weekly to Astypálea on DANE or GA; 1–2 weekly to Amorgós, Náxos, Páros, Sýros on GA or Blue Star.

Sými 1 weekly to Rhodes, Tílos, Níssyros, Kós, Kálymnos, Léros, Pátmos, Pireás on GA; 1–2 daily catamaran or hydrofoil run by ANES to Rhodes.

Catamarans

Two high-speed, long-distance catamarans ply the Dodecanese: The Dodekanisos Express, also known as O Spanos after the supermarket chain which owns it, and the Sea Star. The Dodekanisos Express, based on Rhodes, can carry 4–5 cars and a slightly larger number of two-wheelers; it's a sleek, 2000-built, Norwegian craft, with a limited amount of aft deck space and seating. The Sea Star does not carry vehicles and serves only the route Rhodes–Tílos, with regular extensions to Níssyros. 2003 was the Dodecanese Express's fourth season, and mid-June to mid-Sept departure patterns seem to have settled down as follows: daily except Wed, 8.30am departure from Rhodes to Kós, Kálymnos, Léros and Pátmos (omitted Mon), calling at Lipsí 3 days weekly (southbound or northbound); it returns from Pátmos shortly before 2pm, arriving at Rhodes 6.30pm. On Mon & Fri it makes a stop at Sými, in each direction; on Wed it makes a single journey to Kastellórizo, arriving 11am, returning at 4pm. In spring or autumn there is no Kastellórizo service, there are only two weekly services to Lipsí, and Pátmos is missed out Tues, Wed and Fri as well as Mon. The Dodecanese Express has never called at Astypálea, Agathoníssi, Hálki, Kárpathos or Sámos (Pythagório) and is unlikely to in the future. From May to Oct the Sea Star leaves Rhodes between 7 and 8.30am bound for Tílos, arriving 1hr 15min later. On Sun and Wed it turns around immediately, making another round trip from Rhodes at 5 or 6pm. On Tues it idles at Tílos all day, returning to Rhodes at 5pm. On Mon, Thurs & Fri it sits at Tílos for a few hours before making an afternoon jaunt at 2.30pm to Níssyros, then returning all the way to Rhodes; in peak season, on Fri evening, it runs out to Tílos again, overnights there, and then returns to Rhodes Sat morning.

Hydrofoils

Two hydrofoil companies, Kyriakoulis Maritime and Laoumtzis Flying Dolphins, serve the Dodecanese between mid-May and mid-Oct, operating out of Rhodes, Kálymnos and Sámos (Kyriakoulis only), plus Kós (both companies). Kyriakoulis Maritime has five remaining active craft, inherited from the amalgamation of previously existing companies Samos Hydrofoils and Dodecanese Hydrofoils. Schedules are complicated but fairly predictable. In peak season, there is a daily link Rhodes–Kós and back, north in the morning and south in the evening; this craft no longer calls at any intervening islands. Another craft leaves Kálymnos at 7am for Kós and a selection of islands north to Pythagório on Sámos, returning between 11.45am and 2pm; while the third craft, based in Pythagório, leaves Kós between 1.15 and 2pm, returning to Sámos via Kálymnos, Léros, Lipsí and Pátmos. Twice a week this craft calls at Foúrni and Ikaría as well, and once a week Agathoníssi is served. For current routes and schedules, phone ☎ 22420 25920 (Kós), ☎ 22410 78052 (Rhodes) or ☎ 22730 25065 (Sámos).

Laoumtzis Flying Dolphins, based in Kós, has two craft with a fairly basic pattern. One craft always leaves Kós at around 8am for Rhodes, returning shortly after 4pm. Twice a week the other craft does a run up to Pátmos in the morning, returning in the late afternoon; the other days it's providing a Kós–Bodrum service. For exact details ring ☎ 22420 26388.

International ferries

NB: In all cases below, the cost of Turkish visas, required by most nationals, is not included.

Kálymnos By demand only to Bodrum, Turkey (2hr 30min), departing at 7am; €36.50 day-return. Not recommended owing to the long travel time, involving a mandatory stop in Kós for customs formalities.

Kós 2–14 weekly to Bodrum, Turkey (45min). Greek boat or Laoumtzis hydrofoil leaves 9–10am, returns 4–5pm; €35–40 return, Greek tax inclusive; no cheap day-return or one ways, no Turkish port tax. Identically priced Turkish boat (*Fahri Kaptan*) or hydrofoil departs Bodrum 9am or so, leaves Kós 4.30pm; this provides the only service in winter.

Kastellórizo 1–2 weekly to Kaş, Turkey; €15 one way or day return; €30 if you begin travel from the Turkish side.

Rhodes Daily in summer, 9am to Marmaris, Turkey (1hr) by Greek catamaran, returning about 5pm; €30 one way, €38–43 return, Greek taxes inclusive but excluding €15 Turkish port tax. Anka Travel at Gallías 13 in Neohóri (☎ 22410 26835) handles 1 weekly Turkish ferry (usually Fri), which takes about 3 cars.

Sými 2 weekly on the *Panormitis* catamaran, typically Thurs & Sat, to Datça; this is expensive (over €45 return) and geared mainly to day-trippers' needs.

Flights

NB: All are on Olympic Aviation/Olympic Airways unless stated otherwise.

Astypálea 4 weekly to Athens; 3 weekly to Léros, Kós and Rhodes on the same plane.

Kárpathos 2 daily except Tues to Rhodes; 6 weekly to Kássos; 3–5 weekly to Athens.

Kássos 6 weekly to Kárpathos and Rhodes.

Kastellórizo (Meyísti) 1 daily to Rhodes June–Sept, 5 weekly otherwise.

Kós 3 daily to Athens on Olympic, 4 daily on Aegean; 3 weekly to Astypálea, Léros and Rhodes.

Léros 1 daily to Athens; 3 weekly to Astypálea, Kós and Rhodes.

Rhodes On Olympic, 4–5 daily to Athens; 4 weekly to Iráklion (April–Oct); 3 weekly to Kós, Léros and Astypálea with the same plane; 2 weekly to Sámos and Híos (June–Sept); 2 weekly to Lésvos and Límnos; 2–4 weekly to Thíra; 8–9 weekly to Thessaloníki. On Aegean, 4–5 daily to Athens; 1 daily to Iráklion; 1 daily to Thessaloníki.

The East and North Aegean

CHAPTER 5 **Highlights**

✳ **Vathý, Sámos** The two-wing archeological museum is among the best in the islands. See p.381

✳ **Ikaría** Western Ikaría has superb beaches and an idio-syncratic life-style. See p.393

✳ **Southern Híos** The architec-turally unique mastihohoriá (mastic villages) have a Middle Eastern feel. See p.406

✳ **Néa Moní, Híos** Particularly fine Byzantine mosaics in a monastery which has sur-vived earthquake, massacre and fire. See p.409

✳ **Mólyvos, northern Lésvos** This castle-crowned resort village is arguably the most beautiful on the island. See p.427

✳ **Thermal baths, Lésvos** Those at Loutrá Yéras are especially well-kept and ideal for relaxing in. See p.430

✳ **Mýrina, Limnos** A character-ful port town with a fine castle – and great wines to sample. See p.433

✳ **Samothraki** Remote Samothráki's Sanctuary of the Great Gods is surrounded by natural grandeur. See p.440

✳ **Alykí, Thássos** A beautifully situated beach flanked by ancient and Byzantine arche-ological sites. See p.449

△ Vineyards, Sámos

5

The East and North Aegean

The seven substantial islands and four minor islets scattered off the north Aegean coast of Asia Minor and northeastern Greece form a rather arbitrary archipelago. Although there are some passing similarities in architecture and landscape, the strong individual character of each island is far more striking. Despite their proximity to modern Turkey, members of the group bear few signs of an Ottoman heritage, especially when compared with Rhodes and Kós. There's the occasional mosque, often shorn of its minaret, but by and large the enduring Greekness of these islands is testimony to the four-millennium-long Hellenic presence in Asia Minor, which ended only in 1923. This heritage is regularly referred to by the Greek government in an intermittent propaganda war with Turkey over the sovereignty of these far-flung outposts. Tensions here have often been worse than in the Dodecanese, aggravated by potential undersea oil deposits in the straits between the islands and the Anatolian mainland. The Turks have also persistently demanded that Límnos, astride the sea lanes to and from the Dardanelles, be demilitarized, but so far Greece has shown no signs of giving in.

The heavy military presence can be disconcerting, and despite the growth of tourism, large tracts of land remain off-limits as army or air force bases. But as in the Dodecanese, local tour operators do a thriving business shuttling passengers for inflated tariffs between the easternmost islands and the Turkish coast with its amazing archeological sites and busy resorts. Most of these islands' main ports and towns are not quaint, picturesque spots, but urbanized administrative, military and commercial centres. In most cases you should suppress any initial impulse to take the next boat out, and press on into the interiors.

Sámos ranks as the most visited island of the group, but if you can leave the crowds behind, is still arguably the most verdant and beautiful, even after a devastating July 2000 fire. **Ikaría** to the west remains relatively unspoiled, if a minority choice, and nearby **Foúrni** is a haven for determined solitaries, as are the Híos satellites **Psará** and **Inoússes**, neither of which have any package tourism. **Híos** proper offers far more cultural interest than any neighbours to the south, but its natural beauty has also been ravaged by fires, and the development of tourism was until the late 1980s deliberately retarded. **Lésvos** may not impress initially, though once you get a feel for its old-fashioned, Anatolian ambience, you may find it hard to leave. By contrast virtually no foreigners and few Greeks visit **Áyios Efstrátios**, and with good reason. **Límnos** to the

Thessaloníki

Thessaloníki

Kými

Rafína

Lávrio

Pireás

Páros & Náxos

İstanbul

TURKEY

Kavála
Keramotí
Skála Prínou
Thássos
Thássos
Limenária

Alexandhroúpoli

Kamariótissa
Hóra
Samothráki

Gökçeada (Imbros)

Çanakkale

N

Límnos

Mýrina
Moúdhros

Bozcaada (Tenedos)

0   50 km

Ay. Efstrátios

Mólyvos
Ayvalık
Sígri
TURKEY
Eressós
Ayiássos
Polikhnítos
Mytilíni
Lésvos
Plomári

Skýros

Psará
Mármaro
Inoússes
Inoússes
Volissós
Híos
Híos
Çeşme
İZMİR
Pýrgi

Ándhros

Efes (Ephesus)
Kuşadası

Karlóvassi
Vathý
Pythagório
Sámos

Tínos

Áy. Kírykos
Évdhilos
Ikaría
Foúrni
Arkí
Agathoníssi
Pátmos
Lipsí
Farmakóníssi
Léros

Mýkonos

Sýros

north is much livelier, but its appeal is confined mostly to the area immediately around the attractive port town. To the north, Samothráki and Thássos are totally isolated from the others, except via the mainland ports of Kavála or Alexandhroúpoli, and remain easier to visit from northern Greece, which administers them. **Samothráki** (officially in Thrace) has one of the most dramatic seaward approaches of any Greek island, and one of the more important ancient sites. **Thássos** (technically belonging to eastern Macedonia) is more varied, with sandy beaches, mountain villages and minor archeological sites.

Sámos

The lush and seductive island of Sámos was formerly joined to Asia Minor, until sundered from Mount Mykale opposite by Ice Age cataclysms; the resulting 2500-metre strait is now the narrowest distance between Greece and Turkey in the Aegean, except at Kastellórizo. There's little tangible evidence of it today, but Sámos was also once the **wealthiest island** in the Aegean and, under the patronage of the tyrant Polykrates, home to a thriving intellectual community: Epicurus, Pythagoras, Aristarchus and Aesop were among the residents. Decline set in as the star of Classical Athens was in the ascendant, though Sámos's status improved somewhat in early Byzantine times when it constituted its own *theme* (imperial administrative district). Towards the end of the fifteenth century, the Genoese abandoned the island to the mercies of pirates; following their attacks, Sámos remained **almost uninhabited** until 1562, when an Ottoman admiral received permission from the sultan to repopulate it with Greek Orthodox settlers recruited from various corners of the empire.

The heterogeneous descent of today's islanders largely explains an enduring identity crisis and a rather thin topsoil of indigenous culture. Most of the village names are either clan surnames, or adjectives indicating origins elsewhere – constant reminders of **refugee descent**. Consequently there is no genuine Samiote music, dance or dress, and little that's original in the way of cuisine and architecture. The Samiotes compensated somewhat for this deracination by fighting fiercely for independence during the 1820s, but despite their accomplishments in sinking a Turkish fleet in the narrow strait and annihilating a landing army, the Great Powers handed the island back to the Ottomans in 1830, with the consoling proviso that it be **semi-autonomous**, ruled by an appointed Christian prince. This period, referred to as the *Iyimonía* (Hegemony), was marked by a mild renaissance in fortunes, courtesy of the hemp and (especially) tobacco trades. However, union with Greece in 1912, the ravages of a bitter World War II occupation and mass emigration effectively reversed the recovery until tourism appeared on the horizon during the 1980s.

Today the Samian economy is increasingly dependent on **package tourism**, far too much of it in places; the eastern half of the island, and a large part of the south coast, has pretty much surrendered to the onslaught of holiday-makers, although the more rugged northwestern part has retained some of its undeveloped grandeur. The sedate, couples-orientated clientele is overwhelmingly German, Scandinavian, Swiss and Dutch, with a growing number of Brits, Belgians and even Slovenians; the absence of an official campsite on such a large island, tame nightlife a world away from that in the Dodecanese and Cyclades, and phalanxes of self-catering villas hint at the sort of custom expected.

SÁMOS

▲ *Kuşadası (Turkey)*   ▲ *Kuşadası (Turkey)*

TURKEY

Zoödhóhou Piyís

Kérveli

Kamára

Posidhónio

Kadúna

Áyia Zóni

Paleókastro

Nissí

Psilí Ámmos

Áyia Paraskeví

Kalámi

Áno Vathý

Vathý

Mykáli

Pythagório

Efpalínio Tunnel

Roman Baths

Kokkári

Glyfádha

Hóra

Potokáki

Heraíon

Petrokáravo

Iréon

Mytilíni

Kyriakoú

Tsamadoú

Lemonákia

Tsópela

Timíou Stavroú

Megális Panayías

Mýli

Pándhrossos

Vrondianís

Avlákia

Tzabou

Platanákia

Áyios Konstandínos

Mt. Ámbelos 1153m

Mavratzéi

Pnáka

Vourliótes

Pýrgos

Koumaradhéi

Pagóndas

Spatharéï

Manolátes

Koútsi

Stavrinídhes

Ámbelos

Neohóri

Idhroússa

Kondakéika

Plátanos

Áyios Nikólaos

Kouméika

Bállos

Piáki

Karlóvassi

Órmos Marathókámbou

Méso

Metamórfosis

Lékka

Votsaláki

Limáni Paleó

Kastaniá

Potámi

Kosmadhéi

Marathókambos

Evangelístrias

Psilí Ámmos

Mikró Seitáni

Dhrakéï

Megálo Seitáni

Vársamo

Áyia Triádha

Mt. Kérkis 1437m

Limniónas

Kallithéa

Panayía Makriní

N

0   5 km

▲ *Híos & Lésvos*

▲ *Ikaría & Foúrni*

▼ *Foúrni*

▼ *Pátmos & Foúrni*

▼ *Arkí, Lípsi & Agathonísi*

The heavily developed areas have unsurprisingly been the most afflicted by **repeated wildfires**, in particular one which lasted a week in July 2000, destroying twenty percent of the island's forest and orchards, and over ninety dwellings. If you mention Sámos to other Greeks now, they say *Ah, tó nisí poú kaïke* ("Oh, the island that burned"), and if you take into account other areas that had been torched since 1987, Sámos is indeed about half-scorched. The trees as ever will be a half-century in returning, and the tourist market a good few years in overcoming this stigma. Volunteer fire-lookouts with pumper-trucks have now sprouted at critical points, but it does seem a case of locking the stable after the horse has bolted.

Getting there and getting around

Sámos **airport** lies 14km southwest of Vathý and 3km west of Pythagório; a new, enlarged terminal came on-stream in July 2003. There are no fewer than three **ferry ports**: Karlóvassi in the west, plus Vathý and Pythagório in the east, making the island a major hub for travel in every direction. All ferries between Pireás, Sýros, Mýkonos, Ikaría and Sámos call at both Karlóvassi and Vathý (except for the high-speed catamaran which serves only Vathý), as does a smaller Miniotis Line ferry linking the island with Híos and, at high season, Foúrni and Ikaría. Vathý also receives the weekly NEL sailing between northern Greece and the Dodecanese, via most intervening islands, the weekly DANE ferry between Thessaloníki and Rhodes, plus small boats from Kuşadası. Pythagório sees three regular weekly ferry connections from as far south as Kálymnos in the Dodecanese, as well as hosting the Kyriakoulis **hydrofoil services** to all the Dodecanese down to Kós, and forays over to Foúrni and southern Ikaría.

The **bus terminals** in Pythagório and Vathý lie within walking distance of the ferry dock; at Karlóvassi, you must make your own way the 3km into town from the port. There is no airport bus service; **taxi** fares to various points are stipulated on prominent placards, and in high season taxis to the airport or docks must be booked several hours in advance. The KTEL service itself is excellent along the Pythagório–Vathý and Vathý–Kokkári–Karlóvassi routes, but poor otherwise; with numerous car- and motorbike-rental outlets, it's easy to find a good deal outside July or August and, with tourist numbers down lately by a good third, even all year round.

Vathý

Lining the steep northeastern shore of a deep bay, beachless **VATHÝ** (often confusingly referred to as **SÁMOS**, like the island) is a busy provincial town which grew from a minor anchorage after 1830, when it replaced Hóra as the island's capital. It's an unlikely, somewhat ungraceful resort, which has seen numerous hotels gone bankrupt or converted to apartments since the late 1990s, and is minimally interesting for the most part – although the pedestrianized bazaar, tiers of surviving Neoclassical houses and the hill suburb of **ÁNO VATHÝ**, a separate community of tottering, tile-roofed houses, have some attraction. The only real must is the excellent **archeological museum** (Tues–Sun 8.30am–2.30pm; €3), set behind the small central park beside the restored nineteenth-century town hall. One of the best provincial collections in Greece is housed in both the old Paskhallion building and a modern wing across the way, specially constructed to house the star exhibit: a majestic, five-metre-tall *kouros*, discovered out at the Heraion sanctuary. The *kouros*, the largest free-standing effigy to survive from ancient Greece, was dedicated to

VATHÝ

▲ Pythgório & **Ⓐ**

N

200 m

0

▶ Kokkári

● Áno Vathý & **❶**

Bus Station

THEMISTOKLI SOFOULI

KANARI

P

3 **4**

P

6

SAVVRIS

MYKALIS

Cathedral

Town Hall

ALEX PASKHALI

Street Market

KAPETANI

IMNASTARHOU

Archeological Museum

Cine Olympia

Central Park

KAPETANI

STAMATI

Fishing Port

★ **Taxis**

B

PLATIA PYTHAGORA

KAPETAN

ℹ

PLAVOU NIKOLAOU

GOUNELI

THEMISTOKLI SOFOULI

KAPODISTRIOU

KATODIKI

LYKOURGOU

MANOLI

SOFIA

C

D

A

NIKOLAOU

ERAMMOU

ENDHEKATOU

F

E

Provincial Governorate

Laundry

5

Catholic Church (Frangoklisiá)

7

G

KELAPLOULOU

8

Port Police

● Boats to/from Turkey

● Other Ferries

● High-speed Boat

● Large Ferries (NEL)

▼ Nissi, **❾**, **❿** & **⓫**

ACCOMMODATION
Artemis	B
Pension Avíi	C
Christiana	A
Pension Dreams	D
Emily	F
Galaxy	E
Samos	G

RESTAURANTS
Artemis	8
To Kalami	10
To Kotopoula	2
T'Ostrako	4
Solo Pasta	11

BARS AND CAFÉS
Aeolis	5
Dhiavlos	3
Escape	9
Filarakia	1
NetCafe	6
Silver Club	7

Apollo, but found together with a devotional mirror to Mut (the Egyptian equivalent of Hera) from a Nile workshop, one of only two discovered in Greece to date.

In the compelling **small-objects collection** of the Paskhallion, more votive offerings of Egyptian design prove trade and pilgrimage links between Sámos and the Nile valley going back to the eighth century BC. The Mesopotamian and Anatolian origins of other artwork confirm the exotic trend, most tellingly in a case full of ivory miniatures: Perseus and Medusa in relief, a kneeling, perfectly formed mini-*kouros*, a pouncing lion and a drinking horn ending in a bull's head. The most famous local artefacts are the dozen or so bronze griffin-heads, for which Sámos was the major centre of production in the seventh century BC; mounted on the edge of bronze cauldrons, they were believed to ward off evil spirits.

Practicalities

From the **ferry dock** the shore boulevard – Themistoklí Sofoúli – describes a 1300-metre arc around the bay. About 400m along is pedestrianized Platía Pythagóra, distinguished by its lion statue and some hideous concrete-barricade "sculpture"; about 800m along there's a major turning inland to the **KTEL** terminal, a chaos of buses at a perennially cluttered intersection by the ticket office. The minimally useful **tourist information** office is at 25-Martíou 4 (May–Oct Mon–Fri 9am–2pm; winter sporadic hours), only worth a stop for its comprehensive bus schedules and accommodation listings. If you've arrived with your own vehicle, it's best to use the free lots shown on the map rather than run the risk of the sporadically enforced pay-and-display **parking** scheme in effect along most of the waterfront.

The most useful waterfront **ferry/travel agent** for independent travellers is By Ship, with two branches: one at the base of the jetty (☎22730 80445), primarily handling ships and hydrofoils, and one about 300m southeast (☎22730 25065); between them they sell tickets for most ferry lines (DANE, NEL, GA), as well as seats on Olympic and Kyriakoulis Maritime hydrofoil tickets. Miniotis Lines representation is restricted to helpful Nautica near the dock (☎22730 25133), also the central outlet for NEL. Vathý is chock-a-block with **bike-** and **car-rental** franchises, with supply in excess of demand keeping rates reasonable. For motorbikes, try Aramis (☎22730 22682) at Themistoklí Sofoúli 5, with a large fleet and recovery service; for cars, preferred outlets are Reliable (phone as for By Ship), with branches islandwide, or the similarly far-flung Autoplan, a division of Samina Tours (☎22730 23555). Other amenities include the new **post office** inconveniently out on Themistoklí Sofoúli, six waterfront **banks** with ATMs and a self-serve **laundry** on pedestrianized Lykoúrgou Logothéti.

Accommodation

Most **accommodation** available to independent travellers is clustered in the hillside district of Katsoúni, more or less directly above the ferry dock; except in August, you'll have little trouble finding affordable vacancies. Budget choices include the rock-bottom, somewhat noisy waterfront *Hotel Artemis* (☎22730 27792; ❷) just off "Lion Square"; *Pension Dreams*, up a stair-lane at Áreos 9 (☎22730 24350; ❷), well-kept en suite rooms with fridges; and, best of all, the *Pension Avli* (☎22730 22939; ❷), a wonderful period piece at Áreos 2, the former convent school of the French nuns who ran the local Catholic church until 1973; affable owner Spyros is an excellent source of information on local eating and drinking opportunities.

None of these outfits is a palace by any means; for more luxury, go for proper hotels such as the surprisingly affordable *Galaxy* (☎22730 22665; ❸), at Angéou 1 near the top of Katsoúni, set in garden surroundings and with a small pool, though avoid being sent to the annexe opposite, which is of much lower standard. If they're full, try the sympathetic *Emily*, just downhill at the top of Grámmou (☎22730 24691; open all year; ❹), a small outfit with a roof garden and plenty of parking out front. The *Samos Hotel* (☎22730 28377; ❸) right by the ferry dock but with double glazing against noise, is also open all year, with a little pool in the roof garden. Further afield and a taxi ride uphill, the *Christiana* (☎22730 23084; open July–Sept; ❹), the only hotel in Áno Vathý, has a ravine setting, civil management and an enormous pool.

Eating and drinking

The only **waterfront tavernas** worth a second glance, both open all year, are the new *T'Ostrako* next to the police station at Themistoklí Sofoúli 141, doing shellfish (as the name implies), a few fish of the day and an ample selection of *orektiká*; and *Artemis* near the dock at Kefalopoúlou 4, excellent for a pre-ferry lunch or a leisurely supper, though opt for *mezédhes* (especially their *fáva*) and grills rather than their oven dishes. A third possibility, further out on Kefalopoúlou by the hospital, is *Solo Pasta* (May–Sept), fairly authentic for big portions of exactly the fare described, and patronized by locals. Continuing much further in the same direction, *To Kalami* (aka *Triandafyllos*) in an unpromisingly touristy enclave has good food served up by a friendly family, and spontaneous music and dance sessions one or two nights weekly. Inland, at the Plátanos junction en route to Áno Vathý, *Ta Kotopoula* is a cheap and sometimes cheerful **grill** featuring chicken (as in the name) and other meat from their own farms, much resorted to by the neighbourhood, but service can be abysmal. Way up high in Áno Vathý, *Ta Filarkia* at Ayía Matróna church is the characters' hangout, with the music cranked up loud and, for a couple of euro, *krássomezédhes* (titbits with wine; two orders will fill you up); back on the front, the town's *beau monde* have their *mezédhes* and drinks on the ground floor of the *Aeolis Hotel*.

Vathý's more active **nightlife** revolves around its waterfront bars, the longest lived of these being *Escape*, on a seaview terrace at Kefalopoúlou 9 (north of the jetty), though the real till-dawn action is currently at *Silver Club*, oddly occupying the same building as the Catholic church. Cine Olympia, inland on Yimnasiárhou Katevéni, is plushly fitted and operates all year (summers on the roof), with a variable programme of **films**. There are also two **Internet cafés**, both on Themistoklí Sofoúli: Dhiavlos just around the corner from the KTEL, and NetCafe at no. 175, at the south end of the front.

Around Vathý

The immediate environs of Vathý offer some modest beaches and small hamlets, though you'll usually need your own transport to visit them. Two kilometres east and uphill spreads the vast inland plateau of **Vlamarí**, devoted to vineyards and supporting the hamlets of Ayía Zóni and Kamára (plus an increasing number of distasteful modern villas); from Kamára you can climb up a partly cobbled path to the clifftop **monastery of Zoödhóhou Piyís**, for superb views across the end of the island to Turkey.

Heading north out of Vathý, the narrow road ends after 7km at the pebble bay and fishing port of **AYÍA PARASKEVÍ** (or Nissí), with good swimming. There are, alas, no reliable facilities here other than a fitfully open snack-bar, *Aquarius* (July & Aug only).

As you head southeast from Vathý along the main island loop road, the triple chapel at **Trís Ekklisíes** marks an important junction, with another fork 100m along the left-hand turning. Bearing left twice takes you through the hilltop village of Paleókastro, where the unassuming-looking *Leonidas* on the square does surprisingly competent snacks. Some 3km beyond is another junction; forking left yet again brings you after another 3km to the quiet, striking bay of **Kérveli**, with a small beach, a pair of **tavernas** by the water (the friendly *Sea and Dolphin* has good *mezédhes* and *soúma*, the local spirit, though mains are a bit pricey) and another characterful favourite with simple grills only, *Iy Kryfi Folia*, about 500m uphill along the access road. Taking the right fork leads to **Posidhónio**, with an even smaller beach and another taverna, *Kerkezos*, which takes its cooking more seriously, though it's expensive. A right turn at the junction before Paleókastro leads to the beaches of Mykáli and Psilí Ámmos, the only spots in this section with a bus service. **Mykáli**, a kilometre of windswept sand and gravel, has been encumbered with three package hotels; the best place to try on spec here is *Villa Barbara* (☎22730 25192; ❹), which has apartments behind the *Sirenes Beach* hotel. Far and away the best **eating** on this coast is at *Kalypso*, which has excellent and well-priced *mayireftá* and is reached by its own dead-end access road off the main Mykáli-bound route. **Psilí Ámmos**, further east around the headland, is a crowded, sandy cove backed by several tavernas, the best of which is *Psili Ammos*, on the far right as you face the sea, and *Anatoli* down the sand, which hosts live music at weekends. If you swim to the islet beware of strong currents which sweep through the narrow straits.

Pythagório and around

Most traffic south of Vathý heads for **PYTHAGÓRIO**, the island's premier resort, renamed in 1955 to honour native son Pythagoras, ancient mathematician, philosopher and mystic. Until then it was known as Tigáni (Frying Pan) – in midsummer you'll learn why. The sixth-century BC tyrant Polykrates had his capital here, now subject to sporadic excavations which have forced modern Pythagório to expand northeast and uphill. The village core of cobbled lanes and thick-walled mansions abuts a small **harbour**, fitting almost perfectly into the confines of Polykrates' ancient jetty, but today devoted almost entirely to pleasure craft and overpriced cocktail bars.

Sámos's most complete **castle**, the nineteenth-century *pýrgos* of local chieftain Lykourgos Logothetis, overlooks both the town and the shoreline. Logothetis, together with a certain "Kapetan Stamatis" and Admiral Kanaris of Psará, chalked up decisive victories over the Turks in the summer of 1824. The final battle was won on Transfiguration Day (August 6), and accordingly the church inside the castle precinct is dedicated to this festival. More antiquities include the fairly dull **Roman baths**, signposted as "Thermai", 400m west of town (Tues–Sun 8.30am–2.45pm; free) and a minuscule **archeological collection** in the town hall on Platía Irínis (Tues–Sun 8.45am–2pm; free). Considerably more interesting is the **Efpalínio tunnel** (Tues–Sun 8.45am–2.45pm; €2), a 1040-metre aqueduct bored through the mountain just north of Pythagório at the behest of Polykrates. To get there, take the signposted path from the shore boulevard at the west end of town, which meets the vehicle access road toward the end of a twenty-minute walk.

Further subterranean experience can be had at the monastery of **Panayía Spilianí**, high on the hillside over town. Though most of this has been insensitively restored and touristified, behind the courtyard lies a cool, hundred-metre-long grotto, at one end of which is a shrine to the Virgin (open daylight hours; free). This was the presumed residence of the ancient oracular priestess Fyto, and a pirate-safe hideout in medieval times.

Practicalities

If there are any **accommodation** vacancies – likely of late, with local package tourism down considerably – rooms proprietors meet all incoming ferries and hydrofoils. The **tourist information booth** (June–Sept daily 8am–10pm; ☎22730 62274), on the main thoroughfare, Lykoúrgou Logothéti, can help in finding rooms and sells tickets for the *Nissos Kalymnos* ferryboat. Quietly located at the seaward end of Odhós Pythagóra, south of Lykoúrgou Logothéti, the modest *Tsambika* (☎22730 61642; ❷) or the more comfortable *Dora*, a block west (☎22730 61456; ❸–❹), are two pensions worth considering. Some 50m inland from the north side of the harbour past the customs house, *Lambis Rooms* on Odhós Íras (☎22730 61396; ❷) is another backpackers' transit stop. A peaceful area is the hillside north of Platía Irínis, where *Studios Galini* (☎22730 61167 or 210 98 42 248 in winter; ❹) has high-quality self-catering units with ceiling fans, balconies and kind English-speaking management. The *Evelin* (☎22730 61124, ☎22730 61077; ❸) isn't brilliantly located out by the traffic lights – convenient only for the airport – but it's comfortable, good value and friendly, and has a swimming pool, double glazing against noise and on-site motorbike rental.

Eating out can be frustrating in Pythagório, with value for money often a completely alien concept. For waterside dining, you're best off at the far east end of the quay, beyond the shut-down hotel, where *Remataki* (open all year) features vegetarian dishes such as *angin_áres ala políta* (stewed artichokes with veg); quality has dipped recently but it's still the only spot the locals themselves will be seen in. If you've transport, consider heading 3.5km northwest to the edge of Hóra village, where *Iy Synandisi* (open all year) has a nice line in goat or lamb chops, good bulk wine from Thessaloníki and unusual touches like parsley and parmesan on the fried courgettes. Night-owls gather at the *Labito Club* on Dhespóti Kyrílou, while all-year **Cine Rex** in Mytiliní village, 7km northwest, screens standard first-run fare; the summer premises at the far edge of town are great fun, with free *loukoumádhes* served at intermission.

Buses serving the local area leave from the **stop** that lies just west of the intersection of Lykoúrgou Logothéti and the road to Vathý. Two **banks** (both with ATMs) and the **post office** are also on Lykoúrgou Logothéti. The flattish country to the west is ideal for cycling, a popular activity, and if you want to rent a **motorbike** several outfits on Logothéti will oblige you.

Around Pythagório

The main local beach stretches for several kilometres west of the Logothetis "castle", punctuated about halfway along by the end of the airport runway, and the cluster of nondescript hotels known as **POTOKÁKI**. Just before the turn-off to the heart of the beach sprawls the ultra-luxurious *Doryssa Bay* complex (☎22730 61360, ⓦwww.doryssa-bay.gr; ❻–❽), which includes a meticulously concocted fake village, guaranteed to confound archeologists of future eras. No two of the units, joined by named lanes, are alike, and there's even a *platía* with a (pricey) café. In late September or early October the *Doryssa Bay*'s functions hall hosts an excellent, if poorly publicised, Mediterranean documentary film festival (free screenings). Although you'll have to contend with the hotel crowds and low-flying jets, the sand-and-pebble **beach** here is well groomed and the water clean; for more seclusion head out to the end of the road.

The Potokáki access road is a dead end, with the main island loop road pressing on past the turn-off for the airport and Iréon hamlet. Under layers of alluvial mud, plus today's runway, lies the processional Sacred Way joining the ancient city with the **Heraion**, the massive shrine of the Mother Goddess (Tues–Sun 8.30am–2.45pm; €3). Much touted in tourist literature, this assumes humbler dimensions – one surviving column and assorted foundations – upon approach. Yet once inside the precinct you sense the former grandeur of the temple, never completed owing to Polykrates' untimely death at the hands of the Persians. The site chosen, near the mouth of the still-active Imvrassós stream, was Hera's legendary birthplace and site of her trysts with Zeus; in the far corner of the fenced-in zone you glimpse a large, exposed patch of the paved Sacred Way.

The modern resort of **IRÉON** nearby is a nondescript grid of dusty streets behind a coarse-shingle beach, attracting a slightly younger and more active clientele than Pythagório. Here you'll find assorted rooms and small hotels, most within sight of the water. Tempting, too, are the handful of waterfront **tavernas**, but for the best eating here follow the locals to *Angyra*, a super-hygienic *ouzerí* on an inland corner.

Southern Sámos

Since the circum-island bus only passes through or near the places below once or twice daily, you really need your own vehicle to explore them. Some 5km west of Hóra, a well-marked side road leads up and right to **MAVRATZÉÏ**, one of two Samian "pottery villages", which lost 49 houses to the fire in 2000. The few surviving local potteries specialize in the *Koúpa toú Pythagóra* or "Pythagorean cup", supposedly designed by the sage to leak over the user's lap if they are overfilled. Slightly more practical wares can be found in **KOUMARADHÉÏ**, back on the main road, another 2km along.

From here you can descend a paved road to the sixteenth-century monastery of **Megális Panayías** (theoretically daily 9am–noon & 5–7pm), containing the oldest frescoes on the island, alas now very smudged by damp. This route continues to **MÝLI**, submerged in citrus groves and also accessible from Iréon. Four kilometres above Mýli sprawls **PAGÓNDAS**, a large hillside community with a splendid main square (venue for a lively Pentecost Sunday festival) and an unusual communal fountain house on the south hillside. From here, a scenic paved road curls 9km around the hill to **SPATHARÉÏ** – its surroundings sadly devastated by repeated fires – set on a natural balcony offering the best sea views this side of the island. From Spatharéï, the road loops back 6km to **PÝRGOS**, at the head of a ravine draining southwest and the centre of Samian honey production; a fitfully operating **taverna** (June–Sept) lies 3km west, in the plane-shaded Koútsi ravine which just escaped the July 2000 blaze.

The rugged and beautiful coast south of the Pagóndas–Pýrgos route is largely inaccessible, glimpsed by most visitors for the first and last time from the descending plane bringing them to Sámos. **Tsópela**, a highly scenic sand-and-gravel cove at a gorge mouth, is the only beach here with marked track access and a good seasonal taverna; you'll need a sturdy motorcycle (not a scooter) or jeep to get down there. The western reaches of this shoreline, which suffered comprehensive fire damage in 1994, are approached via the small village of **KOUMÉÏKA**, with a massive inscribed marble fountain and a pair of *kafenía* on its square. Below extends the long, pebble bay at **BÁLLOS**, with sand, a cave and naturists at the far east end. Bállos itself is merely a sleepy collection of summer houses, several simple places to stay and a few tavernas, all on the shore road. The best **accommodation** for walk-ins is the *Hotel Amfilisos* (☎22730 31669, ℗22730 31668; ❹), while the finest **dining** is at *Akrogiali* nearby, with an honourable mention for humbler *Iy Paralia* off to the east. Returning to Kouméïka, the dubious-looking side road just before the village marked "Velanidhiá" is in fact entirely paved and usable by any vehicle – a very useful short cut if you're travelling towards the beaches beyond Órmos Marathokámbou (see p.391).

Kokkári and around

Leaving Vathý on the north coastal section of the island loop road, you've little to stop for until **KOKKÁRI**, Sámos's third major tourist centre after Pythagório and the capital. Sadly, while lower Vathý and Pythagório had little beauty to sacrifice, much has been irrevocably lost here. The town's profile, covering two knolls behind twin headlands, remains unaltered, and one or two families still doggedly untangle their fishing nets on the quay, but in general its identity has been altered beyond recognition, with constant inland expansion over vineyards and the abandoned fields of small boiling-onions that gave the place its name. Since the exposed, rocky beaches here are buffeted by near-constant winds, the promoters have made a virtue of necessity by developing the place as a successful windsurfing resort.

Practicalities

As in Vathý and Pythagório, a fair proportion of Kokkári's **accommodation** is block-booked by tour companies; establishments not completely devoted to such trade include *Lemos* (☎22730 92250; ❹), near the north end of the west beach, and the more modest *Vicky* (☎22730 92231; ❸), facing the same strand. For a guaranteed view of the fishing port, try the *Pension Alkyonis* (☎22730 92225; ❸) or the *Pension Angela* (☎22730 92052; ❸). Otherwise, Yiorgos Mihelios has a range of rooms and flats to rent (☎22730 92456; ❷–❹). If you get stuck, seek assistance from the seasonal **EOT post** (☎22730 92217), housed in a Portakabin near the main church. If money's no object, then it has to be the A-class *Arion* (☎22370 92020, ⓦwww.arion-hotel.gr; ❼), a well-designed bungalow complex on an unburnt patch of hillside 2km west.

Most **tavernas** line the north waterfront, and charge above the norm, though they're steadily losing ground to breakfast, *souvláki/yíros* or cocktail bars. As of writing, none is worth a special mention – you're probably best off patronizing said *yirádhika*. Most (noisy) **bars** ring the little square just west of where the concreted stream (with its family of ducks) meets the sea, but there's also the more elaborate and well-established disco, *Cabana*, on the west beach, drawing clubbers from across the island.

Other amenities include a stand-alone **bank** ATM on the through road, a **post office** in a Portakabin on a seaward lane and, next door, a long-hours, self-service **laundry**; there are also branches of the major Vathý **travel agents**, and a **newsstand/bookstore**, Lexis.

West of Kokkári: the coast

The closest sheltered beaches are thirty-to-forty minutes' walk away to the west, all with sunbeds and permanently anchored umbrellas. The first, **Lemonákia**, is a bit close to the road, though many *Arion* patrons favour it and the taverna's not too bad; 1km beyond, the graceful crescent of **Tzamadhoú** figures in virtually every EOT poster of the island. With path-only access, it's marginally less spoilt, and the far east end of the beach (saucer-shaped pebbles) has become a well-established nudist/gay zone. There's one more pebble bay, 7km west beyond Avlákia, called **Tzaboú**, again with a serviceable snack-bar, but it's not worth a special detour when the prevailing northwest wind is up.

The next spot of any interest along the coast road is **Platanákia**, essentially a handful of tavernas and rooms for rent at a bridge by the turning for Manolátes (see below); best of the **tavernas** is *Iy Apolavsis*, with a limited choice of very good *mayireftá*. Platanákia is actually the eastern suburb of **ÁYIOS KONSTANDÍNOS**, whose surf-pounded esplanade has been prettified. However, there are no usable beaches within walking distance, so the collection of warm-toned stone buildings, with few modern intrusions, constitutes a peaceful alternative to Kokkári, only getting much trade in spring when Dutch hikers frequent the place. In addition to modest 1970s-vintage **rooms**, such as the *Atlantis* just above the highway (T 22730 94329; ❶), there's a new generation of more modern rooms below the road, such as *Kalypso*, by Platanákia (T 22730 94460; ❷). **Eating** out, you're spoilt for choice; besides *Iy Apolavsis*, there's recently expanded *To Kyma* at the east end of the quay, with good bulk wine and *mayireftá*, or (best of all) the *Aeolos* at the far west end of the esplanade (June–Sept), with terrific fish or grilled meat and a few well-chosen baked dishes, served at tables on the jetty or by the tiny beach.

Once past "Áyios", as it's locally abbreviated, the mountains hem the road in against the sea, and the terrain doesn't relent until **Kondakéïka**; its diminutive shore annexe of **Áyios Nikólaos** has an excellent venue for fish meals in *Iy Psaradhes* (T 22730 32489; Easter–Oct), with a terrace lapped by the waves – booking in season is mandatory as it's appeared (deservedly) in so many guides. There's also the reasonable beach of **Piáki**, ten minutes' walk east past the last studio units, evidence of a mild explosion in package development here during the mid-1990s.

Hill villages

Inland between Kokkári and Kondakéïka, an idyllic landscape of pine, cypress and orchards is overawed by dramatic mountains; except for some streaks of damage reaching the sea between Lemonákia and Tzaboú, it miraculously escaped the July 2000 fire. Despite destructive nibblings by bulldozers, some of the trail system linking the various **hill villages** is still intact, and walkers can return to the main highway to catch a bus home. Failing that, most of the communities can provide a bed at short notice.

The monastery of **Vrondianís** (Vróndra), directly above Kokkári, was once a popular destination, but between severe fire damage in 2000 and the army's long, hard-wearing use of it as a barracks, it's closed for renovations at present. **VOURLIÓTES**, 2km west of the monastery, has beaked chimneys and brightly painted shutters sprouting from its typical tile-roofed houses. Restaurateur greed has ruined the formerly photogenic central square; they have cut down two ancient mulberries and jammed tables into every available corner, and it's best to pass over the **tavernas** here in favour of *Iy Pera Vrysi*, at the village entrance, or (even better) the *Piyi Pnaka* taverna, in the idyllic hamlet of the same name just off the ascending Vourliótes road.

MANOLÁTES, further uphill and an hour-plus walk away via a deep river canyon, also has several simple **tavernas** (the pick of these being *Iy Filia* near the village entrance), and is the most popular trailhead for the five-hour round-trip up **Mount Ámbelos** (Karvoúnis), the island's second-highest summit. From Manolátes you can no longer easily continue on foot to Stavrinídhes, the next village, but should plunge straight down, partly on a cobbled path, through the shady valley known as Aïdhónia (Nightingales), towards Platanákia. Manolátes has accommodation with *Studios Angela* at the edge of town (℡22730 94478; ❷), but by far the most characterful base in the area is down in Aïdhónia at the *Hotel Aidonokastro* (℡22730 94686, ℻22730 94404; ❹). Here the kindly, English-speaking Yannis Pamoukis has renovated half the abandoned hamlet of Valeondátes as a unique cottage-hotel, each former house comprising a pair of two- or four-person units with traditional touches.

Karlóvassi

KARLÓVASSI, 35km west of Vathý and the second town of Sámos, is decidedly sleepier and more old-fashioned than the capital, despite having roughly the same population. Though lacking in distinction, it's popular as a base for exploring western Sámos's excellent beaches and walking opportunities. The name, despite a vehement denial of Ottoman legacy elsewhere on Sámos, appears to be a corruption of the Turkish for "snowy plain" – the plain in question being the conspicuous saddle of Mount Kérkis overhead. The town divides into four straggly neighbourhoods: Néo, well inland, whose untidy growth was spurred by the influx of post-1923 refugees; Meséo, across the usually dry riverbed, tilting appealingly off a knoll towards the shore; and picturesque Paleó (or Áno), above Limáni, the small harbour district.

Most tourists stay at or near **Limáni**, the part of town with most of the tourist facilities. Hotels tend to have road noise and not much view; **rooms**, all on the inland pedestrian lane behind the through road, are quieter – try those of *Vangelis Feloukatzis* (℡22730 33293; ❷). The port itself is an appealing place with a working boatyard at the west end and all the **ferry-ticket agencies** grouped at the middle; a shuttle-bus service operates from Néo Karlóvassi, timed to coincide with boat arrivals and departures. **Tavernas** and bars abound on the quay, though the only remarkable one is *Rementzo* (April–Oct), tellingly the locals' hangout, with good fish in season plus *mayireftá*. The local university contingent (a maths and computer science faculty is based here) keeps formal **nightlife** surprisingly lively; try *Popcorn* on the quay.

Immediately overhead is the partly hidden hamlet of **Paleó**, its hundred or so houses draped on either side of a leafy ravine, but no reliable tourist facilities. **Meséo**, just east, is a conceivable alternative base to Limáni, with the *Hotel Aspasia* (℡22730 31201; ❹) well sited 100m west of the wood-fired bakery, with a pool and air-conditioning. Following the street linking the central square to the waterfront, you pass one of the improbably huge, early twentieth-century churches, topped with twin belfries and a blue-and-white dome, which dot the coastal plain here. Just at the intersection with the shore road, well poised for viewing the sunset, you'll find the good-value *ouzerí To Kyma* (April–Oct), where welcoming Ethiopian proprietress Berhane adds a welcome touch to the broad variety of dishes, stressing seafood – most days you'll fight for a table.

Néo has little to recommend it besides a wilderness of derelict stone-built warehouses and mansions down near the river mouth, reminders of the vanished leather industry which flourished here during the first half of the twentieth century. However, if you're staying at Limáni, you'll almost certainly visit one of the several **banks** (all with ATMs), the **post office** or the **bus stop** on the main lower square. There are effectively no **eateries** except the popular, year-round *Dionysos Psistaria*, on the west side of town at the start of the Marathókambos road.

Western Sámos

Visitors tolerate dull Karlóvassi for the sake of western Sámos's excellent **beaches**. Closest of these is **Potámi**, forty minutes' walk away via the coast road from Limáni or an hour by a more scenic, high trail from Paleó. This broad arc of sand and pebbles gets crowded at summer weekends, when virtually the entire population of Karlóvassi descends on the place. Near the end of the trail from Paleó stands *Tò Iliovasilema* (lunch only), a *psistariá* grown complacent on coach tours and recommended only in the absence of anything else; there are also a very few **rooms** signposted locally, and many folk camp rough along the lower reaches of the river which gives the beach its name.

A streamside path leads twenty minutes inland, past the eleventh-century church of **Metamórfosis** – the oldest on Sámos – to a point where the river disappears into a small gorge (a new, guardrailed but still vertiginous stairway takes you up and left here). Otherwise, you must swim and wade 100m in heart-stoppingly cold water through a sequence of fern-tufted rock pools before reaching a low but vigorous waterfall; bring shoes with good tread and perhaps even rope if you want to explore above the first cascade. You probably won't be alone until you dive in, since the canyon is well known to locals and tour agencies. Just above the Metamórfosis church, a clear if precipitous path leads up to a small, contemporaneous **Byzantine fortress**. There's little to see inside other than a subterranean cistern and badly crumbled lower curtain wall, but the views out to sea and up the canyon are terrific, while in October the place is carpeted with pink autumn crocuses.

The coast beyond Potámi ranks among the most beautiful and unspoiled on Sámos; since the early 1980s it has served as a protected refuge for the rare monk seal. The dirt track at the west end of Potámi bay ends after twenty minutes on foot, from which you backtrack 100m or so to find the well-cairned side trail running parallel to the water. After twenty minutes along this you'll arrive at **Mikró Seïtáni**, a small pebble cove guarded by sculpted rock walls. A full hour's walk from the trailhead, through olive terraces, brings you to **Megálo Seïtáni**, the island's finest beach, at the mouth of the intimidating Kakopérato gorge. You'll have to bring food and water, though not necessarily a swimsuit – there's no dress code at either of the Seïtáni bays.

Southwestern beach resorts

The first place you reach on the island loop road south of Karlóvassi is **MARATHÓKAMBOS**, a pretty, amphitheatrical village overlooking the gulf of the same name; there's a taverna or two, but no short-term accommodation; with the new bypass road nearly complete, you won't need to see any of this. Its port, **ÓRMOS MARATHOKÁMBOU**, 18km from Karlóvassi, has emerged as a tourist resort since the 1990s, though some character still peeks through in its backstreets. The harbour has been improved, with *kaïkia* offering day-trips to Foúrni and the nearby islet of Samiopoúla, while the pedestrianized quay has become the focus of attention, home to several **tavernas** – best of these by some way, at the far east end, being the inexpensive *Lekatis*, which gets first crack at the fish from the boats which tie up here. Among the few nonpackaged **accommodation** outfits, try *Studios Avra* (☎22730 37221; ❷), unimprovably perched above the jetty.

The beach immediately east from Órmos is hardly the best; for better ones continue 2km west to **VOTSALÁKIA** (officially signposted as "Kámbos"), Sámos's largest resort, straggling a further 2km behind the island's longest (if not its most beautiful) beach. But for most, Votsalákia is still a vast improvement on the Pythagório area, and the mass of 1437-metre Mount Kérkis overhead rarely fails to impress (see below). As for **accommodation**, Emmanuil Dhespotakis has numerous premises towards the quieter, more scenic western end of things (☎22730 31258; ❸–❹). Also in this vicinity is *Loukoullos*, an unusual *kultúra* **taverna** overlooking the sea where all food is prepared in a wood oven. Other facilities include branches of nearly all the main Vathý travel agencies, offering **vehicle rental** (necessary, as only two daily buses call here) and money exchange.

If Votsalákia doesn't suit, you can continue beyond for 3km to the 600-metre beach of **Psilí Ámmos**, more aesthetic and not to be confused with its name-sake beach in the southeast corner of Sámos. The sea shelves very gently here, and cliffs shelter clusters of naturists at the east end. Surprisingly there is still little development: just three small studio complexes in the pines at mid-beach, and two tavernas back up on the road as you approach, either of these fine for a simple lunch. Access to **Limniónas**, a smaller cove 2km further west, passes the Limnionas Bay Hotel (☎22730 37057; ❻), much the highest-standard accommodation locally with its tiered units arrayed around a garden and pool. Yachts and pleasure *kaïkia* occasionally call at the protected bay, which offers decent swimming away from a rock shelf at mid-strand, especially at the east end where there's a simple **taverna**.

Mount Kérkis and around

Gazing up from a supine seaside position, you may be inspired to climb **Mount Kérkis**. The classic route begins at the west end of the Votsalákia strip, along the bumpy jeep track leading inland towards Evangelistrías convent. After forty-five minutes on the track system, through fire-damaged olive groves and past charcoal pits (a major local industry), the path begins, more or less following power lines up to the convent. A friendly nun may proffer an ouzo in welcome and point you up the paint-marked trail, continuing even more steeply up to the peak. The views are tremendous, though the climb itself is humdrum once you're out of the trees. About an hour before the top there's a chapel with an attached cottage for sheltering in emergencies, and just beyond, a welcome spring. All told, it's a seven-hour outing from Votsalákia and back, not counting rest stops.

Less ambitious walkers might want to circle the flanks of the mountain, first by vehicle and then by foot. The road beyond Limniónas to Kallithéa and Dhrakéï, truly back-of-beyond villages with views across to Ikaría, is paved all the way to Dhrakéï, making it possible to venture out here on an ordinary motorbike. The bus service is better during the school year, when a vehicle leaves Karlóvassi (Mon–Fri 1pm) bound for these remote spots; during summer it only operates two days a week at best (typically Mon & Fri).

From **DHRAKÉÏ**, a lovely trail – minimally damaged by a track – descends ninety minutes through forest to Megálo Seïtáni, from where it's easy enough to continue on to Karlóvassi within another two-and-a-half hours. People attempting to reverse this itinerary often discover to their cost that the bus (if any) returns from Dhrakéï early in the day, at about 2.30pm, compelling them to stay at one of two unofficial **rooms** establishments (summer only) in Dhrakéï, and dine at one of four taverna-*kafenía*. In **KALLITHÉA**, there's only a simple *psistariá* on the tiny square. From Kallithéa, a newer track (from beside the cemetery) and an older trail both lead up within 45 minutes to a spring, rural chapel and plane tree on the west flank of Kérkis, with path-only continuation for another thirty minutes to a pair of cave-churches. **Panayía Makriní** stands detached at the mouth of a high, wide but shallow grotto, whose balcony affords terrific views of Sámos's west tip. By contrast, **Ayía Triádha**, a ten-minute scramble overhead, has most of its structure made up of cave wall; just adjacent, another long, narrow, volcanic cavern can be explored with a torch some hundred metres into the mountain.

After these subterranean exertions, the closest spot for a swim is **Vársamo** (Válsamo) cove, 4km below Kallithéa and reached via a well-signposted dirt road. The beach here consists of multicoloured volcanic pebbles, with two caves to shelter in and a single very friendly **taverna** just inland, run by three generations of women.

Ikaría

Ikaría, a narrow, windswept landmass between Sámos and Mýkonos, is little visited and invariably underestimated. The name supposedly derives from the legendary Icarus, who fell into the sea just offshore after the wax bindings on his wings melted. For years the only substantial tourism was generated by a few **hot springs** on the south coast, some reputed to cure rheumatism and arthritis, some to make women fertile, though others are so highly radioactive that they've been closed for decades.

Ikaría, along with Thessaly on the mainland and Lésvos, has traditionally been one of the Greek Left's strongholds. This tendency dates from the long decades of right-wing domination in Greece, when (as in past ages) the island was used as a place of **exile** for political dissidents. Apparently the strategy backfired, with the Communist transportees favourably impressing and proselytizing their hosts; at the same time, many Ikarians emigrated to North America, and ironically their regular capitalist remittances help keep the island going. It can be a bizarre experience to be treated to a monologue on the evils of US imperialism, delivered by a retiree in perfect Alabaman English. Of late, the Ikarians tend to embrace any vaguely Left cause; posters urge you variously to attend rallies on behalf of Turkish political prisoners or contribute to funding a Zapatista teacher-training school in Chiapas. Athens has historically reacted to this contrarian stance with long periods of punitive neglect, which has only made the islanders even more profoundly self-sufficient and idiosyncratic, and supportive (or at least tolerant) of the same in others. Local pride dictates that outside opinion matters not a bit, and until very recently Ikarians seemed to have little idea what "modern tourists" expected. A lack of obsequiousness, and a studied eccentricity, are often mistaken for hostility.

These are not the only Ikarian quirks, and for many the place is an acquired taste, contrasting strongly (for better or worse) with Sámos. Except for forested portions in the northwest (now fire-denuded near the shore to clear land for hotels), it's not a strikingly beautiful island, with most of the terrain consisting of scrub-covered schist put to good use as building material. The mostly desolate south coast is overawed by steep cliffs, while the north face is less sheer but nonetheless furrowed by deep canyons creating hairpin bends extreme even by Greek-island standards. Neither are there many postcard-picturesque villages, since the rural schist-roofed houses are generally scattered so as to be next to their famous apricot orchards, vineyards and fields.

Until the mid-1990s, the Ikarians resisted most attempts to develop their island for conventional tourism; charter flights still don't land here, as the airport at the northeast tip can't accommodate jets. Since then, however, there's

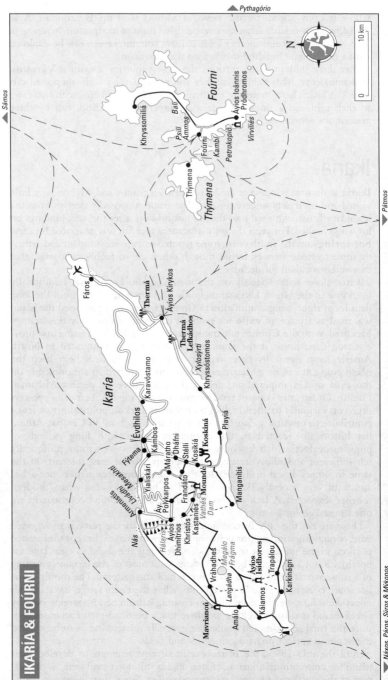

IKARÍA & FOÚRNI

▲ Pythagório

Sámos ▲

▶ Patmos

◀ Náxos, Páros, Sýros & Mýkonos

0   10 km

N

Foúrni

Khryssomiliá

Balí

Psilí
Ámmos

Ayios Ioánnis
Pródhromos

Foúrni
Kambí

Virviliés

Petrokópio

Thýmena

Thýmena

Fáros

Thermá

Ayios Kírykos

**Thermá
Lefkádhos**

Xylosýrti

Khryssóstomos

Ikaría

Karavóstamo

Playiá

Évdhilos

Frýtema
Kámbos

Yialiskári

Máratho
Dháfni

Stélli

Koskiná

Kosíkia

Polýkarpos
Áy.

Frandáto

Vathés
Dam
Moundé

Koskiná

Manganítis

Nás

Ammoúdi

Livádhi
Mesaktí

Hálaris

Áyios
Dhimítrios

Khristós

Kastaniés

Megálo
Frágma

Vráhadhes

Langádha

Áyios
Isídhoros

Trapálou

Karkinágri

Mavrianoú

Amálo

Kálamos

been a slow but steady increase in the quantity and quality of tourist facilities in and around Armenistís, the only resort of consequence.

Áyios Kírykos and around

Passing ferries on the Páros–Náxos–Foúrni–Sámos/Dodecanese line call at the south-coast port and capital of **ÁYIOS KÍRYKOS**, about 1km southwest of the island's main thermal resort. Because of the spa trade, beds are at a premium in town at high season; arriving in the evening from Sámos, accept any reasonable offers of rooms at the jetty, or – if in a group – proposals of a taxi ride to the north coast, which shouldn't cost more than €26 per vehicle to Armenistís. A cream-and-green **bus** supposedly sets out across the island from the main square (summer Mon–Fri only at noon) to Évdhilos, usually changing vehicles there at 1.30pm for the onward trip to Armenistís, but in practice can prove non-existent.

The baths (daily 8am–1pm) in **Thérma** are rather old-fashioned stone tubs, with preference given to those under medical care. A better bet for a less formal soak are the more natural, shoreline hot springs at **Thérma Lefkádhos**, 3km southwest of Áyios Kírykos, below a cluster of villas. Here the seaside spa is derelict, leaving the water to boil up right in the shallows, mixing with the sea between giant volcanic boulders to a pleasant temperature.

A more conventional beach – the largest on the south coast – is found at **Fáros**, 10km northeast of Áyios Kírykos along a good paved road (which also serves the airport). A considerable colony of summer cottages shelters under tamarisks fringing the mixed sand-and-gravel strand, with a reefy zone to cross before deep water; this rather end-of-the-world place looks across to Foúrni and Thýmena, whose beaches (and landscape) it strongly resembles. But the best reason to make the trip out is an excellent, inexpensive and quick-serving **fish taverna**, *Leonidas*, with grilled or fried seafood plus bulk wine (excellent, as it usually is on Ikaría), better than anything in Áyios itself and accordingly popular.

Practicalities

Hydrofoils, the small Miniotis Lines ferries and *kaïkia* for Foúrni use the small east jetty; large ferries and catamarans dock at the main west pier. There are several **hotels**, such as the *Isabella* (℡22750 22839; ③) above the National Bank, or the friendly, basic but spotless *Akti* (℡22750 22694; ②), on a knoll east of the hydrofoil and *kaïki* quay, with views of Foúrni from the garden; both have rooms with and without bathrooms. Otherwise, **pensions** and **rooms** are not especially cheap. Directly behind the base of the ferry jetty and a little to the west there's the well-appointed *Pension Maria-Elena* (℡22750 22835, ℻22750 22223; ④), with sea views. All in a row to the east and suffering some noise from the several *kafenía* and snack-bars below are the *Pension Ikaria* (℡22750 22804; ②), the studios above the *Snack Bar Dedalos* (℡22750 22276; ③) and the clean *dhomátia* run by Ioannis Proestos (℡22750 23176 or 22750 23496; ②).

Eating out, you've less choice than with lodging. It's best to give the obvious quayside eateries a miss in favour of the grilled dishes served up at the *Estiatorio Tzivaeri*, just inland from Ioannis Proestos's rooms, or *Iy Klimataria* just around the corner for less distinguished but year-round *mayireftá*. The front is more glitzy, with *Casino* the last remaining traditional *kafenío*; for further entertainment there's a **summer cinema**, the Rex, with first-run fare. Several **banks** with ATMs, a **post office** on the road out of town and three ferry/hydrofoil **agents** round up the list of essentials. You can **rent** motorbikes and cars here, too, but both are typically cheaper in Armenistís.

Évdhilos and around

The twisting, 41-kilometre road from Áyios Kírykos to Évdhilos is one of the most hair-raising on any Greek island (especially as a taxi passenger), and the long ridge extending the length of Ikaría often wears a streamer of cloud, even when the rest of the Aegean is clear. Karavóstamo, with its tiny, scruffy port, is the first substantial north-coast place, beyond which a series of three beaches leads up to **ÉVDHILOS**. Although this is the island's second town and a regular ferry stop on the Sámos–Náxos–Páros–Sýros line, it's rather less equipped to deal with visitors than Áyios Kírykos. Évdhilos offers just two **hotels** – the *Evdoxia* on the slope southwest of the harbour (T 22750 31502; ❹) and the low-lying *Atheras* (T 22750 31434, F 22750 31926; ❹) with a small pool – plus a few **rooms**, the best of which are run by Apostolos Stenos (T 22750 31365; ❷) just west of town. A **post office** up towards the *Evdoxia*, a pair of **bank ATMs**, and two good **beaches** just to the east, are also worth knowing about, though the nearer beach may be blighted in coming years by a new, much-needed harbour jetty. Among several waterfront **restaurants**, the wood-signed "Kafestiatório" between *O Flisvos* and the Blue Nice **boat-ticket agency** (T 22750 31990) is the most reliable and reasonable option, but for more interesting fare head 1km west of the harbour to **FÝTEMA** hamlet, where just on the roadside *To Inomayerio tis Popis*, alias *To Fytema* (May–Sept), has lots of options for vegetarians, excellent local wine, low prices and pleasant terrace seating, though portions are on the small side.

    KÁMBOS, 1.5km west of Fýtema, offers a small hilltop museum with finds from nearby **ancient Oinoe**; the twelfth-century church of Ayía Iríni lies just below, with the remains of a fourth-century Byzantine basilica serving as the entry courtyard. Lower down still are the sparse ruins of a Byzantine palace (just above the road) used to house exiled nobles, as well as a 250-metre-long sandy beach with a musical drinks *kantína*. *Rooms Dhionysos* are available from the store run by Vassilis Kambouris (T 22750 31300 or 22750 31688; ❷), who also acts as the unofficial and enthusiastic tourism officer for this part of Ikaría, keeping the keys for the church and museum.

    By following the road heading inland from the large church in Évdhilos, you can also visit the Byzantine **castle of Koskiná** (Nikariás), just over 15km south. The road signposted for Manganítis is paved through Kosikiá, 9km away, and for 2km more to the marked side track. You can get a bike or jeep along this to within a short walk of the tenth-century castle, perched on a distinctive conical hill, with an arched gateway and a fine vaulted chapel.

    Beyond this turning, the road creeps over the island watershed and drops precipitously in hairpins towards the south coast; most of this is paved, and with your own vehicle offers an alternative (and much less curvy) way back to Áyios Kírykos in much the same time as via Karavóstomo.

Armenistís and around

Most people carry on to **ARMENISTÍS**, 57km from Áyios Kírykos, and with good reason: this little resort lies below Ikaría's finest (if slightly diminished) forest, with two enormous, sandy beaches battered by near-constant surf from July to September – **Livádhi** and **Mesakhtí** – five and fifteen minutes' walk to the east respectively. The waves, which attract Athenian surfers, are complicated by strong lateral currents (as signs warn), and regular summer drownings have prompted the institution of that Greek rarity, a lifeguard service. Armenistís itself is spectacularly set, facing northeast along the length of Ikaría towards sun- and moonrise, with Mount Kérkis on Sámos closing off the horizon on a clear day. A dwindling proportion of older, schist-roofed buildings, plus fishing boats hauled up in a sandy cove, lend Armenistís the air of a Cornish fishing village. Despite gradual growth it remains a manageable place, reminiscent of similar youth-oriented, slightly "alternative" spots in southern Crete, though gentrification (and a strong package presence) has definitely set in, and the islanders' tolerance doesn't extend to nude bathing. The long-running, semi-official campsite behind Livádhi beach closed in 2001 – a sign of the times – and probably won't reopen, though a few freelance tents still sprout in the rivermouth greenery behind Mesakthí. Several "music bars", often with live Greek gigs, operate seasonally behind Livádhi and at the quay's north end, but for most visitors **nightlife** takes the form of extended sessions in the tavernas and cafés overlooking the anchorage, or the *zaharoplastía* (especially *En Plo*) at the village entrance.

Practicalities

There are easily a score of rooms establishments in the Armenistís area, as well as four bona fide **hotels**. Among the latter, the 1999-built *Erofili Beach*, right at the entrance to "town" (☎22750 71058, ⓦwww.erofili.gr; ❺) is considered the best on the island and has a small pool perched dramatically over Livádhi beach. Runners-up include the *Messakhti Village* complex (☎22750 71331, ⓦwww.messakti-village.com; ❺) just above Mesakhtí beach, with a larger pool, its common areas and private terraces complementing very large if minimally furnished self-catering units suitable for families of three to six, or – on the western edge of Armenistís – the *Daidalos* (☎22750 71390, ⒺDaidalos@aegean-exodus.gr; ❺), the less impersonal and less package-dominated of two adjacent hotels, with another eyrie-pool, unusually appointed rooms and a shady breakfast terrace. If your budget doesn't run to the hotels, among the various **rooms**, the *Kirki* by the *Erofili Beach* (☎22750 71254, Ⓕ22750 71083; ❸) is spartan but en suite, with large private balconies and sea views; on the opposite side of the road, but at the top of the hill, the similar-decor *Armena Inn* (☎22750 71320; ❸) has private parking, seclusion, unobstructed views and cooking facilities in the rooms. Along the shore lane, the *Paskhalia Rooms* (☎22750 71302 or 210 24 71 411 in winter; ❷) are on the small side but en suite and good value, with great views east, while at the far end of Livádhi beach, the *Atsahas Apartments* (☎ & Ⓕ22750 71226; ❸) offer the best standard and setting outside of the hotels.

Discounting the *zaharoplastía* and *souvláki* stalls (a pair each), there are five full-service **tavernas** in Armenistís, of which three have a consistently good reputation. *Dhelfini*, its terrace hovering right above the fishing cove, is the cheap-and-cheerful favourite – come early or very late for a table, and a mix of grills or *mayireftá*. *Paskhalia* (aka *Vlahos* after the helpful managing family) also serves similar fare at its seaview terrace up the hill, and is the most reliable venue for both breakfast and off-season travellers, open until mid-October. Down on the quay itself, *Symposio* is pricier but well worth it for its creative recipes and rich ingredients reflecting the German co-management and chef. Further afield, the *Atsahas*, attached to the namesake apartments, is acceptable as a beach taverna, with generous portions but occasionally under-cooked and over-oiled fare. Just east of Mesakthí in the fishing settlement of **Yialiskári**, looking out past pines to a picturesque church on the jetty, there's another cluster of tavernas overlooking the boat-launching slips, of which

Tramountana and *Kelari* are the most popular, the former purveying superb parrotfish fry-ups. Yialiskári is also home to the area's only **Internet café**, Ic@rian-Sea.

There are now at least four **scooter/mountain-bike rental** agencies in Armenistís; among a like number of **car-rental** outlets, Aventura (☎22750 71117) is the most prominent, with a branch for drop-offs in Évdhilos which could be handy for ferry departures towards Sámos at an ungodly hour (typically 4am), when the buses aren't yet running. Indeed getting away when you need to is the main drawback to staying in Armenistís, since both taxis and buses can be elusive. Theoretically, **buses** head for Évdhilos three times daily mid-June to mid-September, fairly well spaced (typically 7.15am, noon & 7pm, returning an hour or so later) and designed to coincide with ferries; Áyios Kírykos has only one through service year-round at 7.15am, though this can be full with school kids in term-time. If you've a ferry to catch, it's far easier on the nerves to prebook a **taxi**: ring Kostas Stroupas (☎22750 41132), or Yiannis Tsantiris (☎22750 41322).

Ráhes

Armenistís is actually the shore annexe of four inland hamlets – Áyios Dhimítrios, Áyios Polýkarpos, Kastaniés and Khristós – collectively known as **RÁHES**. Despite the modern, mostly paved access roads through the pines (trails shortcut them), the settlements retain a certain Shangri-La quality, with the older residents speaking a positively Homeric dialect. On an island not short of foibles, Khristós (Khristós Rahón in full) is particularly strange inasmuch as the locals sleep until 11am or so, shop and educate their kids until about 4pm, then have another nap until 9pm, whereupon they rise and spend the entire night shopping, eating and drinking until almost dawn. In fact most of the villages west of Évdhilos adhere to this schedule, defying central government efforts to bring them into line with the rest of Greece.

Near the pedestrianized *agorá* of Khristós, paved in schist and studded with gateways fashioned from the same rock, there's a **post office** and a **hotel/restaurant** (☎22750 71269; ❸), but in accordance with the above nocturnal habits, lunchtime can offer pretty slim pickings. The most reliable venue (strictly after 1pm) are the unmarked premises of *Vassilis Yiakas*, at the far southeast end of the pedestrian way – you'll know it from the enormous Victrola and the bare wood floors. The slightly spaced-out demeanour of those serving – plus numbers of old boys shambling around in dirty clothes, with their flies unzipped – may be attributable to overindulgence in the excellent home-brewed **wine** which everyone west of Évdhilos makes. The local festival is August 6, though better ones take place further southwest in the woods at the Langádha valley (August 14–15) or at the Áyios Isídhoros monastery (May 14).

Since the early 1990s, **walking** between Ráhes and the coastal resorts has rocketed in popularity, and locally produced, accurate if somewhat chatty map-guides are now widely available. The black-and-white *Road & Hiking Map of Western Ikaria* (€1.50) shows most asphalt roads, tracks and trails in the west-centre of the island; the more closely focused, colour *Round of Rahes on Foot* (€3) details a loop hike taking in the best the Ráhes villages have to offer. The route sticks mostly to surviving paths, and is well marked; the authors suggest a full day for the circuit, with ample rests, though total walking time won't be more than six hours. More advanced outings involve descending the Hálaris canyon, with its historic bridge, to Nás, or crossing the island to Manganítis via Ráhes.

Nás

By tacit consent, Greek or foreign "New Age" types and beachside naturists have been allowed to shift 3km west of Armenistís by paved road to **Nás**, a tree-clogged river canyon ending in a small but deceptively sheltered sand-and-pebble beach. This little bay is almost completely enclosed by weirdly sculpted rock formations, but for the same reasons as at Mesakhtí it's unwise to swim outside the cove's natural limits. The crumbling foundations of the fifth-century temple of **Artemis Tavropoleio** (Patroness of Bulls) overlook the permanent deep pool at the mouth of the river. If you continue inland along the river past colonies of rough campers defying prohibition signs, you'll find secluded rock pools for freshwater dips – as well as unfortunate evidence of the lack of sanitary facilities. Back at the top of the stairs leading down to the beach from the road are six tavernas, most of them offering rooms. Among the **tavernas**, *O Nas* doesn't abuse its prime position, operating Easter to October, with a good range of lunchtime *mayireftá*; among **rooms**, the *Artemis* (☎ 22750 71485; ❸) overlooks the river canyon, while *Thea* (☎ 22750 71491; ❸) faces out to sea, both places halving the rates out of season.

Satellite islands: Thýmena and Foúrni

The straits between Sámos and Ikaría are speckled with a mini-archipelago of three islets, of which the inhabited ones are Thýmena and Foúrni. More westerly **Thýmena** has one tiny hillside settlement; a regular *kaïki* calls at the quay below on its way between Ikaría and Foúrni, but there are no tourist facilities, and casual visits are explicitly discouraged. Foúrni is home to a huge fishing fleet and one of the more thriving boatyards in the Aegean; thanks to these, and the improvement of the jetty to receive car ferries, its population is stable, unlike so many small Greek islands. The islets were once the lair of Maltese pirates, and indeed many of the islanders have a distinctly North African appearance.

The aforementioned **kaïki** leaves Ikaría at about 1pm several days weekly, stays overnight at Foúrni and returns the next morning; another twice-weekly *kaïki* from Karlóvassi, and the larger car ferries which appear every few days, are likewise not tourist excursion boats but exist for the benefit of the islanders. The only practical way to visit Foúrni on a day-trip is by using the tourist *kaïki*, the *Ayios Nikolaos*, which leaves Áyios Kírykos daily in season at 10am, and returns from Foúrni at 5pm, or on one of the summer morning **hydrofoils** or excursion boats out of Pythagório on Sámos.

Foúrni

Apart from the remote hamlet of **Khryssomiliá** in the north, where the island's longest (and often roughest) road goes, most of Foúrni's inhabitants are concentrated in the **port** and Kambí hamlet just to the south. The harbour community is larger than it seems from the sea, with a friendly ambience reminiscent of 1970s Greece. Among several **rooms** establishments, the most popular are the various premises run by Manolis and Patra Markakis (☎ 22750 51268, ℱ 22750 51355), immediately to your left as you disembark; there are simple rooms, some with balconies (❷), and superb hilltop studios (❸). If they're full you can head inland to the modern blocks of *Evtyhia Amoryianou* (☎ 22750 51364 or 51102; ❷), whose father Nikos Kondylas meets all boats and is a mine of information about the island.

There are two full-service waterfront **tavernas**: local favourite *Rementzo*, better known as *Nikos'*, where, if you're lucky, the local *astakós* or Aegean lobster may be on the menu until mid-August; or the cheaper, less polished *Miltos*, also with good seafood. For breakfast and desserts, repair to the tamarisk terrace at the Markakis family's *To Arhondiko tis Kyras Kokonas*, under their inn. There's surprisingly lively **nightlife** at a half-dozen music bars, clubs and *ouzerís*, often until 5am.

The central "high street", fieldstoned and mulberry-shaded, ends well inland at a little *platía* with more traditional *kafenía* under each of two plane trees; between them stands a Hellenistic sarcophagus found in a nearby field, and overhead is a conical hill, site of the ancient acropolis. There's a **post office**, plus several surprisingly well-stocked shops, but at the time of writing no functioning ATM or other money-changing facilities, so come prepared.

A fifteen-minute trail-walk south from the school, skirting the cemetery and then slipping over the windmill ridge, brings you to **KAMBÍ**, a scattered community overlooking a pair of sandy, tamarisk-shaded coves which you may share with chickens and hauled-up fishing boats. There are two cheap, comparable and sustaining **tavernas**: the *Kambi* with tables on the sand, and *O Yiorgos* clinging to the side of a valley inland. A path continues to the next bay south which, like Kambí cove, is a preferred anchorage for wandering yachts.

Heading north from the harbour via steps, then a trail, you'll find another **beach**: **Psilí Ámmos** in front of a derelict fish-processing plant, with shade at one end. At the extreme north of the island, remote **KHRYSSOMILIÁ** is still best approached by the taxi-boat from the port rather than the atrocious eighteen-kilometre road. The village, split into a shore district and a hillside settlement, has a decent beach flanked by better but less accessible ones. Simple **rooms** and **meals** can be arranged on the spot, though the locals can be less than forthcoming with outsiders. The hamlet and monastery of **Áyios Ioánnis Pródhromos** in the far south of Foúrni is probably a better day-trip target on foot, taxi-boat or by scooter (available for rent), with some good, secluded beaches just below.

Híos

"Craggy Híos", as **Homer** aptly described his putative birthplace, has a turbulent history and a strong identity. It has always been relatively prosperous: in medieval times through the export of mastic **resin** – a trade controlled by Genoese overlords between 1346 and 1566 – and later by the **Ottomans**, who dubbed the place Sakız Adası ("Resin Island"). Since union with Greece in 1912, several shipping dynasties have emerged here, continuing the pattern of wealth. Participation in the maritime way of life is widespread, with someone in almost every family spending time in the merchant navy.

The more powerful ship-owning families, the local government and the military authorities did not encourage tourism until the late 1980s, but the worldwide shipping crisis and the saturation of other, more obviously "marketable" islands eroded their resistance. Since then, numbers of foreigners have discovered a Híos beyond its rather daunting port capital: fascinating villages, important Byzantine monuments and a respectable, if remote, complement of beaches. While unlikely ever to be dominated by tourism, the local scene has a distinctly modern flavour – courtesy of numerous returned Greek-Americans and Greek-Canadians – and English is widely spoken.

Unfortunately, the island has suffered more than its fair share of **catastrophes** during the past two centuries. The Turks perpetrated their most

Lésvos

Psará

Psará

Ayiásmata

Kouroúnia
Víki
Áyio Gála
Kambiá
Amádhes
Yióssonas
Afrodhísia
Kéramos
Nagós
Mármaro
Evangelismoú
Melaniós
Pelinéo
Inoússes
Spartoúnda
1297m
Trýpes
Hálandhra
Áno
Kástro
Inoússi
Parpariá
Kipouriés
Kardhámyla
Fourkeró
Néa
Potamiá
Pityós
Ayía Markélla
Moundhón
Volissós
Límnos
Dhievhá
Langádha
Lefkáthia
Limniá
Sykiádha
Pandoukiós
Managrós

Sidhiroúnda
Panayía
Mersinidhíou
Metóhi
Vrondádhos
Tigáni
Anávatos
Makriá Ámmos
Karyés
Elínda
Avgónyma
Néa Moní
Híos Town
Kastélla
Paralía Lithioú
Áyios
Yeóryios
Kondári
Çeşme
Sikoúsis
Ayii
Lithí
KÁMBOS
Anáryiri
Panayía †
Karfás
Dhídhyma
Krína
Thymianá
Ayía Ermióni
Potámi
Ayía Irini
Eláta
Mégas Limniónas
Liménas Mestón
Véssa
Kallimassiá
Ayía Fotiní
Panayía
Áyios Emilianós
Merikoúnda
Sikelliá †
Katarráktis
Mestá
Armólia
TURKEY
Olýmbi
Kiní
Vounós
Patriká
Nénita
Sykiás
Olýmbon
Kalamotí
Pyrgí
Ayía
Dhýnami
Kómi
Lilikás
Káto Faná
Dhótia
Emboriós
Tower
Mávros Yialós
(Mávra Vólia)
Vroulídhia

N

0   5 km

Sámos, Ikaría, Foúrni & Pátmos

infamous, if not their worst, anti-revolutionary atrocity here in March 1822, massacring 30,000 Híots and enslaving or exiling even more. In 1881, much of Híos was destroyed by a violent **earthquake**, and throughout the 1980s the natural beauty of the island was markedly diminished by devastating forest fires, compounding the effect of generations of tree-felling by boat-builders. Nearly two-thirds of the majestic pines are now gone, with substantial patches of woods persisting only in the far northeast and the centre of Híos.

In 1988 the first charters from northern Europe were instituted, signalling potentially momentous changes for the island. But there are still fewer than five thousand guest beds on Híos, the vast majority of them in the capital or the nearby beach resorts of Karfás and Ayía Ermióni. Further expansion, however, is hampered by the lack of direct flights from most countries (including Britain), and the refusal of property owners to part with land for the extension of the airport runway.

Híos Town

HÍOS, the harbour and main town, will come as a shock after modest island capitals elsewhere; it's a bustling, concrete-laced commercial centre, with little predating the 1881 quake. Yet in many ways it is the most satisfactory of the east Aegean ports, with a large and fascinating marketplace, several museums and some good, authentic tavernas. Although it's a sprawling place of about 30,000 souls, most things of interest to visitors lie within a hundred or so metres of the water, fringed by Leofóros Egéou.

South and east of the main *platía*, officially Plastíra but known universally as Vounakíou, extends the marvellously lively tradesmen's **bazaar**, where you can find everything from parrots to cast-iron woodstoves. Opposite the Vounakíou **taxi rank**, the grandiosely titled "**Byzantine Museum**", occupying the old **Mecidiye Mosque** (Tues–Sun 8.30am–3pm; free), is little more than an archeological warehouse, with a preponderance of Jewish marble gravestones

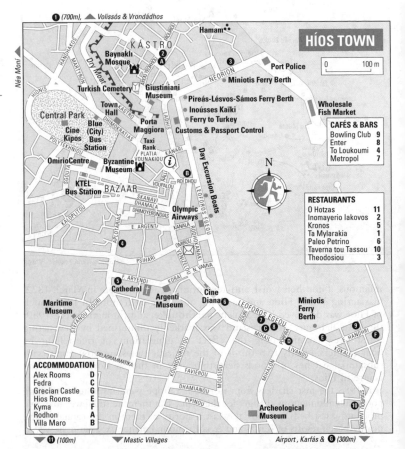

in the courtyard – plus a few Armenian, Genoese and Turkish ones – testifying to the island's varied population in past centuries.

Until the 1881 earthquake, the Byzantine-Genoese **Kástro** was completely intact; thereafter developers razed the seaward walls, filled in much of the moat to the south and made a fortune selling off the real estate thus created around present-day Platía Vounakíou. Today the most satisfying entry to the citadel is via Porta Maggiora behind the town hall. The top floor of a medieval mansion just inside is home to the **Giustiniani Museum** (Tues–Sun 9am–3pm, in summer may close later; €2), with a satisfying (and periodically changing) collection of unusual icons and mosaics rescued from local churches. The small dungeon adjacent briefly held 75 Hiot hostages before their execution by the Ottomans in 1822. The old residential quarter inside the surviving castle walls, formerly the Muslim and Jewish neighbourhoods, is well worth a wander; among the wood and plaster houses you'll find assorted Ottoman monuments in various states of decay: a Muslim cemetery, a small minaretless mosque, a ruined *hamam* (Turkish bath) and several inscribed fountains.

Further afield, three other museums beckon. The **Maritime Museum** at Stefánou Tsoúri 20 (Mon–Sat 10am–1pm; free) consists principally of model ships and oil paintings of various craft, Greek and foreign, all rather overshadowed by the mansion containing them. In the foyer are enshrined the knife and glass–globe grenade of Admiral Kanaris, who partly avenged the 1822 massacre by ramming and sinking the Ottoman fleet's flagship. In the centre of town, the **Argenti Folklore Museum** (Mon–Thurs 8am–2pm, Fri 8am–2pm & 5–7.30pm, Sat 8am–12.30pm; €2), on the top floor of the Korái Library at Korái 2, features ponderous genealogical portraits of the endowing family, an adjoining wing of costumes and rural impedimenta, plus multiple replicas of Delacroix's *Massacre at Hios*, a painting which did much to arouse sympathy for the cause of Greek independence.

The **Archeological Museum** on Mihálon (June–Sept daily 8am–7pm; Oct–May Tues–Sun 8.30am–3pm; €3) finally reopened in late 1999 after an eight-year overhaul. The wide-ranging and well-lit collection, arranged both thematically and chronologically from Neolithic to Roman times, demands at least an hour or so of exploration. Highlights include limestone column bases from the Apollo temple at Faná in the shape of lion's claws; numerous statuettes and reliefs of Cybele (this Asiatic goddess was especially honoured here); Archaic faïence miniatures from Emboriós in the shape of a cat, a hawk and a flautist; terracottas from various eras of a dwarf riding a boar; and figurines (some with articulated limbs) of *hierodouloi* or sacred prostitutes, presumably from an Aphrodite shrine. Most famous of all is an inscribed edict of Alexander the Great from 322 BC, ordering local political changes and setting out relations between himself and the Hiots.

Arrival, information and services

Ferries and **kaïkia** large and small dock at various points as shown on the town map. The **airport** lies 4km south along the coast at Kondári, a €3.50 taxi-ride away; otherwise any blue urban bus labelled "KONDÁRI KARFÁS" departing from the terminal on the north side of the park passes the airport gate, opposite which is a conspicuous stop with shelter. **Ferry** agents cluster to either side of the customs building, towards the north end of waterfront Egéou and its continuation Neoríon: NEL (☎22710 23971) is a few paces south of customs, while Miniotis Lines, at Neoríon 21–23 (☎22710 24670) or Egéou 11 (☎22710 21463), operates small, slow ferries to many neighbouring islands. GA ferries, plus air tickets, are handled by competent Serafim Travel at Kanári 24

(℡22710 23558). Both the Turkish evening ferry to Çeşme, as well as the most regular boat to Inoússes, are represented by Faros Travel at Egéou 18 (℡22710 27240). The helpful municipal **tourist office** (May–Sept daily 7am–10pm; Oct–April Mon–Fri 7am–2.30pm; ℡22710 44389) is at Kanári 18; quality commercial maps and a limited stock of English-language **books** are at Newsstand, at the first "kink" in Egéou near the Cine Diana.

The standard green-and-cream **KTEL buses** leave from a parking area beside their ticket office on the south side of the park, behind the Omírio Cultural Centre. While services to the south of Híos are adequate, those to the centre and northwest of the island are almost nonexistent, and to explore there you'll need to rent a powerful **motorbike** or a car, or share a **taxi** (which are bright red here, not grey as in most of Greece). Three independent or small-chain **car-rental** agencies sit in a row at Evyenías Handhrí 5–7, behind the eyesore *Chandris Hotel*; of these, Vassilakis/Reliable Rent a Car (℡22710 29300 or 694 43 34 898), with a branch at Mégas Limniónas, is particularly recommended. The **post office** is on Omírou, while numerous **banks** all have ATMs. A final Hiot idiosyncrasy is afternoon **shopping hours** limited to Monday and Thursday in summer.

Accommodation

Híos Town has a fair quantity of affordable **accommodation**, rarely completely full. Most places line the water or the perpendicular alleys and parallel streets behind, and almost all are plagued by traffic noise to some degree – listed are the more peaceful establishments.

Alex Rooms Mihaïl Livanoú 29 ℡22710 26054. The friendly proprietor may meet late-arriving ferries; otherwise ring the bell. There's a roof garden above the well-furnished rooms, all en-suite. ❷

Fedra Mihaïl Livanoú 13 ℡22710 41130, ℻22710 41128. Well-appointed *pension* in an old mansion, with stone arches in the downstairs winter bar; in summer the bar operates outside, so ask for a rear room to avoid nocturnal noise. ❹

Grecian Castle Bella Vista shore avenue, en route to airport ℡2710 44740, ⊛www.greciancastle.gr. Opened in 1996 using the shell of an old factory, and popular with package tourists, this is Híos Town's top-rated (A-class) digs. Lovely grounds and a sea-view pool, but the smallish main wing rooms, despite their marble floors, wood ceilings and bug screens, aren't worth the rates charged; the rear "villa" suites are far more pleasant. Std rooms ❻, villa suites ❽

Hios Rooms Egéou 110, cnr Kokáli ℡22710 20198 or 697 28 33 841. Tile- or wood-floored, high-ceilinged rooms, some en suite and relatively quiet for a seafront location, lovingly restored by proprietors Don (New Zealander) and Dina (Greek),

who live on-site. Best is the penthouse "suite" with private terrace. ❷

Kyma East end of Evyenías Handhrí ℡22710 44500, ℮kyma@chi.forthnet.gr. En-suite hotel rooms in a Neoclassical mansion or a modern extension, with TV, huge terraces on the sea-facing side and jacuzzi tubs in some rooms. Splendid service and big breakfasts really make the place. The old wing saw a critical moment in modern Greek history in September 1922, when Colonel Nikolaos Plastiras commandeered it as his HQ after the Greek defeat in Asia Minor, and announced the deposition of King Constantine I. Aug ❺, otherwise ❹

Rodhon Platéon 10 ℡22710 24335. The owners can be awkward, and not all rooms are en suite, but it's just about the only place inside the *kástro*, and pretty quiet. ❷–❸

Villa Maro Roïdhou 15 ℡22710 27003. Modern *pension* tucked onto a tiny plaza just inland from the water; rear rooms unfortunately overlook the public toilets, but all are en-suite, tile-floored and well equipped, plus there's a pleasant breakfast/snack-bar on the ground floor. ❸

Eating

Eating out in Híos Town can be more pleasurable than the fast-food joints and multiple *barákia* on the waterfront (plus American-style pizza parlours inland) would suggest; it is also usually a lot cheaper than on neighbouring Sámos or Lésvos.

O Hotzas Yeoryíou Kondhýli 3, cnr Stefánou Tsoúri, off map. Oldest (and arguably best) taverna in town, with chef Ioannis Linos, the fourth generation of his family, presiding. Menu varies seasonally, but expect a mix of vegetarian dishes (*mavromátika*, cauliflower, stuffed red peppers), and sausages, baby fish and *mydhopílafo* (rice and mussels) washed down by own-brand ouzo or retsina. Allow €14 each. Dinner only, garden in summer; closed Sun.

Inomayerio Iakovos Ayíou Yeoryíou Frouríou 20, Kástro. A good balance of well-executed fishy dishes, grilled titbits, cheese-based recipes and vegetables; local white bulk wine or ouzo. Atmospheric garden seating in a vine-cloaked ruin opposite, or inside Oct–May. Budget €12–14 each. Closed Sun, and no lunch Sept–June.

Kronos Filíppou Aryéndi 2, cnr Aplotariás. The island's best, and own-made ice cream, purveyed since 1929. Limited seating or take away; open noon–midnight.

Ta Mylarakia By three restored windmills in Tambákika district, on the road to Vrondádhos ☎22710 40412. A large, well-priced seafood selection, every kind of Hiot ouzo and limited waterside seating make reservations advisable in summer. Dinner all year, lunch also Oct–April.

Paleo Petrino Egéou 80. Standard, no-nonsense *ouzerí* with such delights as *iliókafto* (sun-dried fish) on the Greek-only menu – mainly patronized by locals. In the cooler months the interior, with 1950s Greek record and film posters, is more pleasant than quayside seating where you often ingest car fumes with your food.

Tavernaki tou Tassou Stávrou Livanoú 8, Bella Vista district. Superb all-rounder with creative salads, better-than-average bean dishes, dolmádhes, snails, properly done chips, a strong line in seafood and good barrel wine. A bit pricier than usual – allow €16 each – but Tassos' and Tsambika's cooking (with son Dhimitris at the grill) is worth it. Open lunch and supper most of the year, with seaview garden seating during warmer months and heated gazebo in winter.

Theodhosiou Ouzeri Neoríon 33. The oldest, least expensive *ouzerí* on the quay, which moved in 2001 to these domed, arcaded premises. A fair amount of meat grills for this type of eatery, plus a long list of seafood standards like shrimp-and-onion fryup. Generally, best avoid fried platters in favour of grilled or boiled ones. Dinner only; closed Sun.

Drinking, nightlife and entertainment

The 1400 or so students at the local technical schools and economics/business management faculties of the University of the Aegean help keep things lively, especially along the portion of the waterfront between the two "kinks" in Egéou. Shooting **pool** is a big thing in Híos Town many bars have several tables.

Bowling Club East end of Egéou. The seven alleys (and to a lesser extent, five pool tables) are very popular with local youth. Open until at least midnight.

Cine Kipos In central park from June to mid-Sept only. Quality/art-house first-run fare, two screenings nightly; watch for flyers around town. During winter, the action shifts to Cine Diana, under the eponymous hotel (two screenings nightly).

Enter Seaward from the *Faidra* hotel. The longest established of several Internet cafés, with ten or so terminals upstairs; a bargain by Greek standards at €2.70/hr.

To Loukoumi Alley off Aplotariás 27/c. Old warehouse refitted as a café (8am–2pm), *ouzerí* (8pm–2am) and occasional events centre. Well executed and worth checking out, but closes May–Sept & Sun.

Metropolis Egéou. The longest-lived and most civilized of the music bars on this stretch of the front, always crowded from sunset until the small hours.

Omirio South side of the central park. Cultural centre and events hall with frequently changing exhibitions; foreign musicians often come here after Athens concerts to perform in the large auditorium.

Beaches near Híos Town

The locals swim at tiny pebble coves near Vrondádhos, north of Híos Town, or from the somewhat grubby town beach in Bella Vista district, but for most visitors the closest decent one is at **KARFÁS**, 7km south beyond the airport and served by frequent blue buses. Once there you can **rent cars** at MG (☎22710 32222) or bikes from Rabbit Moto (☎22710 32501), both uphill from the bus stop. Most large Hiot package hotels are planted here, to the considerable detriment of the 500-metre-long beach itself, sandy only at the south end. The main bright spot is a unique **pension**, *Markos' Place* (☏ 22710 31990 or 697 32 39 706, ⓦ www.marcos-place.gr; ❷; April–Nov), installed in the disestablished **monastery of Áyios Yeóryios and Áyios Pandelímon**, on the hillside south of the bay. Markos Kostalas, who leases the premises from Thymianá municipality, has created a uniquely peaceful, leafy environment much loved by special-activity groups. Guests are lodged in the former pilgrims' cells, with a kitchen available or superior breakfasts laid on by arrangement; individuals are more than welcome (there are several single "cells") as are families (2 "tower" rooms sleep 4 at €45), though reservations are advisable and the minimum stay is four days.

Shoreline **restaurants** aren't brilliant, though *Karatzas* (near mid-beach) and *Giamos* (south end) are striving valiantly to regain credibility after late-1990s bad patches; *Giamos* has the edge in food quality. *Oasis*, between these two on the sand, is a popular breakfast, juice, snack and drinks café-bar; musical *La Notte*, up on the slope near *Markos' Place*, acquits itself well for **nightlife** (especially amongst young Greeks) into the autumn. Generally, though, it's better to strike inland for eating opportunities. *Ouzeri To Apomero* (open daily), in hillside Spiládhia district west of the airport (go around the runway and follow the many luminous green signs) has lovely terrace seating, live music a few nights weekly in summer, and such delights as pancetta with cumin, *garídhes saganáki* and *sheftalyés* (Cypriot-style meat rissoles). Between Thymianá and Neohóri, *Fakiris Taverna* (open all year but weekends only in winter) offers home-marinated aubergine and artichokes, goat baked in tomato sauce and excellent wood-fired pizzas along with well-executed seafood and pork-based *bekrí mezé* in big portions. The easiest way to find it is to head south on the road to Kalimassiá and then turn west onto Ayíou Trýfonos road, just before Neohóri, and proceed about a kilometre.

Some 2km further along the coast from Karfás, **AYÍA ERMIÓNI** is not a beach but a fishing anchorage surrounded by a handful of tavernas (none stand out) and apartments to rent. The nearest proper beach is at **Mégas Limniónas**, a few hundred metres further, smaller than Karfás but more scenic where low cliffs provide a backdrop. Both Ayía Ermióni and Mégas Limniónas are served by extensions of blue-bus routes to either Karfás or Thymianá, the nearest inland village. The coast road loops up to Thymianá, from where you can (with your own transport only) continue 3km south towards Kalimassiá to the turning for **Ayía Fotiní**, a 600-metre pebble beach with exceptionally clean water. Cars are excluded from the shore area; the pedestrian esplanade is lined with various blocks of rooms, less monopolized than formerly by tour companies, plus there's car hire locally. A few tavernas cluster around the point where the side road meets the sea, but there's a better atmosphere – if not necessarily better food – two coves south (meandering, indirect road system in, but a direct 1500-metre walk along the coast), at the seasonal **restaurant** operating in the grounds of the disused little monastery of Áyios Emilianós.

Southern Híos

Besides olive groves, the gently rolling countryside in the south of the island is also home to the **mastic bush** (*Pistacia lentisca*), found across much of Aegean Greece but only here producing an aromatic resin of any quality or quantity. For centuries it was used as a base for paints, cosmetics and the chewable jelly beans, which became a somewhat addictive staple in the

Ottoman harems. Indeed, the interruption of the flow of mastic from Híos to Istanbul by the revolt of spring 1822 was one of the root causes of the brutal Ottoman reaction.

The wealth engendered by the mastic trade supported twenty *mastihohoriá* (mastic villages) from the time the Genoese set up a monopoly in the substance during the fourteenth and fifteenth centuries, but the end of imperial Turkey and the development of petroleum-based products knocked the bottom out of the mastic market. Now it's just a curiosity, to be chewed – try the sweetened Elma-brand gum – or drunk as a liqueur called *mastíha*, though it has had medicinal applications since ancient times. These days, however, the *mastihohoriá* live mainly off their tangerines, apricots and olives.

The towns themselves, the only settlements on Híos spared by the Ottomans in 1822, are architecturally unique, laid out by the Genoese but retaining a distinct Middle Eastern feel. The basic plan consists of a rectangular warren of tall houses, with the outer row doubling as the town's perimeter fortification, and breached by a limited number of arched gateways.

The mastic villages

ARMÓLIA, 20km from town, is the smallest and least imposing of the mastic villages. Its main virtue is its pottery industry; the best workshop, selling useful kitchenware as well as the usual kitsch souvenirs, is Yeoryios Sfikakis, the third outfit on the right as you head southwest. **PYRGÍ**, 5km further south, is the most colourful of these communities, its houses elaborately embossed with *xystá*, geometric patterns cut into whitewash to reveal a layer of black volcanic sand underneath; strings of sun-drying tomatoes add a further splash of colour in autumn. On the northeast corner of the central square the twelfth-century Byzantine church of **Áyii Apóstoli** (Tues–Thurs & Sat 10am–1pm), embellished with much later frescoes, is tucked under an arcade. Of late, vast numbers of postcard racks and boutiques have sprung up on every main thoroughfare, detracting somewhat from the atmosphere. In the medieval core you'll find a **bank** (with ATM), a **post office** and a pair of **tavernas** on the central *platía*. **OLÝMBI**, 7km further west along the bus route serving Armólia and Pyrgí, is the least visited of the mastic villages, but not devoid of interest. The characteristic tower-keep, which at Pyrgí stands half-inhabited away from the modernized main square, here looms bang in the middle of the *platía*, its ground floor occupied by the community *kafenío* on one side, and a taverna-bar on the other; however the best **eating** here is found at *Ayioryitiko* by the Káto Pórta, where the menu can encompass game and mushrooms in the right season, though portions are on the small side.

Sombre, monochrome **MESTÁ**, 4km west of Olýmbi, is considered the finest example of the genre; despite more snack-bars and trinket shops than strictly necessary on the outskirts, Mestá remains just the right side of twee as most people here still work the land. From its main square, dominated by the **church of the Taxiárhis** (the largest on the island), a bewildering maze of cool, shady lanes with anti-seismic buttressing and tunnels, leads off in all directions. Most streets end in blind alleys, except those leading to the six portals; the northeast one still has its original iron gate. There are half a dozen **rooms** in restored traditional dwellings managed by Dhimitris Pipidhis (☎22710 76029; ❸), or apartments through *Dhespina Karambela* (☎22710 76065 or ask at *O Morias eis ta Mesta* taverna; ❹). Alternatively, three separate premises managed by Anna Florádhis's gift shop (☎ & ℻22710 76455; ❸) are somewhat more modernized, and like the other two outfits are nominally open year-round, with heating. Of the two **tavernas** sharing table-space on the main *platía, Mesaionas* is better value and has the more helpful proprietor (she also has rooms: ☎22710 76494; ➌).

The mastic coast – and the Sykiás Olýmbon cave

The closest good **beaches** to Mestá lie just east of its under-used port, Liménas Mestón: **Dhídhyma** (4km away), a double cove with an islet protecting it; **Potámi**, with the namesake stream feeding it; and the least scenic **Ayía Iríni** (8km), which does have a reliable taverna. All of these little bays will catch surf and flotsam when the north wind is up.

From Olýmbi, a paved, six-kilometre road heads to the well-signed **cave of Sykiás Olýmbon** (Easter–Oct Tues–Sun 10am–6pm; admission in groups of 25 or less every 30min; €3), only opened to the public in 2003. For years it was just a small hole in the ground where villagers disposed of their dead animals, but from 1985 on speleologists explored it properly. The cave, with a constant temperature of 18°C, evolved in two phases between 150 million and 50 million years ago, and has a maximum depth of 57m (though tours only visit the top 30m or so). The stalagmite and stalactite formations, with fanciful names like Chinese Forest, Medusa and Organ Pipes, are among the most beautiful in the Mediterranean. Before or after your subterranean tour, you can continue another 1500m on dirt surface to the little cape-top monastery of **Ayía Dhýnami** and two sheltered coves adjacent for a swim: the nearer sandy, the remoter gravel and sand.

Pyrgí village is closest to the two major beach resorts in this corner of the island. The nearest, 6km distant, is **EMBORIÓS**, an almost landlocked harbour with four passable **tavernas** (*Porto Emborios* has the edge with almost year-round operation, home-made desserts and *atherína*-and-onion fry-up). There's a scanty, British-excavated acropolis on the hill to the northeast, vaguely signposted 1km along the road to Kómi; much more accessible – and interesting – is the cruciform **early Christian baptistry**, signposted in a field just in from the water; it's protected by a later, round structure (locked but you can see everything through the grating). For swimming, follow the road to its end at an oversubscribed car park and the beach of **Mávros Yialós** (Mávra Vólia), then continue by flagstoned walkway over the headland to another, more dramatic pebble strand (part nudist) of purpley-grey volcanic stones, twice as long and backed by impressive cliffs.

If you want sand you'll have to go to **KÓMI**, 3km northeast, also accessible from Armólia via Kalamotí; there are just a few **tavernas** (most reliably open of these is *Nostalgia*), café-bars and seasonal apartments behind the pedestrianized beachfront. If summer crowds are too much here, retire 3.5km east beyond Lilikás, where there's a reasonable **taverna** at **Áyios Ioánnis** cove.

Central Híos

The portion of Híos extending west and southwest from Híos Town matches the south in terms of interesting monuments, and good roads (being improved even more with EU funding) make touring under your own power an easy matter. There are also several beaches on the far shore of the island which, though not necessarily the best on Híos, are fine for a dip at the middle or end of the day.

The Kámbos

The **Kámbos**, a vast fertile plain carpeted with citrus groves, extends southwest from Híos Town almost as far as the village of Halkió. The district was originally settled by the Genoese during the fourteenth century, and remained a preserve of the local aristocracy until 1822. Exploring by bicycle or motorbike is less frustrating than going by car, since the web of narrow, poorly marked lanes sandwiched between high walls guarantee disorientation and frequent backtracking. Behind the walls you catch fleeting glimpses of ornate old mansions built from locally quarried sandstone; courtyards are paved in pebbles or alternating light and dark tiles, and most still contain a pergola-shaded irrigation pond filled by a *mánganos* or donkey-powered water-wheel, used before the age of electric pumps to draw water up from wells up to 30m deep.

Many of the sumptuous three-storey dwellings, constructed in a hybrid Italo-Turco-Greek style, have languished derelict since 1881, but an increasing number are being converted for use as private estates or unique **accommodation**. The best and most consistently attended of these is *Mavrokordatiko* (☎22710 32900, 🌐www.mavrokordatiko.com; ➎), about 1.5km south of the airport, with enormous heated, wood-panelled rooms and breakfast (included) served by the *mánganos* courtyard.

Not strictly speaking in Kámbos, but most easily reached from it en route to the *mastihohoriá*, is an outstanding rural Byzantine monument. The thirteenth-century **church of Panayía Krína**, isolated amidst orchards and woods, is well worth the challenge of negotiating a maze of paved but poorly marked lanes beyond Vavýli village, 9km from town. It's closed indefinitely for snail's-pace restoration, but a peek through the apse window will give you a fair idea of the intricately frescoed interior, sufficiently lit by a twelve-windowed drum. All of the late medieval frescoes which overlay the Byzantine work have been removed, and are sometimes displayed in Híos Town's Byzantine and Giustiniani museums (see pp.402–403). The alternating brick and stonework of the exterior alone justifies the trip here, though architectural harmony is marred by the later addition of a clumsy lantern over the narthex, and the visibly unsound structure is kept from collapse by cable-binding at the roofline.

Néa Moní

Almost exactly in the middle of the island, the **monastery of Néa Moní** was founded by the Byzantine Emperor Constantine Monomahos ("The Dueller") IX in 1042 on the spot where a wonder-working icon had been discovered. It ranks among the most beautiful and important monuments on any of the Greek islands; the mosaics, are among the finest surviving art of their age in Greece, and the setting – high up in still partly forested mountains 15km west of the port – is no less memorable.

Once a powerful and independent community of six hundred monks, Néa Moní was pillaged in 1822 and most of its residents (including 3500 civilians sheltering here) put to the sword. Since then many of its outbuildings have languished in ruins, though a recent EU grant has prompted massive restoration work, with the exterior cocooned in scaffolding until further notice. The 1881 tremor caused comprehensive damage, while exactly a century later a forest fire threatened to engulf the place until the resident icon was paraded along the perimeter wall, miraculously repelling the flames. Today the monastery, with its giant refectory and vaulted water cisterns, is inhabited by just a couple of lay workers.

Bus excursions (around €12) are provided once or twice weekly by the KTEL, continuing to Anávatos, Lithí and Armólia; otherwise come by motorbike, or walk from Karyés, 7km northeast, to which there is a regular blue-bus service. **Taxis** from town, however, are not prohibitive, at about €16 round-trip per carload, including a wait while you look around.

Just inside the main gate (daily 8am–1pm & 4–8pm, afternoon hours 5–8pm in summer) stands a **chapel/ossuary** containing some of the bones of those who met their death here in 1822; axe-clefts in children's skulls attest to the savagery of the attackers. The **katholikón**, with the cupola resting on an octagonal drum, is of a design seen elsewhere only in Cyprus; the frescoes in the exonarthex are badly damaged by holes allegedly left by Turkish bullets, but the **mosaics** are another matter. The narthex contains portrayals of the various saints of Híos sandwiched between *Christ Washing the Disciples' Feet* and the *Betrayal*, in which Judas's kiss has unfortunately been obliterated, but Peter is clearly visible lopping off the ear of the high priest's servant. In the dome of the sanctuary (currently hidden by scaffolding), which once contained a complete life-cycle of Christ, only the *Baptism*, part of the *Crucifixion*, the *Descent from the Cross*, the *Resurrection* and the Evangelists Mark and John survived the earthquake.

The west coast

With your own transport, you can proceed 5km west of Néa Moní to **AVGÓNYMA**, a cluster of dwellings on a knoll overlooking the coast; the name means "Clutch of Eggs", an apt description when it's viewed from the ridge above. Since the 1980s, the place has been almost totally restored as a summer haven by descendants of the original villagers, though the permanent population is just seven. A returned Greek-American family runs a reasonable, simple-fare **taverna**, *O Pyrgos* (open all year), in an arcaded mansion on the main square; co-managed *To Arhondiko* and *To Asteria* at the outskirts have far less reliable cooking and opening hours. The classiest **accommodation** option here is *Spitakia*, a cluster of small restored houses for up to five people (☎22710 20513 or 22710 81200, ⓦwww.spitakia.gr; ④), though *O Pyrgos* restaurant also keeps more modernized units in the village (☎22710 42175; ③).

A paved side road continues another 4km north to **ANÁVATOS**, whose empty, dun-coloured dwellings, soaring above pistachio orchards, are almost indistinguishable from the 300-metre-high bluff on which they're built. During the 1822 insurrection, some four hundred inhabitants and refugees threw themselves over this cliff rather than surrender to the besieging Ottomans, and it's still a preferred suicide leap. Anávatos can now only muster two permanent inhabitants, and given a lack of accommodation, plus an eerie, traumatized atmosphere, it's no place to be stranded at dusk – though there's a very good **taverna**, *Anavatos*, at the village entrance (lunch most of the year, also dinner in summer).

West of Avgónyma, the main road descends 6km to the sea in well-graded loops. Turning right (north) at the junction leads first to the beach at **Elínda**, alluring from afar but rocky and murky up close; it's better to continue towards more secluded, mixed sand-and-gravel coves to either side of Metóhi – best of these are **Tigáni** and **Makriá Ámmos**, the latter nudist. **SIDHIROÚNDA**, the only village hereabouts (with a summer **taverna**), enjoys a spectacular hilltop setting overlooking the sea.

All along this coast, as far southwest as Liménas Mestón, are round **watchtowers** erected by the Genoese to look out for pirates – the first swimmable cove you reach by turning left from the junction has the name **Kastélla** (officially Trahíli), again mixed sand and gravel. A sparse weekday-only bus service resumes 9km south of the junction at **LITHÍ**, a friendly village of whitewashed buildings perched on a wooded ledge overlooking the sea. There are tavernas and *kafenía* near the bus turnaround area, but most visitors head 2km downhill to **Paralía Lithíou**, a popular weekend target of Hiot townies for the sake of its large but hard-packed, windswept beach. The better of two **tavernas** here is *Ta Tría Adherfia*; the other, *Kyra Despina*, has a few **rooms** (T 22710 73373; ❸).

Some 5km south of Lithí, the valley-bottom village of **VÉSSA** is an unsung gem, more open and less casbah-like than Mestá or Pyrgí, but still homogeneous. Its honey-coloured buildings are arrayed in a vast grid punctuated by numerous belfries; there's a nameless *kafenío* installed on the ground floor of the tower-mansion on the main through road, while its neighbour *Kostas* (aka *Froso's*) does excellent *yíros*, *loukániko* and *souvláki*.

Northern Híos

Northern Híos never really recovered from the 1822 massacre, and between Pityós and Volissós the desolation left by fires in 1981 and 1987 will further dampen inquisitive spirits. Since the early 1900s the villages have been left all but deserted much of the year, which means correspondingly sparse bus services. About one-third of the former population now lives in Híos Town, venturing out here only during major festivals or to tend smallholdings; others, based in Athens or the US, visit their ancestral homes for just a few intense weeks in midsummer, when marriages are arranged between local families.

The road to Kardhámyla

Blue urban buses run north from Híos Town up to **VRONDÁDHOS**, an elongated coastal suburb that's a favourite residence of the island's many seafarers. Homer is reputed to have lived and taught here, and in the terraced parkland just above the little fishing port and pebble beach you can visit his purported lectern, more probably an ancient altar of Cybele. Accordingly many of the buses heading out here are labelled DHASKALÓPETRA, the "Teacher's Rock".

Some 14km out of town, the tiny bayside hamlet of **PANDOUKIÓS** can offer an excellent if pricey waterside **taverna**, the *Kourtesis*, where lobster can sometimes be had. But **LANGÁDHA**, 2.5km beyond, is probably the first point on the eastern coast road where you'd be tempted to stop, though there is no proper beach nearby. Set at the mouth of a deep valley, this attractive little harbour settlement looks across its bay to a pine grove, and beyond to Turkey. There are a couple of **rooms** outfits, but most evening visitors come for the sustaining seafood at two adjacent **tavernas** on the quay: *Tou Kopelou*, better known as *Stelios'*, and second-choice *Paradhisos*. There is an ad hoc taxi-boat service from here to Inoússes island (20min journey); ring either Mr Tiniakos (T 694 41 68 104) or Mr Boundoulas (T 694 45 14 604) to arrange a shuttle, and expect to pay €30 each way.

Just beyond Langádha an important side road leads 5km up and inland to **PITYÓS**, an oasis in a mountain pass presided over by a tower-keep; people come here from some distance to **eat** at *Makellos* on the southwest edge of the village, a shrine of local cuisine (June–Sept daily; Oct–May Fri–Sun evenings only). Continuing 4km more brings you to a junction allowing quick access to the west of the island and the Volissós area (see p.412).

Kardhámyla and around

Most traffic proceeds to **ÁNO KARDHÁMYLA** and **KÁTO KARDHÁMYLA**, the latter 37km out of the main town. Positioned at opposite edges of a fertile plain rimmed by mountains, they initially come as welcome relief from Homer's crags. Káto, better known as **MÁRMARO**, is larger – indeed the island's second town – with a bank (no ATM), post office and filling station. However, there is little to attract a casual visitor other than some Neoclassical architecture; the port, mercilessly exposed to the *meltémi*, is strictly businesslike, and there are few tourist facilities. A sterling exception is *Hotel Kardamyla* (☎22720 23353, ⓕ22720 23354; ❺ Aug, ❹ otherwise), co-managed with Híos Town's *Hotel Kyma*, offering spacious, fan-equipped **rooms** and a few suites. It has the bay's only pebble beach, and the in-house restaurant is a reliable source of lunch (July & Aug) if you're touring. Worthwhile independent **tavernas** include *Ouzeri Barba Yiannis* (now run by Irini Tsirigou; all year), beside the port authority, or *Iy Vlyhadha* (summer only), facing the bay of the same name west over the headland, with locally produced suckling pig and squid.

For better swimming head west 5km to **Nagós**, a gravel-shore bay at the foot of an oasis, which is where the summertime bus service terminates twice or thrice daily. Lush greenery is nourished by active springs up at a bend in the road, enclosed in a sort of grotto overhung by tall cliffs. The place name is a corruption of *naos*, after a large Poseidon temple that once stood near the springs, but centuries of orchard-tending, antiquities-pilfering and organized excavations after 1912 mean that nothing remains visible. Down at the shore the swimming is good, if a bit chilly; there are two mediocre **tavernas** (there's a better one inland, by the spring) and a few **rooms** to rent. Your only chance of relative solitude in July or August lies 1km west at **Yióssonas**; this is a much longer beach, but less sheltered, rockier and with no facilities.

Volissós and around

VOLISSÓS, 42km from Híos Town by the most direct road (44km via the much easier Avgónyma route), was once the market town for a dozen remote hill villages beyond. Its old stone houses still curl appealingly beneath the crumbling hilltop Byzantine fort, whose towers were improved by the Genoese. Volissós can seem depressing at first, with the bulk of its 250 mostly elderly permanent inhabitants living in newer buildings around the main square, but opinions improve with longer acquaintance. The upper quarters are in the grip of a restoration mania, most of it done in admirable taste but some decidedly twee, with ruins changing hands for stratospheric prices.

Grouped around the *platía* you'll find a **post office**, a **bank** ATM, two well-stocked shops and three mediocre **tavernas**. A filling station operates 2.5km out of town, the only one hereabouts; if reliant on public transport, you should plan on overnighting since the bus only ventures out here on Sundays on a day-trip basis, or on Monday, Wednesday and Friday in the early afternoon (unless you care to travel at 4.30am). This should cause no dismay, since the area has the best beaches and some of the more interesting **accommodation** on Híos. The most reasonable of a few restoration projects are sixteen old houses, mostly in Pýrgos district, available through Omiros Travel (☎22740 21413, ⓕ22740 21521; May–Sept; ❹). Units usually accommodate two people – all have terraces, fully equipped kitchens and features such as tree trunks upholding sleeping lofts.

LIMNIÁ, (sometimes Limiá), the port of Volissós, lies 2km south, with a small ferry coming from and going to Psará several days a week. The most consistent **taverna** here is *O Zikos* (open all year) at the far end of the quay, with good *mayireftá* and seafood. At Limniá you're not far from the fabled beaches either. A 1.5-kilometre drive or walk southeast over the headland brings you to **Managrós**, a seemingly endless sand-and-pebble beach. More intimate, sandy **Lefkádhia** lies just a ten-minute stroll along the cement drive threading over the headland north of the harbour; amenities are limited to a seasonal snack shack on the sand, and Ioannis Zorbas's apartments (℡22740 21436, ℻22740 21720; ❹), beautifully set in a garden where the concrete track joins an asphalt road down from Volissós. This is bound for **Límnos** (not to be confused with Limniá), the next protected cove, 400m east of Lefkádhia, where *Taverna Akroyiali* provides salubrious food and professional service, and the spruce *Latini Apartments* (℡22740 21461, ℻22740 21871; ❹) are graced with multiple stone terraces.

Ayía Markélla, 5km further northwest of Límnos, stars in many local postcards: it's a long, stunning beach fronting the **monastery** of Híos's patron saint, the latter not especially interesting or useful for outsiders, since its cells are reserved for Greek pilgrims. In an interesting variation on the expulsion of the money-changers from the temple, only religious souvenirs are allowed to be sold in the holy precincts, while all manner of plastic junk is displayed just outside. There's a single, rather indifferent taverna to hand as well; around July 22 – the local saint's **festival** and biggest island bash – the "No Camping" signs are doubtless unenforced.

The dirt road past the monastery grounds is passable by any vehicle, with care, and emerges up on the paved road running high above the northwest coast. Turn left and proceed to the remote village of **ÁYIO GÁLA**, whose claim to fame is a **grotto–church** complex, built into a stream-lapped palisade at the bottom of the village. Signs ("Panayía Ayiogaloúsena") point to a lane crossing the water, but for access, except at the festival on August 23, you'll need to find the key-keeper (ask at the central *kafenío*), and descend via a flight of stairs starting beside a eucalyptus tree. Of the two churches inside the cavern, the larger one near the mouth of the grotto dates from the fifteenth century but seems newer owing to a 1993 external renovation. Inside, however, a fantastically intricate *témblon* vies for your attention with a tinier, older chapel, built entirely within the rear of the cavern. Its frescoes are badly smudged, except for a wonderfully mysterious and mournful Virgin, surely the saddest in Christendom, holding a knowing Child.

Satellite islands: Psará and Inoússes

There's a single settlement, with beaches and an isolated rural monastery, on both of Híos's satellite isles, but each is surprisingly different from the other, and of course from their large neighbour. **Inoússes**, the nearer and smaller islet, has a daily *kaïki* service from Híos Town in season; **Psará** has less regular services subject to weather conditions (in theory daily from either Híos or Limniá), and is too remote to be done justice on a day-trip.

Psará

The birthplace of revolutionary war hero Admiral Kanaris, **Psará** devoted its merchant fleets – the third largest in 1820s Greece after those of Ídhra and Spétses – to the cause of independence, and paid dearly for it. Vexed beyond endurance, the Turks landed overwhelming forces in 1824 to stamp out this nest of resistance. Perhaps 3000 of the 30,000 inhabitants escaped in small boats which were rescued by a French fleet, but the majority retreated to a hilltop powder magazine and blew it (and themselves) up rather than surrender. The nationalist poet Dhionysios Solomos immortalized the incident in famous stanzas:

> On the Black Ridge of Psará,
> Glory walks alone.
> She meditates on her heroes
> And wears in her hair a wreath
> Made from a few dry weeds
> Left on the barren ground.

Today, it's a sad, stark place fully living up to its name ("the grey things" in Greek), which never really recovered from the holocaust. The Turks burned whatever houses and vegetation the blast had missed, and the official population barely exceeds four hundred. The only positive recent development was a 1980s revitalization project instigated by a French-Greek descendant of Kanaris and a Greek team. The port was improved, mains electricity and pure water provided, a secondary school opened, and cultural links between France and the island established, though so far this has not been reflected in increased tourist numbers.

Arrival can be something of an ordeal: the regular small ferry from Híos Town can take up to four hours to cover the 57 nautical miles of generally rough sea. Use the port of Limniá to sail in at least one direction if you can; this crossing takes just over an hour at a little over half the price.

Since few buildings in the east-facing harbour community predate the twentieth century, it's a strange hotchpotch of ecclesiastical and secular architecture that greets the eye on disembarking. There's a distinctly southern feel, more like the Dodecanese or the Cyclades, and some peculiar churches of which no two are alike in style.

For **staying overnight**, there's a choice between a handful of fairly basic rooms and three more professional outfits: *Psara Studios* (☎22740 61233; ❹) and *Apartments Restalia* (☎22740 61201, ☎22740 61000; ❹ August, ❷–❸ otherwise), both a bit stark but with balconies and kitchens, or the EOT *xenónas* (☎22740 61293; ❹) in a restored prison. A few **tavernas**, a **post office**, bakery and shop complete the list of amenities; there is no full-service bank.

Psará's **beaches** are decent, improving the further northeast you walk from the port. You quickly pass Káto Yialós, Katsoúni and Lazarétta with its off-putting power station, before reaching **Lákka** ("narrow ravine"), fifteen minutes along, apparently named after its grooved rock formations in which you may have to shelter – much of this coast is windswept, with a heavy swell offshore. **Límnos**, 25 minutes from the port along the coastal path, is big and attractive, but there's no reliable taverna here, or indeed at any of the other beaches. The only other thing to do on Psará is to walk north across the island – the old track there has now been paved – to the **monastery of the Kímisis (Assumption)**; uninhabited since the 1970s, this comes to life only in the first week of August, when its revered icon is carried in ceremonial procession to town and back on the eve of August 5.

Inoússes

Inoússes has a permanent population of about three hundred – less than half its prewar figure – and a very different history from Psará. For generations this medium-sized islet has provided the Aegean with many of her wealthiest shipping families: various members of the Livanos, Lemos and Pateras clans (with every street or square named after the last-named family) were born here. This helps explain the large villas and visiting summer yachts in an otherwise sleepy Greek backwater – as well as a **maritime museum** (daily 10am–1.30pm; €1.50) near the quay, endowed by various shipping magnates. At the west end of the quay, the bigwigs have also funded a large nautical academy, which trains future members of the merchant navy.

On Sundays in season you can make an inexpensive **day-trip** to Inoússes from Híos with the locals' ferry *Inousses II*; on most other days of the week this arrives at 3pm, returning early the next morning. Otherwise, during the tourist season you must participate in the pricier excursions offered from Híos, typically on the *Maria*, with return tickets running up to three times the cost of the regular ferry. Otherwise, in a group, it's feasible to charter one of the water-taxis operating out of Langádha (see p.411).

Two church-tipped islets, each privately owned, guard the unusually well-protected harbour (whose jetty is currently being expanded); the **town** of Inoússes is surprisingly large, draped over hillsides enclosing a ravine. Despite a wealthy reputation, its appearance is unpretentious, the houses displaying a mix of vernacular and modest Neoclassical style. There is just one, fairly comfortable **hotel**, the recently renovated *Thalassoporos* (T22720 55475, F22720 55476; ❸), on the main easterly hillside lane, but no licensed *pensions* or rooms. Aside from the restaurant in the hotel, **eating out** is similarly limited; the most reliable option is the simple *Taverna Pateronisso*, conspicuous at the base of the disembarkation jetty, though every season a few simple *ouzerís* off towards the nautical academy try their luck – the most durable of these is *O Glaros*. Café-bars such as *Naftikos Omilos*, *Karnayio* and (inland uphill) *Trigono* provide a semblance of **nightlife**. Otherwise, be prepared to patronize one of the three shops (one on the waterfront, two up the hill). Beside the museum is a **post office** and a **bank**.

The rest of this tranquil island, at least the southern slope, is surprisingly green and well tended; there are no springs, so water comes from a mix of fresh and brackish wells, as well as a reservoir. The sea is extremely clean and calm on the sheltered southerly shore; among its beaches, choose from **Zepánga**, **Biláli** or **Kástro**, respectively five, twenty and thirty minutes' walk west of the port. More secluded **Fourkeró** (Farkeró in dialect) lies 25 minutes east: first along a cement drive ending at a seaside chapel, then by path past pine groves and over a ridge. As on Psará, there are no reliable facilities at any of the beaches.

At the end of the westerly road, beyond Kástro, stands the somewhat macabre convent of **Evangelismoú**, endowed by a branch of the Pateras family. Inside reposes the mummified body of the lately canonized daughter, Irini, whose prayers to die of cancer in place of her terminally ill father Panagos were answered early in the 1960s on account of her virtue and piety; he's entombed here also, having outlived Irini by some years. The abbess, presiding over about twenty nuns, is none other than the widowed Mrs Pateras; only women are allowed admission, and even then casual visits are not encouraged.

Lésvos (Mytilíni)

Lésvos, the third-largest Greek island after Crete and Évvia, is not only the birthplace of Sappho, but also of Aesop, Arion and – more recently – the Greek primitive artist Theophilos, the Nobel laureate poet Odysseus Elytis and the novelist Stratis Myrivilis. Despite these artistic associations, Lésvos may not at first strike the visitor as particularly beautiful or interesting; much of the landscape is rocky, volcanic terrain, dotted with thermal springs and varying between vast grain fields, salt pans or even near-desert. But there are also oak

LÉSVOS

Limnos, Thessaloníki, Alexandhroúpoli & Kavála

Híos, Sámos, Sýros & Pireás

Ayios Efstátios, Limnos & Kavála

Rafína & Psará

Ayíos Isídhoros

N

0   10 km

and pine forests as well as vast olive groves, some of these over five hundred years old. With its balmy climate and suggestive contours, the island tends to grow on you with prolonged acquaintance.

Lovers of medieval and Ottoman **architecture** certainly won't be disappointed. Castles survive at the main town of Mytilíni, at Mólyvos, Eressós and near Ándissa; most of these date from the late fourteenth century, when Lésvos was given as a dowry to a Genoese prince of the Gattilusi clan following his marriage to the sister of one of the last Byzantine emperors. Apart from Crete and Évvia, Lésvos was the only Greek island where Turks settled significantly in rural villages (they usually stuck to the safety of towns), which explains the odd Ottoman bridge, shed-like mosque or crumbling minaret often found in the middle of nowhere. Again unusually for the Aegean islands, Ottoman reforms of the eighteenth century encouraged the emergence of a Greek Orthodox land- and industry-owning aristocracy, who built rambling mansions and tower-houses, a few of which survive. More common are the bourgeois townhouses of the worthies in Mytilíni town, built early in the twentieth century to French Second Empire models; many of these have often been pressed into service as government buildings or even restored as hotels.

Social and economic idiosyncrasies persist: anyone who has attended one of the extended village *paniyíria*, with hours of music and tables in the streets groaning with food and drink, will not be surprised to learn that Lésvos has the highest alcoholism rate in Greece. Breeding livestock, especially horses, is disproportionately important, and traffic jams caused by mounts instead of parked cars are not unheard of – signs reading "Forbidden to Tether Animals Here" are still common, as are herds of apparently unattended donkeys wandering about. Much of the acreage in olives is still inaccessible to vehicles, and the harvest can only be hauled out by those donkeys – who are duly loaded en masse onto the back of trucks to be transported to the point where the road fizzles out.

Historically, the olive plantations, ouzo distilleries, animal husbandry and fishing industry supported those who chose not to emigrate, but with these enterprises relatively stagnant, mass-market tourism has made visible inroads. However, it still accounts for under ten percent of the local economy: there are still few large hotels outside the capital, Skála Kallóni or Mólyvos; self-catering villas barely outnumber rooms, and the first official campsites only opened in 1990. Foreign tourist numbers have in fact levelled out or even dipped since 1996, the result of stalled plans to expand the airport, unrealistic hotel pricing and the dropping of the island from several German and Dutch tour operators' programmes.

Public **buses** tend to observe schedules for the benefit of villagers come to town on errands, not day-tripping tourists. Carrying out such excursions from Mytilíni is next to impossible anyway, owing to the size of the island – about 70km by 45km at its widest points – and a lingering handful of appalling roads (most others have been improved, along with their signposting). Moreover, the topography is complicated by the two deeply indented gulfs of Kallóni and Yéra, with no bridges across their mouths, which means that going from A to B involves an obligatory change of bus at either Mytilíni, on the east shore, or the town of Kallóni, in the middle of the island. It's best to decide on a base and stay there for a few days, exploring its immediate surroundings on foot or by rented vehicle.

Mytilíni Town

MYTILÍNI, the port and capital, sprawls between and around two bays divided by a fortified promontory, and in Greek fashion often doubles as the name of the island. Many visitors are put off by the combination of urban bustle and (in the traditionally humbler northern districts) slight seediness, and contrive to leave as soon as possible; the town returns the compliment by being a fairly impractical and occasionally expensive place to base yourself.

Nonetheless, Mytilíni offers enough to justify a stopover of a few hours. On the promontory sits the Byzantine-Genoese-Ottoman **fortress** (May–Sept Tues–Sun 8.30am–7pm; Oct–April Tues–Sun 8.30am–2.30pm; €2), comprising ruined structures from all these eras and an Ottoman inscription above a Byzantine double-headed eagle at the south gate. Further inland, the town skyline is dominated in turn by the Germanic-Gothic belfry spire of **Áyios Theodhóros** and the mammary dome of **Áyios Therápon**, both expressions of the post-Baroque taste of the nineteenth-century Ottoman Greek bourgeoisie. They stand more or less at opposite ends of the bazaar, whose main street, Ermoú, links the town centre with the little-used north harbour of Páno Skála. On its way there Ermoú passes several expensive but rather picked-over

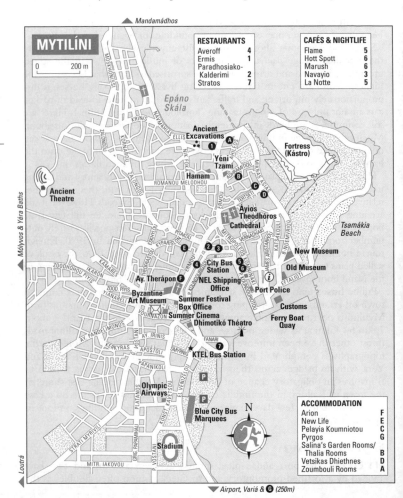

▲ Mandamádhos

MYTILÍNI

0   200 m

RESTAURANTS
Averoff	4
Ermis	1
Paradhosiako-Kalderimi	2
Stratos	7

CAFÉS & NIGHTLIFE
Flame	5
Hott Spott	6
Marush	6
Navayio	3
La Notte	5

Epáno Skála

Ancient Excavations

Yéni Tzami

Hamam

Fortress (Kástro)

Ancient Theatre

◄ Mólyvos & Yéra Baths

Áyios Theodhóros Cathedral

Tsamákia Beach

New Museum
Old Museum

City Bus Station

Ay. Therápon
NEL Shipping Office

Byzantine Art Museum
Summer Festival Box Office

Port Police

Customs

Summer Cinema
Dhimotikó Théatro

Ferry Boat Quay

KTEL Bus Station

Olympic Airways

Blue City Bus Marquees

N

Stadium

◄ Loutrá

ACCOMMODATION
Arion	F
New Life	E
Pelayia Koumniotou	C
Pyrgos	G
Salina's Garden Rooms/Thalia Rooms	B
Vetsikas Dhiethnes	D
Zoumbouli Rooms	A

▼ Airport, Variá & G (250m)

antique shops near the roofless, derelict **Yéni Tzamí** at the heart of the old Muslim quarter, just a few steps east of a superb Turkish **hamam**, restored to its former glory in 2001 but now locked unless a special exhibit is being held. Between Ermoú and the castle lies a maze of atmospheric lanes lined with grandiose Belle Époque mansions and elderly vernacular houses, though most of the ornate townhouses are to be found in the southerly districts of Sourádha and Kióski, on the way to the airport.

Mytilíni's excellent **archeological collection** is housed in **two separate galleries** (May–Sept daily 8am–7pm; Oct–April Tues–Sun 8.30am–3pm; €3), a few hundred metres apart. The newer, upper museum, at the base of 8-Noemvríou, is devoted to finds from wealthy Roman Mytilene, in particular three rooms of well-displayed mosaics from second/third-century AD villas – highlights are a crude but engaging scene of Orpheus charming all manner of beasts, and two fishermen surrounded by clearly recognizable (and edible) sea creatures. Earlier eras are represented in the older wing (same hours as Roman wing, same ticket admits), housed in a former mansion just behind the ferry dock. The ground floor has Neolithic finds from Áyios Vartholoméos cave and Bronze Age Thermí, but the star, late-Classical exhibits upstairs include minutely detailed terracotta figurines: a pair of acrobats, two *kourotrophoi* figures (goddesses suckling infants, predecessors of all Byzantine Galaktotrofoússa icons), children playing with a ball or dogs, and Aphrodite riding a dolphin. A specially built annexe at the rear contains stone-cut inscriptions of various edicts and treaties, plus a Roman sculpture of a drunken satyr asleep on a wineskin.

There's also a worthwhile **Byzantine Art Museum** (Mon–Sat 9am–1pm; €2) just behind Áyios Therápon, containing various icons rescued from rural churches, plus a canvas of the Assumption by Theophilos (see p.421).

Practicalities

The **airport** has a single ATM in arrivals as well as three car rental booths (Europcar, Hertz, and one shared by Budget and Payless) There's no bus link, so a shared taxi for the 7km into Mytilíni Town is the usual shuttle method; Olympic Airways is southwest of the main harbour at Kavétsou 44. As on Híos, there are two **bus stations**: the *iperastykó* (standard KTEL) buses leave from a small station near Platía Konstandinopóleos at the southern end of the harbour, while the *astykó* (blue bus) service departs from a marquee at the top of the harbour. If you're driving, use the enormous free public **car park** a few blocks south of the KTEL – there are no other easily available spaces in the centre. If you're intent on getting over to Ayvalık in Turkey on the Turkish boat *Jale*, book tickets through either Dimakis Tours at Koundouriótou 73 (☎22510 27865) or Picolo Travel at no. 73a (☎22510 27000). NEL Ferries has its own agency at Koundouriótou 47 (☎22510 28480), though tickets (including the high-speed service) are also sold through Dimakis Tours, while GA Ferries are handled by Picolo Travel.

Car rental is best arranged through reputable local-chain franchises like Payless/Auto Moto at Koundouriótou 49 (☎22510 43555, ℮automoto @otenet.gr), Budget at no. 51 (☎22510 29600), Just at no. 53 (☎22510 43080), Egeon at Híou 2 (☎22510 29820) or Alpha in the alley off Koundouriótou 83 (☎22510 26113) – though it's often cheaper to rent at the resort of your choice. Other amenities include the **post office** on Vournázon, behind the central park, and at least five **banks** along Koundouriótou with ATMs, plus a free-standing booth on the quay. Before leaving town, you might visit the **EOT** regional headquarters at James Aristárhou 6 (Mon–Fri 8am–2.30pm) to get hold of their excellent town and island maps, plus other brochures.

Accommodation

Finding **accommodation** can be initially daunting: the waterfront hotels are noisy and exorbitantly priced, with few single rooms to speak of. If you need to stay, it's preferable to hunt down better-value rooms in the backstreets, especially between the castle and Ermoú, with supply usually exceeding demand. Yeoryíou Tertséti street in particular has two possibilities: the friendly if basic *Pelayia Koumniotou* at no. 6 (℡22510 20643; ❷), or the en-suite *Vetsikas/Dhiethnes* at no. 1 (℡22510 24968; ❷). Two other quiet establishments sit between the north harbour and fortress: *Salina's Garden Rooms*, behind the Yéni Tzamí at Fokéas 7 (℡22510 42073; ❷), co-managed with the *Thalia Rooms* across the street (℡22510 24640; ❷). Moving slightly upmarket, *Zoumbouli Rooms*, facing the water on Navmahías Ellís (℡22510 29081; ❸), are en-suite and air-conditioned, but may get more noise from traffic and the *ouzerí* below. *New Life* at the end of Olýmbou, a cul-de-sac off Ermoú (℡22510 42650 or 693 22 79 057; ❸), offers wood-floored, en-suite rooms in an old mansion, or similarly priced ones, but with bizarre modern murals, in the co-managed *Arion* down the street at Árionos 4. The most distinctive place to stay is pricey *Pyrgos*, Eleftheríou Venizélou 49 (℡22510 25069, ⓦwww .pyrgoshotel.gr; ❼), a converted mansion with utterly over-the-top kitsch decor in the communal areas. However the rooms – most with a balcony – are perfectly acceptable; the best ones are the three round units in the tower.

Eating, drinking and nightlife

Dining options in Mytilíni have improved since a late-1990s nadir, when several of the more characterful old-style *ouzerí*s and tavernas shut down in favour of fast-food joints. The obvious, if blatantly touristy, venue for a seafood blowout is the cluster of tavernas on the southerly quay known as Fanári; *Stratos* at the far end is marginally the best, and the only one that doesn't tout aggressively. For *mayireftá* (including early-morning *patsás*), look no further than the *Averoff* on the west quay, a popular place for lunch before an afternoon ferry departure. Finally, there are two recently refurbished, traditional *ouzerí*s at opposite ends of the bazaar. *Paradhosiako-Kalderimi* (closed Sun) occupies two premises around Thássou 2, with seating under the shade of vines; the fare is large-portioned if a bit plainly presented for about €16 per head. For the same or even less (and with friendlier service), you might be better off at the *Ermis* (open daily), best of a cluster of *ouzerí*s up at Páno Skála; a 1999 refit didn't much affect its century-old decor (panelled ceiling, giant mirrors, faded oil paintings), or its claimed two centuries of purveying titbits to a jolly, mixed crowd in the pleasant courtyard.

For **snacks**, **breakfast and drinks**, try *Navayio* at the head of the harbour. With an important university in residence, Mytilíni can offer decent **nightlife and entertainment**, especially along the northeast quay, which the trendy contingent have claimed as their own. Here, all in a row between Budget car rental and the NEL agency, you'll find *Flame* (with bowling upstairs), *La Notte* (a late-night dance club), *Marush* (with video games) and the durable *Hott Spott*. Formal live events constitute the Lesviakó Kalokéri, held in the castle or other venues from mid-July to late August, while the summer cinema Pallas is between the post office and the park on Vournázon. There's also a winter cinema, the Arion, near the KTEL station, and concerts are held in the waterfront Dhimotikó Théatro.

Around Mytilíni

Beyond the airport and Krátigos village, the paved road loops around to **Haramídha**, 14km from town and the closest decent (pebble) beach (the fee-entry town "beach" at Tsamákia is mediocre); the eastern bay has several tavernas. The double cove at **Áyios Ermoyénis**, 3km west and more directly accessible from Mytilíni via Loutrá village, is more scenic and sandy but small and crowded at weekends, with no full-service taverna, just a snack-bar. For other pleasant immersions near Mytilíni, make for **Loutrá Yéras**, 8km along the main road to Kallóní. These public baths (daily: June–Sept 7am–7pm; April–May & Oct 8am–6pm; Nov–March 9am–5pm; €2.50) are just the thing if you've spent a sleepless night on a ferry, with ornate spouts that feed 38°C water to marble-lined pools in vaulted chambers; there are separate facilities for men and women.

The Variá museums

The most rewarding single targets near Mytilíni are a pair of museums at **VARIÁ**, 5km south of town (hourly buses). The **Theophilos Museum** (May–Sept Tues–Sun 9am–2.30pm & 6–8pm; Oct–April may open 9am–2.30pm only; €2 includes key-catalogue) honours the painter, born here in 1873, with four rooms of wonderful, little-known compositions specifically commissioned by his patron Thériade (see below) during the years leading up to Theophilos' death in 1934. A wealth of detail is evident in elegiac scenes of fishing, reaping, olive-picking and baking from the pastoral Lésvos which Theophilos obviously knew best; there are droll touches also, such as a cat slinking off with a fish in *The Fishmongers*. In classical scenes – *Sappho and Alkaeos*, a landscape series of Egypt, Asia Minor and the Holy Land, and episodes from wars historical and contemporary – Theophilos was clearly on shakier ground. In *Abyssinians Hunting an Italian Horseman*, the subject has clearly been conflated with New World Indians chasing down a conquistador.

The adjacent, imposing **Thériade Museum** (Tues–Sun 9am–2pm & 5–8pm; €2) is the brainchild of another native son, Stratis Eleftheriades (1897–1983). Leaving the island at an early age for Paris, he Gallicized his name to Thériade and went on to become a renowned avant-garde art publisher, convincing some of the leading artists of the twentieth century to participate in his ventures. The displays – slightly depleted by a 1999 burglary – consist of lithographs, engravings, wood-block prints and watercolours by the likes of Miró, Chagall, Picasso, Matisse, Le Corbusier, Léger, Rouault and Villon, either annotated by the painters themselves or commissioned as illustrations for the works of prominent poets and authors: an astonishing collection for a relatively remote Aegean island.

Southern Lésvos

The southernmost portion of the island is indented by two great inlets, the gulfs of **Kallóní** and **Yéra**, the first curving in a northeasterly direction, the latter northwesterly, creating a fan-shaped peninsula at the heart of which looms 967-metre Mount Ólymbos. Both shallow gulfs are almost landlocked by virtue of very narrow outlets to the open sea, which don't have – and probably never will have – bridges spanning them. This is the most verdant and productive olive-producing territory on Lésvos, and the stacks of pressing-mills stab the skyline.

With its disused industrial warehouses, **PÉRAMA** is one of the larger places on the Gulf of Yéra, and has a regular **kaïki-ferry** service (no cars) linking it with Koundoroudhiá and blue city buses to/from Mytilíni on the far side. A more likely reason to show up is to patronize one of the better **taverna-ouzerís** in the region: *Balouhanas*, northernmost of a line of eateries on the front, with a wooden, cane-roofed balcony jutting out over the water. The name's a corruption of *balıkhane* or "fish-market" in Turkish, and seafood is a strong point, whether grilled or made into croquettes, as are regional starters like *giouzlemés* (cheese-stuffed fried crepe) and own-made desserts. They're open all year (lunch & dinner); count on €17 per head.

Plomári and around

Due south of Mount Ólympos, at the edge of the "fan", **PLOMÁRI** is the only sizeable coastal settlement in the south, and indeed the second largest municipality on Lésvos. It presents an unlikely juxtaposition of scenic appeal and its famous ouzo industry, courtesy of several local distilleries. Despite a resounding lack of good beaches within walking distance, it's besieged in summer by Scandinavian tourists, but you can usually find a **room** (they are prominently signposted) at the edge of the old, charmingly dilapidated town, or (better) 1km west in **Ammoudhélli** suburb, which has a small pea-gravel beach. Your best bet for an on-spec vacancy is the welcoming *Pension Lida* above the inland Platía Beniamín (☎ & 🖷 22520 32507; ❷), a fine restoration inn occupying adjacent old mansions, with seaview balconies for most units. Rustling up a decent meal presents more difficulties; best stick to the east end of the harbour park-square, where *Berdema* is a reliable and long-established venue for fairly elaborate *mezédhes* and casserole dishes. Ammoudhélli can offer shambolic but friendly *To Ammoudhelli*, perched unimprovably over the beach and open at lunch too; skip the touristy printed menu and ask for the dishes of the day (which can be anything from *ambelofásola* to sardines) and *orektiká* like *tyrokafterí* and grilled octopus – budget €11 each.

Áyios Isídhoros, 3km east, is where most tourists actually stay; pick of the **hotels** here, not completely overrun with package tours, is the *Pebble Beach* (☎22520 31651, 🖷22520 31566; ❹), with many of the large rooms overlooking a slightly reefy section of beach – though avoid those near the in-house bar if you wish to sleep. **Eating** out locally, the clear winner is *Taverna tou Panaï* (all year) at the rear of an olive grove just by the northerly "Áyios Isídhoros" town limits sign; here you'll find big, no-nonsense portions of salubrious meat, seafood and *mayireftá* dishes, and mostly Greeks in attendance.

Melínda, another 700-metre sand-and-shingle beach at the mouth of a canyon, lies 6km west of Plomári by paved road. Here there are three inexpensive **taverna-rooms** outfits, of which *Maria's* (☎22520 93239; ❶) is an endearingly ramshackle place with simple but reasonably priced food and lodging, with *Paradhisos* (☎22520 93220; ❶) of similar standard; *Melinda* (aka *Dhimitris Psaros*; ☎22520 93234; ❶) at the west end of the strand has a more elaborate menu and en-suite rooms. Even more unspoiled (thanks to a formerly dreadful ten-kilometre side road in, now mostly paved), **Tárti**, some 22km in total from Plomári, is a 400-metre-wide cove where Lésvos hoteliers and restaurant owners take *their* holidays. There are three beachfront **tavernas**, plus **rooms** lining the final stretch of road should you want to stay.

The **bus** into Plomári travels via the attractive villages of Paleókipos and Skópelos (as well as Áyios Isídhoros); the road north from Plomári to Ayiássos has paving and public transport only as far as Megalohóri.

Ayiássos and Mylélia

AYIÁSSOS, nestled in a remote, wooded valley under the crest of Mount Ólympos, is the most beautiful hill town on Lésvos, its narrow cobbled streets lined by ranks of tiled-roof houses. On the usual, northerly approach, there's no hint of the enormous village until you see huge knots of parked cars at the southern edge of town (where the bus leaves you after the 26-kilometre run from Mytilíni).

Don't be put off by endless ranks of kitsch wooden and ceramic souvenirs or carved "Byzantine" furniture, aimed mostly at Greeks, but continue past the central **church of the Panayía Vrefokratoússa**, originally built in the twelfth century to house an icon supposedly painted by the Evangelist Luke, to the **old bazaar**, with its *kafenía*, yogurt shops and butchers' stalls. With such a venerable icon as a focus, the local August 15 *paniyíri* is one of the liveliest in Greece, let alone Lésvos. Ayiássos also takes Carnival very seriously; there's a club dedicated to organizing it, opposite the post office. The best **restaurants** are *Dhouladhelli*, on your left as you enter the village from the extreme south (bus stop) end, or the idiosyncratic nocturnal *ouzerí To Stavrí*, at the extreme north end of the village in Stavrí district. At either of these spots you can eat for a fraction of the prices asked at the coastal resorts.

If you're headed for Ayiássos with your own transport, you might visit the **Mylélia water mill**, whose inconspicuously signposted access track takes off 1km west of the turning for Ípios village. The name means "place of the mills", and there were once several hereabouts, powered by a spring, up-valley at Karíni. The last survivor (open daily 9am–6pm), restored to working order, has not been made twee in the least; the keeper will show you the millrace and paddle-wheel, as well as the flour making its spasmodic exit, after which you're free to buy gourmet pastas at the adjacent shop.

Vaterá, Skála Polikhnítou – and spas en route

A different bus route from Mytilíni leads to Vaterá beach via the inland villages of Polikhnítos and Vríssa. **VRÍSSA** itself has a **natural history museum** (daily 9.30am–7pm; €1) dedicated to local paleontological finds – it's not exactly required viewing at present, but a new, more extensive gallery is promised. Until 20,000 years ago, Lésvos (like all other east Aegean islands) was joined to the Asian mainland, the gulf of Vaterá was a subtropical lake, and all manner of creatures flourished here, their fossilized bones constituting the star exhibits.

If you're after a hot bath, head for the small, vaulted **spa house** 1.5km east of Polikhnítos, well restored by an EU programme (management in flux as of writing; €2); there are separate, pink-tinted chambers for each sex. Alternatively there are more **hot springs** at **Áyios Ioánnis**, signposted 3km below the village of Lisvóri. On the far side of the stream here are two pools housed in whitewashed, vaulted chambers (€1.50 fee payable when adjacent snack-bar attended); the left-hand one's nicer, and there's no gender segregation or dress code.

VATERÁ, 9km south of Polikhnítos, is a huge, seven-kilometre-long sand beach, backed by vegetated hills; the sea here is delightfully calm and clean, the strand itself rated as one of the best in Greece. If you intend to stay here you'll probably want your own transport (there's **car rental** locally through Alpha, ☎22520 61132), as the closest well-stocked shops are 4km away at Vríssa, and the bus appears only a few times daily. Development straggles for several kilometres to either side of the central T-junction, consisting mostly of seasonal villas and apartments for locals; at the west end of the strip is one of the very few consistently attended and professionally run hotels, the Greek- and American-owned *Vatera Beach* (☎22520 61212, ⓦwww.vaterabeach.gr; ❺), whose rooms offer air con and fridges. It also has a good attached restaurant with own-grown produce and shoreline tables from where you can gaze on the cape of **Áyios Fokás** 3km to the west, where only foundations remain of a temple of Dionysos and a superimposed early Christian basilica. The little tamarisk-shaded anchorage here has an acceptable fish **taverna**, *Akrotiri/Angeleros*; it's better than most eateries east of the T-junction at Vaterá, many of which only operate July and August, but not so good as the half-dozen tavernas at **SKÁLA POLIKHNÍTOU**, 4km northwest of Polikhnítos itself, where *T'Asteria* and *Exohiko Kendro Tzitzifies* can both be recommended, staying open most of the year. Skála itself is pleasantly workaday, with only a short, narrow beach but one unusual accommodation option, "Soft Tourism" run by Lefteris and Erika (☎22520 42678; ❷). They generally host walking groups April to June and September, but welcome independent travellers during July and August.

East from Vaterá, a mostly paved road leads via Stavrós, and then Akrássi to either Ayiássos or Plomári within ninety minutes, making day-trips there feasible. When leaving the area going north towards Kalloní, use the short cut via the naval base and seashore hamlet at Akhladherí – it's completely paved, despite appearing otherwise on obsolete maps.

Western Lésvos

The main road west of Loutrá Yéras is surprisingly devoid of settlement, with little to stop for before Kalloní other than the traces of an ancient **Aphrodite temple** at **Mésa** (Méson), 1km north of the main road, and signposted just east of the Akhladherí turn-off. At the **site** (Tues–Sun 8am–2.30pm; free) just eleventh-century-BC foundations and a few column stumps remain, plus the ruins of a fourteenth-century Genoese-built basilica wedged inside; it was once virtually on the sea but a nearby stream has silted things up in the intervening millennia. All told, it's not worth a special trip, but certainly make the short detour if passing by. With more time and your own transport, you can turn northeast towards **Ayía Paraskeví** village, midway between two more important monuments from diverse eras: the Paleo-Christian **basilica of Halinádhou**, and the large **medieval bridge** of Kremastí.

KALLONÍ itself is an unembellished agricultural and market town more or less in the middle of the island, with various shops and services (including pharmacies, a **post office** and three **banks** with ATMs). Some 3km south lies **SKÁLA KALLONÍS**, a somewhat unlikely package resort backing a long but coarse-sand beach on the lake-like gulf. It's mainly distinguished as a birdwatching centre, attracting hundreds of twitchers for the March–May nesting season in the adjacent salt marshes. Pick of a half-dozen **hotels** is the human-scale bungalow complex *Malemi* (☎22530 22594, ✉malemi@otenet.gr; ❺), with a variety of units from doubles to family suites, attractive grounds, tennis court and a large pool. **Tavernas** lining the quay with its fishing fleet are generally indistinguishable – though most offer the gulf's celebrated *sardhélles pastés*, salt-cured sardines; the locals themselves tend to favour *O Mimis*, on the square just inland.

Inland monasteries and villages

West of Kalloní, the road winds 4km uphill to the **monastery of Limónos**, founded in 1527 by the monk Ignatios, whose actual cell is maintained in the surviving medieval north wing. It's a huge, rambling complex, with just a handful of monks and lay workers to maintain three storeys of cells around a vast, plant-filled courtyard. The *katholikón*, with its ornate carved-wood ceiling and archways, is built in Asia Minor style and is traditionally off-limits to women; a sacred spring flows from below the south foundation wall. A former abbot established a **museum** (daily 9.30am–6.30pm, may close 3pm off-season;

€1.50) on two floors of the west wing; the ground-floor ecclesiastical collection is, alas, the only wing open as of writing, with the more interesting upstairs ethnographic gallery off-limits indefinitely. Content yourself with an overflow of farm implements stashed in a corner storeroom below, next to a chamber where giant *pithária* (urns) for grain and olive oil are embedded in the floor.

The main road beyond passes through **VATOÚSSA**, a landlocked and beautiful settlement in the heart of Lésvos's westernmost landmass, with a **folk museum** in the ancestral mansion of Grigorios Gogos. Some 8km beyond Vatoússa, a short track leads down to the sixteenth-century **monastery of Perivolís** (daily 8am–1hr before sunset; donation, no photos), built in the midst of a riverside orchard (*perivóli*). Feeble electric light is available to view the narthex's fine if damp-damaged frescoes. In an apocalyptic panel worthy of Bosch (*The Earth and Sea Yield up their Dead*) the Whore of Babylon rides her chimera and assorted sea-monsters disgorge their victims; just to the right, towards the main door, the Three Magi approach the Virgin enthroned with the Christ Child. On the north side you see a highly unusual iconography of *Abraham, the Virgin, and the Penitent Thief of Calvary in Paradise, with the Four Rivers of Paradise gushing forth under their feet*; just right are assembled the Hebrew kings of the Old Testament.

ÁNDISSA, 3km further on, nestles under the arid west's only pine grove (and a newer wind-power farm); at the edge of the village a sign implores you to "Come Visit Our Square", not a bad idea for the sake of a handful of tavernas and *kafenía* sheltering under three sizeable plane trees. You can follow the paved road from directly below Ándissa 6km north to **GAVATHÁS**, a fishing hamlet with a narrow, partly protected beach (there's a bigger, surf-buffeted one at Kámbos just to the east) and a few places to eat and stay – among these *Rooms Restaurant Paradise* (☎22530 56376; ❷), serving good fish and locally grown vegetables.

Just west of Ándissa there's an important junction. Keeping straight leads you past the still-functioning **monastery of Ipsiloú**, founded in 1101 atop an outrider of the extinct volcano of Órdhymnos. The *katholikón*, tucked in one corner of a large, irregular courtyard, has a fine wood-lattice ceiling but had its frescoes repainted to detrimental effect in 1992; more intriguing are portions of Iznik tile stuck in the facade, and the handsome double gateway. Upstairs you can visit a fairly rich **museum** of ecclesiastical treasure (sporadically open; small donation). Ipsiloú's patron saint is John the Theologian, a frequent dedication for monasteries overlooking apocalyptic landscapes like the surrounding parched, boulder-strewn hills.

Signposted just west is the paved, five-kilometre side road to the main concentration of Lésvos's rather overrated **petrified forest** (daily 8am–sunset; €2), a fenced-in "reserve" which is toured along 3km of walkways. For once, contemporary Greek arsonists cannot be blamed for the state of the trees, created by the combined action of volcanic ash from Órdhymnos and hot springs some fifteen to twenty million years ago. The mostly horizontal sequoia trunks average a metre or less in length, save for a few poster-worthy exceptions; another more accessible (and free) cluster is found south of Sígri (see below), plus there is a fair number of petrified logs strewn about the courtyard of Ipsiloú.

Sígri

SÍGRI, near the western tip of Lésvos, has an appropriately end-of-the-line feel; the bay here is guarded both by an Ottoman castle, and the long island of Nissiopí, which protects the place somewhat from prevailing winds. In the past it's been an important NATO naval base and minor ferry port on a seasonal Rafína–Psará–Áyios Efstrátios–Límnos line, but both battleships and ferries are scarce of late, and it's doubtful whether the civilian ferries in particular will resume service. The eighteenth-century **castle** (built atop the ruins of an earlier one) sports the sultan's monogram over the entrance, something rarely seen outside Istanbul, and a token of the high regard in which this productive island was held. The vaguely Turkish-looking **church of Ayía Triádha** is in fact a converted mosque, with a huge water cistern taking up the ground floor by the belfry; this supplied, among other things, the half-ruined hamam just south. The town itself presents a drab mix of vernacular and cement dwellings, while the town beach, south of the castle headland, is narrow and hemmed in by the road. There are much better beaches at **Faneroméni**, 3.5km north by coastal dirt track from the northern outskirts of town, plus another 2km south, just below the fifteen-kilometre dirt track to Eressós (passable with care in 35min); neither beach has any facilities.

Most **accommodation** is monopolized by British tour company Direct Greece, but you might try *Nelly's Rooms and Apartments* (☎22530 54230; ❸), overlooking the castle, or the nearby *Rainbow Studios* (☎22530 54310; ❸). Among several **tavernas**, the best all-rounder, just inland, is Italian-run, ultra-hygienic *Una Faccia Una Razza* (April–mid-Oct), with lovely grilled garlicky vegetables, creative salads, pizza, pasta, grilled seafood and an Italian wine list. The *Australia*, a bit seaward, has the Greek standards and an enviable position under the tamarisks. For **nightlife**, look no further than *Notia* (June–Sept), a jazz bar in operation since 1993.

Skála Eressoú

Most visitors to western Lésvos park themselves at the resort of **SKÁLA ERESSOÚ**, accessible via the southerly turning between Ándissa and Ipsiloú. The three-kilometre beach here runs a close second in quality to Vaterá's, and consequently the place (in a good year, which is rare of late) rivals Plomári and Mólyvos for numbers of visitors, who form an uneasy mix of Brits, Germans, Scandinavians, Greek families, neo-hippies and lesbians. Behind stretches the largest and most attractive agricultural plain on Lésvos, a welcome green contrast to the volcanic ridges above.

There's not much to Skála – just a roughly rectangular grid of perhaps five streets by eight, angling up to the oldest cottages on the slope of **Vígla hill**. The waterfront pedestrian zone (officially Papanikolí) is divided by a café-lined round *platía* midway along dominated by a bust of **Theophrastos**, the renowned botanist who hailed from ancient Eressós. This was not, as you might suppose, on the site of the modern inland village, but atop Vígla hill at the east end of the beach; some of the remaining citadel wall is still visible from a distance. On top, the ruins prove scanty, but it's worth the scramble up for the views – you can discern the ancient jetty submerged beyond the modern fishing anchorage.

Another famous reputed native of ancient Eressós was **Sappho** (ca. 615–562 BC), the ancient poetess and reputed lesbian. There are thus always considerable numbers of gay women here paying homage, particularly at the two hotels devoted to their exclusive use (see opposite), and in the clothing-optional zone of the beach west of the river mouth. Ancient Eressós endured into the Byzantine era, the main legacy of which is the **basilica of Áyios Andhréas** behind the modern church, merely foundations and an unhappily covered floor mosaic; the adjacent museum of local odds and ends is even less compelling.

Skála has countless **rooms and apartments**, but ones near the sea fill early in the day and can be noisy; in peak season you should aim for something quiet and inland, overlooking a garden or fields. Since the millennium, all but one package company have dropped the resort, usually citing a lack of commitment to "family values" – ie, the radical lesbian contingent was a bit hard for the other tourists to handle – so vacancies are now fairly easy to come by. Still, it's wise to entrust the search to Sappho Travel (℡ 22530 52140, ℻ 22530 52000). Jo and Joanna are switched-on and helpful, also serving as the local car-rental station, ferry agent and air-ticket source; they are happy to place walk-ins in accommodation (❷–❹), but suggest you consult their UK-based website, Ⓦ www.lesvos.co.uk, in advance. Otherwise, there are just three bona fide **hotels** in the village, and two of these – the remote *Antiopi* (℡ 22530 53311, Ⓦ www.antiopi.net; rooms ❶, studios ❸) and the seafront *Sappho the Eressia* (℡ 22530 53495, Ⓔ Sappho_sarani@hotmail.com; ❸) – are run exclusively by and for lesbians. The straight alternative is the central, air-conditioned *Galini* (℡ 22530 53138, ℻ 22530 53137; ❹), slightly inland.

Most **tavernas**, with elevated wooden dining platforms, crowd the beach; in the wake of the recent tourism crash, they've been subjected to a harsh winnowing, with more closures or changeovers likely. The *Blue Sardine* at the far west end of the front has historically been an excellent seafood *ouzerí*, but it's up for sale at present; at the extreme east end of the esplanade, *Jay's* does exotic/Western specials like nut and lentil roast, or pork chop in plum sauce, at premium prices. The best Greek cuisine is found at *Eressos Palace*, a few paces inland at the west edge of town, and accordingly well attended by Greek coach tours. In terms of **nightlife**, the gay-women contingent favours *Dhekati Mousa/Tenth Muse*, on the Theophrastos *platía*; out in the bushes west of the stream, aptly named *Primitive* is the most enduring music bar. Skála has a **post office** and a coin-op **laundry** near the church, as well as a **bank** ATM attached to Sappho Travel, and a small **Internet café**, *Cybersurf*, just east of Dhekati Mousa.

If you're returning to the main island crossroads at Kalloní, you can complete a loop from Eressós along the western shore of the Gulf of Kalloní via the hill villages of Mesótopos and Ágra; this route is entirely paved, despite obsolete maps showing it as a track.

Northern Lésvos

The main road north of Kalloní winds up a piney ridge and then down the other side into increasingly attractive country, stippled with poplars and blanketed by olive groves. Long before you can discern any other architectural detail, the cockscomb silhouette of **Mólyvos castle** indicates your approach to the oldest established tourist spot on Lésvos.

Mólyvos (Míthymna)

MÓLYVOS (officially Míthymna), 61km from Mytilíni, is arguably the most beautiful village on Lésvos. Tiers of sturdy, red-tiled houses, some standing defensively with their rear walls to the sea, mount the slopes between the picturesque harbour and the **Byzantine-Genoese castle** (Tues–Sun: summer 8am–7pm; winter 8am–2.30pm; €2), which provides interesting rambles around its perimeter walls and views of Turkey across the straits. Closer examination reveals a score of weathered Turkish fountains along flower-fragrant, cobbled alleyways, a reflection of the fact that before 1923 Muslims constituted over a third of the local population and owned many of the finest dwellings.

The **Komninaki Kralli** mansion, high up in the town, is particularly worth getting into (daily 9am–5pm; free); the lower floor houses an art school, but the wall- and ceiling-paintings on the upper storey (dated 1833) rival those of the Vareltzídena mansion in Pétra (see opposite). A panel in the smallest room portrays some dervish musicians, while other murals depict stylized versions of Constantinople and Mytilíni Town; you can tell the men's and women's quarters apart by the wider recessed "throne" provided for the latter. The contents of the small archeological museum, formerly in the basement of the town hall, have been transferred to Mytilíni while the building undergoes renovation; barely excavated **ancient Mithymna** to the northwest is of essentially specialist interest, though a necropolis has been unearthed next to the bus stop and main car park.

Modern dwellings and hotels have been banned from the municipal core, but this hasn't stopped a steady drain of all the authentic life from the upper bazaar; just one lonely tailor still plies his trade amongst souvenir shops vastly surplus to requirements, and the last traditional locals' *ouzerí* shut in 1989. Once an upmarket resort, Mólyvos is now firmly middle of the road, with the usual silly T-shirts and other trinkets carpeting every vertical surface of a stage-set, albeit an attractive one, for package tourism.

The shingly **town beach** is mediocre, improving somewhat as you head towards the southern end, and a clothing-optional zone. Advertised **boat excursions** to bays as remote as Tsónia (see p.430) seem a frank admission of this failing; there are also five to seven daily minibus shuttles in season, linking all points between Ánaxos and Eftaloú.

Practicalities

Around the tourist office (see below), at the entrance to town, you'll find four **bank** ATMs, plus numerous **motorbike and car rental** places, including Kosmos (T22530 71710) and Alpha (T22530 71942), the latter offering the ability to pick up here and drop off in Vaterá or Mytilíni. The main **post office** is near the top of the upper commercial street; *Centraal*, down near the harbour, is the better equipped of two Internet cafés (€4.40/hr).

The main sea-level thoroughfare of Mihaïl Goútou (closed to cars late June to Aug) heads straight past the tourist office towards the harbour; along or just below it stand a number of bona fide **hotels** or **pensions** not completely taken over by packages. These include the *Hermes* on the beach (T22530 71250; ❸), with variable, marble-floored rooms; the *Molyvos I* next door (T22530 71496, F22530 71640; ❹), with large balconied rooms, and breakfast served on the flagstoned terrace under the palms; and the serviceable *Poseidon* just down from the tourist office (T22530 71981; ❸). For rooms, seek out the modern studio units of *Khryssi Bourdhadonaki* (T22530 72193; ❸), towards Ayía Kyriakí; those of *Panayiotis Baxevanellis* (T22530 71558 or call in at the *El Greco* cake shop; ❶), with a preponderance of double beds and a communal kitchen; or *Studios Voula* below the castle car park (T22530 72017 or 694 52 41 994), which has studios (❸) and a restored four-person house (❺), both with knockout views. Families could consider the high-standard restored stone house offered by Theo and Melinda (T22530 71241, E meltheo@otenet.gr), up near the Komninaki Kralli mansion; it sleeps up to six, and rates vary from €85 (low season) to €140 (high) for the entire premises. Otherwise, rooms can be reserved through the municipal **tourist office** by the bus stop (daily: summer theoretically 8am–3pm & 6.30–8.30pm; spring and autumn 8.30am–3pm; T22530 71347). The official **campsite**, *Camping Methymna* (late June–Sept), lies 2km northeast of town on the Eftaloú road.

The sea-view **tavernas** on the lower market lane of 17-Noemvríou are all much of a muchness, where you pay primarily for the view; it's far better to either head for outlying villages (see below) or descend to the fishing port, where *The Captain's Table* (with green chairs) combines the virtues of fresh seafood, meat grills and vegetarian *mezédhes*, washed down by their very palatable, own-label wine. *To Khtapodhi*, in the old customs house by the port entrance, has fairly consistent quality, a mostly Greek crowd and treats such as *sardhélles pastés*. Many consider the five-kilometre trip east to Vafiós worth it to patronize either *To Petrino*, *Taverna Vafios* or *Taverna Ilias*, but avoid heavy, overly deep-fried dishes at any of these places. Also highly recommended, and open all year (except Nov–mid-Dec), is *Iy Eftalou*, 4km northeast near the spa of the same name (see p.430), where the food (meat/fish grills) and tree-shaded setting are both splendid. For **dessert**, try the pudding and cake shop *El Greco* on the lower market lane, where proprietor Panayiotis is a wonderful raconteur (in several languages).

Midsummer sees a short **festival of music and theatre** up in the castle, and there's also a well-regarded summer **cinema** next to the taxi rank. **Nightlife** centres around the music bars: most durable is the tropical-themed, youth hangout *Congas* (July–Aug only) below the shore road, but the most exciting recent entry on the scene is *Opus 6*, just up from the harbour, with live Greek or Western music every night. State-of-the-art outdoor disco *Gatelousi*, 3km towards Pétra, is the place to be seen on a Saturday night (late June–Aug only).

Pétra and Ánaxos

Since there are political and practical limits to the expansion of Mólyvos, many package companies have shifted emphasis to **PÉTRA**, 5km due south. The place has sprawled untidily behind its broad sand beach and seafront square, but the core of old stone houses, some with Levantine-style balconies overhanging the street, remains. Pétra takes its name from the giant **rock monolith** located some distance inland and enhanced by the eighteenth-century **church of the Panayía Glykofiloússa**, reached via 103 rock-hewn steps. Other local attractions include the sixteenth-century **church of Áyios Nikólaos**, with three phases of well-preserved frescoes, and the intricately decorated **Vareltzídhena mansion** (May–Sept Tues–Sun 8am–7pm; Oct–April Tues–Sun 8am–3pm; free), with naïve wall paintings of courting couples and a stylized view of a naval engagement at Constantinople.

Most small hotels and studios are block-booked, so on-spec arrivals should make a beeline for the Women's Agricultural Tourism Cooperative on the south side of the seafront square (℡22530 41238, ✆womes@otenet.gr), formed by Pétra's womenfolk in 1984 to offer something more unusual for visitors. In addition to operating an excellent, inexpensive restaurant on the square, with both grills and *mayireftá* served at rooftop seating, they arrange rooms or studios (②–③) in a number of scattered premises. For more comfort, try the *Hotel Michaelia* behind the south waterfront (℡22530 41730, ℻22530 22067; ④). Aside from the co-operative's eatery, most tavernas lack distinction, though some people like *Iy Dhrosia* and *To Tyhero Petalo* behind the beach. You're probably better off out of town – either at the *Taverna Petri* (all day May–mid-Oct) in **PETRÍ** village 3km inland, with superb home-recipe *mayireftá* and a view terrace, or at **Avláki**, 1.5km southwest en route to Ánaxos, where there's a competent, signposted taverna/*ouzerí* behind a tiny beach.

ÁNAXOS, 3km south of Pétra, is a higgledy-piggledy package resort fringing by far the cleanest beach in the area: a kilometre of sand cluttered with sunbeds, pedalos and a handful of tavernas that are an improvement on the unmemorable snack-bars of yore. From anywhere along here you enjoy beautiful sunsets between and beyond three offshore islets.

Around Mount Lepétymnos

East of Mólyvos, the villages of 968-metre **Mount Lepétymnos**, marked by tufts of poplars, provide a day's rewarding exploration. The first stop, though not exactly up the hill, might be **Loutrá Eftaloú**, thermal baths 5km along the road passing the campsite. Patronize the hot pool under the Ottoman-era domed structure, not the sterile modern tub-rooms (daily: May & Oct–Nov 9am–1pm & 3–7pm; June–Sept 8am–2pm & 4–8pm; €3.50 for group pool). The spa is well looked after, with the water changed twice daily and mixed up to a comfortable 39–41°C. Still, you'll need to cool down regularly; outside stretches the long, good pebble beach of **Áyii Anáryiri**, broken up by little headlands, with the remotest two coves nudist.

Eftaloú itself has a considerable number of fancy hotels and bungalow complexes, the friendliest and best value (though tour-dominated like the others) being the *Eftalou* (℡22530 71584, ℮parmakel@otenet.gr; ❹), with a pool, well-tended garden and loyal repeat clientele.

The main road around the mountain first heads 6km east to **VAFIÓS**, with its three aforementioned tavernas (see p.429), before curling north around the base of the peaks. This route is entirely paved, but the bus service back towards Mytilíni does not resume until Áryennos, 6km before the exquisite hill village of **SYKAMINIÁ** (**Sykamiá**), birthplace of the novelist Stratis Myrivilis. Below the "Plaza of the Workers' First of May", with its two traditional *kafenía* and views north to Turkey, one of the imposing basalt-built houses is marked as his childhood home. A marked trail shortcuts the twisting road down to **SKÁLA SYKAMINIÁS**, easily the most picturesque fishing port on Lésvos. Myrivilis used it as the setting for his best-known work, *The Mermaid Madonna*, and the tiny rock-top chapel at the end of the jetty will be instantly recognizable to anyone who has read the book.

On a practical level, Skála has a few pensions, such as the central, partly air-con *Gorgona* (℡22530 55301; ❷), with a shaded breakfast terrace, and several **tavernas**. The most durable of these is *Iy Skamnia* (aka *Iy Mouria tou Myrivilí*), with seating under the mulberry tree in which Myrivilis used to sleep on hot summer nights, though newer *Anemoessa* (closest to the chapel, open winter weekends also) has overtaken it quality-wise, with good stuffed squash blossoms complementing fresh seafood. The only local beach is the pebble-on-sand-base one of **Kayiá** 1.5km east.

Continuing east from upper Sykaminiá, you soon come to **KLIÓ**, whose single main street (marked "*kentrikí agorá*") leads down to a platía with a plane tree, fountain, *kafenía* and more views across to Turkey. The village is set attractively on a slope, down which a six-kilometre road, now half-paved, descends to **Tsónia** beach, 600m of beautiful pink volcanic sand.

South of Klió, the route forks at Kápi, from where you can complete a loop of the mountain by bearing west along a completely paved road. **PELÓPI** is the ancestral village of unsuccessful 1988 US presidential candidate Michael Dukakis (who finally visited the island in 2000), and the main street is now named for him. **IPSILOMÉTOPO**, 5km further along, is punctuated by a minaret (but no mosque) and hosts revels on July 17, the feast of Ayía Marína. By the time you reach sprawling **STÝPSI**, you're just 4km shy of the main Kallóni–Mólyvos road; it's also not a bad start-point for rambles along

Lepétymnos's steadily dwindling network of trails (a locally sold guide by Mike Maunder, *On Foot in North Lesvos*, details some).

Mandamádhos and Taxiárhis monastery

The main highway south from Klió and Kápi leads back to the capital through **MANDAMÁDHOS**. This attractive inland village is famous for its pottery, including the Ali Baba-style *pithária* (olive oil urns) seen throughout Lésvos, but more so for the "black" icon of the Archangel Michael, whose enormous **monastery of Taxiárhis** (daily: May–Sept 6am–9.30pm; Oct–April 6.30am–7pm), in a valley just northeast, is the powerful focus of a thriving cult. The image – supposedly made from a mixture of mud and the blood of monks slaughtered in a massacre – is really more idol than icon, both in its lumpy three-dimensionality and in the former rather pagan manner of veneration. First there was the custom of the coin-wish, whereby you pressed a coin to the Archangel's forehead – if it stuck, your wish would be granted. Owing to wear and tear on the image, this practice (along with candle-lighting next to it) has long forbidden, with supplicants referred to an alternative icon by the main entrance.

It's further believed that while carrying out his various errands on behalf of the faithful, the Archangel gets through more footwear than Imelda Marcos. Accordingly the icon used to be surrounded not by the usual *támmata* (votive medallions) but by piles of miniature gold and silver shoes. The ecclesiastical authorities, embarrassed by such "primitive" practices, removed all the little shoes in 1986. Since then, a token substitute has reappeared: several pairs of tin slippers which can be filled with money and left in front of the icon. Just why his devotees should want to encourage these perpetual peripatetics is unclear, since in Greek folklore the Archangel Michael is also the one who fetches the souls of the dying, and modern Greek attitudes towards death are as bleak as those of their pagan ancestors.

Límnos

Límnos is a sizeable agricultural and garrison island whose remoteness and peculiar ferry schedules have until recently protected it from the worst excesses of the holiday trade. Most summer visitors are Greek, particularly from Thessaloníki, though the locals are becoming increasingly used to numbers of northern European visitors flown in by ever more regular charter flights, both in and out of high season. Accommodation tends to be comfortable if a bit overpriced, with a strong bias towards self-catering units, and **backpackers** are explicitly **discouraged**. The bucolic island has been getting trendy of late: there are upscale souvenir shops, village houses restored by mainlanders as weekend retreats and some sort of noon-to-small-hours music bar at every beach.

Límnos's traditional role is as an army posting. Its **military presence** ran to 25,000 soldiers at the nadir of Greco-Turkish relations in the late 1980s, though it is now down to about 10,000; conventional tourism was slow in coming because the islanders made a reliable living off the soldiers and family members coming to visit them. Since the 1960s, the island has been the focus of periodic disputes between the Greek and Turkish governments; Turkey has a long-standing demand that Límnos should be demilitarized, and Turkish aircraft regularly intrude Greek air space overhead, prompting immediate responses from the Greek Air Force squadron here.

LÍMNOS

Samothráki & Alexandhroúpoli

Lávrio, Áyios Efstrátios, Lésvos & Híos

Kavála & Thessaloníki

0   5 km

N

Pláka

Panayiá

Salt Marsh

Kondopoúli

Kalliópi

Kéros

Kabírion (Kavírio)

Hephaestia (Ifestía)

Polyochni (Polyókhni)

Áyios Sózon

Fyssíni

Roussopoúli

Kaminía

Skandháli

Repanídhi

Romanoú

Bourniá Bay

Kótsinas

Város

Lýkhna

Allied War Cemetery

Havoúli

Atsikí

Moúdhros Bay

Moúdhros

Karpássi

Livadhohóri

Kallithéa

Néa Koútali

Tsimándhria

Dháfni

Áyios Dhimítrios

Angariónes

Pedhinó

Dhiapóri

Katálakos

Portianoú

Allied War Cemetery

Thermá

Kondiás

Sardhés

Kornós

Myrína (Kástro)

Thános

Evgátis (Áyios Pávlos)

Káspakas

Platý

Paralía Thánous

Áyios Ioánnis

Avlónas

Rihá Nerá

Paralía Platý

Playísó Mólos

The bays of **Bourniá** and **Moúdhros**, the latter one of the largest natural harbours in the Aegean, almost divide Límnos in two. The west of the island is dramatically bare and hilly, with abundant basalt put to good use as street cobbles and house masonry. Like most volcanic islands, Límnos produces excellent wine from westerly vineyards – good dry whites, rosés and excellent retsina – plus ouzo at Kondiás. The east is low-lying and speckled with marshes popular with duck-hunters, where it's not occupied by cattle, combine harvesters and vast corn fields.

Despite off-islander slander to that effect, Límnos is not flat, barren or treeless; much of the countryside consists of rolling hills, well vegetated except on their heights, and with substantial clumps of almond, jujube, myrtle, oak, poplar and mulberry trees. The island is, however, extremely dry, with irrigation water pumped from deep wells, and a limited number of potable springs. Yet various terrapin-haunted creeks bring sand to several long, **sandy beaches** around the coast, where it's easy to find a stretch to yourself – though there's no escaping the stingless jellyfish that pour out of the Dardanelles, especially in early summer, and die here in the shallows (they've fortunately decreased in recent years). On the plus side, beaches shelve gently, making them ideal for children and quick to warm up, with no cool currents except near the river mouths.

Mýrina

MÝRINA (aka Kástro), the capital and passenger port on the west coast, has the atmosphere of a provincial market town rather than of a resort. With about five thousand inhabitants, it's pleasantly low-key, if not especially picturesque. The main attraction is the Byzantine **castle** (unrestricted access), perched on a craggy headland between the ferry dock and Romeïkós Yialós, the town's chic beach-lined esplanade backed by ornate Neoclassical mansions. In a ruined state despite later additions by the Genoese and Ottomans, the fortress is flatteringly lit at night and warrants a climb at sunset for views over the town, the entire west coast and – in exceptional conditions – over to Mount Áthos, on the mainland 35 nautical miles west (which can also be glimpsed from any suitable height east of town). Also worth exploring is the town's core neighbourhood of old stone houses dating from the Ottoman era. Few explicitly Turkish monuments have survived, though an unassuming **fountain** at the harbour end of the main drag, Kydhá, retains its calligraphic inscription and is still highly prized for its drinking water.

The town's shops and amenities are mostly to be found along Kydhá (also known as Karatzá), which meanders north from the harbour to Romeïkós Yialós – or Garoufalídhou, its perpendicular offshoot, roughly halfway along. As town **beaches** go, Romeïkós Yialós and Toúrkikos Yialós, its less attractive counterpart to the south of the harbour, are not at all bad; Rihá Nerá, the next bay north of Romeïkós Yialós, is even better, with watersports craft on offer.

The **Archeological Museum** (Tues–Sun 8.30am–3pm; €2) occupies a handsome Ottoman mansion right behind Romeïkós Yialós, not far from the site of Bronze Age Myrina. Finds are assiduously labelled in Greek, Italian and English, and the entire premises are exemplary in terms of presentation – the obvious drawback being that the best items have been spirited away to Athens, leaving a collection that's essentially of specialist interest. The south ground-floor gallery is mainly devoted to pottery from Polychni (Polyókhni); the north wing contains more of the same, plus items from ancient Myrina; upstairs features galleries of post-Bronze Age artefacts from Kabirion (Kavírio) and

Hephaestia (Ifestía). The star upper-storey exhibits are votive lamps in the shape of sirens, found in an Archaic sanctuary at Hephaestia, much imitated in modern local jewellery. Rather less vicious than Homer's creatures, they are identified more invitingly as the "muses of the underworld, creatures of super-human wisdom, incarnations of nostalgia for paradise". Another entire room is devoted to metalwork, of which the most impressive items are gold jewellery and bronze objects, both practical (cheese graters, door-knockers) and whimsical-naturalistic (a snail, a vulture).

Practicalities

The modern civilian **airport** is some 20km east of Mýrina, almost at the exact geographic centre of the island, sharing a runway with an enormous air-force base; there's an Olympic-run shuttle bus between town and airport – consult the Olympic office for departure times (☎22540 22078). **Ferries** dock at the southern end of the town, in the shadow of the castle; there are separate agencies for the sailings of NEL boats (☎22540 22460), GA Ferries (☎22540 24617) and the *Saos II/Nissos Limnos* (☎22540 29571).

The **bus station** is on Platía Eleftheríou Venizélou, at the north end of Kydhá. One look at the sparse schedules (only a single daily afternoon departure to most points, slightly more frequently to Kondiás and Moúdhros) will convince you of the need to rent a vehicle from one of many agencies clustered around the harbour area, a couple of them with offices at the airport. **Cars**, **motorbikes** and **bicycles** can be rented from Europcar (☎22540 23125, airport ☎22540 25494), Myrina Rent a Car (☎22540 24476 or 22540 24100), Petrides Tours (☎22540 22039, ✉mapet@lim.forthnet.gr), Holiday (☎22540 23280 or 693 24 81 056, ✉sxas@lim.forthnet.gr), Best (☎22540 22127) or Auto Europe (☎22540 23777); rates for bikes are only slightly above the island norm, but cars are expensive. A motorbike (most obviously from Moto Lemnos, ☎22540 25002) is generally enough to explore the coast and the interior, as there are few steep gradients but many perilously narrow village streets.

All **banks**, most of them along Kydhá, have ATMs; the **post office** and Olympic airlines terminal are adjacent to each other on Garoufalídhou, with a **laundry** across the way by the Hotel Paris. There are **Internet** facilities at *Excite Club*, just behind the port roundabout, and at *Joy*, next to the post office.

Accommodation

Despite Límnos's steady gentrification, you may still be met off the boat with offers of a **room**; there are officially two dozen or so licensed establishments. Otherwise you'll find one or two very decent **hotels** plus some upmarket complexes at beachside locations nearby. In Romeïkós Yialós two or three restored houses serve as *pensions* and small hotels, though most are affected by evening noise from the seafront bars. Just north, the areas of Rihá Nerá and Áyios Pandelímonas are likely bets for **self-catering units**. There's **no official campsite** on Límnos; Greek caravanners and campers have been banished from the north end of Platý beach, though a few tents still sprout furtively at Paralía Thánous and at Kéros (see p.437).

Akti Myrina ☎22540 22681. This self-contained luxury complex of wood-and-stone bungalows (avoid the awful modern annexe) at the north end of Romeïkós Yialóshas all conceivable diversions and comforts and an impressive variety of sports facilities. It is run by, and mainly caters for Italians, who fully occupy it from late June through August, but during low season (May and Sept) they might squeeze you in. Full board ❽

Apollo Pavilion ☎22540 24315, ✉apollo47@otenet.gr. Hidden away at the end of Frýnis – a peaceful cul-de-sac off Garoufalídhou –

this welcoming, if fairly basic, place is the most durable budget establishment in town. It offers multibed rooms in the basement (**②**–**③**) and more comfortable self-catering units upstairs (**④**). **Blue Waters** ☎ 22540 24403, @ bwkon@otenet.gr. The best value place in Romeïkós Yialós, it has smallish but decently appointed rooms. **③**
Hotel Ifestos ☎ 22540 24960, ℱ 22540 23623. Found in the Andhróni district, inland from Rihá Nerá, the hotel has rooms with a mix of sea and mountain views, a pleasant bar-lounge and professional service (something of a rarity in town). **⑤**
Hotel Lemnos ☎ 22540 22153, ℱ 22540 23329. This place, right by the harbour, has smart rooms with air con, fridges and balconies, all of which go some way to offsetting small-hours ferry noise. **④**
Pension Romeïkos Yialos Sakhtoúri 7 ☎ 22540 23787. Located in a fine stone mansion; the rooms here may prove quieter as it is located one block inland. **④**

Eating and drinking

About halfway along Kydhá, *O Plátanos* serves traditional *mayireftá* to big crowds on an atmospheric little square under two plane trees. **Seafood** is excellent on Límnos owing to its proximity to the Dardanelles and seasonal fish migrations; for affordable seaside dining, look no further than *Ostria* at the town end of Toúrkikos Yialós beach, which offers a mix of grills, fish and *ouzomezédhes* from noon until late. There's little to distinguish between the half-dozen tavernas arrayed around the little fishing port nearby, in terms of menu or prices, but *Gláros* at the far end is generally considered the best – and works out slightly more expensive.

Not too surprisingly given the twee setting, the restaurants and ostentatious **bars** on Romeïkós Yialós are pretty poor value, except for a sunset drink in sight of the castle. The tree-shaded tables of *Iy Tzitzífies* on Rihá Nerá are a far better option; most of the extensive menu of fish, *mezédhes* and *mayireftá* is likely to be available on any given day.

Western Límnos

Even though Mýrina's town beaches are fine, if you're looking for more pristine conditions head 3km north past the *Akti Myrina* to Avlónas, unspoiled except for the *Porto Marina Palace* luxury complex flanking it on the south. Some 6km from town you work your way towards **KÁSPAKAS**, its north-facing houses in pretty, tiled tiers, before plunging down to **Áyios Ioánnis**. Here, the island's most unusual – and anonymous – taverna (late June to Aug) features seating in the shade of piled-up volcanic boulders, with a shingle beach just north of the fishing anchorage. If it's shut, *Taverna Iliovasilemata*, signposted to the south, is welcoming with good (if slightly pricey) fish. Arguably the best **taverna** on the island, the *Man-Tela*, is the only reason for visiting the straggly village of **SÁRDHES**, 11km northeast of Mýrina; in a laid-back atmosphere you can feast on free-range poultry, rabbit dishes, home-made pasta and bread, salads and vegetable dishes, plus the best Limnian wine, at very reasonable prices.

PLATÝ, 2km southeast of Mýrina, has had its profile spoiled by the kind of modern villa construction that is blighting many Limnian villages latterly, but it does have two nocturnally popular **tavernas**. By far the better of these is *O Sozos*, just off the main *platía*, where you'll have to show up early for a table (groups should reserve on ☎ 22540 25085). Fine *orektiká*, lamb chops, steamed mussels, grilled *biftéki*, *tsípouro* and local bulk wine are strong points; the bill shouldn't exceed €12. The long sandy beach, 700m below, is popular and usually jellyfish-free, with watersports available; except for the unsightly Mark Warner compound at the south end, the area is still pretty rural, with sheep parading to and fro at dawn and dusk. The single **hotel**, low-rise *Plati Beach* (☎22540 23583 or 694 49 65 189; ❹), has an enviable position in the middle of the beach, but get a room towards the back if you don't fancy noise from the ground-floor bar/restaurant; there are more basic **rooms**, though with fridges and proper showers, available through *Tzimis Taverna* (☎22540 24142; ❷), which divides the lunchtime trade with its neighbour *Grigoris* near the south end of the beach, though both lose out in the evenings to the village-centre tavernas. The highest standard of **studios** in the area, if not the whole island, is the tastefully landscaped *Villa Afroditi* (☎220540 23141, ℱ22540 25031; ❺), with a pleasant pool bar where meals are served, weekly barbecue nights for guests, and one of the best buffet breakfasts in Greece.

THÁNOS, 2km further southeast, seems a bigger, more architecturally char-acterful version of Platý village, with a well-regarded central-*platía* taverna (evenings only) and high-standard mock-trad bungalows at the east edge (☎220540 23162; ❺). **Paralía Thánous**, 1.5km on a paved road below the village, is perhaps the most scenic of the southwestern beaches, flanked by weird volcanic crags and with views on a clear afternoon out to Áyios Efstrátios island. There are two tavernas and a handful of basic **rooms** at *Petradi* (☎22540 24218; ❷). Beyond Thános, the road curls over to the enormous beach at **Evgátis** (Áyios Pávlos), reckoned to be the island's best, with more igneous pinnacles on the west. Despite this rating, it is prone to winds; in addi-tion to the regulation music bar/*kantína* on the sand, there is a full-service taverna across the road, with rooms (❸).

Some 3km further along (11km from Mýrina), **KONDIÁS** is the island's third largest settlement, cradled between two hills tufted with Límnos's only pine forest. Stone-built, red-tiled houses and a row of sail-less windmills combine with the setting to make Kondiás the most attractive inland village, a fact not lost on the urban Greeks restoring fine old houses with varying degrees of taste. You can **stay** in one such house, which sleeps four (❻) and is usually rented by the week by the friendly Greek-South African manage-ment of *Villa Afroditi* in Platý (see p.435); short-term facilities are limited, and aren't much better at the shore annexe of **Dhiapóri**, 2km east. The beach is unappealing (and backed by a huge, fenced-off minefield), the tavernas list-less, with the main interest lent by the narrow isthmus dividing the bays of Kondiás and Moúdhros.

Eastern Límnos

The shores of **Moúdhros Bay**, glimpsed south of the trans-island road, are muddy and best avoided unless you're a clam-digger. The bay itself enjoyed considerable importance during World War I, culminating in the Ottoman surrender aboard the British warship HMS *Agamemnon* here on October 30, 1918. **MOÚDHROS**, the second-largest town on Límnos and the main cargo port, is a dreary place, with only a wonderfully kitsch, two-belfried church to recommend it. The closest decent beach is at **Havoúli**, 4km south by dirt track and still far from the open sea. There are a few **hotels** in Moúdhros, the best of which is the overpriced *Kyma* (☎22540 71333, ℱ22540 71484; ❹). Its more reasonable, but run-of-the-mill, **restaurant** is convenient for a lunch break if you're visiting the archeological sites and beaches of eastern Límnos.

About 800m along the Roussopoúli road, you pass an **Allied military cemetery** (unlocked) maintained by the Commonwealth War Graves Commission; its neat (if rather dry) lawns and rows of white headstones seem incongruous in such parched surroundings. In 1915, Moúdhros Bay was the principal staging area for the disastrous Gallipoli campaign. Of the roughly 36,000 Allied dead, 887 – mainly battle casualties who died after having been evacuated to the base hospital at Moúdhros – are buried here, with 348 more at another signposted graveyard behind the church in Portianoú.

Indications of the most advanced Neolithic civilization in the Aegean have been unearthed at **Polyochni** (**Polyókhni**), 3km from the gully-hidden village of Kamínia (7km east of Moúdhros). The site occupies a bluff over-looking a long, narrow rock-and-sand beach flanked by stream valleys. Since the 1930s, Italian excavations have uncovered five layers of settlement, the oldest from late in the fourth millennium BC, predating Troy on the Turkish coast opposite. The town met a sudden, violent end from war or earthquake in about 2100 BC. The **ruins** (daily 8.30am–3pm; free) are well labelled but of essentially specialist interest, though the *bouleuterion* (assembly hall) with bench seating, a mansion and the landward fortifications are impressive enough. The small but extremely well-presented museum behind the entrance kiosk brings the whole place to life and explains its historic significance. Moreover, during August and September the Italian excavators are normally about, and may be free to show you around the place.

Hephaestia and Kabirion, the other significant **ancient sites** on Límnos, are reached via the village of Kondopoúli, 7km northeast of Moúdhros. Both sites are rather remote, and only reachable with your own transport. **Hephaestia** (present-day Ifestía), 4km from Kondopoúli by rough, signposted track, has little to offer nonspecialists. **Kabirion**, also signposted as Kabirion (modern Kavírio), on the opposite shore of Tigáni Bay and accessed by the same road built to serve the now-bankrupt and derelict Kaviria Palace luxury complex, is more evocative. The **ruins** (daily 8.30am–3pm; free) are those of a sanctuary connected with the cult of the Samothracian Kabiroi (see p.442), though the site here is probably older. Little survives other than the ground plan, but the setting is undeniably impressive. Eleven column stumps stake out a stoa, behind eight spots marked as column bases in the *telestirio* or shrine where the cult mysteries took place. More engaging, perhaps, is a nearby sea grotto identified as the Homeric **Spiliá toú Filoktíti**, where the Trojan war hero Philoctetes was abandoned by his comrades-in-arms until his stinking, gangrenous leg had healed. Landward access to the cave is via steps leading down from the care-taker's shelter, though final access (from a little passage on the right as you face the sea) involves some wading.

The beach at **Kéros** is 2.5km by dirt road below **KALLIÓPI**, which has two snack-bar/**tavernas**, and smart **rooms**, *Keros* (℡22540 41059, ❹), at the edge of town. The beach is the best in this part of the island although it is rather exposed. A 1500-metre stretch of sand with dunes and a small pine grove, plus shallow water, it attracts a number of Greek tourists and foreigners with camper vans and windsurfers; a small snack *kantína* operates near the parking area during July and August only.

On the other side of Kondopoúli, reached via Repanídhi village, the often dirty, hard-packed beach of **Kótsinas** is set in the protected western limb of Bourniá Bay. The nearby anchorage (follow signs to "Kótsinas Fortress") offers a pair of **tavernas**; the better of these is *To Koráli* by the water, which is reliably open at lunch, with a wide range of *mezédhes* and affordable fish. Up on a knoll overlooking the jetty, there's a corroded, sword-brandishing statue of Maroula, a Genoese-era heroine who delayed the Ottoman conquest by a few years, and a large **church of Zoödhóhou Piyís** (the Life-Giving Spring). This is nothing extraordinary, but beside it 63 steps lead down through an illuminated tunnel in the rock to the potable (if slightly mineral) spring in question, oozing into a cool, vaulted chamber.

Áyios Efstrátios (Aï Strátis)

Áyios Efstrátios is without doubt one of the quietest and loneliest islands in the Aegean. Historically, the only outsiders to stay here were compelled to do so – it served as a place of exile for political prisoners under both the Metaxas regime of the 1930s and the various right-wing governments that followed the civil war. It's still unusual for foreign travellers to visit the island, and, if you do, you might be asked why you've shown up.

You may initially ask yourself the same question, for **ÁYIOS EFSTRÁTIOS** village – the only habitation on the island – must be one of the ugliest in Greece. Devastation caused by an earthquake in February 1968, which killed half the population, was compounded by the reconstruction plan: the contract went to a company with junta connections, who prevented the survivors from returning to their old homes and used army bulldozers to raze even those structures that could have been repaired. From the hillside, some two dozen surviving houses of the old village overlook its replacement, whose grim rows of prefabs constitute a sad monument to the corruption of the junta years. If you're curious, there's a pre-earthquake photograph of the village in the *kafenío* by the port.

Architecture apart, Áyios Efstrátios still functions as a traditional fishing and farming community, with the prefabs set at the mouth of a wooded stream valley draining to the sandy harbour beach. Tourist amenities consist of just two basic **tavernas** (one operating July–Aug only), plus a total of three **pensions**. Best of these, in one of the surviving old houses, is the *Xenonas Aï-Stratis* (℡22540 93329; ❸); Andonis Paneras (℡22540 93209; ❸) and Apostolos Paneras (℡22540 93343; ❸) have more conventional **rooms** in the prefabs. These relatively stiff prices for such an out-of-the-way place reflect Aï Strátis' increasing popularity with Greeks, and you may have to ring all three spots for a vacancy in season.

As you walk away from the village – there are few cars and no real roads – things improve rapidly. The landscape, dry hills and valleys scattered with a surprising number of oak trees, is deserted apart from wild rabbits, sheep, an occasional shepherd, and some good beaches where you can camp in seclusion. **Alonítsi**, on the north coast – a ninety-minute walk from the village following a track up the north side of the valley – is a two-kilometre stretch of sand with rolling breakers and views across to Límnos.

South of the village, there's a series of greyish sand beaches, most with wells and drinkable water, although with few real paths in this part of the island, getting to them can be something of a scramble. **Lidharío**, at the end of an attractive wooded valley, is the first worthwhile beach, but again it's a ninety-minute walk, unless you can persuade a fisherman to take you by boat. Some of the caves around the coast are home to the rare Mediterranean monk seal, but you're unlikely to see one.

Ferries on the 2003-inaugurated Kavála–Límnos–Lávrio line call at Áyios Efstrátios three times weekly much of the year; in summer a small Límnos-based ferry, the *Aiolis*, sails every weekday (Mon–Fri) at 3pm from Límnos, returning the next morning. Despite recent harbour improvements, this is still a very exposed anchorage, and in bad weather you could end up stranded here far longer than you bargained for. If an indefinite stay does not appeal, it's best to visit from Límnos on the day-trip offered by the *Aiolis* (usually on Sun).

Samothráki (Samothrace)

Samothráki has one of the most dramatic profiles of all the Greek islands, second only to Thíra's: its dark mass of granite rises abruptly from the sea, culminating in the 1611-metre **Mount Fengári**. Seafarers have always been guided by its imposing outline, clearly visible from the mainland, and in legend its summit provided a vantage point for Poseidon to watch over the siege of Troy. The mostly forbidding coastline provides no natural anchorage, but in ancient times the island was colonized by settlers from Thrace, with more recent migrations from Anatolia and Lésvos swelling the population. Landing is still very much subject to the vagaries of the notoriously unpredictable weather, but it did not deter pilgrims who, for hundreds of years, journeyed to the island to visit the **Sanctuary of the Great Gods** and were initiated into its mysteries. The sanctuary remains the main archeological attraction of the island which, too remote for most tourists, combines earthy simplicity with natural grandeur. The tourist season is relatively short-lived – essentially (late) July and August – but you will find some facilities open as early as Easter and one or two all year round.

Kamariótissa

All ferries and hydrofoils dock at the dull village of **KAMARIÓTISSA**, where you're unlikely to want to spend much time. That said it could be your most convenient base, since some of Samothráki's best **hotels** lie along or just behind the tree-lined seafront and various **rooms** for rent, many of them more than acceptable, can be found in the maze of streets behind; owners often meet incoming vessels. As on most islands with a short season, accommodation can

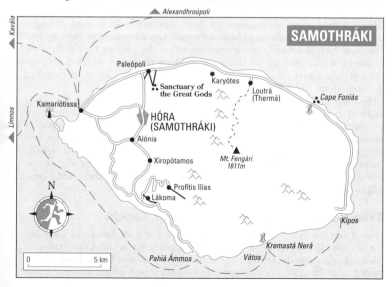

be pricey for what you get, and bargaining is not always productive, especially in midsummer. Along the shore, some way east of your point of arrival, is *Kyma* (☏25510 41263; ❸), where rooms overlooking the pebbly beach can get noise from the string of *barákia* that constitutes Samothráki's main nightlife; avoid the hotel restaurant – the taverna (see below) is much better. Calmer, but somewhat pricier, is the *Niki Beach* (☏25510 41561; ❹) beyond the far north end of the quay. Above, occupying a bluff and visible from out to sea, is the slightly impersonal *Aeolos* (☏25510 41595, ℻25510 41810; ❺); with a large pool and quiet, spacious rooms, it's the island's most comfortable accommodation and offers good half-board deals out of season. Bars and cafés on the harbourfront serve snacks and breakfasts, but the only commendable **taverna** is the *Limanaki*, at the southern end, beyond the docks: excellent Limniot wine from the barrel is perfect with the fish and seafood on offer, which you can virtually watch being unloaded by local fishermen as you order.

Motorbikes and **cars** are in short supply, so it's worth grabbing one immediately on disembarkation – or even reserving a bike in advance from Hanou Brothers (☏25510 41511) or a car from Niki Tours (☏25510 41465), which sells plane tickets as well; also try Kyrkos car rental (☏697 43 71 122). For information about and tickets for **ferries and hydrofoils**, a converted container opposite the docks acts as offices. A fairly reliable timetable for island **buses** is also posted here; these travel up to eight times daily in season (but only twice weekly in deepest winter) along the north coast to Loutrá (Thermá) via Paleópoli, near the site of the Sanctuary, or Karyótes, or directly inland seven times daily to the largest village, Hóra. As with lodging, rented transport is more expensive than on most islands, but if you've the means go for a car as Samothracian roads are often dangerously windswept for bikes. Note that there is currently only one fuel pump on the entire island, 1km above the port, en route to Hóra. Kamariótissa also has a **bank** with an ATM, but no post office.

Hóra

HÓRA, also known as **Samothráki**, is the island's capital. Far larger than implied by the portion visible from out at sea, it's an attractive town of Thracian-style stone houses, some of them whitewashed, clustered around a hollow in the western flanks of Mount Fengári. It is dominated by the Genoese Gateluzzi fort, of which little survives other than the gateway. Half an hour or so can be whiled away at the charming **folklore museum**, which is free, but the opening hours are erratic; it contains a motley collection of clothing, domestic items and miscellany.

Hóra has no reliable short-term accommodation, though asking for unadvertised rooms in the various *kafenía* along the winding commercial street can be productive. On the atmospheric, irregularly shaped *platía*, a couple of **tavernas**, *Iy Platia* and the more down-to-earth *To Kastro*, provide the best suppers on the island, with such delicacies as stuffed squid and *mýdhia saganáki* (mussels with cheese). There have been mutterings of moving the administrative capital down to Kamariótissa, but until further notice the island's **post office** is here.

The Sanctuary of the Great Gods

From Hóra it is 3km to the hamlet of Paleópoli (see p.442) and, in a stony but thickly wooded ravine between it and the plunging northwestern ridge of Mount Fengári, lie the remains of the **Sanctuary of the Great Gods**. Buses from Kamariótissa stop nearby, opposite a small car park on the seashore. From

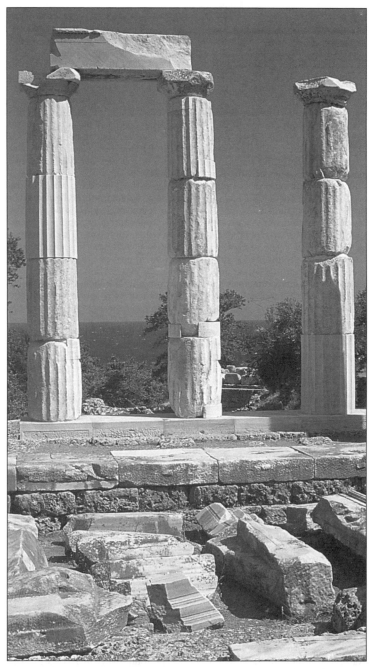

△ Sanctuary of the Great Gods, Samothráki

the late Bronze Age until the early Byzantine era, the mysteries and sacrifices of the cult of the Great Gods were performed on Samothráki, indeed in ancient Thracian dialect until the second century BC. The island was the spiritual focus of the northern Aegean, and its importance in the ancient world was comparable (although certainly secondary) to that of the Mysteries of Eleusis.

The religion of the Great Gods revolved around a hierarchy of ancient Thracian fertility figures: the Great Mother Axieros, a subordinate male deity known as Kadmilos, and the potent and ominous twin demons the Kabiroi, originally the local heroes Dardanos and Aeton. When the Aeolian colonists arrived (traditionally ca. 700 BC) they simply syncretized the resident deities with their own – the Great Mother became Cybele, her consort Hermes and the Kabiroi were fused interchangeably with the *Dioskouroi* Castor and Pollux, patrons of seafarers. Around the nucleus of a sacred precinct the newcomers made the beginnings of what is now the sanctuary.

Despite their long observance, the mysteries of the cult were never explicitly recorded, since ancient writers feared incurring the wrath of the Kabiroi (who could brew up sudden, deadly storms), but it has been established that two levels of initiation were involved. Both ceremonies, in direct opposition to the elitism of Eleusis, were open to all, including women and slaves. The lower level of initiation, or *myesis*, may, as is speculated at Eleusis, have involved a ritual simulation of the life, death and rebirth cycle; in any case, it's known that it ended with joyous feasting, and it can be conjectured, since so many clay torches have been found, that it took place at night. The higher level of initiation, or *epopteia*, carried the unusual requirement of a moral standard (the connection of theology with morality, so strong in the later Judeo-Christian tradition, was rarely made by the early Greeks). This second level involved a full confession followed by absolution and baptism in bull's blood.

The only **accommodation** near the sanctuary is in the tiny hamlet of **PALEÓPOLI**, where the old and basic *Xenia Hotel* (☎25510 41166 or 25510 41230; ❹) offers a downmarket alternative to the smart but overpriced *Kastro Hotel* (☎25510 89400, ⓦwww.kastrohotel.gr; ❺), which comes with pool, restaurant and sea views; there are also some basic but en-suite rooms (❸) down on the seashore below the *kástro*.

The site

The **site** (Tues–Sun 8.30am–8.30pm, or dusk if earlier; €3 combined ticket with museum but no charge for site when museum is closed) is well labelled, simple to grasp and strongly evokes its proud past, while commanding views of the mountains and the sea. You might like to visit the **archeological museum** first (Tues–Sun 8.30am–3pm), and its exhibits spanning all eras of habitation, from the Archaic to the Byzantine, since it explains the significance of the sanctuary. Highlights include a **frieze** of dancing girls from the *propylon* of the Temenos, entablatures from different buildings, and Roman votive offerings such as coloured glass vials from the necropolis of the ancient town east of the sanctuary. You can also see a reproduction of the exquisitely sculpted marble statue, the *Winged Victory of Samothrace*, which once stood breasting the wind at the prow of a marble ship in the Nymphaeum (see opposite). Discovered in 1863 by a French diplomat to the Sublime Porte it was carried off to the Louvre, where it is a major draw, and the well-crafted copy was graciously donated to this museum a mere century later.

The **Anaktoron**, or hall of initiation for the first level of the mysteries, dates in its present form from Roman times. Its inner sanctum was marked by a warning *stele*, now in the museum, and at the southeast corner you can make out the **Priestly Quarters**, an antechamber where candidates for initiation donned white gowns. Next to it is the **Arsinoeion**, the largest circular ancient building known in Greece, used for libations and sacrifices. Within its rotunda are the fourth-century-BC walls of a double precinct where a rock altar, the earliest preserved ruin on the site, has been uncovered. A little further south, on the same side of the path, you come to the **Temenos**, a rectangular area open to the sky where the feasting probably took place, and, edging its rear corner, the conspicuous **Hieron**, the site's most immediately impressive structure. Five columns and an architrave of the facade of this large Doric edifice, which hosted the higher level of initiation, have been re-erected; dating in part from the fourth century BC, it was heavily restored in Roman times. The stone steps have been replaced by modern blocks, but Roman benches for spectators remain *in situ*, along with the sacred stones where confession was heard. To the west of the path you can just discern the outline of the theatre, while just above it, tucked under the ridge is the **Nymphaeum (Fountain) of Nike**, which the *Winged Victory* used to preside over (see opposite). West of the theatre, occupying a high terrace, are remains of the main *stoa*; immediately north of this is an elaborate medieval fortification made entirely of antique material.

The north coast

With its running streams, giant plane trees and namesake hot springs, **LOUTRÁ** (aka **THERMÁ**), 6km east of Paleópoli, is a pleasant place to stay, although less so when it's packed in late July and August, mainly with an incongruous mixture of foreign hippies and elderly Greeks, here to take the sulphurous waters. You have a Hobson's choice of three facilities: the sterile, junta-era main baths (in theory, daily 8am–1pm & 5–7pm; often closed out of season; €3), the *psarováthres* or "fish ponds" – a trio of pleasantly rustic open-air pools with a wooden sun-shade, and a ramshackle hut with a very hot pool (keys from the warden of the main baths). These last two are free with no fixed opening hours, and they're reached by a dirt road starting above and to the right as you face the "improved" spa. For a cold-water but far more appealing contrast, the low waterfalls and rock pools of **Gría Váthra** are signposted 1.5km up the paved side road leading east from the main Thermá access drive.

Loutrá is also the prime base for the tough, six-hour climb up the 1611-metre **Mount Fengári** (known to the ancients as **Sáos**, a name found on some maps to this day), the highest peak in the Aegean islands; the path starts at the top of the village, beside a concrete water tank and a huge open-boled plane tree. Tell your accommodation proprietors that you're going, but no one else, as the police may try to stop you – army teams have been summoned on occasion to rescue ill-prepared climbers on what can be an unforgiving mountain. Fengári is Greek for "moon" and, according to legend, if you reach the top on the night of a full moon your wish will come true – most of those foolhardy enough to attempt this will just hope to get back down safely.

Loutrá is a rather dispersed place, with its winding dead-end streets, all ghostly quiet in winter, and its white-elephant miniharbour – built as an alternative to Kamariótissa, but never used. **Accommodation** includes the *Kaviros Hotel* (☎25510 98277; ❹), just east of the "centre", and, further downhill, 700m from the beach, the *Mariva Bungalows* (☎25510 98258; ❹). None of the tavernas is very inspired, a possible result (or cause) of a predominance in self-catering rooms; *Paradhisos* has the best setting, up under the trees, and charges accordingly. About halfway along the track to Gría Váthra, *Safki*, a summer-only café-bar, occupies the delightful old schoolhouse.

Beyond Loutrá and a ford, on the wooded coastline and reached by a road initially signposted "military camp", are two municipal **campsites**: the first, 1.5km from the village, although large, has no facilities except toilets, while the second, 3km from the village, is more expensive but has hot water, electricity, a small shop, restaurant and bar. The Loutrá bus sometimes goes to either site if you ask nicely.

Beaches on Samothráki's north shore are mostly clean but uniformly pebbly and exposed, but it's still worth continuing along the road east from Loutrá for the views and one or two minor sights. At **Cape Foniás** there's a ruined Gateluzzi watchtower and, 45 minutes' walk inland along the stream, there are **waterfalls** and cold pools much more impressive than those at Gría Váthra, though the sign-posted description of "canyon" is exaggerated. Some 15km from Loutrá along a fine corniche road is **Kípos beach**, a long strand facing the Turkish-held island of Gökçeada (Ímvros to the Greeks) and backed by open pasture and picturesque crags. The water is clean and there's a rock overhang for shelter at one end, a spring, shower and seasonal drinks *kantína*, but no food available.

The south coast

From the warmer south flank of the island, with its fertile farmland dotted with olive groves, there are fine views out to sea – as far as Gökçeada on a clear day. Up to three daily buses go from Kamariótissa via the sleepy village of Lákoma as far as **PROFÍTIS ILÍAS**, an attractive hill village with a number of good **tavernas** – the best being *Paradhisos*, with a wonderful terrace – but no accommodation to speak of, except for some basic **rooms** (❷). From Lákoma it is 8km east to aptly named **Pahiá Ámmos** ("coarse sand"), a long, clean beach with a taverna-rooms outfit (☎25510 94235; ❸) at the west end. The nearest (meagre) supplies are in Lákoma, but this doesn't deter big summer crowds who also arrive by excursion *kaïkia*. These also continue east to **Vátos**, a secluded and sometimes nudist beach also accessible by land, the **Kremastá Nerá** coastal waterfalls, and finally round to Kípos beach (see above).

Thássos

Just 12km from the mainland, **Thássos** has long been a popular resort island for northern Greeks, and since the early 1990s has also attracted a cosmopolitan variety of tourists, in particular Romanians, Serbs, Bulgarians and Hungarians holidaying a tank or so of petrol away from home, plus plenty of the usual Germans and Brits on packages. Although far from unspoiled – vast numbers of rural *bouzoúkia* (music halls) and tavernas lay on music at weekends with cheer-ful vulgarity – it has, however, some areas of outstanding natural beauty, espe-cially inland, and the island's ordinary rural industries have somehow managed to survive. Thássos still makes a substantial living from the pure-white marble that constitutes two-thirds of the landmass, found only here and quarried at dozens of sites (legal and unlicensed) in the hills between Liménas and Panayía. Olives, honey, fruit and nuts (often sold candied) are also important products. The spirit *tsípouro*, rather than wine, is the main local tipple; pear extract, onions or spices like cinnamon and anise are added to home-made batches.

Inhabited since the Stone Age, Thássos was settled by Parians in the seventh century BC, attracted by gold deposits between modern Liménas and Kínyra. Buoyed by revenues from these, and from silver mines under Thassian control on the mainland opposite, the ancient city-state here became the seat of a medium-sized seafaring empire. Commercial acumen did not spell military invincibility however; the Persians under Darius swept the Thassian fleets from the seas in 492 BC, and in 462 BC Athens permanently deprived Thássos of its autonomy after a three-year siege. The main port continued to thrive into Roman times, but lapsed into Byzantine and medieval obscurity.

Sadly, the salient fact of more recent history has been a series of devastating, deliberately set **fires** in the 1980s and 1990s; the worst one, in 1989, began near Rahóni and burned for three days as far as Mariés. Only the northeastern quadrant of the island, plus the area around Astrís and Alykí, escaped, though the surviving forest is still home to numerous pine martens.

Thássos is just small enough to circumnavigate in one full day on a rented motorbike or car. The KTEL will do the driving for you – albeit with little chance for stopping – some four times daily. **Car rental** is dominated by Potos Car Rental (℡ 25930 23969), with branches in all main resorts, or Rent-a-Car Thassos (℡ 25930 22535), also widely represented, as are most of the major international chains, such as Budget at Theayénous 2 in the capital, **Liménas** (℡ 25930 23050). Vigorous bargaining with the local one-off outfits is often productive of 35-percent discounts on official rates – particularly in early June or mid-September. On the other hand, don't bother showing up in Thássos much before or after these dates, as most facilities will be shut, and the weather can be dodgy in any case. Most hotels are closed between October and the end of April, so call ahead to check.

Liménas

Largely modern **LIMÉNAS** (also signposted as Limín or Thássos) is the island's capital, though not the only port. Kavála-based ferries stop down the coast at Skála Prínou, with a KTEL bus always on hand to meet arrivals. At first glance Liménas seems an unlikely resort, plagued as it is with surprisingly clogged vehicle traffic and often noisy bars, but it is partly redeemed by its picturesque fishing harbour and the substantial remains of the ancient city which appear above and below the streets.

With its mineral wealth and safe harbour, **ancient Thassos** prospered from Classical to Roman times. The largest excavated area is the agora, a little way back from the fishing harbour. The site (free) is fenced but not always locked, and is most enjoyably seen towards dusk. Two Roman *stoas* are prominent, but you can also make out shops, monuments, passageways and sanctuaries from the remodelled Classical city. At the far end of the site (away from the sea) a fifth-century-BC passageway leads through to an elaborate sanctuary of Artemis, a substantial stretch of Roman road and a few seats of the *odeion*. The nearby archeological museum is closed indefinitely for extensive expansion.

From a **temple of Dionysos** behind the fishing port, a path curls up to a **Hellenistic theatre**, fabulously positioned above a broad sweep of sea. It's

LIMÉNAS (THÁSSOS TOWN)

ACCOMMODATION

Akropolis	G
Alkyon	C
Amfipolis	A
Athanasia	F
Filoxenia Inn	B
Kipos Studios	D
Lena	E
Myroni & Victoria	H

RESTAURANTS AND BARS

Full Moon	4
Marina's Bar	8
To Perastikon	6
Iy Piyi	7
Platanos	3
Platia Cafe	5
Simi	2
Syrtaki	1

N

Town Beach

Ancient Port (Limenáki)

Ancient Theatre

RO-RO Ferry Dock

Hydrofoil Berth

Taxi Stand

Museum (shut)

Temple of Dionysos

Artemis Shrine

MAIN PLATIA

Byzantine Basilica

Agora

Castle & Apollo Temple

ACROPOLIS

Natural Spring

Temple of Athena Polyouhos

Irakleio

Shrine of Pan

Skála Prínou & Nystéri

Gate of Zeus & Hera

Gate of Hercules

Gate of Silenos

Gate of Parmenon

0   200 m

Panayía & Alykí

currently open, but is a chaos of excavation, with summer-festival performances set to resume in the distant future. On the same corner of the headland as the theatre, you can still see the old-fashioned *kaïkia* being built, and gaze across to the uninhabited islet of Thassopoúla. It's possible to rent boats from the fishing harbour, self-skippered or not, to take you there and elsewhere.

From just before the theatre, the trail winds on to the **acropolis**, where a Venetian-Byzantine-Genoese fort arose between the thirteenth and fifteenth centuries, constructed from recycled masonry of an Apollo temple which stood here. You can continue, following the remains of a massive circuit of fifth-century walls to a high terrace supporting the foundations of the Athena Polyouhos (Athena Patroness of the City) temple, with Cyclopean walls. An artificial cavity in the rock outcrop just beyond was a shrine of Pan, shown in faint relief playing his pipes. From behind the summit, a rock-hewn stairway provided a discreet escape route to the Gate of Parmenon, the only gate in the fortifications to have retained its lintel; it's named from an ancient inscription ("Parmenon Made Me") on a nearby wall slab. From here a track, then a paved lane descend through the southerly neighbourhoods of the modern town, for a satisfying one-hour circuit.

Practicalities
Given the cheap-and-cheerful-package ethos, cuisine is not Liménas's strong point, and eateries are generally overpriced. The picturesque **tavernas** around the old harbour are predictably touristy – sophisticated *Simi* is marginally the best, and serves memorably good wine. Another good option is *Syrtaki*, at the far eastern end of the overly popular town beach. In the town centre, greasy fast food is all too abundant, though a dependable favourite for *mayireftá* is *Iy Piyi*, up at the south corner of the main square, next to the natural sunken spring of the name. *Platanos*, with a pleasant terrace opposite the ferry docks, is the place to head for breakfast, be it English style or ambrosia-like yogurt and honey, and its coffee is highly drinkable. Finally, *To Perastikon* at the northwest corner of the square near *Iy Piyi*, serves the best ice cream on the island. By contrast, there's plenty of choice in local **bars**: *Full Moon* near the *Hotel Amfipolis* is the main Anglophile watering-hole, and comes with a paperback-swap library. *Platia Cafe Bar* on yet another corner of the basilica square, has good music, while *Marina's Bar* near the *Hotel Alkyon* is the best waterfront nightspot, attracting a mainly Greek clientele.

Mountain and motorbikes can be rented from Billy's Bikes (☎25930 22490), Thomai Tsipou (☎25930 22815) or Babis (☎25930 22129). The KTEL office is on the front, virtually opposite the ferry mooring; the service is good, with several daily **buses** to Panayía and Skála Potamiás, Limenária via Potós, Theológos, Kínyra and Alykí. The **taxi** rank is just in front of the bus stop. Thassos Tours (☎25930 23250), at the east end of the waterfront, is the principal airline agent (the closest airport is at Kavála). Several **banks** have ATMs.

Accommodation
Few **hotels** enjoy any calm or decent views but there are some worthy finds; if none from the list below suits, there are also areas in the southwest of town, and some relatively quiet rooms (②–③) just behind the town beach. Note that most of the town hotels are shut from October to early May. The closest **campsite** to town is at Nystéri cove, 2.5km west; the beach is reasonable, and its snack-bar has tables out on a lawn, but the site is small, basic and on hard ground.

See the map opposite for the locations of the following listings; there are no formal addresses here.

Akropolis ☎ 25930 22488, ⓕ 25930 22441.
Occupying a fine traditional house with flagstone
floors and a rear garden-bar, though it can get
traffic noise; worth a try now that package companies don't use it. ❸

Alkyon ☎ 25930 22148, ⓕ 25930 23662. Certainly
the most pleasant of the harbour hotels; English tea
and breakfast, plus friendly, voluble management
make it a home from home for independent British
travellers. Open most of the year; ask also about
their cottage in Sotíras and beach villa at Astrís. ❸

Amfipolis ☎ 25930 23101, ⓕ 25930 22110.
Housed in a folly, this atmospheric hotel is the
town's most exclusive accommodation outfit – and
you pay dearly for the privilege; it has a stylish
drinks terrace. ❺

Athanasia ☎ 25930 23247. Giant and eccentrically furnished rooms with balconies; take the lane
inland from behind the *Xenia Hotel* to reach it. Run
by a friendly fisherman, this place takes the overflow from the *Alkyon.* ❷

Filoxenia Inn ☎ 25930 23331, ⓕ 25930 22231.
Quietly situated behind the archeological museum,
this has immaculate rooms with fridges, designated breakfast areas and a garden with a small
pool. ❹

Kipos Studios ☎ 25930 22469. In a quiet cul-de-
sac next to *Iy Piyi* taverna, this has cool lower-
ground-floor doubles (❸) and four-person galleried apartments of a fair standard (❹); a pool
has been installed in the garden, ostensibly to
make the premises attractive to package companies.

Lena ☎ 25930 23565. Good-value hotel, lightly
refurbished in 1998, near the post office, with
English-speaking management; no packages. ❷

Myroni ☎ 25930 23 256, ⓕ 25930 22132.
Excellent value, well run and allergic to package
companies. It's co-managed with the more modest
(no air con) *Victoria* (☎ 25930 23556; ❸) next
door, with which it shares a common breakfast
room. ❹

Around the coast

Whether you plan to circumnavigate the island clockwise, or in the opposite
direction, plan on a lunch stop at **Alykí**, roughly a third of the way along in
the circuit described below, and the most photogenic spot along the coast.

Panayía, Potamiá and Mount Ipsárion

The first beach east of Liménas, **Makrýammos**, is a purpose-built,
controlled-access compound for package tourists, so carry on to **PANAYÍA**,
the attractive hillside village overlooking Potamiá Bay. It's a large, thriving place
where life revolves around the central square with its large plane trees, fountain and slate-roofed houses. Top **accommodation** choice in both senses is
the *Hotel Thassos Inn* (☎ 25930 61612, ⓕ 25930 61027; ❹), up in the Tris Piyés
district near the Kímisis church, with fine views over the rooftops. Down on
the main road, beside the municipal car park, the newish, clean *Pension Stathmos*
(☎ 25930 61666; ❸) is the quietest of several nearby, with stunning views out
the back; there are also high-standard rooms (☎ 25930 61981; ❷) below the
school basketball courts. There have been complaints about high-pressure
touting tactics from the hotly competing tavernas on the square; for a more
low-key approach, try *Iy Thea*, a view-terrace *pistariá* at the southeast edge of
town en route to Potamiá.

POTAMIÁ, much lower down in the river valley, is far less prepossessing –
with modern red tiles instead of slates on the roofs – and thus little visited,
though it has a lively winter carnival. It also offers the **Polygnotos Vayis
Museum** (Tues–Sat 9.30am–12.30pm, summer also 6–9pm, Sun 10am–1pm;
free), devoted to the locally born sculptor; though Vayis emigrated to America
when young, he bequeathed most of his works to the Greek state. Potamiá also
marks the start of the preferred route up to the 1204-metre summit of **Mount
Ipsárion**. Follow the bulldozer track to the big spring near the head of the
valley extending west of the village (the last source of water), where you'll see
the first red-painted arrows on trees. Beyond this point, cairns mark the
correct turnings in a modern track system; forty minutes above the spring, take

an older, wide track, which ends ten minutes later at a narrow ravine with a stream and the current trailhead. The path is steep, strenuous and unmaintained, and you'll be dependent on cairns and painted arrows. Go early in the day or season, and allow four hours up from Potamiá, and nearly as much for the descent.

Skála Potamiás and Khryssí Ammoudhiá

The onward road from Potamiá is lined with *dhomátia-* and apartment-type accommodation. A side road some 12km from Liménas takes you down to **SKÁLA POTAMIÁS**, at the southern end of the bay, where some fairly uninspired **tavernas** line the harbour front; a road off to the left brings you to sand dunes extending all the way to the far northern end of the bay. An honourable exception amongst the tavernas is *Flor International* (no sign), at the corner where the bus (hourly 7am–8pm to Liménas) turns around; the *Afrodite*, a short way along, is also acceptable for *mayireftá*. Worth a mention also is *Eric's Bar* on the main road just outside the village, where one Stratos Papafilippou has made a career of his uncanny resemblance to footballer Eric Cantona; full English breakfast is available, you can watch Premiership matches on satellite TV and there is now also a heated outdoor swimming pool.

The best places to **stay** are either above the plane-shaded traffic turnaround area by the port, beyond the tavernas – where the *Hera* (☎25930 61467; ❷), just on the left looking inland, or the *Delfini* (☎25930 61275; ❷), 200m straight back, are peaceful but basic – or, if you're prepared to pay rather more, there's the *Miramare* (☎25930 77209; ❹), which has a swimming pool among well-manicured gardens, further up the same lane. Alternatively, head north along the shore towards the sandy beach, for **rooms** (❷–❸), to either side of the *Arion* (☎25930 61486; ❸) and *Anna* (☎25930 61070; ❷) hotels, which represent the best value hereabouts. The north end of this beach is called **Khryssí Ammoudhiá** ("golden sands"), an increasingly chaotic, built-up cluster of tavernas, hotels and a campsite; a direct road (plied by an infrequent bus service) spirals for 5km down from Panayía. Once there, you can choose between the self-catering *Villa Emerald* (☎25930 61979; ❹) or the *Golden Sand* (☎25930 61771 or 25930 61209; ❸), nearer the sands. The *Golden Beach* campsite (☎25930 61472) is the only official one on this side of the island.

Kínyra and Alykí

The dispersed hamlet of **KÍNYRA**, some 24km south of Liménas, marks the start of the burnt zone which overlooks it, though incipient greenery suggests that recovery is underway; it's endowed with a poor beach, a couple of grocery stores and several small hotels. Those not block-booked include *Villa Athina* (☎25930 41214; ❶) at the north end of things, whose top-floor rooms see the water over the olive trees, and the welcoming *Pension Marina* (☎25930 31384; ❶). *Yiorgos* and *Faros* are the best tavernas here. Kínyra is convenient for the superior **beaches** of Loutroú (1km south) and partly nudist Paradise (3km along) – officially called Makrýammos Kinýron – both of which can be reached down poorly signposted dirt tracks. The latter ranks as most scenic of all Thassian beaches, with still-forested cliffs inland and a namesake islet offshore beyond the extensive shallows, with much cleaner water than at Khryssí Ammoudhiá, though a couple of ugly buildings have sprung up over the past few years. A couple of mediocre snack-bars behind the sand overcharge bathers.

The south-facing coast of Thássos has the balance of the island's best beaches. **ALYKÍ** hamlet, 35km from Liménas and just below the main road, faces a perfect double bay which almost pinches off a headland. Alone of Thassian seaside settlements, it retains its original whitewashed, slate-roofed architecture, because the presence of extensive antiquities here has led to a ban on any modern construction. The ruins include an ancient temple to an unknown deity, and two exquisite early-Christian basilicas out on the headland, with a few columns re-erected. The sand-and-pebble west bay gets oversubscribed in peak season, though you can always head off to the less crowded, rocky east cove, or snorkel in the crystal-clear waters off the marble formations on the headland's far side. Dominating the western inlet on the roadward side, well-established **taverna** *Glaros* serves fresh fish and has decent **rooms** (❸) to let. A lively bar and a row of water-edge tavernas also compete for your custom, with *To Limanaki/The Little Mole* winning, if only for its more varied menu – it also tends to open earlier in the year than the others. One kilometre further along the coast, at secluded **Kékes** beach among a pine grove, traditional taverna *Skidhia* also has **rooms** in plain but comfortable bungalows, with air-conditioning and en-suite bathrooms (☎25930 31528; ❸).

Arhangélou Mihaïl to Potós

Some 5km west of Alykí, the **convent of Arhangélou Mihaïl** (open reasonable daylight hours) clings spectacularly to a cliff on the seaward side of the road. Though founded in the twelfth century above the spot where a spring had gushed forth, it has been hideously renovated by the nuns, resident here since 1974; its prize relic is a purported nail from the Crucifixion.

At the extreme south tip of Thássos, 9km further west, **ASTRÍS** (Astrídha) can muster two uninspiring medium-sized hotels, a few rooms and a good beach. Just 1km west is another better but crowded beach, Psilí Ámmos, with watersports on offer. A few kilometres further, **POTÓS** is the island's prime Germanophone package venue, its centre claustrophobically dense, with the few non-block-booked rooms overlooking cramped alleys. However, the kilometre-long beach is still unspoilt. For a less touristy place to eat, the **taverna** *Piatsa*, one of the cheaper and better places, is tucked away at the southern end of the seafront, in a semi-pedestrianized street; next door, *Michael's Place* has great ice cream and breakfasts. Along the harbourfront a string of varyingly trendy **bars and cafés** offer viable alternatives. There are plenty of rental outlets for **cars**, scooters and mountain bikes, including the headquarters of Potos Rent a Car. **Pefkári** with its manicured beach and namesake pine-grove, 1km west, is essentially an annexe of Potós, with a few mid-range **accommodation** options such as *Prasino Veloudho* (☎25930 52001, ℻25930 51232; ❸) and the rather more upmarket *Thassos* (☎25930 51596, ℻25930 51794; ❹). The **campsite**, *Pefkari* (☎25930 51190; June–Sept), with its attractive wooded location and clean facilities, is one of the best on Thássos.

Limenária and the west coast

LIMENÁRIA, the island's second town, was built to house German mining executives brought in by the Ottomans between 1890 and 1905. Their remaining mansions, scattered on the slopes above the harbour, lend some character, but despite attempts at prettifying the waterfront, it's not the most attractive place on Thássos, though it is handy for its **banks** and ATMs, **post office** and seasonal hydrofoil connections. The best **accommodation**, should you take a shine to the place, is the hotel *George* (☎25930 51413, ℻25930 52530; ❹), a relative newcomer with bright and modern rooms at the lower end of the main street leading down to the harbourfront. At the east end of the quay, in some 1960s blocks, are a cluster of very basic hotels such as the *Sgouridis*

(☎25930 51241; ❸). There are also plenty of **rooms** on offer (❷–❸). For eating and drinking, choose from among half-a-dozen each of bars and eateries along the front, of which *Mouragio* is the only one that comes close to having some charm.

The nearest good beach is **Trypití**, a couple of kilometres west – turn left into the pines at the start of a curve right. All development – mostly package villas – is well inland from the broad, 800-metre long strand, although there are umbrellas and sun loungers for rent. The cleft which the name refers to (literally "pierced" in Greek) is a slender tunnel through the headland at the west end of the beach, leading to a tiny three-boat anchorage.

Continuing clockwise from Limenária to Liménas, there's progressively less to stop off for as the western coast is the most exposed and scenically least impressive. The various *skáles* such as Skála Kaliráhis and Skála Sotíros – originally the ports for namesake inland villages – are bleak, straggly and windy. **Skála Marión**, 13km from Limenária, is the exception that proves the rule: an attractive little bay, with fishing boats hauled up on the sandy foreshore, and the admittedly modern low-rise village arrayed in a U-shape all around. There are **rooms** available (❷–❸), a few tavernas and, most importantly, two fine beaches on either side. **Skála Prínou** has little to recommend it, other than ferry connections to Kavála. Buses are usually timed to coincide with the ferries, but if you want to stay, there are several hotels, numerous rooms, quayside tavernas and an EOT **campsite** (☎25930 71171; June–Sept) 1km south of the ferry dock. **Skála Rahoníou**, between here and Liménas, has more accommodation (including the *Perseus* campsite) and fish restaurants, as well as proximity to **Pahýs beach**, 9km short of Liménas, by far the best strand on the northwest coast. Narrow dirt tracks lead past various tavernas through surviving pines to the sand, partly shaded in the morning.

The interior

Few people get around to exploring inland Thássos – with the post-fire scrub still barely chest-high, it's not always rewarding – but there are several worthwhile excursions to or around the **hill villages**, besides the aforementioned trek up Mount Ipsárion from Potamiá (see p.448).

From Potós you can head 10km along a well-surfaced but poorly signposted road to **THEOLÓGOS**, founded in the sixteenth century by refugees from Constantinople and the island's capital under the Ottomans. Its houses, most with oversized chimneys and slate roofs, straggle in long tiers to either side of the main street, surrounded by generous kitchen gardens or walled courtyards. A stroll along the single high street, with its couple of *kafenía*, a soldiers' bar, sandalmaker and traditional bakery, is rewarding and quickly dispels the off-putting effect of vigorous advertising at the outskirts for "Greek Nights" at local tavernas. Two that eschew musical gimmicks and rely on their good fare are the long-running *Psistaria Lambiris*, at the entrance into town, and *Kleoniki/Tou Iatrou*, in the very centre, on the right-hand side past the bus stop and police station. They're at their best in the evening when the *soúvles*, loaded with goat and suckling pig, start turning.

Despite its proximity as the crow flies, there's no straightforward way from Theológos to **KÁSTRO**, the most naturally protected of the anti-pirate redoubts; especially with a car, it's best to descend to Potós before heading up a rough, seventeen-kilometre dirt track from Limenária. Thirty ancient houses and a church surround a rocky pinnacle, fortified by the Byzantines and the Genoese, which has a sheer drop on three sides. Summer occupation by shepherds is becoming the norm after total abandonment in the nineteenth century, when mining jobs at Limenária proved irresistible. There's only one *kafenío* on the ground floor of the former school, one telephone therein, no mains electricity and far more sheep than people.

From Skála Marión an unmarked but paved road (slipping under the main highway bridge to the north) proceeds 11km inland through gnarled old olive trees, to well-preserved **MARIÉS** at the top of a wooded stream valley; of two tavernas here, the well-signed one to the right, *Bethel*, is more of a going concern. From Skála Sotíros, a very steep road heads 3.5km up to **SOTÍRAS**, the only interior village with an unobstructed view of sunset over the Aegean and thus popular with foreigners, who've bought up about half of the houses for restoration. On the ridge opposite are exploratory shafts left by the miners, whose ruined lodge looms above the church. On the plane-shaded square below the old fountain, *O Platanos* taverna is congenially run by Maria and Manolis, who offer grills plus one *mayireftá* dish-of-the-day, good bulk wine and sometimes their potent, home-made *tsípouro*, but only in July and August.

From Prínos (Kalýves) on the coast road, you've a six-kilometre journey inland to the Kazavíti villages, shrouded in greenery that escaped the fires; they're (poorly) signposted and mapped officially as Megálo and Mikró Prínos but still universally known by their Ottoman name. **MIKRÓ KAZAVÍTI** marks the start of the track south for the convent of Ayíou Pandeleímonos, and **MEGÁLO KAZAVÍTI**, 1km beyond, was once the architectural showcase of the island, a fact apparently lost on many of the outsiders who bought holiday homes here and proceeded to carry out appalling renovations, though thankfully some have been done well. On the magnificent *platía*, arguably the prettiest spot on the whole island, are a couple of decent, normal-priced **tavernas**, while *Vassilis*, below in a beautifully restored house, is regarded as a cut above. Some 4km up from its *skála*, **RAHÓNI** is well set at the head of its denuded valley, paired with the small village of Áyios Yeóryios across the way. The road up to the square has plenty of simple tavernas, for example *Iy Dhrosia*.

Travel details

Ferries

To simplify the lists that follow we've excluded two regular sailings in a generally north-to-south route. These are the weekly DANE sailing between Rhodes, Kós, Sámos and Thessaloníki (23hr for the full run, usually over the weekend), and the GA sailing linking Alexandhroúpoli with Límnos, Lésvos, Híos, Sámos, Kós and Rhodes (one-way trip through all ports, again over the weekend, total journey 30hr).

We've also omitted the more convoluted middle-distance schedules kept by the small ferries of Miniotis Lines, based on Híos. These slow and often tardy craft link Híos with Sámos (both northern ports) twice a week year-round, currently Wed & Sun, returning Thurs, & either Sun or Mon. Twice weekly (Thurs & either Sun or Mon, then Mon & Fri), they venture from Sámos (Karlóvassi

or Vathý) to Foúrni and Ikaría (Áyios Kírykos) and back.

Áyios Efstrátios 3 weekly on the *Nissos Limnos* to Límnos, Lávrio and Kavála; 5 weekly by small local ferry to Límnos.

Foúrni 2–3 weekly ferries to Sámos (northern ports), Náxos, Páros and Pireás; 2 weekly to Pátmos, Kós, Rhodes, spring/autumn only; morning *kaïki* to Ikaría on Mon, Wed & Fri; twice weekly (usually Mon & Thurs) morning *kaïki* to Karlóvassi (Sámos).

Híos 11–12 weekly on NEL Lines to Pireás (10hr slow ferry, 4hr high-speed) and Lésvos (3hr 30min/1hr 30min); 2 weekly to Límnos on NEL, usually with a long layover at Mytilíni; 1 weekly to Sámos on NEL. Daily 2pm *kaïki* to Inoússes except Sun morning, and Tues in off-season; 3 weekly on Miniotis Lines – usually Mon, Wed, Fri – from Híos Town to Psará (3hr 30min), 3 weekly on Miniotis from Limniá to Psará, usually Tues, Fri, Sat pm (1hr 30min).

Ikaría At least daily from either Áyios Kírykos or Évdhilos to Sámos (both northern ports) and Pireás, on Hellas Ferries, GA or NEL's catamaran; 3 weekly to Foúrni, Mýkonos and Sýros from Áyios Kírykos on GA; almost daily to Náxos & Páros from Évdhilos or Áyios Kírykos (NEL catamaran or Hellas Ferries); 2 weekly to Rhodes, Kós, Pátmos from Áyios Kírykos, spring/autumn only; daily *kaïki* from Áyios Kírykos to Foúrni; 3 weekly *kaïkia*, usually Mon, Wed & Fri mornings, from Manganítis to Áyios Kírykos.

Lésvos 11–12 weekly on NEL Lines from Mytilíni to Pireás (11hr direct, 13hr 30min via Híos, 7hr 30min high-speed; 16hr 30min via Mýkonos/Sýros); 9–11 weekly to Híos (3hr 30min, or 1hr 30min high-speed); 2 weekly to Límnos (6hr); 2 weekly to Thessaloníki (14hr); 1–2 weekly to Kavála on NEL (12hr); 1 weekly (July–Aug only) to Mýkonos on NEL; 1 weekly to Sámos on NEL (7hr); 1 weekly to Límnos, Skópelos, Skiáthos and Vólos on GA.

Limnos 3–4 weekly on NEL Lines to Lésvos (Mytilíni); 2 weekly to Kavála, 3 weekly to Lávrio, 1 weekly to Alexandhroúpoli and Samothráki direct on the *Nissos Limnos*; 3 weekly to Kavála on NEL; 2 weekly to Thessaloníki, Pireás and Híos on NEL; 1 weekly to Lésvos, Skópelos, Skiáthos, Vólos on GA.

Sámos (Karlóvassi) As for Vathý, but no NEL catamaran service; also 2 weekly *kaïki* departures, usually early Mon & Thurs afternoon, to Foúrni.

Sámos (Pythagório) 3 weekly (Wed, Fri & Sun afternoon) with the *Nissos Kalymnos* to Agathónissi, Arkí, Lipsí, Pátmos, Léros and Kálymnos, with onward connections to all other Dodecanese (see p.372 for the full schedule).

Sámos (Vathý) 1–2 daily, on GA or Hellas Ferries, to Ikaría (Áyios Kírykos or Évdhilos) and Pireás (13–14hr); almost daily to Páros & Náxos, either on NEL high-speed boat or GA conventional ferry; 3 weekly to Pireás by NEL high-speed boat (6hr 30min), 1 weekly direct on NEL conventional boat; 3 weekly to Foúrni on GA; 2–3 weekly to Mýkonos and Sýros on GA; 1–2 weekly to Pátmos and occasionally Lipsí on Hellas Ferries.

Samothráki 2–3 daily ferries to/from Alexandhroúpoli (2hr 30min) in season, dropping to 5–6 weekly out of season. Also 2 weekly late spring & early autumn, up to 3 weekly in July & Aug, to Kavála (and thence other north Aegean islands). Also during July & Aug, 1 weekly (usually Fri) direct to Límnos.

Thássos At least 7 ferries daily, in summer months only (1 daily Oct–May), between Kavála

and Skála Prínou (1hr 15min; 8am–8pm, 6am–7pm to Kavála from the island); 10 daily all year round between Keramotí and Liménas (40min; 7am–10pm, 6am–8.30pm from Thássos).

Hydrofoils

Just one company, Kyriakoulis Maritime, operates in the east Aegean. Based on Sámos and Kós, this offers (late May to late Sept) nearly daily early morning service from Pythagório to Pátmos, Lipsí, Léros, Kálymnos and Kós (in the Dodecanese), returning from Kós in the late afternoon, and conversely morning service from Kós through the same ports, returning from Pythagório at mid-afternoon. Ikaría (Áyios Kírykos) and Foúrni are called at twice weekly, with Agathónissi served just once weekly. From Easter to mid-May, and late Sept to late Oct, official frequencies fall to 4–5 weekly morning departures to the Dodecanese cited, with perhaps 3–4 afternoon departures (but Foúrni/Ikaría are still served twice weekly, and Agathoníssi once).

Samothráki Served by hydrofoil from Alexandhroúpoli April–Nov 4–7 times weekly, usually at 8am (1hr); mid-June to mid-Sept there are 1–2 extra daily departures at 1 and/or 5pm. 2–4 times weekly the morning or early afternoon sailing may continue on to Límnos, but don't rely on this.

Thássos (Liménas) Used to be served all year by hydrofoils from Kavála, but the service is now limited to the summer: 8–15 times daily, 7am–9pm (6am–8pm from Thássos); in the high season there may also be 2–3 daily departures from Kavála to the west-coast resorts of Skála Kaliráhon, Skála Marión and Limenária.

International ferries

Híos–Çeşme (Turkey) 2–13 boats weekly, depending on season. Spring/autumn, about 7 weekly; Thurs evening (Turkish boat) & Sat morning (Greek boat) services tend to run year-round. Passenger fares on the Greek boat (Psara, Miniotis Lines) are €39 one-way, €49 open return (no day-return fare), including Greek taxes; no Turkish taxes. Small cars €70 one way, €110 return, plus small Greek tax. Turkish boat (typically *Ertürk II*) is usually cheaper going from Híos, at €28 one-way, €35 return, Greek taxes inclusive. Small cars €60 one way, €80 return. There are reports of reciprocal tickets between the two lines – ie leave with one company, return with the other – but given the difference in ticket prices this information should be treated cautiously. Journey time 45min.

Mytilíni (Lésvos)–Ayvalık (Turkey) 4–8 weekly May–Oct; winter link unreliable. A single Turkish craft, the *Jale*, departs Mytilíni 8–8.30am most days; there may also be an evening trip Tues, Thurs & Sat in summer. Passenger rates €39 one-way or round-trip, all taxes inclusive. Small cars (the *Jale* carries two) €60 each way. Journey time 1hr 20min.

Vathý (Sámos)–Kuşadası (Turkey) At least 1 daily, late April to late Oct; otherwise a small Turkish boat only by demand in winter, usually Fri or Sat. Greek boat at 8am, 4–5 weekly (passengers only); afternoon (4.45pm) Turkish boats (usually 2 daily in season). Rates are €39 one-way including taxes on both the Greek and Turkish sides, €53 open return; no day-return rate. As of writing the Turkish ferries on this route are not allowed to carry cars between the two countries owing to deficient liability insurance. 2–3 times weekly, there are excursions direct from Pythagório to Kuşadası. Journey time 1hr 30min.

Flights

NB: All flights on Olympic Airways/Aviation unless otherwise specified. Frequencies are for the period May–Oct only.

Híos to: Athens (4 daily on Olympic, 2 daily on Aegean; 50min); Límnos (2 weekly, both via Lésvos; 1hr 35min); Rhodes (2 weekly, 1 via Sámos; 55min–1hr 45min); Thessaloníki (4 weekly, 1 via Lésvos/Límnos; 1hr 10min–2hr 45min).

Lésvos to: Athens (4 daily on Olympic, 3 daily on Aegean; 1hr); to Límnos (5 weekly; 40min); Rhodes (5 weekly, 2 via Híos/Sámos; 1hr 5min–1hr 40min); Thessaloníki (1 daily, sometimes via Límnos, on Olympic; 1 daily direct on Aegean; 1hr 10min–1hr 50min).

Límnos to: Athens (2 daily; 1hr); Lésvos (5 weekly; 35min); Rhodes (5 weekly, 2 via Híos/Sámos; 2hr 5min–2hr 50min); Thessaloníki (4 weekly; 45min).

Sámos to: Athens (3–4 daily; 1hr); Rhodes (2 weekly; 45min); Lésvos (2 weekly, 1 via Híos; 50min–1hr 30min); Límnos (2 weekly, via Lésvos/Híos; 1hr 35min–1hr 55min); Thessaloníki (3 weekly direct; 1hr 20min).

6

The Sporades and Évvia

Highlights

✳ **Lalária beach, Skiáthos** A beautiful beach of smooth white stones, with steep cliffs rising behind it. See p.463

✳ **Skópelos Town** One of the prettiest towns in the Sporades. See p.464

✳ **Glóssa** An unspoilt, authentic Greek town, set high above the port of Loutráki. See p.468

✳ **Skýros** Only recently "discovered" by tourism, this is one of the most traditional islands in the Aegean. See p.472

✳ **The goat dance, Skýros** One of Greece's liveliest and most outrageous festivals. See p.473

✳ **The convent of Ayíou Nikoláou Galatáki** One of Évvia's monastic treasures, decorated with vivid sixteenth-century frescoes. See p.485

✳ **Loutrá Edhipsoú** Greece's biggest spa town, with plenty of Belle Époque hotels (many well restored) to marvel at. See p.487

△ Looking over Skýros Town

6

The Sporades and Évvia

The three northern **Sporades**, Skiáthos, Skópelos and Alónnisos, are scattered (as their Greek name suggests) just off the mainland, their mountainous terrain betraying their origin as extensions of Mount Pílio in Thessaly. They are archetypal holiday islands, with a wide selection of good beaches, transparent waters and thick pine forests. All are very crowded in season, with Skiáthos attracting by far the most package tours. **Skiáthos** has the best beaches, and is still the busiest island in the group, though these days **Skópelos** gets very crowded, too. The quietest of the three, **Alónnisos** also has the wildest scenery, so it's really more for nature lovers than night-owls.

Skýros, the most remote of the Sporades island group and further southeast, retains more of its traditional culture than the other three islands, though development is now well underway. The largest town doesn't yet feel like a resort, but its main street is not without its fast-food and souvenir shops. Unlike on the other three islands, the best beaches are those closest to the main town. Southwest of Skýros, the huge island of **Évvia** (or Euboea) runs for 150km alongside the mainland. It is one of the most attractive Greek islands, with a forested mountain spine and long stretches of rugged, largely undeveloped coast. Perhaps because it lacks any impressive ruins or real island feel owing to its proximity to the mainland, Évvia is explored by few foreign tourists, though Athenians and Thessalians visit the island in force and have erected holiday homes around half a dozen of its major resorts.

The Sporades are well connected by **bus** and **ferry** with Athens (via Áyios Konstandínos or Vólos), and much more sporadically by boat from Thessaloníki; it's easy to island-hop in the northern group. The only connection to Skýros is from Kými on Évvia via a local and rather slow car and passenger ferry. Évvia is linked to the mainland by a couple of bridges at its capital Halkídha, and by six local ferries from various strategic points. Both Skiáthos and Skýros have airports.

Skiáthos

The commercialization of **Skiáthos** is legendary among both foreigners and Greeks: it's a close fourth to that of Corfu (Kérkyra), Mýkonos and Rhodes

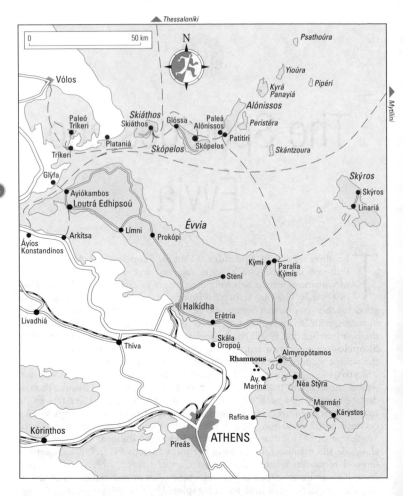

(Ródos). But if you've some time to spare, or a gregarious nature, you might still break your journey here to sample the best, if most crowded, **beaches** in the Sporades. Along the south and southeast coasts, the road serves an almost unbroken line of villas, hotels and restaurants, and although this doesn't take away the island's natural beauty, it makes it difficult to find anything unspoilt or particularly Greek about it all. Nonetheless, you can escape the rush and bustle of the southern coastal strip by heading for the hills: the walking opportunities through most of northern Skiáthos will bring you to some refreshingly deserted vistas, while a rugged vehicle will get you well off the beaten track as well.

If you're planning to camp on Skiáthos, bear in mind that pitching your tent outside official sites is strongly discouraged, since summer turns the dry pine-needles to tinder.

Skiáthos Town

Skiáthos Town, where the ferries dock, looks great from a distance, but tourist

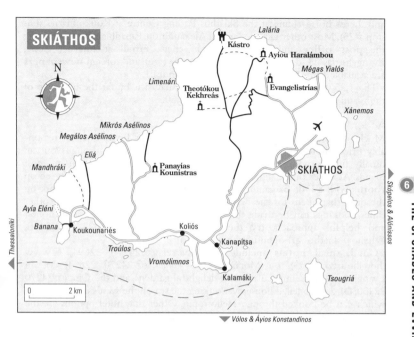

Map labels:
SKIÁTHOS
N
Lalária
Kástro
Ayíou Haralámbou
Mégas Yialós
Limenári
Theotókou Kekhreás
Evangelistrías
Xánemos
Mikrós Asélinos
Megálos Asélinos
Eliá
SKIÁTHOS
Mandhráki
Panayías Kounístras
Skópelos & Alónissos
Ayía Eléni
Thessaloníki
Banana
Koukounariés
Koliós
Troúlos
Kanapítsa
Vromólimnos
Kalamáki
Tsougriá
0   2 km

▼ Vólos & Áyios Konstandínos

development becomes very apparent as you approach, especially to the east side of the port and around Alexándhrou Papadhiamándi where most of the services, the tackier shops, "English" pubs and eateries are located. But it's still possible to find some pockets of charm tucked into the alleys on the older, western side of town – houses, gardens and flowers galore – and with some good restaurants and nightclubs, Skiáthos can be fun in a crowded, boisterous way.

Of the few sights the **Papadhiamándis museum** (Tues–Sun 9.30am–1pm & 5–8pm; €2), housed in the nineteenth-century home of one of Greece's best-known novelists, Alexandros Papadiamantis, is worth a look. The first floor of the two storey building has been maintained as the writer's original house, while the ground floor operates as an exhibition area featuring traditional artefacts from the island. The Galerie Varsakis **antique shop** (open usual shop hours), on Platía Trión Ierarhón near the fishing port, has one of the best **folklore displays** in Greece, and many of the older items would do Athens' Benáki Museum (see p.25) proud; the proprietor neither expects, nor wants, to sell the more expensive of these, which include antique textiles, handicrafts and jewellery.

Practicalities

Buses and **taxis** ply from the area around the **ferry harbour**. To Koukounariés, the bus is the cheapest option (€1.10); it runs at least hourly in summer (every fifteen minutes at peak times), the last bus returning at 1am.

A large number of competing **rental outlets** in town, most on the front behind the ferry harbour, offer bicycles, motorbikes, cars and motorboats. The cheapest, smallest cars go for around €30 per day for one week's rental, while scooters go for between €14 and €18 per day depending on the length of rental. Several travel agents organize "round-the-island" mule trips (€18 a day), and there's horse-riding at the Skiathos Riding Centre at Koukounariés (bus stop #25). Most other facilities are on Alexándhrou Papadhiamándi, including the **post office** and **banks**; you can check **email** at Internet Zone, Evangelistrías 28 (daily 10.30am–2pm & 6pm–1am), and foreign **newspapers** are available from News Stand at Papadhiamándi 21.

The 1:25.000 *Skiathos* **map** published by Anavasi is by far the best map of the island and is available in Skiáthos for €4.50.

Accommodation

Much of the island's **accommodation** is in Skiáthos Town. The few reasonably priced hotels or *pensions* are heavily booked in season, though you can usually find a room, albeit at a slightly more elevated price than on most islands. At other times, supply exceeds demand and you can find very cheap **rooms** with a little bargaining. There is a room-owners' association kiosk on the quay that opens for the best part of the day in high season, but at other times bookings can be made through several tourist agencies. For an honest and helpful approach, try the efficient Heliotropio (☎24270 22430, ✉helio@skiathos.gr) opposite the ferry berth.

Good, small **hotels** include the *Bourtzi* (☎24270 22694, ⓦwww.hotelbourtzi.gr; ⑥), on Moraïtou, and *Pothos* (☎24270 22694; ⑥), on Evanglistrías, both immaculate with delightful gardens, and the *Orsa* (☎24270 22430; ⑥), a remodelled house overlooking the sea on the west side of the port, which can be booked through Heliotropio. Other fine hotel options are the *Alkyon*, on the seafront at the commercial port end (☎24270 22981; ⓦwww.alkyon.gr; ⑥), or the *Meltemi*, on the waterfront, near the taxi rank (☎24270 22493; ⑥). Also overlooking the waterfront, the *Akti Hotel* (☎24270 22024, ⓕ24270 22430; ⑥) is a fine option; its top-floor penthouse, sleeping four, is a good deal if you can land it.

Of the island's three official **campsites**, the closest is that at Xánemos beach, 3km to the northeast of Skiáthos Town next to the airport runway. Apart from being within walking distance of town and close to the beach, there's little to recommend it.

Eating, drinking and nightlife

You're spoiled for choice for places to **eat**, but nothing is particularly cheap apart from the few burger/*yíros* joints. One of the most convenient places for breakfast is *Dinos* on Papadhiamándi, while excellent pizzas can be snared at *Maria's*, tucked away up in the backstreets at Syngroú 6. Of the more traditional and consequently cheaper places to eat, *Mesogeia*, above and to the west of Platía Trión Ierarhón, has excellent moussaka and other home-cooked dishes, while the well-signposted *Alexandros* on Kapodistríou is another decent preferred-by-locals joint. *Karnagio*, at the far end of the old harbour promenade, is the best fish restaurant in town, and prices reflect this. In a pretty old stone building, close to Platía Trión Ierarhón, *1901 En Skiatho* offers up *bouzoúki* and guitar to accompany your meal. For an even smarter culinary experience, *Anemos*, high up overlooking the old harbour, is the decided favourite in the *haute cuisine* stakes with carefully crafted fish dishes, and commendable pasta and roast vegetables.

Nightlife centres on the clubs on or near Polytekhníou. The best places here are *Borzoi*, the oldest club on the island, playing an eclectic sampling of Latino, blues, rock and jazz, or the very Anglicized and rather small *Admiral Benbow*, offering 1970s and 80s British pop hits, draft cider and English ale. Nearer the Papadiamantis Museum on Mitropolítou Ananíou, the long-established and much-loved *Kentavros* plays jazz and blues, while *Adagio* on Evanglistrías prefers the softer tones of classical music. On the east shore, the chic *Remezzo* with its maritime motifs is a perennial favourite for a drink, while the vaguely British *BBC* is another popular watering hole. Almost next door, the flashy *Kahlua* pumps up the rhythm in syncopated competition until the wee hours.

Skiáthos' outdoor **cinema**, Refresh Paradiso, on the ring road, shows new releases in their original language. Another source of entertainment is the little offshore Boúrtzi fortress, transformed into an outdoor **theatre** and home to occasional plays and musical performances during the summer.

Around the island

Other than using the buses or the various rental outlets in town, you can also get your bearings on a **boat trip** around the island (€20 per person; 5–6hr; leaving 10am daily in high season). Longer excursions to the Alónnisos Marine Park cost around €30. You could always make do with a boat trip to the islet of Tsougriá (opposite Skiáthos Town), where there's a good beach and a taverna; boats leave from the fishing harbour beyond the Boúrtzi. Boats to the east coast of the island leave from the quay area in front of the bus station.

The monasteries and Kástro

Founded in the late eighteenth century, the **monastery of Evanglistrías** (daily 8am–noon & 4–8pm) is exceptionally beautiful, even beyond the grandeur of isolation you find in all Greek monasteries. The Greek flag was raised here in 1807, and heroes of the War of Independence such as Kolokotronis pledged their oaths to fight for freedom here. From Skiáthos Town, you can reach Evanglistrías on foot in just over an hour. From the centre, walk 500m along the road towards the airport; where the asphalt veers to the right, take a prominently signposted paved side road that veers left; be careful to stick to this and not to wander off onto the dirt roads.

Beyond Evanglistrías, a mule track continues to the abandoned **Ayíou Haralámbou** monastery, from where it's possible to walk northwest to the ruined capital of Kástro (see below) along another dirt road; this takes about two hours. To reach Kástro from Skiáthos Town, it's quicker to take the direct paved road towards it on a motorbike, or take a *kaïki* ride round the island and get off at the beach below Kástro.

Continuing west from Evanglistrías, first on track, then on *kalderími*, you reach the paved, Kástro-bound road noted above; turn left, and after 200m or so bear right (west) onto the well-used, signposted dirt track heading towards the abandoned fifteenth-century monastery of **Theotókou Kekhreás**, three hours' walk from town. This is claimed to be the oldest monastery on the island and has a colony of bats inside. It's a beautiful walk (or organized donkey-ride), and there are three pebbly beaches below, one with a welcoming stream that provides a cool shower. Back on the paved road, you can continue on to the **Kástro** in about thirty minutes – a spectacular spot, built on a windswept headland. In the past, the entrance was only accessible by a drawbridge, which has been replaced by a flight of steps. The original settlement was built in the sixteenth century, when the people of the island moved here for security from pirate raids. It was abandoned three hundred years later in 1830, following independence from Turkey, when the population moved back to build the modern town on the site of ancient Skiáthos. The ruins are largely overgrown, and only four churches survive intact, the largest still retaining some original frescoes. From outside the gates, a path leads down the rocks to a good pebble

beach; with a stream running down from the hills and a daytime café (with slightly overpriced food and drinks), it makes a good place to camp. For an apparently inaccessible spot, though, it does attract a surprising number of people. All the island excursion boats call here, and even when they've gone, there's little chance of having the ruins or beach to yourself.

Finally, the seventeenth-century **Panayías Kounístras** can be reached by turning right off the paved road that runs north across the island from Tróulos to Asélinos. It's a very pretty spot, with a beautiful carved icon screen, splendid icons, a grape arbour and a taverna.

The beaches

The real business of Skiáthos is **beaches**. There are reputed to be more than sixty of them, but that's hardly enough to soak up the hordes of summer visitors: at the height of the season, the local population of four thousand can be swamped by up to fifty thousand visitors. The beaches on the northeast coast aren't easily accessible unless you pay for an excursion *kaïki*: reaching them on foot requires treks more arduous than those described above. The bus, though, runs along the entire south coast, and from strategic points along the way you can easily reach a good number of beaches. The prevailing summer *meltémi* wind blows from the north, so the beaches on the south coast are usually better protected. Most of the popular ones have at least a drinks/snacks stall; those at Vromólimnos, Asélinos and Tróulos have proper tavernas.

The beaches before the **Kalamáki peninsula** are no great shakes, but at the beginning of the promontory itself are the excellent **Tzaneriá** and **Vromólimnos**, close to Koliós hamlet; Vromólimnos offers windsurfing and waterskiing and is now home to a pumping beach party scene replete with a bungie-jump crane. Overlooking Tzaneriá beach on the eastern side of the Kalamáki peninsula, the Dolphin Diving Centre (☎24270 22599) at the *Nostos* hotel offers **scuba diving**.

Just before Tróulos beach, the last on the south coast before Koukounariés, you can turn right up a paved road, which runs 3.5km north to **Megálos Asélinos**, a very good beach with a bar, reasonable taverna and a decent **campsite**, *Aselinos* (☎24270 49312; April–Oct). A daily bus and excursion boats call here, so it's crowded in season. A fork in the paved road leads to Panayías Kounístras (see above) and continues to **Mikrós Asélinos**, just east of its larger neighbour and somewhat quieter.

The bus only goes as far as **KOUKOUNARIÉS**, a busy resort whose majestic sandy bay of clear, gradually deepening water is backed by acres of pines. Despite its popularity, Koukounariés merits at least one visit if only to assess the claim that it's the best beach in Greece. The three distinct beaches are excellent if you don't mind the crowds; wooden walkways traverse the sand to a series of *kantínas* selling drinks and light snacks. The approach road runs behind a small lake at the back of the pine trees, and features a string of **hotels**, **rooms** and **restaurants**, as well as a good campsite, *Koukounaries* (☎24270 49250; May 15–Sept 15), which is fairly decent with standard facilities. Here, the *Strofilia Apartments* (☎24270 49251, ✉strophilia@n-skiathos.gr; ❻) are particularly nicely furnished. The prominent *Lake Hotel* (☎24270 49362; ❹), right opposite the lake itself, is also decent value. Jet-skis, motorboats, windsurfing and waterskiing are all available off the beach.

Working northwest around coast, "**Banana beach**" (also known as Krasás), the third cove on the far side of Poúnda headland, is one of the island's trendiest beaches with watersports, a couple of bars and tolerance of nude bathing. For the less adventurous, the turnoff from the coast road for neighbouring

Ayía Eléni, leads 1km to a pleasant beach with a drinks kiosk. Further north, **Mandhráki** and **Eliá** beaches have similar facilities, and are accessible by scooter along dirt tracks.

The famed **Lalária** beach, almost at the northernmost point of Skiáthos, can be reached by taxi-boats from the town. Covered in smooth white stones, with steep cliffs rising behind, it's beautiful; the swimming is excellent, but beware of the undertow. The island's three natural grottoes – Skotiní, Galázia and Halkiní – are nearby, and are included in many of the "round-the-island" trips. East of Evanglistrías are the greyish sands of **Mégas Yialós**, one of the less crowded beaches, and **Xánemos**, another nudist beach; both suffer from airport noise.

Skópelos

Bigger, more rugged and better cultivated than Skiáthos, **Skópelos** is almost as busy, but its concessions to tourism are lower key and in better taste than in Skiáthos. Most of the larger beaches have sunbeds, umbrellas and some water-sports, though smaller, secluded coves do exist. Inland, the island is a well-watered place, growing olives, plums, pears and almonds. **Glóssa** and **Skópelos**, its two main towns, are also among the prettiest in the Sporades, clambering uphill along paved steps, their houses distinguished by attractive wooden balconies and grey slate roofs. A number of **nationalities** have occupied the island at various stages of its history, among them the Romans, Persians, Venetians, French and, of course, the Ottomans. The Ottoman pirate-admiral Barbarossa (Redbeard) – actually a Greek renegade from Lésvos – had the entire population of the island slaughtered in the sixteenth century.

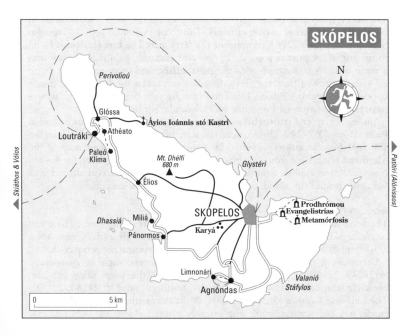

Skópelos Town

The best way to approach **SKÓPELOS TOWN** (Hóra) is by sea: sloping down one corner of a huge, almost circular bay, the main port is revealed slowly as the boat rounds the final headland. Though more and more people seem to have discovered Skópelos Town, the locals are making a tremendous effort to keep it from going the way of Skiáthos. The harbour area is practically wall-to-wall tavernas and cafés, but the shops and eateries in the back alleys tend to be imaginative and tasteful, with wooden, hand-painted name signs. Spread below the oddly whitewashed ruins of a Venetian **kástro** is an enormous number of churches – 123 reputedly, though some are small enough to be mistaken for houses and most are locked except for their annual festival day. Other sights include a **folklore museum** (daily 10.30am–2.30pm & 6–10.30pm; free), featuring a collection of valuable nineteenth- and early-twentieth-century embroidered cloths, traditional costumes, weaving and decorative artefacts, and **photography exhibitions**, held around town in summer.

Outside town, perched on the slopes opposite the quay, are two convents worth visiting for their seclusion and views: **Evanglistrías** (daily 8am–1pm & 4–7pm), which is within view of the town, and **Pródhromou** (daily 8am–1pm & 5–8pm). Also on this promontory, the monastery of **Metamórfosis**, nestled among lush vegetation, was abandoned in 1980 but is now being restored by the monks and is open to visitors. Access is simplest by following an old road behind the line of hotels along the bay to Evanglistrías (an hour's walk). From there it's an extra half-hour's scramble over mule tracks to Pródhromos (with signs to Metamórfosis en route), the remotest and most beautiful of the three. Ignore the new road that goes part way – it's longer, and misses most of the beauty of the walk.

Practicalities

The **ferry quay** is at the middle of a long promenade, lined with an array of boutiques, bars, stores and restaurants. The local hydrofoil agency, Skopelos Shipping (℡24240 22767), is opposite the ferry quay. The **bus station** is 100m to the left of the port as you exit; opposite its entrance, a short road leads into a maze of lanes and signposts to the **post office**, and there are **banks** (with ATMs) about 50m from the ferry quay. You can access the **Internet** at a café opposite the Metro Club on Doulídhis and get your foreign language **newspapers** at International Press, one block inland from the ferry quay.

Among the several **motorbike rental** outlets, friendly service can be had at Panos Bikes (℡24240 23696), near the start of the road towards Glóssa; the 1:40.000 *Skopelos* **map**, published by Anavasi, is by far the best map of the island and is available from International Press, among other places, for €4.50. If you prefer to explore from the sea, day-long **boat cruises** cost around €15 for a trip around the island, or to Alónnisos and the marine park.

Accommodation

There are dozens of **rooms** for rent in the main part of the town. These can be arranged through the Association of Room Owners office (daily 9am–noon & 6–8pm; ℡ & ℻24240 24567), on the seafront opposite the ferry dock.

Alternatively, there are a few pleasant small **hotels**, such as *Andromache* (℡24240 22940; ❹), in a quiet old house near the post office (it's also bookable through Madro Travel by the northern quay ℡24240 22145). The old-style *Georgios* (℡24240 22308; ❹), at the northern end of the promenade, is a fair standby, while the brightly painted *Adonis* (℡24240 22231,

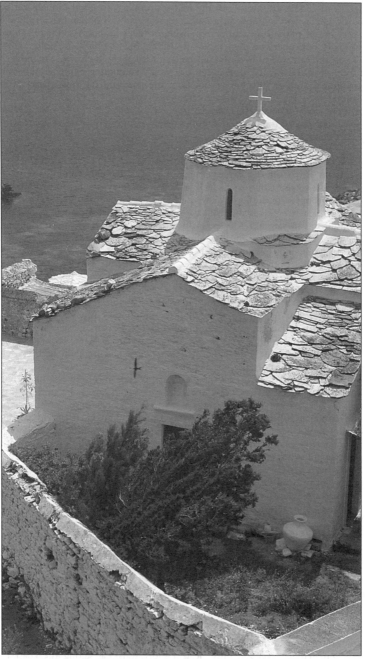

465

△ Skópelos Town

ⓕ24240 23239; ⑤), just above the mid-seafront, is also good though can be noisy. Unless you've booked through a tour operator, you're unlikely to find a space in one of the larger, more **expensive hotels** with pools on the hill above the port, but otherwise there's the cosy *Elli* (ⓣ24240 22943, ⓕ24240 23284; ⑥) on the east side of town or, on the ring road above the town, the modern *Aperitton* (ⓣ24240 22256, ⓕ24240 22976; ⑥), combining contemporary and traditional local architecture, 200m from the port and the town beach; you could also try the first-rate, neo-rustic *Dionysos* (ⓣ24240 23210, ⓔdionysco@otenet.gr; ⑥). *Skopelos Village* (ⓣ24240 22517, ⓕ24240 22958; ⑥), 500m around the bay to the south side, is a comfortable oasis of green with smart bungalows and studios.

Eating, drinking and nightlife

Skópelos Town offers a wide variety of **places to eat**, ranging from the acceptable to the truly excellent. For quick pre-ferry snack or breakfast, *La Frianderie*, opposite the ferry quay, is a French-style delicatessen with a range of fresh baguettes, cakes and drinks. Of the restaurants at the north end of the harbour, the *Molos* and *Klimataria* offer decent meals, as do *To Aktaion* and *Nostos*, a little closer to the harbour, which have exceptionally pleasant staff and large, delicious and reasonably priced portions. A little way inland, two *souvláki* places, both named *O Platanos*, compete for the distinction of having the best *yíros*; the one with blue chairs also has a much wider menu. If you're sick of Greek food, then *Perivoli*, above the two *souvladzídhika* at the east end of town, is the place for an "international-cuisine" gourmet blowout. Signposted down a narrow street at the south side of town is *O Kipos tou Kalou*, a little restaurant in a beautiful quiet garden serving up specialities from Skópelos as well as other generic Mediterranean fare. If you're looking for an out-of-the-way joint, well-signposted *Finikas*, tucked high up in the back streets behind the port, is a good choice.

Nightlife in Skópelos is on the increase, but is more of the late-night-**bar** than the nightclub variety. Look out for the classy *Vengera*, in a restored house in the back streets. The long-standing *Platanos Jazz Club* on the north side of the harbour is still hanging on (just), while on the ring road are two live Greek music clubs – *Bambolo*, not so flash but with good music, and *Rembetiki Istoria*, which features a programme of *rebétika* music; look for signs around town with their opening days and times. Finally, old *rebétika* hand Yiorgos Xintaris performs until late on weekends at the small *Anatoli ouzerí* on top of the *kástro*. If you want to head for something more like a **club**, try the enormous, masted beached galleon, *Karavi*, reaching out over the harbour perimeter road on the south side, the latest gaudy hot spot.

Around the rest of the island

From 7am to 10.30pm, buses (6–8 daily) ply the main paved road between Skópelos Town and Loutráki via Glóssa, stopping at the paths to all the main beaches and villages. Some 4km south of town, **Stáfylos** is the closest beach, and is getting increasingly crowded even though rather small and rocky. The *Pefkos Taverna*, abutting the small car park and overlooking the sea, is the best place to dine down here. Among the newer **room** ventures here, *Mando* (ⓣ24240 23917; ⑤) is friendly and quiet with neat studios set a short way back from the beach up the hill.

When Stáfylos gets too busy, head a short walk east along the coast to **Valanió**, where you've a better chance of escaping the crowds. Nudity is acceptable and although the official campsite has long since closed, you shouldn't be hassled if you stay a night or two. There's spring water and a *kantína* here, too.

Around the coast to the west of Stáfylos and Valanió is the tiny horseshoe-shaped harbour of **AGNÓNDAS**, where you'll find three fish tavernas and rooms to rent. *Pavlina Apartments* (T 24240 23272, pavlinaskopelos@mail.gr; ❸), just back from the beach, have four high-ceilinged, self-contained and tasteful, wood-furnished apartments on offer. *Pavlos* is the best choice of the restaurants, on the waterfront; count on good, solid grills and fresh fish. Next up and reachable by a paved side road is **LIMNONÁRI**, 300m of fine sand set in a closed, rocky bay. The *Limnonari Beach Restaurant*, right on the beach, serves delicious spiral-shaped local *tyrópittes* and rents **rooms** (T 24240 23046; ❹). A little further around the bay, *Ouzeri O Thomas* is another decent option.

Heading up Skópelos's southwest coast, **PÁNORMOS** is very much a full-blown, commercial resort, with rooms, tavernas, a campsite, yacht anchorage and watersports. The beach here is gravelly and shelves steeply, but there are small secluded sandy bays close by. Of places to **stay**, the thirty-room *Panormos Beach Hotel* (T 24240 22711, F 24240 23366; ❻) has a beautiful garden and fine views, and is lovingly looked after; beyond it, the *Adrina Beach* (T 24240 23373, E adrina@otenet.gr; ❼) is one of the most attractive and expensive hotels in the Sporades.

Slightly further on at **MILIÁ**, there's a tremendous, 1500m sweep of tiny pebbles beneath a bank of pines, facing the islet of Dhassía. Though this used to be a fairly quiet and secluded getaway, a very popular party scene has developed here in recent years, with a beach bar attracting scores of hedonistic boys and girls bent on a good time. There's also one fairly standard taverna here, the *Milia Beach*, as well as the *Milia Apartments* (T 24240 23998; ❹).

Further north, **ÉLIOS**, 9km short of the northern port of Glóssa, is a medium-sized, fairly new resort settled by residents of the earthquake-damaged villages above it, with nothing special to offer besides a pleasant beach. If you want to **stay**, try the *Hotel Apartments Zanneta* (T 24240 33140, F 24240 33717; ❻) up on the main bypass road. Beyond here, the renovated village of **Paleó Klíma** marks the start of a beautiful forty-minute **trail** to Glóssa, via the empty hamlet of Áyii Anáryiri and the oldest village on the island, **Athéato** (Mahalás).

West of Skópelos Town, various jeep tracks and old paths wind through olive and plum groves towards **Mount Dhélfi** and the Vathiá forest, or skirt the base of the mountain northeast to **Revýthi** hill with its fountains and churches, and the site of **Karya**, with its *sendoúkia*: ancient rock-cut tombs which may be early Christian. To the northwest of Skópelos Town, **Glystéri** is a small pebble beach with no shade, whose taverna is much frequented by locals on Sundays.

This whole western tract of the island with its pine-clad uplands is prime **walking** territory. Englishwoman and long-time Skópelos resident Heather Parsons runs guided **walking tours** around Skópelos (€15; T 694 52 49 328, W www.skopelos-walks.com), some ending up at beaches and restaurants.

Loutráki, Glóssa and the west

Only hydrofoils now call at the small port of **LOUTRÁKI** ("Glóssa" on schedules), with its narrow pebble beach, small hotels and rooms for rent. The village has been spoiled a little by development at either end, but it's not a bad place to **stay** if you're after peace and quiet; try *O Stelios* (T 24240 33412; ❸), a simple pension above the *Vrahos* taverna; the *Avra* (T 24240 33550; ❹), or any of the rooms advertised just in from the seafront. Though most of the quayside **tavernas** don't offer value for money, there are exceptions: the *Orea Ellas* by the harbour is shaded by beautiful chestnut trees and sells a highly recommended, home-made retsina, while the *Flisvos*, on the far west side of the port, is a friendly place with decent pasta dishes.

High above Loutráki, **GLÓSSA** would perhaps be a preferable base if it had more places to stay. It's a sizeable and quite beautiful, totally Greek town, with several *kafenía*, a taverna and a few **rooms** to let, some of which are hot and musty, with erratic water pressure. *Kostas and Nina's* place (℡24240 33686; ❸) has simple, clean rooms, some with a view; they also rent out studios longer term. Otherwise you could stay at the *Selinounda Apartments* (℡24240 33570; ❹) on the road between Loutráki and Glóssa. The one central **taverna**, popular *To Agnandi*, serves excellent, innovative food and has a roof terrace with wonderful views.

Ninety minutes' walk up to the north coast from Glóssa will bring you to the **beach** called **Perivolioú**. The walk itself is worthwhile, passing a **monastery** next to a stone cairn containing masses of human bones and skulls. There's also a huge hollow oak tree here, in the heart of which is a small tank of drinking water. The beach, when you get there, is nothing out of the ordinary, but there's pure spring water and a cave for shade.

East of Glóssa, a dirt road leads to the splendidly sited church of **Áyios Ioánnis stó Kastrí**, perched on the top of a rock high above a small sandy cove where you can swim. An unsightly house nearby has spoiled the isolation somewhat, but the walk from Glóssa (again, about ninety minutes) is beautiful and peaceful, with hawks and nightingales for company.

Alónnisos

The most remote of the Sporades, **Alónnisos** is also, at first sight, the least attractive, owing to an unfortunate recent history. The vineyards were wiped out by disease in 1950, and the *hóra* was damaged by an earthquake in 1965. Although its houses were mostly repairable, lack of water, combined with corruption and the social control policies of the new junta, were instrumental in the transfer of virtually the entire population down to the previously unimportant anchorage of Patitíri. The result is a little soulless, but what charm may be lacking in the built environment along the coast is made up for by the hospitality of the islanders.

Patitíri and Paleá Alónnisos

PATITÍRI is not the best introduction to the island, though it's trying hard to rectify that via a paved waterfront and a general tidying up of its previous unkempt look; its port, too, is pleasant enough, a pretty cove flanked by pine trees and ringed by busy bars, cafes and restaurants. Patitíri, and the island of Alónnisos in general, attracts fewer casual foreign visitors than Skiáthos or Skópelos, though the number of middle-class Greek visitors has increased sharply in recent years; the island is now considered rather chic and fashionable, and can get very crowded from mid-July to the end of August. It's easy, though, to pick up connections here for beaches and the old town, and there are several good hotels to choose from. The most interesting place to visit is the **Monk Seal Information Centre** (daily 10am–1pm & 7–10pm; free) on the first floor of a building halfway along the seafront. The displays include models, photos, video and slide shows.

Skópelos, Skiáthos, Vólos & Áy. Konstandínos

PALEÁ ALÓNNISOS (Hóra) is a fine but steep fifty-minute walk via the traditional *kalderími* – signposted on the left just outside Patitíri. Alternatively, there's a frequent bus service from Patitíri (€0.90) in the mornings and afternoons. Although some houses are still derelict, much of the village has been painstakingly restored, mainly by English and Germans who bought the properties at knock-down rates. Only a few local families continue to live here, which gives the village a rather odd and un-Greek atmosphere, but it is picturesque and the views make the trip worthwhile.

Practicalities

All Alónnisos's important facilities are in Patitíri; **buses** and **taxis** have adjacent terminals on the waterfront. The **post office** is on the Hóra road, while *kaïkia* leave from the inner ferry quay. You can **rent a scooter** or **motorbike** at I'M Bikes (☎24240 65010) or even a car at reasonable prices. The roads between Patitíri, Stení Vála and the northernmost point on the island are paved, and the dirt roads down to the beaches – with some exceptions – are in good condition: not half as dangerous as the twisting, busy roads on Skiáthos and Skópelos. A couple of the rental places on the waterfront also offer out motorboats and dinghies. The 1:40.000 *Alonissos* **map** published by Anavasi is by far the best of the island, and is available in Patitíri for €4.50.

469

Rooms are easy to find here, as you'll probably be approached with offers as you get off the ferry or hydrofoil. The local room-owners' association (☎ & ℱ24240 66188), on the waterfront, can also find you a room (mostly ❸) in Patitíri or nearby Vótsi. Other options include the *Ioulieta Pension* (☎24240 65463; ❸), *Haravyi* (☎24240 65090, ℱ24240 65189; ❺) and *Pantheon* (☎24240 65139; ❹). Best in the higher price range are *Liadromia* (☎24240 65521, ℯliadromia@alonisso.com; ❻), above the port, while in Hóra, *Konstantina's Studios* (☎ & ℱ24240 66165; ❻) is a small renovated building with eight studios and one apartment, all enjoying exceptionally good views. Also in Hóra, though a little cheaper, is the simple and clean *Fadasia House* (☎24240 65186; ❸), with its own little restaurant.

The **restaurants** along Patitíri's port are reasonably priced, but for the most part the food is nothing special. One exception is *Anaïs*, offering up a selection of ready-made *mayireftá* and grills to order. Recommended *ouzerís* include *To Kamaki*, two blocks up towards the post office from the waterfront, with an amazing selection of seafood *mezédhes*. Heading up to Hóra (where most Greek visitors prefer to dine), you'll pass the family-run *Babis* just outside Patitíri; the food is good, with a special spin on local *píttes*. Up in Hóra proper, the choices are disproportionately wide. On the right as you enter, the quirky *Alon* has spectacular views to the north and simple, good-quality food. Upping the culinary and price stakes, and providing stunning views, there's also *Astrofengia*, at the entrance to the village, combining the cuisines of Greece and the Middle East, and the *Paraport*, up on the main square, offering excellent original fish dishes.

Nightlife is low-key. The best of the seafront bars is *Pub Dennis*, whose ice-cream concoctions are divine, though both *En Plo* and *La Vie* are popular. Club-wise, *Borio* and *Enigma* are fairly European, while *Rembetika*, on the road to the old town, specializes in Greek music.

The island's beaches

Alónnisos is surrounded by some of the cleanest water in the Aegean, but it's lacking in sandy beaches, the two best being **Výthisma** and **Vrysítsa** – though the latter is sited a little too close to the island's rubbish dump for comfort, and is on the more exposed north coast. The rest vary from sandy-gravelly to fine pebbles. There's a very limited **bus service** along the Hóra–Patitíri–Stení Vala route, but *kaïkia* run half-hourly from Patitíri north to Khryssí Miliá, Kokkinókastro, Stení Vála, Kalamákia and Áyios Dhimítrios, and south around the coast to Marpoúnda, Výthisma and Megálos Mourtiás. *Kaïkia* also sail occasionally to Livádhia on Peristéra islet.

At **Patitíri**, there's decent swimming from the rocks around the promontory to the north; pick your way along a hewn-out path past the hotels. To the north, above the headlands, Patitíri merges into two adjoining settlements with reasonable beaches, **ROUSSOÚM YIALÓS** and **VÓTSI**. For better beaches, you'll have to get in a boat or on a bike.

Khryssí Miliá, the first good beach north of Patitíri, has a taverna and pine trees behind the quite decent stretch of sand; there's a couple of new hotels on the hillside above, such as the posh *Milia Bay* (☎24240 66035, ℯmilia-bay@forthnet.gr; ❼), and it can get crowded in summer. At **Kokkinókastro**, over the hill further north, excavations have revealed the site of ancient Ikos and evidence of the oldest known prehistoric habitation in the Aegean. There's nothing much to see, but it's a beautiful spot with a good red-pebble beach, and, in July and August, a daytime bar.

Opposite the island of Peristéra, **STENÍ VÁLA** is a haven for the yachts and flotillas that comb the Sporades, and has almost become a proper village, with two shops, several houses, a bar, rooms and five tavernas, one of which, the *Kyra Tasia* (offically the *Steni Vala*), stays open more or less throughout the year and is famous for its *tyrópita*. The **Monk Seal Treatment and Rehabilitation Centre**, housed in a small hut on the beach, can provide information and insight into the work of the HSPMS (see box below). There's an unofficial campsite (☎24240 65258) in an olive grove by the harbour, a long pebble beach – Glyfa, where boats are repaired – and some stony beaches within reasonable walking distance in either direction. **KALAMÁKIA**, to the north, also has a couple of tavernas and a few rooms, while further on still, at the point where the sealed road ends, **ÁYIOS DHIMÍTRIOS** is rapidly becoming the favourite "remote" beach amongst growing numbers of mainlanders. Backing a curving pebbly beach, the small settlement now has a snack-bar, beach taverna and even a card-phone. There's a good, signposted circular **walking trail** (2hr 30min) from here, that follows the coast for a while before heading up and back to Áyios Dhimítrios via the Kastanórema stream bed.

If you want real solitude you'll need to head north along the paved road that runs the length of the island, though bear in mind that there's nothing in the

The Mediterranean monk seal

The **Mediterranean monk seal** has the dubious distinction of being the European mammal most in danger of extinction – fewer than eight hundred survive worldwide, the majority around the Portuguese Atlantic island of Madeira. Small numbers survive in the Ionian and Aegean seas; the largest population here, of around thirty seals, lives around the deserted islands north of Alónnisos.

Monk seals can travel up to 200km a day in search of food, but they usually return to the same places to rear their **pups**. They have one pup every two years, and the small population is very vulnerable to disturbance. Originally, the pups would have been reared in the open, but increasing disturbance by man has led to the seals retreating to isolated sea caves with partly submerged entrances, particularly around the coast of the remote islet of Pipéri.

Unfortunately, the seals compete with fishermen for limited stocks of fish and, in the overfished Aegean, often destroy nets full of fish. Until recently it was common for seals to be killed by fishermen. This occasionally still happens, but in an attempt to protect the seals, the seas around the northern Sporades have been declared a wildlife reserve, the **Sporades National Marine Park**: fishing is restricted in the area north of Alónnisos and prohibited within 5km of Pipéri. On Alónnisos, the conservation effort and reserve have won a great deal of local support, mainly through the efforts of the **Hellenic Society for the Protection of the Monk Seal** (HSPMS; see above), based at Stení Vála. The measures have been particularly popular with local fishermen, as tight restrictions on larger, industrial-scale fishing boats from other parts of Greece should help restore local stocks, and eventually benefit the fishermen financially.

Despite this, the government has made no serious efforts to enforce the restrictions, and boats from outside the area continue to fish around Pipéri. On a more positive note, the HSPMS, in collaboration with the Pieterburen Seal Creche in Holland, has reared several abandoned seal pups, all of which have been successfully released in the seas north of Alónnisos.

For the moment, your chances of actually seeing a seal are remote, unless you plan to spend a few weeks on a boat in the area. It's recommended that you shouldn't visit Pipéri – this is officially prohibited in any case – or approach sea caves on other islands which might be used by seals, or try to persuade boat-owners to do so.

way of facilities past the turnoff to Steni Vala. This doesn't seem to deter adventurous scooter riders, however. At the northernmost point of Alónnisos, the old shepherds' village of **YÉRAKAS** is a bit of a disappointment, with only a desultory, seldom-used jetty and a scrappy beach.

In the more populated south, **MARPOÚNDA** features a large hotel and bungalow complex and a rather small beach. It's better to turn right before Marpoúnda towards **Megálos Mourtiás**, a pebble beach with several tavernas that's also linked by paved track to Paleá Alónnisos, 200m above. **Výthisma**, the lovely beach just before Megálos Mourtiás, is best reached by boat, the path here having been washed out. Further north, visible from Paleá Alónnisos, **Vrysítsa** is tucked into its own finger-like inlet. There's sand and a taverna, but little else.

Beyond Alónnisos: some minor islets

Northeast of Alónnisos, half a dozen tiny **islets** speckle the Aegean. Virtually none of these has any permanent population, or a ferry service, and the only way you can reach them – at least Peristéra, Kyrá Panayiá and Yioúra – is by excursion *kaïki* (ask at the excursion-boat stands on the harbour), weather permitting. No boats are allowed to take you to the other, more remote islets, as they are protected areas within the Sporades National Marine Park. But though it is possible to be left for a night or more on any of the closer islands, be sure to bring more supplies than you need: if the weather worsens you'll be marooned until such time as small craft can reach you.

Peristéra is the closest islet to Alónnisos, and was joined to it until subsidence (a common phenomenon in the area) created the narrow straits between the two. It's graced with some sandy beaches and there is rarely anyone around, though some Alonissans do come over for short periods to tend the olive groves, and in season there are regular evening "barbecue boats" from the main island. As on Alónnisos, a few unofficial campers are tolerated, but there is only one spot, known locally as "Barbecue Bay", where campfires are allowed.

Kyrá Panayiá is the next islet out and is equally fertile. There are two monasteries here, one still inhabited. Boats call at a beach on the south shore, one of many such sandy stretches and coves around the island. There's no other permanent population besides wild goats.

Nearby **Yioúra** boasts a stalactite cave reputed to be the previous abode of Polyphemus, the Cyclops who imprisoned Odysseus, but you won't be able to check its credentials. No one is allowed within 500m of the island, since, like Pipéri, it lies inside the restricted zone of the marine park.

Pipéri, southeast of Yioúra, is a seabird and monk-seal refuge, and visitable only by scientists who've been granted permission from a ministry of the environment representative. Tiny, northernmost **Psathoúra** is dominated by its powerful modern lighthouse, the tallest in the Aegean, although here, as around many of these islands, there's a submerged ancient town, brought low by the endemic subsidence. Roughly halfway between Alónnisos and Skýros, green **Skántzoura**, with a single empty monastery and a few seasonal shepherds, is a smaller version of Kyrá Panayiá.

Skýros

Despite its proximity to Athens, **Skýros** was a very traditional and idiosyncratic island until fairly recently. Any impetus for change had been neutralized by the lack of economic opportunity (and even secondary schooling), forcing the younger Skyrians to live in Athens and thus leave behind a conservative gerontocracy. A high school was finally provided in the mid-1980s, and the island has been somewhat "discovered" since that time. It's now the haunt of continental Europeans, chic Athenians and Brits, many of whom check into the "New Age" Skýros Centre, to "rethink the form and direction of their lives".

All this notwithstanding, Skýros still ranks as one of the most interesting places in the Aegean. It has a long tradition of painted **pottery** and ornate **woodcarving**, in particular the *salonáki skyrianó* (a handmade set of sitting-room furniture). A very few old men still wear the vaguely Cretan traditional costume of cap, vest, baggy trousers, leggings and *trohádhia* (Skyrian sandals), and some elderly women still wear the favoured yellow scarves and long embroidered skirts, but this is dying out.

The theory that Skýros was originally two islands seems doubtful, but certainly the character of its two parts is very different. The **north** has a greener and more gentle landscape, and away from the port and town retains much of its original pine forest, while the sparsely inhabited **south** is mountainous, rocky and barren; there are few trees and the landscape is more reminiscent of the Cyclades than the Sporades. Compared with Skiáthos, Skópelos and Alónnisos, Skýros isn't a great place for **beaches**. Most of those along the west coast attract a certain amount of seaborne rubbish and, although the scenery is sometimes spectacular, the swimming isn't that good. The beaches along the east coast are all close to Skýros Town, and the best option is probably to stay here rather than head for somewhere more isolated. At the north end of the island, the beaches have been commandeered by a big air-force base, which otherwise keeps a low profile.

Linariá

After crossing a seemingly endless expanse of sea from Kými – an impression due in part to the slowness of the only ferry linking Skýros with the mainland – the boat docks at the tiny port of **LINARIÁ**, a functional place on the island's west coast. Although most of the action is around Skýros Town, Linariá does make for a quiet alternative base and is certainly a pleasant spot to while away time waiting for the ferry. If you decide to **stay**, there are two very

Goat dances and wild ponies

Skýros has some particularly lively, even outrageous, **festivals**. The *Apokriátika* (pre-Lenten) Carnival here is structured around the famous **goat dance**, performed by masked revellers in the village streets. The foremost character in this is the **Yéros**, a menacing figure concealed by a goatskin mask and weighed down by garlands of sheep bells. Accompanying him are **Korélles** and **Kyríes** ("Maidens" and "Ladies" – who are transvestites, as only the men participate) and **Frángi** (maskers in "Western" garb). For further details, read Joy Koulentianou's *The Goat Dance of Skyros*, available in Athens and occasionally on the island.

The other big annual event takes place near Magaziá beach on August 15, when children race domesticated members of the **wild pony** herd, native to Skýros and said to be related to the Shetland pony (if so, it must be very distantly). They are thought to be the diminutive horses depicted in the Parthenon frieze, and at any time of the year you might find some of the tame individuals tethered and grazing near Skýros Town.

reasonable options: *King Lykomides* (☎ 22220 93472, ⓦ www.inskyros.gr /kinglykomides.htm; ❹), right next to the harbour, has thirteen air-conditioned standard rooms with TV, while a little higher up, *Linaria Bay Rooms* (☎ 22220 93274; ❹) has a mixture of rooms and traditional Skyrian studios. For **eating**, try the *Almyra Taverna* for no-nonsense Greek *mezédhes*, the *Psariotis Ouzeri* or the *Filippos* fish taverna, all near the harbour. The splendidly situated *Kavos Bar* welcomes the arrival of the ferry each evening with a rousing musical fanfare, and is open day and night for **drinks** and snacks. In high season, excursion *kaïkia* (€24 including food) offer trips from Linariá to the Pentekáli and Yeránia grottoes, and to the islet of Sarakíno, which has a cave and a very few untamed Skyrian ponies – almost extinct in the wild. See Monika at the port for details.

A good paved road connects Linariá to Skýros Town, 10km away, and then continues round past the airport to Atsítsa, where the Skyros Centre has its main branch; **buses** to Skýros Town, and to Magaziá on the coast below, leave from the quay. Midway up the Linariá–Skýros Town route, a paved side-road strikes off east to Ahíli and Kalamítsa. Most other roads are passable by scooter, apart from the direct track between Skýros Town and Atsítsa.

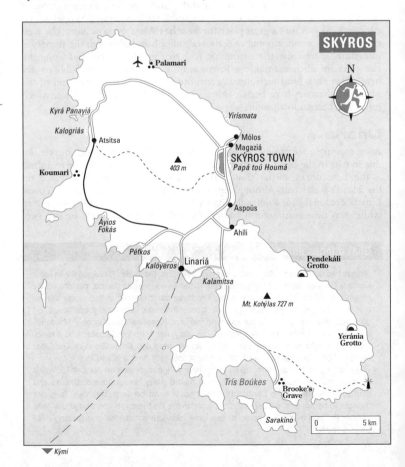

Skýros Town

SKÝROS TOWN (Hóra), with its decidedly Cycladic architecture, sits on the landward side of a high rock that rises precipitously from the coast (according to legend, King Lykomedes pushed Theseus to his death from its summit). With its workaday atmosphere, the town doesn't feel like a resort, but away from the tattier outskirts it's decidedly picturesque. The older and more intriguing parts are higher up, climbing towards the **kástro**, a mainly Byzantine building built on the site of the ancient **acropolis**. There are few traces of the acropolis, although remains of the Classical city walls survive below on the seaward side of the rock. The *kástro* is open to visitors; to reach its upper parts you pass through a rather private-looking gateway into the monastery, then through an attractive shaded courtyard and up a whitewashed tunnel. There's little to see at the top, apart from a few churches in various states of ruin, but there are great views over the town and the island, and the climb up takes you through the quieter, older part of town and its traditionally decorated houses. With their gleaming copper pots, porcelain plates and antique embroideries decorating the hearth, these dwellings are a matter of intense pride among the islanders, who are often found seated in their doorways on tiny carved chairs.

At the northern end of town is the striking and splendidly incongruous **memorial to Rupert Brooke**. It takes the form of a bronze statue of "Immortal Poetry" and its nakedness caused a scandal among the townspeople when it was first erected. Brooke, who visited the south of the island very briefly in April 1915, died shortly afterwards of blood poisoning on a French hospital ship anchored offshore, and was buried in an olive grove above the bay of Trís Boúkes. (The site can be reached on foot from Kalamítsa, by *kaïki* or, less romantically, by taxi.) Brooke, who became something of a local hero despite his limited acquaintance with Skýros, was adopted as the paragon of patriotic youth by Kitchener and later Churchill, who conveniently overlooked his forthright socialist and internationalist views.

Just below the Brooke statue, the **Archeological Museum** (Tues–Sun 8.30am–3pm; €2) has a modest collection of pottery and statues from excavations on the island, and a reconstruction of a traditional Skýros house interior. Nearby, in a nineteenth-century house built over one of the bastions of the ancient walls, the privately run **Faltaïts Museum** (daily 10am–noon & 5.30–8pm/6–9pm in summer; €2) is more interesting, with a collection of domestic items, costumes, embroidery, porcelain and rare books.

Practicalities

The **bus** from Linariá leaves you by the school, 200m below the main square; in season, schedules are guaranteed to meet the ferries, but otherwise services can be limited, and you might be better off getting a taxi. The **post office** and **banks** are both near the square. Skýros Travel (☎22220 91600), on the main street north of the square, can provide **information** or advice, and can find a room or hotel; in high season it's a good idea to phone them in advance. You can access the **Internet** at *Meroi* on the main street, and pick up **foreign newspapers** at International Press opposite the National Bank of Greece. Of the **motorbike and car rental** places in the area, the most prominent and efficient is Pegasus (☎22220 91600) a little way down the hill from the square.

You'll probably be met off the bus with offers of **rooms**, which it's as well to accept. A basic option is the *Elena* (☎22220 91738; ❸) next to the post office, which has very cheap singles with shared bathrooms. There's a rather scruffy **campsite** nearer the beach, at the bottom of the steps below the archeological museum, with basic amenities. If you'd like to stay in a traditional Skyrian house, those of Anna Stergiou (☎22220 91657) and Maria Mavroyiorgi (☎22220 91440) are clean and cosy (both ❸). Alternatively, you could try the pleasant, *Nefeli Hotel & Skyriana Spitia* (☎22220 91964, ☏22220 92061; ❻) on the main road before the square offering rooms or traditionally designed studios.

The square and the main street running by it are the centre of village life, with a few noisy pubs and a wide choice of *kafenía*, tavernas and fast-food places, though only a few are outstanding places to **eat**. Top of the list is *O Pappous ki Ego*, a very pleasant little *ouzerí* with a good range of *mezédhes* and quality Greek music. *To Metopo*, just below the square, is another decent *ouzerí* and is a little cheaper, while *Orestis* on the main street always draws queues for its solid grills, pasta and *mayireftá*. Near the Brooke statue (away from the bustling crowds) and a little more relaxed in style, *Anatolikos Anemos* dishes up Mediterranean and has good views from the patio down to the twin beach annexes of Magaziá and Mólos.

The town's **nightlife** is mostly bar-based until very late, when the few clubs get going. The most popular **bars** are the trendy *Kalypso*, playing jazz and blues, as well as dance-oriented *Kata Lathos* and the rockier *Iroön*. Later on, *Iy Stasis* is one of the most popular places. The best **clubs** include the *Skyropoula*, on the coastal road, and, in town, *Mylos* and the *Stone Club*, while you can listen to live Greek music at *Tzivaeri*.

Magaziá, Mólos and the nearby beaches

A path – and a longer paved road – lead down past the archeological museum towards the small coastal village of **MAGAZIÁ**, coming out by the official campsite. From Magaziá, an 800-metre-long sandy beach stretches to the adjacent village of **MÓLOS**; in recent years, though, a sprawl of new development between the road and the beach has more or less joined the two settlements together. With more of a community feel, Magaziá is still the more lively of the two settlements and has the best selection of rooms; Mólos is more open and scattered, and has a good range of studios as well as the most alluring stretch of **beach**, with umbrellas and loungers for hire and the buzzy *Juicy Beach Bar* attracting a mainly Greek clientele.

The narrow road down to Magaziá beach holds a clutch of very similar **rooms** for rent; of these, the air-conditioned *Georgia Tsakami* (☎22220 91357; ❸), some twenty metres from the beach and opposite a handy car park, is as close as you'll get to the sand and sea. If it's full, try the *Perigiali* (☎22220 91889, ✉perigiali@skyrosnet.gr; ❹) in Magaziá, a very pleasant mix of studios and air-conditioned rooms with phone, surrounding a large garden. Half-way between Magaziá and Mólos, *Pension Galini* (☎22220 91379; ❸) is a quiet and slightly more expensive choice, while the nearby *Motel Hara* (☎22220 91601; ❹) is another quiet option.

The beachfront **tavernas** often compare favourably with those in town: on the Magaziá side, *Stefanos* is reliable and popular, and overlooks the beach. At Mólos, try the *Kokalenia*, a restaurant in a garden and the *ouzerí* at *Balabani's Mill*, all at the end of the beach. It's worth sampling lobster in Skýros: it's a local speciality, often served flaked into pasta as *astakomakaronádha*.

For quieter beaches, carry on past Mólos, or try the excellent and undeveloped unofficial nudist beach, **Papá toú Houmá**, directly below the *kástro*. The path down starts 150m beyond the *Skyropoula* disco, and isn't obvious from above. Further along the road south of here, the beaches are disappointing until **Aspoús**, which has a couple of tavernas and rooms to rent, as well as the smart *Ahillion* hotel (☎22220 93300, ℻22220 93303; ❸). Further south, **Ahíli** had one of the best beaches on the island until it was replaced by the construction of a new marina. Southeast of here, the coast is rocky and inaccessible, although you can take a *kaïki* trip down to the bay of **Trís Boúkes**, passing some picturesque sea caves on the way.

Around the rest of the island

In summer, the bus from Skýros Town visits the more popular beaches, but if you want to branch out on your own, rent a scooter (see p.475). Tracks and footpaths diverge from the main circular road, leading inward and seaward. Among the most interesting places to head for is **Palamári**, the neglected site of an early Bronze Age settlement and a spectacular beach. Travelling from Skýros Town, turn right after the road has begun to descend to the airport plain.

For a taste of the island's wooded interior, a hike following the dirt track from Skýros Town to **ATSÍTSA** is well worth the effort; it takes three to four hours, and is too rough for a scooter. Atsítsa is an attractive bay with pine trees down to the sea, a very good fish taverna (*O Andonis*) and an increasing number of rooms, in addition to the Skýros Centre buildings. The beach here is rocky and isn't great for swimming, but there are small sandy coves fifteen and twenty minutes' walk to the north at **Kalogriás** and **Kyrá Panayiá**, with the seasonal taverna at Kalogriás, *O Yiorgos* being the only source of food here.

Elsewhere in the coniferous north, **Áyios Fokás** and **Péfkos** bays are easiest reached by a turning from the main road near Linariá, while access from Atsítsa is via a reasonable dirt road. Though still pretty undeveloped, Áyios Fokás is home to *Kali Rooms* (☎693 70 90 848; ❸), an excellent, very well-run taverna where you can bed down for the night; in Péfkos, best of the two **rooms** options is *Barba Mitsos* is the more appealing. The bay is beautiful, and the beach quite reasonable.

As for the great southern mountain of **Kohýlas**, exploring is best attempted if you have a four-wheel-drive vehicle, as the tracks are poor away from the main west-coast road via **Kalamítsa** to the naval base at Trís Boúkes (where Rupert Brooke is buried). Kalamítsa beach, just east of Linariá but tricky to get to from there, lacks character, but the *Mouries* taverna between it and Linariá and shaded by mulberry tree, is worth a stop.

Évvia (Euboea)

Évvia is the second-largest Greek island (after Crete), and seems more like an extension of the mainland to which it was once joined. At **Halkídha**, the gateway to the island, the curious old drawbridge link to the mainland has only a forty-metre channel to span, Évvia reputedly having been split from Attica and Thessaly by a blow from Poseidon's trident (earthquakes and subsidence being the more pedestrian explanations). Besides the newer suspension bridge bypassing Halkídha and also linking Évvia to the mainland, there are ferry crossings at no fewer than six points along its length, and the south of the island is closer to Athens than it is to northern Évvia.

Nevertheless, Évvia is an island, in places a very beautiful one. But it has an idiosyncratic history and demography, plus an enduringly strange feel that has

ÉVIA

N

Skiáthos, Skópelos & Alónissos

Skýros

Kávo Dóro
(Kafiréas)

▲ Óhi, 1399 m
Dhrakóspito
⚔ Castel Rosso
Mýli
Kárystos

Dhrakóspita
Stýra
Dhrakóspito

Marmári

Néa
Stýra

Almyropótamos

Panayía

Ayía
Márina

Lépoura
Kálamos

Dystos

Neohóri
Alivéri
Káravos

Amárynthos
Ayios Dhimítrios
Basilica of
Ayía Thékla

Avlonári

Oxýlithos

Paralía Kýmis
Platána
Stómio

Kými

Hiliádhou

Ayía
Irini

Stení

Dhírfys
1743 m

Sarakíniko

Skála
Oropoú

Erétria

Fýla

HALKÍDHA

Néa
Artáki

Ramnous

Pagóndas
Dhervéni Gorge

Paralía
Politikón

Prokópi

Krýa Vrýssi
Kírinthos

Mandoúdhi

Ayíou
Nikoláou
Galatáki

Glýfa

Kírinthos

Strofyliá
Ayía
Anna

Angáli

Paralía Kotsikiás

Elliniká
Psaropoúli

Péfki Vassiliká

Roviés

Limni

Ayiókambos

Loutrá Edhipsoú

Oreí

Yiáltra

Glýfa

Arkítsa

Kaména Voúrla
Áyios Konstandínos

ATHENS

Rafína

Lárissa

Vólos

Kórinthos

Kórinthos

0   25 km

kept it out of the mainstream of tourism. A marked **Albanian influence** in the south, and scattered Lombard and Venetian watchtowers across the island, lend a distinctive flavour. Indeed, Évvia was the longest-surviving south-mainland outpost of the Ottoman Turks, who had a keen appreciation of the island's wealth, as did the Venetians and Lombards before them. The last **Ottoman garrison** was not evicted until 1833, hanging on in defiance of the peace settlement that awarded Évvia to the new Greek state. Substantial Turkish communities, renowned for their alleged brutality, remained in the northwest half of the island until 1923.

Economically, Évvia has always been prized. By Greek standards, it's exceptionally **fertile**, producing everything from grain, corn and cotton to kitchen vegetables and livestock. The classical name, Euboea, means "rich in cattle", but nowadays cows are few and far between; its kid and lamb, however, are highly rated, as is the local retsina. Because of the collapse of much of its mining industry, parts of the island are actively seeking foreign tourism, but for the moment, Greeks predominate, especially in the north around the spa of **Loutrá Edhipsoú**. In July and August, Évvia can seem merely a beach annexe for much of Thessaly and Athens.

The rolling countryside of the **north** is the most conventionally scenic part of the island, echoing the beauty of the smaller Sporades with grain combines whirling on sloping hay meadows between olive groves and pine forest. The **northeast coast** is rugged and largely inaccessible, its few sandy beaches surf-pounded and often plagued by flotsam and jetsam; the **southwest** is gentler and more sheltered, though much disfigured by industrial operations. The **centre** of the island, between Halkídha and the easterly port of Kými, is mountainous and dramatic, while the far **southeast** is mostly dry and very isolated.

Public transport consists of passable bus services along the main roads to Kárystos in the southeast, and Loutrá Edhipsoú in the northwest. Explorations are best conducted by rented car; any two-wheeler will make little impact on the enormous distances involved.

Halkídha

The heavily industrialized island-capital of **HALKÍDHA** (the ancient Chalkis, an appellation still in use today) is the largest town on Évvia, with a population of 50,000. A shipyard, rail sidings and cement works make it a dire place, though things improve in the old Ottoman quarter, **Kástro**, south of Venizélou, and in the area around the Turkish fortress on the mainland. Hardly a trace remains of Halkídha's once-thriving Jewish community, whose presence here dates back around 2500 years.

The entrance to the *kástro* – on the right as you head inland from the old Euripos bridge – is marked by the handsome fifteenth-century **mosque**, nominally a museum of Byzantine artefacts, but permanently locked. Beyond lie the remains of Karababa (the seventeenth-century Ottoman fortress), an arcaded Turkish aqueduct and the unique basilican **church of Ayía Paraskeví** (shut except during services). The church is an odd structure, converted by the Crusaders during the fourteenth century into a Gothic cathedral. In the opposite direction, in the new town, an **archeological museum** at Venizélou 13 (Tues–Sun 8am–2.30pm; €2) has a good display of prehistoric, Hellenic and Roman finds from all over the island.

Halkídha's waterside overlooks the **Évripos**, the narrow channel dividing Évvia from the mainland, whose strange currents have baffled scientists for centuries. You can stand on the bridge that spans the narrowest point and watch the water swirling by like a river; every few hours the current changes and the "tide" reverses. Aristotle is said to have thrown himself into the waters in despair at his inability to understand what was happening, so if you're puzzled you're in good company; there is still no entirely satisfactory explanation.

Practicalities

For most visitors, much the best view of Halkídha is to be had from the bus or train on the way out. **Trains** arrive on the mainland side of the channel, beneath the old fortress; given numerous, quick rail links with Athens, there's little reason to stay overnight. Should you want to, though, the basic *Kentrikon* hotel (☎22210 22375; ❸) is a far better deal than the huge waterfront establishments it backs onto. Most other services of interest lie within sight of the old Évripos bridge. The **bus station** is 400m from the bridge along Kótsou, then 50m right; you should get a connection for any corner of the island as long as you show up by 2pm, later for Kými or Límni.

Halkídha is noted for its superior seafood and *ouzerís*; the waterfront **restaurants** are popular at weekends with Athenians but are not necessarily the best-value options. Two to try are *Ta Pende Fi* at Evvías 61, a classic fish taverna in a peaceful setting, or the more central, long-running *Tsaf* at Papanastasíou 3, off Platía Agorás, again strong on seafood titbits. For the truly impecunious or time-pressured, there's also a handful of acceptable grills serving adequate lunches in the immediate vicinity of the bus station.

Halkídha to Kými

The coast road heading east out of Halkídha offers an exceptionally misleading introduction to the interior of Évvia. The industrial zone gives way to nondescript hamlets, which are succeeded between Erétria and Amárynthos by sequestered colonies of Athenian second homes, rather bleak beaches and large hotels frequented by British and German package-tour visitors. There are some intriguing **Frankish towers** at Fýlla, worth a detour inland from Vasilikó if you have a car, but little else.

The first town along the main road is modern **ERÉTRIA**, a rather dreary resort laid out on a grid plan; for non-package travellers its main asset is a well-advertised ferry service across to Skála Oropoú in Attica. The site of **ancient Eretria** is more distinguished, though much of it lies under the town. A few scanty remains are dotted around the town centre, most conspicuously an **agora** and a **temple of Apollo**, but more interesting are the excavations in the northwest corner, behind the excellent small **museum** (Tues–Sun 8am–2.30pm; €2), opened in 1991 in collaboration with the Swiss School of Archeology. Here a **theatre** has been uncovered; steps from the orchestra descend to an underground vault used for sudden entrances and exits. Beyond the theatre are the ruins of a **gymnasium** and a **sanctuary**, while the museum guard will be happy to unlock the fourth-century-BC **House of Mosaics**, five minutes' walk from the museum. Of the dozen or so hotels in town, one of the more affordable and interesting options is the municipal tourist complex *Dreams Island* (☎22290 61224, ⓦwww.dreams-island.gr; ❺), which occupies a tiny offshore islet linked by causeway to the end of the bay. The handy and central *Pension Diamando* (☎22290 62214; ❸), right in the middle of the long waterfront promenade, is a less expensive option and a little more convenient for the busy nightlife.

Nine kilometres further east, **AMÁRYNTHOS** is a smaller and more pleas-ant resort to stay in. Though the town boasts nothing of particular interest, the seafront square is picturesque enough and there is an ample selection of good eateries, such as *Stefanos* or *Thodoros*, two reliable fish tavernas on the water-front, and *To Limanaki* 200m further west. Two good accommodation options are *Iliaktidhes Hotel Apartments* (☏ 22290 37605; ❹), just off the main road, and the B-class *Stefania Hotel* (☏ 22290 38382, ⓕ 22290 38384; ❺), 1km west of the centre right on the beach.

Moving on east, the enormous modern power plant and virtually intact medieval castle just before **Alivéri** seem incongruously juxtaposed, while more Frankish towers look down from nearby hills. Though Alivéri itself is dreary, the nearby fishing harbour of **KÁRAVOS** has several pleasant watering holes, among them the *Vlahos* taverna. Thereafter, the route heads inland. Beyond Lépoura, where the road branches north and south, the scenery improves dras-tically. Take the north fork towards Kými, and cross some of the most peaceful countryside in Greece. With your own vehicle you can detour east after 5km at Neohóri to the excellent beaches at **Kálamos** and **Korasídha**. There's a grow-ing selection of rooms and tavernas at Kálamos, including the very pleasant *To Egeon* (☏ 22230 41865; ❸), with a downstairs restaurant.

Twelve kilometres north of Lépoura, at Háni Avlonaríou, stands the Romanesque thirteenth- or fourteenth-century **basilica of Áyios Dhimítrios**, Évvia's largest and finest (ask for the key at the café next door). **AVLONÁRI** proper, 2km east, is dominated by a hill that commands most of the island's centre. At its crown is a huge Lombard (or Venetian) tower, rearing above the Neoclassical and vernacular houses that tier the lower slopes. There's a single taverna below the *platía*, though no accommodation.

Avlonári was an archiepiscopal see from the sixth century onwards, and this part of Évvia is particularly well endowed with Byzantine chapels. Back on the road to Kými, a left fork just north of Háni Avlonaríou (the bus goes this way) leads past the hamlet of **Ayía Thékla**, where a small, shed-like **chapel** of that saint, probably slightly later than Áyios Dhimítrios, hides in a lush vale below the modern church. Inside, fresco fragments, depicting large-eyed faces, suggest what has been lost over time. The right fork leads towards the coast and takes you past Oxýlithos, with its somewhat more elaborate chapels of **Áyios Nikólaos** and **Ayía Ánna**, both at least a hundred years older than Áyios Dhimítrios.

The road hits the coast at the fine beach of **Stómio** (known also as just Paralía, or "Beach"), some 1500m of sand closing off the mouth of a river, which is deep, swimmable and often cleaner than the sea. To the north and east you glimpse the capes enclosing the broad bay of Kými. Up on the road, there are a couple of cafés and a small *pension*; most facilities, however, are further round the coast at **PLATÁNA**, where another river is flanked by a line of older houses, many with rooms or flats to rent.

Despite its name, the extremely functional port of **PARALÍA KÝMIS** has no real beach, and is not a particularly congenial place to be stuck overnight waiting for a ferry to Skýros. The most substantial and traditional **taverna** is *To Egeo*, at the south end of the front, while *To Akteon* near the *Beis* hotel is also reasonable. There are a couple of reasonable hotels worth considering, both used to one-nighters: *Coralli* (☏ 22220 22212, ⓕ 22220 23355; ❹) and *Beis* (☏ 22220 22604, ⓕ 22220 22870; ❹).

Most travellers get to **KÝMI** (the main ferry port to Skýros) by bus, which takes the inland route via Ayía Thékla. The upper part of town is built on a green ridge overlooking both the sea and Paralía Kýmis, 4km below. Note that all buses deposit you in the upper town, except for the one or two daily that connect with the ferry. At the bottom of the town, on the harbour-bound road, the **Folklore Museum** (10am–1pm and 6–8.30pm daily; free) has an improbably large collection of costumes, household and agricultural implements and old photos recording the doings of Kymians both locally and in the US, where there's a huge community. Among the emigrants was Dr George Papanikolaou, deviser of the "Pap" cervical smear test, and there's a statue honouring him up in the upper-town *platía*, where you might ask about **rooms**. There are some good tavernas, such as *To Balkoni* on the main road towards the shore, which offers a superb view and the chance to sample the produce of the local vineyards.

To get up into the rugged country west of Kými, you must negotiate jeep tracks through the forest or return to Halkídha for the bus service up to **STENÍ**, a large and beautiful village at the foot of Mount Dhírfys. The village has a couple of decent hotels, the *Dirfys* (☎22280 51217; ❸) and the *Steni* (☎22280 51221; ❸). For a hearty meal, *Sakaflias* on the main square is a good choice, specializing in *tiganópsomo*, a kind of pan-fried cheese pie. It's a good area for hiking, most notably up the peaks of Dhírfys and Xirovoúni, and beyond to the isolated beach hamlets of Hiliádhou and Ayía Iríni, though you'll need a specialist hiking guide to find the routes (see "Books", p.621).

Southeast Évvia

So narrow that you can sometimes glimpse the sea on both sides, the spit of land southeast of Lépoura has a flavour very distinct from the rest of the island. Often bleak and windswept, it forms a geological unit with neighbouring Ándhros to the southeast, with shared slates and marble. Ethnically, the south also has much in common with that northernmost Cyclade: both were heavily settled by Albanian immigrants from the early fifteenth century onwards, and Arvanítika – a **medieval dialect** of Albanian – was until recently the first language of the remoter villages here. Even non-Arvanítika speakers often betray their ancestry by their startlingly fair colouring and aquiline features. For a place so close to Athens, though, the south is often surprisingly untouched by modernity; some of the houses have yet to lose their original slate roofs, while others still lack electricity, and the few fields on the steep slopes are far more often worked by donkeys and horses than by farm machinery.

Immediately southeast of Lépoura, Lake Dhýstos is a shadow of its former self, having been mostly drained and reclaimed as farmland; some migratory birds do still frequent its shallow marshes, however. Atop the almost perfectly conical hill in the centre of its flat basin are the sparse fifth-century-BC ruins of **ancient Dystos** and a subsequent medieval citadel, though they're hard to explore because the surroundings are so swampy.

Beyond the Dhýstos plain, the main road continues along the mountainous spine of the island to Kárystos, at the southern end of the paved road and bus line. If you have your own transport, it's worth stopping off at **STÝRA**, above which are a cluster of **Dhrakóspita** (Dragon Houses), signposted at the north edge of the village and reached by track, then trail. So named because only mythological beings were thought capable of shifting into place their enormous masonry blocks, their origins and uses have yet to be definitively established. The most convincing theory suggests that they are sixth-century-BC temples built by immigrants or slaves from Asia Minor working in the nearby marble and slate quarries.

The shore annexe of **NÉA STÝRA**, 5km downhill from the hill village, is a fairly standard package resort, worth knowing about only for its handy ferry connection to Ayía Marína (which gives access to ancient Ramnous) on the Attic peninsula. Much the same can be said for **MARMÁRI**, 19km south, except in this case the ferry link is with Rafina, and now serves as Kárystos's de facto ferry link too. Here the rather tired *Hotel Delfini* (☏22240 31296, ℗22240 32300; ❸) is at least good value and there are a few decent places to eat; *Zafiris* has shaded tables right on the waterfront, while if you fancy a walk, head for *Tò Akriogiali*, at the far southern end of the waterfront on a platform over the water.

The new road between Marmári and Kárystos completes Évvia's "super-highway", allowing you to enjoy the nether reaches of the island as you cruise down to its last major settlement.

Kárystos and around

Studded with modern buildings, at first sight **KÁRYSTOS** is a rather boring grid (courtesy of nineteenth-century Bavarian town-planners) which ends abruptly to east and west. However, King Otho liked the site so much that he contemplated transferring the Greek capital here, and there are still some graceful Neoclassical buildings dating from that period. Though you're unlikely to want to stay for more than a few days, Kárystos does improve given prolonged acquaintance, with a superb (if often windy) beach to the west, the smaller, sandier **Psilí Ámmos** ten minutes' walk to the east and a lively, genuine working-port atmosphere. Only one plot of fenced-in foundations, in the central bazaar, bears out the town's ancient provenance, and the oldest obvious structure is the fourteenth-century Venetian **Boúrtzi** (locked except for occasional summer-evening art exhibitions) on the waterfront; this small tower is all that remains of once-extensive fortifications. Opposite the Boúrtzi inside the Cultural Centre, a small but interesting **archeological museum** (Tues–Sun 8am–3pm; €1.50) displays finds from the local area – mostly statues and temple carvings, plus a few smaller votive objects. You might find yourself back here in the evenings, when the shore road here is blocked by a gate to allow the locals an undisturbed promenade.

Practicalities

Since the completion of the new road, Marmári, 15km back up the road, has become Kárystos's passenger port, and much to the disgruntlement of the locals, no passenger **ferries** serve the town directly. Frequent **buses** link the two centres, arriving at the bus station, a few blocks inland from the waterfront next to the Town Hall on Kotsíka. The station (☏22240 26303) displays information on the extremely infrequent (once daily at best) departures to the remote villages of the Kavodóro (Kafiréas) cape to the east.

Finding affordable **accommodation** is not a big problem. The most central is the *Als* (☏22240 22202, ℗22240 25002; ❸), right opposite the quay, although it is getting a shade timeworn and can get noisy in high season. Other options are the big *Galaxy* (☏22240 22600; ❹), offering air-conditioned rooms on the west side of the waterfront, or the resort-style *Apollon Suite* (☏22240 22045, ✉apollon-suite@yahoo.com; ❻) on Psilí Ámmos beach. On the shore road in the park beyond the Boúrtzi, the excellent *Karystion* (☏22240 22391, ⓦwww.karystion.gr; ❻) is perhaps the best overall option, with filling breakfasts included in the rates.

You're spoilt for choice when **eating out**. Good choices include the *Kavo Doro*, a friendly and reasonable taverna one block west of the square on Párodos

Sakhtoúri, serving *mayireftá; Ta Kalamia*, at the west end of the esplanade by the start of the beach, is a cheap, filling and popular lunchtime option, while 2km east of town at Aetós, the quiet *Tò Kyma* is an ideal spot for an evening meal or Sunday lunch by the sea. Kotsíka, which runs up from the port, holds are several fine *psistariés*, serving the local lamb and goat for which Kárystos is renowned: *O Panourgias* or the *Karystaki* are two of the better ones.

Mount Óhi

The obvious excursion from Kárystos is inland towards **Mount Óhi** (1399m) Évvia's highest peak after Dhírfys and Xirovoúni. Some 3km straight inland, **MÝLI**, a fair-sized village around a spring-fed oasis, makes a good first stop with a few tavernas. Otherwise, the medieval castle of **Castel Rosso** beckons above, a twenty-minute climb up from the main church (longer in the frequent, howling gales). Inside, the castle is a total ruin, except for an Orthodox **chapel of Profítis Ilías** built over the Venetians' water cistern, but the sweeping views over the sea and the town make the trip worthwhile.

Behind, the ridges of Óhi are as lunar and inhospitable as the broad plain around Kárystos is fertile. From Mýli, it's a three-hour-plus hike up the largely bare slopes, mostly by a path cutting across the new road, strewn with unfinished granite columns, abandoned almost two thousand years ago. The path passes a little-used alpine club shelter (fed by spring water) and yet another *dhrakóspito*, even more impressive than the three smaller ones at Stýra. Built of enormous schist slabs, seemingly sprouting from the mountain, this one is popularly supposed to be haunted.

Halkídha to Límni

Due north from Halkídha, the main road crosses a few kilometres of flat farmland and salt marsh on either side of the refugee settlement of Néa Artáki, after which it climbs steeply through forested hills and the **Dhervéni gorge**, gateway to Évvia's north. With your own transport, you can take a pleasant detour along the side road to the left before Psákhna to the long pebbly beach of **Paralía Politikón**, dotted with places to stay or eat.

The village of **PROKÓPI** lies beyond the narrows, in a valley defined by the rich and beautiful woods that make it famous. A counterpoint, in the village itself is the ugly 1960s pilgrimage **church of St John the Russian**, which holds the saint's relics. The "Russian" was actually a Ukrainian soldier, captured by the Ottomans in the early eighteenth century and taken to Turkey, where he died. According to locals, his mummified body began to promote miracles, and the saint's relics were brought here by Orthodox Greeks from Cappadocian Prokópi (today Ürgüp) in the 1923 population exchange – Evvian Prokópi is still referred to by the locals as Akhmétaga, the name of the old Turkish fiefdom here that was bought right after the War of Independence by Edward Noel, an English nobleman and cousin of Lord Byron.

Following a shady, stream-fed glen for the 8km north of Prokópi, you suddenly emerge at **Mandoúdhi**, much the biggest village in the north of the island. Ignore signs or depictions on certain maps of a beach at Paralía Mandoúdhi; there's nothing more than the abandoned quarries and crushing plants of the town's former magnesite industry. The closest serviceable beach is at **Paralía Kírinthos**, better known as **Krýa Vrýsi** (take a right-hand turning off the main road, 3km beyond Mandoúdhi). At the coast, a river and an inlet bracket a small beach, with the headland south of the river supporting the extremely sparse remains of ancient Kirinthos. The hamlet of **Kírinthos**, just past Mandoúdhi, has some visitors, owing to the craft school there.

Back on the main road, a fork at **Strofyliá**, 8km north of Mandoúdhi, offers a choice of routes: continue north to the coastal resorts that curl round the end of the island (see p.486), east to Pýli and then south to some unspoilt beaches on the way to **Cape Sarakíniko**, or head west for Límni.

Límni

On the west coast 19km from Strofiliá, **LÍMNI** is by far the most practical and attractive base north of Halkídha. The largely Neoclassical, tile-roofed town, built from the wealth engendered by nineteenth-century shipping prowess, is the most appealing on the island, with serviceable beaches and a famous convent nearby. A small **folk art museum** (Mon–Sat 9am–1pm, Sun 10.30–1pm; €1.50) features pottery, coins and sculpture fragments, as well as local costumes, fabrics and furniture.

Buses from Halkídha stop at the north side of the quay. Límni has a **post office** and two **banks**, all inland just off the main through-road into town from Strofyliá.

As yet, Límni gets few package tours, so there's usually space available in its **rooms** or **hotels**, except during August. At the extreme southern – quieter – end of the waterfront, the rather old-fashioned *Limni* (☎22270 31316, ✉hlimni@otenet.gr; ❸) is good value, with singles as well as doubles, while smart rooms with TV can be rented at *Livaditis* (☎22270 31640; ❹), on the northern waterfront. The best **place to eat** in terms of setting, menu and popularity is *O Platanos* (under the enormous quayside plane tree), with the adjacent *Avra* not far behind. Other local favourites include the newer *To Fyki*, also on the waterfront, and *Lambros*, 800m along the way to Katoúnia beach to the south of town.

Around Límni

There are no recommendable beaches in Límni itself, though if you continue 2.5km northwest from the town you reach the gravel strand of **Kohýli**, with a basic but leafy campsite out on the cape, 500m beyond mid-beach. Other congenial places to stay include, most notably, *Denis House* (☎22270 31787; ❺), and the more luxurious *Ostria* (☎22270 32247; ❻), with a pool and breakfast included in the rates.

ROVIÉS, some 14km northwest of Límni, doesn't really stand out (except for its famous olives), but with its medieval tower, rooms, hotels, excellent campsite, grid of weekenders' apartments and services, it's the last place of any size along the scenic coast road to Loutrá Edhipsoú.

The outstanding excursion from Límni is 7km south (under your own steam) to the **convent of Ayíou Nikoláou Galatáki**, superbly set on the wooded slopes of Mount Kandhíli, overlooking the north Evvian Gulf. To get there, veer up and left at the unsigned fork off the coast road; there's no formal scheme for visiting, but don't show up in the early afternoon, as the gates are shut around sunset. Though much rebuilt since its original Byzantine foundation atop a Poseidon temple, the convent retains a thirteenth-century tower built to guard against pirates, and a crypt. One of a dozen or so nuns will show you frescoes in the *katholikón*, dating from the principal sixteenth-century renovation. Especially vivid, on the right of the narthex, is the *Entry of the Righteous into Paradise*: the righteous ascend a perilous ladder to be crowned by angels and received by Christ, while the wicked miss the rungs and fall into the maw of Leviathan.

Below Ayíou Nikoláou Galatáki, and easily combined with it to make a full half-day outing, are the pebble-and-sand beaches of **Glýfa**, arguably the best on this part of Évvia's southwest-facing coast. There are several in succession, leading up to the very base of Mount Kandhíli, some reachable by paths, the last few only by boat. The shore is remarkably clean, considering the number of summer campers who pitch tents here for weeks on end; a single roadside spring, 2km before the coast, is the only facility in the whole zone.

Northern coastal resorts

Returning to the junction at Strofiliá, take the main road north for 8km to **AYÍA ÁNNA** (locally and universally elided to Ayiánna), which has long enjoyed the unofficial status of Évvia's most **folkloric village**, by virtue of traditional costumes worn by the older women and an assiduous local ethnographer, Dimitris Settas, who died in 1989. The place itself is nothing extraordinary, and most passers-by are interested in the prominently marked turn-off for **Angáli beach**, 5km east. Billed as the area's best, it's a broad, long and dark swath of sand protected only at the northern end. For accommodation, the *Agali Hotel* (☎22270 97104, ℱ22270 97067; ❺) is a pretty congenial option, while for eating, *Armata* at the northern end is the only place with tables on the beach. Horseriding on the beach is a well-advertised and popular diversion.

Ten kilometres north of Ayía Ánna, a side road heads downhill for 6km, past the village of Kotsikiá, to **Paralía Kotsikiás**. The small cove, with its taverna and rooms, serves primarily as a fishing-boat anchorage, and its tiny, seaweed-strewn beach is of little interest. **Psaropoúli beach**, 2km below Vassiliká village (13km north of the Kotsikiá turn-off), is more useable in its three-kilometre length, but like Ayía Ánna it's scruffy and shadeless, with a smattering of rooms, self-catering units and tavernas not imparting much sense of community. If you choose to stay, you can't do much better than *Motel Canadiana* (☎22260 43274; ❸), where the road down meets the seafront. **Elliniká**, the next signposted beach, lies just 800m below its namesake village inland; it's far smaller than Angáli or Psaropoúli, but cleaner and certainly the most picturesque spot on this coast, with a church-capped islet offshore as a target to swim to. The approach driveway has a very limited number of facilities: a minimarket and a few studios for rent. *Motel Egeo* (☎22260 42262; ❸) is as good as any if you want to stay, while the newish *O Paradisos* taverna is the best of a fairly limited choice of eating options.

Beyond Elliniká, the road (and bus line) skirts the northern tip of Évvia to curl southwest towards **PÉFKI**, a seaside resort mobbed with Greeks in summer, which straggles for some 2km along a mediocre beach. The best **restaurants**, near the north end of this strip, include *Ouzeri Ta Thalassina*, *Psitopolio O Thomas* and *O Lambros*. **Accommodation** is the usual Evvian mix of self-catering units, and a few seaside hotels such as *Galini* (☎22260 41208, ℱ22260 41650; ❹) and *Myrtia* (☎22260 41202; ❸), both resolutely pitched at mainlanders; the campsite, *Camping Pefki*, 2km north of town behind the beach, is rather pricey and geared to people with caravans. Hydrofoils for the Sporades depart from here once in the morning and once in the afternoon during summer only.

The next resort, 14km southwest, is **OREÍ**, a low-key fishing village, whose cafés are favoured by those in the know as the best places to watch the sunset. It has a fine statue of a Hellenistic bull, hauled up from the sea in 1965. Nearby Néos Pýrgos beach has a selection of rooms and restaurants. Some 7km further along the coast, **AYIÓKAMBOS** has eight daily ferry connections to Glýfa on the mainland opposite, from where there are buses to Vólos.

Ayiókambos is surprisingly pleasant considering its port function, with a patch of beach, two or three tavernas and a few rooms for rent.

The trans-island bus route ends 14km south of Ayiókambos at **LOUTRÁ EDHIPSOÚ**, which attracts older Greeks who come to bathe at the **spas** renowned since antiquity for curing everything from gallstones to depression. The spas themselves are cheap (€1.50 for 20min) and quite an experience; you can always bathe for free at the public beach next to the *Thermae Sylla* hotel, where hot spa water gushes out freely into an artificial set of cascades. The vast number of **hotels**, some old and creaky, which service the summer influx means good deals can be had off-season. On the seafront, the classy 1920s-vintage *Egli* (☎22260 22215, ⓕ22260 22886; ❸) is a good choice, while you can really push the boat out at the 1897-built *Thermae Sylla* (☎22260 60100, ⓦwww.thermaesylla.gr; ❼), a French-style monument atop what's claimed to be the best thermal spring in Greece, thoroughly overhauled in 1998. More affordable options in the side streets near the port are *Valar's* (☎22260 22278, ⓕ22260 23419; ❸), and the more modern *Lito* (☎22260 22081; ❸). For **eating** there is an abundance of tavernas strung along the front; try the leafy restaurant of the *Egli* or the traditional *To Fagadhiko tou Barous*, which offers a wide selection of *mezédhes*.

There are less-regimented **hot springs** at **Yiáltra**, 15km west around the head of Edhipsós bay, where the water boils up on the rocky beach, warming the shallows to comfortable bath temperature. From Loutrá Edhipsoú, the coast road heads southeast to Límni.

Travel details

Ferry services out of Vólos and Áyios Konstandínos to the northern Sporades are run by Hellas Flying Dolphins and GA Lines, while Minoan Lines have an additional service linking Thessaloníki with Crete via Skiáthos and a couple of the more popular Cyclades. Hydrofoils from Vólos and Áyios Konstandínos to the Sporades, as well as the jet ferry between Áyios Konstandínos and the Sporades, only run reliably between early June and mid-September. These craft are pricier than the ferries, but cut journey times virtually in half and are 15 percent faster than the single car-carrying catamaran out of Vólos. The Kými–Skýros route is an overpriced monopoly sailing, served by a single, slow ferry. For more details of all services, as well as ferry company websites, visit ⓦwww.gtp.gr.

Skiáthos, Skópelos and Alónnisos

Ferries

NB: Departure frequencies given are for the June-to-mid-Sept period, and are valid in reverse sense.
Skiáthos to: Iráklion (1–2 weekly), Thessaloníki (1–2 weekly), select Cyclades (1–2 weekly).
Vólos to: Skiáthos (2 daily; 2hr 15min); Skópelos (2 daily; 3hr 30min); Alónnisos (1 daily; 4hr 20min). Also one weekly service on GA Ferries, usually Fri, to Límnos and Lésvos via Skiáthos and Skópelos.

Jet Ferry

Áyios Konstandínos to: Alónnisos (July to mid-Sept 4–6 weekly; 4hr); Skiáthos (July to mid-Sept

1–2 daily; 3hr); Skópelos (July to mid-Sept 1–2 daily; 3hr 30min).

Hydrofoils

Áyios Konstandínos to: Skiáthos, Glóssa, Skópelos and Alónnisos (3 daily in season at 10am, 2pm and 7.15pm; 1–2 daily otherwise).
Vólos to: Skiáthos, Glóssa, Skópelos Town and Alónnisos (4 daily at 9am, 1.15pm, 2.30pm and 7.30pm).

Flights

Athens to: Skiáthos (mid-June to mid-Sept 1 daily, otherwise 3 weekly; 50min).

Skýros

Ferries

Skýros is served from Kými (2hr) by conventional ferry, the *Lykomidis*. Services are at least twice daily from mid-June to early Sept (usually at either 12pm or 1pm and 6pm or 7pm), and once daily (5pm, 6pm or 7pm) the rest of the year; there may be an additional boat on designated peak travel days in July and August – call ☏ 22220 22522 (Kými) or ☏ 22220 91790 (Skýros) for current information. There is a connecting bus service for the late-afternoon boat, from the Liossíon 260 terminal in Athens (departs 10am & 2.45pm).

Flights

Athens to: Skýros (mid-June to mid-Sept 2 weekly; 35min).
Thessaloníki to: Skýros (mid-June to mid-Sept 3 weekly, 40min).

Évvia

Buses

Athens (Liossíon 260 terminal) to: Halkídha (every 30min 5.30am–9.30pm; 1hr 30min); Kými (5 daily; 3hr 15min).
Halkídha to: Kárystos (2 daily; 3hr); Kými (8 daily; 1hr 45min); Límni (5 daily; 1hr 30min); Loutrá Edhipsoú (4 daily; 3hr).

Trains

Athens (Laríssis station) to: Halkídha (19 daily; 1hr 30min).

Ferries

Arkítsa to: Loutrá Edhipsoú (at least hourly July–Sept 15, every 1–2hr otherwise, last at 10–11pm/8–9pm; 45min).

Ayía Marína to: Néa Styýra (summer 12–14 daily; 45min); Alymyropótamos dock (summer 1 daily; 45min).
Glýfa to: Ayiókambos (8–11 daily summer, 4 daily winter; last sailing at 8.30pm/5pm; 30min).
Rafína to: Marmári (4–6 daily in summer, 4 in winter).
Skála Oropoú to: Erétria (March–Oct every 30min 6.45am–7.45pm, then hourly to 11pm; 30min).
NB: Connecting buses from Athens run to Rafína (every 30min; 1hr), Ayía Marína (5 daily; 1hr 15min) and Skála Oropoú (hourly; 1hr 30min), all from the Mavromatéon terminal, and to Arkítsa and Glýfa from the Liossíon 260 terminal.

Hydrofoils

Péfki (to Skiáthos, Glóssa, Skópelos and Alónnisos (2 daily at 10am and 5.45pm).

7

The Ionian Islands

Highlights

* **Kérkyra (Corfu) Town** Venetian fortresses, beautiful churches, fine museums and appealing architecture. See p.494

* **Perouládhes, Corfu** Shaded till early afternoon and backed by sheer vertical cliffs, this beach is an excellent hang-out. See p.504

* **Andípaxi** Some of the Ionian's best swimming and snorkelling is on offer at the exquisite beaches of Paxí's little sister. See p.514

* **Lefkádha's west coast** The archipelago's finest beaches run from Áï Nikítas down to Pórto Katsíki. See p.520

* **Melissáni Cave, Kefaloniá** See dappled sunlight on the water amid rock formations on a boat trip inside this once-enclosed underwater cave. See p.526

* **Mount Énos, Kefaloniá** The highest point in the Ionians has stunning vistas of sea and distant land. See p.530

* **Itháki's Homeric sites** Relive the myths on Odysseus's island. See p.533

* **Boat tour round Zákynthos** The best way to see the impressive coastline is to cruise from Zákynthos Town. See p.538

△ Melissáni Cave, Kefaloniá

7

The Ionian Islands

T he **Ionian** islands, shepherding their satellites down the west coast of the mainland, float on the haze of the Ionian sea, their green, even lush, silhouettes coming as a shock to those more used to the stark outlines of the Aegean. The fertility of the land is a direct result of the heavy rains that sweep over the archipelago – and especially Corfu – from October to March, so if you visit at this time, come prepared.

The islands were the Homeric realm of Odysseus, centred on Ithaca (modern Itháki) and here alone of all modern Greek territory (except for Lefkádha) the Ottomans never held sway. After the fall of Byzantium, possession passed to the **Venetians** and the islands became a keystone in Venice's maritime empire from 1386 until its collapse in 1797. Most of the population must have remained immune to the establishment of Italian as the official language and the arrival of Roman Catholicism, but Venetian influence remains evident in the architecture of the island capitals, despite damage from a series of earthquakes.

On Corfu, the Venetian legacy is mixed with that of the **British**, who imposed a military "protectorate" over the Ionian islands at the close of the Napoleonic Wars, before ceding the archipelago to Greece in 1864. There is, however, no question of the islanders' essential Greekness: the poet Dhionyssios Solomos, author of the national anthem, hailed from the Ionians, as did Nikos Mantzelos, who provided the music, and the first Greek president, Ioannis Kapodhistrias.

Today, **tourism** is the dominating influence, especially on **Corfu** (Kérkyra), which was one of the first Greek islands established on the package-holiday circuit. Parts of its coastline are among the few stretches in Greece with development to match the Spanish *costas*, and in summer even its distinguished old capital, Kérkyra Town, wilts beneath the onslaught. However, the island is large enough to retain many of its charms and is perhaps the most scenically beautiful of the group. Parts of **Zákynthos** (Zante) – which with Corfu has the Ionians' most oversubscribed beaches – have also gone down the same tourist path, but elsewhere the island's pace and scale of development is a lot less intense. Little **Paxí** is rather tricky to reach and lacks the water to support large-scale hotels, but still gets surprisingly packed in August, while **Lefkádha**, connected to the mainland by a causeway and iron bridge, has, a low-key straggle of tourist centres, two major resorts, and some excellent beaches. Perhaps the most rewarding duo for island-hopping are **Kefalloniá** and **Itháki**: the former with a series of "real towns" and a life in large part independent of tourism, the latter, Odysseus's rugged capital, protected by an absence of sand. The Ionian islands' claims to Homeric significance are manifested in the countless bars, restaurants and streets named after characters in the *Odyssey*. Kýthira and Andikýthira lie isolated at the foot of the Peloponnese; both are undeveloped and see few foreign visitors.

491

Corfu (Kérkyra)

Dangling between the heel of Italy and the west coast of mainland Greece, green, mountainous **Corfu (Kérkyra)** was one of the first Greek islands to attract mass tourism in the 1960s. Indiscriminate exploitation turned parts into eyesores, but much of the island still consists of olive groves, mountain or woodland. The majority of package holidays are based in the most developed resorts, but unspoiled terrain is often only a few minutes' walk away.

CORFU (KÉRKYRA)

▲ Eríkoussa

◄ Mathráki & Othoní

▲ Italy

ALBANIA

Perouládhes
Avliótes
Sidhári
Astrakerí
Almyrós
Cape Áyias
Ekaterínis
Almyrós
Andinióti
Lagoon
Aharávi
Loútses
Kassiópi
 Áyios
Stéfanos
Karousádhes
Magouládhes
Ródha
Períthia
Avláki
Áyios Stéfanos
Kerasiá
Kouloúra
Siniés
Kalámi
Arillas
Agrafi
Episkepsi
Mt
Pandokrátor
Afiónas
Kraviá
Áyios Yeóryios
Strinýlas
Agní
Makrádhes
Troumpéta
Spartýlas
Nissáki
Angelókastro
Lákones
Pyrgí
Barbáti
Paleokastrítsa
Skriperó
Ípsos
Liapádhes
Dhassiá
Dhafnila
Vídhos
Gouviá
Kondókali
Érmones
Vátos
Potamós
KÉRKYRA
TOWN
Myrtiótissa
Glyfádha
Pélekas
Kanóni
Pondikoníssi
Pérama
Achílleion
Gastoúri
Aï Górdhis
Ayii
Dhéka
Benítses
Pendáti
Paramónas
Áno
Moraïtika
Moraïtika
Mesongí
Pendanísia
Áyios Matthéos
Boúkari
Prasoúdhi
Áno
Mesongí
Petrití
Gardhíki
Pýrgos
Línia
Aryirádhes
Lefkími
Halikoúna
Korission
Lagoon
Íssos
Áyios
Yeóryios
Perivóli
Ayía Varvára
Kritiká
Neohóri
Sparterá
Kávos
Aï Górdhis
Paleohoríou
Arkoudhilas
Cape
Asprókavos

Igoumenítsa ►
Igoumenítsa ►
Paxí & Pátra ►

N

0   10 km

Corfu is thought to have been the model for Prospero's and Miranda's place of exile in Shakespeare's *The Tempest*, and was certainly known to writers such as Spenser and Milton and – more recently – Edward Lear and Henry Miller, plus Gerald and Lawrence Durrell. Lawrence Durrell's *Prospero's Cell* evokes the island's "delectable landscape", still evident in some of the best beaches of the whole archipelago.

The staggering amount of accommodation (over 5000 places) on the island means that competition keeps prices down even in high season, at least in many resorts outside of Kérkyra Town. Prices at restaurants and in shops also tend to be a little lower than average for the Ionians.

Kérkyra (Corfu) Town

The capital, **KÉRKYRA (CORFU) TOWN**, was renovated for an EU summit in 1994, and is now one of the most elegant island capitals in the whole of Greece. Although many of its finest buildings were destroyed by Nazi bombers in World War II, two massive forts, the sixteenth-century church of Áyios Spyrídhon and buildings dating from French and British administrations remain intact. As the island's major port of entry by ferry or plane, Kérkyra Town is packed in summer.

Arrivals, information and services

Ferries and hydrofoils to and from Italy, the mainland (Igoumenítsa and Pátra) and Paxí dock at the New Port (Néo Limáni) west of the Néo Froúrio (New Fort). The Old Port (Paleó Limáni), east of the New Port, is used only for day-excursions. Most of the ferry offices are on the main road opposite the New Port; ferries to Italy or south towards Pátra become very busy in summer and booking is advisable. The port authority (domestic ☎26610 32655, international ☎26610 30481) can advise on services.

The **airport** is 2km south of the city centre. There are no airport buses, although local **blue buses** #5 and #6 can be flagged at the junction where the airport approach drive meets the main road (500m from terminal). It's a thirty-minute walk on flat terrain into town (follow the road running beside the *Hotel Bretagne* opposite the junction for the shortest route or turn right then follow the sea road). **Taxis** charge at least €6 (but agree the fare in advance) or phone ☎26610 33811 for a radio cab.

The **tourist office** (Mon–Fri 8am–2pm; ☎26610 37520, ⓔe.o.t.corfu @otenet.gr), on Vouleftón near the corner of Polylá, has accommodation and transport details. The **post office** is on the corner of Alexándhras and Zafirópoulou (Mon–Fri 7.30am–8pm). Of the town's several Internet cafés, the best value are *Recorder*, P. Konstandá 1 (Mon–Sat 9am–2pm & 6–11pm; €4.80 per hour), just off Platía Saróko (often anglicized to San Rocco, though it is officially named Platía Yeoryíou Theotóki), and *Hobby Net*, Solomoú 32 (daily 10am–11pm; €5 per hour), near the Old Port.

Getting around

Corfu's **bus** service radiates from the capital. There are **two** terminals: the islandwide green bus service is based on Avramíou (also for Athens and Thessaloníki), and the suburban blue bus system, which also serves nearby resorts such as Benítses and Dhassiá, is based in Platía Saróko. Islandwide services stop between 6 and 8.30pm, suburban ones at around 10pm. Printed English timetables are available for both and can be picked up at the tourist office or the respective terminals. Major **ferry** lines have franchises on the seafront opposite the New Port: ANEK (☎26610 24503, ⓦwww.anek.gr), Blue Star/Strintzis (☎26610 26660, ⓦwww.bluestarferries.com), Fragline (☎26610 38089, ⓦwww.fragline.gr), Minoan (☎26610 25000, ⓦwww.minoan.gr), Ventouris (☎26610 21212, ⓦwww.ventouris.gr) and Italian Ferries (☎26610 36439, ⓦwww.italianferries.it). The Petrakis agency (☎26610 25155, ⓔpetrakis_lines@aias.gr) runs the **hydrofoil** service to Paxí and Igoumenítsa, as well as tours to Albania, Párga and other Ionian islands, which it sells at much cheaper rates than the travel agents in the resorts.

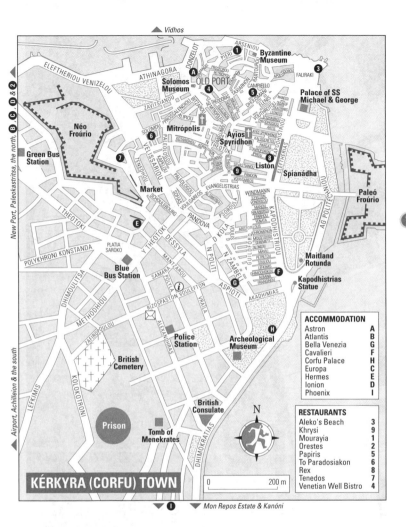

Vídhos

ARSENÍOU

① Byzantine Museum

③ FALIRÁKI

DONZELOT

PIERÍ

ELEFTHERÍOU VENIZÉLOU

ATHINAGÓRA

OLD PORT

A Solomos Museum ④

CAMPIÉLLO

⑤

Palace of SS Michael & George

ZAVITSIÁNOU

Néo Froúrio

⑥ Mitrópolis

Áyios Spyrídhon

⑦

Green Bus Station

Market

Listón

⑨

Spianádha

Paleó Froúrio

E

PLATÍA SAROKO

Blue Bus Station

ⓘ

Maitland Rotunda

F

Kapodhístrias Statue

Police Station

Archeological Museum

H

British Cemetery

British Consulate

N

Prison

Tomb of Menekrates

KÉRKYRA (CORFU) TOWN

0   200 m

Airport, Achílleion & the south

New Port, Paleokastrítsa, the north, B, C, D & ②

⑦

THE IONIAN ISLANDS | Corfu

ACCOMMODATION

Astron	A
Atlantis	B
Bella Venezia	G
Cavalieri	F
Corfu Palace	H
Europa	C
Hermes	E
Ionion	D
Phoenix	I

RESTAURANTS

Aleko's Beach	3
Khrysi	9
Mourayia	1
Orestes	2
Papiris	5
To Paradosiakon	6
Rex	8
Tenedos	7
Venetian Well Bistro	4

ⓘ Mon Repos Estate & Kanóni

Cars can also be rented from international agencies at the airport or in town; try Avis, Ethnikís Andístasis 42 (☎26610 24404, airport 26610 42007), behind the new port, Budget, Venizélou 22 (☎26610 28590; airport ☎26610 44017) or Hertz, Ethnikí Lefkímis (☎26610 38388, airport 35547). Among local companies, Sunrise, Ethnikís Andístasis 14 (☎26610 44325) is reliable for cars, and **bikes** can be rented from Easy Rider, Venizélou 4 (☎26610 43026) or Lazy Bone, Venizélou 52 (☎26610 40580) both in the New Port.

Accommodation

Accommodation in Kérkyra Town is busy all year round, and not always the best value when compared to the rest of the island. Room owners often meet mainland and international ferries, or you can try the Room Owners' Association, near the tourist office at D. Theotóki 2A (Mon–Fri 9am–1.30pm, plus summer Tues, Thurs & Fri 6–8pm; ☎26610 26133, ✉oitkcrf@otenet.gr).

△ Stairs in Kérkyra (Corfu) Old Town

Budget travellers might best head straight for the nearest **campsite** at Dhassiá (see p.501).

Astron Dónzelot 15 ☎26610 39505, ⓔhotel_astron@hol.gr. Tastefully renovated hotel in the Old Port. Good deals available outside the short peak season. All rooms with fan and optional air con. ❻

Atlantis Xenofóndos Stratigoú 48 ☎26610 35560, ⓔatlanker@mail.otenet.gr. Large and spacious air-conditioned hotel in the New Port; rather lacking in character. ❺

Bella Venezia Zambéli 4 ☎26610 46500, ⓔbelvenht@hol.gr. Smart, yellow Neoclassical building just behind the *Cavalieri*, with all the *Cavalieri*'s comforts, but cheaper. ❹

Cavalieri Kapodhistríou 4 ☎26610 39041, ⓦwww.cavalieri-hotel.com. Smart and friendly, with all mod cons, great views and a roof bar open to the public. ❻

Corfu Palace Hotel Leofóros Dhimokratías 2 ☎26610 39485, ⓦwww.corfupalace.com. Luxury hotel with pools, landscaped gardens and excellent rooms. The smartest place on the island. ❼

Europa Yitsiáli 10 ☎26610 39304. Small family hotel one block back from the New Port; a bit disorganized and rundown. Some rooms have TV. ❷

Hermes Markorá 14 ☎26610 39268, ⓕ26610 31747. An old favourite in a busy part of town. The cheapest rooms have shared bathrooms. Overlooks the noisy market. ❷

Ionion Xenofóndos Stratigoú 46 ☎26610 39915, ⓕ26610 44 690. Conveniently located in the New Port, this is a large, functional, friendly and very reasonably priced hotel. Ceiling fans in all rooms. ❸

Phoenix Khryssostómou Smýrnis 2, Garítsa ☎26610 42290, ⓕ26610 42990. Small, stylish hotel between the airport and the seafront. Good value, with complimentary breakfast. ❸

The Town

Kérkyra Town comprises a number of distinct areas. The **Historic Centre**, the area enclosed by the Old Port and the two forts, consists of several smaller districts: **Campiello**, the oldest, sits on the hill above the harbour; **Kofinéta** stretches towards the Spianádha (Esplanade); **Áyii Apóstoli** runs west of the Mitrópolis (orthodox cathedral); while tucked in beside the Néo Froúrio are **Ténedhos** and what remains of the old **Jewish quarter**. These districts form the core of the old town, and their tall, narrow alleys conceal some of Corfu's most beautiful architecture. **Mandoúki**, beyond the Old Port, is the commercial and dormitory area for the port, and is worth exploring as a living quarter of the city, away from the tourism racket. The town's **commercial area** lies inland from the Spianádha, roughly between Yeoryíou Theotóki, Alexándhras and Kapodhistríou streets, with the most shops and boutiques around Voulgaréos, Yeoryíou Theotóki and off Platía Saróko. Tucked below the southern ramparts of the Néo Froúrio is the old morning **market**, which sells fish and farm produce.

The most obvious sights are the forts, the **Paleó Froúrio** and **Néo Froúrio**, whose designations (*paleó* – "old", *néo* – "new") are a little misleading, since what you see of the older structure was begun by the Byzantines in the mid-twelfth century, just a hundred years before the Venetians began work on the newer citadel. They have both been damaged and modified by various occupiers and besiegers, the last contribution being the Neoclassical shrine of **St George**, built by the British in the middle of Paleó Froúrio during the 1840s. Looming above the Old Port, the Néo Froúrio (daily 9am–7pm; €1.50) is the more interesting of the two architecturally. The entrance, at the back of the fort, gives onto cellars, dungeons and battlements, with excellent views over the town and bay; there's a small gallery and café at the summit. The Paleó Froúrio (daily 9am–7pm; €2) is not as well preserved and contains some incongruous modern structures, but has an interesting Byzantine museum just inside the gate, and even more stunning views from the central Land Tower. It also hosts daily son et lumière shows.

Just west of the Paleó Froúrio, the **Listón**, an arcaded street built during the French occupation by the architect of the Rue de Rivoli in Paris, and the green **Spianádha** (Esplanade) it overlooks, are the focus of town life. The cricket pitch, still in use at the northern end of the Spianádha, is another British legacy, while at the southern end the **Maitland Rotunda** was built to honour the first British High Commissioner of Corfu and the Ionian islands. The neighbouring statue of Ioannis Kapodhistrias celebrates the local hero and statesman (1776–1831) who led the diplomatic efforts for independence and was made Greece's first president in 1827. At the far northern end of the Listón, the nineteenth-century **Palace of SS Michael and George**, a solidly British edifice built as the residence of their High Commissioner (one of the last of whom was the future British prime minister William Gladstone), and later used as a palace by the Greek monarchy. The former state rooms house the **Asiatic Museum** (Tues–Sun 8am–3pm; €3) which is a must for aficionados of Oriental culture. Amassed by Corfiot diplomat Gregorios Manos (1850–1929) and others, it includes Noh theatre masks, woodcuts, wood and brass statuettes, samurai weapons and art works from Thailand, Korea and Tibet. Opened in 1996, the adjoining **Modern Art Gallery** (daily 9am–9pm; €1.50) holds a small collection of contemporary Greek art. It's an interesting diversion, as are the gardens and café-bar secreted behind the palace.

In a nearby backstreet off Arseníou, five minutes from the palace, is the museum dedicated to modern Greece's most famous nineteenth-century poet, **Dhionysios Solomos** (Mon–Fri 5–8pm; €1). Born on Zákynthos, Solomos was author of the poem *Ýmnos stín Eleftheria* (*Hymn to Liberty*), which was to become the Greek national anthem. He studied at Corfu's Ionian Academy, and lived in a house on this site for much of his life.

Up a short flight of steps on Arseníou, the **Byzantine Museum** (Tues–Sun 9am–3pm; €3) is housed in the restored church of the Panayía Andivouniótissa. It houses church frescoes and sculptures and sections of mosaic floors from the ancient site of Paleópolis, just south of Kérkyra Town. There are also some pre-Christian artefacts, and a collection of icons dating from the fifteenth to nineteenth centuries.

A block behind the Listón, down Spyrídhonos, is the sixteenth-century **church of Áyios Spyrídhon**, whose maroon-domed campanile dominates the town. Here you will find the silver-encrusted coffin of the island's patron saint, **Spyridhon** – Spyros in the diminutive – after whom about half the male population is named. Four times a year (Palm Sunday and the following Sat, Aug 11 and the first Sun in Nov), to the accompaniment of much celebration and feasting, the relics are paraded through the streets of Kérkyra Town. Each of the days commemorates a miraculous deliverance of the island credited to the saint – twice from plague during the seventeenth century, from a famine of the sixteenth century and (a more blessed release than either of those for any Greek) from the Turks in the eighteenth century.

The next most important of the town's many churches, the **Mitrópolis** (orthodox cathedral), perched at the top of its own square opposite the Old Port, also houses the remains of a saint, in this case St Theodora, the ninth-century wife of Emperor Theophilos. The building dates from 1577 and the plain exterior conceals a splendid iconostasis, as well as some fine icons, including a fine sixteenth-century image of *Saint George Slaying the Dragon* by the Cretan artist Mihaïl Dhamaskinos, and three dark, atmospheric Italianate paintings.

Kérkyra Town's **Archeological Museum** (Tues–Sun 8.30am–3pm; €3), just south round the coast, is the best in the archipelago. The most impressive exhibit is a massive (17m) gorgon pediment excavated from the Doric temple of Artemis at Paleópolis, just south of Kérkyra Town; this dominates an entire room, the gorgon flanked by panthers and mythical battle scenes. The museum also has fragments of Neolithic weapons and cookware, and coins and pots from the period when the island was a colony of ancient Corinth.

Just south of Platía Saróko and signposted on the corner of Methodhíou and Kolokotróni, the well-maintained **British cemetery** features some elaborate civic and military memorials. It's a quiet green space away from the madness of Saróko, and in spring and early summer is alive with dozens of species of orchids and other exotic blooms.

The outskirts

Each of the following sights on the outskirts of the city is easily seen in a morning or afternoon, and best visited from the town rather than outlying resorts.

Around the bay from the Rotunda and Archeological Museum, tucked behind Mon Repos beach, the **Mon Repos** estate (8am–7pm; free) contains the most accessible archeological remains on the island. Thick woodland conceals two **Doric temples**, dedicated to Hera and Poseidon. The Neoclassical Mon Repos **villa**, built by British High Commissioner Frederic Adam in 1824 and handed over to Greece in 1864, is the birthplace of Britain's Prince Philip and was finally opened fully to the public in summer 2001 (daily 8.30am–3pm; free). It contains period furniture *in situ*, various archeological finds, including some fine sculpture, and temporary modern art exhibitions.

The most famous excursion from Kérkyra Town is to the islets of **Vlahérna** and **Pondikoníssi**, 2km south of town below the hill of Kanóni, named after the single cannon trained out to sea atop it. A dedicated bus (#2) leaves Platía Saróko every half-hour, or it's a pleasant walk of under an hour. Reached by a short causeway, the tiny white convent of Vlahérna is one of the most photographed images on Corfu. Pondikoníssi ("Mouse Island") can be reached by a short boat trip from the dock at Vlahérna (€2 return). Tufted with greenery and the small chapel of Panayía Vlahernón, Vlahérna is identified in legend with a ship from Odysseus's fleet, petrified by Poseidon in revenge for the blinding of his son Polyphemus, the Homeric echoes somewhat marred by the thronging masses and low-flying aircraft from the nearby runway. A quieter destination is **Vídhos**, the wooded island visible from the Old Port, reached from there by an hourly shuttle *kaïki* (€1 return).

Four kilometres further to the south, past the resort sprawl of Pérama, is a rather more bizarre attraction: the **Achilleion** (daily 9am–3pm; €6), a palace built in a (fortunately) unique blend of Teutonic and Neoclassical styles in 1890 by Elizabeth, Empress of Austria. Henry Miller considered it "the worst piece of gimcrackery" that he'd ever laid eyes on and thought it "would make an excellent museum for surrealistic art". The house is predictably grandiose, but the gardens are pleasant to walk around and afford splendid views in all directions.

Eating and drinking

Although there are the inevitable tourist traps, Kérkyra Town offers some excellent, quality restaurants. As well as those listed below, there are several decent *psarotavérnes* on the Garítsa seafront, though you need to be careful of the fish prices.

Aleko's Beach Faliráki jetty. Set in the tiny harbour below the palace with great views, this place offers simple, mostly grilled meat and fish dishes at good prices.

Khrysí Sevastianoú 46. A short way west of the Listón, this is one of the town's oldest *estiatória*, serving up delicious oven fare (plus a few grills) to a mostly local clientele.

Mouragia Arseníou 15–17. This unassuming, good-value *ouzerí* near the Byzantine Museum does a range of tasty *mezédhes*, including sausage and seafood such as mussels and shrimp. One of the best seafront establishments.

Orestes Xenofóndos Stratigoú 78, Mandoúki. Probably the best fish and seafood restaurant in town, and better priced than the central or Garítsa equivalents.

Papiris Ayías Theodhóras 25. A well-concealed Campiello restaurant serving fine family cooking such as meats in rich sauces. Justifiably popular with locals.

To Paradosiakon Solomoú 20. Behind the Old Port, this friendly place serves good fresh food, especially home-style oven dishes such as *stifádho* and *kokkinistó*.

Rex Kapodhistríou 66 (the Listón). Pricey owing to its location, but some of the best food in the centre, mixing Greek with north European.

Tenedos 1st Párodhos Solomoú 1, Spiliá. At the foot of the steps to the Néo Froúrio, this place offers an excellent range of *mezédhes*, for example courgette fritters and *yígandes* plus succulent meat dishes to the accompaniment of subtle live guitar music.

Venetian Well Bistro Platía Kremastí. A well-kept secret, tucked away in a tiny square a few alleys to the south of the cathedral, this is the nearest you're likely to get to Greek *nouvelle cuisine*, with large portions, and exotica such as Iraqi lamb and Albanian calves' livers in ouzo. Very expensive.

Nightlife

Kérkyra Town has plenty to offer in the way of **bars** and nightlife. None of the popular Listón cafés is cheap, but among the more reasonable are the *Aegli*, *Europa* or *Olympia*, all guaranteed to be packed from early evening till late. The *Cavalieri* rooftop bar can be heaven at night and stays open till the wee hours, while *En Plo* on Faliráki jetty has a brilliant and breezy setting. For local atmosphere indoors, try *Dirty Dick's*, on the corner of Arseníou and Zavitsiánou, or the expat hangout *Mermaid*, on Ayíon Pandón, just off the Listón.

Corfu's self-proclaimed **disco** strip lies a couple of kilometres north of town, past the New Port, but only revs up after midnight when it becomes classic cruising territory, so lone females beware. Here, at nightclubs such as the *Hippodrome* (the town's biggest disco, with its own pool), *Show*, and the bizarrely decorated *Apokálypsis* and *Coca*, party animals dress up for wild and fairly expensive nights out. Somewhat calmer and smaller watering holes on the same strip include *Ethnik*, *Point* and *Pagoda*. Kérkyra Town's two **cinemas** – the winter Orfeus on the corner of Akadhimías and Aspióti and the open-air summer Phoenix down the side street opposite – both show mostly English-language films.

The northeast and the north coast

The **northeast**, at least beyond the immediate suburbs, is the most typically Greek part of Corfu – it's mountainous, with a rocky coastline chopped into pebbly bays and coves, above wonderfully clear seas. Green **buses** between Kérkyra Town and Kassiópi serve all resorts, along with some blue suburban buses as far as Dhassiá.

Kérkyra Town to Ípsos

The landscape just north of Kérkyra Town is an industrial wasteland, and things don't improve much at the first village you come to, **KONDÓKALI**, overrun by holiday developments. The old town consists of a short street with a number of bars and traditional *psistariés*, the best of which are *Gerekos* and *Takis*, an international restaurant, *Flags*, and the pricey *Lithari* fish taverna.

Neighbouring **GOUVIÁ** is home to Corfu's largest yachting marina. The village boasts a couple of small **hotels**, notably the *Hotel Aspa* (☎26610 91409; ❸) and great-value *Gouvia View* by the beach (☎26610 9167; ❷). For **rooms**, try Maria Lignou (☎26610 91348; ❷) or Karoukas Travel (☎26610 91596, ⓔkaroukas@otenet.gr; ❸). There's a number of decent **restaurants**, including *The Captain's* and *Gorgona* tavernas and *Steki psistariá*, and a couple of pizzerias, *La Bonita* and *Palladium*. The very narrow shingle **beach**, barely 5m wide in parts, shelves into sand; given the sea traffic, the water quality is doubtful.

Two kilometres beyond Gouviá the coastline begins to improve at **DHAFNÍLA** and much larger **DHASSIÁ**, set in adjacent wooded bays with pebbly beaches. Two luxury sister **hotels**, the *Dassia Chandris* and *Corfu Chandris* (both ☎26610 97100–3, ⓦwww.chandris.gr; ❼), dominate Dhassiá, with extensive grounds, pools and beach facilities. Opposite them on the main road, the more reasonable *Hotel Amalia* (☎26610 93523; ❸) has pleasant en-suite rooms and its own pool and garden, while the modest but friendly *Spiros Beach* (☎26610 93666; ❸) is the best bet beside the sea itself. **Rooms** are scarce, although Spyros Rengis's minimarket in Dhassiá has a few (☎26610 90282; ❷), and the Dafnilas supermarket has some of the cheapest going (☎26610 90282; ❶). Dhafníla does, however, have the best **campsite** on the island, *Dionysus Camping Village* (☎26610 91417, ⓕ26610 91760); tents are pitched under terraced olive trees. *Dionysus* also has simple bungalow huts, a pool, shop, bar and restaurant, while the friendly, multilingual owners offer a ten-percent discount to Rough Guide readers.

ÍPSOS, 2km north of Dhassiá, can't really be recommended to anyone but hardened bar-hoppers. The thin pebble beach lies right beside the busy coast road and the resort is generally pretty tacky. Most **accommodation** is pre-booked by package companies, although Premier/Ipsos Travel (☎26610 93661, ⓕ26610 93637; ❸) can offer rooms. *Corfu Camping Ipsos* (☎26610 93579, ⓕ26610 93741) has a bar and restaurant, and offers standing tents. Ípsos is also home to one of the island's major **diving centres**, Waterhoppers (☎26610 93867, ⓔdiverclub@hotmail.com). **Eating** on the main drag is dominated by fast food, though a more traditional meal and a quieter setting can be found in the *Akrogiali psistariá* and *Asteria* taverna, both by the marina to the south of the strip. The northern end is largely devoted to competing bars and discos such as *Albatross Club* and *B52*.

North to Áyios Stéfanos

Ípsos has now engulfed the neighbouring hamlet of Pyrgí, which is the main point of access for the villages and routes leading up to **Mount Pandokrátor** from the south; the road, signposted Spartýlas, is 200km beyond the junction in Pyrgí. A popular base for walkers is the village of **STRINÝLAS**, 16km from Pyrgí. Accommodation is basic but easy to come by: the *Elm Tree* taverna, a long-time favourite with walkers, can direct you to rooms. In summer the main routes are busy, but there are quieter walks taking in the handsome Venetian village of Epískepsi, 5km northwest of Strinýlas – anyone interested in walking the Pandokrátor paths is advised to get the **map** of the mountain by island-based cartographer Stephan Jaskulowski or one of Hilary Whitton-Paipeti's walking books, available locally.

The coast road beyond Ípsos mounts the slopes of Pandokrátor towards **BARBÁTI**, 4km further on. Here you'll find the best beach on this coast, though its charm has been somewhat diminished recently by the construction of the gargantuan *Riviera Barbati* apartment complex. The beach is a favourite with families, and much **accommodation** is prebooked in advance. However, there are some rooms available on spec – *Paradise*

(☎26630 91320, ℻26630 91479; ❷) and *Roula Yeranou* (☎26630 92397; ❶), both on the main road.

The mountainside becomes steeper and the road higher beyond Barbáti, and the population thins drastically. **NISSÁKI** is a sprawling roadside settlement rather than a village, with a number of coves, the first and last accessible by road, the rest only by track – the furthest dominated by the gigantic, expensive and rather soulless *Nissaki Beach Hotel* (☎26630 91232, ✉nissaki@otenet.gr; ❹ half-board). There's a couple of shops and a bakery, and a few travel and **accommodation agencies**. The British-owned Falcon Travel (☎26630 91318, 🌐www.falcon-travel-corfu.com; ❸) rents out apartments above the first beach, a tiny, white-pebble cove with a trio of fine tavernas – try the quayside *Mitsos*. The *Nissaki Holiday Center* (☎26630 91166, ℻26630 91206; ❷), up by the junction, may have some cheaper rooms.

Three pebbly coves no one visiting this coast should miss are Agní, not far past the *Nissaki Beach Hotel*, Kalámi and neighbouring Kouloúra: the first for its trio of fine tavernas, the second for its Durrell connection, the third for its exquisite bay. Crowds flock to **AGNÍ** for the fine eating – *Nicolas* is the oldest taverna and just pips *Toula* and *Agni* for quality. **KALÁMI** is on the way to being spoilt, but the village is still small and you can imagine how it would have looked in the year Lawrence Durrell spent here on the eve of World War II. The **White House**, where Durrell wrote *Prospero's Cell*, is now split in two: the ground floor is an excellent taverna; the upper floor is let through CV Travel (see Basics, p.14). Sunshine Travel (☎26630 91170, ✉info @sunshineclub.gr) and Kalami Tourist Services (☎26630 91062, ✉kalamits @otenet.gr) both have a range of rooms (❷) on their books, or ask at *Matella's* restaurant (☎26630 91371; ❷). The **restaurant** at the White House is recommended, as are *Matella's*, the *Kalami Beach* and *Pepe's*, all tavernas on the beach. Two cocktail bars compete for the happy-hour trade.

The tiny harbour of **KOULOÚRA** has managed to keep its charm intact, set at the edge of an unspoilt bay with nothing to distract from the pine trees and *kaïkia*. The fine sole **taverna** here has to be the most idyllic setting for a meal in the whole of Corfu.

Around the coast to Aharávi

Two kilometres beyond Kouloúra, down a shady lane, the large pebble cove of **Kerasiá** shelters the family-run *Kerasia Taverna*. The most attractive resort on this stretch of coast, however, 3km down a lane from Siniés on the main road, is **ÁYIOS STÉFANOS** (officially Áyios Stéfanos Sinión to distinguish it from a namesake in northwestern Corfu). Most **accommodation** here is of the upmarket prebooked villa sort, and the village has yet to succumb to any serious development; so far only the *Kochili* taverna has independent rooms and apartments (☎26630 81522; ❸). For food, as well as the *Kochili* itself, also recommended are the *Galini* and *Eucalyptus* **tavernas**; the latter, over by the village's small beach, is pricier but serves more adventurous fare such as pork with artichokes. The *Waves* café and *Damianos* cocktail bar are the main spots to idle with a drink.

A thirty-minute walk from the coastguard station above Áyios Stéfanos, along a newly surfaced road, stretches the beach of **Avláki**, a pebble bay that provides lively conditions for the **windsurfers** who visit the beach's windsurf club. There are two **tavernas**, the *Cavo Barbaro* and *Avlaki*, but the only accommodation is taken by upmarket package companies.

Further round the coast is **KASSIÓPI**, a fishing village that's been transformed into a major party resort. The Roman emperor Tiberius had a villa here, and the village's sixteenth-century Panayía Kassópitra church is said to stand on the site of a temple of Zeus once visited by Nero. Little evidence of Kassiópi's past survives, apart from an abandoned Angevin *kástro* on the headland – most visitors come for the nightlife and the five pebbly beaches. Most nonpackage **accommodation** in Kassiópi is rented through village agencies; the largest, Travel Corner (☎26630 81220, ✉info@kassiopi.com; ➋), on the main road near the square, is a good place to start. An independent alternative, the smart *Kastro café-pension* (☎26630 81045; ➍), overlooks the beach behind the castle, while *Edem* (☎26630 81431; ➋) offers bargain rooms one block behind Kalamíonas beach on the west side. International cuisine dominates **eating** in Kassiópi – try the tasty Italian at *Little Italy*, the Tex-Mex at *Poco Loco* or the *Sze Chuan* Chinese – but for something more traditional, head for the *Three Brothers* taverna on the harbour, or the neighbouring *Porto* fish restaurant. At night, Kassiópi rocks to the cacophony of its music and video bars: the flashiest is the gleaming hi-tech *Eclipse*, which also shows DVDs, closely followed by the *Baron*, *Jasmine* and *Visions*, all within falling-over distance of the small town square. The *Axis Club* boasts imported British DJs, and frolics sometimes extend onto the beach until dawn. The village is also home to one of the most reliable diving operations, Corfu Divers (☎26630 81218), which is partly British-run.

The coastline beyond Kassiópi is overgrown and marshy until you get to little-developed **Almyrós** beach, one of the longest on the island, with only a few apartment buildings dotted sporadically behind it. For a peaceful stay you could try *Villa Maria* (☎26630 63359; ➌) and eat at *Liberty's* grill a little further along the beach. The **Andinióti** lagoon, smaller than Korissíon in the south but still a haven for birds and twitchers, backs Cape Ayías Ekaterínis to the east, which marks the northern end of the Corfu Trail (see p.511). With its wide main road, **AHARÁVI**, the next stop west on the main coast road, resembles an American Midwest truck stop, but the village proper is tucked behind this in a quiet crescent of old tavernas, bars and shops. Aharávi makes a quieter beach alternative to the southerly strands, and should also be considered by those seeking alternative routes up onto **Mount Pandokrator**. Roads to small hamlets such as Áyios Martínos and Láfki continue onto the mountain, and even a stroll up from the back of Aharávi will find you on the upper slopes in under an hour.

Accommodation isn't easy to find, but a good place to start is Castaway Travel (☎26630 63541, ✉castaway@otenet.gr) or HN Travel (☎26630 63458, ℻26630 63454). One independent hotel is *Dandolo* (☎26630 63557, ℻26630 63457; ➌), set in lush grounds towards the old village. There's a number of **restaurants** on Aharávi's main drag; go for the *Pump House* steak and pasta joint, *Chris's psistariá*, the large *Manis* taverna, or slightly pricier *Neraïda*, which specializes in meat dishes with mushroom or pepper sauces and trout salad. The bar-restaurants tend to get quite rowdy at night, although the light and airy *Captain Aris* is a pleasant watering hole. For a quieter evening, head for the excellent *Theritas* taverna, the friendly *Mitsouras kafenío* or the cosy *Hole in the Wall* pub, all in the old village.

Ródha, Sidhári and Avliótes

Continuing further west, **RÓDHA** has tipped over into overdevelopment, and can't be wholeheartedly recommended for those after a quiet time. Its central crossroads have all the charm of a service station, and the beach is rocky in parts and swampy to the west. "Old Ródha" is a small warren of alleys between the main road and the seafront, where you'll find the best **restaurants** and **bars**:

the *Taverna Agra* is the oldest in Ródha and the best place for fish, and the *Roda Star Taverna* and *New Port* are also good. For bars, try *Big Ben* or *Five Roses*, both with Sky Sports, or the trendier bar-club *Skouna*. For **accommodation**, the friendly seafront *Roda Inn* (☎26630 63358; ❷) has excellent value en-suite rooms. Both the Anglo-Greek NSK UK Travel (☎26630 63471, ℻26630 63274), on the main drag, and Corfu Nostos Travel on the seafront (☎26630 64602, ✉e.kostali@otenet.gr; ❷) rent rooms and handle car rental. The smart *Roda Beach Camping* (☎26630 93120) is a little way east of the resort, while even pleasanter *Karoussades Camping* (☎ & ℻26630 31415) is to the west towards Sidhári. Myron's good-rate motorbike rental (☎26630 63477) and Kostas horse-riding are also based in Ródha. Several kilometres inland from Ródha, just east of Agrafi, the *Angonari mezedhopolío* serves an excellent range of dishes and great barrelled wine in a relaxed garden with subtle live music.

The next notable resort, **SIDHÁRI**, is constantly expanding and totally dominated by British-package tourists; its small but pretty town square, with a bandstand set in a small garden, is lost in a welter of bars, shops and joints. The beach is sandy but not terribly clean, and many people tend to head just west to the curious coves, walled by wind-carved sandstone cliffs, around the vaunted Canal d'Amour. The biggest accommodation agency is run by young tycoon Philip Vlasseros, whose Vlasseros Travel (☎26630 95695, ℻26630 95969) also handles car rental, horse-riding and excursions, including day-trips to the Dhiapóndia islands (see p.511). Sidhári's **campsite**, *Dolphin Camping* (☎26630 31846), is over 1km inland from the junction at the western end of town. Most **restaurants** are pitched at those looking for a great night out rather than a quiet meal in a taverna. The pricey *Olympic* is the oldest taverna here; also recommended are the *Diamond* and *Sea Breeze* tavernas or *Kavvadias* on the eastern stretch of beach. Asian cuisine and cheap full-on English breakfasts are also readily available. There are no quiet bars in Sidhári, and several **nightclubs** vie for late custom, such as *IQ*, *Ecstasy* and *Caesar's*. Sidhári also has its own waterpark with free entry, a good place to keep the kids happy.

The Sidhári bus usually continues to **AVLIÓTES**, a handsome hill town with several bars and tavernas but few concessions to tourism. The town is note-worthy for two reasons: its accessibility to the stunning beach, bordered by vertical cliffs and shady in the mornings, below the quiet village of Perouládhes, just over 1km away, and the fact that **Áyios Stéfanos** (see p.506) is only about thirty minutes' walk from here, downhill through lovely olive groves.

Paleokastrítsa and the northwest coast

The northwest conceals some of the island's most dramatic coastal scenery, the violent interior mountainscapes jutting out of the verdant countryside. The area's honeypot attraction, **Paleokastrítsa**, is the single most picturesque resort on Corfu, but is suffering from its popularity. Further north, the densely olive-clad hills conceal better, sandier beaches, such as **Áyios Yeóryios** and **Áyios Stéfanos**. Public **transport** all along the west coast is difficult: virtu-ally all buses ply routes from Kérkyra Town to single destinations, and rarely link resorts.

Paleokastrítsa
PALEOKASTRÍTSA, a small village surrounded by dramatic hills and cliffs, has been identified as the Homeric city of Scheria, where Odysseus was washed ashore and escorted by Nausicaa to the palace of her father Alkinous, king of the Phaeacians. It's a stunning site, as you would expect, though one

that's long been engulfed by tourism. The focal point of the village is the car park on the seafront, which backs onto the largest and least attractive of three **beaches**, home to sea taxis and *kaïkia*. The second beach, to the right and signed by flags for Mike's Ski Club, is stony with clear water, and the best of the three is a small unspoilt strand reached along the path by the *Astakos Taverna*. Protected by cliffs, it's undeveloped apart from the German-run Korfu-Diving Centre (☎26630 41604) at the end of the cove. From the first beach you can get a **boat trip** to some nearby seawater caves, known as the "blue grottoes" (€8 for a half-hour trip), worth taking for the spectacular coastal views. Boats also serve as a taxi service to three neighbouring beaches, Áyia Triánda, Palatákia and Alípa, which all have snack-bars.

On the rocky bluff above the village, the **Theotókou monastery** (7am–1pm & 3–8pm; free, donations welcome) is believed to have been established in the thirteenth century. There's also a museum, resplendent with icons, jewelled Bibles and other impedimenta of Greek Orthodox ritual, though the highlight is the gardens, with spectacular coastal views. Paleokastrítsa's ruined castle, the **Angelókastro**, is around 6km up the coast; only approachable by path from the hamlet of Kríni, it has stunning, almost circular views of the surrounding sea and land. For a drink or snack with tremendous views, it's worth stopping at either the *Bella Vista* or *Golden Fox* tavernas on the way up, between Lákones and Makrádhes.

Unfortunately, perhaps owing to the pressure of commerce in such a small space, there's a rather mercenary air about tourism here. **Accommodation** is at a premium, and you may be expected to commit yourself for three to seven days in some places. A good **hotel** is the family-run *Odysseus* (☎26630 41209, Ⓦwww.odysseushotel.gr; ❺), on the road into town, while the nearby modern *Akrotiri Beach* (☎26630 41237, Ⓦwww.akrotiri-beach.com; ❻) is upmarket but unpretentious. There are good-value **rooms** for rent above Alípa beach on the road down into Paleokastrítsa: try at the *Dolphin Snackbar* (☎26630 41035; ❸), the *Green House* (☎26630 41311; ❷) or Michalas tourist bureau (☎26630 41113, Ⓔmichalastravel@ker.forthnet.gr). Above the village, past Nikos' Bikes, the friendly family-run *Villa Korina* (☎26630 44064; ❷) is great value. *Paleokastritsa Camping* (☎26630 41204, Ⓕ26630 41104) is just off the main road into town, a fifteen-minute walk from the centre.

There isn't a huge choice of **restaurants** in the centre of Paleokastrítsa. The *Astakos Taverna* and *Corner Grill* are two traditional places, while *Il Pirata* offers a variety of Italian and Greek dishes, including local fish and seafood, and the seafront *Smurfs* has a good seafood menu despite the name. Also recommended are the very smart *Vrahos*, and the shady *Calm*, which has Internet facilities. **Nightlife** hangouts include the restaurant-bars in the centre, and those straggling up the hill towards Lákones, such as the relaxing *Petrino* bar. By the Lákones turning is Paleokastrítsa's one nightclub, *The Paleo Club*, a small disco-bar with a garden.

Áyios Yeóryios and Áyios Stéfanos

Like many of the west-coast resorts, **ÁYIOS YEÓRYIOS**, 6km north of Paleokastrítsa, isn't actually based around a village, though it is sometimes referred to as Áyios Yeóryios Pagón after the inland village of Payí to avoid confusion with its southern namesake. The resort has developed in response to the popularity of its large sandy bay, and it's a major **windsurfing** centre, busy even in low season. There is one particularly good-value **hotel** at the southern end, the *Alkyon Beach* (☎26630 56204, Ⓕ26630 96206; ❸), some rooms at the Arista supermarket (☎26630 96350; ❶) or *Studio Eleana* (☎ & Ⓕ26630 96366;

❸), both behind the central section of beach, and the *San George* campsite (☎26630 51759), nearly 1km back from the beach towards Kavvadhádhes. *To Vrahos* at the northern end and *Spiros* halfway along are among the better restaurants, both serving Greek and international cuisine. On the way north towards Áyios Stéfanos, the pleasant sandy beach of **Aríllas** has given rise to gradual development, including several tavernas – try *Kostas on the Beach*. Accommodation can be arranged through Arillas Travel (☎26630 51280, ✉arillast@otenet.gr; ❸) or there is the smart *Akti Arilla* hotel (☎26630 51201, ✉aktiaril@otenet.gr; ❹ half-board).

The northernmost of the west-coast's resorts, **ÁYIOS STÉFANOS** is low-key, popular with families and a quiet base from which to explore the northwest and the Dhiapóndia islands, visible on the horizon. Day-trips to Mathráki, Othoní and Eríkoussa (see p.511) run several times a week in season (€15–24 per person), as well as cheaper passenger services (€6–8 return) most days on the Aspiotis lines *kaïki*. Áyios Stéfanos's oldest **hotel**, the *Nafsika* (☎26630 51051, ✉nafsika1@otenet.gr; ❸), has a large restaurant, a favourite with villagers, and gardens with a pool and bar. In recent years it has been joined by the *Hotel San Stefano* (☎26630 51053, 🖷26630 51202; ❸) and **rooms** at the *Sunset* taverna ((☎26630 51185, ✉gizakis@otenet.gr; ❸). For those on a budget, Peli and Maria's gift shop offers bargain **rooms** (☎26630 51424; ❷) and the *Restaurant Evinos* (☎ & 🖷26630 51766; ❷) has small apartments above the village. A number of travel agencies handle accommodation, among them San Stefanos (☎26630 51910, ✉steftrav@otenet.gr; ❷) in the centre. Besides the above-mentioned establishments, good options for **eating** include *Waves* and very reasonable *Mistral* tavernas above the beach, while *O Manthos* taverna serves Corfiot specialities such as *sofríto* and *pastitsádha*. For **nightlife**, there's a couple of lively music bars, *Magnet* and *Athens*, plus the small *Enigma* nightclub.

Central and southern Corfu

Two natural features divide the centre and south of Corfu. The first is the **plain of Rópa**, whose fertile landscape backs on to some of the best beaches on this coast, such as delightful **Myrtiótissa**. Settlements and development stop a little to the south of Paleokastrítsa and only resume around **Érmones** and **Pélekas** – a quick bus ride across the island from Kérkyra Town. Down to the south, a second dividing point is the **Korissíon lagoon**, the sandy plains and dunes that skirt this natural feature being great places for botanists and ornithologists. Beyond, a single road trails the interior, with sporadic side roads to resorts on either coast. The landscape here is flat, an undistinguished backdrop for a series of increasingly developed beaches and, in the far south, **Kávos**, Corfu's big youth resort.

Érmones to the Korissíon lagoon: the west coast

ÉRMONES, around 15km south of Paleokastrítsa by road, is one of the busiest resorts on the island, its lush green bay backed by the mountains above the Rópa River. The resort is dominated by the luxury *Ermones Beach* **hotel** (☎26610 94241, 🌐www.sunmarotelermones.gr; ❽), which provides guests with obligatory full board and a funicular railway down to the beach. More reasonably priced accommodation can be found at the *Pension Katerina* (☎26610 94615; ❷) and *Georgio's Villas* (☎26610 94950; ❸), next to each other on the hillside above the road that leads to the beach. Both the *Maria* and *Nafsica* **tavernas** above the beach provide good, filling *mezédhes* and main dishes. Just inland is the Corfu Golf and Country Club (☎26610 94220), the only golf club in the archipelago, and said to be one of the finest in the Mediterranean.

The nearby small village of **VÁTOS**, on the Glyfádha bus route from Kérkyra Town, has only a shop-cum-café and quaint church, as all the other facilities are to be found on the main road 1km below. Here, the *Olympic Restaurant and Grill* (☎26610 94318; ❷) has rooms and apartments, as well as the only food, while the *Villa Frederiki* (☎26610 94003; ❸), opposite, consists of two large double studios. The Myrtiótissa **path**, now widened and partly paved, is signposted just beyond the extremely handy, if basic, *Vatos Camping* (☎26610 94393), 500m further south.

Far preferable to the gravelly sand of Érmones are the sandy beaches just south of the resort, at Myrtiótissa and Glyfádha. In *Prospero's Cell*, Lawrence Durrell described **Myrtiótissa** as "perhaps the loveliest beach in the world"; it was for years a well-guarded secret but is now a firm favourite, especially with nudists, and gets so busy in summer that it supports three *kantínes*, meaning it's at its best well out of high season. Above the north end of beach is the tiny whitewashed **Myrtiótissa monastery**, dedicated to Our Lady of the Myrtles. There are even a few **rooms** now, just off the approach road at the friendly *Mirtiotissa* taverna (☎26610 94113, ✉sks_mirtia@hotmail.com; ❸), which serves tasty home-style cooking.

The sandy bay of **GLYFÁDHA**, walled in by cliffs, is dominated by the huge *Louis Grand* hotel (☎26610 94140, ⓦwww.louishotels.com; ❼). Far more reasonable **accommodation** is available at the extreme north end of the beach at two good adjacent tavernas; *Glyfada Beach* (☎26610 94258, ℗26610 94257; ❸) and *Glyfada* (☎26610 94224; ❶), whose simple rooms are a real bargain. Nightlife centres on two music bars, the *Kikiriko* and *Aloha*, which pump out heavy-duty sounds all day, as the beach is popular with young Greek and Italian trendies.

PÉLEKAS, inland and 2km south of Glyfádha, has long been popular for its views – the **Kaiser's Throne** viewing tower, just above the town, was Wilhelm II's favourite spot on the island. New developments are beginning to swamp the town, but there are some good **room** deals here, including the friendly *Pension Paradise* (☎26610 94530; ❷), on the way in from Vátos, and the *Alexandros* taverna (☎26610 94215, ✉axel@hol.gr; ❸) and *Thomas* (☎26610 94441; ❸), both on the way towards Kaiser's Throne. Agatha's Tours (☎26610 94283, ℗26610 94602) may have some even cheaper rooms. Among the **tavernas**, the *Alexandros* and *Roula's Grill House* are highly recommended. The colourful *Zanzibar* is a pleasant spot for a drink by the diminutive square, whose Odhiyítria church, renovated in 1884, is worth a peek. Pélekas's sandy **beach** is reached down a short path. Here you'll find *Maria's Place*, an excellent family-run **taverna** with **rooms** (☎26610 94601; ❸), serving fish caught daily by the owner's husband. Sadly, the beach has been rather spoilt by the monstrous *Pelekas Beach* hotel that now looms over it.

Around 7km south of Pélekas, **AÏ GÓRDHIS** is one of the key play beaches on the island, largely because of the activities organized by the startling **Pink Palace** complex (☎26610 53103, ⓦwww.thepinkpalace.com), which dominates the resort. It has pools, games courts, restaurants, a shop and a disco. Backpackers cram into communal rooms for up to ten (smaller rooms and singles are also available) for around €25 a night, including breakfast and evening meal. Other accommodation is available on the beach, notably at *Michali's Place* taverna (☎26610 53041; ❸); the neighbouring *Alex in the Garden* **restaurant** is also a favourite.

Inland from the resort is the south's largest prominence, the humpback of **Áyii Dhéka** (576m), reached by path from the hamlet of Áno Garoúna; it is the island's second-largest mountain after Pandokrátor. The lower slopes are wooded, and it's possible to glimpse buzzards wheeling on thermals over the higher slopes. The monks at the tiny monastery just below the summit lovingly tend a bountiful orchard.

Around 5km south by road from Áï Górdhis, the fishing hamlet of **PENDÁTI** is still untouched by tourism. There is no accommodation here, but *Angela's* café and minimarket and the *Strofi* grill cater to villagers and the few tourists who wander in. Another 4km on, **PARAMÓNAS** has been slowly evolving of late, but remains a low-key resort with some of the best **accommodation** deals on the island: *Sunset* (T 26610 75149, F 26610 75686; ❶), with panoramic views, right above the beach, and the *Paramonas Bridge* restaurant (T 26610 75761; ❷), about 500m inland, are both extremely good value, as are the *Areti Studios* (T 26610 75838; ❷), on the lane in from Pendáti.

The town of **ÁYIOS MATTHÉOS**, 3km inland, is still chiefly an agricultural centre, although a number of *kafenía* and tavernas offer a warm if bemused welcome to passers-by: head for the *Mouria* snack-bar/grill, or the modern *Steki*, which can rustle up tasty *mezédhes*. On the other side of Mount Prasoúdhi, 2km by road, is the **Gardhíki Pýrgos**, the ruins of a thirteenth-century castle built in this unlikely lowland setting by the despots of Epirus. The road continues on to the northernmost tip of splendid and deserted **Halikoúna** beach on the sea edge of the **Korissíon lagoon**, which, if you don't have your own transport, is most easily reached by walking from the village of Línia (on the Kávos bus route) via Íssos beach; other, longer routes trail around the north end of the lagoon from Áno Mesongí and Khlomotianá. Over 5km long and 1km wide at its centre, Korissíon is home to turtles, tortoises, lizards and numerous indigenous and migratory birds. For one of the quietest stays on the island, try *Marin Christel Apartments* (T 26610 75947; ❸), just north of Halikoúna beach, or *Logara Apartments* (T 26610 76477; ❸), 500m inland. *Spiros Halikounas* has the slightly better selection of the two tavernas on this stretch of road. The beach is an idyllic spot for rough camping but only a seasonal canteen operates in the immediate vicinity.

Benítses to Petrití: the east coast

South of Kérkyra Town, there's nothing to recommend before **BENÍTSES**, a once-notorious bonking-and-boozing resort, whose old town at the north end is now reverting to a quiet bougainvillea-splashed Greek village. There's really little to see here, beyond the ruins of a Roman bathhouse at the back of the village, and the small but impressive **Shell Museum** (March–Oct daily 10am–8pm; €2.50). **Rooms** are plentiful: try the Best Travel (T 26610 72037, F 26610 71036) and Achilles Tourist Centre (T 26610 72228, F 26610 72008) agencies (both ❷). Visitor numbers have picked up again after a serious decline but some hotels still offer good deals; the *Corfu Maris* (T 26610 72129, F 26610 71035; ❸), on the beach at the southern end of town, has modern en-suite rooms with balconies and views, while the friendly *Hotel Benitsa* and neighbouring *Agis* in the centre (both T 26610 39269; ❷) offer quiet rooms set back from the main road. Benítses has its fair share of decent **tavernas**, notably *La Mer de Corfu* and the Corfiot specialist *Spiros*, as well as the plush *Marabou*. Lively **bars** such as *Lacey's* and *Tribal* are concentrated behind the crescent-shaped park that separates the old village from the coast road, while larger **nightclubs** like *Casanovas 2000* or *Stadium* are at the southern end of the main strip.

MORAÏTIKA's main street is an ugly strip of bars, restaurants and shops, but its beach is the best between Kérkyra Town and Kávos. Reasonable beachside **hotels** include the *Margarita Beach* (T & F 26610 75267; ●) and the plusher *Three Stars* (T 26610 75263, F 26610 75862; ●). Budget Ways Travel (T 26610 76768, F 26610 75664; ●) offers a range of accommodation and there are **rooms** between the main road and beach, such as those at the *Firefly* taverna (T 26610 75850; ●). Much of the main drag is dominated by souvenir shops and minimarkets, as well as a range of **bars**, including the village's oldest, *Charlie's*, which opened in 1939, and the lively *Very Coco* nightclub. The *Rose Garden* **restaurant** is just off the main road and has a fair mix of vegetarian, Greek and international food, as does the unfortunately named beach restaurant *Crabs*, where the seafood and special salads are excellent. Confusingly, the biggest touristic landmark in the area, the *Messonghi Beach* hotel complex (T 26610 75830, W www.messonghibeach.gr; ●), set in lush landscaped gardens and home to the Nautilus diving centre (daily 5–7pm; T 26610 83295), actually lies just within the limits of Moraïtika, which is separated from neighbouring Mesongí by the Mesongís River. The village proper, **ÁNO MORAÏTIKA**, is signposted a few minutes' hike up the steep lanes inland, and is virtually unspoilt. Its tiny houses and alleys are practically drowning in bougainvillea, among which you'll find two **tavernas**: the *Village Taverna* and the *Bella Vista*, which has a basic menu but justifies its name with a lovely garden, sea views and breezes.

Commencing barely a hundred metres on from the Moraïtika seafront, **MESONGÍ** continues this stretch of package-tour-oriented coast but is noticeably quieter and has a couple of fine accommodation deals. Both the *Hotel Gemini* (T 26610 75221, E geminiht@otenet.gr; ●) and great-value, British-run *Pantheon Hall* (T 26610 75802, E corfudirect@yahoo.co.uk; ●) have pools and gardens, and en-suite rooms with balconies. Mesongí has a number of good **restaurants**: notably the *Memories* taverna, which specializes in Corfiot dishes and serves its own barrel wine, and the upmarket *Castello*. An alternative is to head for the beachside *Bacchus* and *Spanos* tavernas a short walk south on the road to Boúkari. Try the *Dimensions* bar for a relaxed seaside drink.

The quiet road from Mesongí to Boúkari follows the seashore for about 3km, often only a few feet above it. **BOÚKARI** itself comprises little more than a handful of tavernas, a shop and a few small, family-run hotels; the *Boukari Beach*, 1km north of the tiny harbour, is the best of the **tavernas**, offering fresh fish and live lobster. The very friendly Vlahopoulos family who run the taverna also manage two small hotels nearby, the *Penelopi* and newer *Villa Alexandra* (T 26620 51269, W www.boukaribeach.com; ●), as well as good rooms (●) attached to the taverna. Boúkari is out of the way, but an idyllic little strip of unspoilt coast for anyone fleeing the crowds elsewhere on the island, and inland from here is the unspoiled wooded region around **Aryirádhes**, rarely visited by tourists and a perfect place for quiet walks.

Back on the coastline, the village of **PETRITÍ** fronts onto a small but busy dirt-track harbour, but is mercifully free of noise and commerce; its beach is rock, mud and sand, set among low olive-covered hills. The *Pension Egrypos* (T 26620 51949, E egrypos@hol.gr; ●) has **rooms** and a **taverna**. At the harbour, three tavernas serve the trickle of sea traffic: the smart *Limnopoula* guarded by caged parrots, and the more basic but friendly *Dimitris* and *Stamatis*. Back from the village, near the hamlet of Vassilátika, is the elegant *Regina* **hotel**, with gardens and pool (T 26620 52132, F 26620 52135; ●).

THE IONIAN ISLANDS | Corfu

Southern Corfu

Across the island on the west coast, the beach at **ÁYIOS YEÓRYIOS** spreads as far south as Ayía Varvára, and north to encircle the edge of the Korissíon lagoon, around 12km of uninterrupted sand. The resort itself, however, is an unprepossessing seafront sprawl and tourism here has the most mercenary air of anywhere on the island. British package operators have arrived in force, with bars competing to present bingo, quizzes and video nights. The smart *Golden Sands* (☎26620 51225, ⓕ26620 51140; ❸) has a pool, open-air restaurant and gardens, but the best **hotel** bargain is the smaller *Blue Sea* (☎26620 51624, ⓔbluesea@otenet.gr; ❷); both are situated midway along the seafront road. The easiest place to look for good **rooms** is at Stork Tours (☎ & ⓕ26620 51168; ❷), halfway along the seafront. Most **restaurants** are predictably bland but you can eat well enough at *La Perla's*, which serves some Asian cuisine as well as Greek staples in a walled garden; you could also try the cheaper *Makis* and *Sea Gulls* tavernas. **Nightlife** centres around music and pool bars like the *Gold Hart* and *Traxx*, although laid-back *Retreat* and lively *Mad Mike's*, one of the few places off the seafront, have a better atmosphere.

A few minutes' walk north of Áyios Yeóryios, **Íssos** is a far better and quieter beach; the dunes north of Íssos towards the Korissíon lagoon are an unofficial nude bathing area. Facilities around Íssos are sparse: one **taverna**, the *Rousellis Grill*, a few hundred metres from the beach on the lane leading to Línia on the main road; the smart new yellow-and-maroon *Vicky's Apartments* (☎26620 53161; ❹), above a bend in the lane; and the *Friends* snack-bar in Línia itself. An English-run **windsurfing school** operates on the beach.

Anyone interested in how a Greek town works away from the bustle of tourism shouldn't miss **LEFKÍMI**, towards the island's southern tip. The second-largest town after Kérkyra Town, it's the administrative centre of the south of the island as well as the alternative ferry port to or from Igoumenítsa, with half a dozen daily crossings in summer. The town has some fine architecture, including several striking churches: **Áyii Anáryiri** with a huge double belfry, **Áyios Theódhoros**, on a mound above a small square, and **Áyios Arsénios**, with a vast orange dome that can be seen for miles. There are some **rooms** at the *Cheeky Face* taverna (☎26620 22627; ❷), by the bridge over the canal that carries the Himáros River through the lower part of town, and the *Maria Madalena* apartments (☎26620 22386; ❷) further up. For **food** look no further than the home-cooking at the tiny *Maria estiatório*, beside the canal. A few **bars** are tucked in corners of the upper town and see so few tourists that you are likely to receive a friendly welcome: *Hermes* has a leafy garden, while *Mersedes* and *Enigma* both play Greek and foreign sounds in their dimly lit interiors.

There are no ambiguities in **KÁVOS**, 6km south of Lefkími: either you like 24-hour drinking, clubbing, bungee-jumping, go-karts, video bars named after British sitcoms and chips with almost everything, or you should avoid the resort altogether. Kávos stretches over 2km of decent sandy beach, with watersports galore. This is very much Club 18–30 territory; if you want independent **accommodation**, try Pandis Travel (☎26620 61400, ⓕ26620 61401) or Island Holidays (☎26620 61357, ⓕ26620 61426; both ❷), and the nearest to genuine Greek **food** you'll find is at the *Two Brothers psistariá*, at the south end of town. Fast food and British-style Asian cuisine are much easier to come by. *Future* is the biggest **club**, with imported north European DJs, followed by *The Barn*, *42nd St* and *Sex*. Favourite **bars** include *Time*, *Jungle*, *The Face*, *Black Duck* and *Bonkers*, and at night the main drag is one unbroken crowd of young revellers.

Beyond the limits of Kávos, where few visitors stray, a path leaving the road south to the hamlet of Sparterá heads through unspoilt countryside; after around thirty minutes of walking it reaches the cliffs of **Cape Asprókavos** and the crumbling **monastery of Arkoudhílas**. The cape looks out over the straits to Paxí, and down over deserted **Arkoudhílas** beach, which can be reached from Spartterá, 5km by road but only 3km by the signed path from Kávos. Even wilder is **Áï Górdhis Paleohoríou** beach, 3km further on from Spartterá, one of the least visited on the island and not to be confused with the eponymous beach further north. The Cape is also the southern starting point for the **Corfu Trail**, inaugurated in 2001, after years of planning by local walkers. Signposted by yellow waymarkers the trail meanders back and forth over 200km of varying terrain all the way to Cape Ayías Ekaterínis on the north coast and is designed to take at least ten days. Those interested should get a copy of Hilary Whitton Paipeti's *Walking the Corfu Trail* or check out Ⓦwww.travelling .gr/corfutrail for more details.

Corfu's satellite islands

Corfu's three inhabited satellite islands, **Eríkoussa**, **Othoní** and **Mathráki**, in the quintet of **Dhiapóndia islands**, are scattered up to 20km off the northwest coast. Some travel agencies in the northern resorts offer **day-trips** to Eríkoussa only, often with a barbecue thrown in – fine if you're happy to spend the day on the beach. A trip taking in all three islands from Sidhári or Áyios Stéfanos is excellent value: they are between thirty and sixty minutes apart by boat, and most trips allow you an hour on each (longer on sandy Eríkoussa).

Locals use day-trip boats between the islands, so it's possible to pay your way between them. There is also a **ferry** four times a week from Kérkyra Town, the *Alexandros II*, which brings cars and goods to the islands, but given that it has to sail halfway round Corfu first, it's the slowest way to proceed.

Mathráki

Hilly, densely forested and with a long empty beach, beautiful **Mathráki** has the fewest inhabitants of the three islands. Portéllo beach begins at the edge of the tiny harbour, **Plákes**, and extends south for 3km of fine, dark-red sand. A single road rises from the harbour into the interior and the scattered village of **KÁTO MATHRÁKI**, where just one friendly taverna-*kafenío*-shop overlooks the beach and Corfu. The views are magnificent, as is the sense of isolation. However, Mathráki is gradually gearing up towards visitors, and islanders Tassos Kassimis (Ⓣ26630 71700; ❷) and Khristos Aryiros (Ⓣ26630 71652; ❸) already rent **rooms** and **studios** on Portéllo beach. At Plákes the *Port Centre* restaurant specializes in freshly caught fish. The road continues to the village of **Áno Mathráki**, with its single, old-fashioned *kafenío* next to the church, but this is beyond walking distance on a day-visit.

Othoní

Eight kilometres northwest, **Othoní** is the largest, and at first sight the least inviting of Corfu's satellite islands. The island has a handful of places to stay and eat in its port, **ÁMMOS**, but the reception from islanders who aren't in the tourism trade is rather cool. Ámmos has two beaches, both pebbly, one on each side of the jetty. The village *kafenío*, *O Mikros*, serves as a very basic shop, and there's one smart **restaurant**, *La Locanda dei Sogni*, which also has **rooms** (Ⓣ26630 71640; ❸) – though these tend to be prebooked by Italian visitors. Two tavernas, *New York* and tiny *Lakis*, offer decent but fairly limited menus; the owner of the *New York* also offers rooms for rent (Ⓣ26630 71581; ❷). The number of beds on the island has greatly increased with the opening of the

Hotel Calypso (☎26630 72162, ℻26630 71578; ❸), 200m east of the jetty. The island's interior is dramatic, and a road up out of the village leads through rocky, tree-covered hills to the central hamlet, **Horió**, after a thirty-minute walk. Horió, like other inland villages, is heavily depopulated – only about one hundred people still live on the island through the winter – but it's very attractive, and the architecture is completely traditional. On the north coast of the island **Fýki Bay**, accessible via a path from Dhamaskátika, has the longest stretch of sand but there are no facilities and you'll only have time to reach it if you spend at least a night.

Eríkoussa

Some 10km east of Othoní, **Eríkoussa** is the most popular destination for day-trippers. It's invariably hyped as a "desert island" trip, although this is a desert island with a medium-sized hotel, rooms, tavernas and a year-round community. In high season, it gets very busy: Eríkoussa has a large diaspora living in America and elsewhere who return to family homes in their droves in summer, so you may find your *yiásou* or *kaliméra* returned in a Brooklyn accent.

Eríkoussa has an excellent golden sandy beach right by the harbour, with great swimming, and another, quieter, beach reached by a path across the wooded island interior. The island's cult following keeps its one **hotel**, the *Erikoussa* (☎26630 71110, ℻26630 71555; ❸), busy through the season; rooms are en suite with balconies and views. Simpler rooms are available from the *Anemomilos* **taverna** (☎26630 71647; ❷). If you're hoping to stay, phoning ahead is essential, as is taking anything you might not be able to buy – the only shop is a snack-bar selling basic groceries.

Paxí (Paxos) and Andípaxi

Verdant, hilly and still largely unspoilt, **Paxí (Paxos)** is the smallest of the main Ionian islands. Barely 12km by 4km, it has no sandy beaches, no historical sites, only two hotels and a serious water shortage, yet is so popular it is best avoided in high season. It's a particular favourite of yachting flotillas, whose spending habits have brought the island an upmarket reputation, making it just about the most expensive place to visit in the Ionian islands and lending it a rather cliquey air. Pockets of unauthorized camping, however, are tolerated since the closure of the official site. Most accommodation is block-booked by travel companies, though there are local tour operators whose holiday deals are often a fraction of the price. The capital, **Gáios**, is quite cosmopolitan, with delis and boutiques, but northerly **Lákka** and tiny **Longós** are where hardcore Paxophiles head.

Gáios

Most visitors arrive at the new port, 1km north of **GÁIOS**, a pleasant town built around a small square on the seafront overlooking two islands, Áyios Nikólaos and Panayía. Room owners often meet ferries, although it's advisable to phone ahead: try Gáios Travel (☎26620 32033) or Bouas Tours (☎26620 32401, ⓦwww.bouastours.gr), both situated on the seafront (❸). Paxi's two most established seasonal **hotels** are both near Gáios: the *Paxos Beach Hotel* (☎26620 31211, ℻26620 32695; ❺ half-board) which has smart en-suite bungalows on a hillside above a pebbly beach 2km south of town, and the fairly luxurious *Paxos Club Hotel* (☎26620 32450, ⓦwww.paxosclub.gr; ❻), 2km inland from Gáios.

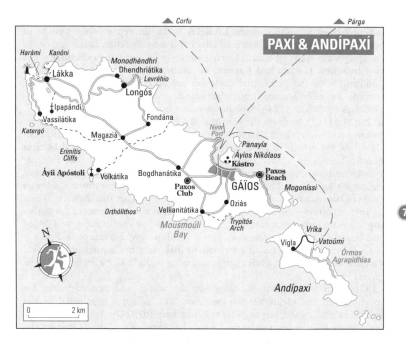

Gáïos boasts a number of decent **tavernas**, most of which are on the pricey side. One exception is the friendly family-run *Acropol*, on a side street off the square, which serves wholesome meat, fish and veg dishes at very reasonable rates. Also recommended are *Dodo's*, set in a garden inland from the Anemoyiannis statue; the *Volcano*, which is the best of those on the square; and *Vassilis*, which has the best selection and prices of the trio to the left of the road up towards the bus stop. *The Cellar* at the top of the square is the best place for a tasty *souvláki*. *Carcoleggio's*, 1.5km out of town towards Bogdhanátika, is popular with locals for its grills. *Gonia*, by the Párga *kaïki* mooring, is the last remaining traditional place for a coffee or drink. Trendier bars include *Remego* on the southern seafront and *Alter Ego* round the quay towards the new port. The *Phoenix* disco out by the new port opens sporadically after midnight and has a terrace for sublunar fun, while the inland *Tango*, beyond the bus stop, is a more regular disco.

Inland are some of the island's oldest settlements, such as Oziás and Vellianitátika, in prime walking country, but with few if any facilities. Noel Rochford's book, *Landscapes of Paxos*, lists dozens of walks, and cartographers Elizabeth and Ian Bleasdale's *Paxos Walking Map* is on sale in most travel agencies.

The rest of the island

Paxí's one main road runs along the spine of the island, with a turning at the former capital Magaziá, leading down to the tiny port of Longós. The main road continues to Lákka, the island's funkiest resort, set in a breathtaking horseshoe bay. Two buses ply the road between Gáïos and Lákka six times a day, most diverting to swing through Longós. The Gáïos–Lákka bus (30min) affords panoramic views, and the route is an excellent walk of under three hours (one way). A taxi between the two costs around €10.

Approached from the south, **LÁKKA** is an unprepossessing jumble of buildings, but once in its maze of alleys and neo-Venetian buildings, or on the quay with views of distant Corfu, you do get a sense of its charm. Lákka's two **beaches**, Harámi and Kanóni, are unfortunately prone to high-season pollution from the yachts that cram the bay. **Accommodation** is plentiful (except in high season) from the island's two biggest agencies: Planos Holidays (☎26620 31744, ⓔplanos@otenet.gr) or Routis (☎26620 31807, ⓕ26620 31161), both on the seafront (❷). Paxí's third bona-fide hotel is the snooty and overpriced *Amfitriti Hotel* (☎26620 30011, ⓦwww.amfitriti -hotel.gr; ❼), which in 2002 sadly replaced the olive groves behind Harámi beach. There's an embarrassment of good **tavernas**, such as the friendly *Nionios* and its new neighbour *Pounentes*, or the more upmarket *Pergola* and exotic *Rosa di Paxos*. There's a similar wealth of bars: the seafront *Romantica* cocktail bar and *Harbour Lights*, *Serano's* in the square, or the friendly *kafenío* of Spyros Petrou – the hub of village life. Lákka is also well situated for **walking**: up onto either promontory, to the lighthouse or Vassilátika, or to Longós and beyond. One of the finest walks – if combined with a bus or taxi back – is an early evening visit to the **Erimítis cliffs**, near the hamlet of Voïkátika: on clear afternoons, the cliffs change colour at twilight like a seafacing Uluru (Ayers Rock).

LONGÓS is the prettiest village on the island, and perfectly sited for morning sun and idyllic alfresco breakfasts. The village is dominated by the upmarket villa crowd, but the Planos office here (☎26620 31530) is the best place to look for accommodation. Longós has some of the island's best restaurants: the seafront *Vassilis*, which does terrific fish dishes, *Nassos*, with a wide variety of fish and seafood, and *Iy Gonia*, a much simpler and cheaper *psistariá*. *To Taxidhi* on the quay is a nice spot for coffee or an early drink, while *Roxi Bar* and *Ores* pander to the night-owls.

Longós has a small, scruffy beach, with sulphur springs favoured by local grannies, but most people swim off **Levrehió** beach in the next bay south, which gets the occasional camper. Islanders are touchy about camping for fear of fires so it's politic to ask at the beach taverna if it's acceptable. Longós is at the bottom of a steep winding hill, making **walking** a chore, but the short circle around neighbouring **Dhendhriátika** provides spectacular views and allows access to the small but excellent **Monodhéndhri** beach, and the walk to **Fondána** and **Magaziá** can be done to coincide with a bus back.

Andípaxi

A mile south, Paxí's tiny sibling **Andípaxi** has scarcely any accommodation and no facilities beyond several beach tavernas open during the day in season. It is most easily reached by the frequent shuttle *kaïkia* from Gáïos (from €5 return). The sandy, blue-water coves have been compared with the Caribbean, but you'll have to share them with *kaïkia* and sea taxis from all three villages, plus larger craft from Corfu (boats from Paxí may also take you to its sea stacks and caves, the most dramatic in the Ionian islands).

Boats basically deposit you either at the sandy **Vríka** beach or the longer pebble beach of **Vatoúmi**. Vríka has a taverna at each end, of which *Spiros* (☎26620 31172) has good food and can arrange self-catering accommodation up in **Vígla**, the island's hilltop settlement, on a weekly basis. Vatoúmi's only facility is the justifiably named *Bella Vista* restaurant, perched on a cliff high above the beach, although a taverna was under construction behind the beach at the time of writing.

For a swim in quieter surroundings the trick is to head south away from the pleasure-craft moorings, although path widening has made even the quieter bays more accessible. Paths also lead inland to connect the handful of homes and the southerly lighthouse, but there are no beaches of any size on Andípaxi's western coastline and thick thorny scrub makes it difficult to approach. In low season, there's also the risk of bad weather keeping pleasure craft in port and stranding you on the island.

Lefkádha (Lefkas)

Lefkádha is an oddity. Connected to the mainland by a long causeway through lagoons, it barely feels like an island, at least on the busier eastern side – and historically in fact it isn't. It is separated from the mainland by a canal cut by Corinthian colonists in the seventh century BC, which has been re-dredged (after silting up) on various occasions since, and today is spanned by a thirty-metre, pontoon-swivel-bridge built in 1986. Lefkádha was long an important strategic base, and approaching the causeway you pass a series of fortresses, climaxing in the fourteenth-century castle of **Santa Maura** – the Venetian name for the island. These defences were too close to the mainland to avoid an Ottoman tenure, which began in 1479, but the Venetians wrested back control a couple of centuries later. They were in turn overthrown by Napoleon in 1797 and then the British took over as Ionian protectors in 1810. It wasn't until 1864 that Lefkádha, like the rest of the Ionian archipelago, was reunited with Greece.

At first glance Lefkádha is not overwhelmingly attractive, although it is a substantial improvement on the mainland just opposite. The whiteness of its rock strata – *lefkás* has the same root as *lefkós*, "white" – is often brutally exposed by road cuts and quarries, and the highest ridge is bare except for ugly military and telecom installations. With the marshes and sumpy inlets on the east coast, mosquitoes can be a midsummer problem. On the other hand, the island is a fertile place, supporting cypresses, olive groves and vineyards, particularly on the western slopes, and life in the mountain villages remains relatively untouched, with the older women still wearing traditional local dress – two skirts (one forming a bustle), a dark headscarf and a rigid bodice. The rugged west coast also boasts some of the finest beaches in the Ionians.

Lefkádha has been the home of various literati, including two prominent Greek poets, Angelos Sikelianos and Aristotelis Valaoritis, and the British writer Lafcadio Hearn. Support for the arts continues in the form of a well-attended international **festival** of theatre and folk-dancing, now extended throughout the summer, with most events staged in the Santa Maura castle. On a smaller scale, frequent village celebrations accompanied by *bouzoúki* and clarinet ensure that the strong local wine flows well into the early hours.

Lefkádha remains relatively undeveloped, with just two major resorts: **Vassilikí**, in its vast bay in the south, claims to be Europe's biggest windsurf centre; **Nydhrí**, on the east coast, overlooks the island's picturesque archipelago, and is the launching point for the barely inhabited island of **Meganíssi**. The completion of the capital's superb new **marina** in 2003, however, with a smart reception centre and ample mooring, refuelling and restocking facilities illustrated the island's efforts to attract more well-to-do visitors.

LEFKÁDHA

N

▶ Vónitsa & Préveza

Santa
Maura
Yíra
Boat-bridge
Faneroméni
Tsoukaládhes
Fríni
LEFKÁDHA
Pefkoúlia
Asproverakáta
Karyótes
Áï Nikítas
Mýlos
SFÁKIÓTES
Spanohóri
Liyiá
Dhrymónas
Lazaráta
Káthisma
Kalamítsi
Karyá
Epískopos
Exánthia
Nikiána
Englouví
Vafkerí
Komíli
Hortáta
Ráhi
Spárti
Nydhrí
Stavrotás ▲
Madhourí (private)
Skorpiós (private)
Dhrágano
Vlyhó
Sývros
Yéni Peninsula
Yialós
Atháni
Áyios Pétros
Katohóri
Dhessími
Ambelákia
Vournikás
Fternó
Paliokatoúna
Spiliá
Vathý
Egremní
Spartohóri
Katoméri
Póndi
Póros
Áy. Ioánnis
Marandohóri
Mikrós
Yialós
Meganíssi
Vassilikí
Sývota
Aviófili
Pórto
Katsíki
Cape Lipsó
Cape Lefkátas
0   5 km

▼ Fiskárdho (Kefalloniá) & Fríkes (Itháki)

Lefkádha Town and around

LEFKÁDHA TOWN sits at the island's northernmost tip, hard by the causeway. Like other southerly capitals, it was hit by the earthquakes of 1948 and
1953, and the town was devastated, with the exception of a few **Italianate
churches**. As a precaution against further quakes, little was rebuilt above two

storeys, and most houses acquired second storeys of wood, giving the western dormitory area an unintentionally quaint look. The town is small – you can cross it on foot in little over ten minutes – and despite the destruction, still very attractive, especially around the main square, Platía Ayíou Spyridhónos, and the arcaded high street of Ioánnou Méla. Much of Lefkádha Town is pedestrian-only, mainly because of the narrowness of its lanes. The centre boasts over half a dozen richly decorated private family churches, usually locked and best visited around services. Many contain gems from the Ionian School of paint-ing, including work by its founder, Zakynthian Panayiotis Doxaras.

The folklore museum has been closed for a number of years but you can catch a glimpse of the old way of life at the quaint little **Phonograph Museum** (daily 9am–1pm & 6–11pm; free), which is dedicated to antique phonographs and bric-a-brac, and sells cassettes of rare traditional music. On the northwestern seafront a new Cultural Centre houses the newly expanded **archeological museum** (Tues–Sun 8.30am–3pm; €2), which contains inter-esting, well-labelled displays on aspects of daily life, religious worship and funerary customs in ancient times, as well as a room on prehistory dedicated to the work of eminent German archeologist Wilhelm Dörpfeld.

Practicalities

The **bus station** is on Dhimítri Golémi opposite the marina. It has services to almost every village on the island, with extensive daily schedules to Nydhrí, Vassilikí and Káthisma beaches on the west coast. Car and motorbike rental is useful for exploring; try EuroHire, Golémi 5 (T26450 26776), near the bus station or I Love Santas (T26450 25250) next to the *Ionian Star* hotel. Most resorts have bicycle-rental outlets, although you'll need stamina to do anything more than local touring.

Hotels have actually dwindled in Lefkádha Town, and currently number just six. All are in busy areas, but the more expensive ones are glazed against the noise and heat. The *Ionian Star* (T26450 24672, Wwww.ionianstar.gr; ❻), Panágou 2, is the plushest hotel with brand-new fittings and a pool. The other smart hotels are the stylish seafront *Nirikos*, Ayías Mávras (T26450 24132, Enirikos@otenet.gr; ❺), the cosy *Santa Maura*, Spyridhónos Viánda 2 (T26450 21308, F26450 26253; ❹), and the large *Lefkas*, Panágou 2 (T26450 23916, F26450 24579; ❻). The *Patras*, Platía Ayíou Spyridhónos (T26450 22359; ❷), is a bargain, as is the recently renovated *Byzantio*, Dörpfeld 40 (T & F26450 21315; ❸). There are simple **rooms** in the dormitory area west of Dörpfeld: the Lefkádha Room Owners Association (T26450 21266; ❷) can help, or try the *Pinelopis Rooms* (T26450 24175; ❷) at Pinelópis 20, off the seafront two short blocks from the pontoon bridge. Lefkádha Town has no campsite, although there are decent sites at Karyótes and Epískopos, a few kilo-metres to the south.

The best **restaurants** are hidden in the backstreets: the *Regantos* taverna, on Dhimárhou Venióti is the local favourite, but opening hours can be erratic. If it's closed, head for the *Lighthouse*, in its own small garden on Filarmonikís or *Romantika* on Mitropóleos, which has nightly performances of Lefkadhan *kantádhes* (hybrid of Cretan folk song and Italian opera ballad). Tasty meat, fish and *mezédhes* at very fair prices can be enjoyed at *Alkyona* and *Sto Molo*, both on Golémi, although you have to contend with the traffic noise.

Of the **bars** in the main square, the *Serano ouzerí*/café is the cheapest, with occasional evening entertainment from buskers, jugglers and even fire-eaters. Further from the action the best spot is the *Cafe Karfakis*, on Ioánnou Méla, an old-style *kafenío* with splendid *mezédhes*. The trendiest bars such as *Excess* and

THE IONIAN ISLANDS | Lefkádha

Il Posto line the seafront west of the bridge. The town's outdoor **cinema**, Eleni, on Faneroménis, has two showings and programmes change daily.

Around Lefkádha Town

The town has a decent and lengthy shingle-and-sandy beach west of the lagoon at **Yíra**, a thirty-minute walk from the centre. In season there's also a bus (hourly 10am–2pm) from the bus station. Roughly 4km long, the beach is often virtually deserted even in high season; there's a **taverna** at either end, and at the western end a couple of **bars** in the renovated windmills, as well as the trendy *Club Milos*. The beach's western extension, **Aïyánnis**, is growing in popularity and now has several restaurants, including *Tilegraphos* (T 26450 24881; ❸), which also lets out some **rooms**.

The uninhabited **Faneroméni monastery** (daily 8am–2pm & 4–8pm; free) is reached by any of the west-coast buses, or by a steep hike on foot from town (30min) through the hamlet of Fríni. There's a small museum and chapel, and an ox's yoke and hammer, used when Nazi occupiers forbade the use of bells. There are wonderful views over the town and lagoon from the Fríni road.

The island's **interior**, best reached by bus or car from Lefkádha Town, offers imposing mountainscapes and excellent walking between villages only a few kilometres apart. **KARYÁ** is its centre, and offers the *Karia Village Hotel* (T 26450 41004; ❹), tucked away above the village, and some rooms: try the Kakiousis family (T 26450 61136; ❷), Olga Lazari (T 26450 61547; ❷) or Haritini Vlahou (T 26450 41634; ❷). The leafy town square has a popular taverna, *Iy Klimataria*, just off the *platía* and two *psistariés* on it, *Ta Platania*, and the smarter *O Rousos*. Karyá is the centre of the island's lace and weaving industry, with a small but fascinating **folklore museum** set in a lacemaker's home (April–Oct daily 9am–10pm; €2.50). The historic and scenic villages of **Vafkerí** and **Englouví** are within striking distance, with the west-coast hamlets of **Dhrymónas** and **Exánthia** a hike over the hills.

The east coast to Vassilikí

Lefkádha's east coast is the most accessible and the most developed part of the island. Apart from the campsite at Karyótes, *Kariotes Beach* (T & F 26450 71103), there's little point stopping before the small fishing port of **LIYIÁ**, which has some rooms and the hotel *Konaki* (T 26450 71127, W www.hotelkonaki.gr; ❺), as well as some restaurants such as the *O Xouras psarotavérna* and the ultra-cheap and excellent garden taverna *Iy Limni*, as you head south. Further on, beyond the *Episcopos Beach* campsite (T 26450 71388), lies **NIKIÁNA**, another fishing village where you'll find the hotel *Pegasus* (T 26450 71766, F 26450 25290; ❺) and the smarter *Ionion* (T 26450 71721, F 26450 71852; ❻), as well as the *Porto Fino* pension (T 26450 71389; ❸). In addition, Nikiána has a selection of fine tavernas, notably *Pantazis*, which also has rooms to let, and *Lefko Akroyiali*, a good fish restaurant further south. Beaches here tend to be pebbly and small.

Most package travellers will find themselves in **NYDHRÍ**, the island's biggest resort by far, with ferry connections to Meganíssi and myriad **boat trips** around the nearby satellite islands. The German archeologist Wilhelm Dörpfeld believed Nydhrí, rather than Itháki, to be the site of Odysseus's capital, and did indeed find Bronze Age tombs on the plain nearby. His theory identifying ancient Ithaca with Lefkádha fell into disfavour after his death in 1940, although his obsessive attempts to give the island some status over its neighbour are honoured by a statue on Nydhrí's quay. Dörpfeld's tomb is tucked away at Ayía Kyriakí on the opposite side of the bay, near the house in which he once lived, visible just above the chapel and lighthouse on the far side of the water.

Nydhrí is an average resort, with some good pebble beaches and a lovely setting, but the centre is an ugly strip with heavy traffic. The best **place to stay** is the *Hotel Gorgona* (T 26450 92197, F 26450 92268; ❸), set in a lush garden away from the traffic a minute along the Ráhi road, which leads to Nydhrí's very own **waterfall**, a 45-minute walk inland. Rooms are best arranged through any of the resort's many travel agencies – try Nidri Travel (T 26450 92514, F 26450 92256; from ❷). The town's focus is the Aktí Aristotéli Onássi quay, where most of the rather ritzy **restaurants** and **bars** are found. The *Barrel* and *Il Sappore* restaurants are pricey but recommended, as is the *Agra* or the *Titanic* on the beach. However, eating is better value on the noisy main drag – try *Agrabeli* or *Ta Kalamia*. Nightlife centres around bars like *No Name* and *The Old Saloon*, and later on *Tropicana* or the *Sail Inn Club*, which claims to be open for 22 hours of the day.

Nydhrí sits at the mouth of a deep inlet stretching to the next village, somnolent **VLYHÓ**, with a few good tavernas and mooring for yachts. Over the Yéni peninsula across the inlet is the large **Dhessími Bay**, home to two campsites: *Santa Maura Camping* (T 26450 95007, F 26450 26087), and *Dessimi Beach Camping* (T 26450 95374, F 26450 95190), one at each end of the beach but often packed with outsized mobile homes. The *Pirofani* beach taverna in between them is excellent.

The coast road beyond Vlyhó turns inland and climbs the foothills of Mount Stavrotás, through the hamlets of Katohóri and Paliokatoúna to **Póros**, a quiet village with few facilities. Just south of here is the increasingly busy beach resort of **MIKRÓS YIALÓS**, more widely known as Póros beach. It boasts a handful of **tavernas**, a few rooms at *Oceanis Studios* (T & F 26450 95095; ❸), plus the posh *Poros Beach Camping* (T 26450 95452, W www.porosbeach .com.gr), which has bungalows (❸), shops and a pool. For food, try the *Rouda Bay* taverna opposite the beach, which also has smart rooms (T 26450 95634, E manolitsis@otenet.gr; ❺).

A panoramic detour off the main road to quiet **Vournikás** and **Sývros** is recommended to walkers and drivers (the Lefkádha–Vassilikí bus also visits); both places have tavernas and some private rooms. It's around 14km to the next resort, the fjord-like inlet of **SÝVOTA**, 2km down a steep hill (bus twice daily). There's no beach except for a remote cove, but some fine tavernas, mostly specializing in fish: the *Palia Apothiki* is the most attractive, but the *Delfinia* and *Ionion* have equally good reputations. Ask at the *Delfinia* or the adjacent Yiannis supermarket for **rooms** (T 26450 31180, F 26450 31050; ❸), or there's a basic unofficial campsite by the bus stop at the edge of the village.

Beyond the Sývota turning, the mountain road dips down towards Kondárena, almost a suburb of **VASSILIKÍ**, the island's premier watersports resort. Winds in the huge bay draw vast numbers of windsurfers, with light morning breezes for learners and tough afternoon blasts for advanced surfers. Booking your **accommodation** ahead is mandatory in high season. Hotels are not cheap: *Pension Hollidays* (T 26450 31011, F 26450 31426; ❸), round the corner from the ferry dock, is a reasonable option with air conditioning and TV in all rooms. Also good value for its rating is slightly more upmarket *Hotel Apollo* (T 26450 31122, F 26450 31142; ❹) nearby. In the centre of town, the two main hotels are the classy *Vassiliki Bay Hotel* (T 26450 31077, F 26450 23567; ❺) and the *Hotel Lefkatas* (T 26450 31801, F 26450 31804; ❹), a large, modern building overlooking the busiest road in town. Rooms and apartments are available along the beach road to Póndi: *Billy's House* (☎26450 31418; ❸) and *Christina Politi's Rooms* (☎26450 31440; ❸) are smart and purpose-built or ask at the central Samba Tours (☎26450 31520, ✉sambatours@otenet.gr; ❸). The largest of the three beach windsurf centres, *Club Vassiliki*, offers all-in **windsurf tuition** and accommodation deals. Vassilikí's only **campsite**, the large *Camping Vassiliki Beach* (☎26450 31308, ℻26450 31458), is about 500m along the beach road; it has its own restaurant, bar and shop.

Vassilikí's pretty quayside is lined with **tavernas** and bars, notably the *Dolphin Psistaria*, the glitzier *Restaurant Miramare*, specializing in fish, and *Alexander*, which has pizza. Quieter spots round the headland include the *Jasmine Garden* Chinese and the leafy *Apollo*. The best place for a **drink** is *Livanakis kafenío* (next to the bakery), now modernized but still genuine and cheap.

The beach at Vassilikí is stony and poor, but improves 1km on at tiny **PÓNDI**; most non-windsurfers, however, use the daily *kaïki* trips to nearby Ayiófili or around Cape Lefkátas to the superior beaches at Pórto Katsíki and Egremní on the sandy west coast (see opposite). There's a gradually increasing number of **places to stay** at Póndi, some with great views of the bay and plain behind, particularly from the terrace of the *Ponti Beach Hotel* (☎26450 31572, ℻26450 31576; ❺), which is very popular with holidaying Greeks, and has a decent restaurant and bar. The *Nefeli* (☎26450 31515, ✉clubnefeli @hotmail.com; ❸), right on the beach, is much better value though. The *Panorama* **taverna** serves delights such as garlic prawns and steak Diana.

The west coast

Tsoukaládhes, just 6km from Lefkádha Town, is developing a roadside tourism business, but better beaches lie a short distance to the southwest, so there's very little reason to stay here. Four kilometres on, the road plunges down to the sand-and-pebble **Pefkoúlia** beach, one of the longest on the island, with two tavernas at the north end, one of which, *Mesoyios*, has rooms (☎26450 97070, ℻26450 97170; ❸) and unofficial camping down at the other end, over 1km away. This part of the island was dealt a severe blow to business in August 2003 when a powerful earthquake buried the main road through to Áï Nikítas, although amazingly there were no fatalities. The road was still closed at the time of writing but should be repaired by the 2004 season.

Jammed into a gorge between Pefkoúlia and the next beach, Mýlos, is **ÁÏ NIKÍTAS**, the prettiest resort on Lefkádha, a jumble of lanes and small wooden buildings. The back of the village is a dust-blown car park, which has completely taken over the former campsite, but this means that the village itself is now a pedestrian zone. The most attractive **accommodation** is in the *Pension Ostria* (☎26450 97483, ℻26450 97300; ❹), a beautiful blue-and-white building above the village, decorated in a mix of beachcomber and ecclesiastical styles. The *Villa Milia* (☎26450 97475; ❸), by the junction, or the *Elena patisserie* (☎26450 97385; ❸) offer better rates than most. Other options are in the alleys that run off the main drag; the best bets are the small *Hotel Selene* (☎26450 97369; ❸) and quieter *Olive Tree* (☎26450 97453, ✉olivetreehotel @hotmail.com; ❸), which is also signposted from the main road. The best tavernas include the *Sapfo* fish taverna by the sea and the *To Agnantio*, just above the main street, which serves excellent traditional cuisine. *Captain's Corner* near the beach is the liveliest drinking venue.

Sea taxis (€1.50 one way) ply between Áï Nikítas and **Mýlos** beach, or it's a 45-minute walk (or bus ride) to the most popular beach on the coast,

Káthisma, a shadeless kilometre of fine sand, which becomes nudist and a lot less crowded beyond the large jutting rocks halfway along. There are two tavernas on the beach: the barn-like *Kathisma* (☎26450 97050, ⓔvatheo@in.gr; ❹), with smart apartments, and the expensive and unfriendly *Akroyiali*. Above the beach the *Sunset* has **rooms** (☎26450 97488; ❸) and the *Balkoni* restaurant commands fine views. Beyond Káthisma, hairpin bends climb the flank of Mount Méga towards the small village of **KALAMÍTSI**, a much cheaper base for this area. Good-value **rooms** or apartments can be found at *Hotel Lenia* (☎26450 99125; ❷), *Hermes* (☎26450 99417; ❷), the smart *Blue and White House* (☎26450 99413; ❸) and the newer *Pansion Nontas* (☎26450 99451; ❸). There are also a few decent **tavernas**, including the *Paradeisos*, set in its own garden with fountain, the more basic *Ionio* and, just north of the village, the aptly titled *Panoramic View*. Three kilometres down a newly paved road is the village's quiet sandy beach.

South of Kalamítsi, past the hamlets of Hortáta, which boasts the excellent *Lygos* taverna with rooms (☎26450 33395, ⓔlola26@ch.gr; ❷), and Komíli, the landscape becomes almost primeval. At 38km from Lefkádha Town, **ATHÁNI** is Lefkádha's most remote spot to stay, with a couple of good tavernas which both have great-value rooms: the *Panorama* (☎26450 33291, ⓕ26450 33476; ❷) and *O Alekos* (☎26450 33484; ❷), the latter only open in high season. Three of the Ionian's choicest **beaches**, each with basic refreshment facilities, are accessible from Atháni: the nearest, reached by a 4km paved road is **Yialós**, followed by **Egremní**, down a steep incline unpaved for the last 2km. Further south an asphalted road leads to the dramatic and popular twin beach of **Pórto Katsíki**, where there are several better-stocked *kantínes* on the cliff above.

Keeping to the main road for 14km from Atháni will bring you to barren **Cape Lefkátas**, which drops abruptly 75m into the sea. Byron's *Childe Harold* sailed past this point, and "saw the evening star above, Leucadia's far projecting rock of woe: And hail'd the last resort of fruitless love". The fruitless love is a reference to Sappho, who in accordance with the ancient legend that you could cure yourself of unrequited love by leaping into these waters, leapt – and died. In her honour the locals termed the place Kávos tis Kyrás ("Lady's Cape"), and her act was imitated by the lovelorn youths of Lefkádha for centuries afterwards. And not just by the lovelorn, for the act (known as *katapondismós*) was performed annually by scapegoats – always a criminal or a lunatic – selected by priests from the Apollo temple whose sparse ruins lie close by. Feathers and even live birds were attached to the victims to slow their descent and boats waiting below took the chosen one, dead or alive, away to some place where the evil banished with them could do no further harm. The rite continued into the Roman era, when it degenerated into little more than a fashionable stunt by decadent youth. These days, in a more controlled modern re-enactment, Greek hang-gliders hold a tournament from the cliffs every July.

Lefkádha's satellites

Lefkádha has four satellite islands clustered off its east coast, although only one, **Meganíssi**, the largest and most interesting, is accessible. **Skorpiós**, owned by the Onassis family, fields armed guards to deter visitors. **Madhourí**, owned by the family of poet Nanos Valaoritis, is private and similarly off-limits, while tiny **Spárti** is a large scrub-covered rock. Day-trips from Nydhrí skirt all three islands, and some stop to allow swimming in coves.

Meganíssi

Meganíssi, twenty minutes by frequent daily ferries from Nydhrí, is a large island with limited facilities but a magical, if bleak landscape. Ferries stop first at **Spiliá**, below **SPARTOHÓRI**, an immaculate village with whitewashed buildings and an abundance of bougainvillea. The locals – many returned émigrés from Australia – live from farming and fishing and are genuinely welcoming. You arrive at a jetty on a pebble beach with a few tavernas and a primitive but free (for a night or two only) campsite behind the excellent *Star Taverna*. The village proper boasts three restaurants: a pizza place called the *Tropicana*, which can direct you to **rooms** (☏26450 51486; ❶–❸), as can *Gakias* (☏26450 51050; ❷); the trio is completed by the traditional taverna *Lakis*. Further west round the coast at Áyios Ioánnis there is a good beach with the *Il Paradiso* taverna and a makeshift campsite, a great spot to unwind in.

The attractive inland village of **KATOMÉRI** is an hour's walk through magnificent country. It has the island's one **hotel**, the *Meganissi*, a comfortable place with a restaurant and pool (☏26450 51240, ℻26450 51639; ❸), and a few café-bars. Ten minutes' walk downhill is the main port of **VATHÝ**, with some accommodation (*Different Studios*: ☏26450 22170; ❸) and several highly rated restaurants, notably the waterside taverna, *Porto Vathi*, which Lefkadans flock to on ferries for Sunday lunch, and the *Rose Garden*. After the high-season madness of Nydhrí, Meganíssi's unspoilt landscape is a tonic, and it's easy to organize a **day-trip** from Nydhrí, getting off at Spiliá, walking via Spartohóri to Katoméri for lunch at the *Meganissi* or down at Vathý, from where you can catch the ferry back. Paths lead from Katoméri to remote beaches, including popular **Ambelákia**, but these aren't realistic on a day-trip.

Kefalloniá

Kefalloniá is the largest of the Ionian islands – a place that has real towns as well as resorts. Like its neighbours, Kefalloniá was overrun by Italians and Germans in World War II; the "handover" after Italy's capitulation in 1943 led to the massacre of over five thousand Italian troops on the island by invading German forces. These events form a key episode in Louis de Bernières' novel, *Captain Corelli's Mandolin*, a tragicomic epic of life on the island, which takes place mostly during the occupation and whose film version was made on the island in 2000.

Until the late 1980s, the island paid scant regard to tourism; perhaps this was partly due to a feeling that Kefalloniá could not easily be marketed. Virtually all of its towns and villages were levelled in the 1953 earthquake, and these masterpieces of Venetian architecture had been the one touch of elegance in a severe, mountainous landscape. A more likely explanation, however, for the island's late emergence on the Greek tourist scene is the Kefallonians' legendary reputation for insular pride and stubbornness, and a good measure of eccentricity.

Having decided on the advantages of an easily exploitable industry, however, Kefalloniá went about it wholeheartedly and it soon started to rival Zákynthos and even Corfu in the tourist stakes. Long favoured by Italians, it began attracting British package companies, for whom an airport terminal was constructed in the mid-Nineties, while virtually every decent beach has been endowed with restaurants. There are definite attractions here, with some **beaches** as good as any in the Ionian islands, and a fine (if pricey) local wine, the dry white

Rombola. Mercifully, the anticipated "Corelli factor" did not lead to the island becoming either oversubscribed or over-expensive. Moreover, the island seems able to soak up a lot of people without feeling at all crowded, and the magnificent scenery speaks for itself, the escarpments culminating in the 1632-metre bulk of **Mount Énos**, a national park.

For **airport** arrival see the Argostóli section on p.528. Kefalloniá's **bus** system is basic but expanding, and with a little legwork it can be used to get you almost anywhere on the island. Key routes connect Argostóli with the main tourist centres of **Sámi**, **Fiskárdho**, **Skála** and **Póros**. There's a useful connection from Sámi to the tiny resort of **Ayía Efimía**, which also attracts many package travellers. If you're using a motorbike, take care, roads can be very rough off the beaten track – although all the major routes have now been surfaced – and the gradients can sometimes be a bit challenging for underpowered machines. The island has a plethora of **ferry** connections, principally from Fiskárdho to Lefkádha and Itháki, and from Sámi to Itháki, Astakós and Pátra, as well as links from Argostóli and Póros to Kyllíni and Pessádha to Zákynthos. Direct sailings between Sámi and one of the Italian ports – usually Brindisi – are offered most years in peak season only, by just one company.

Sámi and around

Most boats dock at the large and functional port town of **SÁMI**, built and later rebuilt near the south end of the Itháki straits, more or less on the site of ancient Sami. This was the capital of the island in Homeric times, when Kefalloniá was part of Ithaca's maritime kingdom: today the administrative hierarchy is reversed, Itháki being considered the backwater. With the only ferry link to Pátra, frequent connections to Itháki and direct (albeit erratic) links to Italy, the town is clearly preparing itself for a burgeoning future. The long sandy beach that stretches round the bay is quite adequate; 2km beyond ancient Sami, lies a fine pebble beach, **Andísamis**.

The town has three big **hotels**: the *Sami Beach* (℡26740 22802, ✉samibeach@otenet.gr; ❺) and friendly *Athina Beach* (℡26740 23067, ℻26740 23040; ❹), both actually situated at the far end of the beach in Karavómylos, and the *Pericles* (℡26740 22780, ℻26740 22787; ❺), over 1km along the Argostóli road, which has extensive grounds, two pools and sports facilities. The best mid-range bet is the comfortable seafront *Kastro* (℡26740 22282, ℻26740 23004; ❸), followed by the *Melissani* (℡ & ℻26740 22464; ❹), up behind the main dock. Both *períptera* on the quay offer rooms, as do a variety of private homes a few blocks back from the front. Sámi's **campsite**, *Camping Karavomilos Beach* (℡26740 22480, ✉valettas@hol.gr), has over 300 well-shaded spaces, a taverna, shop and bar, and opens onto the beach. It is by far the better of the island's two official sites.

Sámi doesn't have a great many **tavernas** beyond those on the seafront; visitors tend to go to the slightly touristic *Adonis* or the *Dolphins*, but cheaper and more genuine choices are *Gorgona* and *O Faros*, both with a good selection of veg and meat dishes, including the famous local meat pie. Better still, head further towards the beach to the *Akroyiali*, where you can sample fresh seafood, succulent meat dishes and good local wine. The inevitably renamed *Captain Corelli's* and *Aqua Marina* are the favourite **bars** in the evenings, while the best place for a snack breakfast or ice cream is *Captain Jimmy's*. The seafront Sami Center (℡26740 22254) rents out **motorbikes** at fair rates.

KEFALLONIÁ AND ITHÁKI

Ithŕki

Sarakíniko
Bay

Lipá

Arethoúsa
Spring

VATHÝ

Perahóri

Áyiou Andhréou
Bay

Stenós
Bay

Loútsa

Dhéxa

Paleohóra

Ω Taxiárhon

Mélos I
Gulf

Mount
Etós

Cave of the
Nymphs

Áyios
Ioánnis

Anoyí

Kióni

Ω Katharón

Alalkomenae

Pisaetós
Bay

Frikes

Pelikáta
Hill

Mount
Nírito

Léfki

Exoyí

Afáles
Bay

Plattřithiés
School of
Homer

Stavrós

Pólis
Bay

Neohóri

Émblisi

Fiskárdho

Fókis

Evretí

Vassilikiádhes

Ayía Efimía

Mánganos

Mazoukáta

Konidharáta

Halikerí

Ayía Ierousalím

Ássos

Dhivaráta

Myrtos

Angónas

Ayía
Kyriakí

Zóla

Áyios
Spyrídhonas

Athéras

N

▲ *Kyllíni*

Skála
Póros
Ratzakli
Tzanáta
Pástra
Markópoulo
Káto
Kateliós

Andísamis
SÁMI

Melissáni Cave
Karavómylos

Dhrogaráti Cave

Áyios
Eleinthérios

*Mount Énos
1632m*

Vlaháta
Moussáta
Lourdháta

Sissiá

Áyios
Yerásimos

Áyios
Yeóryios Fortress

Frangáta

Trapezáki
Pessádha
Spartiá
Keramiés
Koriána

*Mount
Evmorfía
846m*

Dhilináta
Metaxáta
Peratáta

Dhavgáta
Lakíthra

Fársa

ARGOSTÓLI
Dhrápano Causeway

Kourkomeláta
Avythos

Lixoúri
Katavóthres

Lássi
Makrys Yialós
Platýs Yialós

Lépedha

*Mégas
Lákkos*

Mantzavináta

Xi

Ayía Thékli

Kounópetra
*Cape
Akrotíri*

Kipouréon

Petaní

5 km
0

▶ *Áyios Nikólaos (Zákynthos)*
▶ *Kyllíni*

The Dhrogaráti and Melissáni caves

Another good reason to stay in Sámi is its proximity to the Drogharáti and Melissáni caves; the former is 5km out of town towards Argostóli, the latter 3km north towards Ayía Efimía. A very impressive stalagmite-bedecked chamber, **Dhrogaráti** (April–Oct daily 8am–9pm; €3.50) is occasionally used for concerts thanks to its marvellous acoustics – Maria Callas once sang here. **Melissáni** (daily 8am–sunset; €4.10) is partly submerged in brackish water, which, amazingly, emerges from an underground fault which leads the whole way under the island to a point near Argostóli. At that point, known as Katavóthres, the sea gushes endlessly into a subterranean channel – and, until the 1953 earthquake disrupted it – the current was used to drive sea mills. That the water, now as then, still ends up in the cave has been shown with fluorescent tracer dye. The beautiful textures and shades created by the light pouring through the collapsed roof of the cave make it a must.

Ayía Efimía

AYÍA EFIMÍA, 9km north of Sámi, is a friendly little fishing harbour popular with package operators, yet with no major developments. Its two drawbacks are its beaches – the largest, risibly named Paradise beach, is a pathetic 20m of shingle, although there are other coves to the south – and its poor transport connections (only two daily buses to Sámi and Fiskárdho). **Accommodation** here is good at two small, smart **hotels**: *Pyllaros* (℡ 26740 61800, ℻ 26740 61801; ➍) and the better-value *Moustakis* (℡ & ℻ 26740 61030; ➌); and there are also apartments offered by Yerasimos Raftopoulos (℡ 26740 61233, ℻ 26740 61216; ➌). The *Dendrinos* **taverna**, round the headland past the harbour, is the place for island cuisine; the *Pergola* also has a wide range of island specialities and standard Greek dishes. Predictably, the café-bar where the film crew and actors used to hang out has been renamed *Captain Corelli's*, while the *Strawberry zaharoplastío* is the place for a filling breakfast. The town's nightclub is *Paranoia*, 700m out of town towards Fiskárdho. If you are making your own way between here and Sámi, the taverna of the same name at the tiny cove of **Ayía Paraskeví** is famous for its delicious spaghetti with mussel marinade.

Southeast Kefalloniá

Travel **southeast from Sámi** has been made a lot easier by the completion of the asphalt road to **Póros** and the consequent addition of a twice-daily bus route between the two. Continuing south, Póros is connected to **Skála** by another paved coastal road.

Póros

PÓROS was one of the island's earliest developed resorts, and definitely gives the impression of having seen better days. The town's small huddle of hotels and apartment blocks is almost unique on Kefalloniá, and not enhanced by a scruffy seafront and thin, pebbly beach.

Póros does, however, have a regular ferry link to **Kyllíni** on the Peloponnesian mainland, a viable alternative to Sámi–Pátra. Póros is actually made up of two bays: the first, where most tourists are based, and the actual harbour, a few minutes over the headland. There are plenty of rooms, apartments and a few **hotels**. The best deal is at the cosy *Santa Irina* (℡ 26740 72017, ✉ maki@otenet.gr; ➋), by the crossroads inland, whose low rate includes breakfast, while the nearby *Odysseus Palace* (℡ 26740 72036, ℻ 26740 72148; ➎) often gives good discounts. The old-fashioned *Riviera* (☎26740 72327, ℱ26740 72579; ❸) has en-suite rooms on the seafront. Among **travel agents**, Poros Travel by the ferry dock (☎26740 72476, ℱ26740 72069) offers a range of accommodation, as well as services such as car rental and ferry bookings. The main seafront has the majority of the **restaurants** and **bars**. The *Fotis Family* taverna serves good food in a pleasant setting and the *Mythos* café has Internet access. At night, however, the old port is quieter and has more atmosphere, with tavernas such as *Tzivas* and the *Dionissos*, which are strong on local seafood.

The aforementioned road twists 12km around the rocky coastline from Póros to Skála at the southern extremity of the island. It's a lovely, isolated route, with scarcely a building on the way, save for a small chapel, 3km short of Skála, next to the ruins of a **Roman temple**.

Skála

In total contrast to Póros, the resort of **SKÁLA** is a low-rise development set among handsome pines above a few kilometres of good sandy beach. A **Roman villa** (daily: summer 8am–8pm, rest of year 8am–3pm; free) and some mosaics were excavated here in the 1950s, near the site of the *Golden Beach Palace* rooms, and are open to the public.

Its faithful return crowd keep Skála busy until well after Póros has closed for the season, and accommodation can be hard to find. There are studios and apartments at *Dionysus Rooms* (☎26710 83283; ❷), a block south of the high street, and rooms can be found at the *Golden Beach Palace* (☎26710 83327; ❸) above the beach or through Etam Travel Service (☎26710 83101, ℱ26710 83142; ❷). The more upmarket *Tara Beach Hotel* (☎26710 83250, ⓦwww.tarabeach.gr; ❺) has rooms and individual bungalows in lush gardens on the edge of the beach. Skála boasts a number of good **restaurants**: the *Pines*, the *Flamingo*, and, on the beach, the *Paspalis* and *Sunrise*. Drinkers head for *The Loft* cocktail **bar** and the beachside *Pikiona* pool-bar.

Skála to Lourdháta

Some of the finest sandy beaches on the island are just beyond Skála below the village of Ratzaklí, and around the growing microresort of **KÁTO KATELIÓS**, which already has a couple of hotels: the smart *Odyssia* (☎26710 81615, ℱ26710 81614; ❹) and the *Galini Resort* (☎26710 81582, ⓔniko-p-@hotmail.com; ❹), which has good deals on **apartments** for four. There are also some rooms and apartments available through the *Lighthouse* taverna (☎26710 81355; ❷) and *Jimmy's* (☎26710 81363; ❸). Of the half a dozen restaurants and cafés at the seafront, the *Blue Sea* taverna is renowned for the freshness and quality of its fish, the *Arbouro* offers a wide selection of dishes, while the *Cozy* bar is the prime drinking location. The coast around Káto Kateliós is also Kefalloniá's key breeding ground for the loggerhead **turtle** (see box, p.541). Camping on the nearby beaches is discouraged.

The inland village of **MARKÓPOULO**, claimed by some to be the birthplace of homophonous explorer Marco Polo, witnesses a bizarre snake-handling ritual every year on August 15, the **Assumption of the Virgin festival**. The church where this ritual is enacted stands on the site of an old convent. The story goes that when the convent was attacked by pirates, the nuns prayed to be transformed into snakes to avoid being taken prisoner. Their prayers were supposedly answered, and each year the "return" of a swarm of small, harmless snakes is meant to bring the villagers good luck. As Mother Nature is unlikely to keep to such a schedule, some discreet snake-breeding on the part of the village priests must be suspected.

The coastline is largely inaccessible until the village of **VLAHÁTA**, which has some rooms and restaurants, but there's little point in staying up here, when you can turn 2km down to **LOURDHÁTA**, which has a kilometre-long shingle beach, mixed with imported sand. *Adonis* (☎26710 31206; ❸) and *Ramona* (☎26710 31032; ❸) have **rooms** just outside the village on the approach road, while the one **hotel**, the *Lara* (☎26710 31157, ✉larab@hol.gr; ❹), towards the beach, has en-suite rooms with sea views and a pool. Of the two **tavernas** on the tiny plane-shaded village square, *Alexia's* serves some Indian and Middle Eastern dishes and the *Diamond* does a good range of veg items. Further up the hill is the smarter *Spiros* steak-and-grill house and, closer to Vlaháta, *Dionysus*, serving taverna standards; at the beach itself *Klimitis* is good for inexpensive fish. The beachside *Astrabar* is friendly and plays a good mix of English and Greek music into the wee hours. Another fine beach, reached by a turning from Moussáta, west of Vlaháta, is **Trapezáki**, an attractive strand with just one restaurant by the small jetty.

Argostóli and around

ARGOSTÓLI, Kefalloniá's capital, is a large and thriving town, virtually a city, with a marvellous site on a bay within a bay. The stone bridge, connecting the two sides of the inner bay, was initially constructed by the British in 1813. A small obelisk remains, but the plaque commemorating "the glory of the British Empire" has disappeared. The town was totally rebuilt after the 1953 earthquake, but has an enjoyable streetlife that remains defiantly Greek, especially during the evening *vólta* around **Platía Valiánou** (formerly Platía Metaxá) – the nerve centre of town – and along the pedestrianized Lithóstrotou, which runs parallel to the seafront.

The **Korgialenio History and Folklore Museum** (Mon–Sat 9am–2pm; €3), on Ilía Zervoú behind the Municipal Theatre, has a rich collection of local religious and cultural artefacts, including photographs taken before and after the earthquake. Insight into how the island's nobility used to live can be gained from a visit to the **Focas-Cosmetatos Foundation** (Mon–Sat 9.20am–1pm, plus summer 7–10pm; €3), on Valiánou opposite the provincial government building. It contains elegant furniture and a collection of lithographs and paintings, including works by nineteenth-century British artists Joseph Cartwright and Edward Lear. The 2000-refurbished **Archeological Museum** (Tues–Sun 8.30am–3pm; €3), on nearby R. Vergóti, has a sizeable collection of pottery, jewellery, funerary relics and statuary from prehistoric, through Mycenaean to late Classical times. It is well laid out and labelled, rivalling Kérkyra Town's (see p.499) as the best such museum in the Ionians.

Practicalities

Argostóli's modern **Kefalloniá airport** lies 7km south of town. There are no airport buses, and suburban bus services are so infrequent or remote from the terminal that a taxi (at an inflated flat rate of around €10) is the only dependable connection. Those arriving in Argostóli by bus from Sámi or elsewhere will wind up at the KTEL **bus station**, a minute from the Dhrápano causeway and ten minutes' walk south of the main square, Platía Valianoú. Argostóli's friendly **tourist office** (Mon–Fri 7.30am–2.30pm, plus summer Mon–Fri 5–10pm & Sat 9am–1pm; ☎26710 22248, ☏26710 24466), on Andoníou Trítsi at the north end of the seafront, next to the port authority, has information about rooms, piles of brochures and trail guides, and can advise on transport, sites and all resorts around the island. The islandwide

Sunbird agency (☎26710 23723, ⓦwww.sunbird.gr) is a reliable outlet for car or motorbike rental. Excelixis (Mon–Sat 9am–2.30pm & 6–10pm; €5 per hour) at Minoös 3, behind the church on Lithóstrotou, has Internet facilities.

Hotels in Argostóli open all year and are mostly mid-range, the best value of these being the *Ionian Plaza* (☎26710 25581, ⓕ26710 25585; ❹). A good option away from the square is the *Fokas*, Yeroulánou 1–3 (☎26710 22566, ⓕ26710 23109; ❸), while the partly British-run *Mouikis*, Výronos 3 (☎26710 23454, ⓦwww.mouikis.com; ❺) is classy but not cheap; one of the best deals going, if you don't mind sharing a bathroom, is the friendly *Chara* (☎26710 22427; ❶), set in a lovely shady courtyard at the corner of Y. Vergóti and Dhevossétou near Dhrápano bridge. The newly upgraded *pension* attached to the *Tsima Cavo* cafeteria (☎26710 23941; ❸), opposite the Lixoúri ferry ramp, is good value, with TV in all the air-conditioned rooms. In a working town with a large permanent population, **private rooms** aren't too plentiful, but you can call the Room-Owners Association (☎26710 29109) to see what's on offer. Some of the best bargains can be found through waterfront tavernas, such as the *Kalafatis* (☎26710 22627; ❷–❹), not far from the Dhrápano bridge on A. Trítsi or the *Tzivras* (☎26710 24259; ❶–❷), on Vandhórou, just off the waterfront opposite the market. A number of travel agencies also offer rooms, apartments and villas: try Ainos Travel (☎26710 22333, ⓦwww.ainostravel.gr; from ❷), opposite the Archeological Museum, or Myrtos at A. Trítsi 117 (☎26710 25895, ⓔmyrtostr@hol.gr; from ❸). The town's **campsite**, *Argostoli Camping* (☎26710 23487), lies 2km north of the centre, just beyond the Katovóthres sea mills; there's only an infrequent bus service in high season, so you'll probably have to walk and it's rather basic with limited shade.

The aforementioned *Tzivras estiatório* (only open until 5pm) is one of the best places to try Kefallonian cuisine; the upmarket *Captain's Table* **taverna** just off the main square is worth a splurge for its live *kantádhes*, though they are just about as easily heard from the far more reasonable *To Steki* next door. Of the seafront eateries, the *Maïstrato ouzerí* near the square has a good selection of seafood and *mezédhes* and also features gentle live music. For a change of diet, try *Paparazzi*, 50m towards the front from the square, which combines genuine Italian food in the garden with a British-style pub indoors. Local posers hang out at *Polo Central* café-bar and the *Privé* café, both on the square, and the nearby *My Way* club-bar; *Cinema* is a late-night indoor disco by the museum. The quayside bars, particularly the *Aristofanis kafenío* by the Dhrápano bridge, are quiet, cheap and have the best views.

South of Argostóli: beaches and Áyios Yeóryios

Many package travellers will find themselves staying in **LÁSSI**, a short bus ride or twenty-minute walk from town. Lássi sprawls unattractively along a busy main road, but it does have good sandy beaches, particularly at **Makrýs Yialós** and **Platýs Yialós**, although they're right under the airport flight path. **Beaches** such as **Ávythos** are well worth seeking out, although if you're walking beyond **Kourkomeláta** there is a real if occasional risk of being attacked by farm dogs, particularly during the hunting season (Sept 25–Feb 28). There is very little accommodation in the region, and precious few shops or bars. **Pessádha** has a twice-daily ferry link with Zákynthos in summer, but little else, and be warned that the pathetic bus service from Argostóli is no good for connecting up the boats. You'll have to hitch or take an expensive taxi in most cases.

With a scooter, the best inland excursion is to **ÁYIOS YEÓRYIOS**, the medieval Venetian capital of the island. The old town here supported a population of 15,000 until its destruction by an earthquake in the seventeenth century: substantial ruins of its **castle** (summer Tues–Sat 8.30am–7pm & Sun

8.30am–3pm; rest of year Tues–Sun 8.30am–3pm; free), now reopened after extensive renovations, churches and houses can be visited on the hill above the modern village of Peratáta. Byron lived for a few months in the nearby village of Metaxáta and was impressed by the view from the summit in 1823; sadly, as at Mesolóngi, the house where he stayed no longer exists. Two kilometres south of Áyios Yeóryios is a fine collection of religious icons and frescoes kept in a restored church that was part of the nunnery of Áyios Andhréas.

Mount Énos

At 15km from a point halfway along the Argostóli–Sámi road, **Mount Énos** isn't really a walking option, but roads nearly reach the official 1632-metre summit. The mountain has been declared a national park, to protect the *Abies cephalonica* firs (named after the island) which clothe the slopes. There are absolutely no facilities on or up to the mountain, but the views from the highest point in the Ionian islands out over its neighbours and the mainland are wonderful. In low season, watch the weather, which can deteriorate with terrifying speed. Not far before the mountain turning, taking a detour towards Frangáta is doubly rewarded by the huge and lively **Áyios Yerásimos monastery** (daily 8am–1pm & 3–7pm), which hosts two of the island's most important festivals (Aug 15 and Oct 20), and right behind it the **Robola winery** (summer daily 8am–8pm; rest of year Mon–Fri 9am–3pm), which offers a free self-guided tour and generous wine-tasting.

Lixoúri and its peninsula

Half-hourly ferries (hourly in winter) ply between the capital and **LIXOÚRI** throughout the day until midnight. The town was flattened by earthquakes, and hasn't risen much above two storeys since. It's a little drab, but has good restaurants, quiet hotels and is favoured by those who want to explore the eerie quakescapes left in the south and the barren north of the peninsula. **Hotels** are not especially plentiful or cheap, but two comfortable air-conditioned options are the *La Cité* (T 26710 92505, F 26710 92525; ❹), four blocks back from the front, and a beach hotel just south of town, *Summery* (T 26710 91771, E summery@otenet.gr; ❹). Two agencies offer cheaper accommodation (from ❷) in town: A. D. Travel (T 26710 93142, F 26710 92663) on the main road through town, and Perdikis Travel (T 26710 91097, F 26710 92503) on the quay. Among the tavernas, *Akrogiali* on the seafront is excellent and cheap, drawing admirers from all over the island. *Iy Avli*, on the block behind, serves a variety of dishes in a leafy garden, while *Adonis* is a good basic *psistariá* at the back of the square. *Overdose* is the trendy place to drink on the square, but the seafront has a couple of much more genuine *kafenía*.

Lixoúri's nearest beach is **Lépedha**, a two-kilometre walk south. Like the **Xí** and **Mégas Lákkos** beaches (served by bus from Lixoúri and both with restaurants and accommodation), it has rich-red sand and is backed by low cliffs. Those with transport can also strike out for the monastery at **Kipouréon**, and north to the spectacular beach at **Petaní**, where there are two reasonable restaurants. The further of these, *Xougras*, has rooms run by Greek-American Dina (T 26710 97128; ❸), and proves one of the most relaxing places to stay on the island.

The west coast and the road north

The journey between Argostóli and Fiskárdho, by regular bus or rented vehicle, is the most spectacular ride in the archipelago. Leaving town, the road rises into the Evmorfía foothills and, beyond Agónas, clings to near-sheer cliffs as it heads for Dhivaráta, which has a smattering of rooms, such as *Mina Studios* (☎26740 61716, ✉markela1@hol.gr; ❸), a couple of restaurants, and is the stop for **Mýrtos** beach. It's a four-kilometre hike down on foot (you can also drive down), with just one snack-bar on the beach, but from above or below this is the most dramatic beach in the Ionian islands – a splendid strip of pure-white sand and pebbles. Sadly, it's shadeless and gets mighty crowded in high season.

Six kilometres on is the turning for the atmospheric village of **ÁSSOS**, clinging to a small isthmus between the island and a huge hill crowned by a ruined fort. Accommodation is scarce – villagers invariably send you to Andhreas Rokos' rooms (☎26740 51523; ❷) on the approach road, which are great value, or you can opt for the posher *Kanakis Apartments* opposite (☎26740 51631, ℻26740 51660; ❹). Ássos has a small pebble beach, and three tavernas, notably the *Nefeli* and the *Platanos Grill*, on a plane-shaded village square backed by mansions, mostly now restored after being ruined in the quake. It can get a little claustrophobic, but there's nowhere else like it in the Ionian islands.

Fiskárdho

FISKÁRDHO, on the northernmost tip of the island, sits on a bed of limestone that buffered it against the worst of the quakes. Two **lighthouses**, Venetian and Victorian, guard the bay, and the ruins on the headland are believed to be from a twelfth-century chapel begun by Norman invader Robert Guiscard, who gave the place his name. The nineteenth-century harbour frontage is intact, nowadays occupied by smart restaurants and chic boutiques. There is a new **Environmental and Nautical Museum** (summer daily 10am–7pm; donations), housed in a renovated Neoclassical mansion on the hill behind the village. The volunteers who curate it can also arrange **scuba diving**.

The island's premier resort, Fiskárdho is very busy through to the end of October, with **accommodation** at a premium. The cheapest rooms are those of Sotiria Tselenti (☎26740 41204; ❸), 50m back from the tiny square, followed by *Regina's* (☎26740 41125; ❸) with its own café at the back of the village, next to the car park. *Theodora's Café Bar* has rooms in whitewashed houses on the quay (☎26740 41297; ❹), and another reasonable option is the small *Erissos pension* (☎26740 41327; ❸), just off the seafront. Pama Travel (☎26740 41033, ✉pamatravel@otenet.gr; from ❸), on the seafront furthest away from the ferry quay, is another source of rooms and costlier apartments. There's a wealth of good but mostly expensive **restaurants**. Two to try on the seafront are the *Tassia,* which has a vast range of seafood (but check how much fish you are actually ordering), and the *Captain's Table,* serving succulent Greek and Kefallonian fare. On the square, *Alexis* serves pizzas and pastas, while *Lagonderia*, just round the corner, specializes in tasty oven food. *Veggera* and *Occhi di Mare* are two of the most popular harbourside **bars**. The dance spot is *Kastro Club* up at the back of the village. There are two good pebble beaches – **Émblisi** 1km back out of town and **Fókis** just to the south – and a nature trail on the northern headland. Daily **ferries** connect Fiskárdho to Itháki and Lefkádha in season.

Itháki

Rugged **Itháki**, Odysseus's legendary homeland, has yielded no substantial archeological discoveries, but it fits Homer's description to perfection: "There are no tracks, nor grasslands . . . it is a rocky severe island, unsuited for horses, but not so wretched, despite its small size. It is good for goats." In Constantine Cavafy's splendid poem *Ithaca*, the island is symbolized as a journey to life:

When you set out on the voyage to Ithaca
Pray that your journey may be long
Full of adventures, full of knowledge.

Despite the romance of its name, and its proximity to Kefalloniá, very little tourist development has arrived to spoil the place. This is doubtless accounted for in part by a dearth of beaches, though the island is good walking country, with a handful of small fishing ports and inland villages. In the north, apart from the ubiquitous drone of scooters, the most common sounds are sheep bells jangling and cocks (a symbol of Odysseus) crowing.

Itháki's beaches are admittedly minor, mainly pebbly with sandy seabeds, but relatively clean and safe; the real attractions are the interior and sites from the **Odyssey**. Some package travellers will find themselves flying into Kefalloniá and being bused to Fiskárdho (sit on the left for the bus ride of your life), for a short ferry crossing to **Fríkes** or the premier resort **Kióni**. Most visitors, however, will arrive at **Vathý**, the capital.

Vathý

Ferries from Pátra, Astakós and a minority of those from Kefalloniá land at the main port and capital of **VATHÝ**, a bay within a bay so deep that few realize the mountains out "at sea" are actually the north of the island. This snug town is compact, relatively traffic-free and boasts the most idyllic seafront setting of all the Ionian capitals. Like its southerly neighbours, it was heavily damaged by the 1953 earthquake, but some fine examples of pre-quake architecture remain here and in the northern port of **Kióni**. Vathý has a small **archeological museum** on Kalliníkou (Tues–Sun 8.30am–3pm; €1.50), a short block back from the quay. There are banks, a post office, police and a medical centre in town.

Vathý now has four **hotels**, the oldest of which is the air-conditioned *Mentor* (☎26740 32433, ✉mentor@kef.forthnet.gr; ❹) in the southeast corner of the harbour. Further on round the bay are the posh *Omirikon* (☎26740 33598, ℻26740 33596; ❺), and, just beyond it, the much better-value *Captain Yiannis* (☎26740 33419, ℻26740 32849; ❹), complete with tennis court and pool. The small *Odyssey* (☎26740 32268, ℻26740 32668; ❸) is perched on the hillside a short way up the road to Skínos beach. Room owners meet ferries until the end of the season, but you can also call ahead to Vassiliki Vlassopoulou (☎26740 32119; ❸), whose fairly basic rooms overlook pleasant gardens by the church above the quay. The town's two main quayside travel agents, Polyctor Tours (☎26740 33120, ✉polyctor@ithakiholidays.gr) and Delas Tours (☎26740 32104, ✉delas@otenet.gr) both offer a range of accommodation (from ❸) throughout the island.

Even though it's tiny, Vathý has a wealth of **tavernas** and **bars**. Many locals head off south around the bay towards *Paliocaravo* (aka *Gregory's*), popular for its lamb and fish, and the more traditional *Tziribis* and *O Vrachos*. In town, the excellent *O Nikos*, just off the square, fills early, while *To Kohili* is the best of the half-dozen harbourside tavernas. The *Sirenes Ithaki Yacht Club* is upmarket with a nautical theme, but as usual the town's ancient *kafenío* one street back from the front is the spot for a quiet and inexpensive tipple with the locals.

There are two reasonable pebble **beaches** within fifteen minutes' walk of Vathý: **Dhéxa**, over the hill above the ferry quay, and tiny **Loútsa**, opposite it around the bay. Better beaches at **Sarakíniko** and **Skínos** are an hour's trek along recently improved roads leaving the opposite side of the bay. In season, daily *kaïkia* ply between the quay and remote coves.

Odysseus sights

Three of the main **Odysseus** sights are just within walking distance of Vathý: the Arethoússa Spring, the Cave of the Nymphs and ancient Alalkomenae, although the last is best approached by **bus** or **taxi** (no more than €12 round-trip).

The Arethoússa Spring

The walk to the **Arethoússa Spring** – allegedly the place where Eumaeus, Odysseus's faithful swineherd, brought his pigs to drink – is a three-hour round trip along a track signposted next to the seafront telecoms office. The unspoilt landscape and sea views are magnificent, but the walk crosses slippery inclines and might best be avoided if you're nervous of heights. The route is shadeless, so take a hat and plenty of water.

Near the top of the lane leading to the spring path, a signpost points up to what is said to have been the **Cave of Eumaeus**. The route to the spring continues for a few hundred metres, and then branches off onto a narrow footpath through gorse-covered steep cliffs. Parts of the final downhill track involve scrambling across rock fields (follow the splashes of green paint), and care should be taken around the small but vertiginous ravine that houses the **spring**. The spring is sited at the head of a small ravine below a crag known as **Kórax** ("the raven"), which matches Homer's description of the meeting between Odysseus and Eumaeus. In summer it's just a dribble of water.

The spring is a dead end – the only way out is back the way you came. If weather and time allow, you might swim in a small cove a short scramble down from the spring. If you're uneasy about the gradients involved, it's still worth continuing along the track that runs above it, which loops round and heads back into the village of **Perahóri** above Vathý, which has views as far as Lefkádha to the north. On the way, you'll pass **Paleóhora**, the ruined medieval capital abandoned centuries ago, but with vestiges of houses fortified against pirate attacks and some churches still with Byzantine frescoes.

The Cave of the Nymphs

The **Cave of the Nymphs** (Marmarospíli) is about 2.5km up a rough but navigable road signposted on the brow of the hill above Dhéxa beach. The cave is atmospheric, but it's underwhelming compared to the caverns of neighbouring Kefalloniá, and these days is illuminated by coloured lights. The claim that this is the *Odyssey*'s Cave of the Nymphs, where the returning Odysseus concealed the gifts given to him by King Alkinous, is enhanced by the proximity of Dhéxa beach, although there is some evidence that the "true" cave was just above the beach, and was unwittingly demolished during quarrying many years ago.

Alalkomenae and Pisaetós

Alalkomenae, Heinrich Schliemann's much-vaunted "Castle of Odysseus", is signposted on the Vathý–Pisaetós road, on the saddle between Dhéxa and Pisaetós, with views over both sides of the island. The actual site, however, some 300m uphill, is little more than foundations spread about in the gorse. Schliemann's excavations unearthed a Mycenaean burial chamber and domestic items such as vases, figurines and utensils (displayed in the archeological museum), but the ruins actually date from three centuries after Homer. In fact, the most likely contender for the site of Odysseus's castle is above the village of Stavrós (see below).

The road (though not buses) continues to the harbour of **Pisaetós**, about 2km below, with a large pebble beach that's good for swimming and popular with local rod-and-line fishermen. There is just one *kantína* here, serving those awaiting the regular ferries from Sámi on Kefalloniá.

Northern Itháki

The main road out of Vathý continues across the isthmus and takes a spectacular route to the northern half of Itháki, serving the villages of **Léfki**, **Stavrós**, **Fríkes** and **Kióni**. There are only two daily **buses**, though the north of Itháki is excellent scooter country; the close proximity of the settlements, small coves and Homeric interest also make it good rambling terrain. Once a day a *kaïki* also visits the last two of those communities – a cheap and scenic ride used by locals and tourists alike to meet the mainline ferries in Vathý. As with the rest of Itháki there is only a limited amount of accommodation.

Stavrós and around

STAVRÓS, the second-largest town on the island, discounting Perahóri, is a steep two kilometres above the nearest beach (Pólis Bay). It's a pleasant enough town nonetheless, with *kafenía* edging a small square dominated by a rather fierce statue of Odysseus. There is even a tiny **museum** (Tues–Sun 9.30am–2.30pm; free) off the road to Platrithriés, displaying local archeological finds. Stavrós's Homeric site is on the side of **Pelikáta Hill**, where remains of roads, walls and other structures have been suggested as the possible site of Odysseus's castle. Stavrós is useful as a base if both Fríkes and Kióni are full up, and is an obvious stopping-off point for exploring the northern hamlets and the road up to the medieval village of Anoyí (see below). Both Polyctor and Delas handle **accommodation** in Stavrós; the traditional *Petra* taverna (T 26740 31596; ❷) offers rooms, or there's the *Porto Thiaki pension* (T 26740 31245, F 26740 31638; ❸) above the pizzeria. The oldest and best taverna is *Fatouros*, and the *Margarita zaharoplastío* is a good place for a drink or to sample the local sweet *rovaní* (syrupy rice cakes).

A scenic mountain road leads 5km southeast from Stavrós to **ANOYÍ**, which translates roughly as "upper ground". Once the second-most important settlement on the island, it is almost deserted today. The centre of the village is dominated by a free-standing Venetian campanile, built to serve the (usually locked) church of the **Panayía**, which comes alive for the annual *paniyíri* on August 14, the eve of the Virgin's Assumption; at other times enquire at the *kafenío* about access to the church, the Byzantine frescoes of which have been heavily restored following centuries of earthquake damage. On the outskirts of the village are the foundations of a ruined **medieval prison**, and in the surrounding countryside are some extremely strange rock formations, the biggest being the eight-metre-high Iraklis (Hercules) rock, just east of the village. The **monastery of Katharón**, 3km further south along the road, has stunning views down over Vathý and the south of the island, and houses an icon of the *Panayía* discovered by peasants clearing scrubland in the area. Byron is said to have stayed here in 1823, during his final voyage to Mesolóngi. The monastery celebrates its festival on September 8 with services, processions and music.

Two roads push north of Stavrós: one, to the right, heads 2km down to Fríkes, while the main road, to the left, loops below the hill village of **Exoyí**, and on to **Platrithiés**. Just off the start of the road up to Exoyí a signpost points about 1km along a rough track to the supposed **School of Homer**, where excavations still in progress have revealed extensive foundations, a well and ancient steps. The site is unfenced and well worth a detour for its views of **Afáles Bay** as much as the remains. On the outskirts of Platrithiés a track leads down to Afáles, the largest bay on the entire island, with an unspoiled and little-visited pebble-and-sand beach. The landscape around here, thickly forested in parts and dotted with vineyards, provides excellent walking.

Fríkes

At first sight, tiny **FRÍKES** doesn't appear to have much going for it. Wedged in a valley between two steep hills, it was only settled in the sixteenth century, and emigration in the nineteenth century almost emptied the place – as few as two hundred people live here today – but the protected harbour is a natural year-round port. Consequently, Fríkes stays open for tourism far later in the season than neighbouring Kióni, and has a better range of tavernas. There are no beaches in the village, but plenty of good, if small, pebble strands a short walk away towards Kióni. When the ferries and their cargoes have departed, Fríkes falls quiet and this is its real charm: a downbeat but cool place to lie low.

Fríkes's one **hotel** is the upmarket *Nostos* (℡ 26740 31644, ⓦ www .hotelnostos-ithaki.gr; ➍) or you can try the equally comfy *Aristotelis Apartments* (℡ 26740 31079, Ⓕ 26740 31179; ➌). Kiki Travel (℡ & Ⓕ 26740 31726; from ➋) has **rooms** and other accommodation, as do the adjacent souvenir shop (℡ 26740 31735; ➋) and *Ulysses* taverna (℡ 26740 31733; ➌). Phoning ahead is advisable and in peak season chances are slim. Fríkes has a quartet of good seafront **tavernas**, all serving a decent mixture of Greek and international cuisine: the *Symposium*, the *Rementzo*, the *Penelope* and aforementioned *Ulysses*. Tucked in the corner of the harbour, *Café Bemenis* often springs into life late at night as the north's main meeting place for youngsters.

Kióni

KIÓNI sits at a dead end 5km southeast of Fríkes. On the same geological base as the northern tip of Kefalloniá, it avoided the very worst of the 1953 earthquakes, and so retains some fine examples of pre-twentieth-century architecture. It's an extremely pretty village, wrapped around a tiny harbour, and tourism here is dominated by British blue-chip travel companies and visiting yachts.

The bay has a small **beach**, 1km along its south side, a sand-and-pebble strand below a summer-only snack-bar. Better pebble beaches can be found within walking distance towards Fríkes. While the best **accommodation** has been snaffled by the Brits, some local businesses have rooms and apartments to let, among them *Captain's Apartments* (℡ 26740 31481, Ⓕ 26740 31090; ➌), K. Raftopoulos (℡ 26740 31654; ➌) and *Kioni Vacations* (℡ 26740 31668; ➌). A quieter option, a short walk uphill on the main road in the hamlet of Ráhi, are the rooms and studios run by Captain Theofilos Karatzis and his family (℡ 26740 31679; ➋), which have panoramic views.

Kióni's **restaurants** are dotted around the picturesque harbour, but compare unfavourably with those in Fríkes; *Mythos* has a wide selection and is the best of the bunch, the *Avra* fish taverna and *Kioni* pizzeria are adequate, while the upmarket *Calypso* taverna has interesting dishes but is overpriced. Village facilities stretch to two well-stocked shops, a post office and a couple of bars and cafés.

Zákynthos (Zante)

Zákynthos, southernmost of the six core Ionian islands, currently teeters between underdevelopment and indiscriminate commercialization. Much of the island is still green and unspoilt, but the development in some resorts is threatening to spill over into the quieter parts.

The island has three distinct zones: the barren, mountainous northwest; the fertile central plain; and the eastern and southern coasts which house the resorts. The big resort – rivalling the biggest on Corfu – is **Laganás**, on Laganás Bay in the south, a 24-hour party venue that doesn't give up from Easter until the last flight home in October. There are smaller, quieter resorts north and south of the capital, and the southerly Vassilikós peninsula has the best countryside and beaches, including exquisite **Yérakas**.

Although half-built apartment blocks are spreading through the central plain, this is where the quieter island begins: farms and vineyards, ancient villages and the ruins of Venetian buildings levelled in the 1948 and 1953 earthquakes. The island still produces fine wines, such as the white Popolaro, as well as sugar-shock-inducing *mandoláto* nougat, whose honey-sweetened form is best. Zákynthos is also the birthplace of *kantádhes*, which can be heard in tavernas in Zákynthos Town and elsewhere. It also harbours one of the key breeding sites of the endangered **loggerhead sea turtle** at Laganás Bay. The loggerhead (see box on p.541) is the subject of a continuing dispute between tourism businesses and environmentalists, which has caused an international political scandal and even provoked a bomb attack against the environmentalists.

Zákynthos Town

The town, like the island, is known as both **ZÁKYNTHOS** and Zante. This former "Venice of the East" (*Zante, Fior di Levante*, "Flower of the Levant", in an Italian jingle), rebuilt on the old plan, has bravely tried to re-create some of its style, though reinforced concrete can only do so much.

The town stretches beyond the length of the wide and busy harbour, its main section bookended by the grand **Platía Solomoú** at the north, and the church of **Áyios Dhionýsios**, patron saint of the island, at the south. The church is well worth a visit for the dazzling giltwork and fine modern murals inside, and a new **museum**, which has some fine paintings and icons (daily 8.30am–11pm; €0.90). The vestments of St Dhionysios are kept in the restored church of Áyios Nikólaos tou Mólou on Platía Solomoú. The **square** is named after the island's most famous son, the poet Dhionysios Solomos, the father of modernism in Greek literature, who was responsible for establishing demotic Greek (as opposed to the elitist *katharévousa* form) as a literary idiom. He is also the author of the lyrics to the national anthem, an excerpt from which adorns the statue of Liberty in the square. There's an impressive **museum** (daily 9am–2pm; €2.30) devoted to the life and work of **Solomos** and other Zakynthian luminaries in nearby Platía Ayíou Márkou. It shares its collection with the museum on Corfu (see p.498), where Solomos spent most of his life. Another local man of letters, who had a museum dedicated to him by the town council in 1998, is novelist and playwright **Grigorios Xenopoulos**. His eponymous **museum** (Mon–Fri 9am–2pm; free), which occupies the small house he inhabited in Gaïta street, not far from Áyios Dhionýsios church, displays a modest collection of manuscripts, books and photographs, as well as the house's original furniture.

ZÁKYNTHOS

Cape Skinári

Shipwreck Bay

Blue Caves

Mount Astéri 583m

Anafonítria

Volímes

Ávios Nikólaos

Anafonítria

Makrýs Yialós

Skinári

Xygiá

Stenítis Bay

Mariés

Alykón Bay

Kambí

Éxo Hóra

Alykés

Katastári

Mount Vrahiónas 756m

Alikanás

Dhrossiá

Yerakári

Ayía Marína

Tragáki

Pahiá Ámmos

Ávios Léon

Tsiliví

Limniónas

Kiliómeno

Mount Athéras

Plános

Maherádho

Vanáto

Bóhali

ZÁKYNTHOS

Megálo Vounó

Límni Kerioú

Laganás

Argási

Kerí

Kalamáki

Marathiá Caves

Mount Kakavakia 413m

Marathoníssi

Mount Skopós 492m

Dháfni

Pórto Zóro

Áno Vassilikós

Peloúzo

Banana

Ávios Nikólaos

Yérakas

Pórto Róma

0   5 km

Platía Solomoú is home to the town's **library**, which has a small collection of pre- and post-quake photography, and the massive **Byzantine Museum** (Tues–Sun 8am–2.30pm; €3), sometimes referred to as the Zákynthos Museum, most notable for its collection of artworks from the Ionian School, the region's post-Renaissance art movement, spearheaded by Zakynthian painter Panayiotis Doxaras. The movement was given impetus by Cretan refugees, unable to practise under Turkish rule. It also houses some secular painting and a fine model of the town before the earthquake.

Zákynthos's other main attraction is its massive **kástro**, brooding over the hamlet of Bóhali on its bluff above the town. The ruined Venetian fort (daily 8am–7.30pm in summer, 8am–2pm in winter; €1.50) has vestiges of dungeons, armouries and fortifications, plus stunning views in all directions. Its shady carpet of fallen pine needles makes it a great spot to relax or picnic. Below the *kástro* walls, **Bóhali** has a good though expensive taverna with panoramic views. The ugly new **amphitheatre** on the road up from town sometimes hosts concerts. Further towards the *kástro* the **Maritime Museum** (daily 9am–2pm & 6–9pm; €2.50) contains plenty of naval paraphernalia and presents an interesting chronological history of Hellenic seafaring.

Practicalities

Zákynthos is a working town with limited concessions to tourism, although there are hotels and restaurants aplenty, and it's the only place to stay if you want to see the island by public transport. The **bus** station is one block back from the seafront, about halfway along it. On the front nearby, the **tourist police** have a fairly welcoming office (daily 7.30am–9.30pm; ☎26950 27367) in the main police station, which can supply basic information and help people find accommodation. The Room Owners Association (☎26950 49498) can also be contacted for accommodation around town and all over the island. Of the central **hotels**, the *Egli*, on Loútzi (☎26950 28317; ②) is the bargain, tucked in beside the gargantuan and more expensive *Strada Marina* (☎26950 42761, ✉stradamarina@aias.gr; ⑤). There are quieter hotels in the Repára district beyond Platía Solomoú: try either the *Plaza*, Kolokotróni 2 (☎26950 48909, 🖷26950 45059; ④), or the classy *Palatino*, Kolokotróni 10 (☎26950 27780, 🅦www.palatinohotel.gr; ⑤), both near the municipal lido. Cheaper options at the back of town include the functional *Apollo*, Tertséti 30 (☎26950 42838; ③), opposite the post office, and the cosier *Haravyi pension*, Xanthopoúlou 4 (☎26950 23629; ②) further south. Most of the **restaurants** and bars on the seafront and Platía Ayíou Márkou are bedevilled by traffic, although the seafront *Psaropoula* does fine meat and fish, and the pricey but elegant *Komis*, across the quay from Áyios Dhionýsios, serves unusual seafood dishes and is far enough away from the bustle. First stop though, should be the friendly *Arekia* beyond the lido, which offers succulent taverna staples and nightly *kantádhes*. The neighbouring *Alívizos* also specializes in island cuisine and music, and the *Green Boat*, further along, serves up quality fare at a snip. When the bored teens get off their bikes, they go **clubbing** to bars like *Base* on Ayíou Márkou, which plays anything from Miles Davis to Philip Glass, or the *Jazz Café*, on Tertséti which, despite plundering the London jazz club's logo, is actually a techno bar with DJ and token cover charge.

The south and west

The road heading southeast from Zákynthos passes through **ARGÁSI**, the busiest resort on this coast, but with a beach barely a few feet wide in parts. Although independent travellers would be better off basing themselves at one of the places further down, it could be used as a jumping-off point for the Vassilikós peninsula; there are rooms at the *Pension Vaso* (℡26950 44599; ❸) and *Soula* (℡26950 44864; ❸) just off the main road entering the village, and the seafront boasts some smart hotels, among them the *Locanda* (℡26950 45386, ℻26950 23769; ❹) and the joint *Chryssi Akti/Paradise Beach* (℡26950 28679, ℻26950 28699; ❹). Beyond a few indigenous tavernas – try *Three Brothers* or *The Big Plate* restaurant – culture is mainly low-brow with set-piece "Greek nights", one notable exception being the *Venetsiana*, which accompanies traditional food with nightly *kantádhes*. Argási is also home to some of the island's biggest and most popular discos on the town side, such as *Vivlos* and *Barrage*, and a host of cheap and cheerful bars in the village. Up the hill just north of town the Fun Castle (€4.50–7.50, accompanying adults free) has a range of games for kids and a pool, while the small zoo next door (adults €5, children €3) is run by a knowledgable Greek-Australian naturalist, who encourages a hands-on approach to the resident creatures.

The Vassilikós peninsula

The peninsula that stretches southeast of Argási is one of the most attractive parts of the island, with a happy blend of development and natural beauty. Various maps vaguely identify different inland spots as **Vassilikós** villages, but the real interest lies in the series of small beach resorts, mainly situated on the east coast. The first two are recently developed **Kamínia**, with the comfortable *Levantino* rooms (℡26950 35366, ⓦwww.levantino.gr; ❹), and the more established **Pórto Zóro**, a better strand with the good-value eponymous hotel (℡26950 35304, ℻26950 35087; ❸) and restaurant. The only real facilities away from the coast are to be found at the sprawling village of **Áno Vassilikós**, which serves the nearby beaches of **Iónio** and **Banana**. Among accommodation possibilities are the *Vassilikos Apartments* (℡26950 35280; ❸), on the main road, and *Angelika* (℡26950 35201; ❷), by the church just off it. Among the **tavernas**, on the main road, *O Adherfos tou Kosta* is well worth a try, as is the *Logos Rock Club*. Isolated **Áyios Nikólaos** has a good beach and lures day-trippers from Argási, Kalamáki and Laganás with a **free bus** service in season. Its expanding *Vasilikos Beach* (℡26950 35325, ⓔstnicks@otenet.gr; ❹) complex is the focal point of a fast-emerging hamlet with a few restaurants and rooms – the neat white *Christina's* (℡26950 39474; ❷) is one of the best deals on the island.

At the very tip of the peninsula is its star: **Yérakas**, a sublime crescent of golden sand. It's also a key loggerhead turtle breeding ground, and is therefore off-limits between dusk and dawn; the excellent open-air **Turtle Information Centre** provides interesting background on these and other sea creatures. Otherwise, there's little here beyond two tavernas back from the beach – try *To Triodi* – and some pleasant, if remote, cabin accommodation at *Liuba Apartments* (☎26950 35372; ❸). The beach does draw crowds, but the 6am bus out of Zákynthos Town should secure you a few hours of Yérakas to yourself. Compared with Yérakas, **Pórto Róma**, back on the east coast, is a disappointment, a small sand-and-pebble bay with a taverna and bar, some rooms on the approach road and occasional hardy campers, although there is a more genuinely Greek flavour to it. Beaches on the west coast, such as **Dháfni**, require your own transport and have few facilities, but are worth a visit, especially in the quieter months.

Laganás and Kalamáki

The majority of the 400,000 people or so who visit Zákynthos each year find themselves in **LAGANÁS**. The nine-kilometre beach in the bay is good, if trampled, and there are entertainments from watersports to ballooning, and even an occasional funfair. Beachfront bars and restaurants stretch for well over a kilometre, the bars and restaurants on the main drag another kilometre inland. Some stay open around the clock; others just play music at deafening volume until dawn. The competing video and music bars can make Laganás at night resemble the set of *Bladerunner*, but that's how its predominantly English visitors like it. If this is your bag, there's no place better; if it isn't, flee. **Accommodation** is mostly block-booked by package companies. There's a basic campsite on the southern edge of town, where there are also quietish private rooms, or you can contact the Union of Room Owners (daily 8.30am–2pm & 5–8pm; ☎26950 51590). As for hotels, try the old-fashioned *Byzantio* (☎26950 51136; ❷), near the crossroads, *Pension Tasoula* (☎26950 51560; ❸), between the beach and the campsite, or the larger *Ionis* (☎26950 51141, ✉ionishtl@otenet.gr; ❺), on the main drag towards the beach. *Nefeli* and *Zougras* are among the more authentic **tavernas**, the former hosting nightly *kantádhes*, and respectable Chinese and Indian food can be had at *Bee Garden* or *Taj Mahal* respectively. Favourite **bars** include *Kamikazi*, *Must*, *Potters Bar* and *Zeros* nightclub.

Neighbouring **KALAMÁKI** has a better beach than Laganás, and is altogether quieter, although both resorts suffer from airport noise. There are several sizeable, mostly package-oriented hotels, but the upmarket *Crystal Beach* (☎26950 42788, ℻26950 42917; ❻) keeps some rooms aside and the island-wide Spring Tours agency (☎26950 43795, ⊛www.springtours.gr; ❸) can also arrange accommodation. The two *Stanis* tavernas have extensive menus of Greek and international dishes, although the beachside version is geared more to lunches and its sibling more to evening meals. Alternatives include *Afrodite* and *Merlis* or the *Guru* curry house. **Nightlife** centres around bars like *Harvest* and *Down Under* on the Laganás road, and the *Cave Bar* or *Byzantio* discos on the hillside above the village, which play foreign and Greek dance music respectively.

Kerí

The village of **KERÍ** is hidden in a fold above the cliffs at the island's southernmost tip. The village retains a number of pre-quake, Venetian buildings, including the church of the **Panayía Kerioú**; the Virgin is said to have saved the island from marauding pirates by hiding it in a sea mist. Kerí is also famous for a geological quirk, a series of small tar pools mentioned by both Pliny and Herodotus, but these mysteriously dried up in the 1970s. A rough path leaving the southern end of the village leads 1km on to the lighthouse,

Loggerhead turtles

The Ionian islands harbour the Mediterranean's main concentration of **loggerhead sea turtles**. These creatures, which lay their eggs at night on sandy coves, are under direct threat from the tourist industry in Greece. Each year, many turtles are injured by motorboats, their nests are destroyed by bikes ridden on the beaches, and the newly hatched young die entangled in deckchairs and umbrellas left out at night on the sand. The turtles are easily frightened by noise and lights, too, which makes them uneasy cohabitants with rough campers and late-night discos.

The Greek government has passed laws designed to protect the loggerheads, including restrictions on camping at some beaches, but local economic interests tend to prefer a beach full of bodies to a sea full of turtles.

On Laganás, nesting grounds are concentrated around the fourteen-kilometre bay, but Greek marine zoologists striving to protect and study the turtles are in angry dispute with those involved in the tourist industry. Other important locations include the turtles' nesting ground just west of Skála on Kefaloniá, although numbers have dwindled to half their former strength in recent years, and now only about 800 remain. Ultimately, the turtles' main hope of survival may rest in their being appreciated as a unique tourist attraction in their own right.

While capitalists and environmentalists are still at, well, loggerheads, the **World Wildlife Fund** has issued guidelines for visitors:

1. Don't use the beaches of Laganás and Yérakas between sunset and sunrise.

2. Don't stick umbrellas in the sand in the marked nesting zones.

3. Take your rubbish away with you – it can obstruct the turtles.

4. Don't use lights near the beach at night – they can disturb the turtles, sometimes with fatal consequences.

5. Don't take any vehicle onto the protected beaches.

6. Don't dig up turtle nests – it's illegal.

7. Don't pick up the hatchlings or carry them to the water, as it's vital to their development that they reach the sea on their own.

8. Don't use speedboats in Laganás Bay – a 9kph speed limit is in force for vessels in the bay.

with spectacular views of the sea, rock arches and stacks and a taverna. The beach next to **Límni Kerioú** at the southwestern end of Laganás Bay has developed into a laid-back and picturesque resort and is home to the Turtle Beach Diving Centre (T & F 26950 48768). **Rooms** can be found at the friendly *Pension Limni* (T 26950 48716; ❷) or through the local Room-Owners Association (T & F 26950 45105). For **food** there is the *Pirates of Kastello* overlooking the bay from the far end and the *Keri* restaurant, which has good daily specials.

Maherádho, Kiliómeno and Kambí

The bus system does not reach the wild western side of the island, but a rental car or sturdy motorbike will get you there. **MAHERÁDHO** boasts impressive pre-earthquake architecture set in beautiful arable uplands, surrounded by olive and fruit groves. The church of **Ayía Mávra** has an impressive free-standing campanile, and inside a splendid carved iconostasis and icons by Zakynthian painter Nikolaos Latsis. The town's major festival – one of the biggest on the island – is the saint's day, which falls on the first Sunday in June. The other notable church in town, that of the Panayía, commands breathtaking views over the central plain.

KILIÓMENO is the best place to see surviving pre-earthquake domestic architecture, in the form of the island's traditional two-storey houses. The town was originally named after its church, **Áyios Nikólaos**, whose impressive campanile, begun over a hundred years ago, still lacks a capped roof. The *Alitzerini* taverna (usually supper only) still occupies a cave-like house that dates from 1630 and dishes up superb traditional food. The road from Kiliómeno passes through the nondescript village of Áyios Léon, from where two turnings lead through fertile land and down a newly-paved loop road to the impressive rocky coast at **Limniónas**, where there is a tiny bay and a taverna.

Further along the main road another turning leads to the tiny clifftop hamlet of **KAMBÍ**, popular with day-trippers, who come to catch the sunset over the sea. And indeed, there are extraordinary views to be had of the 300-metre-high cliffs and western horizon from Kambí's three clifftop **tavernas**. The best of the three is named after the imposing concrete **cross** above the village, constructed in memory of islanders killed here during the 1940s, either by royalist soldiers or Nazis. The tiny village of **Mariés**, 5km to the north and set in a wooded green valley, has the only other coastal access on this side of Zákynthos, a seven-kilometre track leading down to the rocky inlet of **Stenítis Bay**, where there's a taverna and yacht dock, and another road to the uninspiring **Vrómi Bay**, from where speedboats run trips to Shipwreck Bay (see opposite).

The north

North and inland from Zákynthos Town, the roads thread their way through luxuriantly fertile farmland, punctuated with tumulus-like hills. **Tsiliví**, 5km north of the capital, is the first beach resort here, which has now effectively merged with the hamlet of **PLÁNOS** and matches Argási for development. Unfortunately, this part of the coastline suffers from occasional oil pollution, with nothing but the winter storms to clear it. There's a good, basic **campsite**, *Zante Camping* (☎26950 61710), beyond Plános and, for a prime package-tour location, a surprising variety of accommodation – try the beachside *Anetis Hotel* (☎26950 44590, ℗26950 28758; ❸), which has air conditioning and TV in all rooms; *Gregory's* rooms (☎26950 61853; ❷); or contact Tsilivi Travel (☎26950 44194, ✉akis-125@otenet.gr; from ❷), on the inland road in from town. *The Olive Tree* taverna is the best of a touristy bunch, while the *Mandarin* Chinese is fairly authentic. Pubs such as *The Local* and *Red Lion* tend to be Brit-oriented.

The beaches further along this stretch of coast become progressively quieter and pleasanter, and they all have at least a smattering of accommodation and restaurants to choose from. Good choices include **Pahiá Ámmos**, with the *Pension Petra* (☎26950 61175; ❸) and *Porto Roulis* fish taverna. Also recommended is **Dhrossiá**, where you can find the *Avouris* (☎26950 61716; ❷) and *Drosia* apartments (☎26950 62256; ❸) and eat at another popular fish taverna, *Andreas*.

Alykés and its bay

Ormós Alykón, 12km north of Tsiliví, is a large sandy bay with lively surf and two of the area's largest resorts. The first, **ALIKANÁS**, is a small but expanding village, much of its accommodation being overseas villa rentals; the second, **ALYKÉS**, named after the spooky salt pans behind the village, has the best beach north of the capital. There are **rooms** near the beach, most easily found

through the local branch of Spring Tours (☎26950 83035, ⓦwww
.springtours.gr; from ❷), and a number of **hotels** set back from it, but with sea
views – try the *Ionian Star* (☎26950 83416, ⓦwww.ionian-star.gr; ❹) or the
Montreal (☎26950 83241, ⓦwww.montreal.gr; ❺), although the best deal is off
the crossroads at the *Picadilly* (☎26950 83606; ❷). There are many eating joints,
among the best the *Vineleaf*, which has unusual items such as jalapeño peppers
stuffed with cream, and more standard *Fantasia* and *Golden Dolphin* tavernas.
Alykés is the last true resort on this coast, and the one where the bus service
largely gives out. **Xygiá** beach, 4km north, has sulphur springs flowing into
the sea – follow the smell – which provide the odd sensation of swimming in
a mix of cool and warm water. The next small beach of **Makrýs Yialós**, which
has a good taverna and makeshift campsite, also makes for an extremely pleasant break on a tour of the north.

Áyios Nikólaos, 6km on, is a small working port serving daily ferries to and
from Pessádha on Kefalloniá. Few visitors **stay** here, which perhaps explains
why it hosts one of the most exclusive establishments in the Ionian, the classy
stone *Nobelos* apartments (☎ & ⓕ26950 31131; ❽), as well as the more modest
Panorama (☎26950 31013, ⓔpanorama@can.gr; ❸). Pre-ferry meals can be
had at *La Storia* fish restaurant or *Xagnando* taverna. From here another good
trip is a ride by **kaïki** (around €6) to the extreme northern tip of the island,
where the **Blue Caves** are some of the more realistically named of the many
contenders in Greece. They're terrific for snorkelling, and when you go for a
dip here your skin will appear bright blue. The road snakes onwards through a
landscape of gorse bushes and dry-stone walls until it ends at the lighthouse of
Cape Skinári. With only a taverna and a cafeteria, and a view of the mountainous expanse of Kefalloniá, it's a good spot for unofficial camping, or you
could stay in the unique setting of the converted windmill rented out by *To
Faros* taverna (☎26950 31132; ❺).

Katastári, Ayía Marína and Volímes

The northern towns and villages are best explored with a car or sturdy motorbike, although there are guided coach tours from the resorts and
limited bus services. Two kilometres inland from Alykés, **KATASTÁRI** is the
largest settlement after the capital. Precisely because it's not geared towards
tourism, it's the best place to see Zakynthian life as it's lived away from the
usual racket. Its most impressive edifice is the huge rectangular church of
Iperáyia Theotókos, with a twin belfry and small new amphitheatre for festival
performances. *To Kendro psistariá* does tasty grills at rock-bottom prices.

AYÍA MARÍNA, a few kilometres southwest of Katastári, has a church with
an impressive Baroque altar screen, and a belfry that's being rebuilt from the
remnants left after the 1953 earthquake. As in most Zákynthos churches, the
bell tower stands detached, in Venetian fashion. Just above Ayía Marína is the
Parthenonas taverna, rightly boasting one of the best views on the island. From
here you can see the whole of the central plain from beyond Alykés in the
north to Laganás Bay in the south.

VOLÍMES is the centre of the island's embroidery industry and numerous
shops sell artefacts produced here. With your own transport, you could make it
to the **Anafonítria monastery**, 3km south, thought to have been the cell of
the island's patron saint, Dhionysios, whose festivals are celebrated on August
24 and December 17. A paved road leads on to the cliffs overlooking
Shipwreck Bay (Naváyio), with hair-raising views down to the shipwreck (a
cargo ship which ran aground in the Sixties), and a taverna to recover your
composure in.

Kýthira and Andikýthira islands

Isolated at the foot of the Peloponnese lies the island of **Kýthira**, known as Cerigo under Venetian rule. Administratively it is part of Pireás in mainland Attica – like the Argo-Saronic islands. For the most part, similarities end there. The island architecture of whitewashed houses and flat-roofs looks more like that of the Cyclades, albeit with a strong **Venetian** influence. The landscape is different, too: wild scrub- and gorse-covered hills, or moorland sliced by deep valleys and ravines.

Depopulation has left the land underfarmed and the abandoned fields overgrown, for, since World War II, most of the islanders have left for Athens or Australia, giving Kýthira a reputation of being the classic emigrant island; it is known locally as "Australian Colony" or "Kangaroo Island", and Australia is referred to as "Big Kýthira". Many of the villages are deserted, their *platíes* empty and the schools and *kafenía* closed. Kýthira was never a rich island, but it did once have a military and economic significance – which it likewise lost with Greek independence and the opening of the Corinth Canal. These days, tourism has brought prosperity (and a few luxury hotels), but most summer visitors are Greeks and especially Greek Australians. For the few foreigners who reach Kýthira, it remains something of a refuge, with its undeveloped **beaches** a principal attraction. However, Theo Angelopoulos' film *Taxidhi sta Kythira* ("Journey to Kythira"), and, to a much greater extent, a 1998 popular Greek television serial filmed on the island, have attracted a huge amount of domestic attention and, consequently, holiday-makers from the mainland. Much of the accommodation is now fully booked by Christmas for the entire Greek school-summer-holiday period; outside of this period some accommodation does not open until June and closes early in September. The Association of Rental Room Owners (T & F 27360 31855) have a list of places to stay: in addition to the following, there is accommodation in the villages of Aroniádhika, Dhókana, Dhrymónas, Frátsia, Frilingiánika, Goudhiánika, Kálamos, Kalokerinés, Karvounádhes, Káto Livádhi, Kondoliánika, Mitáta, Mylopótamos, Strapódhi and Travasariánika.

Arrival and getting around

Arrival on the island has changed in recent years. In 1997 a huge all-weather **harbour** was opened at Dhiakófti, and now most large ferries dock here, although the majority of Neápoli ferries go into Ayía Pelayía. The airport is deep in the interior, 8km southeast of Potamós; recent expensive refurbishment did not include extension of the short runway, therefore many of the facilities languish unused due to lack of flights. Further expenditure is unlikely in the near future. The few Olympic Airways flights are met by taxis, as are most high-season boats. Sadly, there was no other **public transport** at the time of writing, with the island buses being only used for school runs, although locals are pressing for the implementation of, at the least, bus services to meet ferries. The only alternative to taxis that often overcharge is to hitch or, more advisedly, rent a **car** or **scooter**. The roads are now well surfaced all over the island and there are reliable petrol stations on the central road at Potamós, Kondoliánika and Livádhi.

Dhiakófti

DHIAKÓFTI, was once an unsung and relatively inaccessible backwater towards the bottom of the northeast coast, but has been catapulted into the

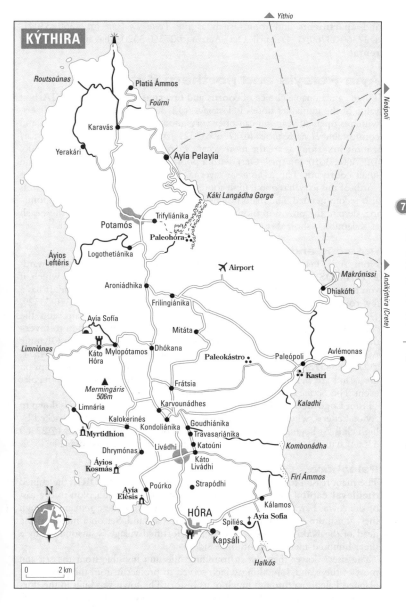

KÝTHIRA

Yíthio

Routsoúnas

Platiá Ámmos

Foúrni

Karavás

Ayía Pelayía

Neápoli

Yerakári

Káki Langádha Gorge

Trifyliánika

Potamós

Paleohóra

Áyios Leftéris

Logothetiánika

Makrónissi

Aroniádhika

Airport

Dhiakófti

Andikýthira (Crete)

Frilingiánika

Ayía Sofía

Mitáta

Limniónas

Káto Hóra

Mylopótamos

Dhókana

Paleokástro

Paleópoli

Avlémonas

Mermingáris 506m

Frátsia

Kastrí

Kaladhí

Limnária

Karvounádhes

Kalokerinés

Goudhiánika

Myrtidhíon

Kondoliánika

Travasariánika

Kombonádha

Dhrymónas

Livádhi

Katoúni

Firí Ámmos

 Áyios Kosmás

Káto Livádhi

Poúrko

Strapódhi

Ayía Elésis

Kálamos

HÓRA

Ayía Sofía

Spiliés

Kapsáli

Halkós

N

0   2 km

forefront of activity by the opening of the harbour, constructed by joining the islet of Makrónisi to the shore by a causeway. Perched on nearby Prasónisi island – and slightly disconcerting when arriving by sea – is a Greek container ship that went aground in 1999. Dhiakófti has a nice sandy beach, and exploitation of the tourist potential is currently fairly low key and seasonal; there are just a few **tavernas**, including the friendly *Notaras* by the causeway, and **apartments** and rooms such as the *Porto Diakofti* (℗27360 33041, ℗27360 33760; ④–⑥; April–Oct). Active (℗27360 33207) has an office for **car rental**.

Ayía Pelayía and northern Kýthira

There's a reasonable choice of **rooms** and **tavernas** in **AYÍA PELAYÍA**; best value of the upmarket hotels is *Venardos* (℗27360 34205, ℗27360 33850; ⑤), which is open all year and can offer very good deals off season. The clean and comfortable *Hotel Kytherea* (℗27360 33321, ℗27360 33825; ④; open all year) is more luxurious, as are the more recent *Filoxenia Apartments* (℗27360 33100, ℗27360 33610; ⑤; April–Oct), with a pool and an imaginative layout around small courtyards. The *Moustakias* taverna, amongst the seafront eating places north of the jetty, has good, fresh food, including fish, while the *Paleo ouzerí* is also recommended. The main beaches are small, rather scruffy and disappointing, despite the provision of blue-and-white-striped changing huts; the beach at Kalamítsa, a short dirt track about 2km away to the south, is better.

Potamós and around

From Ayía Pelayía, the main road winds up the mountainside towards **POTAMÓS**, Kýthira's largest village – a pleasant and unspoilt place which, if you have a rented vehicle, makes a good base for exploring the island. It has a few **rooms** with kitchens, such as those at the *Xenonas Porfyra* (℗27360 33329, ℗27360 33924; ❸) which have a pretty terrace and courtyard, and the *Alevizopoulos* (℗27360 33245; ④) with air conditioning. In addition to **tavernas**, a **bank**, a **post office** and **petrol stations**, facilities include an Olympic Airways office (℗27360 33688) and the Sirene Travel Club (℗27360 34371, ℗27360 34372), the island's agents for the Neápoli ferry. Most of the shops on the island are here, too, as is the **Sunday market**, Kýthira's liveliest regular event. The *Selana* café can provide **Internet** facilities.

From **Logothetiánika**, just south of Potamós, an unpaved road leads down to Áyios Leftéris, where you can **swim** from rocks on the west coast, backed by high cliffs. At Logothetiánika itself, there is a popular taverna, *Karydies* (℗27360 33664) with live music Thursday to Saturday, when booking is advisable.

Paleohóra

The main reason for visiting Potamós is to get to **PALEOHÓRA**, the ruined **medieval capital** (then called Áyios Dhimítrios) of Kýthira, 3km to the east of the town. Few people seem to know about or visit these remains, though they constitute one of the best Byzantine sites around. Set on a hilltop at the head of the **Káki Langádha Gorge**, the fortified village is surrounded by a sheer hundred-metre drop on three sides.

The site is lower than the surrounding hills and invisible from the sea and most of the island, something which served to protect it from the pirates that plagued Paleohóra through much of its history. The town was built in the thirteenth century by Byzantine nobles, and when Mystra (on the mainland) fell to the Turks, many of its noble families also sought refuge here. Despite its seemingly impregnable and perfectly concealed position, the site was discovered and sacked in 1537 by Barbarossa, commander of the Turkish fleet, and the island's seven thousand inhabitants were killed or sold into slavery.

The town was never rebuilt, and tradition maintains that it is a place of ill fortune, which perhaps explains the emptiness of the surrounding countryside, little of which is farmed today. The hills are dotted with Byzantine **chapels**, which suggests that, in its heyday, the area must have been the centre of medieval Kýthira; it is rumoured to have once had eight hundred inhabitants and 72 churches. Now the principal remains are of the surviving churches, some still with traces of frescoes (but kept firmly locked), and the castle. The site is unenclosed and has never been seriously investigated.

If you have your own transport, there's a road to Paleohóra, signposted off the main road from Potamós just north of Aroniádhika: the first 2.4km is asphalt, the remainder driveable gravel. By foot, it's more interesting to take the path from the tiny village of Trifyliánika, just outside Potamós – look out for a rusting sign to the right as you enter the village. The path is overgrown in parts and not easy to follow; the ruins only become visible when you join the road above the gorge.

Karavás

KARAVÁS, 6km north of Potamós, has architecture and a setting more typical of the Ionians, set above a deep, partly wooded valley with a stream. There is nowhere to stay, but there is a popular **restaurant**, *Amir Ali*, providing a large range of *mezédhes* (and sometimes live music) in a shady, streamside setting at the northern end of the village, off the road to Platiá Ámmos; food is also available at the German-run *Maina* ("mynah").

Platiá Ámmos, at the end of the valley, and en route to the lighthouse at the island's northern tip, is a sandy beach with a seasonal fish **taverna**. There is also an *ouzerí*, café, the *Modeas* restaurant, and several **rooms** establishments of which the best is the *Akrotiri* (☎27360 33216; ❸). The little pebble beach at **Foúrni**, 2km south by dirt road, is more attractive.

Kapsáli

KAPSÁLI, in addition to its harbour function, is the one place on Kýthira largely devoted to tourism, although much of it closes down from September to June. Most foreign visitors to Kýthira in summer stay here, and it's a popular port of call for yachts heading from the Aegean to the Ionian islands and Italy, particularly since it is sheltered from the strong north winds of summer. Set behind double pebble-and-sand bays, overlooked by Hóra castle, and backed by high grey cliffs on which the tiny white monastery of Áyios Ioánnis Éngremmos perches, it is certainly picturesque. The larger of its two bays has a line of **tavernas**; *Vlastos* is one of the earliest to open in the season, with fish, local dishes, and its speciality, cockerel (*kókoras*) in wine; *Venetsianiko*, halfway along the front, has good food at reasonable prices, but the best is *Hydragogio* at the Hóra end of the beach which serves up good veggie options. For nightlife the liveliest place is *Shaker*, playing the standard mix of Greek and foreign hits.

The best **accommodation** is in high demand and expensive. Top of the tree is the *Porto Delfino* (☎27360 31940; ❻; April–Oct); a few hundred metres above the bay are *Kalokerines Katikies* (☎ & ℻27360 31265; ❻; May–Oct) and *Hotel Raikos* (☎27360 31629, ℻27360 31801; ❻; May–Sept). The *Afroditi Apartments* (☎27360 31328, ℻27360 31903; ❹; open all year) have more reasonable rates, as do *Megaloudi* rooms (☎27360 31340; ❹). A very basic **campsite** (June–Sept) nestles in the pine trees behind the village.

There's a mobile **post office** in summer, and Panayiotis (☎27360 31600, ✉panayoti@otenet.gr) rents **cars**, **motorbikes** and **scooters**, as well as canoes and pedalboats; you can call off-season (☎29442 63757) and get wheels when most places are closed.

Hóra

HÓRA (or Kýthira Town), a steep 2km haul above Kapsáli, has an equally dramatic site, its Cycladic-style houses tiered on the ridge leading to the Venetian **castle**. Access to the fortress is up a modern pathway, but, to the right of this, the original narrow tunnel entrance is still usable. Within the walls, most of the buildings are in ruins, except the paired churches of Panayía Myrtidhiótissa and the smaller Panayía Orfáni (these were Catholic and Orthodox respectively, under the Venetian occupation), and the office of the archives of Kýthira opposite. There are spectacular views down to Kapsáli and out to sea to the striking chunk of inaccessible islet known as Avgó (Egg), legendary birthplace of Aphrodite. On the cliffs grow the yellow-flowered everlasting (*sempreviva*), used locally for making small dried flower arrangements. Below the castle are both the remains of older Byzantine walls and, in Mésa Vouryó, numerous well-signed but securely locked Byzantine churches. A small **museum** (Tues–Sun 8.30am–3pm; free) at the junction of the Hóra–Kapsáli road, houses modest remnants (labelled only in Greek) of the island's numerous occupiers, in particular Minoan finds from excavations at Paleópoli and an Archaic stone lion, as well as a telling selection of gravestones from the English cemetery. The Stavros bookshop, almost opposite, sells a book of walks (mainly in the southern half of the island; a walk book in German has more complete coverage).

Compared with Kapsáli, Hóra stays quiet and many places are closed out of season. Other facilities include a couple of **banks**, a **post office** and a branch of Panayiotis vehicle rental (☎27360 31004). A few **tavernas** open in summer, of which *Zorba* is by far the best, but the climb from Kapsáli discourages the crowds. A popular bar is *Mercato*, which stays open in winter and also has exhibitions of local art. **Accommodation** is slightly easier to find than in Kapsáli. Options include the *Castello Rooms & Studios* (☎27360 31069; ❸), and the *Hotel Margarita* (☎27360 31711, ☎27360 31325; ❺) in a beautiful 1840s house, with air conditioning in the rooms. The *Xenonas Keiti/Keti/Kaiti* (☎27360 31318; April–Oct; ❸) has nonsmoking rooms in a large 240-year-old characterful house that has seen General Metaxas and George Papandreou as visitors. At **Manitohóri**, 2km further inland, is the more basic *Pension Kythera* (☎27360 31563; June–Aug; ❸).

The southeast coast

The beach at Kapsáli is decent but not large and gets very crowded in July and August. For quieter, undeveloped beaches, it's better to head out to the east coast, towards Avlémonas.

Firí Ámmos, Kombonádha and Halkós beaches, and Spiliés cave

Firí Ámmos, the nearest good sand beach to Kapsáli, is popular but not overcrowded, even in summer. To get there, you can follow paved roads from Kapsáli or Livádhi as far as the *Filio* taverna (June–Sept; with good traditional food and local specialities) in the scattered settlement of Kálamos; the onward road becomes a four-kilometre dirt track to the beach. Firí Ámmos can also be reached by a second dirt track off the Livádhi–Kálamos road, while another, longer, dirt track, off the Káto Livádhi–Frátsia road leads to **Kombonádha**, the next beach north. There are summer canteens at both beaches. Much smaller, but prettier **Halkós** beach near the southeast corner of the island is signposted from the crossroads at the entrance to Kálamos. Between Kálamos and Kapsáli, a short surfaced road leads south to **Spiliés** village; immediately before the village a signed earth road leads down to a small gorge and a large stalagmite cave with an open-roofed church dedicated to Ayía Sofía (not to be confused with the sea cave near Mylopótamos).

Paleópoli and Avlémonas

PALEÓPOLI, a hamlet of a few scattered houses, is accessible by asphalt roads from Aroniádhika, Frátsia and Kondoliánika. The area is the site of the ancient city of **Skandia**, and excavations on the headland of **Kastrí** have revealed remains of an important Minoan colony. There's little visible evidence, apart from shards of pottery in the low crumbling cliffs, but happily, tourist development in the area has been barred because of its archeological significance. Consequently, there's just one solitary **taverna**, the *Skandia* (June–Oct), on the two-kilometre sand-and-pebble **beach** that stretches to either side of the headland. This taverna has a great atmosphere with home cooking and some spontaneous musical evenings.

Paleokástro, the mountain to the west, is the site of ancient Kýthira where there was a sanctuary of Aphrodite, but again, there's little to be seen today. Heading west from Paleópoli, and crossing the river bridge onto the Kondoliánika road, an unpaved road off to the left leads up to a tiny, white-washed church. From there, a rougher track leads down to **Kaladhí**, a beautiful cliff-backed pebble beach with caves, and rocks jutting out to sea.

AVLÉMONAS, on a rocky shoreline 2km east of Paleópoli beach, is a small fishing port with a bleak end-of-the-world feel as you approach from a distance. It becomes much more attractive once reached, and has a remarkable co-ordination of colour schemes throughout the village. There is a small, unimpressive Venetian fortress, and two **tavernas**, of which *Sotiris* is particularly recommended for a wide selection of fresh, well-prepared and reasonably-priced fish dishes. There are a number of **rooms**, including the newer apartments of *Popi Kastrisiou* (☎27360 33735; ❹), and the older, air-conditioned *Schina* studios (☎27360 33060; ❹). The Petrohilos family has a number of rooms or studios, including those of Evdokhia (☎27360 34069; ❷) opposite the *Sotiris*.

North and west of Hóra

LIVÁDHI, 4km north of Hóra, has **rooms** and, on the main road, the *Hotel Aposperides* (☎27360 31656, ℻27360 31688; ❹), which would make a good base if you had transport. Livádhi is also home to the most efficient travel agency on the island, Porfyra Travel, which is the main ANEK/ANEN and Olympic agent (☎27360 31888, ℻27360 31889, 🌐www.kythira.info), with exchange and car rental; they can also arrange accommodation or transfers.

At **Káto Livádhi**, a kilometre to the east of Livádhi, there is a small **museum** of Byzantine and post-Byzantine art (Nov–June Mon–Fri 8.30am–2pm; July–Oct Tues–Sun 8am–8pm; free) next to the large central church. It contains (labelled in Greek only) frescoes, painstakingly removed from island churches, dating from the twelfth to the eighteenth centuries, a seventh-century mosaic floor and some portable icons. Not far away there is also a cooperative pottery workshop (open all day except 2–4pm) and, on the road to Katoúni, a multiple-arched bridge, said to be the longest stone bridge in Greece and a legacy of the nineteenth century when the islands were a British protectorate; like others on the island it was built by a Scottish engineer called McPhail. The best view of it is from beside *Rena's zaharoplastío* in Livádhi. A popular **taverna** nearby is the *Theofilos*.

From Livádhi, a side road heads west to Kalokerinés, and continues 3.6km further to the island's principal monastery, **Myrtidhíon**, set above the wild and windswept west coast, among a dead forest of pines burned in June 2000. The monastery's main icon is said to date from 1160. Beyond the monastery, a track leads down to a small anchorage at **Limnária**; there are few beaches along this rocky, forbidding shore. An early left fork off the Myrtidhíon road out of Livádhi brings you through the hamlet of Poúrko and past the unusual Byzantine church of Áyios Dimítrios. From Poúrko, an increasingly steep road leads up to the **Ayía Elésis**, a nineteenth-century monastery marking the martyrdom of the saint on the hilltop in 375 AD, an event depicted in recent wall-paintings inside the church. For many visitors, however the breathtaking view from the western side of the courtyard is the main reason to visit.

Mylopótamos, Káto Hóra and the Ayía Sofía cave

North of Livádhi, just beyond Dhókana, it is worth making a detour off the main road for **MYLOPÓTAMOS**, a lovely traditional village and an oasis in summer, set in a wooded valley occupied by a small stream. The shady *Platanos kafenío* makes a pleasant stop for a drink above the village's springs and *To Kamari*, in an old restored building, serves snacks and drinks on a lower water-side terrace. Follow the signs for "Katarraktis Neraidha" to find a waterfall, hidden from view by lush vegetation, next to a long-closed café. The valley below the falls is overgrown but contains the remains of the watermill that gave the village its name.

Káto Hóra (aka Kástro Mylopotamoú), 500m down the road, was Mylopótamos's predecessor, and remains half-enclosed within the walls of a Venetian fortress. The fortress is small, full of locked, well-labelled churches, and has a rather domestic appearance: unlike the castle at Hóra, it was built as a place of refuge for the villagers in case of attack, rather than as a base for a Venetian garrison. All the houses within the walls are abandoned – as are many outside – but are open and accessible. Beyond here, a surfaced but briefly pre-cipitous road continues 5km through spectacular cliffscapes to **Limniónas**, a rocky inlet with a small sand beach, but a fire in June 2000 has left the sur-rounding countryside unattractive and bereft of vegetation.

The reason most visitors come to Mylopótamos is to see the **cave of Ayía Sofía**, the largest and most impressive of a number of caverns on the island. A half-hour signposted walk from the village, or a short drive by a new dirt road being constructed off the Limniónas road, the cave is open regularly from mid-June to mid-September (Mon–Fri 3–8pm, Sat & Sun 11am–5pm; €3). When the cave is closed, you can probably find a guide in Mylopótamos; ask at the village, giving a day's notice if possible. The cave is worth the effort to see: the entrance has been used as a church and has an iconostasis carved from the rock, with important Byzantine frescoes on it. Beyond, the cave system comprises a series of chambers which reach 250m into the mountain, although the thirty-minute guided tour (in Greek and English) only takes in the more interesting outer chambers. These include some startling formations such as the "shark's teeth", but you have to ask to be shown "Aphrodite's chambers". A minute new species of disc-shaped insect has been discovered there.

Andikýthira island

Thirteen kilometres to the south of Kýthira, the tiny, wind-blown island of **ANDIKÝTHIRA** has, theoretically, a twice-weekly connection with Crete on the Kýthira–Kastélli–Kýthira run (🆆 www.anen.gr); landings are often impossible due to adverse weather. There are attempts to organize a ferry from

Kýthira on August 17 for the festival of Áyios Mýron, returning the following day, but these are frequently thwarted by the wind. Rocky and poor, the island only received electricity in 1984. Attractions include good birdlife and flora, but it's not the place if you want company: with only seventy or so inhabitants divided among a scattering of settlements – mainly in **Potamós**, the harbour, and **Sohória**, the village – people are rather thin on the ground. A resident doctor and a teacher serve the dwindling community (there are three children at the village school, compared with nearly forty in the 1960s). The only official accommodation is the set of **rooms** run by the local community (☎27360 31390, ℗27360 33471) at Potamós, which also has the sole **taverna**, but you'd be recommended to bring plenty of supplies with you. In Sohória the only provisions available are basic foodstuffs at the village shop.

Travel details

Corfu (Kérkyra)

There are 4–7 daily flights between Corfu and Athens (1hr) on Olympic or Aegean, 4 weekly to Thessaloníki (1hr), and 3 weekly to Préveza, Kefalloniá and Zákynthos. Several ferries (Port Authority ☎26610 32655) per hour (5.15am–10pm) run between Corfu and Igoumenítsa (1hr 15min) in high season. Also 6 daily between Igoumenítsa and Lefkími (40min). Additionally, many ferries between Italy (Brindisi, Bari, Ancona, Trieste and Venice) and Pátra stop at Corfu; stopover is free if specified in advance and there is no problem buying Corfu–Pátra tickets. There are one or two ferries daily to Paxí, and up to 4 hydrofoils daily in season, either direct (1hr) or via Igoumenítsa (1hr 30min). The twice-weekly (Wed & Sat) tour hydrofoil does sometimes take one-way passengers to Kefalloniá.
Buses to Athens via the Igoumenítsa ferry depart 3 or 4 times daily, twice daily to Thessaloníki.

Eríkoussa, Mathráki and Othoní

A car ferry, the *Alexandros II*, runs from Kérkyra Town to all the islands 4 times weekly (Tues & Thurs 7.30am; Fri 4pm; Sun 9am). The ferry leaves from near the BP station on the seafront, midway between the Old and New Ports, although it involves sailing halfway round the island. Quicker access, favoured by islanders without vehicles, is via daily excursions from Sidhári or Áyios Stéfanos run by Nearchos Seacruises (☎26630 95248) or Aspiotis Lines (☎26630 72655).

Itháki (Ithaca)

Seasonal ferries from Fríkes to: Fiskárdho (Kefalloniá; 3 daily; 1hr); Vassilikí (Lefkádha; 2 daily; 2hr 15min). Pisaetós to: Sámi (Kefalloniá; 2 daily; 45min). Vathý to: Astakós (1 daily; 2hr 30min); Pátra (2 daily; 5hr); Sámi (Kefalloniá; 2 daily; 1hr). Off-season, there is 1 daily service on each route, weather permitting – check with Port Authority (☎26740 32909).

Kefalloniá

1–2 daily flights to and from Athens (1hr); 3 weekly to Corfu, Préveza and Zákynthos.
Ferries in season from Sámi to: Astakós (1 daily; 3hr 30min); Pátra (2 daily; 3hr 30min); Pisaetós (Itháki; 3 daily; 40min); Vathý (Itháki; 2 daily; 1hr). Also ferries from Póros to Kyllíni (4 daily; 1hr 15min). Fiskárdho to: Fríkes (Itháki; 1 daily; 1hr); Vassilikí (Lefkádha; 3 daily; 1hr). Argostóli to: Kyllíni (1 daily; 2hr 15min); Lixoúri (every 30min, hourly in winter; 20min). Pessádha to: Áyios Nikólaos (Zákynthos; 2 daily; 1hr 30min). Most routes maintain 1 daily service in winter – check with Port Authorities (Argostóli ☎26710 22224; Sámi ☎26740 22031; Póros ☎26740 72460).
The twice-weekly tour hydrofoils from Sámi to Corfu will often take one-way passengers.
5 daily buses from Argostóli to Athens (6–7hr). 1 daily from Lixoúri, Póros and Sámi.

Kýthira

Ferries to: Andikýthira (2 weekly in season); Kastélli, Crete (4–6 weekly in season; 2hr 15min; 5hr via Andikýthira); Pireás (2 weekly in season). Flights from Athens (1–2 daily; 50min).

Lefkádha

5 buses daily to and from Athens (6–7hr), and 6

buses daily to and from Préveza (30min), passing Áktio airport (25min).

7 ferries daily in season from Nydhrí to Meganíssi; daily connections (several in summer and 1 all year) from Vassilikí to Kefaloniá (Fiskárdho) and Itháki (Fríkes). The weekly cruise boat *Ikaros* may take one-way passengers from Nydhrí to Párga or Paxí.

Paxí

Ferries from Gáïos (Port Authority ☏ 26620 32259) to: Corfu (1–2 daily in season, 2 weekly in winter); Igoumenítsa 1–2 daily in season, 3 weekly in winter. There are up to 3 daily hydrofoils to Corfu and Igoumenítsa daily in season, dwindling to a few weekly in spring or autumn. In summer a kaïki connects daily with Párga.

Zákynthos

Ferries from Zákynthos Town to: Kyllíni (5 daily all year, up to 8 in season; 1hr 30min). Áyios Nikólaos to: Pessádha (Kefaloniá; 2 daily May–Sept; 1hr 30min).

Buses from Zákynthos Town to Athens (5–8 daily, according to season; 6hr).

Flight (on Olympic) from Zákynthos Town to Athens (1–2 daily; 55min), 3 weekly to Kefaloniá, Préveza and Corfu.

Contexts

Contexts

History

T his section is intended to lend some perspective to travels around the Greek islands, and is heavily weighted towards the era of the modern, post-independence nation – especially the twentieth century. More detailed accounts of particular periods are to be found both in the relevant sections of the guide and in specialized histories under "Books", pp.610–623.

Neolithic, Minoan and Mycenaean ages

Other than the solitary discovery of a fossilized Neanderthal skull near Thessaloníki, the earliest evidence of **human settlement** in Greece is to be found at Néa Nikomedhía, near Véria. Here, traces of large, rectangular houses dated to around 6000 BC have been excavated.

It seems that people originally came to this eastern Mediterranean territory in fits and starts, predominantly from Anatolia. These **pre–Hellenes** settled in essentially peaceful farming communities, made pottery and worshipped earth/fertility goddesses – clay statuettes of which are still found on the sites of old settlements. This simple way of life eventually disappeared, as people started to tap the land's resources for profit and to compete and trade.

Minoans and Mycenaeans

The years between around **2000** and **1100 BC** were a period of fluctuating regional dominance, based at first upon sea power, with vast **royal palaces** serving as centres of administration. Particularly important were those at **Knossos** on Crete, and **Mycenae**, **Tiryns** and **Pylos** in the Peloponnese.

Crete monopolized the eastern Mediterranean trade routes during an era subsequently called the **Minoan Age**, with the palace at Knossos surviving two earthquakes and a massive volcanic eruption on the island of Thera (today's Santoríni), at some indefinite point between 1500 and 1450 BC. The most obvious examples of Minoan culture can be seen in frescoes, in jewellery and in pottery, the distinctive red-and-white design on a dark background marking the peak period of Minoan achievement. When Knossos finally succumbed to disaster – natural or otherwise – around 1400 BC, it was the flourishing centre of **Mycenae** that assumed the leading role (and gave its name to the civilization of this period), until it in turn collapsed around 1200 BC.

This is a period whose history and remains are bound up with its **legends**, recounted most famously by Homer and his successors. Knossos was the home of King Minos, while the palaces of Mycenae and Pylos were the respective bases of Agamemnon and Nestor; Menelaos and Odysseus hailed from Sparta and Ithaca. The Homeric and other legends relating to them almost certainly reflect the growing prevalence of violence, revenge and war, instigated and aggravated by trade rivalry. The increasing scale of conflict and militarization is exemplified by the massive Mycenean fortifications of the Peloponnese and central mainland that were built around many of the palaces and dubbed Cyclopean by later ages, after the only beings thought capable of hefting the huge stones.

As the Homeric epics reflect, the Greece of these years was by no means a united nation; its people were essentially divided into splinter groups, defined largely by sea and mountain barriers and by access to **pasture**. Settlements flourished according to their proximity to and prowess on the sea and the fertility of their land; most were self-sufficient, specializing in the production of particular items for **trade**. Olives, for example, were associated with the region of Attica, and minerals with the island of Mílos.

The Dorian and Classical eras

The Mycenaean-era Greek states had also to cope with and assimilate periodic influxes of new peoples and trade. The traditional view of the collapse of the Mycenaean civilization posits a northern "barbarian" people, the **Dorians**, "invaded" from the north, devastating the existing palace culture and inaugurating a "dark age"; a competing theory has the so-called "Sea Peoples", probably based in southwestern Anatolia, conducting a series of raids over several decades. These days, archeologists see the influx more in terms of shifting trade patterns, though undoubtedly there was major disruption of the palace cultures and their sea power during the eleventh century BC.

Two other trends are salient in this period: the almost total supplanting of the mother goddesses by **male deities** (a process begun under the Mycenaeans), and the appearance of an **alphabet** still recognizable by modern Greeks, which replaced the so-called "Linear A" and "Linear B" Minoan/Mycenaean scripts.

City-states: Sparta and Athens

The ninth century BC ushered in the beginnings of the Greek **city-state** (*polis*). Citizens – rather than just kings or aristocrats – became involved in government, took part in community activities and organized industry and leisure. Colonial ventures increased, as did commercial dealings, and a consequent rise in the import trade was gradually to create a new class of manufacturers.

The city-state was the life of the people who dwelt within it, and each state retained both its independence and a distinctive style, with the result that the sporadic attempts to unite in a league against an external enemy were always pragmatic and temporary. The two most powerful states to emerge were Athens and Sparta, who were to exercise rivalry over the next five centuries.

Sparta was associated with the Dorians, who had settled in large numbers on the fertile Eurotas (Évrotas) river plain. The society of Sparta and its environs was highly militaristic and hierarchical, accentuated by the need to defend the exposed and fertile land on which it stood. Rather than build intricate fortifications, the people of Sparta relied upon military prowess and a system of laws decreed by the (semi-legendary) Lycurgus. Males were subjected to military instruction between the ages of seven and thirty, and attended communal refectories even after marriage. Weak babies were known periodically to "disappear"; the majority of the population, the helots, existed in a state of serfdom as they worked to support the elite. Girls too had to perform athletic feats of sprinting and wrestling, and even dwellings were more like barracks than houses.

Athens, the fulcrum of the state of Attica, was dynamic and exciting by contrast, though here too slavery was vital to the economy. Home to the administrations of Solon and Pericles, the dramatic talents of Sophocles and Aristophanes, the oratory of Thucydides and Demosthenes, and the philosophical power of Socrates and Plato, it made up in cultural achievement what it lacked in Spartan virtue. Yet Sparta did not deserve all the military glory. The Athens of the sixth and fifth centuries BC, the so-called **Classical period** in Greek history, played the major part in repelling the armies of the Persian king Xerxes at Marathon (490 BC) and Salamis (480 BC), campaigns later described by Aeschylus in *The Persians*.

Athens also evolved a tradition of **democracy** (*demokratía*), literally "control by the people" – although at this stage "the people" did not include either women or slaves. In Athens there were three organs of government. The Areopagus, composed of the city elders, exercised steadily decreasing authority and eventually dealt solely with murder cases. Then there was the Council of Five Hundred (men), elected annually by ballot to prepare the business of the Assembly and to attend to matters of urgency. The Assembly gave every free man a political voice; it had sole responsibility for law-making and provided an arena for the discussion of important issues.

This was a period of intense creativity, particularly in Athens, whose actions and pretensions were fast becoming imperial in all but name. Each city-state had its **acropolis**, or high town, where religious activity was focused. In Athens, Pericles endowed the acropolis with a complex of buildings, whose climax was the temple of the Parthenon. Meanwhile, the era saw the tragedies of Sophocles performed, and the philosophies of Socrates and Plato expounded.

Religion at this stage was polytheistic, ordering eleven main deities under the aegis of Zeus. Urban temples tended to be dedicated to Zeus, Athena or Poseidon; in the countryside the proliferation of names and sanctuary finds suggests a preference for Apollo, Hera, Dionysos and Artemis.

The Peloponnesian wars

The power struggles between Athens and Sparta, allied with various city-states across the Hellenic world, eventually culminated in the **Peloponnesian wars** of 431–404 BC. After these conflicts, superbly recorded by Thucydides and nominally won by Sparta, the city-state ceased to function so effectively.

This was in part due to drained resources and political apathy, but to a greater degree a consequence of the increasingly commercial and complex pressures on everyday life. Trade, originally spurred by the invention of **coinage** in the sixth century BC, continued to expand; a revitalized Athens, for example, was exporting wine, oil and manufactured goods, getting corn in return from the Black Sea and Egypt.

The amount of time each man had to devote to the affairs of government decreased, and a position in political life became a professional job rather than a natural assumption. Democracy had changed, while in philosophy there was a shift from the idealists and mystics of the sixth and fifth centuries BC to the Cynics, Stoics and Epicureans – followers, respectively, of Diogenes, Zeno and Epicurus.

Hellenistic and Roman Greece

The most important factor in the decline of the city-states was meanwhile developing outside their sphere, in the kingdom of Macedonia to the north. Ruling from the Macedonian capital of Pella, **Philip II** (reigned 359–336 BC) was forging a strong military and unitary force, extending his territories into Thrace and finally establishing control over Athens and southern Greece. His son, **Alexander the Great**, in a brief but glorious thirteen-year reign, extended these gains into Persia and Egypt and parts of modern India and Afghanistan.

This unwieldy empire splintered almost immediately upon Alexander's death in 323 BC, to be divided into the three Macedonian dynasties of **Hellenistic Greece**: the Antigonids in Macedonia, the Seleucids in Syria and Persia, and the Ptolemies in Egypt. Each was in turn conquered and absorbed by the new Roman empire, the Ptolemies – under their queen Cleopatra – last of all.

Roman Greece

Mainland and island Greece were subdued by the Romans over some seventy years of campaigns, from 215 to 146 BC. Once in control, however, **Rome** allowed considerable autonomy to the old territories of the city-states. Greek remained the official language of the eastern Mediterranean and its traditions and culture coexisted fairly peacefully with that of the overlords during the next three centuries.

In central Greece both **Athens** and **Corinth** remained important cities but the emphasis was shifting north – particularly to towns, such as **Salonica** (Thessaloníki), along the new Via Egnatia, a military and civil road engineered between Rome and Byzantium via the port of Brundisium (modern Brindisi in Italy). Among the islands, Rhodes had declined since Hellenistic times but Kós, Lésvos, Thássos and Gortys on Crete remained important centres.

The Byzantine empire and Medieval Greece

The shift of emphasis northwards was given even greater impetus by the decline of the Roman empire and its division into eastern and western empires. In the year 330 AD Emperor Constantine moved his capital to the Greek city of Byzantium, and here emerged Constantinople (modern İstanbul), the "new Rome" and spiritual and political capital of the **Byzantine empire**.

While the last western Roman emperor was deposed by barbarian Goths in 476, this eastern portion was to be the dominant Mediterranean power for some seven hundred years; only in 1453 did it collapse completely.

Christianity

Christianity had been introduced under Constantine, and by the end of the fourth century was the official state religion, its liturgies (still in use in the Greek Orthodox Church), creed and New Testament all written in Greek. However, a distinction must be drawn between perceptions of Greek as a language or culture, and as a concept. The Byzantine empire styled itself Roman, or *Romiós*, rather than Hellenic, and moved to eradicate all remaining symbols of pagan Greece. The Delphic Oracle was forcibly closed, and the Olympic Games discontinued, by the emperor Theodosius I at the end of the fourth century. Schools of philosophy, especially neo-Platonic ones, did however survive until 529.

The seventh century saw **Constantinople** besieged by Persians, and later Arabs, but the Byzantine empire survived, losing only Egypt, the least "Greek" of its territories. From the ninth to the early eleventh centuries it enjoyed an archetypal "golden age" in culture, confidence and security. Bound up with the Byzantines' Orthodox faith was a sense of spiritual superiority, and the emperors saw Constantinople as a "new Jerusalem" for their "chosen people". It was the beginning of a diplomatic and ecclesiastical conflict with the Catholic West that was to have disastrous consequences over the next five centuries. In the meantime the Eastern and Western patriarchs mutually excommunicated each other.

From the seventh until the eleventh centuries **Byzantine Greece**, certainly in the islands, became something of a provincial backwater. Administration was absurdly top-heavy, and imperial taxation led to semi-autonomous provinces ruled by military generals, whose lands were usually acquired from bankrupted peasants. This alienation of the poor provided a force for change, with a disaffected populace ready to turn towards or cooperate with the empire's enemies if the terms on offer were an improvement.

Waves of **Slavic raiders** needed no encouragement to sweep down from the north Balkans throughout this period. At the same time other tribal groups moved down more peaceably from **central Europe** and were absorbed with little difficulty. From the thirteenth century onwards, immigrants from **Albania** repopulated the islands of Spétses, Ídhra, Angístri, Salamína, Ándhros and Évvia, as well as parts of Attica and the Peloponnese.

The crusades: Frankish and Venetian rule

From the early years of the eleventh century, less welcome and less assimilable Western forces began to appear. The **Normans** landed first at Corfu in 1085, and returned again to the mainland with papal sanction a decade later on their way to liberate Jerusalem.

These were only a precursor, though, for the forces that were to descend en route for the **Fourth Crusade** of 1204, when Venetians, Franks and Germans turned their armies directly on Byzantium to sack and occupy Constantinople. These Latin princes and their followers, intent on new lands and kingdoms, settled in to divide up the best part of the empire. All that remained of Byzantium were four small peripheral kingdoms, or **despotates**: the most powerful in Nicaea in Asia Minor, less significant ones at Trebizond on the Black Sea, and (in present-day Greece) in Epirus and around Mystra in the Peloponnese (known in those times as the Morea).

There followed two extraordinarily involved centuries of manipulation and struggle between Franks, Venetians, Genoese, Catalans and Turks. The Paleologos dynasty at Nicaea recovered the city of Constantinople in 1261, but little of its former territory and power. Instead, the focus of Byzantium shifted to the Peloponnese, where the autonomous **despotate of Mystra**, ruled by members of the imperial family, eventually succeeded in wresting most of the peninsula from Frankish hands. At the same time this despotate enjoyed an intense cultural renaissance, strongly evoked in the churches and shells of cities still visible at modern Mystra and Monemvasiá.

Ottoman occupation

Within a generation of driving out the Franks, the Byzantine Greeks faced a much stronger threat in the expanding empire of the **Ottomans**. "Turks" is the generic term used for them in Greece, but the Ottomans were in fact a motley, assimilative crew, who included large numbers of Albanian, Arab, Caucasian and Kurdish Muslims, as well as Christian renegades from Venice, Hungary and the future territory of modern Greece. Torn apart by internal struggles between their own ruling dynasties, the Palaeologi and Kantakuzeni, and unaided by the Catholic West, the Byzantine Greeks were to prove no match for the Ottomans. On Tuesday, May 29, 1453, a date still solemnly commemorated by the Orthodox Church, Constantinople fell to the besieging Sultan Mehmet II.

Mystra was to follow within seven years, and Trebizond within nine, by which time virtually all of the old Byzantine empire lay under Ottoman domination. Only the **Ionian islands**, **Crete** and the **Cyclades**, which remained Venetian for two more centuries (or longer), and a few scattered and remote enclaves – like the Máni in the Peloponnese and Soúli in Epirus – were able to resist the "Turkish" advance.

Ottoman rule

Under what Greeks refer to as the *turkokratía* or era of **Ottoman rule**, the lands of present-day Greece passed into rural provincialism, taking refuge in a self-protective mode of village life based more on pastoralism than cultivation that was only substantially disrupted by World War II. Taxes and discipline, sporadically backed up by the massacre of dissenting communities, were inflicted by İstanbul (as Constantinople was renamed), but large areas passed into the hands of local chieftains who often had considerable independence, provided that revenue was forwarded regularly to the imperial capital. On the larger, more fertile islands such as Crete, Rhodes, Lésvos and Évvia, rule was inevitably stricter, with larger garrisons and more onerous taxes; small islands too impoverished to be exploited were left pretty much to their own devices.

Greek identity, meanwhile, was preserved through the offices of the **Orthodox Church** which, despite instances of enforced conversion, the sultans allowed to continue unhindered. The **monasteries** became the trustees of Byzantine culture, though this had gone into stagnation after the fall of Constantinople and Mystra, whose scholars and artists emigrated west, adding impetus to the Renaissance. Strictly mythical, however, despite nationalist posturings to the contrary, were the so-called "secret (primary) schools" of the Church: poor literacy rates for all confessions was the rule across the Ottoman empire until the eighteenth century, when increasing prosperity prompted the founding of many local schools, sometimes attached to monasteries and usually staffed by learned clerics.

As Ottoman administration became progressively decentralized and inefficient, individual Greeks rose to local positions of considerable influence, and a number of island communities achieved a degree of autonomy. Sými was granted an empire-wide monopoly on sponge-diving in return for a yearly tribute to the sultan. Sámos was declared a "Muslim-free" zone and enjoyed special tax exemptions for two centuries. And on the Albanian-repopulated islands of Ídhra and Spétses, as well as Kássos and Psará, a Greek merchant fleet came into being in the eighteenth century, permitted to trade throughout the Mediterranean. Greeks, too, were becoming organized overseas in the sizeable expatriate colonies of central Europe, which often had affiliations with the semi-autonomous village clusters of Zagóri (in Epirus), Ambelákia (Thessaly) and Mount Pílio.

The struggle for independence

Despite these privileges, by the eighteenth century opposition to Ottoman rule was becoming widespread on the mainland, exemplified most obviously by the **klephts** (brigands) of the mountains, who were often former *armatoles* (guards of the mountain passes) gone over to the "other side". It was not until the nineteenth century, however, that a resistance movement could muster sufficient support and firepower to prove a real challenge to the Ottomans. In 1770 a Russian-backed uprising had been easily and brutally suppressed, but fifty years later the situation was different.

In Epirus the Ottomans were overextended, subduing the expansionist campaigns of local ruler **Ali Pasha**. The French Revolution had given impetus to "freedom movements", and the Greek fighters were provided with financial and ideological underpinnings by the Filikí Etería, or "Friendly Society", a secret group recruited among the exiled merchants and intellectuals of central Europe.

This somewhat motley coalition of klephts and theorists launched their insurrection at several points in the **Peloponnese** during the latter half of March 1821; the blessing of the insurrectionists' banner at the monastery of Ayía Lávra on March 25, 1821 by Archbishop Yermanos of Old Patra is, like the "secret schools", a picturesque myth.

The War of Independence

To describe in detail the course of the **War of Independence** is to provoke unnecessary confusion, since much of the rebellion consisted of local and inconclusive guerrilla campaigns. What is important to understand is that Greeks, though fighting for liberation from the Ottomans, were not fighting as and for a nation. Motives differed enormously: landowners assumed their role was to lead, seeking to retain and reinforce their traditional privileges, while the peasantry saw the struggle as a means towards land redistribution.

Outside Greece, the prestige of, and publicity for, the insurrection were promoted by the arrival of a thousand or so European **Philhellenes**, almost half of them German, though the most important was the English poet, **Lord Byron**, who died while training Greek forces at Mesolóngi in April 1824.

Though Greek guerrilla leaders, above all **Theodhoros Kolokotronis**, "the old man of the Morea", gained significant military victories early in the rebellion, the death of Byron had an immensely important effect on public opinion in the West. Aid for the Greek struggle had come neither from Orthodox Russia, nor from the Western powers of France and Britain, both still ravaged by the Napoleonic wars and suspicious of a potentially anarchic new state. But by 1827, when Mesolóngi fell again to the Ottoman Turks, these three "Great Powers" finally agreed to seek autonomy for certain parts of Greece and sent a combined fleet to put pressure on the sultan's Egyptian army, then ransacking and massacring in the Peloponnese. Events took over, and an accidental naval battle in **Navarino Bay** resulted in the destruction of almost the entire Turkish-Egyptian fleet. The following spring, Russia itself declared war on the Ottomans, and Sultan Mahmud II was forced to accept the existence of an autonomous Greece.

At a series of conferences from 1830 to 1832, Greek independence was confirmed by the Western powers and borders were drawn in 1832. These included just 800,000 of the six million Greeks living within the Ottoman empire, and territories which were for the most part the poorest of the Classical and Byzantine lands: Attica, the Peloponnese and the islands of the Argo-Saronic, Sporades and Cyclades. The rich agricultural belt of Thessaly, Epirus in the west, and Macedonia in the north remained in Ottoman hands. Meanwhile, the Ionian islands were controlled by a British protectorate and the Dodecanese by the Ottomans (and after 1913 by recently unified Italy).

The emerging state

Modern Greece began as a republic, and **Ioannis Kapodistrias**, its first president, concentrated his efforts on building a viable central authority and government in the face of diverse protagonists from the Independence struggle. Almost inevitably he was assassinated – in 1831, by two chieftains from the ever-disruptive Máni – and perhaps equally inevitably the three powers stepped in. They created a monarchy, gave limited aid and set on the throne a Bavarian prince, **Otho (Otto)**. By 1834, Greece also had a national, state-controlled Orthodox Church of its own, independent from the Patriarchate in Constantinople; at the same time, two-thirds of the monasteries and convents were closed down and their assets converted to funding secular public education.

Despite the granting of a constitution in 1844, the king proved an autocratic and insensitive ruler, bringing in fellow Germans to fill official posts and ignoring all claims by the landless peasantry for redistribution of the old estates. In 1862 he was forced from the country by a popular revolt, and the Europeans produced a new prince, this time from Denmark, who requested that Britain cede the Ionian islands as a condition of his accession to the throne. **George I**, in fact, proved more capable and popular: he oversaw the building of the first railways and roads, limited land reforms in the Peloponnese and the first expansion of the Greek borders.

The Megáli Idhéa and expansionist wars

From the very beginning, the unquestioned motive force of Greek foreign policy was the **Megáli Idhéa** (Great Idea) of redeeming ethnically Greek populations outside the country and incorporating the old territories of Byzantium into the kingdom. Wherever or whenever it was impolitic to use regular army units for the task, brigands and guerrilla irregulars conducted raids into Ottoman-held Thessaly and tried to provoke rebellion among the population there.

In 1881 **Thessaly**, along with southern Epirus up to Árta, was ceded to Greece by the Ottomans – though by treaty terms its large estates with their Muslim landlords were to remain intact. Less illustriously, the Greeks failed in 1897 to achieve *énosis* (union) with **Crete** by attacking Ottoman forces on the mainland, and in the process nearly bankrupted the state. The island was, however, placed under a high commissioner, appointed by the Great Powers, and in 1913 did become a part of Greece.

It was also from Crete that the most distinguished modern Greek statesman emerged; **Eleftherios Venizelos**, having led a civilian campaign for his island's liberation, was elected as Greek prime minister in 1910. Two years later he organized an alliance of Balkan powers to fight the **Balkan wars** (1912–13), campaigns that saw the Ottomans virtually driven from Europe, and the Bulgarian competition bested in the culmination of a bitter, four-decade campaign for the hearts and minds of the Macedonian population. With Greek borders extended to include the northeast Aegean islands, northern Thessaly, central Epirus and parts of Macedonia, the Megáli Idhéa seemed to be approaching reality. At the same time Venizelos proved himself a shrewd manipulator of domestic public opinion by revising the constitution and introducing a series of liberal social reforms.

Division, however, was to appear with the outbreak of **World War I**. Venizelos urged Greek entry on the Allied side, seeing in the conflict possibilities for the "liberation" of Greeks in Thrace and Asia Minor, but the new king, Constantine I, who was married to a sister of the German Kaiser, imposed a policy of neutrality. Eventually Venizelos set up a revolutionary government in Thessaloníki, polarizing the country into a state of civil war along Venezelist-Royalist lines, but in 1917 Greek troops entered the war to join the French, British and Serbians in the **Macedonian campaign** against Bulgaria and Germany. Upon the capitulation of Bulgaria and Ottoman Turkey, the Greeks occupied **Thrace** (both western and eastern), and Venizelos presented demands at Versailles for the predominantly Greek region of Smyrna on the Asia Minor coast.

The Katastrofí and its aftermath

This was the beginning of one of the most disastrous episodes in modern Greek history, the so-called **Katastrofí** ("Catastrophe"). Venizelos was authorized to move forces into Smyrna in 1919, but in Turkey itself a new nationalist movement was coalescing under Mustafa Kemal, or **Atatürk** as he came to be known. In 1920 Venizelos lost the elections and monarchist factions took over, their aspirations unmitigated by the Cretan's skill in foreign diplomacy. Despite Allied support for such ventures now having completely evaporated, Greek forces were ordered to advance upon Ankara in an attempt to bring Atatürk to terms.

This so-called **Anatolian campaign** ignominiously collapsed in summer 1922 when Ottoman troops forced the Greeks back to the coast and into a hurried evacuation from **Smyrna**. As they left Smyrna, the Ottomans moved in and systematically massacred much of the Armenian and Greek population before burning most of the city to the ground.

Although an entire Greek army remained intact in eastern Thrace, Britain, hitherto Greece's only backer, let it be known that Greece would be wisest to accept Atatürk's terms, formalized by the 1923 Treaty of Lausanne, which ordered the **exchange of religious minorities** in each country – in effect, the first large-scale regulated ethnic cleansing. Turkey was to accept 390,000 Muslims resident on Greek soil. Greece, mobilized almost continuously for the last decade and with a population of under five million, was faced with the resettlement of over 1,300,000 Christian refugees. Many of these had already read the writing on the wall after 1918 and arrived of their own accord, from Bulgaria and revolutionary Russia as well as Asia Minor; significant numbers were settled on Límnos, Lésvos, Híos, Sámos, Évvia and Crete, as well as around Athens and throughout Macedonia and western Thrace. The Megáli Idhéa had ceased to be a viable blueprint.

Changes, inevitably, were intense and far-reaching. The bulk of the **agricultural estates** of Crete, Évvia, Lésvos and Thessaly were finally **redistributed** – completing a program begun in 1909 – both to Greek tenants and refugee farmers, and huge **shanty towns** grew into new quarters around Athens, Pireás and other cities, a spur to the country's then almost nonexistent industry.

Politically, too, reaction was swift. By September 1922, a group of Venezelist army officers under **Colonel Nikolaos Plastiras**, assembled after the retreat from Smyrna, "invited" King Constantine to abdicate, and in November they executed six of his ministers held most responsible for the debacle. Democracy was nominally restored with the proclamation of a republic, but for much of the next decade changes in government were brought about by factions within the armed forces. Meanwhile, among the urban refugee population, unions were being formed and the Greek Communist Party (KKE) was established.

Venizelos's last gasp — and the rise of Metaxas

Elections in 1928 **returned Venizelos to power**, but his freedom to manoeuvre was restricted by the Great Crash of the following year. He had borrowed heavily abroad and was unable to renegotiate loan terms in 1931. Late 1932 saw a local crash caused by England's abandonment of the gold standard, with Greek currency heavily devalued and Venizelos forced from office. His supporters under Plastiras tried to forcibly reinstate him in March 1933, but their coup was quashed and Venizelos fled to Paris, where he died three years later.

By 1936 the Communist Party had enough electoral support to hold the balance of power in parliament, and would have done so had not the army and the by-then-restored king decided otherwise. **King George II** had been returned by a plebiscite held – and almost certainly manipulated – the previous year, and so presided over an increasingly factionalized parliament. In April 1936 George II appointed **General Ioannis Metaxas** as prime minister, despite the latter's being supported by only six elected deputies. Immediately a series of KKE-organized strikes broke out and the king, ignoring attempts to form a broad liberal coalition, dissolved parliament without setting a date for new elections. It was a blatantly unconstitutional move and opened the way for five years of ruthless and at times absurd dictatorship.

Metaxas averted a general strike with military force and proceeded to set up a state based on **fascist** models of the era. Left-wing and trade union opponents were imprisoned or forced into exile, a state youth movement and efficient secret police set up, and rigid censorship, extending even to passages of Thucydides, imposed. But it was at least a Greek dictatorship, and though Metaxas was sympathetic to Nazi organizational methods and economics, he completely opposed German or Italian domination.

World War II and the Greek civil war

Using a submarine based on Léros in the Dodecanese, the Italians tried to provoke the Greeks into prematurely entering **World War II** by surreptitiously torpedoing the Greek cruiser *Elli* in Tínos harbour on August 15, 1940, but they met with no immediate response. However, when Mussolini occupied Albania and sent an ultimatum on October 28, 1940, demanding passage for his troops through Greece, Metaxas responded to the Italian foreign minister with the apocryphal one-word answer "*óhi*" (no). (In fact, his response, in the mutually understood French, was "*C'est la guerre*".) The date marked the entry of Greece into the war, and the gesture is still celebrated as a national holiday.

Galvanized into brief unity by the crisis, the Greeks drove Italian forces from the country and moreover managed to take control of the long-coveted and predominantly Greek-populated northern Epirus (southern Albania). However, the Greek army subsequently frittered away its strength in the snowy mountains of northern Epirus rather than consolidating its gains or defending the Macedonian frontier, and proposed coordination with the British never materialized.

Occupation and resistance

In April of the following year Nazi mechanized columns swept through Yugoslavia and across the Greek mainland, effectively reversing the only Axis defeat to date, and by late May 1941 airborne and seaborne **German invasion** forces had completed the occupation of Crete and the other islands. Metaxas had died before their arrival, while King George and his new self-appointed ministers fled into exile in Cairo; few Greeks, of any political persuasion, were sad to see them go.

The joint Italian-German-Bulgarian Axis **occupation** of Greece was among the bitterest experiences of the European war. Nearly half a million Greek civilians starved to death over the winter of 1941–42, as all available food was requisitioned, principally by the Germans, to feed occupying armies. In addition, entire villages throughout the mainland and across the islands, especially on Crete, were burned at the least hint of resistance activity. In their northern sector, which included Thássos and Samothráki, the Bulgarians demolished ancient sites and churches to support any future bid to annexe "Slavic" Macedonia.

After the Italians capitulated in September 1943, the Jewish communities in Rhodes, Kós, Crete, Corfu, Vólos, Évvia and Zákynthos in particular were exposed to the full force of Nazi racial doctrine; in the last three places, however, cooperation between courageous church or municipal authorities and the budding Resistance (see below) ensured that most local Jews survived.

With a quisling government in Athens – and an unpopular, discredited royalist government-in-exile in Cairo – the focus of Greek political and military action during the occupation passed largely to the **EAM**, or National Liberation Front. By 1943 it effectively controlled most areas of the country, including Sámos and Lésvos (but not Crete), working with the British on tactical operations, with its own army (ELAS) and navy, and both civil and secret police forces. Initially it commanded widespread popular support and appeared to offer an obvious framework for the resumption of postwar government.

However, most of its highest-ranking members were Communists, and the British prime minister, **Winston Churchill**, was determined to reinstate the monarchy. Even with two years of the war to run, it became obvious that there could be no peaceable post-liberation regime other than a republic. Accordingly, in August 1943, representatives from each of the main Resistance movements (including two non-Communist groups) flew clandestinely to Cairo to request that the king not return unless a plebiscite had first voted in his favour. Both the Greek and British authorities refused to consider the proposal, and the best possibility of averting civil war was lost.

The EAM contingent returned divided, as perhaps the British had intended, and a conflict broke out between those who favoured taking peaceful control of any government imposed after liberation, and the hard-line Stalinist ideologues, who forbade participation in any "bourgeois" regime.

In October 1943, with fears of an imminent British landing force and takeover, ELAS launched a full-scale attack upon its Greek rivals on the mainland; by the following April, they had wiped out all but Epirus-based EDES, their most right-wing rival, suspected of collaboration with the Germans. ELAS's ferocity was spurred by the failure of the Egyptian conference and by half-true reports that British and American agents were being infiltrated into Greece to prevent the establishment of a Communist government when the Germans began withdrawing their forces.

Liberation and civil war

In fact, as the Germans began to leave in October 1944, most of the EAM leadership agreed to join a British-sponsored "official" **interim government**. It quickly proved a tactical error, however. With almost ninety percent of the provinces under their control, the Communists were eventually given only one-third representation in Athens, and a new regular army began to form, based on the extreme-right-wing Mountain Brigade, the Sacred Band and even the fascist Security Battalions, rather than the ELAS officer corps. The king showed no sign of renouncing his claims, and, in November, Allied forces ordered ELAS to disarm. On December 3 all pretences of civility or neutrality were dropped; the police fired on an EAM demonstration in Athens, killing at least sixteen, and fighting broke out between ELAS and **British troops**, in the so-called **Dhekemvrianá** events. Though ELAS quickly quashed all opposition in the countryside, they failed to drive the British and right-wing Greeks from Athens, thus losing their best chance of seizing power. In their fury at being thwarted, ELAS rounded up their most influential and wealthiest opponents in the largest towns, and marched them out to rural areas in conditions that guaranteed their death.

A truce of sorts was negotiated at Várkiza near Athens in February 1945, but the agreement was never implemented. The army, police and civil service remained in right-wing hands, and, while collaborationists were often allowed to retain their positions, left-wing sympathizers, many of whom were merely Venizelist republicans and not communists, were systematically excluded. The elections of 1946 were won by the right-wing parties (the Left unwisely boycotted them), followed by yet another rigged plebiscite in favour of the king's return. By 1947 guerrilla activity had again reached the scale of a full **civil war**, with ELAS reorganized into the Democratic Army of Greece (DSE in Greek).

In the interim, King George had died and been succeeded by his brother Paul (with his consort Frederika), while the **Americans** had taken over the British role, and begun implementing the Cold-War **Truman doctrine**. In March 1947 they effectively took control of Greece, their first significant postwar experiment in anti-Communist intervention. Massive economic and military aid was given to a client Greek government, whose official decrees had to be countersigned by the American Mission chief in order to become valid.

In the mainland mountains US military advisers trained the nationalist army for **campaigns against the DSE**, and in the cities there were mass arrests, court martials and imprisonments – a kind of "White Terror" – lasting until 1951. Over three thousand executions were recorded, including (for their pacifist stance and refusal to swear loyalty oaths) a number of Jehovah's Witnesses, "a sect proved to be under communist domination", according to US Ambassador Grady. To deny the DSE local support, over 700,000 civilians were forcibly evacuated from mountain villages and dumped in squalid internment camps near towns, a move which helped destroy any hope of post-war rural existence.

In the autumn of 1949, with the Yugoslav–Greek border closed after Tito's rift with Stalin, the last DSE guerrillas finally admitted defeat, retreating into Albania from their strongholds on Mount Grámmos. Atrocities had been committed on both sides, including, from the Left, considerably more than three thousand executions, widescale vandalization of monasteries and the dubious evacuation of children from "combat areas". Such errors, as well as the high percentage of openly separatist Slavophones amongst their ranks, and the hopelessness of lightly armed guerrillas fighting an American-backed army equipped with aircraft and heavy artillery, almost certainly doomed the DSE's efforts from the start.

Reconstruction American style 1950–67

After a decade of war that had shattered much of Greece's infrastructure (supposedly not one bridge was left standing by 1948), and had killed twelve percent of the 1940 population, it was a demoralized country that emerged into the Western political orbit of the 1950s. Greece was also perforce American-dominated, enlisted into the Korean War in 1950 and NATO the following year. In domestic politics, the US embassy – still giving the orders – foisted upon the Greeks a winner-takes-all electoral system, which was to ensure victory for the Right over the next twelve years. Overt leftist activity was banned (though a "cover" party for communists was soon founded); those individuals who were not herded into political "re-education" camps on barren islands, or dispatched by firing squads, legal or vigilante, went into exile throughout eastern Europe, to return only after 1974.

The American-backed, highly conservative **"Greek Rally"** party, led by General Papagos, won the first decisive post-civil-war elections in 1952. After the general's death, the party's leadership was taken over – and to an extent liberalized – by **Constantine Karamanlis**. Under his rule, stability of a kind was established and some economic advances registered, particularly after the revival of Greece's traditional German markets. Health and life expectancy improved dramatically, as the age-old scourges of tuberculosis and malaria were finally confronted with American-supplied food and pesticides. Less commendable was Karamanlis's encouragement of the law of **andiparohí**, whereby owners of small refugee shanties or Neoclassical mansions alike could offer the site of their property to apartment-block developers in exchange for two flats (out of eight to ten) in the finished building. This effectively ripped the heart out of most Greek towns, and explains their baleful aesthetics a half-century on.

The 1950s also saw wholesale **depopulation** of remote villages as migrants sought work in Australia, America and western Europe, or the larger Greek cities. This was most pronounced on the remoter islands of Kýthira, Kefaloniá, the northeast Aegean and the Dodecanese, where the longed-for union with Greece in 1948 had ironically conferred the right to emigrate, severely restricted under the Ottomans and Italians.

The main crisis in foreign policy throughout this period was **Cyprus**, where a long terrorist campaign was waged by Greek-Cypriots opposing British rule, and there were sporadic threats of a new Greco-Turkish war. An ultimately unworkable compromise was forced on the island by Britain in 1960, granting independence without the possibility of "self-determination" (ie union with Greece). Much of the traditional Greek-British goodwill was destroyed by the issue, with Britain seen to be acting with regard primarily for its two military bases (over which it still retains sovereignty).

By 1961 unemployment, the Cyprus issue and the imposition of US nuclear bases on Greek soil were changing the political climate, and when Karamanlis was again elected there was strong suspicion of a fraud arranged by the king and army. Strikes became frequent in industry and even agriculture, while King Paul and autocratic, fascist-inclined Queen Frederika were openly attacked in parliament and at protest demonstrations. The far Right grew uneasy about **"communist resurgence"** and, losing confidence in their own electoral influence, arranged the assassination of left-wing deputy **Grigoris Lambrakis** in Thessaloníki in May 1963. (The murder, and its subsequent cover-up, is the subject of Vassilis Vassilikos's thriller *Z*, filmed by Costa-Gavras.) It was against this volatile background that Karamanlis dissolved parliament, lost the subsequent elections and left for exile in Paris.

The new government – the first controlled from outside the Right since 1935 – was formed by **George Papandreou's Centre Union Party**, and had a decisive majority of nearly fifty seats. It was to last, however, for under two years as conservative forces conspired to thwart its progress. In this the chief protagonists were army officers and their constitutional commander-in-chief, the new king, 23-year-old **Constantine II**.

Since power in Greece depended on a pliant military as well as a network of political appointees, Papandreou's most urgent task in order to govern securely and effectively was to reform the armed forces. His first minister of defence proved incapable of the task and, while he was investigating the right-wing plot suspected of rigging the 1961 election, "evidence" was produced of a leftist conspiracy connected with Papandreou's son Andreas (also a minister in the government). When the allegations grew to a crisis, George Papandreou assumed the defence portfolio himself, a move which the king refused to sanction. Papandreou then resigned in order to gain a fresh mandate at the polls but the king would not order new elections, instead persuading members of the Centre Union – chief among them Constantine Mitsotakis – to defect and organize a coalition government. Punctuated by strikes, resignations and mass demonstrations, this lasted for a year and a half until new elections were eventually set for May 28, 1967. They failed to take place.

The colonels' junta 1967–74

It was a foregone conclusion that Papandreou's party would win the polls against the discredited coalition partners. And it was equally certain that there would be some anti-democratic action to prevent them from reassuming power. Disturbed by the party's leftward shift, King Constantine was said to have briefed senior generals for a coup d'état, to take place ten days before the elections. However, he was caught by surprise, as was nearly everyone else, by the coup of April 21, 1967, staged by a group of "unknown" colonels. It was, to quote Andreas Papandreou, "the first successful CIA military putsch on the European continent".

The **colonels' junta**, having dissolved all civilian poles of authority, was sworn in by the king and survived the half-hearted counter-coup which he subsequently attempted to organize. It was an ostensibly **fascist regime**, absurdly styling itself as the true "Revival of Greek Orthodoxy" against Western "corrupting influences", though in reality its ideology was nothing more than warmed-up dogma from the Metaxas era mixed with ultranationalism.

All political activity was banned, independent trade unions were forbidden to recruit or meet, the press was so heavily censored that many papers stopped printing, and thousands of "Communists" were arrested, imprisoned and often tortured. Among the persecuted were both Papandreous, the composer Mikis Theodhorakis (deemed "unfit to stand trial" after three months in custody) and Amalia Fleming (widow of Alexander Fleming). While relatively few people were killed outright, thousands were permanently maimed physically and psychologically in the junta's torture chambers. The best-known Greek actress, Melina Mercouri, was stripped of her citizenship in absentia, and thousands of prominent Greeks joined her in exile.

Culturally, the colonels put an end to genuine popular music (banning, for example, bagpipes on Mýkonos lest visitors think Greece too "primitive", and closing many Athens clubs), while inflicting ludicrous censorship on literature and the theatre, including (as under Metaxas) a ban on production of the Classical tragedies. By contrast, chief colonel Papadapoulos's rambling, illiterate speeches became a byword for bad grammar, obfuscation and Orwellian Newspeak.

The colonels lasted for seven years, opposed (especially after the first two years) by the majority of the Greek people, officially excluded from the Council of Europe, but propped up and given massive aid by US presidents **Lyndon Johnson** and **Richard Nixon**. To them and the CIA the junta's Greece was an ideal client state: human rights considerations were then thought trivial; orders were placed for sophisticated military technology; and foreign investment on terms highly unfavourable to Greece was made available to multinational corporations – for the era, a fairly routine scenario of exploitation of an underdeveloped nation.

Opposition was voiced from the beginning by exiled Greeks in London, the United States and western Europe, but only in 1973 did demonstrations break out openly in Greece – the colonels' secret police had done too thorough a job of infiltrating domestic resistance groups and terrifying everyone else into docility. On November 17 the students of the Polytekhnío (Polytechnic) in Athens began an occupation of their buildings. (Streets in leftist municipalities across Greece, especially the islands, still commemorate the "Heroes of the Polytechnic".) The ruling clique lost its nerve; armoured vehicles stormed the Polytekhnío gates and a still-undetermined number of students (estimates range from tens to hundreds) were killed. Martial law was tightened and junta chief Colonel Papadopoulos was replaced by the even more noxious and reactionary General Ioannides, head of the secret police.

The return to civilian rule 1975–81

The end of the ordeal, however, came within a year as the dictatorship embarked on a disastrous political adventure in **Cyprus**, essentially the last playing of the Megáli Idhéa card. By attempting to topple the Makarios government and impose *énosis* (union with Greece) on the island, they provoked a

Turkish invasion and occupation of forty percent of Cypriot territory. The army finally mutinied, and **Constantine Karamanlis** was invited to return from Paris to take office again. He swiftly negotiated a ceasefire (but no durable solution) in Cyprus, withdrew temporarily from NATO and warned that US bases would have to be removed except where they specifically served Greek interest.

In November 1974 Karamanlis and his **Néa Dhimokratía (New Democracy) Party** were rewarded by a sizeable majority in **elections**, with a centrist and socialist opposition. The latter was the **Panhellenic Socialist Movement (PASOK)**, a new party led by Andreas Papandreou.

The election of Néa Dhimokratía was in every sense a safe conservative option, but to Karamanlis's enduring credit it oversaw an effective and firm return to democratic stability, even legalizing the KKE (Communist Party) for the first time in its history. Karamanlis also held a **referendum on the monarchy**; seventy percent of Greeks rejected the return of Constantine II, so he instituted in its place a French-style presidency, which he himself occupied from 1980 to 1985, and again from 1990 to 1995. Economically there were limited advances, although these were more than offset by inflationary defence spending (the result of renewed tension with Turkey), hastily negotiated entrance into the EC and the decision to let the drachma float after decades of its being artificially fixed at thirty to the US dollar.

Most crucially, Karamanlis failed to deliver vital reforms in bureaucracy, social welfare and education; and while the worst figures of the junta were brought to trial and jailed indefinitely, the face of Greek political life and administration was little changed. By 1981 inflation was hovering around 25 percent, and it was estimated that tax evasion was depriving the state of one-third of its annual budget. In foreign policy the US bases remained, and it was felt that Greece, back in NATO, was still acting as little more than an American satellite. The traditional Right had proved demonstrably inadequate to the task at hand.

PASOK 1981–89

Change ("*Allayí*") and Out with the Right ("*Ná Fíyi íy Dhexiá*") were the slogans of the election campaign that swept **PASOK** and Andreas Papandreou to power on October 18, 1981. This victory meant a chance for Papandreou to form the first socialist government in Greek history and to break a half-century monopoly of authoritarian right-wing rule. With so much at stake, the campaign had been passionate even by Greek standards, and PASOK's victory was greeted with euphoria both by the generation whose political voice had been silenced in the civil war, and by a large proportion of the young. Their hopes ran naïvely and perhaps dangerously high.

The electoral margin, at least, was conclusive. PASOK won 174 of the 300 parliamentary seats and the Communist KKE – though not part of the new government – returned thirteen deputies, one of them composer Mikis Theodhorakis, while Néa Dhimokratía moved into unaccustomed opposition. There appeared to be no obstacle to the implementation of a **radical programme**: devolution of power to local authorities, the effective nationalization of heavy industry, improvement of the woefully skeletal social services, a purge of bureaucratic inefficiency and malpractice, the end of bribery and corruption as a way of life, an independent and dignified foreign policy following expulsion of US bases and finally withdrawal from NATO and the European Community.

A change of style was promised, too, replacing the country's long traditions of authoritarianism and bureaucracy with openness and dialogue. Even more radically, given that Greek political parties had long been the personal followings of charismatic leaders, PASOK was to be a party of ideology and principle, dependent on no single individual member. Or so, at least, thought some of the youthful PASOK cadres.

The new era started with a bang. ELAS was officially recognized; hitherto they hadn't been allowed to take part in any celebrations, wreath-layings or other ceremonies commemorating the wartime Resistance. Peasant women were granted pensions for the first time – 3000 drachmas a month (about US$55 in 1982), the same as their outraged husbands – and wages were indexed to the cost of living. In addition, civil marriage was introduced, family and property law was reformed in favour of wives and mothers, the demanding of dowries was forbidden (though the practice still continues informally), and equal rights legislation was put on the statute book.

These quick, low-cost and popular reformist moves seemed to mark a break with the past, and the atmosphere had indeed changed. Greeks no longer lowered their voices to discuss politics in public or wrapped their leftist newspaper in the respectably conservative *Kathimerini*. At first there were real fears that the climate would be too much for the military who would once again intervene to choke a dangerous experiment in democracy, especially when Andreas Papandreou, imitating his father, briefly assumed the defence portfolio himself. But he went out of his way to soothe military susceptibilities, increasing their salaries, buying new weaponry and being fastidious in his attendance at military functions. Moreover, the resistance of the Polytekhnío students to the 1967–74 junta was mythologized, and PASOK activists could be counted on to form human cordons around party headquarters at the least sign of unrest in the armed forces.

The end of the honeymoon

Papandreou promised a populist bonanza which he must have known, as an academically trained economist, was strictly fantasy. As a result he pleased nobody. He could not fairly be blamed for the inherited lack of investment, low productivity, deficiency in managerial and labour skills and other chronic problems besetting the Greek economy. However, he certainly aggravated the situation early in his first term by allowing his supporters to indulge in violently anti-capitalist rhetoric – which frightened off potential investors – and by the prosecution and humiliation of the Tsatsos family, owners of one of Greece's few competitive businesses (Hercules Cement), for the illegal export of capital, something of which every Greek with any savings was guilty. These were cheap victories, not backed by any rational public investment programme, and the only nationalizations were of hopelessly lame-duck companies.

Faced with a sluggish economy and burdened with the additional expense of (marginally) improved social benefits and wage-indexing, Papandreou's government also had to cope with the effects of **world recession**. Shipping, the country's main foreign-currency earner, was devastated. Remittances from émigré workers fell off as they became unemployed in their host countries, and tourism diminished under the dual impact of the recession and US President Ronald Reagan's warning to Americans to stay away from allegedly terrorist-vulnerable Athens airport.

With huge quantities of imported goods continuing to be sucked into the country in the absence of significant domestic production, the **foreign debt** topped £10 billion in 1986, while inflation remained at 25 percent and the balance of payments deficit approached £1 billion. Greece also began to experience the social strains of unemployment for the first time. Not that it didn't exist before, but it had always been concealed as underemployment because of numerous family-run businesses and the rural/seasonal nature of the economy – as well as by the absence of reliable statistics.

The second term

A modest spending spree, transparently intended to buy votes, continued satisfaction at the discomfiture of the Right, plus the popularity of his Greece-for-the-Greeks foreign policy gave Papandreou a second term with a **June 1985** electoral victory scarcely less decisive than the first; his complacent and frankly dishonest slogan was "Vote PASOK for Even Better Days". By October PASOK had imposed a two-year wage freeze and import restrictions, abolished the wage-indexing scheme and devalued the drachma by fifteen percent. Papandreou's fat was pulled out of the fire by none other than his *bête noire*, the European Community, which offered a huge two-part loan on condition that an IMF-style **austerity programme** was maintained.

The political price of such classic monetarist strategies, accompanied by shameless soliciting for foreign investment, was the alienation of the KKE and most of PASOK's own core constituency. Increasingly autocratic (ironic, given his earlier pledges of openness), Papandreou's response to **dissent** was to fire recalcitrant trade union leaders and expel some three hundred members of his own party. Assailed by strikes, the government stumbled badly, losing ample ground in the municipal elections of October 1986 to Néa Dhimokratía, including the mayoralties of the three major cities – Athens, Thessaloníki and Pátra – the first two retained by them ever since. Papandreou assured the nation that he had learned his lesson, but all that followed were two successive cabinet reshuffles, which saw the departure of most remaining PASOK veterans; the new cabinet was so unsocialist that even the right-wing press called it "centrist".

Similar about-faces took place in **foreign policy**. The first-term anti-US, anti-NATO and anti-EC rhetoric had been immensely popular, and understandable for a people shamelessly bullied by bigger powers since 1830. There was some high-profile nose-thumbing, such as refusing to join EC partners in condemning Jaruzelski's Polish regime or the Soviet downing of a Korean airliner. The "realistic" policies that Papandreou increasingly pursued during his second term were far more conciliatory towards his big Western brothers. Not least was the fact that US bases remained in Greece until 1994, largely owing to the fear that snubbing NATO would lead to Greece being exposed to Turkish aggression, still the only issue that united the main parties to any degree. As for the once-reviled **European Community** (soon to be the European Union), Greece had by now become an established beneficiary, and its leader was hardly about to bite the hand that feeds.

Scandal

Even as late as **mid-1988**, despite the many betrayals and failings of Papandreou, it seemed unlikely that PASOK would be toppled in the 1989 elections. This was due mainly to the lack of a credible alternative. **Constantine Mitsotakis**, a bitter personal enemy of Papandreou's since 1965, when his defection had brought down his father's government and set in motion the events that culminated in the junta, was an unconvincing and unlikeable character at the helm of Néa Dhimokratía. Meanwhile, the liberal centrist parties had disappeared, and the main Communist party, the KKE, seemed trapped in a Stalinist timewarp under the leadership of Harilaos Florakis. Only the **Ellenikí Aristerá (Greek Left)**, the Euro-Communist party spun off from the KKE, seemed to offer any sensible alternative, but they had a precariously small following.

However, a combination of spectacular blunders, plus a general shift to the Right influenced by the cataclysmic events in Eastern Europe, conspired against PASOK. First came the extraordinary **cavortings of the prime minister** himself. Late in 1988, 70-year-old Papandreou was flown to Britain for open-heart surgery. He took the occasion, with fear of death presumably rocking his judgement, to make public a year-long liaison with a 34-year-old Olympic Airways hostess, **Dimitra "Mimi" Liani**. Widespread media images of an old man shuffling about after a young, large-chested blonde, to the public humiliation of Margaret, his American-born wife, and his family, were not helpful (Papandreou soon divorced Margaret and married Mimi). His integrity was further dented when he missed important public engagements in order to relive his youth in flashy nightspots with his new wife.

The real damage, however, was done by a series of **economic scandals**, ranging from illegal arms deals to fraudulent farm-produce sales by assorted ministers. The most serious of these involved a self-made, Greek-American con-man, **Yiorgos Koskotas**, director of the Bank of Crete, who embezzled £120m (US$190m) of deposits and, worse still, slipped through the authorities' fingers on a private jet back to the US, where he had begun his career as a housepainter. Certain PASOK ministers and even Papandreou himself were implicated in this scandal.

United in disgust at this corruption, the other left-wing parties – KKE and Ellinikí Aristerá – formed a coalition, **Synaspismós**, siphoning off still more support from PASOK.

Three bites at the cherry

In this climate, an inconclusive result to the **June 1989 election** was unsurprising. Less predictable, however, was the formation of a bizarre "**kathársis**" **(purgative) coalition** of conservatives and Communists, expressly to cleanse PASOK's Augean stables.

Synaspismós would have formed a government with PASOK, but set an impossible condition for doing so – that Papandreou step down as prime minister. In the deal finally cobbled together between the Left and Néa Dhimokratía, Mitsotakis was denied the premiership, too, in favour of **Ioannis Tzanetakis**, a popular former naval officer who had led a mutiny against the junta.

During the three months that the coalition lasted, *kathársis* turned out to be largely a matter of burying the knife as deeply as possible into the ailing body of PASOK. Andreas Papandreou and three other ministers were officially indicted of involvement in the Koskotas affair – though there was no time to try them before the Greek people returned once again to the polls. In any case, the chief witness and protagonist, Koskotas himself, was still imprisoned in America, awaiting extradition proceedings.

Contrary to the Right's hope that publicly accusing Papandreou and his cohorts of criminal behaviour would pave the way for a Néa Dhimokratía victory, PASOK actually recovered slightly in the **November 1989 elections**, though the result was again inconclusive. This time the Left refused to do deals with anyone, resulting in a caretaker government under the neutral aegis of

Xenophon Zolotas, reluctantly dragged into the prime minister's office from the rectorship of Athens University. His only mandate was to keep the country on the rails while preparations were made for yet another election.

These took place in **April 1990** with the same party leaders *in situ*, and with Synaspismós having completed its about-turn to the extent that in the five single-seat constituencies (the other 295 seats were drawn from multiple-seat constituencies in a complex system of reinforced proportional representation), they supported independent candidates jointly with PASOK. Greek communists are good at about-turns, though; after all, composer Mikis Theodorakis, musical torch-bearer of the Left during the dark junta years, and formerly a KKE MP, was now standing for Néa Dhimokratía, prior to his resignation from politics altogether.

On the night, Néa Dhimokratía scraped home with a majority of one, later doubled with the defection of a centrist, and Mitsotakis finally realized his long-cherished dream of becoming prime minister. The only other memorable feature of the election was the first parliamentary representation for an independent member of the Turkish minority in Thrace, and in Attica for the Greens – a focus for many disaffected PASOK voters.

A return to the Right: Premier Mitsotakis

On assuming power, Mitsotakis prescribed a course of **austerity measures** to revive the chronically ill economy. Little headway was made, though given the world recession that was hardly surprising. Greek inflation was still approaching twenty percent annually, and at nearly ten percent, unemployment remained stubbornly high. Other measures introduced by Mitsotakis included laws to combat strikes and **terrorism**. The latter had been a perennial source of worry for Greeks since the appearance in 1974 of a group called **Dhekaeftá Novemvríou** ("November 17", the date of the colonels' attack on the Polytekhnío in 1973). Before their unmasking in 2002 (see p.579), they (and one or two copycat groups) managed to kill 24 industrialists, politicians and NATO military personnel, rob numerous banks and inflict massive damage to the property of foreign corporations in Athens. It hardly seemed likely that Mitsotakis's laws, however, were the solution. They stipulated that November 17's long-winded, ideologically contorted statements could no longer be published, which led to one or two newspaper editors being jailed for a few days for defiance – much to everyone's embarrassment. The **anti-strike laws** threatened severe penalties but were equally ineffectual, as breakdowns in public transport, electricity and rubbish collection all too frequently illustrated.

As for the Koskotas scandal, the man himself was eventually extradited and gave evidence for the prosecution against Papandreou and various of his ministers. The trial was televised and proved as popular as any soap opera, given its twists of high drama – which included one of the defendants, Agamemnon "Menios" Koutsoyiorgas, dying in court of a heart attack in front of the cameras. The case against Papandreou gradually ran out of steam and he was officially acquitted (by a margin of one vote on the tribunal panel) in early 1992. The two other surviving ex-ministers, Tsovolas and Petsos, were convicted, given jail sentences (bought off with a heavy fine) and barred from public office for a time.

The great showcase trial thus went out with a whimper and did nothing to enhance Mitsotakis's position. If anything, it served to increase sympathy for Papandreou, who was felt to have been unfairly victimized. The indisputable villain of the piece, Koskotas, was eventually convicted of major fraud and is serving a lengthy sentence at the high-security Korýdhallos prison.

The Macedonian question

The last thing the increasingly unpopular Mitsotakis needed was a major foreign policy headache. That is exactly what he got when, in 1991, one of the breakaway republics of the former Yugoslavia named itself **Macedonia**, thereby injuring Greek national pride and sparking off vehement protests at home and abroad. Diplomatically, the Greeks fought tooth and nail against anyone's recognizing the breakaway state, let alone its use of the name "Macedonia", but their position became increasingly isolated, and by 1993 the new country had gained official recognition from both the EU and the UN – albeit under the provisional title of the Former Yugoslav Republic of Macedonia (FYROM).

Salt was rubbed into Greek wounds when the FYROM started using the "Star of Vergina" (and of the ancient Macedonian kings) as a national symbol on their new flag, allegedly printed a banknote portraying the White Tower of Thessaloníki (Solun in Macedonian) and retained passages in its constitution referring to "unredeemed" Aegean territories. Greece still refuses to call its neighbour Macedonia, instead referring to it as Proín Yugoslavikí Dhimokratía Makedhonás, or *Tá Skópia* after its capital.

The ongoing argument for legitimacy hinges mostly on whether the ancient Macedonian kings were pure-bred Hellenes (the Greek position), Hellenized barbarians (the neutral conclusion) or proto-Slavs (the Macedonian claim).

The pendulum swings back

The Macedonian problem effectively led to Mitsotakis's political **demise**. Mitsotakis had also been plagued for many months by accusations of phone-tapping and theft of antiquities to stock his large private collection in Crete, plus links with a complicated contracts scandal focused on the national cement company. In the early summer of 1993 his ambitious and disaffected foreign minister, **Andonis Samaras**, jumped on the bandwagon of resurgent Greek nationalism to set up his own party, **Politikí Ánixi (Political Spring)**. His platform, still right-wing, was largely based on action over Macedonia, and during the summer of 1993 more **Néa Dhimokratía** (ND) MPs defected, making Politikí Ánixi a force to be reckoned with. When parliament reconvened in September to approve severe new budget proposals, the government failed to muster sufficient support, and early **elections** were called for **October 1993**.

On October 11, Papandreou romped to election victory; ND lost in 85 percent of the constituencies and the Synaspismós was replaced as the third party in parliament by Samaras's Politikí Ánixi and the unreconstructed Communists, now under Aleka Papariga. The youthful Miltiades Evert, ex-mayor of Athens, replaced Mitsotakis as head of Néa Dhimokratía, so that – along with ex-KKE head Florakis – two of the dinosaurs of post-junta politics had passed from the scene.

The morning after

Thus a frail-looking Papandreou, now well into his seventies, became prime minister for the third time. He soon realized that he was not going to have nearly so easy a ride as in the 1980s.

PASOK immediately fulfilled two of its pre-election promises by removing restrictions on the reporting of terrorists' communiques and de-privatizing the Athens city bus company. The new government also set about improving the health system, and began proceedings for Mitsotakis to be tried for his purported misdemeanours, though all charges were mysteriously dropped in January 1995, prompting allegations of an under-the-table deal between Papandreou and his old nemesis.

The root of popular dissatisfaction remained **the economy**, still in dire straits. Nor could PASOK claim to have won any diplomatic battles over Macedonia, despite a lot of tough posturing. The only concrete move was the imposition in October 1993 of a **trade embargo** on the FYROM, which merely landed the Greeks in trouble with the European Court of Justice – and succeeded in virtually shutting down the port of Thessaloníki. By contrast, alone among NATO members, Greece was conspicuous for its open **support of Serbia** in the wars wracking ex-Yugoslavia, ostentatiously breaking that particular embargo with supply trucks to Belgrade via Bulgaria.

In autumn 1994, for the first time ever in a PASOK-sponsored reform, provincial governors were directly elected in regional elections, rather than appointed from Athens. The following spring, **presidential elections** were held in parliament to designate a successor to the 88-year-old Karamanlis, who enjoyed just three years of well-deserved retirement before his death in spring 1998. The winner, supported by Politikí Ánixi and PASOK, was **Kostis Stefanopoulos**, ex-head of the dissolved party DIANA (Democratic Renewal). Untainted by scandal, if a bit of a nonentity, he had been nominated by Samaras and accepted by Papandreou in a deal that would allow PASOK to see out its term without ructions.

In November, Greece lifted its embargo on "Macedonia", opening the borders for tourism and trade in return for the FYROM suitably editing its constitution and removing the offending emblem from their flag. Relations, in fact, were instantly almost normalized, with only the name still a moot point; perennial possibilities include "New Macedonia" or "Upper Macedonia", though as of writing the place was still being referred to as the FYROM by most outsiders.

The end of an era

However, the emerging critical issue was the 76-year-old Papandreou's obstinate clinging to power despite obvious signs of dotage. Numerous senior members of PASOK became increasingly bold and vocal in their criticism, no longer fearing expulsion or the sack as in the past.

By late 1995, Papandreou was in intensive care at the Onassis hospital, dependent on life-support machinery. As there was no constitutional provision for replacing an infirm (but alive) prime minister, the country was essentially rudderless for two months, until the barely conscious old demagogue finally faced up to his own mortality and signed a letter **resigning** as prime minister (though not as party leader) in January 1996. The "palace clique" of Mimi Liani and cohorts was beaten off in the parliamentary replacement vote in favour of the allegedly colourless but widely respected technocrat **Kostas**

Simitis, who seemed to be just what the country needed after years of incompetent flamboyance.

Upon assuming office, Simitis indicated that he wouldn't necessarily play to the gallery as Papandreou had with (for a Greek politician) this remarkable statement:

Greece's intransigent nationalism is an expression of the wretchedness that exists in our society. It is the root cause of the problems we have had with our Balkan neighbours and our difficult relations with Europe.

These beliefs were immediately put to the test by a tense armed stand-off with Turkey over the uninhabited Dodecanesian double-islet of **Ímia**, which very nearly degenerated into a shooting war. Simitis eventually bowed to US and UN pressure and ordered a withdrawal of Greek naval forces, conceding "disputed" status to the tiny goat-grazed outcrops – in hindsight a wise decision, but one for which at the time he was roundly criticized in parliament by fire-eating ND MPs and the media.

Papandreou finally succumbed to his illness on June 22, 1996, prompting a moving display of national mourning; it was genuinely the end of an era, with only Karamanlis (who died less than two years later) and junta colonel Papadopoulos (who died, still incarcerated, in June 1999) as the last remaining "dinosaurs" of postwar Greek politics. Already his canonization process proceeds apace, with a spate of streets renamed to honour him in provincial towns where he was always revered, but the long-term **verdict of history** is likely to be harsher. Papandreou the Younger valued sycophancy over ability, and in his declining years was completely manipulated by the "palace clique". Alleged Bank of Crete transactions aside, he also enjoyed indubitable success as a "common cheat" (as described by Karamanlis in his tart memoirs), dying with a huge fortune which he could not possibly have amassed on a public servant's salary.

Simitis two, ND nil

Papandreou's death was promptly followed by PASOK's summer conference, where Simitis ensured his survival as party leader by co-opting his main internal foe, Papandreou's former head of staff, Akis Tsohadzopoulos (subsequently defence and development minister), with a promise of future high office. Following the summer congress, Simitis cleverly rode the wave of pro-PASOK sympathy caused by Papandreou's death and called **general elections** a year early in **September 1996**.

The **results** were as hoped for: 162 seats for PASOK versus 108 for Néa Dhimokratía despite a margin of only three percentage points, the winner's strength artificially inflated by a convoluted electoral law. Given that the two main parties' agendas were virtually indistinguishable, the core issues boiled down to which was better poised to deliver results – and whether voters would be swayed by ND chief Evert's strident Slav- and Turk-baiting nationalism (they weren't). The biggest surprise was the collapse of Samaras's Politikí Ánixi, which failed to clear the three-percent nationwide hurdle for parliamentary representation, but three leftist splinter parties did well: eleven seats and just over five percent for Papariga's KKE; ten seats (including one

Thracian Muslim deputy) with about the same tally for the Synaspismós under new chief Nikos Konstantopoulos; and nine seats at just under five per-cent for the Democratic Social Movement (DIKKI), founded early in the year by rehabilitated ex-minister Tsovolas to push for 1980s-vintage leftist policies. Evert resigned as ND leader, and was succeeded by Karamanlis's nephew Kostas. Néa Dhimokratía was down but by no means out; in the **June 1999** Euro-elections the party finished first nationwide and sent forty percent of Greece's Euro MPs to Strasbourg.

Simitis's first-term problems arose mainly from the economic squeeze caused by continuing **austerity measures**. In December 1996, protesting farmers closed off the country's main road and rail arteries for several weeks, before dis-mantling the blockades in time for people to travel for the Christmas holidays. Much of 1997 saw teachers or students (or both) on strike over proposed edu-cational reforms – essentially about imposing some discipline on the notori-ously lax school regimens. September 1997 also saw a timely boost to national morale and economic prospects with the awarding of the 2004 **Olympic Games** to Athens. Simitis sensibly warned against people treating it as an excuse merely for unbridled money-making projects, and hopefully more sub-stantial and long-lasting benefits will accrue.

Simitis, by nature far more pro-European than his maverick predecessor, devoted himself to the unenviable task of getting the Greek economy in suffi-ciently good shape to meet the criteria for **monetary union**. The *Eforía*, or Greek Inland Revenue, made some highly publicized headway in curbing the largest **black economy** in the EU, by requiring meticulous documentation of transactions and by publicly "outing" the more flagrant tax-dodgers.

After some initial success with his "hard drachma" policy (often propping it up by dumping foreign currency reserves), Simitis was obliged to devalue it upon Greece's **entry to the ERM** in March 1998; however, with other internationally traded currencies badly exposed in the Far East economic crises, the drachma regained prior levels by October 1998. The fact that infla-tion stayed consistently down in single figures for the first time in decades was testament to Simitis's ability as an economist; indeed his nickname, amongst both foes and supporters, was *o loyistís*, "the accountant". Simitis also had the sense to delegate to the capable, and to refrain from meddling, such that his finance minister, Yannos Papantoniou, enjoyed an unprecedented nine years in the job.

Increasingly amicable relations with its Balkan neighbours – Greece is one of the largest foreign investors in Bulgaria and the FYROM, for example – has the potential to generate jobs and trim unemployment, habitually just over nine percent officially (though among recent graduates it remains close to twenty percent). But the most dramatic **improvement in international relations** occurred with old nemesis Turkey, brought about by the severe **earthquake** which struck northern Athens on September 7, 1999, killing scores and render-ing almost one hundred thousand homeless. It came less than a month after the devastating tremor in northwest Turkey, and proved to be the spur for a thaw between the two historic rivals. Greeks donated massive amounts of blood and foodstuffs to the Turkish victims, and were the earliest foreign rescue teams on hand in Turkey; in turn they saw Turkish disaster-relief squads among the first on the scene in Athens. Soon afterwards**, Foreign Minister George Papandreou** (son of Andreas) announced that Greece had dropped its long-time opposition to EU financial aid to Turkey in the absence of a solution to the outstanding Cyprus and Aegean disputes, and further indicated that Greece would no longer oppose Turkish candidacy for accession to the EU.

With his handling of the Turkish détente and progress towards EMU the main campaign issues, Simitis called **elections** five months earlier than required, on **April 9, 2000**. In the event, PASOK squeaked into office for an unprecedented third consecutive term by a single percentage point, 43.7 to ND's 42.7, with 158 seats against 125. The crucial factor that swung the cliff-hanger – not decided until 1am the day after – was voters' mistrust of Karamanlis the Younger's manifest inexperience. The KKE held steady at just over five percent and eleven seats, but Synaspismós barely cleared the three-percent hurdle for its six seats, while DIKKI didn't.

Simitis capped his narrow victory by announcing Greece's official **entry into the euro currency zone** on June 20, at an EU summit in Portugal. He needed this bit of good news, as the country's international reputation had again taken a battering on June 8, when the terror group November 17 emerged from a couple of years' quiescence by assassinating **Brigadier Stephen Saunders**, the UK military attaché, while his car was stalled in Athens traffic. There were various mutterings abroad (again, especially in the US) that adequate security could not be guaranteed for the forthcoming, Greece-hosted Olympics. In July, the Orthodox Church mounted a last-ditch attack on the **new-style national identity cards**, which omitted to state the bearer's religion; government spokesmen proclaimed that the old-style cards were illegal under EU regulations, and an ND-sponsored bill to allow for optional citation of religious faith was defeated in parliament.

Tourism, the most important foreign-exchange earner for the country, had a pretty good year in 1999 despite a slow start occasioned by the Kosovo war, but a well-publicized spate of forest fires during an unusually hot summer, plus the *Express Samina* shipwreck (see box, p.42) conspired to make 2000 an *annus horribilis* for tourist arrival numbers. 2001 was another bad season, even before the September 11 terror incidents (which meant no significant American arrivals for many months); 2002 saw the wettest summer in memory, while 2003 was blighted by murmurings of unwarranted euro-price inflation and an unsavoury sun-sand-and-sex image for the country in wake of the Faliráki incidents (see p.305). After so many lean years, those in the Greek hospitality industry are positively salivating at their prospects for the Olympic summer of 2004.

The run-up to the 2004 Olympics

Though Scotland Yard operatives had been helping their Greek opposite numbers in investigations of the Saunders murder (see above), in the end it was a stroke of luck which led to the **demise of November 17**. On June 29, 2002, a bomb prematurely exploded in the hands of one Stavros Xeros, ostensibly a 40-year-old icon painter but in reality a principal operative of the group. Severely wounded on a Pireás street, Xeros was picked up by police, who following his partial recovery in hospital extracted from him the location of two arms- and explosives-laden safehouses in central Athens, along with the names of numerous other group members. By mid-July, November 17's intellectual godfather, Alexandros Giotopoulos, had been arrested in the act of attempting to leave his hideout on Lipsí island. After a nine-month trial before a tribunal of three judges, in a purpose-built courtroom inside Korýdhallos high-security prison, guilty verdicts – and multiple life sentences – were handed down to fifteen out of the nineteen accused, thus ringing the curtain down on Europe's longest-lived "Red Terrorist" saga.

Notwithstanding the unravelling of November 17 and the kudos which presumably should have accrued to the ruling party, the October 2002

municipal and prefectural elections saw PASOK stumble badly, with opposition Néa Dhimokratía gaining a plurality of mayoral offices and doing nearly as well on the provincial level. Anti-incumbent sentiment, after 19 out of 23 years at the helm, was clearly growing amongst the Greek electorate, although no hint of scandal attached to Simitis personally. On January 7, 2004, Simitis did what he'd long promised, a first for a sitting Greek prime minister – effectively resign, naming Foreign Minister George Papadreou to lead PASOK into the impending election. In doing so, Simitis signalled his belief that one of his main reforms had been completed: the end of personality-based politics, and the completed evolution of an issue-based, centrist, technocratic party.

Despite this, and Papandreou's prompt deselecting of ten MPs in Macedonia who'd been caught with their hands in various cookie jars, PASOK was trounced decisively in the **parliamentary elections** of March 7, 2004. With 45.4 percent of the vote, ND got a comfortable parliamentary majority of 165 seats, versus 40.5 percent and 117 seats for PASOK. The KKE and Synaspismos held steady at twelve and six seats respectively, while extreme-right LAOS and DIKKI failed to clear the three-percent hurdle for parliamentary representation. New Prime Minister Karamanlis – who had never held ministerial office before – listed his immediate priorities as shepherding a satisfactory conclusion to ongoing negotiations over divided Cyprus, designed to get the whole island into the EU on May 1, 2004, and ensuring completion of all preparations for the **2004 Olympics** – to which end he assumed the portfolio of the Culture Ministry (which is overseeing the Games) himself.

As the Olympics approach ever closer, Greece has mounted an increasingly sophisticated public relations campaign for the return of the **Elgin marbles** from the British Museum. Then-Foreign Minister Papandreou travelled to London in June 2000 to state the Greek case and was heard sympathetically by Labour and Liberal Democrat MPs (the Tories walked out), but was ultimately rebuffed by Tony Blair's announcement that the UK had no intention of budging on the issue. But 2003 opinion polls showed a 3:1 majority amongst the British public in favour of some sort of return scheme. Greece has proposed "permanent loan" of the relics in a British Museum "annexe" in Athens (rather than "ownership"), reciprocated by loans of equally significant artefacts from Greece to the London galleries. Designs for a new three-level museum south of the Acropolis pointedly reserve the highest wing for the return of the Parthenon relics. Another potential quid pro quo for a gracious "return" could be vigorous Greek support for a London 2012 bid.

In terms of actual preparations for the Olympics themselves, the odds are that the numerous, cynical skeptics will be largely confounded, though nobody expects, post-September 11, that the Games will be as smooth-running or as friendly as Sydney 2000. At the time of writing, competion of the massive infrastructure projects to make Athens a viable venue is decidedly uneven, with considerable doubt that everything necessary will be done in time. Behind the rictus grins and cheery pronouncements of assorted local and visiting Olympic officialdom, it's difficult to discern the true state of play.

Greek society today

The following summary concentrates on recent, salient trends and can only give a flavour of the massive, ground-level changes which have occurred in

Greece since the late 1980s. First and foremost, it's a conspicuously wealthier, more **consumerist society** than before, with vast disparities in income, and imbued with rampant Thatcherism (in particular a mania for privatizing) long after that ideology has largely subsided in its homeland. Consuming interests in the most literal sense, essentially an over-reaction to wartime privation, have given rise to a nationwide explosion in **slimming centres**, mostly pushing fad diets or amphetamines rather than exercise, and exploiting Greeks' guilt at their record-breaking obesity. Athens, Thessaloníki and most large towns have their legions of **yuppies**, addicted to gourmet wines, properly made cappuccinos, designer accessories, fast cars and **travel**; even small-town agencies promote junkets to Thailand, the Maldives and Cuba (the current trendy favourites). Greek domestic tourism is also heavily marketed, in particular weekend breaks to "name" islands like Corfu, Santoríni, and Rhodes, or outdoor activity expeditions to the mountains; there are numerous Greek-language travel magazines, Sunday supplements and bound guides, advising the yuppies where to spend their cash.

In tandem with this increased materialism, the national **Orthodox Church**, under the reactionary, publicity-seeking Archbishop Khristodhoulos of Athens, has declined from "guardian of the nation" to something of a national embarrassment. Rather than address the pressing social problems and hidden poverty occasioned by Greece's immigration crisis (see p.582), its version of moral leadership has been to organize demos against the new secularized ID cards (see p.579), and (more understandably) to extract from Pope John Paul II, during his May 2001 visit, an apology for the 1204 sacking of Constantinople. But the Church's medieval mindset is best exemplified in its continued ban on cremation, and near-hysteria on the subject of bar codes. Greece is the only EU country where cremation is forbidden; every summer there's a malodorous backlog of corpses awaiting interment at the overcrowded cemeteries, whilst other remains are surreptitiously sent (under threat of excommunication) to be burnt in more accommodating Bulgaria or Romania. Orthodox doctrine is adamant that immolation would compromise the Resurrection, and that the bones of a saint (revered as relics) might thus be destroyed. Bar codes on ID cards and hand- or forehead-stamping for casino patrons and bank employees have really excercised the clergy, in particular Athonite monks. They, and a considerable number of lay believers, see this as a Jewish-Masonic conspiracy, fulfilling Revelations 13:16–17 and 14:9, verses which relate to the Mark of the Beast.

The clergy's rantings notwithstanding, bar-coded Greece is now firmly locked into the **global economy**, and not just in the matter of cross-border shipment of the dead. International franchises such as McDonalds, Next, Häagen Dazs and The Body Shop proliferate in most larger towns; consumer interest rates have plunged while credit cards are aggressively marketed, the Athens stock exchange burgeoned (before crashing spectacularly, prompting a wave of suicides by those who lost their savings), and foreign or multinational companies have flocked to invest. It is they who have largely funded and executed massive infrastructure improvements designed to long outlast the 2004 Olympics: the airport at Spáta, the Athens metro and a mooted tramway for Thessaloníki, the Río-Andírio bridge over the Gulf of Kórinthos and the Via Egnatia expressway across Epirus, Macedonia and Thrace. **Overseas companies** are also quietly **acquiring** more (or less) productive elements of the Greek economy; Britain's Blue Circle, for example, in 1998 purchased Hercules Cement from Italian interests, though after years of trying there are still no takers for red-ink-submerged Olympic Airways, which will probably be allowed to go bust under EU pressure after the Olympics, and reconstituted without its surplus staff. The repeatedly postponed end of cabotage – whereby only Greek companies have been allowed to provide ferry services within Greece – is now set for 2007, and should weed out the flakier shipping companies and have the others pulling their socks up, under threat of potential challenges by the likes of P&O or Fred Olsen. Matters can only get better since the *Express Samina* sinking, which fully exposed the weaknesses in safety, pricing and personnel training of Greek Aegean transport – and most of all the oligopolies which have resulted from domestic companies following overseas examples and engaging in extensive **corporate takeovers**. Hellas Flying Dolphins, the responsible party in the shipwreck, had acquired Ceres Hydrofoils, several smaller steamship outfits and a majority interest in an airline, to become the largest domestic transport company; Alpha Bank absorbed the troubled Ionian/Ioniki Bank in early 1999 and instantly became the second largest banking/insurance group in the country.

It used to be that a lifetime sinecure with the civil service was the goal for most graduates, but no longer – now young people crave a **career** in the private sector, with unlimited salary prospects, and will initially work for low pay which older, less-qualified professionals with families – who often must cobble together part-time jobs – simply can't live on. Yet most Greeks have now become too grand for menial jobs; the late Andreas Papandreou once grumbled that Greece shouldn't remain "a nation of waiters", though it seems he needn't have worried.

Greece may continue to occupy the EU's economic cellar with Portugal, but it's still infinitely wealthier (and more stable) than any of its neighbours, and this has acted as a magnet for **a permanent underclass of immigrants**. Since 1990 they have arrived in numbers estimated variously at 800,000 to well over a million, a huge burden for a not especially rich country of just over ten million native citizens (imagine Britain with six million refugees rather than a few hundred thousand). These days your waiter, hotel desk clerk or cleaning lady is most likely to be Albanian, Bulgarian or Romanian, to cite the three largest groups of arrivals. There are also significant communities of Pakistanis, Egyptians, Poles, Bangladeshis, Syrians, Filipinos, Ukrainians, Russians, equatorial Africans, Kurds and Georgians (not to mention ethnic Greeks from the Caucasus) – a striking change in what had hitherto been a homogeneous, parochial culture.

The **Greek response** to this has been decidedly mixed; the Albanians, making up roughly half the influx, are almost universally detested (except for the ethnic-Greek northern Epirots), and blamed for all manner of social ills. For the first time, crime – especially burglaries – is a significant issue, with a brisk trade in alarms and "beware of guard dog" notices. The newcomers have also prompted the first anti-immigration measures with teeth in a country whose population is more used to being on the other side of such laws – Greece is a member of the Schengen visa scheme and sees itself, as in past ages, as the first line of defence against the barbarian hordes from the Orient. All of the east Aegean islands regularly receive boatloads of people fleeing from every country in Asia, and Greece's single official refugee camp (near Lávrio) is grossly inadequate. In June 2001, as an attempt to cope, legal residence was offered to the estimated half-a-million illegals who could demonstrate two years' presence in Greece, and pay a hefty amount for retroactive social security contributions. But when this initial **amnesty period** ended in early September, fewer than 350,000 of these individuals had applied to be "regularized", and the arduous red tape involved meant that subsequent amnesties netted hardly any more successful applicants.

That said, the "illegals" are unlikely to be deported en masse any time soon; they do the difficult, dirty and dangerous work that Greeks now disdain, especially farm labour, restaurant prep work and rubbish collection. From an employer's point of view, they are cheap – thirty to forty percent less costly than natives – and the **net contributors** to the social welfare system, especially in respect of pensions where Greece, like much of southern Europe, is seeing its population shrinking and aging. The Albanians in particular are also buoying up much of the banking system by their phenomenal saving habits and wiring of funds home, so much so that the National Bank has installed ATMs with Albanian-language instructions.

On a further positive note, these diverse groups, increased travel abroad by the Greeks themselves, touring bands and dance companies and programmes on the private television channels have created a taste for **non–Greek music and foods**. One doesn't always have to wait for the summer festivals to see famous jazz, blues or soul acts in Thessaloníki or Athens, and there are now decent foreign-cuisine restaurants there as well as in many of the major resorts. All of these factors, however, have had the effect of making Greece less identifiably Greek and, it must be said, of making the native Greeks themselves rather less welcoming and more self-absorbed than formerly.

C

Mythology, an A to Z

While all ancient cultures had their **myths**, those of ancient Greece have had the greatest influence on Western civilization. The Trojan War, the wanderings of Odysseus, the adventures of Hercules – these and many other stories have inspired some of the finest literature, music and art.

Homer and his followers were the first bards to codify some of the stories in around 800 BC, but they had existed in the oral tradition for many years, and it was another few centuries before Homeric epics were actually written down and other legends set forth in **Hesiod's** *Theogeny*. With the ritual enactment of the myths in their religious festivals and ceremonies, along with their representation in designs on their pots and the performances of the stories at theatre and drama competitions, Greek myth and culture became inextricably blended.

Many versions of the myths exist, some of which are contradictory and confusing. Below is a summary of the principal **gods** and **heroes**. For further reading Pierre Grimal's *Dictionary of Classical Mythology* is a good reference, but perhaps the best starting point and a way into feeling how the myths might have been told is to read Homer's epics *The Iliad* and *The Odyssey*.

Agamemnon See Atreus, or Trojan War.

Aphrodite When Kronos castrated Ouranos and threw his testicles into the sea off Cyprus, the water spumed and produced Aphrodite, which means "born from sea foam". Her most famous shrines were at Paphos (Cyprus), Knidos on the Anatolian coast and on Lésvos. Aphrodite's magic girdle made people fall in love with the wearer, but her famed adultery with Ares ended badly when she became ensnared in the nets that Hephaistos, her husband, had made to expose her infidelity. She restored her virginity, but later had an affair with Hermes which produced a double-sexed offspring – Hermaphroditos. She particularly favoured the mortal Paris, instigator of the Trojan War.

Apollo The illegitimate son of Zeus and the nymph Leto, Apollo was god of the sun, of plagues and, conversely, of healing. He killed the Python snake that terrorized the land around Delphi, a location with which he subsequently had great associations (his other two main precincts were on the islet of Delos, his purported birthplace, and Letoön in Asia Minor). His shrine at Delphi was, with Olympia, considered one of the centres of the Hellenic world, and through the priestess of the oracle here, the god gave prophecies to pilgrims. Outstandingly beautiful Apollo represented music and poetry, and was usually depicted with either a bow and arrow or a lyre, which was a gift to him from Hermes. He was not generally unlucky in love, but was famously spurned by Daphne.

Ares The god of war and the only legitimate son of Zeus and Hera, Ares had few associations with myths or temples – not surprisingly, given Zeus's famous utterance that Ares was the most hateful of all his offspring. Usually attended by his demon henchmen Deimos (Terror) and Phobos (Fear), Ares was not, however, uniformly victorious – in *The Iliad* he was more than once outwitted by Athena.

Argonauts See Jason and the Argonauts.

Ariadne See Theseus, Ariadne and the Minotaur.

Artemis Apollo's twin sister, Artemis was the goddess of hunting, the moon, unmarried maidens and indeed all of nature beyond the city. Her epithet was "Mistress of the Animals" and she was typically attended by trains of nymphs and lions. Artemis was always described as a virgin endowed with perpetual youth; she also had a dark aspect that involved human sacrifice at some of her rites. Furthermore, she killed the huntsman Orion who tried to rape her, and instigated the death of Actaeon, who had seen her bathe naked, by changing him into a stag and setting his own hounds upon him. Her most important shrines were at Brauron in Attica, at Sparta and at Ephesos in Asia Minor.

Athena Athena did not have a conventional birth – she sprang fully formed out of the head of Zeus ready for battle with armour, helmet and spear. Hephaistos had split Zeus's forehead for the "birth" to occur, and then attempted to ravish her; she remained a virgin, but some of his semen which he flicked off her thigh fell to earth, where it grew up as her son Ericthonius-Erechtheus, legendary first king of Athens. She was accordingly the protectress and namesake of that city and by extension all others, and was regarded as the goddess of both war and certain more peaceable crafts and trades vital to civilized life: olive culture, wool-gathering, spinning, ship-building, chariots and horse tackle. Her many temples are typically on city acropoles or centres; she was ever ready to intervene on behalf of favourite mortals, particularly Odysseus and Hercules.

Atlas See Hercules.

Atreus, House of A dynasty haunted by revenge, murder, incest and tragedy. Atreus hated his younger brother Thyestes, and when their separate claims for the kingship of Mycenae were voiced, the gods promoted Atreus. Atreus banished Thyestes, but learning that his wife had had an affair with him, Atreus feigned forgiveness and recalled him from exile. He then had Thyestes' sons murdered, cut up, cooked and fed to Thyestes. When Thyestes had finished eating, Atreus showed him the heads of his children, clarifying the true nature of the meal. He again banished Thyestes, who took refuge at Sikyon and, sanctioned by the gods, fathered Aegisthus by his daughter, Pelopia. Pelopia then married Atreus, her uncle, and Aegisthus (who did not know who his real father was) was brought up and cared for by Atreus. When Aegisthus came of age, Atreus instructed him to kill Thyestes, but Aegisthus found out the truth, returned to Mycenae and killed Atreus. Atreus's two sons were Agamemnon and Menelaos. Agamemnon paid for his father's crimes by dying at the hands of his wife Clytemnestra (who had committed adultery with Aegisthus while Agamemnon was fighting at Troy). She ensnared him in a net while he took a bath and stabbed him to death. She in turn was killed by her son Orestes, who was pursued by the Furies before being absolved of matricide by Athena.

Bacchus See Dionysos.

Centaurs and Lapiths The centaurs were monstrous beings with the heads and torsos of men and the lower bodies of horses. They lived a debauched life, feeding on raw flesh and enjoying the pleasures of wine, but were also considered particularly skilled in sorcery and herbal healing. There are tales of centaurs battling with Hercules on his quest to complete the Twelve Labours, but the most famous story is of the fight that broke out between them and the Lapiths, a race of heroes and warriors who were the descendants of the river god Pineos (the Piniós still flows near Mount Olympus). Pirithous, a Lapith of partial centaurean descent, invited them all to his wedding. At the feast the latter tried to abduct all the women, including the bride. A bloody brawl followed, of which the Lapiths were the victors; it is depicted on the pediment reliefs at Olympia, as a metaphor for the triumph of reason over barbarism.

Daphne The nymph Daphne was one of the daughters of the river god Pineos. Apollo took a fancy to her and chased her through the woods, but just as he caught up with her, she prayed to her father to save her. He took pity and turned her into a laurel tree, and she became rooted to the spot. Apollo loved her even as a tree and made the laurel sacred, dedicating wreaths of its leaves as a sign of honour. Her name, to this day, is the Greek word for the laurel tree.

Demeter Demeter was the goddess of agriculture, in particular corn, grain and pigs, as well as of death and regeneration. Both her origins and rites were shadowy, though we do know that women were her particular devotees. She exercised her power by making the whole Earth sterile after her daughter Persephone's abduction by Hades. The mother-and-daughter duo were usually revered together, particularly at their major sanctuary at Eleusis.

Dionysos Also known as Bacchus, Dionysos was the god of wine and mystic ecstasy. He was the son of Zeus by Semele, who during conception was consumed by the god in the form of a lightning-bolt; Zeus rescued the unborn child and sewed him up in his thigh for the full gestation period. On birth, he was conveyed by Hermes to a far-off realm to be reared by the nymphs, and as a small boy he was disguised as a girl to hide him from Hera. As a youth, he was abducted by pirates; Dionysos caused the ship to be overgrown with ivy and vines (henceforth his symbols) and in panic the pirates dived overboard to become the first dolphins. Thus at his festivals a commemorative miniature ship was carried or propelled on wheels, suitably decorated. In art he is often shown riding in a chariot drawn by panthers, and followed by a coterie of satyrs, sileni and mortal followers brandishing *thyrsoi* (wands topped with pine cones). Dionysos's semi-mythical women followers, the maenads (see p.589), roamed the countryside at certain seasons in a state of madness; more usually, he was revered in the form of a bearded mask on a column, the antecedent of the comic and tragic masks of theatre. He rescued Ariadne from Náxos following her abandonment there by Theseus.

Eurydice See Orpheus and Eurydice.

Golden Fleece See Jason and the Argonauts.

Hades Hades was the brother of Zeus and Poseidon, and when the cosmos was divided between them he was allotted the underworld. His name means "the invisible", because in the battle with Kronos and the Titans he concealed himself by wearing a magic helmet given to him by the Cyclops. To refer to him as Hades was thought to bring about his awesome anger, so the Greeks called him by his surname Pluto, which means "the rich" and alludes to the wealth that lies hidden underground. His wife was Demeter's daughter, Persephone. Rather than temples, he had suitably mysterious oracles, most notably at Ephyra in Epirus and that of Trophonios at Levadia.

Helen Helen was the daughter of Zeus, who appeared in the form of a swan to her mother Leda. She was believed to be the most beautiful woman in the world. Her husband Menelaos, king of Sparta, entertained the Trojans Paris and Aeneas and was foolish enough to leave them alone with her; Paris abducted her. Some sources say she went willingly, impressed by his beauty and wealth; others say she was raped. In either event her departure from Sparta was the cause of the Trojan War.

Hephaistos The god of fire, Hephaistos was a master craftsman. In his workshop on volcanic Límnos, where he was especially revered, he fashioned everything from jewellery to armour. Elsewhere his cult was less elaborated, except at Athens, where he had a sumptuous temple in honour of his role in siring Erechtheus (see Athena). He was made lame, and there are two conflicting versions of how he sustained his injuries: either they were inflicted when Zeus threw him from Olympus because he had defended Hera in a quarrel, or alternatively when Hera, who bore him, tossed him down to Límnos in disappointment at his ugliness. Clever as well as unprepossessing, he was married to Aphrodite, the most beautiful of the goddesses.

Hera Hera was Zeus's sister, wife and the most powerful of the goddesses – she wreaked her vengeance and jealousy on anyone whom Zeus seduced and the offspring of most of his encounters. Zeus punished her heavily for her anger against Hercules by suspending her from her wrists from Mount Olympus, weighing her ankles down with anvils, and whipping her. Despite her vindictive and irascible Homeric portrayal, she was the protecting deity of wives and marriage. Her totems and sacrificial animals were the cow, the cuckoo and the peacock; her principal temples were on Sámos, near Argos, at modern Perahóra and at Olympia.

Hercules (Herakles) Hercules was the superhero of the ancient world. A mighty hunter and sacrificer, he appealed to young men in particular. His mother was the mortal Alcmene, and his father Zeus. Jealous Hera sent two snakes to kill Hercules while he was still in his cradle, which he duly strangled, all good preparation for his Twelve Labours.

These were commanded by King Eurystheus of the Argolid, who was under the thrall of Hera. The tasks took him to the fringes of the known world, even involving his supporting it on his shoulders while Atlas took a break to lend him a hand in his final task. The Labours were: to kill the Nemean lion; to slay the many-headed Hydra monster at Lerna; to bring back the wild boar of Erymanthus alive; to hunt the Keryneian hind that was sacred to Artemis; to kill the man-eating birds at the Stymphalian Lake; to clean the stables of King Augeas; to bring back the untameable Cretan bull alive; to capture the flesh-eating horses of Diomedes; to fetch the girdle of the Amazon warrior queen; to fetch the herds of Geryon from beyond the edge of the ocean; to capture Cerberus the guard dog of the underworld gates; and finally to fetch the golden apples from the garden of the Hesperides.

Curiously for such a macho figure, Hercules spent a certain amount of time as a slave, or in drag, or both. During a fit of madness sent by Hera, he slew his wife and children at Thebes; in atonement he passed some years dressed as a woman in the court of Queen Omphale of Lydia.

His death was as dramatic as his life. Deianeira, his second wife, gave him a garment that she thought had magic powers and would prevent him from being unfaithful to her. When he put it on, it burned into his flesh; the cloak had, it seemed, been steeped in the blood of the centaur Nessos, who had been slain by Hercules in the act of attempting to rape Deianeira. (With his dying breath, Nessos got posthumous revenge by telling Deianeira that his blood was a love-philtre rather than poisonous.) Unable to bear the pain, Hercules built a funeral pyre and immolated himself. He was fully deified by Zeus – the only mortal or demigod to be so honoured.

Hermes Hermes was the son of Zeus and Maia, the daughter of Atlas. He was born in the Kyllene mountains of Arcadia, where his only major temple existed at Pheneos. A trickster figure, Hermes showed his mettle by inventing the lyre on the day of his birth, then stealing Apollo's sacred cattle, denying the deed to his brother. Zeus effected a reconciliation, and Hermes gave Apollo the lyre in exchange for the cattle and a golden staff.

Hermes was the god of commerce, thievery, herdsmen, travel and boundaries; rather than shrines he had herms, stone cairns or boundary-markers. In his role as Conductor of Souls, Hermes regularly crossed between the living and underworld. He was often depicted wearing winged shoes, a wide-brimmed hat and carrying the herald's staff which showed his position as the divine messenger.

Hippolytos and Phaedra Hippolytos, son of the hero Theseus and the Amazon Hippolyta, was an accomplished hunter who revered Artemis and scorned Aphrodite. Aphrodite sought to teach him a lesson and conspired for Phaedra, the new wife of Theseus, to fall in love with the young man. When she was spurned by Hippolytos she feared he might reveal her advances and so accused him of rape. When Theseus heard this, he called upon Poseidon to kill his son; Hippolytos was then flung from his chariot and torn apart by his horses. Phaedra in shame and remorse hanged herself.

Io A priestess of Hera at Argos, Io was only one of the many mortals who caught Zeus's eye, but before he could get to know her better, Hera got wind of his interest and Zeus hastily transformed Io into a cow. Hera demanded her as a present, and placed her under the guard of Argos, the hundred-eyed monster. Hera then proceeded to torment poor Io the cow by sending a stinging gadfly to goad her on her travels. She made for the sea, first to the Ionian Sea, which was named after her, and then crossed the straits into Asia at the Bosporus (literally, the "Cow Ford"). Before settling in Egypt, she wandered all over Asia, even bumping into Prometheus, who was chained for a few centuries to the Caucasus mountain range.

Jason and the Argonauts Jason, a Greek hero from Iolkos (near present-day Vólos), was the legitimate heir to the Thessalian throne, which had been usurped by his uncle Pelias. The latter received a prophecy that he would die at the hands of a one-sandalled man. When Jason appeared in his court, shod accordingly, the frightened Pelias attempted to get rid of him by sending him on what he hoped would be a fatal quest to the remote Black Sea kingdom of Colchis for the Golden Fleece. He assembled his crew, assorted heroes of the ancient Greek world, and commissioned a ship, called the *Argo* after its maker Argos, and built with the help of Athena and Hera – its prow had the remarkable gift of speech and prophecy. A long, incident-filled journey followed, including landfall at Límnos where the crew repopulated the island, the local women having previously murdered their menfolk. Some of the crew didn't complete the voyage, including Hercules who missed the boat because he was searching for his favourite, Hylas, a beautiful boy who had been abducted by the nymphs. Hera instructed the sea-nereids to carry the *Argo* past the dangerous Wandering Rocks, which would otherwise have smashed the ship. When Jason and his crew finally arrived in Colchis, King Aeëtes would not hand over the Golden Fleece unless Jason completed various labours. The king's daughter, the sorceress Medea (see opposite), fell in love with Jason and undertook to help him; they stole the fleece and fled, pursued by Aeëtes. Medea slowed down their pursuers by tearing up her brother Apsyrtus and casting his body parts into the sea, obliging Aeëtes to collect the pieces. Zeus was greatly angered by this heinous crime and the *Argo* spoke to the crew, telling them that they would have to purify themselves at Circe's island. After more wanderings through treacherous seas, the crew arrived at Iolkos, where Medea fulfilled the prophecy by doing away with Pelias, and then proceeded to Corinth where Jason dedicated the Golden Fleece to Poseidon.

Judgement of Paris The goddess Eris (Strife) began a quarrel between Athena, Hera and Aphrodite by throwing a golden apple between them and saying that it belonged to whichever goddess was the most beautiful. All the gods were too frightened to judge the contest, so Hermes took the goddesses to the top of Mount Ida for Paris, the son of Priam of Troy, to decide. Each used bribery to win his favour: Athena offered him wisdom and victory in combat, Hera the kingdom of Asia, but Aphrodite, the winner of the contest, offered him the love of Helen of Sparta.

Kronos The Titan Kronos was the youngest son of the pre-Olympian deities Gaia and Ouranos, who seized power in the heavens by castrating his father.

Once on the throne, Kronos lived in perpetual fear of the prediction that one of his offspring would one day overthrow him, and so he swallowed all of his children except Zeus – Zeus's mother Rhea had substituted a stone for the bundle that Kronos thought was his baby. Kronos and his Titan brothers were defeated in a cosmic battle by Zeus and his Olympian supporters.

Lapiths See Centaurs and Lapiths.

Maenads The maenads were the possessed or intoxicated female followers of Dionysos. They wore scanty clothes, had wreaths of ivy around their heads and played upon tambourines or flutes in their processions. They had power over wild animals, and in their frenzy they believed they drank milk or honey from freshwater springs. In their orgiastic ecstasies they tore limb from limb those who offended them, did not believe or who spied upon their rites – including Orpheus.

Medea Medea exacted gruesome revenge on any who stood against her. She persuaded the daughters of Pelias (see Jason and the Argonauts) to cut their father up and put him in a boiling cauldron, having convinced them that if they did so she could rejuvenate him. To their extreme disappointment, his body parts did not come back together. Akastos, Pelias's son, banished her and Jason as a punishment; they went together to Corinth, where Jason abandoned her to marry Kreusa the daughter of the local king Kreon. In revenge, Medea orchestrated a gruesome death for Kreusa by sending her a tunic which burst into flames when donned, and then murdered her own two young sons by Jason.

Minotaur See Theseus, Ariadne and the Minotaur.

Mount Olympus See Zeus.

Muses The Muses were the result of nine nights of lovemaking between Mnemosyne (Memory) and Zeus. They were primarily singers and the inspiration for music (to which they gave their name), but also had power over thought in all its forms: persuasion, eloquence, knowledge, history, mathematics and astronomy. Apollo conducted their singing around the Hippocrene fountain on Mount Helikon, or on Mount Olympus itself.

Nymphs There were various subspecies of nymph: meliads were the nymphs of the ash trees; nereids lived in the springs and streams; naïads in the ocean; dryads were individual tree nymphs; oreads were the mountain nymphs; and the alseids lived in the groves. They were thought to be the daughters of Zeus and attended certain deities, particularly Artemis and Poseidon.

Odysseus The word "odyssey" derives from Odysseus's ten-year journey home, which was no less fraught with danger, adventure and grief than the ten-year war against the Trojans which preceded it. Shipwrecked, tormented by the gods, held against his will by bewitching women, almost lured to his death by the hypnotic Sirens, witnessing his comrades devoured by the giant one-eyed Cyclops Polyphemos and all the time missing and desiring his faithful wife Penelope, Odysseus proved himself to be a great and scheming hero. At the end of his arduous journey he arrived in disguise at his palace on Ithaca to find suitors pestering his wife. He contrived a cunning trap and killed them all with a bow which only he could flex.

Oedipus Oedipus was a man profoundly cursed. The Delphic Oracle said that Laius, king of Thebes, should not father any children, for if he did one would kill him. When Oedipus was born Laius abandoned the baby, piercing his ankles with a nail and tying them together: hence the name, which means "swollen foot". But the baby was discovered and brought up at the court of the neighbouring king, Polybos, at Corinth. The same oracle revealed to the adult Oedipus that he would kill his father and marry his mother. When he heard this news he resolved not to return home to Corinth, but east of Delphi he met with Laius, who was heading west to consult the oracle as to how to rid Thebes of the Sphinx. Because the road was narrow, Laius ordered Oedipus to get out of the way, and when one of the guards pushed him, Oedipus drew his sword in anger and, not knowing that Laius was his father, killed him and most of his entourage. He then made his way to Thebes, where Laius had been king, and solved the riddle of the Sphinx. As a reward and in thanks, he was crowned king and offered Laius's widow Iocaste (his mother) in marriage. Plague then fell upon Thebes, because of the crimes of patricide and incest at the heart of the city. The Delphic Oracle instructed Oedipus to expel the murderer of Laius, and in his ignorance he ordered the guilty party cursed and banished. The seer and prophet Teiresias then revealed the full nature of the crime to Iocaste and Oedipus; she hanged herself and he put out his own eyes. He left the city as a vagabond accompanied by his daughter Antigone, and only at his death was granted peace. Attica, the country that received his dead body, became blessed.

Orpheus and Eurydice Orpheus was a great musician who received his lyre from Apollo himself. He played and sang so beautifully that wild beasts were charmed, trees would uproot themselves to come closer, and even the very rocks were moved. He enlisted in the crew of Argonauts and sang for them to row their oars in time. On his return from the *Argo*'s voyage he married the nymph Eurydice. She was bitten by a snake on the banks of the river Pineos and died, and Orpheus was so distraught that he went to the underworld to bring her back to life. His wish was granted by Hades on condition that during the return journey he would not look back at her. As the couple approached daylight, however, his mind became consumed with doubt and, turning around to see if she was behind him, he lost her forever. He preached that Apollo was the greatest god, much to the anger of Dionysos, who set the maenads on him. They tore him apart and cast his head, still singing, into the Thracian river Hebrus; it was finally washed up on the shores of the island of Lésvos, supposedly conferring great musical gifts on the local population.

Ouranos Ouranos was the personification of the sky and by his union with Gaia (Earth) fathered many children, including Kronos (see p.588) and the Titans (see p.592). Gaia became so exhausted by her husband's continual advances that she sought protection from her sons. Kronos was the only one to assist; he cut off Ouranos's testicles with a sickle and threw them into the sea, giving rise to Aphrodite.

Pan The patron of shepherds and flocks, Pan was the son of Hermes and a nymph and, with his beard, horns, hairy body and cloven hooves, was said to be so ugly that his own mother ran from him in fear. He had an insatiable libido, energetically pursuing both sexes. Apollo learned the art of prophecy from Pan, and hunters looked to him for guidance. He enjoyed the cool woodland shade and streams of Arcadia and relished his afternoon naps so much that he wreaked havoc if he was disturbed.

Pandora See Prometheus.

Pegasus See Poseidon.

Penelope See Odysseus.

Persephone Also known as Kore (the Maiden), Persephone was out picking flowers one day when the Earth opened up and swallowed her; she had been abducted by Hades riding his chariot. Her mother Demeter was distraught and when she found out the truth, she left Olympus in protest and made the Earth sterile so that it produced no crops. Zeus ordered Hades to return Persephone, but because she had eaten pomegranate seeds in the underworld she was bound to him. As a compromise, she would be allowed to return to Earth for two-thirds of the year and had to reside with Hades for the remaining third. Thus Demeter divided the year into seasons, so that while Persephone was with Hades the Earth would be wintry and sterile, and while she was on Earth the ground would be fertile for spring, summer and autumn.

Perseus A son of Zeus, and believed to be a direct ancestor of Hercules, Perseus was cast out to sea in a trunk with his mother Danae, because his grandfather feared a prophecy that Perseus would one day kill him. Danae and Perseus were washed up on Sérifos island, where they were discovered by a fisherman who looked after them. When Perseus came of age, the king of Sérifos demanded that he bring back the head of Medusa the gorgon, whose gaze could turn people to stone. Perseus acquired some special aids from Hermes and Athena to perform the task, including a helmet which made him invisible, and winged sandals to fly through the air. He cut off Medusa's head while looking at her reflection in Athena's polished shield. On his return flight he saw and fell in love with Andromeda, who was being offered as a sacrifice to a sea-monster. He rescued her and returned home to find his mother had been raped by the king. He held up the gorgon's head, turned the king to stone and then presented the head as a gift to Athena, who placed it in the middle of her shield. Perseus went on to participate in the king of Lárissa's celebratory games; he competed in the discus-throwing competition, but his throw went off course and killed his grandfather, who was a spectator, thus fulfilling the prophecy.

Phaedra See Hippolytos and Phaedra.

Poseidon Poseidon was the god of the sea, earthquakes and storms, and patron of fishermen. In the battle with Kronos and the Titans, Poseidon, the brother of Zeus, wielded the trident which he later used to shake both sea and land. After the victory he was awarded, by lot, the realm of the ocean, where he dwelt in the depths. He produced some strange offspring, including the Cyclops Polyphemos who had it in for Odysseus, and mated with the gorgon Medusa – which resulted in the winged horse Pegasus. He quarrelled frequently with the other gods, competing with them for power over some of the major cities including Athens, Corinth and Argos. Although he helped destroy Troy, as recounted in *The Iliad*, he also persecuted Odysseus mercilessly on his return home. Among his numerous temples, the most important were those at Isthmía, Soúnio and Póros near Athens; Mykale in Asia Minor; and an oracle at Cape Ténaro.

Prometheus For someone whose name means "forethought", Prometheus showed a distinct lack of it. In his desire to help mankind, he stole fire from the heavens and was immediately punished by Zeus, who bound him in chains, tied him to the Caucasus mountains and then sent an eagle to peck perpetually at his liver. Zeus then dealt with mankind by sending Pandora to Prometheus's brother Epimetheus (whose name means "afterthought") with a box that she had been told never to open. Her curiosity got the better of her and on peeping inside all the evils and one good (hope) were unleashed on the world. Prometheus gave some useful advice to Hercules when he passed by on one of his labours and Hercules rewarded him by setting him free.

Theseus, Ariadne and the Minotaur Theseus's father, Aegeus of Athens, sent him as a child away from Athens for his own safety. At sixteen the hero returned, in full strength and with the weapons that his father had set aside for him. Theseus was destined for a life of action, and his greatest adventure was to kill the Minotaur on Crete. As tribute from Athens, King Minos demanded six men and six women every nine years for sacrifice to the Minotaur – a gruesome beast, half-man half-bull, born from the bestial copulation of the queen Pasiphae with the huge bull sent by Poseidon. The Minotaur was kept in the labyrinth at Crete. Ariadne, Minos's daughter, had fallen in love with Theseus and contrived to help him kill the Minotaur. She gave him a ball of thread so that he would not lose his way in the labyrinth and then accompanied him in his flight from the island, only to be abandoned later on the island of Náxos. Dionysos saw her disconsolate on the shore, took pity on her and married her. Theseus, meanwhile, on his return to Athens forgot to change the black sails to white as a signal to his father that he was alive, and Aegeus – thinking that his son had been killed by the Minotaur – threw himself into the sea which took his name: the Aegean.

Titans The Titans were the six male children of Ouranos and Gaia. Their six sisters, who helped them father numerous gods, were called the Titanides. Kronos was the youngest Titan, and after he had overthrown his father he helped his brothers to power. The Titans lost their grip when they were toppled by the upstart Olympians, led by Zeus, in the cataclysmic battle called the Titanomachia.

Trojan War When Menelaos of Sparta realized that the Trojan Paris had made off with his wife Helen, he called on his brother Agamemnon of Mycenae. Together they roused the might of Greece to get her back. With just about every hero (Ajax, Achilles, Troilus, Hector, Paris, Odysseus, Priam, Diomedes, Aeneas) making an appearance in this epic, the story of the Trojan War is arguably the greatest tale from the ancient world. Homer's *Iliad* dealt with only one aspect of it, the wrath of Achilles. The ten-year war, fought over a woman and which sent many heroes' souls down to Hades, was finally won by the trickery of the Greeks, who used a huge wooden horse left ostensibly as a gift to the Trojans to smuggle an armed platoon inside the city walls. The cunning plan was thought to be the work of Odysseus, who, like many of the surviving heroes, had a less-than-easy journey home.

Zeus was the supreme deity, king of gods and men, but did not get to this position without a struggle. His father, the Titan Kronos, seized power in the heavens by castrating Ouranos the sky god, and in turn lived in fear that one of his own offspring would one day overthrow him. So he swallowed all of his children except Zeus, whose mother, Rhea, came to the rescue and hid him in a cave on the island of Crete, where the warrior Kouretes concealed his cries by smashing their swords and shields together. When he came of age, Zeus poisoned Kronos so that he vomited up all Zeus's siblings; with their help, and the assistance of the Cyclops, he cast Kronos and the Titans from Mount Olympus, the home of the gods. The Cyclops gave Zeus the thunderbolt as a weapon to use in the battle and it became his symbol of power, and emblem of his role as deity of weather and rain. Zeus used his position to maintain cosmic order, control the other gods and men and to get his way with whomever he fancied. Numerous myths tell of his metamorphoses to mate with a variety of mortals out of sight of his jealous wife Hera; all of his liaisons resulted in offspring, which included Hercules, Perseus and Helen.

Wildlife

For anyone who has first seen Greece at the height of summer with its brown parched hillsides and desert-like ambience, the richness of the wildlife – in particular the flora – may come as a surprise. As winter warms into spring, the countryside (and urban waste ground) transforms itself from green to a mosaic of coloured flowers, which attract a plethora of insect life, followed by birds. Islands well away from continental landmasses have had many thousands of years to develop their own individual species. Overall, Greece has around six thousand species of native flowering plants, nearly four times that of Britain but in the same land area. Many are unique to Greece, and make up about one-third of Europe's endemic plants.

Some background

In early antiquity Greece, including the islands, was thickly forested: Aleppo and Calabrian pines grew in coastal regions, giving way to fir or black pine up in the hills and low mountains. But this **native woodland** contracted rapidly as human activities expanded. By Classical times, a pattern had been set of forest clearance, followed by agriculture, abandonment to scrub and then a resumption of cultivation or grazing. Huge quantities of timber were consumed in the production of charcoal, pottery and smelted metal, and for ships and construction work. Small patches of virgin woodland have remained on the largest islands, but even these are under threat from loggers and arsonists.

Greek **farming** often lacks the rigid efficiency of northern European agriculture. Many peasant farmers still cultivate little patches of land, and even town-dwellers travel at weekends to collect food plants from the countryside. Wild greens under the generic term *hórta* are gathered to be cooked like spinach, and grape hyacinth bulbs are boiled as a vegetable. The buds and young shoots of capers, and the fruit of wild figs, carobs, plums, strawberry trees, cherries and sweet chestnuts are harvested. Emergent snails and mushrooms are collected after wet weather. The more resilient forms of wildlife can coexist with these uses, but for many Greeks only those species that have practical uses are regarded as having any value. Nowadays, better access to heavier earth-moving machinery means a farmer can sweep away an ancient meadow full of orchids in an easy morning's work – often to produce a field that is used for forage for a year or two and then abandoned to coarse thistles. Increasingly, the pale scars of dirt tracks crisscross once intact hill- and mountainsides, allowing short-term agricultural destruction of previously undisturbed upland habitats.

During the 1950s the official policy was to drain **wetlands** for conversion to agriculture, and many important areas were lost to wildlife completely. Those lakes, lagoons and deltas that remain on larger islands such as Kefalloniá and Crete are, in theory, now protected for their fragile biodiversity and their environmental and scientific value – but industrial and sewage pollution, disturbance, and misuse are common. Local 4WD vehicles and noisy motorbikes race through the dunes, destroying the surface stability and decimating the nesting chameleons; Greek military planes practice low-level flying over flocks of flamingos; rows of illegally overnighting camper vans disfigure the beaches;

and locals drive out here to dump unwanted televisions and fridges. On Lésvos, one of the island's main tourist attractions, the Kalloní salt-pans, once beloved by rare birds, are being poisoned by sewage. The **Orthodox Church**, whose lands once often provided wildlife with a refuge from hunters, now looks to capitalize on their value for major tourist developments, with plans to develop mass tourism and golf courses around the Toploú Monastery in eastern Crete, already one of Greece's most water-deficient areas.

Since the 1970s, **tourist developments** have ribboned out along coastlines, sweeping away both agricultural plots and wildlife havens as they do so. These expanding resorts increase local employment, often attracting inland workers to the coast; the generation that would have been shepherds on remote hillsides now works in tourist bars and tavernas. Consequently, the pressure of domestic animal grazing, particularly in the larger islands, has been significantly reduced, allowing the regeneration of tree seedlings. Crete, for example, has more woodland now than at any time in the last five centuries, but forest fires remain a threat everywhere. Conflagrations since 1980 have destroyed much of the tree cover in Thássos, southern Rhodes, Kárpathos, Híos and Sámos; the trees may well regenerate eventually, but by then the complex shade-dependent ecology is irrecoverably lost.

Despite an often negative attitude to wildlife, Greece was probably the first place in the world where it was an object of study. Theophrastos (372–287 BC) from Lésvos was the first recorded **botanist** and a systematic collector of general information on plants, while his contemporary, Aristotle, studied the animal world. During the first century AD the distinguished physician Dioscorides compiled a herbal that remained a standard work for over a thousand years.

Flowers

Whereas in temperate northern Europe plants flower from spring until autumn, the arid summers of Greece confine the main **flowering period** to the spring, a narrow climatic window when the days are bright, the temperatures are not too high and the groundwater supply still adequate. **Spring** starts in the southeast, in Rhodes, in early March, and then travels progressively westwards and northwards. Rhodes, Kárpathos and eastern Crete are at their best in March, western Crete in early April, the eastern Aegean from mid- to late April, and the Ionian islands in early May, though a cold dry winter can cause several weeks' delay. In the high mountains the floral spring is held back until the chronological summer, with the alpine zones of central and western Crete in full flower in June.

The delicate flowers of early spring – orchids, fritillaries, anemones, cyclamen, tulips and small bulbs – are replaced as the season progresses by more robust shrubs, tall perennials and abundant annuals, but many of these close down completely for the fierce **summer**. A few tough plants, like shrubby thyme and savory, continue to flower through the heat and act as magnets for butterflies.

Once the worst heat is over, and the first showers of **autumn** arrive, so does a second "spring", on a much smaller scale but no less welcome after the brown drabness of summer. Squills, autumn cyclamen, crocus in varying shades, pink or lilac colchicum, yellow sternbergia and other small bulbs all come into bloom, while the seeds start to germinate for the following year's crop of annuals. By the new year, early-spring bulbs and orchids are flowering in the south.

Seashore

Plants on the **beach** grow in a difficult environment: fresh water is scarce, salt is in excess, and dehydrating winds are often very strong. Feathery **tamarisk** trees are adept at surviving this habitat, and consequently are often planted to provide shade. On hot days or nights you may see or feel them "sweating" away surplus salt water from their foliage.

Sand dunes in the southern and eastern islands support decreasing numbers of the low gnarled trees of the prickly **juniper**. These provide shelter for a variety of colourful small plants, while the sandy depressions or "slacks" behind the dunes – where they have not been illegally ploughed for short-term forage crops – can be home to a variety of plants. Open stretches of beach sand usually have fewer plants, particularly nowadays in resort areas where the bulldozed "spring cleaning" of the beach removes both the winter's rubbish and all the local flora.

Watercourses

Large areas of **freshwater** are naturally scarce, particularly in the warmer south. Many watercourses dry up completely in the hot season, and what seem to be dry river-beds are often simply flood channels which fill irregularly at times of torrential rain. Consequently, there are few true aquatic plants compared with much of Europe. However, species that survive periodic drying-out can flourish, such as the giant reed or **calamus**, a bamboo-like grass reaching up to 6m in height and often cut for use as canes. It frequently grows in company with the shrubby, pink- or white-flowered and highly poisonous **oleander**.

Cultivated land

Arable fields can be rich with colourful weeds: scarlet poppies, blue bugloss, yellow or white daisies, wild peas, gladioli, tulips and grape hyacinths. Small, unploughed **meadows** may be equally colourful, with slower-growing plants such as orchids in extraordinary quantities. The rather dull violet flowers of the mandrake conceal its celebrated history as a narcotic and surgical anesthetic. In the absence of herbicides, olive groves can have an extensive underflora. In the presence of herbicides there is usually a yellow spring carpet of the introduced, weedkiller-resistant *Oxalis pes-caprae*, which now occurs in sufficient quantity to show up in satellite photographs.

C

Flora and fauna field guides

In case of difficulty obtaining titles listed below from conventional booksellers, there is a reliable mail-order outlet for wildlife field guides within the UK. Summerfield Books, Main St, Brough, Kirkby Stephen, Cumbria CA17 4AX (℡017683/41577, ℻41687, ⊛www.summerfieldbooks.com), not only has new botanical titles, but also rare or out-of-print natural history books on all topics. Postage is extra for smaller orders, but they often have special offers on select products. The shop is open Mon–Sat 9.30am–4.30pm.

Flowers

Hellmut Baumann Greek Wild Flowers and Plant Lore in Ancient Greece. Crammed with fascinating ethnobotany, plus good colour photographs.

Marjorie Blamey and Christopher Grey-Wilson Mediterranean Wild Flowers. Comprehensive field guide, with coloured drawings; recent and taxonomically reasonably up to date.

Lance Chilton Plant Check-lists. Small booklets which also include birds, reptiles and butterflies, for a number of Greek islands and resorts. Contact the author directly at ℡ & ℻01485/532710, ⊛www.marengowalks.com.

Pierre Delforge Orchids of Britain and Europe. A comprehensive guide, with recent taxonomy, though beware small inaccuracies in the translation. An updated version (Delachaux & Niestlé) is available in French.

Anthony Huxley and William Taylor Flowers of Greece and the Aegean (o/p). The only volume dedicated to the islands and mainland, with colour photos, but now very dated for taxonomy.

Oleg Polunin Flowers of Greece and the Balkans. Classic, older field guide (reprinted 1997), with colour photographs and line drawings, plus good sections on regional geology, climate, habitats etc; useful if Huxley and Taylor proves difficult to find.

Oleg Polunin and Anthony Huxley Flowers of the Mediterranean. The larger scope means that many Greek endemics get missed out, but recent printings have a brief table of taxonomic changes.

Kit Tan and Gregoris Iatrou Endemic Plants of Greece – The Peloponnese. Hardly pocket size but the first of three volumes planned to cover the entire endemic Greek flora; detailed text and excellent coloured drawings.

Birds

Richard Brooks Birding on the Greek Island of Lesvos. Superb guide with colour

Lower hillsides

The rocky earth makes cultivation on some hillsides difficult and impractical. Agriculture is often abandoned and areas regenerate to a rich mixture of shrubs and perennials – known as **garigue**. With time, a few good wet winters, and in the absence of grazing, some shrubs will develop into small trees, intermixed with tough climbers – the much denser **maquis** vegetation. The colour yellow often predominates in early spring, with brooms, gorse, Jerusalem sage and the three-metre giant fennel followed by the blues, pinks and purples of bee-pollinated plants. An abundance of the pink and white of large rockroses (*Cistus spp.*) is usually indicative of an earlier fire, since they are primary recolonizers of the cleared areas. Strawberry trees (*Arbutus unedo*) are also fire-resistant; they flower in winter or early spring, producing an orange-red edible (though disappointingly insipid) fruit in the autumn. The Judas tree flowers on bare wood in spring, making a blaze of pink against green hillside.

photos which includes a list of birdwatching sites, with detailed maps, plus an annotated species-by-species bird list with much useful information. Revised 2002, plus yearly updates available. Contact the author directly at ©email @richard-brooks.co.uk.

George Handrinos and T. Akriotis Birds of Greece. A comprehensive guide that includes island birdlife.

Lars Jonsson Birds of Europe with North Africa and the Middle East. The ornithologist's choice for the best coverage of Greek birds, with excellent descriptions and illustrations.

Heinzel, Fitter and Parslow Collins Guide to the Birds of Britain and Europe; **Petersen, Mountfort and Hollom** Field Guide to the Birds of Britain and Europe. Though not specific to Greece, these two field guides are very good for Greek birds.

Mammals
Corbet and Ovenden Collins Guide to the Mammals of Britain and Europe. The best field guide on its subject.

Reptiles
Arnold, Burton and Ovenden Collins Guide to the Reptiles and Amphibians of Britain and Europe. A useful guide, though it excludes the Dodecanese and east Aegean islands.

Jiri Cihar Amphibians and Reptiles (o/p). Selective coverage, but includes most endemic species of the Dodecanese and east Aegean isles.

Insects
Michael Chinery Collins Guide to the Insects of Britain and Western Europe. Although Greece is outside the geographical scope of the guide, it will provide generic identifications for many insects seen.

Lionel Higgins and Norman Riley A Field Guide to the Butterflies of Britain and Europe. A thorough and detailed field guide that illustrates nearly all species seen in Greece.

Marine life
B. Luther and K. Fiedler A Field Guide to the Mediterranean (o/p). Very thorough; includes most Greek shallow-water species.

A third vegetation type is **phrygana** – smaller, frequently aromatic or spiny shrubs, often with a narrow strip of bare ground between each hedgehog-like bush. Many **aromatic herbs** such as lavender, rosemary, savory, sage and thyme are native to these areas, intermixed with other less tasty plants such as the toxic euphorbias and the spiny burnet or wire-netting bush.

Nearly 190 species of **orchid** are believed to occur in Greece; their complexity blurs species' boundaries and keeps botanists in a state of taxonomic flux. In particular, the *Ophrys* bee and spider orchids have adapted themselves, through subtleties of lip colour and false scents, to seduce small male wasps. These insects mistake the flowers for a potential mate, and unintentionally assist the plant's pollination. Other orchids mimic the colours and scents of nectar-producing plants, to lure bees. Though all species are officially protected, many are still picked for decoration – in particular the giant *Barlia* orchid – and fill vases in homes, cafés, tavernas and even on graves.

Irises have a particular elegance and charm. The blue-to-violet winter iris is, as the name suggests, the first to appear, followed by the small blue *Iris gynandriris*. The flowers of the latter open after midday and into the night, to wither by the following morning. The widow iris is sombre-coloured in funereal shades of black and green, while the taller, white *Iris albicans*, the holy flower of Islam, is a relic of the Ottoman occupation. On the limestone peaks of Sámos, *Iris suavolens* has short stems, but huge yellow and brown flowers.

Mountains and gorges

The higher **mountains** of the Greek islands have winter snow cover, and cooler weather for much of the year, so flowering is consequently later than at lower altitudes. The **limestone peaks** of islands such as Corfu, Kefaloniá, Crete, Rhodes, Sámos and Thássos hold rich collections of attractive rock plants, flowers whose nearest relatives may be from the Balkan Alps or from the Turkish mountains. Gorges are another spectacular habitat, particularly rich in Crete. Their inaccessible cliffs act as refuges for plants that cannot survive the grazing, competition or more extreme climates of open areas. Many of Greece's endemic plants – bellflowers and knapweeds in particular – are confined to cliffs, gorges or mountains.

Much of the surviving **island forest** covers mountainous areas of Kefaloniá, Évvia, Lésvos and Crete. Depending on the island, the woodland can comprise cypress (widespread at low altitudes), Greek fir (especially on Kefaloniá), oak (on Lésvos, northwestern Híos, southwestern Sámos, Samothráki, Kéa and Crete) and a few species of pine: Calabrian or Aleppo at lower altitudes, black pine at the summits of Thássos, Sámos and (in small quantity) Lésvos. The cypress is native to the south and east Aegean, but in its columnar form it has been planted everywhere with a Mediterranean climate. On Kárpathos, Sými and Crete there are extensive stands of juniper, while shady stream canyons of the largest islands shelter plane, chestnut, and (on Rhodes only) oriental sweetgum. Clusters of introduced poplars indicate past, as well as current, human habitation, as do isolated mulberries, their leaves formerly fed to silkworms. The cooler shade of woodland provides a haven for plants which cannot survive full exposure to the Greek summer. Such species include the wonderful red, pink or white peonies found on Sámos, along with more widespread cyclamens, helleborine orchids, and numerous ferns.

With altitude, the forest thins out to scattered individual conifers and kermes oak, before finally reaching a limit ranging from 1000–1200m (on Samothráki and Sámos) to 1400m (Kefalloniá), for a maximum altitude of about 1800m (Crete). Above this treeline are limited summer meadows, and then bare rock. If not severely grazed, these habitats are home to many low-growing, gnarled, but often splendidly floriferous plants.

Birds

Migratory species which have wintered in East Africa move north in spring through the eastern Mediterranean from mid-March to mid-May, or later, depending on the season and the weather. Some stop to breed in Greece; others move on into the rest of Europe. The southern islands can be the first landfall after a long sea-crossing, and smaller birds recuperate for a few days before moving on north. Larger birds such as storks and ibis often fly very high, and binoculars are needed to spot them as they pass over. In autumn the birds return, but usually in more scattered numbers. Although some species such as quail and turtle dove are shot, there is nothing like the wholesale slaughter that takes place in some other Mediterranean countries.

Swallows, and their relatives the martins, are constantly swooping through the air to catch insects, as are the larger and noisier swifts. Warblers are numerous, with the Sardinian warbler often conspicuous because of its black head, bright red eye and bold habits. Other small insect-eaters include stonechats, fly-catchers and woodchat shrikes.

At **night**, the tiny Scops owl has a very distinct, repeated single-note call, very like the sonar beep of a submarine; the equally diminutive little owl is by contrast also visible by day, particularly on ruined houses, and has a strange repertoire of cries, chortles and a throaty hiss. Certainly the most evocative nocturnal bird is the nightingale, which requires wooded stream valleys and is most audible around midnight in May, its mating season.

Larger **raptors** are rare on the islands – except Crete – but can occur in remoter areas, particularly around mountain gorges and cliffs. Buzzards are perhaps the most abundant, and mistaken by optimistic birdwatchers for the rarer, shyer eagles. Griffon vultures are unmistakable, soaring on broad, straight-edged wings, whereas the lammergeier is a state-of-the-art flying machine with narrow, swept wings, seen over mountain tops by the lucky few; the remaining nine or ten pairs in Crete are now the Balkan's largest breeding population. The lesser kestrels are brighter, noisier versions of the common kestrel, and often appear undisturbed by the presence of humans. Also to be seen in the mountains are ravens, and smaller, colourful birds such as alpine choughs, common choughs, black and white wheatears, wallcreepers and the blue rock thrush.

In **lowland** areas, hoopoes are a startling combination of pink, black and white, particularly obvious when they fly; they're about the only natural predator of the processionary caterpillar, a major pest in pine forests. The much shyer golden oriole has an attractive song but is rarely seen for more than a few moments before hiding its brilliant colours among the olive trees. Rollers are bright blue and chestnut, and as their name suggests have a rolling flight. Multicoloured flocks of slim and elegant bee-eaters, especially on Tílos in spring, fill the air with their soft calls as they hunt insects. Brightest of all is the kingfisher, more commonly seen sea-fishing than in northern Europe.

In those areas of **wetland** that remain undrained and undisturbed, birds flourish. In salt marshes, coastal lagoons, estuaries and freshwater ponds, herons and egrets, ducks, osprey, glossy ibis and spoonbills, black storks, white storks, pelicans and many waders can be seen feeding. Cormorants roost on and dive from coastal cliffs from late summer onwards, while greater flamingos some-times occur, as lone individuals or small flocks, particularly in salt pans in the eastern Aegean between December and May.

Mammals

The island **mammal** population ranges from small rodents and shrews to hedgehogs, hares and squirrels (a very dark form of the red, particularly numer-ous on Lésvos). Rats are particularly common on Corfu and Sámos. Medium-sized mammals include badgers and foxes, but one of the commonest is the fast-moving, ferret-like, stone (or beech) marten, named for its habit of deco-rating stones with its droppings to mark territory. In the White Mountains of Crete an endemic ibex, known to Cretan hunters as the *agrími* or *krí-krí*, is occasionally seen running wild but more often penned as a zoo attraction. When formerly in danger of extinction, a colony of them was established on the offshore islet of Dhía, where they managed in turn to exterminate the rare local flora. Another such project which backfired badly was the (re-)introduc-tion of wild boar to Sámos; producing two septulet litters annually, the creatures quickly became major pests, destroying terraces and crops, and are now being culled by enthusiastic local hunters.

The extremely rare Mediterranean **monk seal** also breeds on some stretches of remote coast in the east Aegean and Sporades; the small world population is now highly endangered since losing many individuals – and most of its main breeding ground – to a toxic algal bloom off Morocco. If spotted, these seals should be treated with deference; they cannot tolerate human disturbance, and on present trends are unlikely to survive much into the new millennium. See p.471 for more about them.

Reptiles and amphibians

Reptiles flourish in the hot, dry summers of Greece and there are many species, the commonest being **lizards**. Most of these are small, slim, agile and wary, rarely staying around for closer inspection. They're usually brown to grey, with subtle patterns of spots, streaks and stripes, though in adult males the undersides are sometimes brilliant orange, green or blue. The more robust green lizards, including long whip-like tails, can be 50cm or more in length, but equally shy and fast-moving unless distracted by territorial disputes with each other.

On some islands, mainly in the central and eastern Aegean, lives the angular, iguana-like **agama**, sometimes called the Rhodes dragon. Occasionally reach-ing a robust 30cm in length, their skin is rough and grey to brown with indis-tinct patterning. Unlike other lizards, they will often stop to study you, before finally disappearing into a wall or under a rock.

Geckos are large-eyed nocturnal lizards, up to 15cm long, with short tails and often rough skins. Their spreading toes have claws and ingenious adhesive pads, allowing them to walk up house walls and onto ceilings in their search for insects. Groups of them lie in wait near bright lights that attract their prey, and small ones living indoors can have very pale, translucent skins. Not always popular locally – one Greek name for them, *miaró*, means "defiler" after their outsized faeces – they should be left alone to eat mosquitoes and other bugs. The **chameleon** is a rare, slow-moving and swivel-eyed inhabitant of eastern Crete and some eastern Aegean islands such as Sámos. Although essentially green, it has the ability to adjust its coloration to match the surroundings; you are only likely to see them crossing roads.

Once collected for the pet trade, **tortoises** can be found on many of the larger islands, though not on Crete. Usually it is their noisy progress through vegetation on sunny or wooded hills that first signals their presence. They spend their often long lives grazing the vegetation and can reach lengths of 30cm. Closely related **terrapins** are more streamlined, freshwater tortoises which love to bask on waterside mud by streams or ponds on many islands. Shy and nervous, they are usually only seen as they disappear under water. They are scavengers and will eat anything, including fingers if handled.

Sea turtles occur mostly in the Ionian Sea, but also in the Aegean. The least rare are the loggerhead turtles (*Caretta caretta*), which nest on Zákynthos and Kefalloniá, and occasionally in Crete. Their nesting grounds are disappearing under tourist resorts, although they are a protected endangered species (see the box on p.541).

Snakes are abundant in Greece and many islands; most are shy and non-venomous. Several species, including the Ottoman and nose-horned **vipers**, do have a poisonous bite, though they are not usually aggressive. They are adder-like and often have a very distinct, dark zigzag stripe down the back. They are only likely to bite if a hand is put in the crevice of a wall or a rock-face where one of them is resting, or if they are molested. Unfortunately, the locals in some areas attempt to kill any snake they see, and thus greatly increase the probability of their being bitten. Leave them alone, and they will do the same for you (but if worst comes to worst, see the advice on p.35). Most snakes are not only completely harmless to humans, but beneficial in that they keep down populations of pests such as rats and mice. There are also three species of legless lizards - slow-worm, glass lizard and legless skink – all equally harmless, which suffer because they are mistaken for snakes.

Frogs and **toads** are the commonest and most obvious amphibians in most of Greece, particularly during the spring breeding season. The green toad has green marbling over a pinkish or mud-coloured background, and a cricket-like trill. Frogs prefer the wettest places, and the robust marsh frog particularly revels in artificial water-storage ponds, whose concrete sides magnify their croaking impressively. Tree frogs are tiny jewels, usually emerald green, with huge and strident voices at night. They rest by day in trees and shrubs, and can sometimes be found in quantity plastered onto the leaves of waterside oleanders. The relatively active Luschan's **salamander** may be seen on Kárpathos, but is usually mistaken for a small lizard.

Insects

Greece teems with **insects.** Some pester, like flies and mosquitoes, but most are harmless to humans. The huge, slow-flying, glossy black carpenter bee may cause alarm by its size and noise, but is rarely a problem.

Grasshoppers and crickets swarm through open areas of vegetation in summer, with several larger species that are carnivorous on the smaller and can bite strongly if handled. Larger still is the grey-brown locust, which flies noisily before crash-landing into trees and shrubs. The high-pitched and endlessly repeated chirp of house crickets can drive one to distraction, as can the summer whirring of cicadas on the trunks of trees. The latter insects are giant relatives of the aphids that infest roses.

From spring through to autumn Greece is full of **butterflies**, particularly during late spring and early summer. There are three swallowtail species, named for the drawn-out corners of the hind-wings, in shades of cream and yellow, with black and blue markings. Their smaller relatives, the festoons, lack the tails, but add red spots to the palette. The rarer, robust brown-and-orange pasha is unrelated but is Europe's largest butterfly. In autumn the black-and-orange plain tiger or African monarch may appear, sometimes in large quantities. In areas of deciduous woodland, look high up and you may see fast-flying large tortoiseshells, while lower down, southern white admirals skim and glide through clearings between the trees. Some of the smallest but most beautiful butterflies are the blues. Their subtle, camouflaging grey and black undersides make them vanish from view when they land and fold their wings.

Some of the Greek **hawkmoths** are equally spectacular, particularly the green-and-pink oleander hawkmoth. Their large caterpillars can be recognized by their tail horn. The hummingbird hawkmoth, like its avian namesake, hovers at flowers to feed, supported by a blur of fast-moving wings. Tiger moths, with their black-and-white forewings and startling bright orange hindwings, are the "butterflies" that occur in huge quantity in sheltered sites of islands such as Rhodes, Níssyros and Páros. The giant peacock moth is Europe's largest, up to 15cm across. A mixture of grey, black and brown, with big eye-spots, it is usually only seen during the day while resting on tree trunks.

Other insects include the camouflaged **praying mantis**, holding their powerful forelegs in a position of supplication until another insect comes within reach. The females are voracious, and notorious for eating the males during mating. **Ant-lion** adults resemble an ineffectually fluttery dragonfly, but their young are huge-jawed and build pits in the sand to trap ants. Hemispherical **scarab beetles** collect balls of dung and push them around with their back legs, while the huge **longhorn beetles** – named for their absurdly extended, whip-like antennae – munch their way through wood in the southern Ionian islands. **Cockroaches** of varying species live in buildings, particularly hotels, restaurants and bakeries, attracted by warmth and food scraps.

Corfu is famous for its extraordinary **fireflies**, which flutter in quantities across meadows and marshes on May nights, speckling the darkness with bursts of cold light to attract partners; look carefully in nearby hedges, and you may spot the less flashy, more sedentary glow-worm.

Centipedes are not often seen, but the fast-moving twenty-centimetre scolipendra should be treated with respect since they can give extremely painful bites. Other non-vertebrates of interest include the **land crabs**, which are found in the southern and eastern islands, especially Crete. They need water to breed, but can surprise when seen crawling across remote hillsides. There are plenty of genuine marine creatures to be seen, particularly in shallow seawater sheltered by rocks – sea cucumbers, sea butterflies, octopus, marine worms, starfish and sea urchins.

Music

Although **music** is central to Greek culture, it's possible to travel through the islands and hear only the most modern versions of older songs and tunes, or pieces composed since 1990 or so, rendered in a style barely resembling the *nisiótika* (island music) of even the 1970s. Much of the live music performed in venues has been dramatically altered over the past three decades by contact with Western pop (and a simultaneous rejection by Greeks of their own traditional music).

A good case in point is Náxos, an island that until the 1970s supported a beautiful, unique musical tradition featuring a large number of fine violinists, some of whom played in the older style, but then went "modern". Although some superb recordings of traditional music have been issued recently, you'll no longer hear this kind of music in Náxos's public places or on local radio stations. At **live-music events** such as *paniyíria* (saints'-day festivals), you may well have your ears blasted by overwhelming amplification, coupled with excessive reverb that radically alters the natural tone of the violin. The use of a pickup on the *laoúto*, the plucked-string instrument still played with the violin on most islands, makes it sound far too much like an electric guitar (and sometimes an electric or acoustic guitar will indeed be substituted). The *bouzoúki*, more at home in Greek urban musical genres, will also often be heard in a band alongside the *laoúto*, as well as *kroustá* (percussion) – anything from the lap-drum known as *toumbéleki* to a modern rock/jazz drum set. Although this commercialized instrumentation is typical nowadays, there are exceptions (see below) which can be found through luck and knowing what to look for.

The social context

Instrumental music, dance and song have been an essential part of **Greek life** from ancient times to the present, and it's difficult to exaggerate its significance for those who have grown up with it. Music and dance form an integral part of weddings, betrothals, baptisms, elections, saint's days observed at local churches or monasteries, name-days (for those who share the name of the saint) observed at private homes or tavernas, Easter and the pre-Lenten Carnival.

Many pieces, which vary from island to island, are specifically associated with **weddings**. Some are processional songs/tunes (*patinádhes*), sung/played while going to fetch the bride from her home, or as the wedding couple leave the church, plus there are specific dances associated with different stages of a wedding ritual. It was common in the past (and in places even today) for the music and dancing that followed a wedding feast to last for up to three days. Some

C

CONTEXTS | Music

Record Stores

If you're stopping over in Athens en route to the islands, the best **record stores** – Tzina (no. 57), Xylouris (no. 39) and Metropolis (nos. 54 & 64) – stand within a few hundred metres of each other on Odhós Panepistimíou, between the university and Platía Omonías. In the UK the best source is Trehantiri, 367 Green Lanes, London N4 (T020/8802 6530, @www.trehantiri.com), which also operates a worldwide mail-order service. In North America, try Down Home Music, 10341 San Pablo Avenue, El Cerrito, CA (T510/525-2129; @www.downhomemusic.com).

songs are sung only at **pre-Lenten Carnivals** (*Apókries* in Greek), accompanied by the shaking of large goat-bells roped together and, in some places, such as Skýros, the wearing of animal skins. Such rituals, widespread across Europe, date back to pre-Christian times. Music also accompanies informal, unpublicized **private gatherings** in homes, *kafenía*, and tavernas with facilities (eg a stage and dance-floor) for musicians and patrons.

Don't be shy about asking people where you can hear *tá paradhosiaká* (traditional music); a few words of Greek go a long way towards inclining locals to help foreign travellers. Learn the Greek names of the instruments you would like to hear, or find someone to translate for you if necessary. Once it's clear that you're a budding *meraklís* (untranslatable, but roughly, aficionado) and past the Zorba-soundtrack stage, people will be flattered by the respect paid to "real" music, and doors will open for you.

The older tradition

Island musical tradition is wonderfully diverse, so only a general overview will be attempted here. Each archipelago has its dances, songs and customs which vary between islands and even between towns on the same island. Different dances go by the same name from place to place (eg *syrtós*), while different lyrics are set to many of the same melodies and vice versa. The same tune can be played so idiosyncratically between neighbouring island groups as to be barely recognizable to an outsider. Compared to Western styles, island music is far less linear and more circuitous, as would be expected from its Byzantine origins and later Ottoman influences. As in all "folk music", pieces are learned by ear. Though transcriptions exist, and there are some who teach with written notes, folk tradition is primarily an aural, hands-on one.

In Crete, **rhymed couplets** called *mantinádhes* are sung in alternation with instrumental interludes; similar satirical couplets are sung in the Dodecanese (eg *pismatiká* on Kálymnos), while on Náxos such couplets are called *kotsákia*, and the short repeating melody to which they are set is called a *kotsátos*. Singers improvise such rhymed couplets on the spot, thinking of new lines during the short instrumental breaks and coming in again when ready with new lines. These often tease the wedding couple, praise the in-laws, lament the loss of a community member or chide a politician. There are also "set" couplets which have entered the traditional canon, sometimes mixed in with newly improvised material.

Many songs (except for the slow table songs, or *epitrapézia*) are in **dance rhythm**, with a vital interaction between dancers and musicians/singers. Dancers and listeners may also join in the song (solo or as a chorus), or even initiate verses. It is customary for the lead dancer to tip the musicians, often requesting a particular tune and/or dance rhythm for his party to dance to.

An excellent introduction to the subject is Yvonne Hunt's *Traditional Dance in Greek Culture* (Centre for Asia Minor Studies, Athens 1996), which, though primarily about dance, also covers important festivals and customs and the social role of music and musicians. A fine bibliography lists works of significant Greek musicological researchers, anthropologists and travellers. This book can be purchased at the Folk Art Museum, Kydhathinéon 17, at the **Museum of Greek Popular Musical Instruments** at Dhioyénous 1–3 in the Pláka district of Athens. This latter museum, in addition to stocking a good selection of folk recordings, also features displays of instruments from every region of Greece. Headphones provided allow you to listen to brief samples of music played on them.

The instruments

The violin (**violí** in Greek) supposedly appeared in Greece during the seventeenth century, migrating from western Europe (followed some decades later by the clarinet, played mainly in mainland Greek music). Although the violin is also played on the Greek mainland, it is the main melodic instrument of the Aegean islands, with the striking exceptions of Crete, Kárpathos, Kássos and Hálki in the southern Aegean, where two kinds of *lýra* still prevail (see below). The violin bridge may be sanded in Greece to a less highly arched form than that used for Western classical music (this is also done in Western folk traditions). An alternate **tuning** known as *álla Toúrka*, more widespread in the past, is still used by some musicians on certain islands (eg Sífnos, Kýthnos and Kós). From high to low, its string values are D, A, D, and G, with a fourth between the two higher-pitched strings instead of the typical all-fifths arrangement. The lowered high string is slacker and "sweeter", and the violin's tonality altered by the modified tuning. Some violinists have reported being pressured to tune *álla Fránga*, ie the standard European tuning with "E" on top.

Playing **styles** vary widely within island groups (or even between villages) but Greek violin technique in general differs radically from that of the classical violin (as well as from more familiar Western folk styles). Modes (related to both the Byzantine and Ottoman systems) are used rather than Western scales, there's a range of possible ornamentation techniques (vibrato being only one of them and used very infrequently), and, in some places, unmetered solos (called *taxímia*) based upon the mode of the melody and subject to modulation into other modes. Some very idiosyncratic violin styles are still found on Sífnos or Kýthnos in the Cyclades, and on Kálymnos or Kós in the Dodecanese, with a few of the finest old-fashioned performers only recently deceased (eg Andonis Xanthakis and Andonis Mougadhis Komis in Sífnos). Bowing patterns in these places can be swift and angular, resulting in a more "fiddle"-like sound than styles that rely on smoother, longer bow-strokes.

The **laoúto** is a member of a family of instruments generally referred to as long-necked lutes. It has a fat, gourd-like back like the oud *(oúti* in Greek, *al-ud* in Arabic) from which the *laoúto* (and lute) derives its name and basic form, but a long fretted neck (the oud has a short, unfretted one) and four sets of double metal strings (the oud has gut ones). The Greek *laoúto* is tuned in fifths (C, G, D, A from lowest to highest), but the G actually has the lowest pitch, since the C is anomalously tuned a fourth higher than the G. On some islands (Sífnos, Kýthnos) the heavier of the lowest-pitched doublet is removed to accentuate the treble end, and make the *laoúto*'s sound less "thunderous".

In most of the Aegean, the *laoúto* is played with the *violí* or *lýra* and sometimes also with the island bagpipe, the *tsamboúna* (see p.608). Typical duos are *violí/laoúto* in the Cyclades or *lýra/laoúto* in Crete and the Dodecanese. In north Aegean islands (such as Lésvos and Samothráki) the *laoúto* may be played with violin and *sandoúri* or even in large ensembles which include brass instruments and accordion. In the hands of a competent player, the *laoúto* is not merely "accompanying" a *violí* or *lýra*, but forms part of a true duo, or *ziyiá*, by virtue of well-chosen rhythmic patterns and melodic notes/phrases that make the whole more dynamic. Conversely, good violin- or *lýra*-playing can be ruined by the slick modern *laoúto* style, much more mechanical even compared to that of the early 1980s, with more frequent chord changes and abrupt attack. The use of electric pickup (see above) alters the instrument's unique tone, and makes open chords impossible as they become "boomy". To make matters worse, the *laoúto* is often drowned out in modern recordings by drums and electric bass. The larger, more deeply pitched Cretan *laoúto* will play melody as

CONTEXTS | Music

All of the following are available on CD unless specified otherwise; similarly, all are Greek label pressings except for the Ziyia entries.

Avthentika Nisiótika tou Peninda (Lyra CD 0168). Good Cretan and Dodecanesian material recorded during the 1950s, from the collection of the late Ted Petrides, musician and dance master.

Dhodhekanisa (Hellenic Music Archives CD AEM 012). Representative Dodecanese songs and dances with native lýra, violí and tsamboúna players.

Ellines Akrites (FM Records). FM's folk pressings are generally to be approached with caution, but Vol. 1 of this 12-CD series (FM 801, "Híos, Mytilíni, Sámos, Ikaría"), Vol. 2 (FM 802, "Límnos, Samothráki, Ímvros, Ténedhos") and Vol. 9 ("Pátmos, Kálymnos, Léros, Kós, Astypálea") feature excellent local musicians (violí/lýra) and singers such as Strais Rallis of Lésvos, as well as violinists Kyriakos Gouvendas of Thessaloníki and the late Gavriel Yiallizis of Kós.

Emilia Hatzidhaki Thalassina Tragoudhia (LP: Panvox 16311, reissued as CD by MBI). The sole easily available collection dedicated to this artist, who otherwise appears only on Nisiótika anthologies.

Nikos Ikonomidhis Perasma stin Amorgo/Passage to Amorgos (Keros Music CD 101). A native of Skhinoússa islet, violinist and lautiéris Ikonomidhis sings traditional pieces from nearby Amorgós on this 2001 recording. His 1991 Perasma sta Kythira/Passage to Kythera (Keros,1982) collection from that lesser-known island is also worth a listen, as is Anatolika tou Egeou/East of the Aegean (Verso CD 101). Despite a persistent, annoying electric bass, Ikonomidhis's playing is so clean and spirited that it is difficult not to enjoy this recording.

Kalimera Theia-Samothrakiki Skopi ke Tragoudia #1/Good Morning Auntie – Tunes and Songs of Samothraki #1 (Hellenic Archives-AEM 014). First in a two-CD set (second CD pending) featuring the local repertoire from this north Aegean island, as well as pieces from neighbouring islands and from Asia Minor.

Anna Karabessini & Effi Sarri CD reissues from old LPs: Yialo Yialo Piyeno (Lyra 0102067), Tis Thalassas (Lyra 10777) and Ena Glendi (Lyra 10717). Two singing sisters from the island of Kós, who were for the Dodecanese what the Konitopoulos family (see below) was for the Cyclades; the fact that they performed only for private gatherings added to their cachet.

Kassos: Skopi tis Lyras/Lyra Tunes (Lyra 0113). A 1990s collection from the bleakest, but one of the more musical, of the Dodecanese.

Kastellorizo (Syrtos 561). Studio production by Manolis Karpathios; of the collected-and-remastered variety, but the only thing easily available for this island.

Irini Konitopoulou-Legaki Athanata Nisiotika 1 (Tzina-Astir 1020). A 1978 warhorse, beloved of bus drivers across the islands. Anefala Thalassina (Lyra 4693) from 1993 is far less commercial and one of the finest recordings from Náxos, featuring Naxian lautiéris Dhimitris Fyroyenis and Yiannis Zevgolis, one the last old-style violinists. Then aged 61, Irini sung her heart out in a richer, deeper voice than she was known for on club stages.

Yiorgos Konitopoulos & Clan Sto Diava tou Egeou (Minos EMI 77) and Yiorgos ke Irini Konitopoulou-Legaki: Apo Limani se Limani (EMI 107243480859231). Reissues of earlier recordings made by violinist Yiorgos with sister Irini, members of a famous (and numerous) Naxian musical family active since the 1960s.

Aryiris Kounadhis Kefalonitikes Arietes (Philips 526 492-2). Sweet without being syrupy, this is one of the very few still-in-print collections of traditional music from Kefalloniá (indeed from any of the Ionians), largely with songs composed by Kounadhis.

Kritiki Mousiki Paradhosi, Iy Protomastores 1920–1953/Cretan Musical Tradition, the First Masters (Aerakis, 10 CDs). The whole set's prohibitively pricey, and some titles are of specialist interest, but discs are available individually; go for No. 1 (Baxevanis, lýra and small orchestra); No. 4 (Stelios Foustalieris, last master of the boúlgari, knowledge of which died with him); No. 5 (Yiannis Demirtzoyiannis, guitarist and epic singer) and No. 6 (Yiorgis Koutsourelis, on melodic laoúto).

Tis Lerou ta Tragoudhia/Songs of Leros (Politistikós ké Morfotikós Sýllogos Néon Lérou/Instructive & Cultural Lerian Youth Society). Double CD produced by Music Folklore Archive. Live field recordings from 1996 and 1998 of island musicians and singers; violí, sandoúri, laoúto and bagpipes in various combinations, plus unaccompanied singing. Each disc finishes with an archival track of bygone greats Emilia Hatzidhaki and Manolis Skoumbouridis, both Lerian.

Lesvos Aiolis: Tragoudhia ke Hori tis Lesvou/Songs & Dances of Lesvos (Panepistimiakés Ekdhóseis Krítis/University Press of Crete, double CD 9/10). Two decades (1974–96) of field recordings of the last traditional music extant on the island, a labour of love supervised by musicologist Nikos Dhionysopoulos. Pricey, but the quality and uniqueness of the instrumental festival tunes and dances especially, and the illustrated booklet, merit the expense (typically around €30).

Lesvos: Mousika Stavrodhromia sto Egeo/Musical Crossroads of the Aegean (University of the Aegean). Pricey five-CD set with an accompanying fat, illustrated booklet. Everything from Asia Minor music played in Lésvos to carols and wedding songs.

Seryiani sta Nisia Mas, Vol 1 (CD, MBI 10371). An excellent retrospective of various nisiótika hits and artists, mostly from the 1950s. The highlight of Vol. 1 (Vol. 2 doesn't exist) is Emilia Hatzidhaki's rendering of "Bratsera".

Skopi tis Kalymnou/Kalymnian Folk Music (Lýkio tón Ellinídhon E2-276-97). Double CD with excellent notes and song translations. Traditional Kalymnian repertoire and native musicians featuring Mikes Tsounias, then 78, on violin, his young grandson playing unison violin on some pieces, plus tsamboúna accompaniment.

Skopi kai Tragoudhia apo tin Apirantho tis Naxou (Aperathítikos Sýllogos TC-CP957). 1983 recording from the famous Náxos mountain village of Apíranthos, featuring native Yiannis Zevgolis (violin) with singer Koula Klironomou-Sidheri, Yiorgos Karapatis on laoúto, plus others on guitar and tsamboúna. Beautiful renditions of traditional Naxian music, with many wistful and nostalgic songs from an era now past.

Songs of...(Society for the Dissemination of National Music, Greece). A thirty-disc-plus series of field recordings from the 1950s–70s, each covering traditional music of one region or type. Lyrics in English, all available in Athens in cassette or CD form, especially at the Museum of Greek Popular Instruments (address as on p.604). Best island discs to date are Mytilene and Chios (SDNM 110); Mytilene and Asia Minor (SDNM 125); Rhodes, Chalki and Symi (SDNM 104); Kassos and Karpathos (SDNM 103); and Amorgos, Kythnos and Sifnos (SDNM105).

Thalassa Thymisou/Sea of Memories: Tragoudhia ke Skopi apo tis Inousses (Navtikó Mousío Inoussón-En Khordais CD 1801/1802). The result of a "field trip" by the En Khordais traditional music school of Thessaloníki to Inoússes, a small islet northeast of Híos, to rescue vanishing traditional material with the help of the islanders' long memories; the result's superb, a mix of live sessions in Inoussan tavernas and some studio recordings. Thorough and intelligent notes, but no translations of the lyrics.

Tragoudhia ke Skopi tis Patmou/Songs and Melodies of Patmos (Politistikón Ídhryma Dhodhekanísou 201). Live 1995 field recordings of well-edited pieces, as

continued overleaf

raw but compelling as you'd hear them at an old-time festival. Local singers and instrumentalists on violí, tsamboúna and sandoúri.

Nikos Xylouris O Arkhangelos tis Kritis,1958–1968 (MBI 10376); Ta Khronia stin Kriti (2CD, MBI 10677/78). The best two retrospectives of the sweet-voiced Cretan singer, with copious notes; the first covers his initial decade of recordings, previously unavailable, with self-accompaniment on the lýra.

Ziyia Fine arrangements and singing of music from across Greece, by a five-member, bi-coastal group from the USA. Their first outing, From the Mountains to the Islands (AgaRhythm, 1993) has more island music than Travels with Karaghiozis (AgaRhythm, 1995), which does however include a lovely piece from Kálymnos.

---

well as chords to accompany violin or *lýra* more often than in other island groups, as well as solo melodies or *taxímia*. In any duo with *violí* or *lýra* and *laoúto,* at least one (and often both) of the musicians sings while the *laoúto* chords continue, the verses alternating with instrumental passages.

The **sandoúri** is a member of the zither family, resembling the hammered dulcimer and played with the *violí* (or *violí* plus *laoúto*) in many of the Dodecanese and also the northeast Aegean islands, where it may also appear in much larger ensembles. It entered these island groups from nearby Asia Minor, principally after 1923 when it was (re)introduced by refugees, especially on Lésvos. The *sandoúri* plays both chords and melody, as well as introductory *taxímia*.While at times only basic chords are played on it to complement the violin, it can fill in with arpeggios, scale runs or melodic tags. It occasionally serves as a solo instrument, and has been recorded as such on the island of Lésvos.

The term **lýra** applies to a family of small, pear- or bottle-shaped instruments which are held upright on the player's thigh with strings facing forward and bowed with the palm facing away from the body. Greek island types are pear-shaped and have three metal strings, with notes played by pressing the finger-nails laterally against the strings. The **Dodecanesian lýra** has a drone string in the middle which fills out the sound, and is bowed continually while playing on either of the outer strings; the bow in some cases has little bells on it which provide rhythmic accompaniment. Its tonal range matches that of the *tsamboúna* played in the Dodecanese and can be played alone, with *laoúto*, with *tsamboúna*, or both of these together, often accompanying vocalists. The **Cretan lýra** is a relatively modern instrument, having supplanted the Dodecanesian type which was used on the island before the 1930s.The contemporary *lýra* is larger and fatter, lacks a drone string and is tuned lower and in successive fifths, thus extending the melodic range by a fifth beyond that of the older instrument.The old belled bow was abandoned, both because it was too heavy for the quick and elaborate tunes now possible, but also because its rhythmic function was replaced by the *laoúto* (and in earlier years by a lute-family member, the *boúlgari*). A fingerboard was added to make fingering easier, as well as a longer, narrow neck, and a modern violin bow replaced the older, more convex bow.Yet despite all these violin-like innovations, the *lýra* retains a tone quality very different from that of the violin; even a skilled violinist can never entirely imitate its sound.

The **tsamboúna** (in Crete, *askomandoúra*) is the Greek-island bagpipe made of goatskin, with no drone and two chanters made of calamus reed. The left chanter does not vary between island groups, having five holes which allow an incomplete diatonic scale from 'do' to 'fa'. The right chanter is of three types, with anywhere from two to five holes depending on the island. In the Dodecanese this bagpipe may be played alone, with another *tsamboúna*, or with a *laoúto* and *lýra*; many songs are accompanied by these various combinations. In the Cyclades (and formerly Híos) the *tsamboúna* is (or was) played with a **toumbáki** or two-headed drum, only one side of which is struck with two wooden (or bone) drumsticks. It is suspended to one side of the player's torso by a strap. The *tsamboúna* and *toumbáki* are quintessential shepherds' instruments, their skins taken from their flocks. Along with the *lýra*, they are the oldest of the instruments played on the islands, though rare now except in some of the places mentioned above. On Náxos the *tsamboúna-toumbáki* duo is still much in demand during the pre-Lenten Apokriátika festivities.

Accordion, clarinet, guitar and *bouzoúki*, all **imported** from the Greek mainland or urban traditions, are sometimes played along with the more traditional instruments on the islands.

Alone of all modern Greek territory, the **Ionian islands** (except for Lefkádha) were never occupied by the Ottomans, but instead by the Venetians, and thus have a predominantly Western musical tradition. The indigenous song-form is both Italianate in names (*kantádhes, ariétes, arékia*), instrumentation (guitar and mandolin – as in Captain Corelli's) and vocals (harmonized choir). Style and nomenclature differ subtly between the various islands: the equivalent of *ariétes* on Kefalloniá are known as *arékia* on Zákynthos. All of the Ionians, especially Corfu, have a tradition of formal musical instruction and excellence, and for many years a disproportionate number of Athens conservatory students were from this archipelago.

Susan Raphael, with Marc Dubin

Books

For each recommended title in this section we only list imprint details when a book is not easily available on-line or at retailers, for example small presses in Greece. An out-of-print but still highly recommended book is indicated by the abbreviation "o/p"; most of these are easily found on used-book dealers' web-sites such as ⊛www.abe.com or ⊛www.bookfinder.com. Books marked ⊡ are particularly recommended, many of them part of a "Modern Greek Writers" series, numbering over thirty titles, issued by the Athenian company Kedros Publishers. One British publisher with a consistent record of publishing or re-issuing excellent social and historical studies of Greece is C. Hurst and Company (⊛www.hurstpub.co.uk).

Travel and memoirs

⊡ **Kevin Andrews** *The Flight of Ikaros* (o/p). An intense and compelling account of an educated, sensitive archeologist wandering the backcountry during the civil war. Half a century on, still one of the best books on Greece as it was before "development"; includes an initial chaper on Páros pre-tourism.

⊡ **James Theodore Bent** *Aegean Islands: The Cyclades, or Life Among the Insular Greeks*. Originally published in 1881 and reissued in 2002, this remains the best account of island customs and folklore; it's also a highly readable, droll account of a year's Aegean travel.

Charmian Clift *Mermaid Singing* (o/p). Clift and family's experiences living on Kálymnos during the 1950s – amongst the first post-war expats to do so. Last reissued in the early 1990s, it is easily found; her *Peel Me a Lotus*, about a subsequent sojourn on Ídhra, may also appeal, and is often co-bound with *Mermaid Singing*.

Gerald Durrell *My Family and Other Animals*. Sparkling, funny anec-dotes of Durrell's childhood on Corfu during the 1930s – and his passion for the island's fauna: toads, tortoises, bats, scorpions, the lot.

Lawrence Durrell *Prospero's Cell* and *Reflections on a Marine Venus*. The elder Durrell lived before World War II with Gerald and the family on Corfu, the subject of *Prospero's Cell*. *Marine Venus* recounts Lawrence's 1945–47 experiences and impres-sions of Rhodes and other Dodecanese islands.

Katherine Kizilos *The Olive Grove: Travels in Greece*. Returned, ambiva-lent Greek-Australian's musings on the country, and İstanbul, with a good initial section on Sýros, Santoríni, Pátmos, Ikaría and Lésvos.

⊡ **Elias Kulukundis** *Journey to a Greek Island* (o/p). More accu-rately, an engaging journey back through time and genealogy by a diaspora Greek two generations removed from Kássos, poorest of the Dodecanese.

Edward Lear *The Corfu Years* (Denise Harvey; Límni, Évvia, Greece). Superbly illustrated journals by the nonsense versifier and noted landscape painter, whose watercolours and sketches of Corfu, Paxí and else-where offer a rare glimpse of the Ionian archipelago during the mid-nineteenth century. His *Cretan Journal* (same imprint) will also be of interest.

Willard Manus *This Way to Paradise: Dancing on the Tables* (Lycabettus Press, Athens). American expatriate's memoir of nearly four decades in Líndhos, Rhodes, beginning long before its descent into mass-tourist tattiness. Wonderful period detail, including hippie/bohemian excesses and often hilarious cameos by the likes of S.J. Perelman, Germaine Greer and Martha Gellhorn.

Melina Mercouri *I Was Born Greek* (o/p). Rollicking autobiography of Greece's best known actress, written in 1971 partly as a polemic against the junta who had stripped her of her Greek citizenship for her resistance activities. La Melina chronicles a suitably dramatic life, including her loves and unlikely friendships (eg, James Watson of DNA fame). To her credit she admits to not being very bright, but the book appears not to have been ghosted – and reads fluently.

Henry Miller *The Colossus of Maroussi*. Corfu, Crete, Athens and the soul of Greece in 1939, with Miller, completely in his element, at his most inspired.

James Pettifer *The Greeks: the Land and People since the War*. Useful, if spottily written and edited, introduction to contemporary Greece – and its recent past, updated to the millennium. Pettifer charts the state of the nation's politics, food, family life, religion and tourism.

Terence Spencer *Fair Greece, Sad Relic: Literary Philhellenism from Shakespeare to Byron* (Denise Harvey, Límni, Évvia). Masterfully traces how the scribblings of poets steeped in the classics, culminating in Byron, and the accounts of early travellers to what's now Greece, gradually fuelled European support for the 1821 Revolution – despite the

misgivings of many of them about the contemporary Greeks themselves. Also demonstrates just how old the Zorba stereotype is (the feckless, "merrie Greeke" was already described in the 1500s).

Tom Stone *The Summer of My Greek Taverna*. An excellent cautionary tale, especially for those entertaining fantasies of a new life in the sun, set in northern Pátmos of the early 1980s; a rather trusting Stone mixes friendship and business at Kámbos beach, with predictable (to everyone else, anyway) results.

Richard Stoneman, ed *A Literary Companion to Travel in Greece*. Ancient and medieval authors, plus Grand Tourists – good for dipping into.

Patricia Storace *Dinner with Persephone*. A New York poet, resident for a year in Athens (with forays to the provinces) puts the country's psyche on the couch, while avoiding the same position with various predatory males. Storace has a sly sense of humour, and in showing how permeated – and imprisoned – Greece is by its imagined past, gets it right ninety percent of the time.

Faith Warn *Bitter Sea: The Real Story of Greek Sponge Diving* (Guardian Angel Press, UK, but widely available on Kálymnos). Short, photo-illustrated potted history of the traditional Kálymnos livelihood, as seen some four decades after Clift's experience (see opposite).

Sarah Wheeler *An Island Apart* (o/p). Entertaining chronicle of a five-month ramble through Évvia, one of the least-visited islands. Wheeler has a sure touch with Greek culture and an open approach to nuns, goatherds and academics; the main quibble is her success in making Évvia seem more interesting than it really is.

The classics

Many of the classics make excellent companion reading for a trip around Greece – especially the historians Thucydides and Herodotus. Reading Homer's *Odyssey* when you're battling with or resigning yourself to the vagaries of island ferries puts your own plight into perspective. Most of the standard undergraduate staples are part of the Penguin Classics paperback series. Routledge and Duckworth both have a huge, steadily expanding backlist of Classical Studies, though many titles are expensive and quite specialized.

Herodotus *The Histories* (trans A.D. Godley). Revered as the father of systematic history and anthropology, this fifth-century-BC Anatolian writer chronicled both the causes and campaigns of the Persian Wars, as well as the contemporary, assorted tribes and nations inhabiting Asia Minor.

★ **Homer** *The Iliad* and *The Odyssey*. The first concerns itself, semi-factually, with the late Bronze Age war of the Achaeans against Troy in Asia Minor; the second recounts the hero Odysseus's long journey home, via seemingly every corner of the Mediterranean. For a verse rendition, Richmond Lattimore's translations have yet to be bettered. For a prose rendition, Martin Hammond's *Iliad* and *Odyssey* currently edge out second-best choices by the father-and-son team of E.V. Rieu (*Iliad*) and D.C.H. Rieu (*Odyssey*).

Ovid *The Metamorphoses* (trans A.D. Melville). Though collected by a first-century-AD Roman poet, this remains one of the most accessible renditions of the more piquant Greek myths, involving transformations as divine blessing or curse.

Plutarch *The Age of Alexander*, *On Sparta* and *The Rise and Fall of Athens*. Another late-antiquity author, writing perhaps with the benefit of hindsight, but with the disadvantage of unreliable sources and much conjecture.

★ **Thucydides** *History of the Peloponnesian War*. Bleak month-by-month account of the conflict, by a cashiered Athenian officer whose affiliation and dim view of human nature didn't usually obscure his objectivity; see George Cawkwell's book (opposite) for a revisionist view.

Xenophon *The History of My Times*. Thucydides' account of the Peloponnesian War stops in 411 BC; this work continues events until 362 BC.

Ancient history and interpretation of the classics

★ **Mary Beard and John Henderson** *The Classics: a Very Short Introduction*. As it says; an excellent overview.

★ **A.R. Burn** *History of Greece*. Probably the best general introduction to ancient Greece, though for fuller analysis you'll do better with one or other of the following more specialized titles.

Paul Cartledge *Cambridge Illustrated History of Ancient Greece*. Large-format, pricey volume packed with information useful for both novices and experts. His more recent work, *The Spartans: The World of the Warrior-Heroes of Ancient Greece*, is the first thorough study of this much-maligned city-state, secretive and a source of speculation from outside even in its own time.

George Cawkwell *Thucydides and the Peloponnesian War*. Revisionist overview of Thucydides' work and relations with main personalities of the war, challenging previous assumptions of his infallibility.

★ **M.I. Finley** *The World of Odysseus*. Reprint of a 1954 warhorse, pioneering in its investigation of the historicity (or otherwise) of the events and society related by Homer. Breezily readable and stimulating, with prejudices apparent rather than subtle.

Michael Grant and John Hazel *Who's Who in Classical Mythology*. A gazetteer of over 1200 mythological personalities, together with historical and geographical background.

★ **Pierre Grimal** (ed) *Dictionary of Classical Mythology*. Though translated from the French, still considered to have the edge on the more recent Grant/Hazel title.

Simon Hornblower *The Greek World 479–323 BC*. An erudite survey of ancient Greece at its zenith, from the end of the Persian Wars to the death of Alexander; now a standard university paperback text.

John Kenyon Davies *Democracy and Classical Greece*. Established, accessible account of the Classical period and its political developments.

Robin Lane Fox *Alexander the Great*. An absorbing study, which mixes historical scholarship with imaginative psychological detail.

Oswyn Murray *Early Greece*. The Greek story from the Mycenaeans and Minoans through to the beginning of the Classical period.

Robin Osborne *Greece in the Making 1200–479 BC*. Well-illustrated paperback on the rise of the city-state.

John Purkis *Teach Yourself Classical Civilisation*. A nice, succinct introduction to the subject.

Tony Spawforth *Greece, an Oxford Archaeological Guide*. An interpretive guide, by the co-author, with Simon Hornblower, of the also-recommended *Oxford Classical Dictionary*.

F.W. Walbank *The Hellenistic World*. Greece under the sway of the Macedonian and Roman empires.

Ancient religion

★ **Walter Burkert** *Greek Religion: Archaic and Classical*. Superb overview of deities and their attributes and antecedents, rites, the protocol of sacrifice and the symbolism of major festivals; especially good on relating Greek worship to its predecessors in the Middle East.

Matthew Dillon *Pilgrims and Pilgrimage in Ancient Greece*. Pricey

hardback exploring not only the main sanctuaries such as Delphi, but also minor oracles, the role of women and children and the secular festivities attending the rites.

Mary Lefkowitz *Greek Gods, Human Lives: What We Can Learn from Myths*. Rather than being frivolous, immoral or irrelevant, ancient religion and its supporting myths, in their bleak indifference of the gods to human suffering, are shown as being more "grown up" than the later creeds of salvation and comfort.

Nano Marinatos and Robin Hagg *Greek Sanctuaries: New Approaches.* The form and function of the temples, in the light of recent scholarship.

Archeology and art

John Beckwith *Early Christian and Byzantine Art.* Illustrated study placing Byzantine art within a wider context.

William R. Biers *Archeology of Greece: An Introduction.* A 1990s-revised and excellent standard text.

⭐ **John Boardman** *Greek Sculpture* (3 vols: *The Archaic Period, The Classical Period, The Late Classical Period*). The definitive references; his earlier *Greek Art* (o/p) is a more concise introduction, part of the "World of Art" series.

Reynold Higgins *Minoan and Mycenaean Art.* A clear, well-illustrated round-up.

Sinclair Hood *The Arts in Prehistoric Greece.* A sound introduction to the subject.

Roger Ling *Classical Greece.* Another useful illustrated introduction.

Colin Renfrew *The Cycladic Spirit.* A fine, illustrated study of the meaning and purpose of Cycladic artefacts.

Gisela Richter *A Handbook of Greek Art.* An exhaustive but readable survey of the visual arts of ancient Greece.

R.R.R. Smith *Hellenistic Sculpture.* A modern reappraisal of the art of Greece under Alexander and his successors.

⭐ **David Talbot Rice** *Art of the Byzantine Era.* Talbot Rice was, with Robert Byron, one of the pioneering scholars in the "rediscovery" of Byzantine art; this illustrated study details all mediums, from ivory miniatures to mosaics, by way of icons, and covers all the ancient Byzantine territories from Armenia to Italy.

Peter Warren *The Aegean Civilizations* (o/p). An illustrated account of the Minoan and Mycenaean cultures.

"Coffee-table" books

⭐ **Chris Hellier** *Monasteries of Greece* (o/p). Magnificently photographed survey of the surviving, active monasteries (including the one on Pátmos) and their treasures, with insightful accompanying essays.

⭐ **Constantine Manos** *A Greek Portfolio.* 1972 classic, now in a reasonably priced reprint: the fruits of a gifted Greek-American photo-

grapher's three-year odyssey in the early Sixties through a country on the edge of modernization, still essentially unchanged from the 1930s. The quality and insight you'd expect from a member of the Magnum co-operative, in elegiac black-and-white photos, strong on Kárpathos and Crete.

Mark Ottaway *The Most Beautiful Villages of Greece.* Not exhaustively inclusive, but easily available and with good photos by Hugh Palmer.

Clay Perry *Vanishing Greece* (Eleftheroudhakis/Newsstand, Athens). Well-captioned photos depict the threatened landscapes and relict ways of life in rural Greece; especially good coverage of Híos.

Suzanne Slesin et al *Greek Style*. Stunning (if sometimes contrived) designer-tweaked interiors from Corfu, Rhodes and Sérifos, among other spots.

Janine Trotereau *Greece from the Air*. Translation of an originally French work, with photos by Yann Arthus.

Byzantine, medieval and Ottoman history

Averil Cameron *The Mediterranean World in Late Antiquity, AD 395–600*. Essentially the early Byzantine years.

Nicholas Cheetham *Medieval Greece* (o/p). A general survey of the period and its infinite convolutions in Greece, with Frankish, Catalan, Venetian, Byzantine and Ottoman struggles for power.

★ **John Julius Norwich** *Byzantium: The Early Centuries*; *Byzantium: the Apogee* and *Byzantium: The Decline*. Perhaps the main surprise for first-time travellers to Greece is the fascination of Byzantine monuments, above all at Mystra. This is an astonishingly detailed yet readable trilogy of the empire that produced them; the one-volume version, entitled *A Short History of Byzantium*, is particularly recommended.

★ **Vangelis Pavlidis** *Rhodes 1306–1522: A Story* (Rodos Image, Rhodes). A caricature-illustrated history of the Knights of St John's occupation of Rhodes, by one of Greece's leading political cartoonists – rigorous research and witty text illuminate a little-known era in the Dodecanese.

Michael Psellus *Fourteen Byzantine Rulers*. A fascinating contemporary

source on the stormy but brilliant period from 976 to 1078.

★ **Steven Runciman** *The Fall of Constantinople, 1453*. This is the standard account of the event; *The Great Church in Captivity* follows the vicissitudes of the Orthodox Patriarchate in Constantinople up to the War of Independence. *Byzantine Style and Civilization* and *Mistra: Byzantine Capital of the Peloponnese* (o/p) are more slanted towards art, culture and monuments.

Apostolos Vacalopoulos *Origins of the Greek Nation; The Byzantine Period 1204–1461* (o/p) and *The Greek Nation, 1453–1669* (o/p). Benchmark studies of the period, remarkably restrained in their attitudes towards the conquering Ottomans. The first volume is as much a study of the origins of the Ottoman ascendancy (Byzantine civil war and decadence) as it is the shifting of Hellenism from the east to exile in Europe, while the sequel is the standard reference for Greek life at the village and island level under the "Turks".

★ **Archbishop Kallistos (Timothy) Ware** *The Orthodox Church*. A good introduction to what is still effectively the established religion of Greece, by the Orthodox archbishop resident in Oxford.

Modern Greece

Timothy Boatswain and Colin Nicolson *A Traveller's History of Greece*. 2001-updated, well-written overview of the important Greek periods and personalities.

David Brewer *The Flame of Freedom: The Greek War of Independence 1821–1833*. A fairly recent history with just a few black-and-white illustrations.

★ **Richard Clogg** *A Concise History of Greece*. A remarkably clear and well-illustrated account of Greece, from the decline of Byzantium to 2000, with the emphasis on recent decades; there are numerous maps and lengthy feature captions to the artwork.

Douglas Dakin *The Unification of Greece, 1770–1923* (o/p). The standard account of the foundation of the Greek state and the struggle to extend its boundaries.

Michael Haag *The Rough Guide History of Greece*. Experienced Hellenophile's illustrated, pocket-sized, chronological gazetteer, with feature boxes and pithy quotes. A good one-stop fill-up if you haven't the appetite for longer or more specialized histories.

★ **John S. Koliopoulos and Thanos M. Veremis** *Greece: The Modern Sequel, from 1831 to the Present*. Thematic rather than chronological study that pokes into corners rarely illuminated by conventional histories, with some tart opinions and debunkings; especially good on brigandage and the Communists, on which Kolipoulos is an expert. That said, best read after you've digested Clogg.

★ **H.A. Lidderdale** (trans & ed) *The Memoirs of General*

Makriyannis, 1797–1864 (o/p). The "Peasant General", one of the few honest and self-sacrificing protagonists of the Greek uprising, taught himself to write at age 32 to set down this apologia of his conduct, in vivid demotic Greek. It's heartbreaking in its portrayal of the incipient schisms, linguistic and otherwise, that tore the country apart until recently.

Dimitri Pentzopoulos *The Balkan Exchange of Minorities and its Impact on Greece*. Reissued 1962 classic which shows, among other things, how Venizelos accepted the inevitability of the Greco-Turkish population exchange, using it to create homogeneous Greek-Orthodox populations in the all-important frontier zones (including Crete) – and conveniently importing a bloc of voters favouring his party.

★ **Michael Llewellyn Smith** *Ionian Vision, Greece in Asia Minor, 1919–22*. Standard work, by a former long-serving UK ambassador to Greece, on the disastrous Anatolian campaign, which led to the exchange of populations between Greece and Turkey. His account evinces considerable sympathy for the post-1920 royalist government pursuing an unwanted, inherited war they know is unwinnable.

Peter Varoulakis *The Greek War of Independence*. A nice counterweight to the Brewer work, with lots of colour reproductions of famous scenes, but with far less text.

C.M. Woodhouse *Modern Greece, A Short History*. Woodhouse, long a Conservative MP for Oxfordshire, was a key figure in liaisons with the Greek Resistance during World

War II. Writing from a more right-wing perspective than Clogg, this history (from the foundation of Constantinople in 324 to 1990), is briefer and a bit drier, but scrupulous with facts.

World War II and its aftermath

David H. Close *The Origins of the Greek Civil War* (o/p). Excellent, readable study that focuses on the social conditions in 1920s and 1930s Greece that made the country so ripe for conflict. Draws on primary sources, slays a few sacred cows along the way, and is relatively objective (though he's no great fan of the Left).

Iakovos Kambanellis *Mauthausen* (Kedros, Athens). Kambanellis was active in the Resistance, caught by the Germans, and sent to Mauthausen, one of the concentration camps reserved for those politicians or partisans who had opposed the Nazis' rise to power. Harrowing atrocities in flashback there are aplenty, but the main thrust of the book is post-liberation, describing the author's awkward romance with a Lithuanian Jew, and how the idealist inmates are slowly disillusioned as they see that the "New World Order" will be scarcely different from the old. The basis of a play, and the Theodhorakis oratorio of the same name.

Mark Mazower *Inside Hitler's Greece: The Experience of Occupation 1941–44*. Somewhat choppily organized, but the standard of scholarship is high and the photos alone justify the price, though there's not a great deal specifically on the islands. Demonstrates how the complete demoralization of the country and the incompetence of conventional politicians led to the rise of ELAS and the onset of civil war.

Peter Murtagh *The Rape of Greece: The King, the Colonels and the Resistance* (o/p). Breezy, journalistic chronicle of the junta years with lots of good anecdotes. Of particular value for the story of Democratic Defense, one of the groups resisting the junta from inside the country, and those who helped them from outside Greece when most of Europe was primarily concerned with coddling the colonels.

Yiannis Roubatis *Tangled Webs: The US in Greece 1947–67*. Traces the comprehensive American involvement in Greece during the lead-up to the military coup.

Marion Sarafis and Martin Eve *Background to Contemporary Greece, vols 1 & 2* (o/p). Useful, not overly academic essays on a wide variety of subjects, from the death of *katharévoussa* to (especially) the civil war; a mild left-wing bias, not surprising since Sarafis was the (English) widow of ELAS commander Stefanos Sarafis.

Adrian Seligman *War in the Islands*. Collected oral histories of a little-known Allied unit: a flotilla of *kaïkia* organized to raid the Axis-held Aegean islands. Boy's Own stuff, with service-jargon-laced prose, but lots of fine period photos and detail.

C.M. Woodhouse *The Struggle for Greece, 1941–49*. A masterly, well-illustrated account of this crucial decade, exploring all of the so-called "three rounds" of resistance and rebellion, and how Greece emerged without a communist government; remarkably objective

considering Woodhouse's role in the British mission to the Greek resistance forces.

Ethnography

★ **Juliet du Boulay** *Portrait of a Greek Mountain Village* (Denise Harvey, Límni, Évvia). An account of the village of Ambéli, on Évvia, during the 1960s. The habits and customs of an all-but-vanished way of life are observed and evoked in an absorbing narrative.

★ **Loring Danforth** (text) and **Alexander Tsiaras** (photos) *The Death Rituals of Rural Greece*. Many visitors and foreign residents find Greek funeral customs – the wailing, the open-casket vigils, the disinterment of the bones after five years – the most disturbing aspect of the culture; this book helps make sense of it all.

★ **Gail Holst-Warhaft** *Road to Rembétika: Songs of Love, Sorrow and Hashish*. The most intriguing Greek urban musical style of the past century, evocatively traced by a Cornell University professor and long-term observer of the Greek music scene; useful discography has been updated to the mid-1990s.

★ **John Cuthbert Lawson** *Modern Greek Folklore and Ancient Greek Religion: A Study in Survivals* (available by print-on-demand basis via the Internet). Exactly as the title states, and still highly applicable a century after its writing; well worth scouring antiquarian dealers for previous editions.

Modern Greek fiction

★ **Maro Douka** *Fool's Gold* (Kedros, Athens). Describes an upper-class young woman's involvement, and subsequent disillusionment, with the clandestine resistance to the junta.

★ **Apostolos Doxiades** *Uncle Petros and the Goldbach Conjecture*. Self-translated from the Greek; an excellent read despite the knotty mathematical puzzle at the heart of the novel.

Eugenia Fakinou *The Seventh Garment*. Greek history, from the War of Independence to the colonels' junta, told through the life stories (interspersed in counterpoint) of three generations of women.

Nikos Kazantzakis Whether in intricate Greek or translated into inadequate English, Kazantzakis can be hard going, yet the power of his writing still shines through. *Zorba the Greek* is a surprisingly dark, nihilistic work, worlds away from the two-dimensional characters of the film. On the other hand, the movie version of *The Last Temptation of Christ* provoked riots amongst Orthodox fanatics in Athens in 1989. *Christ Recrucified* (published in the US as *The Greek Passion*) resets the Easter drama against the backdrop of Christian/Muslim relations, while *Freedom or Death* (published in the US as *Captain Michalis*) chronicles the rebellions of late-nineteenth-century Crete. *The Fratricides* portrays a family riven by the civil war, while *Report to Greco* – perhaps the most accessible of his works – is an autobiographical exploration of his Greekness.

★ **Artemis Leontis** (ed) *Greece: A Traveller's Literary Companion*. An overdue idea, brilliantly executed: various regions of the country as portrayed in (very) short fiction or essays by modern Greek writers. A recommended antidote to the often condescending Grand Tourist accounts.

★ **Stratis Myrivilis** *Life in the Tomb*. A harrowing and unorthodox war memoir, based on the author's experience on the Macedonian front during 1917–18, well translated by Peter Bien. Completing a kind of trilogy are two later novels, set on the north coast of Lésvos, Myrivilis's homeland: *The Mermaid Madonna* and *The Schoolmistress with the Golden Eyes* (Efstathiadis, Athens). Translations of these are not so good, and heavily abridged.

Alexandhros Papadiamantis *The Murderess* (o/p). A landmark novel set on the island of Skiáthos at the beginning of the nineteenth century, in which an old woman, appalled by the fate that awaits them in adulthood, concludes that little girls are better off dead. Also available is a collection of short stories, *Tales from a Greek Island*.

★ **Nick Papandreou** *Father Dancing* (o/p). Thinly veiled roman à clef by the late Andreas's younger son. Papandreou Senior, not too surprisingly, comes across as a gasbag and petty domestic tyrant.

★ **Dido Sotiriou** *Farewell Anatolia* (Kedros, Athens). A perennial favourite since its initial appearance in 1962, this epic chronicles the traumatic end of Greek life in Asia Minor, from World War I to the catastrophe of 1922, as narrated by a fictionalized version of the author's father. In the finale he escapes across the narrow strait of Mykale to Sámos, as so many did during those turbulent years.

★ **Stratis Tsirkas** *Drifting Cities* (Kedros, Athens). Set by turns in the Jerusalem, Cairo and Alexandria of World War II, this unflinchingly honest and humane epic of a Greek army hero secretly working for the Leftist resistance got the author expelled from the Communist Party.

Vassilis Vassilikos *Z* (o/p). A novel based closely enough on events – the 1963 political assassination of Gregoris Lambrakis in Thessaloníki – to be banned under the colonels' junta, and brilliantly filmed by Costa-Gavras in 1968.

★ **Alki Zei** *Achilles' Fiancée* (Kedros, Athens). An often moving portrait of the friendships and intrigues amongst a collection of communist exiles floating between Athens, Rome, Moscow, Paris and Tashkent in the years between the civil war and the colonels' junta. Largely autobiographical, it captures the flavour of the illusions, nostalgia and party-line schisms endemic in this community.

Greece in foreign fiction

★ **Louis de Bernières** *Captain Corelli's Mandolin*. Set on Kefaloniá during the World War II occupation and aftermath, this accomplished 1994 tragicomedy quickly acquired cult, then word-of-mouth bestseller status, but has lately become a *succès de scandale*. When the islanders, Greek Left intellectuals and surviving Italian partisans woke up to its virulent anti-communism and disparaging portrayal of ELAS, there was a furore, with de Bernières eventually obliged to eat large quantities of humble pie in the UK press. It also seems the novel is closely based on the experiences of still-alive-and-kicking Amos Pampaloni, an artillery captain on Kefalloniá in 1942–44 who later joined ELAS, and who accuses de Bernières of distorting the roles of both Italians and ELAS on the island. The Greek translation has been suitably abridged to avoid causing offence, and the movie (starring Nicholas Cage and Penelope Cruz), watered down to a pallid love story as a condition for filming on the island, sank without trace after a few weeks in 2001.

John Fowles *The Magus*. Fowles' biggest and best novel: a tale of mystery and manipulation – plus Greek island life – inspired by his stay on Spétses as a teacher during the 1950s.

Mary Renault *The King Must Die*; *The Last of the Wine*; *The Masks of Apollo* and *The Praise Singer*. Mary Renault's imaginative reconstructions are more than the adolescent's reading they're often taken for, with impeccable research and tight writing. The quartert above retell, respectively, the myth of Theseus, the life of a pupil of Socrates, that of a fourth-century-BC actor, and the the fortunes of poet Simonides at the court of Samian tyrant Polykrates. The life of Alexander the Great is told in *Fire from Heaven*, *The Persian Boy* and *Funeral Games*, available separately or in one economical volume.

Evelyn Waugh *Officers and Gentleman*. This volume of his wartime trilogy includes an account of the Battle of Crete and subsequent evacuation.

Modern Greek poetry

With two Nobel laureates in the twentieth century – George Seferis and Odysseus Elytis – modern Greece has an extraordinarily intense and dynamic poetic tradition. Translations of all of the following are excellent.

C.P. Cavafy *Collected Poems*. The complete works, translated by Edmund Keeley and Philip Sherrard, of perhaps the most accessible modern Greek poet, resident for most of his life in Alexandria. For some, *The Complete Poems of Cavafy*, translated by Rae Dalven, or *The Poems of C. P.*

Cavafy by John Mavrogordato, are superior versions.

Odysseus Elytis *The Axion Esti*; *Selected Poems* (o/p) and *The Sovereign Sun* (o/p). The major works in good English versions. Easier to find is *Collected Poems*, which includes virtually everything except *The Axion Esti*.

Modern Greek Poetry (Efstathiadis, Athens). Despite the publisher's reputation for shoddy work, this in fact is a decent anthology of translations, predominantly of Seferis and Elytis.

Yannis Ritsos *Exile and Return, Selected Poems 1967–1974* (o/p). A fine volume of Greece's foremost

Leftist poet, from the junta era when he was internally exiled on Sámos.

George Seferis *Collected Poems, 1924–1955* (o/p). Virtually the complete works of the Nobel laureate, with Greek and English verses on facing pages. More recent, but lacking the parallel Greek text, is *Complete Poems*.

Specific guides

Archeology

★ A.R. and Mary Burn *The Living Past of Greece: A Time Traveller's Tour of Historic and Prehistoric Places* (o/p). Unusual in extent, this covers sites from Minoan through to Byzantine and Frankish, with good clear plans and lively text.

★ Paul Hetherington *The Greek Islands: Guide to Byzantine and Medieval Buildings and their Art*. A gazetteer of most major island sites, with some colour photos and useful plans, though there are some peculiar omissions of worthy monuments.

Evi Melas (ed) *Temples and Sanctuaries of Ancient Greece: A Companion Guide* (o/p). An excellent collection of essays on the main sites, written by archeologists who have worked at them.

Alexander Paradissis *Fortresses and Castles of Greece* (Efstathiadis, Athens). Three exhaustive and extremely prolix volumes, widely available in Greek bookshops; the third volume (if available separately) covers strictly the islands.

Hiking

★ Lance Chilton Various walking pamphlets (Marengo Publications, UK). Small but thorough guides to the best walks at various island charter resorts, accompanied by three-colour maps. Areas covered to date include: Áyios Yeóryios, Corfu; Yeoryioúpolis and Plakiás, Crete; Kálymnos; Líndhos, Rhodes; Kokkári, Sámos; and Sými. Obtain in specialist UK shops or online at ⊛www.marengowalks.com.

Marc Dubin *Trekking in Greece* (o/p). Though many sections are showing their 1988–92 age (and the depredations of bulldozers), still an

excellent walkers' guide, expanding on the hikes covered in this book. Includes day-hikes and longer treks on the islands, plus extensive preparatory and background information.

★ Loraine Wilson *The White Mountains of Crete*. Nearly sixty walks and treks, from easy to gruelling, by the doyenne of foreign trekking guides in Crete; implicitly trustworthy directions and prudent warnings. The book's marred only by rudimentary maps (buy the Harms series) and rather bizarre transliterations of Greek phrases.

Regional guides

★ **Johan de Bakker** *Across Crete* (World Discovery Guide Books, Netherlands). Planned three-volume coverage of Crete, assessing the modern sites in comparison with extracted accounts of eighteenth- and nineteenth-century travellers; only the superb Vol 1, *From Khaniá to Herákleion*, available thus far.

Marc Dubin *The Rough Guide to the Dodecanese and the East Aegean*. Exhaustive coverage of the islands described in Chapters Four and Five of this book, by a part-time resident of Sámos.

Nick Edwards *The Rough Guide to the Ionian Islands*. Exhaustive coverage of the islands described in Chapter Seven of this book, by a well-travelled ex-classicist.

John Fisher and Geoff Garvey *The Rough Guide to Crete*. An expanded and practical guide to the island by two Cretophiles, who contributed the Crete chapter to this book.

Lycabettus Press Guides (Athens, Greece). This series takes in several of the more popular islands; most, despite decade-long intervals between revisions, pay their way both in interest and usefulness – in particular those on Páros, Kós, Pátmos, Ídhra and the travels of Saint Paul.

★ **Oliver Rackham and Jennifer Moody** *The Making of the Cretan Landscape*. It's hard to classify this academic-press product written for the casual visitor. As the title says, but much more, taking in geology, natural history, agricultural practices, place names, architecture and demography, all arranged by topic. Not error-free – nothing this ambitious could be – but impressive.

Nikos Stavroulakis *Jewish Sites and Synagogues of Greece* (Talos Press, Athens). A lavishly illustrated alphabetical gazetteer of all Jewish monuments in the Greek islands, with town plans and full histories of the communities that created them.

Yachting

H.M. Denham *The Aegean* and *The Ionian Islands to the Anatolian Coast* (o/p). Long the standard references if you were out yachting; still found in secondhand bookshops and on websites, but a bit obsolete.

Rod Heikell *Greek Waters Pilot*. Rather better than the preceding, which it has superseded; updated to 2001 conditions.

Bookshops

Athens has a number of excellent central **bookshops**, at which many of these recommendations should be available (at fifty-percent mark-up for foreign-published titles). Outlets include Eleftheroudhakis, Panepistimíou 17 plus other branches; Compendium, Níkis 28, off Sýndagma; and Iy Folia tou Vivlíou, in the arcade at Panepistimíou 25.

In London, the Hellenic Bookservice, 91 Fortess Rd, Kentish Town, London NW5 1AG (☎020/7267 9499, ℻7267 9498, ⊛www.hellenicbookservice.com), is the UK's premier walk-in Greek bookshop: knowledgeable and well-stocked specialist dealers in new, secondhand and out-of-print books. Rivals Zeno's have premises at 57A Nether St, North Finchley, London N12 7NP (☎020/8446 1985, ⊛www.thegreekbookshop.com).

Food and wine

Rosemary Barron *Flavours of Greece*. The leading cookbook among many contenders, by an internationally recognized authority on Greek cuisine. Contains over 250 recipes; now in paperback too.

Andrew Dalby *Siren Feasts: A History of Food and Gastronomy in Greece*. This analysis of ancient texts demonstrates just how little Greek cuisine has changed in three millennia; also excellent on the introduction and etymology of common vegetables and herbs.

[★] **Alan Davidson** *Mediterranean Seafood*. A 1972 classic, revised in 2002, this amazingly erudite and witty book catalogues 99.9 percent of all known edible species, complete with legends, anecdotes, habits, local names and a suggested recipe or two for each.

[★] **James Davidson** *Courtesans and Fishcakes*. The politics, class characteristics and etiquette of consumption and consummation – with wine, women, boys and seafood – in ancient Athens, with their bearing on both historical events and modern attitudes.

[★] **Nico Manessis** *The Illustrated Greek Wine Book* (Olive Press Publications, Corfu; available at select retailers in Greece or through ⓦwww.greekwineguide.gr). Covers almost all the wineries, from mass-market to micro, with very reliable ratings (up to the year 2000); also fascinating features on grape varieties, traditional retsina-making, and even how Greeks were instrumental in introducing vines to the New World. Pricey but worth it.

Nikos Stavroulakis *Cookbook of the Jews of Greece* (Lycabettus Press, Athens; Cadmus Press, US). Tasty if often fiddly recipes interspersed with their relation to the Jewish liturgical year, plus potted histories of the communities which produced them.

[★] **Traditional Greek Recipes** (Grecocard, Greece). As it says; the best of a huge pile of glossy pictorial cookbooks pitched at the tourist market.

Language

Language

Greek

S o many Greeks have lived or worked abroad in North America, Australia and, to a much lesser extent, Britain, that you will find someone who speaks **English** in the tiniest island village. Add to that the thousands attending language schools or working in the tourist industry – English is the lingua franca of most resorts, with German second – and it is easy to see how so many visitors come back having learned only half a dozen restaurant words.

You can certainly get by this way, but it isn't very satisfying, and the willingness and ability to say even a few words will transform your status from that of dumb *touristas* to the more honourable one of *xénos/xéni*, a word which can mean foreigner, traveller and guest all rolled into one.

Learning basic Greek

Greek is not an easy language for English-speakers – translators' unions in the UK rate it as harder than German, slightly less complex than Russian – but it is a very beautiful one, and even a brief acquaintance will give you some idea of the debt owed to it by Western European languages. Greek **grammar** is predictably complicated; **nouns** are divided into three genders, all with different case endings in the singular and in the plural, and all adjectives and articles have to agree with these in gender, number and case. To simplify life for beginners, all adjectives are arbitrarily cited in the neuter form in the boxed lists on p.629. **Verbs** are even more complex; they come in two conjugations, in both active and passive voices, with passively constructed verbs often having transitive sense. As a novice, the best thing is simply to say what you know the way you know it, and dispense with the niceties.

Teach-yourself Greek courses

Breakthrough Greek (Pan Macmillan; book and 4 cassettes). Excellent, basic teach-yourself course; no Greek lettering, but good for classicists who need to unlearn bad habits.

Greek Language and People (BBC Publications, UK; book and 2 cassettes available). More limited in scope but good for acquiring the essentials, and the confidence to try them.

Anne Farmakides *A Manual of Modern Greek* (Yale UP; McGill UP; 3 vols). If you have the discipline and motivation, this is one of the best for learning proper, grammatical Greek; indeed, mastery of just the first volume will get you a long way.

Hara Garoufalia *Teach Yourself Holiday Greek* (Hodder & Stoughton, UK; book and cassette available). Unlike many quickie courses, this provides a good grammatical foundation, but you'll need a dictionary (see p.628) to supplement the scanty vocabulary lists.

David Hoton et al *Greek: A Comprehensive Grammar of the Modern Language* (Routledge). A bit technical in terminology, so not for rank beginners, but it covers just about every conceivable construction.

Niki Watts *Greek in Three Months* (Hugo, Dorling Kindersley; book and 4 cassettes). Delivers as promised; equals or exceeds *Breakthrough Greek*.

Phrasebooks and dictionaries

Greek, a Rough Guide Phrasebook Up to date and accurate pocket phrasebook with actually useful phrases. The English-to-Greek section is sensibly transliterated, though the Greek-to-English part requires basic mastery of the Greek alphabet. Feature boxes fill you in on cultural know-how.

The Oxford Dictionary of Modern Greek. A bit bulky in its wide format, but generally considered the best Greek–English, English–Greek paperback dictionary.

Collins Pocket Greek Dictionary. Very nearly as complete as the Oxford and probably better value for money. The inexpensive *Collins Gem Greek Dictionary* (UK only) is palm-sized but exactly the same in contents – the best day-pack choice.

Oxford Greek–English, English–Greek Learner's Dictionary. If you're planning a prolonged stay, this pricey, hardbound, two-volume set is unbeatable for usage and vocabulary. There's also a more portable one-volume Learner's *Pocket Dictionary*.

The Greek alphabet: transliteration and accentuation

On top of the usual difficulties of learning a new language, Greek presents the additional problem of an entirely separate **alphabet**. Despite initial appearances, this is in practice fairly easily mastered – a skill that will help enormously if you are going to get around independently (see the alphabet box opposite). In addition, certain combinations of letters have unexpected results. This book's transliteration system should help you make intelligible noises, but you have to remember that the correct **stress** (marked throughout the book with an acute accent or sometimes dieresis) is crucial. With the right sounds but the wrong stress people will either fail to understand you, or else understand something quite different from what you intended – there are numerous pairs of words with the same spelling and phonemes, distinguished only by their stress.

The **dieresis** is used in Greek over the second of two adjacent vowels to change the pronunciation that you would expect from the table opposite; often in this book it can function as the primary stress. In the word *kaïki* (caique), the presence of the dieresis changes the pronunciation from "cake-key" to "ka-ee-key" and additionally the middle "i" carries the primary stress. In the word *païdhákia* (lamb chops), the dieresis again changes the sound of the first syllable from "pay" to "pah-ee", but in this case the primary stress is on the third syllable. It is also, uniquely among Greek accents, used on capital letters in signs and personal-name spellings in Greece, and we have followed this practice on our maps.

Set out below is the Greek alphabet, the system of transliteration used in this book, and a brief aid to pronunciation.

Greek	Transliteration	Pronounced
A, α	a	a as in father
B, β	v	v as in vet
Γ, γ	y/g	y as in yes except before consonants or a, o or ou when it's a breathy g, approximately as in gap
Δ, δ	dh	th as in then
E, ε	e	e as in get
Z, ζ	z	z sound
H, η	i	i as in ski
Θ, θ	th	th as in theme
I, ι	i	i as in ski
K, κ	k	k sound
Λ, λ	l	l sound
M, μ	m	m sound
N, ν	n	n sound
Ξ, ξ	x	x sound, never z
O, o	o	o as in toad
Π, π	p	p sound
P, ρ	r	r sound
Ϟ, σ, ς	s	s sound, except z before m or g; single sigma has the same phonic value as double sigma
T, τ	t	t sound
Y, υ	y	y as in barely
Φ, φ	f	f sound
X, χ	h before vowels, kh before consonants	harsh h sound, like ch in loch
Ψ, ψ	ps	ps as in lips
Ω, ω	o	o as in toad, indistinguishable from o

Combinations and diphthongs

AI, αι	e	e as in hey
AY, αυ	av/af	av or af depending on following consonant
EI, ει	i	long i, exactly i or h
EY, ευ	ev/ef	ev or ef, depending on following consonant
OI, οι	i	long i, exactly like i or h
OY, ου	ou	ou as in tourist
ΓΓ, γγ	ng	ng as in angle; always medial
ΓΚ, γκ	g/ng	g as in goat at the beginning of a word, ng in the middle
ΜΠ, μπ	b/mb	b at the beginning of a word, mb in the middle
ΝΤ, ντ	d/nd	d at the beginning of a word, nd in the middle
ΤΣ, τσ	ts	ts as in hits
ΤΖ, τζ	tz	dg as in judge, j as in jam in some dialects

Greek words and phrases

Essentials

Yes	Né	Here	Edhó
Certainly	Málista	There	Ekí
No	Óhi	This one	Aftó
Please	Parakaló	That one	Ekíno
OK, agreed	Endáxi	Good	Kaló
Thank you (very much)	Efharistó (polý)	Bad	Kakó
I (don't) understand	(Dhén) Katalavéno	Big	Megálo
Excuse me	Parakaló, mípos	Small	Mikró
Do you speak English?	Miláte angliká?	More	Perisótero
Sorry/excuse me	Signómi	Less	Ligótero
Today	Símera	A little	Lígo
Tomorrow	Ávrio	A lot	Polý
Yesterday	Khthés	Cheap	Ftinó
Now	Tóra	Expensive	Akrivó
Later	Argótera	Hot	Zestó
Open	Anikhtó	Cold	Krýo
Closed	Klistó	With (together)	Mazí (mé)
Day	Méra	Without	Horís
Night	Níkhta	Quickly	Grígora
In the morning	Tó proï	Slowly	Sigá
In the afternoon	Tó apóyevma	Mr/Mrs	Kýrios/Kyría
In the evening	Tó vrádhi	Miss	Dhespinís

Other needs

To eat/drink	Trógo/píno	Bank	Trápeza
Bakery	Foúrnos, psomádhiko	Money	Leftá/Khrímata
Pharmacy	Farmakío	Toilet	Toualéta
Post office	Tahydhromío	Police	Astynomía
Stamps	Gramatósima	Doctor	Yiatrós
Petrol station	Venzinádhiko	Hospital	Nosokomío

Requests and questions

To ask a question, it's simplest, though hardly elegant, to start with *parakaló*, then name the thing you want in an interrogative tone.

Where is the bakery?	Parakaló, o foúrnos?	May I have a kilo of oranges?	Parakaló, éna kiló portokália?
Can you show me the road to . . . ?	Parakaló, ó dhrómos yiá . . . ?	Where?	Poú?
We'd like a room for two	Parakaló, éna dhomátio yiá dhýo átoma?	How?	Pós?
		How many?	Póssi, pósses or póssa?

How much?	Póso?	How much (does it cost)?	Póso káni?
When?	Póte?		
Why?	Yiatí?	What time does it open?	Tí óra aníyi?
At what time . . . ?	Tí óra . . . ?		
What is/ Which is . . . ?	Tí íne/Pió íne . . . ?	What time does it close?	Tí óra klíni?

Talking to people

Greek makes the distinction between the informal (*essý*) and formal (*essís*) second person, as French does with "tu" and "vous". Young people, older people and country people often use *essý* even with total strangers, though if you greet someone familiarly and they respond formally, it's best to adopt their usage as the conversation continues, to avoid offence. By far the most common greeting, on meeting and parting, is *yiá sou/yiá sas* – literally "health to you". Incidentally, as across most of the Mediterranean, the approaching party utters the first greeting, not those seated at sidewalk *kafenío* tables or doorsteps – thus the silent staring as you enter a village.

Hello	Hérete	Speak slower, please	Parakaló, miláte pió sigá
Good morning	Kalí méra		
Good evening	Kalí spéra	How do you say it in Greek?	Pós léyete stá Elliniká?
Good night	Kalí níkhta		
Goodbye	Adío	I don't know	Dhén xéro
How are you?	Tí kánis/Tí kánete?	See you tomorrow	Thá sé dhó ávrio
I'm fine	Kalá íme	See you soon	Kalí andhámosi
And you?	Ké essís?	Let's go	Páme
What's your name?	Pós se léne?	Please help me	Parakaló, ná mé voithíste
My name is . . .	Mé léne . . .		

Greek's Greek

There are numerous words and phrases which you will hear constantly, even if you rarely have the chance to use them. These are a few of the most common.

Éla!	Come (literally) but also Speak to me! You don't say! etc.	Po-po-po!	Expression of dismay or concern, like French *O là là!*
Oríste!	Literally, "Indicate!"; in effect, "What can I do for you?"	Pedhí moú	My boy/girl, sonny, friend, etc.
Embrós! or Léyete!	Standard phone responses	Maláka(s)	Literally "wanker", but often used (don't try it!) as an informal term of address.
Tí néa?	What's new?		
Tí yínete?	What's going on (here)?	Sigá sigá	Take your time, slow down
Étsi k'étsi	So-so		
Ópa!	Whoops! Watch it!	Kaló taxídhi	Bon voyage

Accommodation

Hotel	Xenodhohío	Hot water	Zestó neró
Inn	Xenón(as)	Cold water	Krýo neró
Youth hostel	Xenónas neótitos	Air conditioning	Klimatismós
A room . . .	Éna dhomátio . . .	Fan	Anamistíra
for one/two/three people	yiá éna/dhýo/tría átoma	Can I see it?	Boró ná tó dhó?
for one/two/three nights	yiá mía/dhýo/trís vradhiés	Can we camp here?	Boroúme na váloume ti skiní edhó?
with a double bed	mé megálo kreváti	Campsite	Kámping/ Kataskínosi
with a shower	mé doús	Tent	Skiní

On the move

Aeroplane	Aeropláno	How many kilometres?	Póssa hiliómetra?
Bus, coach	Leoforío, púlman	How many hours?	Pósses óres?
Car	Aftokínito, amáxi	Where are you going?	Poú pás?
Motorbike, scooter	Mihanáki, papáki		
Taxi	Taxí	I'm going to . . .	Páo stó . . .
Ship	Plío/vapóri/karávi	I want to get off at . . .	Thélo ná katévo stó . . .
High-speed catamaran	Tahýplio	The road to . . .	O dhrómos yiá . . .
Hydrofoil	Dhelfíni	Near	Kondá
Train	Tréno	Far	Makriá
Train station	Sidhirodhromikós stathmós	Left	Aristerá
		Right	Dhexiá
Bicycle	Podhílato	Straight ahead	Katefthía, ísia
Hitching	Otostóp	A ticket to . . .	Éna isitírio yiá . . .
On foot	Mé tá pódhia	A return ticket	Éna isitírio mé epistrofí
Trail	Monopáti		
Bus station	Praktorío leoforíon, KTEL	Beach	Paralía
		Cave	Spiliá
Bus stop	Stássi	Centre (of town)	Kéndro
Harbour	Limáni	Church	Eklissía
What time does it leave?	Ti óra févyi?	Sea	Thálassa
What time does it arrive?	Ti óra ftháni?	Village	Horió

Numbers

1	énas/éna/mía	7	eftá
2	dhýo	8	okhtó
3	trís/tría	9	ennéa (or more slangy, enyá)
4	tésseres/téssera		
5	pénde	10	dhéka
6	éxi	11	éndheka

12	dhódheka	90	enenínda
13	dhekatrís	100	ekató
14	dhekatésseres	150	ekatón penínda
20	íkossi	200	dhiakóssies/dhiakóssia
21	íkossi éna (all	500	pendakóssies/
	compounds written		pendakóssia
	separately thus)	1000	hílies/hília
30	triánda	2000	dhýo hiliádhes
40	saránda	1,000,000	éna ekatomírio
50	penínda	first	próto
60	exínda	second	dhéftero
70	evdhomínda	third	tríto
80	ogdhónda		

Days of the week and the time

Sunday	Kyriakí	Twenty minutes to four	Tésseres pará íkossi
Monday	Dheftéra		
Tuesday	Tríti	Five minutes past seven	Eftá ké pénde
Wednesday	Tetárti		
Thursday	Pémpti	Half past eleven	Éndheka ké misí
Friday	Paraskeví	In half an hour	Sé misí óra
Saturday	Sávato	In a quarter-hour	S'éna tétarto
What time is it?	Tí óra íne?	In two hours	Sé dhýo óres
One/two/three o'clock	Mía iy óra/dhýo iy óra/trís iy óra		

Months and seasonal terms

NB: You may see *katharévoussa*, or hybrid, forms of the months written on schedules or street signs; these are the spoken demotic forms.

January	Yennáris	September	Septémvris
February	Fleváris	October	Októvrios
March	Mártis	November	Noémvris
April	Aprílis	December	Dhekémvris
May	Maïos	Summer schedule	Therinó dhromolóyio
June	Ioúnios	Winter schedule	Himerinó dhromolóyio
July	Ioúlios		
August	Ávgoustos		

A food and drink glossary

Basics			
Aláti	Salt	Hortofágos	Vegetarian
Avgá	Eggs	Katálogo/lísta	Menu
(Horís) ládhi	(Without) oil	Kréas	Meat
		Lahaniká	Vegetables
		O logariasmós	The bill

Méli	Honey
Neró	Water
Psári(a)	Fish
Psomí	Bread
Olikís	Wholemeal bread
Sikalísio	Rye bread
Thalassiná	Seafood
Tyrí	Cheese
Yiaoúrti	Yogurt
Záhari	Sugar

Cooking terms

Akhnistó	Steamed
Makaronádha	Any spaghetti/pasta-based dish
Pastó	Marinated in salt
Psitó	Roasted
Saganáki	Cheese-based red sauce; also any fried cheese
Skáras	Grilled
Stí soúvla	Spit-roasted
Stó foúrno	Baked
Tiganitó	Pan-fried
Tís óras	Grilled/fried to order
Yakhní	Stewed in oil and tomato sauce
Yemistá	Stuffed (squid, vegetables, etc)

Soups and starters

Avgolémono	Egg and lemon soup
Dolmádhes	Stuffed vine leaves
Fasoládha	Bean soup
Fáva	Purée of yellow peas, served with onion and lemon
Florínes	Canned red sweet Macedonian peppers
Hortópita	Turnover or pie stuffed with wild greens
Kafterí	Cheese dip with chili added
Kápari	Pickled caper leaves
Kopanistí, khtypití	Pungent, fermented cheese purée
Krítamo	Rock samphire

Mavromátika	Black-eyed peas
Melitzanosaláta	Aubergine/eggplant dip
Revythokeftédhes	Chickpea (garbanzo) patties
Skordhaliá	Garlic dip
Soúpa	Soup
Taramosaláta	Cod roe paté
Trahanádhes	Crushed wheat and milk soup, sweet or savoury
Tyrokafterí	Cheese dip with chilli, different from kopanistí
Tzatzíki	Yogurt and cucumber dip
Tzirosaláta	cured mackerel dip

Vegetables

Angináres	Artichokes
Angoúri	Cucumber
Ánitho	Dill
Bámies	Okra, ladies' fingers
Bouréki, bourekákia	Courgette/zucchini, potato and cheese pie
Briám	Ratatouille
Domátes	Tomatoes
Fakés	Lentils
Fasolákia	French (green) beans
Horiátiki (saláta)	Greek salad (with olives, feta etc)
Hórta	Greens (usually wild), steamed
Kolokythákia	Courgette/zucchini
Koukiá	Broad beans
Maroúli	Lettuce
Melitzánes imám	Aubergine/eggplant slices baked with onion, garlic and copious olive oil
Patátes	Potatoes
Piperiés	Peppers
Pligoúri, pinigoúri	Bulgur wheat
Radhíkia	Wild chicory - a common hórta
Rýzi/Piláfi sáltsa	Rice (usually with sauce)

Rókka	Rocket
Saláta	Salad
Spanáki	Spinach
Vlíta Notchweed	another common hórta
Yígandes	White haricot beans

Fish and seafood

Astakós	Aegean lobster
Atherína	Sand smelt
Bakaliáros	Cod or hake, usually latter
Barbóuni	Red mullet
Fangrí	Common bream
Foúskes	*Uovo de mare* (Italian), *violet* (French); no English equivalent for this invertebrate.
Galéos	Dogfish, hound shark, tope
Garídhes	Shrimp, prawns
Gávros	Mild anchovy
Glóssa	Sole
Gónos, Gonákia	Any hatchling fish
Gópa	Bogue
Kalamarákia	Baby squid
Kalamária	Squid
Karavídhes	Crayfish
Kefalás	Axillary bream
Koliós	Chub mackerel
Koutsomoúra	Goatfish (small red mullet)
Kydhónia	Cockles
Lakérdha	Light-fleshed bonito, marinated
Marídhes	Picarel
Melanoúri	Saddled bream
Ménoula	Sprat
Mýdhia	Mussels
Okhtapódhi	Octopus
Pandelís	Corvina; also called sykiós
Platý	Skate, ray
Sardhélles	Sardines
Sargós	White bream
Seláhi	Skate, ray
Skáros	Parrotfish
Skathári	Black bream
Skoumbrí	Atlantic mackerel
Soupiá	Cuttlefish
Spiníalo or spinóalo	marinated foúskes
Synagrídha	Dentex
Tsipoúra	Gilt-head bream
Vátos	Skate, ray
Xifías	Swordfish
Yermanós	Leatherback

Meat and meat-based dishes

Arní	Lamb
Bekrí mezé	Pork chunks in red sauce
Biftéki	Hamburger
Brizóla	Pork or beef chop
Hirinó	Pork
Keftédhes	Meatballs
Kokorétsi	Liver/offal roulade, spit-roasted
Kopsídha	(Lamb) shoulder chops
Kotópoulo	Chicken
Kounélli	Rabbit
Loukánika	Spicy course-ground sausages
Moskhári	Veal
Moussakás	Aubergine, potato and lamb-mince casserole with bechamel topping
Païdhákia	Rib chops, lamb or goat
Papoutsákia	Stuffed aubergine/ eggplant "shoes"- like *moussakás* without bechamel
Pastítsio	Macaroni "pie" baked with minced meat
Pastourmás	Cured, highly spiced meat; traditionally camel, nowadays beef
Patsás	Tripe and trotter soup
Psaronéfri	Pork tenderloin medallions
Salingária	Garden snails
Soutzoukákia	Minced meat rissoles/beef patties

Spetzofáï	Sausage and pepper red-sauce stew
Stifádho	Meat stew with tomato and boiling onions
Sykóti	Liver
Tiganiá	Meat chunks, usually pork, fried in its own fat
Tziyéro sarmás	Lamb's liver in cabbage
Youvétsi	Baked clay casserole of meat and kritharáki (short pasta)

Sweets and dessert

Baklavás	Honey and nut pastry
Bougátsa	Salt or sweet cream pie served warm with sugar and cinammon
Galaktobóureko	Custard pie
Halvás	Sweetmeat of sesame or semolina
Karydhópita	Walnut cake
Kréma	Custard
Loukoumádhes	Dough fritters in honey syrup and sesame seeds
Pagotó	Ice cream
Pastélli	Sesame and honey bar
Ravaní	Spongecake, lightly syruped
Ryzógalo	Rice pudding

Fruit and nuts

Akhládhia	Big pears
Aktinídhia	Kiwis
Fistíkia	Pistachio nuts
Fráoules	Strawberries
Karpoúzi	Watermelon

Kerásia	Cherries
Krystália	Miniature pears
Kydhóni	Quince
Lemónia	Lemons
Míla	Apples
Pepóni	Melon
Portokália	Oranges
Rodhákino	Peach
Sýka	Figs
Stafýlia	Grapes

Cheese

Ayeladhinó	Cow's-milk cheese
Féta	Salty, white cheese
Graviéra	Gruyère-type hard cheese
Katsikísio	Goat cheese
Kasséri	Medium-sharp cheese
Myzíthra	Sweet cream cheese
Próvio	Sheep cheese

Drinks

Alisfakiá	Island sage tea
Boukáli	Bottle
Býra	Beer
Gála	Milk
Galakakáo	Chocolate milk
Gazóza	Generic fizzy drink
Kafés	Coffee
Krasí	Wine
áspro	white
kokkinélli/rozé	rosé
kókkino/mávro	red
Limonádha	Lemonade
Metalikó neró	Mineral water
Portokaládha	Orangeade
Potíri	Glass
Stinyássas!	Cheers!
Tsáï	Tea
Tsáï vounoú	"Mountain" (mainland sage) tea

Katharévoussa, dhimotikí and dialects

Greek may seem complicated enough in itself, but problems are multiplied when you consider that since the early 1800s there has been an ongoing dispute between two versions of the language: **katharévoussa** and **dhimotikí**.

When Greece first achieved independence in the nineteenth century, its people were almost universally illiterate, and the language they spoke – *dhimotikí*, "demotic" or "popular" Greek – had undergone enormous change since the days of the Byzantine empire and Classical times. The vocabulary had assimilated countless borrowings from the languages of the various invaders and conquerors, such as the Turks, Venetians and Slavs.

The finance and inspiration for the new Greek state, as well as some of its early leaders, came largely from the diaspora – Greek families who had been living in the sophisticated cities of central and eastern Europe, in Constantinople or in Russia. With their European notions about the grandeur of Greece's past, and lofty conception of Hellenism, they set about obliterating the memory of subjugation to foreigners in every possible field. And what better way to start than by purging the language of its foreign accretions and reviving its Classical purity?

They accordingly created what was in effect a new form of the language, *katharévoussa* (literally "cleansed" Greek). The complexities of Classical grammar and syntax were largely reinstated, and Classical words, long out of use, were reintroduced. To the country's great detriment, *katharévoussa* became the language of the schools and the prestigious professions, government, business, the law, newspapers and academia. Everyone aspiring to membership in the elite strove to master it, and to speak it – even though there was no consensus on how many of the words should be pronounced.

The *katharévoussa/dhimotikí* debate remained a highly contentious issue until the early 1980s. Writers – from Solomos, Makriyiannis and Papadiamantis in the nineteenth century to Seferis, Kazantzakis and Ritsos in the twentieth – have all championed the demotic, or some approximation of it, in their literature. Advocacy of demotic became increasingly linked to left-wing politics, while crackpot right-wing governments forcibly (re)instated *katharévoussa* at every opportunity. Most recently, the **colonels' junta** (1967–1974) reversed a decision of the previous government to use *dhimotikí* as the medium of instruction in schools, bringing back *katharévoussa*, even on sweet wrappers, as part of their ragbag of notions about racial purity and heroic ages.

Dhimiotikí returned once more after the fall of the colonels and now seems here to stay; perhaps the final blow to the classicizers was the official decision, in 1981, to do away with breath marks (which in fact no longer signified anything) and abolish the three different stress accents in favour of a **single accute accent** (though there are still plenty of pre-1981 road-signs displaying the older system). *Dhimotikí* is used in schools, on radio and TV, and after a fashion in newspapers (with the exception of the extreme right-wing *Estia*). The only institutions which refuse to bring themselves up to date are the Church and the legal professions – so beware rental contracts and official documents.

This is not to suggest that there is now any less confusion. The Metaxas dictatorship of the 1930s, elaborating on attempts at the same by previous regimes, changed scores of village names from Slavic, Turkish or Albanian words to Greek ones – often reviving the name of the nearest ancient site – and these official **place names** still hold sway on most road signs and maps – even though the local people may use the *dhimotikí* or non-Greek form. Thus you will see "Plomárion" or "Spétsai" written, while everyone actually says "Plomári" or "Spétses"; Pándhrossos on Sámos, and Platáni on Kós, are still preferably known to locals as Arvanítes and Kermedés respectively.

Dialects and minority languages

If the lack of any standardized Greek were not enough, the islands still offer considerable linguistic diversity, both in their regional variants and minority languages. Ancient **dialects** are alive and well in many remote areas, and some of them are quite incomprehensible to outsiders. The dialect of Sfákia in Crete is one such; those of Náxos and Lésvos are other strong Aegean dialects, which owe much to migration from Crete and influences from Asia Minor respectively. The dialect of Sámos and that of adjacent Híos are completely different from one another, Híos being considered a more pure "Ionian" (and this thousands of years after the Ionians arrived from the mainland), while the rough "Samian" variant owes much to the diverse origins of its settlers. Arvanítika – a form of medieval Albanian – was until well into the twentieth century the first language of many villages of southern Évvia, northern Ándhros, and much of the Argo-Saronic area; it is still (just) spoken (and sung) among the oldest generation. On Rhodes and Kós there is a dwindling Turkish-speaking population, probably not in excess of seven thousand persons as of writing.

A glossary of words and terms

Acropolis Ancient, fortified hilltop.

Agora Market and meeting place of an ancient Greek city; also the "high street" of a modern village (**agorá** in modern Greek).

Amphora Tall, narrow-necked jar for oil or wine.

Áno Upper; common prefix element of village names.

Apse Curved recess at the east end of a church nave.

Archaic period Late Iron Age period, from around 750 BC to the start of the Classical period in the fifth century BC.

Architrave Horizontal masonry atop temple columns; same as **entablature**.

Arhondikó A lordly stone mansion, as in Kastoriá or Pílio.

Astykó (Intra) city, municipal, local; adjective applied to phone calls and bus services.

Áyios/Ayía/Áyii Saint or holy (m/f/plural). Common place-name prefix (abbreviated Ag or Ay), often spelled **Agios** or **Aghios**.

Basilica Colonnaded, "hall-" or "barn-" type church adapted from Roman models, most common in northern Greece.

Bema Rostrum for oratory (and later the chancel) of a church.

Bouleuterion Auditorium for meetings of an ancient town's deliberative council.

Capital The flared top, often ornamented, of a column.

Cavea Seating curve of an ancient theatre.

Cella Sacred room of a temple, housing the cult image.

Classical period Essentially from the end of the Persian Wars in the fifth century BC until the unification of Greece under Philip II of Macedon (338 BC).

Conch Concave semi-dome surmounting a church apse, often frescoed.

Corinthian Decorative columns, festooned with acanthus florettes; a temple built in this order.

Dhimarhío Town hall.

Dhomátia Rooms for rent in purpose-built blocks or (seldomly these days) private houses.

Dorian Northern civilization that displaced and succeeded the Mycenaeans and Minoans through most of Greece around 1100 BC.

Doric Minimalist, unadorned columns, dating from the Dorian period; a temple built in this order.

Drum Cylindrical or faceted vertical section, usually pierced by an even number of narrow windows, upholding a church cupola.

Entablature The horizontal linking structure atop the columns of an ancient temple.

Eparhía Greek Orthodox diocese, also the smallest subdivision of a modern province, analogous to a county.

Exedra Display niche for statuary.

Exonarthex The outer vestibule or entrance hall of a church, when a true **narthex** is present.

Forum Market and meeting place of a Roman-era city.

Frieze Band of sculptures around a temple. Doric friezes consist of various tableaux of figures (**Metopes**) interspersed with grooved panels (**triglyphs**); Ionic ones have continuous bands of figures.

Froúrio Medieval castle; nowadays, usually means a modern military headquarters.

Garsoniéra/es Studio villa/s, self-catering apartment/s.

Geometric period Post-Mycenaean Iron Age era named for the style of its pottery; begins in the early eleventh century BC with the arrival of Dorian peoples. By the eighth century BC, with the development of representational styles, it becomes known as the **Archaic period**.

Hellenistic period The last and most unified "Greek empire", created in the wake of Alexander the Great's Macedonian empire and finally collapsing with the fall of Corinth to the Romans in 146 BC.

Heroön Shrine or sanctuary, usually of a demigod or mortal; war memorials in modern Greece.

Hokhláki Mosaic of coloured pebbles, found in church or house courtyards of the Dodecanese and Spétses.

Hóra Main town of an island or region; literally it means "the place". An island *hóra* is often known by the same name as the island.

Ierón Literally, "sacred" – the space between the altar screen and the apse of a church, reserved for priestly activities.

Ikonostási Screen between the nave of a church and the altar, supporting at least three icons.

Ionic Elaborate, decorative development of the older **Doric** order; Ionic temple columns are slimmer, with deeper "fluted" edges, spiral-shaped capitals and ornamental bases.

Iperastykó Long-distance – as in phone calls and bus services.

Kafenío Coffee house or café; in a small village the centre of communal life and probably serving as the bus stop, too.

Kaïki (plural **kaïkia**) Caique, or medium-sized boat, traditionally wooden and used for transporting cargo and passengers; now refers mainly to island excursion boats.

Kalderími A cobbled mule-track or footpath.

Kámbos Fertile agricultural plain, usually near a river mouth.

Kantína Shack, caravan or even a disused bus on the beach, serving drinks and perhaps sandwiches or quick snacks.

Kástro Any fortified hill, but most often the oldest, highest, walled-in part of an island *hóra*, intended to protect civilians.

Katholikón Central chapel of a monastery.

Káto Lower; common prefix element of village names.

Kendrikí platía Central square.

Kouros Nude Archaic statue of an idealized young man, usually portrayed with one foot slightly forward of the other.

Megaron Principal hall or throne room of a Mycenaean palace.

Meltémi North wind that blows across the Aegean in summer, starting softly from near the mainland and hitting the Cyclades, the Dodecanese and Crete full on.

Metope See **Frieze**.

Minoan Crete's great Bronze Age civilization, which dominated the Aegean from about 2500 to 1400 BC.

Moní Formal term for a monastery or convent.

Mycenaean Mainland civilization centred on Mycenae and the Argolid from about 1700 to 1100 BC.

Naos The inner sanctum of an ancient temple; also, any Orthodox Christian shrine.

Narthex Western vestibule of a church, reserved for catechumens and the unbaptized; typically frescoed with scenes of the Last Judgement.

Neolithic Earliest era of settlement in Greece, characterized by the use of stone tools and weapons together with basic agriculture. Divided arbitrarily into Early (ca. 6000 BC), Middle (ca. 5000 BC) and Late (ca. 3000 BC).

Néos, Néa, Néo "New" – a common prefix to a town or village name.

Nomós Modern Greek province – there are more than 52 of them. Island bus services are organized according to their borders (most obvious on Crete, with its four provinces).

Odeion Small theatre, used for musical performances, minor dramatic productions or councils.

Orchestra Circular area in a theatre where the chorus would sing and dance.

Palaestra Gymnasium for athletics and wrestling practice.

Paleós, Paleá, Paleó "Old" – again a common prefix in town and village names.

Panayía Virgin Mary.

Pandokrátor Literally "The Almighty"; generally refers to the stern portrayal of Christ in Majesty frescoed or in mosaic in the dome of many Byzantine churches.

Paniyíri Festival or feast – the local celebration of a holy day.

Paralía Beach or seafront promenade.

Pediment Triangular, sculpted gable below the roof of a temple.

Pendentive Any of four triangular sections of vaulting with concave sides, positioned at a corner of a rectangular space to support a circular or polygonal dome; in churches, often adorned with frescoes of the four Evangelists.

Períptero Street kiosk.

Peristereónes Pigeon towers, in the Cyclades.

Peristyle Gallery of columns around a temple or other building.

Pinakothíki Picture gallery, ancient or modern.

Pithos (plural **pithoi**) Large ceramic jar for storing oil, grain, etc. Very common in Minoan palaces and used in almost identical form in modern Greek homes.

Platía Square, plaza.

Polygonal masonry Wall-building technique of the Classical and Hellenistic period, which used unmortared, closely joined stones; often called "Lesvian polygonal" after the island where the method supposedly originated. The much-(ab)used term "Cyclopean" refers only to Mycenean/Bronze Age mainland sites such as Tiryns and Mycenae itself.

Propylaion Monumental columned gateway of an ancient building; often used in the plural, **propylaia**.

Pýrgos Tower or bastion; also tower-mansions found in the Máni or on Lésvos.

Skála The port of an inland island settlement, nowadays often larger and more important than its namesake, but always younger since built after the disappearance of piracy.

Squinch Small concavity across a corner of a columnless interior space, which supports a superstructure such as a dome.

Stele Upright stone slab or column, usually inscribed with an edict; also an ancient tombstone, with a relief scene.

Stoa Colonnaded walkway in Classical-era marketplace.

Távli Backgammon; a favourite café pastime, especially among the young. There are two more difficult local variations (*févga* and *plakotó*) in addition to the standard international game (*pórtes*).

Témblon Wooden altar screen of an Orthodox church, usually ornately carved and painted and studded with icons; more or less interchangeable with **ikonostási**.

Temenos Sacred precinct, often used to refer to the sanctuary itself.

Theatral area Open area found in most of the Minoan palaces with seat-like steps around. Probably a type of theatre or ritual area.

Tholos Conical or beehive-shaped building, eg a Mycenaean tomb.

Triglyph See **Frieze**.

Tympanum The recessed space, flat or carved in relief, inside a pediment.

Acronyms

ANEK Anónymi Navtiliakí Etería Krítis (Shipping Co of Crete, Ltd), which runs most ferries between Pireás and Crete, plus many to Italy.

DANE Dhodhekanisiakí Anónymi Navtiliakí Etería (Dodecanesian Shipping Company Ltd), which runs many ferries between Rhodes and Pireás via intervening islands.

DIKKI Democrat Social Movement, a more left-leaning spinoff from PASOK; now moribund.

EAM National Liberation Front, the political force behind ELAS.

ELAS Popular Liberation Army, the main Resistance group during World War II and the basis of the Communist army during the civil war.

ELTA Postal service.

EOS Greek Mountaineering Federation, based in Athens, controlling a few refuges on Crete.

EOT Ellinikós Organismós Tourismoú, National Tourist Organization.

FYROM Former Yugoslav Republic of Macedonia.

KKE Communist Party, unreconstructed.

KTEL National syndicate of bus companies. The term also refers to individual bus stations.

LANE Lasithiakí Anónymi Navtiliakí Etería (Lasithian Shipping Company Ltd), based in eastern Crete.

ND Conservative (Néa Dhimokratía) party.

NEL Navtiliakí Etería Lésvou (Lesvian Shipping Co).

OTE Telephone company.

PASOK Socialist party (Pan-Hellenic Socialist Movement).

Rough Guides

advertiser

...music & reference

ROUGH GUIDES ADVERTISER

Also! More than 120 Rough Guide music CDs are available from all good book
and record stores. Listen in at www.worldmusic.net

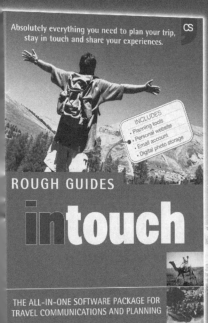

Absolutely everything you need to plan your trip, stay in touch and share your experiences.

INCLUDES
• Planning tools
• Personal website
• Email account
• Digital photo storage

ROUGH GUIDES

intouch

THE ALL-IN-ONE SOFTWARE PACKAGE FOR TRAVEL COMMUNICATIONS AND PLANNING

A NEW CONCEPT IN TRAVEL

ROUGH GUIDES

ROUGH GUIDES ADVERTISER

OUGH GUIDES SOFTWARE
are your adventures on the move

gh Guides have launched **intouch**, a new
one software package for planning your
and staying in touch with people back
before, during and after your travels.

e an itinerary and budget using on-screen
mation and maps, and take advantage
e diary to keep family and friends
med of your whereabouts.

iary can be linked to your mobile
e so that you can send a text message,
ch will automatically send an email or
SMS to those listed on your account.

You can also post photos and diary entries
online and then download them to make a
journal on your return.

Rough Guides **intouch** is easy to install and
you don't need to take anything with you -
just hit the synchronize button and then
use it from any internet café in the world.

Rough Guides **intouch** includes:
Planning tools
Free email address
Free personal website
Digital photo storage   And much more......

5 OFF your purchase of Rough Guides **intouch** if you buy online at
www.roughguidesintouch.com   reference code: Rough Guide Books

mended retail price £24.99 available through leading retailers e.g. WH Smith, Waterstones and PC World

649

ROUGH GUIDES ADVERTISER

ROUGH GUIDES ADVERTISER

654

small print

and

Index

A Rough Guide to Rough Guides

In the summer of 1981, Mark Ellingham, a recent graduate from Bristol University, was travelling round Greece and couldn't find a guidebook that really met his needs. On the one hand there were the student guides, insistent on saving every last cent, and on the other the heavyweight cultural tomes whose authors seemed to have spent more time in a research library than lounging away the afternoon at a taverna or on the beach.

In a bid to avoid getting a job, Mark and a small group of writers set about creating their own guidebook. It was a guide to Greece that aimed to combine a journalistic approach to description with a thoroughly practical approach to travellers' needs – a guide that would incorporate culture, history and contemporary insights with a critical edge, together with up-to-date, value-for-money listings. Back in London, Mark and the team finished their Rough Guide, as they called it, and talked Routledge into publishing the book.

That first *Rough Guide to Greece*, published in 1982, was a student scheme that became a publishing phenomenon. The immediate success of the book – with numerous reprints and a Thomas Cook prize shortlisting – spawned a series that rapidly covered dozens of destinations. Rough Guides had a ready market among low-budget backpackers, but soon also acquired a much broader and older readership that relished Rough Guides' wit and inquisitiveness as much as their enthusiastic, critical approach. Everyone wants value for money, but not at any price.

Rough Guides soon began supplementing the "rougher" information about hostels and low-budget listings with the kind of detail on restaurants and quality hotels that independent-minded visitors on any budget might expect, whether on business in New York or trekking in Thailand.

These days the guides – distributed worldwide by the Penguin group – offer recommendations from shoestring to luxury and cover more than 200 destinations around the globe, including almost every country in the Americas and Europe, more than half of Africa and most of Asia and Australasia. Our ever-growing team of authors and photographers is spread all over the world, particularly in Europe, the USA and Australia.

In 1994, we published the *Rough Guide to World Music* and *Rough Guide to Classical Music*; and a year later the *Rough Guide to the Internet*. All three books have become benchmark titles in their fields – which encouraged us to expand into other areas of publishing, mainly around popular culture. Rough Guides now publish:

- Travel guides to more than 200 worldwide destinations
- Dictionary phrasebooks to 22 major languages
- History guides ranging from Ireland to Islam
- Maps printed on rip-proof and waterproof Polyart™ paper
- Music guides running the gamut from Opera to Elvis
- Restaurant guides to London, New York and San Francisco
- Reference books on topics as diverse as the Weather and Shakespeare
- Sports guides from Formula 1 to Man Utd
- Pop culture books from *Lord of the Rings* to Cult TV
- World Music CDs in association with World Music Network

Visit **www.roughguides.com** to see our latest publications.

Rough Guide Credits

Editors: Sally Schafer, Helena Smith and Polly Thomas
Layout: Umesh, Ajay and Jessica
Cartography: Ashutosh Bharti, Miles Irving, JP Mishra, Rajesh Mishra and Animesh Pathak
Picture research: Veneta Bullen and Joe Mee
Proofreader: Madhu Mohapatra
Editorial: London Martin Dunford, Kate Berens, Claire Saunders, Geoff Howard, Ruth Blackmore, Gavin Thomas, Richard Lim, Lucy Ratcliffe, Clifton Wilkinson, Alison Murchie, Fran Sandham, Alexander Mark Rogers, Karoline Densley, Andy Turner, Ella O'Donnell, Keith Drew, Andrew Lockett, Joe Staines, Duncan Clark, Peter Buckley, Matthew Milton; **New York** Andrew Rosenberg, Richard Koss, Yuki Takagaki, Hunter Slaton, Chris Barsanti, Steven Horak
Design & Pictures: London Simon Bracken, Dan May, Diana Jarvis, Mark Thomas, Jj Luck, Harriet Mills; **Delhi** Madhulita Mohapatra, Umesh Aggarwal, Ajay Verma, Jessica Subramanian

Production: Julia Bovis, John McKay, Sophie Hewat
Cartography: London Maxine Repath, Ed Wright, Katie Lloyd-Jones, Miles Irving; **Delhi** Manish Chandra, Rajesh Chhibber, Jai Prakash Mishra, Ashutosh Bharti, Rajesh Mishra, Animesh Pathak, Jasbir Sandhu, Karobi Gogoi
Cover art direction: Louise Boulton
Online: New York Jennifer Gold, Cree Lawson, Suzanne Welles, Benjamin Ross; **Delhi** Manik Chauhan, Narender Kumar, Shekhar Jha, Rakesh Kumar
Marketing & Publicity: London Richard Trillo, Niki Smith, David Wearn, Chloë Roberts, Demelza Dallow, Kristina Pentland; **New York** Geoff Colquitt, Megan Kennedy
Finance: Gary Singh
Manager India: Punita Singh
Series editor: Mark Ellingham
PA to Managing Director: Julie Sanderson
Managing Director: Kevin Fitzgerald

Publishing Information

This fifth edition published July 2004 by
Rough Guides Ltd,
80 Strand, London WC2R 0RL.
345 Hudson St, 4th Floor,
New York, NY 10014, USA.
Distributed by the Penguin Group
Penguin Books Ltd,
80 Strand, London WC2R 0RL
Penguin Putnam, Inc.
375 Hudson Street, NY 10014, USA
Penguin Books Australia Ltd,
487 Maroondah Highway, PO Box 257,
Ringwood, Victoria 3134, Australia
Penguin Books Canada Ltd,
10 Alcorn Avenue, Toronto, Ontario,
Canada M4V 1E4
Penguin Books (NZ) Ltd,
182–190 Wairau Road, Auckland 10,
New Zealand
Typeset in Bembo and Helvetica to an original design by Henry Iles.

Printed and bound in China

© Lance Chilton, Marc Dubin, Mark Ellingham, Nick Edwards, John Fisher and Natania Jansz 2004

No part of this book may be reproduced in any form without permission from the publisher except for the quotation of brief passages in reviews.

672pp includes index
A catalogue record for this book is available from the British Library

ISBN 184353259X

The publishers and authors have done their best to ensure the accuracy and currency of all the information in **The Rough Guide to The Greek Islands**, however, they can accept no responsibility for any loss, injury, or inconvenience sustained by any traveller as a result of information or advice contained in the guide.

3   5   7   9   8   6   4   2

Help us update

We've gone to a lot of effort to ensure that the fifth edition of **The Rough Guide to The Greek Islands** is accurate and up-to-date. However, things change – places get "discovered", opening hours are notoriously fickle, restaurants and rooms raise prices or lower standards. If you feel we've got it wrong or left something out, we'd like to know, and if you can remember the address, the price, the phone number, so much the better.

We'll credit all contributions, and send a copy of the next edition (or any other Rough Guide if you prefer) for the best letters. Everyone who writes to us and isn't already a subscriber will receive a copy of our full-colour thrice-yearly newsletter. Please mark letters: **"Rough Guide to The Greek Islands Update"** and send to: Rough Guides, 80 Strand, London WC2R 0RL, or Rough Guides, 4th Floor, 345 Hudson St, New York, NY 10014. Or send an email to **mail@roughguides.com**

Have your questions answered and tell others about your trip at **www.roughguides.atinfopop.com**

SMALL PRINT

657

Acknowledgements

Don Bapst would like to thank John Van Lerberghe and the entire staff of the Mýkonos Accommodation Center; Despina Kitini and the entire staff of Náxos Tourist Information Centre; the lovely family who animates *Popi's* restaurant on Náxos each evening; fellow travellers Derick, Augie and Gwawr; Emm. A. Lignos of the Folklore Museum on Santoríni; Tassos Nomikos at the *Hotel Nisaki* on Sýros; and the highly accommodating families and staff who run the *Hotel Anna Platanou* on Páros, the *Hotel Poseidon* on Íos, and the *San Georgio* on Thíra. Extra special thanks go out to my dear friends Anna, Spiros and Agis in Athens, Norman on Santoríni, and Dimitri in Chicago, without whom I'd have never discovered the true beauty of Greece.

Andrew Benson gives special thanks to Persephone in Thássos and Panayiotis in Límnos, the tourist office in Édhessa – an example to all tourist offices in Greece – and everyone at Olymbiádha, Stavroúpoli and Marónia. *Heretismoús ke filákia* to Peter, Jerry and all my friends in or near Haniá, for years of true hospitality. Thanks to Geoff and Kate at HQ for their continuing trust. And to Sally for grappling bravely with unruly accents and other challenges.

Marc Dubin thanks Thanos, Nancy and Susanna at *Marble House* in Athens; Roy and Effi Hounsell in Koukoúli; Kostas and Marianthi Pappas in Lykiádhes; Thanasis and Toula Nakas in Kastráki; Khristos in Sarakíniko for the fine wine and music; Jill Sleeman in Moúressi; the management of the *Hotel Akti* in Náfpaktos; Theo and Melinda Kosmetos in Mólyvos; Markos Kostalas and Theodhore and Güher Spordilis on Híos; Alexis, Sonia and Dionysia Zikas on Kós; David, Lisa, Iain, Lynn and Nigel on Tílos; Efi, Spyros, John, Constance, Sotiris, Marianne and Kim on Rhodes; Nikos, Wendy and Adriana on Sými; Elina Scoutari on Pátmos; the Vavoulas family and Faith Warn on Kálymnos, the managements of the hotels *Porphyris* (Níssyros), *Irini* (Tílos), *Krithoni Paradise* (Léros) and *Maltezana Beach* (Astypálea) for their support; and once again to Pamela for patience back in London, being force-fed at endless tavernas, and coming along to Tílos, Níssyros and Kós as well as Sámos.

Nick Edwards would like to thank all his friends in Athens, especially Jonathan Sim and Yiannis Karapapas, and his friends in the Ionians, particularly Maria of the *Hotel Gorgona* in Nydhrí. Thanks to Maria E for keeping me going during the write-up.

John Fisher would like to thank Alexandros Stivanakis, Dimitris Koutoulas, Calli Travlos and the staff of the GNTO in London, Yiannis Mikhas and all at the prefecture of Pireás, Leonidas Tsagaris and Lena Zolota.

Irwin Lane thanks Angelique Kenalli for an acute dose of hospitality and support during my time in Athens.

The editor would also like to thank Keith Drew for checking the maps and Clifton Wilkinson, Helena Smith and Kate Davie for all their support and advice.

Readers' letters

Kathy Abbott, Verna Alexander, Roger Alsop, Monika and Kevin Atherton, Zaynab Ayub, Michael Bance, Jef Barnes, Mary Bateman and William Matthews, Ibrahim Bayoumi, Yiannis Bikakis, Robin and Pippa Blackall, R. J. C. Blackshaw, M. Bloomfield, Katharina Bolesch, Dimitris Bolos, Judith Bonhiver, Gregory Bouras, Andrea Bradford, Andrew Briggs, Allan Brigham, Sue Broadfield, Garry Brooks, Amanda Brown, Kendall P. Brown, Candy Burns, E. Butterworth, Lynne Campbell, Steve Cant, Alison Chapman, Clare and Gerald Chapman, Liz Clarke, Diana Coode and Lee Barnett, Fleur Conn and Christian Nielsen, Pam Cooper, Jane Maw Cornish, A. Cullings-Wells, Malcolm Davies, Michael Davies, Jo Day, Michael Dite, Barbara Dorf, Holly Downing, Maggie Duckham, Harvey Florman, Liz Fogarty, Geoff Ford, Marco Gandini, Frances Gill, Mike Glynn, Sue Good, Mike Gordon, Margaret Green, Ed Gregory, Paul Gregory, Mike and Ruth Hall, Wendy Harper, Julie Harrison and Jon Weidner, Edward Hatton, Maria and Chris Hawkes, Colin and Carol Hawkins, Allan M. Healy, Maxim Heijndijk, Emma Hicks, A. Hill, Helen Hines, Mark Holmström, Anouk van Hoofstadt, Jennifer Horne and Don Noble, Charles Howard, Kurt Jewkes, Georgina Jones, Vesna Kann, Richard and Jennie Kellner, Paul and Lindsay Kelly, Kerry King, John Kirkaldy, Diana van Laan, Ioannis Lambrou, Leda and David Lassman, David G. Lees, H. M. Lewis, Simon Loft, S. Lucas, Charly Lynn, Ian Mace, Gordon MacKenzie, Julie MacSwan, Kerry Malaperiman, Malcolm Mallison, Brit Ragnhild Manengen, John Marsh, Massimiliano Mattioli, Pat and David Maxwell, Andy McCosh, Peter

SMALL PRINT

McCoy, Anthony McElvaney, Brian McMahon, Phil Meade, Alf B. Meier, Alf Meir and Roberta Jacobson, Ton Mensenkamp, Chris Moore, Maire Morton, Jean Nantais, Tomi Nicholson, Richard O'Connell, Michael O'Flaherty, Emma Owens, Tolis Papazoglou and Robin Payne, Laura Pavlou-Mudie, Ruth and John Pigneguy, J. M. Polkinghorne, D. J. S. Pullin, Susan Raphael, Jake Rayson, Julia Ritter, Dan Robinson and Wendy Finch-Turner, Wanda Root, Sandy Rose, Nick Roussis, H.H. Saffery, Tina Salmon, S. Saxby-Soffe, Alexander Schouvaloff, Carola Scupham, Claude Seban, Nic Shannon, Hugh Sharp, Irene Sharp, Paul Sharrocks, Clive Smith, Graham Smith, Tim Smithier, Margaret Stewardson, Danièle Stewart, Jacqui Swenson, Roger Theobald, Richard F. Thomas, Susan A. Thompson, David Thornton, Michael Tippett, Thora Togher, Branka Trajkovski, David Tricker, Dave and Yvonne Waldron-Kelly, Jeffrey Walter, Kevin Walters, Graham Whitehouse, Veryan Wilkie-Jones, Claire Wilson, Chris Wood, A. Wormell, Chris & Jan Wright, Duncan K Young.

Photo Credits

Cover credits

Main (front) Santoríni © Robert Harding
Front (small top) Páros © Robert Harding
Front (small lower) Lésvos © Robert Harding
Back (top) Folégrandhros © Robert Harding
Back (lower) Asklepion, Kós © Robert Harding

Colour Introduction

Mólyvos at sunset © Marc Dubin
View over caldera, Santoríni © Travel Ink/Roger Rowland
Pomegranate tree © Travel Ink/Richard Rawlingson
Kaïkí-building, Pátmos © Marc Dubin
Travelling fisherman © Geoff Garvey
Wayside shrine © Neil Setchfield
Blue amulet © Trip/Helene Rogers
Departing ferry © Peter Wilson
Beach scene, Kós © Neil Setchfield

Things not to miss

01 Sými Harbour © Trip/Mark Azavedo
02 Váï beach, Crete © Peter Wilson/Axiom
03 Windsurfing off Vassilikí, Lefkádha © Axiom/Jack Moscrop
04 Hikers in Samarian Gorge, Crete © Robert Harding/Mark Vivian
05 Hellenistic acropolis, Lindos © Marc Dubin
06 Village weaver, Lasíthi plateau © Robert Harding
07 Paleohóri beach, Mílos © Marc Dubin
08 Melissáni Cave, Kefalloniá ©Travel Ink/Peter Whalley
09 View over Firá, Santoríni © T. Bognar/TRIP
10 Dhíkeos peak, Kós © Marc Dubin
11 Kérkyra (Corfu) old town © Travel Ink/Ian Booth
12 Tomatoes drying, Híos © Marc Dubin
13 Mýkonos island at sunset © Alamy Images
14 A boat excursion to Kós © Alamy Images
15 Loggerhead sea turtle © Corbis
16 Mountain vineyards, Sámos © Robert Harding
17 Ídhra © Travel Ink/Ian Booth

18 Kárpathos, Ólymbos © Marc Dubin
19 Monastery of Ayíou Ioánnou Theológou, Pátmos © Trip/B Seed
20 Hozoviotíssas monastery, Amorgós © Robert Harding
21 Greek food and wine © Alamy Images
22 Naoússa harbour, Páros © Robert Harding/Ellen Rooney
23 The Queen's Megaron, Knossos © Corbis/Roger Wood
24 Temple of Aphaea, Égina © Robert Harding/Ellen Rooney
25 Volcano floor, Níssyros © Neil Setchfield
26 Haniá old town © Axiom/Peter Wilson
27 Ápella beach, Kárpathos © Travel Ink/Marc Dubin
28 Longós, Paxí © Marc Dubin
29 Mólyvos, Lésvos © Travel Ink/S. Hines
30 Dovecotes, Tínos © Rainer Reisenberger

Black and white photos

Moored yachts at Spétses harbour front © Alamy Images (p.90)
Póros harbour © Peter Wilson (p.102)
Dovecotes, Tínos © Rainer Reisenberger (p.112)
Temple of Apollo, Náxos © Robert Harding (p.173)
Haniá old town © Axiom/Peter Wilson (p.208)
Interior, Archeological Museum, Iráklion © Neil Setchfield (p.217)
Hóra, Astypálea at sunset © Marc Dubin (p.282)
Icon in shop, Rhodes © Neil Setchfield (p.322)
Vineyards, Sámos © Robert Harding (p.376)
Sanctuary of the Great Gods, Samothráki © Marc Dubin (p.441)
Skýros © Robert Harding (p.456)
Skópelos Town © Travel Ink/Ian Booth (p.465)
Melissáni Cave, Kefalloniá © Travel Ink/Peter Whalley (p.490)
Stairs in Kérkyra (Corfu) Old Town © Axiom/Steve J Benbow (p.496)
Wild flower (turban buttercup) © Marc Dubin (p.593)

Index

Map entries are in colour.

663

INDEX

O

669

INDEX

671

Map symbols

maps are listed in the full index using coloured text

---·---·---	International boundary	⸖	Marshland
------	Chapter division boundary	🇽	Waterfall
▬▬▬	Motorway	ᐱᐱ	Spring/spa
═══	Major paved road	◓	Cave
━━	Minor paved road	⊙	Statue/memorial
────	Unpaved road	🎿	Ski area
··········	Road under construction	⌂	Refuge
▬▬▬	Pedestrianized street	⚐	Campsite
- - - - -	Footpath	◉	Accommodation
⊪⊪⊪⊪⊪	Steps	▪	Restaurant
━▬━▬━	Railway	✕	Airport
— — —	Ferry route	🅿	Parking
▬▬▬	Waterway	Ⓜ	Metro station
🕌	Mosque	★	Bus/taxi stop
✡	Synagogue	🕯	Lighthouse
☩	Church	ⓘ	Information office
⛪	Monastery or convent	⊠	Post office
∴	Archeological site	◆	Point of interest
♛	Castle	⊞	Hospital
⸌	Hill	⊠—⊠	Gate
▲	Peak	⬭	Stadium
⛰	Mountains	▪	Building
⸮	Gorge	⇥	Church
⬇	Viewpoint	⊹⊹⊹	Christian cemetery
) (	Bridge	▨	Park
@	Internet	⸽	Beach
▄▄▄	Wall		